encyclopedia of the world's endangered languages

The concern for the fast-disappearing language stocks of the world has arisen particularly in the last decade, as a result of the impact of globalization. This encyclopedia appears as an answer to a felt need: to catalogue and describe those languages, making up the vast majority of the world's six thousand or more distinct tongues, which are in danger of disappearing within the next few decades.

Endangerment is a complex issue, and the reasons why so many of the world's smaller, less empowered languages are not being passed on to future generations today are discussed in the encyclopedia's introduction. This is followed by regional sections, each authored by a notable specialist, combining to provide a comprehensive listing of languages which, by the criteria of endangerment set out in the introduction, are likely to disappear within the next few decades. These languages make up ninety per cent of the world's remaining language stocks.

The encyclopedia provides in a single resource: expert analysis of the current language policy situation in every multilingual country and on every continent, detailed descriptions of little-known languages from all over the world, and clear alphabetical entries, region by region, of all the world's languages currently thought to be in danger of extinction.

The *Encyclopedia of the World's Endangered Languages* will be a necessary addition to all academic lingustics collections and will be a useful resource for a range of readers with an interest in development studies, cultural heritage and international affairs.

Christopher Moseley has recently retired from two decades spent covering Baltic affairs for BBC Monitoring, part of the BBC World Service. He now works as a freelance translator and editor, with a particular lifelong interest in the languages and literatures of the Baltic and Nordic areas. He is the editor of the *Journal of the Foundation for Endangered Languages*. His other books include *Atlas of the World's Languages* (Routledge, 2007), *Colloquial Latvian* (Routledge, 1996) and *Colloquial Estonian* (Routledge, 1994).

encyclopedia of the world's endangered languages

edited by
christopher moseley

LONDON AND NEW YORK

First published 2007
by Routledge
2 Park Square, Milton Park, Abingdon, Oxon OX14 4RN
www.routledge.co.uk

Simultaneously published in the USA and Canada
by Routledge
270 Madison Avenue, New York, NY 10016
www.routledge.com

Routledge is an Imprint of the Taylor and Francis Group, an informa business

© 2007 Routledge

Typeset in Times New Roman and Helvetica by
Taylor & Francis Books
Printed and bound in Great Britain by
TJ International Ltd, Padstow, Cornwall

British Library Cataloguing in Publication Data
A catalogue record for this book is available from the British Library

Library of Congress Cataloging-in-Publication Data
A catalog record for this book has been requested

ISBN13: 978-0-7007-1197-0

Contents

Maps

General introduction

Christopher Moseley

If we trace the history of linguistics as a science, from the realms of mere speculation as recently as the eighteenth century to its status as a relatively exact science, with many distinct specialisations, at the beginning of the twenty-first, and compare that history with the history of demographic, political and economic change across the globe over the same brief period in the span of man's existence as a speaking animal, then it begins to become clear why the concept of 'endangerment' is so new to the realms of linguistics. This volume arose as an answer to a felt need: to document a diversity that is fast attenuating, in a world where 'diversity' in other spheres – the natural world, the cultural world and even in race relations – is a quality which has enjoyed a heightened appreciation only within the past two generations or so.

Linguistics may be a relatively exact science now, but it is still very much a science whose object of study moves and changes more rapidly than its practitioners can follow it. It is also the science that is perhaps most closely bound up with the expression of human emotion, a science where the objective is in constant collision with the subjective. Everybody has an opinion about language to some extent, and except in purely monolingual societies, everybody is made aware at some point of externally imposed policies, other people's prejudices, and an almost instinctive sense of 'appropriateness' about language use. Even monoglots are not free from the strictures imposed by society on their language use; they, too, must learn to graduate and refine their use of the different registers within a language. In more fragmented language communities, dialect differences must be distinguished. Language is a badge of the individual's place in the community.

There are well over 6,000 languages spoken in the world today. This is itself a fact that is only recently established by linguistic science, and there is some debate still about the exact number. Not only is the difference between a 'language' and a 'dialect' a perennial bone of contention, but even in the late twentieth century, new languages remained to be discovered, identified and classified – often misclassified, when the data about them was only sketchy. Whatever the exact number, even though perhaps some few genuinely new cases remain to be discovered, it is not a number that is growing. It is diminishing, and diminishing at a rate that should worry anyone who regards diversity as healthy in the same way that we may worry about the accelerating endangerment to the world's rare flora and fauna, or the shrinking of the polar ice-caps.

There are no grounds for complacency, then, and the book you hold in your hands is one attempt to document as accurately as possible the true state of that endangerment. The languages described and listed in this volume are all at least to some extent under threat of extinction within the next two generations of their native speakers. The ultimate reasons for their decline are many, but the most immediate reason is a simple, stark truth: knowledge of the language as a tool of everyday communication is not being passed from one generation to another.

It is easy enough to take the view that this state of affairs simply does not matter. It is especially easy for native speakers of the language in which these lines are being written and read – but it is in many cases easy even for speakers of tiny minority languages that have barely any currency outside the immediate environment. The need to communicate is an urgent imperative, and the ability to communicate fluently is intimately bound up with self-esteem. If we can communicate on an equal footing with those people with whom we must come into daily contact, what does it matter if we have to dress our thoughts in another's language? The end justifies the means. Only the fittest survive.

Language has always been a powerful weapon in the subjugation of peoples and nations. Empires have come and gone by the sword, but their true staying power, their lasting influence over many generations, long after the trappings of government and formal administration have disappeared, lies in the power of language. At the centre of each empire lies a tradition of book learning – literacy, whereby a nation's traditions can be passed in a stable and unchanged form from one generation to another, which in turn implies the power to legislate, the power to standardise language and conquer dialect differences, the power to institute formal education, the power to expand and amplify the findings of science. Without these things, a society remains fragmented and weak, and a language remains variable and dependent on the accidents of geography and demography. With them, it has the opportunity to conquer even numerically stronger opponents. The secrets of shipbuilding, arms making, colonial administration, trade regulation, are all passed on in written form.

Empires have spread out in various forms from or within other continents, but in Europe the process of colonial conquest whose linguistic fruits we see today began over five hundred years ago, and it is no coincidence that it began in the same century as the invention of movable type. The acquisition of printing multiplied and accelerated the opportunities for conquering the hearts and minds of those who did not have it. In the twentieth century, within our own living memory, attempts have been made to redress the balance; once the United Nations made possible the (at least theoretically) equal representation of sovereign nations in a world forum, the movement to banish colonialism was able to gain a stronger foothold, but whereas all the other trappings of colonial administration fell gradually away in what is habitually called the Third World, language lingered on. It served to unite countries that were in many cases the artificial creations of European overlords dividing their spoils at the conference table. The tongues of former masters were pressed into service to educate the vital infrastructure of the new civil service, to pass on the vital data of technology, and to engage in trade with powerful partners.

But it would be a gross oversimplification to lay the blame for minority language attrition only at the feet of colonial powers. There is a hierarchy, a pecking order, within multilingual states that obtains quite independently of any former external conquest. This is true even of some of the colonial powers themselves: Britain, France and Spain themselves all have minority language situations, and for some of the languages indigenous to those countries (Cornish and Manx in Britain, for example), the late twentieth-century attempt to reverse the trend of language attrition has come far too late for their first-language native speakers. And it is true of states that have retained their sovereignty over long centuries: Thailand and Ethiopia are two examples of multilingual nation-states that spring to mind. In both of these cases, a single national language centred around the court and the capital has consistently been used as a tool to forge national unity, without snuffing out the many languages of purely local currency that have survived within their borders.

There are many pitfalls in trying to generalise on a global scale about what causes language attrition. The economic factors that lead to language death are undeniably important, but they are not uniform. We can say with some certainty that urbanisation is a killer of languages, especially if rapid economic change takes place over one or two generations and attracts the rural poor to urban centres in search of work. Not only does urbanisation fragment families, especially in post-colonial states, where the breadwinner may be constrained to move to the city from a subsistence economy to earn a livelihood in a new major-language environment, but it generally fails to provide an institutional basis for maintenance of the non-local languages within the new urban environment.

Economic factors, however, do not merely attract small linguistic populations to the urban centres and erode the nutrients from the soil of their continued existence; they also contribute to the linguistic invasion of even the most settled speech communities. Increased local and national wealth brings with it the opportunity and the desire to 'plug in' to global communications networks, with all the linguistic baggage that this implies. In the late twentieth and early twenty-first centuries, more than ever, the key to linguistic hegemony lies in the possession of the media. And here we confront a painful moral dilemma of our age: should we deny the populations of what we have come to see as unspoiled rural Arcadias the access they crave to the knowledge we have at our fingertips, which is only available through the medium of a few standardised major languages? Even if 'we' wanted to, 'we' could do nothing to prevent it. The agents of change are no longer the bands of conquistadors of 500 years ago, who changed the linguistic map of 'Latin' America forever; they are the faceless mortals who sit at millions of computer screens dotted all over the globe.

Allied to this problem is another, to which linguists cannot be indifferent; should the effort to rescue a language from annihilation come from inside or outside the speech community? Linguists who are outsiders must be sufficiently well trained as anthropologists, sufficiently observant and methodical as scientists, and sufficiently compassionate and sensitive as human beings, to be able to tackle both of these problems head-on. When a language is on the threshold of extinction, its speakers may well be demoralised in other, non-linguistic ways as well – economically deprived, dependent on aid, malnourished, unable or unwilling to draw on their cultural or religious traditions: any combination of these factors is possible. While it is not reasonable to expect the linguist to provide for all of these needs, it is impossible to act as if one were unaware of them. Likewise, the linguist may also be acting out of motives that are other than strictly linguistic. Much pioneering fieldwork among speakers of minority and endangered languages has been done by field-workers with missionary aims, for instance notably by the Summer Institute of Linguistics. The Institute's publication *Ethnologue* is the most comprehensive compendium of the world's languages that has yet been produced, and frequent reference will be made to its findings in the pages of this volume.

In the past decade leading up to the publication of this encyclopedia there have been various initiatives to foster awareness of the accelerating rate of the loss of languages. The UNESCO Red Book, which appeared in 1993, was a pioneering effort in this direction. Then in 1995 the University of Tokyo set up a Clearing House for endangered languages, the emphasis being on recording newly discovered instances of disappearing languages rather than taking action to preserve them. There swiftly followed the creation of 'activist' groups on both sides of the Atlantic in 1995: in the USA, the Endangered Languages Fund (ELF), and in Britain, the Foundation for Endangered Languages (FEL). These bodies have taken an active part in the actual preservation of endangered languages, by acting as charitable grant-giving bodies which make awards to scholars who are doing valuable investigative work; they stipulate that the published results of the work undertaken shall benefit the community concerned. The prestige of the study of endangered languages was further enhanced in 2002 with the creation of the first university chair in the subject by the Rausing Foundation at the School of Oriental and African Studies in London. This foundation, too, is engaged in giving grants for research projects that it deems will assist in language recovery.

Training of linguists in language documentation is a crucial issue for the future, and courses like the one offered in London are a valuable and all too rare asset, if the task of reclaiming disappearing languages is to be met. Perhaps new disciplines within linguistics and in cross-fertilisation with other scientific disciplines will arise in the near future as a result of the academic interest in endangered languages; one possible pointer to the future was indicated in an article on 'Ecolinguistics' – the comparison of language attrition with ecological decline, by Professor Bill Sutherland in *Nature* (May 2003). Fruitful collaboration with the disciplines of anthropology and sociology may result in a better understanding of the power relations between strong and weak languages within and beyond national boundaries. And the full implications of the economic causes and effects of language switching have yet to be understood.

The serious study of language endangerment and attrition is still in its infancy. It is an ironical fact that the estimated number of languages in the world was put as much lower at a time when the real number was much higher than it is now, as David Crystal points out in the introductory chapter of his book *Language Death* (2000). The estimated number, he notes, has grown from around a thousand, a conjectural figure, mentioned in 1874, to the 4,500 or so listed in the first attempt to catalogue them all, the Voegelins' *Classification and Index of the World's Languages* (1977), and on to the 6,703 entries cited in the 1996 edition of *Ethnologue*. The *Atlas of the World's Languages* (Moseley and Asher (eds) 1994) mapped well over 6,000 languages.

In compiling this volume, inevitably we have come up against the age-old question of 'what is a language, as opposed to a dialect?' Since in the case of endangered languages the adage 'a language is a dialect with an army and a navy' cannot possibly apply, we have had to err on the side of generosity: sometimes there is so little information to go on that the question is left in doubt. *Ethnologue* is fairly firm about the distinction, based on percentages of mutual intelligibility and common lexicon, but the section editors in this volume have also had to consider historical and geographical factors: 'dialects' that have sprung from a language may have developed in isolation from each other and been subjected to different endangering factors, acquired different levels of prestige. We have necessarily favoured 'splitting' over 'lumping' rather than run the risk of omitting what might emerge as a unique disappearing language, for want of information.

The size of this volume alone should give an indication of the extent of the problem of language endangerment. Arbitrary cut-off points in terms of sheer numbers of speakers cannot be made to apply throughout the world, so in the following pages you will find languages with mere hundreds of speakers referred to as potentially endangered, while those with thousands or tens of thousands might be described as severely endangered. Complex factors are involved, but reduced to a nutshell the deciding factor is *rate of attrition,* or the likelihood of a language being passed on to the next generation. But in strictly quantifiable terms, Crystal constructed a table in his *Language Death* based on the alarming statistic that 96 per cent of the world's languages are spoken by 4 per cent of its population. Tabulating the world's languages in terms of numbers of their speakers, from '1–9' (181 contenders) at the lowest level to 'more than 100 million' (eight contenders) at the highest, he established that the median number of speakers for a language is 6,000, and that if 20,000 speakers were taken as a danger-level (which is a moot point, but would not be far from the average for the languages included in this book), then two thirds of the world's languages are in danger.

That fact alone stands as an urgent reason for compiling an encyclopedia such as this. For each language given an entry in this volume, our editors have tried to assess the level of endangerment that faces the language, given the circumstances described in the entry. Generally speaking they follow a five-grade scale as described by the late Stephen Wurm:

- *potentially endangered*, which usually implies lack of prestige in the home country, economic deprivation, pressure from larger languages in the public sphere and social fragmentation in the private, to the extent that the language is not being systematically passed on in the education system;
- *endangered*, where the youngest fluent speakers tend to be young adults, and there is a disjunction in passing on the language to children, especially in the school but even in the home environment;
- *seriously/severely endangered*, with the youngest fluent speakers being among the older generation aged fifty and over, implying a loss of prestige and social value over a generation ago;
- *moribund*, with only a tiny proportion of the ethnic group speaking the language, mostly the very aged;
- *extinct*, where no speakers remain. This last category, in terms of this encyclopedia, means that a language whose existence is remembered by living people in the community merits inclusion, because there is at least the faint or theoretical possibility of revival.

This encyclopedia does not claim to be a manual for language rescue, and it contains no recipes for language preservation. But it does, I hope, make an eloquent case for maintaining the irreplaceable treasure-house of the world's language stocks in all their variety, against all the odds stacked against them and wherever possible. Humankind is the poorer for the loss of even a single language.

Humankind – not just its speakers, who may themselves be past caring about the fate of their own tongue. Why? To cite but a few reasons, speakers of languages indigenous to a particular area tend to have a unique and intimate knowledge of the flora and fauna and the natural resources of their own habitat, one which often outstrips the widespread Western languages in its ability to divide up and classify the natural world. This would be reason enough for their preservation if language was just the business of naming things; but language is much more than that. It also reflects man's affective relation to the perceived cosmos, and Western linguists have come to appreciate this more and more ever since the work of the American linguist Benjamin Lee Whorf on the Hopi world-view. If you would like to explore indigenous cosmologies and their reflection in human language further, you will find plenty of references in the short reading list appended at the end of this introduction. Human relations, too, family and clan structure, are uniquely reflected in language: kinship terminology is remarkably diverse from one language group to another. Australian aboriginal languages, for instance – collectively among the most endangered languages in the world – contain intricate sets of kinship terms which not only reflect the structure of family and clan relations but govern human behaviour, and as their societies fragment and their languages atrophy, the niceties of kinship terminologies are among the first features to be lost.

And what are the causes of language attrition? Time and time again in the entries listed in this book you will find recurring factors which tend to lead to language loss. Most are man-made; some are imposed by nature, often with brutal suddenness. At the time of writing these lines, one of the worst natural calamities in recorded history is still a fresh memory: the *tsunami* wave which struck the shorelines of the Indian Ocean, decimating populations in numbers which may never be known. Who knows what the effect on the world's language stocks will be? Particularly close to its epicentre were the Andaman and Nicobar islands, whose aboriginal populations speak a number of endangered languages (some of them actually language isolates, with no known relatives) which you will find listed in the chapter on South Asia in this volume.

To enumerate some of the other more immediate reasons for language loss, some are a conspiracy between man and nature: for instance epidemic disease, which decimates communities, or soil erosion, which may force them to shift or change livelihood. And if the soil is not taken over by natural forces, it may simply be seized by economically more powerful groups. Dispersing a minority population is usually a sure way of dissolving its language.

Cohesion of the nation-state, especially a recently formed one, is in some cases the altar on which minority languages are sacrificed. Throughout Africa and Latin America in particular, but also in parts of Asia and the Pacific, colonial languages are used as a political tool to weld a nation together. Direct political prohibition of an indigenous language is not the usual method of denigrating or suppressing it; rather subtler means tend to be used to ensure small languages are not passed on, such as excluding them from the education system or the press, or religious life. Even stridently anti-'colonialist' nation-states, such as Zimbabwe, use the language of the 'oppressor' to enforce a single-nation identity in the face of multilingualism. It must be said, though, that the plight of minority languages in Zimbabwe is not necessarily any worse than in its more democratic neighbour states, and it would be rash to blame colonial languages in general for the attrition of indigenous ones. The ex-colonial situation is complex; as Adegbija points out (in Fishman 2000, pp. 284–7), nation-states in Africa tend to inflate the prestige of certain big indigenous languages along-side the ex-colonial administrative ones (Bambara in Mali; Yoruba, Hausa, Igbo in Nigeria, and so on) with the consequent denigration of the indigenous 'minnows' by these 'big fish'.

Over the centuries and millennia, civilisations rise and fall, and leave their tide-marks on the linguistic composition of their successor nations. For instance, modern Mexico, a largely Spanish-speaking nation but with a patchwork of surviving indi-genous languages, has experienced huge fluctuations in population in the centuries before and since the arrival of the conquistadors 500 years ago. (For more detail on this fluctuation see Garzón and Lastra in Robins and Uhlenbeck 1995, p. 100.) But unlike so many African nations, Mexico has not fostered any particular indigenous language for a prestigious role in either national or regional life. In this respect Mexico is following the general Latin American pattern, to which the only real exception is found in Paraguay, where Guaraní enjoys equal status with Spanish and is flourishing in most areas of communication.

Colonial attitudes to indigenous languages are of course also reflected in the present state of knowledge of, and data collection on, threatened indigenous languages. In so many parts of the world conquered by Europeans, colonial administrators' attitudes to indigenous languages ranged from indifference to contempt. But this was not the case everywhere: in India, for example, the methodical Linguistic Survey conducted between 1886 and 1927 has saved for posterity, if not all the languages themselves, then at least data that is invaluable to modern scholars and which, in some cases, has not been bettered since by scholars in independent India and Pakistan. The modern Indian situation is rather unique, wherein certain languages are designated 'Scheduled' as part of the system of 'Scheduled tribes', whereas others are ignored by statisticians and scholars alike.

Language planning at the national level is conducted in widely varying ways. Con-trast the multi-layered situation in post-colonial India with that in post-colonial Papua New Guinea, which has the greatest concentration of distinct languages of anywhere in the world, and yet few of its languages are seriously endangered, owing to weak central administration, haphazard communication over mountainous terrain, under-developed infrastructure, natural multilingualism among contiguous sedentary popu-lations, and where there is a drift towards a 'metropolitan' language, it is only towards the standardised colonial (English) language in a restricted number of domains, the main thrust being towards Tok Pisin (PNG pidgin).

Papua New Guinea is one area, then, where a wide variety of indigenous languages are assured a future for some foreseeable time. But for those parts of the world where languages are disappearing before linguists' eyes, as fast as the ice-shelf of Antarctica under global warming, it might seem, the temptation is to set about rescuing lan-guages before it is too late.

Language rescue cannot be imposed from outside; and it is not usually the business of linguists to interfere in political processes. Ultimately communities must help themselves, with informed decisions and the perspective of more than one generation.

But before the community can help itself, the language must be *codified* – set down in some permanent form. Initially this process may require outside help, but not always. Let us not forget Sequoia, inventor of the Cherokee syllabary in the nineteenth century, who made it possible for his fellow-speakers to read and write their own language. Usually, though, those who first codify a minority language are outsiders – ideally, trained linguists with the capacity to pick up the salient phonetic, semantic and syntactic subtleties of an unfamiliar tongue. Often they will have an ulterior motive, a missionary one perhaps, but purely from the point of view of codification that is no bad thing. Exhaustive analysis of a language is required before the translation of the Christian Gospels can begin. Once the turning point of codification has been reached, a language may possibly be on the road to recovery, because codification implies that a language can be passed on at more than just the individual level, and thus acquires a certain increase in prestige for its own speakers.

Once a language is on the road to recovery, what other factors can promote its survival? Not all the factors promoting survival are purely linguistic ones. As David Crystal points out in *Language Death*, causes of survival include:

- increased prestige within the dominant community (witness the revival of Basque and Welsh in recent years, to cite European examples);
- increased wealth relative to the dominant community (witness the strong Catalan economy, and hence language, in Spain);
- increased legitimate power, or stronger rights, within the dominant community (but this may be the result of legislation by supranational bodies, such as the European Union);
- a strong presence in the educational system – at least regionally, but ideally at a national level;
- literacy – which implies a codified written language.

Other, longer lists of preconditions for advancement have been posited by linguists, but these are the basic ones.

Joshua Fishman, in his book *Can Threatened Languages be Saved?* (Fishman (ed.) 2001, and earlier in *Reversing Language Shift*, 1991), a book dedicated to the theme of reversing language shift, posited what he called the GIDS or Graded Intergenerational Disruption Scale – a quantifying measure that has been cited a lot subsequently. Fishman sees two major phases as necessary: the attainment of diglossia, and the stages beyond diglossia. Within each of these phases are four stages. Within the first major phase there is progression through reconstruction of the language and adult acquisition of it; cultural interaction in the language, primarily involving the older generation; mother-tongue transmission in the home, family and community; and schools for literacy acquisition. In the post-diglossia phase, the minority imposes the curriculum and staff on schools and provides some education in the minority language; the language penetrates the local and regional work sphere; it reaches the mass media and public offices; and finally, it becomes a part of the education system, the workplace, the mass media and government operations.

The destruction or decay of a language follows certain reasonably well defined paths. Patterns borrowed from the encroaching language impose themselves on the receding one in a particular order. At the present of stage, it would be unwise to state too categorically whether syntax, phonology, grammar or vocabulary are eroded first in an endangered language; what we can say is that the erosion occurs at all levels over time. Unique elements are lost in the process – features that at first may appear to be of curiosity only to linguists, but which have implications for the study of human thought and society itself.

This implies that linguistic fieldworkers must be hypersensitive to the nuances of language shift at several levels at once. The late Ken Hale, who more than most linguists had direct experience of language diversity, put it this way:

> The loss of local languages, and of the cultural systems which they express, has meant irretrievable loss of diverse and interesting intellectual wealth, the priceless products of human mental industry. The process of language loss is ongoing. Many linguistic fieldworkers have had, and will continue to have, the experience of bearing witness to the loss, for all time, of a language and of the cultural products which the language served to express for the intellectual nourishment of its speakers.
>
> (quoted from Grenoble and Whaley 1998)

Elements of language lost through attrition, for example, may involve a blunting of fine distinctions in, say, the pronoun system. In the Kiwai language of Papua New Guinea, the system of first person singular and plural actors vs. patients has largely been lost through contact with neighbouring languages which lack that feature. (Wurm, cited in Robins and Uhlenbeck 1995, pp. 10–11). Sometimes an endangered language may take on the morphology of its 'oppressor', as happened with the language or dialect continuum of the Aleutian Islands under Russian influence. Insufficient research has been done so far to categorically list the order of disappearance of the elements of eroding languages (phonology, morphology, grammar, lexicon, syntax) and the factors affecting this order, but it is one of the urgent tasks facing the burgeoning study of language endangerment.

Arrangement of this book

The encyclopedia is arranged into geographical regions, each the work of a separate regional editor.

A general introduction to the chapter describes the linguistic situation in the region as a whole, and this is followed by individual entries on each language in alphabetical order, giving the linguistic affiliation, demographic data, the degree of endangerment and the causes of the threat to it. The texts in each chapter are accompanied by maps showing some of the denser and more complex concentrations of endangered languages, to give the reader some geographical bearings.

Further reading

You will find bibliographies at the end of each chapter of the encyclopedia, but for more general reading on the subject of language endangerment, the following are especially recommended:

Mark Abley, *Spoken Here: Travels among Threatened Languages* (2003) is a very readable and entertaining excursion across the world by a sympathetic and knowledgeable observer, who keenly feels the personal effects of language loss on the individual.

David Crystal, *Language Death* (2000) is an excellent general introduction to all aspects of the theme of language endangerment and loss, and why it is important.

Suzanne Romaine and Daniel Nettle, *Vanishing Voices* (2001) is also a very readable account of the emerging scope of the language endangerment problem world-wide that is becoming apparent to linguistic science.

Leanne Hinton and Ken Hale (eds) *The Green Book of Language Revitalization in Practice* (2001) is intended as a practical guide to the solutions to language attrition and loss, and although its geographical coverage is patchy, it offers numerous practical solutions and invaluable experience.

Similarly practical, but with a more academic bias, is Joshua A. Fishman (ed.) *Can Threatened Languages be Saved?* (2000), which sets out clearly the theoretical basis for classifying degrees of endangerment.

R. H. Robins and E. Uhlenbeck, *Endangered Languages* (1995) was something of a pioneering work in this young field, and although some of its findings have been superseded to some extent, it achieved a global coverage of the issue quite effectively.

Lenore A. Grenoble and Lindsay Whaley, *Endangered Languages and Community Response* (1998) takes a more academic approach to the subject but is full of examples which are otherwise little documented.

For an overview of the world as seen from the point of view of the 'big' languages as they rise and fall over time, Nicholas Ostler's *Empires of the Word* (2005) is highly recommended.

Also recommended are the annual *Proceedings* volumes of the Foundation for Endangered Languages, each on a different theme, the outcome of the Foundation's annual conferences.

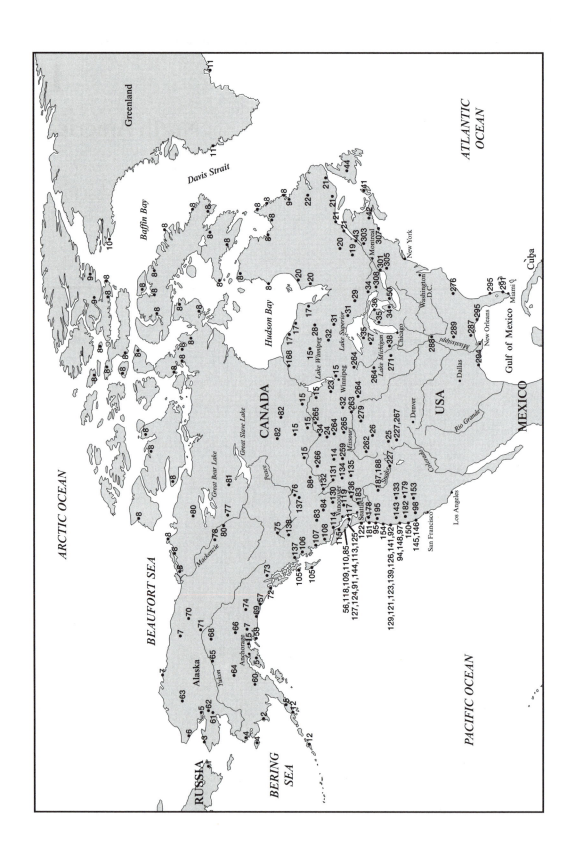

1

North America

Victor Golla

Introduction

The languages treated in this chapter are the indigenous languages of North America, defined as the territory of the United States and Canada, the immediately adjacent areas of northern Mexico (including Baja California), and Greenland. Although some of these languages are more immediately threatened than others, only a handful are spoken by more than 10,000 people and all must be considered endangered in the long term.

Origins

Even taking into account recent archaeological discoveries in South America, incontrovertible evidence of human activity in the western hemisphere can be dated no earlier than 12,500 years before the present (Dillehay 2000). This indicates that the Americas were the last major land mass to be reached by our species after its expansion from Africa about 100,000 years ago, contrasting with a date of at least 40,000 BP for the human settlement of Australia. However, American Indian languages show considerably greater diversity in their grammars and vocabularies than the indigenous languages of Australia, and some have argued that 12,500 years is too short a time to have produced so many distinct language families exhibiting such deep-seated typological differences (Nichols 1990).

The current state of our knowledge of American prehistory does not allow a resolution of this question. It seems clear, however, that part of the reason for the diversity of the languages of the Americas generally, and of North America specifically, lies in the long-term operation of social processes that promote a multitude of small linguistic communities. While precise figures are impossible to determine, it is likely that at the time of European contact the average number of speakers of a North American language was only a few thousand. During the historical period only a handful of North American languages were spoken by groups significantly larger than this, and most of these appear to have been the result of post-contact cultural changes (the spread of Cree and Ojibwe was largely due to the fur trade, while the Cherokee and Navajo nations are political artifacts of the eighteenth and nineteenth century). Traditional alliances such as the League of the Iroquois or the Creek Confederacy were typically multilingual, and even trade languages or lingua francas were rare and largely post-contact. In California and Oregon, where the tendency to local identity was amplified by a complex geography and ecology, some language communities appear to have numbered only a few hundred speakers. Even where trade and intermarriage were common, adjoining tribes usually had clear linguistic boundaries and multilingualism was frequent.

Survival

The social forces that have generated a multitude of small, distinct language communities appear also to have promoted their survival for many generations after the European penetration and domination of the continent. Until recent decades, the number of North American languages that continued to be spoken was remarkably high, despite remarkably small numbers of speakers. In the classification adopted here, 312 distinct indigenous languages are recognized as having been been spoken during the past 500 years in North America. Of these, only sixty-five became extinct, or were last documented, before about 1930. Most of these were spoken in the areas along the Atlantic and Gulf of Mexico where Europeans almost totally displaced indigenous populations.

The rate of attrition has accelerated considerably during the last seventy years. Of the 247 languages that survived past 1930, a little under one fourth (fifty-eight) have already ceased to be spoken as first languages, a loss of about nine languages per decade, and more will follow soon. This sudden decline is an index of the economic and political integration of indigenous people into the general North American population and their absorption into general North American political and economic culture. Since the passage of the Indian Reorganization Act of 1934, native identity in the United States has largely been defined through federally recognized tribal governments which, although unique to American Indians, are thoroughly Euro-American in their underlying values and modes of operation. A similar transformation took place in Canada, although somewhat later and at a slower pace. This was followed by the incorporation of many reservation communities into the national economies of the US and Canada in the postwar years. The consequent peripheralization of traditional cultural activities led to the replacement of native languages by English (or French in parts of Canada) as the general code of community interaction, further encouraged by the growth of satellite television and the internet in the 1980s and 1990s.

However, despite the loss of speakers, many North American Indian languages endure. A few speech communities remain remarkably intact, with the traditional language still acquired by most children and used for most social purposes. These communities are either geographically remote (such as Attikamek Cree) or protected by strong social boundaries (such as Picuris and Santo Domingo Pueblos). In most communities language use is rapidly eroding, and all are vulnerable to the homogenizing trend of North American society.

The languages that are still spoken can be divided into five groups according to the size of their speech communities and their prospects for long-term survival:

2

1 Languages with only one known native speaker, and consequently on the verge of extinction. At the time of writing there were five languages in this category: Eyak, Klamath-Modoc, Northern Pomo, Tolowa, and Unami Delaware.

2 Languages with more than one native speaker but fewer than ten, and rapidly approaching extinction. Included here are thirty-six languages: Achumawi, Arikara, Central Pomo, Central Sierra Miwok, Chiwere, Coeur d'Alene, Eastern Pomo, Holikachuk, Ipai Diegueño, Kawaiisu, Kiksht, Kiliwa, Kings River Yokuts, Kiowa Apache (Plains Apache), Klallam, Konkow, Lake Miwok, Luiseño, Lushootseed, Mandan, Northern Sierra Miwok, Osage, Patwin, Pawnee, Sarcee (Tsuut'ina), Serrano, Southern Pomo, Southern Sierra Miwok, Tubatulabal, Tule-Kaweah Yokuts, Tuscarora, Wappo, Western Abenaki, Wichita, Wintu-Nomlaki, and Yuchi (Euchee).

3 Languages with from ten to 100 speakers, none of them children. These languages are severely endangered, but will probably continue to have a few first-language speakers for at least another generation. About one third (forty-four) of surviving languages fall into this category, and include: Ahtna, Bella Coola, Caddo, Cahuilla, Columbian, Comanche, Comox, Copper Island Aleut Creole, Gros Ventre (Atsina), Haida, Han, Hare, Hupa, Ingalik (Deg Xinag), Karuk, Kashaya, Kumeyaay Diegueño, Kutenai, Lower Tanana, Makah, Menominee, Mohave, Mono, Naukanski Yupik, Nez Perce, Nitinaht, Nootka (Nuuchahnulth), Northern Straits Salish, Omaha-Ponca, Onondaga, Paipai, Panamint (Tümpisa Shoshone), Potawatomi, Sechelt, Sekani, Spokane-Kalispel, Squamish, Tahltan, Tanacross, Tanaina (Dena'ina), Upper Kuskokwim, Valley Yokuts, Washo, and Yurok.

4 Languages with more than 100 speakers but fewer than 1,000, some of them still spoken by at least a few children. These languages are endangered, but most will survive for two or more generations. There are forty-seven languages in this category: Alabama, Aleut, Assiniboine (Nakota), Babine, Bearlake, Beaver, Cayuga, Chickasaw, Chilcotin (Tsilhqot'in), Cocopa, Gwich'in (Kutchin), Haisla, Halkomelem, Heiltsuk-Oowekyala, Hidatsa, Jicarilla, Kaska, Kiowa, Koasati (Coushatta), Koyukon, Kwakiutl (Kwak'wala), Lillooet (St'at'imcets), Maliseet-Passamaquoddy, Maricopa, Maritime Tsimshianic, Michif, Mountain, Nass-Gitksan, Northern Paiute (Paviotso), Northern Tutchone, Okanagan, Oneida, Pacific Yupik (Alutiiq), Picuris, Quechan (Yuma), Sahaptin, Sauk-Fox (Mesquakie), Seneca, Shawnee, Shuswap (Secwepemc), Southern Tutchone, Taos, Thompson, Tipai Diegueño, Tlingit, Upper Tanana, and Winnebago (Ho-Chunk).

5 Languages with 1,000 or more speakers, all of them being acquired by children. There are fifty-five languages in this category, with the largest (Navajo) having about 120,000 speakers; the average number of speakers is between 9,000 and 10,000. Of the fifty-five languages, twenty-one are sub-languages of two widespread Algonquian languages, Cree and Ojibwe, and of three equally widespread Eskimo languages, Greenlandic, Inuktitut, and Inupiaq. None of these languages is seriously endangered and most are likely to survive for at least a century, although in the longer term their status is far from secure. Included in this category are: Acoma-Laguna, Arapaho, Blackfoot, Carrier, Central Alaskan Yup'ik, Central Siberian Yupik,Cherokee, Cheyenne, Chipewyan, Choctaw, Cree-Montagnais-Naskapi (eight sub-languages), Creek (Muskogee), Crow,

3

Dogrib, Greenlandic (two sub-languages), Hopi, Inuktitut (two sub-languages), Inupiaq (two sub-languages), Jemez, Kickapoo, Mescalero-Chiricahua, Micmac, Mikasuki, Mohawk, Navajo, Ojibwe (seven sub-languages), Rio Grande Keresan, Shoshoni, Sioux, Slave, Southern Tiwa, Stoney, Tewa, Upland Yuman, Upper Piman (O'odham), Ute-Chemehuevi, Western Apache, Yaqui (Yoeme), and Zuni.

Extinct languages

As noted above, sixty-five languages are known to have become extinct before 1930. No memory of these languages being fluently spoken survives among modern descendants. Equally important, the last speakers died before the advent of tape recorders or easily portable phonograph disc recorders, and thus no significant documentation of their spoken reality exists beyond the written transcriptions of linguists, anthropologists, missionaries, and (not infrequently) untrained amateur collectors. The future study, and possible revitalization, of these languages must depend on archival research, and the prospects vary with the abundance of documentation. As many as fifty of the sixty-five are little more than scholarly curiosities, attested only in a few wordlists that sometimes date back (as with Laurentian and Virginia Algonquian) four centuries or more. Fewer than a dozen can be called well attested, in the majority of cases owing to the the diligent work of survey linguists working for the Bureau of American Ethnology in the late nineteenth and early twentieth century. This includes the extensive documentation of Eastern Atakapa and Biloxi by Albert S. Gatschet; of Kathlamet and Pentlatch by Franz Boas; and of Chochenyo, Mutsun and Rumsen – three Costanoan languages – by J. P. Harrington. The thorough and accurate data collected by Edward Sapir on Takelma and Yana, much of which he analyzed and published, put these languages in a class by themselves, in many ways making them better known than dozens of languages still spoken. Mention should also be made of three extinct languages that were extensively (if not exclusively) documented by seventeenth-century missionaries: Timucua by Spanish missionaries in Florida; Massachusett-Narragansett by John Eliot, a New England divine; and Old Algonquin by the Jesuits in Canada.

Classification

The classification adopted here is a modified version of the 'Consensus Classification' published in Volume 17, Languages, of the *Handbook of North American Indian Languages* (Goddard 1996a: 4–8), differing from it principally in the omission of a few languages of northen Mexico that fall outside the purview of this chapter. It divides the 312 languages of North America to fifty-eight classificatory units, including:

Fourteen major language families, made up of several languages with significant sub-grouping: (1) ESKIMO-ALEUT, (2) ALGIC, (3) NA-DENE, (5) WAKASHAN, (7) SALISHAN, (17) UTIAN, (19) PLATEAU PENUTIAN, (27) COCHIMÍ-YUMAN, (33) UTO-AZTECAN, (34) KIOWA-TANOAN, (45) SIOUAN-CATAWBA, (47) CADDOAN, (52) MUSKOGEAN, and (57) IROQUOIAN.

Eighteen minor language families, made up of a small number of relatively closely related (usually contiguous) languages: (6) CHIMAKUAN, (8) TSIMSHIANIC, (9) CHINOOKAN,

(12) COOSAN, (14) KALAPUYAN, (15) WINTUAN, (16) MAIDUAN, (18) YOKUTS, (22) SHASTAN, (23) PALAIHNIHAN, (24) POMOAN, (26) SALINAN, (28) GUAICURIAN, (30) YUKIAN, (32) CHU-MASHAN, (35) KERESAN, (38) COMECRUDAN, and (49) ATAKAPAN.

Twenty-five classificatory isolates, individual languages or dialect areas that cannot be assigned to a larger unit: (4) HAIDA, (10) ALSEAN, (11) SIUSLAW, (13) TAKELMAN, (20) KARUK, (21) CHIMARIKO, (25) YANA, (29) WASHO, (31) ESSELEN, (36) ZUNI, (37) COA-HUILTECO, (39) COTONAME, (40) ARANAMA, (41) SOLANO, (42) KARANKAWA, (43) KOOTENAI, (44) CAYUSE, (46) TONKAWA, (48) ADAI, (50) CHITIMACHA, (51) TUNICA, (53) NATCHEZ, (54) YUCHI, (55) TIMUCUAN, (56) CALUSA, and (58) BEOTHUK.

This classification is admittedly a conservative one, reflecting only the relationships which are considered to be proven by the majority of scholars. Most of the units it recognizes were included in the first general classification of North American languages, over a century ago (Powell 1891), the only significant additions being seven families: Eskimo-Aleut, Algic (Yurok, Wiyot and Algonquian), Na-Dene (Tlingit, Eyak, and Athabaskan), Plateau Penutian, Kiowa-Tanoan, Siouan-Catawba, and Uto-Aztecan. (The present classification also follows modern opinion in splitting one of Powell's families, Yakonan, into Alsean and Siuslaw.)

Many proposals for more inclusive groupings have been made, the most influential by Sapir (1921; 1929), Voegelin and Voegelin (1965), and Greenberg (1987), summarized in Goddard (1996b: 308–23) and Campbell (1997: 66–80).

Sapir proposed that all attested North American languages could be grouped into six phyla: Eskimo-Aleut, Na-Dene (expanded to include Haida), Algonkin-Wakashan, Hokan-Siouan, Penutian, and Aztec-Tanoan. An outline of his evidence – as much morphological and typological as it is lexical – is laid out in Sapir (1929). Subsequent research indicated that some of the relationships within Sapir's framework were more promising than others, and that similar evidence for different interconnections could be adduced. The most active researcher in this area in the 1950s and 1960s was Haas (see Haas 1969), and some of her proposals, together with others, were brought together in a revised version of Sapir's scheme that was published by Voegelin and Voegelin (1965). This classification recognizes seven phyla: American Arctic-Paleosiberian (connecting Eskimo-Aleut with Chukchi-Kamchatkan), Na-Dene, Macro-Algonquian, Macro-Siouan, Hokan, Penutian, and Aztec-Tanoan, with nine smaller classificatory units ranging from the Salish and Wakashan families to the Beothuk and Kutenai language isolates.

The most recent large-scale reassessment of North American historical relationships is contained in the hemisphere-wide classification proposed by Greenberg (1987). Working with the multilateral comparison of raw vocabulary resemblances, Greenberg found evidence for the ultimate relationship of nearly all indigenous American languages in a stock he called 'Amerind'. This stock, in turn, is divided into phyla, ... of which encompass most of the languages of North America: Almosan-Keresiouan, Hokan, and Penutian. Standing outside of Amerind, however, are Sapir's Eskimo-Aleut and Na-Dene groups, which in a subsequent classification of the languages of Eurasia (2000) Greenberg linked to ... and ... respectively.

Whatever their differences, all of the larger-scale classifications of North American languages agree on including the following four groupings, which may be considered the most promising (or at least most enduring) of the higher-order classifications for the continent:

1. Macro-Siouan: (45) SIOUAN-CATAWBA, (47) CADDOAN, and (57) IROQUOIAN.
2. Hokan. Originally proposed by Dixon and Kroeber (1913), this relationship among the isolates and minor families of California and the Southwest is now generally considered by its proponents to include (20) KARUK, (21) CHIMARIKO, (22) SHASTAN, (23) PALAIHNIHAN, (24) POMOAN, (25) YANA, (26) SALINAN, (27) COCHIMÍ-YUMAN, and (29) WASHO. It is sometimes extended to include (28) GUAICURIAN, (31) ESSELEN, and (32) CHUMASHAN, and at least some of the poorly documented long-extinct language isolates and small families in Texas and Northern Mexico that have been called 'Coahuiltecan' – (37) COAHUILTECO, (38) COMECRUDAN, (39) COTONAME, (40) ARANAMA, (41) SOLANO, and (42) KARANKAWA.
3. Penutian. Also originally proposed by Dixon and Kroeber (1913) as a relationship among four California families – (15) WINTUAN, (16) MAIDUAN, (17) UTIAN, and (18) YOKUTS – it was expanded by Sapir to include a number of isolates and small families to the north of California, specifically (8) TSIMSHIANIC, (9) CHINOOKAN, (10) ALSEAN, (11) SIUSLAW, (12) COOSAN, (13) TAKELMAN, (14) KALAPUYAN, and (19) PLATEAU PENUTIAN. In addition to these, proponents of the Penutian phylum sometimes also include (36) ZUNI.
4. Aztec-Tanoan: (33) UTO-AZTECAN and (34) KIOWA-TANOAN.

Loss of classificatory diversity

Of the fifty-eight classificatory units, exactly half (twenty-nine) are now extinct – sixteen having become extinct before 1930 and thirteen since then. Much of this loss is due to the extinction of classificatory isolates, only six of which survive, although half of the eighteen minor families are also extinct. In addition, several branches of major families have been lost: Southern New England Algonquian within Algonquian; Tsamosan within Salishan; Costanoan within Utian; Cochimí within Cochimí-Yuman; and Catawban within Siouan-Catawba.

This loss of diversity will almost certainly accelerate in the near future. A major subdivision of Na-Dene will be extinguished with the death of the one remaining speaker of Eyak, and five of the nine remaining small language families – Chinookan, Maiduan, Palaihnihan, Wintuan, and Yukian – survive in the speech of less than a score of very elderly people.

Documentation and scholarship

North American Indian languages are relatively well documented, at least by comparison to the indigenous languages of South America and New Guinea. A missionary tradition of translating the Christian scriptures into Indian languages, beginning in New England and New France in the seventeenth century and continuing through the twentieth century, has left many important monuments. In addition to full translations of the Bible into such languages as New England Algonquian, Plains Cree, Creek, and Gwich'in, extensive dictionaries and detailed grammars were produced, and in at least two important instances – a syllabic script for Plains Cree that was later extended to a number of Canadian languages, and an alphabetic orthography for Creek that became widespread in Oklahoma – major, enduring traditions of literacy were introduced by missionary work.

A tradition of secular scholarship began during the Enlightenment, focusing on classification and typology (Thomas Jefferson was an early collector of Indian vocabularies).

Except for important advances in understanding family relationships, these efforts remained relatively superficial until the 1870s. With the founding of the Bureau of American Ethnology in 1879 under the direction of the explorer and linguist John Wesley Powell, documentation of Indian languages became a government priority and a team of trained fieldworkers was sent out to collect extensive vocabularies and other materials. An accurate and comprehensive classification of all North American languages was published by the BAE before the end of the century (Powell 1891) and at least a few languages received detailed attention (such as Albert Gatschet's documentation of Klamath-Modoc and several languages of the Southeast; J. Owen Dorsey's studies of the Dakotan languages; and, most significantly, Franz Boas's work on Chinookan, Wakashan, and Salishan languages in the Northwest).

In 1897, Boas established a research program at Columbia University that focused on American Indian languages and cultures, and in the ensuing decades substantial efforts were made to collect thorough lexical and grammatical data, and representative traditional texts, from dozens of languages. These were often chosen for study because of their classificatory distinctness and dwindling numbers of speakers, and the richness of the data that has been preserved from a number of languages that are now extinct owes much to this deliberate strategy. This is especially the case with the work of Boas's student, Edward Sapir, whose accurate and penetrating descriptive work on Wishram Chinook, Takelma, Yana, Southern Paiute, Nootka, and several Athabaskan languages has made these languages among the best known of all indigenous American languages. From 1925 to 1939 Sapir himself trained a new generation of descriptive linguists, many of whom carried out detailed studies of North American Indian languages, including Fang-Kuei Li, Harry Hoijer, Mary Haas, and Morris Swadesh. Special mention must be made of John Peabody Harrington, a fieldworker for the Bureau of American Ethnology from 1915 to 1953, whose personal dedication to collecting accurate and extensive data from languages that were close to extinction was legendary.

Academically trained linguists continue to produce important descriptive studies of North American Indian languages, and at the beginning of the twenty-first century nearly every North American Indian language that continues to be spoken has its own small tradition of study. An international organization (the Society for the Study of the Indigenous Languages of the Americas, SSILA) represents the body of American Indian language scholars, most of whom are professional linguists or anthropologists. Annual meetings are held by SSILA and by smaller regional groups, including specialists in Athabaskan, Algonquian, Salishan, Siouan and Caddoan, and Iroquoian languages.

In many instances, linguists are helping tribal members interpret and use the accumulated documentation of their language in education programs and more general revitalization efforts.

Retention efforts and secondary survival

The perception is widespread among North American Indian tribes that the loss of a group's traditional language is a serious threat to their communal identity. Consequently, as the rate of extinction of languages has accelerated, particularly in the last thirty years, many groups have made considerable efforts to preserve some knowledge of their traditional languages. To date, most of these efforts have focused on second language learning, relying on a variety of techniques from classroom teaching to immersion camps and one-on-one 'master-apprentice' tutoring (Hinton 2001a). In recent years the use of the internet as a language teaching tool in dispersed communities has been rapidly expanding (the Choctaw tribe has been particularly innovative). Documentation of the speech of surviving first-language speakers has also been a high priority, frequently involving collaborations between professional linguists and community-based educators.

The last two decades have seen a number of initiatives, both in the United States and in Canada, to provide institutional and governmental support for indigenous language retention efforts. The training of teachers has been a high priority. In the United States the most significant teacher-training initiative has been the American Indian Language Development Institute (AILDI), now located at the University of Arizona in Tucson, which for over twenty years has offered a one-month summer workshop for Indian language teachers, primarily for languages in the Southwest. Similar workshops have been organized in Oklahoma and Oregon. More loosely organized, but of considerable importance, is an annual conference of Indian language teachers, administrators, and curriculum developers (Stabilizing Indigenous Languages). In Canada, native language teaching programs are offered at the University of Alberta, the University of Regina in Saskatchewan, and Lakehead University in northern Ontario, all focused on Cree and Ojibwe.

During the 1990s the governments of both countries began funding tribal language education programs, in the United States under the Native American Languages Act (1992) and in Canada under the Aboriginal Language Initiative (1998). In both schemes, a limited amount of funding (approximately $3–4 million each year in both countries) is allotted by grants directly to tribes. Additionally in Canada, several aboriginal languages have official status in the Northwest Territories and in Nunavut, and separate funding is available through the Canadian federal government to support language education projects in those jurisdictions. Similarly, Greenlandic is the official language of Greenland.

During the past twenty years probably the majority of tribes in the United States and Canada have instituted some sort of language retention or revitalization effort. The results of these efforts vary considerably from tribe to tribe, but in a small but significant number of cases a sustained tradition of second-language use has developed (for example, in the Coeur d'Alene communities).

In this context there are emerging what might be termed *heritage speech communities*. These are groups of second-language learners who have acquired some degree of fluency in a linguistic code based on a specific moribund or extinct language, and who are actively passing on knowledge of this code to others. The age of the learners varies from early childhood to middle aged, but heritage communities typically recruit new speakers through educational programs – school-based teaching, summer camps, tribally-sponsored pre-school and adult classes – and focus on children and young adults. In most heritage communities there is a core of deeply committed individuals who act as teachers and custodians of the heritage code and who usually collaborate with linguists and other professionals in designing a teaching curriculum (including, most importantly, an orthography) and preparing and using dictionaries and other reference materials, including audio-visual documentation of the surviving first-language speakers. These tribal language scholars are often cultural activists who take a more general role in the preservation and revitalization of what are perceived to be defining features of traditional culture.

The degree of structural continuity between the heritage codes that are being acquired in these circumstances and the indigenous codes on which they are based varies from community to community, and not infrequently from individual to individual within a community. The influence of the first language of the learners (English, or sometimes French) ranges from relatively subtle phonological and morpho-syntactic restructuring to situations in which the heritage code is essentially a dialect of English (or French) with an Indian vocabulary. Much depends on the extent to which surviving first-language speakers are directly involved in the teaching of the heritage code.

The existence of such speech communities makes the distinction between survival and extinction sometimes difficult to draw. A language that has no first-language speakers, but that is being actively taught as a second language and has a definable heritage speech community, may be better considered to be *secondarily surviving* rather than extinct. Since many of the North American languages that are on the verge of extinction as first languages are associated with (often vigorous) heritage communities, it can be anticipated that the number of secondarily surviving languages will grow considerably in the next few decades. In addition, some languages that at present must be considered extinct may attain secondary survival status as communities of heritage learners create and learn codes based on the extant documentation (Hinton 2001b).

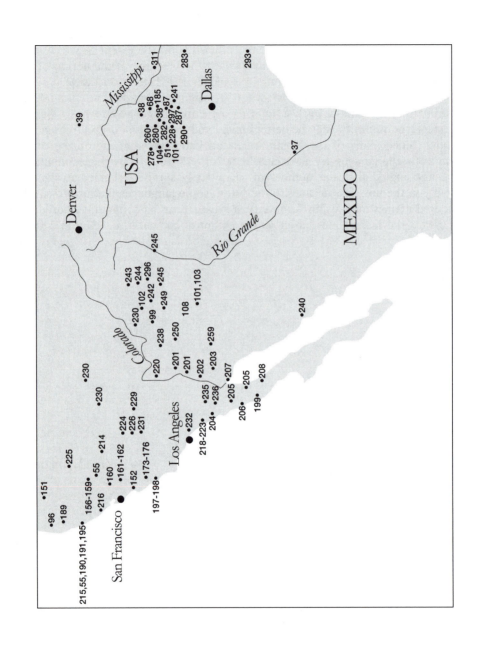

Classificatory list of languages

The classification used here is taken, with some modifications, from Goddard (1996a: 4–8). Languages and classificatory units that were extinct before 1930 are indicated by *italics*; those that have become extinct since 1930 are indicated by an asterisk (*).

(1) Eskimo-Aleut

Eskimoan

WESTERN ESKIMO (YUPIK)

1 *Sirenikski
2 Naukanski Yupik
3 Central Siberian Yupik
4 Central Alaskan Yup'ik
5 Pacific Yupik (Alutiiq)

EASTERN ESKIMO (INUIT)

6 Seward Peninsula Inupiaq
7 North Alaska Inupiaq
8 Western Canadian Inuktitut
9 Eastern Canadian Inuktitut
10 West Greenlandic
11 East Greenlandic

Aleut

ALEUT

12 Aleut

ALEUT-RUSSIAN MIXED LANGUAGE

13 Copper Island Aleut Creole

(2) Algic

Algonquian

BLACKFOOT

14 Blackfoot

CREE-MONTAGNAIS

15 Plains Cree

16 Woods Cree
17 Swampy Cree
18 Moose Cree
19 Attikamek
20 East Cree
21 Montagnais
22 Naskapi

CREE-FRENCH MIXED LANGUAGE

23 Michif

ARAPAHO

24 Gros Ventre (Atsina)
25 Arapaho

CHEYENNE

26 Cheyenne

MENOMINEE

27 Menominee

OJIBWE

28 Severn Ojibwe (Oji-Cree)
29 Northern Algonquin
30 Southern Algonquin (Nipissing Algonquin)
31 Southwestern Ojibwe (Anishinaabemowin)
32 Saulteaux
33 *Old Algonquin*
34 Nishnaabemwin (Eastern Ojibwe and Ottawa/Odawa)

POTAWATOMI

35 Potawatomi

SAUK-FOX-KICKAPOO

36 Sauk-Fox (Mesquakie)
37 Kickapoo

SHAWNEE

38 Shawnee

*MIAMI-ILLINOIS

39 *Miami-Illinois

MICMAC

40 Micmac (Mi'kmaq)

ABENAKI

41 Maliseet-Passamaquoddy
42 *Eastern Abenaki
43 Western Abenaki

ETCHEMIN

44 *Etchemin*

SOUTHERN NEW ENGLAND ALGONQUIAN

45 *Massachusett-Narragansett*
46 *Loup*
47 *Mohegan-Pequot*
48 *Quiripi-Unquachog*

DELAWARE

49 *Mahican*
50 *Munsee
51 Unami

NANTICOKE-CONOY

52 *Nanticoke-Conoy*

VIRGINIA ALGONQUIAN

53 *Virginia Algonquian*

CAROLINA ALGONQUIAN

54 *Carolina Algonquian*

Ritwan

*Wiyot

55   *Wiyot

Yurok

56   Yurok

(3) Na-Dene

Tlingit

57   Tlingit

Eyak

58   Eyak

Athabaskan

AHTNA

59   Ahtna

TANAINA

60   Tanaina

KOYUKON-INGALIK

61   Ingalik (Deg Xinag)
62   Holikachuk
63   Koyukon

TANANA

64   Upper Kuskokwim (Kolchan)
65   Lower Tanana
66   Tanacross
67   Upper Tanana

TUTCHONE

68   Northern Tutchone
69   Southern Tutchone

KUTCHIN-HAN

70   (Gwich'in) Kutchin
71   Han

CENTRAL CORDILLERA

72   Tagish
73   Tahltan
74   Kaska

SOUTHEASTERN CORDILLERA

75   Sekani
76   Beaver

DENE

77   Slave (South Slavey)
78   Mountain Slavey
79   Bearlake (North Slavey)
80   Hare (North Slavey)
81   Dogrib
82   Chipewyan (Dene Soun'line)

BABINE-CARRIER

83   Babine
84   Carrier

CHILCOTIN

85   Chilcotin (Tsilhqot'in)

NICOLA

86   Nicola

TSETSAUT

87   Tsetsaut

SARCEE

88   Sarcee (Tsuut'ina)

KWALHIOQUA-CLATSKANIE

89 *Kwalhioqua-Clatskanie*

OREGON ATHABASKAN

90 *Upper Umpqua*
91 *Tututni
92 *Galice-Applegate
94 Tolowa

CALIFORNIA ATHABASKAN

95 Hupa
96 *Mattole
97 *Eel River
98 *Kato (Cahto)

SOUTHERN ATHABASKAN (APACHEAN)

99   Navajo
100 Western Apache
101 Mescalero-Chiricahua
102 Jicarilla
103 *Lipan
104 Kiowa Apache (Plains Apache)

(4) Haida

105 Haida

(5) Wakashan

Northern Wakashan

106 Haisla
107 Heiltsuk-Oowekyala
108 Kwakiutl (Kwak'wala)

Nootkan

109 Nootka (Nuuchahnulth)
110 Nitinaht (Ditidaht)
111 Makah

(6) *Chimakuan

112 *Chemakum*

113 *Quileute

(7) Salishan

Bella Coola

114 Bella Coola (Nuxalk)

Central Salish

115 Comox
116 *Pentlatch*
117 Sechelt
118 Squamish
119 Halkomelem
120 *Nooksack
121 Northern Straits Salish
122 Klallam
123 Lushootseed
124 *Twana

*Tsamosan

125 *Quinault
126 *Lower Chehalis
127 *Upper Chehalis
128 *Cowlitz*

*Tillamook

129 *Tillamook

Interior Salish

130 Lillooet
131 Thompson
132 Shuswap (Secwepemc)
133 Okanagan
134 Spokane-Kalispel
135 Coeur d'Alene
136 Columbian

(8) Tsimshianic

137 Maritime Tsimshianic
138 Nass-Gitksan

(9) Chinookan

139 *Lower Chinook
140 *Kathlamet*
141 Kiksht

(10) *Alsean

142 *Alsea
143 *Yaquina*

(11) *Siuslaw

144 *Siuslaw

(12) *Coosan

145 *Hanis
146 *Miluk

(13) Takelman

147 *Takelma*

(14) *Kalapuyan

148 *Tualatin-Yamhill
149 *Central Kalapuyan
150 *Yoncalla

(15) Wintuan

151 Wintu-Nomlaki
152 Patwin

(16) MAIDUAN

153 *Maidu
154 Konkow
155 *Nisenan

(17) Utian

Miwok

WESTERN MIWOK

156 *Coast Miwok
157 Lake Miwok

EASTERN MIWOK

158 *Bay Miwok*
159 *Plains Miwok
160 Northern Sierra Miwok
161 Central Sierra Miwok
162 Southern Sierra Miwok

Costanoan

NORTHERN COSTANOAN

163 *Karkin*
164 *Ramaytush*
165 *Chochenyo*
166 *Tamyen*
167 *Awaswas*
168 *Chalon*

SOUTHERN COSTANOAN

169 *Mutsun*
170 *Rumsen*

(18) Yokuts

171 *Palewyami*
172 *Buena Vista*
173 Tule-Kaweah
174 Kings River
175 *Gashowu
176 Valley Yokuts

(19) Plateau Penutian

Klamath

177 Klamath-Modoc

Sahaptian

178 Sahaptin
179 Nez Perce

*Molala

180 *Molala

(20) Karuk

181   Karuk

(21) *Chimariko

182   *Chimariko

(22) *Shastan

183   *Shasta
184   *New River Shasta*
185   *Okawnuchu*
186   *Konomihu*

(23) Palaihnihan

187   Achumawi
188   *Atsugewi

(24) Pomoan

189   *Northeastern Pomo
190   *Southeastern Pomo
191   Eastern Pomo
192   Northern Pomo
193   Central Pomo
194   Southern Pomo
195   Kashaya

(25) Yana

196   *Yana*

(26) *Salinan

197   *Antoniano
198   *Migueleño

(27) Cochimí-Yuman

Yuman

PAI

199   Paipai
200   Upland Yuman

RIVER YUMAN

201   Mohave
202   Quechan (Yuma)
203   Maricopa

DIEGUEÑO-COCOPA

204   Ipai
205   Kumeyaay
206   Tipai
207   Cocopa

KILIWA

208   Kiliwa

Cochimí

209   *Northern*
210   *Southern*

(28) Guaicurian

211   *Guaicuri (Waikuri)*
212   *Huchiti*
213   *Pericú*

(29) Washo

214   Washo

(30) Yukian

215   *Yuki
216   Wappo

(31) Esselen

217   *Esselen*

(32) *Chumashan

218   *Obispeño*
219   *Purisimeño*
220   *Ineseño*
221   *Barbareño*
222   *Ventureño*
223   *Island Chumash*

16

(33) Uto-Aztecan

Numic

WESTERN NUMIC

224 Mono
225 Northern Paiute

CENTRAL NUMIC

226 Panamint
227 Shoshoni (Shoshone)
228 Comanche

SOUTHERN NUMIC

229 Kawaiisu
230 Ute-Chemehuevi

Tubatulabal

231 Tubatulabal

Takic

SERRANO-GABRIELINO

232 Serrano
233 *Kitanemuk
234 *Gabrielino (Tongva)

CUPAN

235 Cahuilla
236 *Cupeño
237 Luiseño

Hopi

238 Hopi

Tepiman

239 Upper Piman (O'odham)

Taracahitic

240 Yaqui (Yoeme)

(The Uto-Aztecan languages of Mexico, including other languages in the Tepiman and Taracahitic subfamilies, are treated in the chapter on Central and South America.)

(34) Kiowa-Tanoan

Kiowa

241 Kiowa

Jemez

242 Jemez

Tiwa

243 Taos
244 Picuris
245 Southern Tiwa

Tewa

246 Tewa

Piro

247 *Piro*

(35) Keresan

248 Acoma-Laguna
249 Rio Grande Keresan

(36) Zuni

250 Zuni

(37) Coahuilteco

251 *Coahuilteco*

(38) Comecrudan

252 *Comecrudo*
253 *Mamulique*
254 *Garza*

(39) Cotoname

255 *Cotoname*

(40) Aranama

256 *Aranama*

(41) Solano

257 *Solano*

(42) Karankawa

258 *Karankawa*

(43) Kootenai

259 Kutenai (Kootenai, Ktunaxa)

(44) Cayuse

260 *Cayuse*

(45) Siouan-Catawba

Siouan

MISSOURI RIVER

261 Hidatsa
262 Crow

MANDAN

263 Mandan

DAKOTAN

264 Sioux
265 Assiniboine
266 Stoney

DHEGIHA

267 Omaha-Ponca
268 Osage
269 *Kansa
270 *Quapaw

CHIWERE-WINNEBAGO

271 Chiwere
272 Winnebago (Ho-Chunk, Hochank)

SOUTHEASTERN

273 *Ofo*
274 *Biloxi*
275 *Tutelo*

Catawban

276 *Catawba
277 *Woccon*

(46) *Tonkawa*

278 *Tonkawa

(47) Caddoan

Northern Caddoan

279 Arikara
280 Pawnee
281 *Kitsai
282 Wichita

Southern Caddoan

283 Caddo

(48) Adai

284 *Adai*

(49) Atakapan

285 *Western Atakapa*
286 *Eastern Atakapa*

(50) *Chitimacha

287 *Chitimacha

(51) *Tunica

288 *Tunica

(52) Muskogean

Western Muskogean

289 Choctaw
290 Chickasaw

Eastern Muskogean

291 Hitchiti-Mikasuki
292 *Apalachee*
293 Alabama
294 Koasati
295 Creek (Muskogee)

(53) *Natchez

296 *Natchez

(54) Yuchi

297 Yuchi (Euchee)

(55) Timucuan

298 *Timucua*
299 *Tawasa*

(56) Calusa

300 *Calusa*

(57) Iroquoian

Northern Iroquoian

301 Tuscarora
302 *Nottoway*
303 *Huron-Wyandotte
304 *Laurentian*
305 Seneca
306 Cayuga
307 Onondaga
308 *Susquehannock*
309 Mohawk
310 Oneida

Cherokee

311 Cherokee

(58) Beothuk

312 *Beothuk*

Catalogue of languages

Languages extinct before 1930

Information on the documentation of extinct languages summarizes the bibliographical data that can be found in Mithun (1999).

Adai [284] was originally spoken in west-central Louisiana, between the Red and Sabine Rivers, and during the eighteenth century it was the language of the Spanish mission of Adayes, west of Natchitoches. After the closing of the mission in 1792 the remnants of the tribe migrated to Texas and apparently joined one or more Caddoan groups. The language is known from a single vocabulary of 275 words collected around 1804. Although it was earlier thought to be Caddoan, Adai is now considered a classificatory isolate.

Apalachee [292] was an Eastern Muskogean language that was spoken in the late seventeenth century in northern Florida around present-day Tallahassee and Apalachee Bay. It is attested mainly in a letter written in 1688 to Charles II of Spain, published in 1860, the original of which is lost. This difficult document has been analyzed in detail by several scholars and a vocabulary of about 120 items recovered.

Aranama [256] was spoken at the Franciscan mission of Espíritu Santo de Zúñiga, established in 1754 on the lower Guadalupe River in southeastern Texas. Only two words of Aranama are attested, and its relationship is unknown.

Atakapa is the general term for the languages and dialects of the Atakapan family, formerly spoken for 200 miles along the Gulf of Mexico between Galveston Bay in Texas and Vermillion Bay in Louisiana. There were several dialects, clustering in two emergent languages divided roughly at the Sabine River, **Western Atakapa [285]** and **Eastern Atakapa [286]**. Western Atakapa was extensively documented by Gatschet in 1885, and a dictionary, grammatical sketch, and collection of texts were published. The last speakers of any variety of Atakapa died early in the twentieth century. Although a few scholars think Atakapa belongs to a 'Gulf' stock, most consider it a classificatory isolate.

Awaswas. See *Costanoan*

Bay Miwok [158], sometimes referred to as Saclan, was a language of the Eastern Miwok branch of the Utian family, and was formerly spoken in parts of Contra Costa County, California, west of Mt Diablo. About eighty words are documented in a manuscript from the Mission period.

Beothuk [312] was the aboriginal language of Newfoundland. Although the English began settling on the island in the early sixteenth century and were in contact with the original inhabitants for over 300 years, Beothuk is attested in only three vocabularies, totaling about 325 words, all collected between 1791 and 1828. These lists, furthermore, are error-ridden and difficult to assess. Although the last known Beothuk survivor died in 1829, Frank Speck interviewed a woman in 1911 who claimed to be the daughter of a Beothuk man and a Micmac woman, and who remembered six words. But since these do not correspond to any words in the earlier recordings they may be spurious, or possibly an attestation of another, otherwise unknown language. It has long been conjectured that Beothuk is distantly related to the Algic family, but the Beothuk data are too poor to allow a definite conclusion and the language is best considered a classificatory isolate.

Biloxi [274] was a language of the Southeastern subgroup of Siouan, spoken in the seventeenth and early eighteenth century on the lower Pascagoula River and Biloxi Bay in southern Mississippi. The language was extensively documented by Dorsey in 1892–3 from a remnant of the tribe living in Rapides Parish, Louisiana. A search for speakers in 1934 was fruitless, although a short wordlist was collected from a woman who had spoken the language in her youth.

Buena Vista Yokuts [172], formerly spoken in at least two local varieties around Buena Vista Lake in Kern County, California, was a distinctive emergent language in the Yokuts complex. Its vocabulary is partially documented in several wordlists. There have been no speakers since the 1930s.

Calusa [300] was a language spoken in the sixteenth century in the far southwest of Florida, directly attested only in a handful of words cited in a book published in 1575. The data are too scant to allow the language to be classified.

Carolina Algonquian [54], also known as Pamlico, was the Algonquian language spoken in the vicinity of Pamlico Sound, North Carolina. It is known only from two short wordlists, one from the Roanoke colony in the 1580s, the other collected in 1709. The language became extinct in the eighteenth century.

Cayuse [260] was spoken in the early nineteenth century in the plateau region of northeastern Oregon and southeastern Washington. It is a classificatory isolate; an earlier classification that linked Molala (now considered Plateau Penutian) and Cayuse in the 'Waiilatpuan' family has been abandoned. By 1850 the remnants of the Cayuse had settled among the Nez Perce and the Umatillas, where the Cayuse fell out of use. A few people retained some fluency in the language as late as the early 1930s, but Cayuse was totally extinct by the 1960s. It is documented only in a few wordlists. Cayuse is considered one of the heritage languages of the Umatilla Reservation, and some attempts have been made to teach the language, but the paucity of documentation makes this a difficult task.

Chalon. See *Costanoan*

Chemakum [112], one of the two languages of the Chemakuan family, was spoken in a small territory between Hood Canal and Port Townsend, on the east side of the Olympic Peninsula in northwest Washington. In the nineteenth century, when it was first noted, Chemakum was being replaced by Salish (Klallam and Lushootseed) and was not well documented. Boas found three speakers in 1890, and the language was extinct by the 1940s.

Chochenyo. See *Costanoan*

Coahuilteco (Pajalate) [251] was spoken in the eighteenth century at the Franciscan mission in San Antonio, Texas. It is primarily documented in an eighty-eight-page bilingual Spanish-Coahuilteco confessor's manual published in Mexico in 1760, which apparently represents one dialect (Pajalate) of a language spoken widely in southern Texas and Coahuila. Although in the past Coahuilteco was often joined to several other extinct languages of Texas and Mexico in a family called 'Coahuiltecan' it is now considered a classificatory isolate. There is no attestation of the language after the end of the eighteenth century.

Cochimí was a chain of dialects that were formerly spoken in the central portion of the peninsula of Baja California, from about 150 miles south of the US border to about 200 miles north of Cabo San Lucas. Cochimí is usually classified as a branch of the Cochimí-Yuman family coordinate with the Yuman languages. Two dialect clusters or emergent languages can be identified: **Northern Cochimí [209]**, spoken by nomadic bands in the extremely arid Central Desert and later associated with the missions at Santa María Cabujacamang, Santa Gertrudis, and San Francisco de Borja; and **Southern Cochimí [210]**, spoken by more settled groups at the oases and in the highlands south of the 28th parallel and best attested from the missions of San Javier Viggé, San José Comondú, and San Ignacio Kadakaaman. Most of the scanty documentation of Cochimí comes from the Jesuit missions (1697–1767), although there are some nineteenth-century vocabularies. As late as 1925 Harrington was able to find a person who remembered a few Northern Cochimí forms, but the language was essentially extinct by that time.

Comecrudan was a family of three languages that were formerly spoken along the lower Rio Grande River in southern Texas and northern Mexico. **Comecrudo [252]** is documented by two short wordlists collected in 1829 and 1861 and by a substantial vocabulary collected in 1886. **Mamulique [253]** and **Garza [254]** are attested in one short wordlist from 1829. Although earlier thought to be part of a 'Coahuiltecan' family Comecrudan is not now considered to be related to any other family.

Costanoan is one of the two branches of the Utian family, and includes eight languages that were spoken in a compact area along the coast of California from north of San Francisco to south of Monterey. All Costanoan languages are extinct, and some are very poorly documented. Three of the four languages formerly spoken around San Francisco Bay, **Karkin [163]**, **Ramaytush [164]** and **Tamyen [166]**, have been extinct since the mid-nineteenth century and are known only through short vocabularies. The fourth language, **Chochenyo [165]**, formerly spoken along the eastern shore of the bay, was moderately well documented by Harrington early in the twentieth century, although very little of his material has been published. **Awaswas [167]**, spoken around Santa Cruz, and **Chalon [168]**, spoken in the Salinas Valley near Mission Soledad, became extinct early along and are very scantily attested. **Mutsun [169]** was the language of the area around Mission San Juan Bautista. It survived until the 1930s and is well documented, both from the Mission period and in the twentieth century by Harrington. The Mission materials have been published, and there is an unpublished grammar and dictionary based on Harrington's materials. **Rumsen (Rumsien) [170]** was the language of the Monterey area. It is moderately well documented, mostly by Harrington, and a full dictionary has been prepared based on all extant Rumsen materials. There are several organized groups of Costanoan descendants, and some interest in the revival of both Mutsun and Rumsen. One tribal scholar has acquired a moderate second-language fluency in Rumsen.

Cotoname [255] was formerly spoken along the lower Rio Grande River in southern Texas and northern Mexico, adjacent to the Comecrudan languages. It is attested by two short vocabularies, collected in 1829 and 1886. Although earlier thought to be part of a 'Coahuiltecan' family Cotoname is now considered to be a classificatory isolate.

Cowlitz [128], one of the four languages of the Tsamosan division of the Salishan family, was formerly spoken along the Cowlitz River in southwestern Washington. Cowlitz descendants live in scattered locations in and around their former territory. The language is very poorly documented, and no speakers are known to remain.

Esselen [217] was the language spoken in the late eighteenth century in the upper Carmel Valley and around Big Sur, on the central California coast south of Monterey. It is a classificatory isolate usually considered to belong to the Hokan stock. The small population was divided among three missions and the language did not survive long into the nineteenth century. Esselen is directly documented in three vocabularies collected between 1786 and 1832, as well as by a catechism and a short translation. Additional material was obtained between 1830 and 1930 from Costanoan speakers who remembered something of Esselen. The total extant corpus is about 300 words.

Etchemin [44] was an Algonquian language spoken along the coast of Maine, extinct since the seventeenth century. Nothing is known of it for certain besides a list of numbers, which indicate it was distinct from adjoining Algonquian languages.

Garza. See *Comecrudan*

Guaicurian was a family composed of three languages that were formerly spoken in the southernmost part of the peninsula of Baja California. Only one of the languages, the most northerly, is directly attested. **Guaicura (Waikuri) [211]** is documented in the eighteenth-century report of a Jesuit who had served in the mission at San Luis Gonzaga; he supplies only the Lord's Prayer, the Twelve Articles of the Creed, a verb paradigm, and a few additional words. The existence of the other two languages, **Huchití [212]**, spoken at La Paz and Santa Rosa, and **Pericú [213]**, spoken at San José del Cabo, and the fact that they bore a similarity to Guaicura, is known indirectly from mission reports.

Huchití. See *Guaicurian*

Karankawa [258] was spoken until the mid-nineteenth century along the south Texas coast from Galveston to Corpus Christi. It is attested in several vocabularies, collected between 1698 and 1888, one of the most extensive from a white woman in Massachusetts who had spent her childhood near the last Karankawa-speaking community. Although earlier thought to be part of a 'Coahuiltecan' family, Karankawa is now considered to be a classificatory isolate.

Karkin. See *Costanoan*

Kathlamet [140] was the Chinookan language formerly spoken along the lower Columbia River from the vicinity of Astoria upstream about fifty miles. It was documented by Boas in the 1890s, primarily in narrative texts. The language has been extinct since shortly after the beginning of the twentieth century.

Kaw. See *Kansa*

Konomihu. See *Shasta*

Kwalhioqua-Clatskanie [89] was an Athabaskan language formerly spoken in two separate areas along the lower Columbia River, the Kwalhioqua to the north of the river, the Clatskanie to the south, separated by the territory of the Lower Chinook and Cathlamet. The Kwalhioqua area, along the Willapa River in what is now southwestern Washington, included two subgroups, the Willapa and the Suwal. The language, attested in several vocabularies collected between 1841 and 1910, shows some connection to the Athabaskan languages of southwestern Oregon and Northwestern California, but also has a number of distinctive traits. The Kwalhioqua-Clatskanie people were dispersed among Coast Salish tribes in the nineteenth century and their language was extinct before the 1930s.

Laurentian [304] was a Northern Iroquoian language spoken in the sixteenth century along the St Lawrence River in Quebec. It is known only from the wordlists collected by the explorer Jacques Cartier during his two visits in 1534 and 1536. Examination of the data suggests they represent more than one dialect. By the time Champlain visited the area in 1603 the Laurentians had vanished.

Loup [46] was an Algonquian language of the Southern New England group, spoken in central Massachusetts and parts of northern Connecticut. It is attested only in two wordlists ('Loup A' and 'Loup B'), which indicate dialect differences. The language became extinct in the eighteenth century.

Mahican [49] was an emergent language in the Delaware dialect complex of Algonquian. It was spoken in the upper Hudson River from Lake Champlain south to Dutchess County, and in the eighteenth century was the dominant language at the mission village of Stockbridge in western Massachusetts. There is a fair amount of documentation, principally by Moravian missionaries. The Mahicans were removed to the west in the nineteenth century, and the language was last spoken in Wisconsin in the 1930s.

Mamulique. See *Comecrudan*

Massachusett-Narragansett [45] was a complex of Southern New England Algonquian dialects spoken around Massachusetts Bay from southern Maine to Cape Cod, as well as around Narragansett Bay and on Martha's Vineyard. Several varieties of Massachusett-Narragansett are quite well documented from the Colonial period, including the dialect of the mission town of Natick, which Eliot documented in a grammar

(1666) and a full translation of the Bible (1663), and the Narragansett dialect of Rhode Island (Williams 1643). The language fell into disuse in most areas during the eighteenth century, but a variety continued to be spoken on Martha's Vineyard until the end of the nineteenth century. A number of speakers of Massachusett-Narragansett were literate in Eliot's orthography and a number of native documents, mostly of a legal or commerical nature, survive from the Colonial period. Members of the Aquinnah Tribe, at Gay Head on Martha's Vineyard, and the Mashpee Tribe, on Cape Cod, have formed a Wampanoag Language Reclamation Committee that offers classes in Wampanoag to tribal members.

Mohegan-Pequot [47] was an Algonquian language of the Southern New England group, spoken in eastern Connecticut and the eastern part of Long Island. There is scattered documentation, but dialect diversity is poorly known. The last speaker, a Mohegan, died in 1908.

Mutsun. See *Costanoan*

Nanticoke-Conoy [52] was the Algonquian language of Chesapeake Bay and the Delmarva Peninsula. The Indian inhabitants of this area were scattered by the mid-eighteenth century, some taking refuge with the Delawares, others with the Iroquois. Although Nanticoke was spoken on the Six Nations Reserve in Canada as late as the 1860s, it is documented only by a few short vocabularies.

Nicola [86] was an Athabaskan language formerly spoken in the Nicola and Similkameen Valleys of south-central British Columbia, adjoining Thompson Salish territory. It is documented only by fragmentary wordlists that are insufficient to allow its relationship to other Athabaskan languages to be clearly determined, although it appears closest to Chilcotin. Nicola was presumably extinct before the beginning of the twentieth century.

Nottoway [302] was a Northern Iroquoian language, closely related to Tuscarora. It was spoken in colonial times and into the nineteenth century along the Nottoway River in southeastern Virginia, adjacent to the original territory of the Tuscaroras in North Carolina. It is attested only in two early-nineteenth-century wordlists.

Ofo [273] was a language of the Southeastern subgroup of Siouan, spoken in the 1670s on the east bank of the Mississippi River below the mouth of the Ohio, in present-day western Tennessee. The Ofos moved south to the Yazoo River in the 1690s and were subsequently absorbed into nearby tribes. The only documentation of Ofo is a vocabulary collected in 1908 from a woman of Ofo descent, living among the Tunicas in Louisiana, who had learned some of the language from her grandmother.

Okwanuchu. See *Shasta*

Old Algonquin [33] was the Algonquian language spoken in the early French missions in the lower Ottawa Valley and along the St Lawrence, and is attested in a number of unpublished seventeenth- and eighteenth-century documents. It went out of use in the nineteenth century. Although it was part of the Ojibwe dialect complex, Old Algonquin was quite distinct from the Ojibwe dialects that are today called Northern and Southern Algonquin.

Palewyami Yokuts [171], formerly spoken along Poso Creek in Kern County, California, was the most divergent of the languages or emergent languages in the Yokuts complex. Its vocabulary is partially documented in several wordlists, the longest and most reliable collected by Harrington in the 1920s. There have been no speakers of Palewyami since the 1930s.

Pentlatch [116] was a Central Salish language formerly spoken on the east coast of Vancouver Island to the south of the Island Comox. The last speaker died in 1940. The only documentation of the language was made by Boas in 1886, who collected a fair amount of data most of which remains unpublished.

Pericú. See *Guaicurian*

Piro [247] was a Kiowa-Tanoan language, formerly spoken in a number of now-abandoned pueblos in the Rio Grande Valley south of Isleta. After the Pueblo Revolt of 1680 most of the Piros, together with some Isletas and other Southern Tiwas, moved south to the vicinity of El Paso and established new settlements, only one of which, Ysleta del Sur, still remains. No speakers of Piro survived into the twentieth century and documentation is sparse, although small amounts continue to be discovered in Spanish mission records. Another language, Tompiro, attested in many of the same early sources, is probably a dialect of Piro.

Quiripi-Unquachog [48] was an Algonquian language of the Southern New England group, spoken in western Connecticut and central Long Island. Documentation is sparse (although it includes an Unquachog vocabulary collected on Long Island by Thomas Jefferson). The language was extinct by the early nineteenth century.

Ramaytush. See *Costanoan*

Rumsen. See *Costanoan*

Shasta is often used as the cover term for all of the Shastan languages, a family of four languages that were formerly spoken along the Klamath River and its tributaries in the mountainous interior of northwestern California. Three of these languages have been extinct for several generations and are poorly known: **New River Shasta [184]**, spoken in a remote area near the head of Salmon River and New River, is known only from brief wordlists collected early in the twentieth century. **Okawnuchu [185]**, spoken along the upper Sacramento River, near Mt Shasta, is even less well attested. **Konomihu [186]**, spoken along the Salmon River, centering in the area around Forks of Salmon, was documented by Harrington, who worked with the last speakers in the 1920s; most of his material remains unpublished. A fourth Shastan language, **Shasta (proper) [187]**, survived until recently.

Solano [257] was spoken early in the eighteenth century at the Franciscan mission of San Francisco Solano, at Eagle Pass on the Rio Grande River in southern Texas. It is attested only in a twenty-one-word vocabulary in the mission records. Solano is considered to be a classificatory isolate.

Susquehannock [308] was a Northern Iroquoian language, spoken in the seventeenth and eighteenth century along the Susquehanna River in southeastern Pennsylvania and northeastern Maryland. It is known only from a list of about eighty words appended to a Delaware catechism compiled by a Swedish Lutheran missionary in 1696.

Takelma [147] was a language formerly spoken in the valley of the upper Rogue River in southwestern Oregon. The Takelmas were displaced from their homeland by the Rogue River War of 1855–6 and the survivors eventually settled on the Grand Ronde and Siletz Reservations in northwestern Oregon. There may have been several distinct local dialects, but only one is reflected in most of the documentation, the largest part of which comes from Sapir's work in 1906 with a single speaker. He published a full grammar and a collection of narrative texts, the latter with a lexicon. There are some other less extensive materials, the latest collected in the 1930s. The language was extinct by the 1940s. Takelma is a classificatory isolate, but likely to be part of the Penutian stock.

Tamyen. See *Costanoan*

Tawasa. See *Timucua*

Timucua [298] was a large complex of dialects spoken in the sixteenth and seventeenth century over much of the northern half of the Florida peninsula, as well as in parts of Georgia and Alabama. It is well documented from Spanish missionary sources, most importantly in the work of Pareja, a Franciscan missionary at St Augustine after 1590; his various works constitute more than 2,000 pages of Timucua text. The documentation (in which several dialects are represented) has been extensively analyzed, and a full dictionary published. An isolated and divergent dialect, **Tawasa [299]**, spoken in east-central Alabama and attested only in a short vocabulary from 1797, is probably best treated as a closely related language. Most scholars consider Timucua to be a classificatory isolate, although some evidence suggests a relationship to one or more South American languages.

Tsetsaut [87] was an Athabaskan language formerly spoken on Portland Canal, on the north coast of British Columbia adjacent to Nass-Gitksan territory. It is known exclusively from a single vocabulary collected by Boas in 1894, but the data are sufficient to show that Tsetsaut formed its own distinct subgroup within the Athabaskan family. The language has been extinct for over a century and the Tsetsaut people have been absorbed into neighboring tribes.

Tutelo [275] was a language of the Southeastern subgroup of Siouan, spoken in the seventeenth century in the Shenandoah Valley and elsewhere in western Virginia. In the mid-eighteenth century the Tutelos became affiliated with the Iroquois and moved northward, eventually settling on the Six Nations Reserve in Ontario with the Cayuga. Most of the rather scant documentation of Tutelo comes from the late nineteenth and early twentieth century. A man who had spoken Tutelo in his youth recognized some words as late as 1982, but the language is now presumed to be extinct. A grammatical outline and a lexicon based on all extant sources has been compiled.

Upper Umpqua [90] was a language of the Oregon Athabaskan subgroup formerly spoken in the upper drainage of the Umpqua River in southwestern Oregon. After the Rogue River War of 1855–6 the Upper Umpquas were forcibly resettled in northern Oregon on the Grand Ronde and Siletz Reservations, and the language rapidly fell out of use. It is sparsely documented in vocabularies collected between 1840 and 1941. The last speaker died in the 1940s. The Cow Creek Band of Umpquas, who in 1986 were allowed to reestablish a reservation near former Upper Umpqua territory, claim Takelma rather than Upper Umpqua as their heritage language.

Virginia Algonquian [53] is the name given to the Algonquian language attested in two vocabularies collected at Jamestown between 1607 and 1611. It presumably was the language of the Powhatan confederacy in tidewater Virginia. There may have been speakers as late as 1790, but no further documentation exists.

Waikuri. See *Guaicurian*

Woccon [277] was one of the two languages in the Catawban branch of the Siouan-Catawba family. It was spoken in the early eighteenth century in eastern North Carolina, and is attested only in a vocabulary of 143 words that was printed in 1709. The relationship between Woccon and Catawba (proper) is not close.

Yana [196] was spoken in several distinct dialects in the rugged country west of Mt Lassen in the northern Sacramento Valley. It is a classificatory isolate, usually considered to belong to the Hokan stock. There were three principal dialects: Northern Yana, spoken in a small area around Montgomery Creek; Central Yana, on Cow Creek; and Southern Yana, spoken in the southern two-thirds of the territory. Curtin collected substantial material in the 1880s, much of it unpublished. All three dialects were extensively documented by Sapir between 1907 and 1915. His Northern and Central Yana materials have been published, including a volume of narrative texts, a grammatical sketch of the Northern dialect, and a comprehensive dictionary. His documentation of the Southern dialect, collected from the last survivor of the Yahi group, Ishi, is now being prepared for publication. At least one speaker of Yana survived until about 1940 and Harrington collected a moderate amount of data, all unpublished.

Languages still spoken or recently extinct

Accurate information on the current state of language survival in indigenous North American communities is difficult to come by. The most reliable general source of data on number of speakers is the *Ethnologue*, a survey of the languages of the world published by SIL International and frequently updated (Grimes 2000). Also informative are US and Canadian census reports (the most recent available figures are from 1990 for the US and 1996 for Canada). Neither source, however, consistently notes degrees of fluency or distinguish first-language from second-language speakers, and information on retention or revitalization efforts are usually lacking. Most of the information in the list of languages below was gathered between 1999 and 2001 directly from the linguists and educators best placed to know the relevant facts about the various speech communities.

Several individuals, in addition to providing information on specific languages, aided in the gathering of data from other languages in certain areas or language groups. For such valuable assistance special thanks go to: Margaret Seguin Anderson, Alice Anderton, M. Dale Kinkade, Michael Krauss, Jack Martin, John McLaughlin, Pamela Munro, Douglas Parks, William Poser, Keren Rice, John Ritter, and Akira Yamamoto.

The sources of information on specific languages or groups of languages are as follows:

Anderson, Margaret Seguin – Northern British Columbia
Anderton, Alice – Oklahoma
Bakker, Peter – Mitchif
Beaumont, Ron – Sechelt
Beck, David – Bella Coola
Burton, Strang – Halkomelem (Upriver)
Buszard-Welcher, Laura – Potawatomi
Caldwell, Alan – Menominee
Callaghan, Catherine – Miwok
Carlson, Barry – Spokane-Kalispel
Costa, David – Miami-Illinois
Dayley, Jon – Panamint, Shoshoni
de Reuse, Willem – Apache
DeLancey, Scott – Klamath
Demers, Richard – Lummi
Denham, Kristin – Lushootseed
Doak, Ivy – Coeur d'Alene
Elzinga, Dirk – Ute-Chemehuevi (Chemehuevi)
Enrico, John – Haida
Fowler, Catherine – Northern Paiute
Furbee, Louanna – Chiwere
Gardiner, Dwight – Thompson
Givón, Tom – Ute-Chemehuevi (Ute)
Graczyk, Randy – Crow
Hargus, Sharon – Babine, Sahaptin, Sekani
Howe, Darin – Nootka
Ignace, Marianne Boelscher – Shuswap
Jacobs, Peter – Squamish
Kinkade, M. Dale – Lower Chehalis, Upper Chehalis, Pentlatch
Kinkade, M. Dale – Northwest Coast
Koontz, John – Omaha-Ponca
Krauss, Michael – Eskimo-Aleut, Alaskan Athabaskan, Eyak
Leavitt, Robert M. – Maliseet-Passamaquoddy
Leer, Jeff – Tlingit
Macaulay, Monica – Menominee
Martin, Jack – Muskogean

29

Mattina, Anthony – Okanagan
Mattina, Nancy – Columbian
McKenzie, Marguerite – Cree-Montagnais-Naskapi
McLaughlin, John – Numic
Miller, Amy – Quechan, Diegueño
Mixco, Mauricio – Cochimí-Yuman
Montler, Tim – Klallam, Northern Straits Salish
Morgan, Lawrence – Kutenai
Munro, Pamela – Muskogean, Takic, Yuman
Parks, Douglas – Caddoan
Pearson, Bruce – Shawnee, Delaware, Wyandotte
Poser, William – British Columbia languages
Powell, Jay – Quileute, Quinault
Rementer, Jim – Delaware
Rice, Keren – Slavey, Northwest Territories, Canada in general
Rice, Sally – Chipewyan
Rigsby, Bruce – Tsimshianic, Sahaptin
Ritter, John (YNLC) – Yukon languages
Rude, Noel – Nez Perce, Sahaptin
Shepherd, Alice – Wintu
Silver, Shirley – Shasta, Palaihnihan
Tarpent, Marie-Lucie – Tsimshianic
Tatsch, Sheri – Nisenan
Thomason, Sally – Spokane-Kalispel (Flathead)
Underriner, Janne – Klamath
Valentine, Rand – Ojibwe
Valiquette, Hilaire – Keresan
Wash, Suzanne – Miwok
Watanabe, Honoré – Comox
Wolfart, H. C. – Cree, Ojibwe
Yamamoto, Akira – Yuman languages

The Regional Editor is profoundly indebted to each of these individuals. In addition, some supplementary facts about language survival and retention activites in certain communities were gleaned from articles in Davis (1994). However, the responsibility for the interpretation of the data in every case lies with the Regional Editor.

Abenaki [42, 43] is a nearly extinct Eastern Algonquian dialect complex, originally spoken from Massachusetts to the St Lawrence River valley, including most of present-day northern New England and parts of Quebec. Two dialect areas, or emergent languages, are usually distinguished. **Eastern Abenaki** was spoken in southern and central Maine and adjacent Quebec. The only surviving Eastern Abenaki group is the Penobscot community at Old Town, on Indian Island, on the Penobscot River of north-central Maine. The last fluent Penobscot speaker died in 1993, but the dialect is extensively documented in the (largely unpublished) work of Frank Siebert. **Western Abenaki** was spoken in Vermont and New Hampshire and adjacent Quebec. The largest modern community is in Quebec, at the Odanak Reserve on the St François River, where a handful of elderly fluent speakers survive. A dialect intermediate between Eastern and Western Abenaki was spoken at Bécancourt, on the St Lawrence River, but there are no surviving fluent speakers. In addition about 2,000 people of Western Abenaki descent live in Vermont around the northern end of Lake Champlain; attempts are underway there to revive the language and teach it in the Vermont school system. Western Abenaki was extensively documented by Gordon Day, who published a comprehensive dictionary.

Achumawi [187] is one of the two languages of the Palaihnihan family of northeastern California; the other is Atsugewi, which has been extinct since 1988. Both Achumawi and Atsugewi are heritage languages of the Pit River Tribe, which is organized into eleven bands representing the tribal groups with traditional territory along Pit River. Achumawi, the language of nine of these bands, is spoken by fewer than ten elderly people, most of them semi-speakers or passive speakers. There are noticeable differences among local varieties. Instructional materials were prepared for a language program in the 1980s but this program is apparently no longer in operation.

Acoma-Laguna [248] is the Keresan language spoken by members of the Pueblos of Acoma and Laguna in northwestern New Mexico, west of Albuquerque. Acoma-Laguna is partially intelligible to speakers of most Rio Grande Keresan varieties, but is usually considered a separate language. At Acoma about half of the total population of approximately 4,000 are speakers; most are over thirty. No children are acquiring the language. A bilingual education program existed for a number of years at Sky City Elementary School, but was discontinued around 1990. Retention effotrs were renewed in 1997 and a summer immersion camp was started in 1998. At Laguna there are about 2,000 speakers out of a total population of approximately 7,000; most are over forty. No children are acquiring the language. Laguna is taught as a second language at Laguna Elementary School; the Pueblo sponsors a language preservation project and a dictionary is in preparation by the Summer Institute of Linguistics.

Ahtna [59] is the language of eight communities along the Copper River and in the upper Susitna and Nenana drainages in south-central Alaska. The total Ahtna population is about 500 with perhaps eighty speakers. The first extensive linguistic work on Ahtna was begun in 1973 by James Kari, who published a comprehensive dictionary of the language in 1990.

Ajachemem. See *Luiseño*

Alabama [293] is an Eastern Muskogean language spoken by 250 to 300 residents of the Alabama-Coushatta Indian Reservation near Livingston, in the Big Thicket area of East Texas. Alabama speakers share the reservation with a smaller number of Koasati (Coushatta) speakers, and some individuals have learned to speak or understand both of these related languages. Until recently there were also a few elderly speakers of Alabama among the 900 enrolled members of the Alabama-Quassarte Tribe, an administrative subdivision of the Muskogee Creek Nation, in Okfuskee County, Oklahoma. In Texas, Alabama is the language of choice among those fifty and above and is used at home and at the Senior Citizen Center. The youngest speakers are probably in their teens. Some speakers of Koasati have learned to understand Alabama. A writing system has only recently been developed and literacy in Alabama is extremely low, although a full dictionary of the language was published in 1993 to aid language preservation. While Alabama is used in homes on the reservation, English is used for school and church services. Efforts have been made to teach Alabama to young children in summer programs and to introduce it in preschool.

Aleut [12] is the only language of the Aleut branch of the Eskimo-Aleut family. Its speakers are indigenous to the Aleutian Islands, the Pribilof Islands, and the Alaska Peninsula west of Stepovak Bay. The only major internal division occurs at Atka Island, separating Eastern from Western dialects. The traditional ethnonym is Unangan ('Aleuts' was introduced by Russian explorers, who used the same term for the Pacific Yupik Eskimos). Of a current population of about 2,200 Aleuts, about 150–60 speak the language. In the early nineteenth century Russian Orthodox missionaries promoted native literacy and helped foster a remarkably bilingual society. The most notable of these missionaries, Ivan Veniaminov, developed a writing system and translated religious material into Aleut. In modern times the outstanding contributor to Aleut linguistics was Knut Bergsland, who worked with Aleut speakers to design a modern writing system and develop bilingual curriculum materials, including school dictionaries, for both dialects, a comprehensive dictionary, and a detailed reference grammar.

Alsea [142] and **Yaquina [143]**, the two closely related languages that constitute the Alsean family, were formerly spoken by adjacent tribes in a small territory on the central coast of Oregon. The remnants of both tribes were removed to the Siletz Reservation in 1875, where they were absorbed into the heterogeneous population and their languages fell into disuse. Some Yaquina vocabulary was documented in the 1880s, but the language appears to have become extinct soon afterward. Alsea was more thoroughly documented, primarily by Frachtenberg in 1910–13, who published a volume of narrative texts with a lexicon. Much archival material exists, including a grammatical sketch. At least one speaker survived into the 1940s, but the language has been extinct for at least fifty years.

Alutiiq. See *Pacific Yupik*

Antoniano. See *Salinan*

Arapaho [25] is an Algonquian language of the High Plains, the heritage language of both the Northern Arapaho of the Wind River Reservation in central Wyoming and of the Southern Arapaho members of the Cheyenne-Arapaho Tribe in west-central Oklahoma. Approximately 1,000 of the 5,953 Northern Arapaho tribal members are first-language speakers, most over fifty; there are no first-language speakers of Arapaho in Oklahoma. Bilingual education efforts were begun on the Wind River Reservation in the early 1980s, and a substantial amount of pedagogical material was produced, including videotaped language lessons. Only modest progress was made in reintroducing the language to children, however, until the establishment in 1993 of the Arapaho Language Lodge, a remarkably successful immersion program. In a related development, in the mid-1990s the Disney studios produced an Arapaho-language version of the classic children's film *Bambi*, using the voices of Arapaho children.

Arikara [279] is a Northern Caddoan language, formerly spoken in earthlodge villages along the Missouri River in central and north-central South Dakota, downstream from the Mandan villages. The modern Arikara, one of the Three Affiliated Tribes, share the Fort Berthold Reservation in North Dakota with the Mandan and Hidatsa. They now live in the Eastern Segment of the reservation, primarily in the communities of White Shield and Parshall. There are fewer than ten fluent speakers, all elderly, in a population of approximately 2,000. Extensive instructional material, including an introductory textbook, was prepared in the late 1970s for use in Arikara classes at Mary College in Bismarck and at Fort Berthold Community College. Since the 1990s the American Indian Studies Research Institute at Indiana University has been developing printed and multimedia/interactive instructional materials at the elementary and secondary levels for use in the White Shield School. Extensive documentary records, including sound recordings, are archived at the American Indian Studies Research Center.

Assiniboine (Nakon) [265] is an emergent language in the **Dakotan** dialect complex of Siouan, spoken (with little variation) on two reservations in Montana – Fort Belknap and Fort Peck – and on three reserves in Saskatchewan – Whitebear, Carry the Kettle, and Mosquito-Grizzly Bear's Head. Other Indian languages are present in all of these communities. On the Saskatchewan reserves Cree is widely spoken and many of the Assiniboine speakers are fluent in it. In Montana, Assiniboines share the Fort Belknap Reservation with the Algonquian-speaking Gros Ventre (Atsinas), and the Fort Peck Reservation with speakers of Sioux. In a total Assiniboine population of approximately 3,500 there are no more than 150 first-language speakers, none under forty and most elderly. Courses in Assiniboine are taught at Fort Belknap Community College.

Atsina. See *Gros Ventre*

Atsugewi [188] is one of the two languages of the Palaihnihan family of northeastern California. It is the heritage language of two of the eleven bands that constitute the Pit River Tribe, the Atsugewi of Hat Creek and the Aporige (Apwaruge) of Dixie Valley. Atsugewi has been well documented in recent decades, principally by Talmy, who published a major study of its semantic structure. There have been no known speakers since 1988, and no revitalization effort is under way.

Attikamek (Tête de Boule) [19] is the Western Cree dialect spoken on the Manouane/ Manuan, Obedjiwan/Obidjewan, and Weymontachingue/Wemontachie Reserves, north of Trois-Rivières in south-central Quebec. The entire native population of about 3,000 is fluent in the language, and most children are monolingual before entering school. Schooling is carried out using Attikamekw as the language of instruction in the primary grades, and extensive work is being carried out to provide a dictionary and a reference grammar solely in the language.

Babine (or **Bulkley Valley/Lakes District Language**) **[83]** is the Athabaskan language spoken on Bulkley River and in the Lake Babine area of central British Columbia, to the north and west of the Carrier dialect complex. Although there is a tradition of grouping Babine with Carrier (it has sometimes been referred to as 'Northern

Carrier'), there is a sharp linguistic and cultural boundary between the two speech communities. Babine has two clearly differentiated dialects. The western dialect (usually called **Wetsuwet'en**) includes the Bulkley River communities (Hagwilget, Moricetown, Smithers, Houston, and Broman Lake) and the Nee-Tahi-Buhn and Skin Tayi bands at Burns Lake. It has about 100 fluent speakers, none of them children. An additional 100 or more are passive speakers, including a few children. Although Wetsuwet'en has been offered for credit by the University of Northern British Columbia since 1996 and is taught in local schools in Moricetown and Smithers, there is little indigenous literacy. The eastern dialect ('**Babine proper**') includes the Lake Babine and Takla Lake communities as well as former residents from Lake Babine who have settled in Burns Lake. It has up to 200 speakers of all degrees of fluency out of a total population of 250. However, there are few speakers under twenty-five, and although some children have a passive knowledge none are active speakers. There are no fluent second-language speakers, and literacy in the language is very low.

Bannock. See *Northern Paiute*

Barbareño. See *Chumash*

Bearlake [79] is an emergent Athabaskan language within the North Slavey group of Slavey dialects of the Dene complex. It is spoken as a first language by about 580 people (450 of whom use it actively at home) in two communities in the Northwest Territories, Déline, formerly Fort Franklin (460 speakers out of a total population of 615), and Tulita, formerly Fort Norman (up to 120 speakers out of 450 total). At Déline, Bearlake is the lingua franca of a dialectally mixed community and many speakers are also fluent in Dogrib. At Tulita, an unknown number of the speakers of Bearlake are also fluent (or primarily fluent) in Mountain.

Beaver [76] is an Athabaskan language, spoken in eastern British Columbia (in the communities of Doig, Blueberry, Hudson Hope, and Prophet River) and in northwestern Alberta (in the communities of Horse Lakes, Clear Hills, Boyer River, and Rock Lane). There are about 300 speakers. Although Beaver is partially intelligible to speakers of emergent languages in the Dene dialect complex, for political and geographical reasons it is not usually considered a Dene language.

Bella Coola [114] is a Salishan language spoken by members of the Bella Coola Band in a single community (Bella Coola) on the north-central coast of British Columbia. The term **Nuxalk** (derived from the native name for Bella Coola Valley) was adopted by the Band around 1980 to designate the language and its speakers. Isolated geographically from other Salishan languages, Bella Coola has been heavily influenced by the Wakashan languages that adjoin it (Haisla, Heiltsuk-Oowekyala). There are about twenty native speakers, the youngest in their sixties. Nuxalk College offers occasional language classes and the band has sponsored immersion camps and other revitalization programs. There are a few second-language speakers, all literate. The language has been the focus of considerable linguistic work, most notably by Philip W. Davis, Ross Saunders, and Hank Nater. Nater's dictionary and grammar use the community's practical writing system, but most of the documentation of the language and its traditional literature is in a scientific orthography.

Blackfoot [14] is an Algonquian language of the northern High Plains, spoken principally on the Blackfoot, Peigan, and Blood Reserves in southern Alberta, and on the Blackfeet Reservation in northwestern Montana. There are three shallowly differentiated dialects, representing old tribal subdivisions: **Siksika**, spoken primarily on the Blackfoot Reserve; **Kainaa**, or **Blood**, spoken on the Blood Reserve; and **Piegan** (spelled 'Peigan' in Canada), spoken on the Peigan Reserve in Alberta and the Blackfeet Reservation in Montana. While the number of fluent speakers of Blackfoot has declined in the past generation, there are still several thousand speakers of the language, including hundreds who no longer reside on tribal land. In Canada, 5,605 first-language speakers of Blackfoot were counted in the 1996 census, out of a total combined Band membership of over 15,000. In some locations Blackfoot remains the principal means of communication for older adults. In the United States the 1990 census counted 1,062 first-language speakers in a tribal enrollment of approximately 13,000. In Canada, education efforts have focused on the Siksika dialect. A standard orthography for Blackfoot was adopted in 1975 by the education committees of the three Canadian Bands, and was subsequently used in a full dictionary of the language. All of the schools on the three reserves in Canada have Blackfoot language classes, and the Blood Tribe has an extensive language program that includes immersion-based instruction. In Montana, the Piegan Institute, a non-profit group, operates successful immersion schools on the Blackfeet Reservation.

Bulkley Valley/Lakes District Language. See *Babine*

Caddo [283] is the sole surviving member of the Southern branch of the Caddoan family, remotely related to members of the Northern branch. The modern Caddo Tribe was formerly an aggregate of numerous autonomous bands speaking distinctive dialects, and organized into at least three confederacies that were distributed over a vast area of eastern Texas, southeastern Oklahoma, southwestern Arkansas, and northern Louisiana. During the nineteenth century the remnants of those groups settled in present Caddo County, Oklahoma, primarily in the vicinity of Anadarko and Binger. Currently, the language is spoken by fewer than twenty-five elderly members of the tribe, and only remnants of the former dialectal diversity survive. Since the 1970s the Caddo Tribe has devoted significant resources to recording and archiving songs, oral history, and language, and recently the Tribe's heritage department, the Kiwat Hasinay Foundation, has been concerned with the long-term archiving and preservation of this record.

Cáhita. See *Yaqui*

Cahuilla [235] is a Uto-Aztecan language of the Takic subfamily, the heritage language of several small tribes in the inland area of southern California, including the Morongo, Agua Caliente (Palm Springs), Cabazon, Augustine, Torres-Martinez, Santa Rosa, Cahuilla, Ramona, and Los Coyotes. There are approximately thirty fluent first-language speakers of Cahuilla in a combined reservation population of about 2,300. A practical orthography was introduced in 1980 and extensive teaching materials were prepared, including a full introductory textbook. The Malki Museum, on the Morongo Reservation in Banning, published this textbook and several others on Cahuilla language and traditional culture.

35

Carrier [84] is the general term for a complex of Athabaskan dialects in central British Columbia, adjoining (but clearly distinct from) Babine on the northwest and Chilcotin on the south. Carrier (locally called **Dakelh**) is spoken in a number of local varieties, traditionally divided into 'Upper Carrier' (the communities to the north of Fort St James, around Stuart and Trembleur Lakes) and 'Lower Carrier' in communities to the south. More recent research indicates that Lower Carrier should be split into a Fraser/Nechako dialect group (Prince George, Cheslatta, Stoney Creek, Nautley, and Stellakoh) and a Blackwater dialect group (Ulkatcho, Kluskus, Nazko, Red Bluff, and Anahim Lake). A Carrier lingua franca was established by Catholic missionaries (most notably Father A. G. Morice) in the nineteenth century, based on the dialect around Fort St James, and a syllabic writing system introduced. This standardized variety (although not the syllabic orthography) remains the focus of educational efforts, many of them sponsored by the Yinka Dene Language Institute in Vanderhoof, near Prince George, a collaborative venture between First Nations and schools in the Athabaskan-speaking area of central British Columbia. While Carrier has up to 1,000 speakers out of a total population of about 4,000 and until recently was one of the more vigorously surviving British Columbia languages, it can no longer be characterized as 'enduring'. The youngest fluent speakers are over twenty-five (in many communities much older) and it is not being acquired by children as a first language.

Catawba [276] was one of the two languages in the Catawban branch of the Siouan-Catawba family; the other, **Woccon**, has been extinct since the eighteenth century. During Colonial times the Catawbas were one of the most important tribes of the Southeast, but went into decline in the late eighteenth century and scattered. Some joined the Choctaws in Oklahoma, others joined the Cherokee. A small group, the Catawba Nation of York County, South Carolina, remained near their old homeland, where the language continued to be spoken through the mid-twentieth century. Although the last fluent speaker died in 1959, Catawba is well documented, and the Catawba Nation's Cultural Preservation Program is engaged in a vigorous language revitalization effort.

Cayuga [306] is a Northern Iroquoian language, originally spoken by a tribe of the Iroquoian Confederacy (Six Nations) situated west of Onondagas and east of the Senecas, between Cayuga and Owasco Lakes. After the American Revolution many of the Cayugas fled to Canada, where their modern descendants make up part of the population of the Six Nations Reserve at Grand River, Ontario. There are about 100 first-language speakers of Cayuga in Ontario, the youngest around forty years of age. Other Cayugas joined the Seneca, where their language was gradually replaced by Seneca, and yet others moved westward with other Iroquois, eventually settling in northeastern Oklahoma. A dialect of Cayuga was spoken in Oklahoma as late as the 1980s but is now apparently extinct.

Central Alaskan Yup'ik [4] (the apostrophe denotes a long p) is the most vigorously surviving native language in Alaska. Of a total population of about 21,000, 10,000 are speakers, and the language is still being acquired by children in seventeen of the sixty-eight villages in which it is spoken. Five regional dialects can be distinguished, one spoken by a majority of speakers and four minority dialects. Early work by Russian Orthodox, Jesuit and Moravian missionaries resulted in a modest tradition of literacy.

A modern writing system was introduced in the 1960s and school bilingual programs were established in Yup'ik villages beginning in 1972. Since then a wide variety of bilingual materials has been published, as well as a comprehensive dictionary, a practical classroom grammar, and story collections and narratives, including a full novel.

Central Siberian Yupik [3] is spoken in Alaska in two villages on St Lawrence Island, Gambell and Savoonga. Almost the entire adult population (1,200 on the island, about 200 more in Nome and Anchorage) speaks the language and a decreasing number of children acquire it as their first language. A modern orthography was developed in the 1960s and curriculum materials, including a preliminary dictionary and a practical grammar, are available for the schools. The St Lawrence Island dialect is nearly identical to the Chaplinsky Yupik spoken on the Chukotka Peninsula on the Russian side of the Bering Strait, principally in the town of Chaplino. There are about 300 speakers of Chaplinsky in a population of about 900, none under thirty. Much linguistic and pedagogical work was published in a Cyrillic orthography from the 1930s through the 1950s, but this ceased when bilingual programs were replaced by a strict Russian-only policy in 1958.

Central Sierra Miwok. See *Eastern Miwok*

Chaplinsky Yupik. See *Central Siberian Yupik*

Chemehuevi. See *Ute-Chemehuevi*

Cherokee [311] is an Iroquoian language spoken in two slightly divergent dialects by up to 10,000 of the more than 122,000 members of the Cherokee Nation of Oklahoma, and about 1,000 of the approximately 10,000 members of the Eastern Band of Cherokees in North Carolina. In addition, an undertermined – but relatively high – percentage of the 7,500 members of the United Keetoowah Band of Oklahoma and Arkansas are speakers of the Oklahoma variety. A number of the speakers reported for the Cherokee Nation may in fact be Keetoowahs; the political independence of the Keetoowahs is in dispute and the membership rolls of the two tribes overlap. The Keetoowah population is largely rural and culturally conservative, and at least a few children are reported to be fluent speakers. At least three distinct dialects of Cherokee are known to have been spoken in the eighteenth and early nineteenth century, but modern dialect differences primarily reflect the split in the historic Cherokee community in the late 1830s, when the Cherokee Nation was removed from Georgia to eastern Oklahoma. The North Carolina group is descended from Cherokees who took refuge in the southern Appalachians rather than undergo the 'Trail of Tears' to Oklahoma. Cherokee is written in a traditional syllabic orthography, devised by George Guest (Sequoyah) in the 1820s and later promoted by missionaries and progressives in the Cherokee Nation both before and after removal. The Sequoyah syllabary remains a badge of Cherokee tribal identity, both in Oklahoma and North Carolina, but is no longer in active use for general literacy. The Cherokee Nation sponsors a language preservation project, and a dictionary has been published under its auspices (in both syllabic and roman orthographies). The language is regularly taught at the University of Oklahoma and at Northeastern Oklahoma University in Tahlequah, and adult classes are held in a number of locations.

Cheyenne [26] is an Algonquian language of the High Plains, spoken on the Northern Cheyenne Reservation in southeastern Montana, and in scattered communities in central Oklahoma. There are a number of differences between the Northern Cheyenne and Southern Cheyenne dialects, but they are not significant. The language is widely spoken in Montana, with about 1,700 first-language speakers out of a total Cheyenne population of 4,000, including at least some children. There are an additional 400 speakers in Oklahoma, most of them middle aged or older. A bilingual education program is sponsored by the Northern Cheyenne Tribe and summer immersion camps have been held since 1998. The language is also taught at the tribally controlled Dull Knife Memorial College in Lame Deer, Montana, and at St Labre Indian School in Ashland, Montana. A standard orthography, based on a missionary writing system, has been used in teaching programs and in published language materials since the early 1970s.

Chickasaw [290] is a Western Muskogean language, closely related to Choctaw, spoken by about 600 members of the Chickasaw Nation of south-central Oklahoma. The youngest speaker is in her mid-forties, though most are in their fifties or older. The language is in use among those who are middle-aged and elderly, and is not being learned by children or by second-language learners. A writing system has only recently been developed, and literacy in Chickasaw is extremely low, though some speakers of Chickasaw are able to read Choctaw. There is a full published dictionary. While Chickasaw is used in some homes, English is used for school and church services (though some Chickasaw speakers attend services in Choctaw). Chickasaw is used at political and senior citizen events. Few courses are offered in Chickasaw, and there is no use of Chickasaw in media.

Chilcotin (Tsilhqot'in) [85] is an Athabaskan language of south-central British Columbia, spoken in several communities along the Chilco and Chilcotin Rivers in the vicinity of Williams Lake, including Alexis Creek, Anaham, Nemaiah Valley, Stone, and Toosey, as well as at Alexandria on the Fraser River. Although Chilcotin adjoins Carrier on the north and there are several communities in which both languages are spoken, they are quite distinct and are not mutually intelligible. Until the 1980s Chilcotin had been considered to be in a relatively healthy state, with many children acquiring it as their first language; in 1979 the language was estimated to have 1,725 speakers, a high percentage of the population. A survey conducted in 1988, however, showed that while a sizeable proportion of Chilcotin children over ten were speakers of the language, younger children spoke only English. Current estimates of the number of speakers range between 400 and 1,200, with the youngest in their mid-teens. There are no fluent second-language speakers, and no literacy program.

Chimariko [182] was spoken in a small territory along the Trinity River and its tributaries in the mountainous interior of northwestern California. It is a classificatory isolate, but usually considered part of the Hokan stock. At the time of contact many Chimarikos were bilingual in Hupa, the adjoining Athabaskan language, and most Chimariko survivors joined the Hupas. The language was extensively documented by Harrington in the 1920s, who worked with the last fluent speakers. None of his material has been published, although some earlier, less accurate material has. The last speaker died around 1950. Modern Chimariko descendants, organized as the

Tsnungwhe Tribe, consider both Hupa and Chimariko to be their heritage languages, but emphasize Hupa for cultural revitalization.

Chinook. See *Kiksht*

Chipewyan (Dene Soun'line) [82] is an Athabaskan language of the Dene complex spoken in a number of communities scattered across a large area in the forest and tundra of northern Alberta, Saskatchewan, and Manitoba, and the eastern Northwest Territories. Among the principal settlements are Cold Lake and Fort Chipewyan, Alberta, and Fort Resolution and Lutselk'e, NWT. Making an accurate estimate of the number of first-language Chipewyan speakers is difficult because many are also speakers of Cree. The Government of Canada estimates a total of 1,865 speakers, the majority in Alberta and Saskatchewan. A recent survey at Cold Lake found only 200 fluent speakers out of 1,800–802,000 Band members, but the proportion is much higher in some remote communities such as Wollaston Lake, Saskatchewan, where most children are reported to be more fluent in Chipewyan than in English. In the Northwest Territories, where Chipewyan has official language status, there are 370 speakers (185 of whom use the language at home) in the communities of Lutselk'e, Ft Smith, and Ft Resolution. The most important revitalization initiative is the Daghida Project at Cold Lake, involving school and community programs, university-level courses, the development of resource materials, as well as linguistic and psycho-linguistic research. Literacy in Chipewyan is rudimentary and there is no standard orthography.

Chitimacha [287], the heritage language of the Chitimacha Tribe of Cheranton, St Mary Parish, Louisiana, was originally spoken throughout the Bayou country at the delta of the Mississippi River. Although attested in several wordlists in the nineteenth- and early twentieth century, Chitimacha is primarily documented in the extensive data collected by Swadesh in 1932–4 from the last two fluent speakers, most of which remains unpublished. The last speaker died in 1940. Although a few scholars think Chitimacha belongs to a 'Gulf' stock, most consider it a classificatory isolate.

Chiwere [271] is a moribund Siouan language of the Chiwere-Winnebago subgroup. Two tribal dialects can be distinguished: **Otoe-Missouria (Jiwere)** is the dialect of the Otoe-Missouria Tribe of the Red Rock region of North Central Oklahoma. **Iowa (Baxoje)** is the dialect of the Iowa Tribe of Perkins, Oklahoma, and of the Iowa Tribe of Kansas and Nebraska at White Cloud, Kansas. The total Chiwere population is about 1,150, but in 1999 only four passive first-language speakers of the Otoe-Missouria dialect remained, none fluent. Language programs have been started in both Oklahoma communities (with tribal employees charged with language preservation and renewal activities), and classes are conducted in the Red Rock high school. No organized activities are reported from the Kansas community. There are about twenty second-language learners, all of whom are at best semi-speakers. There is no tradition of literacy in the language, and its primary function is as a symbol of cultural heritage.

Choctaw [289] is a Western Muskogean language, closely related to Chickasaw, with 9,000 to 11,000 speakers in various locations in Mississippi, Oklahoma and Louisiana. The Mississippi Band of Choctaws has around 5,000 fluent speakers in seven small communities scattered throughout the state (the tribal headquarters is in Philadelphia, Mississippi). The use of Mississippi Choctaw is vigorous at all ages, and many children are monolingual in Choctaw before attending school. The Choctaw Nation of Oklahoma counts at least 4,000 speakers among its more than 20,000 members, most of them middle-aged or elderly. Some Chickasaw speakers in Oklahoma are also bilingual in Choctaw. Choctaw serves a much more restricted range of social functions in Oklahoma than it does in Mississippi, but is prominent in church services. The Oklahoma Choctaws are a widely dispersed group with many tribal members living outside the state, and recent language preservation efforts have emphasized the development of distance learning, including both closed-circuit television and interactive internet courses. In 1999–2000, about 350 learners were actively participating in the internet courses. In Louisiana a small number of Choctaw speakers are found in two small state-recognized tribes, the Clifton Choctaws and the Jena Band. Literacy among all Choctaw speakers is low, though many are competent in the orthography of the Choctaw Bible. In addition to the television and internet courses sponsored by the Choctaw Nation, courses are offered at the University of Oklahoma.

Chumash is the general term for the six languages of the extinct Chumashan family, formerly spoken along the south-central coast of California from Morro Bay to Malibu, as well as in the interior of Santa Barbara and Ventura Counties. Most of the languages are referred to by the Franciscan mission community with which they were associated. **Obispeño [218]**, spoken at San Luis Obispo mission, was quite distinct from the rest. The other languages, except for Island Chumash, were at least partially mutually intelligible and probably constituted a dialect complex with emergent languages structured around the mission communities. **Purisimeño [219]** was spoken at the mission of La Purisima Concepción near Lompoc as well as in the Santa Maria area. **Ineseño [220]** was spoken at Santa Ynez mission and throughout the upper valley of the Santa Ynez River. **Barbareño [221]**, was spoken at Santa Barbara mission and along the southern coast of Santa Barbara County from Point Conception to Carpinteria. **Ventureño [222]** was spoken at San Buenaventura mission and in most of Ventura County. **Island Chumash [223]** was originally spoken on the three largest Channel Islands – San Miguel, Santa Rosa, and Santa Cruz – but with the establishment of the missions the island communities were relocated on the mainland, primarily at San Buenaventura. All of the Chumash languages were poorly documented before the twentieth century, but after 1913 they became the focus of much of Harrington's work. He extensively documented all of the languages, and continued the work until his death in 1961. The last Chumash speaker, a fluent Barbareño, died in 1965. Much of Harrington's documentation has been been organized and analyzed. A full grammar and dictionary of Ineseño exist, as well as a detailed study of the Barbareño documentation and a sketch and lexicon of Island Chumash; other works are in preparation. Although only descendants of the Santa Ynez mission community are currently organized as a recognized tribe, there is considerable interest among all Chumash descendants in restoring their traditional culture and language. The Chumash Living Language Revitalization Project, established in 1999, is a collaboration between linguists and community members.

Coast Miwok [156] was a language of the Western Miwok branch of the Utian family formerly spoken in Marin County and southern Sonoma County, California, immediately to the north of San Francisco. The Coast Miwoks were brought into the Franciscan missions at San Rafael and Sonoma and their culture and language largely destroyed before 1835. Remnants of the language, mostly vocabulary, were collected from survivors between 1840 and 1964. Several local dialects were represented, with the Bodega Bay dialect (Bodega Miwok) somewhat divergent from the others (Marin Miwok). The last known person to have direct knowledge of the language died in the 1970s. A compilation has been made of the extant documentation of Marin Miwok, and a dictionary of Bodega Miwok has been published. The Federated Coast Miwok Tribe, organized in 1992, has recently achieved federal recognition, and some cultural revitalization efforts are under way.

Coast Tsimshian. See *Maritime Tsimshianic*

Cochiti. See *Rio Grande Keresan*

Cocopa [207] is a Yuman language, which together with Diegueño forms the Diegueño-Cocopa subgroup of the family. It was originally spoken by the people of the lowermost Colorado River and its delta. It is spoken today by between 150 and 300 of the approximately 700 members of the Cocopah Tribe, who have a reservation near Yuma, Arizona, and an equal or greater number of Mexican Cucapás in communities in Baja California and Sonora. In Arizona, most Cocopas over fifty are fluent, and a number of younger people are semi-speakers, including at least some children. There is a summer program with some language retention activities, and a course in Cocopa is offered at Yuma Community College.

Coeur d'Alene [135] is a moribund Interior Salish language spoken on the Coeur d'Alene Reservation in northern Idaho. There are only four surviving first-language speakers, ranging in age from the mid-seventies to 101 (the oldest member of the tribe). The language has been taught in the high school for the past five years, and the tribe has an official language program, which provides access to language materials and conducts a well-attended weekly fluency class. In addition, a three-semester college extension course in Coeur d'Alene has been taught since 1996. These educational efforts have been quite successful – approximately 120 students have completed the high school and/or college courses – and there are many second-language speakers (none fully fluent), ranging in age from three to sixty and beyond. The tribe adopted an official writing system in 1996, which is used by all who are teaching and learning the language. A full Coeur d'Alene dictionary is nearing completion.

Columbian [136] is an Interior Salish language, originally spoken in a number of local dialects along the Columbia River in north-central Washington. Most of the approximately twenty-five remaining first-language speakers refer to their dialect as **Nxa'amxcin** and live on or near the Colville Reservation. All are elderly, ranging in age from their late sixties to their mid-eighties with most well over seventy. A few other speakers elsewhere may represent other dialects. The Colville Confederated Tribes began a language preservation program for Nxa'amxcin in 1995, focusing on documentation and analysis rather than revitalization. Informal classes have been held but no second-language speakers have been produced. An analytical dictionary with grammatical notes is being readied for publication. No orthography has been developed

41

for teaching purposes, and many elders object to the idea of Nxa'amxcin literacy. The language is used infrequently in public, due in part to the stronger presence of other languages (Okanagan and Nez Perce) in the reservation community.

Colville. See *Okanagan*

Comanche [228] is a Central Numic language, formerly spoken in the southern Plains from Kansas and Colorado to the Rio Grande. Before the eighteenth century the ancestors of the Comanches were Shoshoni speakers in what is now Wyoming, but the Comanche dialect became quite distinct after the groups separated and they are now mutually intelligible only with difficulty. In the late nineteenth century the Comanches were placed on reservation lands in southwestern Oklahoma, north of Lawton, where the tribe maintains a current membership of about 8,500. No more than 100 are speakers of Comanche, all older than fifty. There are no major dialect divisions, although there are minor variations from town to town which are sometimes attributed to old band divisions. Courses in Comanche have been taught through the University of Oklahoma.

Comox [115] is a Central Salish language, spoken at the northern end of the Strait of Georgia in British Columbia, both on the mainland and on the east coast of Vancouver Island. **Island Comox** and **Mainland Comox** dialects are recognized, the latter divided into three varieties associated respectively with the Homalco, Klahoose, and Sliammon Bands. The last fluent speaker of Island Comox died in the mid-1990s. Although in the early 1980s Mainland Comox was reported to be spoken fluently by about one third of the population, in 2000 it was estimated that there were sixty or fewer active first-language speakers, most of them fifty-five or older, in a total population of 1,500. There are community-based language projects on both the Homalco Reserve at Campbell River and the Sliammon Reserve at Powell River, and there is a Comox language program in the Powell River school system.

Coos. See *Hanis*

Copper Island Aleut Creole [13] is a mixed language (Aleut and Russian) spoken on the Commander Islands (Copper Island and Bering Island), the westernmost islands of the Aleutian chain, near Kamchatka. As of the late 1980s, there were fifteen fluent speakers of Copper Island Aleut, all living on Bering Island. The language originated in the nineteenth century among the children of Russian fur traders and Aleut women, and is characterized by a mixture of Aleut nouns with Russian verbs. All speakers are middle-aged or elderly, and are bilingual in Russian.

Cree-Montagnais-Naskapi [15–21] is a chain of Algonquian dialects extending across Canada from the Rockies to the coast of Labrador. A major distinction is usually drawn between the **Western Cree** dialects (**Plains Cree**, **Woods Cree**, **Swampy Cree**, **Moose Cree** and **Attikamek**) and the **Eastern Cree** dialects of northern Quebec and Labrador (**East Cree**, **Montagnais**, **Naskapi**) primarily on the basis of differing pronunciation. Although there is some degree of mutual intelligibility across the entire chain, a language boundary is often drawn between Eastern Cree and Western Cree ('Cree proper'); Montagnais is also significantly different from East Cree and Naskapi.

Most dialects are thriving, and in some communities a few older speakers are monolingual. In the 1996 Canadian census 102,215 individuals reported that a Cree-Montagnais-Naskapi dialect was their mother tongue, and about half of these (49,850) said that they used it as their home language. The language is strongest in the more northerly, isolated communites, many of which are not accessible by road. Two types of orthography are widely used: an older syllabary developed by missionaries in the nineteenth century and still used in many communities for both religious and secular purposes, and three versions of a roman-based orthography. The Western Cree roman system, promoted relatively recently by linguists at the University of Manitoba, is used primarily in literature and in educational materials. Montagnais uses a French-based roman spelling, recently standarized, as does Atikamek.

Creek (or **Muskogee**) **[295]** is an Eastern Muskogean language spoken by 4,000 to 6,000 residents of the the former territory of the Muscogee (Creek) Nation and Seminole Nation in east-central Oklahoma, and by fewer than 200 members of Seminole Tribe of Florida, most of them living on the Brighton Reservation. The dialect of Creek spoken by the Florida Seminoles is distinct. There are also some differences between the dialects of the tribal groups in Oklahoma. Except for the elderly, almost all Creek speakers also speak English. As of 2001, the youngest speaker in Oklahoma was eighteen, the youngest in Florida forty-four. An alphabet devised by missionaries in the nineteenth century is widely used, and while full literacy in Creek is infrequent many Christian Creeks can read the Bible and hymns. A full dictionary was published in 2000. Creek is routinely used among those in their sixties and above, and is also widely used at church services, for hymns, and for ceremonial speeches. In the early 1990s, there were weekly radio broadcasts in Creek in Oklahoma. Several schools have attempted to introduce Creek in the first few years of primary education, and it has been taught in one elementary school in Florida since 1979. Courses are offered in Creek at the University of Oklahoma and other institutions, and approximately 100 adults study Creek formally each year.

Crow [262], a Siouan language of the Missouri River subgroup, is spoken on the Crow Reservation in southeastern Montana and in adjacent off-reservation communities. Principal towns on the reservation are Crow Agency, Lodge Grass, Pryor, Wyola and St Xavier, and the total tribal enrollment is about 8,500. There are 3,000–4,000 first-language speakers, mostly over the age of thirty. There are a few children, teenagers and young adults who are Crow speakers, and a larger number who are semi-speakers and/or understand the language. A practical orthography has been developed, but few Crow speakers (perhaps several dozen) are literate in the language. There have been bilingual programs in the reservation schools since the 1960s, and these programs have produced a number of language booklets and a small dictionary. The New Testament in Crow is in the final stages of translation. In recent years increasing efforts have been directed toward language preservation through summer immersion programs and early childhood programs.

Cupeño [236], a language of the Cupan division of the Takic subfamily of Uto-Aztecan, was originally spoken near Warner's Hot Springs, in Riverside County, California, but in 1902 the Cupeños were resettled with speakers of Luiseño on the rancheria at Pala. The last fluent speaker of Cupeño died in 1987 at the age of ninety-four, although several people still remember a few words and phrases and there is one elderly semi-speaker. The language has been extensively documented by Hill, who prepared a full grammar. There is a collection of texts and a dictionary for community use.

Dakelh. See ***Carrier***

Dakota. See ***Sioux***

Dakotan is a Siouan dialect complex, within which three relatively well defined dialect areas may be distinguished: **Stoney [266]**, currently spoken in southwestern Alberta; **Assinibone [265]**, in southern Saskatchewan and northern Montana; and **Sioux [264]**, spoken widely in North and South Dakota, Minnesota, and in southern Manitoba and Saskatchewan. Intelligibility between these dialect areas is low, although speakers can communicate after a while with some difficulty, and they are perhaps best considered emergent languages. Sioux is further divided into three major dialects, Santee-Sisseton (Dakota), Yankton-Yanktonai, and Teton (Lakota), between which there is a fair degree of mutual intelligibility.

Delaware (Lenape) [50, 51] is an Eastern Algonquian dialect complex, originally spoken along the Hudson and Delaware Rivers, and in southern New Jersey, but since the eighteenth century in more westerly locations. Three emergent languages are recognized in the complex, one of which, **Mahican**, is long extinct. **Munsee (Munsi) [50]**, originally the language of the lower Hudson River, including the New York City metropolitan area, is the heritage language of the Delaware First Nation, on the Moraviantown Reserve, near Thamesville, Ontario. **Unami [51]**, originally spoken in eastern Pennsylvania, southern New Jersey, and northern Delaware, is the heritage language of the Delaware Tribe, at Bartlesville, Oklahoma, and the Delaware Tribe of Western Oklahoma, at Anadarko. As of 2001 only one fluent first-language speaker remained, a speaker of Unami who lived in Bartlesville. There are regular language classes held in Bartlesville and Moraviantown, and there are between six and eight second-language learners, with varying degrees of fluency, in each of the three communities. The language is mostly used as a badge of tribal identity, and to pray at religious/ceremonial functions. The Lenape Language Project, sponsored by the Delaware Tribe at Bartlesville, plans to integrate classes with existing child-care programs and is developing CD-ROMs in the language.

Dene, in older Canadian usage synonymous with 'Athabaskan', is now used as the name of a complex of Athabaskan dialects and emergent languages in the Mackenzie River drainage of northwestern Canada, primarily in the Northwest Territories but also extending into parts of northern British Columbia, Alberta, Saskatchewan, and Manitoba. Three major Dene languages are distinguished, **Slavey, Dogrib [81]**, and **Chipewyan [82]**. Slavey can be further divided into **Bearlake** and **Hare** (together constituting **North Slavey [80]**), **Mountain**, and **Slave** or **South Slavey [77]**. There is a moderate degree of mutual intelligibility across the Dene complex, but this extends as well to some adjacent Athabaskan languages (particularly Beaver, Sekani and Kaska) that are not usually called Dene. The group is defined as much on a social and political basis (the Athabaskan languages of the Northwest Territories) as on a linguistic basis.

Diegueño is the general term for a complex of Yuman dialects spoken on the coast of southern California and northern Baja California. Three emergent languages are recognized within this complex: **Ipai [204]**, or Northern Diegueño, is spoken by a small number of elderly people in four communities in northwestern San Diego County, including Mesa Grande, Santa Ysabel, San Pasqual, and Barona. **Kumeyaay [205]** is spoken in several locations in central and southern San Diego County, the most important of these being Campo. There are between forty and fifty fluent speakers. (In recent years the entire Diegueño dialect complex has also been referred to as Kumeyaay, creating some confusion.) **Tipai [206]** is spoken by approximately 100 people in several communities in northern Baja California, as far south as Ensenada and Santa Catarina, and also in California by the Jamul community near San Diego. The distinction between Kumeyaay and Tipai is perhaps more political and social than it is linguistic, and is greatly influenced by the US-Mexican border. Several Diegueño groups have instituted language classes, and a dictionary and pedagogical grammar were published for the Mesa Grande variety of Ipai in the 1970s.

Ditidaht. See *Nitinaht*

Dogrib [81] is an Athabaskan language of the Dene complex spoken in the Northwest Territories between Great Slave Lake and Great Bear Lake. It is the first language of 2,470 people (of whom about 1,350 regularly use it in the home), primarily in five small communities: Detah (105 speakers out of a total population of 190), Rae Lakes (210 out of 260), Rae-Edzo (1,010 out of 1,655), Snare Lake (100 out of 135), and Wha Ti (325 out of 415). There are also about 220 speakers in the city of Yellowknife, as well as an unknown number of speakers in the dialectally mixed community of Déline (Fort Franklin), where Bearlake is the lingua franca. Dogrib is one of the official languages of the Northwest Territories.

East Cree [20] is the Eastern Cree dialect spoken in northwestern Quebec, along the east coast of James and Hudson Bay and inland. There is a distinction between northern and southern subdialects, the latter with coastal and inland varieties. The northern dialect is spoken in Whapamagostui (Great Whale River), Chisasibi (Fort George), and Wemindji (Paint Hills); southern dialects are spoken in Nemaska (Nemiscau), Waskaganish (Rupert House), Eastmain, Waswanipi, Ouje-bougamau and Mistissini. Of a population of about 12,000, all but a small number are speakers. Schooling is in Cree to grade four, using the syllabic orthography, and in French in the upper grades, with a Cree maintenance program. Local radio service is provided in Cree in each community.

Eastern Canadian Inuktitut. See *Inuktitut*

Eastern Eskimo. See *Inuit*

Eastern Miwok, one of the two branches of the Miwok languages of north-central California, consists of five languages: **Bay Miwok** and **Plains Miwok** are extinct. East and south of the Plains Miwok, in the Sierra Nevada mountains as far south as Yosemite Valley, was the territory of the Sierra Miwoks. Their descendants (who refer to themselves as 'Mewuk') now live in a scattering of small communities, the largest at

45

the Jackson and Tuolumne Rancherias. Of the three emergent languages that are usually distinguished in the Sierra Miwok dialect complex, the most visible today is **Northern Sierra Miwok [160]**, spoken at the Jackson Rancheria near Westpoint. It is estimated that there are between six and twelve speakers, only one of whom has active conversational fluency. There is a sustained community interest in language revival, and several of the speakers meet regularly as an informal language class/forum. Elementary curricular materials were prepared in the 1980s for a (now-terminated) bilingual program in the San Juan Unified School District in Carmichael, and a practical orthography was established. Extensive documentation of Northern Sierra Miwok has been made in recent years, including numerous audiotapes and videotapes of speakers. Both of the other two Sierra Miwok languages, **Central Sierra Miwok [161]**, and **Southern Sierra Miwok [162]** have a few semi-speakers or passive speakers, but no overt community activity is focused on their survival or revitalization.

Eel River Athabaskan [97] was a complex of closely related local dialects of California Athabaskan that were formerly spoken along the Eel River and its major tributaries in Humboldt and Mendocino Counties. At least four dialect clusters can be distinguished: Sinkyone, Nongatl, Lassik, and Wailaki. Some documentation exists for all of these, most extensively for Wailaki, although much of it is unpublished. Semi-fluent speakers of one or more Eel River Athabaskan varieties survived into the 1970s.

Eyak [58], the only member of its branch of the Na-Dene family, was spoken in the nineteenth century along the south-central Alaska coast from Yakutat to the Copper River. Today, about fifty of the approximately 500 members of the Eyak Village corporation recognize Eyak or part-Eyak ancestry (most of the others are Chugach). As of 2001 there was only one remaining speaker, born in 1920 and living in Anchorage. Comprehensive documentation of Eyak has been carried out since the 1960s by Michael Krauss, most of it unpublished. The Eyak narrative tradition is well documented in a collection of traditional stories and historic accounts by one of the last speakers.

Flathead. See *Spokane-Kalispel*

Gabrielino (Tongva) [234], a language of the Serrano-Gabrielino division of the Takic subfamily of Uto-Aztecan, was the language of the community at San Gabriel mission. The Gabrielino were originally a large and powerful tribe whose territory included most of Los Angeles and Orange County. Several local dialects were distinguished including Gabrielino (proper), spoken in the Los Angeles basin; Fernandeño, spoken in San Fernando Valley; and the variety spoken on Santa Catalina Island. The Gabrielino were nearly destroyed by missionization, but a few speakers survived into the twentieth century and the language was extensively documented, primarily by Harrington beween 1914 and 1933. Nearly all of the documentation remains unpublished, but it helps sustain intermittent language revival efforts by the community of Tongva-Gabrielino descendants.

Galice-Applegate [92] was a language of the Oregon Athabaskan subgroup formerly spoken along Galice Creek and Applegate River, tributaries of the Rogue River in southwestern Oregon. There were at least two distinct dialects, but only the Galice

Creek dialect is well documented. After the Rogue River War of 1855–6 the Galice-Applegate people were forcibly resettled in northern Oregon on the Grand Ronde and Siletz Reservations, where the language fell into disuse. Although the language is not well attested otherwise, the speech of the last speaker of Galice Creek, who died in the 1960s, was extensively documented by Hoijer, who published a grammatical sketch and lexicon.

Gitksan. See *Nass-Gitksan*

Gosiute. See *Shoshoni*

Greenlandic [10, 11] is the English name for the **Inuit (Eastern Eskimo)** dialects of Greenland (the Inuit term is Kalaallisut). Of the seventy-nine Inuit communities in Greenland, all but seventeen are on the west coast, including the largest, Nuuk (Gothåb), which has an Inuit population of 8,500. There is a significant dialect difference between the west coast settlements and those on the east coast, leading to a distinction between **West Greenlandic [10]** and **East Greenlandic [11]**. The five Thule communities in the far northwest of the island constitute a third dialect cluster, sometimes called **Polar Eskimo**. This dialect is closer to the speech of Baffin Island than to West or East Greenlandic, and is usually considered to be a variety of Eastern Canadian Inuktitut that has been influenced by standard Greenlandic. Greenland, which became an autonomous province associated with the Danish Commonwealth in 1979, has a population of about 56,000, approximately 10,000 of whom are Danes. The remaining 46,000 are Inuit, nearly all of them speakers of Greenlandic. Another 7,000 speakers of Greenlandic live in Denmark, most of them in Copenhagen. A writing system was introduced by early Danish missionaries; the literacy rate is very high and there has been a flourishing literature in Greenlandic for over 200 years. Since Home Rule in 1979 Greenland's official language has been Greenlandic (standardized to the Nuuk dialect of West Greenlandic, and written in a roman orthography), although Danish still predominates in administration, the media and education.

Gros Ventre (Atsina) [24], a moribund Algonquian language of the High Plains, is a highly differentiated dialect of Arapaho, with which it is mutually intelligible. It is the heritage language of approximately 1,000 Gros Ventre who live on the Fort Belknap Reservation in north-central Montana, which they share with the Siouan Assiniboine. The Gros Ventre are descendants of Arapahos who allied with the Blackfeet in the eighteenth century. (They are occasionally confused with the completely unrelated Hidatsa, whom the French also called Gros Ventre, apparently because the symbols for the two tribes in Plains Indian Sign Language are quite similar.) Fewer than ten elderly first-language speakers remain, none of them fully fluent; the last traditional speaker died in 1981. The language was intensively documented in a University of Colorado project in the 1970s, and a full dictionary was prepared, although not published. Courses in Gros Ventre are taught at Fort Belknap Community College in Harlen, Montana.

Gwich'in (Kutchin) [70] is an Athabaskan language spoken in northeastern Alaska in the villages of Arctic Village, Venetie, Fort Yukon, Chalkyitsik, Circle, and Birch

Creek, as well as in Aklavik, Inuvik, Tsiigehtchic (formerly Arctic Red River) and Fort McPherson in the Northwest Territories, and in Old Crow in the Yukon Territory. A distinction is made between Western (Alaskan) and Eastern (Canadian) dialects, with the latter often called **Loucheux**. The Gwich'in population of Alaska is about 1,100, and of that number about 300 are speakers of the language; the Canadian population is about 1,900, with perhaps as many as 500 speakers. Gwich'in has had a written literature since the 1870s, when Archdeacon Robert McDonald translated the entire Bible (1886), the Book of Common Prayer, and a hymnal into a variety of Eastern Gwich'in he called **Tukudh**. Middle-aged and older speakers still use McDonald's Bible, but younger speakers find its orthography and style difficult. Modern writing systems have been developed both in Alaska (in the 1960s by Richard Mueller) and in Canada (in the mid-1970s by the Yukon Native Language Centre), and there are many publications in both, including story collections and linguistic material. Gwich'in has been taught in the school at Old Crow since the early 1970s, and in 1996 Old Crow students launched a website, 'Old Crow: Land of the Vuntut Gwich'in.'

Haida [105], a classificatory isolate (sometimes grouped with Na-Dene), is the aboriginal language of the isolated Queen Charlotte Islands (known locally as *Haida Gwaai*), which lie about seventy-five miles off the coast of British Columbia, immediately south of Alaska. There are two Haida villages on the Queen Charlottes, each with a distinct dialect: Masset (pop. 750) and Skidegate (pop. 500). Between fifty and 100 first-language speakers, none younger than fifty, are divided between the two communities; only those over seventy are active speakers. The language is taught at Skidegate in a community-based immersion program, and has been offered for university credit in partnership with the University of Northern British Columbia. This has not so far produced any fluent second-language speakers, although there is some beginning literacy; at least one non-native linguist has acquired second-language proficiency. Language use is restricted to formal gatherings. About 600 additional Haida people live in Alaska (representing an eighteenth-century migration from Masset), in the villages of Hydaburg, Kasaan, and Craig on the southern half of Prince of Wales Island, as well as in the city of Ketchikan. Only about fifteen Alaskan Haidas, all very elderly, are active speakers of the language. A modern writing system was developed for the Alaska dialect in 1972.

Haisla [106] is the northernmost Northern Wakashan language, spoken in northwestern British Columbia immediately adjacent to Coast Tsimshianic. The principal Haisla community is Kitamaat, where out of a total population of 600 there are estimated to be between fifty and 150 fluent speakers, none under the age of twenty-five. Haisla has been taught in Kitamaat by the University of Northern British Columbia since 1994, and a small number of people have acquired second-language fluency and literacy. No children read or write the language.

Halkomelem [119] is a Central Salish language, spoken in southwestern British Columbia in a number of small communities along the lower Fraser River and on the east coast of Vancouver Island. The combined population of all Halkomelem groups is 6,700, of whom about 120 speak the language with some degree of fluency, with another 100 passive speakers. Three dialects are recognized: (1) **Island Halkomelem**, on the southeast coast of Vancouver Island, is spoken in local varieties at Malahat,

Cowichan, Halalt, Chemainus, Penelakut, Nanaimo, and Nanoose. There are up to 100 active speakers, and several community language programs. (2) **Downriver Halkomelem**, at the mouth of the Fraser River in and around the city of Vancouver, has six elderly first-language speakers. The language is being revived on the Musqueam Reserve through a program based at the (closely adjacent) University of British Columbia. On the Tsawwassen Reserve language courses are offered for adults through Simon Fraser University; the Katzie Reserve has a program for elementary school children; and both the Tsawwassen and Katzie bands have summer immersion camps in language and culture for children. Although no fluent speakers have resulted from these programs, several people have acquired good transcription and pronunciation skills and are teaching the language to others. (3) **Upriver Halkomelem** (Sto:lo), in the Fraser River valley, has between five and ten fluent speakers, the youngest over seventy. Band-sponsored language classes have produced an additional ten to twnety second-language speakers, a few of whom are able to read and write the language. The principal use of the language is for religious ceremonies and songs, and literacy is restricted to language class settings.

Han (Hän) [71] is a moribund Athabaskan language spoken in the village of Eagle, Alaska, and in Dawson City, Yukon Territory. Of the total Alaskan Han population of about fifty people, perhaps twelve speak the language. In Dawson City only a handful of fluent speakers remain. Han is closely related to Gwich'in, and some older speakers make use of Archdeacon McDonald's Tukudh (Eastern Gwich'in) Bible (1886) and prayer book. A modern writing system was established in the 1970s and considerable documentation has been carried out, both by the Alaska Native Language Center and by the Yukon Native Language Centre in Whitehorse; more than a dozen publications are currently available. A Han Language program has been in operation since 1991 at Robert Service School in Dawson City, and the Tr'ondëk Hwëch'in (formerly the Dawson First Nation) sponsors an adult language class and organizes cultural gatherings.

Hanis [145] and **Miluk [146]** were the two languages of the Coosan family, formerly spoken in a small territory along the south-central coast of Oregon around Coos Bay. Both languages are often referred to as 'Coos', although they were quite distinct. Although some Hanis and Miluk people were removed to reservations between 1855 and 1875, most remained in their traditional territory, where more than 150 descendants still reside. The Confererated Tribes of Coos, Lower Umpqua, and Siuslaw was recognized in 1984, with tribal headquarters at Coos Bay. Extensive documentation of both Hanis and Miluk exists, from several linguists, including a number of sound recordings made by Jacobs in the 1930s. A number of narrative texts have been published in both languages, and a grammatical sketch of Hanis. The last fluent speaker of Miluk died in 1939, and the last speaker of Hanis in 1972. The Confederated Tribes have a language program and some educational materials on Hanis and Miluk have been prepared for use by tribal members.

Hano. See *Tewa*

Hare [80] is an emergent Athabaskan language within the North Slavey group of Slavey dialects of the Dene complex. It is spoken as a first language by about seventy people (thirty of whom use it actively at home) in two communities in the Northwest Territories, Colville Lake (thirty speakers out of a total population of ninety), and Fort Good Hope (forty-five speakers out of 645 total).

Havasupai. See *Upland Yuman*

Heiltsuk-Oowekyala [107] is a Northern Wakashan language, spoken on the coast of British Columbia south of Haisla and Coast Tsimshianic and north of Kwakiutl. It has two deeply differentiated dialects, or emergent languages, **Heiltsuk** (also known as **Bella Bella**) and **Oowekyala**. Heiltsuk is principally spoken in two communities, Bella Bella (population 1,200) and Kitasoo (or Klemtu, population 370), the latter on former Southern Tsimshian territory. There are between 100 and 200 fluent speakers, none under the age of thirty-five. A local teaching program at Bella Bella is linked with Simon Fraser University, and a small number of people have achieved second-language fluency and some degree of literacy. Oowekyala – the dialect of the Oowe-keeno people – is spoken by a few residents of a community at the lower end of Wannock River, at the head of Rivers Inlet.

Hidatsa [261] is a Siouan language of the Missouri River subgroup, originally spoken in a group of villages along the Missouri River in central North Dakota upstream from the Mandan villages. The modern Hidatsas (sometimes called **Gros Ventres**) are one of the Three Affiliated Tribes and share the Fort Berthold Reservation of North Dakota with the Mandans and the Arikaras. Their principal reservation settlement is Mandaree. There are about 200 fluent speakers, the youngest in their late twenties. The language is used conversationally by most older Hidatsas, but it is rarely used in public settings except in announcements at rodeos and pow-wows, where it is a badge of tribal identity in the larger reservation community. No children are first-language speakers, although a few may have passive knowledge. Curriculum for a language program is under development.

Hitchiti. See *Mikasuki*

Holikachuk [62] is a moribund Athabaskan language of west-central Alaska, formerly spoken by a group that lived at Holikachuk on the Innoko River, but which is now located at Grayling on the lower Yukon River. Holikachuk is intermediate between Ingalik and Koyukon, and was only identified as a separate language in the 1970s. The total population is about 200, of whom six or seven speak the language.

Hopi [238] is the traditional language of Hopi Pueblo and constitutes an independent branch of the Uto-Aztecan family. At least 5,000 of the approximately 7,350 members of the tribe are fluent speakers, including many children. Four dialects are usually distinguished: (1) the First Mesa villages of Walpi and Sichomovi (the language of a third First Mesa village, Hano, is Tewa) and the town of Polacca; (2) the Second Mesa village of Shipaulovi; (3) the Second Mesa village of Mishongnovi (also called Toreva); and (4) the Third Mesa villages of Oraibi, Hotevilla, Bacabi, and New Oraibi, as well as the settlement of Moencopi forty miles to the west. The language is superbly documented, most notably in a tribally sponsored dictionary published in 1997 that focuses on the Third Mesa dialect. Hopi is the medium of instruction in tribal schools, and is taught at Northern Arizona University in Flagstaff.

Hualapai. See *Upland Yuman*

Hupa [95], the only surviving language of the Calfornia Athabaskan subgroup, is spoken on the Hoopa Valley Reservation in northwest California. There are fewer than twelve fluent first-language speakers, all elderly, who use the language primarily in educational and ceremonial settings. A tribally sponsored language program, in operation since the early 1980s, has produced a dictionary and other pedagogical materials, using a standardized practical orthography. The language is taught at both the K-8 and high school levels, and up to thirty second-language speakers exist with varying degrees of fluency. Traditional literature is well documented in publications by Goddard, and by Sapir and Golla.

Huron-Wyandotte (Wendat) [303] was a Northern Iroquoian language that was originally spoken in the Georgian Bay area of Ontario, near Lake Huron. A variety of this language was the lingua franca of the Huron Confederacy in the seventeenth century and extensively documented by Jesuit missionaries. After the Huron Confederacy was destroyed by the Iroquois around 1650 in a war over control of the fur trade, some Hurons settled at Lorette, near Quebec City, where their French-speaking descendants still live. Others moved to Ohio, from where they were removed to Kansas and Oklahoma in the nineteenth century, where they are now organized as the Wyandotte Tribe of Oklahoma, with about 3,600 members. The Oklahoma group was the last to retain its language, but the last native speaker died around 1960. The last speakers, both in Quebec and in Oklahoma, were extensively documented by Barbeau early in the twentieth century; forty analyzed texts were published, but much remains in manuscript. The communities in both Oklahoma and Quebec have limited language programs. In Oklahoma the program teaches words and phrases in the local elementary school and, with the help of a linguist, is planning publication of a collection of stories, along with a dictionary and handbook.

Ineseño. See *Chumash*

Ingalik (Deg Xinag) [61] is an Athabaskan language of west-central Alaska, spoken at Shageluk and Anvik and by the Athabaskans in the multilingual community at Holy Cross on the lower Yukon River. Of a total population of about 275, about forty speak the language. A collection of traditional folk tales by the elder Belle Deacon was published in 1987, and a literacy manual in 1993.

Innu-aimun is a socio-political designation for the Cree dialects of Labrador, specifically the Eastern Naskapi spoken at Davis Inlet and the Montagnais spoken at Sheshatshiu. The term is also sometimes used to refer to all Montagnais dialects. An occasional newspaper in both English and Innu-aimun, as well as community radio, is provided for the two Labrador communities.

Inuit (Eastern Eskimo) consists of a chain of dialects spoken in at least 165 settlements from Norton Sound in Northwestern Alaska to the East Coast of Greenland. The dialects at the opposite ends of this chain are not mutually intelligible, but the location of 'language' boundaries is largely arbitrary. Mainly for political and cultural reasons three languages are distinguished, **Inupiaq** in Alaska, **Inuktitut** in Canada, and

Greenlandic in Greenland. Each of these is subdivided into dialect clusters or emergent languages. Despite these dialect and national differences, all speakers of Inuit recognize a common linguistic heritage and there is increasing communication among them. In Greenland and in the newly established territory of Nunavut in Canada, Inuit is the official language and standardization is under way.

Inuktitut [8, 9] is the collective name for the dialects of **Inuit (Eastern Eskimo)** spoken on the northern coast of Canada, from the Mackenzie Delta in the west to Labrador in the east. (It is also sometimes used for Eastern Eskimo dialects in general, synonymous with Inuit.) The dialects of **Western Canadian Inuktitut [8]** are usually distinguished from **Eastern Canadian Inuktitut [9]**, the boundary falling between the Central Arctic coast and Baffin Island, but there is no sharp discontinuity. All of the Inuktitut speakers of the newly formed territory of Nunavut, which encompasses dialects belonging to both the Western and Eastern divisions, can understand one another's speech. A more socially significant difference between Inuktitut communities is whether indigenous literacy is in a roman orthography or in Inuit syllabics. A syllabic writing system, introduced by Anglican missionaries in the late nineteenth century and modeled on the syllabary earlier developed for Cree, is now the preferred writing of Inuktitut in much of the central Canadian area, with a roman orthography in common use only in Labrador and from Cambridge Bay westward. In Nunavut, the Inuinnaqtun dialect of the western Kitikmeot region is written in a roman orthography, while in the rest of the territory syllabics are used, and this distinction more than phonological or lexical dialect differences is the principal obstacle to standardization. The Inuktitut population in Canada is about 31,000, a high proportion being speakers. In the 1996 Canadian census 26,960 people indicated Inuktitut was their first language, 18,495 of them in the Northwest Territories (and Nunavut) and 7,685 in Quebec. Literacy is high, both in roman and syllabic orthographies. Since the establishment of Nunavut as a preponderantly aboriginal territory within Canada in 1999, Inuktitut has enjoyed official status in that jurisdiction. It is government policy to insure that Inuktitut is used in all public offices and is taught from grades K to 12 in all Nunavut schools. The government of Nunavut also offers Inuktitut language classes to new employees from other parts of the country.

Inupiaq [6, 7] Inupiaq is the collective term for the dialects of **Eastern Eskimo** (q.v.) spoken in Alaska and immediately adjacent parts of Northern Canada. There are two major dialect groups, **Seward Peninsula Inupiaq (Qawiaraq) [6]** and **North Alaskan Inupiaq [7]**. Seward Peninsula Inupiaq includes the local dialects of the southern Seward Peninsula and Norton Sound area, and of the villages surrounding Bering Strait and on King and Diomede Islands. North Alaskan Inupiaq includes the Malimiut dialect around Kotzebue Sound and the North Slope dialect spoken along the Arctic Coast as far east as the Mackenzie Delta. The Seward Peninsula and North Alaskan dialect groups differ significantly from each other and a fair amount of experience is required for a speaker of one to understand a speaker of the other. There are about 13,500 Inupiat (the plural form, referring to the people collectively) in Alaska, of whom about 3,000, mostly over age forty, speak the language.

Iowa (Baxoje). See *Chiwere*

Ipai. See *Diegueño*

Jemez [242], sometimes known as **Towa**, is the Kiowa-Tanoan language of the Pueblo of Jemez (pronounced He-mish), forty-five miles northwest of Albuquerque. The residents of the former Pueblo of Pecos, east of Santa Fe, moved to Jemez early in the nineteenth century and some Pecos descendants retain separate traditions and – to an undocumented extent – a distinctive variety of Towa. Nearly the entire Jemez population of about 3,000 speaks the language, including most children. Attitudes toward language are conservative and traditional, and traditional Pueblo law forbids writing Jemez or teaching it to outsiders.

Jicarilla [102] is an emergent language within the Southern Athabaskan dialect complex, spoken on the Jicarilla Reservation in northeastern New Mexico. There are about 300 first-language speakers and an equal or greater number of semi-speakers out of a total Jicarilla tribal population of 3,100.

Juaneño. See *Luiseño*

Kalapuya is the general term for the three languages of the Kalapuyan family, **Tualatin-Yamhill [148]**, **Central Kalapuyan (or Santiam) [149]**, and **Yoncalla [150]**, formerly spoken throughout most of the Willamette River valley of western Oregon. All three languages had well differentiated local dialects. The Kalapuya people suffered a catastrophic demographic decline after contact with whites, and in 1856 the few survivors were settled on the Grand Ronde Reservation, where most abandoned their native language for other Indian languages or Chinook Jargon. The best documented varieties of Kalapuya are the Tualatin dialect of Tualatin-Yamhill and a variety of Santiam, but Jacobs was able to collect a substantial amount of data for all three languages, much of it from elderly speakers in the 1920s and 1930s. This documentation remains largely unpublished except for an extensive collection of narrative texts (without interlinear glossing). Most Kalapuyan varieties were extinct before 1940, but a speaker of Santiam lived into the 1950s.

Kansa [269] was a language of the Dhegiha subgroup of Siouan closely related to Osage. Kansa was spoken before the mid-nineteenth century by the Kansa or Kaw tribe in northeastern Kansas, which was removed in 1873 to a small reservation in Oklahoma. Dissolved in 1902, the Kaw Nation was reconstituted in 1959 with a headquarters at Kaw City, Oklahoma, and now has a membership of about 1,700. There have been no fluent speakers of the language since the early 1980s, but about a dozen people claim some knowledge of it. A language revitalization program has been started.

Karuk [181], a classificatory isolate of the Hokan stock, is the heritage language of the Karuk Tribe of the Klamath River in northwestern California. There are fewer than a dozen fluent first-language speakers, and a larger number of semi-speakers and passive speakers. Up to thirty people have some degree of second-language fluency, including a near-traditional command of the language on the part of a small group of tribal scholars and cultural revival activists. In addition, many children have acquired a degree of familiarity with Karuk in school-based programs at both the primary and the secondary level, and through a tribally sponsored summer immersion camp. Several pairs of speakers and learners have participated in the master-apprentice program. The tribe has a Language Committee that coordinates some of these activities, and a standard writing system was adopted in the 1980s. One tribal scholar has published extensively in Karuk.

Kashaya. See *Pomo*

Kaska [74] is an Athabaskan language spoken in the southeastern Yukon at Ross River, Watson Lake and Upper Liard, and in northern British Columbia at Lower Post, Fireside, Good Hope Lake, Dease Lake and Muncho Lake. In all these communities there is perhaps a total of 250 fluent speakers and another 150 passive speakers. Kaska territory adjoins that of **Tahltan** (as well as to extinct Tagish) on the southwest and **Sekani** on the southeast, and a high degree of mutual intelligibility exists between these languages and the adjoining dialects of Kaska. The Yukon Native Language Centre conducts annual Literacy Workshops and produces teaching and learning materials. Kaska is taught at schools in Watson Lake and Ross River in the Yukon, and at Lower Post and Good Hope Lake in British Columbia. In 1997 the Kaska Tribal Council, working with the linguist Pat Moore, published a two-volume topical noun dictionary.

Kato (Cahto) [98] was the California Athabaskan language that was formerly spoken in Cahto Valley, near Laytonville. It was extensively documented around 1905–10 by Goddard, who published a grammatical sketch and a volume of narrative texts. The last fluent speaker died in the 1960s, but a few individuals remain who have fragmentary memories of the language. Kato is the heritage language of the Cahto Tribe of Laytonville Rancheria, and there is some interest in language revitalization.

Kaw. See *Kansa*

Kawaiisu [229] is the Southern Numic language of a small unrecognized tribe of the Tehachapi region between the Mohave Desert and the San Joaquin Valley in south-central California. Fewer than ten speakers were reported in 1994, but this is a significant proportion of the total population of this culturally conservative group, which is less than 100.

Keweevkapaya (Yavapai). See *Upland Yuman*

Kickapoo [37] is a Central Algonquian language, mutually intelligible with Sauk-Fox but spoken since the mid-nineteenth century in separate locations. These include reservations in Kansas and in Oklahoma, and a culturally conservative community in the Mexican state of Coahuilla (with land and US federal recognition in the Rio Grande River valley of southern Texas). There are estimated to be around 1,100 first-language speakers of Kickapoo, about 700 of them in Mexico, 400 in Oklahoma, and only a few in Kansas.

Kiksht [141] is the only surviving language of the Chinookan family, originally spoken along the Columbia River from its mouth upriver to the vicinity of The Dalles. Kiksht (or **Upper Chinook**) was the language spoken upstream from Portland and originally included a string of dialects, of which only the easternmost, **Wasco-Wishram**, is still spoken. The Wasco variety is represented by five elderly speakers on the Warm Springs Reservation in north-central Oregon. The Wishram variety is spoken by two elders on the Yakima Reservation in eastern Washington. Kiksht has been extensively documented by linguists, most significantly by Sapir in 1905, and a full dictionary has been prepared (although not yet published). Wasco language classes are given at Warm Springs and a large amount of instructional material exists.

Kiliwa [208] is a Yuman language, forming its own distinct subgroup. Originally spoken on the Baja California peninsula south of Paipai, fewer than ten surviving speakers of Kiliwa now share the Santa Catarina community with speakers of Paipai. No language retention efforts are reported.

King's River. See *Yokuts*

Kiowa [241] is the only Kiowa-Tanoan language not spoken in a Pueblo community. It is the traditional language of the Kiowas, a Plains tribe now settled in southwestern Oklahoma, mainly in Caddo, Kiowa, and Comanche counties. There is no reservation, but the Kiowa Tribe has its headquarters in Carnegie, Oklahoma. There are fewer than 400 speakers, most over the age of fifty, out of a population of about 6,000. Parker McKenzie (1897–1999), a self-taught Kiowa linguist, devised a practical phonetic alphabet and published several important works on his language, some of them in collaboration with John P. Harrington.

Kiowa Apache (Plains Apache) [104] is a nearly extinct Southern Athabaskan language, distinctly different from the rest of the Southern Athabaskan dialect complex. It is spoken in Caddo County, western Oklahoma, by the descendants of an Apache band that joined the Kiowas in the eighteenth century. Only three very elderly first-language speakers remain, together with a few semi-speakers, but there are no second-language speakers. There is no tradition of writing the language, and there are no education efforts being made at this time, although there were some limited attempts to teach the language in previous years.

Kitanemuk [233] was a language of the Serrano-Gabrielino division of the Takic subfamily of Uto-Aztecan, closely related to Serrano. It was formerly spoken in the Tehachapi Mountains and Antelope Valley in the interior of southern California, immediately south of the San Joaquin Valley. It was extensively documented by Harrington in 1916–17, and a grammar and dictionary were prepared on the basis of his materials. The last speakers probably died in the 1940s.

Kitsai [281] was the Northern Caddoan language of a tribe that formerly lived south of the Wichitas in east Texas, but which joined the Wichitas in Oklahoma in 1858. Kitsai continued to be spoken alongside Wichita for two or three generations, and then died out. The language was moderately well documented in 1929–30 from the last speaker, who died in 1940.

Klallam (Clallam) [122] is the Central Salish language of the north shore of the Olympic Peninsula in the State of Washington, closely related to **Northern Straits**

Salish (the two languages are sometimes grouped together as 'Straits Salish'). The principal Klallam communities are at three small reservations, Port Gamble, Lower Elwha, and Jamestown. There is also a Klallam community on the Becher Bay Reserve on Vancouver Island. There are very few first-language speakers remaining (two of them at Becher Bay), none fully fluent. The language is used in ceremonies and for tribal identity and there is considerable interest in revival. Klallam is taught as the 'heritage language' in public K-12 schools, as well as in the Headstart program, and language material is available on the internet. At present there are six second-language speakers at varying levels of fluency, and the number is growing; all are literate in Klallam.

Klamath-Modoc [177] is the Plateau Penutian language originally spoken, in shallowly differentiated dialects, by both the Klamaths of south-central Oregon and the Modocs of the Tule Lake area in adjacent northeastern California. After the Modoc War of 1872–3 about 150 Modocs were relocated in Oklahoma, the remainder merging into the Klamath community. The Modoc dialect is extinct in Oklahoma. The Klamath dialect has continued to be spoken in and around the former reservation community of Chiloquin, Oregon. (The Klamath Tribe was terminated in 1954, and although it was re-recognized in 1986 the Klamath Reservation was not restored.) In 2001 only one very elderly first-language speaker survived. Revitalization efforts have been made at Chiloquin, in informal liaison with anthropologists and linguists from the University of Oregon who have drawn on the extensive documentation of the language by Gatschet in the late nineteenth century and Barker in the 1950s. These efforts have included language lessons in the tribal Head Start program, weekly classes in the local primary school and after-school program, and weekly community meetings. About half a dozen adult second-language speakers have been produced, two of whom are moderately fluent.

Koasati (Coushatta) [294] is an Eastern Muskogean language, closely related to Alabama. It is spoken by 300 to 400 members of the Coushatta Tribe of Louisiana (living near Elton, in Allen Parish), and by up to 100 residents of the Alabama-Coushatta Indian Reservation near Livingston, Texas, where Alabama is the dominant language; some speakers of Alabama have also learned to speak Koasati. There are speakers of all ages in the Louisiana community, which is culturally quite conservative. Until recently there were also a few elderly speakers of Koasati among the 900 enrolled members of the Alabama-Quassarte Tribe, an administrative subdivision of the Muskogee Creek Nation, in Okfuskee County, Oklahoma. Although a full dictionary of Koasati was published in 1994, no writing system is in general use, and literacy in the language is extremely low.

Kolchan. See ***Upper Kuskokwim***

Konkow [154] is a Maiduan language, spoken in the Feather River and Oroville area of Butte and Yuba County, California, at the eastern edge of the Sacramento Valley. The principal modern Konkow community is at the Mooretown Rancheria. There are a few elderly speakers, who participate in a Konkow Language Preservation Group.

Koyukon [63] is the Athabaskan language of eleven villages along the Koyukuk and middle Yukon rivers of central Alaska, the most widespread Athabaskan language in the state. It is spoken in three dialects, Upper, Central, and Lower. About 300 speak the language, out of a total population of about 2,300. Koyukon was painstakingly documented by the Jesuit missionary Jules Jetté in the early twentieth century. Since the 1970s, native Koyukon speaker Eliza Jones has produced much linguistic material for use in schools and by the general public, and (together with James Kari) has edited a comprehensive dictionary based on Jetté's manuscripts.

Kumeyaay. See *Diegueño*

Kutchin. See *Gwich'in*

Kutenai (Kootenai, Ktunaxa) [259], a classificatory isolate, is the heritage language of three politically independent groups in Montana, Idaho and British Columbia (the name Ktunaxa is now official in Canada). The Montana Kootenai are part of the Confederated Salish and Kootenai Tribes, and are concentrated at the northern end of the Flathead Reservation, around Elmo. The Kootenai Tribe of Idaho has a reservation near Bonners Ferry in the Idaho panhandle. The communities in British Columbia are represented by the Ktunaxa/Kinbasket Tribal Council and include the Lower Kootenay Band, with a reserve near Creston; the Tobacco Plains Band with a reserve at Grasmere; the St Mary's Band with a reserve near Cranbrook; and the Columbia Lake Band with a reserve at Windermere. Most elders of the neighboring Shuswap Band, the Kinbaskets, near Invermere, have a working knowledge of the Kutenai language. An ethnographic and linguistic distinction is usually drawn between the Bonners Ferry and Creston groups (**Lower Kutenai**) and the others (**Upper Kutenai**), but dialect diversity is actually very limited. The language is spoken by elders in all the communities, and there were monolingual speakers at Tobacco Plains and Bonners Ferry as recently as the 1980s. With a few exceptions, the youngest first-language speakers are in their fifties, and even some of them have more of a passive knowledge of the language than active fluency. Retention efforts are underway in most locations. The language is on the curriculum of Salish Kootenai College in Pablo, Montana, and community classes have been organized for young children, high-school-age students, and adults, most notably at the Columbia Lake Reserve in Canada.

Kwakiutl (Kwak'wala) [108] is the southernmost of the three Northern Wakashan languages, spoken in a number of local varieties on the central coast of British Columbia from Smith Sound to Cape Mudge, and on the northern third of Vancouver Island. The principal communities are Campbell River, Cape Mudge, Fort Rupert, Mamaleleqala, Nimpkish (Alert Bay), Nuwitti, Qualicum, Quatsino, Tanakteuk, Tlowitsis-Mumtagilia, Tsawataineuk, and Tsulquate. Out of a total population of approximately 3,500 there are between 200 and 400 speakers, none under the age of thirty-five. There is some second-language fluency, and an impressive degree of literacy. Kwakiutl was extensively documented by Boas, whose principal consultant, George Hunt, became literate in his native language. (Boas's use of the term 'Kwakiutl' was inconsistent, ranging from the local variety of Campbell River to all of Northern Wakashan. To avoid confusion, **Kwak'wala**, a version of the Kwakiutl word for 'Kwakiutl language', has been adopted in local English and by some scholars to designate what is here defined as Kwakiutl.)

Kwak'wala. See *Kwakiutl*

Laguna. See *Acoma-Laguna*

Lake Miwok. See *Western Miwok*

Lakota. See *Sioux*

Lenape. See *Delaware*

Lillooet (St'at'imcets) [130] is an Interior Salish language of southwestern British Columbia, and is spoken in two major dialect clusters, Upper Lillooet, in and around Fountain and Lillooet on the Fraser River, and Lower Lillooet, in and around Mount Currie, near Pemberton, on the Lillooet River. The bands associated with these two areas are culturally and politically distinct. There are about 200 speakers divided between the two areas, and vigorous language retention programs at both Mt Currie and Lillooet.

Lipan [103] was an emergent language within the Southern Athabaskan dialect complex, spoken in the eighteenth century by several bands of Plains Apaches who lived in south-central Texas. During the nineteenth century the Lipan amalgamated with other Apache groups and today their descendants share the Mescalero Reservation in southeastern New Mexico with the Mescalero and the Chiricahua. There were two or three elderly speakers living as late as 1981, but the language is now extinct. It is very poorly documented.

Loucheux. See *Gwich'in*

Lower Chehalis [126], one of the four languages of the Tsamosan division of the Salishan family, was formerly spoken in a number of local varieties along the lower Chehalis River and around Grays Harbor and Shoalwater Bay on the coast of southwest Washington. Most Lower Chehalis descendants live on the Shoalwater Bay Reservation, although some live at the Quinault Reservation. Few speakers of Lower Chehalis survived into the twentieth century, and the language is not well documented, although a substantial number of sound recordings of one of the last fluent speakers was made around 1940. One very elderly and incapacitated man may have some limited fluency, and a few others may have a passive knowledge of words and phrases, but the language is extinct as a medium of communication.

Lower Chinook [139] was the Chinookan language formerly spoken at the mouth of the Columbia River from Shoalwater Bay in the north to Tillamook Head in the south, and for about ten miles upstream. After a brief period of prosperity after the establishment of a fur-trading post at Astoria in 1811, they suffered a steep demographic decline, and by the end of the nineteenth century the surviving Lower Chinooks had been incorporated into the Lower Chehalis Salish to the north. Boas collected extensive data on the language in the 1890s and published a grammatical sketch. The last speaker died in the 1930s.

Lower Tanana [65] is an Athabaskan language belonging to the Tanana series. It was originally spoken in a number of villages on the Tanana River in the vicinity of Fairbanks, but now is spoken only at Nenana and Minto. The native population of these two villages is approximately 380, of whom about thirty elderly people speak the language. Michael Krauss did the first major linguistic fieldwork on this language beginning in 1961, and this was continued by James Kari. Recent publications in the language include the 1992 edition of stories told by Teddy Charlie as recorded by Krauss in 1961, and a preliminary dictionary compiled by Kari in 1994.

Luiseño [237] is a Uto-Aztecan language of the Takic subfamily, originally spoken by the native peoples of the southern California coast north of the Diegueño and south of the Gabrielino, in the area dominated by the missions of San Luis Rey and San Juan Capistrano. The dialects of the two mission communities differed, but were mutually intelligible; the **Juaneño (Ajachemem)** dialect is now extinct. Both dialects were extensively documented by J. P. Harrington in the 1930s. Approximately 2,500 descendants of the San Luis Rey and San Juan Capistrano communities currently live at the La Jolla, Rincon, Pauma, Pechanga, and Pala Reservations, and in the town of San Juan Capistrano. Between 5 and 10 elderly speakers or semi-speakers of Luiseño remain, and there is some interest in studying the language in the master-apprentice format or through Harrington's documentation. The San Juan Capistrano community has a language revival program for the Ajachemem dialect.

Lummi. See *Northern Straits Salish*

Lushootseed [123] is a complex of closely related Central Salish dialects spoken in the Puget Sound area of Washington (older sources refer to it as Puget Sound Salish). The principal modern communities in which Lushootseed is the heritage language include the Upper Skagit, Swinomish, Suquamish, Muckleshoot, Puyallup, and Nisqually Reservations, and especially the Tulalip Reservation near Marysville. Lushootseed is now spoken as a first language by fewer than five elderly people out of a total population of over 18,000, but there are efforts to revive the language. It is taught in the school on the Tulalip Reservation (including an immersion class), and there are several second-language speakers, some quite fluent and most of them literate in the language. In recent years a substantial amount of Lushootseed material, including sound files, has become available on the internet.

Maidu [153], also known as **Northeastern Maidu** or **Mountain Maidu**, is the Maiduan language of the people who traditionally occupied the northern Sierra Nevada and the Honey Lake Valley, east and south of Lassen Peak in northeastern California. Some Maidu descendants are members of the small Susanville and Greenville Rancherias, but most live away from tribal land in scattered locations in Plumas and Lassen County. Only a few semi-speakers of Maidu remain, but there is considerable interest in revitalization and William Shipley, a linguist who documented the language in the 1950s and acquired second-language fluency, is working closely with several language learners. All three of the Maiduan languages (Maidu, Konkow, and Nisenan) are sometimes referred to collectively as 'Maidu', but they differ considerably in their grammars and are not mutually intelligible.

Makah [111] is the Southern Wakashan language spoken by the Makah Tribe, at Neah Bay on the northwest tip of the Olympic Peninsula in Washington State. Of the other two Southern Wakashan languages, Nootka and Nitinaht, both spoken on Vancouver Island, Makah appears to be closer to the latter. About a dozen elderly first-language speakers survive. Since the late 1970s the Makah Cultural and Research Center has sponsored language education and related cultural activities at Neah Bay, including the production of various linguistic resource materials.

Maliseet-Passamaquoddy [41] is an Eastern Algonquian language spoken in the St Croix and St John River valleys along the border between the state of Maine and the Canadian province of New Brunswick. There are about 500 first-language speakers. Most of those in Maine are members of the Passamaquoddy tribe, while in Canada they identify themselves as Maliseet, but dialect differences between the two groups are minimal. The principal communities in Maine are Pleasant Point and Indian Township, with fewer than 100 fluent speakers between them. In New Brunswick there are 355 first-language speakers at Tobique, Woodstock, Kingsclear, St Mary's, and Oromocto; another forty live elsewhere in Canada. There are also some speakers of both dialects residing with the Penobscots of Indian Island, at Old Town, Maine, and in an urban community in Bridgeport, Connecticut. Nearly all speakers are middle-aged, with the most fluent in their sixties and older. Both US and Canadian communities have initiated a variety of teaching programs, including school and community-based classes, and 'language nests' where speakers and non-speakers of all ages share stories and songs in an informal setting. Maliseet is also taught at the University of New Brunswick.

Mandan [263] is a moribund Siouan language, originally spoken in a cluster of villages along the Missouri River in south-central North Dakota, located between the Hidatsa villages to the north and the Arikara villages to the south. The modern Mandans are one of the Three Affiliated Tribes who share the Fort Berthold Reservation in North Dakota, the others being the Hidatsas and the Arikaras. Their primary settlement is Twin Buttes. There are fewer than ten remaining first-language speakers of Mandan, all elderly, and no fluent second-language speakers. The Circle Eagle Project of the Three Affiliated Tribes Museum is sponsoring documentation and educational efforts in collaboration with Minot State University, including a weekly language class conducted by a fluent speaker at Twin Buttes Elementary School.

Maricopa [203] is a Yuman language of the River subgroup, originally spoken by several small tribes along the lower Gila and Colorado Rivers. It is now spoken by a minority – perhaps as few as 100 – of the approximately 800 members of the Maricopa (or Pee-Posh) tribe of Arizona, most of whom live at the Maricopa Colony at Laveen, on the Gila River Reservation south of Phoenix, and in the community of Lehi on the Salt River Reservation northeast of Phoenix. There is a language program being organized at Lehi, where the language is referred to as 'Piipaash'.

Maritime Tsimshianic [137], the more southerly of the two branches of theTsimshianic language family of northwestern British Columbia, has two deeply differentiated dialects, or possibly emergent languages. **Southern Tsimshian** (or **Sküüxs**), originally spoken along the coast south of the Skeena River and on a few islands, now has only one fully fluent speaker, who lives in the village of Klemtu on Swindle Island. **Coast Tsimshian** (or **Sm'algyax**, often referred to simply as **Tsimshian**), is spoken near

Terrace on the lower Skeena River and on the coast near the Skeena estuary, as well as at one location in southern Alaska. In the Canadian communities it is estimated that there are between 250 and 400 fluent speakers of Coast Tsimshian out of a total population of 6,780, almost none under forty. The highest proportion of speakers is in Kitkatla and Hartley Bay, where perhaps one person in five is fluent, although most are aged fifty or older. Two children in Hartley Bay are learning the language from their grandfather. The language is taught in school programs in some communities, and through the University of Northern British Columbia. About fifty people have some degree of second-language fluency and some literacy. The Alaska settlement is at (New) Metlakatla on Annette Island – Tlingit territory – where a utopian religious community was established in 1887 under the leadership of the missionary William Duncan. Of the 1,300 Coast Tsimshians currently living at Metlakatla, about seventy of the most elderly speak the language. In 1977 the Metlakatlans adopted a standard practical orthography, but there are no fluent second-language speakers, and no appreciable literacy. There is a long history of documentation of Coast Tsimshian, including the work of Boas, who carried out research at Port Simpson, British Columbia, in the early 1900s and published a grammar and a large number of narrative texts.

Mattole [96] was a language of the California Athabaskan subgroup formerly spoken along the Mattole and Bear Rivers near Cape Mendocino. The Mattole River and Bear River dialects were distinct. The Mattole dialect was documented by Li in 1927 and the material published; more fragmentary materials exist for the Bear River dialect. The last speaker died in the 1950s, although a few individuals retain some memory of the language. A tribal scholar of Hupa background has some interest in reviving the language.

Menominee [27] is a Central Algonquian language, spoken on the Menominee Reservation in northern Wisconsin in the towns of Keshena, Neopit, South Branch, and Zoar. It is spoken as a first language by about thirty-five people, none under fifty years old, and by an additional twenty-five (none under fifty) who have acquired second-language fluency. About sixty-five people have studied the language or have otherwise acquired a basic understanding. There is no uniform writing system for the language, and very little written other than pedagogical material and reference works. The language is used for restricted communication among elders, for religious/ceremonial functions, and in educational settings. Although the tribal legislature passed a resolution requiring Menominee to be used in tribal government where possible, and that it be taught in all reservation schools, this resolution has been difficult to implement due to the small number of fluent speakers. A master-apprentice program has been set up to train language teachers, and educational videos are being prepared.

Mescalero-Chiricahua [101] is an emergent language within the Southern Athabaskan dialect complex, spoken with very little dialectal variation by people whose tribal identity is either Mescalero or Chiricahua. Over 1,500 members – slightly under half – of the Mescalero Tribe of New Mexico are first-language speakers of Mescalero-Chiricahua, most of them Mescaleros, although perhaps a dozen identify as Chiricahuas. The principal Chiricahua community is at Fort Sill, in southwestern Oklahoma, where they settled early in the twentieth century. At most three fluent speakers remain at

Fort Sill, together with a few semi-speakers. The language was extensively documented by Hoijer in the 1930s.

Miami-Illinois [39] was an Algonquian dialect complex spoken in the eighteenth century and earlier by groups in what is now Illinois and northern Indiana. At least three clusters of dialects were preserved after the relocation of these tribes to Kansas in the nineteenth century: (1) Peoria-Kaskaskia; (2) Piankashaw-Wea; and (3) Miami. Speakers of at least some varieties survived into the twentieth century, but there have been no fluent first-language speakers since 1962. Although no modern linguistic study was made of Miami-Illinois before it became extinct, a considerable amount of earlier documentation exists, including several dictionaries. Relying on this data, a Miami tribal scholar has acquired second-language fluency in the language and has made it the medium of communication in his home. His two youngest children are acquiring Miami-Illinois as their first language. Miami University of Ohio has established an institute for the study of Miami culture and language, and courses in Miami have been offered there and at the Woodland Indian Cultural Center at Prophetstown, Indiana.

Michif (Mitchif) [23] is a mixed language (Cree and French) spoken by some Métis, an ethnic group of the northern Great Plains, descendants of the children of Indian woman and French fur traders. Several hundred thousand Métis live in numerous rural and urban communities in Manitoba, Saskatchewan, and Alberta, and on the Turtle Mountain Reservation and surrounding towns in North Dakota. Although all Métis now speak English, some traditionally speak Cree, others Ojibwe, yet others French, and many are bi- or multilingual. Michif – historically a mixture of Cree verbs and French nouns – was spoken only by a small minority of Métis families, and many of these families have now lost it. Scattered as they are, it is difficult to estimate the current number of speakers, but it is probably around 200, nearly all over seventy years old. The language has been taught for decades at Turtle Mountain Community College in Belcourt, North Dakota, where it has also been used occasionally on the local radio. Local schools in the Turtle Mountain area also incorporate it occasionally into their bilingual programs. Some teaching material was produced in the 1980s, and a commercial dictionary was published in 1983. In Manitoba and Saskatchewan Métis organizations have organized Michif courses for adults, and the Manitoba Métis Federation has a language officer. The Gabriel Dumont Institute in Saskatoon has produced a series of children's books in Michif, as well as cultural videos. None of these efforts has resulted in second-language speakers. Some speakers have acquired Michif literacy through the teaching material, but do not use it in print or in correspondence.

Micmac (Mi'kmaq) [40] is an Eastern Algonquian language spoken in over twenty-five reserves scattered across the provinces of Nova Scotia, New Brunswick, Prince Edward Island, and Quebec, as well as in the United States. There are 8,145 first-language speakers in a total Micmac population of about 20,000, the most important speech communities being at Restigouche, Quebec; Big Cove, New Brunswick; and Eskasoni, on Cape Breton Island, Nova Scotia. There is also a large expatriate community of Micmacs in the United States, primarily in Boston, where perhaps a quarter of all first-language speakers reside. A distinctive pictographic script ('Micmac Hieroglyphs') devised by seventeenth-century missionaries, and apparently based on indigenous mnemonic designs, is still used in the Catholic liturgy on the Eskasoni Reserve and in a few other places. The standard orthography now in use has its origins in nineteenth-century missionary work. Recently there has been renewed interest in the language and it is being introduced into the reserve schools. A curriculum is being developed by the Mi'kmaq Resource Centre at the University College of Cape Breton.

Migueleño. See *Salinan*

Mikasuki [291] is the only surviving dialect of the Eastern Muskogean language known as **Hitchiti** (or **Hitchiti-Mikasuki**). It is spoken in Florida by most of the 400 enrolled members of the Miccosukee Tribe, as well as by many of the 2,700 members of the Seminole Tribe. There are five Seminole reservation communities, with Mikasuki the dominant language at the Big Cypress, Immokalee, Hollywood, and Tampa reservations, while the Florida Seminole dialect of Creek is dominant at the Brighton Reservation. Until the 1980s, many Miccosukee and Seminole children spoke little English when entering school. This situation has shifted in recent years, and many children now learn English at home. Some Creek speakers in Florida have learned to speak Mikasuki, but there are no formal courses in the language. Although an alphabet was devised in the 1950s, literacy is low. Mikasuki still has a full range of social functions, and is spoken by tribal leaders, in churches, and at ceremonial grounds, as well as in some schools.

Miluk. See *Hanis*

'Mingo'. See *Seneca*

Miwok is the general common name for the languages of the Miwokan language family, spoken aboriginally in north-central California from San Francisco Bay to the Sierra Nevada. Seven languages are usually distinguished, subdivided linguistically into **Western Miwok** and **Eastern Miwok**.

Modoc. See *Klamath-Modoc*

Mohave (Mojave) [201], a Yuman language of the River subgroup, is the heritage language of the Fort Mojave Tribe, near Needles, California, and of the Mohave members of the Colorado River Indian Tribes, near Parker, Arizona. In the two communities combined there are fewer than 100 fluent first-language speakers, nearly all of them elderly, in a total Mohave population of over 2,000. A practical orthography has been developed and language classes are offered in both communities, drawing on a rich documentation that includes a published dictionary. At Fort Mojave the language program is sponsored by the Ahamakav Cultural Society.

Mohawk [309] is a Northern Iroquoian language, originally spoken by the easternmost tribe of the Six Nations (Iroquoian Confederacy) in the Mohawk River Valley of New York, between present Schenectady and Utica. There are six modern Mohawk communities, located primarily in Canada: Caughnawaga (Kahnawake) and Oka (Kanehsatake) in the vicinity of Montreal; St Regis (Ahkwesahsne) on the St Lawrence River at the US–Canadian border; the Six Nations Reserve (Grand River) in southern Ontario; the Tyendinaga Reserve on the Bay of Quinté near Kingston; and a small settlement at Gibson (Wahta) east of Georgian Bay. Mohawk is the most vigorous of the Six Nations languages, with about 3,850 fluent first-language speakers. Of these, 600 are at Caughnawaga, 100 at Oka, 3,000 at St Regis, eighty-seven on the Six Nations Reserve, two on the Tyendinaga Reserve, and fewer than fifty at Gibson. A small number of children are native speakers. There are also several hundred second-language speakers, produced by successful immersion schools in Caughnawaga, Oka, St Regis, and on the Six Nations Reserve.

Molala [180] was formerly spoken along the western slopes of the Cascades of central Oregon, from the upper Rogue River to the vicinity of Mt Hood. It is a Plateau Penutian language, distantly related to Klamath and Sahaptian; an earlier classification that linked Molala and Cayusein the 'Waiilatpuan' family has been abandoned. The Molala were displaced and suffered a severe decline in population after the white occupation of their territory in the mid-nineteenth century. The survivors were settled on the Grand Ronde Reservation, where their language and tribal identity was lost. The last speaker died in 1958. Molala was extensively documented by linguists between 1910 and 1930, most importantly by Jacobs, but very little of the material has been published

Monachi. See *Mono*

Mono [224] is a Western Numic language spoken in central California both on the western side of the Sierra Nevada, between Yosemite National Park and Kings Canyon National Park, and on the eastern side in Owens Valley from Lone Pine north to Big Pine. Mono has two main geographical divisions. **Western Mono** (or **Monachi**) is spoken in several communities that are close by (and socially connected to) Yokuts communities. The most important of these are at North Fork and Auberry (Big Sandy Rancheria), each of which has at least ten fully fluent speakers, the youngest in his fifties. There are also a few speakers at Tollhouse (Cold Springs Rancheria) and Dunlop. In addition, 100 or more people have some passive or second-language knowledge of the language. The Mono Language Program, a collaborative effort with UCLA, has produced a dictionary and a CD-ROM. Local language retention efforts are coordinated by the Sierra Mono Museum in North Fork and are integrated with other cultural revitalization activities. **Eastern Mono** (or **Owens Valley Paiute**) is spoken in the Owens Valley communities of Bishop, Big Pine, Lone Pine, and Fort Independence. All Eastern Mono speakers are elderly and number not more than thirty in a total population of about 1,000. Each of the communities has sponsored language revival programs. There are some shallow dialect differences in the Mono speaking area, but they do not coincide with the Western–Eastern geographical division; all speakers can understand one another with little difficulty.

Montagnais [21] is an Eastern Cree dialect, spoken by over 10,000 people in an area stretching from Lac St Jean across southeastern Quebec, along the north shore of the St Lawrence into Labrador. Three main subdialects are distinguished: **Western** (Matsheuiatsh, Les Escoumins, Betsiamites), **Central** (Matimekush at Schefferville and Uashat/Maliotenam at Sept-Iles) and **Eastern** (Mingan, La Romaine, Nastashquan,

Pukuashipu (St Augustine) and Sheshatshiu, Labrador). The more westerly dialects have a significantly lower percentage of speakers. French is the second language for all communities except Sheshatshiu, and an extensive Montagnais-French dictionary has codified the standard roman spelling. The language is taught in all schools, and a one-year program in Montagnais language and culture has been introduced at the post-secondary level to promote adult literacy.

Moose Cree [18] is the Western Cree dialect spoken by about 3,000 people at Fort Albany, Kasechewan, and Moose Factory, on the southwestern shore of James Bay in northern Ontario. While speakers of all ages in Kasechewan are fluent, the language is in serious decline in Moose Factory, where many young adults have little or no knowledge of it. The boundary between Swampy Cree and Moose Cree overlaps, most notably at Fort Albany and Kasechewan, where two communities based on dialect and religion have recently developed. Extensive teaching materials, including audio tapes and a set of texts, have been published in a generalized Moose Cree/Swampy Cree dialect, using a roman orthography. Although useful for the language learner, these materials have had relatively little effect on local standardization and literacy, since the Ontario dialects use the syllabic writing system. Although syllabic literacy is taught in all schools, the rate of literacy is low and the primary native language medium is radio.

Mountain [78] is an emergent Athabaskan language within the Slavey dialects of the Dene complex. In the Northwest Territories it is the principal language of Fort Wrigley (100 speakers out of 170 total population), as well as of some of the population of Tulita (Fort Norman), in many cases people who also speak Bearlake. There are also speakers of Mountain Slavey in the Yukon at Fort Liard and at Ross River.

Munsee. See *Delaware*

Nambe. See *Tewa*

Naskapi [22] is a distinct dialect of Eastern Cree, spoken in two varieties, Western (in Quebec) and Eastern (in Labrador). **Western Naskapi** is the first language of nearly 800 people in Kawawachikamach, near Schefferville, Quebec (the second language being English), although many young adults also speak the neighboring variety of Montagnais and some French. A trilingual lexicon was published in 1994, and there is an ongoing community language program. The syllabic orthography is taught in school to grade two but literacy remains low. **Eastern Naskapi** is the first language of over 500 speakers at Utshimassits (Davis Inlet), Labrador, with English the second language. The Montagnais roman orthography is used, and there is a high degree of literacy, with the language being taught as a subject at school. The Eastern Naskapi of Davis Inlet and the variety of Montagnais spoken at Sheshatshiu, although quite distinct, are often grouped together as **Innu-aimun**.

Nass-Gitksan [138], the more northerly of the two branches of the Tsimshianic language family of northwestern British Columbia, consists of two emergent languages. (1) **Nisqa'a (Nisgha)** is spoken in four village communities along the Nass River and has between 400 and 500 speakers, with no first-language speakers under thirty. It has been taught in public schools since 1976, and has been offered for credit at the local community college (Wilp Wilxo'oskwhl Nisga'a, the Nisqa'a House of Learning) and, since 1992, through the University of Northern British Columbia. There is some second-language fluency and considerable literacy. (2) **Gitksan** is spoken in six village communities along the Skeena River upriver from the Coast Tsimshians. It has about the same number of speakers as Nisqa'a (400 to 500), but there is a small number of families in which children and young people are fluent speakers. Gitksan is taught in public schools in some communities, and is offered for credit through the University of Northern British Columbia. There are no fully fluent second-language speakers of Gitksan, but many people have become familiar with the writing system and a few speakers have achieved considerable literacy. There is extensive documentation of both Nisqa'a and Gitksan, some of it by Boas, who worked at Kincolith in 1894 and published a volume of Nisqa'a texts.

Natchez [296] was spoken in the seventeenth- and early eighteenth century along the Mississippi River in the vicinity of present-day Natchez, Mississippi. The Natchez tribe was destroyed by the French in a series of wars that ended in 1731, and many of the survivors took refuge with the Creeks and the Chickasaws, moving with them to Oklahoma in the 1830s, where they also intermarried with the Cherokees. Four Natchez wordlists were collected in Oklahoma during the nineteenth century, but the most important documentation was made during the twentieth century, by Swanton in 1907–15 and by Haas in 1934–6, who between them worked with all the surviving speakers; much of this material remains unpublished. The last known speaker died in 1965. Although Natchez is best treated as a classificatory isolate, there is some evidence that it is distantly related to the Muskogean family.

Naukanski Yupik [2] is a Western Eskimo language of Siberia, linguistically the link between Central Alaskan Yupik and Central Siberian Yupik. Originally spoken in the village of Naukan on the easternmost point of East Cape, facing the Diomede Islands of Alaska, the community was relocated in 1958 to the nearby villages of Lavrentiya, Uelen, and Lorino. There are about sixty speakers, all over forty, in a total population of 300.

Navajo [99] is a well established language within the Southern Athabaskan dialect complex. Some degree of mutual intelligibility exists between Navajo and the other emergent languages of the complex, in particular Western Apache, but the Navajo and Apache communities have been politically and culturally distinct since at least the early eighteenth century. In 1990 an estimated 115,000 people living on the Navajo Nation in northern Arizona and northeastern New Mexico had fluency in Navajo, about 75 percent of the reservation population, to which must be added a somewhat lower percentage of the 12,000 to 15,000 Navajos living off-reservation. A conservative estimate of the total number of fluent speakers in 1990 would be about 120,000. In 2001, although the population has increased, the number of speakers is probably smaller. Until World War II Navajo was the universal language of communication on the reservation, and there are still several thousand elderly near-monolingual speakers. As late as 1981, 85 percent of Navajo children acquired Navajo as their first language, but the percentage has declined rapidly in recent years and some surveys show it now to be as low as 25 percent. In response to this decline an immersion program was started at Fort Defiance Elementary School in 1986, and is being adopted at other schools. A standard writing system was introduced by the BIA in 1940 and a high percentage of Navajo speakers are literate in their language. The language is used in a wide range of functions and the Navajo people are justifiably proud of the important role their language played as a code during World War II. There are several Navajo literary figures, including poets, and a full standard dictionary is available. Navajo is formally taught at a number of institutions, including Diné College, Northern Arizona University, the University of Arizona, and the University of New Mexico.

Nez Perce [179] is a Plateau Penutian language, together with Sahaptin forming the Sahaptian branch of that family. Two dialects are distinguished, **Upriver** and **Downriver**, correlated with the original settlement pattern along the Snake River and its tributaries in eastern Washington and Idaho. The Upriver dialect is spoken fluently by a handful of elders at Kamiah and Lapwai on the Nez Perce Reservation in north-central Idaho, and by several more on the Colville Reservation in eastern Washington. The Downriver dialect is mainly preserved by a few speakers on the Umatilla Reservation in Oregon (most of them descendants of Cayuse speakers who adopted Nez Perce in the nineteenth century). In addition to these fully fluent speakers there are between thirty and forty speakers and semi-speakers of varying degrees of fluency, most of them in Idaho. The Nez Perce Tribe sponsors a language program, and a class in Nez Perce is also given under tribal sponsorship on the Umatilla Reservation. Nez Perce is well documented and has a full, published dictionary.

Nisenan [155], also known as **Southern Maidu**, was the Maiduan language traditionally spoken in a number of local village dialects along the Yuba River in the Sierra Nevada foothills east of Sacramento, California. Nisenan descendants live at Auburn Rancheria in Placer County, Shingle Springs Rancheria in El Dorado County, and in other scattered locations in the area. Nisenan was documented by Uldall in the 1920s as well as by more recent linguists, and a grammar, dictionary, and collection of texts have been published. There are no fluent speakers of Nisenan, but a language program is under way at Shingle Springs, with classroom instruction.

Nishnaabemwin [34] is an emergent language within the Ojibwe dialect complex, spoken at a number of reserves in southern Ontario as well as at various locations in Michigan. Nishnaabemwin represents the linguistic and social fusion of two historically distinct communities, the **Ottawa (Odawa)** and the **Eastern Ojibwe**. The homeland of the Ottawa dialect is on the north shores of Lake Huron, and the most vigorous community of speakers is at the Wikwemikong Reserve on Manitoulin Island, Ontario; there are also several hundred speakers in Michigan, with the largest community at the Isabella Reservation. A number of Ottawas were relocated in Oklahoma during the nineteenth century, but the language does not survive there. The principal Eastern Ojibwe communities are at Walpole Island on the Detroit River, on Parry Island, and at Curve Lake, near Peterborough. In both Ontario and in Michigan there is considerable dialect mixture between Nishnaabemwin and Southwestern Ojibwe (here usually called 'Chippewa') and the distinction is sometimes hard to make. The most clearly defined (and most vigorously surviving) variety is the Odawa of Manitoulin Island, where perhaps half of the population of over 3,000 has some fluency in the language.

67

Nisqa'a. See *Nass-Gitksan*

Nitinaht (Ditidaht) [110] is the Southern Wakashan language of two groups on the west coast of Vancouver Island immediately to the south of Nootka territory, now organized as the Ditidaht and Pacheenaht Bands. Although the Nitinahts were traditionally part of the Nootkan interaction sphere (and the Dididaht Band is currently represented on the Nuu-chah-nulth Tribal Council), the Nitinaht language is sharply discontinuous from the chain of Nootka dialects and closer to Makah. There are a dozen or so fluent speakers, all elderly, but no educational or revitalization efforts separate from Nootka.

Nooksack [120] was a Central Salish language formerly spoken in the vicinity of Bellingham in northwest Washington, between Halkomelem and Lushootseed. The language has been well documented by several linguists, although much of the documentation remains unpublished. The last fluent speaker died in 1977 and the last person with any degree of first-language competence died in 1988.

Nootka (Nuuchahnulth) [109] is the Southern Wakaskan language of the west coast of Vancouver Island, from Cape Cook to Barkley Sound. Modern Nootkas are organized in fifteen bands, all represented by the Nuuchahnulth Tribal Council (a name adopted in 1985). There is a handful of speakers in most communities, totaling over fifty but fewer than a hundred, out of a population of around 5,000. The language is used primarily in ceremonies and in some political meetings. A school-based teaching program has existed for over a decade at Port Alberni (Sheshaht Band) and about a dozen individuals are literate, although no fluent second-language speakers have been produced. Between 1910 and 1935 Nootka linguistics and traditional literature was extensively documented by Edward Sapir, and later Morris Swadesh. One of their consultants, Alec Thomas, became literate and collected extensive materials of his own.

North Alaska Inupiaq. See *Inupiaq*

North Slavey. See *Bearlake* and *Hare*

Northeastern Pomo [189] was the Pomoan language that was formerly spoken around Stonyford, on the west side of the Sacramento Valley north of Clear Lake. The Northeastern Pomo were isolated from other Pomo speakers by territory belonging to the Patwin, with whom they culturally identified; bilingualism in Patwin was common. The last fluent speaker died in 1961.

Northern Algonquin (Algonquine du Nord) [29] is a distinct regional dialect within the Ojibwe dialect complex, spoken in southwestern Quebec at Lac Simon, Grand Lac Victoria, La Barriere, and a few other communities. There are perhaps as many as 1,000 fluent speakers.

Northern Paiute (Paviotso) [225] is a Western Numic language formerly spoken in the western Great Basin from roughly the John Day River in Oregon south through the western third of Nevada, to the vicinity of Mammoth, California. Today limited numbers of speakers are found in reservation communities and colonies in Oregon, Nevada, California and Idaho, as well as in urban locations in these states. Principal communities are at Warm Springs and Burns, Oregon; Fort McDermitt, Owyhee, Winnemucca, Pyramid Lake, Reno-Sparks, Lovelock, Fallon, Yerington, and Walker River, Nevada; Lee Vining and Fort Bidwell, California. A variety (called **Bannock**) is also spoken by a few elderly people at Fort Hall, Idaho, where otherwise Shoshoni is the heritage language. There are two major dialects, with the Truckee River in west-central Nevada serving as the general dividing line. In addition, most of the individual communities have developed recognizable local varieties. Fluency in all communities except Fort McDermitt is confined to speakers aged sixty years and above, with roughly 300 speakers total. Fort McDermitt has a fluency rate above 50 percent (roughly 400 speakers), with about 20–30 percent of children acquiring it as their first language. Semi-speakers from all areas add another 400 to these figures. During the past twenty-five years nearly all communities have started teaching programs, but few have continued. Beginning in the 1990s, Warm Springs, Reno-Sparks and Pyramid Lake began more sustained efforts. They have produced phrase books, some audio and video tapes, dictionaries, and a series of lessons, all designed to be used in class-room settings within the communities. These materials use a standard orthography, with some variations due to local dialect differences and other idiosyncracies. A few communities have also used the master-apprentice approach and other activities, but none has an immersion school. All of these efforts have increased language awareness and resulted in some language activity, but no new fluent speakers. The state of Nevada approved the awarding of high school credit in Great Basin languages in 1998, but thus far only the tribal high school at Pyramid Lake and the state high school at McDermitt have regularly scheduled classes.

Northern Sierra Miwok. See *Eastern Miwok*

Northern Straits Salish [121] is the Central Salish language of the southern tip of Vancouver Island, the San Juan Islands, and the mainland immediately to the south of the US–Canadian border. At least three dialects continue to be spoken in a number of small communities. (1) The **Saanich** dialect on Vancouver Island has fewer than twenty first-language speakers, the youngest nearly sixty years old. However, there are up to 100 second-language speakers of varying degrees of fluency, and Saanich is frequently used in ceremonies and for tribal identity. A distinctive orthography based on English capital letters has been quite successful; literacy is high among first-language speakers and universal among second-language speakers. The local school has produced books of traditional stories, and there is a significant amount of Saanich material available on the internet. (2) The **Samish** dialect of the San Juan Islands has about five remaining speakers, but their speech is mixed with other dialects or with Halkomelem and they do not form a distinct speech community. The Samish community in Anacortes, Washington, is developing a second-language teaching program. (3) The **Lummi** dialect of the mainland has no active first-language speakers, and if passive first-language speakers exist they are likely to be elderly. However, sustained efforts have been made to develop second-language speakers on the Lummi Reservation. These have been quite successful and speakers number in the hundreds, some of whom are moderately fluent. Revival of Lummi is linked to a general revival of traditional customs, and much attention is given to the use of language in such contexts as naming ceremonies. The Tribe requires its employees to have some knowledge of Lummi. Literacy is a crucial part of the second-language efforts, and an non-phonemic roman orthography is in wide use.

Northern Tutchone [68] is an Athabaskan language (closely related to Southern Tuchone) spoken in the Yukon communities of Mayo, Pelly Crossing, Stewart Crossing, and Carmacks. There are about 200 speakers out of a total population of 1,100. Early documentation of Northern Tutchone was carried out in the 1890s by the Anglican Archdeacon Thomas Canham, but most of his materials remain in manuscript. A practical orthography was developed by John Ritter of the Yukon Native Language Centre in the 1970s and literacy workshops have been held since 1984. More than twenty publications in and on Northern Tutchone are currently available from the Yukon Native Language Centre. There have been Northern Tutchone school programs in Mayo, Pelly Crossing and Carmacks for more than a dozen years.

Nuuchahnulth. See *Nootka*

Nuxalk. See **Bella Coola**

Nxa'amxcin. See **Columbian**

Obispeño. See **Chumash**

Oji-Cree. See **Severn Ojibwe**

Ojibwe [28–34] is a Central Algonquian dialect complex, varieties of which are spoken in a large number of communities in the north-central United States, and in Canada from Alberta to Quebec. There are approximately 43,000 Ojibwe speakers, the majority of them in Canada (where 31,625 first-language speakers were counted in the 1996 census). At least six regional dialects or emergent languages can be distinguished: **Severn Ojibwe**, **Northern Algonquin**, **Southern Algonquin (Nipissing)**, **Southwestern Ojibwe**, **Saulteaux**, and **Nishnaabemwin (Eastern Ojibwe** and **Ottawa/Odawa)**. The first two are classified as Northern Ojibwe; the last three as Southern Ojibwe. Southern Algonquin (Nipissing) is intermediate between Northern and Southern Ojibwe. A standard practical orthography is used for all of the Southern Ojibwe dialects, and two general reference dictionaries exist. There are numerous local and university-level language education courses in Ojibwe. The Native Language Instructors' Program at Lakehead University in Thunder Bay, Ontario, trains language teachers and produces Ojibwe curricular materials in all dialects, with an emphasis on Severn Ojibwe, Saulteaux, and Nishnaabemwin.

Okanagan [133] is an Interior Salish language, spoken in a number of communities in southern interior British Columbia and northeastern Washington. There are seven Okanagan reserves in British Columbia: Vernon, Douglas Lake, Westbank, Penticton, Keremeos (Lower Similkameen), Hedley (Upper Similkameen), and Oliver (Osoyoos). Except for the Westbank Reserve, which may have as few as a dozen fluent speakers, all of the Okanagan reserves have at least fifty speakers of varying degrees of fluency, the Vernon Reserve perhaps over 100. There is a large Okanagan community on the

Colville Reservation of Washington with perhaps as many as 400 speakers, representing largely the Methow, Southern Okanagan, Colville, and Sanpoil-Nespelem dialects. Adding a few dozen who live away from the reserves, the total number of first-language speakers with conversational fluency is about 800, the youngest in their early thirties. There are substantial Okanagan preservation and revitalization efforts in both Canada and the United States, most notably the En'owkin Centre in Penticton, BC, and the Colville Language Preservation Program in Nespelem, Washington. There are possibly as many as 2,000 second-language speakers; at least half of these are literate in Okanagan, as are also many first-language speakers.

Omaha-Ponca [267] is a Siouan language of the Dhegiha subgroup and – in two shallowly differentiated dialects – is the heritage language of both the Omaha Tribe of Nebraska and of the two Ponca tribes, the Northern Ponca of Nebraska and the Southern Ponca of Oklahoma. Most of the remaining speakers of the **Omaha** dialect live in Macy and Walthill in rural southeastern Nebraska. There are fewer than fifty fluent first-language speakers, the youngest about sixty, and a larger number of semi-speakers and second-language learners. A language program has been instituted at the Umonhon Nation Public School Culture Center in Walthill, and the language is also taught at the tribal college and at the University of Nebraska at Lincoln. The Omaha dialect was extensively documented by the ethnographer Alice Fletcher, working with tribal member Francis La Flesche, and a few speakers are literate in the Fletcher-LaFlesche orthography, which has status in the community. The language is used mainly for religious and ceremonial functions; ability to give formal thanks and to pray in Omaha are highly valued, but the language is not essential to modern tribal identity. The **Ponca** dialect is spoken by about thirty-five elderly people in the Red Rock area of south central Oklahoma. A language program has been initiated under Ponca tribal auspices in the Red Rock high school.

Oneida [310] is a Northern Iroquoian language, originally spoken by a tribe of the Iroquoian Confederacy (Six Nations) situated east of Onondagas and west of the Mohawks, south of Oneida Lake. Most of the modern Oneidas live in two widely separated reservation communities, about 3,000 on the Thames River near London, Ontario, and 11,000 at Green Bay, Wisconsin. In addition, a few hundred Oneidas continue to live in upstate New York, some on a small tract of land near the town of Oneida, and others dispersed into neighboring white and Indian communities. There are about 200 fluent speakers of Oneida in Ontario and perhaps a dozen in Wisconsin; there are no reliable estimates for the New York Oneidas, but some speakers are reported.

Onondaga [307] is a Northern Iroquoian language, spoken in upstate New York by the central tribe (the 'firekeepers') of the Iroquoian Confederacy (Six Nations). Most modern Onondagas (about 1,600) live on a reservation in their old homeland, south of the city of Syracuse, but there is a smaller community on the Six Nations Reserve in southern Ontario. There are about a dozen elderly speakers of Onondaga in New York, the youngest in their seventies, and about forty more are reported in Ontario.

Osage [268] is a Siouan language of the Dhegiha subgroup, spoken in the eighteenth century by people living along the Osage River in Missouri. Since the 1870s the Osage

71

Tribe has been settled in the northeastern corner of Oklahoma, around Pawhuska. Osage land has proved to be rich in oil, and a number of Osage families are quite wealthy. There are ten or fewer fluent speakers of Osage, all over sixty-five, in a total tribal membership of 11,000, although there are a number of semi-speakers and second-language speakers. A revitalization program has been in existence since the 1970s and tapes and other teaching materials have been prepared.

Otoe-Missouria. See *Chiwere*

Ottawa. See *Nishnaabemwin*

Owens Valley Paiute. See *Mono*

Pacific Yupik (Alutiiq) [5], spoken on the south coast of Alaska from the Alaska Peninsula to Prince William Sound, is a distinct language within the Yupik branch of Eskimo, although closely related to Central Alaskan Yup'ik. Speakers call themselves 'Aleuts' in English, reflecting the early Russian use of *Aleuty* to designate all of the native people of the south coast of Alaska; *Alutiiq* is the Pacific Yupik version of the same word, and *Sugpiaq* has also been used in recent decades. Two dialects of Pacific Yupik are distinguished, **Koniag** in the west (on the upper part of the Alaska Peninsula and Kodiak Island) and **Chugach** in the east (on the Kenai Peninsula). Of a native population of about 2,900 about 300 still speak the language. Some early work on Pacific Yupik literacy was done by Russian Orthodox missionaries. The Alaska Native Language Center has produced both a grammar and a dictionary of Koniag for classroom use.

Paipai [199] is a Yuman language spoken in several small communities in northern Baja California, near San Miguel, Santa Catarina, and San Isodoro. There are probably fewer than 100 speakers, most of them over fifty. Paipai is most closely related to the Upland Yuman languages of western Arizona, from which it is separated, for historical reasons that are not clear, by the River Yuman languages (Mohave, Quechan, and Maricopa) and Cocopa.

Panamint (Tümpisa Shoshone) [226] is the Central Numic language formerly spoken in the region between the Sierra Nevada in California and the Nevada valleys east of Death Valley. Panamint has two main dialects, although intervening varieties show a gradation between them. **Eastern Panamint** includes the community around Beatty, Nevada. **Western Panamint** includes the communities permanently living in Lone Pine and Darwin, California. The Timbisha community in Death Valley and Lone Pine is transitional between Eastern and Western Panamint. There are no monolinguals and no speakers who did not also learn English as small children. The 'pure' Eastern and Western dialects from Lone Pine and Beatty are almost extinct. The majority of no more than twenty speakers speak the Timbisha variety and all are elderly. There are very few, if any, passive speakers since there is a strong tendency to marry outside the tribe. There is interest in revitalizing the language, but funding is scarce and will require distance education techniques due to the widely scattered nature of the tribe. Literacy is very low.

Patwin [152] is one of the two languages of the Wintuan family of northern California, and was originally spoken in two major dialects or dialect clusters along the Sacramento

River from Colusa south to the Delta and in the foothills of the Coast Range to the west. Descendants live on small rancherias at Cortina and Colusa, and on the Rumsey (Cache Creek) Rancheria west of Woodland. In 1997 at least one speaker of the Hill dialect remained. The language was documented by several linguists between 1920 and 1980, but very little of the material has been published.

Paviotso. See *Northern Paiute*

Pawnee [280], a Northern Caddoan language closely related to Arikara, is spoken in two dialects, **Skiri** and **South Band**. The language was spoken in villages along the Platte River in central Nebraska until 1874, when the tribe was relocated to what is now Pawnee County in north-central Oklahoma, where they reside today. There are fewer than ten speakers, all elderly and most speaking the South Band dialect, in a total tribal population of about 2,500. The Pawnee Nation, working with the American Indian Studies Research Institute at Indiana University, is developing both printed and multimedia/interactive materials for teaching Pawnee in the local high school and in adult education. Documentary materials, including extensive sound recordings, are archived at the American Indian Studies Research Institute.

Pend d'Oreille. See *Spokane-Kalispel*

Penobscot. See *Abenaki*

Picuris [244] is a Kiowa-Tanoan language spoken by nearly all of the 225 members of the small and isolated Pueblo of Picuris, fifty miles north of Santa Fe, New Mexico. Together with Taos and Southern Tiwa, Taos belongs to the Tiwa branch of the Kiowa-Tanoan family, but these languages are not mutually intelligible.

Plains Cree [15] is the dialect of Western Cree spoken in a large number of communities in the central prairies of Alberta and Saskatchewan. Northern and southern dialects are distinguished on the basis of phonology and morphology. Plains Cree has become the prestige dialect of Western Cree, largely because a considerable amount of nineteenth- and early twentieth-century religious literature was published in it, using the syllabic script. In recent decades Plains Cree has been the dialect most often used in teaching and for the publication of indigenous literature.

Plains Miwok [159] was a language of the Eastern Miwok branch of the Utian family of California, formerly spoken along the lower Cosumnes and Moquelumne Rivers to the southeast of Sacramento, from Ione to Stockton. Plains Miwok descendants now reside at the Ione Rancheria and the Wilton Rancheria. The language has been extensively documented by Callaghan and a full dictionary published. Although the last fluent speaker died in the late 1990s, some passive knowledge of the language is retained by a few individuals and there is interest in revival.

Pojoaque. See *Tewa*

Pomo is the general name for the languages of the Pomoan family of northern California. The seven Pomo languages were spoken in a compact territory north of San Francisco, including the Russian River and adjoining coast in Mendocino and Sonoma counties, and most of the region around Clear Lake. All are distinct languages and are (or were) mutually unintelligible. Two of the Pomo languages are extinct, **Northeastern Pomo** and **Southeastern Pomo**, and the remaining five are moribund, spoken by a handful of elderly people who live at various locations at or near the twenty small reservations or rancherias in the area. **Northern Pomo [192]** has a single elderly speaker at Sherwood Rancheria, near Willits. **Central Pomo [193]** has several speakers in the Hopland area and at Manchester and Point Areana on the coast. **Southern Pomo [194]** has speakers in the Cloverdale and Geyserville area. **Eastern Pomo [191]** has speakers on the west side of Clear Lake. None of these speakers is younger than sixty. **Kashaya [195]** (or **Southwestern Pomo**) is the most vigorously surviving Pomo language, and is still spoken by several dozen people near the mouth of the Russian River and in the Fort Ross area. Extensive linguistic documentation exists for all Pomo languages except Southern Pomo and Northeastern Pomo. Small-scale language education programs have been started for Kashaya and Eastern Pomo, and practical orthographies have been devised.

Ponca. See *Omaha-Ponca*

Potawatomi [35] is an Algonquian language closely related to the Ojibwe dialect complex. It has about fifty first-language speakers in several widely separated communities in the US and Canada. These include the Hannahville Indian Community (Upper Peninsula of Michigan), the Pokagon and Huron Bands (southern Michigan), the Forest County Band (northern Wisconsin), the Prairie Band (eastern Kansas), and the Citizen Potawatomi Nation of Oklahoma. A few Potawatomi speakers also live among the Eastern Ojibwe (Nishnaabemwin) in Ontario, particularly at the Walpole Island Reserve. The largest speech communities are in the Forest County and Prairie Bands, each with about twenty speakers, several conservatively fluent. While most community functions are now conducted in English, Potawatomi is highly valued and remains the language of ceremonial and religious activities. The language is taught in tribal Head Start and K-12 schools in most Potawatomi communities, as well as in adult language programs. Since 1996 an intertribal Potawatomi Language Scholar's College, hosted by Haskell Indian Nations University in Kansas, has offered classes in conversation, grammar, writing, and pedagogy. About 250 second-language learners participate in these various programs. Several writing systems are in use.

Purisimeño. See *Chumash*

Quechan (Yuma) [202] is a Yuman language of the River subgroup, spoken by 150 to 200 of the 3,000 members of the Quechan Indian Nation of southeastern California, adjacent to Yuma, Arizona. Most fluent speakers are middle aged or elderly, but fluency in the language retains considerable social prestige, particularly in ceremonial contexts, and there are a number of younger semi-speakers. Language retention is largely a traditional concern and there is no systematic attempt to teach Quechan in the schools, although there is a Quechan culture course at the high school where some vocabulary is taught.

Quileute [113], one of the two languages of the Chemakuan family, was spoken on the west coast of the Olympic Peninsula in northwest Washington, in a territory south of the Makah and north of the Quinault. The Quileutes now live on two small reservations, Quileute (at La Push) and Lower Hoh River, which have a combined population of less than 500. The language has been extensively documented by Powell, who published a grammar and a dictionary. The tribe began a language education program in the 1970s and several workbooks were published. Although as recently as 1986 ten first-language speakers of Quileute remained, the last speaker died in 1999. Three or four people in their fifties have a limited second-language command of some vocabulary and phrases.

Quinault [125], one of the four languages of the Tsamosan division of the Salishan family, was spoken on the west coast of the Olympic Peninsula in western Washington, in a small territory south of the Quileute. A substantial part of this territory is now the Quinault Reservation, centered on the community of Taholah, which the descendants of the Quinault-speaking groups share with several other tribes, including the closely related Lower Chehalis. The last first-language speaker of Quinault died recently. Up to half a dozen second-language speakers in their fifties have limited knowledge of vocabulary and phrases. A language program has been started at the Taholah school, but has had little success.

Rio Grande Keresan [249] is a complex of Keresan dialects spoken by members of five New Mexico Pueblos located near the Rio Grande or Jemez River north of Albuquerque: Zia, Santa Ana, San Felipe, Santo Domingo, and Cochiti. There is considerable local variation, but all varieties are mutually intelligible, as well as partially intelligible to speakers of Acoma-Laguna. Rates of language retention vary considerably from community to community, as do attitudes toward language preservation efforts. In general, outsiders are discouraged from learning the language, and this is especially strongly enforced at Santo Domingo and San Felipe. At Zia there are about 500 speakers out of a total population of approximately 800; there are relatively few speakers under twenty, but at least some children acquire the language. The language is taught at Zia Elementary School and at Jemez Valley High School, but only to Zia children. At Santa Ana there are about 385 speakers out of a total population of approximately 650. At San Felipe an estimated 90 percent of the population of over 2,600 speak the language, and most children acquire it. There is no language program and the language is not written. At Santo Domingo nearly all of the Pueblo's population of approximately 2,850 are speakers. Parents are expected by the community (and obliged by the Pueblo officers) to teach the language to their children, but no language classes are conducted in the Santo Domingo School. At Cochiti about half of the total population of approximately 1,200 speak the language, few if any of them children. It is taught at Cochiti Elementary School and, in 1996, the Pueblo began a community-based language revitalization program featuring a Keres-only summer school.

Saanich. See *Northern Straits Salish*

Sahaptin [178] is a Plateau Penutian language of marked dialectal diversity spoken along the Columbia River and adjacent Plateau in eastern Oregon and Washington. Together with Nez Perce it forms the Sahaptian branch of the Plateau Penutian family. **Southern Sahaptin** (or 'River') varieties were originally spoken along the Columbia River from The Dalles to the Umatilla River, and included Tenino, Wayam, and

Umatilla. **Northwest Sahaptin** varieties were spoken in the Yakima River drainage and included Klickitat, Taitnapam, Upper Nisqually, Yakima, and Kittitas. **Northeast Sahaptin** varieties were spoken on the Columbia River above Southern Sahaptin and along the lower Snake River, and included Walla Walla, Wanapam, and Palouse. The principal surviving Sahaptin communities are on the Warm Springs Reservation in northern Oregon (about fifty speakers of Tenino); on the Umatilla Reservation in northeastern Oregon, near Pendleton (twenty-five to fifty speakers of Umatilla and Walla Walla); and at Toppenish on the Yakima Reservation in south-central Washington (about twenty-five fluent speakers and a larger number of less-fluent speakers of Yakima). There is also a small Wanapam-speaking community near Priest Rapids Dam on the Columbia River. In some of these communities other native languages are spoken (Wasco and Northern Paiute at Warm Springs, Nez Perce at Umatilla), to an extent reflecting the pervasive multilingualism of the Plateau in the traditional period. A scattering of Sahaptin speakers can also be found among speakers of Okanagan and Nez Perce on the Colville Reservation in northeastern Washington. The Warm Springs and Umatilla tribes both have language programs working with all of the languages spoken on the respective reservations. At Warm Springs these include classes for the Tenino dialect of Sahaptin, and at Umatilla for both the Umatilla and Walla Walla dialects. In Toppenish, Heritage College is now offering two levels of (Yakima) Sahaptin, there is sporadic broadcasting of the language on the radio, and the Yakima tribal museum offers occasional classes. There is some literacy in Sahaptin, but each of the three major communities uses a separate orthography.

Salinan is an extinct language family of the central California coast. It consisted of two closely related languages or dialect clusters, a northern one, **Antoniano [197]**, primarily associated with Mission San Antonio de Padua, near Jolon in southern Monterey County, and a southern one, **Migueleño [198]**, primarily associated with Mission San Miguel, in northern San Luis Obispo County. Both languages are attested in a number of documents from the late eighteenth and early nineteenth century, including an extensive vocabulary of Antoniano prepared by Franciscan missionaries that was later published. They were also moderately well documented by at least three linguists in the twentieth century, including Harrington. J. Alden Mason published a grammar with texts and vocabulary, but much valuable material, including some sound recordings, remains in archives. The last speakers of both languages died in the late 1950s or early 1960s.

Samish. See *Northern Straits Salish*

San Felipe. See *Rio Grande Keresan*

San Ildefonso. See *Tewa*

San Juan. See *Tewa*

Sanpoil-Nespelem. See *Okanagan*

Santa Ana. See *Rio Grande Keresan*

Santa Clara. See *Tewa*

Santee-Sisseton. See *Sioux*

Santiam. See *Kalapuya*

Santo Domingo. See *Rio Grande Keresan*

Sarcee (Tsuut'ina) [88] is the only northern Athabaskan language spoken by a Plains group and, primarily on phonological grounds, constitutes its own subgroup within the Athabaskan family. It is spoken fluently by fewer than ten elderly people on or near the Sarcee Reserve, east of Calgary, Alberta, along with a small number of semi-speakers and passive speakers. One of the fluent speakers employs an orthography of his own devising but there is no generally accepted standard. There is a school program taught by a semi-speaker.

Sauk-Fox (Mesquakie) [36] is a Central Algonquian language, spoken by about 200 members of the Mesquakie Tribe in Iowa, by fifty or more members of the Sac and Fox Tribe of central Oklahoma, and by a few Nemaha Sauks on the Kansas-Nebraska border. The Mesquakie variety is often called 'Fox' and the other two 'Sauk', but the differences are more social than linguistic. Kickapoo was originally part of the same dialect complex, but for historical and social reasons it is treated as a separate language. Sauk-Fox is one of the few Native American languages to have been extensively documented by native speakers, first by William Jones, an anthropologist working under Boas, and slightly later by Alfred Kiyana (1877–1918), a tribal member who wrote hundreds of pages of Sauk-Fox narratives in a syllabic orthography.

Saulteaux [32] (pronounced 'Sodoe') is an emergent language of the Ojibwe dialect complex, closely related to Southwestern Ojibwe. The name 'Saulteaux' refers to the historical origin of the group at Sault Ste Marie and around Lake Superior; they moved westward onto the prairies with the expansion of the fur trade in the eighteenth and nineteenth century. Today, most varieties of Saulteaux are spoken in southern Manitoba in the vicinity of Lake Winnipeg, including a large urban population in the city of Winnipeg, although there are speakers as far west as British Columbia. The Saulteaux spoken north and east of Lake Winnipeg, and into Northern Ontario, shows considerable influence from Severn Ojibwe, including use of the syllabic orthography. These varieties are sometimes called **Northern Ojibwe**. Most Saulteaux varieties have a number of borrowings from Cree and other features that show Cree influence. Up to 10,000 people may be speakers of Saulteaux.

Sechelt [117] is a Central Salish language spoken by members of the Sechelt Band on the north coast of the Strait of Georgia, British Columbia. Out of a total population of over 700 there are up to forty-five speakers of varying degrees of fluency (only fifteen fully fluent), the youngest in his fifties, with an additional ten to fifteen who can carry on limited conversations. Sechelt is used for restricted communication among elders, and as a badge of tribal identity; Sechelt names are frequently given. There is a strong desire to revive use of the language and it is taught in the local school, but there are no fluent second-language speakers. A few (all involved in teaching the language) are literate.

Sekani [75] is an Athabaskan language, spoken in two remote communities in north-central British Columbia, Ware and Fort McLeod, as well as by some residents of the Beaver community of Prophet River and the Tahltan community of Iskut. A fair degree of mutual intelligibility exitsts between Sekani and Beaver, Kaska, and Tahltan. There are about fifty speakers. It is not spoken by children as a first language. There are few if any first-language speakers under thirty-five, no fluent second-language speakers, and no native-language literacy.

Seminole is sometimes used loosely to refer to Oklahoma Seminole Creek, a variety of Creek spoken in the Seminole Nation of Oklahoma. **Florida Seminole** is a closely related variety of Creek that is spoken by some members of the Seminole Tribe of Florida, although most speak **Mikasuki**.

Seneca [305] is a Northern Iroquoian language, originally spoken by the westernmost tribe of the Six Nations Iroquois Confederacy in western New York and adjacent Pennsylvania. It is now spoken by about 100 people in three reservation communities in New York: Cattatraugus, on Lake Erie; Allegany, in Salamanca; and Tonawanda, near Buffalo. The youngest speaker is in his fifties. A tribal language program has been in existence for a number of years, and several people have acquired a second-language fluency. Extensive educational material on Seneca – putatively a West Virginia variety called 'Mingo' – has been disseminated on the internet without the permission of the Seneca people and should be used with caution.

Serrano [232], a language of the Serrano-Gabrielino division of the Takic subfamily of Uto-Aztecan, was originally spoken in much of the Mojave Desert and the San Bernardino Mountains of southern California. Serrano descendants live mainly at the San Manuel Reservation near San Bernardino; also a number of Serranos have inter-married with the Cahuillas at the Morongo and Soboba Reservations. Only a very few older people are speakers, none completely fluent. The language is well documented, including materials collected by Harrington, but little is published. There is an active language program at San Manuel.

Severn Ojibwe (Oji-Cree) [28] is a well defined regional dialect within the Ojibwe dialect complex, spoken in northwestern Ontario in communities on Severn River, Winisk River, and Sandy Lake. First-language use of Severn Ojibwe is high, but Cree also has cultural prominence in these communities. Speakers employ a script derived from the Cree syllabary and the the Cree translation of the Bible is used in the local Anglican liturgy. The complex interrelationship of linguistic identity, script, and religion in Severn Ojibwe society has been described by Lisa Valentine.

Seward Peninsula Inupiaq. See ***Inupiaq***

Shasta (proper) [183], the only Shastan language to survive into the twentieth century, was originally spoken in several dialects across a relatively large territory that included Scotts Valley, near modern Etna and Fort Jones; Shasta Valley, around Yreka; and the Klamath River between Karuk and Klamath-Modoc territory. Substantial documentation exists for the Scotts Valley dialect, including a full grammar based on Silver's work with the last speakers in the 1950s and 1960s; most of this material remains unpublished. Many modern Shastas have merged their political and cultural identity with the Karuk Tribe and consider Karuk their heritage language, and no Shasta language program is active.

Shawnee [38] is an Algonquian language that was spoken in the early historical period in the Ohio Valley, mainly in the present state of Ohio. Today most of the descendants of the Shawnee live in Oklahoma, organized in three distinct groups. The Absentee Shawnee Tribe, located in and around the town of Shawnee, near the Citizen Potawatomi Nation, has about 2,000 members. At least 100 Absentee Shawnees are fluent speakers of the language, constituting the largest Shawnee-speaking community. The language remains in use on ceremonial occasions, and informal language classes for adults are offered on an irregular schedule. The Eastern Shawnee Tribe, whose 1,500 members live in Ottawa County near the Oklahoma Seneca community, has only a few elderly Shawnee speakers. The Loyal Shawnee (or 'Cherokee Shawnee'), a group of about 8,000, reside in the Cherokee region of northeastern Oklahoma, mainly around Whiteoak. Although fewer than a dozen Loyal Shawnees are speakers, the tribe has a language preservation project and offers language classes, primarily for adults.

Shoshoni (Shoshone) [227] is a Central Numic language, formerly spoken in a wide band stretching from Lida, Nevada northeast through Nevada, Utah, Idaho, and Wyoming as far north as Lemhi, Idaho and as far east as Wind River, Wyoming. Although there are a few large reservations which are exclusively (or at least half) Shoshoni, there are dozens of smaller reservations and communities scattered throughout the region. Shoshoni was a dialect continuum without rigid isoglosses to separate the dialects, but several major clusters of varieties can be identified. **Western Shoshoni** includes the communities throughout Nevada except for the Gosiute and Duck Valley communities. **Northern Shoshoni** includes the Duck Valley and Fort Hall communities as well as the smaller communities of northern Utah and southern Idaho. **Eastern Shoshoni** includes the Wind River community in Wyoming. **Gosiute** includes the Gosiute and Skull Valley communities in Utah. The largest speech community is at Fort Hall. Altogether, there are around 1,000 actively fluent speakers of Shoshoni, and perhaps another 1,000 with more restricted competence. While a few children still learn Shoshoni as a first language in the Duck Valley and Gosiute communities, the majority of speakers are over fifty. There are about the same number of passive speakers. There is a strong interest in maintaining or revitalizing the language in most communities, but the efforts are scattered and there has been little inter-community coordination. Funding is limited and sometimes very hard to obtain. Idaho State University offers a two-year Shoshoni language program which satisfies university second-language requirements and publishes a Shoshoni language newsletter. The classes are regularly full and about one third of the students are passive speakers who want to achieve a speaking fluency and literacy; about one third are Shoshoni, but don't have a knowledge of the language; and about one third are non-Shoshoni who want to learn it as a second language. Literacy is increasing. There are two major orthographies in use – one used in the Western Shoshoni and Gosiute areas, another used in Northern Shoshoni areas.

Shuswap (Secwepemc) [132] is an Interior Salish language spoken in east-central British Columbia along the Fraser River and its tributaries, upstream from Lillooet and

Thompson territory and adjoining Chilcotin and Carrier territory on the north. The modern Shuswaps are organized into seventeen bands, with the largest settlement at Kamloops on the Thompson River. There are between 200 and 500 fluent first-language speakers, most of them over fifty, in a total population of over 6,000. The Secwepemc Cultural Education Society, formed in 1983 with support from all seventeen bands, has made efforts to revitalize the language through classes at all levels from prescool to adult education, including an immersion program. A standard practical orthography has been adopted and a range of pedagogical and reference materials are available. However, these initiatives have produced few if any fluent second-language speakers and most younger people learn only a few words.

Sioux [264] is the cover term for the varieties of the **Dakotan** dialect complex other than Assiniboine and Stoney. Three Sioux dialect groups can be distinguished, from east to west: the **Santee-Sisseton (Dakota)** dialect is spoken in at least fifteen widely dispersed reservation communities in Minnesota, Manitoba, and Saskatchewan, and in the eastern parts of Nebraska and the Dakotas. The **Yankton-Yanktonai** dialect is primarily spoken on the Yankton and Crow Creek reservations in South Dakota, and on the northern part of the Standing Rock Reservation in North Dakota, although it also has speakers on the Devils Lake and Fort Peck reservations in North Dakota and on a few reserves in Saskatchewan. **Teton (Lakota)** is the dialect of the Cheyenne River, Lower Brule, Pine Ridge, Rosebud, and Sisseton reservations of South Dakota, as well as of the southern part of the Standing Rock Reservation in South Dakota and of the Wood Mountain Reserve in Saskatchewan. There are also substantial off-reservation communities of Sioux speakers, particularly in Rapid City, Minneapolis, and other urban centers in the upper Midwest. Together, there are nearly 25,000 first-language speakers of all Sioux dialects in a total population of 103,000. Of these an estimated 4,755 reside in Canada. There are teaching programs for Sioux – particularly for Lakota – at every level, from preschool through university. A substantial Lakota language program has been developed at Sinte Gleska College on the Rosebud Reservation, and courses in Lakota are offered at a number of American colleges and universities. In addition to the second-language speakers produced by these programs, a number of Sioux men acquire a speaking knowledge of the language for ritual purposes when they are in their teens or later. This acquisition takes place in relatively traditional settings. Orthographies exist for all Sioux dialects, but nowhere are they fully standardized; the most frequently used systems are those derived from mission schools, especially the one developed by Catholic missionaries on the Rosebud Reservation. Ella Deloria, a speaker of the Yankton dialect, wrote extensively in her language.

Sirenikski [1], a recently extinct language of the Yupik branch of Eskimo, was spoken in the villages of Sireniki and Imtuk on the Chukchi Peninsula in Russia. The last speaker died in 1997. Quite divergent from the other Yupik languages, it shows influence from Chukchi. It is sometimes considered a third branch of Eskimo, alongside Inuit and Yupik.

Siuslaw [144] was a language formerly spoken in two closely related local dialects, **Siuslaw** (proper) and **Lower Umpqua**, by adjacent tribes in a small territory on the central coast of Oregon. It is a classificatory isolate, usually considered part of the Penutian stock. Although some Siuslaw people were removed to reservations between 1855 and 1875 most remained in their traditional territory, where more than 100 descendants still reside. The Confererated Tribes of Coos, Lower Umpqua, and Siuslaw was recognized in 1984, with tribal headquarters at Coos Bay. Frachtenberg extensively documented both dialects of Siuslaw, and a set of texts, a vocabulary, and a grammatical sketch have been published for Lower Umpqua, and other materials exist in manuscript. Although a linguist worked with a speaker as late as 1954, the language was extinct by the 1970s. The Confederated Tribes have a language program and some Siuslaw-Lower Umpqua educational materials have been prepared for use by tribal members.

Sküüxs. See ***Maritime Tsimshianic***

Slave [77], or **South Slavey**, is an emergent Athabaskan language within the Slavey dialect area of the Dene complex. Slave is spoken as a first language by about 3,260 people in a number of communities in the Northwest Territories and in adjacent parts of northern British Columbia and Alberta. In the Northwest Territories, where it is one of the offical languages, Slave has 1,260 speakers, about half of whom use it in the home. The principal communities include: Fort Liard (310 speakers out of a total population of 510), Fort Providence (280 out of 750 total), Fort Simpson (290 out of 1255 total), Hay River Dene (eighty-five out of 250 total), Jean Marie River (thirty out of fifty-five total), Nahanni Butte (fifty out of seventy-five total), and Trout Lake (fifty-five out of sixty-five total). It may also be spoken by some of the 100 Slavey speakers at Fort Wrigley, most of whom speak Mountain. There are also up to sixty speakers of Slave in the town of Hay River. In northern British Columbia there are reported to be approximately 500 Slave speakers, with the principal community at Fort Nelson. In Alberta Slave is spoken by about 1,500 people at Meander River, Chateh Lake (Assumption) and at a few other places on the upper Hay River. Slave is one of the official languages of the Northwest Territories.

Slavey is the general term for a group of Athabaskan dialects or emergent languages of the Dene complex, including **Bearlake** and **Hare** (together constituting **North Slavey**), **Mountain**, and **Slave** or **South Slavey**.

Sm'algyax. See ***Maritime Tsimshianic***

South Slavey. See ***Slave***

Southeastern Pomo [190] was the Pomoan language that was formerly spoken at the east end of Clear Lake California, and is the heritage language of the Elem Indian Colony at Sulphur Bank and the Lower Lake Rancheria. The language was extensively documented in 1939–40 by Halpern and again in the 1960s by Moshinsky; a grammar has been published, but much remains in archives. The last fluent speaker died in the 1990s.

Southern Algonquin (Nipissing) [30] is an emergent language within the Ojibwe dialect complex, primarily spoken at the River Desert Reserve, on the Gatineau River at Maniwaki, Quebec. Although speakers identify themselves and their language as

Algonquin, Southern Algonquin is distinctly different from Northern Algonquin, as well as from the (extinct) Old Algonquin that was spoken in the Ottawa Valley in the seventeenth century.

Southern Paiute. See **Ute-Chemehuevi**

Southern Sierra Miwok. See **Eastern Miwok**

Southern Tiwa [245] is a Kiowa-Tanoan language spoken by members of the Pueblos of Sandia and Isleta, on the Rio Grande near Albuquerque, New Mexico. At Sandia Pueblo, fifteen miles north of Albuquerque, only middle-aged and elderly people are fully fluent, although some younger people use the language and at least a few children still acquire it. In all there are about 100 speakers in a total population of about 500. Since the 1960s the Pueblo has engaged in a variety of efforts to preserve the language. At Isleta Pueblo, fifteen miles south of Albuquerque, there are approximately 1,500 speakers in a membership of about 4,000.

Southern Tsimshian. See **Maritime Tsimshianic**

Southern Tutchone [69] is an Athabaskan language (closely related to Northern Tutchone) spoken in the southwestern Yukon in settlements at Aishihik, Burwash Landing, Champagne, Haines Junction, Kloo Lake, Klukshu, and Lake Laberge, as well as in the city of Whitehorse. There are about 200 speakers out of a total population of 1,400. The first systematic description of the language was by Daniel Tlen, a Burwash native, who returned to his home community in the 1970s after studying linguistics. He compiled language lessons, a basic noun dictionary, and a collection of stories and songs. Literacy workshops have been held since 1984, and the Yukon Native Language Centre currently has more than two dozen print and multimedia titles in and on Southern Tutchone. Southern Tutchone is taught in schools at Kluane Lake and Haines Junction, and three elementary schools in Whitehorse have native language programs which include Southern Tutchone.

Southwestern Ojibwe (Anishinaabemowin) [31] is an emergent language of the Ojibwe dialect complex, closely related to Saulteaux in Manitoba and to Nishnaabemwin in Michigan and Southern Ontario, a relationship which reflects the historical dispersion of Southern Ojibwe speakers across the Great Lakes and beyond during the fur trade from the seventeenth to the nineteenth century. Southwestern Ojibwe is spoken in a large number of communities in Northern Ontario, Michigan. Wisconsin, and Minnesota, as well as on reservations in North Dakota and Montana. These include twenty-five separate tribal entities in the United States and a roughly equal number of communities in Canada. Different groups refer to themselves and their language as Ojibwe, Chippewa, Chippeway, and Anishinabe, but local varieties do not differ substantially. Language retention varies, with Northern Ontario communities generally having a higher proportion of first-language speakers; use of the language is relatively strong in Minnesota, but much less so in Wisconsin and Michigan, where it is spoken only by middle-aged and elderly people. In addition to a number of community-based language programs, Southwestern Ojibwe is taught at the University of Manitoba, the University of Minnesota, and the University of Wisconsin.

Spokane-Kalispel [134] is an Interior Salish language, spoken in Washington, Idaho, and Montana in three major dialects. (1) The **Spokane** dialect is spoken on the Spokane Reservation in northeastern Washingon. It has only two fluent first-language speakers, a married couple in their seventies, both of whom are literate in a phonetically based orthography. The wife is the driving force in a language revival program that is expanding to provide instruction at all grade levels in the reservation school. She has also collaborated with linguists on two editions of a Spokane dictionary and taught her language at university level. A small number of partly fluent Spokanes are literate in the language and act as assistant teachers. A large data base of traditional literature is being incorporated into the school curriculum. These programs have not yet created any second-language speakers. (2) The **Flathead** dialect (also known as **Salish** or **Selish**, in this context referring to a specific language and not the entire language family) is spoken on the Flathead Reservation in western Montana by members of the Confederated Salish and Kootenay Tribes. There are about sixty fluent first-language speakers of Flathead, one in his forties, another about fifty-five, all others sixty-five or older. A subdialect is said to characterize Flathead speakers of **Pend d'Oreille** descent, but no separate statistics are available. Flathead is still used for general communication among fluent elders, with extensive code-switching to English. It is also a badge of tribal identity, and is used for prayers, especially at traditional wakes. Regular language classes are held in some reservation schools and at the tribal college, and educational videos and other materials have been produced. However, literacy in Flathead is rare. The Salish Culture Committee holds a week-long language camp each summer, where elders speak the language to the students. (3) The **Kalispel** dialect primarily survives on the Kalispel Reservation in northeastern Washington, where a handful of fluent speakers remain. There are also a few speakers living on the Spokane Reservation and in the nearby community of Chewelah, but information on them is scant. The Kalispel Tribe has recently begun a language documentation and revitalization program.

Spokane. See *Spokane-Kalispel*

Squamish (Skwxwu'mesh snichim) [118] is the Central Salish language of the Squamish reserves on Howe Sound and Burrard Inlet, British Columbia, on the Strait of Georgia immediately north of the city of Vancouver. There are fewer than twenty first language speakers, the youngest in their late sixties, out of a total population of 2,000. A Band-sponsored language program has offered K-12 classes in the local public schools for the last twenty-five years, and probably more than three quarters of the Band population has acquired some knowledge of the language in this setting. Although conversationally fluent second-language speakers are rare, many use Squamish in ceremonial contexts and at other community gatherings and this type of use is significantly increasing. There is a standard practical orthography, and many are literate. One first-language speaker (now deceased) wrote hundreds of pages of stories, legends and history, as well as pedagogical material. The Squamish Language Program is producing a bilingual dictionary and other materials, including audiotape lessons.

St'at'imcets. See *Lillooet*

St Lawrence Island Yupik. See *Central Siberian Yupik*

Stoney [266] is an emergent language in the **Dakotan** dialect complex of Siouan, historically related to – but clearly distinct from – Assiniboine. It is spoken on five reserves in Alberta located along the eastern base of the Rocky Mountains west of Calgary and Edmonton: Alexis, Paul, Bighorn, Morley, and Eden Valley. The principal community is Morley, midway between Calgary and Banff. The language is vigorous, with between 1,000 and 1,500 speakers in a total population of 3,200.

Swampy Cree [17] is the dialect of Western Cree spoken in northeastern Manitoba and on the west coast of James Bay and Hudson Bay in Ontario. The boundary between Swampy Cree and Moose Cree overlaps, most notably at Attawapiskat, but the two dialects can readily be distinguished. A distinction is made between an **Eastern Swampy Cree** subdialect, spoken at Fort Albany, Attawapiskat and Peawanuck (Winusk), and a **Western Swampy Cree** subdialect spoken in all other communities, including York Factory, Fox Lake, Shamattawa, Churchill, and Norway House. Fort Severn, on the boundary, shows features of both subdialects, as well as of neighbouring Ojibwe. Of a population of approximately 2,800, most are speakers.

Tagish [72] is an Athabaskan language, closely related to Tahltan and Kaska, that was spoken until the mid-nineteenth century around the lakes at the head of the Yukon River south of Whitehorse. In the later nineteenth century the Tagish community shifted to Tlingit and by the mid-twentieth century only a handful of older people remembered Tagish from their childhood. Tagish has been moderately well documented by several linguists during the last few decades. As of 2001 there remains one semi-fluent speaker and another elderly speaker who is deaf. Despite the marginality of the language and the dominance of Tlingit, there is some community interest in relearning the language. Curricular materials, including audiotapes, have been produced by the Yukon Native Language Centre.

Tahltan [73] is an Athabaskan language of northwestern British Columbia, closely related to Kaska (with which it is easily mutually intelligible) and to (nearly extinct) Tagish in the southern Yukon. It is principally the language of the remote community of Telegraph Creek, on the upper Stikine River, where there are five fluent speakers and perhaps fifteen passive speakers out of a total population of 100. It is also spoken in the mixed Sekani-Tahltan community of Iskut, at Kinaskan Lake. No children are reported to speak or understand it.

Tanacross [66] is an Athabaskan language belonging to the Tanana series, spoken at Healy Lake, Dot Lake, and Tanacross on the middle Tanana River of central Alaska. The total population is about 220, of whom about sixty speak the language. A practical alphabet was established in 1973.

Tanaina (Dena'ina) [60] is the Athabaskan language of the Cook Inlet area of southern Alaska. Distinct local dialects are associated with the Kenai Peninsula, the Upper Inlet area above Anchorage, and coastal and inland areas of the west side of Cook Inlet. Of the total population of about 900 people, about seventy-five speak the language. An orthography was developed by the Alaska Native Language Center in the 1970s, and Peter Kalifornsky, a native speaker, wrote extensively in Tanaina.

Tanana is a series of Athabaskan varieties spoken in east-central Alaska and adjacent Canada, from the upper Kuskokwim River to the headwaters of the Tanana River. Four languages are usually distinguished in the series: **Upper Kuskokwim**, **Lower Tanana**, **Tanacross**, and **Upper Tanana**. Speakers of adjacent languages can usually understand one another, although with some difficulty. None of the varieties of Tanana is flourishing; in most communities fewer than a third of the population are speakers, few or none of them children.

Taos [243] is a Kiowa-Tanoan language spoken by members of the Pueblo of Taos, 70 miles north of Santa Fe, New Mexico. Together with Picuris and Southern Tiwa, Taos belongs to the Tiwa branch of the Kiowa-Tanoan family; although close, these languages are not mutually intelligible. There are approximately 800 speakers in a Pueblo population of 1,600. Taos Pueblo, located next to a world-famous art colony, is probably one of the best known American Indian tribes, but a rule of secrecy is adhered to by all members of the Pueblo never to reveal anything to outsiders that is intrinsic to Taos culture. As a result, any language education and retention efforts that the Pueblo may be engaged in are not publicly known.

Tesuque. See *Tewa*

Teton. See *Sioux*

Tewa [246] is a Kiowa-Tanoan language spoken in distinct local varieties at seven Pueblos in northern New Mexico and Arizona. These include Santa Clara, San Juan, San Ildefonso, Nambe, Tesuque, and Pojoaque in New Mexico, and in Arizona the village of Hano on the First Mesa at Hopi. There are approximately 1,200 speakers of Tewa in the New Mexico Pueblos out of a total enrollment of approximately 4,500. There are about 300 additional speakers at Hano, where at least some children are acquiring the language. At San Juan, the largest of the New Mexico Tewa pueblos, as few as thirty fully fluent speakers remain in a population of about 2,000; most adults are semi-speakers, and no children are acquiring Tewa. The efforts of an SIL missionary at San Juan between 1965 and 1983 resulted in a dictionary and a standard orthography, and these are being used in a language preservation project that focuses on computer technology.

Thompson [131] is an Interior Salish language spoken along the Fraser River Canyon in southwest British Columbia and along the adjacent Thompson and Nicola Rivers. A shallow dialect distinction exists between Upper Thompson varieties in the northern part of Thompson territory and Lower Thompson varieties in the south. The principal modern settlements are at Lytton on the Fraser River and at Lower Nicola and Merritt in Nicola Valley. There are about 150 first-language speakers in a total population of over 5,000. Although a full dictionary and other extensive documentation exists for Thompson, including a detailed ethnobotanical study, language preservation efforts are not strong and no standard orthography exists. The Nlakapmx Tribal Council in Lytton has recently begun a language education program and is developing a teaching curriculum.

Tillamook [129], a Salishan language usually classified as its own subgroup, was formerly spoken in several local varieties along the northwest coast of Oregon, from the

Nehalem River to the Siletz River. Tillamook descendants have not organized as a tribe and are widely scattered. The language is moderately well documented, and a grammatical sketch has been published. The last speaker died in 1970.

Timbisha. See *Panamint*

Tipai. See *Diegueño*

Tlingit [57] is the traditional language of the Tlingit people on the southeastern coast of Alaska from Yakutat to Ketchikan, and constitutes a separate branch of the Na-Dene family alongside Eyak and the Athabaskan languages. The total Tlingit population in Alaska (organized as the Sealaska Regional Corporation, divided into sixteen village communities) is about 10,000, of whom perhaps as many as 500, none of them children, are fluent speakers of the language. An additional 185 Inland Tlingit speakers live in Canada in several communities in the southern Yukon and northern British Columbia. Most Inland Tlingits are descendants of Athabaskans who adopted Tlingit culture in the nineteenth century in connection with the fur trade, and their distinct dialect has low prestige on the coast. The only other well marked local variety is the phonologically archaic Tongass dialect, formerly spoken in the Ketchikan area but now nearly extinct. A practical writing system for Tlingit was developed in the 1960s, and the language has been well documented in a number of publications, including a verb dictionary and a noun dictionary. There is an especially rich documentation of traditional Tlingit literature and oratory in a series of publications by Nora and Richard Dauenhauer.

Tolkapaya (*Yavapai*). See *Upland Yuman*

Tolowa [94], the only surviving language of the Oregon Athabaskan subgroup, is spoken by a few individuals at the Smith River Rancheria near Crescent City, California. It is nearly extinct as a first language (one elderly semi-speaker survives in 2001) but there is one fully fluent second-language speaker in his forties and a growing number of younger speakers with more restricted competence. A full dictionary and some pedagogical materials have been published in a practical orthography in which all second-language speakers are literate.

Tonkawa [278] was spoken in the eighteenth century at San Gabriel Mission, between Austin and Waco in east-central Texas, and apparently by many groups in that region. After a tangled relationship with whites and other Indians in the first half of the nineteenth century, the Tonkawas were removed to Oklahoma, ultimately to a reservation in Kay County. The tribe currently has a membership of less than 200, none of whom speak the language. Tonkawa is attested in three nineteenth-century vocabularies, but was mainly documented by Hoijer's extensive fieldwork with one of the last fluent speakers in 1928–9. Publications resulting from his research included a grammar, grammatical sketch, dictionary, and collection of texts. Although earlier thought to be part of a 'Coahuiltecan' family, Tonkawa is now considered to be a classificatory isolate.

Tsimshian is a name commonly used for at least two different language units. On the one hand it is the term associated in much of the older literature with the entire Tsimshianic language family. More narrowly, it is often used as a synonym for Coast Tsimshian (Sm'algyax), an emergent language in the Maritime Tsimshianic area of Tsimshianic.

Tsuut'ina. See ***Sarcee***

Tualatin-Yamhill. See ***Kalapuya***

Tubatulabal [231], a Uto-Aztecan language that constitutes an independent branch of the family, is the heritage language of the unrecognized Tubatulabal tribe of Kern County, California. There are approximately 900 Tubatulabals, about half of them still living in the tribe's traditional territory in the Kern River Valley of the southern Sierra Nevada. Only a handful of elderly people – fewer than five – are speakers of the language. No retention or revitalization activities are reported, although a cultural center, developed in partnership with the US Forest Service, has stimulated interest in traditional culture.

Tukudh. See ***Gwich'in***

Tule-Kaweah. See ***Yokuts***

Tümpisa Shoshone. See ***Panamint***

Tunica [288], the heritage language of the Tunica-Biloxi Tribe of Marksville, Avoyelles Parish, Louisiana, was spoken in the seventeenth and eighteenth century along the Mississippi River near Vicksburg, Mississippi. Some materials on Tunica were collected in the late nineteenth and early twentieth century, but the principal documentation is by Haas, who collected extensive data between 1933 and 1939 and published a grammar, a grammatical sketch, a dictionary, and a collection of texts. The last speaker, with whom Haas worked, died after 1950. Although a few scholars think Tunica belongs to a 'Gulf' stock, most consider it a classificatory isolate.

Tuscarora [301], a Northern Iroquoian language, was spoken until the early eighteenth century in eastern North Carolina. After 1711–13 many Tuscaroras moved north to join the League of the Iroquois in New York, settling near the Seneca. After the American Revolution part of the group fled to Canada, joining other Iroquois on the Six Nations Reserve in Ontario. Only two or three speakers of Tuscarora remain, all over eighty. The documentation is extensive, including substantial materials collected for the BAE between 1880 and 1939 by J. N. B. Hewitt, himself of Tuscarora descent. No retention or revitalization efforts are known.

Tututni [91] was a language of the Oregon Athabaskan subgroup formerly spoken along the southwest Oregon coast from the Coquille River to a few miles north of the California border. There were several distinct local varieties, the best attested of which are Coquille, Euchre Creek, and Chasta Costa. After the Rogue River War of 1855–6 the Tututnis were forcibly resettled in northern Oregon on the Grand Ronde and Siletz Reservations, where Tututni continued to be spoken for several generations. The last fluent speaker died in 1983. The language is moderately well documented, although most of the documentation remains unpublished. In the 1990s the Confederated Tribes of the Siletz Reservation adopted Deene, a standardized form of Oregon Athabaskan based on Tolowa rather than Tututni, as the heritage language of the group.

Twana [124] was a Central Salish language formerly spoken along Hood Canal on the east side of the Olympic Peninsula in northwestern Washington. The Twana were concentrated on the Skokomish Reservation in 1859, where dialect differences were lost but the language and culture survived for several generations. The language has been moderately well documented by several linguists. A language program was begun on the Skokomish Reservation in the 1970s and educational materials, including a dictionary, were published. The last fluent speaker died in 1980.

Unami. See *Delaware*

Upland Yuman [200] is a Yuman language, closely related to Paipai, spoken by three historically and culturally distinct groups in western Arizona, the Hualapai, the Havasupai, and the Yavapai, the last traditionally divided into four regional subtribes. Each community speaks a distinct variety, with the Yavapai varieties forming a well defined dialect, although all varieties are mutually intelligible with little difficulty. **Hualapai (Walapai)** is spoken at the Hualapai Indian Reservation in Peach Springs by approximately 1,000 people, slightly more than half the total population. Speakers are of all ages and at least some children continue to acquire Walapai as their first language. There has been an active bilingual education program in the Peach Springs schools for over twenty years and extensive teaching materials have been prepared, as well as a full reference grammar and dictionary. **Havasupai** is spoken by more than 500 people of all ages, nearly the entire population of the village of Supai in Havasu Canyon, at the western end of the Grand Canyon. The tribally controlled school offers bilingual education courses and there is extensive literacy in the dialect. **Yavapai** is spoken in four small reservation communities, Prescott, Fort McDowell, Camp Verde, and Clarkdale. Local varieties, however, reflect pre-reservation subtribes and include **Yavepe, Tolkapaya, Keweevkapaya**, and **Wipukpaya**, speakers of which are found in all four communities. None of the Yavapai varieties are thriving, and most of the estimated 100 to 150 speakers (out of a total population of about 1,000) are middle-aged or older. Yavapai is taught in the reservation school in Prescott. During the nineteenth century the Yavapais were allied with the Western Apaches, and there are small numbers of Western Apache speakers at the Camp Verde Reservation and the Fort McDowell Reservation.

Upper Chehalis [127], one of the four languages of the Tsamosan division of the Salishan family, was formerly spoken on the upper Chehalis River in southwestern Washington. Most Upper Chehalis descendants live on the Chehalis Reservation, west of Centralia, which they share with the descendants of several other groups. The language has been well documented by Kinkade, and a grammar and dictionary have been published. The last active speaker died at the age of ninety in 2001.

Upper Kuskokwim (or **Kolchan**) **[64]** is an Athabaskan language belonging to the Tanana series, spoken in the villages of Nikolai, Telida, and McGrath in the Upper

Kuskokwim River drainage of central Alaska. Of a total population of about 160 people, about forty still speak the language. Raymond Collins began linguistic work at Nikolai in 1964, when he established a practical orthography. Since then he has worked with Betty Petruska to produce many small booklets and a school dictionary for use in a bilingual program.

Upper Piman (O'odham) [239] is the northernmost of the languages of the Tepiman subfamily of Uto-Aztecan, and the only one spoken in the United States. There are between 14,000 and 15,000 fluent speakers of all ages in Arizona, and many additional speakers in Mexico. Two major dialects are distinguished, **Tohono O'odham** (or **Papago**) and **Akimel O'odham** (or **Pima**). Most Akimel O'odham speakers live on the Gila River, Salt River, and Ak Chin Reservations, in the vicinity of Phoenix. Most Tohono O'odham speakers in the United States live on the Papago Reservation in southern Arizona west of Tucson, with the tribal headquarters at Sells; there are also speakers on the San Xavier and Gila Bend Reservations. Both dialects of O'odham are well documented, with published dictionaries and grammars. A practical writing system is well established and some literary works have been published in Tohono O'odham. The language is taught at the University of Arizona.

Upper Tanana [67] is an Athabaskan language belonging to the Tanana series, spoken mainly in the Alaska villages of Northway, Tetlin, and Tok, but also in the Beaver Creek area of the Yukon. Each of these communities has a different local variety. The Alaskan population is about 300, of whom at most 100 speak the language. During the 1960s, Paul Milanowski established a writing system and produced several booklets and a school dictionary for use in bilingual programs. In the Beaver Creek school the Upper Tanana language is taught to about twenty students from kindergarten to grade 9. Eight publications in and on Upper Tanana are currently available from the Yukon Native Language Centre.

Ute. See *Ute-Chemehuevi*

Ute-Chemehuevi [230] is a dialect chain within Southern Numic that extends from central Colorado westward across Utah and southern Nevada to the eastern Mojave Desert in California. There are three major regional varieties, all mutually intelligible. **Ute** (Colorado and central Utah) is spoken by about 900 people in and around three reservation communities: (1) Southern Ute (Ignacio, Colorado), where there about 100 first-language speakers, the youngest about fifty-five, out of a total population of 1,300. (2) Ute Mountain Ute (Towaoc, Colorado), where there about 500 first-language speakers, the youngest about twenty-five, out of a total population of 1,500. (3) Uintah and Ouray (Northern) Ute (Fort Duchesne, Utah), where there about 300 first-language speakers, the youngest about forty-five, out of a total population of 2,000. There are tribally sponsored language programs at all three reservations, and substantial reference materials have been produced for Southern Ute, but efforts to date have resulted in few if any second-language speakers or literate first-language speakers. **Southern Paiute** (southern Utah and Nevada) is spoken in ten widely separated communities in Utah, Arizona, and Nevada. The five Utah communities constitute the Paiute Tribe of Utah and have a total population of about 600. The San Juan Paiute Tribe is settled on the Navajo Reservation in Utah and Arizona and has a population of 220. The Kaibab Paiute Tribe, with a reservation north of the Grand Canyon, has a population of 212. The three southern Nevada tribes (Moapa, Las Vegas, and Pahrump) have a combined population of over 400. The language is spoken to a varying extent in all communities, but only in the San Juan tribe are children still acquiring it as their first language. There are no active language education programs, although there is considerable interest in recording and videotaping traditional storytellers. Southern Paiute is extensively documented, most importantly in the work of Edward Sapir, who published a full grammar and dictionary of the language as well as a set of narrative texts. **Chemehuevi** (southern California) is spoken on the Colorado River Indian Reservation at Parker, Arizona (which the Chemehuevis share with Mohaves, Navajos, and Hopis), and on the neighboring Chemehuevi Reservation in California. There are fewer than twenty first-language speakers, with the youngest nearly forty. The Arizona Chemehuevis have started a language revitalization program, but there are few materials and no agreement on orthography. One woman is learning Chemehuevi as a second language from her mother in a master-apprentice program.

Ventureño. See *Chumash*

Wappo [216] is the only surviving Yukian language, a small family of the Coast Range northern California. Wappo was originally spoken from Napa Valley to Clear Lake, in a compact, mostly mountainous, territory hemmed in by speakers of the Pomo languages to the west, Lake Miwok to the north, and Patwin to the east and south. During the nineteenth century most of the surviving Wappos joined these surrounding groups. There are at most three speakers of Wappo, all elderly, and probably none of them fully fluent. The language has a moderate amount of published documentation, but no thorough modern description. Since there is no modern group for which Wappo is the heritage language, no retention effort is under way and the language is likely to become extinct soon.

Wasco-Wishram. See *Kiksht*

Washo [214] is a Hokan language spoken by members of the Washoe Tribe of Nevada and California, whose traditional homeland centers on Lake Tahoe in the High Sierra. There are several dozen fluent first-language speakers, all middle-aged or elderly, in a total population of over 1,500, divided among four small reservations in both Nevada and California. The Washoe Tribe sponsors a language retention project that emphasizes master-apprentice learning and (since 1994) a small but successful immersion school, where students use Washo as the medium of instruction from kindergarten through 8th grade. A number of children and young adults have acquired moderate second-language fluency in these initiatives. Curricular materials have also been prepared for use in community classes and for a course that is given from time to time at at the University of Nevada in Reno.

Western Apache [100] is an emergent language within the Southern Athabaskan dialect complex, spoken as a first language by up to 14,000 people in several reservation communities in southeastern Arizona. Of these, about 6,000 live on the San Carlos Reservation and 7,000 on the Fort Apache Reservation (White Mountain Apache

Tribe), making up about 65 percent of the population of those two tribes. Much smaller numbers of speakers are found at the Tonto Reservation at Payson, at the Camp Verde Reservation (shared with the Yavapais), and at the Fort McDowell Reservation near Scottsdale (shared with the Yavapais and the Mojaves). A few children at San Carlos and Fort Apache speak Western Apache as their first language, but most children and young adults are passive speakers or semi-speakers. There are several dozen second-language speakers, mostly children raised by grandparents and a few older whites. A practical orthography was adopted in 1972, based on the Navajo orthography, and literacy in Western Apache is promoted in the reservation schools. The language is widely used at San Carlos and Fort Apache, and is broadcast on local radio stations. A number of publications have been issued by the White Mountain Cultural Center at Fort Apache, and some self-teaching materials are available.

Western Canadian Inuktitut. See *Inuktitut*

Western Eskimo. See *Yupik*

Western Miwok, one of the two branches of the Miwok languages of north-central California, consists of two languages: **Coast Miwok**, originally spoken in Marin and Sonoma counties, is extinct. **Lake Miwok [157]** has two or three semi-speakers, none of them actively using the language, who live at the Middletown Rancheria, on ancestral Lake Miwok territory to the southeast of Clear Lake.

Wetsuwet'en. See *Babine*

Wichita [282] is a Northern Caddoan language, spoken by the Wichita Tribe, formerly a confederacy of autonomous bands that until the late nineteenth century lived in an area extending from central Oklahoma through central Texas. Today they live in Caddo County in central Oklahoma, primarily in and around the town of Anadarko, an area in which the Caddo, Delaware, and Kiowa also live. There are fewer than ten elderly speakers of the language in a total tribal population of approximately 2,100. Extensive efforts have been made to document and preserve the language, most recently the Wichita Documentation Project funded by the Volkswagen Foundation, the results of which will be housed in a data archive in the Netherlands.

Winnebago (Ho-Chunk, Hochank) [272] is a Siouan language of the Chiwere-Winnebago subgroup, spoken in central Wisconsin. Winnebago has over 250 fluent first-language speakers, divided between the Winnebago Tribe of northeastern Nebraska and the Ho-Chunk Nation of central Wisconsin. The number may be higher; 2,000 speakers were reported by reliable sources in 1980. The Ho-Chunk Culture Committee has been engaged in language maintenance activities since 1990, and a linguistic consultant assembled a substantial reference dictionary that is so far unpublished.

Wintu-Nomlaki [151] is one of the two languages of the Wintuan family of northern California, and was originally spoken in the northern half of the Sacramento Valley, on the upper Sacramento River below Mt Shasta, and in the upper drainage of the Trinity River and on Hayfork Creek in Trinity County. There were two major dialects, **Nomlaki**, spoken along the Sacramento River south of Red Bluff, and **Wintu**, spoken

91

elsewhere in the territory. There appears to have been no significant difference between the variety of Wintu spoken in the Trinity-Hayfork area and the Sacramento Valley variety. At least one fluent, traditional speaker of the Wintu dialect remains, although elderly, as well as several semi-speakers. Three master-apprentice pairs have been sponsored.

Wipukpaya (*Yavapai*). See *Upland Yuman*

Wiyot [55] was an Algic language of the Humboldt Bay region of northwestern California, distantly related to the Algonquian languages as well as to adjacent Yurok. It is the heritage language of the Wiyot tribe, whose principal modern community is at Table Bluff Rancheria near Ferndale. The language was extensively documented by Reichard in 1922–3 and Teeter in 1956–9; the last speaker died in 1961. Two grammars have been published, and a full dictionary is in preparation. A modest language revival program is under way at Table Bluff.

Woods Cree [16] is the dialect of Western Cree spoken in communities in the forested interior of northwestern Manitoba and north-central Saskatchewan (Lac La Ronge, Montreal Lake, Lac La Ronge, Peter Ballantyne). The use of roman orthography has been recently gaining ground at the expense of the older syllabic system, due to university language and teacher education programs. While younger speakers still use the language, it is losing ground to English.

Wyandotte. See *Huron-Wyandotte*

Yankton-Yanktonai. See *Sioux*

Yaqui (Cáhita, Yoeme) [240] is a language of the Taracahitan subfamily of Uto-Aztecan, primarily spoken along the lower Yaqui River in southern Sonora, Mexico. In the early twentieth century many Yaquis fled to the United States to escape political persecution and settled in southern Arizona. About 8,000 Yaquis are now members of the Yaqui Tribe of Arizona, which since 1964 has had a reservation at New Pascua, southwest of Tucson. Although older Arizona Yaquis speak their language fluently or are bilingual in Yaqui and Spanish, younger tribal members have largely switched to English, and a retention program has been instituted in the local schools. A standard orthography has been developed and a dictionary published.

Yaquina. See *Alsea*

Yavapai. See *Upland Yuman*

Yavepe (*Yavapai*). See *Upland Yuman*

Yoeme. See *Yaqui*

Yokuts is a large complex of dialects, spoken aboriginally in the San Joaquin Valley of south-central California and the foothills of the Sierra Nevada to the east. There were over forty local varieties of Yokuts, each associated with a small independent community, often only a single village or close-knit group of villages. Although the classification is somewhat arbitrary, six emergent languages are usually distinguished, three of which (Palewyami, Buena Vista, and Gashowu) are extinct. Still spoken are: **Tule-Kaweah [173]**, a cluster of dialects originally spoken in the Sierra Nevada foothills along the Tule and Kaweah Rivers, east of Porterville. Fewer than ten speakers of the Wukchumne (Wikchamni) dialect of Tule-Kaweah remain, most of them on the Tule River Reservation. A Wukchumne preschool has been started, weekly adult classes are given by elders, and several speakers and learners have participated in master-apprentice teaching. **Kings River [174]**, a cluster of dialects originally spoken in the Sierra Nevada foothills east of Fresno. Half a dozen elderly speakers or semi-speakers of the Choinumne (Choynimni) dialect live in scattered locations in and around their traditional homeland. **Valley Yokuts [176]**, a large complex of shallowly differentiated dialects spoken mainly in the San Joaquin Valley. There are speakers of at least three Valley Yokuts dialects, including up to twenty-five fluent and semi-fluent speakers of Yowlumne (Yawelmani) on the Tule River Reservation, a few semi-speakers of Chukchansi at the Picayune and Table Mountain Rancherias in the foothills northeast of Fresno, and a few speakers of Tachi at the Santa Rosa Rancheria near Lemoore. Some language revival activity has occurred in the Chukchansi and Tachi communities, and several Yowlumne speakers and learners have participated in master-apprentice teaching.

Yoncalla. See *Kalapuya*

Yuchi (Euchee) [297] is a classificatory isolate, possibly distantly related to the Siouan languages. Originally an independent tribe located in central Tennessee, the Yuchis have been politically associated with the Muscogee Creeks since the early nineteenth century and most of the 1,500 members of the group live among the Creeks in northeastern Oklahoma, near Sapulpa, Hectorsville, and Bristow. They maintain distinct traditions, however, and the language is still spoken fluently by five to seven elderly people, only one younger than seventy-five. The Euchee Language Program, established in the mid-1990s, emphasizes collaboration among linguists, learners, and speakers.

Yuki [215] was a complex of distinct but closely related dialects that were spoken in northern Mendocino and Lake Counties, California, from Round Valley to the coast. Together with Wappo, the Yuki dialects form the Yukian family. The major dialects were **Coast Yuki**, spoken along a short stretch of the rugged coast between Fort Bragg and Rockport; **Huchnom**, spoken along the South Eel River north of Willits; and **Yuki** (proper), or **Round Valley Yuki**, spoken in a number of village communities in and around Round Valley. Yuki was documented by several linguists during the twentieth century, most extensively by Kroeber. A compilation of the vocabulary of Round Valley Yuki has been published, but Kroeber's archival materials are yet to be analyzed. The last fluent speaker died around 1990. Yuki descendants share the Round Valley Reservation with several other tribes, and no language revitalization effort is known to be under way.

Yupik (Western Eskimo). See *Central Alaskan Yup'ik, Naukanski Yupik, Pacific Yupik, Central Siberian Yupik*

Yurok [56], an Algic language distantly related to the Algonquian languages, is the traditional language of the Yurok Tribe of northwestern California and of three nearby independent rancherias of Yurok heritage, Reseghini, Big Lagoon, and Trinidad (Cher-Ae). Only a dozen or fewer elderly people have full first-language fluency in a combined tribal enrollment of well over 4,000, although there are perhaps three times as many semi-speakers and passive speakers, all middle-aged or older. In addition, several individuals, not all of them Indians, have acquired second-language fluency, and many younger Yuroks have an acquaintance with the language through local school programs that have been in place since the 1970s at both the primary and secondary level. A distinctive writing system based on English phonetics ('Unifon') has been widely employed in classroom teaching, but other orthographies are also in use, including one recently adopted by the Yurok Tribe for use in a dictionary that is being planned.

Zia. See *Rio Grande Keresan*

Zuni [250], a classificatory isolate, is the language of Zuni Pueblo in western New Mexico. Zuni remains the primary language of most of the more than 9,000 tribal members, although almost all are bilingual in English. The Zuni Tribe has formally adopted a practical orthography and has collaborated with the public school district in developing a literacy program designed to help preserve the language in written form.

References

Campbell, Lyle (1997) *American Indian Languages: The Historical Lingustics of Native America.* New York and Oxford: Oxford University Press.

Davis, Mary B. (ed.) (1994) *Native America in the Twentieth Century: An Encyclopedia.* New York and London: Garland Publishing.

Dillehay, Thomas D. (2000) *The Settlement of the Americas: A New Prehistory.* New York: Basic Books.

Goddard, Ives (1996a) Introduction. *Handbook of North American Indians* 17: 1–16. Washington DC: Smithsonian Institution.

——(1996b) The Classification of the Native Languages of North America. *Handbook of North American Indians* 17: 290–323. Washington DC: Smithsonian Institution.

Greenberg, Joseph H. (1987) *Language in the Americas.* Stanford CA: Stanford University Press.

Grimes, Barbara F. (ed.) (2000) *Ethnologue: Languages of the World.* 14th edn. Dallas TX: SIL International.

Haas, Mary R. (1969) *The Prehistory of Languages.* The Hague: Mouton.

Hinton, Leanne (2001a) The Master-Apprentice Language Learning Program. In: Hinton, Leanne and Ken Hale (eds) *The Green Book of Language Revitalization in Practice.* San Diego and London: Academic Press, pp. 217–26.

——(2001b) The Use of Linguistic Archives in Language Revitalization: The Native California Language Restoration Workshop. In: Hinton, Leanne and Ken Hale (eds) *The Green Book of Language Revitalization in Practice.* San Diego and London: Academic Press, pp. 419–23.

Mithun, Marianne (1999) *The Languages of Native North America.* Cambridge and New York: Cambridge University Press.

Nichols, Johanna (1990) Linguistic Diversity and the First Settlement of the New World. *Language* 66: 475–521.

Powell, John Wesley (1891) *Indian Linguistic Families North of Mexico.* Bureau of American Ethnology, Seventh Annual Report, 1–142. Washington DC: Government Printing Office.

Sapir, Edward (1921) A Bird's-Eye View of American Indian Languages North of Mexico. *Science* 54: 408. Reprinted in Bright, William (ed.) *Collected Works of Edward Sapir* 5: 93–4, 1990, Berlin: Mouton de Gruyter.

——(1929) Central and North American Languages. *Encyclopedia Britannica*, 14th edn, 5: 138–41. Reprinted in Bright, William (ed.) *Collected Works of Edward Sapir* 5: 95–104, 1990.

Voegelin, C. F. and Florence M. Voegelin (1965) Classification of American Indian Languages. *Anthropological Linguistics* 7(7), fascicle 2, 121–50.

USA

Gulf of Mexico

*NORTH ATLANTIC
OCEAN*

Cuba

MEXICO

Hispaniola

Jamaica

CARIBBEAN SEA

Caracas

VENEZUALA

Orinoco

Bogota

COLUMBIA

Quito

Manaus

Belem

Amazonas

Madeira

Xingu

Lima

PERU

BRAZIL

Salvador

La Paz

Brasilia

BOLIVIA

PARAGUAY

Rio de Janeiro

Asunsion

PACIFIC OCEAN

Parana

CHILE

URUGUAY

Santiago

Buenos Aires

Montivideo

ARGENTINA

*SOUTH ATLANTIC
OCEAN*

Falkland Islands

South Georgia

SCOTIA SEA

2

Latin America

Willen Adelaar

Introduction

Diachronic survey of the linguistic development of the area

Central and South America present an extraordinary linguistic diversity, both from a genetic and from a typological point of view. At the time of the European invasion this region had apparently preserved most of its original language groups, which were existing in a sort of numerical equilibrium. Large movements of linguistic unification, as we know them from Africa, Asia and Europe, were either absent, or had produced limited effects. The classification of the numerous linguistic isolates and families of native Latin America, the reconstruction of the proto-languages, and the tracing of past migrations based on linguistic data are tasks that will occupy linguists for many decades to come. The existence of possible genetic connections between South and North America, let alone other areas of the world, is a question that has hardly been touched. The only classification that proposes such connections (Greenberg 1987) has not gained the acceptance of most of the linguists working in the indigenous Latin American field.

The indigenous languages spoken today in Central and South America include only a relatively small portion of the languages existing in that area at the moment of the first contact. During the past five centuries massive language extinction has occurred, leading into oblivion numerous languages of which even the names were not recorded. In large parts of South America and the Caribbean islands the indigenous languages have disappeared completely, leaving a fragmentary and uneven picture of the original language situation. The reasons for this extinction were manifold. Ruthless oppression, including countless massacres and widespread overexploitation of the human workforce, accompanied the conquest by the Spanish and Portuguese invaders. It led to the physical disappearance of many nations, in particular in the first half of the sixteenth century. On the greater Caribbean islands and in eastern Panama a numerous indigenous population became extinct in the first decades of the sixteenth century. The conquerors also brought an unprecedented wave of epidemic illnesses which had previously been unknown in the continent. These illnesses decimated and demoralised scores of ethnic groups already affected by widespread oppression and violence. The combination of these events brought about a demographic collapse of catastrophic dimensions. Ethnic groups with a limited number of language speakers, who had managed to survive throughout the centuries, often fell below a critical size, making it impossible for them to continue their existence as a group. Even so the demographic reduction was more significant in some areas than in others. As a general rule, coastal areas were more radically affected than parts of the mountainous interior. It goes without saying that such events had a devastating effect on the existing linguistic diversity. Scores of languages disappeared in early post-contact days, often leaving no more than a name or a mention in one of the chronicles.

After the stabilisation of colonial power in the Spanish domains, a relatively benevolent and somewhat protective administration, stimulated and supported by the church, allowed some of the plagued indigenous groups to recover demographic strength. This occurred in Middle America and in the Central Andes, areas which had previously harboured organised states with intensive agriculture and large populations. A special case is Paraguay, where Jesuit missionaries established indigenous protectorates (*reducciones*), in which the Indian identity and language (*Guaraní*) were preserved. Protective measures included the recognition for official use of some of the more widely used native languages, largely to the detriment of smaller local languages that were frequently abandoned. The imposed expansion of the Quechua language, associated with the former Inca empire, led to an early extinction of the highland languages of Ecuador and northern Argentina. Elsewhere, e.g. in central Chile, northern Peru, the Colombian highlands, and on the coast of Ecuador and Peru the imposition of Spanish had a similar effect. Meanwhile, in marginal areas of the Spanish domain exploitation and warfare continued to take their toll. This was the case, for instance, in northern Mexico and in parts of what is now Colombia and Venezuela.

In the eastern part of South America, the Portuguese established in Brazil were less sensitive to the interests and survival of the indigenous population. Ruthless exploitation of indigenous manpower, obtained by slaving raids that did not even spare the eastern borders of the Spanish domain, reduced the native population to a dramatic extent. Existing enmities between the different tribes were used in order to achieve their destruction and enslavement. In Brazil, genocidal practices have continued well into the twentieth century, leaving the eastern half of the country nearly empty of speakers of native languages.

The independence of the Latin American countries brought a further deterioration of the situation of the indigenous peoples. Renewed genocidal activity, especially in the far south of the continent, led to the extermination of many peoples and their languages. Notorious is the fate of the indigenous populations of Tierra del Fuego, of central and southern Argentina, Uruguay, and the southern and central states of Brazil. The indigenous populations of Middle America and the Andes were impoverished and became increasingly subject to discrimination. The status of their languages was lower than ever, if the existence of these languages was not simply denied. In the twentieth century conservative elites in countries such as Guatemala and El Salvador stimulated and organised massive killings of largely acculturated Indians in a reaction to ongoing social development and in defence of their own vested interests. In the case of El Salvador such actions led to the destruction of the Pipil language and culture in 1930s. The trauma caused by the marginalisation of the indigenous population during the nineteenth and most of the twentieth century brought along thoroughly negative consequences for the survival of the native languages, which can still be felt today.

Language endangerment and problems of language preservation in the area

In spite of notable differences in the number of speakers, vitality, visibility and generational distribution, all the indigenous languages of South and Central America must be characterised as endangered. There is one exception: Paraguayan Guaraní is spoken by almost the entire population of Paraguay, and it has been recognised as an official language at the same level as Spanish in the national constitution of that country. Most of its growing number of speakers consider themselves non-Indians, lexical concepts have been redefined following European models, and a certain amount of morphophonemic simplification has occurred in the past under the guidance of the missionaries. Nevertheless, from most points of view, Paraguayan Guaraní is a typical Amerindian language, not a mixed language or a jargon.

The other Amerindian languages in Latin America all face the danger of becoming extinct within a few generations. Some languages are on the verge of extinction because they are only used by aged speakers. These speakers form a vanishing minority within an ethnic group now generally using some other language. Other languages are spoken by all generations of an ethnic group, but the number of speakers as a whole is too small to eventually secure their survival as a separate ethnolinguistic group. If the size of the speaker group is critically small, any change in social conditions or migrational movement can lead to immediate extinction. It should be emphasised that Latin America harbours dozens of relatively vital linguistic groups that elsewhere in the world would be considered non-viable for numerical reasons. Their capacity of survival has often defied earlier expectations of extinction. Nevertheless, it is hard to imagine that these languages can survive without heavily protective measures.

The larger Amerindian languages in Latin America, some of which are spoken by millions of speakers, are facing a different type of threat, consisting in a failure of transmission of the language from one generation to the next. Such generational language shift has its roots in past neglect, discrimination and oppression, through which speakers came to associate their ancestral language with absence of social opportunities. Although a last generation of speakers may be visibly attached to the language and the traditions associated with it, they are also generally aware of the social disadvantages of belonging to a vernacular language group, which makes them want a different option for their children. In addition, the national language is overtly favoured by school and television, both likely to reach the youngest generation in the first place. Generational language shift is difficult to influence in view of the size of the group in question. Small speaker groups can be reached more easily.

Quechua, the largest indigenous language of the Americas, is typically threatened by generational language shift. Although it has several millions of speakers, it has disappeared or is about to disappear from areas such as Central Peru, where its presence has a long history. Quechua may not become extinct soon, but the territory

99

where it is spoken has become much reduced. Here and there continuous Quechua-speaking areas are becoming Spanish-speaking areas leaving a few Quechua-speaking islands, a development which turns Quechua from a language of regional communication into a relic community language. Many of the interesting dialectal varieties, crucial for the reconstruction of Quechua internal history (Quechua dialects may vary beyond the level of mutual understandability), are becoming extinct, a process that causes considerable loss of diversity without, for the moment, destroying the language itself. Migration of Quechua speakers into Spanish-speaking areas, such as the Lima agglomeration, has also become an important factor. No matter how large the migrating groups are, it is unlikely that they will for very long continue to speak Quechua in their new environment. Similar observations as for Quechua can be made for some of the more widely spoken Mexican languages, such a Mixtec and Zapotec, for instance.

In spite of the pessimistic views outlined above, it would be a mistake not to mention some more positive developments. In particular, during the last two decades of the twentieth century, there has been a remarkable tendency towards a reappraisal of indigenous cultural and linguistic values. Indigenous groups have entered the political scene of the national states in which they live and have begun to use their language and cultural identity as an instrument of emancipation and empowerment. This is particularly visible in relatively small countries with a predominantly indigenous population, such as Bolivia, Ecuador and Guatemala. In several Latin American states new legislation has created a legal and administrative framework more favourable for the future development and continued existence of indigenous groups, including their languages and traditions. The Colombian constitution of 1901 is a good example of that tendency.

Even in countries where the indigenous population is minoritarian it can be advantageous for ethnic groups to be recognised as such. When legally recognised, Brazilian indigenous groups often enjoy territorial rights, although the pressure from local farmers remains problematic. Programmes for bilingual education have gained importance over the last decades. Their initial aim to propagate the national language by use of the vernacular has been replaced by the quest for a more equilibrated situation of 'intercultural' bilingualism, in which the indigenous language remains the first language and both cultures are meant to be on an equal footing. It is needless to say that such programmes do not reach everyone, but their influence can certainly be felt in a change of attitude among both indigenous, and non-indigenous groups.

Notwithstanding these improvements, the negative historical factors and social traumas outlined before cannot easily be eliminated. Internal disagreements about standardisation options, for instance, a unified language against conservation of the dialects, as well as the choice of a suitable orthography, continue to block progress in several countries.

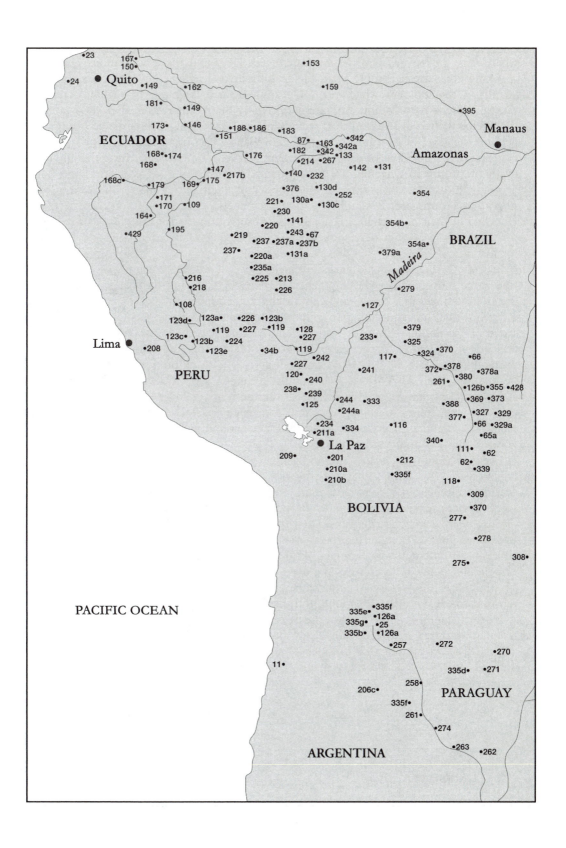

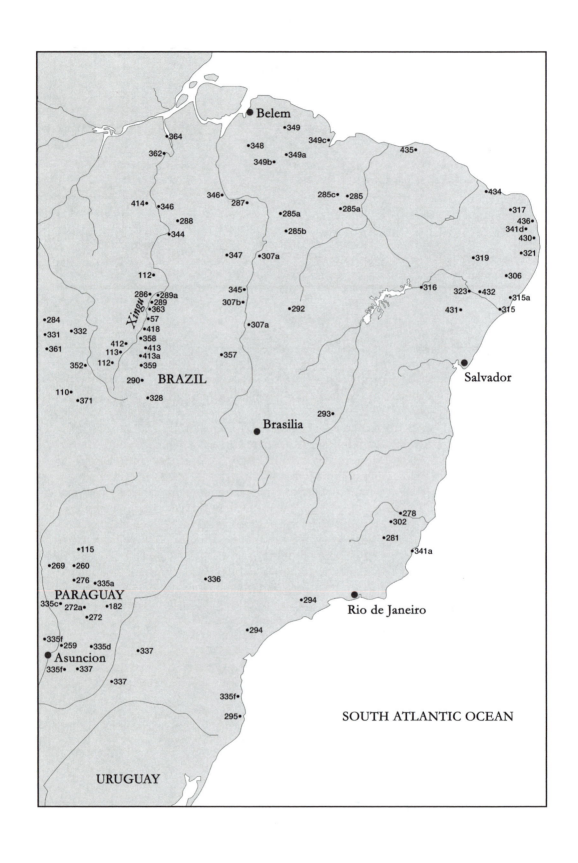

South America

Mily Crevels

Classification is generally taken from Grimes (ed.) (2000) or Dixon & Aikhenvald (eds) (1999). Demographic figures, location of the groups, speaker numbers and other relevant information are generally taken from Censabella (1999), Fabre (1998), the internet, and various other sources, including personal communication with Ana Fernández Garay (**Argentina**); the 1994 *Censo Indígena Rural de las Tierras Bajas*, Albó (1995), Díez Astete and Murillo (1998), Lema (1997), the internet, and various other sources, including personal communications with Antoine Guillaume, Simon van der Kerke, Jeanette Sakel, and Lucrecia Villafañe (**Bolivia**); Instituto Socioambiental (2004a,b,c), Ricardo (ed.) (2000), Fabre (1998), Moore (fc.), Aikhenvald (2002), Dixon & Aikhenvald (eds.) (1999), the internet, and various other sources, including personal communications with Patience Epps, Sérgio Meira, Denny Moore, and especially Hein van der Voort (**Brazil**); Fabre (1998), Sánchez C. (2003), Salas (1996), the internet, and various other sources (**Chile**); Arango Ochoa & Sánchez Gutiérez (1998), González de Pérez & Rodríguez de Montes (eds.) (2000), Gómez-Imbert (2000), Instituto Colombiano de Antropología (2004), Landaburu (2004), Fabre (1998), Dixon & Aikhenvald (eds.) (1999), the internet, and various other sources, including personal communications with Natalia Eraso Keller, Sérgio Meira and Frank Seifart (**Colombia**); Gnerre (2000), Juncosa (2000) and Fabre (1998), the internet, and various other sources, including personal communication with Rafael Fischer (**Ecuador**); Grenand (2000), Queixalós (2000), the internet, and various other sources (**French Guiana**). Forte (2000), the internet, and various other sources (**Guyana**); Melià (1997), Museo Etnográfico Andres Barbero, the internet, and various other sources (**Paraguay**); Pozzi-Escot (ed.) (1998), García Rivera (2000), Solís Fonseca (2000), the internet, and various other sources including personal communication with Astrid Alexander-Bakkerus (**Peru**); Carlin (2001), Boven & Morroy (2000), and personal communication with Eithne Carlin (**Suriname**); the 1992 Indigenous Census, González Ñañez (2000), Mosonyi & Mosonyi (2002), and various other sources, including the internet.

Achagua **[75]** Colombia, Department of Meta, on the right bank of the Meta River, between Puerto López and Puerto Gaitán, community of Umapo. *Arawakan*, Maipuran,

Northern Maipuran, Inland. Once one of the most representative groups of the Meta region, today the Achagua are suffering a strong process of acculturation, which has led them to the brink of extinction. The Achagua language is still very viable and apart from their own language the Achagua generally speak Piapoco as well as Spanish. Nevertheless, the language is to be considered seriously endangered with only about 280 persons in the ethnic group (possibly extinct in Venezuela).

Aché (or *Axé, Aché-Guayaki, Guayakí*) [337] Paraguay, Eastern, Department of Caaguazú, District of San Joaquín, Cerro Morotï reservation; Department of Caazapá, District of Abaí, Ypetimi (Cantina Cue) reservation; Department of Alto Paraná, District of Naranjal¡ San Alfred (Puerto Barra) reservation; Department of Canindeyú, District of Ygatymí, Chupa Pou and Arroyo Bandera reservations. *Tupian*, Tupi-Guarani, Tupi (I). The Aché being physically and culturally distinct from other Tupi-Guarani groups in the region, may point to the fact that they were not a Tupian group originally, but a distinct ethnic group that was assimilated by a Tupi-Guarani group. With about 515 speakers out of an ethnic group of 640 members the language is to be considered endangered.

Achuar-Shiwiar (or *Shiwiar-Maina*) [168] Peru, between the rivers Morona and Tigre, in the northwest of the department of Loreto on the border with Ecuador. *Jivaroan*, Shuar. The language is potentially endangered with an ethnic group of about 2,800–3,000 persons, of whom the majority are monolingual speakers (more in Ecuador). Children acquire the language and there is a bilingual education programme.

Achuar-Shiwiara (or *Achiar Chicham*) [168] Ecuador, between the rivers Macuma and Conambo, delimited in the north by the imaginary line between the communities of Copataza, Montalvo and Conambo, and in the south by the Peruvian border. Jivaroan. There are about 4,000 speakers out of an ethnic group of 5,000. In Ecuador, the language is potentially endangered (more in Peru).

Aguano (or *Uguano, Aguanu, Awano, Santa Crucino*) [109a] Peru, Lower Huallaga and Upper Samiria rivers, the right bank tributary of the Marañon River. *Unclassified* (Arawakan?). In 1959 the ethnic group consisted of forty families in Santa Cruz de Huallaga who did not use the Aguano language. Today the language is probably extinct.

Aguaruna (or *Aguajún, Awajún, Ahuajún*) [168b] Peru, the high jungle in the northern part of the spurs of the Andes, mostly along the Marañon River and its tributaries. *Jivaroan*, Shuar. The Aguaruna have a long history of revenge killings and head shrinking and permanent Catholic missions were only established in the twentieth century. Until 1964 the only access to the Aguaruna territory was by trail from the coast or by river from the city of Iquitos. According to SIL, church, school, community meetings, and daily conversations predominantly take place in Aguaruna. There is a bilingual education programme and native speakers have written many Aguaruna texts. Most children acquire the language and, therefore, the language is potentially endangered with an estimated 39,000 speakers out of an ethnic group of the same size.

Aikanã (or *Aikaná, Masaká, Kasupá, Huarí, Corumbiara, Mondé, Tubarão*) [328] Brazil, southeastern Rondônia, Terra Indígena Tubarão/Latundê, Posto Indígena Rio

Guaporé, Terra Indígena Kwazá do São Pedro, Vilhena, Porto Velho. *Unclassified.* The Kasupá sometimes claim to form a separate ethnic group. The language is one of the first of the region that was recorded, in a brief word list from 1913 in Nordenskiöld (1915). The name *Corumbiara* is very confusing since it is also encountered as referring to the Kanoê and the Mekens. The name *Mondê* may also refer to the Salamãi. With about 150 speakers out of an ethnic group of about 200 the language is to be considered seriously endangered in view of the reduced number of its ethnic group.

Ajurú (or *Wayurú*, *Wayoró*) [371] Brazil, southwestern Rondônia state, three villages in the Posto Indígena Rio Guaporé, Municipality of Guajará-Mirim. *Tupian*, Tupi-Tupari. The Ajurú were first contacted more than a century ago by rubber tappers. Today they live in constant contact with national society. The language is seriously endangered with perhaps ten speakers out of an ethnic group of seventy-seven (2001), living among majority populations of Makurap and Jeoromitxí.

Akawaio (or *Kapón*) [401b] Guyana, lowland and upland forests, the Mazaruni River Basin, north of Patamona. *Cariban*, Northern, East-West Guiana, Macushi-Kapon, Kapon. The ethnic group consists of about 5,000 members (more in Venezuela and Brazil). The language is potentially endangered.

Akawaio (or *Kapón*) [401b] Venezuela, Bolivar State, on the upper course of the Kamarang River, and in Monagas State near to the border of the Amacuro Delta Territory. *Cariban*, Northern, East-West Guiana, Makushi-Kapon, Kapon. Akawaio, Patamona, and Ingarikó belong to the Cariban subbranch Kapón, which at its turn is closely related to Pemón and Makushi. The 1992 Indigenous Census registered approximately 810 Akawaio (more in Guyana and Brazil), which classifies the language as endangered.

Akuntsun (or *Akuntsu*, *Akunt'su*, *Akunsu*) [370] Brazil, southeastern Rondônia, Terra Interditada Igarapé Omeré. *Tupian*, Tupi-Tupari. The Akuntsun group was first contacted in 1995 on the headwaters of the Omeré River, together with a neighbouring group of four Kanoê. The two groups avoid each other. The language is seriously endangered with only seven monolingual speakers.

Akuriyo [385] Suriname, south and southwest area, on the Tapanahoni and Sipaliwini rivers, in the Trio villages Tëpu (Përëru Tëpu), Kwamalasamutu, and in Palumeu. *Cariban*, Northern, East-West Guiana, Wama. The Akuriyo were the last of the indigenous groups in Suriname to leave their nomadic way of life in the forest, and they are now living among the Trio. There are ten elderly speakers out of an ethnic group of fifty. The language is moribund.

Amahuaca (or *Ameuhaque*, *Amaguaco*) [224] Peru, Department of Ucayali, Province of Coronel Portillo, along the Mapuya, Curuija, Sepahua and Inuya rivers. *Panoan*, South-Central. Only children in the most distant communities still acquire the language. Amahuaca is to be considered seriously endangered with about 189 speakers out of an ethnic group of 500–1,000. There is no bilingual education programme.

Amanayé (or *Amanaié*, *Ararandeuara*) **[349]** Brazil, southeastern Pará State, right bank of the Capim River, locality of Barreirinha; Terra Indígena Saraua. *Tupian*, Tupi-Guarani, Oyampi (VIII). Since it is not known how many speakers are left in the ethnic group of approximately 192 (2001) the language is to be considered seriously endangered.

Anambé **[349a]** Brazil, southeastern Pará State, on right bank of the Upper Cairari River, Moju Municipality, Terra Indígena Anambé. *Tupian*, Tupi-Guarani, Oyampi (VIII). In the 1980s only Anambé older than forty years of age still spoke the language, while the 20–30 year old Anambé understood the language but no longer spoke it. SIL reports six active speakers (2000) out of an ethnic group of 132 members (2000). It is very probable that the number of the ethnic group included non-indigenous persons as well. The language is to be considered moribund.

Andoa-Shimigae **[174]** Peru, Department of Loreto, Province of Alto Amazonas, Pastaza District, Santo Tomás de Andoa(s), near to the border with Ecuador, on the Pastaza River. *Zaparoan*. The language is possibly extinct with five speakers reported by SIL in 1975 out of an ethnic group of 150 in the 1950s.

Andoke (or *Andoque*) **[191]** Colombia, Department of Amazonas, on the Aduche River, right tributary of the Caquetá. *Language Isolate*. The Andoke are one of the very few surviving groups of the Amazonian cultural complex located between the Caquetá and Putumayo rivers. At the beginning of the twentieth century, the Andoke group, which counted some 10,000 members, almost disappeared due to the massacres effected by the Iquitos-based rubber company Casa Arana. Although children speak more and more Spanish, ethnic pride and appreciation of tradition is still very strong among the Andoke. With approximately 520 members in the ethnic group, the language is to be considered endangered.

Angaité **[272]** Paraguay, Department of Presidente Hayes, Pozo Colorado, Puerto Pinasco, Menno and Fernheim districts, Department of Concepción, District of Concepción, and Department of Boquerón, District of General Eugenio A. Garay. *Mascoyan*. After the bankruptcy of the tannin factories on the Upper Paraguay River in the past decades, the Angaité were forced to look for other employment, mainly on cattle farms, where it is difficult to maintain their identity and cultural background. The language is to be considered endangered with approximately 1,085 speakers out of an ethnic group of 1,650 persons.

Añún (or *Añuu*, *Paraujano*) **[104]** Venezuela, Zulia State, between Maracaibo and the La Guajira Peninsula; especially near the Laguna de Sinamaica, a few miles to the southwest of Sinamaica in four settlements: El Barco, Caño Morita, La Boquita and Boca del Caño; Santa Rosa de Agua, El Moján, and the islands Toas and San Carlos. *Arawakan*, Maipuran, Northern Maipuran, Caribbean. The language is closely related to Guajiro, but out of an ethnic group of approximately 17,440 members there are only 20–30 speakers left, most of whom speak Spanish and Guajiro as well. The language is seriously endangered.

Aparaí (or *Apalaí*, *Aka Wama*) **[386]** Brazil, northern Pará State, mainly on the upper and middle course of the Paru de Leste River, Parque Indígena do Tumucumaque and

Terra Indígena Rio Paru D'Este. *Cariban*, Northern, East-West Guiana, Wayana-Trio. In Brazil, the Aparaí have been living together in the same villages and intermarrying with the Wayana for at least a century. Because of the high incidence of intermarriage, the Aparaí and Wayana have been registered as a single group of 415 members (1998). Since it is not known how many speakers of Aparaí are among these 415 persons, the language is to be considered seriously endangered (a few more families in French Guiana).

Apiaká (or *Apiacá*) [357] Brazil, northern Mato Grosso State, on the Arinos, Juruena, and Teles Pires rivers, Terra Indígena Apiaká-Kayabí, and in the towns of Juara, Porto dos Gaúchos, Cuiabá, and Belém (Pará). *Tupian*, Tupi-Guarani, Kawahib (VI). In the nineteenth century, the Apiaká formed a group of some 2,700 members, but after two centuries of contact and an intense depopulation process they have lost their traditional way of life and no longer speak their language, having switched to Portuguese. The language is to be considered extinct within the ethnic group of approximately 192 (2001).

Apinajé (or *Apinayé*, *Apinaié*, *Timbira Ocidentais*) [287] Brazil, extreme north of the Tocantins State, at the confluence of the Araguaia and Tocantins rivers, eight villages in the Terra Indígena Apinajé. *Macro-Ge*, Ge, Northern Ge. In the second half of the twentieth century, the Apinajé group suffered an enormous decline in population due to the invasion of their territory by hundreds of migrant families with the construction of the Belém-Brasília and Trans-Amazon highways. Apart from their mother tongue, most Apinayé men speak Portuguese fluently today. The women all understand Portuguese, even if they do not speak it. The language is to be considered endangered with an ethnic group of 1,262 (2003).

Apolista (or *Lapachu*) [125] Bolivia, Department of La Paz, Province of Bautista Saavedra, Charazani area north of Lake Titicaca. *Arawakan*, Maipuran, Southern Maipuran. The language is possibly extinct.

Apurinã (or *Popingaré*, *Kangitê*, *Kaxiriri*, *Cacharary*) [122] Brazil, Amazonas State, Juruá, Jutaí, and Purus rivers region, Terra Indígena Acimã, Terra Indígena Água Preta/Inari, Terra Indígena Alto Sepatini. *Arawakan*, Maipuran, Southern Maipuran, Purus. The Apurinã dialect Kaxiriri should not be confused with Kaxariri, a Panoan language. Apurinã is potentially endangered with an ethnic group of 2,799 (1999).

Arabela (or *Chiripuno*) [174] Peru, Department of Loreto, Province of Maynas, along the Arabela River (tributary of the Curaray River), near the border with Ecuador, in the villages of Buena Vista and Flor de Coco. *Zaparoan*. According to SIL, a bilingual education programme ran from 1963 till 1990, when the teachers decided to stop teaching Arabela. Recently small groups of Ecuadorian Záparo have been going into Peru to contact their relatives, the Arabela. In the 1930s and/or 1940s, the Arabela were held as forced labourers on an Ecuadorian farm along the Curaray River. The Arabela who are nowadays in Peru succeeded in escaping, but a small group stayed on in Ecuador. The language is to be considered seriously endangered with an estimated 55–100 speakers out of an ethnic group of 300.

Araona [240] Bolivia, northwest, Department of La Paz, Province of Iturralde, headwaters of the Manupare River, in the community of Puerto Araona near the Municipality of Ixiamas. *Tacanan*, Araona-Tacana, Araona. The Araona descend from an Araona and a Cavineña family that survived the rubber boom. Evangelisation has banned the traditional religious ideology. At the same time, there exists a strong resistance to adopt western ideology. Increasing knowledge of Spanish, especially among the male members of the Araona group. Although the percentage of monolingual speakers in the Araona group is still higher than in any other indigenous group of Bolivia, the language is to be considered seriously endangered due to the fact that the ethnic group consists of no more than approximately 90 members.

Arapaso (or *Arapaço*) [160a] Brazil, northwestern Amazonas State, Upper Rio Negro region, Vale de Uaupés, Terra Indígena Alto Rio Negro and Terra Indígena Médio Rio Negro II. *Tucanoan*, Eastern Tucanoan, Northern. Arapaso is considered a dialect of Tukano. All Arapaso are bilingual in Tukano and even switching to this language. The younger generations have received schooling in Portuguese. Due to these facts Arapaso is to be considered seriously endangered. There are 328 members in the ethnic group (2001).

Arara do Acre (or *Arara*, *Shawanauá*) [226] Brazil, northwestern Acre State, Municipality of Cruzeiro do Sul, on the Rio Humaitá off the Juará River, Terra Indígena Arara-Igarapé Humaitá and Terra Indígena Jaminawa-Arara do Rio Bagé. *Panoan*, Unclassified. It has been postulated that Arara do Acre may be a dialect of Panoan Katukina or the same language as Sharanahua, which is spoken in Peru. Another view is that Arara do Acre, Shanenawá, Yaminawa, and Yawanawá are all dialects of one language (*Arara*). With an ethnic group of 200 (1999) the language is to be considered seriously endangered.

Arara do Aripuanã (or *Arara do Beiradão*) [428] Brazil, northwestern Mato Grosso State. *Unclassified* (for lack of information). Since the 150 members (1994) of the ethnic group only speak Portuguese, the language is to be considered extinct.

Arara do Pará (or *Arara*, *Ukarãngmã*, *Ukarammã*) [414] Brazil, Pará State, Terra Indígena Arara and Terra Indígena Cachoeira Seca. *Cariban*, Northern, Northern Brazil. With the construction of the Trans-Amazon highway at the beginning of the 1970s the Arara group – which was considered to be extinct since the 1940s – was 'rediscovered'. The road literally split up the Arara territory and caused the subgroups to disperse. After many years and intents to attract these subgroups, two of them were contacted in 1981 and 1983 and finally settled in a village near to the Laranjal creek in the TI Arara. A third, more distant group was contacted in 1987 and lives today in a village near to the Cachoeira Seca creek on the Upper Iriri River in the TI Cachoeira Seca. Since the ethnic group only consists of 195 persons (1998), the language is to be considered seriously endangered (1998).

Arawak (or *Lokono*) [105] French Guiana, immediately behind the coastline in the northeast and in the area of Cayenne, communities of Balaté, Saint-Sabat, Larivot, and Sainte-Rose de Lima. *Arawakan*, Maipuran, Northern Maipuran, Caribbean. In French Guiana the two Arawakan languages, Arawak and Palikur, seem to be the most endangered, since the settlements of the two groups are located nearby urban centres. It is not clear how many speakers are left in the ethnic group of 350–600 (more in Suriname, Guyana, and Venezuela). The language is to be considered seriously endangered.

Araweté (or *Araueté*) **[344]** Brazil, southern Pará State, Terra Indígena Araweté-Igarapé, one village on the banks of the Igarapé Ipixuna River, a right bank tributary of the Middle Xingu River. *Tupian*, Tupi-Guarani, Kayabi-Arawete (V). Kayapó and Parakanã attacks forced the Araweté to move from their original habitat, the Upper Bacajá River, to the Middle Xingu region in the 1960s. While adult Araweté are reported to still be practically monolingual speakers of the language, the Araweté under thirty speak and understand some Portuguese. In 1977, the Brazilian Federal Agency for Indian Affairs (FUNAI) only registered 120 Araweté after more than one third of the population contacted in 1976 had died from attacks by the Parakanã and white man's diseases. Although by 2000 the ethnic group amounted to 278 persons, the language is to be considered seriously endangered.

Arekuna (or *Pemón*) **[400]** Guyana, upland savanna, Upper Mazaruni District, in the border village of Paruima, and in Kaikan. *Cariban*, Northern, East-West Guiana, Macushi-Kapon, Kapon. The vast majority of the Arekuna ($\pm 20,000$) live in the Gran Sabana region of Venezuela. Most of the Arekuna migrated to Guyana at the beginning of last century to form the communities of Paruima and Kaikan in the Upper Mazaruni District. There are about 500 in the ethnic group (more in Venezuela and Brazil). In Guyana, the language is endangered.

Arikapú (or *Aricapú*) **[325]** Brazil, southern and western Rondônia State, Posto Indígena Rio Guaporé, Terra Indígena Rio Branco. Macro-Ge, *Yabutian*. The Arikapú language was first documented (under the name *Mashubi*) in a brief word list by Fawcett from 1913 (in Rivet 1953). Recent research has shown thst Yabutian languages Arikapú and Jeoromitxí are almost certainly Macro-Ge languages. Several speakers of Jeoromitxí and Tuparí assert at least partial Arikapú ethnic identity. The language is moribund with probably no more than two speakers out of an undetermined ethnic group.

Aruá **[379]** Brazil, southern Rondônia State, Terra Indígena Rio Branco, Posto Indígena Rio Guaporé. *Tupian*, Monde. The language is seriously endangered with twelve speakers out of an ethnic group of thirty-six, living among majority populations of Tuparí, Makurap and Jeoromitxí.

Asháninca (or *Asháninka*) **[123b]** Peru, Department of Junín and to the north of the Department of Cuzco, on the rivers Apurímac, Ene, Mantaro, Perené, Tambo, Lower Urubamba, Lower Perené and tributaries. *Arawakan*, Maipuran, Southern Maipuran, Campa. In 1987, the guerrilla movement Sendero Luminoso ('Shining Path') began recruiting Asháninka youths by force. In the following years the guerrilla movement started a campaign of genocide in the Apurímac, Ene, Perene, and Tambo valleys against the Asháninka, who were enslaved and worked to death cultivating coca. At least 2,000 Asháninka were assassinated for trying to escape these concentration camps, or even for falling ill. Another 5,000 Asháninka were held captive, of which in 1992–3 some 3,550 were freed by the Army and by Asháninka self-defence units. There are about 20,000 speakers out of an ethnic group of the same size. There is an intercultural bilingual education programme. The language is potentially endangered.

Asháninka (or ***Kampa***) **[123b]** Brazil, Acre State, border area with Peru, between the Amônia, Arara, and Breu rivers, all three tributaries of the Juruá River, and the Envira, a tributary of the Tarauacá River, Terra Indígena Rio Amônia. *Arawakan*, Maipuran, Southern Maipuran, Campa. In order to preserve their culture and territory, the Asháninka are keen on combining economic activities with a controlled use of natural resources. With an ethnic group of 813 members (1999) the language is to be considered endangered in Brazil (more in Peru).

Ashéninca (or ***Asháninca, Asháninka, Axininca***) **[123a]** Peru, on the rivers Ucayali, Apurucayali, Yurúa and their tributaries. *Arawakan*, Maipuran, Southern Maipuran, Campa. Based on dialect differences the following subgroups are distinguished: Campa del Pichis, Campa del Perené, Campa del Alto Ucayali, Campa del Gran Pajonal, and Campa del Apurucayali. Except for a few areas, all children are generally learning the language. There is a bilingual education programme. There are about 20,000 speakers out of an ethnic group of the same size. The language is potentially endangered in Peru (more in Brazil).

Asurini do Tocantins (or ***Asurini, Asurini do Trocará, Akuáwa, Akwawa***) **[346]** Brazil, Pará State, Municipality of Tucuruí, Terra Indígena Trocará. *Tupian*, Tupi-Guarani, Tenetehara (IV). The original habitat of the Asurini do Tocantins was located on the Xingu River, where they lived with the Parakanã. Conflicts with other indigenous groups caused the Asurini to leave the Xingu region at the beginning of the twentieth century, moving to the east and settling on the headwaters of the Pacajá River and later on the Trocará River banks, where they still live. The language of the Asurini do Tocantins is closely related to both Parakanã and Suruí do Tocantins and lately these three languages have been considered to be dialects of the same language *Akwawa*. Today practically all adult Asurini are fluent in Portuguese, while youngsters and children almost exclusively use Portuguese. With an ethnic group of 303 members the language is to be considered seriously endangered.

Asurini do Xingu (or ***Asurini, Asurinikin, Surini, Awaeté***) **[353]** Brazil, Pará State, right bank of the Xingu River, Terra Indígena Koatinemo, one village. *Tupian*, Tupi-Guarani, Kayabi-Arawete (V). Many Asurini do Xingu were killed in conflicts with the Kayapó and Araweté between 1930 and 1971, the year in which the Asurini do Xingu were first contacted. By 1982 another 50 per cent of the Asurini population had died due to the effects of white man's diseases and the ethnic group had been reduced to fifty-two persons. In 2002, the ethnic group consisted of 106 members. Today all Asurini under forty years of age are bilingual in Portuguese. The language is to be considered seriously endangered.

Atacameño (or ***Kunza, Likanantai, Ulipe, Lipe***) **[11]** Chile, Antofagasta (II Region), in the Salar de Atacama region. *Language Isolate*. The language was spoken until 1900 in several oases of the Atacama desert. There have been reports of its survival until the 1950s in remote locations on the Andean mountain plateaux in the northwestern border area with Argentina and Bolivia. Many traditions, song texts and a certain fragmentary knowledge of the language and its pronunciation subsist until today in prayers and invocations. Today the language is to be considered extinct.

Atikum (or *Aticum*) **[321]** Brazil, Pernambuco State, interior, Area Indígena Atikum, twenty villages. *Language Isolate*. By 1961, there were only two elders left who were still able to provide some lexical items on the language. The ethnic group amounts to 2,743 members (1999), but the language is to be considered extinct today.

Aushiri (or *Tekiraka*) **[146]** Peru, Department of Loreto, Province of Maynas, Puerto Elvira (Lake Vacacocha, Rio Negro). *Language Isolate*. In the 1930s there were about twenty-five Aushiri in the area of Lake Vacacocha and another group of 30–40 in the region of the Tiputini River (Shiripuno River, Ecuador). Today the language is probably extinct, since all speakers have switched to Quechua.

Avá-Canoeiro (or *Canoeiro*, *Carijó*, *Índios Negros*, *Cara Preta*) **[347]** Brazil, Goiás State, Terra Indígena Avá-Canoeiro, municipalities of Minaçu and Colinas do Sul; Tocantins State, in the Terra Indígena Inãwebohona (in the Boto Velho or Inãwebohona village), in the Posto Indígena Canoanã in the interior of the Terra Indígena Parque do Araguaia, located on the banks of the Javaés River on the Bananal Island, and in the municipalities of Formoso do Araguaia, Lagoa da Confusão, Sandolândia and Pium. *Tupian*, Tupi-Guarani, Tenetehara (IV). In addition to the groups of the Tocantins and Araguaia river areas, which were first contacted after the 1970s, two Avá-Canoeiro subgroups remain uncontacted in Goiás and Tocantins, respectively. The language is seriously endangered with an estimated total of forty members in the ethnic group, including the uncontacted subgroups.

Ava-Guaraní (or *Chiripá*, *Ava-Chiripá*, *Chiripá-Guaraní*, *Ava-katu-ete*) **[335d]** Paraguay, Department of Canindeyú, Salto del Guairá, Corpus Christi, Curuguaty, Ygatymí, Ypejhú, and General F. Caballero A. districts, Department of Alto Paraná, Hernandarias, Itakyry, and Minga Porã districts, Department of San Pedro, General Isidro Resquín and Guayaibí districts, Department of Caaguazú, Yhú and Mariscal. F. S. López districts, Department of Concepción, District of Concepción, Department of Amambay, District of Capitán Bado, Department of Boquerón, District of Pedro P. Peña. *Tupian*, Tupi-Guarani, Guarani (I). Many factors have caused the Ava-Guaraní to become the most acculturated group of Paraguay. While they were forced to work under miserable circumstances on maté plantations from the nineteenth century onwards, the deforestation of their traditional habitat forced them to look for alternative ways of subsistence from the 1960s onwards. The construction of the road between Coronel Oviedo and the Paraná River and the hydroelectric power plant ITAIPU on the Brazilian-Paraguayan border, have also led to a substantial change in the Ava-Guaraní habitat. With approximately 2,060 speakers (29.8 per cent) out of an ethnic group of 6,920, the language is to be considered endangered in Paraguay (more in Brazil). According to the 1992 *Censo Nacional de Población y Vivienda*, however, the majority of the ethnic group (67.3 per cent) does speak a variety of Paraguayan Guaraní, one of the two official languages of Paraguay.

Awa Pit (or *Awapit*, *Awá*, *Awa-Cuaiquer*, *Cuaiquer*, *Coaiquer*, *Cuayquer*, *Kwaiker*, *Kwayquer*) **[20]** Colombia, Department of Nariño, area around Barbacoas, from the

111

Upper Telembí River to the Ecuadorian border; Indian reservations of Cuambí-Yaslambi and Cuaiquer del Alto Albí in the Municipality of Ricaurte. Barbacoan, Pasto. The Awa form one of the groups that have suffered and suffer most under the Colombian civil war. The presence of petrol companies, paramilitaries, guerrilla forces, the cultivation of illicit crops and subsequent widespread fumigation of their territory has had extremely disruptive effects on the Awa society that nowadays is coping with a very serious acculturation process. With approximately 12,940 members in the ethnic group the language is potentially endangered in Colombia (more in Ecuador).

Awa Pit (or *Awa-Cuaiquer, Kwaiker, Cuaiquer, Coaiquer*) [20] Ecuador, northwest of Ecuador, on the western slopes of the Andes, near the Colombian border, between the Mira and San Juan rivers in the Province of Carchi; other communities are also located in the Province of Imbabura, Esmeraldas. *Barbacoan*, Pasto. It is estimated that there are about 1,000 Awa Pit speakers out of an ethnic group of about 2,200 Awa-Cuaiquer. In the early 1920s the Ecuadorian Awa-Cuaiquer migrated from Altaquer in Colombia to Ecuador. Traditionally they had little contact with the outside world, although the majority is bilingual in Awa Pit and Spanish, having learned Spanish from their parents and grandparents, who had learned the language in Colombia. Women and pre-school-aged children know less Spanish than adult men. It seems, however, that the Ecuadorian Awa-Cuaiquer very much want to acculturate, both ethnically and linguistically, and that this in combination with other factors may eventually lead to the disappearance of the Awa-Cuaiquer as a viable ethnic and linguistic society. In Ecuador, the language is endangered (more in Colombia).

Aweti (or *Aueti*) [359] Brazil, Mato Grosso State, southern part of the Parque Indígena do Xingu, two villages. *Tupian*, Maweti-Guarani. The Aweti are one of the ten groups that belong to the so-called Upper Xingu culture area. Although these groups speak different languages, they share a good deal of cultural traits. Recent data show that Aweti and Sateré-Mawé probably form a separate subbranch within the Tupian linguistic family. In 1954, after yet another outbreak of measles, the Aweti group was reduced to only twenty-three members. In 2002, the ethnic group consisted of approximately 138 members, of whom only a few, mostly men, speak Portuguese. The language is to be considered seriously endangered.

Aymara (or *Aimara, Aymará*) Bolivia, Chile, and Peru, along the shore of Lake Titicaca (except for its western end), extending to the south, southwest and southeast, including some areas close to the Pacific coast in the departments of Moquegua and Tacna (Peru) and the Tarapacá region (Chile); parts of the departments of Cochabamba, Oruro and Potosí (Bolivia). *Aymaran*. In spite of an estimated 2 to 3 million speakers, Aymara is to be considered potentially endangered due to the lack of intergenerational transmission of the language.

Aymara [209] Chile, north, highland and valleys of I and II regions, among others in the localities of Caquena, Parinacota, Visviri, Putre, and Enquelga; along the coast in Arica and Iquique. *Aymaran*. About half of the ethnic group of 48,500 has some kind of knowledge of the language, but less than a third transmits it to its children. Due to acculturation processes, the Aymara language is especially being lost at a rapid pace in

the coastal areas and the valleys. Intercultural bilingual education is being implemented in some schools in the highland. In Chile, the language is to be considered
endangered (more in Bolivia and Peru).

Ayoreo (or *Ayoreode*) [275] Bolivia, Gran Chaco region, Department of Santa Cruz,
provinces of Ñuflo de Chávez, Chiquitos, Sandóval and Busch, the city of Santa Cruz
de la Sierra. *Zamucoan*. In spite of their sedentary life nowadays, the Ayoreo basically
still are a nomadic group. This renders a biased outcome of the 1994 Indigenous
Census, in which approximately 770 speakers are reported out of an ethnic group of
860 (more in Paraguay). With the loss of their own religion and its partial substitution
by Christian elements the Ayoreo live in an ideological void, which causes serious
problems in their social communication. Although especially women still show great
linguistic fidelity, the language is to be considered endangered.

Ayoreo (or *Moro*, *Pyta Jovai*) [275] Paraguay, Department of Boquerón, Mariscal
Estigarribia (Campo Loro), General Eugenio A. Garay, and Menno districts,
Department of Alto Paraguay, District of La Victoria (Pto. María Auxiliadora).
Zamucoan. Even before their contact with Western society, the Ayoreo were persecuted
relentlessly. In the first half of the twentieth century young men could get their discharge
from military service by killing an Ayoreo. The first contact took place in 1956, when the
whites captured an Ayoreo boy. As far as known, the last uncontacted Ayoreo came out
of the forest in 1998. With approximately 815 speakers out of an ethnic group of the
same size the language is to be considered endangered in Paraguay (more in Bolivia).

Bakairí (or *Bacairí*, *Kurâ*) [412] Brazil, northern Mato Grosso State, southwest to the
Upper Xingu area, Terra Indígena Bakairi, Municipality of Nobres, and Terra Indígena Santana, Municipality of Paranatinga. *Cariban*, Southern, Xingu Basin. In the
past, the Baikirí used to control the access of scientific expeditions into the Upper
Xingu area, where part of them lived. Apart from their mother tongue, all Bakairí
speak Portuguese. Between 1965 and 1999 the Baikarí population grew from 261 to
950. The language is to be considered endangered.

Banawá Yafí (or *Banawá*) [130d] Brazil, Amazonas State, upriver from the Jamamadi,
Terra Indígena Banawa/Rio Piranhas. *Arauan*, Madi. Half of the Banawá population
lives on the Banawa River, others on small creeks and scattered locations. Banawá is
one of the three Madi dialects – the others being Jamamadi and Jarawara. Even though
all members of the ethnic group of approximately 215 (1999) speak the language, and
most of them are monolingual, Banawá Yafí is to be considered seriously endangered.

Baniva (or *Baniva del Guainía*) [92] Colombia, Department of Guainía, along the Aqui
River, in Tâalapu, Patânasri, and Apîya Weêni; in La Sabanita on the Tomo River.
Arawakan, Maipuran, Northern Maipuran, Inland. Although the size of the Baniva
group in Colombia is not exactly known, there are supposedly not many speakers of
the language left. In Colombia, the language is to be considered seriously endangered
(more in Venezuela and Brazil).

Baniva (or *Baníwa*, *Banibo*, *Baniva-Yavitero*, *Baniva del Guainía*) [92] Venezuela, Bolivar
State, Cedeño District, Municipality of La Urbana, on the right bank of the Orinoco,

113

opposite the Apure State; Amazonas State, village of Maroa, along the Guainía River; in the settlements of La Comunidad and Tirikín on the Lower Guainía; along the Atabapo River; Puerto Ayacucho. *Arawakan*, Maipuran, Baniva-Yavitero. *Arawakan*, Maipuran, Northern Maipuran, Inland. Until the 1960s the Baniva lived in their traditional settlements on the Guainía and Atabapo rivers, but today the majority of the group has migrated to Puerto Ayacucho. The language is very similar to Yavitero. The highly acculturated ethnic group consists of about 1,190 persons, of whom about one third speak the language. The language is to be considered endangered (more in Colombia and Brazil).

Baniwa (or ***Baniwa do Içana, Baniva, Baniua, Walimanai, Wakuenai***) (not to be confused with Baniva del Guainía) **[92]** Brazil, northwestern Amazonas State, border area with Colombia and Venezuela, on the Lower and Middle Içana River and its tributaries Cuiari, Aiairi, and Cubate, as well as on the Upper Rio Negro/Guainía, and in the cities of São Gabriel da Cachoeira, Santa Isabel, and Barcelos, on Terra Indígena Alto Rio Negro, Terra Indígena Marabitanas/Cue-Cue, Terra Indígena Médio Rio Negro I, and Terra Indígena Médio Rio Negro II. *Arawakan*, Maipuran, Northern Maipuran, Inland. Since language use is still vigorous among the Baniwa, the language is potentially endangered with 5,141 members (2002) in the ethnic group (more in Colombia and Venezuela).

Bará (or ***Waimajã, Waípinõmakã***) **[158]** Brazil, northwestern Amazonas State, Upper Tiquié River, Terra Indígena Pari Cachoeira, municipalities of Bittencourt and Iauareté, Terra Indígena Pari Cachoeira II, Municipality of Iauareté, Terra Indígena Pari Cachoeira III, Municipality of Bittencourt. *Tucanoan*, Eastern Tucanoan, Central, Bará. All Bará are at least bilingual in another Tucanoan language. In Brazil, the language is to be considered seriously endangered with an ethnic group of thirty-nine (2001) (more in Colombia).

Bará (or ***Waimaja, Waimasa, Waymasa, Waimaha, Barasano del Norte, Northern Barasano***) **[158]** Colombia, Department of Vaupés, on the Upper Colorado, the headwaters of the Papurí, the Tiquié and along the Inambú, Yapú. *Tucanoan*, Eastern Tucanoan, Central, Bara. The Bara form part of the whole of Eastern Tucanoan groups that are known for practising linguistic exogamy and for their general multilingualism. They principally maintain relations with the Barasana, Taiwano, Tatuyo, Tuyuca, and Desano. The ethnic group consists of about 100 members, subdivided into the following clans: Waimaja, Wamutañara, Pamoa, Bará, Wañaco, and Bupua-Bara. Due to the reduced number of the ethnic group, the language is to be considered seriously endangered in Colombia (more in Brazil).

Barasana (or ***Barasano, Pãnerã, Hanera, Panenoá***) **[161a]** Brazil, northwestern Amazonas State, Terra Indígena Alto Rio Negro. *Tucanoan*, Eastern Tucanoan, Central, Southern. The Eastern Tucano groups are in general exogamous with respect to language, which means that strict marriage rules are governed by language affiliation (cf. Sorensen 1967). Children grow up speaking their mother's and their father's language and having at least passive knowledge of the languages of the other women in the village. In Brazil, the Barasana language is seriously endangered with an ethnic group of sixty-one (2001) (more in Colombia).

Barasana (or ***Barasano***, ***Barasano del Sur***, ***Southern Barasano***, ***Pãnerã***) **[161a]** Colombia, Department of Vaupés, near to the Brazilian border, on the Pira-Panará River and its tributaries. Tucanoan, Eastern Tucanoan, Central, Southern. Barasana and Taiwano are sometimes considered two varieties of the same language, which differ mainly in pitch-stress on words (cf. Barnes 1999). The Barasana form part of the whole of Eastern Tucanoan groups that are known for practising linguistic exogamy and for their general multilingualism. Apart from intergroup relations, the Barasana principally maintain relations with the Taiwano, Tatuyo, Bará, Macuna, and Cabiyarí. The language is potentially endangered with about 1,890 members in the ethnic group.

Baré **[89]** Brazil, northwestern Amazonas State, Xié river area, Terra Indígena Alto Rio Negro, Terra Indígena Marabitanas/Cue Cue, Terra Indígena Médio Rio Negro I, Terra Indígena Médio Rio Negro II, Terra Indígena Rio Téa. *Arawakan*, Maipuran, Northern Maipuran, Inland. In the nineteenth and early twentieth centuries Baré was the most widespread language in the Upper Rio Negro region, along the Baria River and the Casiquiare Channel and Orinoco. Since the early twentieth century speakers of the Baré language have been switching to the local lingua franca Nheengatu (Língua Geral). Baré is spoken by just two semi-speakers out of an ethnic group of 2,790 (1998). The language is moribund in Brazil (more in Venezuela).

Baré **[89]** Venezuela, Amazonas State, in San Carlos de Río Negro and Santa Rosa de Amanadona along the Río Negro, in Solano and on the mouth of the Pasimoni River along the Caño Casiquiare. *Arawakan*, Maipuran, Northern Maipuran, Inland. Baré, the most deviant of the Arawakan languages spoken in Amazonas State, is spoken by just a few elders in an ethnic group of approximately 1,220 members. The language is moribund (more in Brazil).

Barí (or ***Motilón***) **[37]** Colombia, Department of Norte de Santander, Serranía de los Motilones, Upper Catatumbo and Oro River region, Reserva Indígena Motilón-Barí and Resguardo Indígena Gabarra-Catalaura. *Chibchan*, Motilon. At the time of the first arrival of the Spaniards the Barí group dominated a vast territory that included the whole eastern and southern part of Lake Maracaibo. They were first called *Motilón* by Fray Pedro Simón in the chronicles on the 1548 Zulia River expedition. In the course of time the Barí have characterised themselves through their continuous resistance against the presence of outsiders. First against the conquistadors, then against the missionaries, and from the beginning of the twentieth century onwards against the petrol companies. With approximately 3,540 members in the ethnic group the language is potentially endangered (more in Venezuela).

Barí (or ***Motilón***) **[37]** Venezuela, Zulia State, southern zone of the Sierra de Perijá, limiting with the Yukpa territory in the north and the Catatumbo River in the south. *Chibchan*, Motilon. Since regular contacts between the Barí and national society only started a little more than thirty years ago, a significant part of the ethnic group of about 1,520 members is still monolingual. The language is potentially endangered (more in Colombia).

Baure **[117]** Bolivia, Department of Beni, provinces of Iténez and Mamoré, between the Iténez and Rio Blanco rivers, municipalities of Baures, Huacaraje and Magdalena, southeast of Magdalena, mainly in the villages of Baures and El Carmen. *Arawakan, Maipuran, Southern Maipuran.* The Baure are one of the tribes that belonged to the Mojo culture area, in which thousands and thousands of artificial hillocks with a height up to 60 feet were built along with hundreds of artificial rectangular ponds up to three feet deep, all part of a system of cultivation and irrigation. When the Spaniards first contacted the Baure at the end of the seventeenth century, they encountered many villages and farms in the area, and even the remains of great hydraulic works, which provided a clear token of the technical and organisational skills of the indigenous people of the region. Today there are about forty speakers of Baure, all of whom are over fifty years old, out of an ethnic group of aprroximately 630. The language is to be considered seriously endangered.

***Betoye* [47a]** Colombia, Department of Arauca, Municipality of Tame, communities of Roqueros, Gananeros, Velazqueros, Julieros, Cajaros, Bayoneros, El Refugio, Matacandelas, and Zamuro. *Chibchan.* The language is extinct, but has left substrate traces in the local Spanish. The ethnic group consists of approximately 750 members.

***Bora* [183]** Colombia, Department of Amazonas, near the mouth of the Cahuinarí River, on the Caquetá and Igará-Panará rivers, La Providencia. *Boran.* Bora and Miraña are the two dialects that form the Boran linguistic family together with the closely related Muinane language. The mean age of the speakers is over thirty. Children no longer acquire the language. Although it is not clear how many speakers are exactly left in the ethnic group of approximately 650 (more in Peru), the language is to be considered seriously endangered.

***Bora* [182]** Peru, northeast, along the Ampiyacu and Yaquasyacu rivers, some along the Marañón near Iquitos and partly along the Putumayo. *Boran.* Together with Miraña and Muinane, Bora forms the Boran linguistic family. The mean age of the youngest speakers is 20–30, and although there are bilingual primary and secondary schools, unfortunately the classes are generally taught in Spanish. Nevertheless, there still is a strong linguistic awareness among the Bora. In Peru, the language is endangered with an estimated 2,000 speakers out of an ethnic group of 3,000 (more in Colombia and possibly Brazil).

***Bororo* [278]** Bolivia, Department of Santa Cruz, part of the Province of Angel Sandoval, near the Bolivian–Brazilian border. *Macro-Ge*, Bororo, Bororo Proper. In 1976, there were still four reported speakers of Bororo, who are descendants of a group of 120 men brought from Brazil by the German farmer Reck when he settled in Bolivia. It is assumed that this group has assimilated with the Chiquitano. In Bolivia, the language is possibly extinct (more in Brazil).

***Bororo* (or *Eastern Bororo, Boe, Boe Wadáru*) [278]** Brazil, Mato Grosso State, Terra Indígena Meruri, Terra Indígena Perigara, Terra Indígena Sangradouro-Volta Grande, Terra Indígena Tadarimana, Terra Indígena Jarudori, and Terra Indígena Teresa Cristina. *Macro-Ge*, Bororo, Bororo Proper. Until the end of the 1970s the use of the Bororo language was prohibited by the Salesian Indigenous Mission school system in the villages of Meruri and Sangradouro. After a re-evaluation of their school system, however, the Salesian missionaries implemented bilingual education, resulting in a revitalisation of the Bororo language. Today the language is spoken by almost all Bororo. The language is to be considered endangered with an ethnic group of approximately 1,024 (1997).

Cabiyarí (or *Kawillari, Kabiyari, Kawiri, Cauyari, Cabuyari*) [78] Colombia, Department of Vaupés, on the banks of the Middle Apaporis River and its tributary Canarí, and along the surrounding lagoons. *Arawakan*, Maipuran, Northern Maipuran, Inland. Like other (Tucanoan) groups in the same area, the Cabiyarí practise linguistic exogamy. They principally maintain relations with the Barasana, Taiwano, and Tatuyo. In the first two cases, they acquire the language of their in-laws; in the last case, it has been observed that one of the Tatuyo clans, the Yukáa, have acquired Cabiyarí. With only about 280 members in the ethnic group the language must be considered seriously endangered.

Cahuarano (or *Cahuarana*) [175] Peru, Department of Loreto, Province of Maynas, headwaters of the Nanay River. *Zaparoan*. Today the language is possibly extinct with only five speakers reported by SIL in 1975.

Callahuaya (or *Kallawaya*) [211a] Bolivia, Department of La Paz, Province of Bautista Saavedra, in the neighbourhood of Charazani and Curva. *Unclassified Mixed Language*. Callawaya is a professional secret language spoken by herb doctors. Most of its lexical roots have their origin in a dialect of the extinct Puquina language, the affixes being Quechua. In the 1960s most of the speakers were already in their sixties and in 2002 the language has been reported possibly extinct.

Campa Caquinte (or *Poyenisati*) [123d] Peru, Department of Junín, on the Poyeni River (tributary of the Tambo River); Department of Cuzco, on the Agueni River (tributary of the Mipaya River that flows into the Urubamba). *Arawakan*, Maipuran, Southern Maipuran, Campa. There are about 250–300 speakers out of an ethnic group of the same size. There is a state bilingual school in the community of Tsoroja. The language is to be considered endangered.

Candoshi-Shapra (or *Candoshi*) [132] Peru, between the west bank of the Morona and Pastaza rivers; a few along the Upper Chambira. *Language Isolate* (last surviving member of the linguistically important *Murato* or *Chirino* family, which extended into Ecuador). Children acquire the language and there is a language maintenance programme, as well as a bilingual education programme. The people take great pride in their culture and language, which is widely used by all generations. The language is endangered with approximately 1,120–3,000 speakers out of an ethnic group of the same size.

Canela (or *Kanela, Canela Ramkokamekrá, Kanela Ramkokamekrá, Kanela Apanyekra, Canela Apanyekra*) [285] Brazil, Maranhão State and southeastern Pará State. *Macro-Ge*, Ge, Northern Ge, Timbira. Canela is spoken by its two subgroups Ramkokamekrá and Apanyekra. The Kenkateye subgroup, which split from the Apanyekra in approximately 1860, was massacred and dispersed in 1913. The Canela and Krahô speak the same language, which is also mutually intelligible with the one spoken by the Krikatí, Gavião Pukobiê and the Gavião Perkatêjê in the Tocantins River area, all of which are Eastern Timbira groups. With 1,337 Canela

Ramkokamekrá (2001) and 458 Canela Apanyekra (2000) the language is to be considered endangered.

Canichana **[147]** Bolivia, Department of Beni, Province of Cercado, 60km to the north of Trinidad in the village of San Pedro Nuevo, and in Trinidad. *Unclassified* (for lack of information). At the time of the first contact with the Spaniards (1693), the Canichana were known as a fierce and belligerent group that continuously attacked the Cayubaba and Itonama. In 1696, the Jesuits established the Mission of San Pedro, which due to its central position soon became the capital of the province. The Mission of San Pedro used to be the most prosperous of all Jesuit missions, but rapidly declined after the expulsion of the Jesuits in 1767. In 2001, three elders of 75–80 years still remembered some words and one or two phrases. The Canichana ethnic group consists of approximately 580 persons. The recent strong feelings of ethnic revival among the Canichana have emerged too late to revive the language as well. The language is on the brink of extinction.

Capanahua (or ***Kapanawa, Capabaquebo, Capacho***) **[219]** Peru, along the rivers Buncuya and Tapiche. *Panoan*, North-Central. Children generally do not acquire the language; about one third of the children have passive knowledge of the language. There are about 50–120 speakers who use the language on a daily basis out of an ethnic group of 350–400. The language is seriously endangered.

Carabayo (***Yuri***) **[163]** Colombia, Department of Amazonas, on the right bank of the Caquetá and on the San Bernardo River. *Unclassified*. Since the ethnic group consists of approximately 200 persons, the language is to be considered seriously endangered.

Carapana (or ***Karapana***) **[159]** Colombia, Department of Vaupés, on the Ti (Upper Papurí), Pirá, and Vaupés rivers. *Tucanoan*, Eastern Tucanoan, Central, Tatuyo. The semi-nomadic Carapana form part of the whole of Eastern Tucanoan groups, which are known for practising linguistic exogamy and for their general multilingualism. They principally maintain relations with the Tatuyo and Bará groups. The language is endangered with about 410 members in the ethnic group (more in Brazil).

Carib (or ***Karinya, Kariña, Kaliña, Kari'na, Kalihna, Galibi***) **[384]** Suriname, various villages along the coast and up to about 30km inland from the coast. *Cariban*, Carib, Northern, Galibi. Carib villages in the west and central part of Suriname are struggling with a progressive loss of language, culture and tradition. Young people only speak the English-based creole language Sranantongo and Dutch. The situation in the east is better. In the village of Galibi, for instance, which is located on the mouth of the Maroni River, the Carib language and culture are still preserved. However, even there the language is spoken less and less by children. In Suriname, there are about 1,200 speakers out of an ethnic group of 3,000 (more in Venezuela, Guyana, French Guiana, and Brazil). The language is endangered.

Carijona **[388]** Colombia, Department of Amazonas, near La Pedrera, Department of Guaviare, on the Upper Vaupés, near Miraflores. *Cariban*, Southern, Southeastern Colombia. The language is moribund with six speakers near La Pedrera and a few more near Miraflores. The ethnic group consists of some 290 members.

Cashibo-Cacataibo (or *Uni*) [216] Peru, in the Department of Huánuco (central jungle) and Coronel Portillo. Along the Aguaytía, Zungaruyacu, Pachitea, San Alejandro, and Chanintía rivers; between the Ucayali River and the Cordillera Azul. *Panoan*, Western. All children acquire the language. There are about 1,150–1,500 speakers out of an ethnic group of the same size. The language is endangered.

Cashinahua (or *Caxinahua*, *Cachinawa*, *Kaxinawa*) [225] Peru, along the rivers Curanja and Purús. *Panoan*, Southeastern. All children acquire Cashinahua and they learn to read and write it at the bilingual schools, but sometimes this is not possible because the teachers who are assigned to the schools are not native speakers of the language. In Peru, the language is to be considered endangered with about 750–1,000 speakers out of an ethnic group of the same size (more in Brazil).

Cauqui [208] Peru, Department of Lima, Province of Yauyos, in the village Cachuy. *Aymaran*. The Cauqui language used to be seen as a dialect of Jaqaru, but nowadays it is more and more considered to be a separate language. With eleven speakers (1998), the language is moribund.

Cavineña [241] Bolivia, north, departments of Beni and Pando, provinces of Ballivián, Vaca Diez and Madre de Dios, southeast of Riberalta, along the Beni River. *Tacanan*. There are approximately 1,180 speakers out of an ethnic group of 1,740. The language is highly conserved in the Cavineña communities and forms a uniting factor for the different communities of the ethnic group. However, the Cavineña are becoming increasingly bilingual in Spanish. In Riberalta, for instance, children no longer acquire the language, which, therefore, is to be considered endangered.

Cayubaba (or *Cayuvava*) [334] Bolivia, Department of Beni, Province of Yacuma, west of the Mamoré River, north of Santa Ana, in the municipality of Exaltación, mainly in the village of Exaltación. *Language Isolate*. Before the Cayubaba were brought together in the Mission of Exaltación in 1704, they used to live on the drained savannas in settlements of about 100 inhabitants divided over twenty houses. Exaltación became a thriving commercial centre during the rubber boom (1870–1910), when most of the rubber transported over the Mamoré River was shipped at its port. Like other groups, the Cayubaba were massively recruited for the rubber exploitation and decimated as a consequence of this. Today the group faces an extremely rapid process of ethnic extinction. With four elderly speakers and a few semi-speakers left out of an ethnic group of about 790 members the language is moribund.

Chácobo [234] Bolivia, northwest, Department of Beni, south of Riberalta, provinces of Yacuma, Vaca Diez, and Ballivián, municipalities of Riberalta, Exaltación, and Reyes, on the rivers Ivón, Nenicito and Yata. *Panoan*, Southern. There are approximately 550 speakers out of an ethnic group of 770. The small Chácobo group seems to have been growing steadily since 1965, when SIL only reported 165 Chácobo. Although language use is still vigorous in remote areas, such as the Alto Ivón community, the language is to be considered endangered.

Chamacoco (or *Yshyrö*, *Ishir*) [276] Paraguay, Department of Alto Paraguay, District of Fuerte Olimpo (Puerto Esperanza, Puerto Diana, and Santa Teresita), Department

119

of Central, District of Luque (Laurelty 1ª Compañía). *Zamucoan*. The Chamacoco group consists of three culturally and linguistically distinct subgroups: the Xorshio, which have disappeared, the Ebitoso on the Upper Paraguay River and the Tomarajo in the interior. The language is endangered with about 910 speakers out of an ethnic group of the same size.

Chamicuro (or *Chamekolo*) [109] Peru, Province of Loreto, Pampa Hermosa, on a tributary of the Huallaga river. *Arawakan*, Maipuran, Western Maipuran (relatively isolated within the Maipuran Arawakan family). The language is moribund with two elderly speakers out of an ethnic group of 10–20.

Chané [126a] Bolivia, Department of Santa Cruz, Province of Cordillera. *Arawakan*, Maipuran, Southern Maipuran. Chané is the Arawakan language formerly spoken by the Izoceño who have shifted completely to Guaraní-Chiriguano. In the 1920s, Erland Nordenskiöld, the first anthropologist to visit the Izoceño, still found many Indians speaking Chané apart from Guaraní-Chiriguano. In 1980, the anthropologist Jürgen Riester only met with three elders who still knew a few words of Chané. In Bolivia, the language is possibly extinct (as it is in Argentina).

Chané [126a] Argentina, Province of Salta, in the missions of Tartagal, Pocitos and Pichanal. *Arawakan*. Chané is the Arawakan language formerly spoken by the Izoceño who have shifted completely to Chiriguano (Tupian). Originally the Chané were descendants of Arawakan groups of peasants, who were pushed out of the Guianas by Cariban groups, and who trekked south in search of better grounds. In spite of the total linguistic assimilation of the Chané language by the Chiriguano language, the Chiriguano variant spoken by the Chané still has a great number of Arawakan loans. In 1995, the indigenous census of the Province of Salta registered 758 persons in the ethnic group (more in Bolivia). The language, however, is extinct in Argentina.

Cha'palaachi (or *Chachi*, *Cayapa*, *Cha'palaa*) [23] Ecuador, north coastal jungle, Province of Esmeraldas, between the Cayapa, Santiago, Onzole and Canandé rivers. *Barbacoan*, Cayapa-Colorado. There are about 7,600 Chachi in the ethnic group, of which elders and pre-school-aged children are mostly monolingual speakers of Cha'palaachi. The Chachi often clash over limited resources with the Afro-Ecuadorians who occupy the same region. According to Chachi tradition, they are originally from the Province of Imbabura in the highlands, but fled towards the coast when faced with the Inka and Spanish conquests. Traditionally their economy was based on hunting, gathering and fishing, but now they engage in agriculture both for household consumption as well as growing coffee and cacao for export. The language is potentially endangered.

Chayahuita (or *Chahui*, *Chayabita*, *Shayabit*) [169] Peru, along the Paranapura River and its tributaries Cahuapanas, Sillay, Supayacu and Shanusi. *Cahuapanan*. Most children acquire the language, but those that live near to Yurimaguas and along the Marañón River are stimulated by their parents to speak Spanish only. Bilingual education has been implemented in some communities, and there are about 30–40 persons who know how to read in Chayahuita. The language is potentially endangered with approximately 7,870–12,000 speakers out of an ethnic group of the same size.

Chimane (or ***Tsimane'***) **[244a]** Bolivia, Department of Beni, Province of Ballivián, municipalities of San Borja and Rurrenabaque, on the Maniqui River, Yucumo-Rurrenabaque,
Bosque de Chimanes, Parque Nacional Isiboro-Sécure. *Mosetenan*. Tsimane' forms
together with Mosetén the small linguistic family Mosetenan, and although they are
mutually intelligible, there are some dialects with quite some lexical and grammatical
differences. The language is very viable, and especially women and elders speak very
little Spanish. Children do not acquire Spanish until they are fifteen, unless they
attend a school in one of the so-called *colla* (highland Indian) communities. There are
approximately 5,320 speakers out of an ethnic group of 5,910. The Tsimane' have a
complex religious system with their own vision of the cosmos, complete with a rich
mythology and the shaman as a central figure. The language is to be considered
potentially endangered.

Chimila (or ***Ette Taara***) **[36]** Colombia, Department of Magdalena, Sierra Nevada de
Santa Marta region, lowlands near Valledupar. *Chibchan*, Aruak. At the arrival of the
Spaniards, the Chimila group, which is said to have consisted of some 10,000 members,
occupied vast territories from the Río Frío and the northwestern foothills of the Sierra
Nevada de Santa Marta to Mompox and the Ciénaga de Zapatosa; from the east bank of
the Magdalena River to the Ariguaní and Cesar river basins. Today the Chimila group is
limited to a marginal territory on the San Ángel savannas in the Department of Magdalena. In the past the Chimila language has erroneously been classified as Arawakan
(Reichel-Dolmatoff 1946). Although the language is still used vigorously in the ethnic
group of around 900 members, Chimila is to be considered endangered.

Chipaya **[210b]** Bolivia, east, Department of Oruro, Province of Atahuallpa (cantons
of Santa Ana de Chipaya and Ayparavi). *Uru-Chipayan*. The Chipaya have a profound
religious world in which complex rituals are maintained. In spite of the numerous loans
from Aymara the language is maintained at a notable level. There are about 1,200
speakers out of an ethnic group of 1,800. The language is potentially endangered.

Chiquitano **[277]** Bolivia, Department of Santa Cruz, provinces of Ñuflo de Chávez
(cantons of Concepción and Santa Rosa del Palmar), Velasco (cantons of San Ignacio,
Santa Rosa de Roca and San Miguel), Chiquitos, Angel Sandoval and Germán Busch.
Macro-Ge. Recent research has shown that it is almost certain that the Chiquitano language (previously classified as an isolate) is a Macro-Ge language. There are about 5,880
speakers out of an ethnic group of 47,080. Speakers are massively switching to Spanish: for
each eight elders there is only one youngster who still speaks Chiquitano. Therefore, the
language is to be considered endangered.

Chiquitano (or ***Chiquito, Língua, Linguará, Anenho***) **[277]** Brazil, Mato Grosso State,
border area with Bolivia, municipalities of Vila Bela, Cáceres, and Porto Espiridião.
Macro-Ge. The Chiquitano that live in Brazil maintain close relations with their relatives in Bolivia. In Brazil, the ethnic group consists of approximately 2,000 members
(2000), but since it is not known how many of these still speak Chiquitano, the language is to be considered endangered (more in Bolivia).

Chiriguano (or ***Ava, Guaraní-Chiriguano, Eastern Bolivian Guarani***) **[335c]** Argentina,
provinces of Salta and Jujuy. *Tupian*, Tupi-Guaraní, Guarani (I). Proceeding from the

121

Lower Amazon region and having crossed the whole Gran Chaco from east to west, the Chiriguano settled in the fifteenth century in regions near to the Andes, belonging today to Argentina and Bolvia. Having resisted the advance of the Incas in the sixteenth century, the belligerent Chiriguano were feared by the Spaniards with whom they exchanged Chané slaves for firearms. Having assimilated the languages of various ethnic groups, Chiriguano consists today, according to Dietrich (1986), of four dialects: Chriguano, Chané, Izoceño and Tapieté. The ethnic group consists of about 21,000 persons, but it is not clear how many of these are speakers. In Argentina, the language is potentially endangered (more in Bolivia and Paraguay).

Cholón (or *Seeptsá*) [195] Peru, Department of San Martín, Province of Mariscal Cáceres, valley of the Huallaga River, near the villages of Sion, Valle, and Juanjui. *Hibito-Cholonan.* Cholón is related to Hibito, which was spoken in the same area and became extinct in the nineteenth century. The Cholón language is possibly extinct, with two speakers reported by SIL in 1986.

Chorote [257] Argentina, Province of Salta, departments of Rivadavia and San Martín. *Mataco-Mataguayan.* The Chorote, who are nomadic hunter-gatherers and fishermen, used to occupy much bigger parts of the Central and Southern Chaco, but they were probably pushed to the northwest by Guaicuruan groups that at their turn were displaced by the Spaniards. There are two varieties of Chorote: Yofuáha, spoken near to the Pilcomayo River, and Yowúwa, spoken in the interior of Paraguay. The Chorote language is used vigorously amongst its speakers. However, it is not known how many speakers there are in the ethnic group of about 2,000 persons. The language is to be considered endangered (more in Paraguay).

Chorote (or *Iyo'wujwa*) [257] Bolivia, southeast, Department of Tarija. *Mataco-Mataguayan.* SIL only mentions a few families in Bolivia in 1982. In Bolivia, the language is possibly extinct (more in Argentina and Paraguay).

Chulupí-Ashlushlay (or *Nivaglé*, *Nivaklé*, *Guisnai*) [258] Bolivia, Department of Tarija, Province of Gran Chaco, north of the Pilcomayo River, on the Bolivian–Paraguayan border. *Mataco-Mataguayan.* In 1976, there were 100 Chulupí reported in Bolivia. Nowadays the language is possibly extinct in Bolivia (more in Argentina and Paraguay).

Cinta Larga [378] Brazil, eastern Rondônia, Terra Indígena Roosevelt, Parque Indígena Aripuanã; western Mato Grosso, Terra Indígena Aripuanã. *Tupian*, Tupi-Monde. First contacts in the early 1970s were devastating because of introduced epidemic diseases and logging by Westerners. At the present, diamond fever in the Roosevelt Basin has got completely out of hand and destroyed the ecology of a vast area and the lives of many Westerners and Indians and their families. With 645 speakers out of an ethnic group of the same size the language is to be considered endangered.

Cocama (*Cocama-Cocamilla*, *Kokama*) [342] Colombia, on the Island of Ronda in the Amazon River opposite the city of Leticia, in Leticia, and in the villages of Naranjales, Palmeras and San José. *Tupian*, Tupi-Guarani, Tupi (III) (unclassified mixed language according to some linguists). With possibly only a few semi-speakers left in the ethnic group of approximately 770 members the language is moribund in Colombia (more in Peru and Brazil).

Cocama-Cocamilla (or ***Xibitoana***, ***Huallaga***, ***Pampadeque***) **[342a]** Peru, along the Huallaga, Lower Marañón, Lower Ucayali, Amazonas, and Lower Nanay rivers. *Tupian*, Tupi-Guarani (unclassified mixed language according to some scholars). The members of the Cocama-Cocamilla group have practically all switched to *castellano sharapa*, the variant of Spanish that is spoken in the jungle. The youngest speakers are all over forty years old, and, in Peru, the language is seriously endangered with about 250 speakers out of an ethnic group of 15,000 (more in Brazil and Colombia).

Cofán (***Kofán***) **[167]** Colombia, southeast Colombia, Department of Putumayo, on the border with Ecuador, along the rivers Guamués, Aguarico, and Churuyaco. *Language Isolate*. The Cofán are one of the groups hardest hit by the Colombian civil war. The widespread fumigation of their territory – part of Plan Colombia, a primarily military offensive funded partially by the US that aims to undermine the stability of guerrilla forces in Colombia's civil war, and the clashes between the leftist insurgent Revolutionary Armed Forces of Colombia (FARC) and the right-wing paramilitaries of the United Self-Defence Forces of Colombia (AUC) caused an exodus of the Cofán to Ecuador (Province of Sucumbíos). In Colombia, the language is endangered with an ethnic group of around 1,450 (more in Ecuador).

Cofán (or ***A'ingae***) **[167]** Ecuador, Province of Sucumbíos, along the Aguarico River in the settlements of Sinangué, Doriño, and Dureno and along the Bermejo River in the Ecuadorian Amazon; part of the territory is included in the Cayambe Coca Reservation. *Language Isolate*. Although the language is still viable – there are about 800 A'ingae speakers out of an ethnic group of 800 Cofán – an accelerated loss of the language is taking place, on the one hand because of mixed marriages, and on the other hand because of the complete loss of the Cofán cultural identity. The Cofán remained relatively isolated from Western society until the 1950s when SIL missionaries began efforts to evangelise them. Since then, outside forces have disrupted their culture as well as that of the Siona and Secoya. They occupy a region where intensive petroleum exploitation has taken place, especially in the 1970s with the Texaco-Gulf consortium. Roads, pipelines, and penetrating colonists have had devastating effects on their territory. Nowadays the ongoing guerrilla war in Colombia is chasing the Colombian Cofán into Ecuador. In Ecuador, the language is endangered (more in Colombia).

Cubeo **[153]** Colombia, southeast, Department of Vaupés, northwestern Vaupés River area, on the Vaupés, Cuduyarí and Querarí rivers. *Tucanoan*, Central Tucanoan. Although the Cubeo have been in contact with the outside world since the sixteenth century (explorers, rubber hunters, etc.), the Cubeo language and culture have remained largely intact. With an ethnic group of approximately 6,035 the language is potentially endangered in Colombia (more in Brazil).

Cuiba (or ***Cuiva***, ***Kuiva***) **[69]** Colombia, between the Meta, Casanare, and Capanaparo rivers, western part of the Department of Arauca: Resguardo Los Iguanitos, Municipality of Tame, Lower Cusay, to the north of the city of Tame; northwestern part of the Department of Casanare: Resguardo Caño Mochuelo-Hato Corozal, municipalities of

Hato Corozal and Paz de Ariporo, between – to the north – the city of Tame (Department of Arauca) and – to the south – Paz de Ariporo; north-northwestern part of Vichada: Resguardo Santa Teresita del Tuparro, Municipality of Cumaribo, to the northwest of the centre of the Municipality of Cumaribo, between the rivers Tomo and Vichada, about 200km to the west of the Orinoco River; Resguardo La Pascua, municipalities of Puerto Carreño and Guacacías. *Guahiban*. Territorial criteria have led to the distinction of various, formerly nomadic, subgroups of Cuiba, like, for instance, Amorúa, Masiwar (or Masiguare, Maibén), Siripu, Chiricoa, and Casibara-Iguanito. The language is potentially endangered with an ethnic group of about 2,275, which is mainly located in the Department of Casanare (more in Venezuela).

Cuiba (or *Cuiva*, *Kuiva*) [69] Venezuela, Apure State, along the Upper Capanaparo River and its tributary Riecito. *Guahiban*. The Cuiba hunter-gatherers live in semi-nomadic bands and most of them are still monolingual. There are approximately 650 speakers out of an ethnic group of the same size (more in Colombia). Nevertheless, the language is to be considered endangered in Venezuela due to the reduced number of its ethnic group.

Culina (or *Kulino*, *Kurina*, *Madija*) [128] Peru, along the Upper Purús River. *Arauan*. The community has very little contact with speakers of Spanish. Brazilian merchants often visit them. About 10 per cent speak some Spanish. There are two bilingual schools with three teachers. All children acquire the language, which, nevertheless, is to be considered endangered due to the reduced size of the ethnic group of 400 members (more in Brazil).

Culle (or *Culli*) [429] Peru, highland zone of the Department of La Libertad, between the Marañón River in the east and the Chicama River Basin in the north; in the southwest up to the Santa River, and in the southeast along the Marañón up to Huacaibamba opposite to Piscobamba, and in the departments of Ancash (Province of Pallasca) and Cajamarca (Province of Cajabamba). *Unclassified* (for lack of information). The last known groups of Culle speakers were located in 1915 in the Province of Pallasca in the extreme north of the Department of Ancash, in the village of Aija near Cabana, and in the 1950s in Tauca (Province of Pallasca). Today the language is probably extinct.

Cuna (or *Kuna*, *Tule*) [41] Colombia, along the east and west banks of the Gulf of Urubá, Darién region, Department of Antioquia: Caiman Nuevo, Neoclí; Department of Chocó: Arquía. *Chibchan*. In spite of long-standing cultural contact with the non-indigenous society, the Cuna have maintained their language, social organisation, and religious beliefs. Due to bad sanitary services, the Colombian Cuna have been decimated by tuberculosis, malaria, and parasites. In Colombia, the Cuna language is endangered with an ethnic group of approximately 1,170 members (more in Panama).

Curripako (or *Curripaco-Baniva*, *Kurripako*, *Baniva del Isana*) [86a] Colombia, on the Guainía, Isana and Inirida rivers. *Arawakan*, Maipuran, Northern Maipuran, island. The ethnic group amounts to around 7,060 persons, a number that probably includes at least some members of the Baniva group. In Colombia, the language is potentially endangered (more in Venezuela and Brazil).

Damana (or ***Sanka***, ***Malayo***, ***Arsario***, ***Wiwa***) **[33]** Colombia, Department of Cesar, to the northeast of Valledupar, bordering the departments of Guajira and Magdalena, on the northeastern slope of the Sierra Nevada de Santa Marta, between the Guatapuri, Barcino, Guamaca, Cesar and Badillo rivers. *Chibchan*, Aruak. Like other Sierra groups, the Damana avoided contact with national society in the past by retreating to less accessible zones. Dispersed over twenty-six communities, there are around 1,850 speakers out of an ethnic group of the same size. The language is potentially endangered.

Dâw (or ***Kamã***) **[135b]** Brazil, Amazonas State, Upper Rio Negro/Vaupés region, Terra Indígena Médio Rio Negro I, one community across the river from São Gabriel da Cachoeira, a county seat just below the confluence of the Vaupés and Negro rivers. *Makuan*. Dâw shares a great part of its lexicon with Kuyabi. The language is seriously endangered with approximately eighty-five speakers out of an ethnic group of the same size.

Deni **[129]** Brazil, Amazonas State, between the Purus and Juruá rivers, to the northeast of the Cunhua, Upper Cunhua and Xiruã rivers, Terra Indígena Camadeni and Terra Indígena Deni. *Arauan*, Deni-Kulina, Deni. In 2001, after they had become aware of the fact that their land had been sold to the Malaysian logging giant WTK, the Deni decided to take control of their traditional lands in a move to have their territory recognised by the Brazilian federal government. With the help of Greenpeace they marked their most vulnerable borders, cutting thirty-three miles of trail through thick jungle and 135 miles along the banks of rivers and creeks. In October 2001, their land was finally recognised. Although most Deni speak some Portuguese, their native language is still well conserved. With an ethnic group of 736 (2002) the Deni language is to be considered endangered.

Desano (or ***Desana***, ***Dessano***, ***Wira***, ***Umúkomasá***) **[157]** Brazil, northwestern Amazonas State, Terra Indígena Alto Rio Negro Rio Negro, region along the border with Colombia, sixty communities and sites along the margins of the Tiquié River and its tributaries. *Tucanoan*, Eastern Tucanoan, Central, Desano. Like other Eastern Tucanoan groups the Desano practise linguistic exogamy and, therefore, also speak Tukano as well as another Tucanoan language spoken by their mothers. In Brazil, the language is to be considered potentially endangered with an ethnic group of 1,531 (2001) (more in Colombia).

Desano **[157]** Colombia, Department of Vaupés, near to the Vaupés, Papurí, Abiyú, Macú-Panará, and Viña rivers. *Tucanoan*, Eastern Tucanoan, Central, Desano. The Desano are known for their excellent handicraft, especially reed baskets and clay pots. Belonging to the whole of Eastern Tucanoan groups that are known for practising linguistic exogamy, the Desano also speak Tucano as well as another Tucanoan language spoken by their mothers. Although many Desano are bilingual in Spanish, they use the Desano language almost exclusively in their own villages. Desano shares about 90 per cent of its lexicon with Siriano. With approximately 2,140 persons in the ethnic group the language is to be considered potentially endangered (more in Brazil).

Emberá (or ***Epenã***, ***Epérã Pedée*** (***Ember-Tadó***), ***Chamí***, ***Catío*** (***Katío***), ***Sambú***) **[8x]** Colombia, Department of Antioquia: mainly on the banks of the Murrí and its tributaries; Department of Córdoba: on the banks of the San Jorge y Sinú; Department of Chocó:

125

on almost all the big rivers, especially in the river basins of the Atrato and the Baudó, along the Middle and Upper San Juan, and in the Tadó area; Department of Risaralda: on the Camí River (Chami); Department of Cauca: on the Saija and its small tributaries; Department of Caldas: along the network of rivers in the Dabeiba region (tributaries of the San Juan River); Department of Nariño: on the Morondó and Satinga rivers. *Chocoan.* Emberá forms a dialect continuum with different names according to the area in which the respective dialects are spoken: **Cholos** on the Pacific Coast, **Chamí** in Risaralda, **Catío** in Antioquia and **Epérã** in Nariño and Cauca. 50 per cent of the Colombian Emberá live in the Department of Chocó. The language is potentially endangered, with approximately 71,410 members in the ethnic group (more in Ecuador).

Emérillon (or *Teko*) **[350c]** French Guiana, southern border area, along the Upper Maroni and Oyapock rivers. *Tupian,* Tupi-Guarani, Oyampi (VIII). The Emérillon form the only ethnic group in French Guiana that is not represented in one of the neighbouring countries as well. Halfway through the twentieth century, they were on the brink of extinction, but nowadays the Emérillon seem to be recovering at the demographic and linguistic levels. There are about 400 in the ethnic group. The language is endangered.

Enawê-Nawê (or *Salumã*) **[126b]** Brazil, northwestern Mato Grosso State, Terra Indígena Enawê-Nawê, one big village near the Iquê River, a tributary of the Juruena River. *Arawakan,* Maipuran, Central Maipuran. First contacted officially by the Anchieta Mission in 1974, the Enawê-Nawê kept on living relatively isolated from national society. Interference from outside was consciously limited to health services and the protection of their territory. Through this approach the Anchieta Mission not only managed to keep epidemics away from the Enawê-Nawê, but also enabled them to maintain their traditional way of life. Today most Enawê-Nawê are still monolingual. With an ethnic group of 320 members (2000) the language is to be considered endangered.

Enlhet (or *Enslet, Enxet, Enthlit, Enlhet-Lengua, Lengua*) **[271]** Paraguay, Department of Presidente Hayes, Pozo Colorado (Paz del Chaco, Nueva Vida), Benjamín Aceval, Puerto Pinasco, Menno, and Fernheim districts, and Department of Boquerón, Mariscal Estigarribia, Menno (Pesempoo), Fernheim, and Neuland districts. *Mascoyan.* Although the Enlhet were once self-sufficient hunter-gatherers, most of them now live as exploited labourers on vast cattle ranches and in Mennonite colonies. Enlhet or Lengua is one of the five members of the Mascoyan family, which is entirely spoken on the Paraguayan Chaco. The other languages belonging to the Mascoyan family are Angaité, Guaná, Sanapaná, and Toba-Maskoy. The language is potentially endangered with an ethnic group of approximately 9,500 members, of which 98.6 per cent speak the language according to the 1992 census.

Êpera (or *Êpera Pedede, Êpena Pedee, Embera, Embera del Sur, Embera Chami*) **[8]** Ecuador, northwest. *Chocoan.* Êpera forms part of the Embera dialect continuum that is mainly spoken in Colombia. In 1964, a group of Êpera from the Colombian Chocó region immigrated to the Ecuadorian Chocó region. Today, with only 60–150 members in the ethnic group, the language is to be considered seriously endangered in Ecuador (more in Colombia).

Ese Ejja (or ***Chama***, ***Huarayo***) **[242]** Bolivia, departments of La Paz, Beni and Pando, provinces of Iturralde, Ballivián, Vaca Diez and Madre de Dios, on the Beni and Madre de Dios rivers. *Tacanan*, Tiatinagua. The Bolivian Ese Ejja are divided into two clans: the Equijati near to Riberalta and the Hepahuatahe in the Rurenabaque region. There are about 500 speakers out of an ethnic group of 580. Although the language is maintained at a high level, it is to be considered endangered in Bolivia because of the relatively small Ese Ejja ethnic group (more in Peru).

Ese Ejja (or ***Huarayo***, ***Guarayo***, ***Chama***, ***Tambopata Guarayo***, ***Guacanahua***, ***Echoja***, ***Chuncho***) **[242]** Peru, along the rivers Madre de Dios and Tambopata and their headwaters in three settlements: Sonene, Palma Real and Infierno. *Tacanan*, Tiatinagua. All the children acquire the language as long as their mother is Ese Ejja. Due to its small size, the language is seriously endangered in Peru, with 225 speakers out of an ethnic group of the same size (more in Bolivia).

Galibi (or ***Galibi do Oiapoque***, ***Kaliña***) **[384]** Brazil, Amapá State, on the right bank of the Oiapoque River, to the south of the city of Saint Georges, between the Morcego and Taparabu streams, Terra Indígena Galibi, in the village of São José dos Galibi. *Cariban*, Northern, Galibi. In 1950, the Galibi of the Oiapoque migrated from villages on the Mana River in French Guiana to their current location. The language is still spoken by the elders, who also know French, since they were educated in this language. Many Galibi also speak Patuá, the Creole language used as a lingua franca in the region. Many Galibi live outside the village of São José in the cities of Amapá, Belém and Brasília. In Brazil, Galibi is seriously endangered with twenty-eight members in the ethnic group in São José (more in Venezuela, French Guiana and Suriname).

Galibi (or ***Kali'na***, ***Kaliña***) **[384]** French Guiana, northwestern part of the coast, along the Maroni River, along the Lower Mana to the east of the mouth of the Maroni, in the area of Iracoubo and Organabo between Kourou and Mana. *Cariban*, Northern, Galibi. With the exception of the situation in Iracoubo, the Galibi, who like the Arawak group live close to urban centres, do not seem to be losing their language. There are about 2,000 in the ethnic group (more in Venezuela, Guyana, Suriname, and Brazil). The language is potentially endangered.

Gavião (or ***Digüt***) **[378a]** Brazil, eastern Rondônia State, Terra Indígena Igarapé Lourdes. *Tupian*, Monde. Like the traditional cultures of many indigenous nations everywhere in Rondônia, the culture of the Gavião has been much under attack by Western missionaries. At the present ecologically sustainable economic projects, such as copaiba oil extraction, are being developed. With 360 speakers out of an ethnic group of the same size, the language is to be considered endangered.

Gavião Perkatêjê (or ***Gavião***, ***Parkatejê***, ***Gavião do Pará***, ***Gavião do Mãe Maria***) **[285a]** Brazil, southeastern Pará State, Municipality of Bom Jesus do Tocantins, Terra Indígena Mãe Maria, village of Kaikoturé. *Macro-Ge*, Ge, Northern Ge, Timbira. In the first half of the twentieth century the Gavião Perkatêjê were subdivided in three groups according to their location in the Tocantins River Basin: the ***Parkatêjê*** 'down-river people', the ***Kyikatêjê*** 'up-river people', and the ***Akrãtikatêjê*** 'mountain people' who occupied the headwaters of the Capim River. Although the descendants of these three subgroups live together in the same village today, they are still recognised as such. Portuguese has been gaining ground at an accelerated pace since the 1980s, but the Gavião Perkatêjê language is still used in ceremonies, songs, and speeches. The language is to be considered seriously endangered with an ethnic group of 338 (1998).

Gavião Pukobiê (or ***Pykopjê***, ***Gavião do Maranhão***) **[285b]** Brazil, Maranhão State, Municipality of Amarante do Maranhão, Terra Indígena Gobernador. *Macro-Ge*, Ge, Northern Ge, Timbira. With an ethnic group of just 250 members (1998) the language is to be considered seriously endangered.

Guahibo (or ***Sikuani***, ***Sikwani***, ***Vichadeño***, ***Amorúa***, ***Tigrero***) **[68]** Colombia, Department of Vichada, between the Meta and Guaviare rivers and to the north of the Meta, Casanare and Arauca rivers. *Guahiban*. Vichadeño, Amorúa, and Tigrero are considered dialects of Guahibo. The Guahibo vary from good Guahibo-Spanish bilinguals to about 40 per cent completely monolingual (Grimes 2000). With about 20,550 members in the ethnic group the language is potentially endangered (more in Venezuela).

Guahibo (or ***Hiwi***, ***Jiwi***, ***Sikuani***) **[68]** Venezuela, in the south of Apure State, northwest of Amazonas State, and around San Juan de Manapiare; basically the territory includes the banks of the rivers Vichada, Tuparro, Tomo, Meta, part of the Capanaparo and Arauca, and part of the middle course of the Orinoco on the Colombian border. *Guahiban*. In 1992, the ethnic group consisted of about 11,600 members, most of whom were monolingual speakers of Guahibo (more in Colombia). The language is potentially endangered.

Guajá (or ***Awá***, ***Avá***) **[349b]** Brazil, Maranhão State, Terra Indígena Alto Turiaçu and Terra Indígena Caru, four settlements. *Tupian*, Tupi-Guarani, Oyampi (VIII). The Guajá are one of the last hunter-gatherer groups in Brazil. In addition to those Guajá that were contacted and settled by the FUNAI in the 1970s and 1980s there still are a few uncontacted Guajá groups, which amount to approximately thirty persons. Currently there are about 234 Guajá living in four settlements in the reserves. The language is to be considered endangered.

Guajajara (or ***Tenetehára***, ***Ze'egete***) **[348]** Brazil, central Maranhão State, regions of the Pindaré, Grajaú, Mearim, and Zutiua rivers, in eleven Terras Indígenas at the eastern margin of the Amazon Basin, especially Terra Indígena Araribóia, Terra Indígena Bacurizinho, and Terra Indígena Cana Brava. *Tupian*, Tupi-Guarani, Tenetehara (IV). The Guajajara are one of the most numerous indigenous groups of Brazil. Since the end of the seventeenth century they have had very variable contacts with the Western world, ranging from submissions to revolts against the Westerners and culminating in their 1901 revolt against the Capuchin Mission. The Guajajara language, which is closely related to Tembé, is still the dominant language in the villages. However, Portuguese is understood by most of the ethnic group and as such used as a lingua franca. The language is potentially endangered with an ethnic group of 13,100 (2000).

Guajiro (or ***Goajiro***, ***Wayuunaiki***, ***Wayuu***) **[68a]** Colombia, Department of La Guajira, all over the peninsula, especially in the municipalities of Uribia, Manaure, and Maicao, but also in Riohacha, Barrancas, Fonseca, San Juan del Cesar, Villanueva,

Urumita, and El Molino. *Arawakan*, Maipuran, Northern Maipuran, Caribbean. Guajiro is one of the most vigorously spoken indigenous languages in Latin America today. The ethnic group consists of some 144,000 members, 20.5 per cent of the total indigenous population of Colombia. Quite a few Guajiro, especially the younger generations, understand and speak Spanish fluently. Nevertheless, their mother tongue still forms an important factor of ethnic and cultural identity for them. The language is to be considered potentially endangered (more in Venezuela).

Guajiro (or *Goajiro*, *Wayuu*, *Wayuunaiki*) **[103]** Venezuela, Zulia State, La Guajira Peninsula, to the northwest and west of Lake Maracaibo; to the north of the cities Sinamaica and Maracaibo, towards the Colombian border; a little to the north of Guana, and in Maracaibo. *Arawakan*, Maipuran, Northern Maipuran, Caribbean. Guajiro is taught at university level, and it is one of the most vital indigenous languages spoken in Latin America today. The ethnic group consists of approximately 168,730 members, all of whom speak the language (more in Colombia). Although most Guajiro are bilingual in Spanish, they still successfully pass the language on to their children. The language is to be considered potentially endangered.

Guambiano (or *Coconuco*, *Guanaca*, *Totoró*) **[19]** Colombia, Department of Cauca, on the western slopes of the Andean Cordillera Central, in the municipalities of Silvia, Jambaló, Totoró, Caldono and Toribío, and on the banks of the Piendamó River. *Barbacoan*, Coconucan. It is not clear how many speakers there are in the ethnic group of about 20,780 – 3 per cent of the total indigenous population of Colombia. The speakers are mostly bilingual in Spanish. While Guambiano is to be considered endangered, the closely related Totoró language is no longer spoken in its ethnic group consisting of about 3,550 members.

Guaná (or *Kashika*) **[269]** Paraguay, Department of Concepción, District of San Lázaro, in Valle Mi on the banks of the Apa River, Department of Alto Paraguay, on the Riacho Mosquito. *Mascoyan*. Among other things, work in the tannin factories on the Upper Paraguay River has caused the Guaná to become one of the most acculturated groups in the Chaco today. Their language is seriously endangered with approximately twenty-eight (33.3 per cent) speakers out of an ethnic group of eighty-four. According to the 1992 census, however, the majority of the Guaná group (66.7 per cent), does claim to speak a variety of Paraguayan Guaraní.

Guajiro (or *Goajiro*, *Wayuu*, *Wayuunaiki*) Venezuela, Zulia State, La Guajira Peninsula, to the northwest and west of Lake Maracaibo; to the north of the cities Sinamaica and Maracaibo, towards the Colombian border; a little to the north of Guana, and in Maracaibo. *Arawakan*, Maipuran, Northern Maipuran, Caribbean. Guajiro is taught at university level, and it is one of the most vital indigenous languages spoken in Latin America today. The ethnic group consists of approximately 168,730 members, all of whom speak the language (more in Colombia). Although most Guajiro are bilingual in Spanish, they still successfully pass the language on to their children. The language is to be considered potentially endangered.

Guaraní Chiriguano (or *Guaraní boliviano* (Eastern Bolivian Guaraní), *Ava*, *Izoceño*, *Guaraní Chirigauno*, *Mbya*) **[335f]** Bolivia, departments of Santa Cruz, Tarija and

129

Chuquisaca, provinces of Cordillera, Luis Calvo, Hernando Siles, O'Connor and Grand Chaco. *Tupian*, Tupi-Guarani, Guarani (I). There are approximately 33,670 speakers out of an ethnic group of 36,920. Bilingual education is being implemented on a large scale. The language is potentially endangered (more in Argentina and Paraguay).

Guaraní Correntino (or ***Guaraní Goyano***) **[335b]** Argentina, provinces of Corrientes, Chaco, Misiones, Formosa, and in Buenos Aires, Rosario, and Córdoba. *Tupian*, Tupi-Guarani, Guarani (I). This variety of Guaraní, which is closely related to Paraguayan Guaraní, is spoken by non-indigenous *criollo* speakers in a colloquial setting, which impedes an exact estimate of its number of speakers (100,000–1,000,000). Its idiolect Guaraní Goyano has a very high percentage of Spanish loans. The language is potentially endangered.

Guaraní-Ñandeva (or ***Ñandeva, Tapieté***) **[335d]** Paraguay, Department of Boquerón, District of Mariscal Estigarribia (Laguna Negra), District of General Eugenio A. Garay (Pykasú), and District of Fernheim (Filadelfia and Lichtefelde). *Tupian*, Tupi-Guarani, Guarani (I). The Guaraní-Ñandeva or Tapieté fought in the Chaco War (1932–5) against Bolivia and after the war the army assisted the group to settle in the Nueva Asunción region, thus creating a border population that could defend the border with Bolivia. But once the official assistance was over, the Guaraní-Ñandeva scattered and migrated to the labour zones of the Mennonite market. With about 110 speakers out of an ethnic group of 1,825 the language is seriously endangered in Paraguay (more in Argentina and Bolivia). According to the 1992 census, the vast majority of the Guaraní-Ñandeva population (86.5 per cent) does speak a variety of Paraguayan Guaraní.

Guarayo (or ***Guarayu***) **[338]** Bolivia, Department of Santa Cruz, provinces of Guarayos and Ñuflo de Chávez, Ascensión and San Pablo (cantons of Ascensión), Yotaú (Canton of El Puente), Urubichá, Yaguarú and Salvatierra (Canton of Urubichá). *Tupian*, Tupi-Guarani, Guarayu-Siriono-Jora (II). According to Métraux (1942: 95), the Guarayo and the Pauserna belonged to the same ethnic group. This group was split up at the end of the nineteenth century, when the Guarayo decided to settle down in the missions. The 1994 Indigenous Census has shown a stable situation and even a slight increase in the number of younger speakers of Guarayo. There are approximately 5,930 speakers out of an ethnic group of 7,230 (more in Paraguay). The language is to be considered potentially endangered.

Guarayo (or ***Guaraní Occidental***) **[335f]** Paraguay, Department of Boquerón, District of Mariscal Estigarribia, in Machareti and District of Pedro P. Peña; Department of Concepción. *Tupian*, Tupi-Guarani, Guarani (I). With about thirty speakers out of an ethnic group of 1,255 the language is to be considered seriously endangered in Paraguay (more in Bolivia). According to the 1992 census, the vast majority of the Guarayo group (79.9 per cent) does speak a variety of Paraguayan Guaraní.

Guató **[309]** Brazil, extreme northwestern Mato Grosso do Sul State, on the border between Bolivia and Mato Grosso and Mato Grosso do Sul states, north of Corumbá and southwest of Pto. Jofre, Municipality of Corumbá, Terra Indígena Guató. *Macro-Ge*,

Guato. The language is moribund with only about five speakers out of an ethnic group of 372 members (1999).

Guayabero (or ***Mitua***, ***Jiw***) **[70]** Colombia, east, Department of Guaviare, on the upper course of the Guaviare, to the east of San José del Guaviare in Barrancón, Barranco Salado, Barranco Colorado or Barrranco Alto or Bellavista, Barranco Ceiba, Laguna Araguato, Laguna Barajas, Macuare and La Fuga. *Guahiban*. Guayabero is not mutually intelligible with the other Guahiban languages. With an ethnic group of approximately 1,060 members the language is to be considered endangered.

Gününa Yajich (or ***Gününa Küne***, ***Pampa***) **[245a]** Argentina, Province of Chubut, central zone, Gan Gan, Aguada del Guanaco, Sacanana, La Jarilla, Laguna Fría, Yalalaubat, Lefi Niyeo, Pirrén Mahuida, and Marrauf. *Chonan*. Gününa Yajich was the language of the Gününa Küne or Gennaken, the northernmost group of the Tehuelche (Chonan) complex in Patagonia. The language has also been classified as an isolate, because it is quite deviant from other Chonan languages. It became extinct in the 1960s or 1970s. Today its ethnic group, called Pampa, has 200 members who have assimilated with the Mapuche.

Harakmbut (or ***Harakmbut Hate***, ***Harakmbut Ate***, ***Amarakaeri***) **[54b]** Peru, departments of Madre de Dios and Cuzco, headwaters of the Madre de Dios (E'ori or 'Oriwe) to the Piñi Piñi River on the left bank, the entire right bank of the Upper and Lower Madre de Dios to the Inambari (Arasa) River, headwaters of the Inambari, mouth of the Los Amigos (Ami'ko) River, mouth of the Manu River (Hakwe 'de las casas'). *Harakmbut-Katukinan*. Based on dialect differences the following subgroups are distinguished: Amarakaeri, Toyoeri, Wachipairi, Arasaeri, Pukirieri, Kisamberi, and Sapiteri. Most children acquire the language, which is to be considered endangered with about 1,620 speakers out of an ethnic group of the same size.

Hoti (or ***Jodi***, ***Yuwana***) **[427]** Venezuela, jungle area on the borderline between Amazonas and Bolivar states, to the north and northwest of San Juan de Manapiare, between the Kaima, Cuchivero, Parucito, and Asita rivers. *Language Isolate*. Although already mentioned by Koch-Grünberg (1913), the Hoti were not contacted by Westerners until 1961. In the past genetic relationships have been postulated with Yanomaman, Cariban, and Saliba-Piaroan, but these hypotheses have never been supported by factual data. Lately there have also been indications that the Hoti language may be related to Makuan (cf. Henley *et al.* 1996). With about 640 speakers out of an ethnic group of the same size, the language is to be considered endangered.

Huambisa (or ***Huambiza***) **[168c]** Peru, north, in the high jungle on the spurs of the Andes, along the Santiago and Morona rivers. *Jivaroan*, Shuar. According to SIL, church and community meetings usually take place in Huambisa, and some texts and a bilingual vocabulary are available for bilingual education. Most children acquire the language, which is potentially endangered with about 8,000 speakers out of an ethnic group of the same size.

Huaorani (or ***Waorani***, ***Wao***, ***Waotededo***, ***Wao Tiriro***, ***Auca***, ***Sabela***) **[181]** Ecuador, eastern jungle, between the Napo River in the north, the Curaray and Cononaco rivers in the south, the Peruvian border in the east, and the headwaters of the Curaray and Nushiño in the west. *Language Isolate.* Among the indigenous groups of Ecuador the Huaorani (sometimes called Auca, which is Quichua for 'savages') remain the most isolated from Western civilisation. Since the earliest recorded contact with European society in the 1600s, violence and bloodshed have characterised their relationships with the outside world. Although there are about 1,200 speakers out of an ethnic group of 1,200, the language is to be considered endangered due to the emerging Huaorani-Quichua bilingualism brought about by mixed marriages and bilingual education programmes taught by Quichua teachers who do not speak Huaorani.

Huilliche **[249a]** Chile, X Region (south of the Mapuche), from Valdivia to Chiloé, mountain valleys, San Juan de la Costa area in the Province of Osorno. *Araucanian.* Huilliche is related to Mapuche, but barely intelligible with it. Most members of the ethnic group speak Spanish as a first language. Huilliche is used mainly among friends and for ceremonial purposes. Nowadays the language is to be considered seriously endangered with several thousand speakers, mainly over sixty years old, reported in 1982 by SIL.

Huitoto (or *Witoto*) **[188]** Peru, northeast, along the Napo, Ampiyacu, and Putumayo rivers. *Witotoan.* Huitoto has three dialects: Murui (Bue), Mïnïca, and Munánï (Nïpode). There is a bilingual programme in two or three schools on the Ampiyacu River. The Huitoto who live in Peru today descend from a group of Huitoto that had been forced to move from Colombia to Peru during the rubber boom at the beginning of the twentieth century. During that period they worked for the rubber company Casa Arana and, therefore, not only became one of the most hated groups, but also one of the most decimated indigenous groups in the Amazon due to the atrocities committed by the same Casa Arana. Children do acquire Huitoto, but many of them do not use the language. In Peru, the language is to be considered endangered with approximately 1,130 speakers out of an ethnic group of 3,000 (for both Peru and Colombia).

Hup (or *Hupdá*, *Hupdé*, *Hupdá Makú*, *Jupdá Macú*, *Makú-Hupdá*, *Macú De*) **[134]** Brazil, northwestern Amazonas State, Vaupés/Upper Rio Negro region, on the Tiquié and Vaupés rivers, Terra Indígena Alto Rio Negro. *Makuan.* The Maku linguistic family is also known as Maku-Puinave, but its relationship with Puinave is unclear. An alternate family name – suggested because Maku is considered a very offensive ethnic slur by speakers – is Guaviaré-Japurá or Nadahup (Patience Epps p.c.). Hup has at least three main dialectal areas, of which one is distinct enough that speakers claim to have some difficulty in understanding each other. Hup shares a large percentage of its lexicon with Yuhup. Although they are sometimes considered the same language for this reason, they are best considered different languages. In Brazil, the language is endangered with about 1,000 speakers out of an ethnic group of the same size (more in Colombia).

Hup (or *Hupda*, *Hupdë*, *Macú of Tucano*) **[134]** Colombia, Department of Amazonas, Colombian–Brazilan border area, where the Taraira flows into the Apaporis. *Makuan.* Hup and Yuhup are sometimes considered the same language. While they do share a large percentage of their lexicon, they are best considered different languages on the basis of phonological and grammatical differences, and speakers' claims that they cannot understand each other. With 235 speakers in an ethnic group of the same size the Hup language is seriously endangered in Colombia (more in Brazil).

Hyxkaryana (or *Hixkariana, Hyskariana, Hiskariana*) [393] Brazil, Amazonas State, from the Upper Nhamundá River to the Mapuera and Jatapú rivers, Municipality of Faro, Terra Indígena Nhamundá-Mapuera, in the multi-ethnic village of Cassauá, close to the Wai Wai. *Cariban*, Southern, Southern Guiana. Most Hyxkaryana speak their native language. Population estimates range from 804 (1991) to 1,116 (1987). The language is to be considered endangered.

Ika (or *Arhuaco, Bíntukua*) [35] Colombia, northeast, southern slopes of the Sierra Nevada de Santa Marta. *Chibchan*, Aruak. Kogi, Damana, and Chimila are the languages most closely related to Ika. Although Ika is usually classified as Chibchan, a family coordinate with Chibchan, called Aruakan, has been posited consisiting of Ika and its three sister languages (cf. Shafer 1962). The language is potentially endangered with an ethnic group of approximately 14,300.

Ikpeng (or *Txikão*) [418] Brazil, Mato Grosso, Parque Indígena do Xingu, left bank of the Upper Xingu in the Uaví River mouth area, to the north of the Kaiabi settlements. *Cariban*, Northern, Northern Brazil. Originating from the Iriri River, the Ikpeng arrived via the Tapajós River in the Xingu Park in 1967, where they are now settled in their own village since the 1970s. The language is to be considered endangered with an ethnic group of 319 (2002).

Inga (or *Ingano*) [205c] Colombia, Department of Putumayo, Sibundoy, Yunguillo, and Condagua valleys; Department of Nariño, Aponte; on the Upper Caquetá and Putumayo rivers. *Quechuan*, Quechua IIB. One of the most characteristic aspects of the Inga group is that it is dispersed over various regions in Colombia, having adopted commerce as a survival strategy. The language is to be considered endangered with an ethnic group consisting of about 17,855 persons.

Ingarikó (or *Ingaricó, Akawaio, Akwaio, Arawaio, Kapóng, Kapón*) [401] Brazil, northern Roraima State, Terra Indígena Raposa/Serra do Sol, near the Cotingo River, Serra do Sol. *Cariban*, Northern, East-West Guiana, Macushi-Kapon, Kapon. Ingarikó, Patamona, and Akawaio (Guyana, Venezuela) belong to the Cariban subbranch Kapón, which in its turn is closely related to Pemón and Makushi. Portuguese is becoming dominant among the younger generation. In Brazil, the language is to be considered endangered with an ethnic group of 675 members (1997) (more in Venezuela and Guyana).

Iñapari [120] Peru, Department of Madre de Dios, on the Piedras River, near to Puerto Maldonado. *Arawakan*, Maipuran, Southern Maipuran, Purus. The language is moribund with four speakers over forty-five years of age reported by SIL in 1998.

Iquito (or *Amacacore, Quiturran, Puca-Uma*) [175] Peru, Department of Loreto, Province of Maynas, on the Nanay River, to the northwest of Iquitos, in San Antonio de Pintoyacu, Atalaya, and Saboya. *Zaparoan*. In the 1990s all the monolingual speakers and many bilingual speakers of Iquito died of malaria. Today there are 22–6 elderly speakers out of an ethnic group of about 230, which makes the language seriously endangered.

Iranxe (or *Irantxe*, *Manoki*, *Menky*, *Myky*, *Munku*) [332] Brazil, western Mato Grosso, Brasnorte Municipality, Terra Indígena Manoki in the Cravari River area and Terra Indígena Umutina on the banks of the Papagaio River; Diamantino Municipality, Terra Indígena Menku. *Language Isolate*. In the past century the Iranxe were practically decimated as a result of massacres and diseases from their contacts with Westerners. The fate of the Myky, an Iranxe subgroup that was not contacted until 1971, was practically the same as that of the Iranxe. The area surrounding the Iranxe territory is being affected by landholding speculation and, therefore, both groups are making claims to increase their territory. Including seventy-eight Myky, the Iranxe ethnic group consists of 326 members (2000). The language is to be considered endangered.

Itonama (or *Sihnipadara*) [26] Bolivia, Department of Beni, Province of Iténez, in Magdalena and Huacaraje; Province of Mamoré, in San Ramón. *Language Isolate*. The last speakers – less than five including semi-speakers and rememberers – are all well into their eighties and reside in Magdalena. The number of the ethnic group must be considerably lower than the 5,090 registered by the 1994 Indigenous Census, since group membership rather than ethnicity seems to have played a crucial role in this census. Thus, anyone born in Magdalena – or anywhere else in the Province of Iténez for that matter – is considered to be, or considers himself to be Itonama, including whites, mestizos and criollos. The language is moribund.

Jamamadi (or *Yamamadi*, *Kanamanti*) [130a] Brazil, Acre and Amazonas states, Middle Purus region; on the Curiá and Saburrun (Sabuhã) streams, tributaries of the Piranhas River and on the Mamoriazinho, Capana, Santana, and Teruini streams, tributaries of the Purus, in five homologated indigenous areas. *Arauan*, Madi. Jamamadi is one of the three Madi dialects – the others being **Jarawara** and **Banawá Yafí**. Most Jamamadi are monolingual. With an ethnic group of 800 (2000) the language is to be considered endangered.

Jaqaru (or *Cauqui*) [208] Peru, Department of Lima, Province of Yauyos, in the villages Tupe, Aiza, and Colca. *Aymaran*. There are about 725 speakers, all of whom are over 20–25 years of age. The language is to be considered endangered.

Jarawara (or *Jarauara*) [130c] Brazil, Amazonas State, Middle Purus region, Terra Indígena Jarawara/Jamamadi/Kanamanti. *Arauan*, Madi. Jarawara is one of the three Madi dialects – the others being Jamamadi and Banawa Yafi. Most Jarawara are monolingual speakers of their language and only a few speak Portuguese. Nevertheless, the language is to be considered seriously endangered with only 160 members in the ethnic group (2000).

Javaé (or *Karajá*) [307b] Brazil, Tocantins State, on the banks of the Javaés River on the eastern shore of the Ilha do Bananal and in its interior, Terra Indígena Parque Araguaia. *Macro-Ge*, Karaja. With Karajá and Xambioá, Javaé forms the Karaja subbranch within the Macro-Ge linguistic family. With an ethnic group of 919 members (2000) the language is to be considered endangered.

Jebero (or *Xebero*, *Shihuilu*) [170] Peru, northeast, Department of Loreto, Province of Alto Amazonas, in the District of Jeberos, between the Marañon and Huallaga rivers.

Cahuapanan. Children acquire the language, if their parents are bilingual in Jebero and Spanish, but usually they shift to Spanish because of the absence of a bilingual educational programme. In the 1970s the ethnic group of 3,000 members was reported to be dissolving due to a progressive *mestization* process. Recent data show that competent speakers are all at least over thirty years of age. The language is to be considered endangered.

Jeoromitxí (or ***Djeoromitxí***, ***Jabutí***, ***Quipiu***) **[324]** Brazil, southern and western Rondônia State, Posto Indígena Rio Guaporé, Terra Indígena Rio Branco. *Macro-Ge Yabutian*. Recent research has shown that the Yabutian languages Arikapú and Jeoromitxí are almost certainly Macro-Ge languages. The language is seriously endangered with around forty speakers out of an ethnic group of approximately sixty-five. Several speakers of Jeoromitxí assert at least partial Arikapú ethnic identity.

Jiahui (or ***Jahói***, ***Djahui***, ***Diahoi***, ***Diarroi***) **[354a]** Brazil, Middle Madeira River, southern Amazonas State, Municipality of Humaitá, Terra Indígena Diahui, in the village of Ju'i. *Tupian*, Tupi-Guarani, Kawahib (VI). The Jiahui form part of a bigger group of peoples that call themselves ***Kagwahiva***. In the 1970s the Jiahui were driven out of their traditional territory and subsequently almost disappeared because of conflicts with neighbouring groups, ranchers who occupied their land and illegal timber extractors. The few remaining Jiahui went to live with the Tenharim or in nearby cities. Today they have reclaimed their traditional land, where they built the village Ju'i. Including the Jiahui that are living with the Tenharim and those that are in Humaitá and Porto Velho, the ethnic group amounts to some fifty members (2000). The language is to be considered seriously endangered.

Jorá **[340a]** Bolivia, Department of Beni, Province of Iténez, in the area of the Jorá Lagoon, east of the San Joaquín River and the Bolsón de Oro Lagoon. *Tupian*, Tupi-Guarani, Guarayu-Siriono-Jora (II). In 1951, a small group of fourteen Jorá still survived at the Bolsón de Oro Lagoon, to the east of Magdalena and the San Joaquín River. They stayed near an abandoned Jorá village of which the major part of the inhabitants had been exterminated a year and a half before during one of the punitive expeditions undertaken by whites, criollos and mestizos in order to 'reduce' and 'domesticate' one of the last Bolivian tribes that had the audacity to defend its hunting grounds and crops. In 1955, only five Jorá were left, and today the ethnic group, and therefore the language, is possibly extinct.

Juma (or ***Yuma***) **[354b]** Brazil, Amazonas State, upper courses of the Ipixuna, Mucuim, Tabocal, and Jacaré rivers (tributaries of the Purus), on the Igarapé Tapiu (right tributary of the Içuã), Municipality of Canutama between the cities of Humaita and Lábrea, Terra Indígena Juma. *Tupian*, Tupi-Guarani, Kawahib (VI). The Juma form part of a bigger group of peoples that call themselves ***Kagwahiva***. The Juma subgroup probably amounted to some 12,000–15,000 individuals in the eighteenth century. After successive massacres and the explosive expansion of extracting industries, however, their population had been reduced to a few dozen people by the 1960s. In 2002, the ethnic group consisted of five persons belonging to one family, all of whom are married to Uru-Eu-Wau-Wau. Presently they live with the Uru-Eu-Wau-Wau in the Upper Jamary village. Although the remaining Juma are monolingual, it is highly probable that their language will become moribund.

135

Juruna (or *Juruûna*, *Geruna*, *Yuruhuna*, *Yuruna*, *Yudjá*, *Yudya*) **[363x]** Brazil, Lower and Middle Xingu region, Mato Grosso State, Parque Indígena do Xingu; Pará State, Altamira, Terra Indígena Paquiçamba. *Tupian*, Yuruna. The Juruna are a canoe people that inhabit the islands and peninsulas of the Lower and Middle Xingu River. In the past they were one of the most important groups of the Xingu, but, just as in the case of many other groups, they were decimated as the rubber tappers advanced into their territory. In the Xingu Park most adult men speak Portuguese, while approximately half of the women understand it. Elders are less fluent in Portuguese, but with the introduction of bilingual education the younger generations all speak Portuguese. In 1989, there was only one speaker of Juruna left in the Terra Indígena Paquiçamba. The language is seriously endangered with an ethnic group of approximately 278 (2001), of whom about thirty-five live in the TI Paquiçamba.

Kaapor (or *Ka'apor*, *Urubu-Kaapor*, *Kaapor*, *Kaaporté*) **[349c]** Brazil, northern Maranhão State, roughly between the Rio Gurupi in the north, the southern tributaries of the Rio Turiaçu in the south, the Igarapé do Milho in the west, and the BR-316 highway in the east, Terra Indígena Alto Turiaçu. *Tupian*, Tupi-Guarani, Oyampi (VIII). All Kaapor still use their native language as a first language, even though about 40 per cent of the ethnic group speaks Portuguese. The Kaapor also use a standard sign language to communicate with the deaf, who until approximately 1985 made up 2 per cent of the population. The language is endangered, with an ethnic group consisting of 800 members (1998).

Kadiweu (or *Kadiweo*, *Caduveo*, *Cadiuéu*, *Ejiwajigi*, *Mbaya-Guaycuru*) **[260]** Brazil, western Mato Grosso do Sul, near to the border with Paraguay, between the Paraguai and Nabileque rivers in the west, the Serra da Bodoquena in the east, the Neutaka River in the north, and the Aquidavão River in the south, Municipality of Porto Murtinho, in the villages of Bodoquena, Campina, Tomázia, and São João. *Guaycuruan*. Although a good number of Kadiweu speak Portuguese fluently, most members of the ethnic group still use Kadiweu as a first language. Some elders, women, and especially children are still monolingual. The language is endangered, with 1,592 members (1992) in the ethnic group.

Kaiabi (or *Kayabi*, *Caiabi*) **[352]** Brazil, Mato Grosso and Para states, Terra Indígena Apiaká-Kayabi, Terra Indígena Kayabi, and Parque Indígena do Xingu *Tupian*, Tupi-Guarani, Kayabi-Arawete (V). In the Xingu Park almost all Kaiabi are bilingual in Portuguese. Many Kaiabi living outside the park no longer speak their native language. In 1999, the ethnic group amounted to 1,000 members, which classifies the Kaiabi language as endangered.

Kaingang (or *Caingangue*, *Kanhgág*) **[294]** Brazil, São Paulo, Paraná, Santa Catarina, and Rio Grande do Sul states, in thirty-two Indigenous Lands, representing only a small part of their traditional territory. *Macro-Ge*, Ge, Southern Ge. The Kaingang language consists of the following dialects: Kaingang do Paraná, Kaingang Central, Kaingang do Sudoeste, and Kaingang do Sudeste. Language use varies quite a bit in the different Indigenous Lands. Apart from communities where all members speak Kaingang as a first language, there are communities in which everybody speaks Portuguese as a first language, or communities in which the majority of the population is bilingual in Portuguese. However, the past years have shown a growing interest in maintaining and/or revitalising the Kaingang language. With 25,875 members in the ethnic group (2003), the language is potentially endangered.

Kaiowa (or ***Kaiova, Paï-Tavyterã***) **[335a]** Brazil, southern Mato Grosso do Sul State, from the Apa, Dourados, and Ivinhema rivers in the north to the Mbarakaju mountains and the tributaries of the Jejui River (Paraguay) in the south. *Tupian*, Tupi-Guarani, Guarani (I). Language use is still vigorous among the Kaiowa. In Brazil, the language is potentially endangered with an ethnic group of some 18,000–20,000 members (more in Paraguay).

Kakua (or ***Cakua, Bará-Makú, Makú of Cubeo, Makú of Guanano, Makú of Desano***) **[157]** Colombia, near the Brazilian border in the Department of Vaupés, along the tributaries of the Vaupés, Papurí and Querarí rivers. *Makuan*. The Kakua are one of the seven traditionally nomadic hunter-gatherer groups belonging to the Makuan family. These Makuan groups have a low socio-economic status among other (Eastern Tucanoan, Arawakan) groups in the region who practise slash-and-burn agriculture. They are generally endogamous and are excluded from the marriage network in the Vaupés region. Kakua and Nukak share about 90 per cent of their lexicon and supposedly are mutually intelligible. With just about 150 speakers out of an ethnic group of the same size, the language is to be considered seriously endangered.

Kalapalo (or ***Calapalo***) **[413]** Brazil, Mato Grosso, Upper Xingu area, Upper Kuluene River area, Parque Indígena do Xingu, 75km to the southeast of Posto Leonardo Villas Boas. *Cariban*, Southern, Upper Xingu, Kalapalo. The Kalapalo are one of the four Cariban groups currently living in the Xingu Indigenous Park, the others being the Matipú, Kuikuro and Nahukwá. Although they speak dialects of the same language (Upper-Xingu Carib or Kalapalo), each of these groups sees itself as distinct from the others. Most Kalapalo still speak their native language, which is endangered with an ethnic group of 417 (2002).

Kamaiurá (or ***Camaiurá***) **[430]** Brazil, Mato Grosso, Parque Indígena do Xingu, one village about 9km to the north of Posto Leonardo Villas-Bôas, near to the south bank of Lake Ipavu, 6km from the Kuluene River. *Tupian*, Tupi-Guarani, Kamayura (VII). The Kamaiurá language is still used vigorously. In 2002, the ethnic group consisted of 355 members, which classifies the language as endangered.

Kambiwá (or ***Cambiuá***) **[430]** Brazil, Pernambuco State, Inajá Municipality, Terra Indígena Kambiwá. *Unclassified* (for lack of information). In 1961, there were only two elders left who still remembered a few Kambiwá words and phrases. By that time the whole ethnic group had already switched to Portuguese. Today the ethnic group consists of some 1,578 members (1999), but the language is to be considered extinct.

Kamsá (or ***Camsá, Camëntsa***) **[51]** Colombia, Department of Putumayo, Valle de Sibundoy, south of Sibundoy and Colón, and in Moncoa. *Language Isolate*. Since the Kamsá share the Valle de Sibundoy with the Inga, many of them speak Inga apart from Kamsá and Spanish. Moreover, they also seem to share features at the cultural and socio-political level. The Kamsá are actively trying to preserve their language and culture by organising workshops, publishing texts on cultural topics, and by performing

137

autochthonous drama and music. The language is potentially endangered with approximately 4,020 members in the ethnic group.

Kanamarí (or **Canamarí**, **Tüküná**, **Tâkâna**) **[141]** Brazil, southwestern Amazonas State, Solimões River are, Maraã Municipality, Terra Indígena Kanamari do Rio Juruá, Terra Indígena Mawetek, Terra Indígena Vale do Javari. *Harakmbut-Katukinan.* The Kanamarí were one of the few tribes that used permanent facial tattoos and were noticed for their ability as *curandeiros*, 'healers'. Other tribes in the area have been known to reject the Kanamarí because they are rapidly acculturating. The Kanamarí language, however, is still used vigorously by the members of the ethnic group, which totalled 1,327 persons in 1999. The language is to be considered endangered.

Kanoê (or **Canoé**, **Kapixaná**) **[370]** Brazil, western and southeastern Rondônia, Terra Interditada Igarapé Omeré, Posto Indígena Rio Guaporé, Área Indígena Sagarana, Guajará-Mirim. *Unclassified.* The first documents on Kanoê are from 1928 by Nimuendajú (1955). A group of four Kanoê at Omeré was only contacted in 1995, since when two children were born, of whom one died, along with two adults. The tragic history of the Kanoê after first contact with Western society has been documented only very sparsely, like that of most peoples of Rondônia. The language is moribund with five speakers out of an ethnic group of around ninety-five people (2002).

Kantaruré [431] Brazil, northern Bahia State, Terra Indígena Kantaruré, in the Batida and Pedras communities. *Unclassified* (for lack of data). The Kantaruré claim to be descendants of the Pankararu. However, the fact that they are completely acculturated and only speak Portuguese impedes their linguistic identification. Today the ethnic group totals some 353 members (2003). The language is extinct.

Kapinawá (or **Capinaauá**) **[432]** Brazil, Pernambuco State, Buique, Ibimirim, and Tupanatinga municipalities, Terra Indígena Kapinawá. *Unclassified* (for lack of data). Today all 422 members of the ethnic group speak Portuguese. The language is extinct.

Karajá (or **Carajá**, **Iny**) **[307a]** Brazil, Goiás, Mato Grosso, Pará, and Tocantins states, Araguaia River valley, including the Ilha do Bananal, twenty-nine villages divided over various indigenous lands close to the lakes and tributaries of the Araguaia and Javaés rivers, as well as in the interior of the Ilha do Bananal. *Macro-Ge*, Karaja. Although the Karajá have a long-standing history of contact with Western society, they still preserve their language and culture. However, Portuguese is becoming dominant in some villages, such as Aruanã in Goiás State. With Javaé and Xambioá, the Karajá language forms the Karaja subbranch within the Macro-Ge linguistic family. The language is potentially endangered with an ethnic group of approximately 2,500 (1999).

Karapanã (or **Carapanã**, **Muteamasa**, **Ukopinõpõna**) **[159]** Brazil, northwestern Amazonas State, Terra Indígena Alto Rio Negro, São Gabriel and Pari-Cachoeira. *Tucanoan*, Eastern Tucanoan, Central, Tatuyo. Carapana shares a big part of its lexicon with Tatuyo (Colombia). In Brazil, the language is seriously endangered with an ethnic group consisting of only forty-two members (2001) (more in Colombia).

Kariña (or *Galibi*, *Carib*, *Kalina*) **[384]** Guyana, North West District, coastal river heads and coastal lowland forests. *Cariban*, Northern, Galibi. The coastal and, therefore, reasonably accessible Kariña communities face the reality of the loss of their native language for a number of geographic and historical reasons. Despite this prognosis, the significant Kariña communities which are located in the remote wetland forested areas of the Guyana North West – who speak Kariña as a first language – ensure that there is no immediate threat of extinction in the short term. There are 3,000 in the ethnic group (more in Suriname, French Guiana, Venezuela, and Brazil). The language is endangered.

Kariña (or *Cariña*, *Kari'ña*, *Kalihna*, *Galibi*) **[141]** Venezuela, Monagas and Anzoategui states, northeast near the Orinoco River mouth, plus a few communities in Bolivar State, just south of the Orinoco. *Cariban*, Northern, Galibi. The Kariña are one of the groups that are in closest contact with the urban society of Caracas. Especially during the last decades they have been subjected to an intense acculturation process, which in its turn has resulted in considerable language loss among younger generations. Although a considerable number of the approximately 11,140 members of the ethnic group do speak the language, it has to be classified as endangered due to the lack of intergenerational transmission (more in French Guiana, Suriname, Guyana, and Brazil).

Karipuna **[232]** Brazil, northwestern Rondônia State, Upper Madeira River, Terra Indígena Karipuna. *Tupian*, Tupi-Guarani, Kawahib (VI). A group by this name that spoke a Panoan language disappeared in the first half of the twentieth century. Nowadays this name refers to a small Tupi-Kawahib speaking group that immigrated from Amazonas State somewhere during the second half of the twentieth century. The Karipuna form part of a bigger group of peoples that call themselves *Kagwahiva*. There are about ten speakers out of an ethnic group of approximately twenty-one (2001). Consequently, the language is seriously endangered.

Kariri (or *Cariri*, *Kipea*, *Kiriri*, *Dzubukuá*) **[315]** Brazil, Ceará State, Terra Indígena Kariri. *Unclassified* (for lack of consensus). The Kariri linguistic family consisted of two languages: **Kipea** (or **Kariri**) and **Dzubukuá** (or **Kiriri**), not to be confused with other languages in the region in which the names Kariri or Kiriri occur. While it is not known how many persons belong to the Kariri ethnic group, the Kariri language family is definitely extinct.

Karitiana **[367]** Brazil, northwestern Rondônia State, Terra Indígena Karitiana, Terra Indígena Karipuna. *Tupian*, Tupi-Arikem. The Karitiana were first contacted at the end of the seventeenth century, after which they withdrew into isolation again until the beginning of the twentieth century. The Karitiana group came into contact with *seringueiros* ('rubber tappers') and subsequently suffered great losses due to epidemics and forced labour in the rubber business. Today the language is seriously endangered with around 206 speakers (2001) out of an ethnic group of the same size.

Karo (or *Arara*, *Arara Karo*, *Arara de Rondônia*, *Arara Tupi*, *Ntogapíd*, *Itogapúk*, *Ramarama*, *Uruku*, *Urumi*, *Ytangá*) **[376]** Brazil, eastern Rondônia State, in the southern part of the Terra Indígena Igarapé de Lourdes, in the villages Iterap and

Paygap. *Tupian*, Tupi-Ramarama. Karo is the only member of the Tupi-Ramarama subbranch. The language is spoken by almost everyone in the two villages. Portuguese is learned as a second language and only used in contact situations. However, due to the reduced number of the Karo ethnic group (170 persons in 2004), the language is to be considered seriously endangered.

***Katawixí* [142]** Brazil, Amazonas State, Jacareúba River, a right-bank tributary of the Purus River, Municipality of Canutama, Terra Indígena Jacareúba/Katawixi. *Harakmbut-Katukinan*. The size of this isolated group is not exactly known, but with an estimated ten persons (SIL 1986), the language is seriously endangered.

Katukina do Biá (or ***Pedá Djapá*, *Tüküná***) **[140]** Brazil, Amazonas State, Juruá, Jutaí and Purus rivers area, Terra Indígena Rio Biá. *Harakmbut-Katukinan*. With one reported speaker (SIL 1976) within an ethnic group of 289 (2000) the language is to be considered moribund.

Katukina do Acre (or ***Katukina Pano*, *Panoana Katukina*, *Katukina***) **[221]** Brazil, Upper Juruá River region, Acre State, Tarauacá Municipality, Terra Indígena Rio Gregório; Tarauacá and Ipixuna municipalities, Terra Indígena Rio Campinas, on the border of the Amazonas and Acre states. *Panoan*, Southeastern. All Katukina do Acre speak their native language among themselves. Portuguese is only used for communication with the outside world. Despite their long-standing contact with outsiders, less than half of the Katukina do Acre are fluent in Portuguese. The language, which is possibly intelligible with Marubo, is to be considered endangered with 318 members in the ethnic group (1998).

Kawésqar (or ***Qawésqar*, *Alacalufe***) **[248]** Chile, Tierra del Fuego Archipelago, Isle of Wellington, Puerto Edén, Punta Arenas, and Puerto Natales. *Unclassified*. Although Kawésqar has traditionally been classified as a language isolate, some authors have pointed out a possible relationship with the Chonan languages or Mapuche. The ethnic group consists of less than 100 persons, of which most are bilingual in Spanish. The language is to be considered seriously endangered.

Kaxararí (or ***Caxarari*, *Kaxariri***) **[213]** Brazil, Terra Indígena Kaxararí on the border between the federal states of Rondônia and Amazonas. *Panoan*, Eastern. The language is the only representative of the Panoan family in Rondônia. It is not known how many speakers there are among the 269 (2001) members of the ethnic group. The language is to be considered seriously endangered.

Kaxinawá (or ***Caxinauá*, *Cashinahuá*, *Cashinahua*, *Huni-Kuin***) **[225]** Brazil, Acre State, spread over approximately eleven Indigenous Lands, among which Terra Indígena Igarapé do Caucho, Terra Indígena Kaxinawá do Rio Jordão, Terra Indígena Kaxinawá Nova Olinda. *Panoan*, Southeastern. In Brazil, the language is to be considered potentially endangered with an ethnic group of 3,964 members (1999) (more in Peru).

Kaxuyana (or ***Kaxuyâna*, *Kaxuiâna*, *Katxuyana*, *Kashuyana*, *Warikyana*, *Warikiana***) **[390]** Brazil, northern Pará State, Terra Indígena Parque Tumucumaque. *Cariban*, Southern, Southern Guiana. Traditionally the Kaxuyana language was spoken in the Middle

Trombetas River Basin. Today the language is seriously endangered with only sixty-nine, mostly bilingual (Kaxuyana-Tiriyó), persons in the ethnic group (1998).

Kayapó (or **Kaiapó, Caiapó, Mebêngokrê**) **[288]** Brazil, Central Brazilian plateau, southern Pará State and northern Mato Grosso State. *Macro-Ge*, Ge, Northern Ge. Among the Kayapó subgroups the knowledge of Portuguese varies quite a bit, depending on the degree of contact of each group with the Western world. Apart from the nineteen communities that are in more or less regular contact with the outside world, there still are three or four small isolated Kayopó groups totalling approximately 30–100 individuals. The language is potentially endangered with an ethnic group of approximately 7,096 members (2003), including the subgroups Gorotire, A'ukré, Kikretun, Mekrãnotí, Kubenkránkén, Kokraimôro, Metuktire, Xikrin (1,052 in 2000), Kararaô.

Kiriri (or **Katembri, Kariri, Kariri de Mirandela**) **[323]** Brazil, northern Bahia State, Banzaê and Quijingue municipalities, Terra Indígena Kiriri. *Unclassified* (for lack of data). In the early 1960s, 100 words were registered from the only elder who could still remember the language vaguely. Today the ethnic group totals 1,401 members (2003), but the language is extinct.

Kogui (or **Cogui, Kogi, Kággaba**) **[32]** Colombia, north side of the Sierra Nevada de Santa Marta, in the valleys of the Ancho, Palomino, Don Diego and Jerez rivers; also to the northeast, on the Barcino River, and to the south on the Guatapuri River. *Chibchan*, Aruak. The Kogui are the most traditional group of the Sierra Nevada de Santa Marta area with a very strong religious tradition. The language is still transmitted to children. With about 9,765 speakers out of an ethnic group of the same size the language is to be considered potentially endangered.

Kokama (or **Kocama, Cocama**) **[342]** Brazil, Amazonas State, Rio Solimões region, Terra Indígena Acapuri de Cima, Terra Indígena Espírito Santo, Terra Indígena Evaré I, Terra Indígena Kokama. *Tupian*, Tupi-Guarani (unclassified mixed language according to some scholars). In Brazil, the language is to be considered moribund with perhaps five speakers out of a group of 622 ethnic Kokama (1989) (more in Peru and Colombia).

Koreguaje (or **Coreguaje, Ko'reuaju**) **[148]** Colombia, Department of Caquetá, in twenty-seven settlements along the rivers Orteguazo, Peneya, and Cauquetá. *Tucanoan*, Western. Nowadays the speakers of Koreguaje represent a fusion of various ethnic groups, since it is not only spoken by the Koreguaje themselves but also by Inga, Witoto, Carijona, and Tama (a probably extinct group that assimilated with the Koreguaje). With an ethnic group of approximately 2,110 members the language is to be considered potentially endangered.

Korubo or **Caceteiros [433]** Brazil, State of Amazonas, Javari River Basin, Terra Indígena Vale do Javari, near the Ituí, Itaquai and Quixiti rivers. *Panoan*, Unclassified. The Korubo are also known as Caceteiros, a name referring to their traditional weapon, a long, lethal wooden tube through which poisoned darts can be blown. A FUNAI expedition first contacted part of the Korubo group in 1996. This group of twenty-two persons split off from the original group, which resists any further contact

141

and continues to hide itself. The language is seriously endangered with an ethnic group of about 250 (2000).

Krahô (or ***Craô, Kraô, Mehim, Mãkrare, Quenpokrare, Timbira***) **[285a]** Brazil, northeastern Tocantins State, Goiatins and Itacajá municipalities, Terra Indígena Krâolandia, five villages. *Macro-Ge*, Ge, Northern Ge, Timbira. Although Krahô is still learned as a first language by children, boys, men and a growing number of women have become fluent in Portuguese. The language is potentially endangered, with an ethnic group of 1,900 (1999).

Krenak (or ***Crenaque, Nakrehé, Krenak-Nakrehé, Borun***) **[281]** Brazil, northeastern Minas Gerais State, east bank of the Doce River, between the towns of Resplendor and Conselheiro Pena, Terra Indígena Fazenda Guaraní, Terra Indígena Krenak. *Macro-Ge*, Krenak. Victims of several massacres in the past, the Krenak are the last surviving Botocudo do Leste (Eastern Botocudo). Only women over forty-five years of age still speak the language. Men, youngsters and children have all switched to Portuguese. The language is to be considered seriously endangered with perhaps ten speakers out of an ethnic group of 150 (1997).

Krikatí (or ***Krinkatí, Krikatí-Timbira, Timbira***) **[285c]** Brazil, Maranhão, between the cities of Imperatriz to the northwest and Grajaú to the east, Terra Indígena Krikatí. *Macro-Ge*, Ge, Northern Ge, Timbira. The Timbira dialect Krikatí is endangered with an ethnic group of approximately 620 members (2000).

Kubeo (or ***Cubeo, Cobewa, Kubéwa, Pamíwa***) **[153]** Brazil, northwestern Amazonas State, Vaupés River area, Terra Indígena Alto Rio Negro, between the Vaupés River and the headwaters of the Ayarí. *Tucanoan*, Central Tucanoan. In Brazil, the Kubeo language is to be considered endangered due to its reduced ethnic group of 287 members (2001) (more in Colombia).

Kuikuro (or ***Kuikuru***) **[413]** Brazil, Mato Grosso, Upper Xingu area, Parque Indígena do Xingu, on the Culuene River, in the villages of Ipatse and Ahukugí, and in the Yawalapití (Arawakan) village, near the mouth of the Tuatuari River. *Cariban*, Southern, Upper Xingu, Kalapalo. The Kuikuro are one of the four Cariban groups currently living in the Xingu Indigenous Park, the others being the Matipú, Kalapalo and Nahukwá. Although they speak dialects of the same language (Upper-Xingu Carib or Kalapalo), each of these groups sees itself as distinct from the others. Most Kuikuro still speak their native language. With about 415 (2002) members in the ethnic group, the Kuikuro language is endangered.

Kulina (or ***Culina, Madihá, Madiha, Madija***) **[128]** Brazil, Acre State, on the Juruá and Purus rivers, Terra Indígena Alto Rio Purus, Terra Indigena Jaminawa/Elvira, Terra Indígena Kaxinawá, Terra Indigena Kulina do Igarapé do Pau, Kulina do Rio Envira. *Arauan*, Deni-Kulina, Kulina. Like the Deni and Madi, the Kulina ethnic group is semi-acculturated. In the more remote villages in the jungle Kulina is still spoken as a first language, but Portuguese is becoming dominant in the villages close to the cities. With an ethnic group of approximately 2,537 members (2002) the language is potentially endangered (more in Peru).

142

Kulina do Acre (or *Kulina Pano*, *Culina*) **[214]** Brazil, Amazonas State, Terra Indígena Vale do Javari, between the Curuça and Ituí rivers, southwest of the city of Atalaia do Norte and east of the Javari River, 100km from border with Peru. *Panoan, Unclassified*. The language is seriously endangered with an ethnic group of only twenty persons (1996).

Kuripako (or *Curipaco*, *Coripaco*) **[92a]** Brazil, Amazonas State, Upper Içana River. *Arawakan*, Maipuran, Northern Maipuran, Inland. Although the Kuripako are related to the Baniwa and speak a dialect of the Baniwa language, they do not consider themselves a Baniwa subgroup. With an ethnic group of 1,115 members (2001) the language is to be considered endangered in Brazil (more in Colombia and Venezuela).

Kurripako (or *Kurripaco*, *Curripaco*, *Corripako*, *Baniva-Kurripako*, *Baniwa del Isana*) **[86a]** Venezuela, zone of Victorino, not far from Maroa on the Guainía River, and in the San Fernando de Atabapo zone. *Arawakan*, Maipuran, Northern Maipuran, Inland. Kurripako is more related to Piapoko and Warekena than to Baré and Yavitero, the other two Arawakan languages in Amazonas State. The language has the following three dialects: **Ôjo-Kjárru**, **Âja-Kurri**, and **Êje-Kjénim**. With about 2,810 members in the ethnic group the language is to be considered potentially endangered (more in Colombia and Brazil).

Kuruaya (or *Kuruaia*, *Curuaia*) **[362]** Brazil, Pará State, Municipality of Altamira, on the right bank of the Curuá River, Terra Indígena Curuá, in the Cajueiro village; Terra Indígena Xipaia, in the town of Altamira. *Tupian*, Munduruku. The Cajueiro village has a young population that speaks Portuguese and only knows a few words of their mother tongue. In 2000, there was just one elder in the village who spoke Kuruaya fluently. There are eight elders of Kuruaya and Xipaya descendance in Altamira who still speak the native language. In Altamira, there has been a great deal of intermarriage between the Kuruaya and Xipaya, with the result that they are sometimes considered to form a single ethnic group. This complicates a precise demographic census. Currently there are 115 persons (2002) living in the Cajueiro village, but the Kuruaya ethnic group is obviously bigger. The language, however, is seriously endangered.

Kuyabi (or *Kuyawi*) **[135c]** Brazil, Amazonas State south shore of the Middle Rio Negro, village of Bom Jardim. *Makuan*. Martins and Martins (1999) consider Kuyabi to be closely related to Nadëb, since both languages share a large percentage of their lexicons. This relationship, however, is not mentioned by other sources. The language is seriously endangered with approximately twenty speakers.

Kuyubí (or *Kujubim*, *Cojubím*, *Kaw Ta Yo*) **[380]** Brazil, southwestern Rondônia. *Chapacuran*. The Rio Cautario is possibly named after the autodenomination of the Kuyubí. The language is moribund with possibly three speakers out of a scattered ethnic population of twenty-seven in 2001.

Kwazá (or *Koaiá*, *Coaiá*, *Quaia*) **[327]** Brazil, southeastern Rondônia State, Área Indígena Tubarão-Latundê, Terra Indígena Kwazá do Rio São Pedro, Chupinguaia, Vilhena. *Unclassified*. The Kwazá were first mentioned in 1913 by their Kepkiriwat neighbours to Rondon (1916). Today the speakers' community consists of two separate families. The language is seriously endangered with twenty-five speakers, of whom a number assert Aikanã ethnic identity.

Latundê (or *Lakondê*) **[329a]** Brazil, southeastern Rondônia State, Terra Indígena Tubarão-Latundê, Vilhena. *Nambikwaran*, Northern Nambikwara. The language is practically identical with Lakondê, of which the last speaker lives in Vilhena. The Latundê were first contacted by the Aikanã in 1975, and by Westerners in 1976. They became nearly extinct due to the general incompetence of the representatives of responsible Western institutions. Nowadays there are approximately twenty speakers out of an ethnic group of the same size, a number of whom also speak Portuguese.

Leko (or *Ríka*, *Buruwa*) **[201]** Bolivia, Department of La Paz, provinces of Franz Tamayo, Nor-Yungas, Caranavi y Larecaja, municipalities of Apolo and Guanay, Trapiche Ponte. *Language Isolate*. The Leko ethnic group may be facing extinction due to the intense acculturation process they have been submitted to, primarily caused by the growing presence of the Andean population in the region. Nevertheless, there seems to be a growing sense of ethnicity among the Leko, which has resulted initially in their political organisation. Out of an ethnic group of 80 there are about twenty semi-speakers who are all over sixty years old. The language is to be considered moribund.

Lokono (or *Arawak*) **[105]** Guyana, west coast, white sand plateaux near the coast, and middle river basins flowing northwards below the falls; northeast along the Corantyne River; about ninety settlements. *Arawakan*, Maipuran, Northern Maipuran, Caribbean. There are probably less than 1,550 speakers out of an ethnic group of 15,500 (more in Suriname, French Guiana, and Venezuela). The language is endangered.

Lokono (or *Arawak*) **[105]** Suriname, coastal area, several villages between coast and about 30km inland, mainly on the savanna. *Arawakan*, Maipuran, Northern Maipuran, Caribbean. The Lokono villages show a progressive loss of language, culture and tradition. Young people are no longer interested in learning their own language, and the daily spoken language in these villages is Sranantongo, an English-based creole language, and sometimes Dutch. In Suriname, there are about 700 speakers out of an ethnic group of 2,000 (more in Guyana, French Guiana, and Venezuela). The language is endangered.

Lokonó (or *Aruaco*, *Arawak*) **[105]** Venezuela, coastal area near Guyana, Amacuro Delta, Bolivar State. *Arawakan*, Maipuran, Northern Maipuran, Caribbean. The language is spoken in a few small communities that have undergone a strong acculturation process. It is not known how many speakers there are in the ethnic group of about 250 persons (more in French Guiana, Suriname, and Guyana). Apart from Lokonó, speakers usually speak Spanish and English as well. In Venezuela, the language is to be considered seriously endangered.

Macaguaje (or *Makaguaje*) **[148a]** Colombia, Department of Putumayo, on the Lower Putumayo, in El Hacha on the Ecuadorian border and on the tributaries of the Caquetá, such as the Mecaya and Senseya. *Tucanoan*, Western Tucanoan, Northern,

Siona-Secoya. Although the Macaguaje group still consists of about fifty members, the language may be extinct.

***Macaguane-Hitnu* [68a]** Colombia, Department of Arauca, Arauca, Agualinda and San José de Lipa between the Lipa, Ele and Cuiloto rivers, and other scattered locations. The language is no longer spoken on the Caño Colorado and the Caño Cangrejo, and in La Cabaña and La Vigía. *Guahiban.* It is not known how many speakers are precisely left in the ethnic group of approximately 540. The language is to be considered endangered.

Machiguenga (or ***Matsiguenga, Matziguenga, Matsigenka, Niagantsi***) **[123c]** Peru, along the Upper and Lower Urubamba and its tributaries, along the Manu River and its tributaries, on the left-bank tributaries of the Madre de Dios, and some families on the headwaters of the Colorado River. *Arawakan,* Maipuran, Southern Maipuran, Campa. According to SIL, in Quillabamba, Koribeni, Chirumbia, and in some other areas along the Upper Urubamba, Quechua and Spanish are replacing Machiguenga. Children no longer acquire the language. Nevertheless, Machiguenga is not endangered on the Manu River, where the Machiguenga teachers from the Urubamba River area are interested in implementing a formalised bilingual education programme. The language is potentially endangered with approximately 5,910 speakers out of an ethnic group of 13,000.

***Machineri* [119]** Bolivia, Department of Pando, Province of Nicolás Suárez, Municipality of Bolpebra, in San Miguel on the Acre River. *Arawakan,* Maipuran, Southern Maipuran. There are 140 speakers out of an ethnic group of 155. The negative social pressure they had to deal with in Brazil in 1985 caused this group of Machineri to move from the State of Acre (Brazil) into the Department of Pando (Bolivia) on the other side of the Acre River. They have settled in San Miguel, a rubber plantation managed by Brazilians with whom they speak Portuguese all the time. In Bolivia, the language is to be considered seriously endangered (more in Brazil).

Machineri (***Manchineri, Yine***) **[119]** Brazil, Acre State, Sena Madureira and Assis municipalities, Terra Indígena Mamoadate. *Arawakan,* Maipuran, Southern Maipuran. In 1985, negative social pressure caused a group of Machineri to move from the State of Acre into the Department of Pando (Bolivia) on the other side of the Acre River. Currently the the Machineri ethnic group totals 459 persons in Brazil (1999) (more in Bolivia). The language is to be considered endangered.

Macuna (or ***Makuna***) **[154]** Colombia, Department of Vaupés, on the banks of the Comeña River, and the mouth of the Apaporis and Pirá-Paraná. *Tucanoan,* Eastern Tucanoan, Central, Southern. The Macuna share their territory with other groups, such as the Carijona, Cubeo, Miraña, Tanimuca, Yucuna and Matapí. They form part of the whole of Eastern Tucanoan groups, which are known for practising linguistic exogamy and for their general multilingualism. The Macuna principally maintain relations with the Barasana and Tuyuca. The Macuna Group assimilated the Yahuna, of which in 1988 less than twenty survived on the Umuña River, a tributary of the Apaporis, and three on the Apaporis River itself. Today all have switched to Macuna and the Yahuna language (Tucanoan, Eastern Tucanoan, Unclassified) has probably

145

become extinct. With about 920 members in the ethnic group the language is to be considered endangered (more in Brazil).

Maká (Maca) **[259]** Paraguay, Nueva Colonia Indígena Maká, located in the Mariano Roque Alonso District at a distance of 20km from the city of Asunción; Puerto Botánico (Asunción); Cuatro Vientos (Chaco). *Mataco-Mataguayan*. The Maká were first contacted by the whites in 1927. During the Chaco War (1932–5) the Maká fought against Bolivia and by way of 'thanks' they were relocated after the war to Colonia Fray Bartolomé de las Casas on the west bank of the Paraguay River, opposite to Puerto Botánico (Asunción). They remained there until 1985 when they were brought to their current location. With about 985 speakers out of an ethnic group of 1,060 the language is to be considered endangered.

Mako (or *Maco, Maku, Sáliba-Maco, Maco-Piaroa, Wirö*) **[426]** Venezuela, savannas, on the right bank of the Orinoco River between the Ventuari and the Cunucunúma rivers, south to the Piaroa area. *Saliba-Piaroan*. Mako has been considered a dialect of Piaroa (cf. Migliazza 1985). With an ethnic group of 345 members the language is to be considered endangered.

Makuna (or *Macuna, Yeba-Masã*) **[154]** Brazil, northwestern Amazonas State, Terra Indígena Alto Rio Negro, Xié River area. *Tucanoan*, Eastern Tucanoan, Central, Southern. In Brazil, the language is seriously endangered with an ethnic group of 168 (2001) (more in Colombia).

Makurap (or *Macurap*) **[372]** Brazil, southwestern Rondônia, Terra Indígena Rio Branco, Posto Indígena Rio Guaporé, Guajará-Mirim. *Tupian*, Tupi-Tupari. The Makurap language used to be a lingua franca in southwestern Rondônia during a number of decades in the twentieth century. Today the language is seriously endangered with around fifty speakers out of an ethnic group of approximately 130.

Makushi (or *Pemon*) **[399]** Guyana, southwestern border area, in the north Rupununi savannas, twenty settlements. *Cariban*, Northern, East-West Guiana, Macushi-Kapon, Macushi. There are 7,750 in the ethnic group (more in Brazil and Venezuela). The language is potentially endangered in Guyana.

Makushi (or *Macushi, Makuxi*) **[399]** Venezuela, eastern border area with Guyana and Brazil. *Cariban*, Northern, East-West Guiana, Macushi-Kapon, Macushi. Makushi, Kapón and Pemón are three closely related Cariban subbranches. The number of Makushi in Venezuela is not entirely clear, since the 1992 Indigenous Census probably included them in the Pemón group. According to Grimes 2000, the ethnic group consists of 600 members (more in Brazil and Guyana). In Venezuela, the language is to be considered endangered.

Makuxí (or *Macuxi, Macushi, Pemon*) **[399]** Brazil, Roraima State, on more than twenty Indigenous Lands, among which Terra Indígena Raposa/Serra do Sol. *Cariban*, Northern, East-West Guiana, Macushi-Kapon, Macushi. The Makuxí, Wapixana, Ingarikó and Taurepang had fought for decades for the legal recognition of their Indigenous Land Raposa/Serra do Sol, when in 2002 a judgment from Brazil's highest court finally made this possible. In Brazil, most Makuxí still speak their language, which is potentially endangered with a population of some 16,500 persons (2000) (more in Guyana and Venezuela).

Mandahuaca (or *Mandawaca*, *Mandawaka*) **[80]** Venezuela, Amazonas State, to the east of the Baré group, from the Baria River to the Caño Casiquiare. *Arawakan*, Maipuran, Northern Maipuran, Inland. The language is sometimes considered a dialect of Baré. It is not clear how big the ethnic group is, since the usually cited number of 3,000 (Gaceta Indigenista 1975) probably includes Baré, Baniva, and Mandahuaca. It is possible that the language is extinct in Venezuela (possibly more in Brazil).

Manjui (or *Chorote*, *Yojwaja*, *Yowúwa*) **[257]** Paraguay, border area between Paraguay, Argentina and Bolivia, Department of Boquerón, District of Pedro P. Peña. *Mataco-Mataguayan*. The Manjui or Chorote can be subdivided into two main groups and their language consequently into two dialects: Yofuáha, spoken on the south bank of the Pilcomayo River, downstream from the second dialect, and Yowúwa, spoken in the interior of Paraguay. There were bands of uncontacted Manjui until well into the 1970s. The Manjui language is to be considered seriously endangered, even though all of the approximately 230 members of the ethnic group speak the language (more in Argentina).

Mapoyo (or *Mapoio*, *Wánai*) **[409]** Venezuela, southwestern part of Bolivar State, on the savanna between the Caño Caripo to the north and the Villacoa River to the south, near to the road that connects Caicara del Orinoco with Puerto Ayacucho, in the Palomo community, 60km to the south of La Urbana. *Cariban*, Northern, Western Guiana. There are only a few semi-speakers left in the ethnic group consisting of less than 200 members. The language is moribund.

Mapuche (or *Ranquel*, *Manzanero*, *Pehuenche*, *Huilliche*) **[249]** Argentina, provinces of Neuquén, Río Negro, Chubut, La Pampa, and Buenos Aires. *Araucanian*. In Argentina, children no longer speak Mapuche, which is generally spoken by women who have remained in their houses instead of going out of the reservation to earn their living. The language competence of the speakers varies from fluent to passive. It is not clear how many speakers are left within the ethnic group of 40,000 to 50,000 (more in Chile). In Argentina, the language is to be considered endangered due to the lack of intergenerational transmission.

Mapuche (or *Mapadungu*, *Araucano*) **[249]** Chile, central-south, mainly in the IX Region (provinces of Cautín and Malleco), but also in the VIII and X regions (provinces of Arauco, Bío-Bío, Valdivia, and Osorno), in the cities of Santiago, Temuco, and Concepción. *Araucanian*. Traditionally, Mapuche has been considered to have the following four varieties: **Picunche**, **Moluche** (or **Araucano**), **Pehuenche**, and **Huilliche**. While the first three are closely related, Huilliche diverges considerably. There are about 250,000 speakers out of an ethnic group of more than 600,000 (more in Argentina). Today Intercultural Bilingual Education programmes may contribute to the survival and extension of Mapuche. The language is potentially endangered in Chile.

Marubo **[220]** Brazil, Amazonas State, Javari River Basin, Terra Indígena Vale do Javari, on the upper course of the Curuçá and Ituí rivers, Atalaia do Norte Municipality.

147

Panoan, North-Central. The Marubo have been in contact with the Western world for approximately 150 years. Nevertheless, they have preserved their culture and language. Marubo vocabulary has a ritual counterpart, used in myths and curing chants. While the younger generation is becoming fluent in Portuguese, older people tend to know a few words of Quechua and Spanish, picked up in the past when Peruvian rubber tappers explored their terrirory and the Marubo were forced to work in the rubber-tapping industry until the early 1990s. With an ethnic group of about 1,043 (2000) the language is endangered.

Mashco (or ***Mashco-Piro***) **[119]** Peru, Department of Ucayali, Province of Purús, Upper Purús region. *Unclassified* (for lack of evidence). The Mashco form an uncontacted group that has been sighted regularly since the 1960s. Yine attempting to contact the Mashco on the Río de las Piedras claim that they speak a language closely related to Yine. The size of the ethnic group and, therefore, the number of speakers is still unknown. Nevertheless, the language is to be considered endangered (more in Brazil).

Matipú **[413]** Brazil, Mato Grosso, Upper Xingu area, in the south of the Parque Indígena do Xingu, near the Kurisevo and Buriti rivers, two villages. *Cariban*, Southern, Upper Xingu, Kalapalo. The Matipú are one of the four Cariban groups currently living in the Xingu Indigenous Park, the others being the Kalapalo, Kuikuro and Nahukwá. Although they speak dialects of the same language (Upper-Xingu Carib or Kalapalo), each of these groups sees itself as distinct from the others. Most Matipú still speak their native language, which is seriously endangered with an ethnic group of 119 (2003).

Matís **[237a]** Brazil, State of Amazonas, Javari River Basin, Terra Indígena Vale do Javari, one village on the banks of the Ituí River. *Panoan, Unclassified*. The Matís group was first contacted in the early 1970s and erroneously thought to be Matsés or Marubo. Contact with the Western world led to the death of more than half of the group. The Matís, who are masters of curare, are also known as the *jaguar men*, because their tattoos and ornaments make them look like jaguars. The Matís language, culture and traditional costume are still fully preserved. Nevertheless, the language is to be considered seriously endangered due to the reduced size of its ethnic group of 239 members (2000).

Matsés (or ***Matsé, Mayoruna, Matsés-Mayoruna***) **[237]** Brazil, Amazonas State, Javari River Basin, Terra Indígena Vale do Javari, Terra Indígena Lameirão; Solimões River area, Terra Indígena Mayoruna. *Panoan*, Northern. An interesting characteristic of the Matsés, or so-called *cat people*, is the large number of captives that they have integrated in their group. In Brazil, the Matsés still speak their native language, but in the last decade both missionary and military contact have been steadily increasing, which causes them to quickly acculturate to a new lifestyle. With an ethnic group of approximately 829 persons (2000) the language is endangered (more in Peru).

Matsés-Mayoruna (or ***Matsés, Mayoruna***) **[237]** Peru, Department of Loreto, along the Lower Yaquerana River (also called the Upper Yavarí) and its tributaries, the Lower Yavarí, and along the Chobayacu and Gálvez rivers. *Panoan*, Northern. There is a bilingual education programme with schoolteachers who are bilingual Matsés speakers. Some Matsés can speak Spanish or Portuguese as a second language. In Peru, the language is endangered with 890–93,000 speakers (including Brazil) out of an ethnic group of the same size.

Mawayana **[406]** Suriname, south, among the Trio in Kwamalasamutu on the Sipaliwini River. *Arawakan*, Maipuran, Mawayana. The Mawayana are mixed with Waiwai and live among the Waiwai group in Guyana; only a few are in Suriname. In the 1960s Door-to-Life missionaries, who had been active among the Waiwai in neighbouring Guyana, came to evangelise the Surinamese Amerindians of the interior. They brought with them a few Waiwai, as well as Mawayana and Tunayana Amerindians who had been living among the Waiwai, and whose task was to learn Trio in order to convert them. The Tunayana and Mawayana have remained in Suriname and now speak Trio as their primary language. In Suriname, there are ten speakers out of an ethnic group of sixty (more in Guyana and Brazil). All speakers are over seventy years old. The language is moribund.

Maxakalí (or ***Maxacalí***, ***Monacóbm***, ***Kumanuxú***, ***Tikmuún***) **[278]** Brazil, northeastern Minas Gerais State, 100 miles inland from the coast, Mucuri Valley, on the headwaters of the Umburanas River, Bertópolis Municipality, Terra Indígena Maxakali/Unificacão, in two Indigenous Areas, Água Boa and Pradinho, which have been grouped together to form the Maxakalí Indigenous Land. *Macro-Ge*, Maxakali. Language use is still vigorous among the Maxakalí. Portuguese is spoken in those places that are in closer contact with the Western world, like for instance Água Boa. In Pradinho, however, only the men speak some Portuguese. The language is endangered with an ethnic group of approximately 802 members (1997).

Maya (or ***Maya-Quixito***) **[220a]** Brazil, Amazonas State, Terra Indígena Vale do Javari, border area with Peru on the upper course of the Quixiti River (tributary of the Javari), to the southwest of the city of Atalaia do Norte, between the Itui and Javari rivers. *Panoan, Unclassified*. The language of this isolated group does not seem to be mutually intelligible with Matsés and is distinct from Marubo. In Brazil, the language is endangered with an ethnic group of about 400 persons (possibly more in Peru).

Mbyá **[335f]** Brazil, rural and coastal areas of the Paraná, Santa Catarina, and Rio Grande do Sul states, in the São Paulo, Rio de Janeiro, and Santa Cristina states, and in several villages located within the Atlantic forest. *Tupian*, Tupi-Guarani, Guarani (I). While most children, women and elders are still monolingual speakers of Mbyá, only those Mbyá that represent the interests of the group before national society are relatively fluent in Portuguese. With an ethnic group of about 6,000 members (2003) the language is to be considered potentially endangered (more in Argentina and Paraguay).

Mbyá **[335f]** Argentina, Province of Misiones. *Tupian*, Tupi-Guarani, Guarani (I). The Mbyá arrived in the region where they are today at the end of the nineteenth century. Before that time the area was inhabited by other groups, such as the Kaingang, a Ge group that migrated to Brazil. The Mbyá kept coming from Paraguay to the Province of Misiones until 1980. The ethnic group consists of 2,500–3,500 members. Language use is vigorous among the groups that have arrived recently, but among those that have been arriving since the end of the nineteenth century the use of Spanish is becoming more and more predominant. The language is endangered (more in Paraguay and Brazil).

Mbyá [335f] Paraguay, Department of Caaguazú, Caaguazú, Repatriación, Yhú, Dr. J. E. Estigarribia, Raúl A. Oviedo, and Mariscal. F. S. López districts, Department of Caazapá, Abaí and Tavaí districts, Department of Alto Paraná, Presidente Franco, Hernandarias, Itakyry, Yguasú, and San Cristóbal districts, Department of San Pedro, San Estanislao, Tacuatí, General Isidro Resquín, and Itacurubi del Rosario districts; Department of Guairá, District of Independencia, Department of Itapúa, Capitán Meza, Jesús, Obligado, San Cosme y Damián, Edelira, and Alto Verá districts, Department of Misiones, San Ignacio and Yabebeyry districts, Department of Central, District of Luque, Department of Canindeyú, Ypejhú and Ygatimi districts. *Tupian*, Tupi-Guarani, Guarani (I). The deforestation of their traditional habitat and the occupation of their territories by so-called landless farmers have led the Mbyá to scatter all over Paraguay. Today they can be seen in rags, begging in the main cities of Paraguay, such as Asunción, Encarnación, and Ciudad del Este. Unlike the Ava Guaraní and the Paï-Tavyterä who only use their language in cultural and religious contexts, the Mbyá still use their language in day-to-day speech. Out of an ethnic group of approximately 4,745 members 2,445 speak the language, which is to be considered potentially endangered in Paraguay (more in Argentina and Brazil). Nearly half of the Mbyá ethnic group (42.5 per cent) speaks a variety of Paraguayan Guaraní.

Mehinako (or *Mehinaku*, *Meinaku*, *Meinacu*) [112] Brazil, Mato Grosso, Parque Indígena do Xingu, Tuatuari and Kurisevo rivers area, in the Jalapapuh Community. *Arawakan*, Maipuran, Central Maipuran. The Mehinako villages used to be located to the north of the current Awetí villages, on the Tuatuari River, but attacks by the Ikpeng caused them to move to their current location Jalapapuh. All Mehinako still speak their mother tongue, which is closely related to Waurá. However, with just about 199 persons (2002) in the ethnic group, the language is to be considered seriously endangered.

Mekens (or *Mekém*, *Sakurabiat*, *Sakiráp*, *Sakirabiat*, *Guaratira*, *Guarategaja*, *Siokweriat*, *Kampé*) [373] Brazil, southeastern Rondônia, near to the headwaters of the Mekens and Verde rivers, Municipality of Cerejeira, Terra Indígena Rio Mequens. *Tupian*, Tupi-Tupari. Mekens is one of the five surviving languages of the Tupari linguistic branch of the Tupi family. The rubber boom has had devastating effects on the Mekens population. Measles and influenza reduced the group from thousands in the early 1930s and 1940s to its current size of sixty-six persons (2003) on the Rio Mekens Indigenous Land. With a mere twenty-three speakers and a lack of intergenerational transmission, the language is to be considered seriously endangered.

Miguelenho (or *Uomo*) [65a] Brazil, southern Rondônia, Costa Marques vicinity. *Chapacuran*. The ethnic group is named after the São Miguel River. The language is moribund with one speaker in an ethnic group of fifty.

Miranha (or *Mirãnha*, *Miraña*) [182] Brazil, Amazonas State, Middle Solimões River, Alvarães Municipality, Terra Indígena Méria and Uarini Municipality, Terra

Indígena Miratu; Japurá River, Maraã Municipality, Terra Indígena Cuiú-Cuiú. *Boran*. The Brazilian Miranha no longer use their native language, although today there still are former speakers and their descendants. The Brazilian Miranha are aware of the fact that the language is still spoken in Colombia and consequently they would like to establish contact with the Colombian Miraña. Although the ethnic group consists of 613 members (1999) in Brazil, the language is no longer spoken (more in Colombia).

Miraña [182] Colombia, Department of Amazonas, on the lower part of the Caquetá River, near the mouth of the Cahuinarí. *Boran*. Miraña and Bora are the two dialects that form the Boran linguistic family together with the closely related Muinane language. There are less than 100 speakers – among whom are less than ten children – of Miraña out of an ethnic group of about 660 (more in Brazil). The language is seriously endangered.

Mirity-Tapuya (or *Miriti-Tapuia*, *Buia-Tapuya*) [161b] Brazil, northwestern Amazonas State, Terra Indígena Alto Rio Negro, Terra Indígena Médio Rio Negro II. *Tucanoan*, Miriti. With an ethnic group of approximately ninety-five members (1998) the language is seriously endangered.

Mocoví (or *Moqoyt La'qa:tqa*) [263] Argentina, southern half of the Chaco Province, departments of 12 de Octubre, 9 de Julio, Chacabuco, Cte. Fernández, Maipú, Mayor Luis Fontana, O'Higgins, Quitilipi, San Lorenzo, and Tapenagá; and in the northern half of the Santa Fe Province, departments of Garay, Obligado, San Javier, San Justo, and Vera. *Guaicuruan*. In general, the Mocoví language is preserved to a higher degree in the Chaco Province than in the Province of Santa Fe, where the pressures of the so-called *criollo* society are much bigger. By the early 1990s already less than 50 per cent of the Mocoví maintained their ancestral language. It is not known how many speakers are left in the ethnic group of 2,800–8,000. The language, however, is to be considered endangered due to its reported low vitality.

Mojo (or *Moxo*, *Mojeño*, *Moxeño*) [116] Bolivia, Department of Beni, Province of Moxos, around San Ignacio de Moxos (Ignaciano) and Department of Beni, Provinces of Cercado, Moxos (TIPNIS) and Ballivián, Trinidad (Trinitario). *Arawakan*, Maipuran, Southern Maipuran. The Mojo language consists of the two subgroups Ignaciano and Trinitario. For both groups an alarmingly rapid loss of language is reported among the youth. There is an estimated total of 10,000 speakers for both subgroups. The 1994 census gives an approximate number of 20,800 for the whole Mojo ethnic group. The language is to be considered endangered due to the dramatic loss of language use among the youngsters.

Moré (*Itene*, *Iténez*) [62] Bolivia, Department of Beni, Province of Mamoré, at the confluence of the Mamoré and Iténez (Guaporé) rivers, in the village of Monte Azul. *Chapacuran*. Between 1762 and 1763 the Jesuits brought the belligerent Moré together in the mission of San Miguel. Hardly a year later the mission ceased to exist and the Moré returned to their former, free way of life. Today there are approximately seventy-five speakers of around seventy years old out of an ethnic group of 200. The language is to be considered seriously endangered.

Moré [62] Brazil, western Rondônia, Guajará-Mirim, Porto Velho. *Chapacuran.* According to Angenot de Lima (2002), twelve out of eighty-six speakers and thirty out of 200 members of the ethnic group live in Brazil, whereas the majority of speakers and members of the ethnic group live in Bolivia. In Brazil, the Moré language is to be considered seriously endangered (more in Bolivia).

Mosetén [244] Bolivia, Department of La Paz, Province of Sud Yungas, also known as Alto Beni, i.e. the Upper Beni River. *Mosetenan.* Mosetén forms together with Tsimane' the small linguistic family Mosetenan. Although Tsimane' and Mosetén are mutually intelligible; there are some dialects with quite a few lexical and grammatical differences. There are about 580 speakers out of an ethnic group of 1,200. Some children still speak the language, which is to be considered endangered.

Movima [333] Bolivia, Department of Beni, Province of Yacuma, in Santa Ana del Yacuma and El Perú. *Language Isolate.* Including fluent speakers and persons with only a passive competence, there are about 2,000 speakers out of an ethnic group of 6,530. There is a strong movement among the Movima to revitalise the use of their language. Hopefully the efforts of a few teachers in combination with solid linguistic description of the language, will lead to the preservation of the Movima language. In view of the fact that all fluent speakers are way over fifty years old, the language is to be considered seriously endangered.

Muinane (or *Bora Muinane*) [183]: Colombia, Department of Amazonas, near the headwaters of the Cahuinari River, in the communities of La Sabana and Villa Azul; Department of Caquetá, on the banks of the Caquetá River, near Araracuara. *Boran.* In the literature the Boran Muinane are often confused with the Witotoan Muinane. With an ethnic group of some 550 members, the language is to be considered endangered.

Mundurukú (or *Mundurucú*) [361] Brazil, southwestern Pará State, on the creeks and tributaries of the Tapajós River, Santarém, Itaituba and Jacareacanga municipalities; eastern Amazonas State, on the Canumã River, Nova Olinda Municipality, and near the Trans-Amazon highway, Municipality of Borba; northern Mato Grosso State, Rio dos Peixes area, Juara Municipality; in total on six Indigenous Lands. *Tupian,* Munduruku. Traditionally a warrior people, the Mundurukú used to dominate the Tapajós Valley region culturally. The Mundurukú living in small villages on the banks of the Tapajós are mostly bilingual in Portuguese, but in the Sai Cinza village and in villages on the Cururu, Kabitutu and other tributaries of the Tapajós, children, women and elders usually only speak Munduruku. In villages near to towns Portuguese is becoming the dominant language. With an ethnic group of 10,065 (2002) the language is potentially endangered.

Munichi (or *Muniche*) [164] Peru, Department of Loreto, village of Muniches on the Paranapura River. *Language Isolate.* The language is moribund, with three speakers reported by SIL in 1988.

Nadëb (or *Nadöbö, Anodöb, Makunadöbö, Guariba, Guariba-Tapuyo, Kabori, Xiriwai*) [135a] Brazil, northwestern Amazonas State, Middle Rio Negro area, on the Uneiuxi and Japurá rivers, Terra Indígena Paraná Boá-Boá (Lago Jutaí), Terra Indígena Rio Téa, Terra Indígena Uneiuxi, and Terra Indígena Alto Rio Negro. *Makuan.* Pozzobon (1994) reports that the Nadëb are divided into two groups, one living in the vicinity of the town Santa Isabel do Rio Negro, and the other living in the interfluvial regions (Riacho Escondido). Those living near Santa Isabel are reported to be partially assimilated into the local Brazilian culture, and may be losing their native language. Those in Riacho Escondido were all full speakers at the time of the article. With around 400 speakers out of an ethnic group of the same size, the language is endangered.

Nahua (or ***Yora***, ***Yaminahua***, ***Parquenahua***) **[227]** Peru, Department of Ucayali, in Sepahua on the Urubamba River and in Serjali on the Upper Mishagua (Lower Urubamba); Department of Madre de Dios on the Upper Manu, Lower Cashpajali, and Panagua rivers in the Manu National Park. *Panoan,* South-Central. The Nahua or Yora were contacted in 1984, which resulted in the death of more than half of the group. There are about 170 contacted Nahua left, but the group seems to be growing again. Members of the Yaminahua group, who had been contacted twenty years earlier and whose language is quite similar to Nahua, facilitated the contact. The Yaminahua within the contacted Nahua group have imposed themselves as leaders and are forcing their language on the Nahua. The language is seriously endangered with 170 speakers out of an ethnic group of the same size. The possibility exists that there are another 400 uncontacted speakers on the Upper Piedras River.

Nahukwá (or ***Nahukuá***, ***Nafuquá***) **[413a]** Brazil, Mato Grosso State Parque Indígena do Xingu, on the Karaunánya River, tributary of the Kuluene River. *Cariban,* Southern, Upper Xingu, Kalapalo. The Nahukwá are one of the four Cariban groups currently living in the Xingu Indigenous Park, the others being the Kalapalo, Matipú and Kuikuro. Although they speak dialects of the same language (Upper-Xingu Carib or Kalapalo), each of these groups sees itself as distinct from the others. The Nahukwá have been living with the Matipú for a few years. Most still speak their native language, which is seriously endangered with an ethnic group of only about 105 members (2002).

Nambikwara **[329]** Brazil, western Mato Grosso, Terra Indígena Nambikwara; southeastern Rondônia State, Vilhena. *Nambikwaran.* The Nambikwara linguistic family consists of three main groups: **Northern Nambikwara** (a.o. Mamindê, Latundê, Nakarotê), **Southern Nambikwara** (a.o. Sararé) and **Sabanê**. **Northern Nambikwara** and **Southern Nambikwara** are collective names for groups of languages that are mutually intelligible. Sabanê is represented by a single language, which is very different from all other Nambikwaran languages. Although first contacts occurred in the eighteenth century, the first large-scale contact with the outside world was with the Rondon expedition of 1911. The number of speakers given for the Nambikwara totals 1,145 (1999), which would classify the language family as endangered. However, it should be kept in mind that this is the number for all Nambikwaran languages, of which most are seriously endangered.

Ñandeva (or ***Chiripá***, ***Ava-Chiripá***, ***Ava-Guaraní***) **[182]** Brazil, Mato Grosso do Sul and Paraná states, Iguatemi River and its tributaries, also near the juncture of the Iguatemi

153

and Paraná rivers. *Tupian*, Tupi-Guarani, Guarani (I). Just as in the case of the other Guarani groups in Brazil, language use is still vigorous among the Ñandeva. With an ethnic group of 8,000–10,000 members the Ñandeva language is to be considered potentially endangered in Brazil (more in Paraguay).

Nanti (or *Cogapacori, Kogapakori, Kugapakori*) **[123e]** Peru, southeast, on the head-waters of the Camisea and Timpia rivers, in the communities Montetoni and Mar-anxejari. *Arawakan*, Maipuran, Southern Maipuran, Campa. Nanti is closely related to Machiguenga. With about 250 speakers out of an ethnic group of the same size, the language is to be considered seriously endangered.

Naruvoto **[400a, not mapped]** Brazil, Mato Grosso State. *Cariban*. The exact affiliation and location of this Carib group remains unclear. Instituto Socioambiental (2004c) mentions an ethnic group of seventy-eight (2003), which would classify the language as seriously endangered.

Ñengatú (or *Nheengatu, Yeral, Geral*) **[341c]** Venezuela, Amazonas State, border area with Brazil, Río Negro area, on the Lower Guainía in, among others, San Pedro and Bultón. *Tupian*, Tupi-Guarani, Tupi (III). This Tupí-Guaraní-based creole with heavy Arawakan and Portuguese influences was used as a lingua franca from the end of the sixteenth century onwards. Used by the Jesuits as a tool for catechisation and coloni-sation purposes, the language was spoken by the Kurripako, Baniva, Baré, Tucano, Warekena, Puinave, Guahibo and Yavitero. Although today there are very few – if any – speakers of the language left in Venezuela, the 1992 Indigenous Census registered 774 'ethnic' Yeral. The language is to be considered seriously endangered in Venezuela (more in Brazil).

Nheengatu (or *Língua Geral, Língua Geral Amazônica*) **[341c]** Brazil, Amazonas State, Upper Rio Negro, Vaupés area; Lower Rio Negro, São Gabriel da Cachoeira Municipality, especially between the Curicuriari and Maré rivers. *Tupian*, Tupi-Guarani, Tupi (III). Nheengatu is a creolised version of Tupinambá (Tupi-Guarani), which was spread from the east coast by white merchants and mis-sionaries. From the late seventeenth century up to the middle of the nineteenth century it was the lingua franca of the whole Amazon region. In the Vaupés area, it is being replaced by Tukano as a lingua franca and today it is only understood by older people. All speakers of Nheengatu know Tukano as a second language. Despite some 3,000 reported speakers in 1977 (SIL), the language is to be considered endangered.

Nivaclé (or *Nivaklé, Nivaglé, Chulupí, Ashluslay*) **[258]** Argentina, Province of Salta, departments of Rivadavia and San Martín, on the outskirts of Tartagal, and in Misión La Paz. *Mataco-Mataguayan*. The first whites that contacted the Nivaclé were the anthropologists Hermann and Nordenskiöld in 1908. It was not until after the Chaco War (1932–5) that the Nivaclé accepted living under the regime of Catholic and Protestant missions, where they continued their traditional lifestyle in spite of the opposition of the missionaries. Estimates of the number of the ethnic group vary from 200 to 1,200 persons (more in Paraguay), who all speak the language. Nevertheless, Nivaclé is to be considered endangered.

Nivaclé (or *Nivaklé*, *Nivaglé*, *Niwaqlé*, *Chulupí*, *Ashluslay*) [258] Paraguay, Department of Boquerón, Pedro P. Peña, Mariscal Estigarribia, Menno, Fernheim (Filadelfia), and Neuland (Cayin'ô Clim) districts, Department of Presidente Hayes, Pozo Colorado and Villa Hayes districts. *Mataco-Mataguayan*. The Nivaclé can be subdivided into the following four groups: the **Tovoc Lhavós** 'river people', the **Yita'a Lhavós** 'forest people', the **Jotoy Lhavós** (to the north of the Mennonite colonies), and the **Tavashay Lhavós**, who are in close contact with the Maká. The 1992 census registered 7,725 speakers of Nivaclé out of an ethnic group of approximately 7,930 members (more in Argentina). In Paraguay, the language is to be considered potentially endangered.

Nomatsiguenga (or *Inato*, *Ina'o*, *Inthome*, *Intsome*) [123c] Peru, between the Ene and Perené rivers, in the Province of Satipo, District of Pangoa. *Arawakan*, Maipuran, Southern Maipuran, Campa. All children acquire the language, which is potentially endangered with an estimated 4,000–4,500 speakers out of an ethnic group of approximately the same size. There is a bilingual education programme.

Nonuya [187] Colombia, on the Middle Caquetá, Villa Azul, and on the Lower Putumayo. *Witotoan*. Just like the other indigenous groups of the region, the Nonuya fell victim to the rubber boom in the first half of the twentieth century. Through the activities of the English-Peruvian rubber company Casa Arana, tens of thousands of Indians either died from hard labour or murder, or had to flee from their territories. Today the Nonuya language is moribund, with two speakers out of an ethnic group of approximately 200 persons.

Nukak [139] Colombia, departments of Guaviare and Guainía, between the Guaviare River and the Upper Inírida. *Makuan*. Most Makuan groups did not enter into contact with white people until the twentieth century. The Nukak, however, were first contacted in 1988. Nukak and Kakua are sometimes considered the same language, because they share a large percentage of their lexicon and supposedly are mutually intelligible. With some 380 members in the ethnic group, the language is to be considered endangered.

Nukini (or *Nuquini*, *Nukuíni*) [237b] Brazil, northwestern Acre State, from the Upper Môa to the Rio Sungarú in Juruá, Municipality of Mâncio Lima, Terra Indígena Nukini. *Panoan*, South-Central, Unclassified. While the Nukini ethnic group consists of 458 members (2001), it is not clear whether the language is still spoken.

Ocaina [186] Colombia, on the Igará-Panará and the Lower Putumayo rivers. *Witotoan*, Witoto, Ocaina. During the rubber boom many Ocaina were slaughtered and all were exposed to the white man's diseases. During a border dispute between 1930 and 1935 landowners transported many Ocaina across the Putumayo River into Peru. In the late 1950s about 200 were living in Peru and possibly three to four families in Colombia. In Colombia, the Ocaina language is seriously endangered today, with approximately 125 members in the ethnic group (more in Peru).

Ocaina [186] Peru, northeast, along the Yaguasyacu, Ampiyacu, Putumayo and Algodón rivers. *Witotoan*, Witoto, Ocaina. At the end of the nineteenth century, the

155

Witotoan group, to which the Ocaina belong, was estimated to be over 50,000 people. During the rubber boom many were slaughtered and all were exposed to the white man's diseases. By the first decade of the twentieth century only 7,000–10,000 had survived, among them 2,000 Ocaina. Originally living in Colombia, land-owners transported many Ocaina during a border dispute in 1930–5 across the Putomayo River into Peru. As a result of mixed marriages with Bora and Witoto (Murui), and because of the spreading Castellanisation, Ocaina speakers have been switching to Bora, Witoto and Spanish. Today the language is seriously endangered, with approximately fifty speakers out of an ethnic group of 150 (more in Colombia).

Ofaié (or *Opayé*, *Ofayé-Xavante*) [308] Brazil, Mato Grosso do Sul State, Brasilândia Municipality, Terra Indígena Ofaié-Xavante. *Macro-Ge*, Ofaye. It is estimated that at the beginning of the twentieth century there were still about 1,000 Ofaié living in their traditional territory on the Ivinhema, Verde and Pardo rivers, right-bank tributaries of the Panará, as well as on the Anhandui, tributary of the Pardo river, in the south of Mato Grosso do Sul. Today the ethnic group consists of approximately fifty-six persons (1999), of whom perhaps twenty-five still speak the Ofaié language. Therefore, the Ofaié language is to be considered seriously endangered.

Omagua (or *Kambeba*, *Kambewa*, *Cambeba*) [343] Brazil, Amazonas State, Solimões River area, Tefé Municipality, Santa Cruz on the right bank of the Solimões River, and Terra Indígena Kokama; Maraã Municipality, Terra Indígena Jaquiri; Alvarães Municipality, Terra Indígena Igarapé Grande. *Tupian*, Tupi-Guarani, Tupi (III). The language is seriously endangered with perhaps a few speakers in the ethnic group of 156 members (2000) (more in Peru).

Omagua (or *Omagua-Yeté*, *Ariana*, *Pariana*, *Anapia*, *Macanipa*, *Yhuata*, *Umaua*, *Cambeba*, *Campeba*, *Cambela*, *Canga-Peba*, *Agua*, *Omaguino*) [343] Peru, Department of Loreto, San Joaquín de Omaguas, San Salvador de Omaguas, El Porvenir, Grau, and other settlements on the left bank of the Lower Marañón, near to the mouth of the Ucayali. *Tupian*, Tupi-Guarani, Tupi (III). Persons above forty years of age used to understand their parents, but do not speak the language themselves. Although the ethnic group was reported to have approximately 630 members in 1976, the language is moribund in Peru (more in Brazil).

Ona (or *Selk'nam*) [246a] Chile, Isla Grande de Tierra de Fuego. *Chonan*. The Ona nomadic hunters were the first to succumb to the impact of foreign culture. Whereas in 1880 the ethnic group consisted of about 4,000 members, there were only two direct descendants of the Ona left in 1980. Today the language may be considered extinct in Chile and Argentina.

Orejón (or *Coto*, *Orechón*, *Payagua*, *Tutapi*) [151] Peru, Department of Loreto, along the Yanayacu, Sucusari, Putumayo, and Algodón rivers. *Tucanoan*, Western Tucanoan, Southern. During the rubber boom at the turn of the twentieth century the Orejón experienced great suffering and the loss of many lives. The younger generation has abandoned the language and most of the Orejón culture. The language is seriously endangered, with approximately 220 speakers out of an ethnic group of 290.

Oro Win (*Oro Towati*) **[66]** Brazil, western Rondônia State, Terra Indígena Pacaás-Novos. *Chapacuran.* The first encounter between the Oro Win and Westerners took place in 1963 on the headwaters of the Pacaás Novos River. The group was almost exterminated after two attacks by outsiders. Today the language is moribund with five speakers in the ethnic group of fifty (2000).

Pacahuara (or *Pacaguara*) **[233]** Bolivia, Department of Beni, Province of Vaca Díez, near the Chácobo community of Alto Ivón. *Panoan,* Southern. There are eighteen speakers out of an ethnic group of nineteen. It is thought that there are still another fifty Pacahuara in about eight families scattered between the Rio Negro and Pacahuaras rivers in the Province of Federico Román, Department of Pando. The Pacahuara form a sad example of how Western 'civilisation' has exterminated native cultures in South America. The language is moribund.

Páez (or *Nasa Yuwe*) **[15]** Colombia, eastern slopes of Central Andes Range, Tierradentro zone between the departments of Huila and Cauca. *Language Isolate.* With approximately 118,845 members – 16.93 per cent of the total indigenous population of Colombia – the Páez form the second largest ethnic group of Colombia after the Guajiro. With about 40,000 speakers, most of whom are bilingual in Spanish, the language is potentially endangered.

Paï-Tavyterä (or *Kaiova*, *Kaiowa*, *Avá*) **[335c]** Paraguay, Eastern, Department of Amambay, Pedro J. Caballero, Bella Vista, and Capitán Bado districts, Department of Concepción, Concepción, Horqueta, and Yby Yaa'ú districts, Department of Canindeyú, Ygatymí and Itanará districts, and Department of San Pedro, District of Guayaibi. *Tupian,* Tupi-Guarani, Guarani (I). Among the Paï-Tavyterä many suicides have been registered in the past years. This may be attributed to the fact that the cultivation and commercialisation of soy has robbed many communities of their territories and forced them into small urban spaces. In Paraguay, the language is endangered with just about 600 speakers out of an ethnic group of 8,025 (more in Brazil). The vast majority of the ethnic group (91.63 per cent), however, claims to speak a variety of Paraguayan Guaraní according to the 1992 census.

Palikur (or *Paliku'ene*, *Aukwayene*, *Aukuyene*) **[107a]** Brazil, on the border with French Guiana in the extreme north of Amapá State, on the banks of the Urucauá River, right-bank tributary of the Uaçá between the Uaçá and the curipi rivers, Oiapoque Municipality, Terra Indígena Uaçá I and II, in ten villages. *Arawakan,* Maipuran, Eastern Maipuran. The Palikur language is called *Pa'ikwaki* by its speakers. Many Palikur also speak or understand Patuá, the Creole language used as a lingua franca in the region. The majority of the educated younger generation and some men speak Portuguese. With an ethnic group of approximately 918 members (2000) the language is endangered (more in French Guiana).

Palikur **[107a]** French Guiana, in the central coast area, and on the Lower Oyapock River. *Arawakan,* Maipuran, Eastern Maipuran. There are about 500 in the ethnic group (more in Brazil). Like Arawak, Palikur is seriously endangered in French Guiana, since it is spoken near urban centres.

157

Panará (*Krenhakarore, Krenakore, Krenakarore, Kreen-Akarore, Índios Gigantes*) [286] Brazil, northern Mato Grosso State, Parque Indígena do Xingu; southwestern Pará State, on the Iriri River, Terra Indígena Panará, Nãspotiti village. *Macro*-Ge, Ge, Northern Ge. The Panará group, last descendants of the Southern Kayapó, was decimated by the white man's diseases after the first contacts with Western society in 1973. In 1975, they were brought by aeroplane from their traditional territory on the Peixoto de Azvedo River to the Xingu Indigenous Park, but after twenty years of forced dislocation they were able to recover part of their traditional territory on the Iriri River in the border area between Mato Grosso and Pará states. All Panará speak their native language and many also speak Kayapó or Suyá, or both. Nearly all understand some Portuguese, but only a few men speak it relatively fluently. With 250 members (2003) the ethnic group is growing once again, but the language remains seriously endangered.

Panare (or *E'ñepa, Mapoyo*) [421] Venezuela, Bolivar State: District of Cedeño, on the Cuchivero and Guaniamo rivers. Amazonas State: in the interethnic communities of Caño Culebra (Panare-Hoti), Coromoto II (Panare-Piaroa) and Majagua (Panare-Yabarana-Piaroa-Yekuana, and non-indigenous), in all communities of the Municipality of Atures on the Orinoco. *Cariban*, Northern, Western Guiana. Up to a few years ago the ethnic group of approximately 3,130 members had had few contacts with the outside non-indigenous world, but recent invasions into their territory by *criollo* settlers have led to growing bilingualism in Spanish among the speakers. The language is potentially endangered.

Pankararu (or *Pancararu, Pankaru, Pankararé, Pancararé*) [317] Brazil, Pernambuco State, Petrolândia and Tacaratu municipalities, Terra Indígena Pankararu (Pankararu); Bahia State, Glória and Nova Glória municipalities, Terra Indígena Brejo do Burgo, Terra Indígena Pankararé (Pankararé); Serra do Ramalho Municipality, Terra Indígena Vargem Alegre (Pankaru). *Language Isolate*. The three Pankararu subgroups, Pankararu (4,146 in 1999), Pankararé (1,500 in 2001) and Pankaru (eighty-four in 1999) total some 5,730 persons who today all speak Portuguese. The Pankararu language is extinct.

Parakanã (or *Paracanã, Apiterewa*) [346] Brazil, southeastern Pará State, Terra Indígena Parakanã, Terra Indígena Apyterewa, Terra Indígena Trincheira/Bacajá. *Tupian*, Tupi-Guarani, Tenetehara (IV). The Parakanã language is closely related to both Asurini do Tocantins and Suruí do Tocantins and lately these three languages have been considered to be dialects of the same language *Akwawa*. Most Parakanã still speak their mother tongue and with approximately 753 members (2001) in the ethnic group the language is to be considered endangered.

Parecí (or *Paresí, Arití, Halití*) [110] Brazil, western Mato Grosso State, on the Jubá, Guaporé, Verde, Papagaio, Burití and Juruena rivers, Terra Indígena Est. Parecis, Terra Indígena Estivadinho, Terra Indígena Figueiras, Terra Indígena Juininha, Terra Indígena Pareci, Terra Indígena Rio Formoso, Terra Indígena Umutina, and Terra Indígena Utiariti. *Arawakan*, Maipuran, Central Maipuran. The Parecí are closely related to the Saraveca of Bolivia. It is unclear how many speakers are left in the ethnic group of about 1,293 persons (1999).

Parintintin [354] Brazil, southern Amazonas State, Juruá, Jutaí and Purus rivers area, Municipality of Humaitá, Terra Indígena Ipixuna, Terra Indígena Nove de Janeiro. *Tupian*, Tupi-Guarani, Kawahib (VI). The Parintintin form part of a bigger group of peoples that call themselves **Kagwahiva**. With an ethnic group of 156 members (2000) the language is to be considered seriously endangered.

Patamona (or **Kapon**, **Akawaio**) [401a] Brazil, northern Roraima State, Terra Indígena Raposa/Serra do Sol. *Cariban*, Northern, East-West-Guiana, Macushi-Kapon, Kapon. In Brazil, the Patamona language is seriously endangered with an ethnic group of some fifty members (1991) (more in Guyana and Venezuela).

Patamona (or **Kapon**) [401a] Guyana, west-central, upland savanna in the Pakaraima Mountains. *Cariban*, Northern, East-West Guiana, Macushi-Kapon, Kapon. Patamona, Ingarikó and Akawaio belong to the Cariban subbranch Kapón, which at its turn is closely related to Pemón and Macushi. There are 5,000 in the ethnic group (more in Venezuela and Brazil). The language is potentially endangered in Guyana.

Patamona (or **Kapón**) [401a] Venezuela, eastern border area with Guyana and Brazil. *Cariban*, Northern, East-West Guiana, Macushi-Kapon, Kapon. With no more than 200 members in the ethnic group, Patamona is to be considered seriously endangered in Venezuela (more in Guyana and Brazil).

Pataxó (or **Pataxó do Norte**, **Pataxó do Sur**, **Hã Hã Hãe**) [302] Brazil, Bahia State, on more than ten Indigenous Lands. *Macro-Ge*, Maxakali. The Pataxó group can be subdivided into the **Pataxó** (or **Pataxó do Norte**) and the **Hã Hã Hãe** (**Pataxó do Sur**). One of the last speakers, if not the last, of Pataxó was encountered in 1982 in the Indigenous Park of Paraguaçu. Today all Pataxó speak Portuguese and the language is to be considered extinct. With 2,790 Pataxó and 1,865 Pataxó Hã Hã Hãe, the ethnic group totals 4,655 persons (1998).

Paumarí (or **Palmarí**) [131] Brazil, Amazonas State, Middle Purus Basin with its tributaries Ituxi, Sepatini and Tapauá, on six Indigenous Lands. *Arauan*. The Paumarí are the Arauan group that has been most in contact with Westerners. Today only the older peoples still speak Paumarí, while the younger ones speak either Portuguese or a mixture of Portuguese and Paumarí. The language is seriously endangered, with approximately 290 speakers out of an ethnic group of 870 (2000).

Paunaca [118] Bolivia, Department of Santa Cruz, Province of Ñuflo de Chávez. *Arawakan*, Maipuran, Southern Maipuran. In spite of the complete 'chiquitanisation' (assimilation by Chiquitano) of other Arawakan groups such as the Sarareca– there are still about five speakers out of an ethnic group of 150 of the Arawakan language Paunaca in Concepción de Ñuflo de Chávez and in two settlements north of it. The language is moribund.

Pauserna-Guarasug'we [339] Bolivia, departments of Beni (Province of Alto Iténez) and Santa Cruz (Province of Velasco) where the Paraguá river flows into the Iténez (or Guaporé). *Tupian*, Tupi-Guarani, Pauserna. In the early 1960s, the German anthropologist Riester witnessed the last days of the Pauserna-Guarasug'we as an ethnic group. The 1994 census reports an ethnic group of forty-six without any speakers. In Bolivia, the language is possibly extinct (possibly more in Brazil).

Pemón (or ***Arekuna***, ***Arecuna***, ***Taurepang***, ***Taurepan***, ***Kamarakoto***) **[400]** Venezuela, Bolivar State, southeast, Gran Sabana, from the Caroní and Paragua rivers until the border area with Guyana. *Cariban*, Northern, East-West Guiana, Macushi-Kapon, Kapon. With approximately 19,130 members, the Pemón form the biggest Cariban group in Venezuela. This Cariban subbranch can be divided into three dialect subgroups: **Arekuna**, **Taurepang**, and **Kamarakoto**. Some of the adults are still monolingual, but the younger generation is becoming bilingual in Spanish. The language is potentially endangered (more in Brazil and Guyana).

Pepojivi (or ***Playero***, ***Guahibo Playero***) **[68b]** Colombia, Arauca River, border area with Venezuela, Arauca Division, on the banks of the Arauca River from Gaviotas Island to Arauca. *Guahiban*. There are about 150 to 160 speakers out of an ethnic group of the same size. In Colombia, the language is seriously endangered due to the reduced size of its ethnic group (more in Venezuela).

Pepojivi (or ***Playero***, ***Guahibo Playero***) **[68b]** Venezuela, western zone of Apure State, to the north of the Arauca River and the Colombian Pepojivi settlements. *Guahiban*. There are about 200 speakers out of an ethnic group of the same size. The language is endangered (more in Colombia).

Piapoco (or ***Piapoko***, ***Tsáçe***) **[76]** Colombia, in the region of the Lower Vichada River and its tributaries, on the Meta and Guaviare rivers. *Arawakan*, Maipuran, Northern Maipuran, Inland. There are about 4,470 speakers out of an ethnic group of the same size (more in Venezuela). Piapoco-Guahibo bilingualism, and even Piapoco-Guahibo-Spanish trilingualism is augmenting. The language is to be considered potentially endangered.

Piapoko (or ***Piapoco***, ***Tsáçe***) **[76]** Venezuela, Amazonas State: on the banks of the Orinoco, near the mouth of the Guaviare and Atabapo rivers, in the settlements of Laja Lisa and Primavera, Kupaven River; the neighbourhood of Punta E'Lara in San Fernando de Atabapo, Municipality of Atabapo; along the Atabapo; settlements of Agua Blanca and Picatonal, Municipality of Atures; settlement of El Diamante, on the cross-road Puerto Ayacucho-El Burro (Municipality of Atures de Amazonas); Bolivar State: near the Villacoa River (Municipality of Cedeño). *Arawakan*, Maipuran, Northern Maipuran, Inland. The language is closely related to Warekena. In 1992, there were approximately 1,330 speakers out of an ethnic group of the same size (more in Colombia). Piapoko is to be considered potentially endangered.

Piaroa (or ***Uwotjüja***, ***U'wuthuja***, ***Wuöthuja***, ***De'aruwa***) **[426]** Venezuela, northwest zone of Amazonas State, west to east from the Orinoco River to the Manapiare River, and north to south from the Suapure River to the Ventuari. *Saliba-Piaroan*. The genetic relationship between Piaroa and Sáliva remains putative and needs to be investigated more thoroughly. Because of the strong ethnic conscience of its speakers, the Piaroa language is conserved to a high degree. In 1992 the Indigenous Census registered 11,540 Piaroa (more in Colombia). In Venezuela, the language is potentially endangered.

Piaroa **[426]** Colombia, extreme east of the Department of Vaupés, especially on the border with Venezuela, on the banks of the smaller tributaries of the Manaveni, Vichada, Guaviare, and Zama rivers, Selva de Matavén, Resguardo Matavén Fruta. *Saliba-Piaroan*. Lately the Piaroa living in the Resguardo Matavén have been trying to take measures to safeguard their way of life for the future. Thus, attempts will be made to restrict large-scale hunting and fishing. The ethnic group consists of some 800 members (more in Venezuela). In Colombia, the language is to be considered endangered.

Pilagá (or ***Pitelaya Laqtak***) **[261]** Argentina, Province of Formosa, departments of Patiño and Bermejo. *Guaicuruan*. There are about 4,000 speakers out of an ethnic group of the same size. Depending on age, level of formal education, and frequency of use of Spanish, the language exhibits several grades of vitality. The language is potentially endangered.

Pirahã (or ***Mura-Pirahã***) **[252]** Brazil, Amazonas State, Tapajós and Madeira rivers area, on the Maici River, a tributari of the Marmelos which again flows into the Madeira, Terra Indígena Pirahã. *Muran*. Pirahã seems to be the only surviving member of the Mura linguistic family. The Pirahã group has managed to retain its culture and language partly through rejecting the surrounding Western culture. Most men understand Portuguese, though not all can express themselves in this language. Women understand very little Portuguese and never use it to express themselves. The language is endangered with an ethnic group of some 360 members (2000).

Piratapuya (or ***Piratapuia***, ***Pira-Tapuia***, ***Piratapuyo***, ***Waíkana***) **[161]** Brazil, northwestern Amazonas State, Terra Indígena Rio Negro, Terra Indígena Médio Rio Negro I, Terra Indígena Médio Rio Negro II, Terra Indígena Rio Téa. *Tucanoan*, Eastern Tucanoan, Northern. Piratapuya shares a great part of its lexicon with Wanano. As is the case with other Eastern Tucanoan groups, marriage is exogamous among the Piratapuya and marrying someone from the same language group is considered incestuous. Interestingly enough, Piaratapuya and Wanano are considered each other's kin and, therefore, cannot intermarry (cf. Aikhenvald 2002). With an ethnic group of 1,004 (2001) the language is to be considered endangered (more in Colombia).

Piratapuyo (***Piratapuya***) **[161]** Colombia, Department of Vaupés, along the Lower Papurí River. *Tucanoan*, Eastern Tucanoan, Northern. The language is endangered, with an ethnic group consisting of about 630 members (more in Brazil).

Pisamira (or ***Pápiwa***) **[161c]** Colombia, Department of Vaupés, in the village of Yacayacá, on the right bank of the Vaupés River, about 35km to the southeast of Mitú. *Tucanoan*, Eastern Tucanoan, Central, Bara. The language is seriously endangered with about twenty-five speakers out of an ethnic group of fifty-five (more in Brazil).

Potiguara (or ***Potyguara***) **[341d]** Brazil, north coast of Paraíba State, Baía de Traição, Marcação and Rio Tinto municipalities, Terra Indígena Potiguara, Terra Indígena Jacaré de São Domingos and Terra Indígena Potyguara de Monte-Mór. *Unclassified*

161

(for lack of data). The Potiguara are said to have spoken a Tupi-Guarani language, but according to Fabre (1998) the language cannot be classified for lack of data. Today all Potiguara speak Portuguese and the language may be considered extinct. Including the historically related Pitaguari group (Ceará State, Maracanaú Municipality, Pitaguari Mountain, Terra Indígena Pitaguari), the ethnic group now totals 8,446 persons (2002).

Poyanawa (***Poianáua***) **[230]** Brazil, Acre, on the Upper Rio Môa, tributary of the Jumá, Mâncio Lima Municipality, Terra Indígena Poyanawa. *Panoan*, South-Central, Yaminahua-Sharanahua. The language is moribund with two speakers out of an ethnic group of 403 (1999).

Puinave (or ***Wántyinhet***) **[138]** Colombia, Department of Guainía, near to the Inírida River and its tributary Bocón; on the banks of the Orinoco, and along the Guaviare. *Language Isolate*. Puinave has sometimes been linked to the Makuan languages, postulating a Maku-Puinavean linguistic family. As long as a genetic relationship between Puinave and Makuan still remains to be proven, Puinave may best be considered a language isolate. The language is potentially endangered, with approximately 5,380 members in the ethnic group (more in Venezuela).

Puinave **[138]** Venezuela, Amazonas State, lower part of the Guaviare and Inírida river basins down to the San Fernando de Atabapo region. *Language Isolate*. Puinave has sometimes been linked to the Makuan languages, postulating a Maku-Puinavean linguistic family. A genetic relationship between Puinave and Makuan, however, still remains to be proven. Although the Puinave language and culture are conserved within the ethnic group of approximately 775 members, bilingualism is incipient. In Venezuela, the language is to be considered endangered (more in Colombia).

Puroborá **[380]** Brazil, southern Rondônia, Costa Marques vicinity and possibly in Guajará-Mirim. *Tupian*, Purobora. Despite the fact that the Puroborá are one of the earliest mentioned ethnic groups of Rondônia (early twentieth century), the language has been poorly documented until now. With two possible speakers in an ethnic group of fifty the language is moribund.

Quechua (or ***Quichua***) Colombia, Ecuador, Peru, Bolivia, and Argentina, from the departments of Caquetá, Nariño and Putumayo in southern Colombia discontinuously to the Province of Santiago del Estero in the lowlands of Argentina. *Quechuan*. The numerous Quechua dialects may differ considerably and are often not mutually intelligble. Even though the number of Quechua speakers is estimated between 8.5 million and 10 million, the language is to be considered potentially endangered due to the lack of intergenerational transmission in many regions, resulting in a language shift to Spanish.

Quichua Santiagueño **[206c]** Argentina, north central Argentina, Province of Santiago del Estero and southeast Province of Salta. *Quechuan*, Quechua IIC. Language use is still fairly vigorous and the estimated number of speakers runs from 60,000 to 100,000. According to Stark (1985), the vitality of the language has to be attributed to the fact that it has long been conceptualised as a non-Indian *criollo* language, and that this belief is tied to the historical interpretation that *Quichua Santiagueño* was brought to Santiago del Estero by the Spaniards, an assumption which has served to disassociate the language from its Indian past. During the past decades many speakers of the dialect migrated to the cities of Buenos Aires, Rosario, Córdoba and Mendoza. The language is potentially endangered.

Resígaro (or ***Resígero***) **[87]** Peru, in the northeastern Bora and Ocaina communities Puerto Isago and Brillo Nuevo. *Arawakan*, Maipuran, Northern Maipuran, Inland (heavily influenced by Bora). The Resígaro group seems to have dissolved within the Bora and Ocaina communities in which they settled. The language is moribund, with fourteen reported speakers by SIL in 1976.

Reyesano (or ***Maropa***) **[239]** Bolivia, Department of Beni, Province of Ballivián, southwest of the Beni River, in Santa Rosa and Reyes. *Tacanan*, Araona-Tacana, Cavineña-Tacana, Tacana Proper. Including semi-speakers and rememberers, the 1994 census registered 245 speakers out of an ethnic group of 1,130. Recent reports, however, state that there are only about ten elderly speakers left. The language is seriously endangered.

Rikbaktsá (or ***Erikbaktsá***, ***Erigpaktsá***, ***Orelhas de Pau***, ***Canoeiros***) **[284]** Brazil, northwestern Mato Grosso State, Juruena River Basin, Terra Indígena Erikbaktsa, Terra Indígena Japuíra, and Terra Indígena do Escondido. *Macro-Ge*, Rikbaktsa. The Rikbaktsá are also known as *Canoeiros*, 'Canoe People', because of their great ability with canoes or *Orelhas de Pau*, 'Wooden Ears', after the large wooden plugs in their earlobes. Known as ferocious warriors until the 1960s, more than 75 per cent of the Rikbaktsá population died from influenza, chickenpox and smallpox epidemics during and after the so-called 'pacification' process effected by Jesuit missionaries and financed by rubber planters between 1957 and 1962. Today the Rikbaktsá are bilingual in Portuguese. The younger generation is more fluent in Portuguese, because they speak it more regularly. The older generation, on the other hand, has more difficulties speaking Portuguese and only uses it for communication with the Western world. With an ethnic group of approximately 909 (2001) the language is endangered.

Sabanê **[331]** Brazil, western Mato Grosso State, Terra Indígena Pirineus de Souza, southeastern Rondônia State, Terra Indígena Tubarão-Latundê, Vilhena. *Nambikwaran*. There are about ten speakers out of an ethnic group of 40. The language is seriously endangered.

Salamãi (or ***Sanamãika***, ***Mondé***) **[377]** Brazil, Rondônia State, Terra Indígena Tubarão-Latundê, Terra Indígena Sagarana, Porto Velho. *Tupian*, Monde. In traditional times, the group lived in the Pimenta Bueno Basin and entered into alliances with Aikanã, Kwaza and especially Kanoê groups. The language was recorded in various word lists throughout the twentieth century, but apart from lexical and phonological documentation, the language must be considered as lost. With two semi-speakers out of an ethnic group of about ten, Salamãi is moribund.

Sáliba (or ***Sáliva***) **[425]** Colombia, Department of Vichada, Municipality of Puerto Carreño: protected area of Santa Rosalia; Department of Casanare, Municipality of

Orocué: protected areas of El Consejo, El Duya, Paravare, San Juanito, El Saladillo, El Suspiro and the reservation of Macucuana; Municipality of Paz de Ariporo: protected areas of Morichito and Caño Mochuelo (Hato Corozal). *Saliba-Piaroan*. In the Orocué area the language is only conserved to a high degree among elderly women; men, youngsters and children understand everything that is said in Sáliba, but no longer express themselves in the language. Since it is not clear how many speakers are precisely left in the ethnic group of about 1,300 members, the language is to be considered endangered in Colombia (more in Venezuela).

Sáliva (or *Sáliba*) [425] Venezuela, Amazonas State, Municipality of Atures del Edo, San Pedro del Orinoco. *Saliba-Piaroan*. The Sáliba were mainly to be found in the Barraguán region on the Middle Orinoco, where they maintained close relationships with the Piaroa, a group to which they are genetically and linguistically related. In Venezuela, the language is seriously endangered with an ethnic group of approximately eighty members (more in Colombia).

Sanapaná (or *Sa'apan*, *Kasnapan*) [270] Paraguay, Department of Presidente Hayes, Pozo Colorado (La Esperanza and Nueva Promesa) and Menno districts, Department of Alto Paraguay, District of Fuerte Olimpo. *Mascoyan*. Like the related Enlhet, the Sanapaná mainly live on scattered cattle ranches and in Mennonite colonies. Having worked since the 1900s in the tannin factories on the Upper Paraguay River, they had to search for new employment locations after the bankruptcy of these companies in the past five decades. With about 785 speakers out of an ethnic group of 1,065 the language is to be considered endangered.

Sánema (or *Sánïma*, *Sánuma*) [424] Venezuela, Amazonas and Bolivar states, along the Caura, Erebato and Ventuari rivers, and along the Upper Auaris extending west to the Upper Padamo River area. *Yanomaman*. There are at least three mutually intelligible varieties of Sánema. The percentage of monolinguals is still relatively high, but in some areas up to 25 per cent of the population is bilingual in Yekuana (Cariban). With an ethnic group of approximately 1,980 members the language is to be considered potentially endangered (more in Brazil).

Sánuma (or *Sánïma*, *Sánema*) [424] Brazil, Roraima State, Terra Indígena Yanomami, on the Auaris River and its tributaries. *Yanomaman*. Sánuma is the most deviant dialect at the lexical level within the language family that it forms together with Yanomami, Yanomam and Ninam. In Brazil, the language is to be considered endangered with an ethnic group of approximately 500 members (more in Venezuela).

Sapé (*Kariana*, *Kaliana*, *Caliana*) [144] Venezuela, Bolivar State, three settlements on the Paragua and Karun rivers. *Language Isolate*. The traditional Sapé habitat was on the Middle and Upper Paragua, where they claim that at the turn of the century they were a small tribe of about 100–200 people. Epidemics, and the invasion of the Upper Paragua by the Yanam, decimated and caused the dispersal of their population. Most Sapé have intermarried with Pemón (Cariban), and a few with Uruak and Yanam (Yanomaman). These linguistically mixed marriages, especially with the economically more powerful Pemón, have led to a language shift from Sapé to Pemón. The language is to be considered moribund with five reported speakers in 1985 out of an ethnic group of twenty-eight (1992).

***Saraveca* [111]** Bolivia, Department of Santa Cruz, northeastern part of the Province of Velasco. *Arawakan*, Maipuran, Central Maipuran. The Saraveca seem, or until very recently seemed, to avoid contact with the national society. By 1962 most of the Saraveca had switched to Chiquitano. The language is possibly extinct.

***Sateré-Mawé* (or *Sataré-Maué, Sateré, Mawé*) [360]** Brazil, Middle Amazon River, border area between Amazonas and Pará states, municipalities of Maués, Barreirinha, Parintins (Amazonas), and Itaiutuba (Pará), Terra Indígena Sateré-Mawé/Andirá-Marau. *Tupian*, Maweti Guarani. Recent data show that Awetí and Sateré-Mawé probably form a separate subbranch within the Tupian linguistic family. The present state of the Sateré-Mawé language is very good, with speakers of both sexes and all ages. There are one or two villages in which Portuguese speakers abound and some people do not speak Sateré-Mawé; in some other villages, all inhabitants speak Sateré-Mawé, but knowledge of Portuguese is widespread; in some other villages, only a few people know Portuguese, with Sateré-Mawé being the only known language. In the short run, the language is healthy, despite a few signs of danger; in the long run, however, it is clearly under pressure from Portuguese and thus potentially endangered. The ethnic group consists of approximately 7,134 members (2000).

***Secoya* (or *Siona-Secoya, Pai Coca*) [149]** Ecuador, on the Aguarico and Cuyabeno rivers, in the communities of San Pablo Cantesioya and Seqoya. *Tucanoan*, Western Tucanoan, Northern, Siona-Secoya. Together with the Siona, the Secoya live in the northeastern Amazon nearby the Cofán. At the beginning of the twentieth century, the Secoya began to merge with the Siona, particularly due to intermarriage, and by the 1970s they were considered to be only one ethnic group (the Siona-Secoya). Recently, however, recognising the advantages of maintaining their distinct ethnic identities, they manifest themselves as two separate groups again: the Secoya and Siona. Their territory has been devastated by oil exploration, and in November of 1993, the Secoya and Siona fought back by suing Texaco for more than one billion dollars for a variety of environmental abuses, including dumping more than 3,000 gallons of oil a day into their lagoons. With an ethnic group of about 300 speakers, the language is to be considered endangered in Ecuador (more in Peru).

***Secoya* (or *Siona-Secoya*) [149]** Peru, along the rivers Santa María, Yubineto, Angusilla, Yaricaya and Cuyabeno (Aguarico). *Tucanoan*, Western Tucanoan, Northern, Siona-Secoya. In 1941 the Secoyas were separated by a war between Ecuador and Perú that divided the Secoya homelands. Their cultural and ancestral lands are now imperiled by geopolitical borders, the encroachment and harassment of the petroleum companies, and the impact of colonization. In Peru, the language is to be considered endangered with about 680 speakers out of an ethnic group of the same size (more in Ecuador).

***Selk'nam* (or *Ona*) [246a]** Argentina, Isla Grande de Tierra de Fuego, northwestern zone. *Chonan*. The Selk'nam hunter-gatherers and fishermen were massacred indiscriminately and systematically by nutria and seal hunters, and by farm owners who paid mercenaries for each pair of indigenous ears they brought them. At the beginning of the twentieth century the ethnic group had disintegrated and in the 1970s the last speakers died. The language is extinct in Argentina and Chile.

Selk'nam (or ***Ona***) Chile, Isla Grande de Tierra de Fuego. *Chonan.* The Selk'nam nomadic hunters were the first to succumb to the impact of foreign culture. Whereas in 1880 the ethnic group consisted of about 4,000 members, there were only two direct descendents of the Ona left in 1980. Today the language may be considered extinct in Chile and Argentina.

Shanenawá (or ***Katukina Shanenawá***) [235] Brazil, Acre State, Terra Indígena Katukina/Kaxinawa, Feijó Muncipality, on the Envira River, in the village of Morada Nueva. *Panoan*, Southeastern. The Shanenawa are considered to be a subgroup of the Katukina do Acre. Another view is that Shanenawá, Arara do Acre, Yaminawa and Yawanawá are all dialects of one language (***Arara***). With about 178 persons in the ethnic group the language is to be considered seriously endangered (1998).

Sharanahua (or ***Marinahua***, ***Mastanahua***) [226] Peru, along the Upper Purús River in the southeast of Peru near the Brazilian border. *Panoan*, South-Central, Yaminahua-Sharanahua. Wanting to assimilate to the mestizo culture, the Sharanahua have dropped many of their customs, including their traditional celebrations, music and dances. Nowadays they speak their language exclusively in their homes. There is a bilingual education programme. In Peru, the language is endangered with approximately 350–500 speakers out of an ethnic group of the same size.

Shipibo-Conibo (or ***Shipibo***, ***Caliseca***, ***Sinabo***, ***Manamabobo***, ***Manava***, ***Xipibo***, ***Chama***) [218] Peru, on the banks of the Ucayali River, more or less from Bolognesi along the Upper Ucayali to the south of the Department of Ucayali, to Contamana along the Lower Ucayali, more to the north of the Department of Ucayali; some settlements on the rivers Aguaytía, Pisqui, Lower Pachitea, Callería, Tamaya and on the shores of the lakes Imiríaand Yarinacocha. *Panoan*, North-Central. The rubber boom at the turn of the twentieth century did not have such a devastating effect on the Shipibo-Conibo group as on other indigenous groups. This may have been due to the fact that they lived on one of the major rivers with many outlets. Despite many years of contact and their proximity to the city of Pucallpa, the Shipibo-Conibo have preserved their language and culture. The language is potentially endangered, with about 16,100 speakers out of an ethnic group of the same size.

Shuar (or ***Shuar Chicham***) [168a] Ecuador, southeast, between the Pastaza and Marañón rivers, east of the present city of Cuenca along the contested border region with Peru, a rocky region covering approximately 25,000 square miles along the lower eastern slopes of the Andes. *Jivaroan.* Although the Shuar are the second largest and one of the most studied Amazonian groups, their language has barely been studied. They have a long history of survival and defence against outsiders, and have long had a reputation as headhunters and savages and as very well organised enemies of the Spaniards. In 1964, the Shuar, with support from Salesian missionaries, founded the first ethnic federation in the Ecuadorian Amazon. With an estimated 35,000 speakers of Shuar out of an ethnic group of the same size, the language is to be considered potentially endangered.

Sikiana (or *Sikiâna*, *Chikena*) **[391]** Brazil, northwestern Pará, near the border with Suriname, on the Cafuini, Turuna and Itapi rivers, Parque Indígena do Tumucumaque. *Cariban*, Northern, East-West Guiana, Waiwai, Sikiana. The status of the Sikiana ethnic group and language are unclear, since they are only mentioned by SIL and do not figure in Brazilian census numbers. With a reported ethnic group of thirty-three (SIL 1986) the language should be considered seriously endangered.

Sikiuyana **[391]** Suriname, south, among the Trio in Kwamalasamutu on the Sipaliwini River. *Cariban*, Northern, east-West Guiana, Wauwai, Sikiana. The Sikiuyana are relative latecomers to the Trio community of Kwamalasamutu. Nowadays they all speak Trio as their primary language. There are fifteen elderly speakers out of an ethnic group of fifty. The language is moribund.

Siona **[149a]** Colombia, Department of Putumayo, on the border with Ecuador, along the Putumayo River and its tributaries, between Poñuna Blanca and Poñuna Negra, in the Resguardo Buenavista as well as in El Tablero. *Tucanoan*, Western Tucanoan, Northern, Siona-Secoya. White man's diseases and atrocities committed during the rubber era reduced the number of Siona, the majority of whom now live in the Resguardo Buenavista near Puerto Asís. The language is to be considered endangered, with an ethnic group of approximately 700 members (more in Ecuador).

Siona (or *Pai Coca*, *Kokakañú*) **[149]** Ecuador, along the rivers Shushufindi, Eno, Aguarico, and Cuyabeno, in the communities of Biaña, Puerto Bolívar, and Orawaya. *Tucanoan*, Western Tucanoan, Northern, Siona-Secoya. At the beginning of the twentieth century, the Siona began to merge with the Secoya, particularly due to intermarriage, and by the 1970s they were considered to be a single ethnic group (the Siona-Secoya). Recently, however, recognising the advantages of maintaining their distinct ethnic identities, they manifest themselves as two separate groups again: the Siona and Secoya. Their territory has been devastated by oil exploration, and in November 1993 the Siona and Secoya fought back by suing Texaco for more than one billion dollars for a variety of environmental abuses, including dumping more than 3,000 gallons of oil a day into their lagoons. With about 250 speakers, the language is to be considered seriously endangered in Ecuador (more in Colombia).

Siriano **[157]** Colombia, along the Papurí, Paca and Vaupés rivers. *Tucanoan*, Eastern Tucanoan, Central, Desano. Although Siriano is closely related to Desano, with 90 per cent cognates, the two languages diverge in their use of grammatical suffixes. With an ethnic group of about 715 members, the language is to be considered endangered (more in Brazil).

Siriano **[157]** Brazil, northwestern Amazonas State, Terra Indígena Alto Rio Negro. *Tucanoan*, Eastern Tucanoan, Central, Desano. The Siriano are yet another Eastern Tucanoan group known for practising linguistic exogamy. Apart from another Tucanoan language spoken by their mothers, the members of these groups usually speak another Tucanoan language, usually Tukano, which is used as a lingua franca in the region. Siriano shares a big part of its lexicon with Desano. In Brazil, the language is seriously endangered with an ethnic group of seventeen (2001) (more in Colombia).

167

Sirionó [340] Bolivia, departments of Beni and Santa Cruz, provinces of Cercado (El Iviato) and Guarayos (along the Rio Negro). *Tupian*, Tupi-Guarani, Guarayu-Siriono-Jora (II). There are approximately 400 speakers out of an ethnic group of 420. More than half of the Sirionó ethnic group is under fifteen years of age, which implies that in a few years' time the group may become twice its current size. In the Bolivian Amazon, the Sirionó form the group with the highest percentage of bilinguals (92.2 per cent in 1994). More and more children, however, do not acquire the language, which is to be considered endangered.

Suruí (or *Paiter, Suruí de Rondônia*) [375] Brazil, eastern Rondônia State (Cacoal Municipality) and western Mato Grosso State (Rondolândia and Aripuanã municipalities), Terra Indígena Sete de Setembro, Parque Indígena Aripuanã. *Tupian*, Monde. In spite of being surrounded by Western settlers, due to the proximity of the highway BR 364, the Suruí have maintained their original lifestyle to a great extent. With approximately 920 speakers out of an ethnic group of the same size (2003) the language is to be considered endangered.

Suruí do Tocantins (or *Suruí do Paraná, Aikewara*) [346] Brazil, southeastern Pará State, São João do Araguaia Municipality, about 100km from the city of Marabá, Terra Indígena Sororó. *Tupian*, Tupi-Guarani, Tenetehara (IV). The language of the Suruí do Tocantins is closely related to both Parakanã and Asurini do Tocantins and lately these three languages have been considered to be dialects of the same language *Akwawa*. Most Suruí do Tocantins still speak their native language, but with an ethnic group of 185 (1997) the language is to be considered seriously endangered.

Suyá (or *Suiá, Mẽkisêdjê, Kisêdjê*) [289] Brazil, Mato Grosso State, Parque Indígena do Xingu and Terra Indígena Wawi, on the Suyá-Missu River, in the villages of. Ngôsokô, Roptôtxi and Beira Rio. *Macro-Ge*, Ge, Northern Ge. Although the Suyá have never really formed part of the Upper Xingu region, contact with the Xingu peoples made them take over a number of cultural traits they did not have before, such as hammocks, canoes and manioc, so that today they are considered marginal representatives of the Upper Xingu culture area (Seki 1999). With about 334 speakers out of an ethnic group of the same size the language is endangered (2002).

Tacana [238] Bolivia, Department of La Paz, Province of Iturralde (cantons of Tumupasa and Ixiamas, north of La Paz); some groups scattered along the banks of the Orton, Beni and Madre de Dios rivers. *Tacanan*, Araona-Tacana, Cavineña-Tacana, Tacana Proper. There are about 1,820 speakers out of an ethnic group of 5,060. In 1965, there were still 3,000 to 4,000 speakers of Tacana reported. This implies a massive shift to Spanish, which is spoken by 100 per cent of the Tacana population. The language is hardly spoken by children under ten years of age and, therefore, is to be considered endangered.

Taiwano (or *Taibano, Eduria*) [161d] Colombia, Department of Vaupés, on the middle part of the Pira-Paraná River and on the Cananarí. *Tukamoan*, Eastern Tucanoan, Central Southern. Barasana and Taiwano are considered to be two varieties of the same language, which differ mainly in pitch-stress on words. With only nineteen members, the ethnic group is on the brink of extinction and the language, therefore, moribund.

Tanimuca-Letuama (or ***Opaina***, ***Ufaina***, ***Retuarã***) **[150a]** Colombia, departments of Vaupés and Amazonas, on the Apoporis River near the mouth of the Pirá and on the Mirití-Paraná and its tributaries. *Tucanoan*, Western Tucanoan, Tanimuca. The language consists of two mutually intelligible dialects, Tanimuca and Letuama. The Tanimuca and Letuama also form part of the whole of Tucanoan, groups that are known for practising linguistic exogamy and for their general multilingualism. Apart from inter-group relations, they principally maintain relations with the Arawakan Yucuna (Mirití River area) and the Eastern Tucanoan Macuna (Apoporis River area). The language is no longer spoken in the communities near the non-indigenous villages. Despite the strong influence of Yucuna and Macuna, the language is still spoken on all occasions. With an ethnic group of approximately 1,800 members, the language is to be considered endangered.

Tapayuna (or ***Suyá Orientais***, ***Novos Suyá***, ***Beiço-de-Pau***) **[289a]** Brazil, Mato Grosso State, Parque Indígena do Xingu, Colider Municipality. *Macro-Ge*, Ge, Northern Ge. In 1969, after a disastrous contact with the white 'pacificators', forty-one surviving Tapayuna were transferred from their territory between the Arinos and Sangue rivers to the Suyá group in the Xingu Indigenous Park. In 1980, the Tapayuna felt strong enough to build their own village on the right bank of the Xingu River, where it flows together with the Suyá-Missu River. All Tapayuna speak their native language, which is considered a dialect of Suyá. Nevertheless, the language is seriously endangered, with an ethnic group of only fifty-eight people (1995).

Tapeba (or ***Tapebano***, ***Perna-de-Pau***) **[434]** Brazil, Ceará State, Caucaia Municipality, on the Ceará River, about 20km to the west of Fortaleza, Terra Indígena Tapeba. *Unclassified* (for lack of data). The Tapeba group may have originated from intertribal unions principally between the Potiguara, Tremembé and Kariri. Since all 2,491 Tapeba (1999) speak Portuguese today and nobody seems to speak the anchestral language, it may be assumed that it is extinct.

Tapiete (or ***Tapieté***) **[335g]** Bolivia, Department of Tarija, Province of Gran Chaco, Municipality of Villa Montes, in the communities Samaihuate and Cutaiqui, on the left bank of the Pilcomayo River. *Tupian*, Tupi-Guarani, Guarani (I). There are some seventy speakers out of an ethnic group of eighty. Most elders and women are monolingual speakers of Tapiete. Due to the small number of the ethnic group, Tapiete men are obliged to marry Weenhayek women, and, therefore, more and more children are trilingual Tapiete-Weenhayek-Spanish. In spite of its viability, the language is seriously endangered because of the small number of speakers and the progressive intermarriage with the Weenhayek group (more in Argentina and Paraguay).

Tapieté (or ***Ñandevá***) **[335g]** Argentina, Province of Salta, Misión Tapieté near Tartagal; District of San Martín, Curbita near the Pilcomayo River. *Tupian*, Tupi-Guarani, Guarani (I). It has been assumed that the Tapieté descend from a Chaco (Mataco-Mataguayan) group that was assimilated by the Chiriguano at a late stage. Although the language has been considered a dialect of Chiriguano with many loans from other

169

Chaco languages (cf. Dietrich 1986), further linguistic research needs to corroborate this. In 1995, the ethnic group consisted of 384 members (more in Bolivia). Today only persons older than twenty years use the language in every day conversation, which implies that intergenerational transmission no longer takes place. The language is endangered.

Tapirapé (or *Tapi'irape*) [345] Brazil, Tocantins State, Terra Indígena Parque Araguaia; Mato Grosso, Terra Indígena Tapirapé/Karajá and Terra Indígena Urubu Branco. *Tupian*, Tupi-Guarani, Tenetehara (IV). At the beginning of the twentieth century the Tapirapé group still consisted of some 1,500–2,000 members. Diseases and attacks by the Kayapó decimated the group, which moved from the north and the east to a village at the confluence of the Tapirapé and Araguaia rivers. The Tapirapé maintain commercial relations with the nearby Karajá, who, for instance, build canoes for them. Today the ethnic group consists of 438 members (2000), which classifies the language as endangered.

Tariana (or *Tariano*) [85] Brazil, northwestern Amazonas State, Vaupés River area, Upper Rio Negro, Terra Indígena Alto Rio Negro and Terra Indígena Médio Rio Negro II. *Arawakan*, Maipuran, Northern Maipuran, Inland. Tariana is the only Arawakan language spoken in the multilingual context of the Vaupés linguistic area (cf. Aikhenvald 1996). The language has been influenced heavily by the Tucano languages in the region. With about 100 speakers out of an ethnic group of 1,914 (2001) the language is to be considered seriously endangered (more in Colombia).

Tariana (or *Tariano*) [85] Colombia, Department of Vaupés, on the Lower Papurí River, Mitú; Department of Amazonas, Leticia. *Arawakan*, Maipuran, Northern Maipuran, Inland. Since there are no known speakers left in the ethnic group of approximately 330 members, the language is possibly extinct in Colombia (more in Brazil).

Tatuyo [155a] Colombia, Department of Vaupés, on the Upper and Middle Pirá and its tributaries, on the Ti (Upper Papurí), and in the village of Yapú on the Papurí. *Tucanoan*, Eastern Tucanoan, Central, Tatuyo. The Tatuyo form part of the whole of Eastern Tucanoan groups, which are known for practising linguistic exogamy and for their general multilingualism. They principally maintain relations with the Bará, Carapana, Macuna, Barasana, and Taiwano. The language is endangered, with about 300 speakers out of an ethnic group of the same size.

Taurepang (or *Taulipang*, *Pemon*, *Arekuna*) [400b] Brazil, Roraima State, Lavrado region, Terra Indígena Raposa/Serra do Sol, Monte Roraima. *Cariban*, Northern, East-West Guiana, Macushi-Kapon, Kapon. Taurepang is considered to be a dialect of the Cariban subbranch Pemón, which at its turn is closely related to the Cariban subbranch Kapón, to which Ingarikó, Patamona, and Akawaio (Guyana, Venezuela) belong. Most Taurepang still speak their native language, which is to be considered seriously endangered (more in Guyana and Venezuela).

Taushiro (or *Pinche*) [179] Peru, Department of Loreto, Province of Loretos, Tigre District: along the mountain streams Aucayacu and Quebrada de Legia, and the Tigre

River basin. *Unclassified* (for lack of information). In the 1950s there still were fifty speakers of Taushiro, by the 1960s this number had been reduced to thirty. Due to an epidemic disease in the same decade and to the fact that most survivors have inter-married with non-Taushiro speakers and have adopted Spanish or a variety of Que-chua, the language is now moribund with seven speakers out of an ethnic group of twenty.

Tehuelche (or ***P'e:nk'enk***, ***Aonek'enk***) **[245]** Argentina, from the Santa Cruz River to the Strait of Magellan. *Chonan*. Except for the southernmost group located in southern Patagonia, most Tehuelche subgroups were assimilated by Mapuche speakers, and lost their language for that reason. Whereas estimates on the number of the ethnic group vary from 100–1,000 persons, there are only three speakers left. The language is moribund.

Tembé (or ***Timbé***, ***Tenetehára***, ***Turiwara***) **[348]** Brazil, Pará State, Terra Indígena Alto Rio Guamá, on the right bank of the Upper Guamá River, between the *igarapés* (small Amazonian waterways) Tauari to the south and Pitomba to the north, Terra Indígena Turé-Mariquita, Terra Indígena Tembé, on the left bank of the Acará-Miri River; Maranhão State, Terra Indígena Alto Turiaçu, on the banks of the Gurupi River. *Tupian*, Tupi-Guarani, Tenetehara (IV). The Tembé seem to have assimilated the closely related Turiwara group. The Tembé language, which is closely related to Guajajara, is seriously endangered. Out of an ethnic group of 880 – 820 Tembé (1999) and sixty Turiwara (1998) – there are only about 100 speakers left (SIL 1995), who all live in the Gurupi River area.

Tenharim (or ***Kagwahiva***) **[354]** Brazil, southern Amazonas State, Middle Madeira River, Terra Indígena Marmelos, Terra Indígena Tenharim do Igarapé Preto, and Terra Indígena Sepoti. *Tupian*, Tupi-Guarani, Kawahib (VI). The Tenharim form part of a bigger group of peoples that call themselves ***Kagwahiva***. Apart from their identical self-denomination, these Kagwahiva groups speak dialects of the same language and are organised according to an identical social system. Other groups belonging to the Kagwahiva are the Parintintin, Jahui, Uru-Eu-Wau-Wau, Amondawa, Karipuna, and Juma. Practically all Tenharim are bilingual in Portuguese, but the language has almost disappeared on the Igarapé Preto and Sepoti River. On the Marmelos River Tenharim is still used within the group, while Portuguese is spoken with outsiders. The language is seriously endangered within the ethnic group of 585 (2000).

Terêna (or ***Terena***) **[115]** Brazil, southern Mato Grosso do Sul State, east of the Para-guay River, Miranda and Aguidauana rivers area, Avaí Municipality, near Baurú, on ten Indigenous Lands; São Paulo State, Terra Indígena Araribá and Terra Indígena Icatu. *Arawakan*, Maipuran, Southern Maipuran, Bolivia-Parana. The Terêna are the last survivors of the Guaná nation. The Guaná lived with the Guaycuruan Mbayá – whose descendants are the Kadiweu today. Until the second half of the eighteenth century these groups lived in the Chaco region to the west of the Paraguay River. At that time they crossed this river to settle in the area that today forms part of southern Mato Grosso del Sur State. Bilingual intercultural education has been implemented successfully in all municipal schools in the Terêna region. The language is potentially endangered, with an ethnic group of 16,000 (2001).

171

Teteté **[150]** Ecuador, Province of Sucumbíos, eastern jungle near the Colombian border, in the area of the Cofán and the Cuyabeno Reservation, east of Lake Agrio. *Tucanoan*, Western. With two speakers reported by SIL in 1969, the language is possibly extinct today.

Teushen (or ***Tehuesh***) **[246c]** Argentina, between the rivers Chubut and Santa Cruz, extending to the north up to the Río Negro. *Chonan*. At the end of the nineteenth century only the elders remembered their ancestral language, since it had been replaced by then by Tehuelche. The language became extinct in the first decade of the twentieth century.

Ticuna (or ***Tikuna***, ***Tukuna***, ***Magüa***) **[162]** Brazil, Amazonas State, Upper Solimões River area, on more than twenty Indigenous Lands, in more than ninety villages. *Language Isolate*. Despite their long-standing contact with mainstream society, the Ticuna conserve many important traditional cultural practices, including initiation rites, shamanism, mythology, arts and language. The large size of their group, their cultural awareness and living traditions, make the Ticuna the dominant culture of the Upper Solimões River. With an ethnic group of 32,613 (1998) the language is potentially endangered (more in Colombia and Peru).

Ticuna **[162]** Colombia, along the west bank of the Amazon River, in the so-called *Trapecio amazónico*, on the banks of the Loretoyacu, Atacuari, Amacayacu, and the Arara. *Language Isolate*. The Ticuna share their territory with other groups, such as the Bora, Cocama, Witoto, and Yagua. In Colombia, the language is potentially endangered with an ethnic group of approximately 6,585 members (more in Peru and Brazil).

Ticuna **[162]** Peru, on the Amazon River, from the Cajacuma Island (north of San Pablo) up to the Brazilian border. *Language Isolate*. Although many of the Ticuna in Peru are learning Spanish, Ticuna is still used at home and in public. In Peru, the language is potentially endangered with about 6,000–8,000 speakers out of an ethnic group of the same size (more in Brazil and Colombia).

Tingui-Botó **[315a]** Brazil, Alagoas State, Feira Grande Municipality, Terra Indígena Tingui-Botó, in Olho D'Água do Melo. *Unclassified* (for lack of data). The name Tingui-Botó is a recent autodenomination for a group of which the origin is unclear and which may be composed of members of distinct ethnic groups. All 350 Tingui-Botó (2002) are native speakers of Portuguese today and the language they possibly spoke, ***Dzubukuá*** (or ***Dzboku'a***), is extinct.

Tinigua **[52]** Colombia, Department of Meta, between the Upper Guayabero and Yarí rivers, on the Ariari River, in the Sierra de la Macarena. *Language Isolate*. Tinigua used to form a small independent linguistic family with the extinct language ***Pamigua***. Today the language is moribund with only two male speakers left.

Tiriyó (or ***Trio***, ***Tarëno***, ***Tirió***, ***Tirio***, ***Tarona***, ***Yawi***, ***Pianokoto***) **[386]** Brazil, northern Pará State, mostly on the West Paru River, but also on the Marapi and East Paru rivers, Terra Indígena Parque Tumucumaque. *Cariban*, Carib, Northern, East-West

Guiana, Wayana-Trio. By Amazonian standards, the Tiriyó language is still healthy. Although a few speakers or 'understanders' of Portuguese already exist, most of the population in Brazil is monolingual and all children still learn the language. With an ethnic group of 735 members (1998) the language is to be considered endangered (more in Suriname).

Toba (or ***Namqom***) **[262]** Argentina, provinces of Chaco, Formosa, Salta; due to recent migrations also in Santa Fe (Rosario), and in the Gran Buenos Aires District. *Guaicuruan*. With 36,000–60,000 members the Toba form the biggest Guaycuran group, but the exact number of speakers is unknown. The degree of speakers' competence varies considerably according to location, age, and attitude towards the language, which is to be considered potentially endangered.

Toba **[262]** Bolivia, Department of Tarija, on the left bank of the Pilmacayo River, between Villa Montes and the border with Paraguay. *Guaycuruan*. From 1916 onwards the Toba were pushed to the right (south) bank of the Pilmacayo, until they were finally pushed out of Bolivia. After the Chaco war (1936) there was not a single Toba settlement left. (Grimes 2000), however, mentions that there are possibly 100 speakers of Toba in Bolivia. Nevertheless, the language is to be considered possibly extinct in Bolivia (more in Argentina and Paraguay).

Toba-Maskoy (or ***Enenxet***) **[272]** Paraguay, Chaco region, Department of Presidente Hayes, Pozo Colorado (Casanillo) and Fernheim districts, Department of Alto Paraguay, Fuerte Olimpo and La Victoria (Padre Livio Farriña) districts, and Department of Boquerón, Mariscal Estigarribia and Menno districts; East, Department of Concepción, District of San Lázaro. *Mascoyan*. It is hypothesised that around 1870 some Argentinean Toba chiefs fled from the persecutions that took place in their territory and settled on the Riacho Mosquito in the Alto Paraguay Department. Here they supposedly transfigured culturally and linguistically, thus becoming Toba-Maskoy. With about 1,280 speakers out of an ethnic group of 2,055, the language is to be considered endangered.

Toba-Qom (***Qom-Lik***, ***Emok-Lik***, ***Takshika***) **[272a]** Paraguay, Department of Presidente Hayes, District of Benjamín Aceval, Región Oriental, near Villa del Rosario. *Guaycuruan*. Culturally the Guaycuruan Toba-Qom share a lot of characteristics with the Mascoyan Enlhet. Their complicated cultural history has led to a special ethnic, linguistic, and cultural mix. After having worked on farms for decades, they now group together in four major communities: one in the Región Oriental near Villa del Rosario and three others in the Benjamín Aceval District in the Department of Presidente Hayes. In Paraguay, the language is endangered with approximately 755 speakers out of an ethnic group of 780 (more in Argentina).

Torá **[67]** Brazil, Amazonas State, Lower Marmelos River (right-bank tributary of the Madeira), Auxiliadora Municipality, Terra Indígena Torá. *Chapacuran*. The Torá are the nothernmost Chapacuran group. A 'punitive expedition' undertaken against the group in the eighteenth century almost led to their extinction. Today the Torá no longer speak their language, which possibly has become extinct. The ethnic group consists of fifty-one members (1999).

Toromona (or *Toromono*) **[243]** Bolivia, Department of La Paz, Province of Iturralde, between the upper Madidi and the River Heath. *Tacanan*. It is not clear whether this group really exists. Up till now they have never been contacted and possibly all rumours concern an uncontacted group of Araona. If the Toromona exist, their language is to be considered seriously endangered in view of the reduced ethnic group, which in the past has been estimated at twenty-five.

Tremembé **[435]** Brazil, Ceará State, Itarema Municipality, 150km northwest of Fortaleza, in Almofala on the Atlantic coast, Terra Indígena Córrego João Pereira and Terra Indígena Tremembé de Almofala. *Unclassified* (for lack of data). All 1,511 Tremembé (1999) are native speakers of Portuguese today. The language is extinct.

Trio **[386]** Suriname, south, in Palumeu on the Palumeu River; in Pëlelutëpu (Tëpu) on the Upper Tapanahoni River; and in Kwamalasamutu and Sipaliwini on the Sipaliwini River. *Cariban*, Carib, Northern, East-West Guiana, Wayana-Trio. In Suriname, the whole ethnic group of 1,000–1,200 (more in Brazil) speaks the language. However, the language is endangered because of its relatively low number of speakers.

Truká **[436]** Brazil: Pernambuco State, Cabrobó Municipality, Terra Indígena Truká. *Unclassified* (for lack of data). All 1,333 Truká (1999) are native speakers of Portuguese today. The language is extinct.

Trumai **[436]** Brazil, Mato Grosso State, Parque Indígena do Xingu, some villages along the banks of the Xingú River source. *Language Isolate*. The Trumai are the last group that arrived in the Xingu Indigenous Park. They have changed their location several times in the last 100 years, moving from the Lower Culuene River up to the northern parts of the Upper Xingu, and from there to the Middle Xingu (Guirardello 1999). According to Seki (1999), the frequent change of location by groups forms an important problem in the Xingu area. Intertribal hostilities and warfare cause some groups to become weaker, seeking protection with other groups, which in the long run may lead to language loss. The Trumai language is seriously endangered, with about fifty speakers out of an ethnic group of 120 (2002).

Tsafiqui (or *Tsafiki*, *Tsáchila*, *Tsachela*, *Colorado*) **[24]** Ecuador, southeastern part of the Province of Pinchincha, along the Chihuepe, Baba, Tahuazo, and Poste rivers. *Barbacoan*, Cayapa-Colorado. The Tsáchila live in the forest at the foot of western Andes Mountains and form the best-known indigenous group on the coast of Ecuador. They used to be called 'Colorado' because of their way of combing and colouring their hair with achiote. The ethnic group numbers about 2,000, and, whereas in 1975 still less than 50 per cent of the speakers were bilingual in Tsafiqui and Spanish, the increased contact with the outside world has led to almost 100 per cent bilingualism. The language is to be considered endangered.

Tsohom Djapá (or *Txunhuã-Djapá*, *Tsunhum Djapá*, *Tyonhwak Dyapa*, *Tucano*) **[141]** Brazil, Amazonas State, Terra Indígena Vale do Javari, between the Igarapé Davi in the south and the Jandiatuva in the northwest. *Harakmbut-Katukinan*. The language is seriously endangered, with an ethnic group of approximately 100 members (1985).

Tucano [160] Colombia, Department of Vaupés, on the banks of the Papurí River and its tributaries, in the villages of Acaricuara (on the banks of the Paca River), Montfort and Piracuara (on the banks of the Papurí); in Mitú, the Upper Vaupés region, and in the area of San José del Guaviare. *Tucanoan*, Eastern Tucanoan, Northern. Welch and West (2000) mention the fact that there are many more speakers of Tucano than the number of 1,500–2,000 that they give for the ethnic group, since it is used as a lingua franca in the Paca and Papurí rivers region. This might explain the much higher number of 6,840 given for the ethnic group by Arango and Sánchez (1998). In Colombia, the language is potentially endangered (more in Brazil).

Tukano (or *Tucano, Ye'pãmasa, Dasea*) [160] Brazil, northwestern Amazonas, Terra Indígena Alto Rio Negro, Terra Indígena Balaio, Terra Indígena Marabitanas/Cue-Cue, Terra Indígena Médio Rio Negro I, Terra Indígena Médio Rio Negro II, Terra Indígena Apaporis, Terra Indígena Rio Téa, and Terra Indígena Uneiuxi. *Tucanoan*, Eastern Tucanoan, Northern. As is the case with other Easten Tucanoan groups, marriage is exogamous among the Tukano. Marrying someone from the same language group is considered incestuous. Language is acquired through patrilineal descent. In the Vaupés area, Tukano has been gradually replacing Nheengatu as a lingua franca. With an ethnic group of approximately 4,604 persons (2001) the language is to be considered potentially endangered (more in Colombia).

Tumbalalá [not mapped] Brazil, northern Bahia State, between the Curaçá and Abaré municipalities, on the border with Pernambuco State, and on the banks of the São Francisco River. The Tumbalalá were only recognised as an indigenous community in 2001. They are native speakers of Portuguese and cannot be linked to an extinct indigenous language. Nevertheless, they contend to use *Kariri* words in their rituals. Kariri was once spoken over the whole Lower and Middle São Francisco River area. The size of the Tumbalalá ethnic group is not precisely clear yet, but it varies between 180 and 400 families (2001).

Tunayana [385a] Suriname, south, among the Trio in Kwamalasamutu on the Sipaliwini River. *Cariban*. Until very recently, the Tunayana were thought to be a mythical tribe. The Tunayana are mixed with *Waiwai*. In the 1960s Door-to-Life missionaries, who had been active among the Waiwai in neighbouring Guyana, came to evangelise the Surinamese Amerindians of the interior. They brought with them a few Waiwai, as well as Mawayana and Tunayana Amerindians who had been living among the Waiwai, and whose task was to learn Trio in order to convert them. The Tunayana and Mawayana have remained in Suriname and now speak Trio as their first language. There are ten elderly speakers out of a group of eighty. The language is moribund.

Tunebo (or *Uwa-Tunebo*) [38] Venezuela, extreme west of Apure State, Paéz District, Municipality of Urdaneta, to the south of San Cristobal, on the Arauca River, near to the Colombian border, east of the Guahibo territory. *Chibchan*, Chibchan Proper, Tunebo. Possibly extinct in Venezuela (more in Colombia).

Tuparí [369] Brazil, southern and western Rondônia State, Posto Indígena Rio Guaporé, Terra Indígena Rio Branco. *Tupian*, Tupi-Tupari. Although the traditional culture of this group is one of the best documented of the Amazon River Basin through the work of Caspar (1975), a published description of the language is still lacking. With about 150 speakers out of an ethnic group of 200, the language is to be considered seriously endangered.

Tupinamba (or ***Coastal Tupi***) **[341a]** Brazil, northern Espírito Santo State, Aracruz Municipality, near the cities of Aracruz, Santa Cruz and Vila do Riacho, Terra Indígena Caieiras Velhas, Terra Indígena Pau-Brasil and Terra Indígena Comboios (Tupiniquim); Maranhão State, Amarante do Maranhão Municipality, Terra Indígena Governador (Tabajará). *Tupian*, Tupi-Guarani, Tupi (III). The Tupiniquim and the Tabajará are descendants of the Tupinamba. Today they are all native speakers of Portuguese and the Tupinamba language may be considered extinct. While the size of the Tabajará group remains unclear, the Tupiniquim group definitely is much bigger, totalling some 1,386 members.

***Tuxá* [316]** Brazil, Bahia State, Terra Indígena Ibotirama, Terra Indígena Nova Rodelas (urban area), Terra Indígena Riacho do Bento; Pernambuco State, Terra Indígena Tuxá de Inajá/Fazenda Funil. *Language Isolate*. In 1961, two elders were contacted who still remembered some words of the Tuxá language. Today all 1,630 Tuxá (1999) are native speakers of Portuguese and the language is extinct.

***Tuyuca* [158]** Brazil, northwestern Amazonas State, Vaupés region, Terra Indígena Alto Rio Negro and Terra Indígena Apaporis. *Tucanoan*, Eastern Tucanoan, Central, Bara. Tuyuca seems to share a great deal of its lexicon with Yurutí (Colombia). In Brazil, the language is to be considered endangered, with an ethnic group of 593 (2001) (more in Colombia).

***Tuyuca* [158]** Colombia, southeast, Vaupés region, Department of Vaupés, on the Upper Tiquié, Papurí and the Inambú, and along the headwaters of the Comeyaca. *Tucanoan*, Eastern Tucanoan, Central, Bara. The Tuyuca form part of the whole of Eastern Tucanoan groups, who are known for practising linguistic exogamy and for their general multilingualism. They principally maintain relations with the Makuna and Bará. The language is endangered, with an ethnic group of about 570 members (more in Brazil).

Umutina (***Omotina***, ***Barbados***) **[279]** Brazil, western Mato Grosso State, on the Bugres River (a tributary of the Paraguay), about 130km to the northeast of Cuiabá, Alto Paraguai and Barra dos Bugres municipalities, Terra Indígena Umutina. *Macro-Ge*, Bororo. Contrary to Bororo, the Umutina language is moribund, with one speaker out of an ethnic group of 124 (1999).

Urarina (or ***Kacha Ere***, ***Shimacu***, ***Itucale***, ***Cimarrón***) **[171]** Peru, Department of Loreto, Province of Urarinas, District of Urarinas, along the Chambira River (headwater of the Marañon River) and along all its headwaters; several groups along the rivers Urituyacu (also headwater of the Marañon) and Corrientes. *Language Isolate*. There is a bilingual education programme, but in almost all bilingual schools Spanish is used exclusively, because the teachers are not native speakers of Urarina. The language is potentially endangered, with approximately 3,000 speakers out of an ethnic group of the same size.

Uru (or *Uru'wit'u*, *Iruito*, *Uru murato*, *Murato*, *Kotsuñ*, *Uchusuma*, or the official name *Uchumataqu*) **[210a]** Bolivia, departments of La Paz and Oruro, provinces of Jesús de Machana and Poopó. *Uru-Chipayan* (heavily influenced by Aymara on all grammatical levels). In Bolivia, there are still three groups of Uru origin: the Chipaya, the Iru Itu (banks of the River Desaguadero), and the Murato (around lake Poopó). Of these three groups only the Chipaya have conserved their ancestral language. Already in the 1950s and 1960s it was reported that there were no speakers of Iru Itu left. The 1994 census, however, has shown to everyone's surprise that fifty-nine of the 142 Iru Itu (40 per cent) contended to know the Uru language, which in reality is only spoken by a few elders. The approximately 450 Murato have shifted completely to Aymara, conserving some Uru terminology which has to do with their work as fishermen. The language is moribund.

Uruak (*Awake*, *Arutani*) **[143]** Venezuela, Bolivar State, headwaters of the Paragua and Uraricaa rivers. *Language Isolate*. Most members of the Uruak group have inter-married with Yanam (Yanomaman), some with Pemón (Cariban), and very few with Sapé of the Paragua River area. The language is moribund, with five reported speakers in 1985 out of an ethnic group of forty-five (1992) (possibly more in Brazil).

Uru-Eu-Wau-Wau **[355]** Brazil, central Rondônia State, Upper Madeira River, Terra Indígena Uru-Eu-Wau-Wau. *Tupian*, Tupi-Guarani, Kawahib (VI). Bloody conflicts with Western invaders of their territory both preceded and followed official first peaceful contact in 1981. The linguistically defined Uru-Eu-Wau-Wau consist of two ethnic groups, the *Jupa'u* (also called Uru-Eu-Wau-Wau) and the *Amondawa*. The language is seriously endangered, with approximately 170 speakers (87 Jupaú and 83 Amondawa in 2003) out of an ethnic group of the same size.

Uwa-Tunebo **[38a]** Colombia, in the north of the Department of Boyacá, on the slopes of the eastern Cordillera; also in the departments of Norte de Santander, Santander, Arauca, and Casanare. *Chibchan*, Chibchan Proper, Tunebo. Since 1993, the Uwa people have been fighting a battle against the American oil company Occidental Petroleum Corporation, to prevent it from drilling for oil on their ancestral lands. The Uwa case has been followed by the international media since 1997 and has become the symbol for the wide range of battles currently being fought in and outside Colombia by indigenous groups. With an ethnic group of approximately 7,010 persons, the language is to be considered potentially endangered in Colombia (possibly extinct in Venezuela).

Vilela **[274]** Argentina, Province of Chaco, the area of Napalpí and Quitilipi. *Lule-Vilelan*. Vilela was spoken in the Bermejo River area in the eastern Gran Chaco. It is a member of the otherwise extinct Lule-Vilela family. The descendants of the last surviving Vilela group live in the eastern Chaco area, where they are mixed with the Toba and Mocoví. It has been reported that they deny having knowledge of the language, or are unwilling to supply information on it. The language, however, is to be considered moribund, with only two semi-speakers out of an ethnic group consisting of 45 households (cf. Domínguez *et al.* submitted).

Waimiri-Atroari (or *Kiñá*, *Kinja*) **[395]** Brazil, border area Roraima State and Amazonas states, Terra Indígena Waimiri-Atroarí. *Cariban*, Northern, East-West-Guiana.

Although the history of contact between the Waimirí Atroarí and the Western world goes back to the seventeenth century, all Waimirí Atroarí still speak their native language. Portuguese is considered a contact language and the number of bilinguals is quite low, about 20 per cent of the population, mostly males. The Waimirí Atroarí maintain close relationships with the Waiwai. With an ethnic group of 931 (2001) the language is to be considered endangered.

Waiwai [392] Guyana, southwest, in the dense tropical forests of the upper Essequibo River basin: only one community at Gunn's Strip in the far south of the country. *Cariban*, Northern, East-West Guiana, Waiwai. Most of the Waiwai (1,366) migrated from Guyana to Brazil in the aftermath of the 1969 Rupununi Uprising. They settled in the states of Pará, Roraima and Amapá in Brazil. The settlements in the two countries maintain links, particularly for trade and religious worship. Among the Waiwai of Guyana live the Mawayana, a group that speaks an Arawakan language heavily influenced by Cariban. There are about 240 in the ethnic group (more in Brazil), which makes the language seriously endangered.

Waiwai (or *Wai Wai*) [392] Brazil, Roraima, Terra Indígena Trombetas/Mapuera, one village on the Jatapuzinho River; Pará and Amazonas states, Terra Indígena Nhamundá-Mapuera, one village on the Mapuera River (Pará), and a few among the Hyxkaryana on the Nhamindá River (Amazonas). *Cariban*, Northern, East-West Guiana, Waiwai. The people who are now called Waiwai by the outside world are remnants of various groups, such as the Mawayana, Hyxkaryana, Sikiana, and others. All of these tribe remnants have their own language or dialect. Nearly all that live among the Waiwai speak the Waiwai language fluently. The language is potentially endangered, with an 'ethnic' group of 2,020 (2000), including the subgroups Karafawyana, Xerey, Katuena, and Mawayana (more in Guyana).

Wanano (or *Wanana*, *Guanano*, *Uanano*) [161] Brazil, northwestern Amazonas State, on the border with Colombia, Terra Indígena Alto Rio Negro. *Tucanoan*, Eastern Tucanoan, Northern. Wanano shares a great part of its lexicon with Piratapuya. As is the case with other Easten Tucanoan groups, marriage is exogamous among the Wanano and marrying someone from the same language group is considered incestuous. Interestingly enough, Wanano and Piaratapuya are considered each other's kin and, therefore, cannot intermarry (Aikhenvald 2002). With an ethnic group of 447 (2001) the language is to be considered endangered (more in Colombia).

Wanano (or *Guanano*) [161] Colombia, Department of Vaupés, on the border with Brazil, middle part of the Caiarí River, in Santa Cruz, Villa Fátima, Yapima, Carurú, Tayasú, Ibacaba and Yapima. *Tucanoan*, Eastern Tucanoan, Northern. Forming part of the whole of Eastern Tucanoan groups known for practising linguistic exogamy, the Wanano also maintain close relations with the Arawakan Tariana and Baniva, but not with the Piratapuyo Tucano, Tuyuca, and Siriano. The language is endangered, with an ethnic group of about 1,170 (more in Brazil).

Wapishana [101] Guyana, southwest, south Rupununi savannas, to the northwest of the Waiwai; a few villages. *Arawakan*, Maipuran, Northern Maipuran, Wapishana. The Wapishana were divided by an arbitrary border in 1904 after litigation between

Brazil and Great Britain (Guyana's colonizer at the time). In Guyana there are 6,900 Wapishana in the ethnic group (more in Brazil). The language is potentially endangered.

Wapixana (or ***Wapishana***, ***Wapisiana***, ***Uapixana***, ***Vapidiana***) **[101]** Brazil, Roraima State, on twenty-three Indigenous Lands. *Arawakan*, Maipuran, Northern Maipuran, Wapishana. The ancestors of the Wapixana were the first of Roraima's indigenous groups to encounter Western explorers, who penetrated the area on several occasions during the eighteenth century. By the 1970s, it was reported that 60 per cent of Brazil's Wapixana were 'integrated' and spoke Portuguese as their first language, and that the rest were largely bilingual and in permanent contact with the state. Today the Wapixana ethnic group totals 6,500 persons (2000), nevertheless, the language must be considered endangered (more in Guyana).

Warao **[27]** Guyana, coastal swamps of the North West Region. *Language Isolate.* In the 1980s, in particular when the Guyanese economy went into steep decline, many Warao from Guyana trekked to the Amacuro Delta on the Venezuelan side. There the Warao renewed links with their kinsfolk across the border, and many of them recounted later that the circumstances forced them to communicate in their language. In Guyana, the Warao who live in closer contact to coastal society are more acculturated than those residing close to the border areas with Venezuela, and, therefore, face the reality of the loss of their native language. However, in view of the big Warao populations of Venezuela, and the cross-border traffic between Guyanese and Venezuelan Warao, there is no immediate threat of extinction of the language. In Guyana, there are 5,000 in the ethnic group. The language is potentially endangered.

Warao **[27]** Venezuela, delta area of the Orinoco River (Delta Amacuro State), extending also to Sucre and Monagas states in the west, and the Guyana border area in the east. *Language Isolate.* Warao has a slightly diverging western and eastern dialect, divided by the Caño Mánamo. Yet another dialect is spoken on Mariusa Island. The Warao language has been documented extensively, and in the past decades it has been taught at university level. The language is potentially endangered, with an ethnic group of about 24,000 members (more in Guyana).

Warekena (or ***Werekena***, ***Uarequena***) **[79]** Brazil, northwestern Amazonas State, Xié River area; Lower Rio Negro, São Gabriel da Cachoeira Municipality, especially between the Curicuriari and Maré rivers, Terra Indígena Alto Rio Negro and Terra Indígena Marabitanas/Cue-Cue. *Arawakan*, Maipuran, Northern Maipuran, Inland. Warekena is considered a dialect of ***Baniva del Guainía*** (Venezuela) and is no longer used for everyday communication. The remaining speakers are all bilingual in Nheengatu and many also speak Portuguese, Spanish and Baniwa do Içana or Kuripako. With a few dozen speakers out of an ethnic group of 491 (1998) the language is to be considered seriously endangered (more in Venezuela).

Warekena (or ***Guarequena***, ***Guarekena***, ***Uarekena***) **[79]** Venezuela, Amazonas State, settlement of Guzmán Blanco (also known as Wayanápi) and in San Miguel de Davipe on the Caño Itíni Wíni (San Miguel, Conorochite) along the Guainía River, in Quiratare and Capihuara (Capivara), Caño Casiquiare as well as along the

179

Atabapo River and in certain neighbourhoods of Puerto Ayacucho. *Arawakan,* Maipuran, Northern Maipuran, Inland. Warekena is considered to be a dialect of **Baniva del Guainía**. It is not exactly known how many speakers are left in the ethnic group of no more than 500 members (more in Brazil). The speakers are all over fifty years of age and bilingual in Spanish, some of them even speakers of three or four languages, a regional phenomenon. The language is to be considered seriously endangered.

Wari' (or **Pakaa Nova**, **Pacaás Novos**) **[66]** Brazil, western Rondônia State, Terra Indígena Igarapé Lage, Terra Indígena Ribeirão, Terra Indígena Rio Negro/Ocaia, Terra Indígena Pacaás-Novos, Terra Indígena Sagarana. *Chapacuran.* After many bloody conflicts with Westerners during the second rubber boom in the 1940s, the first peaceful contact of the Wari' with missionaries of the Brazilian New Tribes Mission and the SPI (Serviço de Proteção ao Índio 'Indian Protection Service', the governmental agency preceding FUNAI) took place in 1956. The 'pacification' process took more than a decade until 1969, because the Wari' were dispersed over a vast territory on the Lage River – a right-bank tributary of the Mamoré – and its affluents, on the headwaters of the Ribeirão River, on right-bank tributaries of the Pacaás Novos River (Upper Ouro Preto, Manato', Igarapé Santo André, Rio Negro, and its affluent, the Ocaia River), and on the Dos Irmãos River. Once settled at the SPI posts, the Wari' returned to the forest whenever they felt threatened by epidemics, which had decimated their population during the contact period. Today there are around 1,930 speakers out of an ethnic group of the same size (1998).

Wariapano (or **Huariapano**, **Panobo**) **[217b]** Peru, Department of Loreto, on the Lower Ucayali River, Contamana area, Cashiboya, among the Shetebo who speak a dialect of Shipibo-Conibo. *Panoan, Unclassified.* The language is possibly extinct due to the fact that the last known speaker died in 1991.

Wassú [not mapped] Brazil, Alagoas State, Joaquim Gomes Municipality, 70km to the north of the city of Maceió, Terra Indígena Wassu-Cocal. The Wassú form a group of which the origin is unclear and which may be composed of members of distinct ethnic groups. All 1,447 (1999) Wassú are native speakers of Portuguese today and the language they possibly spoke is extinct.

Waunana (or **Waunán**, **Wounaan**, **Wou Meu**, **Waunméu**, **Waumeo**, **Chocó**, **Noanama**) **[7]** Colombia, Department of Chocó: on the banks of the Middle and Lower San Juan River, especially to the north of Buenaventura. *Chocoan.* Together with Emberá, a language that consists of a dialect continuum, Waunana forms the Chocoan linguistic family, which does not seem to be related to any other family. Waunana and Emberá are not mutually intelligible. The ethnic group consists of about 7,970 persons. With the exception of elders, most Waunana are bilingual in Spanish and want their children to become proficient in this language. In Colombia, Waunana is to be considered potentially endangered (more in Panama).

Waurá (or **Uará**, **Waujá**) **[112]** Brazil, Mato Grosso State, Parque Indígena do Xingu, Piyulaga Lake area. *Arawakan,* Maipuran, Central Maipuran. The Waurá are famous for their fine pottery, the graphic designs of their baskets, their feather artwork and their ritual masks. They seem to have come from the northwest and were the first settlers in the Xingu area. All Waurá still speak their mother tongue, which is closely related to Mehinako. With an ethnic group of approximately 321 members (2002) the language is to be considered endangered.

Wayampi (or *Wajãpi*, *Oyampi*, *Wayãpy*, *Waiãpi*, *Guaiapi*) **[350]** Brazil, Amapá State, Amapari River area, between the Inipiku River (Mapari) in the west, the Karapanaty (Aroã) in the south, and the Onça and Kumakary (Água Preta) *igarapés* (small Amazonian waterways) in the east, Mazagão and Macapá municipalities, Terra Indígena Waiãpi. *Tupian*, Tupi-Guarani, Oyampi (VIII). Outside the Wayampi Indigenous Land there may be two other uncontacted Wayampi subgroups on the headsprings of the Amapari and Anakui rivers (Amapá State), and on the Upper Ipitinga River (Pará State), respectively. Although all Wayampi still speak their native language, knowledge of Portuguese is growing fast, especially among men. With an ethnic group of 525 members (1999) the language is to be considered endangered (more in French Guiana).

Wayana (or *Waiana*, *Uaiana*) **[406]** Brazil, northern Pará State, mainly on the upper and middle course of the Paru de Leste River, Parque Indígena do Tumucumaque and Terra Indígena Rio Paru D'Este. *Cariban*, Northern, East-West Guiana, Wayana-Trio. In Brazil, the Wayana have been living together in the same villages and intermarrying with the Aparaí for at least a century. Because of the high incidence of intermarriage, the Wayana and Aparai have been registered as a single group, Wayana-Aparaí, of 415 members (1998). Most Wayana still speak their native language, but since it is not known how many speakers of Wayana are among these 415 persons, the language is to be considered seriously endangered (more in French Guiana and Suriname).

Wayana **[406]** French Guiana, along the Upper Maroni River. *Cariban*, Northern, East-West Guiana, Wayana-Trio. Some Aparaí families, and some Akuriyo and Tiriyó individuals have been signalled recently in Wayana communities. The Wayana have continued to gain speakers from Suriname, partly as a result of the war in Suriname's interior, but also because of the better socio-economic conditions that prevail in French Guiana. There are about 1,000 in the ethnic group (more in Suriname and Brazil). The language is endangered.

Wayana **[406]** Suriname, southwest Marowijne District, on the Upper Tapanahoni River; northwest of the Trio settlements on the Lawa and Tapanahoni rivers. *Cariban*, Carib, Northern, East-West Guiana, Wayana-Trio. Wayana is still actively spoken in the geograhically distant and isolated villages. Although Dutch is taught at school in some villages, everybody speaks Wayana outside the schools. In trade relations with non-indigenous people the English-based creole language Sranantongo is used. However, the Wayana have continued to lose speakers to French Guiana, partly as a result of the war in the interior, but also because of the better socio-economic conditions that prevail there. The whole ethnic group of 500 (more in French Guiana and Brazil) speaks the language, which is endangered.

Wayãpi (or *Wayampi*, *Oayampi*, *Oyampi*) **[350]** French Guiana, along the Upper Oyapock, in two settlements, one near Camopi, and the other more to the south along the

181

headwaters of the Oyapock River (Trois-Sauts). *Tupian*, Tupi-Guarani, Oyampi (VIII). Many Wayãpi understand the Emérillon language, but nobody is able or wants to speak it. At the end of the seventeenth century, the group migrated from the Lower Xingu (Brazil) to the Guianas. There are about 500 in the ethnic group (more in Brazil). The language is endangered.

Weenhayek (or ***Mataco***) **[256]** Bolivia, Department of Tarija, Province of Gran Chaco, along the southwest bank of the Pilcomayo River. *Mataco-Mataguayan*. There are about 1,810 speakers out of an ethnic group of 2,020. Perhaps Mataco is the clearest example of language recuperation instead of language loss. The 1994 Indigenous Census shows an increase in language use among the youngsters compared to the elders. The reason for this increase is not quite clear, but it cannot be ascribed to a lack of knowledge of Spanish, since the biggest part of the population, with the exception of some elderly women, already knows this language. The language is to be considered endangered in Bolivia (more in Argentina).

Wichi (or ***Mataco***) **[256]** Argentina, Province of Chaco, Department of General Güemes, Province of Formosa, departments of Bermejo, Matacos, Patiño, and Ramón Lista, Province of Salta, departments of San Martín, Rivadavia, Orán, Metán, and Anta. *Mataco-Mataguayan*. Wichi forms a dialectal continuum consisting of the following three dialects: **Noctén**, spoken in the Bolivian towns Yacuiba, Villa Montes, and Crevaux; **Vejoz**, spoken between the Tartagal zone and the Bermejo River (Argentina); **Guisnay**, spoken on the right bank of the Pilcomayo, near to the current Argentinean-Bolivian border. Although the language seems to be very vital with a high number of monolinguals, it is not exactly known how many speakers there are in the ethnic group of 35,000–60,000 (more in Bolivia). The language is to be considered potentially endangered.

Witoto (or ***Huitoto***, ***Uitoto***) **[188]** Brazil, Amazonas State, Alvarães Municipality, Terra Indígena Méria; Uarini Municipality, Terra Indígena Miratu; Tefé Municipality, Santa Cruz. *Witotoan*. The size of the Witoto ethnic group in Brazil is not clear, nor is the number of speakers. Grimes (1992) lists 261 Witoto for Brazil, which would imply that the language is seriously endangered (more in Peru and Colombia).

Witoto (or ***Huitoto***, ***Witoto Murui***, ***Witoto Mïnïca***, ***Witoto Muinane***) **[188]** Colombia, on the rivers Cara-Paraná (Murui dialect), on the rivers Igará-Paraná, Caquetá and Putumayo (Mïnïca dialect), and on the Caquetá above Arraracuyara (Nïpode dialect) *Witotoan*. The Witoto became one of the most decimated indigenous groups of the Amazon due to the atrocities committed by the rubber company Casa Arana during the rubber boom at the beginning of the twentieth century. In Colombia, the language is potentially endangered with an ethnic group of about 6,245 (more in Peru and Brazil).

Xakriabá (or ***Xacriabá***, ***Xikriabá***) **[293]** Brazil, Minas Gerais State, Terra Indígena Riachão/Luiza do Vale, Terra Indígena Xakriabá and Terra Indígena Xakriabá Rancharias. *Macro-Ge*, Ge, Central Ge. Today all 6,000 members (2000) of the Xakriabá ethnic group are native speakers of Portuguese. The language is probably extinct.

Xambioá (or *Karajá do Norte, Ixybiowa, Iraru Mahãdu*) [307a] Brazil, Tocantins State, Terra Indígena Xambioá, on the right bank of the Lower Araguaia River, in the villages of Xambioá and Kurehe. *Macro-Ge*, Karaja. *Xambioá, Karajá*, and *Javaé* are the three languages that form the Karaja subbranch in the Macro-Ge linguistic family. Prolonged contact with Western society has caused Portuguese to become the dominant language in the village of Xambioá. The Xambioá language is to be considered seriously endangered, with an ethnic group of 185 (1999).

Xavante (or *A'uwe, Awen, Akwe, Akwen*) [290] Brazil, southeastern Mato Grosso State, between the Serra do Roncador and the Mortes, Culuene, Couto de Magalhães, Boti, and Garças river valleys, in more than seventy villages on eight Indigenous Lands. *Macro-Ge*, Ge, Central Ge. The first attempt to 'pacify' the Xavante took place in the nineteenth century in western and northern Goiás State, when they were relocated in a number of official village settlements with other indigenous and non-indigenous groups. Eventually they escaped back to the jungle and were relatively undisturbed until halfway through the twentieth century. By the end of the 1950s all Xavante subgroups, which had since migrated to Mato Grosso State, had been contacted. Most Xavante still speak their native language, which is potentially endangered with an ethnic group of approximately 9,602 (2000).

Xerente (or *Akwen, Akwe, Awen*) [292] Brazil, Tocantins State, to the east of the Tocantins River, 70km to the north of the city of Palmas, Terra Indígena Xerente and Terra Indígena Funil, in thirty-three villages. *Macro-Ge*, Ge, Central Ge. After 250 years of contact with the Western world, the ethnic identity of the Xerente has not been affected yet. All Xerente speak their native language and children are monolingual up to five years of age. Although the Xerente are fluent in Portuguese, the Xerente language is used in all contexts of daily life in the villages. Nevertheless, the language is to be considered endangered with an ethnic group of 1,814 members (2000).

Xetá (or *Hetá*) [336] Brazil, Paraná State, Serra dos Dourados, south to the Lower Ivaí River, southeast to its confluence with the Paraná, São Jerônimo da Serra Municipality, Terra Indígena Barão de Antonina I and Guarapuava. *Tupian*, Tupi-Guarani, Guarani (I). The Xetá have probably been assimilated by the Kaingang, with whom they live. Whereas Grimes (1992) still mentioned three speakers out of an ethnic group of 100–250 Xetá, the number for the ethnic group totalled eight persons in 1998. It is not clear whether there are any speakers left. The language is moribund.

Xipaya (*Xipaia, Shipaya*) [364] Brazil, Pará State, Altamira Municipality, Terra Indígena Curuá; on the left bank of the Iriri River, Terra Indígena Xipaia, in the village of Tukamã, and in the town of Altamira. *Tupian*, Juruna. In Altamira, the high percentage of intermarriage between the Kuruaya and Xipaya complicates a precise demographic census, since the two groups are sometimes considered to form a single ethnic group. Although there are still eight elders of Kuruaya and Xipaya descendance in Altamira who speak the native language, it is to be considered moribund. The ethnic group consists of 595 members (2003), probably including Kuruaya as well.

Xokleng (or *Shokleng, Laklanô*) [295] Brazil, Santa Catarina State, on the rivers Hercílio and Plate, approximately 260 kms northwest of Florianópolis and 100km west of

Blumenau, in the municipalities of José Boiteux, Victor Meirelles, Doutor Pedrinho and Itaiópolis, Terra Indígena Ibirama. *Macro-Ge*, Ge, Southern Ge. The Xokleng of TI Ibirama are survivors of the brutal colonisation process in the south of Brazil, which started halfway through the nineteenth century and almost completely exterminated their ethnic group. In spite of their confinement to a determined area in 1914, the Xokleng continued fighting to survive the invasion of the Itajaí River valley, even after the almost complete disappearance of the natural resources of their territory, which was further aggravated by the construction of the Barragem Norte (Norte Dam). In the past two decades the number of Xokleng speakers has dropped alarmingly due to, among other things, intermarriage with non-indigenous people and countless social, political and cultural disruptions caused by the construction of the Barragem Norte. The vast majority of the young people only speak Portuguese. Today the ethnic group consists of approximately 757 (1998) persons and the language is to be considered endangered.

Xokó (or *Xocó*, *Chocó*, *Kariri-Xocó*, *Kariri-Shoko*, *Cariri-Chocó*, *Xukuru-Kariri*, *Xucuru-Kariri*, *Xucuru-Cariri*) [323] Brazil, Northeast, Sergipe State, Terra Indíge Caiçara/Ilha de São Pedro (the Xokó); Alagoas State, Lower São Francisco River, near the town of Porto Real do Colégio, Terra Indígena Kariri-Xocó (the Kariri-Xokó); Terra Indígena Mata da Cafurna, Terra Indígena Quixabá, Terra Indígena Sitio Cajazeiras to the south of Palmeira dos Indios, and Terra Indígena Xukuru-Kariri (the Xukuru-Kariri). *Unclassified* (for lack of data). The Xokó, Kariri-Xokó and Xukuru-Kariri are all descendants of indigenous groups that used to inhabit northeast Brazil. It is not clear whether these three groups used to speak three different languages, or just one. In 1961, only a few dozen words were registered from an elder in Porto Real do Colegio and two other men in Palmeira dos Indios. Although the language is extinct today, the ethnic group still consists of approximately 250 Xokó (1987), 1,500 Kariri-Xokó (1999), and 1,820 Xukuru (1996), totalling 3,570 members.

Xukuru [319] Brazil, Pernambuco State, Pesqueira Municipality, 200km to the west of Recife, Terra Indígena Xukuru. *Unclassified* (for lack of data). According to Loukotka (1968), the Xukuru linguistic family consisted of two languages: **Xukuru** and **Paratió**. In 1961, just a few words were registered from an elder. Although the Xukuru language family is extinct, the ethnic group is blooming with 6,363 members (1999).

Yabarana (or *Yavarana*) [409] Venezuela, Amazonas State, in the north between the Parucito and Manapiare river basins and along the middle basin of the Ventuari River, in the communities of Chirinos and Majagua to the north of San Juan de Manapiare; also in La Esmeralda (Upper Orinoco). *Cariban*, Northern, Western Guiana. The language has two divergent dialects: **Guaiquiare** and **Orechicano**. It is not known how many speakers are left in the ethnic group of about 320 members, which has been partially assimilated by the Piaroa, the strongest group in the zone. Due to this assimilation process, the language is to be considered seriously endangered.

Yagua (or *Yawa*) [176] Colombia, Department of Amazonas, on the Tucuchira River near Leticia. *Peba-Yaguan*. Yagua is the sole surviving language of the Peba-Yaguan family, which consisted of three more languages: **Peba**, **Masamae**, and **Yameo**. With an ethnic group of about 295 persons, the language is endangered in Colombia (more in Peru).

Yagua (or *Yawa*, *Iahua*) **[176]** Peru, northeast, along the headwaters of the Amazon River from Iquitos up to the Brazilian border. *Peba-Yaguan*. Yagua is the sole surviving language of the Peba-Yaguan family, which consisted of three more languages: **Peba**, **Masamae** and **Yameo**. Children who live near to the big 'mixed' villages usually no longer acquire Yagua, but those that live in more isolated areas still do at a very young age. In Peru the language is potentially endangered, with 4,000 speakers out of an ethnic group of 5,000 (more in Colombia).

Yahgan (or *Yámana*) **[247]** Argentina, extreme south of Isla Grande de Tierra del Fuego (Fireland), from the southwest corner that forms the border with Chile (Lapataia, Parque Nacional Tierra del Fuego, and Ushuaia) to the area of the Moat *estancia* (estate) to the northeast of Picton Island. *Language Isolate*. Although Yahgan is generally considered a language isolate, Viegas Barros (1994) postulates a distant relationship with Kawésqar. Yahgan, the southern most language in the world, used to have five dialects: the **Wollaston Island dialect**, spoken in the southeast of the territory; the **southern dialect**, spoken in the southwest and subdivided into a western variety, Hatuwaia, and an eastern variety, Ufyargo; the **eastern dialect**, spoken on Navarino Island; the **central dialect**, spoken from Gable Island to Punta Davide; and the **western dialect**, spoken between Punta Davide and Brecknock Peninsula, bordering the Kawésqar area. In the last decades of the twentieth century the language became extinct in Argentina, and today it only has one speaker left in Chile.

Yahgan (or *Yámana*, *Háusi Kúta*) **[247]** Chile, most southern part of the Tierra del Fuego Archipelago and canals, between the Brecknock Peninsula and Cape Horn. *Language Isolate*. In the nineteenth century the Yahgan ethnic group is said to have amounted to 3,000 members. In the 1990s only three Yahgan women survived in the Ukika hamlet, near Puerto Williams on Isla Navarino. All three were over sixty years of age and had only spoken the language in their childhood. Today just one of them is still alive, which implies the pending extinction of the Yahgan language (extinct in Argentina).

Yaminahua **[227]** Bolivia, Department of Pando, Province of Nicolás Suárez, headwaters of the rivers Alto Yuruá and Purús, in Puerto Yaminawa. *Panoan*, South-Central. There are about 140 speakers out of an ethnic group of 160. During the rubber boom the Yaminahua were practically exterminated. Nowadays they form a small group that wanders between Peru, Brazil and Bolivia, more and more on the brink of extinction. The biggest group of Yaminahua (120) now resides permanently at Puerto Yaminahua where the *Escuela (Ecola) de la Misión Suiza* used to be installed. The language is seriously endangered in Bolivia (more in Brazil and Peru).

Yaminahua (or *Jaminahua*) **[227]** Peru, along the Purús, Yurua, and Mapuya rivers, and in Sepahua. *Panoan*, South-Central, Yaminahua-Sharanahua. There are two intercultural bilingual schools sponsored by the Ministry of Education. In Peru, the language is endangered with approximately 400 speakers out of an ethnic group of the same size (more in Bolivia and Brazil).

Yaminawa (*Jaminawá*, *Iaminawá*, *Xixinawá*, *Yawanawá*, *Bashonawá*, *Marinawá*) **[227]** Brazil, Acre State, Terra Indígena Alto Rio Purus, Terra Indígena Cabeceira do Rio Acre, Terra Indígena Jaminawa do Igarapé Preto, Terra Indígena Jaminawa Arara do

185

Rio Bagé, Terra Indígena Mamoadate. *Panoan*, South-Central, Yaminahua-Sharanahua. In the last decade more and more Yaminawa have come to the city of Rio Branco, where they generally end up in slum areas or under bridges with all the imaginable serious consequences. Except for the older generation, all Yaminawa are bilingual in Portuguese. Yaminawa, Arara do Acre, Shanenawá, and Yawanawá are considered dialects of one language (*Arara*). In Brazil, the language is endangered with an ethnic group of 612 members (1999) (more in Bolivia and Peru).

Yanam (or *Ninam*) [423] Brazil, Roraima State, Terra Indígena Yanomami, Mucajaí, Upper Uraricaá and Paragua rivers. *Yanomaman*. The Yanam are generally monolingual, but children are beginning to learn Portuguese. Despite a reported 400 speakers in Venezuela and Brazil out of an ethnic group of the same size, the Yanam language is to be considered seriously endangered.

Yanam (or *Ninam*) [423] Venezuela, Bolivar State, between the Upper Paricaa and Paragua rivers. *Yanomaman*. There are three dialects of Yanam. The drastic changes in the contact situation and the mortality rate of the Yanam Indians during the last decades could bring about the extinction of the Yanam language within the next generation. In 1985 the population had already been reduced to half of what it was in 1970. Despite a reported 400 speakers in Venezuela and Brazil out of an ethnic group of the same size, the Yanam language is to be considered seriously endangered.

Yanesha' (or *Amuesha*) [108] Peru, eastern foothills of the Andes, departments of Pasco and Junín, headwaters of the Pachitea and Perené rivers. *Arawakan*, Maipuran, Western Maipuran (heavily influenced by Quechua and old varieties of Quechua I – phonologically and lexically special). There is a bilingual education programme, but in some areas (Lower Palcazú) children no longer acquire the language, while they still do in other areas (Upper Perené and Upper Palcazú). The language is to be considered potentially endangered, with about 8,000 speakers out of an ethnic group of 10,000.

Yanomam [422b] Brazil, Roraima State and northern Amazonas State, Terra Indígena Yanomami. *Yanomaman*. The Yanomam language is potentially endangered, with about 3,800 speakers in Venezuela and Brazil out of an ethnic group of the same size.

Yanomam [422b] Venezuela, Amazonas State, headwaters of the Upper Parima and Orinoco rivers area. *Yanomaman*. Yanomam has two main dialects, and it is not in immediate danger of extinction if its speakers are helped in their adaptation to the oncoming contact situation with the rapidly penetrating national society. The language is potentially endangered, with about 3,800 speakers in Venezuela and Brazil out of an ethnic group of the same size.

Yanomami (or *Yanomamõ*, *Yanomama*, *Yanoama*, *Ianomãmi*, *Ianoama*, *Xirianá*) [422a] Brazil, Roraima State, Terra Indígena Yanomami, Waicá post, Uraricuera River and Catrimani River; Amazonas State, Toototobi post. *Yanomaman*. Yanomami forms a dialect continuum with Yanomam, Yanam, and Sánuma. These four groups together are one of the largest indigenous nations in the Americas that still retains its traditional way of life. Having had very little contact with outside society before the 1980s, the number of monolingual Yanomami is still quite high. The language is to be considered potentially endangered, with about 11,700 speakers out of an ethnic group of the same size, including Yanomam, Sánuma and Yanam (2000).

Yanomami (or *Yanomamï*, *Yanomamö*, *Yanoama*) **[422a]** Venezuela, south, states of Amazonas and Río Negro, in the Parima mountains, the valley of the Padamo River, on the Ocamo and Upper Orinoco rivers, and to the south of the Orinoco River. *Yanomaman*. The Yanomami were first contacted by a Salesian priest in 1957 and today their way of life is threatened by many outside factors, which in the long run may lead to the loss of their identity. The language is to be considered potentially endangered in Venezuela, with about 15,000 speakers out of an ethnic group of the same size (more in Brazil).

Yaruro (or *Pumé*) **[166]** Venezuela, Apure and Amazonas states, on the banks of the Orinoco, Sinaruco, Meta, and Apure rivers. *Language Isolate*. Due to contact with national society, the majority of the speakers manage Spanish quite well, but at the same time the Yaruro language is conserved at a satisfactory level. In 1992, the size of the ethnic group amounted to approximately 5,420. The language is to be considered potentially endangered.

Yatê (or *Iatê*, *Fulniô*, *Carnijó*) **[306]** Brazil, Pernambuco State, Sertão, Municipality of Águas Belas, in two villages. *Macro*-Ge, Yatê. While adult and elderly Fulniô still speak their mother tongue Yatê, children and youngsters prefer to speak Portuguese, a language today spoken by all Fulniô. Although the Yatê language is steadily losing ground to Portuguese, it still plays an important role in Fulniô society. With an ethnic group of 2,930 (1999) the language is to be considered endangered.

Yauna **[152]** Colombia, Department of Amazonas, on the Apaporis and Mirití rivers, in the Yaigojé Rió Apaporis reservation. *Tucanoan*, Eastern Tucanoan. With about ninety-five ethnic Yauna living in Miraña and Tanimuca communities, the language is to be considered seriously endangered.

Yavitero (or *Baniva-Yavitero*, *Banibo*) **[91]** Venezuela, Amazonas State, Yavita region, border area between Venezuela, Brazil, and Colombia *Arawakan*, Maipuran, Northern Maipuran, Inland. The Yavitero language is practically extinct with only one known elderly female speaker (Mosonyi & Mosonyi 2000). It is not clear how many persons are still left in the ethnic group, which was submitted to violent extermination practices in the 1930s.

Yawalapiti (or *Iaualapiti*) **[113]** Brazil, Mato Grosso State, Parque Indígena do Xingu, on the Tuatuari River, a few kilometres to the south of Posto Leonardo Villas Boas. *Arawakan*, Maipuran, Central Maipuran. Although Yawalapiti shares about 80 per cent of its lexicon with Mehinako and Waurá, its grammar is very different so that it has to be considered a separate language. The language is moribund, with perhaps eight speakers out of an ethnic group of 208 (2002).

Yawanawá (or *Yauanauá*, *Iauanauá*) **[235a]** Brazil, Acre State, Gregório River, Terra Indígena Rio Gregório. *Panoan*, South-Central, Yaminahua-Sharanahua. Yawanawá,

187

Arara do Acre, Shanenawá, and Yaminawa are all considered dialects of one language (*Arara*). With an ethnic group of 450 (1999) the language is to be considered endangered.

Yekuana (*Ye'kuana*, *Yekwana*, *Yecuana*, *Makiritare*, *Maiongong*, *So'to*) [410] Brazil, northwestern Roraima State, near the border with Venezuela, Terra Indígena Yanomami. *Cariban*, Southern, Southern Guiana. Most of the Yekuana – also commonly referred to as Makiritare – still speak their mother tongue. In Brazil the ethnic group amounts to approximately 430 persons (2000), which classifies the language as endangered (more in Venezuela).

Yekuana (or *Ye'kuana*, *Yecuana*, *De'kwana*, *Maquiritare*, *Maiongong*) [410] Venezuela, Amazonas State: in the east along the Cunucunuma River and the upper basins of the Padamo, Ventuari and Cuntinamo rivers. Bolivar State: communities of Caaji Atai'ña, Wasaiña and Santa María de Erebato along the Merevari River; Boca de Cushime, Boca de Kanarakuni and Boca de Guaña, Parroquia Aripao. *Cariban*, Southern, Southern Guiana. The Yekuana live in direct contact with the Sánema. Within their solid ethnic group of 4,470 all members speak the language. Whereas children and youngsters are now becoming bilingual in Spanish, most adults and elders hardly speak any Spanish. In Venezuela, the language is potentially endangered (more in Brazil).

Yine (or *Piro*, *Apurinña*, *Yinerï Tokani*) [119] Peru, southeast, Department of Ucayali: on the mouth of the Cushabatay River (tributary of the Ucayali); departments of Ucayali and Cuzco: Urubamba River (especially the lower zone), Manu River (tributaries on the right), the Upper Madre de Dios in the area of the mouth of the Manu River; Department of Madre de Dios: Acre River. *Arawakan*, Maipuran, Southern Maipuran, Purus. Like many other groups, the Yine suffered greatly during the rubber boom at the turn of the twentieth century. SIL has been involved in establishing bilingual schools in Yine communities since 1953. Today there is a bilingual education programme in the communities on the Urubamba River. The language is potentially endangered with approximately 2,150–3,500 speakers out of an ethnic group of the same size (including Mashco-Piro).

Yucuna-Matapí (or *Yukuna*) [84a] Colombia, Department of Amazonas, along the Mirití-Paraná River. *Arawakan*, Maipuran, Northern Maipuran, Inland. The Matapí used to live on the headwaters of the Popeyacá and Yapiyá – tributaries of the Mirití and Apoporis rivers. It seems that at the beginning of the twentieth century the majority of the Matapí either moved to Brazil or perhaps were sold as slaves. The few that remained in the region went to live with their allies, the Yucuna, and adopted the Yucuna language. The language is endangered, with some 600 ethnic Yucuna and 200 Matapí.

Yuhup [134a] Brazil, Amazonas State, between the Tiquié river to the north and the Curicuriari and Apaporis rivers to the south, Terra Indígena Alto Rio Negro, Terra Indígena Médio Rio Negro I and Terra Indígena Rio Apaporis. *Makuan*. Yuhup shares a large percentage of its lexicon with *Hup*. They are sometimes considered the same language for this reason, but they are best considered different languages. In Brazil, the language is endangered with about 370 speakers out of an ethnic group of the same size (more in Colombia).

Yuhup (or *Yuhup Makú*) **[134a]** Colombia, Department of Amazonas, between the Tiquié, Apaporis, and Taraira rivers. *Makuan*. Although Yuhup shares about 90 per cent of its lexicon with *Hup*, these languages are best considered different languages on the basis of phonological and grammatical differences, and the lack of mutual intelligibility. Today the nomadic Yuhup are in the process of settling down, substituting their ways of subsistence, formerly based on hunting and gathering, with horticulture and fishing. In Colombia the language is seriously endangered, with only about 130 speakers out of an ethnic group of the same size (more in Brazil).

Yuki (or *Yuqui*, *Yukí*, *Mbiá*, *Bía*) **[335f]** Bolivia, Department of Cochabamba, in between the rivers Chimoré and Ichilo, Biá Rekuaté. *Tupian*, Tupí-Guaraní, Guarayu-Siriono-Jora (II). In 1995, there were about 125 speakers out of an ethnic group of 155. The New Tribes Mission started to contact the nomadic Yuki in 1965, but it was not until 1971 that a group of Yuki settled at the Chimoré River. They became completely dependent on the missionaries who provided them with medicine, clothing and even food. In 1986 and 1989 two other unknown groups of Yuki mountain nomads in the Víbora River region (Ichilo) and the Tres Cruces region (Ichilo) were contacted and brought to the Mbia-Recuaté Community. Used to a subsistence system based on hunting and gathering, the Yuki have a very hard time adapting to cultivating and producing their own food, which greatly contributes to the miserable state in which they live nowadays. It is said that there is yet another uncontacted nomadic group of Yuki of about fourteen persons. The language is to be considered seriously endangered.

Yuko (or *Yuco*, *Yukpa*, *Yucpa*, *Japrería*) **[382]** Colombia, foothills of the Serranía de Parijá: in protected areas (Iroka) and in the settlements Menkue, La Bodega and El Vallito; northern part of the eastern Cordillera, parallel to the borderline between Colombia and Venezuela. *Cariban*, Northern, Coastal. Inside the protected areas the language is used all the time; outside the areas, for instance in settlements like Menkue, La Bodega and El Vallito, the language is only spoken when there are no outsiders present. With approximately 3,530 members in the ethnic group the language is potentially endangered (more in Venezuela).

Yukpa (or *Yucpa*, *Japrería*) **[382]** Venezuela, Zulia State, Cesar region, northern part of the Sierra de Perijá, on the border with Colombia, approximately between the rivers Palmar in the north and Tucuco in the south. *Cariban*, Northern, Coastal. The Yukpa form the only surviving Cariban group in the west of Venezuela. Most adults are still monolingual, but the younger generation is becoming more and more bilingual in Spanish. Yukpa can be subdivided into three dialect groups: **Macoíta**, **Irapa** and the more divergent dialect **Japrería**. There are more than 4,000 speakers out of an ethnic group of the same size (more in Colombia). The language is potentially endangered.

Yuracaré (or *Yurakaré*) **[212]** Bolivia, Department of Cochabamba, provinces of Chapare and Carrasco; Department of Beni, Province of Moxos; Department of Santa Cruz, Province of Ichilo. *Language Isolate*. In the past decades the Yuracaré have lost more and more of their profound ethnic identity due to the systematic acculturation methods of the New Tribes Mission. There are about 2,670 speakers out of an ethnic

189

group of 3,330. The language is to be considered endangered, since most speakers are over twenty-five years old.

***Yurutí* [153a]** Colombia, border area with Brazil, along the Yi and its tributaries, and the Upper Paca. *Tucanoan*, Eastern Tucanoan, Central, Bara. The Yurutí are very attached to their language and prefer to use it – instead of the local lingua franca Tucano – in everyday communication with members of other groups in the region (Kinch and Kinch 2000). Nevertheless, the language is to be considered endangered, since the ethnic group consists of only about 610 members (more in Brazil).

***Záparo* (or *Kayapi*) [173]** Ecuador, Province of Pastaza, between the Curaray River and the lower course of the Bobanaza – principally along the Conambo River – in the Montalvo area. *Zaparoan*. The Záparo form the smallest indigenous group in the Ecuadorian Amazon. Their history demonstrates the devastating impact of Western civilisation as their numbers collapsed from possibly more than 100,000 to approximately 120. Today the Záparo may well be on their way to extinction and their language moribund. About twenty elderly Záparo still have some variable degree of knowledge of the language. While all Záparo speak Quichua, about one third of the ethnic group speaks Achuar as well. Recently small groups of Ecuadorian Záparo have been going into Peru to contact their relatives, the Arabela. In the 1930s and/or 1940s, the Arabela were held as forced labourers on an Ecuadorian farm along the Curaray River. The Arabela who are nowadays in Peru managed to escape, but a small group stayed on in Ecuador. It is possible that this small group of Arabela still exists, although by now its members will probably have become speakers of Quichua.

***Zenú* [10a]** Colombia, Department of Córdoba, Municipality of San Andrés de Sotavento, Tuchin, Cerro Vidales, El Campano, La Cruz de Guayabo, Fleca, and Comején. *Chocoan*. Today the language is no longer spoken by the approximately 33,910 ethnic Zenú.

***Zo'é* (or *Poturu*) [358a]** Brazil, Northern Pará State, between the Cuminapanema and Erepecuru rivers, Oriximiná Municipality, Terra Indígena Cuminapanema/Urukuriana. *Tupian*, Tupi-Guarani, Oyampi (VII). After many short and tense contact episodes between the New Tribes Mission and the Zo'é, definitive contact took place in 1987 when the Zo'é approached the Mission's base, Esperaça. During the whole contact process (1982–90) many Zo'é fell victim to previously unknown diseases, which resulted in great demographic losses. In 1997, all Zo'é were still monolingual speakers of their native language. Now that the Zo'é have definitively come out of isolation the language is seriously endangered, with only 152 members in the ethnic group (1998).

***Zoró* (*Pageyn*) [379a]** Brazil, Mato Grosso State, Aripuanã area, Terra Indígena Zoró. *Tupian*, Monde. The Zoró were in close contact with the Gavião and Karó groups during the twentieth century. Although Zoró, Gavião and Cinta Larga are dialects of the same language (**Cinta-Larga**), each of these groups sees itself as distinct from the others. Today all Zoró still speak their mother tongue. Nevertheless, the language is endangered, with an ethnic group of approximately 414 persons (2001).

***Zuruahã* (or *Sorowaha*, *Suruwaha*) [131a]** Brazil, Amazonas State, Juruá, Jutaí and Purus rivers area, Terra Indígena Terra Indígena Zuruahã. *Arauan*. The Zuruahã were only contacted in 1980 and today they still maintain their traditional way of life. The ethnic group consists of 143 members (1995). Although all Zuruahã are still monolingual, the-language is to be considered seriously endangered due to the reduced number of its ethnic group.

References

Aikhenvald, Alexandra Y. (1996) 'Areal diffusion in Northwest Amazonia: the case of Tariana'. *Anthropological Linguistics* 38: 73–113.

——(2002) *Language contact in Amazonia.* Oxford: Oxford University Press.

Albó, Xavier (1995) *Bolivia plurilingüe: Una guía para planificadores y educadores.* 3 vols. La Paz: UNICEF-CIPCA.

Angenot de Lima, Geralda (2002) *Description phonologique, grammaticale et lexicale du Moré, langue amazonienne de Bolivie et du Brésil.* 2 vols. Porto Velho: Editora da Universidade Federal de Rondonia.

Arango Ochoa, Raúl and Enrique Sánchez Gutiérrez (1998) *Los pueblos indígenas de Colombia 1997. Desarrollo y territorio.* Bogotá: Tercer Mundo Editores and Departamento Nacional de Planeación.

Barnes, Janet (1999) 'Tucano'. In: R.M.W. Dixon and Alexandra Y. Aikhenvald (eds) *The Amazonian languages.* Cambridge: Cambridge University Press. 207–26.

Boven, Karin and Robby Morroy (2000) 'Indigenous languages of Suriname'. In: Francisco Queixalós and Odile Renault-Lescure (eds) *As Línguas Amazônicas Hoje.* São Paulo: Instituto Socioambiental. 377–84.

Carlin, Eithne B. (2001) 'Of riches and rhetoric: languages in Suriname'. In: R. Hoefte and P. Meel (eds) *Twentieth-century Suriname: Continuities and Discontinuities in a New World Society.* Kingston: Ian Randle Publishers.

Caspar, Franz (1975) *Die Tuparí: Ein Indianerstamm in Westbrasilien.* Monographien zur Völkerkunde herausgegeben vom Hamburgischen museum für Völkerkunde VII. Berlin/New York: Walter de Gruyter.

Censabella, Marisa (1999) *Las lenguas indígenas de la Argentina: Una mirada actual.* Buenos Aires: Eudeba.

Censo Indígena 1992. República de Venezuela. Oficina Central de Estadística e Informática.

Dietrich, Wolf (1986) *El idioma Chiriguano: Gramática, textos, vocabulario.* Madrid: Instituto de Cooperación Iberoamericana (Ediciones Cultura Hispánica).

Díez Astete, Álvaro and David Murillo (1998) *Pueblos indígenas de Tierras Bajas: Características principales.* La Paz: PNUD.

Dixon, R. M. W. and Alexandra Y. Aikhenvald (eds) (1999) *The Amazonian languages.* Cambridge: Cambridge University Press.

Domínguez, Marcelo, Lucí Golluscio, and Analía Gutiérrez (subm.). 'Los vilelas del Chco: desestructuración y estrategias identitarias' (submitted for publication to *Indiana.* Berlin: Ibero-Amerikanische Institut Preussischer Kulturbesitz.

Fabre, Alain (1998) *Manual de las lenguas indígenas sudamericanas.* 2 vols. Munich/ Newcastle: Lincom Europa (Lincom Handbook in Linguistics 05).

Forte, Janette (2000) 'Amerindian languages of Guyana'. In: Francisco Queixalós and Odile Renault-Lescure (eds) *As línguas Amazônicas hoje.* São Paulo: Instituto Socioambiental. 317–33.

Gaceta Indigenista, (1975) Caracas.

García Rivera, Fernando Antonio (2000) 'Estado de las lenguas en el Perú'. In: Francisco Queixalós and Odile Renault-Lescure (eds.) *As línguas Amazônicas hoje.* São Paulo: Instituto Socioambiental. 333–42.

Gnerre, Maurizio (2000) 'Conocimiento científico de las lenguas de la Amazonía del Ecuador'. In: Francisco Queixalós and Odile Renault-Lescure (eds) *As línguas Amazônicas hoje*. São Paulo: Instituto Socioambiental. 277–86.

Gómez-Imbert, Elsa (2000) 'Introducción al estudio de las lenguas del Piraparaná (Vaupés)'. In: María Stella González de Pérez and María Luisa Rodríguez de Montes (eds) *Lenguas indígenas de Colombia: Una visión descriptiva*. Santafé de Bogotá: Instituto Cara y Cuervo. 321–56.

González Ñañez, Omar (2000) 'Las lenguas del Amazonas Venezolano'. In: Francisco Queixalós and Odile Renault-Lescure (eds) *As línguas Amazônicas hoje*. São Paulo: Instituto Socioambiental. 385–418.

González de Pérez, María Stella and María Luisa Rodríguez de Montes (eds) (2000) *Lenguas indígenas de Colombia: Una visión descriptiva*. Santafé de Bogotá: Instituto Cara y Cuervo.

Grenand, Françoise (2000) 'La Connaissance Scientifique des Langues Amérindiennes en Guyane Française'. In: Francisco Queixalós and Odile Renault-Lescure (eds) *As línguas Amazônicas hoje*. São Paulo: Instituto Socioambiental. 307–16.

Grimes, Barbara F. (ed.) (1992) *Ethnologue: Languages of the World*. 12th edn. Dallas: Summer Institute of Linguistics.

——(ed.) (2000) *Ethnologue: Languages of the world*. 14th edn. Dallas TX: Summer Institute of Linguistics.

Guirardello, R. (1999) 'A reference grammar of Trumai'. Doctoral dissertation, Rice University, Houston TX.

Henley, Paul, Marie-Claude Mattéi-Müller and Howard Reid (1996). 'Cultural and linguistic affinities of the foraging people of North Amazonia: a new perspective'. *Anthropológica* 83: 3–37. Caracas.

Instituto Colombiano de Antropología (2004) *Introducción a la Colombia amerindia*. Banco de la República, Biblioteca Luís Ángel Arango, Biblioteca Virtual, online version: http://www.lablaa.org/blaavirtual/letra-a/amerindi/

Instituto Nacional de Estadística (1996) *Censo indigena rural de Tierras Bajas, Bolivia: 1994*. La Paz.

Instituto Socioambiental (2004a) 'Indigenous peoples in Brazil: encyclopedia'. Online version: http://www.socioambiental.org/pib/english/whwhhow/wichpe.shtm

——(2004b) 'Enciclopédia dos povos indígenas'. Online version: http://www.socioambiental.org/pib/portugues/quonqua/cadapovo.shtm

——(2004c) 'General table of the indigenous peoples in Brazil'. Online version: http://www.socioambiental.org/pib/english/whwhhow/table.asp

Juncosa, José E. (2000) 'Mapa lingüístico de la Amazonía Ecuatoriana'. In: Francisco Queixalós and Odile Renault-Lescure (eds) *As línguas Amazônicas hoje*. São Paulo: Instituto Socioambiental. 263–75.

Kinch, Rodney and Pamela Kinch (2000) 'El yurutí'. In: María Stella González de Pérez and María Luisa Rodríguez de Montes (eds) *Lenguas indígenas de Colombia: Una visión descriptiva*. Santafé de Bogotá: Instituto Cara y Cuervo. 469–87.

Koch-Grünberg, Theodor (1913) 'Abschluss meiner Reise durch Nordbrasilien zum Orinoco, mit besonderer Berücksichtigung der von mir besuchten Indianerstämme'. *Zeitschrift für Ethnologie* 45: 448–74.

Landaburu, Jon (2004) 'Clasificación de las lenguas indígenas de Colombia'. Online version: http://www.banrep.gov.co/blaavirtual/letra-l/lengua/clas3.htm

Lema, Ana María (ed.) (1997) *Pueblos indígenas de la Amazonía boliviana*. La Paz: CID-Plural.

Martins, Silvana and Valteir Martins (1999) 'Makú'. In: R. M. W. Dixon and Alexandra Y. Aikhenvald (eds) *The Amazonian languages*. Cambridge: Cambridge University Press. 251–68.

Melià, Bartolomeu (1997) *Pueblos indígenas en el Paraguay. Demografía histórica y análisis de los resultados del Censo Nacional de Población y Viviendas, 1992.* Paraguay: Dirección General de Estadística, encuestas y censos.

Migliazzi, Ernest C. (1985) 'Languages of the Orinoco-Amazon region: Current status'. In: Manelis Klein, Harriet E. and Louisa R. Stark (eds) *South American Indian languages: Retrospect and Prospect.* Austin TX: University of Texas Press. 17–139.

Moore, Denny (fc.) 'Endangered languages of lowland tropical South America'. In: Mathias Brenzinger (ed.) *Language diversity endangered.* Berlin/New York: Mouton de Gruyter.

Mosonyi, Esteban Emilio and Jorge Carlos Mosonyi (2002) *Manual de lenguas indígenas de Venezuela.* Caracas: Fundación Bigott.

Museo Etnográfico *Andres Barbero* (2004) Online version: http://www.museobarbero.org.py/

Nimuendajú, Curt (1955) 'Vocabulários Makuší, Wapičána, Ipurinã' e Kapišanã'. *Journal de la Société des Américanistes,* n.s. 44: 179–97.

Nordenskiöld, Erland (1915) *Forskningar och äventyr i Sydamerika.* Stockholm: Albert Bonniers Förlag.

Pozzi-Escot, Inés (ed.) (1998) *El multilingüismo en el Perú.* Cuzco: CBC-SID.

Pozzobon, Jorge (1994) 'Indios por opção'. *Porto e Virgula* 17: 34–9. Porto Alegre: Instituto Socioambiental.

Queixalós, Francisco (2000) 'Langues de Guyane Française'. In: Francisco Queixalós and Odile Renault-Lescure (eds) *As línguas Amazônicas hoje.* São Paulo: Instituto Socioambiental. 299–306.

Reichel-Dolmatoff, Gerardo (1946) 'Etnografía chimila'. *Boletín de Arqueología* 2(2): 95–156. Bogotá.

Ricardo, Carlos Alberto (ed.) (2000) Povos indígenas no Brasil, 1996/2000. São Paulo: Instituto Socioambiental.

Rivet, Paul (1953) 'La langue Mašubi'. *Journal de la Société des Américanistes de Paris* 42: 119–25.

Rondon, Cândido Mariano da Silva (1916) 'Conferencias realizadas nos dias 5, 7 e 9 de Outubro de 1915 pelo Sr. Coronel Cândido Mariano da Silva Rondon, no Theatro Phenix de Rio de Janeiro sobre trabalhos da Expedição Roosevelt e da Commissão Telegráfica'. *Commissão de Linhas Telegraphicas Estratégicas de Matto Grosso ao Amazonas,* Publicação no. 42. Rio de Janeiro: Typ.

Salas, Adalbert (1996) 'Lenguas indígenas de Chile'. In: Jorge L. Hidalgo, Virgilio F. Schiappacasse, Hans F. Niemeyer, Carlos del S. Aldunate and Pedro R. Mege (eds) *Etnografía. Sociedades indígenas contemporáneas y su ideología.* Santiago de Chile: Editorial Andrés Bello (Culturas de Chile, vol. 2) 257–95.

Sánchez Cabezas, G. (2003) 'Vigencia de las lenguas aborigines de Chile'. Paper presented at the 51th International Congress of Americanists, Santiago de Chile, 14–18 July 2003.

Seki, Lucy (1999) 'The Upper Xingu as an incipient linguistic area'. In: R. M. W. Dixon and Alexandra Y. Aikhenvald (eds) *The Amazonian languages.* Cambridge: Cambridge University Press. 417–30.

Shafter, Robert (1962) 'Aruacan (not Arawakan)', *Anthropological Linguistics* 4 (4): 31–40.

Solís Fonseca, Gustavo (2000) 'La Lingüística Amerindia Peruana de la Selva'. In: Francisco Queixalós and Odile Renault-Lescure (eds) *As línguas Amazônicas hoje.* São Paulo: Instituto Socioambiental. 343–60.

Sorensen, A. P. Jr (1967) [1972] 'Multilingualism in the Northwest Amazon'. *American Anthropologist* 69: 670–84. Repr. pp. 78–93 of *Sociolinguistics,* eds J. B. Pride and J. Holmes, Harmondsworth: Penguin, 1972.

Stark, Louisa R. (1985) 'History of the Quichua of Santiago del Estero'. In: Harriet E. Manelis Klein and Louisa R. Stark (eds) *South American Indian languages: Retrospect and Prospect.* Austin TX: University of Texas Press. 732–52.

Viegas Barros, P. (1994) 'La clasificación de las lenguas patagónicas. Revisión de hipótesis del grupo lingüístico "andino-meridional" de Joseph Greenberg'. *Cuadernos del Instituto Nacional de Antropología* 15: 167–84. Buenos Aires.

Welch, Betty and Birdie West (2000) 'El tucano'. In: María Stella González de Pérez and María Luisa Rodríguez de Montes (eds) *Lenguas indígenas de Colombia: Una visión descriptiva.* Santafé de Bogotá: Instituto Cara y Cuervo. 419–36.

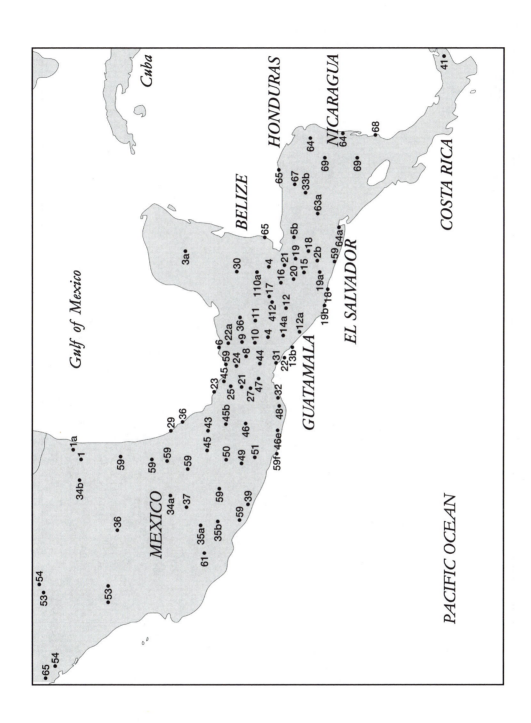

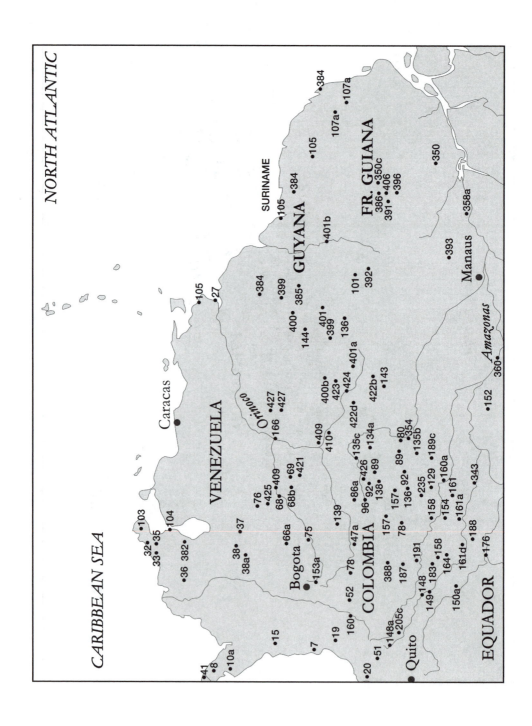

Meso-America

Willem Adelaar and J. Diego Quesada

Acatec (*Akateko*) **[10a]** Guatemala. *Mayan*, Kanjobalan branch. 20,000 speakers in San Miguel Acatán, Huehuetenango; also a few speakers in Mexico (Chiapas).

Achí **[19a]** Guatemala. *Mayan*, Quichean branch. The language of Rabinal and neighbouring communities in Baja Verapaz. Generally treated as a dialect of Quiché.

Aguacatec (*Awakateko*) **[16]** Guatemala. *Mayan*, Mamean branch. 16,000 speakers in Aguacatán, Huehuetenango.

Amuzgo **[48]** Mexico. *Oto-Manguean*, Amuzgo branch. Language spoken in a border area of the states of Guerrero (16,205 speakers) and Oaxaca (2,454 speakers) not far from the Pacific coast. In Garza Cuarón and Lastra (1991) Guerrero Amuzgo and Oaxaca Amuzgo are listed as separate languages. Amuzgo is said to have the highest percentage of monolinguals (38 per cent) among all native languages of Mexico, with a total number of speakers of 28,228 (INEGI 1993).

Ayapanec (*Ayapa Zoque*) **[22a]** Mexico. *Mixe-Zoquean*, Zoquean branch. Language spoken by about forty people in Jalpa de Méndez, Tabasco. Highly endangered (Garza Cuarón and Lastra 1991; Wichmann 1995).

Bocotá (*Buglere*, *Bukutá*, *Guaymí Sabanero*) Panama. *Chibchan*, Guaymían branch. 2,500 speakers. Most speakers live in the Province of Veraguas. The language is rather healthy in Veraguas. However, a small group of Bocotás has moved to the southern Province of Chiriquí, and have come to live among the Guaymí. For that reason, they are most often confused with them; in fact, they are called Guaymí Sabanero. They even migrate together, so that there are also some Bocotás living in Costa Rica. The Chiriquí dialect of Bocotá is seriously endangered, so that a situation of dialect death, similar to that of the Teribe, could occur.

Boruca or *Brunka* Costa Rica. *Chibchan*, Isthmian. Practically extinct. There remain only three elderly speakers. It was spoken in the Boruca Reservation, in the Province of Puntarenas. Language attitude was apparently the ultimate reason for decay, as younger generations utterly despised the language. The Boruca sense of identity is in their craftsmanship, not the language.

Bribri Costa Rica. *Chibchan*, Viceita branch. 6,000 speakers. It is spoken in the Talamanca mountain region, which divides the provinces of Puntarenas in the Pacific and Limón in the Atlantic. Dialectal differences reflect this geographic fact. There is extensive bilingualism but the language is not seriously endangered, there being a strong tradition.

Cabécar Costa Rica. *Chibchan*, Viceita branch. According to lexico-statistical analyses, the temporal separation of Bribri and Cabécar is only 1,100 years. Like Bribri, dialectal variation includes Atlantic and Pacific dialects. Cabécar is the only language of Costa Rica that has monolingual speakers, basically women.

Cacaopera [64a] El Salvador. *Misumalpan*. This language used to be spoken in Cacaopera (department of Morazán) and Lislique (department of La Unión) in eastern El Salvador. It was closely related to the (extinct) Matagalpa language of Nicaragua. Cacaopera is reportedly extinct.

Cahita [66] Mexico. *Uto-Aztecan*, Taracahita branch. 462 speakers (Manrique 1997).

Cakchiquel (*Kaqchikel*) Guatemala. *Mayan*, Quichean branch. 406,000 speakers in the departments of Chimaltenango, Escuintla, Guatemala, Sacatepéquez, Sololá, Suchitepéquez.

Chatino [47] Mexico. *Oto-Manguean*, Zapotecan branch. Language spoken in the southern part of Oaxaca by 20,543 people (Garza Cuarón and Lastra 1991). Chatino has a high percentage of monolinguals (30 per cent) and 28, 987 speakers according to INEGI (1993).

Chiapanec [41] Mexico. *Oto-Manguean*, Mangue branch. Language spoken near Tuxtla Gutiérrez, state of Chiapas, until the 1950s. It is now presumably extinct. Close relatives of Chiapanec (the Mangue group) were spoken in Nicaragua until 1900.

Chichimeca-Jonaz [34a] Mexico. *Oto-Manguean*, Oto-Pame branch. About 877 speakers in San Luis de la Paz (state of Guanajuato) (Garza Cuarón and Lastra 1991). Manrique (1997) gives 1,582 speakers.

Chicomuceltec [1a] Mexico. *Mayan*, Huastecan branch. This language is reported extinct by most sources, but Manrique (1997), based on the 1990 INEGI census, lists twenty-four speakers.

Chinantec [21a] Mexico. *Oto-Manguean*, Chinantecan branch. Highly fragmented language spoken in the northern part of the state of Oaxaca in the former districts of Tuxtepec and Choapan. Merrifield (1994) distinguishes 14 Chinantec languages. The total number of speakers (77,087 in 1980) is increasing (Garza Cuarón and Lastra 1991). INEGI (1993) reports 109,100 speakers for Chinantec.

Chocho (***Chuchona, Chocholteco***) |45| Mexico. *Oto-Manguean*, Popolocan branch. The language is spoken in a border area of the states of Oaxaca and Puebla. Together with the closely related Popoloca dialects it has 12,310 speakers (Garza Cuarón and Lastra 1991). There is a rich legacy of colonial documents in Chocho illustrating its historical bifurcation from neighbouring Popoloca. INEGI (1995) lists 12,554 Chocho speakers, which presumably include the speakers of Popoloca as well.

Chol (***Ch'ol***) |6| Mexico. *Mayan*, Cholan branch. Historically important language associated with the city-state of Palenque of the classic Mayan civilisation. The language has played a crucial role in the decipherment of the Mayan writing system. Chol has 96,776 speakers divided over the main dialects of ***Tila*** and ***Tumbalá*** in the northern part of the state of Chiapas (Garza Cuarón and Lastra 1991). INEGI (1993) reports 128,240 speakers of Chol.

Chontal (***de Tabasco***) [32] Mexico. *Mayan*, Cholan branch. Language spoken in the state of Tabasco by about 60,000 people (Garza Cuarón and Lastra 1991). This number of speakers is based on Schumann. INEGI (1995) indicates a much lower number: 36,267 speakers.

Chortí (***Ch'orti'***) |56| Guatemala. *Mayan*, Cholan branch. 52,000 speakers in eastern Guatemala (departments of Chiquimula and Zacapa) and a few in Honduras (near ruins of Copán). The language was closely connected to the development of Mayan hieroglyphic writing.

Chuj |11| Guatemala. *Mayan*, Chujean branch. 29,000 speakers in the department of Huehuetenango (San Mateo Ixtatán, Nentón); also a few thousand in Mexico.

Cochimí Mexico. *Hokan*, Yuman branch. Endangered language spoken by some 220 people in Baja California Norte (Ensenada) according to Garza Cuarón and Lastra (1991). Manrique (1997) reports 148 speakers. No monolinguals (INEGI 1993).

Cora Mexico. *Uto-Aztecan* language of the Cora-Huichol group. 12,240 speakers in Nayar, state of Nayarit (Garza Cuarón and Lastra 1991). INEGI (1993) lists 11,923 speakers.

Cucapá Mexico. *Hokan*, Yuman branch. Endangered language spoken by 178 people in Baja California Norte (Mexicali) according to Garza Cuarón and Lastra (1991). Manrique (1997) reports 136 speakers.

Cuicatec |50| Mexico. *Oto-Manguean* language, Mixtecan branch. The language is spoken by 14,155 people in northern Oaxaca (Garza Cuarón and Lastra 1991). It is closely related to Mixtec. INEGI (1993) indicates a lower number of 12,677 speakers.

Cuitlatec Mexico. *Unclassified language* or *isolate*, spoken in the western part of the state of Guerrero until the 1950s. The language was typologically divergent (with some influence from neighbouring Tarascan) and is now reported extinct.

Cuna (***Tule***) Panama. *Chibchan*. There are approximately 70,000 speakers, the second largest group of Chibchan affiliation. Most of them live on the San Blas Islands and

199

on the mainland, but some 10,000 have moved to Panama City, and the port of Colón. The Cunas are famous for their *molas*. The language is also spoken by some 1,000 speakers around the Gulf of Urabá in Colombia.

Emberá (***Atrato***, ***Darien***, ***Cholo***) Panama. *Chocoan*. 8,000 people, Province of Darien, in the lowland jungle, though most speakers (around 40,000) live in Colombia. Dialectal differences do not have to do with the political frontier (that is, there is no Colombian or Panamanian Emberá), but rather between two varieties of the San Juan River and those of its tributaries; the latter are the ones who have migrated to Panama. Emberá has a rich dialectal variation; the following dialects are recognised: the one in Panama or Northern, Antioquian, also called Dabeiba, Chami, Baudó, and the one on the southern coast of Buenaventura.

Garífuna (***Black Carib***, ***Central American Carib***) Honduras. *Arawakan*, Northern branch. Originally from the island of St Vincent. Approximately 100,000 speakers. Also spoken in Belize, Guatemala and Nicaragua. In Honduras it is spoken in the Departments of Cortés and Gracias a Dios. There is a high degree of bilingualism with English-based Caribbean Creole.

Guarijío (***Varohío***) Mexico. *Uto-Aztecan* language closely related to Tarahumara of the Taracahita branch. About 300 speakers in the state of Chihuahua (Garza Cuarón and Lastra 1991). There are two distinct varieties of Guarijío: ***Mountain Guarijí***o and ***Lowland Guarijío***.

Guatuso or ***Maleku Jlaika*** Costa Rica. *Chibchan*, Pota Branch. 300 speakers. Spoken in the northern lowlands, in the Province of Alajuela. There are two main reservations: Tonjibe and Margarita. There is a radio station which broadcasts in both Spanish and Guatuso, with the aim of rescuing the already endangered language.

Guaymí (***Ngabére***, ***Ngobe***, ***Move***) Panama. *Chibchan*, Guaymían branch. There are approximately 150,000 speakers, mostly in Panama, in the Provinces of Chiriquí, Bocas del Toro and Veraguas. The Guaymí constitute one of the most marginal(ised) groups of Panama, despite (or perhaps due to) their ever-increasing population size. Semi-nomadic, and polygamous, the Guaymí have 'invaded' other indigenous territories of Panama, e.g. Teribe, thereby clashing with the local groups; others have migrated to Costa Rica and established themselves at the skirts of the Talamanca mountain range. There are some 5,000 speakers in Costa Rica.

Huastec (***Tenek***) [1] Mexico. *Mayan*, Huastecan branch. Language spoken by 103,788 people in the states of San Luis Potosí and Veracruz (Garza Cuarón and Lastra 1991). The other Huastecan language, Chicomuceltec (in the state of Chiapas), is presumably extinct. Huastecan is the most divergent branch of Mayan, which may be due to its early geographical separation from the Mayan heartland. The number of speakers listed by INEGI (1993) is 120,739.

Huave [31] Mexico. *Linguistic Isolate*. Spoken in the coastal region of southeastern Oaxaca (in San Mateo del Mar and four other towns). The language had 9,972 speakers in 1980 (Garza Cuarón and Lastra 1991). It is surrounded by Zapotec speakers. INEGI (1993) gives 11,955 speakers.

Huichol (*Wixarika, Wixaritari*) [53] Mexico. *Uto-Aztecan* language of the Cora-Huichol group. 51,850 speakers in the state of Nayarit (Nayar) and in the state of Jalisco (Mesquitic, Zapopan, Guadalajara) (source: Garza Cuarón and Lastra 1991). The INEGI census (1993) reports a much lower figure: 19,363 speakers. Strong ethnic identity associated with pilgrimages to a holy place called Wirikuta.

Itzá (*Itzaj*) [3c] Guatemala. *Mayan*, Yucatecan branch. 3,000 speakers near the shores of Lake Petén (department of El Petén). Descendants of the last Maya stronghold conquered by Spaniards in 1697.

Ixcatec [44] Mexico. *Oto-Manguean*, Popolocan branch. A highly endangered, historically important language, spoken in Santa María Ixcatlan, Oaxaca. Only a few elderly speakers can still be found (Michael Swanton, pers. comm.). Other Ixcatec listed in statistical overviews (as many as 1,220 in INEGI 1995, Manrique 1997) are presumably Mazatec speakers.

Ixil [17] Guatemala. *Mayan*, Mamean branch. 71,000 speakers in the department of El Quiché (Chajul, Nebaj, etc.).

Jacaltec (*Popti'*) [12c] Guatemala. *Mayan*, Kanjobalan branch. 32,000 speakers near Jacaltenango (department of Huehuetenango) and a few in Mexico (Chiapas).

Jicaque or **Tol [33b]** Honduras. *Language Isolate*. 300 speakers. It is spoken in the department of Morazán, and by some elderly speakers in the department of Yoro. It has an extinct variant, which used to be spoken in the Departments of Atlántida and Colón. There are varying degrees of bilingualism in Spanish; adult male leaders are more fluent, while women and children are more limited.

Kanjobal (*Q'anjob'al*) [12] Guatemala. *Mayan*, Kanjobalan branch. 112,000 speakers in the department of Huehuetenango and a few thousand in Mexico (also in Florida, US).

Kekchí (*Q'eqchi'*) [21] Guatemala. *Mayan*, Quichean branch. 361,000 speakers in Alta Verapaz, El Petén and Izabal. This predominantly monolingual group has expanded considerably during the last century. Originally a highland group, it now occupies a large part of the tropical lowlands.

Kickapoo Mexico. *Algonquian*, language spoken by a group of descendants of North American Indian refugees in the state of Coahuila (Ranchería Nacimiento in the district of Melchor Muzquiz). 400 Mexican speakers reported by Garza Cuarón and Lastra (1991). Manrique (1997) mentions 232 speakers in Mexico.

Kiliwa Mexico. *Hokan*, Yuman branch. Endangered language spoken by some ninety people in the state of Baja California Norte (Ensenada). Source: Garza Cuarón and Lastra (1991). Manrique (1997) reports forty-one speakers. No monolinguals (INEGI 1993).

Kumiai Mexico. *Hokan*, Yuman branch. Endangered language spoken by a few people in the state of Baja California Norte (Tecate and Ensenada, also in the US). There are ninety-six Mexican speakers according to Manrique (1997). No monolinguals (INEGI 1993).

Lacandón **[3b]** Mexico. *Mayan*, Yucatecan branch. Highly endangered language of a formerly isolated group located in the Usumacinta basin in the eastern part of the state of Chiapas. The language has about 200 speakers and is closely related to Yucatec. Manrique (1997) mentions 104 speakers of Lacandón.

Lenca **[63a]** Honduras. *Language Isolate*. Practically extinct. There remain some semi-speakers in the Departments of La Paz, Intibucá, Lempira, Comayagua, Santa Barbara, Valle and Morazán. An extinct dialect variant (***Chilanga***) used to be spoken in El Salvador.

Lower Pima (***Pima Bajo***) Mexico. *Uto-Aztecan* language, Piman branch. Spoken, among other places, in Yécora, Sonora. 553 speakers in 1980 (Garza Cuarón and Lastra 1991).

Mam **[15]** Guatemala. Mayan, Mamean branch. 686,000 speakers in southwestern Guatemala (departments of Huehuetenango, Quetzaltenango and San Marcos) and 28,000 in Mexico (eastern Chiapas).

Matlaltzinca **[35a]** Mexico. *Oto-Manguean* language of the Oto-Pame branch. The language is spoken by 1,792 people in San Francisco Oztotilpan, state of México (Garza Cuarón and Lastra 1991). Manrique (1997) lists 1,452 speakers.

Mayo Mexico. *Uto-Aztecan* language of the Taracahita branch, spoken by 56,387 people (1980) in Sinaloa (El Fuerte) and Sonora (Etchojoa, Huatabampo, Navojoa). (Garza Cuarón and Lastra 1991). INEGI (1993) lists 37,410 speakers.

Mazahua **[37]** Mexico. *Oto-Manguean* language of the Oto-Pame branch, mainly spoken in the state of México and in Michoacán (Zitácuaro). 194,125 speakers according to Garza Cuarón and Lastra (1991). The number given by INEGI (1993) is much lower, namely 127,826.

Mazatec **[43]** Mexico. *Oto-Manguean* language of the Popolocan branch. The number of speakers (124,176 in 1980) is increasing. The (internally diversified) Mazatec language is spoken in northern Oaxaca by a very traditional people. Statistic information from Garza Cuarón and Lastra (1991). INEGI (1993) lists 168,374 speakers for Mazatec.

Miskito **[64]** Nicaragua. *Misumalpan*. It is spoken by some 150,000 people in Nicaragua, in the Department of Zelaya, now part of the Autonomous Northern Atlantic Region, with a concentration in the city of Puerto Cabezas, and towns and villages of Prinzapolka, Tronquera, San Carlos (Río Coco), Waspam, Leimus, Bocana de Paiwas, Karawala, Sangnilaya, Wasla, Sisin, Rosita, Bonanza, Siuna, Bihmuna, and all along the Rio Coco area. There are some other 30,000 speakers in Honduras, in the

Department of Gracias a Dios. The language is rather healthy, to the point that even mestizo speakers of Spanish learn it.

***Mixe* [27]** Mexico. *Mixe-Zoque*, Mixean branch. Fragmented language group in the state of Oaxaca, subdivided into four languages: **North Highland Mixe (*Totontepec*), South Highland Mixe, Midland Mixe** and **Lowland Mixe** (Wichmann 1995). The total number of Mixe speakers, which is increasing, is 74,083 (Garza Cuarón and Lastra 1991). INEGI (1993) reports 95,264 speakers for Mixe.

***Mixtec* [49]** Mexico. *Oto-Manguean*, Mixtecan branch. Highly fragmented language group of a historically important nation covering a large territory in western Oaxaca, eastern Guerrero and Puebla. In 1990, Mixtec had 386,874 speakers in Mexico (INEGI 1993), of which about two thirds lived in Oaxaca. Many speakers have migrated to the US. Possibly, more than thirty mutually unintelligible varieties of Mixtec have to be distinguished. The number of speakers is increasing moderately, and there are about 21 per cent monolinguals. Garza Cuarón and Lastra (1991) mention a number of 323,137 Mixtec speakers in 1980.

***Mopan* [4]** Guatemala. *Mayan*, Yucatecan branch. 5,000 speakers in Guatemala (El Petén) and a few thousand in Belize (Toledo district).

***Motocintleco* (*Mochó*) [12a]** Mexico. *Mayan*, Kanjobalan branch. Highly endangered language located in the state of Chiapas (Mototzintla) with about. 500 speakers. No monolinguals (INEGI 1993; Garza Cuaron and Lastra 1991).

Nahuatl* (*Aztec, Mexicano*) [59]** Mexico. *Uto-Aztecan*, Nahuatl branch. Historically important language subdivided into many local varieties, distributed over a number of Mexican states (Federal District, Colima, Durango, Guerrero, Jalisco, Hidalgo, México, Michoacán, Nayarit, Oaxaca, Puebla, San Luis Potosí, Tabasco, Veracruz). A closely related language (Pipil***) is spoken in El Salvador. Some varieties are endangered. Uto-Aztecan family. With 1,197,328 speakers (INEGI 1993) it is the largest indigenous language in Mexico. Garza Cuarón and Lastra give a higher number of 1,376,898. Nahuatl probably has the richest and most diverse preserved written literature of all Native American languages.

Naolan Mexico. *Unclassified Language*. Spoken in the ranchería (hamlet) of San Juan de Naolan, a five-hour walk from Ciudad Tula, state of Tamaulipas. The existence of this language was reported by Robert J. Weitlaner in the 1940s. Apparently, there have been no further reports since then (source: website Cd. Tula Tamaulipas).

***Ocuiltec* [35b]** Mexico. *Oto-Manguean*, Oto-Pame branch. In San Juan Atzingo, state of Mexico. The language is closely related to Matlaltzinca and has ninety-three speakers (Garza Cuarón and Lastra 1991). Manrique (1997) mentions 755 speakers.

***Oluta Popoluca* [45]** Mexico. *Mixe-Zoque*, Mixean branch. Highly endangered language spoken by 121 people in Oluta, state of Veracruz (Garza Cuarón and Lastra 1991). The language is of particular importance for the reconstruction of Mixe-Zoquean (Wichmann 1995).

Ópata Mexico. This *Uto-Aztecan* language is generally considered extinct, but the 1990 census lists twelve speakers (Manrique 1997).

Otomí Mexico. *Oto-Manguean*, Oto-Pame branch. Dialectally fragmented language spoken in the states of Guanajuato, Hidalgo, Mexico, Querétaro and Tlaxcala. There are four major dialects: ***Mezquital, Eastern, Toluca*** and ***Tula*** (Bartholomew 1994). Otomí has 306,190 speakers according to Garza Cuarón and Lastra (1991). INEGI (1993) lists 280,238 speakers.

Paipai Mexico. *Hokan*, Yuman branch. Endangered language spoken by some 240 people in the state of Baja California Norte (Ensenada). (Garza Cuarón and Lastra 1991).

Pame [34b] Mexico. *Oto-Manguean*, Oto-Pame branch. The northern variety is still used by 5,649 speakers in the state of San Luis Potosí (Santa Catarina, Tamasopo, Rayón, Alaquines). The southern variety is extinct (Garza Cuarón and Lastra 1991).

Papabuco [46e] Mexico. *Oto-Manguean*, Zapotec branch. The 1990 census (see Manrique 1997) mentions nineteen speakers of this language in San Juan Elotepec, Oaxaca. However, Smith-Stark (1994) reports that they are probably central Zapotec speakers.

Paya or *Pech* [67] Honduras. *Chibchan*. Spoken in the Department of Olancho. The Paya territory is gradually shrinking due to pressure from Mestizo settlers and infrastructure works. Substantial intermarriage with Miskito (Misumalpan) people has brought cultural and linguistic assimilation. There remain only 600 speakers out of 2,500 ethnic Paya. The youngest speakers are forty years old, but most are over sixty. There is a lot of interest in the community in preserving the Pech language, and some work is being done to preserve it.

Pima-Papago Mexico. *Uto-Aztecan*, Piman branch. 236 speakers in 1980 in the state of Sonora (Garza Cuarón and Lastra 1991). More in the US (Arizona).

Pipil [59e] El Salvador. *Uto-Aztecan*, Nahuatl branch. There may be some twenty speakers left in the department of Sonsonate (Izalco).

Pochutec [59f] Mexico. *Uto-Aztecan*, Nahuatl branch. Highly divergent Nahuatlan dialect spoken in Pochutla, on the Pacific coast of Oaxaca, until well into the twentieth century. Now presumably extinct.

Pocomam (*Poqomam*) [20b] Guatemala. *Mayan*, Quichean branch. 32,000 speakers in the departments of Escuintla, Guatemala and Jalapa.

Pocomchí (*Poqomchi'*) [20a] Guatemala. *Mayan*, Quichean branch. 50,000 speakers in the departments of Alta and Baja Verapaz.

Popoloca (*Ngiwa*) [45b] Mexico. *Oto-Manguean*, Popolocan branch. This language is spoken in the area of Tehuacán, state of Puebla. Together with the closely related Chocho it has 12,310 speakers (Garza Cuarón and Lastra 1991). Popoloca is rapidly losing ground and therefore highly endangered.

Quiché (*K'ichee'*) **[19a]** Guatemala. *Mayan*, Quichean branch. 926,000 speakers in El Quiché, Quetzaltenango, Retalhuleu, Sololá, Suchitepéquez and Totonicapán. Quiché is the largest indigenous language of Guatemala and the largest Mayan language with a rapidly growing community. It is also the language of the most admired literary work written in any Amerindian language: the Popol Vuh. In spite of recent growth, the long-term perspectives are not as good as they might seem, because of endemic repression in the country.

Rama **[68]** Nicaragua. *Chibchan*, Pota branch. Twenty-four speakers, living around Rama Cay, in the Autonomous Southern Atlantic Region. The Ramas were at the brink of extinction before 1979; the Sandinista Revolution gave them (and other indigenous groups) new hope of survival when the Atlantic coast of Nicaragua was given the status of 'autonomous region' and new laws for the protection of the indigenous groups were passed. However, with the collapse of the revolutionary process, the Ramas lost institutional support and are currently involved in land disputes, being pressured by Mestizo settlers to abandon the riverbanks and forests they occupy.

Sacapultec (*Sakapulteko*) **[19b]** Guatemala. *Mayan*, Quichean branch. 21,000 speakers in Sacapulas (department of El Quiché).

Sayula Popoluca **[25]** Mexico. *Mixe-Zoque*, Mixean branch. Language spoken by 3,025 speakers in Sayula, state of Veracruz (Garza Cuarón and Lastra 1991; Wichmann 1995).

Seri (*Comcáac*) Mexico. *Unclassified* or *Hokan*. Language of a group located in El Desemboque and Punta Chueca (near Hermosillo, State of Sonora). About 500 speakers according to Garza Cuarón and Lastra (1991); 561 according to Manrique (1997). The group has recovered from near extinction (Beck Moser 1996).

Sierra Popoluca or *Soteapan Zoque* **[23]** Mexico. *Mixe-Zoque*, Zoquean branch. Language spoken by 19,819 people in Soteapan and neighbouring towns in the state of Veracruz.

Sipacapa (*Sipakapense*) **[19c]** Guatemala. *Mayan*, Quichean branch. 3,000 speakers in Sipacapa (department of San Marcos).

Soltec Mexico. The 1990 census (see Manrique 1997) mentions fifty-one speakers of this *Zapotecan* language mainly in San Miguel Sola de Vega, Oaxaca. However, Smith-Stark (1994) reports that its last speaker died about 1900.

Sumu or *Tawahka* or *Ulwa* **[69]** Nicaragua. *Misumalpan*. 8,000 speakers. It is spoken west of the Miskitu territory, in the Department of Jinotega, around the Huaspuc (Waspuk) River and tributaries. Also spoken in Honduras, in the Department of Gracias a Dios, by some 1,000 speakers, as a different dialect: *Ulua*. In Nicaragua, there are two dialects: *Panamaca* and *Taguasca*.

Takaneko **[14a]** Guatemala. *Mayan*, Mamean branch. Spoken in Tacaná (department of San Marcos).

Tarahumara (Rarámuri) **[54]** Mexico. *Uto-Aztecan* language of the Taracahita branch, spoken mainly in the state of Chihuahua by a well-preserved, highly traditional group. It had 62,419 speakers in 1980 (Garza Cuarón and Lastra 1991). The INEGI (1993) estimate is 54,431.

Tarascan (Purépecha) **[61]** Mexico. *Linguistic Isolate.* Historically important language spoken in the state of Michoacán by 118,614 speakers (Garza Cuarón and Lastra 1991), especially near Lake Pátzcuaro. The INEGI (1993) estimate is 94,835. The Tarascan language is both genetically and typologically alien to its Mesoamerican environment. Andean connections have been suggested. The power of the Tarascan empire extended far beyond its linguistic area, which explains the presence of Tarascan place names (e.g. Querétaro).

Tektiteko (Teko) **[14]** Guatemala. *Mayan*, Mamean branch. 2,500 speakers in Tectitán (Huehuetenango). Also 107 speakers in Mexico (Chiapas) according to Manrique (1997).

Tepecano Mexico. *Uto-Aztecan* language related to Tepehuán and formerly spoken in the state of Jalisco (now possibly extinct).

Tepehua **[30]** Mexico. *Totonacan.* According to McKay (1994), a language group subdivided into three languages: Huehuetla Tepehua (in the state of Hidalgo), Tlachichilco Tepehua (in the state of Veracruz) and Pisa Flores Tepehua (in Ixhuatlán de Madero, state of Vera Cruz). The total number of speakers is 8,487, each of the three languages having a few thousand speakers. (Garza Cuarón and Lastra 1991). The INEGI (1993) estimate is 8,702.

Tepehuán **[53]** Mexico. *Uto-Aztecan* language of the Piman branch. Subdivided in Northern Tepehuán with 14,900 speakers (1980) in the states of Chihuahua (Guadalupe y Calvo) and Durango (Vicente Guerrero), and Southern Tepehuán with 2,903 speakers (1980) in the states of Durango (Mezquital, Pueblo Nuevo) and Nayarit (Huajicori). Information taken from Garza Cuarón and Lastra (1991). INEGI (1993) has 18,469 speakers, and lists Tepehuán as the fastest growing indigenous language of Mexico (6 per cent yearly between 1970 and 1990). This may also be the result of statistical shortcomings in the past.

Tequistlatec (Chontal de Oaxaca) **[32]** Mexico. *Unclassified* or *Hokan.* In area of Tequisistlán, southeastern Oaxaca. Coastal (Huamelula) and Highland varieties, listed as separate languages in Garza Cuarón and Lastra (1991). Coastal Chontal had 1,985 speakers and Highland Chontal 6,101 in 1980. The language is surrounded by Zapotec.

Teribe (Tiribí, Térraba, Naso) Panama. *Chibchan.* 1,000 speakers. Teribe is spoken in the Province of Bocas del Toro. The language is relatively healthy in the main villages of Sieyllik and Sieyking. In the Province of Puntarenas, Costa Rica, near the Boruca Reservation live nearly 500 descendants of them, known as Térrabas. Originally, both groups lived along the Teribe river, but in 1695, the Spanish missionaries relocated a clan, the Térrabas who were apparently in favour of Christianisation. After the relocation both groups lost contact until in 1992 a re-encounter took place. It was already too late for revitalisation of the moribund Térraba dialect, which is now extinct; linguistic and cultural orphanhood accelerated the process of decay.

Texistepec Zoque (*Texistepec Popoluca*) **[24]** Mexico. *Mixe-Zoque*, Zoquean branch. Highly endangered language with about 100 speakers in Texistepec (state of Veracruz) (Wichmann 1995; Reilly 2002).

Tlapanec (*Yopi*) **[39]** Mexico. *Oto-Manguean*, Tlapanec branch. Language spoken, among other places, in Malinaltepec in the eastern part of the state of Guerrero by 55,068 (Garza Cuarón and Lastra (1991)). INEGI (1993) estimates their number at 68,483. The language of the closely related Subtiaba in Nicaragua is extinct. In the past, Tlapanec has also been classified as Hokan.

Tojolabal **[10]** Mexico. *Mayan*, Chujean branch. According to Garza Cuarón and Lastra (1991) the language has 22,331 speakers in the eastern part of the state of Chiapas (Altamirano, Comitán, Margaritas). INEGI (1993) has a much higher number: 36,011. Strong political associations have emerged since the Zapatista Movement of 1994.

Totonac **[29]** Mexico. *Totonacan*. Language group subdivided into four languages: Papantla Totonac, North-Central Totonac, South-Central Totonac and Misantla Totonac, together spoken by 186,058 people (1980) distributed over the states of Puebla (86,788), (northern) Veracruz (111,305) and Hidalgo (209). Misantla Totonac is now reduced to a few hundred speakers. Information from McKay (1994). INEGI (1993) puts the number of Totonac speakers at 207,876.

Trique (*Triqui*) **[51]** Mexico. *Oto-Manguean* language of the Mixtecan branch. Its two main dialects, Copala (4,342 speakers) and Chicahuaxtla (4,056 speakers), are listed as separate languages in Garza Cuarón and Lastra (1991). The Trique speaking area is part of Oaxaca state. INEGI (1993) gives a total number of 14,981 Trique speakers.

Tuzantec **[13b]** Mexico. *Mayan*, Kanjobalan branch. Highly endangered language located in the state of Chiapas (Tuzantán) with about 300 speakers (Garza Cuarón and Lastra 1991).

Tzeltal **[9]** Mexico. *Mayan*, Tzeltalan branch. The language was spoken in the central part of the state of Chiapas by 261,084 speakers in 1990 (INEGI 1993) including a high percentage of monolinguals (36 per cent). Tzeltal is one of the fastest growing indigenous languages in Mexico. Strong political associations have emerged since the Zapatista Movement of 1994.

Tzotzil **[8]** Mexico. *Mayan*, Tzeltalan branch. The language is spoken in the central part of the state of Chiapas in the area of Chamula and Zinacantán. Tzotzil is one of the fastest growing indigenous languages in Mexico, with an estimated 229,203 speakers in 1990 (INEGI 1993). Strong political associations have emerged since the Zapatista Movement of 1994. High percentage of monolinguals (34 per cent).

Tzutuhil (*Tz'utujiil*) **[19d]** Guatemala. *Mayan*, Quichean branch. 80,000 speakers near Lake Atitlán in the departments of Sololá and Suchitepéquez.

Uspantec (*Uspanteko*) **[18]** Guatemala. *Mayan*, Quichean branch. 2,000 speakers in San Miguel Uspantán (El Quiché).

Waunana Panama. *Chocoan*. It is spoken in the Pacific coast region, in the Provinces of Panama and Darien, by approximately 2,500 speakers. There are many monolingual speakers. The main group of Waunana speakers lives in Colombia near the lower San Juan River.

Xinka or *Szinka* **[62]** Guatemala. *Linguistic Isolate*. Spoken until recently in southeastern Guatemala. There were different varieties corresponding to the areas of Chuquimulilla, Guazacapán and Jumaytepeque (department of Santa Rosa). The Xinca languages may be extinct or on the verge of extinction. The Xinka were not part of the Mayan cultural area.

Yaqui Mexico. *Uto-Aztecan* language of the Tarachita branch, closely related to Mayo. The language is spoken by some 9,282 speakers in Guaymas (state of Sonora) and in Sinaloa (Garza Cuarón and Lastra 1991). The Yaqui are a historically prominent people that suffered heavy persecution until well into the twentieth century. INEGI reports 10,984 speakers in Mexico (there may also be speakers in the US).

Yucatec (*Maya, Mayathan*) **[3a]** Mexico. *Mayan*, Yucatecan branch. Historically important language, inheritor of the Late Mayan civilisation. With over 713,250 speakers it is the second in importance of Mexico's indigenous languages (INEGI 1993). The daily language is heavily influenced by Spanish, but a puristic variety is used in literature. A 'classical' variety is used by shamans (*h-men*) and in folk literature (the Chilam Balam books). Yucatec is spoken in the states of Yucatán, Quintana Roo and Campeche. About 8 per cent are monolinguals. It is also spoken in parts of Belize.

Zapotec **[46]** Mexico. *Oto-Manguean*, Zapotecan branch. Mainly in central and eastern Oaxaca. 403,457 speakers in Mexico in 1990 (INEGI 1993). Garza Cuarón and Lastra (1991) mention a slightly higher figure for 1980 (422,937). Many speakers live in the US (California). This historically important language group is highly fragmented and possibly includes more than forty mutually unintelligible varieties. About 12 per cent of the Zapotec speakers are monolinguals.

Zoque **[22]** Mexico. *Mixe-Zoque*, Zoquean branch. Language group subdivided into two languages: Chimalapa Zoque (in the state of Oaxaca) with 5,231 speakers and Chiapas Zoque (in the state of Chiapas) with 25,744. The Zoquean languages have been associated with the historical Olmec people, whose culture flourished before the present era (Garza Cuarón and Lastra 1991; Wichmann 1995). INEGI (1993) estimates the number of Zoque speakers at 43,160.

References

Bartholomew, Doris (1994) 'Panorama of studies in Otopamean languages'. In: Bartholomew, Doris, Yolanda Lastra and Leonardo Manrique, *Panorama de los estudios de las lenguas indígenas de México*. Part I, pp. 335–77. 2 vols. Quito: Abya-Yala.

Bartholomew, Doris, Yolanda Lastra and Leonardo Manrique (1994) *Panorama de los estudios de las lenguas indígenas de México*. 2 vols. Quito: Abya-Yala.

Beck Moser, Mary (1996) *Seri de Sonora*. Archivo de lenguas indígenas de México. Mexico City: El Colegio de México.

Garza Cuarón, Beatriz and Yolanda Lastra (1991) 'Endangered languages in Mexico'. In: R. H. Robins and E. M. Uhlenbeck, *Endangered Languages*, pp. 93–134. Oxford and New York: Berg.

Greenberg, Joseph (1987) *Language in the Americas*, Stanford: Stanford University Press, 1987.

INEGI (Instituto Nacional de Estadística, Geografía e Informática) (1993) *La población hablante de lengua indígena en México (XI Censo General de Población y Vivienda, 1990)*. Aguascalientes: INEGI.

——(1995) *Oaxaca: Hablantes de lengua indígena: Perfil sociodemográfico*. Aguascalientes: INEGI.

Manrique Castañeda, Leonardo (1997) 'Clasificaciones de las lenguas indígenas de México y sus resultados en el censo de 1990'. In: Beatriz Garza Cuarón (ed.) *Políticas lingüísticas en México*, pp. 39–65. Mexico City: La Jornada.

McKay, Carolyn J. (1994) *A grammar of Misantla Totonac*. Salt Lake City UT: University of Utah Press.

Merrifield, William R. (1994) 'Progress in Chinantec language studies'. In: Bartholomew, Doris, Yolanda Lastra and Leonardo Manrique, *Panorama de los estudios de las lenguas indígenas de México*. Part II, pp.187–236. 2 vols. Quito: Abya-Yala.

Proyecto Lingüístico Francisco Marroquín (May 2004) website: http://www.langlink.com/plfm/language.html

Reilly, Ehren M. (2002) 'A survey of Texistepec Popoluca verbal morphology'. Unpublished undergraduate thesis. Carleton College, Northfield, Minnesota.

Smith-Stark, Thomas C. (1994) 'El estado actual de los estudios de las lenguas Mixtecanas y Zapotecanas'. In: Bartholomew, Doris, Yolanda Lastra and Leonardo Manrique (1994) *Panorama de los estudios de las lenguas indígenas de México*. Part II, pp. 5–186. 2 vols. Quito: Abya-Yala.

Wichmann, Søren (1995) *The relationship among the Mixe-Zoquean languages of Mexico*. Salt Lake City UT: University of Utah Press.

Yax Te' (May 2004) website: http://www.csuohio.edu./yaxte/languages.html

3

Europe and North Asia

Tapani Salminen

An outline of the chapter

The coverage of this chapter is defined geographically with certain ethnolinguistic considerations. In broad terms, it includes languages spoken in Europe (including Malta and Cyprus), Anatolia, Caucasia, Central Asia, Mongolia, Manchuria and Siberia. The exact border line is drawn so that the contiguous areas of Turkic and Mongolic languages are included in this chapter while Indo-Iranian and Semitic languages spoken on the border regions belong to adjacent chapters. This means, for instance, that languages spoken in Tajikistan are not represented here insofar as they are Iranian, even though Tajikistan is one of the Central Asian countries. Eastern Turkestan (Sinkiang) and Inner Mongolia are largely included in this chapter while Tibet is not. Enclaves of Indo-Iranian and Semitic languages within the above-mentioned geographical boundaries are, however, dealt with here, and Turkic and Mongolic languages spoken inside the areas of other chapters are found there. All Eskimo-Aleut languages, including those spoken in Siberia, are dealt with in Chapter 1 on North America, and the entry on Ainu is found in Chapter 5 on East and Southeast Asia. The special cases as well as the overall contents of the chapter are explained in the following list of language families, which also serves as an index to the subsequent survey of linguistic history and diversity of the area:

1 the *Basque* language;
2 the *Uralic* (or Finno-Ugrian) language family;
3 the *Indo-European* language family *except* the Indo-Iranian branch (see Chapter 4); the Romani and Lomavren languages of the Indic subbranch as well as the Ossete language and the Tat languages of the Iranian subbranch are, however, included in this chapter;
4 the Cypriot Arabic and Maltese languages of the Arabic branch of the *Semitic* language family (see Chapters 4 and 7 for the other Semitic languages);
5 the *Kartvelian* language family;
6 the *Abkhaz-Adyge* language family;

7   the *Nakh-Daghestanian* language family;
8   the *Turkic* language family *except* the Khalaj and Kashkay languages (see Chapter 4) and the Salar and Saryg Yugur languages (see Chapter 5);
9   the *Mongolic* language family *except* the Mogol language (see Chapter 4) and the Shira Yugur language and the Monguor branch (see Chapter 5);
10 the *Tungusic* language family *except* the Manchu branch (see Chapter 5);
11 the *Nivkh* language;
12 the *Yeniseian* language family;
13 the *Yukagir* language family;
14 the *Chukotkan* language family;
15 the *Kamchatkan* language family.

Languages belong to the same language family, if the similarities among them, as formulated by Watkins in *The Indo-European languages* (1998: 26), 'require us to assume they are the continuation of a single prehistoric common language'. Watkins is discussing Indo-European, but obviously, any group of languages must meet this definition to be called a language family. The above classification can be regarded as very firm in this respect, none of the families being in any way controversial. Notably, the genetic connection between the Nakh languages and the Daghestanian languages, that is, their belonging to a single Nakh-Daghestanian language family, has been definitively demonstrated (see Nichols 2003).

On the other hand, no solid evidence has been presented for the genetic affinity between Abkhaz-Adyge and Nakh-Daghestanian, although such a 'North Caucasian' family is propagated by people involved in long-range comparisons and frequently quoted in general handbooks. Another alleged macro-family, typically included in overall classifications, often even without a question mark, is, of course, 'Altaic', consisting of Turkic, Mongolic and Tungusic, and extending to Korean and Japanese in more extreme versions. Furthermore, a 'Chukotko-Kamchatkan' family, incorporating Chukotkan and Kamchatkan, is often taken for granted, and other combinations such as Uralic plus Yukagir are occasionally called language families as well. In all of these cases, it is possible and indeed plausible to explain the shared features on the basis of areal influence and typological similarity rather than genetic affinity, and the extant material rather supports the idea of ancient contacts between genetically unrelated languages. The basic issue here is that these groups contrast markedly with established language families such as Uralic and Indo-European which, although internally diverse, can only be explained as deriving from a single proto-language. For a recent attempt to establish a genetic connection between Chukotkan and Kamchatkan, see Fortescue 2005.

In the particular case of Altaic, the best recent elaboration of the plausibility of the areal rather than genetic explanation actually comes from a firm supporter of the genetic hypothesis. Dybo in the entry on the '*altajskie jazyki*' in the *Jazyki Rossijskoj Federacii i sosednih gosudarstv* I (1997: 79–86) presents a large number of lexical comparisons which according to her represent cognate words inherited from Proto-Altaic. Two things are, however, conspicuously missing. First, while there are several words related to fundamental concepts such as body parts in the Altaic corpus, the most basic words in the relevant semantic fields remain restricted to a single family without cognates in the other Altaic families. Second, the material in the Altaic corpus shows only shallow phonological differentiation of shared lexicon, which cannot be the case of words deriving from Proto-Altaic, as the alleged proto-language, if valid, must have gone through a drastic series of changes not only in morphology and lexicon but also in its sound system. Schönig in the chapter on 'Turko-Mongolic relations' in *The Mongolic languages* (2003) discusses the matter further.

While 'North Caucasian', 'Altaic' and 'Chukotko-Kamchatkan' appear in literature both as presumed genetic and factual areal units, there are other labels that only have a conventional meaning. For instance, it is a matter of consensus that the term 'Caucasian languages' only refers to a geographic group including the Kartvelian (South Caucasian), Abkhaz-Adyge (Northwest Caucasian) and Nakh-Daghestanian (Northeast Caucasian) languages, as apparently no one would suggest that the Kartvelian family was related to the others. Similarly, 'Paleoasiatic (or Paleosiberian) languages' is only used as a cover term for Chukotkan, Kamchatkan, Nivkh, Yeniseian and Yukagir, because they simply represent languages not belonging to any larger family in Siberia.

The one and only language in the area that can be called genuinely mixed, Copper Island Aleut, based on Aleut and Russian, as explained by Golovko in the *Mixed languages* (1994: 113–21), in its mixed nature second only to Michif, described by Bakker in the same volume (13–33), is dealt with in Chapter 1.

There are several other languages that can be called mixed with regard to their lexicon, although their grammar derives from a single language. Examples are Town Frisian, which can be described as a variety of Dutch heavily influenced by West Frisian, and Äynu in Sinkiang, which is an in-group language whose speakers use it besides their native Uygur (see Wurm 1997). A whole group of languages are those with Romani lexicon incorporated into the grammar of local languages, including, in Europe, Angloromani, Scandinavian Traveller languages, Caló or Hispanoromani, Dortika or Hellenoromani, and Šatrovački in the central Balkans. The earlier English, Scandinavian, Iberian and Greek dialects of Romani appear to be extinct but their lexical resources serve to form these special varieties. Bosha, in Caucasia, is similarly based on Armenian, with influences from Lomavren, an extinct language closely related to Romani. Furthermore, there are a number of secret or in-group languages such as Hantyrka, Rotwelsch and Yeniche in Central Europe, Polari and Shelta (Cant) or Yola in the British Isles, and Quinqui in Spain. A few pidgin languages such as Taymyr Pidgin (Govorka) that is still spoken on Taymyr peninsula, or the extinct Russenorsk and Russian-Chinese Pidgin, are also known from the area. Since all of the languages mentioned in this paragraph are typically used as second languages, they are not further discussed in this presentation as it is difficult to characterise languages without native speakers as endangered. Case studies on most of these and several other similar languages are presented in the *Mixed languages* (1994). No creole languages seem to have been recorded in the area.

Also excluded from this presentation are sign languages, classical languages that represent the proto-form of a group of modern languages, notably Latin, and artificial languages such as Esperanto and Volapük, despite the fact that there may be grounds for characterising some of them as endangered.

More crucially, dialects, irrespective of their endangerment status, have not, as a rule, been included in this presentation. Contrary to the frequently repeated claims about the impossibility of distinguishing between language and dialect on a purely linguistic basis, it is maintained here that in the overwhelming majority of cases linguistic criteria lead to an unambiguous solution, and while borderline cases, such as large dialect continua, may exist, they are in reality much rarer than is often assumed and their documentation is typically anecdotal. Notably, the linguistic concept of language is only concerned with spoken varieties, or vernaculars, and does *not* depend on their social status or level of cultivation, and the presence or absence of a corresponding literary tradition plays no role at all in defining a language. The foundation of this concept lies in the nature of language boundaries as opposed to dialect boundaries. A single language is typically a contiguous network of intergradating varieties, while two separate languages, even when closely related, are divided by a unique boundary, which has historically emerged through the recurring process of extinction of transitional dialects. Language boundaries must be corroborated by the more commonly cited criterion of mutual intelligibility to the extent that dialects of a single language must be mutually intelligible, but, obviously, there should be no requirement of total mutual unintelligibility between closely related languages. The point is that while mutual intelligibility occurs in all possible shades, rendering it useless as a criterion on its own, dialect and language boundaries represent two reasonably distinct states of affairs, which function differently with regard to historical change, areal contacts, and bilingualism or diglossia.

Needless to say, there is another, equally legitimate but different concept of language, based on sociolinguistic criteria such as literary use or administrative divisions. From a sociolinguistic point of view, it is entirely plausible to recognise Bosnian, Croatian and Serbian as separate entities following the separation of literary traditions, while from a linguistic perspective these traditions are based not only on a single language conventionally referred to as Serbo-Croat but more exactly on varieties of the same dialect group within it. Similarly, national boundaries mark Alsatian, Aranese and Torne Valley Finnish as mediums of separate language communities, and thus languages in the sociolinguistic sense, while they continue to function as parts of strictly linguistic units, Alemannic, Gascon and Finnish, respectively. Also, only five Jewish languages, Italkian, Judezmo, Juhur, Krimchak, and Yiddish, are recognised here, because they represent markedly distinct units as spoken languages in contrast with other varieties often referred to as Jewish languages but probably better described as dialects, registers or literary traditions; most notable of the spoken varieties not listed below are Shuadit (Judeo-Provençal; recently extinct) and Yevanic (Judeo-Greek; nearly extinct).

It is important to understand that all minority language communities, including those demarcated by cultural, political and administrative boundaries and thus qualifying as distinct languages in the sociolinguistic sense such as Alsatian, Aranese and Torne Valley Finnish mentioned above, or Valencian as opposed to Catalan spoken in Catalonia, Rhenish Franconian in France and Luxemburgian in Belgium to name just a few other examples, need and deserve equal support and full recognition of their language rights, irrespective of the fact that they have no specific entries in this presentation. Crucially, decisions about the use and cultivation of the native language must have the support of the local population without unwanted interference from external authorities.

The details of distinguishing between language and dialect in allegedly or factually problematic cases are presented in the following discussion on the classification of the languages dealt with in this chapter. In anticipation, it can be immediately said that the majority of the cases where handbooks typically state that the status of a particular variety is unclear derive from confusing linguistic and sociolinguistic, or synchronic and diachronic criteria. To name a few examples, there should be no doubt at all that Frisian, Mordvin, Nenets and Saami do *not* constitute single languages but can only be understood as groups of closely related but distinct languages. Notably, even in this presentation which seeks to recognise all units defined by unambiguous language boundaries as separate languages, many languages with highly divergent dialects remain, for instance, Albanian, Armenian, Chuvash, Dargwa, Estonian, Kryts, Nanay, Nivkh, North Frisian, Ossete and Romani.

On the other hand, some concessions have been made in a number of cases where some transitionality or intergradation is found between two closely related varieties that nevertheless are generally viewed as separate languages. Such pairs of what could be called co-languages or twin languages include Bulgarian-Macedonian, Galician-Portuguese and Azerbaijani-Turkish. The point is that a shallow language boundary can be found between the members of these pairs, but the boundaries do not follow national borders but, in the above-mentioned cases, Macedonian is spoken in south-western Bulgaria, Galician in northern Portugal, and Azerbaijani in eastern Turkey.

Of course, national borders do not generally correlate with language boundaries except on the level of official terminology referring to literary traditions rather than spoken languages. For instance, Luxemburgian is spoken not only in Luxembourg but in all neighbouring countries, Belgium, France and Germany, while it is usually not called Luxemburgian but Moselle Franconian or simply Franconian in those countries. Similarly, the border between the Netherlands and Germany does not correspond to any language boundaries, but Low Saxon is spoken across the border in the Netherlands, while Dutch in the form of the Brabantish dialect extends to Germany, and the Limburgian-Ripuarian language area covers parts of both countries.

It can be argued that in a number of cases the present classification is over-differentiating, for instance Mari, Komi (including Permyak), Occitan (covering all Oc languages), French (covering all Oïl languages), Sardinian, Abkhaz (including Abaza), Circassian and Koryak (including Alutor) could basically be treated as single languages rather than groups of closely related languages, but the current solutions have simply turned out to be the most fruitful in the preparation of this presentation.

While dialects as such are excluded from this presentation, there exists a special type of varieties which still to some extent function within larger language units as dialects, but are geographically or ethnologically clearly detached from them and have started to develop independently, especially because of their different language environment. They include, for example, the Algherese dialect of Catalan, the Norman dialects of the Channel Islands, Cimbrian and other Germanic enclaves in Italy, Dolgan as a distinct ethnolinguistic variety of Yakut, or the ancient forms of Greek in Italy known as Griko. Quite obviously, such varieties need to be discussed in the context of language endangerment, and they also require a specific label, for which I here suggest 'outlying dialect'; other possible terms could be 'diaspora dialect' or 'isolated dialect', but they appear slightly restrictive.

While the list of distinct languages presented below is supposed to be reasonably comprehensive, the decision about what counts as an outlying dialect is obviously a more relative issue. Some omissions are therefore inevitable, and several examples come immediately to mind. To give an idea, Neo-Chuvan, a dialect of Russian with notable lexical influences from aboriginal Siberian, especially Yukagir languages, is not included here because it seems too integrated into Russian-speaking society, to the extent that it might be considered a specific register rather than a dialect, but it remains a borderline case nevertheless. Another example would be Tazy (in Chinese pinyin *Dazi*), a dialect of Northern Chinese, influenced, in particular, by Udege, and spoken mainly in the village of Mikhaylovka in Ol'ga County in Maritime (Primor'ye) Region in the Russian Federation by 100 to 200 people. Tazy is even included in the *Krasnaja kniga jazykov narodov Rossii* (1994), but since it has only been isolated from the rest of Northern Chinese for decades rather than centuries, it does not yet qualify as an outlying dialect. In Europe, the list of outlying dialects could probably be augmented by several others that are no less distinct than those dealt with below, for instance, Luxemburgian in the Bistriţa (Bistritz) region in Romania, or other Germanic varieties, collectively known as 'Transylvania Saxon'.

On the other hand, there are a number of languages whose origin can straightforwardly be tracked to an outlying dialect but which have later become fully-fledged languages. They include Kalmyk, Khamnigan Mongol, Manchurian Kirghiz, Sibe and Vojvodina Rusyn, which are *not* called here outlying dialects of Oyrat, Buryat, Khakas, Manchu or Eastern Slovak, respectively.

Remarks on classification

Basque language

Basque is probably the world's best-known language isolate, in other words it constitutes a family of its own. Language isolates and small language families are by no means rare in the world, but since Europe is dominated by a couple of large families, Basque may appear as a kind of an anomaly, although it simply represents a state of affairs that was much more widespread in early historical times, as witnessed by Etruscan and other attested non-Indo-European languages of Western and Southern Europe. The dialects of Basque are less distinct than occasionally suggested in popular sources, and continue to form a cohesive network typical of a single language.

Uralic language family

The traditional classificatory scheme into which the Uralic (or Finno-Ugrian) languages are cast, found in practically all handbooks, is a binary or an almost binary model, reminiscent of the classification proposed for the Indo-European languages by Schleicher and still occasionally referred to, for instance, by Gamkrelidze and Ivanov (1995). Especially since the critique by Häkkinen (1984), however, it has become increasingly clear that there is little factual basis for maintaining the binary classification, and that its long-standing popularity is simply due to the conservativeness of the field of Uralic studies, at the same time when the classification of Indo-European languages has been thoroughly and critically examined, and the binary model found severely problematic. There are no less than three recent handbooks of the family, namely *The Uralic languages* (1988), the *Jazyki mira: ural'skie jazyki* (1993) and *The Uralic languages* (1998), but they can all be said to suffer from a number of shortcomings, not least in questions of classification.

In its structure, Uralic is actually very similar to the Indo-European family. It consists of nine distinct and cohesive branches: Saami, Finnic, Mordvin, Mari, Permian, Hungarian, Mansi, Khanty and Samoyed. The intermediate subgroups of the binary model, including Finno-Saami, Volgaic (Mordvin and Mari), Finno-Volgaic, Finno-Permian, Ob-Ugrian (Mansi and Khanty), Ugrian (Hungarian and Ob-Ugrian), and, finally, Finno-Ugrian, the last one covering all languages except those of the Samoyed branch, are not based on shared innovations but their only meaningful, yet unreliable, justification derives from lexicostatistic calculations with Finnish as their starting-point. From the point of view of historical phonology, in particular, even the branches that appear closest to each other in the binary model, such as Saami and Finnic, or Mansi and Khanty, are so distant that their differentiation must have started directly from Proto-Uralic. The Samoyed branch is lexically innovative, though not to much greater extent than the other branches, but in other respects, Samoyed deserves no special position in the classification of the family. The statement of Comrie (1981: 93–4) that 'the initial division of Uralic into Samoyedic and Finno-Ugric is a major division, and in many ways the modern Samoyedic and Finno-Ugric languages are very different from one another' is therefore patently untrue both diachronically and synchronically. The rejection of the binary classification does not imply that there are no important similarities between branches such as Saami and Finnic, or the Ugrian branches, Hungarian, Mansi and Khanty, but they can be better explained by assuming language contacts than positing separate proto-languages, and, crucially, there are similarities of the same kind and extent across the alleged intermediate subgroups.

Another conservative feature of Uralic studies is that, following historical criteria or administrative decisions, units that are from a synchronic point of view clearly groups of closely related languages are called single languages with highly divergent dialects. Since the latter concept must be seen as an anomaly, the actual number of Uralic languages included in this presentation is, in almost every branch, notably higher than in conservative assessments. There are thus altogether forty-seven languages in the family, of which forty are living languages.

Consequently, there are no less than ten living Saami languages plus one that has become extinct. The internal diversity of the Saami branch easily matches that of, for instance, the Slavonic or Romance branches of the Indo-European family. Saami is very much a language chain, but the boundaries between languages are mostly clear, and often deep, except that in the part of the chain from Pite Saami via Lule Saami to North Saami there is admittedly some transitionality. The boundaries between Skolt Saami and Akkala Saami, on the one hand, and Akkala Saami and Kildin Saami, on the other, are also relatively shallow.

In older terminology that is better avoided today, calques such as 'Baltic Finnic' or 'Balto-Finnic' were often used for Finnic in the current sense of the branch of closely related languages including Estonian and Finnish, while 'Finnic' was supposed to cover all 'Finno-Ugrian' languages except 'Ugrian', and thus synonymous to 'Finno-Permian'. To be able to give a consistent view of the Finnic branch, Ingrian, Karelian, Olonetsian and Lude must all be granted language status, in contrast to administrative solutions where Karelian, Olonetsian and Lude are subsumed under 'Karelian'. In the northern Finnic language chain from Finnish via Karelian, Olonetsian and Lude to Veps, each pair of neighbouring languages are close to one another, yet language boundaries are clear, and Karelian, for instance, is not necessarily more similar to Olonetsian than it is to (Eastern) Finnish. Võro-Seto is here recognised as a regional language in relation to Estonian; it may also be called an incipient language (cf. Salminen 2003).

Another term reflecting the older usage was 'Volga-Finnic' instead of current 'Volgaic'. This is another intermediate subgroup, uniting the Mordvin and Mari branches, but the relatively few common features shared by them can be rather easily explained on the basis of language contacts. Both Mordvin and Mari were formerly regarded as single languages but they actually consist of two languages each.

In the Permian branch, Komi (Komi proper, or Zyryan) and Permyak are very closely related but differ in a number of diagnostic features. Understandably they constitute a subbranch as opposed to Udmurt.

Hungarian is a single language, but with an outlying dialect, Csángó Hungarian. By contrast, both Mansi and Khanty are branches consisting of four and three closely related languages, respectively. In the case of the two surviving Khanty languages, the relationship is actually more distant than, for instance, that between English and Swedish.

The history of the internal classification of the Samoyed branch reminds us of that of the whole language family in that it has usually also followed a binary model, involving a primary division into northern and southern branches. There is little foundation for such a scheme, but Samoyed is actually a chain of seven distinct branches, four of which are single languages, while Enets, Nenets and Selkup are subbranches consisting of closely related but separate languages despite their administrative treatment as single languages.

Indo-European language family

The difference in the traditions of classifying Uralic and Indo-European languages, despite the factual similarity in the structure and time depth of the families, is evident in, for example, Campbell (1998: 168–9). That the Indo-European family is currently represented by nine branches, Slavonic (Slavic), Baltic, Germanic, Celtic, Romance, Albanian, Hellenic (Greek), Armenian and Indo-Iranian, is almost uncontroversial. Slavonic and Baltic branches are often regarded as united, but this view could perhaps be challenged by claiming that the two groups of Baltic, West Baltic and East Baltic, should be elevated to the status of primary branches instead, and since West Baltic is extinct, we are in any case left with nine branches of modern languages. The term Romance, of course, corresponds to the entity that was created when the first language boundaries emerged within the proto-language of the branch, Latin.

The internal classification of the Slavonic branch is rather well-established and the individual languages are aptly presented in *The Slavonic languages* (1993). The closeness of East Slavonic languages is often exaggerated, and here, by contrast, Rusyn is recognised as a language distinct of Ukrainian. There may be a couple of regional languages awaiting recognition, for instance, Upper Silesian, included in parentheses in the checklist of languages below.

As to the classification of the (East) Baltic languages, only the recognition of Latgalian as a regional language in relation to Latvian needs to be mentioned.

The division of the Germanic languages into three primary branches appears solid, and problems are found at lower levels of classification. They revolve around the question of which varieties are to be subsumed under the German language. The solution offered here excludes the westernmost, and most distinct, Franconian varieties as well as Alemannic and Bavarian from German in the narrow sense, which then consists of the East Central German dialects, historically mainly based on Thuringian, plus East Franconian and Rhenish Franconian. A great deal of arbitrariness is inevitably involved in this simple answer to such a complex question, but it seems to be consistent with both the historical development and the synchronic functioning of the varieties in question; cf. König (2001: 92). Outside this area, a number of regional languages are recognised but the list is not to be regarded as anything like the last word. The traditional classification of Germanic, referring more to literary traditions than spoken languages, forms the basis of the recent handbook *The Germanic languages* (1994), while *Germanische Rest- und Trümmersprachen* (1989) focuses on languages that enter the discussions more rarely, such as Cimbrian and Norn.

The extant Celtic languages offer few problems for classification, and the picture becomes extremely clear from the presentations in *The Celtic languages* (1993), which unlike most volumes of its kind, offers in-depth analyses of issues in language endangerment and language revival as well.

The classification of the Romance languages is arguably more complicated than that of any other language group, as can be seen from the discussions in *The Romance languages* (1988), Posner (1996), *The dialects of Italy* (1997), or, indeed, the vast compendium *Lexikon der Romanistischen Linguistik* (1988–2002), but Romance specialists also seem to enjoy emphasising this state of affairs quite eagerly. Haiman and Benincà (1992), for instance, discuss the position of the Raeto-Romance languages rather tendentiously, occasionally confusing early historical developments and more recent contact phenomena, which allows them to undermine the position of Raeto-Romance as a distinct branch, and similar statements have been aired on other forums about Occitano-Romance, in particular. These two branches, as well as Istro-Romance represented by the often neglected Istriot alone, are here recognised as well-founded subbranches alongside the less controversial Ibero-Romance, Gallo-Romance, Sardinian, Italo-Romance, Dalmatian and Romanian subbranches. The division of Romance into separate languages in this presentation can certainly be regarded as generous, but the language boundaries found between them turn out to be much clearer than is often assumed in discussions focusing on the relativity of the issue based on the idea of extensive dialect continua. Importantly, there is no obstacle to recognising larger units as languages in the sociolinguistic sense; for instance, Occitan is also in my view a valid concept of a literary language that largely unites the Oc languages described here. Incidentally, the classification of the Oc languages, itself a subbranch of Occitano-Romance, turns out to be less problematic than that of the Oïl languages, in which case the current treatment of Poitevin-Saintongeais, Gallo, Norman, Picard and Walloon as separate languages, but Lorrain and Champenois among the dialects of French, must be seen as highly tentative.

Albanian is here classified as a single language, although there are major differences between the Geg and Tosk dialects. Two outlying dialects, of Tosk to be precise, are found in Italy and Greece.

Rather than a single Greek language, there is a Hellenic branch consisting of (Modern) Greek and Tsakonian, and Cypriot Greek could also be seen as a distinct regional language. The outlying dialects of Greek, Griko (in Italy), Pontic Greek, Mariupolitan Greek and Cappadocian Greek, approach the status of separate languages.

Armenian is currently classified as a single language, although the differences between West Armenian and East Armenian are quite notable. No outlying dialects of Armenian are recognised here, which is possibly an omission, as at least Homshetsma, mentioned on various occasions by Vaux, could well be described as such.

Of the many languages of the Indo-Iranian branch, only those spoken in enclaves within the geographic area are covered by this chapter, namely Romani and Lomavren belonging to the Indic subbranch, and Juhur and Tat as well as Ossete of the Iranian subbranch. The classification of Indo-Iranian languages is discussed in the Middle East and South Asian chapters.

Semitic language family

Since Malta and Cyprus are included in this chapter, two Semitic, and more exactly Arabic languages, Cypriot Arabic and Maltese, are considered here. Arabic was introduced to these islands only in the Middle Ages. Discussion on the classification of Arabic and Semitic can be found in Chapter 4.

Kartvelian language family

Few people would claim today that Georgian is *the* Kartvelian language, but the language status of Laz, Mingrelian and Svan is generally recognised. The only exception is that Laz and Mingrelian, which undoubtedly belong together historically, are occasionally called dialects of 'Zan'. There is, however, little question about Laz and Mingrelian currently functioning as distinct languages.

Abkhaz-Adyge language family

The internal classification of the Abkhaz-Adyge family is uncontroversial in that it involves three branches, Abkhaz, Ubykh and Circassian (or Adyge). There are some grounds for regarding these three units as single languages, but the division of both Abkhaz and Circassian into two languages is also based on appropriate linguistic criteria. It must be noted, though, that the boundary between Abkhaz and Abaza does not follow the administrative border, but Abaza, as defined linguistically, only covers the Tapanta dialect group, while the other dialect spoken on the Russian side of the border belongs to Abkhaz proper.

A specific feature of this language family is that a very large portion of the speakers live outside their indigenous territory after the large-scale migration to Turkey, the Middle East and the Balkans in the nineteenth century to avoid Russian hegemony.

Nakh-Daghestanian language family

The primary division within Nakh-Daghestanian is, indeed, between Nakh and Daghestanian (Nichols 2003), although some schemes have dissolved the Daghestanian branch into a number of branches at the same level as Nakh. An open question is whether or not Dargwa and Lak form a subbranch together. The position of Khinalug and perhaps some other languages customarily included in the Lezgian subbranch has raised doubts as well, but the discussion of these matters must be left to better-informed commentators. The boundaries of the Nakh-Daghestanian languages are well-established both in literature and in reality. The only unorthodox decision made here is the treatment of Inkhokvari as an independent language rather than a co-dialect of Khvarshi, but the grounds for this as presented by Starostin seem convincing. On the other hand, this presentation remains on the conservative side in regarding Dargwa as a single language rather than a group of closely related languages.

Turkic language family

The Turkic family is fundamentally divided into two distinct branches, known as Bulgar Turkic and Common Turkic, although this division is often not highlighted in the literature, presumably because the Bulgar Turkic branch, although it represents the first historically attested Turkic expansion from Asia to Europe, is survived by a single modern language, Chuvash. There are two recent handbooks covering all of Turkic, namely *The Turkic languages* (1998) and the *Jazyki mira: tjurkskie jazyki* (1997), of which the latter in general offers more information about the less well-known Turkic languages. The shortcomings of the English-language handbook are compensated by the article 'Discoveries on the Turkic linguistic map' (http://www.srii.org/Map.pdf) by Johanson.

The classification of the Common Turkic branch into subbranches is a relatively complex matter, as evident from the detailed treatment by Schönig (1997–8), but in Central Asia and Europe, three major groups can be recognised as follows. First, the Oguz subbranch consists of Gagauz, Turkish, Azerbaijani, Kashkay, Khorasan Turk, Turkmen and Salar, of which Kashkay is spoken in Iran (and in a broad sense may also cover Iraqi Turk) and Salar in China, which means that they are dealt with in the Middle East and East Asian chapters. Second, the Karluk subbranch includes Uzbek and (Modern) Uygur. Third, the Kipchak subbranch incorporates three subgroups, namely those including (i) Crimean Tatar, Karaim, Kumyk and Karachay-Balkar, (ii) Tatar and Bashkir, and (iii) Nogay, Karakalpak and Kazakh.

In some classifications, Kirghiz, and occasionally Southern Altay as well, are included in Kipchak, but in the present scheme, they form the fourth subbranch of Common Turkic. Siberian Turkic in general appears to be a strictly geographic concept, and besides the one including Southern Altay with Kirghiz, three distinct subbranches of Common Turkic are attested in Siberia and adjacent regions. To the Yenisey Turkic, or Khakas, subbranch belong Northern Altay, Shor, Chulym Turk and Khakas, as well as Manchurian Kirghiz, which has clearly developed into a full language from being originally an outlying dialect of Khakas. The two other Siberian subbranches of Common Turkic are also known by their principal languages, Sayan Turkic by Tuvan and Lena Turkic by Yakut. There are further two peripheral subbranches, Khalaj in Iran, often included in Oguz but apparently distinct from it and dealt with in Chapter 4, and Saryg Yugur in China, the entry on which can be found in Chapter 5.

Altogether, there are thus nine reasonably clear-cut subbranches of Common Turkic, although the situation becomes complicated if administrative considerations are taken into account beside linguistic facts. Uzbek, for instance, contrary to the above divisions, conventionally includes dialects called Oguz Uzbek and Kipchak Uzbek. The status of these dialects, especially with respect to the neighbouring dialects of Turkmen and Kazakh, respectively, remains obscure even on the basis of the recent handbooks mentioned above. It seems therefore necessary to rely on the older but still indispensable compendium *Philologiae Turcicae Fundamenta I* (1959), in which Wurm simply regards Kipchak Uzbek as a Kazakh dialect, while Oguz Uzbek refers to Uzbek dialects that have been influenced by secondary contacts with Turkmen. Similar questions arise elsewhere as well, most notably in the cases of Crimean Tatar (see Doerfer in *Philologiae Turcicae Fundamenta I*) and Urum (see Podolsky 1985a; 1985b).

In this introduction, only the major Turkic languages have been mentioned, but the explicit classification found in the list of languages includes all of the languages and outlying dialects that belong to the Turkic family, and the less well-known of them have their own entries below.

Mongolic language family

The classification of the Mongolic family has become increasingly clear thanks to a number of recent studies, summarised in *The Mongolic languages* (2003). Essentially, there are five branches in the family, including a central or core group and four peripheral or satellite groups. The core branch consists of the principal language of the family, Mongolian, which includes Khalkha, Chakhar and Khorchin among its dialects, as well as Khamnigan Mongol, Buryat, Ordos and the Kalmyk-Oyrat language complex. Besides the core branch, one of the satellite branches, Dagur, is dealt with in this chapter. Of the other satellite branches, Shira Yugur, a single language, and Monguor, consisting of four languages, appear in Chapter 5, while the fifth branch, Mogol, has an entry in Chapter 4. In addition to the volume mentioned above, the *Jazyki mira: mongol'skie jazyki, tunguso-man'čžurskie jazyki, japonskij jazyk, korejskij jazyk* (1997) presents a survey of Mongolic, and it also covers the next language family, Tungusic.

Tungusic language family

The classification of the Tungusic family is perhaps slightly less complicated than is often tacitly assumed, at least if a binary classification is not required, as the family consists of four rather distinct branches (Janhunen 1996: 78; 2004). The first, North Tungusic branch, comprises, on the one hand, Even and, on the other, Evenki with closely related Negidal and Solon. The second branch consists of Udege and Oroch, and the third one of Nanay, Ulcha and Orok. These two branches are usually grouped together as Amur Tungusic, but there appear to be few features that could be regarded as shared innovations. The fourth branch is that of Manchu and Sibe, originally an outlying dialect of Manchu but by now rather a fully separate language, both dealt with in Chapter 5. The language boundaries within Tungusic are also somewhat clearer than could be expected on the basis of recent literature (cf. Grenoble and Whaley 2003, and the Tungusic Research Group website http://www.dartmouth.edu/~trg/), the main source of confusion being the idiosyncratic system of ethnonyms used in China. The details are presented in the entries on Evenki and Solon, but to explain the situation briefly, 'Ewenke' is the official Chinese term for the group of people whose traditional language is Solon, while 'Oroqen' is used for the majority of Evenki-speaking groups. On the diversity of the dialects of Nanay, known as 'Hejen' in China, see the respective entry.

Nivkh language

Nivkh is here seen as a single-language family, or language isolate, although differences between Amur and Sakhalin dialects as well as within Sakhalin dialects themselves are known to be extensive. Nevertheless, the northern Sakhalin dialects are closer to those on Amur, and in that sense, Nivkh can be seen as constituting a network of dialects rather than a group of two languages. The *Jazyki mira: paleoaziatskie jazyki* (1997) is the best general source currently available, but an English-language handbook of Nivkh and the other Paleoasiatic language families is under preparation.

Yeniseian language family

Ket is often considered to be an isolate, but it is rather the principal surviving member of what used to be a larger family. The other language that survived until recently, Yug, was previously considered a dialect of Ket, but there is little question of its being a separate language. Ket and Yug constitute, however, a distinct northern branch within the family, as opposed to the two other, more southerly branches, all languages of which became extinct long ago. There are some controversies about the classification of the Yeniseian languages, but the scheme proposed by Werner in the *Jazyki mira: paleoaziatskie jazyki* (1997) appears to be well-founded. According to it, Arin and Pumpokol constitute the second, and Assan and Kott the third branch of the family. That Assan and Kott were very close to each other is clear, rather the question is if they were distinguishable at all, but Werner has been able to identify a number of specific traits in the respective corpora. Arin and Pumpokol, on the other hand, are so different from each other that their belonging to the same branch is not immediately obvious, but a substantial if small set of common innovations supports the classification.

The Yeniseian languages are particularly interesting from the areal and typological points of view. They represent the only language family in Siberia with a fully developed and apparently ancient tone system, and they also have an extremely complicated morphological structure involving, among other things, the category of grammatical gender.

Yukagir language family

Yukagir is to be understood as a family of two languages, Tundra Yukagir and Forest Yukagir, the differences between them being great enough to invalidate claims of their being dialects of a single language. There are several small corpora of material from extinct members of the family, but with certain reservations mainly concerning terminological issues, all of them can be seen representing older stages of the extant languages. Two varieties known as Chuvan and Omok, both of which became extinct long ago, are particularly often regarded as distinct languages, but the solution adopted here is to classify them as dialects of Tundra Yukagir instead.

Chukotkan language family

Also called Chukchi-Koryak, the Chukotkan family is often seen as a union of only two languages, Chukchi and Koryak. Kerek, however, although it has been classified as a dialect of both Chukchi and Koryak, has a number of diagnostic features which clearly mark it as a separate language, and its superficial similarity with Chukchi can also be due to secondary contacts. Alutor, by contrast, is so close to Koryak that they could perhaps be seen as a single language complex, but the solution adopted here recognises Alutor and Koryak as two separate if closely related conglomerations of dialects. The details of the actual division remain to be sorted out, but here I follow the position of Skorik in the *Jazyki narodov SSSR V* (1968: 235) in incorporating the distinct Palana and Karaga dialects into Alutor rather than, as suggested by Zhukova in the same volume (292), into Koryak.

Kamchatkan language family

Itelmen (Western Kamchadal) is the only surviving member of the Kamchatkan family which also comprises the extinct Southern Kamchadal and Eastern Kamchadal. The differences between the three languages are, indeed, well beyond what could be called dialectal. Notably, the ethnonym Kamchadal is also used to refer to the old Russian-speaking immigrant population of Kamchatka, which may or may not have absorbed Itelmen speakers in the past.

Furthermore, three languages of the Yupik subbranch of the Eskimo branch of the Eskimo-Aleut language family are or were spoken to the west of the Bering Strait, Sirenik and East Cape Yupik exclusively, and Central Siberian Yupik also on St Lawrence Island in Alaska, but their entries are included in Chapter 1 alongside the other Eskimo-Aleut languages. The Yupik subbranch has further two languages, Central Alaskan Yupik and Pacific Gulf Yupik, spoken exclusively in Alaska. The other subbranch of the Eskimo branch is Inuit, of which the westernmost language, Seward Peninsula Inupiaq, was formerly spoken on the Great Diomede Island belonging to the Russian Federation; the last of the Inuit-speaking elders born on the island before the entire population was relocated on the continent seem to have died by the 1990s. Aleut, which constitutes the other branch of the family, is not autochthonous to the present Russian territory but its presence there derives from a nineteenth-century resettlement on the Commandor Islands whence Aleuts were brought to Bering Island from Atka and to Copper Island from Attu. The entries on Aleut and the mixed language Copper Island Aleut are therefore also included in Chapter 1; the few remaining speakers of Siberian Aleut and Copper Island Aleut, all elderly, are concentrated in the village of Nikol'skoye on Bering Island in Kamchatka Province.

Assessing the levels of endangerment

Europe differs from other parts of the world in that the number of very safe languages, spoken by majority populations of independent nation-states, is exceptionally high. The assimilative policies of the same nation-states are largely responsible for another peculiar feature of Europe, namely that almost all of the other languages spoken there are endangered, in other words, the number of safe minority languages is remarkably low. In Caucasia, by contrast, there are several indigenous languages that cannot be regarded as endangered at all, and, as a rule, the level of endangerment of the smaller languages is not particularly severe. Siberia is more like the most critical areas of the world because almost all of its native languages are endangered, and in many cases nearing extinction, although not on an equally drastic pace as in North America or Australia. In this section, the areas covered in the chapter are discussed from the point of view of deciding where to draw the line between safe and endangered languages.

Except for the bald fact that most of the minority languages in Europe are endangered, their status is quite different from what is known from other parts of the world.

In particular, the level of integration of European minority communities to main-stream societies is very high, because, typically, their only distinctive features are, indeed, the language and the related aspects of culture. It is therefore possible to assimilate more or less fully to the majority community, and escape various forms of discrimination, by adopting the majority language. Stable functional bilingualism would obviously contribute to both avoiding marginalisation and maintaining the native language, but the deeply-rooted ideologies of nation-states have largely favoured, and forced, a language shift instead. Political awareness within European minority communities is currently on a high level, but activists too rarely focus on basic issues of language maintenance at home and with peers, and direct their atten-tion to literacy projects, media coverage, and higher education instead. From the point of view of descriptive linguistics, European minority languages are relatively well stu-died (cf. Pogarell 1983), and most of them have native speakers trained as linguists, but there are also many lacunae in our knowledge. Primary source materials are typi-cally scattered, and in this study I have largely relied on secondary sources. For-tunately, there are several recent publications devoted to European languages that have proved useful. There is a wealth of up-to-date sources covering the languages of the Russian Federation or all of the Soviet Union, notably Comrie (1981), Kibrik in the *Endangered languages* (1991: 257–73), the *Jazykovaja situacija v Rossijskoj Feder-acii: 1992* (1992), the *Krasnaja kniga jazykov narodov Rossii* (1994), Kazakevitch in the *Lectures on language situation* (2002), and the *Jazyki Rossijskoj Federacii i sosednih gosudarstv* being currently published, yet the superb five-volume series *Jazyki narodov SSSR* (1966–8) continues to be valuable. On the languages of France, which used to be and still largely is one of the more problematic areas, we now have the books *Vingt-cinq communautés linguistiques de la France* (1988) and Sibille (2000), and *Languages in Britain and Ireland* (2000) covers the British Isles. As for other recent sources, the *Linguistic minorities in Central and Eastern Europe* (1998) lacks linguistic detail, while the *Minority languages today* (1981 [2nd edn 1990]), the *Encyclopedia of the languages of Europe* (1998), the *Minor languages of Europe* (2001), and the *Language death and language maintenance* (2003) provide rather uneven data on a selection of endangered languages. The *Ethnologue* (13th edn 1996), employed extensively by experts on lan-guages of other parts of the world, rarely contains unique information about the lan-guages of Europe or other areas dealt with in this chapter. Besides the printed publications, there are plenty of the electronic sources of various quality available, of which the *Euromosaic* and the *GeoNative* sites proved most fruitful for the present purpose.

There are thirty languages that have a dominant position in at least one European country: Albanian, Belarusian, Bulgarian, Czech, Danish, Dutch, English, Estonian, Finnish, French, German, Greek, Hungarian, Icelandic, Italian, Latvian, Lithuanian, Macedonian, Maltese, Norwegian, Polish, Portuguese, Romanian, Russian, Serbo-Croat, Slovak, Slovene, Spanish, Swedish and Ukrainian. Consequently, these lan-guages are in no way endangered, with the possible exception of Belarusian, which clearly is under pressure from Russian, but whose speaker base is nevertheless broad enough to keep it in the group of safe languages.

Several other languages meet the criteria for being safe in that, although there are other languages competing with them for dominance in their areas, they are widely spoken by all generations. Faroese and Luxemburgian, while having relatively low numbers of speakers, are clearly within this group because of their position as the most commonly spoken languages in the respective autonomous and independent states. Catalan and Tatar, with millions of speakers, are the largest minority languages in Europe and also have a strong position in their autonomous regions. Bashkir, Basque, Chuvash, Galician, Welsh and West Frisian are spoken by slightly smaller minority nations, but appear to be supported by both communities and authorities to the extent that their position is quite stable. Low Saxon, Rusyn and Scots arguably have a weaker status in the countries where they are spoken, but seem not to qualify as endangered languages because they have millions of speakers and show a reasonably stable diglossia with dominant languages, backed up by substantial and old literary and other cultural traditions.

The last group of European languages that in this presentation have been deemed to be on the safe side also involve a diglossic situation. They represent what are often called regional languages in a specific sense, meaning that they are intimately related to the dominant language of their area and, because of the lack of an established literary tradition, they can from a sociolinguistic point of view be regarded as dialects. Linguistically, however, their language status is in most cases reasonably clear. Eastern Slovak is, obviously, related to Slovak, and Western Flemish to Dutch, while Latgalian is a regional language with regard to Latvian, Jutish to Danish, Scanian to Swedish, and Extremaduran to Spanish. German is the umbrella language, so to speak, for Alemannic and Bavarian, while Limburgian-Ripuarian is diglossic with both German and Dutch, Venetan and South Italian (Neapolitan) and Sicilian have the same relationship with Italian. These regional languages are supposedly not losing ground, at least not very fast, to dominant languages in their most important domain as the spoken medium among family and friends. If the area of a language extends to several countries, the differences in its status are typically sharp. For instance, Alemannic covers the extremely safe Swiss German as well as Alsatian in France, which is under strong pressure from French.

No less than fifty-five presumably non-endangered European languages have been mentioned above. This figure must be contrasted with the seventy-three languages and twenty-four outlying dialects spoken in Europe that have been classified as endangered here, as can be seen in their respective entries below; the languages known to have disappeared from Europe in the modern era are summarised in the following section on extinct languages. The level of endangerment is discussed to some detail in each entry, but some general guidelines concerning the reasons why some apparent borderline cases have been regarded as endangered languages are given here.

Irish is clearly a special case, as it is an official and widely cultivated language of an independent country, but as the first language, it is used by a tiny fraction of Irish society. Romani and Yiddish, by contrast, have millions of speakers worldwide, but they are everywhere under strong pressure from dominant languages. Emilian-Romagnol, Friulian, Ligurian, Lombard and Piedmontese, regional languages of northern Italy, also have large numbers of speakers but a language shift has been so rapid in their regions that they rather fall in the category of endangered languages. The same is true about Eastern Mari, Erzya, Komi, Moksha and Udmurt, the major Uralic languages in east-central Russia, whose status is thoroughly discussed by Lallukka (1990) and corroborated by the preliminary results of the 2002 census in the Russian Federation. North Saami, Romansh and Scottish Gaelic have some official support and a reasonably stable position at least in their core areas but assimilation is still taking place and the overall numbers of speakers are smaller. Other larger minority languages such as Corsican, Gagauz, Kalmyk, Kashubian, Nogay and Walloon, as well as Campidanese Sardinian and Logudorese Sardinian, are also losing speakers on a scale that makes it necessary to define them as endangered.

All the other European languages undoubtedly belong to the category of endangered languages. It is, of course, important to keep in mind that even in their cases, endangered is not synonymous with dying, and I, for one, would never use the word 'moribund' in the context of language endangerment. It may be useful to point out that symbols characterising the level of endangerment of European languages in the map that I prepared for the *Atlas of the world's languages in danger of disappearing* (2nd edn 2001) do not match with the definitions given to them elsewhere in the book, a state of affairs that was beyond my control.

In Caucasia, despite the many ethnic and political conflicts, there are several indigenous languages that cannot be regarded as endangered at all, and, as a rule, the level of endangerment of the smaller languages is not particularly severe. The dominant languages in the area including Anatolia are, besides Russian, the four state languages, Armenian, Azerbaijani, Georgian and Turkish. Besides them, the twelve main indigenous languages of northern Caucasian republics, Adyge, Avar, Chechen, Dargwa, Ingush, Lak, Lezgian, Kabard-Cherkes, Karachay-Balkar, Kumyk, Ossete and Tabasaran, are maintained well by the population, and the bilingualism in Russian, in contrast with the major Uralic languages in east-central Russia having similar numbers of speakers, appears both functional and stable. The status of Abkhaz in Georgia is more problematic, and the closely related Abaza is clearly less secure than the above-mentioned larger languages of northern Caucasia, but even in their case the speakers appear loyal enough to the native languages to keep them on the safe side.

If the number of non-endangered languages in Caucasia and adjacent Anatolia is eighteen, there remain twenty-nine languages and two outlying dialects (Pontic Greek and Trukhmen) that are endangered to various extents. Of these, Mingrelian is perhaps functioning as a regional language in a diglossic relationship with Georgian, but its position seems quite weak. Nogay is another language with a larger number of speakers but it is spoken in widely scattered areas and appears to be losing ground to Russian. The smaller languages in Daghestan are relatively stable in spite of the low numbers of speakers, as only Agul, Juhur, Rutul and Tsakhur have close to 20,000 speakers, but even they are under growing pressure from dominant languages. There is little question about all the other languages, spoken by much smaller nations, belonging to the category of endangered languages.

In Central Asia and Mongolia, the number of languages is much smaller. Kazakh, Kirghiz, Mongolian, Turkmen and Uzbek are the dominant languages in the area covered by this chapter, and regional languages that appear to be relatively safe are Karakalpak, Khorasan Turk, Ordos and Uygur. This leaves only Oyrat and Dukha as well as two outlying dialects, Ili Turk and Sinkiang Dagur, in the group of endangered languages. The speaker base of Oyrat is still reasonably broad, but it has a very subordinate position in modern society, so regarding it as endangered seems justified. A useful summary of the complex ethnolinguistic situation in Sinkiang is provided by Rybatzki (1994).

In Siberia and Manchuria, by contrast, only two languages, Tuvan and Yakut, supported by reasonably large nations with a certain level of autonomy, can be regarded as non-endangered, although they are clearly under pressure from Russian

227

like all other Siberian languages. This means that as many as thirty-eight indigenous languages and three outlying dialects (Baraba Tatar, Dolgan and Manchurian Ölöt) are classified as endangered here. In most cases, there is no question about their being endangered, and a large number of indigenous languages are not only endangered but are nearing extinction. The three co-official languages of the other autonomous republics in Siberia, especially Buryat, and to lesser extent Khakas and Southern Altay, as well as the most prominent indigenous language in Manchuria, Dagur, still have relatively large numbers of speakers, but a shift to Russian or Northern Chinese has been the constant trend, which has brought them into the category of endangered languages. Besides the publications covering all languages of the Russian Federation, there are a few others with a focus on Siberia and Manchuria, notably the *Arctic languages* (1990), Janhunen (1991; 1996), Vakhtin (1993; 2001), and the *Northern minority languages* (1997).

Extinct languages

Recently (or possibly) extinct languages have their own entries below. In Europe, this category includes Manx and Alderney French, and in Caucasia and Anatolia, Ubykh and Cappadocian Greek. In Siberia, there are seven such languages, Kamas, Kerek, Southern Khanty, Southern Mansi, Western Mansi, Sirenik (see Chapter 1), and Yug; and in Central Asia there is one recently extinct outlying dialect, Ongkor Solon.

Another group of extinct languages comprises those that were still spoken and at least fragmentarily attested after the beginning of modern times. They are also incorporated into the checklist of languages below. In what follows they appear divided into geographic sections and in an approximate chronological order of their extinction moving back in time.

In Europe, *Dalmatian* was spoken in Krk (Veglia) on the coast of Dalmatia until the death of the last speaker in 1898; earlier it was also spoken in Zarar (Zada) and Dubrovnik (Ragusa). *Norn* was spoken in the Shetland Islands until approximately 1880; earlier it was also spoken in the Orkney Islands and adjacent mainland Scotland. *Kemi Saami* was spoken in Sodankylä and Kuolajärvi (Salla) counties in Lapland Province in Finland till the mid-nineteenth century. *Old Prussian* was spoken in Samland and Kurische Nehrung in East Prussia probably till the end of the eighteenth century. *Cornish* was spoken in Cornwall, England, until the death of the last speaker, which probably took place in 1777; Cornish is currently being revived and exists in three different versions; revived Cornish cannot be regarded as endangered as the number of users seems to be constantly growing. *Polabian* was spoken in the Elbe River basin in northeastern Germany until approximately 1750. *Gothic* was spoken in the Crimea in the Ukraine perhaps till the early eighteenth century. *Cuman* was spoken in Hungary till the early seventeenth century; earlier it was spread over a large area of Eastern Europe. *Mozarabic* was spoken in southern Spain until extinction in early modern times. Two extinct outlying dialects of endangered languages, Krevin and Slovincian, are presented in the respective entries on Vote and Kashubian.

From Caucasia, only *Lomavren* needs to be mentioned here. Here it refers to the original Indic language, closely related to Romani, that became extinct when it was replaced by the Armenian-based variety here conventionally called Bosha. The time of extinction seems to be unknown.

In Siberia, *Eastern Kamchadal* was spoken on the eastern coast of central Kamchatka and in the basin of the river Kamchatka, and may have survived till the first decades of the twentieth century. *Southern Kamchadal* was spoken in the southern part of Kamchatka, possibly mainly on the eastern coast, and became extinct by the end of the nineteenth century. *Kott* was spoken in the basin of the river Kan, an eastern tributary to the upper Yenisey, till the 1850s. *Mator* was spoken on the northern slopes of the Eastern Sayan mountains, extending from the eastern part of the Minusinsk region in the west (dialects Mator proper and Taygi) to the Baykal region in the east (Karagas Samoyed) till the 1840s. *Pumpokol* was spoken on the upper Ket', an eastern tributary to the upper Ob', till the early nineteenth century. *Yurats* was spoken in the tundra zone to the west of the lower Yenisey basin till the early nineteenth century. *Arin* was spoken in the upper Yenisey basin, to the north of the Minusinsk region, till the late eighteenth century. *Assan* was spoken to the east of the Kott territory perhaps till the late eighteenth century. Two extinct outlying dialects of endangered languages, Kamas (not Kamas Samoyed) and Arman, are presented in the respective entries on Khakas and Even.

Languages that only survived into the Middle Ages are not discussed in this presentation. To give just a couple of examples, Cumbric, Khazar and Langobardic would belong to this group. Needless to say, languages that disappeared even earlier, such as Etruscan, Gaulish, Hittite, Hurrian or Oscan, are left out as well.

Notes on language names

Most languages spoken in the area have their established names in English, but especially in the case of the minority languages of the Russian Federation there appear variant names and spellings. Occasionally they derive from a lack of familiarity with earlier studies in these languages, but there occur truly controversial and problematic issues as well, and I try to shed light on them in this section.

Most minority languages of the Russian Federation as well as some others have had their old, often derogatory names changed in the twentieth century. Conservative linguists in other countries may still employ them, regarding them as cherished relics of scholarly tradition, but, in my view, there is really nothing quaint about them. While the modern names are recommended for current usage, it is, of course, important to recognise the old ones, because they are found in many sources, so here is a checklist of old and new names: Cheremis → Mari; Gilyak → Nivkh; Gold → Nanay; (Western) Kamchadal → Itelmen; Karagas → Tofa; Lamut → Even; Lappish (or Lapp) → Saami; Oyrot → Altay; Ostyak → Khanty; Ostyak Samoyed → Selkup; Tavgi (or Tavgi Samoyed) → Nganasan; Tungus → Evenki; Vogul → Mansi; Votyak → Udmurt; Yenisey Ostyak → Ket (and Yug); Yenisey Samoyed → Enets; Yurak (or Yurak Samoyed) → Nenets; Zyryan → Komi. Obviously, most names in this list refer to groups of languages. Notice that 'Ostyak' in its widest sense referred not only to Khanty but also to the distantly related Selkup and the unrelated Ket (and Yug). Also notice that Karagas is still used as the name of a dialect of the extinct Mator language, and that Southern Kamchadal and Eastern Kamchadal are valid names for the extinct languages related to Itelmen.

Furthermore, many old language names contained the word 'Tatar', for instance, Karachay-Balkar was known as Mountain Tatar, Khakas as Abakan Tatar or Yenisey Tatar, and Shor as Kuznetsk Tatar. Beyond the Russian Federation, there are a few notable name changes. Romani is nowadays preferred over Gypsy, and Eskimo is not used in language names, although it continues to be valid as the name of a branch.

Different spelling conventions abound in words borrowed from Russian, and this can be seen in geographic names as well, for instance the above-mentioned language names referred to the river Yenisey and the mountain range Altay, but these are also commonly spelled as Yenisei and Altai, respectively. Here the former spelling is adopted consistently, hence, for example, the language names Nanay, Nogay, Oyrat and Uygur contain a vowel plus 'y' instead of a vowel plus 'i' used in spellings like 'Nanai', etc., Azerbaijani being an established exception. This is also a feature of the transliteration system for Russian place-names used in this presentation: since there is no risk of confusion, the letter 'y' has two different functions in that it represents both the Russian 'back i' (a vowel variant) and the 'short i' (a glide), as in the Russian name of the capital of the Republic of Chechenia, Groznyy.

The letter 'y' is also part of the transliterations of the Russian vowel letters 'yu' and 'ya', hence the language names Buryat pro 'Buriat' and Koryak pro 'Koriak'. An apostrophe marks the Russian soft sign letter in regular transliterations, but it must be omitted from language names, for example Itelmen pro 'Itel'men' and Mansi pro 'Man'si'. The digraph 'gh' is avoided in language and place names alike, as there is no point in employing it in words deriving from Russian, hence the language names Adyge, Agul, Dagur, Godoberi, Khinalug, Lezgian, Negidal, Nogay, Udege, Uygur, Yug and Yukagir instead of 'Adyghe', etc., Kirghiz being an established exception. Some people would use 'x' for velar fricative but 'kh' is clearly more suitable for English terminology, including the language names Abkhaz, Akhvakh, Botlikh, Budukh, Hinukh, Tsakhur, Ubykh, Khakas, Khamnigan, Khanty, Khinalug, Khvarshi and Nivkh rather than 'Abxaz', etc. Double 'ss', typically copied from German spelling, is avoided, as it is sometimes added to the language names Cherkes, Kamas, Karagas, Khakas, Nganasan and Tabasaran yielding 'Cherkess', etc.

Suffixes that lack any function are avoided, so that, to give a few examples, the language and branch names Kabard, Mordvin, Ossete, Samoyed, Serbo-Croat, Slovene and Vote appear instead of 'Kabardian', 'Mordvinian', 'Ossetic' (or 'Ossetian'), 'Samoyedic', 'Serbo-Croatian', 'Slovenian' and 'Votic' (or 'Votian'). A special case involves the names with an Iranian-based 'i' at the end, which is not used in the language names Ili Turk, Juhur and Tat, pro 'Ili Turki', 'Juhuri' and 'Tati', but is by necessity and convention found in Azerbaijani.

Randomly nativised or otherwise manipulated versions of language names that have already been established as Russian borrowings in English are not recommended, so that, for example, the language names Evenki, Selkup, Sirenik and Tuvan are used in this presentation instead of 'Ewenki', 'Sölkup' (or 'Sölqup'), 'Sirenikski' and 'Tyvan'. A colonial spelling 'Chukchee' persists strangely in scholarly literature in place of the modern spelling, Chukchi. Other non-recommended variants based on recent Russian colloquialisms include 'Evenk' for Evenki, 'Khant' for Khanty, and 'Tof' for Tofa. The current names of the Finnic languages Ingrian and Vote should also not be replaced with 'Izhor(ian)' or 'Vod'.

In the names of a few Caucasian languages, exceptions are made to these conventions when English spellings seem to be well-established, so that 'h' and 'w' are used when Russian would suggest 'g' and 'v', respectively, hence the languages names Hinukh pro 'Ginukh', Hunzib pro 'Gunzib', and Dargwa pro 'Dargva'. Lezgian is likewise used instead of suffixless 'Lezgi'. For Saami, there is a widely used alternative spelling Sámi.

The language checklist

The following list summarises the genetic classification of the languages dealt with in this chapter. Language families, marked in boldface, and major branches appear as separate paragraphs, and the different levels of subbranches are represented by the number of horizontal bars between languages; some subbranches have specific names followed by a colon, while some do not. Outlying dialects are separated by the + sign, and a number of other varieties that are clearly worth mentioning and in many cases languages in the sociolinguistic sense, while classified here as dialects on the basis of linguistic criteria, are included within parentheses, also separated by the + sign. The languages and outlying dialects with an entry in the next section are marked in italics, and the extinct, or in a few specially discussed cases possibly extinct, varieties are followed by an asterisk. Alternative names are given in parentheses.

There are altogether 172 entries, of which twenty-one represent outlying dialects of non-endangered languages. Besides that, there are fourteen outlying dialects of endangered languages dealt with in the entries on the languages in question and with references in their place in the alphabetic order.

Basque

Uralic

Saami: Western Saami: *South Saami* | *Ume Saami* | *Pite Saami* | *Lule Saami* | *North Saami* || Eastern Saami: *Inari Saami* | Kemi Saami* | *Skolt Saami* | *Akkala Saami* (Babino Saami) | *Kildin Saami* | *Ter Saami*

Finnic: *Livonian* | *Võro-Seto* | Estonian | *Vote* (+ Krevin*) | Finnish (+ Torne Valley Finnish + Finnmark Finnish) | *Ingrian* | *Karelian* | *Olonetsian* | *Lude* | *Veps*

Mordvin: *Erzya* | *Moksha*

Mari: *Western Mari* | *Eastern Mari*

Permian: *Udmurt* || Komi: *Permyak* + *Yazva Komi* (Eastern Permyak) | *Komi*

Hungarian + *Csángó Hungarian*

Mansi: *Northern Mansi* | *Eastern Mansi* | *Western Mansi** | *Southern Mansi**

Khanty: *Northern Khanty* | *Southern Khanty** | *Eastern Khanty*

Samoyed: *Nganasan* || Enets: *Tundra Enets* | *Forest Enets* || Yurats* || Nenets: *Tundra Nenets* | *Forest Nenets* || Selkup: *Northern Selkup* | *Central Selkup* | *Southern Selkup* || *Kamas** (+Koybal) || Mator* (+-Taygi+Karagas)

Indo-European

Slavonic: South Slavonic: Bulgarian (+ Pomak) | Macedonian || Serbo-Croat (+Forlak) + *Burgenland Croatian* + *Molise Croatian* || Slovene + *Resian Slovene* |||

West Slavonic: Lechitic: Polabian* | *Kashubian* (+ Slovincian*) | Polish (+ Upper Silesian) || *Sorbian* || Czech-Slovak: Czech | Slovak | Eastern Slovak | *Vojvodina Rusyn* (Bachkan) ||| East Slavonic: Rusyn (Ruthenian) (+ Lemko [Lemke] + Boyko + Hutzulian) | Ukrainian | Belarusian (+ Polissian [Palesian]) | Russian

Baltic: West Baltic: Old Prussian* ||| East Baltic: Lithuanian || Latvian | Latgalian

Germanic: West Germanic: Anglo-Saxon: Scots (+ Northumbrian) | English || Frisian: West Frisian | *Saterlandic* (Sater Frisian) | *North Frisian* || Low Saxon + *Plautdietsch* || Low Franconian: Dutch + Afrikaans (see Chapter 7) | Western Flemish || Central Franconian: Limburgian-Ripuarian | Luxemburgian (Moselle Franconian) || German (+ Rhenish Franconian + East Franconian) + Pennsylvania German (see Chapter 1) | *Yiddish* (Judeo-German) || Alemannic (+ Alsatian + Swabian) + *Töitschu* || Bavarian + *Cimbrian* (+ Mòcheno*) + *Gottscheerish* ||| North Germanic (Scandinavian): West Scandinavian: Icelandic | Faroese | Norn* | Norwegian (+ Jemtian) || East Scandinavian: *Dalecarlian* | Swedish (+ Gutnish) | Scanian | Danish | Jutish ||| Gothic*

Celtic: Gaelic (Goidelic): *Irish* (Irish Gaelic) | *Manx** (Manx Gaelic) | *Scottish Gaelic* || Brythonic: Welsh | Cornish* | *Breton*

Romance: Ibero-Romance: Portuguese | Galician (+ Fala) || *Asturian-Leonese* (+ Sanabrese + Mirandese + Cantabrian) || Extremaduran | Spanish (Castilian) (+ Llanito) | *Judezmo* (Ladino, Judeo-Spanish) | Mozarabic* || *Aragonese* ||| Occitano-Romance: Catalan (+Valenciano) + *Algherese Catalan* || *Gascon* (+ Aranese) || Oc (Occitan): *Limousin* | *Auvergnat* | *Languedocian* | *Provençal* (+ Niçard) | *Alpine Provençal* + *Gardiol* ||| Gallo-Romance: Oïl: *Poitevin-Saintongeais* | French (+ Lorrain + Champenois + Burgundian [Morvan] + Franc-Comtois) | *Gallo* | *Norman* + *Alderney French* + *Guernsey French* + *Jersey French* (+ Sark French) | *Picard* | *Walloon* || *Francoprovençal* + *Faetar* || *Piedmontese* | *Ligurian* (+ Monégasque) | *Lombard* | *Emilian-Romagnol* | Venetan ||| Raeto-Romance: *Romansh* | *Ladin* | *Friulian* ||| Sardinian: *Logudorese Sardinian* | *Campidanese Sardinian* ||| Italo-Romance: *Corsican* + *Gallurese Sardinian* + *Sassarese Sardinian* | Italian (Tuscan + Central Italian) | *Italkian* (Judeo-Italian) || South Italian (Neopolitan + Camponian + Abrizzian + Apulian + Lucanian) | Sicilian (+ Calabrian + Salentine [Otrantan] ||| *Istriot* ||| Dalmatian* ||| Romanian: *Istro-Romanian* | *Aromanian* (Macedo-Romanian) | *Megleno-Romanian* | Romanian (Daco-Romanian)

Albanian + *Arvanite Albanian* + *Arbëreshë Albanian*

Hellenic: Greek (+ Cypriot Greek) + *Griko* (Italiot Greek) + *Pontic Greek* + *Mariupolitan Greek* (Tauro-Romaic) + *Cappadocian Greek** || *Tsakonian*

Armenian

Indo-Iranian (Aryan): Iranian: South-West Iranian: Tat: *Tat* | *Juhur* (Judeo-Tat) || see Chapter 4 for the other South-West Iranian languages ||| North-west Iranian (see Chapter 4) ||| South-East Iranian (see Chapter 4) ||| North-east Iranian: Ossete || Yagnob (see Chapter 4) |||| Indic (Indo-Aryan): *Romani* | Lomavren* | Domari (see Chapter 4) ||| see Chapter 4 for the other Indic languages

Semitic

Arabic: Maltese | *Cypriot Arabic* | see Chapters 4 and 7 for the other Arabic and Semitic languages

Kartvelian

Georgian || *Svan* || Zan: *Mingrelian* | *Laz* (Chan)

Abkhaz-Adyge

Abkhaz: Abaza | Abkhaz || *Ubykh** || Circassian (Adyge): Adyge (West Circassian) (+ Shapsug) | Kabard-Cherkes (East Circassian)

Nakh-Daghestanian

Nakh: *Bats* || Chechen-Ingush: Chechen | Ingush

Daghestanian: Avar-Andi-Tsezic: Avar || Andi: *Andi* | *Botlikh* | *Godoberi* | *Karata* | *Akhvakh* | *Bagvalal* | *Tindi* | *Chamalal* || Tsezic: *Tsez* (Dido) | *Hinukh* | *Khvarshi* | *Inkhokvari* | *Bezhta* (Kapucha) | *Hunzib* ||| Lak ||| Dargwa (+ Kaytag + Kubachi + Megeb) ||| Lezgian: Lezgian | Tabasaran | *Agul* | *Rutul* | *Tsakhur* | *Kryts* (Kryz) | *Budukh* | *Archi* | *Udi* || *Khinalug*

Turkic

Chuvash

Common Turkic: Khalaj (see Chapter 4) ||| Oguz: *Gagauz* (+ Balkan Gagauz) | Turkish + *Crimean Turkish* + *Urum* | Azerbaijani (Azeri) | Kashkay (+ Aynallu + Iraqi Turk) + Afshar (see Chapter 4) | Khorasan Turk | Turkmen + *Trukhmen* | Salar (see Chapter 5) ||| Karluk: Uzbek + *Ili Turk* | Uygur (+ Lopnor) ||| Kipchak: *Crimean Tatar* | *Krimchak* (Judeo-Crimean Tatar) | Cuman* (+ Armeno-Kipchak*) | *Karaim* | Kumyk | Karachay-Balkar || Tatar (+ Siberian Tatar) + *Baraba Tatar* | Bashkir || *Nogay* + *Alabugat Tatar* + *Karagash* + *Yurt Tatar* | Karakalpak | Kazakh (+ Kipchak Uzbek) ||| Kirghiz || *Southern Altay* ||| Yenisey Turkic: *Northern Altay* | *Shor* | *Chulym Turk* | *Khakas* (+ Kamas*) | *Manchurian Kirghiz* (Fuyü Kirghiz) ||| Saryg Yugur (see Chapter 5) ||| Sayan Turkic: Tuvan (+ Toja) | *Dukha* (Tuha) | *Tofa* ||| Lena Turkic: Yakut + *Dolgan*

Mongolic

Dagur + *Sinkiang Dagur* ||| *Khamnigan Mongol* | *Buryat* || Mongolian | Ordos || *Kalmyk* | *Oyrat* + *Manchurian Ölöt* ||| Shira Yugur (see Chapter 5) ||| Monguor: Mongul (Huzhu Monguor) | Manguer (Minhe Monguor) | Bonan | Santa (see Chapter 5) ||| Mogol (see Chapter 4)

Tungusic

North Tungusic: *Even* (+ Arman*) || *Evenki* (+ Orochen) | *Negidal* || *Solon* + *Ongkor Solon** ||| *Udege* | *Oroch* ||| *Nanay* | *Ulcha* || *Orok* (Uilta) ||| Manchu: Manchu (+ Jurchen*) | Sibe (see Chapter 5)

Nivkh

Yeniseian

Ket | *Yug** || Arin* | Pumpokol* || Assan* | Kott*

Yukagi

Tundra Yukagir (+ Chuvan* + Omok*) | *Forest Yukagir*

Chukotkan

Chukchi || *Kerek** || Koryak: *Alutor* (+ Palana Koryak + Karaga Koryak) | *Koryak*

Kamchatkan

Itelmen (Western Kamchadal) | Southern Kamchadal* | Eastern Kamchadal*

Alphabetical list of languages

Agul **[125]** Caucasia: southern Daghestan. Spoken in fifteen villages in Agul County and five villages in Kurakh County, amongst them Richa, Burkikhan, Tpig, Kurag, Burshag, and Fite, in the Republic of Daghestan and in a number of expatriate communities elsewhere in the Russian Federation. In 1989, nearly 18,000 speakers were reported. Despite the relatively large number of speakers of all ages, there are reasons such as the presence of more dominant neighbouring languages, notably Dargwa, Lak, Tabasaran and Lezgian, as well as the increasing influence of Russian, for regarding the language as definitely endangered. Literary experiments took place in the nineteenth century and again in recent years, and there is now one local newspaper in Agul. Until recently, Agul had no role in school curriculum but now it can be taught as a subject in local schools.

Akhvakh **[115]** Caucasia: western Daghestan. Spoken in six villages in Akhvakh County and in the villages of Ratlub, Tlyanub and Tsegob in Kakhib County in the Republic of Daghestan in the Russian Federation, as well as in the expatriate community of Akhvakh-dere in Kuba (Quba) County in Azerbaijan. There may be up to 5,000 speakers, including many children, but because of the small size of the community and the dominant position of Avar, the language must be regarded as definitely endangered. There is no literacy in it.

Akkala Saami (or *Babino Saami*) **[8]** Northern Europe: Kola peninsula. Earlier spoken in the village of Babino in southern Murmansk Province in the Russian Federation, from where the speakers were forcibly translocated to Lovozero, the centre of Lovozero County. There were eight speakers in the early 1990s, all elderly, and according to a recent report, now only one speaker is known to be living. Some descendants of Akkala Saami speak Kildin Saami, but most have shifted to Russian. Nearly extinct.

Alabugat Tatar. See *Nogay*

Alderney French. See *Norman*

Algherese Catalan [in Algherese *alguerès*] **[60]** Italy: an outlying dialect of Catalan spoken by an old immigrant community deriving from the mid-fourteenth century in the town of Alghero in northwestern Sardinia. The number of speakers is probably between 20,000 and 30,000. Some children learn the language, but they may stop using it at school age. For many speakers, the influence of Italian or Logudorese Sardinian is strong. Endangered.

Alpine Provençal **[66]** In France, Alpine Provençal is spoken in the departments of Ardèche (except the north and the western border areas), Drôme (except the north), Hautes-Alpes, the northern parts of Alpes de Haute-Provence, and the southernmost parts of Isère by perhaps over 100,000 speakers, but most of them are middle-aged or elderly. In Italy, it is spoken in the upper valleys of Piedmont (Val Mairo, Val Varacho, Val d'Esturo, Entraigas, Limoun, Vinai, Pignerol, Sestriero) by approximately 100,000 speakers of all ages, but younger people are shifting to Italian. Definitely endangered. Often regarded as a single language with Provençal. – *Gardiol* **[67]** Italy: spoken in

Guardia Piedmontese in Calabria. Gardiol is an outlying dialect of Alpine Provençal, which has been under strong South Italian influence for a long time. There are a few hundred mainly older speakers. Severely endangered.

Alutor [in Russian *aljutorskij jazyk*] (spelling 'Alyutor' better avoided) **[179]** Siberia: spoken in the region of the Kamchatkan Isthmus, including most of Olyutor and Karaga counties and the north of Tigil' County in Koryak Autonomous District in the Russian Federation. Includes three dialect groups, Alutor proper, Karaga, and Palana, all of which are often considered dialects of Koryak. There are much fewer than 2,000 speakers, including very few if any children; most speakers are elderly; cf. Koryak. Kibrik reports in the *Endangered languages* (1991: 268) that of the 400 ethnic Alutor living in the village of Vyvenka in Olyutor County, 'fewer than 100 speak the language'. Alutor dialects are still used for interethnic communication by many of the neighbouring ethnic groups in central and northern Kamchatka, including speakers of Even and Itelmen. There has never been a specific Alutor literary language, and the use of written Koryak has turned out to be impossible. Severely endangered.

Andi **[110]** Caucasia: western Daghestan. Spoken in nine villages, including Andi, Muni (Munib), and Kvankhidatl', in Botlikh County in the Republic of Daghestan in the Russian Federation. The number of speakers is usually given as being below 10,000, but the actual figure may be as high as 20,000, and includes many children. Nevertheless, for reasons such as the dominant position of Avar the language must be regarded as definitely endangered. Andi is not a written language, and Russian and Avar are used in schools.

Aragonese [in Aragonese *aragonés*] **[59]** Spain: originally spoken in most parts of the historical province of Aragón and adjacent parts of Navarra. Today Aragonese is spoken mainly in the high valleys of the Pyrenees, notably Aragon River (Somontano), Sobrarbe and Ribagorza, in the northern part of the Huesca (Uesca) region in the northeast of Aragón, main towns being Graus and Sabiñánigo (Samianigo). The number of active speakers is perhaps below 10,000, but there are several times more people with some knowledge of the language. Few children learn the language, but Aragonese is also actively studied as a second language. Definitely endangered.

Arbëreshë Albanian **[96]** Italy: an outlying dialect of (Tosk) Albanian deriving from the language of fifteenth- and sixteenth-century (or even earlier) refugees spoken in nearly fifty scattered villages mainly in Avellino, Potenza, Taranto, Cosenza, Catanzaro and Palermo provinces by probably under 100,000 speakers out of a much larger ethnic population. In some places, there may be children learning the language, but many stop using it at school age. Speakers' competence is likely to vary greatly. Definitely endangered.

Archi **[130]** Caucasia: southern Daghestan. Spoken in the village of Archi (Archib) in Charoda County in the Republic of Daghestan in the Russian Federation by up to 1,000 speakers, including a number of children. Within its family, Archi is highly divergent. There is no literacy in it, and Avar and Russian are used in school and for wider communication. It has been influenced by Lak and Avar. Definitely endangered.

236

Aromanian (or *Aromunian*, or *Macedo-Romanian*) **[93]** the Balkans. Spoken in two larger areas, one in Thessaly and Epirus in northern Greece and another in the central parts of Albania, as well as in several small pockets in the Republic of Macedonia, Greek Macedonia and Bulgaria. In Serbia, especially between Niš and Kladovo, and elsewhere in former Yugoslavia, there are traditionally Aromanian-speaking immigrant groups deriving from the eighteenth century known by the names Vlach and Tsintsars; since the early twentieth century, there have also been many Aromanian immigrants in Romania. The total number of speakers has been estimated at 350,000, but because of a rapid language shift especially in Greece, the factual figure may be lower; on the other hand, recent data from Albania suggest up to 400,000 speakers there alone. In any case, the largest number of speakers is probably now found in Albania, followed by Greece and the Republic of Macedonia. Some children learn the language, but many stop using it at school age. Severely endangered.

Arvanite Albanian **[95]** Greece: an outlying dialect of (Tosk) Albanian spoken in old immigrant communities that occupy extensively the rural areas in Attica, Boeotia (Voiotía), southern Euboea (Évvoia), northern Andros (Ándros), Corinthia, Argolis and a few smaller sections of Peloponnese and central Greece. There are perhaps 50,000 speakers, but a language shift has proceeded rapidly and regular use is probably confined to a much smaller number of people. Very few if any children learn the language. All idiolects are heavily influenced by Greek. Severely endangered.

Astrakhan Nogay. See *Nogay*

Asturian-Leonese (also known as *Bable*; in Portugal known locally as *Mirandese* [*mir-andês*]) **[57]** Spain earlier in most parts of the historical provinces of Asturias and León, extending to the northeastern corner of Portugal. Asturian-Leonese (or simply *Asturian* [*asturianu*]) survives mainly in Asturias around Oviedo (Uviéu) where some children learn the language, and to much lesser extent in the western parts of León Province (*Leonese*) and in the Sanabria region in Zamora Province (*Sanabrese*) in the autonomous region of Castille-León, where probably all speakers are elderly. The number of speakers in Spain is not known exactly but a reasonable estimate is 100,000. Though not recognised as official, the language is to some extent used in the school system in Asturias. In Portugal, the language is spoken in the Miranda do Douro region and in two towns in the Vimioso region by some 10,000 to 15,000 people; it was officially recognised there in 1999, and it has gained some presence in education, media and public life since then. Nevertheless, Asturian-Leonese is increasingly endangered both in Portugal and Spain.

Auvergnat [in Auvergnat *auvernhàs* or *auvernhat*] **[63]** France: spoken in an area covering the departments of Cantal (except Aurillac region), Haute-Loire, and Puy-de-Dôme, and extending to the Gannat region in Allier, the Saint-Bonnet-le-Château region in Loire, and the western border areas in Ardèche. There may be over 100,000 people able to speak Auvergnat, but very few if any children learn it. Even the language of the most competent speakers is likely to be heavily influenced by French. Severely endangered.

Bagvalal (also called *Bagulal*) **[116]** Caucasia: western Daghestan. Spoken in the villages of Khushtada, Tlondoda, Kvanada and Gemerso in Tsumada County and the villages of Tlissi and Tlibisho in Akhvakh County as well as in a number of expatriate communities elsewhere in the Republic of Daghestan in the Russian Federation. The number of speakers lies somewhere between 4,000 and 6,000. Because of the small size of the community and the dominant position of Avar, the language must be regarded as definitely endangered. There is no literacy in it.

Baraba Tatar **[142]** Siberia. An outlying dialect of Tatar spoken in the Baraba steppes in the western parts of Novosibirsk Province in the Russian Federation. Baraba Tatar has more recently been influenced by mainstream Siberian Tatar. There are 8,000 members of the ethnic group, but only the elderly speak Baraba Tatar, while the younger generations use Tatar and Russian. Schools operated in Tatar until 1964 when they were shifted to Russian. Baraba Tatar must be regarded as severely endangered.

Bats (also called ***Batsbi***) [in Georgian *tsova-tush*] **[110]** Caucasia: northeastern Georgia. Spoken in the village of Zemo-Alvani in Akhmeta County. The number of speakers is usually given as 3,000, but active users may be far fewer. Modern Bats is heavily influenced by Georgian with most speakers, and a more traditional variety of Bats is perhaps only known by a small group of elders. There is no literacy in it, but Georgian is used in school and for wider communication.

Bezhta (also called ***Kapucha***) **[123]** Caucasia: western Daghestan. Spoken in the villages of Bezhta, Tlyadal, and Khasharkhota in Tsunta County in the Republic of Daghestan in the Russian Federation. There may be up to 7,000 speakers, including many children, but because of the small size of the community and the dominant position of Avar, the language must be regarded as definitely endangered. There is no literacy in it, but Avar and Russian are used in school and for wider communication.

Botlikh **[112]** Caucasia: western Daghestan. Spoken in the villages of Botlikh and Miarsu in Botlikh County in the Republic of Daghestan in the Russian Federation. There are approximately 4,000 speakers, including many children, but because of the small size of the community and the dominant position of Avar, the language must be regarded as definitely endangered. There is no literacy in it, but Avar and Russian are used in school and for wider communication.

Breton [in Breton *brezhoneg*] **[56]** France: spoken mainly in western Brittany. In the 1950s, there were over a million speakers, but only 240,000 speakers were reported in 1997. The transmission of the language to children stopped almost completely between 1950 and 1970. Now a small number of children are learning the language, but it is not clear if they continue to use it in adulthood. Regular users are mostly fully competent, although French influence is felt strongly. Severely endangered.

Budukh **[129]** Caucasia: northern Azerbaijan. Spoken in the village of Budukh and in the expatriate communities of Deli-Kaya and Pirusti in Kuba (Quba) County and elsewhere in Azerbaijan. There are approximately 1,000 speakers, including some children; higher figures found in literature probably refer to members of the ethnic group. There is no literacy in it, but Azerbaijani is used in school and for wider communication. Definitely endangered.

Burgenland Croatian **[40]** Austria: an outlying dialect of Serbo-Croat spoken in Burgenland. It is said to differ extensively from Serbo-Croat dialects spoken in Croatia. There were approximately 28,000 speakers in the 1970s, now probably much less. It is possible that a number of children still learn the language, but many families have shifted to the majority language. Speakers' competence is not known exactly, but varies within different areas, and, presumably, between age groups. Definitely endangered.

Buryat [in Chinese pinyin *Buliyate*] **[159]** Siberia, China and Mongolia. Two old dialect groups, Western Buryat in Cisbaykalia, to the north of the Eastern Sayan mountains and in the Angara region, and Eastern Buryat in Transbaykalia, extending from Lake Baykal in the west to the Onon basin in the east, can be distinguished. Western Buryat is spoken mainly in Ust'-Orda (Ust'-Ordynskiy) Buryat Autonomous District and elsewhere in Irkutsk Province in the Russian Federation; an outlying dialect of Western Buryat is spoken in the Barguzin valley of Transbaykalia. Eastern Buryat is spoken in the Republic of Buryatia and in Aga (Aginskiy) Buryat Autonomous District and elsewhere in Chita Province in the Russian Federation, as well as by recent immigrant groups in adjacent regions of Mongolia and China. Old Bargut and New Bargut are earlier branches of Eastern Buryat in Manchuria deriving from the seventeenth and eighteenth centuries, respectively. Old Bargut [in Chinese pinyin *Chen Baerhu*] is spoken in the northern part and New Bargut [in Chinese pinyin *Xin Baerhu*] in the southwestern part of the Barga steppe region in Chen Baerhu Banner and Right and Left Xin Baerhu banners, respectively, in Hulun Buir League in Inner Mongolia in China. There are probably over 400,000 speakers of all dialects, including many children, but Buryat is everywhere under pressure from dominant languages, Russian, Chinese and Mongolian. In many rural areas of the Russian Federation, children are learning the language, but in cities Russian is normally spoken even between Buryat speakers. Among the Western Buryat there are relatively few child speakers, and Russian influence has been stronger on Western Buryat than on Eastern Buryat. Speakers in China and Mongolia, especially among the Old Bargut, are shifting to Mongolian. Buryat has a literary standard in Cyrillic script based on Eastern Buryat, which replaced the earlier use of Written Mongolian; Written Mongolian serves as the literary language for the Buryat population in China. In China and Mongolia all Buryat varieties are officially counted as varieties of Mongolian. Buryat as a whole is moderately endangered, the Buryat-speaking territory continually shrinking and there being very few monolinguals, but the situation of dialects such as Western Buryat is even more alarming, and Old Bargut may be regarded as severely endangered.

Campidanese Sardinian **[86]** Italy: spoken in southern Sardinia. The number of speakers is perhaps approximately 500,000; cf. Logudorese Sardinian. Many children learn the language, but often stop using it at school age. Definitely endangered.

Cappadocian Greek **[100]** an outlying dialect of Greek spoken in a few isolated communities in the interior of Cappadocia in central Turkey, notably in Sille (Silli) near Konya, villages near Kayseri, and Faras (Pharasa) and adjacent villages, before the genocide of 1915 and the subsequent population exchanges, after which most survivors settled in Greece. Cappadocian Greek is extinct in Turkey and in Greece, and the Greek dialects still spoken in the regions of Tsalka in Georgia and Alaverdi in

Armenia, which derive partly from Cappadocian Greek, have apparently assimilated to Pontic Greek. Recently extinct.

Central Selkup **[37]** Siberia: in the basin of the upper Ob' and on its tributaries, from the Chaya in the south to the Tym in the north, with each river basin having a dialect of its own, mainly in the eastern parts of Kargasok and Parabel' counties in Tomsk Province in the Russian Federation. There are a couple of hundred speakers at best, probably all elderly. There exists a movement of national awakening, but it seems mainly concerned about social and ecological problems rather than the fate of the native language. There have been attempts to create a written standard in Cyrillic script. Critically endangered.

Chamalal [in Russian *čamalinskij jazyk*] **[118]** Caucasia: western Daghestan. Spoken in the villages of Upper Gakvari, Lower Gakvari, Agvali, Tsumada, Richaganik, Gadyri, Gigatl', and Kvankhi in Tsumada County in the Republic of Daghestan in the Russian Federation. The number of speakers lies somewhere between 4,000 and 6,000. Because of the small size of the community and the dominant position of Avar, the language must be regarded as definitely endangered. There is no literacy in it, but Avar and Russian are used in school and for wider communication.

Channel Islands French. See ***Norman***

Chukchi [in Russian *čukotskij jazyk*] (also known as ***Luoravetlan***) **[177]** Siberia: in and around Chukotka from the Arctic coast to the Bering Sea region, covering most parts of Chukchi Autonomous District, adjacent regions in Koryak Autonomous District and Lower Kolyma (Nizhnekolymskiy) County in the Republic of Sakha (Yakutia) in the Russian Federation. There are two geographical and economical groups known as the Maritime or Coastal or Sea Chukchi and the Inland or Reindeer Chukchi, but there is no corresponding dialectal division. In 1989, 11,000 speakers were reported, but the figure may be slightly inflated. Chukchi is often thought to be rather safe, but there are actually very few children speaking the language. There used to be phonological, possibly also lexical and grammatical, differences between men's speech and women's speech, but the differences are now being levelled in favour of the men's variety. Chukchi has a written standard in Cyrillic script, but it is little used in education. Definitely or even severely endangered.

Chulym Turk (also called ***Chulym Tatar*** or ***Middle Chulym language***) **[150]** Siberia: on the middle Chulym, a tributary to the upper Ob', mainly in Tegul'det County in Tomsk Province and Tyukhtet County in Krasnoyarsk Region in the Russian Federation. Two extinct Turkic varieties known by the special names Küärik and Kecik can apparently be regarded as dialects of Chulym Turk. The number of fluent speakers is only thirty-five; all of them are middle-aged or older. There are a few others with strong interference from Russian and Siberian Tatar, which is spoken on lower Chulym. Critically endangered.

Cimbrian (or ***Cimbro***) [in German *Zimbrisch*] **[51]** Italy: an outlying dialect of Bavarian spoken in the towns of Giazza (Ljetzan) in Verona Province, Roana (Rowan), Mezzaselva (Mitterballe) and Rotzo (Rotz) in Vicenza Province, and Luserna (Lusern) in Trento Province. Earlier spoken in two larger areas known as Sette comuni (Sieben Gemeinden) established in the twelfth century, including Roana and Rotzo as well as Lavarone (Lafraun) from which Luserna was founded in the sixteenth century, and Tredici comuni (Dreizehn Gemeinden) established in the thirteenth century, of which only in Giazza the language has survived up till today. In Luserna, Cimbrian is still the language used by the whole community of some 500 people, while the couple of hundred speakers in Giazza, and the approximately 1,500 speakers in Sette comuni are mostly middle-aged or older. Although a number of children apparently learn Cimbrian in Luserna, the language cannot be regarded as safe even there. Speakers are all fluent in Italian and Venetan, many knowing German as well, and modern Cimbrian tends to be heavily influenced by these languages. Although Cimbrian has some presence in school and media, and there have been attempts to promote it more actively in recent decades, it is definitely endangered. Another outlying dialect of Bavarian known as *Mòcheno* has been spoken in the Fersina Valley (Fersental, Valle del Fèrsina, or Val dei Mòcheni) in Trento Province. Although there are reports that Mòcheno still has 400 speakers in Fierozzo (Florutz), 1,000 in Palù (Palai), and 460 in Frassilongo (Gereut), it seems more likely that they currently use a local variety of Venetan with numerous Germanic substate influences, and at least Matzel in *Germanische Rest- und Trümmersprachen* (1989) refers to Mòcheno as extinct.

Corsican [87] France: spoken by approximately two thirds of the total population of 250,000 people of the island of Corsica (Corse). Also spoken on Maddalena Island off the northeast coast of Sardinia. There are tens of thousands of speakers in expatriate communities elsewhere in France and other parts of the world. The position of Corsican is much stronger than that of any other minority language in France, but it is nevertheless increasingly endangered. – *Gallurese Sardinian* [88] Italy: spoken in northeastern Sardinia. Gallurese Sardinian is an outlying dialect of Corsican. The number of speakers is perhaps approximately 100,000; cf. Logudorese Sardinian. Many children learn the language, but often stop using it at school age. Definitely endangered. – *Sassarese Sardinian* [89] Italy: spoken in northwestern Sardinia. Sassarese Sardinian is here treated as another outlying dialect of Corsican. It has been influenced by other Romance languages, notably Logudorese Sardinian, Ligurian and Tuscan, so profoundly that it can also be called a mixed dialect. The number of speakers is perhaps approximately 100,000; cf. Logudorese Sardinian. Many children learn the language, but often stop using it at school age. Definitely endangered.

Crimean Tatar [139] Eastern Europe. Originally spoken in the Crimea, but most speakers were deported from there mainly to Central Asia after the Second World War. There are also Crimean Tatar speakers in the southern parts of the Dobruja region in northeastern Bulgaria and adjacent Romania. Crimean Tatar was spoken across the central parts of the Crimea, while speakers of Nogay in the northern steppe area and those of Crimean Turkish in the southern coastal region have been officially subsumed under the Crimean Tatar. In 1989, 250,000 speakers were reported from the Soviet Union, including over 40,000 in the Ukraine, where they lived both in the traditional area in the Crimea and elsewhere, especially in Kherson Province, 180,000 in Uzbekistan plus a few from Tajikistan, and 20,000 in the Russian Federation, mostly settled in Krasnodar Region; since then, many more have returned to the Crimea. It is unlikely, however, that these figures represent the number of fully fluent speakers reliably:

241

Comrie writes in the *Atlas of the world's languages* (1994) that 'Maria S. Polinsky advises me that the number of solid first language speakers of Crimean Tatar may not exceed 100,000'. In Bulgaria, the official term 'Tatar' refers principally to Crimean Tatar, and the number of 'Tatar' speakers lies somewhere between 6,000 and 11,000. In Romania there are up to 25,000 'Tatar' speakers, which covers speakers of both Crimean Tatar and Nogay. In some communities, children learn the language, but many stop using it in adulthood. Probably all speakers exhibit strong influence of related Turkic languages, Russian or Bulgarian, and younger people may be less competent in Crimean Tatar. Definitely endangered.

Crimean Turkish **[135]** Eastern Europe: an outlying dialect of Turkish originally spoken in a number of villages in the Yalta region along the southern shores of the Crimea, but the speakers shared the fate of the Crimean Tatars, as explained above. There are a few thousand speakers at best, but even this rough figure is based on a best guess rather than a reliable estimate. Definitely endangered.

Csángó Hungarian **[23]** Eastern Europe: an outlying dialect of Hungarian spoken in the Moldova region in Romania, primarily in Bacău, Neamţ and Iaşi counties; formerly, there were also a few Csángó-speaking villages east of the river Prut in the Republic of Moldova. The number of speakers is in the range of some tens of thousands. Csángó Hungarian derives from the Middle Ages; there are also Hungarian speakers in Moldova who are not Csángó but are mainly seventeenth- and eighteenth-century immigrants from the Szekler community in Transylvania. There are still young people able to speak Csángó Hungarian in a few villages, but they rarely use it amongst themselves. The attitude of Romanian authorities towards the language continues to be hostile. Severely endangered.

Cypriot Arabic (also called ***Cypriot Maronite Arabic***) **[105]** Cyprus: spoken mainly in the Kormakiti village in the north. There are far fewer than 2,000 speakers out of many thousand Maronites. Probably no children learn the language, and younger speakers, if there are any left, are more fluent in Greek. Greek influence has been strong for a long time to make Cypriot Arabic a hybrid language. Many people, especially the young, have moved to the government-controlled, Greek-speaking area from the self-declared Turkish Republic of Northern Cyprus. Severely endangered.

Dagur (also spelled ***Daur***) [in Chinese pinyin *Dawoer*] **[156]** Manchuria: spoken in central and northwestern Manchuria in China, mainly in Morin Dawa Daur and Ewenki autonomous banners in Hulun Buir League in Inner Mongolia (in the Nonni and Imin basins) and in Heilongjiang Province (in the Nonni basin) as well as within a small population in the Aihui region (in the middle Amur basin); cf. Janhunen in the *Northern minority languages* (1997: 128–9). In earlier times the Dagur language area covered parts of adjacent Siberia. There are probably more than 50,000 speakers. In Hulun Buir (especially in the Imin basin) the language is being retained well, while it has ceased to be transmitted to children among most groups in Heilongjiang, where (as in the cities of Nenjiang and Qiqihar) most or all speakers are middle-aged or older. Speakers are generally fluent within those communities retaining the language. Many attempts have been made to write Dagur in various systems (Manchu, Mongolian, Roman, Cyrillic), and a project of a new literary language is currently being planned. Increasingly endangered. – *Sinkiang Dagur* (also called *Turkestan Dagur*) Sinkiang: spoken in the Ili (Yili) region of Sinkiang, in Tacheng Prefecture in Xinjiang Uygur Autonomous Region in China. Sinkiang Dagur is an outlying dialect of Dagur. Dagur speakers were translocated to Sinkiang from Manchuria in 1763. The number of speakers is not known exactly but it lies in the range of a few thousand. Sinkiang Dagur is possibly being learnt by some children. Speakers are in many cases reportedly fluent but under the influence of neighbouring languages. There is widespread multilingualism in Kazakh, Uygur, Chinese and other languages. Definitely endangered.

Dalecarlian [157] Northern Europe: Sweden. Spoken in the central parts of Dalarna Province by approximately 10,000 people. Its most characteristic dialect (occasionally referred to as 'Elfdalian') is spoken in the south of Älvdalen County by 3,000 speakers. In Älvdalen, Dalecarlian is maintained quite well and it has recently created literary standard, while in other areas younger people are shifting to Swedish/ Because of the small size of the comunity the language must be regarded as definitely endangered.

Dolgan [155] Siberia: southern Taymyr peninsula. Spoken mainly in Dudinka and Khatanga counties in Taymyr (Dolgan and Nenets) Autonomous District as well as in Anabar County in the Republic of Sakha (Yakutia) in the Russian Federation. Dolgan is an outlying dialect of Yakut with deep influences from Evenki. In 1989, 5,500 speakers were reported, and it is one of the few smaller languages in Siberia with a substantial number of child speakers. Nevertheless, because of the small size of the community and the dominant position of Russian, Dolgan must be regarded as definitely endangered.

Dukha (also spelled *Tuha*) [in Mongolian known as *tsaatan*] [153] Mongolia: spoken by a semi-nomadic group living to the northwest of Lake Khövsgöl, mainly in the Tsaagannuur district of Khövsgöl League in the northernmost region of Mongolia, in an area bordering the Republic of Tuva in the west and the Republic of Buryatia in the northeast. Dukha is closely related to but clearly distinct from Tuvan, although this is not always made clear in general handbooks. The number of speakers lies between 100 and 200, and because of the geographic isolation and the traditional way of life, practically all of the members of the group continue to speak the native language, and at least until the 1970s children used to be monolingual in it. Given the very small population, Dukha must nevertheless be regarded as definitely endangered.

Eastern Khanty [30] Siberia: spoken along the western and eastern tributaries to the middle Ob', from the Vas'yugan to the Pim, mainly in Nefteyugansk, Surgut and Nizhnevartovsk counties in Khanty-Mansi Autonomous District and the adjacent parts of Tomsk Province in the Russian Federation. Eastern Khanty dialects include Salym Khanty, Surgut Khanty and Vakh-Vas'yugan Khanty. There are probably a couple of thousand speakers, including some children, but many of them shift to Russian at school age; most active speakers are therefore middle-aged or older. Definitely endangered.

Eastern Mansi (also called *Konda Mansi*) [25] Siberia: in the basin of the river Konda, a western tributary to the lower Irtysh, mainly in Konda County and the southern parts of Sovetskiy County in Khanty-Mansi Autonomous District in the Russian Federation. The number of speakers is not known exactly, but most likely there are only a handful of elderly speakers, and some reports are even more pessimistic. Nearly extinct.

Eastern Mari (often called ***Meadow Mari*** after the largest dialect group) **[20]** Eastern Europe: east-central Russia. Spoken mainly in central and eastern parts of the Republic of Mariy-El and parts of Bashkortostan, Tatarstan, the Udmurt Republic, and Yekaterinburg, Perm' and Orenburg provinces, in the Russian Federation. In 1989, 540,000 speakers were reported for both Mari languages, the large majority of them, approximately 500,000, speaking Eastern Mari. Many children learn the language, but only those living in remote rural areas continue to use it actively; in eastern diaspora areas in Bashkortostan practically all children learn the language. In many publications, the term 'Eastern Mari' is reserved to the diaspora groups outside the Republic. Increasingly endangered.

Emilian-Romagnol **[81]** Italy: spoken in the region of Emilia-Romagna, parts of the provinces of Pavia, Voghera, and Mantua in southern Lombardy, the Lunigiana district in northwestern Tuscany, the Republic of San Marino, and the Pesaro-Urbino province in the region of Marche. The number of speakers is probably between one and two million but the domains of use of Emilian-Romagnol have been constantly narrowing. Increasingly endangered. Emilian and Romagnol can also be viewed as two separate languages.

Erzya **[17]** Eastern Europe: Central Russia. Spoken mainly in the eastern parts but also in small pockets in the northwest and south of the Republic of Mordovia in the Russian Federation; also several areas in Nizhniy Novgorod, Samara, Saratov and Orenburg provinces, Tatarstan and Bashkortostan. In 1989, 770,000 speakers were reported for the two Mordvin languages; approximately 500,000 of them were speakers of Erzya. Quite a lot of children learn the language, but most of them use it only with elderly relatives, which means that they will have little use for it in the future. The situation is actually better in the Eastern diaspora areas than in the Republic. Increasingly endangered.

Even **[163]** Siberia: in northeastern Siberia, from the Lena to the Anadyr', including areas in Allaykhovskiy, Momskiy, Tomponskiy, Middle Kolyma (Srednekolymskiy), Verkhoyansk, Ust'-Yansk, Kobyay, Lower Kolyma (Nizhnekolymskiy), Upper Kolyma (Verkhnekolymskiy), Oymyakonskiy, Abyy, Bulun and Eveno-Batantay counties in the Republic of Sakha (Yakutia), Ola, Northern Even (Severo-Evenskiy), Omsukchan, Ten'kinskiy and Yagodnoye counties in Magadan Province, Okhota County in Khabarovsk Region and Bilibino and Anadyr counties in Chukchi Autonomous District in the Russian Federation, plus a small diaspora group in the Bystraya region of central Kamchatka in Kamchatka Province and several areas in Koryak Autonomous District. In 1989, 8,000 speakers were reported, but the figure is probably slightly inflated, so that the approximate number of speakers may be given as 7,000. There are very few or no child speakers; most speakers are middle-aged or older; the whole population is bi- or multilingual in Russian, Yakut or Koryak. Two orthographical standards, both in Cyrillic script, conforming to Yakut and Russian, respectively, have limited use. Severely endangered. – *Arman* was an archaic outlying dialect of Even spoken in a small coastal pocket at the Okhotsk Sea, to the south west of Magadan city, that became extinct recently, though no exact date is available.

Evenki **[164]** Siberia (including parts of the Russian Far East), Manchuria and Mongolia. Evenki is the widest-spread language of Siberia, spoken by a population sparsely covering the whole taiga zone from the Yenisey in the west to the lower Amur and Sakhalin in the east, and from Taymyr and the lower Lena in the north to Baykal and the upper Amur in the south where the language area extends to the Khingan region of northern Manchuria. In the Russian Federation, the largest numbers of Evenki communities are found in the Republic of Sakha (Yakutia), Evenki Autonomous District including adjacent regions of Taymyr (Dolgan and Nenets) Autonomous District and Krasnoyarsk Region and Khabarovsk Region including settlements in Maritime (Primor'ye) Region and Sakhalin Province, but the level of native language maintenance is higher in the remote parts of Amur and Chita provinces, as explained by Atknine in the *Northern minority languages* (1997); Evenki is also spoken, in declining numbers, in a few localities in Irkutsk and Tomsk provinces and the Republic of Buryatia. In the Russian Federation, 10,000 speakers were reported in 1989. The majority of them are middle-aged or older but Evenki is still learnt by some of the children in some localities, notably in the Tunguska region in Evenki Autonomous District and in the middle Amur region. In official Chinese terminology, 'Evenki' [in Chinese pinyin *Ewenke*] refers almost exclusively to the closely related but distinct Solon, while all long-established varieties of Evenki are subsumed under 'Orochen' [in Chinese pinyin *Elunchun*, in nativised pinyin *Oroqen*]. The official Oroqen nationality has 8,196 ethnic members, but Evenki is only spoken by at most 30 per cent of the group, mainly middle-aged to elderly. They represent four dialects of Evenki: the remaining speakers of *Orochen* proper, all over fifty years old, live scattered around Oroqen Autonomous Banner in Hulun Buir League in northeastern Inner Mongolia, while the speakers of the other dialects live along the Amur basin in northwestern Heilongjiang Province: *Kumarchen* (or *Manegir*), in the Kumara basin on the upper Amur, still has some child speakers, but the closely-related *Selpechen*, in the Fa and Selpe basins on the middle Amur, has no speakers under fifty, and *Birarchen* (or *Birar*), in the Xun and Zhan basins, is only spoken by a small number of elderly people. Only two recent immigrant groups of Evenki speakers belong to the official Ewenke nationality: the Manchurian Reindeer Tungus (also known as 'Yakut Ewenke'), numbering less than 1,000 people, who migrated from Russia to Chen Barag Banner in Hulun Buir League in Inner Mongolia in the early nineteenth century, and the Khamnigan (also known as Tungus Ewenke) who are originally from the Onon-Argun region of Transbaykalia on the Siberian and Mongolian sides of the border but who settled mainly in Chen Baerhu Banner in Hulun Buir League after the October Revolution in 1917; today, there are approximately 1,000 Evenki-speaking Khamnigan who also speak Khamnigan Mongol as a second language. Altogether, there are a couple of thousand speakers of Evenki in China, including very few children except among the Khamnigan where Evenki is learnt consistently as the home language by most children. In spite of the vast area, the dialectal differences within Evenki are small, and the case for regarding Evenki and Orochen, and possibly also Birarchen and Kumarchen, as separate languages is weak; notably, some Evenki-speaking groups living to the north of the Amur are also occasionally referred to as Orochen.

245

Not only Russian and Northern Chinese but also more prominent indigenous languages, notably Yakut and Buryat, are spoken as a second, or often the first, language in Evenki communities. Evenki has a written norm in Cyrillic script, used for elementary-school textbooks and occasional other publications; the language has been taught in China at a few elementary schools in IPA transcription, but with poor results. Severely endangered in the Russian Federation and China, possibly extinct in Mongolia.

Faetar. See **Francoprovençal**

Forest Enets (also called **Bay**) **[33]** Siberia: spoken in the forest zone on the lower Yenisey, now concentrated in the village of Potapovo in Dudinka County in Taymyr (Dolgan and Nenets) Autonomous District in the Russian Federation. In the last 150 years, the speakers of Forest Enets have gradually moved approximately 500 kilometres northwards along the Yenisey basin. The number of speakers is currently perhaps between 30 and 40, and practically all of them are middle-aged or older. The last speakers are mainly trilingual, speaking also Russian and Tundra Nenets. Critically endangered.

Forest Nenets **[36]** Siberia: spoken in Pur County and the southern parts of Nadym County in Yamal Nenets Autonomous District and the adjacent parts of Nizhnevartovsk, Surgut and Beloyarskiy counties in Khanty-Mansi Autonomous District in the Russian Federation. There are approximately 1,500 speakers; cf. Tundra Nenets. A few children learn the language, but many shift to Russian at school age. In some areas there is notable Khanty influence, and younger people may prefer Russian. Definitely endangered.

Forest Yukagir (also called **Southern Yukagir** or **Kolyma Yukagir** or **Odul**) **[176]** Siberia: spoken in the forest zone, on the sources of the Kolyma, divided between the Republic of Sakha (Yakutia) and Magadan Province in the Russian Federation, now largely concentrated in the village of Nelemnoye as well as in the county centre Zyryanka in Upper Kolyma (Verkhnekolymskiy) County in the Republic of Sakha, previously in a much wider area in the upper Kolyma region. There are less than fifty speakers, all middle-aged and older, fluent speakers are found among those over sixty years old; cf. Tundra Yukagir. Speakers are typically multilingual. Of the two Yukagir languages, Forest Yukagir seems to be dying even more rapidly than Tundra Yukagir. Critically endangered.

Francoprovençal **[76]** In France, most or all speakers of Francoprovençal are elderly, but they are still found in almost all departments within the traditional area of the language: in Savoy (Savoie and Haute-Savoie), Francoprovençal is spoken by approximately 35,000 speakers, in Ain (mainly in the region of Bresse) by 15,000, in Rhône by 1,000, in Loire by 5,000, in the northern and central parts of Isère by 2,000, and in the southern parts of the departments of Jura and Doubs by 2,000; the original area extended to the northernmost parts of Ardèche and Drôme as well. In Italy, Francoprovençal (locally called *Harpitan*) is spoken in the Aosta Valley and in the Alpine valleys to the north and east of Val di Susa in Piedmont by perhaps 70,000 speakers of all generations but with a notable shift to Italian among younger people.

In Switzerland, Francoprovençal was earlier spoken everywhere in Suisse romande except the Canton of Jura where the Franc-Comtois dialect of French was spoken, but it survives mainly in mountain villages of Valais and Fribourg, perhaps also Vaud, being most actively used in the village of Evolène in Valais. Definitely endangered in Italy; severely endangered in France and Switzerland. – *Faetar* [77] Italy: spoken at Faeto and Celle San Vito in Foggia Province in Apulia Region. Faetar is an outlying dialect of Francoprovençal, which has been under strong South Italian influence for a long time. Approximately 700 speakers were reported in 1995, probably including a few children, as the population remains loyal to the language. Because of the small size of the community and the continuing emigration, Faetar is definitely endangered.

Friulian [in Friulian *furlan*] [84] Italy: spoken in the Autonomous Region Friuli-Venezia Giulia except Trieste Province and western and eastern border regions, and in Portogruaro area in Venezia Province in Veneto Region. The estimates about the number of speakers range from 350,000 to 500,000 or as many as 720,000. Many children learn the language, but often stop using it at school age, especially in towns where a shift to Venetan is evident. Most idiolects are heavily influenced by Venetan and Italian. Increasingly endangered.

Gagauz [134] Eastern Europe. Spoken primarily in a relatively compact area known as Bujak, deriving from eighteenth- and nineteenth-century immigration, covering the towns and surrounding areas of Comrat, Ceadîr-Lunga, Basarabeasca, Taraclia and Vulcăneşti in the south of the Republic of Moldova, constituting the Gagauz autonomous area, and the adjacent Izmail region of Odessa (Odesa) Province in the Ukraine. A separate group known as Maritime Gagauz occupies the original Gagauz territory, covering the coastal region to the north of, and inland from, Varna in Bulgaria. Scattered Gagauz settlements are or were found in other parts of Bulgaria as well as in Romania, Serbia and Central Asia. There are further at least three groups, collectively known as *Balkan Gagauz* (often subsumed under 'Balkan Turkic'), whose linguistic connections with Gagauz proper remain somewhat obscure, namely (i) *Macedonian Gagauz* in southeastern Macedonia, apparently both within the Republic of Macedonia and in the northern parts of the Province of Macedonia in Greece; (ii) *Surguch* in the region of Edirne (Adrianople) in Turkey; and (iii) *Gajal* in the region of Deli Orman in Bulgaria. In 1989, 140,000 speakers were reported from the Republic of Moldova and 25,000 speakers from the Ukraine; the number of Maritime Gagauz in Bulgaria was reported as 12,000 in 1990 but more recent estimates indicate only 5,000 speakers. Balkan Gagauz has probably few speakers now: early in the twentieth century, there were approximately 4,000 Macedonian Gagauz, approximately 7,000 Surguch, and an unknown number of Gajal; the total number of Gagauz speakers is close to 200,000. Some children learn the language, but in many areas, the communities are shifting to dominant languages; there are probably no children speaking Balkan Gagauz. Many speakers have been strongly influenced by neighbouring languages, both by closely related Turkish and non-related languages like Russian, Bulgarian, Romanian and Greek. Increasingly endangered.

Gallo [69] France: spoken in the eastern parts of Brittany and in the department of Loire-Atlantique (Pays de Loire region) by a small portion of the population. Very few if any children learn the language. Even the language of the most competent speakers is likely to be heavily influenced by French. Severely endangered.

Gallurese Sardinian. See *Corsican*

Gardiol. See *Alpine Provençal*

Gascon [61] In France, Gascon is spoken in the departments of Landes, Gers and Hautes-Pyrénées, the eastern parts of Pyrénées-Atlantiques, the western parts of Haute-Garonne and Ariège, and the southern and western parts of Gironde, by perhaps 250,000 speakers, and it is still used actively by many people especially in the Béarn region (Pyrénées). Nevertheless, everywhere in France, as stated by Field in FEL IV (2000: 86), it 'has nearly ceased to be used for the primary socialization of children'. In Spain, Gascon (known as *Aranese*) is spoken by most of the 4,800 people living in the Aran Valley in the Pyrenees. At least elderly speakers both in Béarn and Aran appear to be fully competent; elsewhere in France, French influence is increasingly strong, and this may be so for many speakers in Béarn, too; in Aran, there is notable Catalan and Spanish influence. Definitely endangered in Spain; severely endangered in France.

Godoberi [113] Caucasia: western Daghestan. Spoken in the large village of Godoberi and two small villages Zibirkhali and Beledi in Botlikh County in the Republic of Daghestan in the Russian Federation. The number of speakers lies somewhere between 2,500 and 4,000, with relatively few child speakers. Because of the small size of the community and the dominant position of Avar, the language must be regarded as definitely endangered. There is no literacy in it, but Avar and Russian are used in school and for wider communication.

Gottscheerish (also called *Granish*) [52] Slovenia: originally spoken in the Gottschee (Kočevje) region in northern Slovenia, but the speakers were resettled during the Second World War, and now live scattered practically all around the world. Gottscheerish is an outlying dialect of Bavarian that was flourishing in Gottschee but is now only known by the oldest members of the community in exile. Critically endangered.

Griko (also called *Italiot Greek*) [97] Italy: spoken in the Salento peninsula in Lecce Province in southern Apulia and in a few villages near Reggio di Calabria in southern Calabria. Griko is an outlying dialect of Greek largely deriving from Byzantine times. The Salentine dialect is still used relatively widely, and there may be a few child speakers, but a shift to South Italian has proceeded rapidly, and active speakers tend to be over fifty years old. The Calabrian dialect is only used more actively in the village of Gaddhiciano, but even there the youngest speakers are over thirty years old. The number of speakers lies in the range of 20,000. South Italian influence has been strong for a long time. Severely endangered.

Guernsey French. See *Norman*

Hinukh (also spelled *Ginukh*) [120] Caucasia: western Daghestan. Spoken in the village of Ginukh in Tsunta County, and by an immigrant community in the village of Monastyrskoye in Kizlyar County, in the Republic of Daghestan in the Russian

Federation. The number of speakers is somewhere between 200 and 500, with few child speakers. There is no literacy in it, but Avar and Russian are used in school and for wider communication. Hinukh is also influenced by the closely related Tsez language. Definitely endangered.

Hunzib (also spelled *Gunzib*) [124] Caucasia: western Daghestan. Spoken in the villages of Gunzib, Nakhada and Garbutl' (Gorbutl') in Tsunta County in the Republic of Daghestan in the Russian Federation. The number of speakers is somewhere between 600 and 800, with few child speakers. There is no literacy in it, but Avar and Russian are used in school and for wider communication. Hinukh is also influenced by the closely related Bezhta language. Definitely endangered.

Ili Turk [138] Sinkiang: spoken in the eastern parts of the Ili Valley in Xinjiang Uygur Autonomous Region in China. Ili Turk is an outlying dialect of Uzbek with deep influences from other Turkic languages. It is the language of thirty or so families, where younger generations are shifting to Kazakh or Uygur. Ili Turk is not officially recognised, and its speakers tend to be fluent in Kazakh and Uygur. Definitely endangered. For detailed information, see Zhào and Hahn 1989.

Inari Saami [6] Northern Europe: Lapland. Spoken in central Inari County of Lapland Province in Finland. There are approximately 300 speakers. Very few children used to learn the language; before the founding of the first Inari Saami language nest in 1997, the number of child speakers was down to five or so. Since then, however, the programme, which at the moment runs two language nests, has proved remarkably successful, and a substantial portion of Inari Saami youth are now growing as functional bilinguals who may even use the native language not only with elderly relatives or language nest tutors but also amongst themselves. This positive trend is fortunately supported to some extent by recent changes in the local school system. At the same time, a number of adults who have not learnt Inari Saami in childhood have started to study it actively in evening classes. Given the small size of the community and the overwhelming presence of Finnish-language media, the situation is still precarious, but clearly, most Inari Saami people value their native language highly and are committed to its survival. Despite the positive trends, it must be said that the language is being heavily influenced by Finnish, and continues to be severely endangered.

Ingrian [in Russian *ižorskij jazyk*, in Estonian *isuri keel*, in Finnish *inkeroinen*] [13] Northern Europe: northwestern Russia. Spoken in three small areas on the southern shore of the Gulf of Finland in St Petersburg (Leningrad) Province in the Russian Federation: the cape of Kovashi (Hevaa) in Lomonosov County, the cape of Soykin (Soikkola) in Kingisepp County, and the cape of Kurkola in the lower Luga River area in the same county; a fourth area was formerly found along the Oredezh River in Gatchina County. In 1989, 300 speakers were reported; the actual number is lower, and most of them prefer other languages. There are probably no younger speakers, so practically all speakers are middle-aged or older. Most idiolects are heavily influenced by Finnish and Russian. Severely endangered.

Inkhokvari (also spelled *Inkhokari*) [122] Caucasia: western Daghestan. Spoken in the villages of Kvantlyada, Santlyada, Inkhokari (Inkhokvari) and Khvayni in Tsumada

249

County in the Republic of Daghestan in the Russian Federation. The number of speakers is somewhere around 1,000. Inkhokvari is customarily, but with little foundation, regarded as a single language with Khvarshi. There are child speakers, but because of the small size of the community and the dominant position of Avar, the language must be regarded as definitely endangered. There is no literacy in it.

Irish (also known as *Irish Gaelic*) **[53]** the Republic of Ireland: four principal areas in the west, two in County Donegal, one each in Galway and Kerry counties, plus eight small pockets, also in Mayo, Cork and Waterford counties; formerly also in Northern Ireland. There were 29,000 first language speakers in the four principal areas, plus less than a thousand in each of the pockets in 1976; perhaps less than 20,000 today; the official census figures include many English speakers who have learned Irish at school. A number of children learn the language, but their number appears to be decreasing in the Irish-speaking areas. At the same time, Irish is being used widely as a second language in all parts of the Republic of Ireland as well as in Northern Ireland. Shannon in FEL III (2000: 109–16) explores the place of Irish in schools, while Hindley's (1990) controversial treatment may be offered as an alternative approach. Definitely endangered in the Republic of Ireland; extinct as a first language in Northern Ireland.

Istriot (also called *Istro-Romance*) **[91]** Croatia spoken in the southwest of the Istrian peninsula, mainly in the towns of Rovinj (Rovigno), Bale (Valle), Vodnjan (Dignano) and Gali\u017eana (Gallesano). Jahn in FEL II (1998: 48) estimates that there are 400 first-language and 400 second-language speakers in Istria, plus 500 others living outside Istria. There are young speakers in Bale and middle-aged speakers in Gali\u017eana, but elsewhere speakers are elderly. All idiolects tend to be heavily influenced by Venetan, but Istriot is also actively cultivated in the form of folkloristic poetry. Severely endangered.

Istro-Romanian (also spelled *Istrio-Romanian*) **[92]** Croatia: spoken in the northeast of the Istrian peninsula, in the village of \u017dejane to the north of U\u010dka mountain, and a few villages to the south of it, the main one of these being Su\u0161njevica. Jahn in FEL II (1998: 48) gives an estimate of 300 first-language and 100 second-language speakers in Istria, plus 1,000 others living outside Istria. Other sources contain highly inflated figures, such as 450 to 500 for \u017dejane and 800 to 1,000 for the southern villages. There are no children and few younger speakers. All speakers are bilingual in Serbo-Croat, which has had a strong influence on the language. Severely endangered.

Italkian (or *Judeo-Italian*) **[90]** Italy, mainly in urban areas in Rome and central and northern Italy; also in Corfu, Greece (*Corfiote Italkian*). There appear to be some speakers in Rome, but generally very few in Italy are fluent in the language. In Corfu, although the total population counts less than 50 individuals, Italkian is still in some sort of use. Critically endangered.

Itelmen **[181]** Siberia: in a small pocket on the western coast of central Kamchatka, mainly in the villages of Kovran and Upper Khayryuzovo in the south of Tigil' County in the southern corner of Koryak Autonomous District in the Russian Federation. In 1989, 500 speakers were reported, but currently there are perhaps less than 100 speakers, all elderly; the figure of the 1989 Soviet census suggesting 2,500 ethnic

Itelmen is highly inflated. There is noticeable areal influence of Palana Koryak. Critically endangered.

Jersey French. See **Norman**

Judezmo (or ***Judeo-Spanish***, or ***Ladino***) **[58]** since the Middle Ages, Judezmo, the traditional language of Sephardic Jews, has been spoken in dispersed communities mainly in Greece and Turkey, primarily in the historical provinces of Macedonia and Thrace, but also elsewhere in the Balkans, as well as in North Africa, especially Morocco (where known as ***Haketía***). It is now spoken in a few locations in Turkey, where speakers are largely concentrated in Istanbul (traditionally in the quarters of Balat and Hasköy), by probably less than 10,000 speakers, in resettled communities in Israel where the majority of the speakers live, and in the United States and several European countries. In Greece or elsewhere in the Balkans there are very few if any Judezmo speakers left after the Holocaust, and in Morocco the language is extinct. According to Hetzer in the *Minor languages of Europe* (2001: 144), 'one can say that less than 400,000 people still have a certain command of' the language worldwide, but 'most of them [are] older than 50 years'. Other estimates suggest a total of some 200,000 speakers, and Judezmo is not the dominant language for most speakers. Younger speakers are very few. Severely endangered.

Juhur (also called ***Judeo-Tat***) **[102]** Caucasia: northern Azerbaijan and parts of Daghestan and other regions of northern Caucasia. Still spoken, though in diminishing numbers, in its most original area in Azerbaijan, mainly in the villages of Krasnaya Sloboda in Kuba (Quba) region and Vartashen (Vardashen, currently Oguz) in Vartashen (Vardashen) region, but the great majority of speakers live in communities that started to form in the eighteenth century, especially in the town of Derbend and surrounding rural areas in the Republic of Daghestan in the Russian Federation, but also in other towns in Daghestan such as Makhachkala, Majalis, Pyatigorsk and Buynaksk and elsewhere in northern Caucasia, in particular in Nal'chik in the Kabard-Balkar Republic and, until recently, in Groznyy in the Republic of Chechenia; there are some speakers in Baku in Azerbaijan as well. Juhur is customarily, but with little foundation, regarded as a single language with Tat. While there are apparently Christian Tats speaking Tat rather than Juhur in Daghestan, most members of the Tat nationality in the Russian Federation appear to only nominally distinct from the Mountain Jew nationality, whose traditional language is Juhur. In 1989, the joint figure of reported native language speakers from the Russian Federation was nearly 25,000, of them 15,000 from Daghestan, to which are added 5,000 speakers belonging to the Mountain Jew nationality from Azerbaijan. Since then, however, thousands of Juhur speakers have emigrated to Israel, where they live in places like Sderot, Haderah and Or Akiva. A Juhur literary language based on Derbend dialect is in use in Daghestan. In Azerbaijan, Azerbaijani is used as a literary language. Definitely endangered.

Kalmyk (also spelled ***Kalmuck*** or ***Kalmuk***) **[160]** Eastern Europe: southeastern Russia. Spoken in the Kalmyk Republic and the adjacent part of Astrakhan, Rostov and Volgograd provinces and Stavropol' Region in the Russian Federation. Kalmyk may be historically seen as an outlying dialect of Oyrat, but now it clearly functions as a distinct language, although the differences are largely limited to lexicon. In 1989, 150,000 speakers were reported. A few children learn the language, but most of them tend to prefer Russian. Definitely endangered.

Kamas (or ***Kamas-Koybal***) **[151a]** Siberia: formerly spoken in the eastern part of the Minusinsk region, in modern Krasnoyarsk Region in the Russian Federation, where the area of Kamas became gradually restricted to the Kan and Mana river basins and their sources on the northwesternmost slopes of the Eastern Sayan mountains. The last Kamas-speaking community lived here in a single village, Abalakovo. The last speaker, Klavdia Plotnikova, died in September 1989. She was trilingual in Khakas and Russian, with rather rudimentary native language skills. Recently extinct.

Karagash. See ***Nogay***

Karaim **[141]** Eastern Europe. Originally spoken in the Crimea in the Ukraine, where small communities of ethnic Karaim remain near Yevpatoriya; since medieval times Karaim has been translocated in the west Ukrainian towns of Luts'k (Lutsk) and Halych (Galich) and in Trakai (Troki) and a few other places in Lithuania. In 1989, 500 speakers were reported, including 200 in Lithuania, and 100 in the Crimea, but in reality there are about fifty speakers in Lithuania plus a small number who have settled in Poland, only six in Halich, and none in the Crimea. Two thirds of the speakers are over sixty years old, but recent revitalisation efforts in the Lithuanian community give some hope to the language, and while severely endangered, it is not immediately nearing extinction, as described by Csató in the *Minor languages of Europe* (2001).

Karata **[114]** Caucasia: western Daghestan. Spoken in nine villages, including Karata and Tokita (Tukita), in Akhvakh County in the Republic of Daghestan in the Russian Federation. There are at least 5,000 speakers, but because of the small size of the community and the dominant position of Avar, the language must be regarded as definitely endangered. There is no literacy in it.

Karelian [in Karelian and Finnish *karjala*] **[14]** Northern and Eastern Europe: northwestern and west-central Russia. Spoken in several separate areas in the Russian Federation: northern and central regions of the Republic of Karelia, mainly in Loukhi, Kem', Kalevala and Muyezerskiy counties, the western parts of Belomorsk, Segezha and Medvezh'yegorsk counties, the southwestern part of Kondopoga County and the Porosozero region of Suoyarvi (Suojärvi) County; small pockets in the vicinity of Tikhvin and Novgorod; in Tver' Province, mainly around Tolmachi, Maksatikha and Ves'yegonsk. In Finland, Karelian is spoken by people evacuated, in 1940 and 1944, from former Finnish territories north of Lake Ladoga including Suojärvi, Suistamo and Korpiselkä counties, currently the central parts of Suoyarvi (Suojärvi) County in the Republic of Karelia, and in two border villages in Suomussalmi County in Oulu Province. In the Russian Federation, there are possibly approximately 35,000 speakers; the combined figure for Karelian, Olonetsian, and Lude in 1989 was 63,000 which may actually be too low, because many speakers outside the Republic may not have been registered as such. There are in any case more Karelian speakers in Tver' Province than in the Republic of Karelia. A number of children learn the language, but most if not all of them become more fluent in Russian and largely stop using

Karelian later in life. Following the initiative of the local cultural society (in Finnish, Uhtua-Seura) and the participation of a Finnish linguist (Annika Pasanen), two language nests have recently, in 1999 and 2002, started to operate in the northwestern county centre of Kalevala (Uhtua). A language shift in the county centre has proceeded rapidly, so that people under thirty years of age possess little knowledge of Karelian, those between 30 and 70 generally have a passive command but prefer Russian in most contexts, and only those seventy years and older use the native language in all its traditional functions. The situation is, however, much better in smaller villages of the county such as Vuokkiniemi and Jyskyjärvi, where speakers of all ages can be found. The trend is everywhere such that most Karelian speakers change to Russian when addressing young people, but there are also dedicated individuals who use Karelian as much as possible. Since the language nests have not yet produced any clear changes to the better, the choice of home language remains the decisive factor in the survival of Karelian. Speaking Karelian still bears a major stigma, so it is not surprising that shifting to Russian is seen as the easy and perhaps inevitable solution. Since the value of the native language is also felt strongly, a dilemma arises, and people escape to sweeping the problem of language maintenance under the carpet, and end up in a state of collective self-betrayal where the language is claimed to be in active use in families while everybody knows that this is not the case. In Finland, there are a few thousand speakers, all elderly; even those who are fluent in Karelian use mostly Finnish. A literary language existed in Tver' Province in the 1930s, and it has been revived recently. Another literary variant, based on the northern dialects, is now used in the Republic of Karelia. Definitely endangered in the Russian Federation; critically endangered in Finland.

Kashubian (also spelled ***Cassubian***) **[43]** Poland: dispersed in an area northwest, west and southwest of Gdansk, mainly in Wejherowo, Lebork, Bytów (Betowo), Pock (Puck), Kartuzy, Koscierzyna and Chojnice districts. The number of speakers is not known exactly, but may be around 50,000, including quite a lot of child speakers in some areas. Definitely endangered. – An outlying dialect called ***Slovincian*** was spoken in the parishes of Schmolsin and Garde in Pomerania in present-day Poland, until extinction in approximately 1900.

Kerek **[178]** Siberia: originally spoken in a large belt along the Bering Sea coast between the Olyutor Bay and the Anadyr Bay, later only in the villages of Meyno-pil'gino and Khatyrka in Beringovskiy County in Chukchi Autonomous District in the Russian Federation. There were three elderly speakers in 1991; in the early 1950s there were approximately 100 speakers. The language of the last speakers showed strong interference from Chukchi, the language which the Kerek community had adopted, as well as from Russian. Possibly extinct.

Ket (also called ***Northern Ket*** or ***Imbat Ket***; cf. Yug) **[173]** Siberia: spoken on the middle and upper Yenisey and its tributaries, mainly between the Yeloguy and Turu-khan basins, today concentrated in the villages of Farkovo, Serkovo, Kellog, Kanga-tovo, Baklanikha, Vereshchagino, Surgutikha, Verkhneimbatsk, Bakhta, Goroshikha and Maduyka in Turukhansk County in the north of Krasnoyarsk Region and, along the Podkamennaya Tunguska, in the village of Sulomay in Baykit County in the west of Evenki Autonomous District in the Russian Federation. In 1989, over 500 speakers were reported, which is confirmed by some specialists, for instance Vajda (2003: 394) mentions 600 or so remaining native speakers, although Georg in the *Language death and language maintenance* (2003) provides a much more pessimistic evaluation. There are generally very few child speakers, but the situation varies depending on locality; in any case, most speakers are middle-aged or older. Severely endangered.

Khakas* [151]** Siberia: in the western half of the Minusinsk steppe region on the upper Yenisey in southern Siberia, mainly in the Republic of Khakasia but also in Uzhur and Sharypovo counties in Krasnoyarsk Region and in adjacent parts of the Republic of Tuva in the Russian Federation. Khakas is a conglomeration of several closely related dialects: Kacha, Sagay, Kyzyl, Koybal, Beltir and Shor. The Koybal dialect of Khakas is spoken by the descendants of the speakers of the Koybal dialect of Kamas, and the Shor dialect of Khakas derives from the migration (in the sixteenth to nineteenth centuries) of part of the speakers of Mrassu Shor across the Kuznetskiy Alatau to the Minusinsk region. In 1989, 60,000 speakers of Khakas were reported. In some rural areas, the language is being learnt by children, but in cities Russian is typically the only language even in families with Khakas-speaking parents; most speakers are therefore middle-aged or older, and Khakas has become the language of a small minority, approximately 10 per cent, of the total population of Khakasia. Nevertheless, it has recently been introduced as the language of instruction in a few schools, including one in Abakan, the local capital. Khakas has a written standard in Cyrillic script with some use even in newspapers and belletristics. Definitely endangered. – ***Kamas was an outlying dialect of Khakas spoken by the last speakers of Kamas (Samoyed) and their descendants until recently when it as well became extinct.

Khamnigan Mongol [in Chinese pinyin *Hamunikan*] **[158]** Manchuria, earlier and more originally in the Onon-Argun region of Transbaykalia in adjacent Siberia and Mongolia. Khamnigan Mongol may be historically seen as an archaic outlying dialect of Buryat, but is better classified as a distinct language, which furthermore exists in a complex symbiotic relationship with Evenki. It is currently spoken mainly in Chen Baerhu Banner in Hulun Buir League in Inner Mongolia in China by approximately 1,500 people. Khamnigan Mongol is learnt consistently by almost all children as either the first language (in monolingual families) or as the community language (in families bilingual in Khamnigan Mongol and Evenki). Although vigorous for the moment, the survival of Khamnigan Mongol in the long run is threatened by the increasing influx of Han Chinese settlers. Both Chinese and Mongolian are also present through radio and television as well as printed material. Khamnigan Mongol is spoken as the community language by all speakers, but grammatical and lexical interference from Modern Written Mongolian is occasionally present in the speech of educated people. Modern Written Mongolian is used as the literary language. Definitely endangered in Manchuria, possibly extinct in Mongolia and Siberia.

***Khinalug* [132]** Caucasia: northern Azerbaijan. Spoken in the village of Khinalug in Kuba (Quba) County in Azerbaijan. The number of speakers lies somewhere between 1,000 and 2,000, and includes some children. Within its family, Khinalug is highly divergent. There is no literacy in it, but Azerbaijani is used in school and for wider communication. Definitely endangered.

***Khvarshi* [121]** Caucasia: western Daghestan. Spoken in the village of Khvarshi in Tsumada County in the Republic of Daghestan in the Russian Federation by a few hundred speakers. Khvarshi is customarily, but with little foundation, regarded as a single language with Inkhokvari. There are child speakers, but because of the very small size of the community and the dominant position of Avar, the language must be regarded as definitely endangered. There is no literacy in it.

Kildin Saami [9] Northern Europe: Kola peninsula. Earlier spoken in many locations in the eastern parts of Kola County and the western parts of Lovozero County in central Murmansk Province in the Russian Federation, from which they were forcibly concentrated to the county centre Lovozero. In 1989, combined 800 speakers were reported for the four Saami languages on Kola peninsula, the vast majority of them being Kildin Saami speakers. Today there are perhaps 650 speakers, amongst them probably no children. There are some younger speakers, but most are middle-aged or older. Kildin Saami has had small-scale use as a literary language, first in the 1930s, and again in the 1990s. Severely endangered.

Komi (or, to make a distinction from the Komi subbranch comprising both Komi and Permyak, **Zyryan Komi**; the Russian-based term 'Komi-Zyryan' better avoided) [22] Eastern Europe: northeastern Russia. Spoken in the Komi Republic and parts of Nenets Autonomous District, Arkhangel'sk Province, Yamal Nenets Autonomous District, Murmansk Province and other regions in the Russian Federation. In 1989, 240,000 speakers were reported. Quite a lot of children learn the language, but many of them stop using Komi later in life. Increasingly endangered. Often considered a single language with Permyak.

Koryak (also known as **Nymylan**) [180] Siberia: in northern Kamchatka, from the Okhotsk Sea to the Bering Sea, extending to the upper Anadyr basin in the north, mainly in Penzhinskiy County in Koryak Autonomous District in the Russian Federation. In 1989, a combined figure 5,000 speakers was reported for Koryak and Alutor; a rough estimate would give that slightly more than one half of them, or approximately 3,000 people, speak Koryak. There are very few child speakers, although the situation may vary depending on locality; there are some younger speakers but most are middle-aged or older. Koryak has a written standard in Cyrillic script, but education is only conducted in Russian. Often considered a single language with Alutor. Severely endangered.

Krimchak (also spelled **Krymchak**; also called **Judeo-Crimean Tatar**) [140] the Crimea: speakers lived originally among Crimean Tatar speakers, with Simferopol as the main centre. More than two thirds of the population were murdered by Germans during the Second World War. There are now 1,200 ethnic Krimchaks in the Crimea, and 600 elsewhere. In 1989, 500 speakers were reported from the Soviet Union, including 100 in the Crimea, but the figures seem meaningless, as only people born in the 1930s or earlier appear to retain fluency in Krimchak; they number perhaps 200, and even they use Krimchak rarely. Critically endangered.

Kryts (also spelled **Kryz**; also called **Jek**) [128] Caucasia: northern Azerbaijan. Spoken in the villages of Kryz, Jek, Khaput, Yergyuj and Alyk in Kuba (Quba) County and in expatriate communities elsewhere in Azerbaijan. The number of speakers lies somewhere between 5,000 and 8,000, and includes many children, but decreasingly so.

255

There is no literacy in it, but Azerbaijani is used in school and for wider communication. Definitely endangered.

Ladin (also called ***Dolomitic Ladin***) **[83]** Italy: spoken in several towns and villages in the Dolomites, including Badia and Marebbe in the Badia valley and Gardena in the Gardena valley in Bolzano Province (South Tyrol), Fassa in the Fassa valley in Trento Province, and Livinallongo in the Cordevole valley in Belluno Province. The number of speakers lies in the range of 20,000. Some children learn the language, but many stop using it at school age; besides, the total number of speakers is low. Definitely endangered.

Languedocian [in Languedocian *lengadocian*] **[64]** France: spoken in an area from Bordeaux in the northwest to Montpellier in the southeast, and from Toulouse in the southwest to Rodez in the northeast, covering the departments of Aveyron, Lot, Lot-et-Garonne, Tarn-et-Garonne, Tarn, Aude, Hérault, the eastern parts of Haute-Garonne and Ariège, the southern parts of Dordogne, the Aurillac region of Cantal, the western parts of Gard, and smaller areas in Lozère, Pyrénées-Orientales, and Gironde. There may well be over a million people able to speak Languedocian, but very few children learn the language, which makes the language severely endangered despite the large number of speakers and the continuing cultivation of the Occitan literary language which is essentially based on Languedocian.

Laz (or ***Chan***) **[108]** Turkey and Georgia. Spoken along the Black Sea coast in the northeast of Turkey and the southwestern corner of Georgia, including the towns of Pazar (Atina), Ardeşen, Çamlıhemşin and Fındıklı in Rize Province and Arhavi (Arkabi/Arxave), Hopa (Xopa), Borçka and Sarp (Sarpi) in Artvin Province in Turkey; Sarpi is partly in the Republic of Ajaria on the Georgian side; there are also Laz villages, founded by refugees of the 1877–8 war, in the western parts of Turkey mainly in Sakarya, Kocaeli and Bolu provinces. The number of speakers in Turkey is 20,000 to 30,000, in Georgia 1,000 to 2,000, and in an expatriate community in Germany approximately 1,000. A language shift to Turkish and Georgian has proceeded increasingly rapidly. There is no literacy in Laz. Definitely endangered.

Ligurian **[79]** in Italy, Ligurian is spoken in Liguria and adjacent areas of Piedmont, Emilia and Tuscany by well over a million speakers, but the shift to Italian has been even more marked than in other parts of northern Italy. Ligurian, under the name ***Monégasque***, is also the traditional language of Monaco, where it was reportedly spoken by 5,000 people, presumably second language speakers, in 1988, after being regarded as nearly extinct in the 1970s, and its area extended to the eastern corner of the department of Alpes-Maritimes in France until the twentieth century. Ligurian is still used in the town of Bonifacio in Corsica by 300–400 mainly elderly speakers, and more actively in the towns of Carloforte on the San Pietro island and Calasetta on the Sant'Antioco island off the southwest coast of Sardinia. Increasingly endangered.

Limousin [in Limousin *lemosin*] **[62]** France: spoken in the departments of Corréze and Haute-Vienne, most of Creuse, the northern parts of Dordogne, and the eastern parts of Charente. There may well be over 100,000 people able to speak Limousin, but very few if any children learn it. In the northern dialects there are many inherent French features, but in all areas, even the most fluent speakers exhibit strong interference from French. Severely endangered.

***Livonian* [11]** Latvia: along the northern coast of Curonia in the northwest, but also scattered elsewhere; formerly also in the historical province of Livonia east of the Gulf of Riga. In 1989, fifty speakers were reported from Latvia and about the same number in parts of the Russian Federation, but these figures were clearly inflated. There is possibly only one speaker with full native competence, which makes the language nearly extinct. At the same time, there are several younger descendants of Livonian speakers who have learnt Livonian as second language and cultivate it actively.

Logudorese Sardinian (also called ***Logudorese-Nuorese***) **[85]** Italy: central Sardinia. The number of speakers is perhaps approximately 500,000; the total number of Sardinian speakers appears to be slightly over 1,000,000, although many of them use Italian more often. Many children learn the language, but often stop using it at school age. Definitely endangered.

***Lombard* [80]** In Italy, Lombard is spoken in the region of Lombardy (except the southernmost border areas) and in the Novara province in Piedmont, as well as in twelfth- and thirteenth-century immigrant settlements in the south of Italy and Sicily. There are still several million speakers, but particularly in towns and among younger generations the use of Lombard has diminished drastically. In Switzerland, Lombard is spoken in Ticino Canton and in the Mesolcina District and two districts south of St Moritz in Graubünden (Grigioni) by perhaps 300,000 speakers. Increasingly endangered.

Lude [in Lude *liüdi*, in Russian *ljudikovskij jazyk*, in Finnish *lyydi*] **[15]** Northern Europe: northwestern Russia. Spoken along a narrow strip streching from north to south in the Republic of Karelia in the Russian Federation, covering the central parts of Kondopoga County, the eastern parts of Pryazha County, the northernmost corner of Onega (Prionezhskiy) County and the Mikhaylovskoye (Kuujärvi) region in the east of Olonets County. There are a couple of thousand speakers at best, including very few children. Severely endangered.

***Lule Saami* [4]** Northern Europe: Lapland. Spoken in Jokkmokk County and parts of Gällivare and other adjacent counties in Norrbotten Province (Lule Lappmark) in Sweden and in the Tysfjord region in northern Nordland Province in Norway. The number of speakers lies somewhere between 1,000 and 2,000. A small number of children learn the language, and while the trend seemed highly alarming a few years ago, the use of Lule Saami has recently been activated to some extent. Younger speakers may nevertheless prefer Swedish or Norwegian. Definitely endangered.

Manchurian Kirghiz (also called ***Fuyü Kirghiz***) [in Chinese pinyin *Jierjisi* or *Fuyu Keerkezi*] **[152]** Manchuria: still spoken on the eastern bank of the lower Nonni, in Fuyu County in Heilongjiang Province in China; extinct since the early twentieth century in the Imin region of Hulun Buir League in Inner Mongolia. Manchurian Kirghiz may be historically seen as an outlying dialect of Khakas, but must now be regarded as a distinct language. There are less than ten elderly speakers left. For several generations, the speakers of Manchurian Kirghiz seem to have been bilingual in Manchurian Ölöt; knowledge of Dagur has also been common, but today all the local languages are being replaced by Northern Chinese. Nearly extinct.

Manchurian Ölöt. See *Oyrat*

Manx (also known as *Manx Gaelic*) [54] Western Europe: originally spoken in the Isle of Man. The last speaker, Ned Maddrell, died in 1974. Native Manx people, though monolingual in English, regard themselves as a separate people. There are people living in the Isle of Man who have now learned Manx as a second language. Extinct as a first language.

Mariupolitan Greek (or *Crimean Greek*; also called *Tauro-Romaic*) [in Russian *tavro-rumejskij jazyk*, in Mariupolitan Greek *ruméka*] [99] Eastern Europe: an outlying dialect of Greek originally spoken in the south of the Crimea, from where its speakers moved to the shores of the Azovan Sea in the Ukraine in the 1770s, and founded the city of Mariupol' (Zhdanov) and several villages in what is now Donets'k (Donetsk) Province. In 1989, 20,000 speakers of Greek were reported from the Ukraine. Mariupolitan Greek is now influenced by Russian and Ukrainian, but earlier also by Crimean Tatar. Definitely endangered.

Megleno-Romanian (also called *Meglenitic*) [94] Greece and the Republic of Macedonia: originally spoken in the area where the Vardar (Axios) River crosses the Macedonian-Greek border northwest of Salonika. According to a count by Atanasov (1989), there were 5,000 speakers, only 70 per cent of whom, however, remained in the area. Many speakers were deported to Turkey during the Balkan population exchanges, and some others emigrated to Romania where they established a few villages. There are probably few if any child speakers. Severely endangered.

Mingrelian (or *Megrel*) [in Mingrelian *margali*] [107] Georgia: western lowlands. The number of speakers is usually given as 500,000. The closely related Georgian is generally used as a literary language, and the position of Mingrelian among younger generations is precarious. Increasingly endangered.

Moksha [18] Eastern Europe: central Russia. Spoken mainly in the western parts of the Republic of Mordovia in the Russian Federation, and in the adjacent parts of Ryazan' and Penza provinces; also in pockets in Tatarstan and Orenburg Province. In 1989, there were approximately 250,000 speakers; cf. Erzya. Quite a lot of children learn the language, but the typical pattern is that they only use it with elderly relatives. Increasingly endangered.

Molise Croatian [42] Italy: an outlying dialect of Serbo-Croat deriving from the language of fifteenth- and sixteenth-century refugees from Dalmatia spoken mainly in the villages of Montemitro (Mundimitar), San Felice del Molise (Filić, or Stifilić) and Acquaviva Collecroce (Kruč, or Živa voda) in Campobasso Province in southern Molise. There are over 1,000 speakers among the approximately 2,300 inhabitants of the three villages, plus a number in expatriate communities; the figure of 3,500 speakers reported by Vincent in *The world's major languages* (1987: 282) seems exaggerated. There are a few younger speakers in Montemitro, while in Acquaviva and especially in San Felice most speakers are middle-aged or older. Severely endangered.

Nanay (called *Hejen* [in Chinese pinyin *Hezhe*] in China) **[170]** Siberia (the Russian Far East) and Manchuria: in the middle and lower Amur basin, in Nanay, Amursk, Komsomol'sk, Solnechnyy, Ul'cha and Khabarovsk counties in Khabarovsk Region and Pozharskoye and Ol'ga counties in Maritime (Primor'ye) Region as well as in Poronaysk County in Sakhalin Province in the Russian Federation, and in the lower Sungari and Ussuri basins in Tongjiang, Fuyuan and Raohe counties in the northeast of Heilongjiang Province in China. Nanay comprises three dialect groups: besides Nanay proper (with many subdialects, one of which was formerly known as 'Sama-gir'), there are *Kur-Urmi Nanay* (or *Kile*, or *Kili*, or *Kiler*), a special northern group in the region of the Kur and Urmi rivers, to the north of the middle Amur basin, with Evenki influences in its phonology, and *Sungari Nanay* (or *Kilen*; includes Ussuri Nanay and Upper Amur Nanay, also called *Akani*), which is connected with Udege and spoken in China and by the small Nanay-speaking population on the river Bikin in Pozharskoye County on the Russian side. In 1989, nearly 6,000 speakers were reported from the Russian Federation, but the actual figure is much smaller, and practically all speakers are middle-aged or older. There are perhaps 3,000 speakers of Nanay proper, and a hundred or so speakers of Kur-Urmi Nanay. There are fewer than forty elderly speakers concentrated in three villages in Tongjiang and Raohe counties in China, all now over sixty years old, out of 4,640 ethnic group members; about half speak Sungari Nanay and half speak Nanay proper. There is a written standard in Cyrillic script used for native language teaching in schools in the Russian Federation, but the language of instruction is Russian. Severely endangered in the Russian Federation, critically endangered in China.

Negidal (also called *Ilkan Beye* or *El'kan Beye* or *Elkembey*) **[165]** Siberia: in the Amgun' basin, to the west of the lower Amur, in a number of villages including Tyr, Beloklinka and Kal'ma in Ul'cha County and Vladimirovka in the County of Polina Osipenko in Khabarovsk Region in the Russian Federation. The number of speakers is well below 200. Practically all speakers are elderly, and only a few of them appear fully fluent in all stylistic varieties of the language. Critically endangered.

Nganasan **[31]** Siberia: the northernmost language of the Eurasian continent; origin-ally spoken on central Taymyr, in the regions of the Pyasina and Taymyra river sys-tems, now largely concentrated in the villages of Ust'-Avam and Volochanka in Dudinka County and Novaya in Khatanga County in Taymyr (Dolgan and Nenets) Autonomous District in the Russian Federation; there is, however, a group of approximately 100 people who continue to lead a semi-nomadic life in the region of the river Dudypta near Ust'-Avam. In 1989, 1,100 speakers were reported, but the actual number is much smaller, perhaps only 500, which includes very few children except in the semi-nomadic group, whose members have, at least until recently, been using Nganasan more actively. As an example of cruel destiny playing havoc in a small, self-sustainable group such as this, they have lost the special breed of reindeer necessary for survival in their severe environment, and may therefore be forced to change their way of life even in the case that Russian authorities do not meddle with them. Outside this group, only people aged forty or more are fully fluent. There are a few old speakers with little knowledge of Russian, or only with a knowledge of a special Russian-based Taymyr pidgin also known as Govorka. Middle-aged and younger speakers are fully bilingual in Russian, with interference features easy to detect because of the intricate system of morphophonological alternations typical of traditional Nganasan. Some knowledge of Dolgan is also common. Severely endangered.

Nivkh [173] Siberia (the Russian Far East): traditionally spoken along the Tatar Strait around the mouth region of the Amur River in Khabarovsk Region and on both the northwestern and the eastern coast of Sakhalin in Sakhalin Province in the Russian Federation. Nivkh consists of Amur Nivkh and Sakhalin Nivkh, of which Sakhalin Nivkh comprises three dialects, geographically identified as North Sakhalin, East Sakhalin and South Sakhalin; North Sakhalin shows features transitional towards Amur Nivkh. In the 1960s and 1970s, the Amur Nivkhs were forced to move to various settlements, and only in the single village of Aleyevka on the Amur River in Komsomol'sk County, a distinct Nivkh community may be said to exist; other villages with Nivkh population include Vlas'yevo, Baydukovo, Makarovka and Tneyvakh in the same county. On Sakhalin, the original Nivkh villages were liquidated around the same time, and the people were sent to live in three larger settlements: those from the Schmidt peninsula in the north to the village of Nekrasovka and smaller neighbouring villages such as Moskal'vo, Chir-Unvd and Viakhtu in Okha County, those living in the northwestern corner of the island to the village of Rybnovsk (Rybnoye) in the same county, and those inhabiting the eastern shore and the basin of the river Tym' to the town of Nogliki in Nogliki County; a small group lives in the town of Poronaysk in Poronaysk County. In 1989, 1,200 speakers were reported, but the number of active users is probably in the range of a few hundred. There are no younger speakers in the Amur region, and very few, if any, on Sakhalin, though Sakhalin Nivkh appears to be somewhat more vigorous than Amur Nivkh; nevertheless, most speakers are middle-aged or older. Several of the Nivkh speakers who used to live in the territory of modern Poronaysk County in the southern part of Sakhalin were evacuated to Hokkaido, Japan, after 1945; a few of these emigrants survived until recently. There is a written standard based on Amur Nivkh, also used in Nekrasovka, and a recently created literary standard based on the East Sakhalin dialect is being propagated with some success, both in Cyrillic script. Sakhalin Nivkh is severely endangered and Amur Nivkh critically endangered.

Nogay [143] Caucasia and Eastern Europe: spoken in several areas in northern Caucasia and southern Russia as well as in the northern parts of the Dobruja region in Romania, and before the deportations to Central Asia after the Second World War around Perekop in the northern steppe area of the Crimea. In 1989, approximately 70,000 speakers were reported from the Russian Federation, where they live in parts of the Karachay-Cherkes Republic, Nogay, Tarumovka, Kizlyar and Babayurt counties in the Republic of Daghestan, Shelkovskaya County in the Republic of Chechenia, and Neftekumsk, Mineral'nyye Vody and Kochubeyevskoye counties in Stavropol' Region. The speakers of Crimean Nogay are counted among the Crimean Tatar. In the Dobruja region in Romania there are up to 25,000 'Tatar' speakers, which covers speakers of both Crimean Tatar and Nogay. Children living in more remote areas are likely to learn Nogay, but many of them shift to other languages at school age. Because of the small, scattered communities, and the overwhelming dominance of other languages everywhere in its traditional area, Nogay is increasingly endangered. – *Alabugat Tatar* [144] Eastern Europe: south-eastern Russia. Spoken in the village of Severnyy at the station of Ulan-Khol in Lagan' County in the Kalmyk Republic in the Russian Federation. Alabugat Tatar is an outlying dialect of Nogay with deep influences from Tatar and other Turkic languages and, in particular, Kalmyk. There were over 400 members of the ethnic group, presumably all speakers, in 1987. They have traditionally employed the Tatar literary language, and the school operated in Tatar until 1960 when it was shifted to Russian. Because of the small size of the community and the increasing influence of Russian the language must be regarded as definitely endangered. – There are two outlying dialects of Nogay spoken in Astrakhan Province in the Russian Federation, collectively known as *Astrakhan Nogay*; the schools in their areas operated in Tatar until 1962, but since then the Russian influence has been growing and they are now clearly endangered: *Karagash* has been influenced especially by Kazakh. It is spoken in Krasnoyarskiy and Kharabali counties by a few thousand speakers. – *Yurt Tatar* has been influenced especially by Tatar. It is spoken in Volga (Privolzhskiy), Nariman and Volodarskiy counties as well as in the suburbs of the city of Astrakhan by several thousand speakers; a small group known as Kundor Tatars lives in the village of Tuluganovka in Volodarskiy County.

Norman [70] France: spoken in the regions of Upper Normandy (Haute-Normandie) and Lower Normandy (Basse-Normandie) by a small portion of the population. Very few if any children learn the language. Even the language of the most competent speakers is likely to be heavily influenced by French. Severely endangered. – There are three outlying dialects of Norman spoken on the Channel Islands, collectively known as *Channel Islands French*: *Alderney French* [*auregnais*] [71] was spoken on the island of Alderney in the Bailiwick of Guernsey. The last native speakers died around 1960. Recently extinct. – *Guernsey French* [*guernesiais*] [72] is spoken on the island of Guernsey in the Bailiwick of Guernsey by perhaps 5,000 speakers, practically all of them middle-aged or older. Severely endangered. – *Jersey French* [*jèrriais*] [73] is spoken on the island of Jersey, which constitutes the Bailiwick of Jersey, and on the island of Sark in the Bailiwick of Guernsey [*sercquiais*]. In 1989, less than 6,000 speakers were reported from Jersey; the number of speakers on Sark is below 100. There are some younger speakers but most are middle-aged or older. Severely endangered.

North Frisian [47] Germany: western coast of Schleswig north of Husum including the Halligen Islands and the adjacent islands of Föhr, Amrum, Sylt, and Helgoland; formerly extended to adjacent Denmark. There are approximately 8,000 speakers; language use is most active on western Föhr and in the village of Risum-Lindholm on the mainland. A small number of children learn the language, but few of them continue to use it in adulthood. Most idiolects are heavily influenced by Low Saxon and German. Severely endangered in Germany; extinct in Denmark.

North Saami [5] Northern Europe: Lapland. Spoken in most parts of Finnmark and Troms provinces and in the northernmost corner of Nordland Province in Norway, in Kiruna and Pajala counties and parts of Gällivare and other adjacent counties in Norrbotten Province (Torne Lappmark) as well as, because of resettlements in the twentieth century, also in more southerly regions in Sweden, and in Utsjoki and Enontekiö counties, western parts of Inari County, and Vuotso region of Sodankylä

County in Lapland Province in Finland. Formerly extended to Petsamo region in Murmansk Province in the Russian Federation. Includes three dialect groups, Torne Saami, Finnmark Saami and Sea Saami. In Norway, the number of speakers is above 10,000, in Sweden perhaps 5,000, and in Finland approximately 1,500. In the core area in central Finnmark Province, where North Saami has an official status, many children learn the language and are likely to continue to use the language in adulthood, and in the adjacent parts of Sweden and Finland, there are also child speakers. In other regions, however, North Saami is still giving away to dominant languages. Despite the recent positive trends in parts of its range, North Saami must be regarded as definitely endangered in Sweden, Norway and Finland; extinct in the Russian Federation.

Northern Altay **[148]** Siberia: in the northeastern river valleys of the Altay area in southern Siberia. Northern Altay is a conglomeration of three closely related dialects: **Tuba**, **Kumandy** and **Chalkan** Tuba is spoken in Turochak, Choya and Mayma counties in the Republic of Altay in the Russian Federation by a couple of thousand people, including few children. Kumandy is spoken in Krasnogorskoye, Solton, Kytmanovo and Tselinnoye counties in Altay Region and in adjacent counties in the Republic of Altay as well as in the towns of Tashtagol and Sheregesh in Kemerovo Province by several thousand people, but only rarely among younger generations. Chalkan (Kuu) is spoken in the villages of Kurmach-Baygol, Suranash, Malyy Chibechen' and Itkuch in Turochak County by approximately 2,000 people. Altogether, there are probably less than 10,000 speakers. The transmission of the language to children is becoming rare but has probably not stopped completely. Southern Altay is used as the written standard. Definitely endangered.

Northern Khanty **[28]** Siberia: spoken in the lower Ob' basin and on its tributaries, mainly in Beloyarskiy and Oktyabr'skoye counties and in the adjacent parts of Berezovo County in Khanty-Mansi Autonomous District and in Shuryskary County and the southern parts of Ural (Priural'skiy) County in Yamal Nenets Autonomous District in the Russian Federation. Northern Khanty dialects include Ob' Khanty, Shuryskary and Berezovo Khanty, Kazym Khanty, Sherkaly Khanty and Niz'yam Khanty. In 1989, 14,000 speakers were reported for Khanty as a whole, and since a clear minority of them speak Eastern Khanty, the number of Northern Khanty speakers is possibly more than 10,000. Northern Khanty is still used as a family language, but the boarding school system often forces a shift to Russian among younger generations. Separate written norms in Cyrillic script exist for some of the dialects, but they have very limited use. Definitely endangered.

Northern Mansi **[24]** Siberia: on the western tributaries to the lower Ob', mainly along the Sos'va, and in the central and northern Ural mountains, within the forest zone, mainly in Berezovo County and the northern parts of Sovetskiy County in Khanty-Mansi Autonomous District, formerly also in adjacent parts of the Komi Republic and Yekaterinburg Province in the Russian Federation. Northern Mansi dialects include Sygva Mansi, Sos'va Mansi, Ob' Mansi, and Upper Loz'va Mansi. In 1989, 3,400 speakers were reported for Mansi as a whole; since this figure includes a maximum couple of hundred Eastern Mansi speakers, there are approximately 3,000 speakers of Northern Mansi. There are very few, if any, child speakers; most speakers are middle-aged or older. There is a written standard in Cyrillic script, but its use is limited to school textbooks. Severely endangered.

Northern Selkup (also called ***Taz Selkup***) **[36]** Siberia: in the basin of the river Taz (flowing to the Arctic Ocean), as well as in the Baykha-Turukhan river system, to the west of the upper Yenisey, partly within the tundra zone, mainly in Krasnosel'kup County in Yamal Nenets Autonomous District, the northern parts of Turukhansk County in Krasnoyarsk Region and the northeastern corner of Nizhnevartovsk County in Khanty-Mansi Autonomous District in the Russian Federation. In 1989, 1,800 speakers were reported for all three Selkup languages; the number of Northern Selkup speakers lies somewhere between 1,000 and 1,500, and includes, in the remotest areas, some children. Most children are monolingual speakers of Russian, but Selkup is probably used in some families for internal communication. A written standard in Cyrillic script has recently been reintroduced and is being used, with modest success, in elementary-level school instruction. Severely endangered.

Olonetsian [in Olonetsian *livvi*, in Russian *livvikovskij jazyk*, in Finnish *aunus*] **[14a]** Northern Europe: northwestern Russia. Spoken northeast of Lake Ladoga in the southwest of the Republic of Karelia in the Russian Federation in an area which includes Olonets County (except the eastern corner), the western parts of Pryazha County and the southwestern part of Kondopoga County. In Finland, Olonetsian is spoken by people evacuated, in 1940 and 1944, from former Finnish territories north of Lake Ladoga including Salmi and Impilahti counties, currently the eastern parts of Pitkyaranta (Pitkäranta) County and the southern corner of Suoyarvi (Suojärvi) County in the Republic of Karelia. In the Russian Federation, there are possibly approximately 25,000 speakers. A few children learn the language, but most if not all of them become more fluent in Russian and largely stop using Olonetsian later in life. A literary language written in the Latin alphabet has recently been developed. In Finland, there are a few thousand speakers, all elderly, and even those who are fluent in Olonetsian use mostly Finnish. Definitely endangered in the Russian Federation; critically endangered in Finland.

Ongkor Solon. See ***Solon***

Oroch [in Oroch *naani*] **[169]** Siberia (the Russian Far East): spoken in the northern section of the Sikhote Alin mountain range, to the east of the lower Amur, now in two isolated groups in Khabarovsk Region in the Russian Federation, one mainly in Vanino County, near the town of Sovetskaya Gavan' along the rivers emptying into the Tatar Strait, including the villages of Datta and Us'ka-Orochskaya on the Tumnin River, and the other on the Amur River in Komsomol'sk County. In 1989, 150 speakers were reported, all middle-aged or older; among the languages of the so-called 'Peoples of the Far North', Oroch has the lowest proportion of native speakers, approximately 20 per cent, in relation to the corresponding ethnic group. Critically endangered.

Orok [in Orok *ulta* or *uilta*; in Japanese *Orokko* or *Uiruta*] **[172]** Siberia: spoken in the northern and central parts of the eastern shore of Sakhalin, in Nogliki, Poronaysk and Aleksandrovsk counties in Sakhalin Province in the Russian Federation, now mainly

263

in the village of Val in Nogliki County, but many Oroks have moved to the county centres Nogliki and Poronaysk. There used to be Orok speakers also in the southern part of the island, from where people were evacuated to Hokkaido, Japan, after 1945; the descendants of this small emigrant population have by now lost the Orok language. In 1989, eighty speakers were reported, but the actual number is below forty, all middle-aged or older. Among the languages of the so-called 'Peoples of the Far North', Orok has the smallest number of native speakers out of the smallest size of the corresponding ethnic group. A project aiming at creating a literary norm for Orok in Cyrillic script and teaching the language at elementary schools has recently been launched in cooperation with Japanese scholars; earlier, the Japanese syllabic script (katakana) has also been used to transcribe Orok material. Critically endangered.

Oyrat [161] Mongolia and Central Asia: spoken mainly in Kobdo and Ubsu leagues in the west of Mongolia and in Jungaria region (Bortala, Hoboksar, Tarbagatai and Bayangol) in the north of Xinjiang Uygur Autonomous Region in China, and by smaller groups in the Kukunor region in Qinghai in China, Alashan League in the west of Inner Mongolia in China and the Issyk-Kul' region in Kyrgyzstan. Oyrat includes nine dialect groups known by tribal names, including Torgut, Khoshut, Ölöt and Dörbet. The number of Oyrat speakers can only be estimated because they are officially counted as Mongolians both in Mongolia and China; in Mongolia there are approximately 150,000, in Sinkiang less than 130,000, and in other areas only a few thousand speakers. In the Issyk-Kul' (Issyk Köl) region, where the Oyrats are officially called Kalmyks, Oyrat is only spoken by the oldest generation, constituting a few of hundred speakers. In most areas, Oyrat continues to be used as a community language but it is under severe pressure from Mongolian, Uygur and Northern Chinese. As a whole, it is increasingly endangered, and in Kyrgyzstan critically endangered. – *Manchurian Ölöt* [in Written Mongolian *Yeke Mingghan*, in Modern Mongolian *Yikh Mianggan*] [162] Manchuria: still spoken on the eastern bank of the lower Nonni, in Fuyu County in Heilongjiang Province in China; extinct since the early twentieth century in the Imin region of Hulun Buir League in Inner Mongolia. Manchurian Ölöt is an outlying dialect of Oyrat. There are probably less than 1,000 speakers, most of them elderly, all in the Nonni region. There have been attempts to support Manchurian Ölöt by teaching Standard and Written Mongolian at a local school. Severely endangered.

Permyak (also called *Permyak Komi* or *Permian Komi*; the Russian-based term 'Komi-Permyak' better avoided) [21a] Eastern Europe: east-central Russia. Spoken in Permyak Komi Autonomous District and the adjacent parts of Kirov (Vyatka) and Perm' provinces in the Russian Federation. In 1989, 110,000 speakers were reported. Quite a lot of children learn the language, but only in remote rural areas they tend to continue to use the language in adulthood. Definitely endangered. Often considered a single language with Komi. – *Yazva Komi* (also called *Eastern Permyak*) [21b] an outlying dialect of Permyak, is spoken in the Yaz'va Valley in Krasnovishera County in northeastern Perm' Province. There are a couple of hundred speakers at best, possibly all elderly, out of a population of some 4,000. Severely endangered.

Picard [74] In France, Picard is spoken in the regions of Picardy (Picardie) and Nord-Pas-de-Calais by a small but notable portion of the population. In Belgium, it is spoken by an estimated 200,000 people in the area extending from Tournai to Mons in the western part of the province of Hainaut. A few children learn the language, and the future of Picard seems slightly less bleak than that of other Oïl languages of France. It is nevertheless severely endangered.

Piedmontese [78] Italy: spoken in Piedmont Region except the Novara Province, the western Alpine valleys and southern border areas, as well as in the border area of Savona Province in Liguria. There are a couple of million speakers, but particularly in towns and among the young the use of Piedmontese has diminished drastically. Increasingly endangered.

Pite Saami (also called *Arjeplog Saami*) [3] Northern Europe: Lapland. Traditionally spoken in most parts of Arjeplog County in Norrbotten Province (Pite Lappmark) in Sweden. There are less than twenty elderly speakers. Nearly extinct.

Plautdietsch [48] an outlying dialect of Low Saxon which derives from the concentration of Mennonites in the area of the Vistula Delta in what is now northern Poland and their subsequent emigration to the Ukraine and further to the Americas. Most speakers in the Ukraine were deported during the Second World War to Central Asia and Siberia. Many Central Asian and Siberian speakers have recently emigrated to Germany or other countries. Plautdietsch still has a couple of hundred thousand speakers, including a number of younger people, mainly in the Americas, where the approximate numbers of speakers are for Argentina 4,000, Belize 6,000, Bolivia 60,000 to 80,000, Brazil 8,000, Costa Rica 2,000, Canada 80,000 to 100,000, Mexico 40,000, Paraguay 40,000, Uruguay 2,000, and the United States 10,000. In Europe, Central Asia and Siberia, the transmission of the language to children has all but stopped. Plautdietsch may be regarded as the last remnant of West Prussian Low Saxon. Definitely endangered.

Poitevin-Saintongeais [68] France: spoken in the region of Poitou-Charentes and in the department of Vendée in Pays de la Loire region as well as in northern Gironde in Aquitaine region by a small portion of the population. Very few if any children learn the language. Even the language of the most competent speakers is likely to be heavily influenced by French. Severely endangered.

Pontic Greek [98] an outlying dialect of Greek which at the beginning of the twentieth century was spoken along the entire Black Sea coast of Turkey and adjacent Georgia: western Pontic was spoken from Inebolu to Ünye, and eastern Pontic in Trebizond (Trabzon, Trapezunt) area and in Chaldia, especially around Gümüşhane. Most speakers in Turkey emigrated to Greece after the First World War; Muslims remained, and are to some extent still found around the towns of Of and Sürmene. There was significant migration to southern Russia and Caucasia in the eighteenth and nineteenth centuries, where Pontic Greek is now healthiest, but many of these populations are now migrating to Greece. In 1989, 40,000 speakers of Greek were reported from the Russian Federation, including 15,000 in Krasnodar Region and the same number in Stavropol' Region; 60,000 speakers were reported from Georgia, and 2,500 from Armenia; the Greek dialects spoken in the regions of Tsalka in Georgia and Alaverdi in Armenia derive partly from Cappadocian Greek but seem to have assimilated to Pontic. The total number of Pontic Greek speakers can only be guessed but it may still

265

be closer to 200,000 than 100,000. There are probably a few child speakers, but most speakers are middle-aged or older. In Greece, Pontic Greek retains mainly symbolic functions. Definitely endangered in the Russian Federation and Caucasia, severely endangered in Turkey, and critically endangered in Greece.

Provençal **[65]** France: spoken in the departments of Alpes-Maritimes (except the eastern corner), Bouches-du-Rhône, Var and Vaucluse, in the southern parts of Alpes de Haute-Provence, and the eastern parts of Gard, by approximately 200,000 speakers, most of them middle-aged or elderly. A small number of children learn the language, but they usually shift entirely to French at school age. Definitely endangered. Often regarded as a single language with Alpine Provençal.

Resian Slovene **[42]** Italy: an outlying dialect of Slovene spoken in the five villages that constitute the municipality of Resia in the northeastern part of Udine Province in the Autonomous Region Friuli-Venezia Giulia by the majority of the approximately 1,400 inhabitants of the municipality. In the westernmost villages of San Giorgio, Gniva and Prato there are few, if any child speakers, but in the villages of Oseacco and Stolvizza children are still learning the language to some extent. The language of younger men in particular is quite heavily influenced by Italian. Definitely endangered.

Romani **[104]** dispersed in many European countries, most densely in East-Central and Eastern Europe and in the Balkans. Many speakers were murdered by Germans during the Second World War. Seven Romani dialects are still spoken: (1) ***Vlach*** in Albania, Bosnia and Hercegovina, Hungary, the Republic of Moldova, Romania, the Ukraine, Yugoslavia and neighbouring countries; (2) ***Balkan Romani*** in Bulgaria, Greece, the Republic of Moldova, the Republic of Macedonia, Romania, Turkey, the Ukraine and Yugoslavia; (3) ***Welsh Romani*** in Wales; (4) ***Finnish Romani*** in Finland; (5) ***Sinte*** in Austria, Croatia, the Czech Republic, France, Germany, Italy, the Netherlands, Poland, Slovenia, Switzerland and Yugoslavia; (6) ***Carpathian Romani*** in the Czech Republic, Hungary, Poland, Romania, Slovakia, and the Ukraine; (7) ***Baltic Romani*** in Belarus, Estonia, Latvia, Lithuania, Poland, Russia and the Ukraine. There are at least three and a half million speakers in total (see Matras 2002). In 1989, 130,000 speakers were reported from the Russian Federation, 30,000 from the Ukraine, 10,000 from the Republic of Moldova, and 30,000 from other parts of the Soviet Union. Welsh and Finnish Romani have few speakers left; the situation of Sinte may actually be similar; other dialects have large numbers. There are many children who learn Romani, and they would have all chances to continue to use it through adulthood, were it not that practically all national governments are hostile to the Romani language and culture. In many countries, such discriminatory policies have already led to a situation where children no longer learn the language. Increasingly endangered.

Romansh [in German often *Bündnerromanisch*] **[126]** Switzerland: Graubünden (Grischun), mainly in Surselva, Seumeir, and Unterengadin. Perhaps little more than half of the official number of 65,000 speakers (1986) use the language actively. Many children learn the language, but most of them become more fluent in German and may not use Romansh actively later in life. Increasingly endangered.

Rutul (also known as *Mukhad*) **[126]** Caucasia: southern Daghestan and northern Azerbaijan. Spoken in seventeen villages, including Rutul, Shinaz, Ikhrek, Myukhrek, Luchek, Amsar and Borch, in Rutul County and in the village of Khnov in Akhty County in the Republic of Daghestan in the Russian Federation, and in adjacent villages in Kakh (Qax) and Sheki (Šäki) counties in Azerbaijan. In 1989, 19,000 speakers, almost all in Daghestan, were reported from the Soviet Union, including many children, but because of the small size of the community and the dominant position of Russian, Azerbaijani and Lezgian, the language must be regarded as definitely endangered. Until recently, there was no literacy in it, but a Rutul primer was published a few years ago.

Sassarese Sardinian. See *Corsican*

Saterlandic (also called *Sater Frisian* or, earlier more correctly but now possibly creating confusion with neighbouring dialects of Low Saxon, *East Frisian*) [in Saterlandic. *seeltersk*] **[46]** Germany: spoken in the towns of Strücklingen (Strukelje), Ramsloh (Romelse) and Scharrel (Schäddel) in Saterland region west of Oldenburg; East Frisian was also spoken on the island of Wangerooge till the early twentieth century. Although the commonly cited figure is 2,000, there are probably much less than 1,000 speakers, including few if any child speakers. While there may be some younger speakers, most are middle-aged or older. All idiolects are likely to be heavily influenced by Low Saxon and German. Severely endangered.

Scottish Gaelic **[55]** Scotland: rural areas of the Western Isles (Lewis, Harris, North Uist, South Uist, Barra) and Skye, and a few locations in the rest of the Inner Isles and the Highland mainland (mainly Sutherland, Ross and Cromarty, Inverness, and Argyll counties). There are 20,000 to 30,000 active users; more than 50,000 others claim knowledge of the language. Scottish Gaelic is also spoken elsewhere in Scotland, and by one to several thousand speakers in immigrant communities in Nova Scotia and Prince Edward Island in Canada. A number of children learn the language, but there are serious problems in language maintenance even in the core areas. Definitely endangered.

Shor **[149]** Siberia: spoken along the rivers flowing from the southwestern slopes of the Kuznetskiy Alatau mountains in the southern parts of Kemerovo Province in the Russian Federation. Shor is a conglomeration of two historically distinct dialects, identified by river names as Kondoma Shor (the southern dialect, close to Northern Altay) and Mrassu Shor (the northern dialect, close to Khakas). The Shor-speaking territory, known as Shoria, briefly held the status of an autonomous district (1925–39), but was subsequently turned into one of the greatest industrial regions of the Soviet Union (the so-called Kuzbass region). In 1989, less than 10,000 speakers were reported. There are probably no child speakers, except possibly in a few rural families, and most speakers are middle-aged or older. The Shor community is surrounded by Russian-speaking immigrants, but there have recently been signs of increased national and linguistic consciousness. A written standard in Cyrillic script is based on Kondoma dialect. Severely endangered.

Sinkiang Dagur. See *Dagur*

267

Skolt Saami [in Finnish *koltta*] **[7]** Northern Europe: Lapland and Kola peninsula. Spoken in Sevettijärvi region in Inari County in Lapland Province in Finland, mainly by people evacuated from former Finnish territory of Petsamo, now Pechenga County in Murmansk Province in the Russian Federation. Earlier spoken also in the western parts of Kola County in western Murmansk Province, from where the speakers were forcibly translocated to Lovozero, the centre of Lovozero County. The number of speakers in Finland is around 300. There were approximately twenty speakers in the Russian Federation in the early 1990s. Formerly also spoken in easternmost Finnmark Province of Norway. In Finland, very few children learn the language, and in the Russian Federation, there are only elderly speakers. Skolt Saami has been used as a literary language since the 1970s. It is severely endangered in Finland, nearly extinct in the Russian Federation, and extinct in Norway.

Solon [in Chinese pinyin *Suolun* or *Suolun Ewenke*] **[166]** Manchuria: spoken in central and northwestern Manchuria in China, in Morin Dawa Daur and Ewenki autonomous banners and adjacent areas of neighbouring banners in Hulun Buir League in northeastern Inner Mongolia (in the Imin basin) as well as in Heilongjiang Province, mainly in Nahe (Nehe) County (in the Nonni basin), west and south of the Evenki. Solon speakers are included in the official Ewenke nationality; cf. Evenki. There are perhaps fewer than 10,000 speakers, out of 21,000 ethnic group members, and in many places they are over fifty years old. As to child speakers, the situation varies greatly, with some groups in Heilongjiang adopting other languages (Dagur, Chinese). On the Inner Mongolian side the language is generally being retained better, with some children learning it, depending on locality. Most if not all speakers also speak Dagur, and many speak Northern Chinese. The function of literary languages is fulfilled by both Chinese and Modern Written Mongolian; attempts have also been made to write Solon in various systems of transcription (Mongolian, Roman, IPA). Severely endangered. – **Ongkor Solon** (also called **Sinkiang Solon** or **Turkestan Solon**) **[167]** Sinkiang: spoken in the Ili (Yili) region, in Kazakh Autonomous District in Xinjiang Uygur Autonomous Region in China. Ongkor Solon is an outlying dialect of Solon: Solon speakers were translocated to Sinkiang from Manchuria together with Dagurs in 1763. The last fluent speaker, of the male sex, was seventy-nine in 1990, and his death was announced recently. There may still be a few people who know some isolated phrases or words. Recently extinct.

Sorbian (also called **Lusatian** or **Wendish**) **[44]** Germany: Lusatia (Lausitz [Łužica or Łužyca]) region around Cottbus (Chośebuz) and in the Spreewald (Błota) area in Brandenburg (lower Lusatia) and in and around Bautzen (Budyšin) in Saxony (upper Lusatia). There are two literary languages, Lower Sorbian and Upper Sorbian, based on different dialects but the language area is unified by a large area of transitional dialects, which speaks for the recognition of a single spoken language. Although the number of Sorbian speakers is occasionally reported as high as 70,000 or even 110,000, the factual number is much lower, and lies somewhere between 20,000 and 30,000; about one third in lower and two thirds in upper Lusatia. Among the Upper Sorbian Catholics, constituting some 10,000 people between the towns of Bautzen, Hoyerswerda and Kamenz, most children still learn the language and continue to use it in adulthood unless they are forced to move away because of unemployment, while elsewhere shift to German has been proceeding rapidly since the Second World War, so that there are now very few child speakers among the Upper Sorbian Protestants, and none among the Lower Sorbians who are all Protestants. Most active speakers among Protestants are therefore elderly, although Sorbian is still studied as a second language at school starting from the age of fifteen. Contrary to recent trends among European minority languages, Sorbian has lost much of its former public support after the unification of Germany. Sorbian schools are being closed one after another, officially for financial reasons, but anti-minority feelings are apparent in the background. For instance, the government of Saxony is currently planning to close down the Sorbian Secondary School at Crostwitz (Chróścicy), which would severely disrupt, if not destroy, the Upper Sorbian school network. Definitely endangered; in lower Lusatia, severely endangered.

South Saami [1] Northern Europe: Lapland and central Scandinavia. Spoken in Vilhelmina County and parts of neigbouring counties in Västerbotten Province (Åsele Lappmark), in Strömsund, Krokom, Åre, Berg and Härjedalen counties in Jämtland Province, and in Idre region in Älvdalen County in Dalarna Province in Sweden, and in southern parts (up till Rana) in Nordland Province, many parts of Nord-Trøndelag and Sør-Trøndelag provinces, and in Engerdal region in Hedmark Province in Norway. There are a few hundred speakers, many of whom prefer Swedish or Norwegian, out of a much larger ethnic population. In some families, children may learn the language, but it is nevertheless severely endangered.

Southern Altay [147] Siberia: in the central and southwestern river valleys of the Altay area in southern Siberia. Southern Altay is a conglomeration of three closely related dialects: *Altay, Telengit,* and *Teleut* (or *Telengut*) [in Chinese pinyin *Tielingute*]. In 1989, a combined figure of 61,000 speakers for Southern Altay and Northern Altay was reported, which means that Southern Altay is spoken by approximately 50,000 people, as long as the figure is not notably inflated. Southern Altay is mainly spoken in the Republic of Altay in the Russian Federation. Teleut specifically is still spoken in Shebalino County in the Republic of Altay, but the bulk of Teleut speakers were dispersed by political developments in the seventeenth and eighteenth centuries, and Teleut is now mainly spoken to the north of the actual Altay region, concentrated in the Bachat region in Belovo, Gur'yevsk and Novokuznetsk counties in the western part of Kemerovo Province and in the Chumysh region in Tselinnoye County in the eastern part of Altay Region. A small diaspora group (probably since the eighteenth century) of Teleut origin has been registered within the Altai District of northern Sinkiang, China, but it is not known if they continue to speak the language. Southern Altay is probably still being learnt by some proportion of children, and even in the case of the widely dispersed Teleut communities consisting of a couple of thousand people, the transmission of the language to children has probably not stopped entirely. Triggered by both social and ecological problems, there is currently a rise of nationalism, which may improve the position of the native language. The speakers of Teleut, in particular, have recently shown interest in national renaissance, which might lead to the revigoration of the native language. Increasingly endangered.

Southern Khanty [29] Siberia: formerly spoken in the lower Irtysh basin and on its tributaries, within Uvat County in Tyumen' Province and Konda and Khanty-Mansiysk counties in Khanty-Mansi Autonomous District in the Russian Federation. Dialects included Dem'yanka Khanty, Konda Khanty and Irtysh Khanty. There are probably no speakers left, but no confirmation is available; in any case, the transmission of the language to children stopped long ago. Southern Khanty was assimilated to both Siberian Tatar and Russian. Possibly extinct.

Southern Mansi (also called ***Tavda Mansi***) **[27]** Siberia: last speakers lived in the region of the lower Tavda, a tributary to the lower Tobol'-Irtysh, in the border area of Nizhnyaya Tavda County in Tyumen' Province and Tavda County in Yekaterinburg Province in the Russian Federation. Earlier Southern Mansi was spoken over a much larger area covering the southern parts of Yekaterinburg Province and adjacent parts of neighbouring regions. Southern Mansi became extinct before the middle of the twentieth century. The language, as recorded from the last generations of speakers, reveals interference from Siberian Tatar, but the very last speakers seem to have adopted Russian.

Southern Selkup **[38]** Siberia: spoken mainly in the basin of the river Ket', an eastern tributary to the upper Ob', in Kolpashevo and Upper Ket' (Verkhneketskiy) counties in Tomsk Province and adjacent parts of Krasnoyarsk Region in the Russian Federation; formerly spoken further to the south. Consists of two dialect groups, Upper Ob' Selkup, which is practically extinct, and Ket' Selkup, which still has a small number of speakers, probably much less than one hundred, all elderly. Critically endangered.

Svan **[106]** Caucasia: northwestern Georgia. Spoken in an area known as Svanetia, mainly within Mestiya and Lentekhi counties in Georgia, and possibly in small enclaves in the adjacent regions in the Kabard-Balkar Republic in the Russian Federation. The number of speakers is usually given as 40,000, but in reality it may be down to a few thousand, because many people who have shifted to the closely related Georgian still claim Svan ethnicity. While the situation is poorly known, it is possible that there are very few child speakers left. There are certainly some younger speakers, but most speakers appear to be middle-aged or older. There is no literacy in Svan, but Georgian is used as a literary language. Definitely endangered.

Tat **[102]** Caucasia: northern Azerbaijan. Spoken in Syazan, Divichinsk, Kuba, Konakhkend, Semakh and Ismail regions in the northeast of Azerbaijan as well as on Apsheron peninsula and Baku. Apart from the Jewish Tats traditionally speaking the closely related but distinct Juhur (Judeo-Tat) language, the Tat nationality is divided into two groups, the Muslim Tats and the Christian (or Armenian) Tats. Many of the Christian Tats settled in Daghestan already in the eighteenth and nineteenth centuries, and the people in the last Christian Tat communities in Azerbaijan, in the villages Kilvar in Divichinsk region and Madras in Shemakh region, were forced to move to Armenia in the late 1980s. The 1989 census reports 5,000 speakers of Tat in Azerbaijan, 4,000 of them in Baku, but these figures are far from trustworthy. There may possibly still be some child speakers, but a shift to Azerbaijani has proceeded rapidly among Muslim Tats. Tat is not written, but the speakers in Azerbaijan use Azerbaijani in school and for wider communication. Definitely endangered.

Ter Saami **[10]** Northern Europe: Kola peninsula. Earlier spoken in the eastern parts of Lovozero County in Murmansk Province in the Russian Federation, from where the speakers were forcibly translocated to Lovozero, which lies outside the native territory. There were six speakers in the early 1990s, all elderly. Some descendants of Ter Saami speak Kildin Saami, but most have shifted to Russian. Nearly extinct.

Tindi [117] Caucasia: western Daghestan. Spoken in the villages of Tindi, Angida, Aknada, Echeda and Tissi in Tsumada County in the Republic of Daghestan in the Russian Federation. The number of speakers lies somewhere between 4,000 and 6,000, with relatively few child speakers. Because of the small size of the community and the dominant position of Avar, the language must be regarded as definitely endangered. There is no literacy in it.

Tofa [155] Siberia: originally spoken by nomadic groups on the northern slopes of the Eastern Sayan mountains, now in the villages of Alygdzher, Nerkha and Verkhnyaya Gutara in Nizhneudinsk County in Irkutsk Province in the Russian Federation, to the south of the city of Nizhneudinsk. In 1989, 300 speakers were reported, and the actual figure was probably lower, and currently there are perhaps no more than forty fluent speakers plus the same number of passive speakers in Alygdzher and Nerkha. All known fluent speakers are above forty years of age, but the situation may be slightly better in Verkhnyaya Gutara. Critically endangered.

Töitschu [50] Italy: an outlying dialect of Alemannic or, more precisely, of Walser (Highest Alemannic), spoken in the village of Issime (Eischeme) in the upper Lys valley. Another Walser dialect, Titsch, is spoken in the villages of Gressoney-Saint-Jean and Gressoney-La-Trinité, but it appears to be very closely related to and in constant contact with cross-border Alemannic in Switzerland; the same may be true of other varieties of Walser spoken outside Valais (Wallis) Canton, notably in the village of Bosco-Gurin in Ticino Canton as well as in Graubünden and parts of Austria. Töitschu is a typical, rather independent outlying dialect that has been influenced by Francoprovençal and Piedmontese. The combined number of speakers of both Töitschu and Titsch in the Aosta Valley is reportedly 600. Definitely endangered.

Trukhmen (also called *Caucasian Turkmen*) [137] northern Caucasia and Eastern Europe: an outlying dialect of Turkmen spoken since the eighteenth century in southern Russia, mainly in Stavropol' Region and Astrakhan Province in the Russian Federation. A figure of 18,000 speakers has been reported, and a few children probably learn the language, but the situation is poorly known. Definitely endangered.

Tsakhur [127] Caucasia: northern Azerbaijan and southern Daghestan. Spoken in sixteen villages in Zakatala (Zaqatala) and Kakh (Qax) counties in Azerbaijan as well as in thirteen villages in Rutul County in the Republic of Daghestan in the Russian Federation. In 1989, 13,000 speakers were reported from Azerbaijan and 6,000 from the Russian Federation, but the actual figures may be even higher. Most children are speakers, but because of the relatively small size of the community and the dominant position of Azerbaijani and Russian, the language must be regarded as definitely endangered. Tsakhur was used as a literary language in the mid-1930s and again in the 1990s, and in recent years it has been studied as a subject in local schools.

Tsakonian [101] Greece, eastern Peloponnese: southern Tsakonian is still spoken in villages around Leonidio, but practically all speakers are elderly, while northern

271

Tsakonian barely survives in the villages of Kastanitsa and Sitena. There was also an outlying dialect called Propontis Tsakonian spoken by colonists in northeastern Turkey, in the villages of Havoutsi and Vatka on the mouth of the Gönen river, but after the speakers were settled in Greek Macedonia following the 1922 population exchanges, it became extinct. There are a couple of hundred people with some fluency in Tsakonian at best, mainly in Leonidio region but still a few in Kastanitsa as well. Northern Tsakonian has undergone earlier influence from Greek than southern Tsakonian, but there is also significant influence discernible in southern Tsakonian. Critically endangered.

Tsez (or ***Dido***) **[119]** Caucasia: western Daghestan. Spoken in several villages, including Khutrakh, Kidero, Khupri, Shaitl, Mikok, Tsebari, Asakh, Shapikh and Sagada, in Tsunta County in the Republic of Daghestan in the Russian Federation, and in a number of expatriate communities elsewhere in Daghestan as well as in Turkey. The number of speakers is probably between 7,000 and 8,000. Because of the small size of the community and the dominant position of Avar, the language must be regarded as definitely endangered. Until recently, there was no literacy in it, but a Tsez primer was published in 1993.

Tundra Enets (also called ***Madu*** or ***Somatu***) **[32]** Siberia: in the tundra zone on the lower Yenisey, now concentrated in the village of Vorontsovo in Ust'-Yeniseysk County in Taymyr (Dolgan and Nenets) Autonomous District in the Russian Federation. Historically, there has occurred a northward movement comparable to that of Forest Enets. The number of speakers is perhaps around thirty, and all of them are middle-aged or older. The last speakers are bilingual in Russian, but there may also be individuals with a knowledge of Nganasan. Critically endangered.

Tundra Nenets **[34]** Siberia and northern Russia: spoken in northwestern Siberia across a vast area in the Russian Federation, covering Yamal, Nadym and Taz counties and the northern parts of Ural (Priural'skiy) County in Yamal Nenets Autonomous District as well as most parts of Ust'-Yeniseysk County in Taymyr (Dolgan and Nenets) Autonomous District, and in the northernmost parts of European Russia including Nenets Autonomous District, the Kolguyev Island, the northern parts of Mezen' County and formerly the Novaya Zemlya Islands in Arkhangel'sk Province, as well as Vorkuta Territory and at least formerly the northern parts of Inta Territory and Usinsk, Ust'-Tsil'ma and Izhma counties in the Komi Republic. In 1989, 27,000 speakers were reported for the two Nenets languages; of these approximately 25,000 were speakers of Tundra Nenets. In Siberia, many children learn the language, but often shift to Russian at school age, yet most young people are still fluent in the language. On the European side, very few children learn the language, young people tend to prefer Russian, and most speakers there are middle-aged or older. Definitely endangered.

Tundra Yukagir (also called ***Northern Yukagir*** or ***Wadul***) **[176]** Siberia: spoken in the tundra zone, in a belt extending from the lower Indigirka in the west close to the lower Kolyma basin in the east, in the Republic of Sakha (Yakutia) in the Russian Federation, now largely concentrated in the villages of Andryushkino and Kolymskoye in Lower Kolyma (Nizhnekolymskiy) County. Previously Tundra Yukagir was spoken in a much wider area in the Lena-Yana-Indigirka-Kolyma region. In 1989, 400 speakers were reported for both Yukagir languages, but the figure is clearly inflated. There are fewer than 150 speakers of Tundra Yukagir, including elderly people who have it as their first language and middle-aged people who are typically more fluent in Russian and Yakut. In Andryushkino there may be a few younger speakers. All the remaining speakers are multilingual in Russian, Yakut, Even or Chukchi. Attempts are currently being made to create a written standard in Cyrillic script, with either Russian or Yakut-based orthographical principles, for both Tundra Yukagir and Forest Yukagir. Critically endangered.

Ubykh [109] originally spoken in northern Caucasia, on the Black Sea coast north from Khosta in what is now the southernmost part of Krasnodar Region, but practically the entire Ubykh nation, some 50,000 people, migrated to Turkey in 1864. The last speaker, Tevfik Esenç, from the village of Hacı Osman Köyü near the Sea of Marmara, died in October 1992. Recently extinct.

Udege (also spelled ***Udihe*** or ***Udehe***) [168] Siberia (the Russian Far East): in the southern and central sections of the Sikhote Alin mountain range, to the east of the Ussuri river, now mainly concentrated in four villages: Krasnyy Yar in Pozharskoye County and Agzu in Terney County in Maritime (Primor'ye) Region, and Gvasyugi in the County of Lazo and Arsen'yevo (Rassvet) in Nanay County in Khabarovsk Region in the Russian Federation. In 1989, under 500 first-language speakers out of 1,900 ethnic group members were reported, but the actual number is currently much smaller, possibly below 100, all of them elderly. A shift to Russian has proceeded in Udege communities faster than almost anywhere else in Siberia, and many characteristic features of the language have been lost. Earlier there were speakers of Udege between the Ussuri and Sungari basins in northeastern Manchuria in China, locally known as *Kyakala* [in Chinese pinyin *Qiakala*]. Manchurian Udege became extinct probably in the early twentieth century, but no exact date is available; it was initially replaced by Manchu and finally by Northern Chinese. The Udege were earlier also called *Tazy*, a term which today primarily refers to a local Chinese-speaking population. Critically endangered in the Russian Federation, extinct in China.

Udi [131] Caucasia: northern Azerbaijan and eastern Georgia. Earlier spoken across a large area in northern Azerbaijan, but now mainly in the villages of Vartashen (Vardashen, currently Oguz) in Vartashen County and Nij (Niç) in Kutkashen (currently Qabala) County, recently also in Sheki (Šäki) County and part of Zakatali County. Since the 1920s Udi has also been spoken in the village of Okt'omber (formerly Zinobiani) in Kvareli County in Georgia, the dialect of which is closely related to that of Vartashen from where the speakers fled. In 1989, 5,500 speakers were reported from Azerbaijan and a few hundred from Georgia, but the actual numbers may be lower; many Udi may have emigrated from Vartashen to Russia. There are relatively few child speakers, and the language is definitely endangered. Literary experiments took place in the nineteenth century, in the 1930s, and again in recent years. Until recently, Azerbaijani, Georgian and Russian were used exclusively in school, and they continue to be used for wider communication.

Udmurt [21] Eastern Europe: east-central Russia. Spoken in the Udmurt Republic and parts of Tatarstan, the Republic of Mariy-El, Bashkortostan, and Kirov (Vyatka) and

Perm' provinces in the Russian Federation. In 1989, 520,000 speakers were reported. Many children learn the language, but only those living in remote rural areas continue to use it actively. Increasingly endangered.

Ulcha (also spelled *Olcha*) [in Ulcha *naani*] **[171]** Siberia (the Russian Far East): spoken in the lower Amur basin, in Ul'cha County in Khabarovsk Region in the Russian Federation. In 1989, less than 1,000 first-language speakers out of 3,200 ethnic group members were reported, all middle-aged or older, and the shift to Russian continues to proceed rapidly. Critically endangered.

Ume Saami **[2]** Northern Europe: Lapland. Traditionally spoken in Arvidsjaur County and the southeastern corner of Arjeplog County in Norrbotten Province (Pite Lappmark) and in Malå and Sorsele counties and the northern Tärna region in Storuman County in Västerbotten Province (Lycksele Lappmark) in Sweden. Formerly also spoken in Rana County in Nordland Province in Norway. There are less than twenty speakers, all elderly. Nearly extinct in Sweden; extinct in Norway.

Urum (or *Greek Tatar*) **[136]** Eastern Europe and Caucasia: an outlying dialect of (Crimean) Turkish originally spoken in the south of the Crimea, now in a few villages in Donets'k (Donetsk) Province in the southeast of the Ukraine and in some places, notably Trialeti, in Georgia and perhaps elsewhere in Caucasia. The number of speakers is not known exactly, but may range in some tens of thousands. A language shift to dominant languages has proceeded rapidly, leaving few child speakers. Definitely endangered.

Veps **[16]** Northern Europe: northwestern Russia. Veps comprises three dialect areas: Northern Veps is spoken in the eastern part of Onega (Prionezhskiy) County in the southeast of the Republic of Karelia in the Russian Federation; Central Veps is spoken in a larger area across the boundary of St Petersburg (Leningrad) and Vologda provinces, mainly in the southern part of Podporozh'ye County, the eastern corner of Tikhvin County and the northeastern part of Boksitogorsk counties in St Petersburg Province, and the western parts of Babayevo and Vytegra counties in Vologda Province; Southern Veps is spoken in the southeastern part of Boksitogorsk County. In 1989, 6,000 speakers were reported, but the figure may actually be slightly too low. In a couple of villages, some children learn the language, but many stop using it at school age. Veps was used as a literary language in the mid-1930s and again in the 1990s, and in recent years it has been studied as a subject in local schools. Severely endangered.

Vojvodina Rusyn (or *Bachkan*) **[45]** the Balkans. Vojvodina Rusyn can be historically seen as an outlying dialect of Eastern Slovak with Rusyn influences, but it is now better regarded as a distinct language. It is spoken by less than 20,000 speakers in the Bačka region in Vojvodina Province in Serbia. There are probably some child speakers but also various negative factors. Definitely endangered.

Võro-Seto (or simply *Võro*) [in Estonian *Võru Keel*] Northern Europe: Estonia and northwestern Russia. Spoken in the southeastern corner of Estonia and in Pechory County in the rest of Pskov Province in the Russian Federation by approximately

50,000 speakers of all ages, but younger people are shifting to the majority language. Definitely endangered.

Vote [in Russian *vodskij jazyk*, in Estonian *vadja keel*, in Finnish *vatja*] (variants such as 'Votic' better avoided) **[12]** Northern Europe: northwestern Russia. Spoken in a few inland villages south of the Gulf of Finland in Kingisepp County in the west of St Petersburg (Leningrad) Province in the Russian Federation. There are probably less than twenty-five speakers left now, concentrated in the villages of Krakol'e (Jõgõperä) and Peski-Luzhitsy (Liivtšülä-Luuditsa), until recently also in Kotly (Kattila) and Mezhniki (Rajo). All of them are elderly, and prefer Russian in daily communication. The above mentioned villages belong to the area of the Western dialect; the last speakers of Eastern Vote, in Icipino (Itšäpäivä), died probably in the 1960s, and those of the distinct, Ingrian-influenced dialect of Kurovitsy (Kukkusi) in the 1980s. All modern idiolects are heavily influenced by Ingrian, Finnish and Russian. Nearly extinct. – An outlying dialect known as *Krevin*, originally spoken by prisoners captured in the fifteenth century, survived in the territory of present-day Latvia until the early nineteenth century.

Walloon **[75]** In Belgium, Walloon is spoken in the greater part of the province of Liège, in the southern part of the province of Brabant, in the province of Namur, in the northern part of the province of Luxemburg and in the eastern part of the province of Hainaut by an estimated 600,000 people, although the number of active speakers may be half that number. In France, it is spoken in the north of the department of Ardennes (town of Givet) by a small number of people, mostly elderly. In Luxembourg, it was formerly spoken in two or three villages (Doncols, Sonlez), where the last speakers died in the 1970s. In Belgium, a number of children learn the language, but many are likely to shift entirely to French. Increasingly endangered in Belgium; severely endangered in France; extinct in Luxemburg.

Western Mansi **[26]** Siberia: formerly spoken in the region of the source rivers of the Tavda, a tributary to the lower Tobol'-Irtysh, within Ivdel' and Gari counties in Yekaterinburg Province in the Russian Federation. Dialects included Pelym Mansi, Middle and Lower Loz'va Mansi and Vagil'sk Mansi. There are probably no speakers left, but when the last ones died is not known. Possibly extinct.

Western Mari (often called ***Hill Mari*** after the largest dialect group) **[19]** Eastern Europe: east-central Russia. Spoken in westernmost parts of the Republic of Mariy-El and adjacent parts of Kirov (Vyatka) and Nizhniy Novgorod provinces in the Russian Federation. There are probably less than 50,000 speakers, including few children; cf. Eastern Mari; interference from Russian is generally stronger than in Eastern Mari. Definitely endangered.

Yazva Komi (Eastern Permyak). See ***Permyak***

Yiddish (or ***Judeo-German***) **[49]** the traditional language of Ashkenazi Jews, Yiddish was earlier spoken in large areas mainly in Eastern and East-Central Europe, but most speakers were murdered by Germans during the Second World War. Before the war, there were 11–12 million speakers, while in the 1960s, 4 million were estimated. In

Europe, Yiddish is currently spoken in a few places in Belarus and the Ukraine, as well as by a small number of individuals in Alsace, the Netherlands and Switzerland, and in Jewish Autonomous Province (capital Birobijan) in eastern Siberia in the Russian Federation. In 1989, 150,000 speakers were reported from the Soviet Union, but the number of actual users was probably much smaller. Most speakers now live in North America and Israel. More than 1,000,000 people in North America and approximately 200,000 in Israel have knowledge of Yiddish, and there are several communities where children still learn the language, but the general trend is alarming. Definitely endangered in Europe, increasingly endangered worldwide.

Yug (also called *Southern Ket* or *Sym Ket*; cf. Ket) **[175]** Siberia: originally spoken in the basins of the rivers Sym, Kas and Dubches, western tributaries to the middle Yenisey opposite to the Podkamennaya Tunguska, later in the villages of Vorogovo in Turukhansk County and Yartsevo in Yeniseysk County in Krasnoyarsk Region in the Russian Federation. There are probably no speakers left. Possibly extinct.

Yurt Tatar. See *Nogay*

Acknowledgements

I wish to express my gratitude to all colleagues of mine who have provided information for the purpose of this study, first to Juha Janhunen, whose work forms the basis of much of the Siberian and Manchurian data, and further to a large number of specialists, including Jarmo Alatalo (Selkup), Ole Stig Andersen (Ubykh), Lars-Göran Andersson (Dalecarlian), Viktor D. Atknine (Evenki), Peter Bakker (Romani and mixed languages), Mariana Bara (Istro-Romanian, Aromanian and Megleno-Romanian), Sarah Benor (Jewish languages), Martin Böhler (Tsakonian), Jørgen Giorgio Bosoni (Lombard), Wayles Browne (Rusyn, Vojvodina Rusyn), Juris Cibuls (Latgalian), Xavier F. Conde (Galician), Karen H. Ebert (North Frisian), Onno Falkena (West Frisian), Andrei Filtchenko (languages of western Siberia), A. N. Garkavec (Urum and other Turkic languages), Luís Gomes (Asturian-Leonese), Godehard Gottwald (Sorbian), Ekaterina Gruzdeva (Nivkh), Reinhard F. Hahn (Low Saxon and Plautdietsch, Sorbian, languages of Sinkiang), Mikko Hakalin (Cypriot Arabic, Karaim, Old Prussian), Panu Hallamaa (Eskimo-Aleut and Finnic), K. David Harrison (Chulym Turk, Dukha, and Tofa), Christian Heinen (Luxemburgian), Eugene Helimski (Enets and Nganasan), Lorint Hendschel (Walloon), Katalin Henriksson (Csángó Hungarian), Davyth Hicks (Cornish, Manx), Stephanie Hughes (Rhenish Franconian), Geraint Jennings (Jersey French), Seth Jerchower (Italkian and other Jewish languages), George Jochnowitz (Jewish languages), Thede Kahl (Megleno-Romanian), Timo Kalmu (languages of eastern Siberia and northern China), Paweł Kąsk (Kashubian), Olga Kazakevitch (Selkup and other Siberian languages), Aleksandr E. Kibrik (Alutor), Tomas Kindahl (Rusyn), Olavi Korhonen (Saami in Scandinavia), Iacovos Koumi (Cypriot Greek), Lars-Gunnar Larsson (Saami in Scandinavia), Larisa Leisiö (Nganasan), Marina Lublinskaya (Tundra Nenets and Nganasan), Walter Lupani (Germanic in Italy), Kaur Mägi (Forest Nenets), Peter Mansfield (Tsakonian), Kazuto Matsumura (languages of the Russian Federation), Lars Narvselius (Scanian), Nick Nicholas (Hellenic languages and languages of Greece), Ilia Nikolaev (Ingrian), Irina Nikolaeva (Udege), Karl Pajusalu (Võro-Seto), Annika Pasanen (Inari Saami and Karelian), Gabriela Popa (Megleno-Romanian), Raija Pyöli (Olonetsian), Elisabetta Ragagnin (Dukha), Leif Rantala (Saami in Kola Peninsula), Torkel Rasmussen (Saami), Gabriele Romagnoli (Molise Croatian), Esa-Jussi Salminen (Udmurt), Gábor Sandi (Francoprovençal), Elena K. Skribnik (Buryat), Sven-Erik Soosaar (Tundra Nenets), Han Steenwijk (Resian Slovene), Jan-Olof Svantesson (Mongolic languages), Jon Todal (Saami), Eva Toulouze (Forest Nenets), Tom Trier (Rusyn), Manuel Trinidad (Extremaduran), Trond Trosterud (languages of Scandinavia), Nikolai Vakhtin (Siberian languages), Philippe Verdy (Gallo), Tiit-Rein Viitso (Livonian, Vote), Dusan Vitanovics (Rusyn), Chris Wilson (Cornish), David Wilson (Scots), Peter Wiens (Plautdietsch), and Birger Winsa (Torne Valley Finnish). I also wish to thank all the other scholars who have helped me with more general problems connected with this study, notably Daniel Abondolo, Florian Blaschke, David Bradley, Lyle Campbell, Paul Fryer, Victor Golla, Riho Grünthal, Joachim Otto Habeck, Michael E. Krauss, Jarel Kuga de Deaton, Ulla-Maija Kulonen, Ago Künnap, Ariadna I. Kuznecova, Jouni Maho, Lubor Mojdl, Nicholas Ostler, Donall Ó Riagain, Merja Salo, Pekka Sammallahti, Tove Skutnabb-Kangas, Seppo Suhonen, and the late Larry Trask and Stephen A. Wurm. Obviously, none of the above mentioned should be held responsible for any errors found in this presentation.

277

Bibliography

Arctic languages: an awakening (1990) ed. Dirmid R. F. Collis, Paris: Unesco.

Atlas of the world's languages (1994) general eds Christopher Moseley and R. E. Asher, London and New York: Routledge.

Atlas of the world's languages in danger of disappearing, 2nd edn, revised, enlarged and updated (2001) ed. Stephen A. Wurm, cartographer Ian Heyward, Paris: Unesco.

Campbell, Lyle (1998) *Historical linguistics: an introduction*, Edinburgh: Edinburgh University Press.

The Celtic languages (1993) ed. Martin J. Ball with James Fife, London: Routledge.

Comrie, Bernard (1981) *The languages of the Soviet Union*, Cambridge: Cambridge University Press.

The dialects of Italy (1997) eds Martin Maiden and Mair Parry, London: Routledge.

Encyclopedia of the languages of Europe (1998) ed. Glanville Price, Oxford and Malden: Blackwell.

Endangered languages (1991) eds Robert H. Robins and Eugenius M. Uhlenbeck, Oxford and New York: Berg.

Ethnologue: languages of the world, 13th edn (1996) ed. Barbara F. Grimes, Dallas TX: Summer Institute of Linguistics.

FEL II = *Endangered languages: what role for the specialist? Proceedings of the Second FEL Conference* (1998) ed. Nicholas Ostler, Edinburgh: Foundation for Endangered Languages.

FEL III = *Endangered languages and education: Proceedings of the Third FEL Conference* (1999) ed. Nicholas Ostler, Maynooth: Foundation for Endangered Languages.

FEL IV = *Endangered languages and literacy: Proceedings of the Fourth FEL Conference* (2000) eds Nicholas Ostler and Blair Rudes, Charlotte: Foundation for Endangered Languages.

Forbescue, Michael (2005) *Comparative Chukotko-kamchatkan dictionary*, Trends in Linguistics: Documentation 23, Berlin and New York: Mouton de Gruyter.

Gamkrelidze, Thomas V. and Vjačeslav V. Ivanov (1995) *Indo-European and the Indo-Europeans: a reconstruction and historical analysis of a proto-language and a proto-culture*, Trends in Linguistics: Studies and Monographs 80, Berlin and New York: Mouton de Gruyter.

The Germanic languages (1994) eds Ekkehard König and Johan van der Auwera, London: Routledge.

Germanische Rest- und Trümmersprachen (1989) ed. Heinrich Beck, Ergänzungsbände zum Reallexikon der germanischen Altertumskunde 3, Berlin: de Gruyter.

Grenoble, Lenore A. and Lindsay J. Whaley (2003) 'The case for dialect continua in Tungusic: plural morphology', in *Current trends in Caucasian, East European and Inner Asian linguistics: papers in honor of Howard I. Aronson*, eds Dee Ann Holisky and Kevin Tuite, Current Issues in Linguistic Theory 246, Amsterdam and Philadelphia: John Benjamins, 97–122.

Haiman, John and Paola Benincà (1992) *The Rhaeto-Romance languages*, London and New York: Routledge.

Häkkinen, Kaisa (1984) 'Wäre es schon an der Zeit, den Stammbaum zu fällen?' *Ural-Altaische Jahrbücher*, Neue Folge 4: 1–24.

Hindley, Reg (1990) *The death of the Irish language*, London and New York: Routledge.

Janhunen, Juha (1991) 'Ethnic death and survival in the Soviet North', *Journal de la Société Finno-Ougrienne* 83: 111–22.

——(1996) *Manchuria: an ethnic history*, Mémoires de la Société Finno-Ougrienne 222, Helsinki.

——(2004) 'Tungusic: an endangered language family in Northeast Asia', *International Journal of the Sociology of Language* 170: 25–38.

Jazyki mira: tjurkskie jazyki (1997) Moskva: Indrik.

Jazyki mira: mongol'skie jazyki, tunguso-man'čžurskie jazyki, japonskij jazyk, korejskij jazyk (1997) Moskva: Indrik.

Jazyki mira: paleoaziatskie jazyki (1997) Moskva: Indrik.

Jazyki mira: ural'skie jazyki (1993) Moskva: Nauka.

Jazyki narodov SSSR I: *Indoevropejskie jazyki* (1966) general ed. V. V. Vinogradov, Moskva: Nauka.

Jazyki narodov SSSR II: *Tjurkskie jazyki* (1966) general ed. N. A. Baskakov, Moskva: Nauka.

Jazyki narodov SSSR III: *Finno-ugorskie i samodijskie jazyki* (1966) general eds V. I. Lytkin and K. E. Majtinskaja, Moskva: Nauka.

Jazyki narodov SSSR IV: *Iberijsko-kavkazskie jazyki* (1967) general eds E. A. Bokarev and K. V. Lomtatidze, Moskva: Nauka.

Jazyki narodov SSSR V: *Mongol'skie, tunguso-man'čžurskie i paleoaziatskie jazyki* (1968) general ed. P. Ja. Skorik, Leningrad: Nauka.

Jazyki Rossijskoj Federacii i sosednix gosudarstv: ènciklopedija I: *A–I* (1997) Moskva: Nauka.

Jazyki Rossijskoj Federacii i sosednix gosudarstv: ènciklopedija II: *K–R* (2001) Moskva: Nauka.

Jazykovaja situacija v Rossijskoj Federacii: 1992 (1992) general eds V. M. Solncev and V. Ju. Mixal'čenko, Moscow [with a detailed English summary: The language situation in the Russian Federation: 1992].

König, Werner (2001) *dtv-Atlas Deutsche Sprache*, 13. durchgesehene Auflage, München: Deutscher Taschenbuch Verlag.

Krasnaja kniga jazykov narodov Rossii: ènciklopedičeskij slovar'-spravočnik (1994) ed. V. P. Neroznak, Moskva: Academia.

Lallukka, Seppo (1990) *The East Finnic minorities in the Soviet Union: an appraisal of the erosive trends*, Annales Academiæ Scientiarum Fennicæ B 252, Helsinki: Suomalainen Tiedeakatemia.

Language death and language maintenance: theoretical, practical and descriptive approaches (2003) eds Mark Janse and Sijmen Tol, Current Issues in Linguistic Theory 240, Amsterdam and Philadelphia: John Benjamins.

Languages in Britain and Ireland (2000) ed. Glanville Price, Oxford: Blackwell.

Lectures on language situation: Russia, Estonia, Finland (2002) ed. Kazuto Matsumura, ICHEL Linguistic Studies 6, Tokyo.

Lexikon der Romanistischen Linguistik I–VII (1988–2002) eds Günter Holtus, Michael Metzeltin and Christian Schmitt, Tübingen: Niemeyer.

Linguistic minorities in Central and Eastern Europe (1998) eds Christina Bratt Paulston and Donald Peckham, Multilingual matters 109, Clevedon: Multilingual Matters.

Matras, Yaroz (2002) *Romani: a linguistic introduction*, Cambridge: Cambridge University Press.

Minority languages today: a selection from the papers read at the first International conference on minority languages held at Glasgow University from 8 to 13 September 1980 (1981 [2nd edn 1990]) eds Einar Haugen, J. Derrick McClure and Derick Thomson, Edinburgh: Edinburgh University Press.

Minor languages of Europe: a series of lectures at the University of Bremen, April–July 2000 (2001) ed. Thomas Stolz, Bochum-Essener Beiträge zur Sprachwandelforschung 30, Bochum: Brockmeyer.

Mixed languages: 15 case studies in language intertwining (1994) eds Peter Bakker and Maarten Mous, Studies in language and language use 13, Amsterdam: IFOTT.

The Mongolic languages (2003) ed. Juha Janhunen, London and New York: Routledge.

Nichols, Johanna (2003) 'The Nakh-Daghestanian consonant correspondences', in *Current trends in Caucasian, East European and Inner Asian linguistics: papers in honor of Howard I. Aronson*, eds Dee Ann Holisky and Kevin Tuite, Current Issues in Linguistic Theory 246, Amsterdam and Philadelphia: John Benjamins, 207–64.

Northern minority languages: problems of survival (1997) eds Hiroshi Shoji and Juha Janhunen, Senri Ethnological Studies 44, Osaka: National Museum of Ethnology.

Philologiae Turcicae Fundamenta I (1959) eds Jean Deny, Kaare Grønbech, Helmuth Scheel and Zeki Velidi Togan, Wiesbaden: Steiner.

Podolsky, Baruch (1985a) 'Notes on the Urum language', *Mediterranean Language Review* 2: 99–112.

——(1985b) 'Notes on the Urum (Greek-Tatar) language', *Rocznik orientalistyczny* 44: 59–66.

Pogarell, Reiner (1983) *Minority languages in Europe: a classified bibliography*, Berlin: Mouton.

Posner, Rebecca (1996) *The Romance languages*, Cambridge: Cambridge University Press.

The Romance languages (1988) eds Martin Harris and Nigel Vincent, London: Croom Helm.

Rybatzki, Volker (1994) 'Xinjiang im 19. und 20. Jahrhundert', *Journal de la Société Finno-Ougrienne* 85: 149–82.

Salminen, Tapani (2003) 'Languages, language boundaries and language communities in Europe and beyond', in *I Seminari Internacional de Llengües Minoritaries: ponencies i comunicacions = Ist International Seminar on Lesser Used Languages: proceedings*, ed. Angel V. Calpe Climent, Serie Filologica 26, Valencia: Real Academia de Cultura Valenciana, 53–62.

Schönig, Claus (1997–8) 'A new attempt to classify the Turkic languages' (1–3), *Turkic Languages* 1 (1997): 117–33, 262–77; 2 (1998): 130–51.

Sibille, Jean (2000) *Les langues régionales*, Dominos 220, Paris: Flammarion.

The Slavonic languages (1993) eds Bernard Comrie and Greville G. Corbett, London: Routledge.

The Turkic languages (1998) eds Lars Johanson and Éva Á. Csató, London: Routledge.

The Uralic languages (1998) ed. Daniel Abondolo, London and New York: Routledge.

The Uralic languages: description, history and foreign influences (1988) ed. Denis Sinor, Handbuch der Orientalistik 8: Handbook of Uralic studies 1, Leiden: Brill.

Vajda, Edward J. (2003) 'Tone and phoneme in Ket', in *Current trends in Caucasian, East European and Inner Asian linguistics: papers in honor of Howard I. Aronson*, eds Dee Ann Holisky and Kevin Tuite, Current Issues in Linguistic Theory 246, Amsterdam and Philadelphia: John Benjamins, 393–418.

Vakhtin = Vaxtin, Nikolaj (1993) *Korennoe naselenie Krajnego Severa Rossijskoj Federacii*, Sankt-Peterhburg: Izdatel'stvo Evropejskogo Doma.

Vakhtin = Vaxtin, N. B. (2001) *Jazyki narodov Severa v XX veke: očerki jazykovogo sdviga*, Sankt-Peterhburg: Dmitrij Bulanin.

Vingt-cinq communautés linguistiques de la France 1: *Langues régionales et langues non territorialisées* (1988) Geneviève Vermes, Paris: L'Harmattan.

The world's major languages (1987) ed. Bernard Comrie, London and Sydney: Croom Helm.

Wurm, Stephen A. (1997) 'Two Turkic-based hybrid languages in northwestern China', *Turkic Languages* 1: 241–53.

Zhào Xiāngrú and Reinhard F. Hahn (1989) 'The Ili Turk people and their language', *Central Asiatic Journal* 33: 260–89.

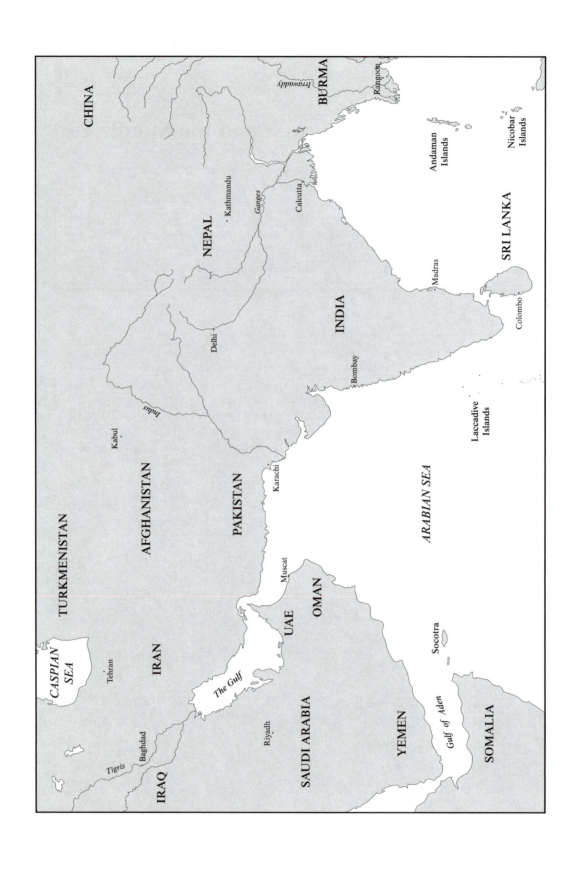

4

South Asia and the Middle East

George van Driem

South Asia is an ethnolinguistically inordinately complex portion of the planet. The topography of the greater Himalayan region has impeded migrations of peoples throughout prehistory. The result is an intricate patchwork of language phyla and language isolates enmeshed in a geographically complex pattern. Languages of the Altaic and Daic language families have encroached upon the periphery of the Himalayan region, whereas the Indian subcontinent is the home of Indo-European, Dravidian, Tibeto-Burman and Austroasiatic languages. Moreover, South Asia is the home to the language isolates Andamanese, Nahali, Kusunda and Vedda. Burushaski, which was traditionally viewed as a language isolate, but has been shown to be a member of the Karasuk language family, is distantly related to the Yenisseian languages.

The Indo-European family tree of *Stammbaum* has traditionally been emblematic of comparative linguistics. The family tree model is still a valid model of linguistic phylogeny, particularly with all of the qualifications and nuances which were already explicitly formulated from the earliest days of historical linguistics and later enhanced in the writings of *Junggrammatiker*, though these nuances have often been ignored by laymen as well as some linguists. Yet even the Indo-European family tree has come to look less like a tree today and increasingly resembles a bed of flowers sprouting forth from a common primordial substrate, despite the recognition of higher-order branches such as Indo-Iranian, Balto-Slavic and Italo-Celtic. Below family trees will be depicted of the three major language families which are either wholly or largely confined to the Indian subcontinent and the greater Himalayan region, namely Tibeto-Burman, Austroasiatic and Dravidian.

A situation exists in Tibeto-Burman which is comparable with the Indo-European model in that a number of higher-order groupings have been proposed, such as Sino-Bodic, but these will not be discussed here. Instead, the most empirically defensible picture of the language family is represented as a patch of fallen leaves on the forest floor, rather than as a tree. At the present state of the art, the branches of the tree cannot yet be clearly discerned, but the 'leaves' or subgroups which have fallen from the Tibeto-Burman tree have finally all been identified. As hitherto undescribed languages become grammatically and lexically documented in ever greater detail, we can begin to make out the shadows which the branches of the family tree cast between the leaves on the forest floor. This picture of Tibeto-Burman is represented in Figure 4.1.

In Figure 4.1, this patch of leaves on the forest floor has fallen from a single tree, which we know as Tibeto-Burman. We cannot see the branches of the tree, but we are beginning to see the shadows they cast between the leaves on the forest floor. This schematic geographical representation provides an informed but agnostic picture of Tibeto-Burman subgroups. The extended version of the Brahmaputran hypothesis

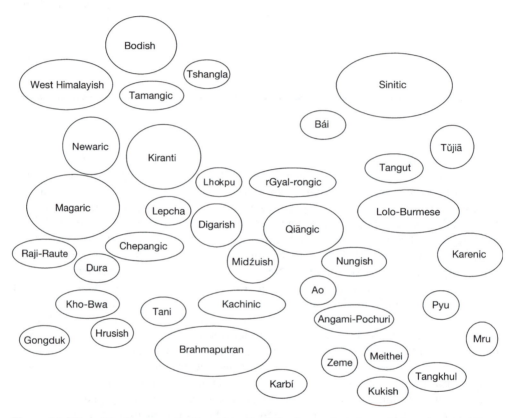

Figure 4.1 This patch of leaves on the forest floor has fallen from a single tree, which we know as Tibeto-Burman. We cannot see the branches of the tree, but we are beginning to see the shadows they cast between the leaves on the forest floor. This schematic geographical representation provides an informed but agnostic picture of Tibeto-Burman subgroups. The extended version of the Brahmaputran hypothesis includes Kachinic, but for the sake of argument this diagram depicts the short variant of Brahmaputran, viz. excluding Kachinic. Kachinic comprises the Sak languages and the Jinghpaw dialects. Likewise, Tangut is separately depicted, although Tangut is likely to be part of Qiāngic. Digarish is Northern Mishmi, and Midźuish is Southern Mishmi, i.e. the Kaman cluster. Bái is listed as a distinct group, whereas it may form a constituent of Sinitic, albeit one heavily influenced by Lolo-Burmese. Tǔjiā is a heavily sinicised Tibeto-Burman language of indeterminate phylogenetic propinquity spoken by about three million people in an area which straddles the provinces of Sìchuān, Húběi, Húnán and Guìzhōu. The Sino-Bodic hypothesis encompasses at least the groups called Sinitic, Kiranti, Bodish, West Himalayish, rGyal-rongic, Tamangic, Tshangla and Lhokpu and possibly Lepcha. Other hypotheses, such as the inclusion of Chepang and perhaps Dura and Raji-Raute within Magaric, are discussed in the handbook (van Driem 2001).

includes Kachinic, but for the sake of argument this diagram depicts the short variant of Brahmaputran, i.e. excluding Kachinic. Kachinic comprises the Sak languages and the Jinghpaw dialects. Likewise, Tangut is separately depicted, although Tangut is likely to be part of Qiāngic. Digarish is Northern Mishmi, and Midźuish is Southern Mishmi, i.e. the Kaman cluster. Bái is listed as a distinct group, whereas it may form a constituent of Sinitic, albeit one heavily influenced by Lolo-Burmese. Tŭjiā is a heavily sinicised Tibeto-Burman language of indeterminate phylogenetic propinquity spoken by about 3 million people in an area which straddles the provinces of Sìchuān, Húběi, Húnán and Guìzhōu. The Sino-Bodic hypothesis encompasses at least the groups called Sinitic, Kiranti, Bodish, West Himalayish, rGyal-rongic, Tamangic, Tshangla and Lhokpu and possibly Lepcha. Other hypotheses, such as the inclusion of Chepang and perhaps Dura and Raji-Raute within Magaric, are discussed in the handbook (van Driem 2001).

Unlike Indo-European, the original Tibeto-Burman theory of language relationship was for a time eclipsed by other fanciful theoretical language families, which have since been shown to be without a sound empirical basis. These are the defunct 'Turanian' family and the obsolete 'Indo-Chinese' or 'Sino-Tibetan' family. The field has now returned to the original Tibeto-Burman model, which is defined as the family of languages comprising Tibetan, Burmese and Chinese and all languages which can be demonstrated to be genetically related to these three languages (Figures 4.2 and 4.3).

Currently, the most informed and authoritative Austroasiatic *Stammbaum* is the language family tree presented by Diffloth (2001, 2005), reproduced here. In Figure 4.2, the Austroasiatic family tree is presented with a tentative calibration of time depths for the various branches of the language family (Diffloth 2001, 2005). The precise phylogenetic propinquity of Pearic, after Khmeric loan layers have been stripped off, remains uncertain except that Diffloth observes that Pearic is Mon-Khmer and not 'une espèce de vieux khmèr', as earlier scholars once maintained. This diagram arranges in a tree-shaped phylogeny the fourteen recognised branches of Austroasiatic, i.e. North Munda, South Munda, Khasian, Pakanic, Palaungic, Khmuic, Vietic, Katuic, Bahnaric, Khmeric, Pearic, Monic, Aslian and Nicobarese.

Austroasiatic splits up into three major nodes, i.e. Munda, Khasi-Khmuic and a new 'Mon-Khmer'. In this new tripartite division, Munda is still one of the primary branches of Austroasiatic, representing the native heart of the Indian subcontinent. The Khasi-Khmuic branch represents 'Inland Austroasiatic', and a more precisely delineated Mon-Khmer represents 'Littoral Austroasiatic'. The new Mon-Khmer comprises Khmero-Vietic and Nico-Monic. Each of the two sub-branches of Mon-Khmer is further subdivided, with Nico-Monic consisting of Asli-Monic and Nicobarese, and Khmero-Vietic breaking up into Vieto-Katuic and Khmero-Bahnaric. The greatest genetic affinity of Pearic is not with the Munda or Khasi-Khmuic branches, but with Mon-Khmer. A comparable picture is available of the structure and subgrouping of the Dravidian language family. One of the better informed family trees is depicted in Figure 4.3. Yet the view diagrammed here is not the only version of the Dravidian language family, and some specialists prefer instead to group Brahui, Malto, Kurukh and perhaps Koraga together within a single North Dravidian branch.

In Figure 4.3, the family tree of the Zagrosian or Elamo-Dravidian language family as envisaged by McAlpin (1981) represents the theory that the Dravidian languages are genetically related to Elamite. Another widely held view of the Dravidian language family groups Brahui, Malto, Kurukh and perhaps Koraga together in a single North Dravidian branch.

The rugged alpine topography of the Himalayas has made the Indian subcontinent the ethnolinguistically most complex area in the world, rivalled only by New Guinea. In terms of antiquity of human habitation, one would expect Africa to be ethnolinguistically more complex, but much ancient diversity on the Dark Continent has in fact been wiped out by subsequent linguistic dispersals, such as the Bantu expansion. The inaccessibility of many recesses within the Himalayas and the remoteness of

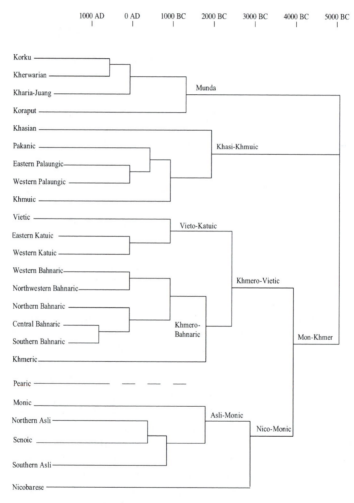

Figure 4.2 Austroasiatic with Gérard Diffloth's tentative calibration of time depths for the various branches of the language family (modified from Diffloth 2001, 2005). The precise phylogenetic propinquity of Pearic, after Khmeric loan layers have been stripped off, remains uncertain except that Diffloth observes that Pearic is Mon-Khmer and not 'une espèce de vieux khmèr', as earlier scholars once maintained. This diagram arranges in a tree-shaped phylogeny the fourteen recognised branches of Austroasiatic, i.e. North Munda, South Munda, Khasian, Pakanic, Palaungic, Khmuic, Vietic, Katuic, Bahnaric, Khmeric, Pearic, Monic, Aslian and Nicobarese.

286

insular habitats such as the Andamans have shielded many older language groups and strata of population from assimilation and extinction. However, with the advent of modern mobility, telecommunications and the rampant destruction of natural habitats, these lesser disturbed pieces of the puzzle of population prehistory have suddenly become highly exposed to socio-economic upheavals on an unprecedented scale.

Not only can ideas and memes go extinct, but entire conceptualisations of reality are wiped off the map when languages go extinct. Many languages of South Asia have become extinct in documented history. For example, Pyu is an extinct Tibeto-Burman language of the Irrawaddy basin in what today is Burma. The language had an epigraphic tradition which endured well into the twelfth century. The Pyu had an advanced Bronze Age culture and system of rice agriculture until they were overrun by the Burmese and other groups. Numerous languages have gone the way of Pyu. Rangkas was recorded in the Western Himalayas as recently as the beginning of the twentieth century, but is now extinct. August Schleicher wrongly believed that the survival and extinction of languages was characterised by 'die Erhaltung der höher entwickelten Organismen im Kampfe ums Dasein' (1863: 28). However, the survival of individual languages is primarily determined by factors which have nothing to do with their intrinsic worth as a system for the articulation of human thought, but by economic, ecological and demographic factors affecting the individual language communities. The success of one language in outcompeting another has little or, in some cases, nothing to do with its grammatical propensities or lexical richness and refinement. Instead, the extinction of a language is a function of the histories of peoples, regions and language communities.

In addition to the socio-economic and demographic changes which cause language communities to assimilate to larger, often more exploitative groups, there are also trends and fashions within the linguistic establishment that impede the documentation of endangered languages. The most obvious has been the detrimental influence of

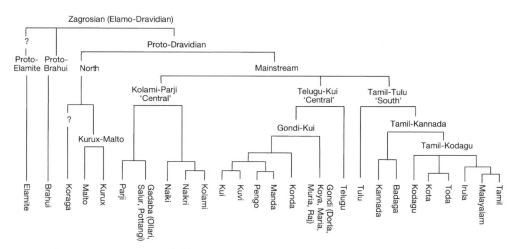

Figure 4.3 The family tree of the Zagrosian or Elamo-Dravidian language family as envisaged by McAlpin (1981) represents the theory that the Dravidian languages are genetically related to Elamite. Another widely held view of the Dravidian language family groups Brahui, Malto, Kurukh and perhaps Koraga together in a single North Dravidian branch.

287

Chomskyite formalism on the field of linguistics as a whole since the 1960s, leading to vast amounts of public and private funding and human resources being channelled away from research on languages. More recently, some funding bodies have undertaken to prescribe codes of conduct or research regimens. Linguists have been working on endangered languages for many decades, but now that 'endangered languages' has become a buzz phrase, there is also suddenly no shortage of people who would tell these linguists how precisely to go about conducting their work.

Where linguists have previously been working effectively, ethically and constructively with native language communities, now they will have to conduct their work with the meddlesome prompting of people sitting on the sideline. The codes of conduct currently being drafted have generally been inspired by the extreme situation which exists in North America and Australia, where colonial European populations have on a grand scale wiped out native peoples along with the languages they once spoke, and in their place set up modern Western societies with litigious Anglo-Saxon legal customs. The situation on the ground is already utterly different from one Asian country to the next. Therefore, codes of conduct inspired by the situation in North America and Australia are singularly inappropriate in other parts of the world. In practice, codes of conduct are more than superfluous, for they can actually hamper sound and ethical field research.

In a similar vein, in addition to conventional grammatical analysis and lexical documentation, it is helpful to document a language in the form of an audio recording. In fact, I have never met a field linguist who did not do this as a matter of course. Yet it serves no purpose to prescribe a format of audiovisual documentation to which the fieldworker must adhere in order to be eligible for funding. Recruiting a capable field linguist willing to document endangered languages is already a big challenge. Most people trained in linguistics are either not up to the task or unwilling to suffer the discomfort or brave the dangers involved. Putting extra hurdles in place, however well intentioned, merely obstructs the documentation of what remains of humankind's endangered linguistic heritage.

Endangered language isolates of the Indian subcontinent

Each of the languages endangered with extinction discussed in this section represent so-called language isolates, i.e. languages which have not been demonstrated to belong to any other major language family or linguistic phylum. There is a theory connecting the Nahali language to Austroasiatic, although even this theory recognises that Nahali, if Austroasiatic, would constitute the only representative of its own distinct major branch of this large linguistic phylum. The Karasuk theory, advanced by myself on the basis of specific morphological evidence, holds that Burushaski forms a language family together with the Yenisseian languages.

Andamanese languages

All native languages spoken by the indigenous negrito peoples of the Andaman Islands are either extinct or threatened with imminent extinction. As a result of British colonial policies, just three of over a dozen native languages of the Andamans were driven extinct, along with the people who spoke them. The three surviving

Andamanese languages are Önge, spoken on Little Andaman, Sentinelese, spoken on North Sentinel Island, and Jarawa, spoken in the interior of South Andaman. The 1981 census enumerated thirty-one speakers of Jarawa, ninety-seven speakers of Önge, and a comparably small Sentinelese language community holding out on Sentinel Island. No reliable recent data are available. Historically the Andamanese used to give outsiders visiting the islands a hostile reception, but in view of their tragic history the prompt slaying of outsiders was in retrospect the best policy that the Andamanese could have had. Since the beginning of the twentieth century, Urdu or Hindi had established itself as the dominant language because it was the *lingua franca* between the inmates of the penal colony established on the Andamans by the government of British India. Today Bengali, Tamil, Malayalam and Telugu are also significant minority languages spoken by the colonists who have settled the islands.

Vedda

The earliest Western account of the aboriginal Veddas of Ceylon and their language was written by Ryklof van Goens of the Dutch East India Company in 1675. Subsequently most Veddas were assimilated by the Tamil and Sinhalese speaking populations of the island, both linguistically and through acculturation and intermarriage. Policies implemented by the Ceylonese government in the 1950s and 1960s led to the displacement, fracturing and impoverishment of the last remaining Vedda language communities. The individuals who survived the devastation of their communities have been absorbed into modern Sinhalese society in terms of both lifestyle and language. It is not known whether there are still any surviving speakers of the original, albeit heavily Indo-Aryanised Vedda language, but the places to look would be at the Mahaweli Vedda Settlement Area at Hennanigala on the Kudu Oya, or in isolated households around either Dambana or Polonnaruwa. The Rodiya language, another language of Ceylon, is almost certainly extinct.

Nahali

The Nahali are mainly settled in and around the Gawilgarh Hills south of the Tapti river in Nimar and Ellichpur Districts of Madhya Pradesh, especially around the village of Tembi 40km east of Burhanpur. The Gawilgarh Hills form part of the Vindhya and Satpuḍā chain, which separates the Deccan Plateau from the Gangetic plain. There are less than 2,000 speakers of Nahali. The Nahali language – also written as Nihali or Nehali – has been heavily influenced by the Austroasiatic language Korku. It should be possible to do fieldwork using Hindi as the contact language.

Kusunda

Kusunda is the language of an ancient aboriginal relict group of Nepal. The four remaining Kusunda clans, which designated themselves by the Indo-Aryan names of Siṃha, Śān, Śāhī and Khān, split up in the middle of the twentieth century. Kusunda speakers could still be found in the 1960s and 1970s, but the remaining Kusunda are generally individuals which have married into a sedentary agriculturalist community. Several individuals are known to remember the language of their parents, though none speak Kusunda as the language of daily communication. Individual Kusunda are known to be found around Damaulī and near Gorkhā in central Nepal as well as further west in Dāṅg and Surkhet. For those interested in finding the last speakers, more detailed clues and reports on their possible whereabouts are given in my handbook (van Driem 2001).

Burushaski

Burushaski is spoken in the high alpine valleys of Hunza-Nager and Yasin in northern Pakistan by about 80,000 people who call themselves *Burúšo* and their language *Burúšaski*. Some 50,000 Burúsho live in Hunza and Nager and some 30,000 live in Yasin. A considerable Burúsho population has also settled in Gilgit itself. The Burúsho area is surrounded on all sides by tracts of land where Iranian, Indo-Aryan, Turkic and Tibetan languages are spoken. The Burúsho for centuries enjoyed a high degree of local autonomy. In 1891, Hunza was conquered by the British after a bloody three-day struggle, and in 1947 the region became part of Pakistan. In 1972 President Bhutto abolished the autonomous Nager kingdom, and in 1974 the kingdom of Hunza was abolished. Between 1964 and 1968 the Karakoram highway was built, which has rendered the area easily accessible to outsiders. In addition to many older Ṣiṇā loans, Burushaski has become swamped with Urdu and English loan words. Bilingualism has led to the attrition of native morphosyntactic complexity in the speech of the younger generation. In 1992, Hermann Berger predicted that at the present rate of assimilation the language would be fully extinct within several decades.

Endangered Austroasiatic languages of the Indian subcontinent

The Austroasiatic language family is the most ancient linguistic phylum of mainland South and Southeast Asia. With the exception of the four languages Khmer, Vietnamese, Khasi and Santhali, each of the over two hundred Austroasiatic languages is threatened with extinction. Even the Mon language, which has an epigraphic and literary tradition dating back to the seventh century, is threatened with imminent extinction. The Austroasiatic languages of South Asia are the Nicobarese languages of the Nicobar Islands, Khasi and the Munda languages of the Indian subcontinent.

Nicobarese languages

Over 20,000 people presently inhabit the Nicobar Islands, but not all of these speak a native language of the Nicobar Islands. The precise linguistic situation on the Nicobars is currently kept hidden from the scrutiny of foreign scholars by the Indian government. The names and locations of the language communities are known, however. Pû is spoken on Car Nicobar Island, Tatet on Chowra Island, Taihlong on Teressa Island, Powahat on Bompoka Island, Nancowry on the islands of Nancowry and Camorta, Lâfûl on Trinkut Island, Téhñu on Katchall Island, Lo'ong along the coast of Great Nicobar Island, Ong on Little Nicobar Island, Lâmongshé at Condul, and Miloh at Milo. The language Shompen, the most aberrant and idiosyncratic of the Nicobarese languages, constitutes a group unto itself. Shompen is spoken in the hinterland of

Great Nicobar Island by the Shompen tribe. The 1981 census enumerated 223 members of the Shompen tribe.

South Munda languages

The Munda languages are divided into a southern and a northern branch. Despite the large number of speakers of a few of the Munda languages, bilingualism is widespread. At the present breakneck speed of assimilation, most Munda languages will not survive to the end of this century. All Munda language communities are under heavy demographic and socio-economic pressure to assimilate linguistically to the local Indo-Aryan majority language. We shall turn to the South Munda languages first. Juang has approximately 17,000 speakers in the Kyonjhar and Dhekānāl districts of Orissa. The Kharia dialects have over 190,000 speakers, concentrated mainly in the Choṭā Nāgpur, especially in Rāñcī district of Bihar, and in scattered communities in Orissa, West Bengal, Bihar, Assam and Madhya Pradesh. The language known variously as Sora, Saora or Savara has over 300,000 speakers in the Korāpuṭ and Gañjām districts of southern Orissa and in neighbouring parts of Andhra Pradesh. Pareng or Gorum is spoken by approximately 10,000 people in Nandpur and Poṭṭangī tālukā in Korāpuṭ. Remo or Bonda has approximately 2,500 speakers in the Jayapur hills of Korāpuṭ. Gutob or Sodia (also known as Gadaba, but not to be confused with the Dravidian language also named Gadaba) has just over 40,000 speakers in Kalāhāṇḍī, Korāpuṭ, Viśākhāpaṭnam and Bastar districts. The language known as Geta?, Gta?, Dideyi or Didam has about 3,000 speakers in the hills and plains on either side of the Sileru river in East Godāvarī district of Andhra Pradesh.

North Munda languages

Santhali or Santali is the only Munda language community with millions of speakers that may be large and resilient enough to resist the forces of linguistic assimilation in the course of the present century. Korku, the westernmost Munda language, has approximately 200,000 speakers in southwestern Madhya Pradesh and neighbouring parts of Maharashtra, especially in the Satpuḍā range and Mahādev hills. The diverse Muṇḍārī or Horo dialects, including Hasada?, Naguri, Latar and Kera?, together have approximately 750,000 speakers in the districts Rāñcī, Siṃhabhūm, Manbhūm, Hazārībāg and Palāmū of Bihar and in northern Madhya Pradesh and Orissa. Ho or Kol has just over 400,000 speakers in Siṃhabhūm district in Bihar. Bhumij may have as many as 150,000 speakers in scattered communities in Bihar, Orissa and Madhya Pradesh. The language of the semi-nomadic Birhor is moribund, with less than two thousand speakers in Siṃhabhūm, southern Palāmū, southern Hazārībāg, and northern and northeastern Rāñcī. The Koḍa dialects, which have been utterly neglected by scholars and evangelists alike, are spoken by about 25,000 people in scattered enclaves throughout the Choṭā Nāgpur. Turi is spoken by several thousand people living as small artisanal groups in West Bengal, Palāmū, Rāñcī, Siṃhabhūm, Rāygaḍh and Chattīsgaḍh. The Asur dialects count some 7,000 speakers on the Netarhaṭ plateau in southern Palāmū and northern Rāñcī as well as further south around Gumlā. The dialects collectively referred to as Korwa, Koroa or Ernga together have over 35,000 speakers in the Jaśpurnagar tahsil of Rāygaḍh district and in Sargujā district of Madhya Pradesh and in Palāmū and Hazārībāg districts of Bihar.

Endangered Dravidian languages of the Indian subcontinent

Other than the four major Dravidian languages Kanarese, Tamil, Malayalam and Telugu, most minor Dravidian languages are spoken by small tribes and have not been systematically committed to writing. Kanarese, Tamil and Malayalam are South Dravidian languages. Telugu is the only Central Dravidian language not threatened with extinction.

South Dravidian languages

Iruḷa, Toda, Kota and Badaga are minor South Dravidian languages spoken in the Nilgiri Hills in the west of Tamil Nadu. Of these Iruḷa, Toda and Kota are most closely related to Tamil and Malayalam, whereas Badaga can be said to be a major variant of Kannada. Iruḷa has only about 5,000 speakers. Kota and Toda are each spoken by about 1,000 people, Kota in the Kōttagiri portion of the Nilgiris, and Toda in the vicinity of Udagamaṇḍalam or 'Ootacamund', affectionately known as 'Ooty'. Although a close relative of Kota, Toda is aberrant and is said to have non-Dravidian features. Badaga has over 100,000 speakers. Another relative of Tamil and Malayalam is the Koḍagu language, spoken by about 100,000 speakers in the 'Coorg' or Koḍagu district of Karnataka in the vicinity of 'Mercara' city or Maḍkeri. Tuḷu is a totally distinct South Dravidian language with over a million speakers around the coastal city of Mangalore or Maṅgalūru and along the coast from Kāsargoḍu in Kerala up as far as North Kanarā district in Karnataka. Tuḷu is written in an adapted form of the Grantha script, like Malayalam, and schoolbooks and Bible translations have been printed in Tuḷu since 1842. The Kuruba language is spoken by the thousand or so members of the Betta-Kuruba tribe in the hilly parts of Coorg. The Betta-Kuruba tribe constitute merely one tenth of all ethnic Kuruba, for other Kuruba tribes have adopted Kannada. The Koraga and Bellari languages each have roughly 1,000 speakers in the area around Kuṇḍāpura or 'Coondapoor' and Uḍupi or 'Udipi' in South Kanarā district of Karnataka. The recently discovered Koraga language is spoken by untouchables who are bilingual in Kannada. Kurru (including Korava, Yerukula, Yerukala and Kaikudi) is spoken by an estimated 100,000 nomadic tribesmen in Andhra Pradesh and neighbouring portions of Karnataka and Tamil Nadu.

Central Dravidian languages

Central Dravidian comprises the minor languages of the Telugu-Kūi group (Gōṇḍi, Koṇḍa, Maṇḍa, Pengo, Kūvi and Kūi) and the Kolami-Parji group (Kolami, Naikri, Naiki, Gadaba and Parji). Over two million speakers of Gōṇḍi, who call themselves either *Kōi* or *Kōya,* live in scattered communities in Madhya Pradesh, Maharashtra, Orissa and the north of Andhra Pradesh. Koṇḍa or Kūbi is spoken by the more than 15,000 members of the Konda Dora tribe in the districts of Viśākhāpaṭnam and Śrīkākulam in Andhra Pradesh and the neighbouring district of Korāpuṭ in Orissa. Maṇḍa and Pengo are spoken in Korāpuṭ and Kalāhāṇḍī districts in Orissa by an estimated 1,500 speakers. The languages Kūi or Kū?i and Kūvi are spoken by more than half a million members of the Kondho (also Kondh, Kandh or Khond) tribes in Gañjām, Kalāhāṇḍī, Baudh-Kondhamāl and Korāpuṭ districts in Orissa and in Viśākhāpaṭnam district in Andhra Pradesh. Christian missionaries have printed religious tracts in Kūi and Kūvi using the Roman and Oriya scripts. Kolami is spoken by about 70,000 people in the hills of Yavatmāl and Vardhā districts in Maharashtra and in Adilābād district in Andhra Pradesh. An estimated 1,500 Yerku tribesmen in the hills of Canda district in Maharashtra speak the related language Naiki. There are roughly 50,000 speakers of Parji in Bastar district in Madhya Pradesh in the vicinity of Jagdalpur. In neighbouring Korāpuṭ district in Orissa, there are roughly 40,000 speakers of the various dialects of Gadaba, not to be confused with the Muṇḍā language of the same name, currently more usually called Gutob.

Northern Dravidian languages

The Northern Dravidian languages are all minor languages, i.e. Brahui, Malto and Kurukh. Brahui [brā?ūī] is spoken in Pakistan, mainly in Kalat and the adjacent districts of Hyderabad, Karachi and Khairpur, and in small communities in adjacent portions of Afghanistan and Iran. The language is spoken by about half a million members of the so-called indigenous Brahui tribes of the Kalat, the Sarawan tribes north of the Kalat and the Jhalawan tribes south of the Kalat. Brahui has been a written language for over three centuries, but a truly flourishing literary tradition has never developed. Brahui, like the Indo-Aryan language Urdu, is written in an adapted form of the Persian script. Traditionally, Brahui is considered to be either a separate branch of Dravidian or a member of North Dravidian alongside Malto and Kurukh. More than 100,000 people speak the Dravidian language of Malto, mainly in the Rājmahal Hills of central Bihar.

Kurukh, also written Kuṛux, and also known as Oraon or Uraon, is spoken by roughly 1.5 million speakers, mainly in the hill tracts of the Choṭā Nāgpur in the states of Bihar, Madhya Pradesh, Orissa and West Bengal but also in scattered communities elsewhere in these states and even as far east as Assam and as far north as the foot of the Himalayas in the eastern Nepalese Terai, where about 15,000 people speak the Dhangar and Jhangar dialect. There are also a few scattered Uraon settlements on the Indian side of the Indo-Bhutanese border at intervals from the area south of Samtsi in the west to the area south of Samdrup Jongkhar in the east. Moreover, scattered Uraon communities are found throughout Assam, where they are referred to as 'Adibasis', and so lumped together with the various linguistically unrelated Austroasiatic Muṇḍā groups with whom they share their geographical provenance and their dark, at times nearly negroid appearance. The term Ādivāsī used in northeastern India literally means 'aboriginal', but, ironically and confusingly, the groups thus designated are, in fact, not aboriginal to northeastern Indian, but aboriginal to the Choṭā Nāgpur.

Endangered languages of Bhutan and Sikkim

The contrast between Bhutan and Sikkim in terms of the language endangerment situation could not be greater. With the possible exception of Singapore, Bhutan is the most anglophone country in all of Asia. The position of English in education, government and daily life is such that even Dzongkha itself, the national language which is actively propagated by the Royal Government of Bhutan, occupies a precarious position alongside English. On the other hand, the Royal Government of Bhutan fosters a policy of studying, documenting and preserving the native languages of the country as part of the national cultural heritage. Sikkim, on the other hand, has been swamped by colonists from Nepal and lost sovereignty in 1975 when it was annexed by India. The indigenous population groups of Sikkim, the Lepcha and the Dränjop, have been reduced to a minority of less than 10 per cent in their own native homeland. Nepali, an allochthonous language, has expanded in Sikkim to the detriment of all native languages, and Nepali has also made inroads into Bhutan. In comparison with Sikkim and Nepal, the sociolinguistic situation in Bhutan is characterised by far greater stability. In Bhutan, languages under threat are faced with encroaching endangerment and gradual extinction, but not with the cataclysmic upheaval and immediate endangerment which threatens almost all of the native language communities of Nepal. The only exception is Lhokpu, the most endangered language in Bhutan, which is threatened by linguistic assimilation to the surrounding communities of Nepali colonists in southwestern Bhutan. Here too Nepali is spreading at the expense of a native language. The least endangered language in Bhutan is the Tshangla or Shâchop language. Tshangla is a Tibeto-Burman tongue which constitutes a subgroup in its own right, spoken by a highly robust language community native to the eastern part of the kingdom. A Tshangla dialect is also spoken in an enclave around Pemakö, further east on the Indo-Tibetan border.

South Bodish languages

The four South Bodish languages are Dzongkha, Dränjoke, J'umowa and Cho-ca-nga-ca-kha. Dzongkha is the national language of the kingdom of Bhutan, but is actually native to just eight out of twenty districts, all located in western Bhutan. Propagation of a standard form of the language highly influenced by the Classical Tibetan liturgical language or 'Chöke'. The preeminent role of English in Bhutan threatens Dzongkha even though there are an estimated 160,000 native speakers of the language. The normative influence of Chöke threatens authentic grassroots forms of Dzongkha.

The sister language of Dzongkha, Dränjoke, used to be the national language of the Kingdom of Sikkim. However, since before Sikkim was annexed by India in 1975, the land has been overwhelmed by a Nepali-speaking immigrant population which now constitutes over 90 per cent of the populace. As a result, young Dränjop are almost all raised in Nepali, and Dränjoke is now moribund.

J'umowa is spoken in the southernmost portion of the Chumbi valley, a sliver of former Sikkimese territory which was ceded to Tibet and is now wedged in between Sikkim and Bhutan. The Chumbi valley is known in Tibetan as Gro-mo or 'Dr'omo' and in Dzongkha as Gyu-mo or 'J'umo'. The English name for the Chumbi Valley is derived from the genitive adjectival form J'umbi, 'of or pertaining to the Chumbi valley'. Based on the Tibetan pronunciation of the valley, the language is also known as 'Tromowa' or 'Dr'omowa'. This language, only spoken in the lower portion of the valley, is now moribund. Cho-ca-nga-ca-kha is spoken by approximately 20,000 speakers in Monggar and Lhüntsi districts on both banks of the Kurichu. This language is under threat from Tshangla and Dzongkha. The closeness of Cho-ca-nga-ca-kha to Dzongkha means that assimilation to the Bhutanese national language is an easy process which involves the language being shorn of all its most interesting features, some of which are Kurichu linguistic substrate traits.

East Bodish languages

The East Bodish languages are the most archaic branch of Bodish, more conservative in some respects than Old Tibetan. East Bodish comprises Dakpa, Black Mountain, Bumthang, Kurtöp, Kheng, Nupbikha, 'Nyenkha, Dzala and Chali. Of these languages, four can be seen as dialects of a single Greater Bumthang language, i.e. Bumthang, Nupbikha, Kheng and Kurtöp. Yet all the other East Bodish languages are quite distinct, and their diversity reflects a great time depth. The particular language endangerment situation of Bhutan has already been discussed above in light of the country's relative sociolinguistic stability.

Bumthang is the native language of Bumthang district in central Bhutan, where four dialects of the language are spoken by an estimated 30,000 people. The dialect spoken in Trongsa is called Nupbikha 'language of the west', i.e. west of Bumthang. Kheng is the language of an estimated 40,000 people in Kheng district, now also known as Zh'ämgang, south of Bumthang in central Bhutan. Kurtöp is spoken by approximately 10,000 people in Lhüntsi district, to the west of the Kurichu all the way north to the Tibetan border. The Kurtöp area is therefore east of the Bumthang area, whilst the Kurichu separates the Kurtöp area from the Dzala language area of northeastern Bhutan.

The other East Bodish languages are all quite distinct languages. 'Nyenkha is also known as Henkha, but the most popular name is probably Mangdebi-kha because this highly divergent East Bodish language is spoken by an estimated 10,000 people in the Mangde river valley. Chali is spoken by about a thousand people in a small enclave north of Monggar on the east bank of the Kurichu, consisting mainly of Chali itself and neighbouring Wangmakhar. Dzala is spoken by about 15,000 people in northeastern Bhutan in Trashi'yangtse district and in Lhüntsi district east of the Kurichu. Chinese sources have reported over 40,000 speakers of the same language in the portion of Tibet just north of northeastern Bhutan and the adjacent part of Arunachal Pradesh. Dakpa is spoken by a few thousand people in Tawang, which now makes up the northwestern corner of Arunachal Pradesh, and in a few villages in eastern Bhutan abutting Tawang. The Black Mountain language is spoken by about 500 people in six different villages scattered throughout the southern jungle heartland of the Black Mountains in central Bhutan. This language is decidedly the most divergent and aberrant of all East Bodish languages. The language may, in fact, not be East Bodish at all, but represent another Tibeto-Burman language on its own which has been extensively relexified by East Bodish.

Lhokpu

Lhokpu constitutes a group unto itself within the Tibeto-Burman language family. The Lhokpu language is spoken in the hills of Samtsi District in southwestern Bhutan in two distinct language communities. The robust western community in the hills one day's march to the northwest of Samtsi bazaar comprises approximately 1,340 speakers in the villages of Sanglung, Sataka and Loto Kucu and Lotok. The eastern community comprises approximately 1,270 speakers in Tâba, Dramte and several associated hamlets near Jenchu, upstream from the town of Phüntsho'ling on the Indo-Bhutan border. Language retention is better in the western community because there are fewer Nepali settlements nearby. The entire Lhokpu population is effectively bilingual in Nepali, and most of the hill tracts of southwestern Bhutan as well as a portion of the western Bhutanese duars used to be Lhokpu territory. The Royal Government of Bhutan has recognised the urgent language endangerment situation of the Lhokpu due to the influx of Nepali settlers into their traditional homeland, and Lhokpu is currently being grammatically and lexicographically documented under the auspices of the Royal Government of Bhutan.

Lepcha

The Lepcha have their own indigenous script and a literary tradition which dates back to the early eighteenth century. Lepcha is the language of the original populace of Sikkim. The kingdom of Sikkim once comprised present-day Sikkim as well as most of the present-day Darjeeling District. Outside of this area, Lepcha is also still spoken decreasingly within roughly 100 Lepcha households in Ilām district in eastern Nepal. The language is also spoken in Kalimpong or 'British Bhutan', i.e. the territory wrested from Bhutan which now forms the easternmost part of Darjeeling District. Lepcha is furthermore spoken in a few Lepcha villages in Samtsi District of southwestern Bhutan. Zongu District in Sikkim is the only remaining area where the Lepcha have not been outnumbered by Nepali colonists. The entire Lepcha area is bilingual. Despite spirited attempts to preserve the language, Lepcha has already effectively been lost everywhere in favour of Nepali. There are very few remaining households where the younger generation actively speaks the language, and these households are few and far between. The total number of fluent Lepcha speakers does not exceed a few thousand.

Gongduk

Gongduk is a previously unknown Tibeto-Burman language which was first discovered for scholarship in May 1991. The language, which has turned out to constitute a distinct and unique branch unto itself within the great Tibeto-Burman language family, is spoken by a dwindling population of just over 1,000 people in a remote enclave along the Kurichu in Monggar district in east-central Bhutan. Gongduk is one of the two languages in Bhutan which has retained complex conjugations which reflect the ancient Tibeto-Burman verbal agreement system. The language community has survived intact for so long because of its remoteness and the relative general stability of language communities in Bhutan over time. Whereas some language communities are remote in the sense that they are many days on foot from a motorable road, the Gongduk-speaking enclave has until recent historical times also been several days on foot from the nearest neighbouring language communities. This means that travellers had to carry their own provisions and sleep outdoors to reach the Gongduk area. This still holds true for two of the three approaches to the language community. Yet Bhutan has been transformed in recent decades by a network of narrow but motorable roads and a growing infrastructure of educational and health care facilities set up by a caring central government. The Gongduk language community is opening up to the outside world, and a growing staff of civil servants who do not speak the language are now stationed there on a semi-permanent basis. Although there is still a fair number of genuine monolinguals, the situation is rapidly changing, and the future prospects for the survival of Gongduk are not good. The Royal Government of Bhutan has recognised the urgent language endangerment situation of the Gongduk, and the language is currently being grammatically and lexicographically documented under the auspices of the Royal Government of Bhutan.

Endangered languages of Arunachal Pradesh

The Kho-Bwa languages

The four languages of the enigmatic Kho-Bwa cluster in western Arunachal Pradesh, just east of Bhutan, are all threatened with imminent extinction. These are Khowa or Bugun, Sulung or Puroit, Lishpa and Sherdukpen. Khowa is spoken by an estimated 800 people, more than half of whom reside in the two villages of Wanghoo and Singchung near the district headquarters at Bomdila in West Kameng district. Sulung is spoken by about 4,000 people, half of whom inhabit a small area which straddles the northeastern hills of East Kameng and the northwestern hills of Lower Subansiri district. In this area, they occupy the northern and more inaccessible parts of the upper reaches of the Par river. The Sulung have been compelled to lead a semi-nomadic existence because they were lowest in the pecking order established by the perennial internecine tribal warfare traditionally waged in the region. The Sulung were often enslaved by rival groups. Therefore, their actual area of dispersal extends from the Bhareli river to the Subansiri, and small settlements of Sulung are interspersed with the villages of more numerous groups such as the Tani and Hruso. Lishpa is spoken by about 1,000 people in Kameng district who pass themselves off as 'Monpa'. Sherdukpen is spoken by less than 2,000 people who live mainly in the villages of Rupa, Shergaon and Jigaon in the southwestern corner of Kameng district, but are also settled in the area in and around the Tenga valley south of Bomdila. Culturally the Sherdukpen are distinct from the other Kho-Bwa language communities because they have adopted a Tibetan Mahāyāna Buddhist *Hochkultur*.

Hrusish languages

All three Hrusish languages are endangered with imminent extinction. The Hruso or 'Aka' population is estimated at less than 3,000 speakers. The Hruso live in the southeast of Kameng, where they are concentrated in the Bichom river valley. Like the Bhutanese to the west and the neighbouring Nishi tribes to the east, the Hruso or Aka have historically observed the practice of raiding the plains to take back slaves to the hills. Dhímmai or 'Miji' is still spoken by about 4,000 people. The Dhímmai inhabit about twenty-five villages and hamlets in the northeastern and north-central region of Kameng, i.e. in the Bichom river valley to the north of Hruso territory and also in the Pakesa river valley. There are only about 1,000 speakers of Levai or 'Bongro', who live in Kameng and also part of Subansiri.

Tani languages

Tani languages, formerly known as 'Abor-Miri-Dafla' languages, are spoken by the many Adi and Nishi tribes and a few other groups such as the Milang which are not thus classified. An estimated 5,000 speakers of Milang live on the eastern fringe of the Tani area, abutting the territory of the Idu Mishmis. The Milang inhabit the three villages of Milang, Dalbing and Pekimodi in the upper Yamne valley in Mariyang subdivision of East Siang district.

Bangni, Nishi, Tagin and Apatani form a cluster. Bangni, traditionally known as Western Dafla, is spoken by roughly 23,000 people. In the north, the Bangni area straddles the Indo-Tibetan border. Nishi, formerly known as Eastern Dafla, is spoken by roughly 30,000 people. Nah is spoken in just seven villages of Taksing administrative circle in Upper Subansiri district. Sarak or 'Hill Miri' is spoken just east of the Apatani area by an estimated 9,000 people. An estimated 25,000 Tagin inhabit the northeastern quadrant of Subansiri district and Subansiri and adjoining parts of West Siang, including the towns of Denekoli and Taliha. The Tagin were driven to their present abode by the bellicose Pailibo and Ramo tribes. Apatani is the most divergent member of the Nishi group and has been exposed to the most Tibetan influence. An estimated 14,000 Apatani inhabit an enclave in the fertile valley of the Apatani Plateau in lower central Subansiri district, between the Nishi and Hill Miri, midway between the Panior and Kamla rivers.

Gallong, Bokar, Pailibo and Ramo form a cluster. Gallong, one of the two Tani languages which is endangered but not threatened with immediate extinction, is spoken by approximately 40,000 people in the southern half of West Siang district as far down as where the plains of Lakhimpur District begin in Assam. The largest Gallong village is Bagra with a population exceeding 3,000 near the West Siang district headquarters at Along. Approximately 3,500 speakers of Bokar live in forty villages in the Monigong Circle of Machukha subdivision in West Siang district just below the peaks of the Indo-Tibetan border, as well as in several villages on the Tibetan side of the ridge. Just over a thousand speakers of Pailibo live along the banks of the Siyom or Yomgo river, in nine villages in the Tato Circle and two villages in the Payum circle of West Siang district. Less than 800 speak Ramo in the upper Siyom valley in Mechukha subdivision of West Siang district to the northwest of the Pailibo area. Exclusively Ramo villages are located between Machukha and Tato, whereas elsewhere Ramo are mixed with Bokar and Memba settlers.

The remaining languages belong to the Minyong-Padam cluster, although nothing is in fact known about the Ashing language except its name. Its inclusion, therefore, is just a matter of geographical convenience. Whereas Padam is one of the two Tani languages which is endangered but not threatened with immediate extinction, Tangam is nearly extinct because most of the people who spoke the language became the victims of genocide. The endangerment situation therefore varies widely from language community to language community. Approximately 20,000 speakers of Minyong occupy the swathe of territory along the west bank of the lower Siang river, downstream of the Bori and Karko language communities and to the east of the Gallongs. Not much more than 2,000 speakers of Bori are settled along the Siyom and Sike rivers in an area enclosed by the Luyor hills on the east, the Piri hills on the west and on the north by the closing together of these two ranges. The totally undocumented Ashing language is spoken by less than 1,000 people who inhabit the northernmost headwaters of the Siang river near the Tibetan border, beginning from the village of Ramsing in the south and extending up as far as Tuting village in the north. Pango and Bomdo are the most numerous Ashing settlements. An estimated 2,000 speakers of Shimong remain on the left bank of the Siang in the northernmost portion of what used to be known administratively as the Siang Frontier Division. Yingkiong is the administrative centre in the Shimong area. Less than 200 speakers of Tangam remain in the northernmost portion of Siang district inhabiting the three villages of Kuging, Ngering, Mayum and a few neighbouring hamlets in the north-eastern corner of the Adi tribal region of Arunachal Pradesh, along the upper reaches of the rivers Siang and Nigong. The Tangam were once numerous but were killed *en masse* by neighbouring tribes. Karko is spoken by a small tribe of just over 2,000 people found mainly in Karko village and surrounding hamlets, such as Ramsing and Gosang. About 600 speakers of Panggi live in the lower Yamne valley above the con-fluence of the Yamne and the Siang, in the villages of Geku, Sumsing, Sibum, Jeru and Pongging. Padam, formerly known as the 'Bor Abor' or 'Great Abor', is spoken by probably over 40,000 people in the tract of land between the Dibang, Siang and Yamne valleys in East Siang, from the Assam border in the south to the Sidip river in the north. Mishing or 'Plains Miri' is spoken by less than 4,000 Hin-duised people living in scattered settlements on the plains closely skirting the hills of Arunachal Pradesh. All the language communities of Arunachal Pradesh are threa-tened by Hindi, which has been propagated in the area by the government of India since the 1970s.

Midźuish languages

The Midźuish languages are referred to in older writings by the antique term 'North-ern Mishmi'. The two Midźuish languages, Kaman and Zaiwa, are both endangered. Approximately 9,000 people speak Kaman or 'Miju Mishmi' along the upper reaches of the Lohit on both banks of the river around Parsuram Kund in Lohit district, and across the border in Tibet. Less than 200 people of the Zakhring and Meyor clans speak the Zaiwa language in the vicinity of Walong. This 'Zaiwa Mishmi' is not to be confused with the utterly different Burmic language also named Zaiwa, which is spoken in parts of Yúnnán and Burma.

Digarish languages

The two Digarish languages, Idu and Taraon, are both endangered with imminent extinction. There are only an estimated 9,000 speakers of Idu, once known as Chuli-kata 'cropped hair' Mishmi. An estimated 6,000 speakers of Taraon are concentrated in the area between the Delei and Lati rivers in the east, the Kharem in the south and the Digaru in the west.

Endangered languages of the Brahmaputran Plain and associated hill tracts

Brahmaputran is a major trunk of the Tibeto-Burman language family, comprising the three branches Konyak, Bodo-Koch and Dhimalish, and may include a fourth branch, Kachinic or Jinghpaw. The Kachinic languages are all endangered, not only by Mandarin, Burmese and Assamese, but also by the Jinghpaw creole which is used as a *lingua franca* between diverse Kachinic language communities. This form of Jinghpaw has been grammatically simplified and is shorn of the native morphosyntactic complexity which characterises the various local grassroots Jinghpaw languages. More information on the Jinghpaw languages can be found in Chapter 5 on Southeast Asia. The Bodo-Koch branch of the Tibeto-Burman family consists of Chutiya, Bodo-Garo and the Koch languages. A number of Bodo-Koch languages mentioned and even scantily documented in British sources in the nineteenth and twentieth century have since then become extinct, e.g. Hâjong.

Deori Chutiya

There was once a large number of ethnic Chutiya, but the only group that had retained the original language at the dawn of the twentieth century was the priestly Deori clan, who formerly officiated at sacrificial ceremonies for the Ahom kings. The 1971 census only counted 2,683 ethnic Deori in Arunachal Pradesh and 9,103 Chutiya in Assam. Today there are reportedly only few households in Lakhimpur and Sibsagar districts of upper Assam who still speak the language, and one would have to make an effort to locate them.

Bodo-Garo languages

The Bodo-Garo cluster consists of Kokborok, Tiwa, Dimasa or 'Hills Kachari', Hojai, 'Plains Kachari', Bodo, Mech and Garo. The most divergent languages within this cluster are believed to be Dimasa, Tiwa and Kokborok. Dimasa is hardly documented and today very much under threat of extinction. The Dimasa live in the northern Cachar hills and portions of the adjacent plains, where they have largely been linguistically assimilated to their Bengali and Assamese neighbours. Dimasa is only spoken in isolated households, and local sleuthing would be required to find them. There is no description of Hojai, but old sources suggest some affiliation with the Dimasa. Dimasa and Hojai are distinct from Plains Kachari, but the speakers of all three dialects refer to themselves as 'Bodo'. Plains Kachari or simply Kachari is the dialect spoken in Darrang district, upriver from Bodo proper and downriver from the Chutiya territory. The surviving Kachari language communities are rapidly being assimilated. The dialect spoken further downriver in areas such as Goalpara is generally referred to simply as Bodo. There is still a considerable number of Bodo speakers, but their communities are presently assimilating linguistically to Bengali and Assamese under heavy demographic and socio-economic pressure. Meche is a Bodo-Koch language often mentioned in British sources, but now perhaps extinct. If there are still households speaking Meche, they must be sought by a locally savvy linguist in Jalpaiguri district and neighbouring parts of Goalpara. The original Meche territory stretched from what today is Jhāpā district in the eastern Nepalese Terai all the way across the Bhutanese duars as far as modern Goalpara district

Kokborok, formerly known as 'Hill Tippera', is spoken in the low rolling hills of Tripurā. At the time that India gained its independence from Great Britain, at least 70 per cent of the people in Tripurā were Kokborok and a mere 30 per cent were Bengali colonists. Today the Kokborok constitute just a 30 per cent minority in their own tribal homeland, having been swamped by Bengali immigrants, especially from the area which now constitutes the country of Bangladesh. Bengali colonists now make up over 85 per cent of the population. There are an estimated 800,000 ethnic Kokborok, but the vast majority have abandoned their ancestral language or are in the process of doing so. Tiwa, also known as 'Lalung', is spoken by about 35,000 people settled in Kamrup and Marigaon districts and in the Karbi Anglong, formerly known as the Mikir Hills. Garo is the only Bodo-Koch language not threatened with imminent extinction. About 200,000 of the 250,000 people living in the western half of the Meghālaya, known as the Garo Hills, speak Garo. An additional 50,000 Garo speakers live in the Assamese districts of Goalpara and Kamrup and in Mymensing District of Bangladesh, which all skirt the Garo Hills. Some Garo even live further south in the Bangladeshi hinterland, e.g. about 15,000 in Modhupur.

The Koch languages

The Koch languages are Pānī Koch, A'tong, Ruga and Rabha. Koch proper is still spoken by only approximately 300 people along the western fringe of the Garo Hills near Dalu in the vicinity of Garobadha. The speakers are known as Wanang or Pānī Koch 'Water Koch'. Several thousand speakers of A'tong live in the southeast of the Garo Hills and reside in and around Somasvarī and Bāghmārā. The A'tong speak a Koch language, but identify themselves as 'Garo' and are already bilingual in their native A'tong and in Garo. The Ruga or Rugha are a small group in the south of the Garo Hills. No data are available on the number of Rugha speakers. The Rabhas inhabit the territory where the Brahmaputra meanders around the highlands of the Meghālaya and bends south towards the Bay of Bengal after flowing westward across the plains of Assam. The prehistoric Rabha ethnic area may originally have extended as far east as Guwahati. There are at least 150,000 ethnic Rabha in Assam, and in 1993 the Rabha Hasong Demand Committee even put the number of ethnic Rabha as high as 375,000. Yet there are no more than several thousand speakers of the Rabha language. Most Rabhas speak Bengali or Assamese. Rabha is only still actually spoken in a number of villages in Goalpara District between Goālpārā proper and Phulbārī, including Bardāmāl, Mātiā, Majerburi and Mākuri. However, even here the younger generation is already fully bilingual in Assamese, and most young Rabhas have a better command of Assamese than they have of Rabha.

Dhimalish languages

Dhimalish includes the Toto and Dhimal languages. Toto is spoken by a small tribal group at the town of Totopārā in Baksā or Mādārīhāt subdivision of Jalpāīgudī district in the Indian state of West Bengal nearby the Bhutanese border town of Phüntsho'ling. In November 1994, there were 176 Toto families with a total number of 992 Toto speakers. Although this language of the Bhutanese duars is officially spoken on the Indian side of the border today, the Royal Government of Bhutan has recognised the precarious situation of this community and commissioned a grammatical investigation of the language, which is currently being prepared for publication. On the basis of British sources, it is known that the range of Toto-speaking settlements was once far larger than it is today.

The Dhimal live in Jhāpā and Morań districts in the eastern Nepalese Terai. There are two distinct Dhimal language communities, an eastern conglomeration of sixteen villages in Jhāpā district to the east of the Kankāīmāī or Māī river, with an estimated 3,000 speakers, and a western tribe of over 25,000 speakers to the west of the river inhabiting about twenty-four villages in western Jhāpā and fifty-one villages in Moran district. The current Dhimal population has recently been estimated as high as 35,000 people, though the 1991 census somehow only counted 16,781 Dhimal. The language is rapidly being lost in favour of Nepali, however, because the Dhimal are a 10 per cent minority in their own native areas. The groups in the same region which are sometimes identified as *Jhāṅgaḍ Dhimāl* are speakers of the Dravidian language Jhangar.

Konyak languages

The 'Northern Naga' or Konyak languages are spoken in Arunachal Pradesh, Nagaland and adjacent areas of Burma. Two clusters can be distinguished, the first comprising the languages Konyak, Wancho, Phom, Khiamngan and Chang, and the second comprising Tangsa and Nocte. Tangsa, Nocte and Wancho are spoken in Arunachal Pradesh, whereas Konyak, Phom and Chang are spoken to the southwest in Nagaland. There are approximately 30,000 Wanchos in approximately forty-one villages grouped into eleven confederacies, known as *jan*, in the southwestern tip of Tirap district between the foothills and the Patkoi range. To the south of the Wancho, in Nagaland, live approximately 70,000 speakers of Konyak. South of the Konyak live about 19,000 speakers of Phom. To the southeast of the Phom, approximately 16,000 Chang occupy the hinterland of Nagaland, stretching back into the high range which divides India from Burma. An unknown number of speakers speak Khiamngan, and the precise wherabouts of this language community is unknown. There were about 20,000 Tangsa in Changlang and Miao subdivisions of Tirap district. The Jogli, Moklum and Lunchang languages are dialects of Tangsa, divergent enough to warrant separate documentation and each spoken by well over 1,000 people. The Noctes live in central Tirap to the northeast of the Wanchos and to the west of the Tangsas. There are approximately 28,000 Nocte.

Karbí

Karbí or Mikir is spoken in the Karbi Anglong or 'Mikir Hills' of Assam as well as in the neighbouring districts of Kamrup, Nowgong and Sibsagar. The language is not a Brahmaputran language, but a taxon unto itself within the Tibeto-Burman language family. There are over 150,000 Mikir, the vast majority of whom reside in the Karbi Anglong. Half of the Karbí are bilingual in Assamese, and amongst the younger generation the ancestral language is being abandoned at an alarming rate in favour of Assamese.

Endangered Tibeto-Burman and Daic languages of the Indo-Burmese borderlands

Ao languages

The Ao languages are spoken in central Nagaland. These are Chungli Ao, Mongsen Ao, Sangtam, Yimchungrü, Lotha, Yacham and Tengsa. Lotha is the most robust with about 35,000 speakers. All the other Ao languages together have about 65,275 speakers. Over one third of the population of Nagaland are not indigenous Tibeto-Burmans, but Indo-Aryan settlers. Due to the many languages spoken in Nagaland, the increased mobility of all population groups and the use of Assamese and Naga-mese, a low-status Assamese-based creole, as *lingua franca*, all the Ao languages are threatened with extinction.

Angami-Pochuri languages

There are two language clusters, one consisting of Angami, Chokri, Kheza and Mao, and the other of Pochuri, Ntenyi, Maluri, Sema and Rengma. There are roughly 30,000 speakers of Angami and an estimated 65,000 speakers of Sema. The other languages are all spoken by far smaller populations. For example, there are about 9,000 speakers of Rengma.

Zeme languages

The linguistic territory of the Zeme languages lies in the southwestern corner of Nagaland and the northwestern portion of Manipur, where the languages Zeme, Liangmai, Nruanghmei, Mzieme, Puiron, Khoirao and Maram are spoken. There are no good population counts for these language communities. There were twenty-six Zeme-speaking villages in 1901, whereas the 1971 census returned 406 Khoirao, 19,968 Maram and 17,360 Rongmai. All Zeme languages are threatened with extinction. The direction of linguistic assimilation is generally towards Meithei, a robust Tibeto-Burman language which is the official language of Manipur, spoken by over one million people.

Tangkhul languages

Tangkhul territory covers the northeastern quadrant of Manipur. The two languages are Tangkhul in the north and Maring in the south. The 1971 census returned 58,167 ethnic Tangkhul in Manipur, and no separate data were available on Maring. Tang-khul is being lost in favour of Meithei and is nearly extinct. It is not known whether Maring is already extinct or still survives in certain households.

Mizo-Kuki-Chin languages

Some languages of this branch are not yet endangered, e.g. Mizo, also known as Lushai, spoken by 300,000 people. Precise numbers for other language communities are unavailable, but it is certain that all these languages are vanishing fast. Thadou, Kom, Chiru, Gangte, Lamgang, Anal and Paite are spoken by dwindling numbers of speakers in Manipur, where these communities are being linguistically assimilated to the Meithei-speaking majority. The small Lakher language community in southern Mizoram is assimilating to the Mizo-speaking minority. The Simte, Zo, Vaiphei, Tiddim Chin, Falam Chin, Haka Chin and various Southern Chin language commu-nities in Burma are being linguistically assimilated by the Burmese-speaking majority. The small Hrangkol, Chorei, Bawm, Kom and Hmar language communities in Tri-pura, southern Assam and the northern tip of Mizoram are all assimilating to the Assamese or Bengali-speaking majority.

Mru

Mru is a Tibeto-Burman language in a class by itself. The estimated 40,000 speakers of Mru in the central hills of the Chittagong in southeastern Bangladesh are losing their language in favour of Bengali.

Sak languages

The Kachinic branch consists of the Sak languages and the Jinghpaw dialects. The Sak languages, formerly also known as 'Luish' languages, are Sak, Kadu, Andro and Sengmai. Andro and Sengmai went extinct in the course of the twentieth century. The descendants in Manipur now speak Meithei. In 1911, Kadu was still spoken by at least 11,000 people in the portion of the Burmese district of Katha adjacent to Manipur. It is unknown whether there are any hamlets or households in which the language is still spoken. The Chakmas of the northern Chittagong hill tracts have adopted Bengali, but the Chak, Cak or Sak in the southern Chittagong hill tracts still speak their ancestral Tibeto-Burman tongue. The Sak are separated from the Chakma by bands of territory inhabited by speakers of the Mru language and of the Arakanese dialect of Burmese. A mere 1,500 speakers of Sak were counted in 1981 in the area of Alaykhyong, Baichiri, Nakhali and Nakhyongchari near the Burmese border east of Cox's Bazar.

Daic languages

Ahom is an ancient Daic language introduced into the lower Brahmaputra valley in what today is northeastern India with the incursion of a Daic tribe in 1228. A Daic élite led by prince Sukāphā imposed its language and culture upon a Bodo-Koch populace, but their language ultimately went extinct and all that survives are chronicles known as *Buranjis*. Subsequently other Daic groups migrated into north-eastern India, such as the Khampti and Tai Phake or 'Phākial', who arrived in the mid-eighteenth century. Today the Khampti predominantly inhabit the south-eastern corner of Lakhimpur district in Assam and neighbouring portions of Lohit district in Arunachal Pradesh, and an unknown but dwindling number of ethnic Khampti still speak their ancestral Daic language. The roughly 2,000 Buddhist speakers of Tai Phake inhabit the six villages of Nam Phakial, Tipam Phakial, Bar Phakial, Namman, Namchai and Lang in Tinsukia and Dibrugarh districts. The Tai Phake are already all bilingual and speak Assamese in addition to their native language.

The Tai Nora are a Northern Shan group who fled to the Patkoi Hills to escape persecution by the Jinghpaw at the beginning of the nineteenth century, later moving to Jorhat subdivision of Sibsagar district. Most of the Tai Nora have lost their native Daic tongue, whereas the few Tai Nora who continue to speak the language usually identify themselves and their language as Khamyang. The Tai Rong or Tai Long 'Great Tai' are a Shan group who settled in northeastern India in 1825, likewise settling in Jorhat. The approximately 2,000 speakers of Aiton or 'Shām Doāniyās' are also a Northern Shan group who fled to avoid persecution in the nineteenth century and settled in small numbers in Lakhimpur and Sibsagar districts and the Naga Hills.

Endangered languages of Nepal

The 1971 census returned 220,000 speakers of all the Rai languages taken together. After the Nepalese Revolution did away with repressive language policies in 1990, it became popular to identify oneself as a speaker of one's ancestral language even when one no longer spoke it. In the 1991 census, 80 per cent of the 525,551 Rai people reportedly still spoke their native language, but this outcome is the product of collective wishful thinking. All Rai languages are moribund and will go extinct within one or two generations at the present rate, being lost in favour of Nepali. A comparable situation exists amongst the Limbu. The Kiranti languages consist of the Limbu group, Eastern Kiranti, Central Kiranti and Western Kiranti. Sometimes the Limbu and Eastern Kiranti languages are grouped together under the heading of Greater Eastern Kiranti languages.

The Limbu group

There are an estimated 300,000 ethnic Limbu in eastern Nepal and a portion of western Sikkim. It is sometimes claimed that language retention is as high as 80 per cent, but these figures belie the dire situation of these languages. The most conservative Limbu language, Phedāppe, will probably go extinct when today's generation of young adults takes the language to the grave with them because virtually nobody in the Phedāppe language community is currently raising their children in Limbu. The linguistic situation is comparable in the even smaller Chathare language community. The situation is slightly better in the larger Pāñcthare language community to the west of the Tamor. Yet even the prospects for Pāñcthare as well as Tamarkhole, the Limbu dialect spoken in northeastern Limbuvān, look bleak. Under the currently prevailing sociolinguistic conditions Limbu is likely to be completely extinct by the end of this century unless measures are taken to revitalise the language through the primary school system.

Eastern Kiranti languages

Eastern Kiranti consists of the Upper Aruṇ and Greater Yakkha languages. The languages of the Greater Yakkha cluster are Yakkha, Chiliŋ and the Athpahariya dialects. Yakkha is on the verge of extinction. There are reportedly only a few isolated households where the language is still spoken on a daily basis, though there is a slightly larger number of elderly Yakkha throughout the former Yakkha territory who can remember the language, but have no fellow speakers with whom to speak it. Chiliŋ is a Rai language spoken by about 3,000 people in the hamlets and villages of Āṅkhisallā in Dhankuṭā district. The language has managed to survive surprisingly well amongst the approximately 600 households where it is spoken. Language retention amongst the Chiliŋ younger generation is still relatively good, but under the present sociolinguistic conditions it is highly unlikely that the next generation of speakers will be raised in the language. The Athpahariya dialects are spoken by the indigenous people of Dhankuṭā district, who are now vastly outnumbered by settlers from outside. There is significant dialectal diversity within the Athpahariya dialects area. For example, the Belhare variety is somewhat distinct. Comprehensive grammatical and lexical documentation of the Athpahariya dialects is a matter of great urgency. There are probably only several hundred elderly speakers, and these languages are all now on the verge of extinction.

The Upper Aruṇ or Yakkhaba languages are Yamphu, Lohorung and Mewahang. The Yamphu is spoken by less than 3,000 people in the upper Aruṇ valley in the north of Saṅkhuvā Sabhā district. Lohorung is spoken by an estimated 4,000 people in a language community in the central portion of Saṅkhuvā Sabhā district on the left bank of the Aruṇ. Mewahang is spoken by a comparable number of speakers north of the Saṅkhuvā river and to the east of the Aruṇ. The southern portion of the Mewahang area is flooded with Indo-Aryan colonists as well as Newar, Ghale and other Tibeto-Burman migrants from more westerly parts of Nepal. These language communities are all bilingual in Nepali. In terms of language they have fared surprisingly well until today. Yet these communities are now being subjected to unprecedented upheaval due to the economically motivated emigration of their members to urban centres elsewhere and the likewise economically motivated influx of monied outsiders into these areas. Not only are indigenous languages of the Himalayas endangered by the construction of roads into their areas, the socio-economic detrimental effects of roads on indigenous populations are often observed, studied and reported. In Nepal roads have generally benefitted outsiders moving in and had deleterious economic effects on local people, but this is a message which development banks, aid organisations and governments do not want to hear.

Central Kiranti

The Central Kiranti languages comprise the Khambu group and the Southern Kiranti languages. The Khambu group encompasses Kulung, Sampang, Nachiring and probably Sām. Kulung is spoken by an estimated 15,000 people, mainly in Solukhumbu district but also in neighbouring portions of Saṅkhuvā Sabhā district. Nachiring is spoken downstream from the Kulung area, just above the confluence of the Hoṅgu and the Dūdhkosī and in the swathe of territory which lies between Hulu and the Rāva river in Khoṭāṅg district. There are only an estimated several hundred speakers of the language, all quite elderly and often isolated from other speakers. Sampang is spoken in the Khārtamchā, Phedī and Pātheka areas of Khoṭāṅ district and in adjacent parts of Bhojpur district to the east. Although there may be over a thousand speakers, increasingly fewer members of the younger generation are learning the language. The Sām inhabit the territory which straddles both Saṅkhuvā Sabhā and Bhojpur districts along the Irkhuvā river, a western tributary of the Aruṇ. It is uncertain whether there are any remaining speakers of the language, but patient sleuthing in the area could uncover a remaining Sām-speaking household.

The Southern Kiranti languages are Bantawa, Chintang, Dungmali, Chamling and Puma. They are spoken in the lower hills region between the Dūdhkosī and the Aruṇ. The Sunkosī which runs through this area cuts through Chamling territory, but in the east, where the river has already descended onto the plains, it more or less coincides with the southern border of Bantawa territory. Two of the Southern Kiranti languages, Bantawa and Chamling, are respectively the largest and second largest Rai language in terms of numbers of speakers. Yet hardly any young people speak these languages. Bantawa is the language native to Bhojpur district. Dungmali is spoken in the northeastern quarter of Bhojpur district, north of the Pikhuvā river, covering the territory on the right bank of the Aruṇ across the river from Yakkha territory.

Chintang is spoken in just the two villages of Chintāṅ and Ḍāṇḍāgāū in Dhankuṭā district, just west of the Chiling language area further along the same ridge. Chamling is spoken in Khoṭāṅ and Udaypur districts, south of the Rāva Kholā and east of the Dūdhkosī, and on both banks of the Sunkosī, especially to the northeast of the river. The number of ethnic Chamling have been estimated to be as high as 30,000, but language retention is poor in most areas. Language retention amongst the younger generation is reported to be highest in communities on the southwest bank of the Sunkosī, such as Balamtā. Puma is spoken in Dipluṅ and Cisopānī in the southeastern corner of Khoṭāṅ district, about 10km north of the Sunkosī to the west of the Buṅvā river.

Western Kiranti

Western Kiranti consists of the Thulung, Tilung, the Chaurasiya group, the Upper Dūdhkosī languages and the Northwestern Kiranti languages. Thulung is spoken mainly in the southern part of Solukhumbu district and in the territory surrounding the confluence of the Solu river and the Dūdhkosī. Thulung is so distinct within Kiranti that it is viewed as a group on its own, termed Midwestern Kiranti. The number of Thulung has been estimated at 8,000, but the language is being lost. Tilung is a Kiranti language about which very little is known except the name and the approximate location. The language is spoken only by an indigenous minority in the triangle of land between the lower course of the Dūdhkosī and the part of the Sunkosī below the confluence in the southwestern portion of Khoṭāṅ district. There are few remaining speakers.

The Chaurasiya group comprises the languages Ombule or 'Wambule' and Jero. Ombule is spoken around the confluence of the Dūdhkosī and Sunkosī. The Jero-speaking area is contiguous with Ombule territory and lies to the northwest of the Ombule area on both sides of the Sunkosī. There are approximately 15,000 Chaurasiya people, speaking either Jero or Wambule, and language retention is rapidly waning in the younger generation.

The Upper Dūdhkosī languages are Dumi, Kohi and Khaling. There are less than eight speakers of Dumi east of the Lidim river, all of whom are very elderly. There are unsubstantiated reports of middle-aged speakers around Aiselukharka on the west bank of the Lidim. The Dumi homeland is the area between the Rāva and the Tāp rivers. Kohi is an undescribed Rai language related to Dumi. The language is still spoken in and around the village of Suṅdel along the upper headwaters of the Rāva in Khoṭāṅ district. Language retention amongst the young is still good, but the language community is very small. Khaling is spoken by about 15,000 people in Solukhumbu district in the mountains on either side of the Dūdhkosī from Bupsā above Jumbhiṅ as far downstream as Kilimpī, just above the confluence of the Hoṅgu river and the Dūdhkosī.

The Northwestern Kiranti languages are Hayu, Bahing, Sunwar and perhaps Surel. If there are any elderly speakers of Hayu remaining, they would most likely be found in the villages of Muḍhājor, Barḍāṇḍā, Māneḍihī, Adhamarā or in some neighbouring hamlet. Hayu was once spoken in a corridor of land, along the Mahābhārat Lek range alongside the Sunkosī above its confluence with the Likhu river, primarily in Rāmechāp and in neighbouring portions of Sindhulī and Kābhrepālañcok districts. Bahing is also on the verge of extinction. The language has been lost or language retention is poor in most Bahing villages. There are a few exceptional villages with exceptional households, however, within the Bahing homeland area in Okhaldhuṅgā district and neighbouring parts of Solukhumbū. Sunwar is the most northwesterly of the Kiranti languages, and it is now spoken only by a small and dwindling minority out of the approximately 30,000 ethnic Sunwar. The Sunwar homeland is the river valleys of the Likhu and Khimtī, tributaries of the Sunkosī and Tāmākosī respectively. The Surel live in the village of Surī near Hāleśvara in Dolakhā district. Their language is spoken by at least several hundred people, and some claim that it represents a more archaic stage of the Sunwar language.

Newaric

The Newaric languages are Newar, Barām and Thangmi. Newar is the Tibeto-Burman language of the urbanised civilisation of the Kathmandu Valley. The language has an epigraphic tradition dating back to 1171 AD. Land deeds survive in Newar from as early as 1114 AD, and the Newar literary tradition dates back to 1374. There are over a million Newar. None the less Newar is a language endangered with imminent extinction. All Newars are bilingual in Newar and Nepali. Nepali is a language originally not native to the Nepali capital. Today the native Newar are vastly outnumbered in their native homeland of the Kathmandu Valley.

At a Tibeto-Burman workshop held at the University of California at Santa Barbara on 28 July 2001, the Newar scholar Dayā Ratna Śākya went as far as to proclaim that 'the more educated the Newar, the less likely he is able to speak Newar'. This is a damning observation to have to make about the language that has been the daily means of communication for a society that yielded one of the most advanced premodern societies and has produced sublime art and a refined culture and acted as the midwife for the birth of numerous schools of philosophy. The drastic sociolinguistic changes which have overwhelmed the culturally and technologically advanced Newar language community since the conquest of the Kathmandu Valley by Pṛthvī Nārāyaṇ Śāh in 1768 may serve as a metaphor for the convulsive changes which are now overwhelming language communities all over the world as they increasingly come under siege by expansive languages such as English.

There is a large Newar language community, but few families are raising their children in Newar. It has even been claimed that none do so. Though the language community is still large in absolute terms, the language may already have reached the point of no return. The prospects may be slightly better for other Newar dialects, which are at any rate not mutually intelligible with the Newar language of Kathmandu and Pāṭan. The situation is in fact not much better for the Newar dialect spoken in Bhaktapur, but the highly divergent Paharā and Citlāṅg dialects and the Dolakhā Newar language could conceivably hold out for another generation. The Paharā and Citlāṅg dialects are spoken by rural groups at localities within the Kathmandu Valley and surrounding hill tracts, whereas the Dolakhā Newar language is spoken far away in Dolakhā district.

Barām is still spoken in just one village in Gorkhā district in central Nepal, i.e. Dāṇḍāgāũ near Pīpal Dāṇḍā in the Tākukot area. Ethnic Barām can be found throughout Gorkhā district as well as in Dhādiṅ and Nuvākot districts. However, in these areas only a few very elderly and isolated individuals can be found with some fragmentary recollection of the language. There are only a few hundred speakers of

Barām, but the fluent speakers are all middle-aged to elderly and together number far less than a hundred. Thangmi is spoken by approximately 30,000 people, mainly in the northern portion of Dolakhā district, but also in eastern Sindhupālcok. Language retention is poor amongst the younger generation.

Shingsaba

Shingsaba or Lhomi are a cis-Himalayan Bodish group with a distinct language. Not much is known about the language, but Shingsaba may not even be a Bodish language, but one heavily influenced by Tibetan. The language may have some affinity with the Kiranti or Tamangic languages. Just over 4,000 speakers were reported in the 1970s. The Shingsaba live in villages on the steep slopes of the upper Aruṇ upstream from the Hedāṅnā area in Saṅkhuvā Sabhā district as far as the Tibetan border, e.g. in the villages of Cyāmṭaṅ and Kimāthaṅkā. The Shingsaba area is surrounded by the towering Lumbā-Sumbā Himāl, Umbhak Himāl and Kumbhakarṇa Himāl.

Magaric

Magaric includes the Magar dialects spoken by the southern Magar septs and Kham or Northern Magar. According to the 1991 census data on language retention, only 430,264 out of 1,339,308 ethnic Magar or one third of the Magar population in Nepal still speak the Magar language, but this return is higher than the real number. Actual language retention is sadly just a fraction of this number. The Magar have been a highly mobile group since the dawn of the Gorkha conquest in the eighteenth century, and most Magar communities have abandoned their language in favour of Nepali. The language is primarily still spoken in small communities found between the Bherī and Marsyāṅdī, especially in the districts Pālpā, Syāṅjā, Tanahū and Gorkhā. The original home of the Magar was known as Bāhra Magarānt 'the twelve Magar regions', which comprised all the mid-hill regions of Lumbinī, Rāptī and Bherī zones. The Magar still live in these areas as well as in adjacent parts of Gaṇḍakī and Dhavalāgiri zones. There is great dialectal variation within Magar, and because of major differences in grammar and lexicon the various dialects merit separate studies. Northern Magar or Kham is also a distinct language spoken by at least 30,000 people in the upper valleys of Rukum and Rolpā districts in west-central Nepal and in adjacent portions of Bāgluṅ district, separated from the Magar area proper by several days' walk. Most Magar dialects are on the verge of extinction, with few children being raised in Magar anywhere. The prospects for Kham are slightly better in the short term.

Chepangic

Chepangic consists of Chepang and Bhujeli. Chepang is spoken by only 25,097 out of 36,656 ethnic Chepang or two thirds of the Chepang, who live in Makvānpur, Citvan and Dhādiṅ districts, south of the Triśulī river, north of the Rāptī river and west of the highway connecting Heṭaūḍā to Kathmandu. Chepang proper is spoken to the east of the Nārāyaṇī river, whilst Bhujelī is spoken by at least 2,000 people in Tanahū district to the west of the Nārāyaṇī. The Chepang have until recently lived as semi-nomadic hunter-foragers, but their habitat has been largely deforested and rendered accessible by roads and settlers from elsewhere in Nepal. The work of Christian missionaries has pitted the converted against the traditionalist Chepang. Therefore, the Chepang are now entering modern Nepalese society as a fragmented and socio-economically depressed group, compelled to assimilate both linguistically and culturally in order to survive at all.

Raji and Raute

The Raji and Raute are two groups who have until recently lived as semi-nomadic hunter-gatherers in the western Nepalese Terai and the adjoining portion of Pithaurāgaḍh district in Uttarkhaṇḍa. The Raji and Raute groups have been compelled to abandon their traditional lifestyle and adopt a sedentary existence by Nepalese and Indian government resettlement programmes. This has left most Raji and Raute destitute and prey to alcoholism and other social ills. Just 472 Raji were counted in 1988 in the Indian district of Pithaurāgaḍh, where they had been resettled in four villages in Dhārcūlā tehsil, four villages in Ḍiḍihāṭ tehsil and one village in Campāvat tehsil. The 1991 census of Nepal returned 3,274 Raji and 2,878 Raute by ethnicity, and 2,959 Raji by mother tongue. The Raji are primarily settled in Dāṅ-Deukhurī district. Since 1979 the Raute have been settled at two places in Ḍāḍeldhurā district. In addition, several hundred Raute still lead a nomadic lifestyle, led by the septuagenarian headman Man Bahādur Raskoṭī. This traditional group has resorted to modest forms of trading in jungle commodities and crafts, since much of their original forest habitat has been destroyed. Unverified reports would indicate that the resettled groups have largely lost the ancestral language, whereas the itinerant band of Raute is still known to speak Raute. Traditionally the Raute used to migrate from Pyūṭhān in the east to Ḍoṭī district in the west. Most recently, the itinerant group has been operating in Surkhet.

Dura

The Dura language is a Tibeto-Burman language which was spoken until the 1970s in the heartland of Lamjuṅ between the Pāūdī and Midim rivers. The last speakers passed away in the 1980s. The surviving Dura data have been collated in Leiden. The precise position which Dura occupied within the Tibeto-Burman language family has yet to be determined.

Gurung

Gurung is a Tamangic language. The Tamangic group includes Gurung, Tamang, Thakali, 'Narpa, 'Nyishangba, Gyasumdo, Chantyal, Kaike and perhaps Ghale. According to the 1991 census data on language retention, 227,918 out of 449,189 ethnic Gurung or about one half of the Gurung population still speaks the Gurung language. Gurungs live in the districts Gorkhā, Kāskī, Lamjuṅ, Parbat, Syāṅjā, Tanahũ and Dhādiṅ. Gurung comprises three dialects with a low degree of mutual intelligibility between them: (1) a relatively homogeneous western Gurung dialect in Kāskī and Parbat; (2) a heterogeneous eastern dialect group in Lamjuṅ, Gorkhā and Tanahũ; and (3) a southern dialect in Syāṅjā. All Gurung language communities are abandoning the language in favour of Nepali. Probably no young children are being raised in the language, so that all dialects of the language are likely to go extinct after the present generation of speakers expires.

Tamang

According to the 1991 census data on language retention, 904,456 or nearly 90 per cent of the 1,018,252 ethnic Tamang reported Tamang as their first language. Though already in a precarious position, Tamang is not yet as endangered as the other Tamangic languages. Tamang language communities are found dispersed throughout central and eastern hill regions of Nepal, especially in the districts Kābhrepālañcok, Makvānpur, Sindhupālcok, Nuvākoṭ, Dhādiṅ, Sindhulī, Rāmechāp, Bāgmatī, Dolakhā and Rasuvā. A majority of 83 per cent of the population in the sparsely populated district of Rasuvā in Bāgmatī zone is Tamang-speaking. There is a clear distinction between the western and eastern dialects of Tamang, whereby the Triśulī river demarcates the linguistic boundary between the two varieties, with transitional dialects found in western Makvānpur. 'Murmi' is an obsolete term for Tamang. The *Humlī Tāmāṅ* 'Tamangs of Humlā' and *Mugulī Tāmāṅ* 'the Tamangs of Mugu' are not linguistically Tamangs, but Limirong Tibetans and Mugu Tibetans respectively.

Thakali

The Thakali are a Tamangic language community in the Kālī Gaṇḍakī river valley, an affluent area because of the trade in salt and other commodities between Tibet and India in olden days and today because of tourism. The majority of the ethnic Thakali are economically successful, no longer speak Thakali and have moved out of their native homeland to Kathmandu and abroad. Many of the remaining Thakali speakers are originally outsiders of other ethnic groups who have settled in the Thakali portion of the Kālī Gaṇḍakī river valley in order to make a livelihood and have assimilated as best they can to the Thakali both linguistically and culturally. Particularly, the Towa, who were originally speakers of the 'Loke dialect of Tibetan, have moved from the neighbouring Bāhra Gāũ area and mastered the Thakali language, though they are looked down upon by the Thakali, who refer to them by the derogatory name *arangsi karangsi*. Thakali was spoken by 7,113 people according to the 1991 census. A comparable number of people speak Seke, a related and mutually intelligible dialect spoken in an enclave further upstream, surrounded on all sides by Tibetan-speaking settlements. The speakers of Seke are known as *Shopa*.

Manangba

The Manangba dialects include 'Nyishangba, Gyasumdo and 'Narpa, spoken respectively in the upper Manang valley, the lower Manang valley, and in the 'Nar and Phu valleys, east of the Annapūrṇā Himāl massif. The 1971 population estimate for the 'Nar-Phu dialect area was approximately 500, whilst the 1971 census put the number of Manangba in Manang proper at approximately 2,600. The latter figure revealed that at the time the Manangbas already effectively constituted merely one third of the population of their native homeland in the Manang valley. A sociolinguistic detail relevant to any field linguist is that the speakers of Manangba dialects generally resent the qualifications Manangba or *Manāṅe*, both of which have acquired a derogatory connotation. Instead, these people prefer to be known as 'Gurungs'.

Kaike and Chantyal

Kaike is another Tamangic language spoken by approximately 2,000 people in several villages in Dolpo district. The language is also known as 'Tārālī Khām' or 'Tārālī Magar'. This name is taken from the toponym Tārākoṭ 'star fort', the main town in Tichurong, where these people live. Chantyal is spoken in the hills south of the Thakali area between the Myāgdī and Bherī rivers on the steep western and southern slopes of the Dhaulāgiri massif. The Chantyal until recently worked the copper mines of the area. Approximately only 2,000 of the 10,000 ethnic Chantyal still speak the language. The ethnic Chantyal are divided into two groups, one in the northeast, in Myāgdī district, and the other in the southwest, in Bāgluṅ district, the two areas being separated by a ridge. The Bāgluṅ Chantyal had ceased to speak Chantyal by the nineteenth century. The Myāgdī Chantyal still speak the language in certain villages, e.g. Maṅgale Khānī, Dvārī, Ghyā̃s Kharka, Caurā Khānī, Gurjā Khānī, Kuhine Khānī, Thārā Khānī, Pātle Kharka, Mālāmphār and Malkābāṅ, as far as the Rāhughāṭ Kholā.

Ghale

Ghale is a Tibeto-Burman language which may, in fact, not be Tamangic, but may phylogenetically constitute a group on its own within the Tibeto-Burman language family. The number of Ghale speakers was estimated at 12,000 in 1975. The language is spoken in the northern portion of Gorkhā district, where there are thirty-three Ghale villages and hamlets, and in an adjacent portion of Dhādiṅ district. The main Ghale speech community lies in the area surrounding and north of the town of Bārpāk, which has about 650 houses. Traditionally, the Ghale have been ethnically classed with the Gurung, with whom they may intermarry. The designation 'Ghale Gurung' is even heard, though others deny that they are Gurung. The inaccessibility of the area has protected the language thus far. Yet even in this remote northern part of Gorkhā district, language death is inevitable, given the present pace of linguistic assimilation to Nepali in Nepal.

Endangered Tibeto-Burman languages of the western Indian and Pakistan Himalayas

West Himalayish

The ten West Himalayish languages are spoken in scattered enclaves in the western Indian Himalayas, between Jammu and Kashmir in the west-northwest and the modern state of Nepal in the east-southeast. Rangkas was recorded at the beginning of the twentieth century, but is now extinct. Zhangzhung went extinct even earlier, and used to be spoken to the north of the Himalayas across a large portion of western Tibet until it was wiped out by Tibetan towards the end of the first millennium AD. All surviving West Himalayish languages are severely endangered.

The three languages Manchad, Tinan and Bunan are spoken in Lahul district in what today is the Indian state or Himachal Pradesh. Manchad is spoken along the Candra or Upper Chenab river by approximately 15,000 people who have adopted the Hindu religion, and whose language has adopted many Indic loanwords. The term 'Manchad' means 'lower valley' in the local Tibetan dialect. The language has also been called 'Paṭanī' or 'Paṭṭanī' after the Paṭan or Paṭṭan valley, where it is spoken from

Tandi as far upstream as Thirot. Tinan is spoken on the Chenab immediately downstream from the Manchad area, from Tandi as far downstream as Sissu Nullah, particularly in the area known as Gondhla. The 1981 census counted 1,833 speakers of Tinan. Bunan is spoken in the Gahar or Gahr valley which covers both banks of the Bhāgā river from Tandi northeast to Kyelong. The Bhāgā is a tributary emptying into the Chenab from the north. The 1981 census enumerated 3,581 speakers of Bunan.

Kanashi is a special language within this branch of the family, spoken in just the one village of Malāṇa near Kulu in Kulu district of Himachal Pradesh. Kinnauri is spoken in Kinnaur district of Himachal Pradesh. It is unknown what percentage of the 59,154 people enumerated in the 1981 census for Kinnaur district actually still spoke the language. Rangpo or Rongpo is spoken along the northeastern fringe of Garhwal, confined to the area of the Nītī and Māṇā valleys in Jośīmaṭh subdivision of Cāmolī district, north of Badrināth along the upper course of the Alaknandā river and around the lower course of the Dhaulī-Gaṅgā river above its confluence with the Alaknandā at Jośīmaṭh. There are an estimated 12,000 remaining speakers of Rangpo. Darma and Byangsi are spoken further west in the Indian-Nepalese borderlands, straddling the Indian districts of Almoḍā and Pithaurāgaḍh in the area that used to be known as Kumaon as well as in the Nepali district of Dārculā. Darma is spoken in the uppermost portion of the Darmā valley, drained by the river Dhaulī and bounded in the north by Tibet. At the beginning of the twentieth century, 1,761 speakers of the language were counted. No more recent statistic is available. Immediately to the east of the Darmā valley lies the Mahākālī river valley, which is the home to the Byangsi. The 1991 census counted 1,314 Byangsi in Nepal. A form of Byangsi was recorded by Sten Konow under the name 'Chaudāngsī'.

Central Bodish languages

Europeans call German and English 'languages', rather than treating them respectively as a hinterland dialect and an insular dialect of Dutch. However, Westerners tend to treat languages in other parts of the world as 'dialects' which are just as distinct from each other phonetically, phonologically, morphologically and lexically as German and English are from Dutch. The same applies to what are generally referred to in the West as 'Tibetan dialects'. The Standard or Central dialect of Tibetan, spoken in Lhasa, is not an endangered language, even though the language is undergoing heavy lexical and even grammatical influence from Mandarin, the language of the occupying forces. Kham and 'Amdo Tibetan also still represent lively language communities. However, many other 'Tibetan dialects' are endangered. Linguistically, it is more correct to refer to these languages as Central Bodish languages, and not as 'Tibetan dialects'. These include the many diverse languages spoken in the western extremity of Tibet, parts of which now lie in the modern states of Pakistan and India, as well as the languages spoken in the sBas-yul 'hidden lands', as the high alpine valleys on the southern flank of the Himalayas have been referred to from the Tibetan perspective.

The Central Bodish languages of western Tibet are in many respects the most conservative of the Tibetan languages and also amongst the most endangered. They are spoken in the parts of Tibet which are now located in the modern states of Pakistan and India, in the areas of sBal-ti 'Bälti', Bu-rig 'B'urik' or 'Purik', La-dwags 'Lada' of 'Ladakh', sBi-ti 'Biti' or 'Spiti', and Zangs-dkar 'Z'angkar'. In the western Indian

Himalayas, the languages of the 'hidden lands' include Jāḍ, spoken mainly in Bagorā village, just 17km south of Uttarkāśī on the banks of the Bhāgīrathī, where the Jāḍ were resettled after the Indo-Chinese conflict of 1962. Some settlements are also found in Purolā, Rājgaḍhī, and Bhaṭvārī sub-divisions. Their original homes lay on the Indo-Tibetan border.

In Nepal, several Central Bodish languages are spoken in enclaves on the southern slopes of the Himalayas which show characteristics divergent from Central Tibetan proper. These include the dialects spoken by the Limirong Tibetans in the extreme northwest of Karṇālī zone in the district of Humlā, the Tibetans of Mugu and the Karmarong Tibetans in northwestern Nepal, the dialect of Dol-po 'D'ölpo', the dialect of Mustang known as 'Loke, the dialect of the Nupri or *Lārkyā Bhoṭe* below Manāslu Himāl in Gorkhā district, the dialect of the Tsum in a few villages along a tributary of the Buḍhī Gaṇḍakī known as the Shar, the community of *Khaccaḍ Bhoṭe* 'mule Tibetans' north of Dhāibuṅ and northeast of Nuvākoṭ, the 'Langthang Tibetans south of the 'Langthang Himāl and north of Jugal Himāl and Gosāĩkuṇḍ, the well known Sherpa in the mountains surrounding Mt Everest and in Solu Khumbu, and a small population living at Ha-lung, known in Nepali as Olāṅcuṅ Golā, and at Tāpke Golā and Thudam in the northeastern extremity of Nepal around the headwaters of the Tamor.

In Bhutan, three endangered Central Bodish language communities account for nearly 15,000 people. The Brokpas of Säphu Geo in 'Wangdi Phodr'a district in the north of the Black Mountains speak a dialect called Lakha 'language of the mountain passes' or Tshangkha. There are an estimated 8,000 speakers. Brokkat is a Central Bodish language spoken by the Brokpa community of 300 speakers at Dur in Bumthang district in central Bhutan. A Central Bodish language is spoken by approximately 5,000 people at Mera and Sakteng in eastern Bhutan. A number of Tibetan enclaves are also spoken in Arunachal Pradesh, south of the McMahon line on the Indian side of the Indo-Tibetan border.

Other Bodish languages

Jirel is a poorly documented Bodish language spoken by about 3,000 people in the Jirī and Sikrī valleys of Dolakhā district in northern central Nepal The name *Jirel* is the Nepali adjectival form of the place name Jirī. Kāgate is spoken in the mountains between the Likhu and Khimṭī rivers in the northeastern part of Rāmechāp district by the *Kāgate Bhoṭe* 'paper Bhutiya' because their ancestors used to manufacture paper. The Kāgate call themselves 'Śyu:ba', which likewise signifies 'paper maker', and pass themselves off as 'Tamang' to outsiders. The number of speakers was estimated at about one thousand in 1974. There is another group of 'Sherpas', who are not recognised as Sherpas by the Sherpa proper, mentioned above. Whilst the Sherpas around Mt Everest and in Solu Khumbu speak a Central Bodish language, the Sherpa of Yolmo or 'Ölmo', an area known in Nepali as Helambū, north of Sindhupālcok, speak a distinct Bodish language.

Endangered Indo-European languages of South Asia

Indo-European languages are spoken throughout the north of the Indian subcontinent and on Sri Lanka. All of these are Indo-Iranian languages belonging to Iranian,

Nuristani and Indo-Aryan branches. Nuristani sometimes still goes by the name 'Kafiri', and Indo-Aryan is sometimes still called 'Indic'.

Iranian languages

Older stages of Iranian, such as Avestan, Old and Middle Persian, Pehlevi, Parthian, Sogdian, Chorasmian, Bactrian, Sarmatian and Khotanese, have gone extinct or have effectively been superseded by later stages of Iranian. The modern languages Persian or Fārsī, Darī, Tājikī, Kurdish, Baluchi or Balōčī, and Pashto or Pakhto are flourishing. Yet a number of Iranian languages are spoken only by small and dwindling language communities. Ossetian is spoken in the north-central Caucasus. Tātī is spoken in parts of Azerbaijan, and Āzarī, Tāleshī, Semnānī, Gīlakī and Māzanderānī are spoken in the southwestern Caspian littoral. Gurānī is spoken in several areas in the Zagros east of the Tigris, Zāzā or Dimli is spoken in eastern Turkey and western Iran. There is considerable dialectal heterogeneity in southwestern, southeastern and central Iran. Other endangered Iranian languages of eastern Afghanistan and neighbouring parts of Pakistan include Parācī, spoken in three valleys along the southern flank of the Hindu Kush, and Ōrmuṛī, spoken in the area around Barakī-Barak in Afghanistan and at Kāṇīgrām in Pakistan. The archaic and highly endangered Pāmir languages spoken by communities along the Āb-i Panja river in southern Tajikistan, in Badakhshan province of northeastern Afghanistan and neighbouring portions of Chinese Turkestan, include Śughnī, Rośanī, Bartangī, Rośorvī, Sariqōlī, Yāzghulāmī, Wakhī, Zēbākī, Sanglīcī and Iśkāśmī. Closely related to Paśtō are Yidgha, spoken in the Lutkuh valley of Pakistan, and Munjī, spoken in the Munjān valley of northeastern Afghanistan. Yaghnōbī is still spoken by a small community in an alpine valley around the headwaters of the Yaghnōb in Tajikistan. There are no reliable up-to-date statistics for the precise numbers of speakers of these endangered language communities.

Nuristani languages

All Nuristani languages were already faced with imminent extinction before Afghanistan was turned into a war zone by the Soviet Union under Brezhnev and later by the Taliban and warring Islamists from countries like Saudi Arabia and Pakistan. The Nuristani languages are spoken by tribesmen whose ancient Indo-Aryan ancestors took refuge in the inaccessible mountain valleys of the Hindu Kush in Nuristan. These tribes have no literary tradition of their own and were collectively called *Kāfirī* ('infidels') until they were converted to Islam after Nuristan was conquered by the Afghans in 1896. The Nuristani languages from north to south are Kati, Prasun, Waigali, Ashkun, Gambiri and Zemiaki. Kati, formerly also known as Bashgali, is perhaps still spoken by about 20,000 speakers. All the other Nuristani language communities are much smaller than Kati. Prasun, the most aberrant of the Nuristani languages, is spoken in six villages in the high alpine valley along the headwaters of the Peč, wedged in between the Kati-speaking areas in the Ktiwī valley and the upper Bashgal valley. Waigali is spoken in the Waigal valley, a northern tributary of the Peč. Gambiri or Tregāmī 'three villages dialect' is spoken not only at Gambīr, Kaṭār and in the Tregām valley southeast of lower Waigal in the direction of the Kunar river. The Ashkun-speaking area lies between the Peč and the Alingar and in valleys along the upper drainage of these two rivers and their minor tributaries. Zemiaki, first identified as a

315

sixth quite distinct Nuristani language by Edelman and Grünberg-Cvetinovič in 1999, is spoken in a small enclave south of the Peč river, south of the Waigali area but immediately surrounded on all sides by Dardic language communities. The Nuristani languages are not only highly important from the point of view of understanding the population prehistory of South and Central Asia, they exhibit numerous peculiar typological features of great interest to cognitive linguistics.

Dardic languages

The most endangered Indo-Aryan languages are the heterogeneous and archaic Dardic languages, spoken in small alpine communities. The five clusters of Dardic languages are the Ṣiṇā cluster, the Kōhistānī cluster, the Kunar group, the Citrāl group and Paśaī. Ṣiṇā and Kashmiri are not themselves endangered, but other languages of the Ṣiṇā group are threatened with extinction. These are the archaic Phalūṛa and Sāwī dialects, related to Ṣiṇā, and the endangered Ḍumākī language is of great historical importance because it is believed to be related to the language of the gypsies. Ḍumākī is spoken by less than 600 elderly Ḍoma in Hunza, who traditionally belong to the lowly minstrel and blacksmith castes in what is now northern Pakistan. The Kōhistānī languages are Baśkarīk, Torwālī, Maiyã, Tirāhī, and the language of Woṭapūr and Kaṭārqalā. Baśkarīk or Gāwrī is spoken around the headwaters of the Swāt and in the Panjkora valley. Torwālī is spoken in the upper Swāt valley. Maiyã is spoken between Ṣiṇā and Pashto-speaking territory. Tirāhī is spoken in a few villages southeast of Jalalabad in eastern Afghanistan. The language of Woṭapūr and Kaṭārqalā is spoken in a few villages on the Peč in eastern Afghanistan. The Citrāl languages are Khowār and Kalaṣa. Khowār, the language of the Khō tribe, is the main language of the great Citrāl valley. Kalaṣa is spoken by members of the Kalaṣ tribe in the western side valleys of southern Citrāl. The nearly extinct languages of the Kunar group are spoken by small communities found around the confluence of Citrāl and the Bashgal, i.e. Damēlī, Gawar-Bātī, Ningalāmī and Śumāśtī. Gawar-Bātī or Narisātī is spoken in a few villages on the Kunar river. A divergent language is or used to be spoken by a dwindling number of speakers at Ningalām on the Peč. Another divergent but related language is or used to be spoken at Śumāśt. Damēlī is likewise spoken in just one village. The Paśaī language is spoken in lower Kunar and in Laghmān and was once spoken over a larger area than it is today.

Western Pahāḍī and Central Pahāḍī

The three branches of Indo-Aryan known as Western Pahāḍī, literally 'montane', Central Pahāḍī and Eastern Pahāḍī do not together form a linguistic taxon, as the nomenclature misleadingly suggests, but merely share the feature of designating groups of alpine language communities. Western Pahāḍī languages are spoken from the western portion of Dehrā Dūn district in Uttar Pradesh, through Himachal Pradesh all the way west into Jammu and Kashmir. The 1961 census of India distinguished over sixty highly divergent and poorly documented Western Pahāḍī languages known by a welter of local dialect names, including Baṅgāṇī, Jaunsarī, Sirmaudī, Baghāṭī, Mahāsuī (formerly known as Kiūṇṭhalī), Haṇḍūrī, Kuluī, Maṇḍeālī in the area formerly known as *Maṇḍe Rājya,* Cameālī in the area once known as *Cambā-Rājya,* Kāṅgḍī, Bharmaurī (or Gāḍī), Curāhī, Paṅgvālī, Bhadravāhī, Bhalesī,

Khaśālī and Pāḍrī. The Central Pahāḍī languages are the Garhwali and Kumaoni dialects (*Gaḍhvālī* and *Kumāunī*), spoken in Garhwal and Kumaon, together forming an area known today as Uttarākhaṇḍ. All the Western and Central Pahāḍī languages are endangered because these areas are increasingly being linguistically assimilated by larger language communities, e.g. Urdu, Panjabi, Hindi. Eastern Pahāḍī is represented by the successful and growing Nepali language. The success and spread of Nepali not only has conferred upon the language the dubious honour of being a 'killer language' throughout Nepal, Sikkim and parts of Bhutan, but ironically also of threatening the archaic and divergent western dialects of Nepali itself.

Indo-Aryan languages with possible allophylian substrate

The Tharu in the Terai speak Indo-Aryan dialects collectively known as *Thāruvānī*, which is not a language as such but a cover term for various Terai dialects of Bhojpuri, Maithili and especially Awadhi as spoken by ethnic Tharu. The original pre-Indo-Aryan languages spoken by the Tharu are extinct, but survive in the form of substrate words used within households, so that doublets exist for certain words. For example, in Citvan Thāru alongside Indo-Aryan *yaṅkhī*, 'eye', there exists a form *tẽḍ*, 'eye', reminiscent of the Manchad form *tira*, 'eye'. These original Tharu substrate words are being lost because not every household preserves them. The differences between the Tharuwani dialects and the local Indo-Aryan languages spoken by the high castes have never been properly or systematically studied and documented. Varieties of Tharuwani have been investigated by Christian missionaries, but they have kept their linguistic findings to themselves and used their knowledge mainly for the production of hymnals and Christian literature. As the Tharu are being continuously assimilated into mainstream culture, the vestiges of their ancestral language and the peculiar features of Tharuwani are being lost through increasing linguistic assimilation to the mainstream Awadhi, Maithili, Bhojpuri and Nepali language communities.

Three other Indo-Aryan languages of Nepal are in the throes of death. Most speakers of the Danuwar, Darai and Majhi or Bote language communities have already assimilated linguistically and culturally to modern Nepali mainstream culture. The main Darai settlements are in Citvan, Tanahū, Gorkhā, Navalparāsī and Pālpā districts. According to the 1991 census data on language retention, only 6,520 out of 10,759 ethnic Darai or less than two thirds of the Darai still speak the Darai language, which exhibits biactantial verbal morphology. The Danuwar or *Danuvār* are native to Sindhulī and Udaypur districts in the Inner Terai, but Danuwar are also settled in the hills of Kābhrepālañcok and Sindhupālcok districts and in the Terai districts of Sarlāhī, Mahottarī, Dhanuṣā and Sirāhā. According to the 1991 census data on language retention, only 23,721 out of 50,574 ethnic Danuwar or roughly just half of the Danuwar still speak the Danuwar language. The group known as Majhi or Bote live along the Nārāyaṇī or Saptagaṇḍakī river and its tributaries in the districts of Bāgluṅ, Parvat, Syāñjā, Gulmī, Pālpā, Kāskī, Gorkhā, Tanahū, Parsā, Citvan and Navalparāsī, as well as in the Terai and hills of the districts of Rāmechāp, Sindhulī, Sindhupālcok, Kābhrepālañcok and Dhanuṣā. The 1991 census data on language retention show that only 11,322 out of 55,050 ethnic Majhi, or just one fifth of the Majhi, still speak the Majhi language.

A number of other inadequately documented Indo-Aryan languages spoken in the hills of Nepal, the Nepalese Terai and Manipur have now nearly vanished. The *Kumāle* or

317

Kumhāle language is spoken by a potter's caste in the central Terai and adjacent central hills. The total number of speakers was estimated at 3,500 in the early 1950s, but only 1,413 speakers of the language were counted in the 1991 census. The original language of the *Bãtar* in the eastern Terai, especially Morań District, may have already vanished. A dwindling number of *Ganagāĩ* in eastern Bihar, the eastern Nepalese Terai and West Bengal still speak Ańgikā. In Manipur, the Indo-Aryan language known as Bishnupriya Manipuri or *Viṣṇuprīya Maṇipurī,* served as an Indo-Aryan contact language and *lingua franca* between the thirteenth and nineteenth centuries, which had undergone influence of the Meithei language native to the region. In 1964, there were still reportedly 114 speakers of Bishnupriya Manipuri.

Bibliography

Diffloth, Gérard (2001) Tentative calibration of time depths in Austroasiatic branches. Paper presented at the Colloque 'Perspectives sur la Phylogénie des Langues d'Asie Orientales' at Périgueux, 30 August 2001.

—— (2005) The contribution of linguistic palaeontology to the homeland of Austroasiatic, pp. 77–80 in Laurent Sagart, Roger Blench and Alicia Sanchez-Mazas, eds., *The Peopling of East Asia: Putting Together the Archaeology, Linguistics and Genetics.* London: RoutledgeCurzon.

van Driem, George (2001) *Languages of the Himalayas: An Ethnolinguistic Handbook of the Greater Himalayan Region, Containing an Introduction to the Symbiotic Theory of Language,* 2 vols, Leiden: Brill.

McAlpin, David Wayne (1981) 'Proto-Elamo-Dravidian: The Evidence and its Implications', *Transactions of the American Philosophical Society*, vol. 71, part 3, Philadelphia PA: American Philosophical Society

Schleicher, August (1863) *Die Darwinsche Theorie und die Sprachwissenschaft: Offenes Sendschreiben an Herrn Dr. Ernst Häckel, a.o. Professor der Zoologie und Direktor des zoologischen Museums an der Universität Jena*, Weimar: Böhlau.

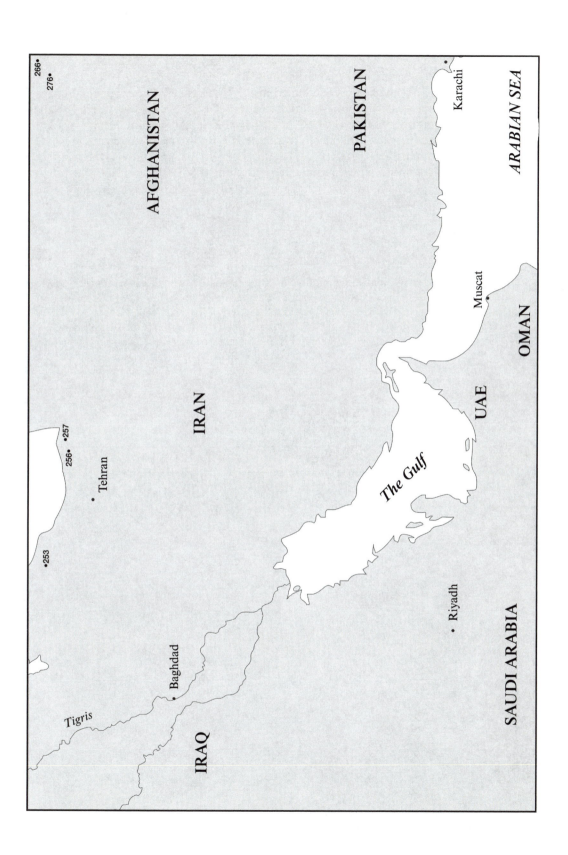

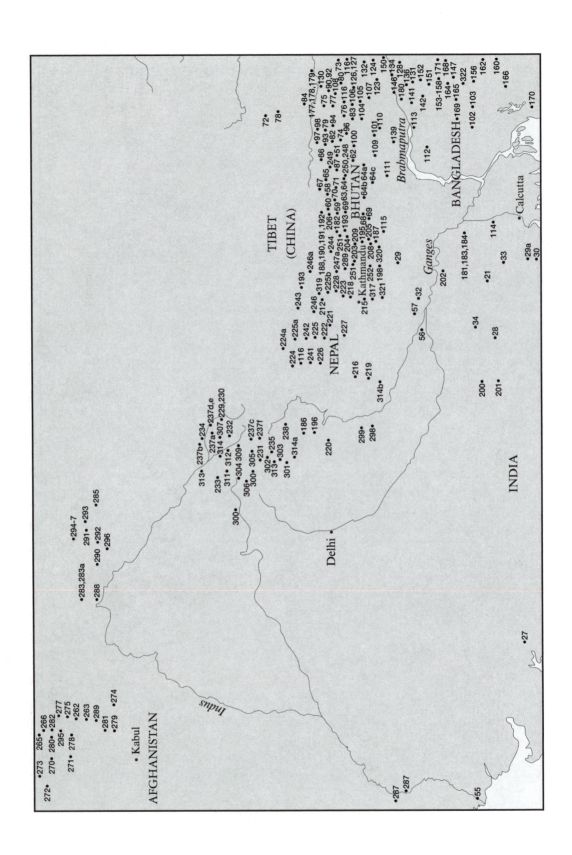

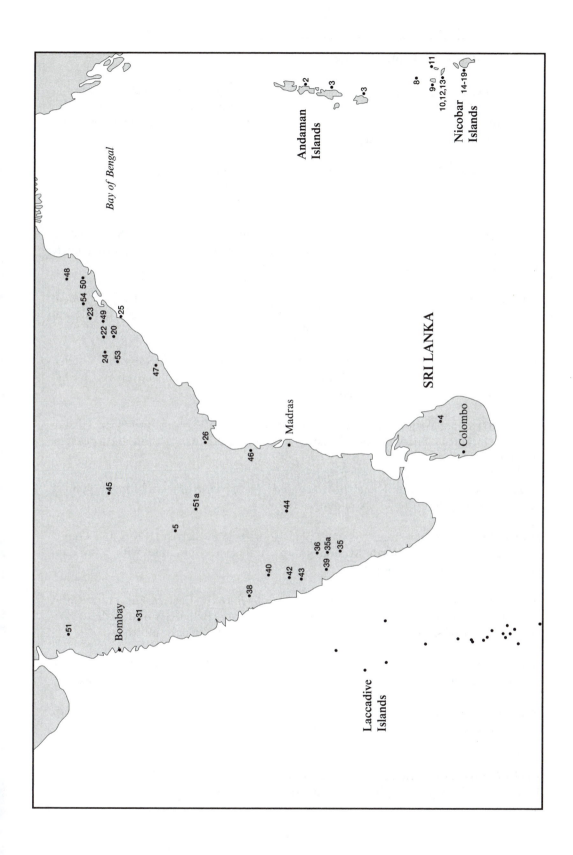

Alphabetical list of languages

Aiton (*Shām Doāniyā*) [180] India: Assam state, Lakhimpur and Sibsagar districts and Naga hills. *Tibeto-Burman*, Daic branch. This Shan ethnic group settled there to flee persecution in the nineteenth century from Burma; numbers unknown but now dwindling; severely endangered.

Anal [154] India: Manipur state. *Tibeto-Burman*, Mizo-Kuki-Chin branch. Number of speakers unknown, but rapidly losing ground to Meithei, the state majority language; severely endangered.

Angami [131] India: western Nagaland state, Kohima district; Manipur, Maharashtra states. *Tibeto-Burman*, part of Angami-Pochuri language cluster. Approximately 30,000 speakers; endangered.

Aṅgikā [321] India: Bihar and West Bengal states; also Nepal, eastern Terai. *Indo-European*, further affiliation uncertain. Number of speakers over 725,000 but declining, owing to general use of Hindi and Maithili. Endangered.

Apatani [82] India: Arunachal Pradesh state, Apatani Plateau in Subansiri district. *Tani language cluster*, one of the Western Tani group known collectively as 'Nishi'. About 14,000 speakers; endangered.

Ashing [87] India: Arunachal Pradesh state, headwaters of Siyang river near Tibetan border. Nothing is known about it except its name. Less than a thousand speakers; endangered.

Ashkun [280] Afghanistan: Kunar province. *Indo-European*, Nuristani branch. Number of speakers may be up to 7,000; endangered.

Asur [187] India: Bihar state, Netarhaṭ plateau of Palāmū district, Rāñcī and Gumlā districts. *Austroasiatic*, North Munda group. A dialect continuum with a total of about 7,000 speakers; endangered.

Athpahariya [111] Nepal: Dhankuta district. *Tibeto-Burman*, Eastern Kiranti group. A continuum of dialects rather than a single language, and Belhare is one of these varieties. Number of speakers small and fast declining for all dialects; moribund.

A'tong [33] India: Meghalaya state, southeastern Garo hills. *Tibeto-Burman*, Koch language cluster. Several thousand speakers, generally bilingual in Garo. Endangered.

Badaga [35a] India: Tamil Nadu state, Nilgiri Hills. *Dravidian*, South Dravidian group, closely related to Kannada. Over 100,000 speakers, but with no official status; potentially endangered.

Baghāṭī [301] India: Himachal Pradesh state, Simla district. *Indo-European*, Western Pahadi branch. May be up to 4,000 speakers. Endangered; little is known about the language.

Bahing [208] Nepal: Okhaḷḍhuṅgā and Solukhumbu districts. *Tibeto-Burman*, Northwestern Kiranti branch. Only a few elderly speakers remain; moribund.

Bälti (*sBalti*) [237a] India: Jammu and Kashmir state. *Tibeto-Burman*, Central Bodish branch. Number of speakers unknown, but may be up to 67,000; endangered.

Baṅgāṇī [298] India: Uttar Pradesh state. *Indo-European*, Western Pahadi branch. Little is known about the language.

Bangni (*Western Dafla*) [79] India: Arunachal Pradesh state, across the Indo-Tibetan border. *Tani language cluster.* About 23,000 speakers; endangered.

Bantawa [195] Nepal: Bhojpur district. *Tibeto-Burman*, Southern Kiranti branch. The major language of the district formerly, but first-language speakers dwindling; endangered.

Barām [212] Nepal: Gorkhā district. *Tibeto-Burman*, Newaric branch. A few middle-aged and elderly speakers remain in one village. Moribund.

Bartangi [266] Afghanistan: Badakhshan province. *Indo-European*, Iranian branch; may be a dialect of Śughnī (q.v.) Number of speakers unknown; endangered.

Baśkarīk (*Gāwrī*) [286] Pakistan: headwaters of Swāt river and Panjkora valley. *Indo-European*, Dardic branch, Kohistani group. There may be up to 1,500 speakers; endangered.

Bãtar [320] Nepal: Moraṅ district. *Indo-European*, further affiliation uncertain. Moribund or may be already extinct.

Bawm [166] India: Mizoram and Assam states; also spoken in Bangladesh and Burma. *Tibeto-Burman*, Mizo-Kuki-Chin branch. Number of speakers unknown; population is shifting to Assamese; severely endangered.

Bellari [42] India: Karnataka state, South Kanarā district, near Udupi. *Dravidian*, South Dravidian group. About a thousand speakers; severely endangered.

Bhadravāhī [311] India: Jammu and Kasmhir state. *Indo-European*, Western Pahadi branch. There may be up to 69,000 speakers; potentially endangered.

Bhalesī [312] India: Jammu and Kashmir state. *Indo-European*, Western Pahadi branch. Little is known about the language; may be a dialect of Bhadravāhī above.

Bharmaurī (*Gādī*) [308] India: Himachal Pradesh state, Chamba district; Uttar Pradesh; Jammu and Kashmir. *Indo-European*, Western Pahadi branch. Bharmaurī is regarded by some as a dialect of Gādī. Number of speakers up to 120,000; potentially endangered.

Bhujeli [218] Nepal: Tanahū district. *Tibeto-Burman*, Chepangic branch. At least 2,000 speakers, but the language is giving way to Nepali, the language of incoming settlers; severely endangered.

Bhumij [29a] India: scattered communities in Bihar, Orissa and Madhya Pradesh states. *Austroasiatic*, North Munda group. Possibly as many as 150,000 speakers in total, but with widespread bilingualism. Potentially endangered.

Birhoṛ [30] India: Bihar state, Siṃhabhūm, Palāmū, Hazārībāg, Rāñcī districts. *Austroasiatic*, North Munda group; its speakers are semi-nomadic people, assimilating into the Bihari speech community. Less than 2,000 speakers; moribund.

Bishnupriya Manipuri [322] India: Manipur state and elsewhere. *Indo-European*, previously regarded as a Bengali-Meithei creole. There were 114 speakers remaining in 1964; moribund.

Black Mountain [63] Bhutan: Black Mountains of central Bhutan. *Tibeto-Burman*, East Bodish group, but very divergent from other members of this group, possibly not of this group. About 500 speakers in the jungle area; endangered.

Bodo [107] India: Assam, Cachar district. *Tibeto-Burman*, Bodo-Garo language cluster. Speakers of Dimasa and Hojai (q.v.) also refer to themselves by this name. Number of speakers unknown, but rapidly assimilating with Bengali- and Assamese-speaking communities. Highly endangered.

Bokar [84] India: Arunachal Pradesh state, West Siang district, and across Tibetan border. *Tani language cluster*. About 3,500 speakers; endangered.

Bori [91] India: Arunachal Pradesh state, on Siyom and Sike rivers. Part of Minyong-Padam subgroup within *Tani language cluster*. About 2,000 speakers; endangered.

Brahui [55] Pakistan: Kalat district and parts of Hyderabad, Karachi and Khairpur districts; also small communities in Afghanistan and Iran. *Dravidian*, North Dravidian group. Approximately half a million speakers. The language has been written for three centuries, in a Persian-based script like Urdu, but its written use is not widespread. Potentially endangered.

Brokkat [250] Bhutan: Bumthang district, Dur village. *Tibeto-Burman*, Central Bodish branch. Number of speakers around 300; endangered.

Brokpa [248] Bhutan: Sakteng valley, 'Wangdi Phodr'a district. *Tibeto-Burman*, Central Bodish branch. Number of speakers may be as high as 5,000; endangered.

Bumthang [64a] Bhutan: Bumthang district. *Tibeto-Burman*, East Bodish group. Spoken by about 30,000 people in four distinct dialects. Potentially endangered.

Bunan [231] India: Himachal Pradesh state, Lahul district. *Tibeto-Burman*, West Himalayish branch. 3,581 speakers in 1981, endangered.

Bu-rig (*Purik*) [237b] India: Kashmir, Kargil district. *Tibeto-Burman*, Central Bodish branch. Number of speakers unknown, but may be up to 132,000; declining and endangered.

Burushaski [7] Pakistan: Hunza-Nager and Yasin valleys. *Language Isolate.* Heavily admixed with Urdu and English elements in recent times. Owing to the high degree of local autonomy up to the mid-twentieth century, the language was not declining in use until recently, but the current speech community (estimated at around 80,000) is believed to be dwindling fast. Potentially endangered.

Byangsi [236] India/Nepal borders: Mahākālī river valley. *Tibeto-Burman*, West Himalayish branch. Nepalese census of 1991 recorded 1,314 ethnic Byangsi; endangered.

C(h)am(b)eālī [306] India: Himachal Pradesh state, Chamba district. *Indo-European*, Western Pahadi branch. Number of speakers 129,654 in 1991 census; potentially endangered.

Chali [67] Bhutan: north of Monggar area, east of Kurichu river. *Tibeto-Burman*, East Bodish group. About 1,000 speakers; endangered.

Chamling [198] Nepal: Bhojpur district. *Tibeto-Burman*, Southern Kiranti branch. The second largest language of the district formerly, with 30,000 members of ethnic group, but first-language speakers dwindling; endangered.

Chantyal [227] Nepal: Myāgdī and Bāgluṅ districts. *Tibeto-Burman*, Tamangic branch. Spoken by only about one fifth of the 10,000 reported ethnic Chantyal. Extinct in some districts already; endangered.

Chathare Limbu [182] Eastern Nepal. *Tibeto-Burman*, Limbu group. Total Limbu population about 300,000, but transfer to younger speakers is not taking place. Severely endangered.

Chepang [217] Nepal: Makvānpur, Citvan and Dhādiṅ districts. *Tibeto-Burman*, Chepangic branch. Census figures show 25,097 speakers, which is two thirds of the ethnic group, but their forest habitat is now largely uninhabitable and they are being forcefully assimilated among Nepali speakers.

Chiling [186] Nepal: Āṅkhisallā and Dhankuṭā districts. *Tibeto-Burman*, Eastern Kiranti group. About 3,000 speakers, but number dwindling; endangered.

Chintang [196] Nepal: Dhankuṭā district. *Tibeto-Burman*, Southern Kiranti branch. Spoken in only two villages and severely endangered.

Chiru [151] India: Manipur state. *Tibeto-Burman*, Mizo-Kuki-Chin branch. Number of speakers unknown, but rapidly losing ground to Meithei, the state majority language; severely endangered.

Cho-ca-nga-ca-kha [61] Bhutan: Monggar and Lhüntsi districts. *Tibeto-Burman*, South Bodish group. A close relative of the national language Dzongkha, with which it is being assimilated. About 20,000 speakers; endangered.

Chokri [132] India: Nagaland state, around Cheswezumi village. *Tibeto-Burman*, Angami-Pochuri language cluster. Closely related to Angami; number of speakers unknown but may be up to 20,000; endangered.

Chorei [165] India: Manipur, Assam and Tripura states. *Tibeto-Burman*, Mizo-Kuki-Chin branch. Number of speakers is unknown but small, and shifting to Assamese or Bengali; severely endangered.

Chungli Ao [124] India: Nagaland state. *Tibeto-Burman*; the closely related Ao sub-group has a total number of about 65,275. Transfer to an Assamese-based creole is general among Ao speakers; severely endangered.

C(h)urahi [309] India: Himachal Pradesh, Chamba district. *Indo-European*, Western Pahadi branch. Number of speakers 110,552 in 1991 census; potentially endangered.

Dakpa [62] India and Bhutan: Arunachal Pradesh state, Tawang district, straddling the Bhutanese border. *Tibeto-Burman*, East Bodish group. A few thousand speakers; endangered.

Damēlī [293] Pakistan: Damel valley. *Indo-European*, Dardic branch. Spoken in one remaining village; severely endangered.

Danuwar [316] Nepal: Inner Terai district. *Indo-Aryan*, further affiliation uncertain. Distinct from but related to the language of the same name spoken in India (Madhya Pradesh, Maharashtra). Number of speakers in 1991 census was 23,721, less than half of the ethnic group, which is rapidly assimilating to the Nepali-speaking community. Severely endangered.

Darai [317] Nepal: Inner Terai district. *Indo-Aryan*, further affiliation uncertain. Number of speakers in 1991 census was 6,520, just over half of the ethnic group, which is rapidly adopting Nepali. Severely endangered.

Darma [235] India and Nepal: Himachal Pradesh state, Almoḍā and Pithaurāgaḍh districts in India and Dārculā district in Nepal. *Tibeto-Burman*, West Himalayish branch. 1,761 speakers recorded at beginning of twentieth century but no figures since then; thought to be endangered.

Deori Chutiya [101] India: Assam state, Lakhimpur and Sibsagar districts (formerly also Arunachal Pradesh). *Tibeto-Burman*, Bodo-Koch branch; Deori and Chutiya are two separate clans sharing a common language. Rapidly declining, a few thousand speakers left; severely endangered.

Dhimal [115] Nepal: Jhāpā and Moraṅ districts. *Tibeto-Burman*, Dhimalish language cluster. Estimates of number of speakers vary from 16,000 to 35,000, but the language is giving way to Nepali and is a minority in its own districts. Severely endangered.

Dhímmai (*Miji*) [76] India: Arunachal Pradesh state, Kameng district, Bichom and Pakesa river valleys. *Hrusish language cluster*. About 4,000 speakers; severely endangered.

Dimasa (*Hills Kachari*) **[104]** India: Assam, North Cachar district. *Tibeto-Burman*, Bodo-Garo language cluster. Speakers largely assimilated into Bengali and Assamese communities; a few isolated households remain. Probably moribund.

Dimli (*Zaza*) **[261]** Iran and Turkey: upper Euphrates river. *Indo-European*, Iranian branch. Total number of speakers in both countries about 1,000,000. No institutional support in either country.

Dol-po (*D'ölpo*) Nepal: Dolpa district up to Tibetan border. *Tibeto-Burman*, Central Bodish branch. Closely related to Tibetan. Number of speakers unknown but may be around 5,000; endangered.

Dränjoke [241] India: Sikkim. *Tibeto-Burman*, South Bodish group. Former national language of the kingdom of Sikkim before it was annexed by India in 1975, since when it has been swamped by immigration from Nepal. Number of first-language speakers unknown, but already moribund.

Dumākī [285] Pakistan: Hunza valley. *Indo-European*, Dardic branch. Less than 600 elderly speakers remain, concentrated mostly in one village; moribund.

Dumi [204] Nepal: upper reaches of Dūdhkosī river. *Tibeto-Burman*, Western Kiranti branch. Fewer than eight speakers remain, all elderly; moribund.

Dungmali [197] Nepal: northeastern Bhojpur district. *Tibeto-Burman*, Southern Kiranti branch. Number of speakers unknown; endangered.

Dura [221] Nepal: Lamjuṅ, between Pāudī and Midim rivers. *Tibeto-Burman*, further affiliation unidentified. Last speakers died sometime after 1980; recently extinct. Some data were collected on the language.

Dzala [66] Bhutan: Trashi'yangtse and Lhüntsi district in the northeast. *Tibeto-Burman*, East Bodish group. About 15,000 speakers; potentially endangered.

Dzongkha [58] Bhutan. *Tibeto-Burman*, South Bodish group. The official national language of Bhutan, but marginalised by the official use of English. 260,000 speakers. The language is potentially endangered.

Falam Chin [161] India: Assam, Tripura and Mizoram states; also spoken in Burma. *Tibeto-Burman*, Mizo-Kuki-China branch. Numerous dialect divisions. Number of speakers in India unknown, but may be about 23,000; severely endangered.

Gadaba [54] India: Orissa state, Korāpuṭ district. *Dravidian*, Central Dravidian group. Approximately 40,000 speakers of its various dialects; potentially endangered. Not to be confused with the unrelated South Munda language also known as Gutob (see below).

Gallong [83] India: Arunachal Pradesh state, West Siang district up to border of Assam. *Tani language cluster*. About 40,000 speakers; endangered.

Gambiri (*Tregami*) [281] Afghanistan: Kunar province, Tregam valley. *Indo-European*, Nuristani branch. About a thousand speakers in a few villages; endangered.

Gangte [152] India: Manipur state. *Tibeto-Burman*, Mizo-Kuki-Chin branch. Number of speakers unknown, but rapidly losing ground to Meithei, the state majority language; severely endangered.

Garhwali [314a] India: Kashmir and Uttar Pradesh. *Indo-European*, Central Pahadi branch. Number of speakers over two million, but with little institutional support or prestige the language is potentially endangered.

Garo [109] India: Meghalaya state, Garo Hills; Assam state, Goalpara and Kamrup districts; Bangladesh, Mymensing district and in Modhupur. *Tibeto-Burman*; the most viable of the Bodo-Garo language cluster, with a total of about 265,000 speakers, but endangered.

Gawar-Bātī (*Narisātī*) [294] Pakistan: southern Chitral valley. *Indo-European*, Dardic branch. Spoken by up to 1,500 people in a few villages on the Kunar river. Endangered.

Geta? (*Gta?, Dideyi, Didam*) [26] India: Andhra Pradesh state, East Godāvarī district, both sides of Sileru river. *Austroasiatic*, South Munda group. About 3,000 speakers, bilingualism widespread; endangered.

Ghale [228] Nepal: Gorkhā and Dhādiṅ districts. *Tibeto-Burman*, possibly Tamangic but affiliation uncertain. About 12,000 speakers in 1975, and slowly declining despite the remoteness of the community; potentially endangered.

Gilaki [257] Iran: Gilaki region of Caspian littoral. *Indo-European*, Iranian branch. About 3,265,000 speakers but unwritten and with no institutional support; potentially endangered.

Gōṇḍi [45] India: scattered parts of Madhya Pradesh, Maharashtra, Orissa, northern Andhra Pradesh states. *Dravidian*, Central Dravidian group. Over two million speakers in total, but potentially endangered.

Gongduk [70] Bhutan: Monggar district, one enclave along the Kurichu river. A distinct group within *Tibeto-Burman*, only discovered by scholars in 1991, retaining many archaic Tibeto-Burman features. Approximately 1,000 speakers. Now that Bhutanese infrastructure is opening up this remote territory to outsiders, it is potentially endangered.

Gurani (*Hawrami*) [260] Iran: Kordestan province. *Indo-European*, Iranian branch. Also spoken in Iraq. Number of speakers unknown; thought to be endangered.

Gurung [222] Nepal: Gorkhā, Kāskī, Lamjuṅ, Parbat, Syāṅjā, Tanahŭ and Dhādiṅ districts. *Tibeto-Burman*, Tamangic branch. About half of the 449,189 (1991 census) ethnic Gurung retain the language. Three main dialects. Shift to Nepali is widespread; endangered.

Gutob (*Sodia*, *Gadaba*) **[25]** India: Orissa state, Kalāhāṇḍī, Korāpuṭ, Viśākhāpaṭnam, Bastar districts. *Austroasiatic*, South Munda group. Over 40,000 speakers, widespread bilingualism, potentially endangered.

Gyasumdo [225b] Nepal: lower Manang valley. *Tibeto-Burman*, Manangba branch. Number of speakers unknown; endangered.

Haka Chin [162] India: Mizoram, Assam and Meghalaya states; also spoken in Burma. *Tibeto-Burman*, Mizo-Kuki-Chin branch. Numerous dialect divisions. Number of speakers unknown, but Haka is the most widely spoken of the Chin sub-branch. Endangered.

Ha-lung Tibetan [247a] Nepal: near headwaters of Tamor river. *Tibeto-Burman*, Central Bodish branch. Regarded as a dialect of Tibetan in Nepal. Number of speakers unknown; endangered.

Haṇḍūrī [303] India: Himachal Pradesh state, Simla and Solan districts. *Indo-European*, Western Pahadi branch. Only a few speakers remain; moribund.

Hayu [207] Nepal: formerly in Sindhulī and Kābhrepālañcok districts. *Tibeto-Burman*, Northwestern Kiranti branch. Only a few elderly speakers remain, if any; moribund.

Hmar [168] India: Assam, Manipur and Mizoram states. *Tibeto-Burman*, Mizo-Kuki-Chin branch. Number of speakers unknown, but there is general bilingualism in Assamese; severely endangered.

Ho (*Kol*) **[29]** India: Bihar state, Siṃhabhūm district. *Austroasiatic*, North Munda group. Over 400,000 speakers, but widespread bilingualism. Potentially endangered.

Hojai [105] India: Assam state, Cachar hills. *Tibeto-Burman*, Bodo-Garo language cluster. Not described, probably closely related to Dimasa. Severely endangered or moribund.

Hrangkol [164] India: Manipur, Assam and Tripura states. *Tibeto-Burman*, Mizo-Kuki-Chin branch. Number of speakers is unknown but small, and shifting to Assamese or Bengali; severely endangered.

Hruso (*Aka*) **[75]** India: Arunachal Pradesh state, Kameng district, Bichom river valley. *Hrusish language cluster*. Less than 3,000 speakers; severely endangered.

Idu [99] India: Arunachal Pradesh state, near Digaru river. *Digarish language cluster*. Estimated to have 9,000 speakers; severely endangered.

Iruḷa [35] India: western Tamil Nadu state, Nilgiri Hills. *Dravidian*, South Dravidian group, closely related to Tamil and Malayalam. Unwritten; about 5,000 speakers; potentially endangered.

329

Iškāšmī [273] Afghanistan: Sanglech valley; Tajikistan. *Indo-European*, Iranian branch. Number of speakers may exceed 1,000; grouped together with its close relative Sanglīcī (q.v.); endangered.

Jāḍ [237f] India: Himachal Pradesh state, on Bhāgīrathī river, resettled from Tibetan border in 1962. *Tibeto-Burman*, Central Bodish branch; considered a dialect of Tibetan by some. Number of speakers unknown; endangered.

Jarawa [3] India: spoken in the interior of South Andaman, Andaman Islands. *Language Isolate*. One of three surviving Andamanese languages of more than a dozen known during British colonial times. Extremely endangered; thirty-one speakers recorded in 1981 census of India.

Jaunsarī [299] India: Uttar Pradesh state. *Indo-European*, Western Pahadi branch. Little is known about the language.

Jero [203] Nepal: along Sunkosī river. *Tibeto-Burman*, Western Kiranti branch, Chaurasiya group. The two Chaurasiya languages have a total of 15,000 speakers; endangered.

Jirel [251] Nepal: Dolakha district. *Tibeto-Burman*, Bodish branch. Poorly documented. Number of speakers may be around 8,000; endangered.

Juang [20] India: Orissa state, Kyonjhar and Dhekānāl districts. *Austroasiatic*, South Munda group. About 17,000 speakers recorded, rapidly declining and bilingualism widespread. Potentially endangered.

J'umowa [60] India and Tibet: between Sikkim and Bhutan in the Chumbi valley. *Tibeto-Burman*, South Bodish group. Number of speakers unknown, but moribund or extinct.

Kachari (*Plains Kachari*) [106] India: Assam state, northern Cachar district, Darrang district. *Tibeto-Burman*, Bodo-Garo language cluster. Speakers being rapidly assimilated into Bengali and Assamese communities. Severely endangered.

Kadu [171] India: Manipur state and across into Burma. *Tibeto-Burman*, Kachinic branch, Sak subgroup. No known speakers left; moribund or possibly extinct.

Kāgate [252] Nepal: Ramechhap district. *Tibeto-Burman*, Bodish branch. Possibly around 1,000 speakers in 1974; endangered.

Kaike [226] Nepal: Dolpo district. *Tibeto-Burman*, Tamangic branch. About 2,000 speakers; endangered.

Kalaṣa [292] Pakistan: southern Chitral district. *Indo-European*, Dardic branch. Number of speakers unknown, but in the thousands; endangered.

Kaman (*Miju Mishmi*) [97] India and Tibet: Arunachal Pradesh state, Lohit district, banks of the Lohit river. Part of the small *Midźuish language cluster*. About 9,000 speakers; endangered.

Kanashi [232] India: Himachal Pradesh state, Kulu district. *Tibeto-Burman*, West Himalayish branch. Number of speakers unknown, but spoken in only one village; endangered.

Kāṅgḍī [307] India: Himachal Pradesh state. *Indo-European*, Western Pahadi branch. Little is known about the language.

Karbí (*Mikir*) [123] India: Assam state, Karbi Anglong, Kamrup, Nowgong and Sibsagar districts. A separate subgroup within the *Tibeto-Burman* family. Speakers number over 150,000, but bilingualism in Assamese is widespread and there is a rapid process of shift to that language.

Karko [93] India: Arunachal Pradesh state, Siang district. Part of Minyong-Padam subgroup within *Tani language cluster*. About 2,000 speakers; endangered.

Kati (*Bashgalī*) [277] Afghanistan: Bashgal valley; Pakistan. *Indo-European*, Nuristani branch. The largest number of speakers in this branch, about 20,000; endangered.

Khaccaḍ Bhoṭe [244] Nepal: Dhāibuṅ area. An ethnonym, meaning 'mule Tibetans' rather than a language name. *Tibeto-Burman*, Central Bodish branch. Regarded as a dialect of Tibetan in Nepal. Number of speakers unknown; endangered.

Khaling [206] Nepal: Solukhumbu district. *Tibeto-Burman*, Western Kiranti branch. About 15,000 speakers; endangered.

Kham [216] Nepal: Rukum and Rolpā districts. *Tibeto-Burman*, Magaric branch; also known as Northern Magar. About 30,000 speakers, and though endangered, faring better than the Magar dialects.

Khampti [176] India: Assam state, Lakhimpur district; Arunachal Pradesh, Lohit district. *Tibeto-Burman*, Daic branch. Number of speakers unknown but dwindling; severely endangered.

Kharia [21] India: Bihar, West Bengal, Orissa, Assam and Madhya Pradesh states. *Austroasiatic*, South Munda group. A dialect continuum in scattered communities over a wide area; bilingualism with majority languages is widespread. The total number of speakers is over 190,000. Potentially endangered.

Khaśālī [313] India: Jammu and Kashmir state. *Indo-European*, West Pahadi branch. Little is known about the language.

Kheng [64b] Bhutan: Kheng district, also known as Zh'ämgang, south of Bumthang. *Tibeto-Burman*, East Bodish group. About 40,000 speakers; potentially endangered.

Kheza [133] India: eastern Nagaland, Kohima district. *Tibeto-Burman*, Angami-Pochuri language cluster. Number of speakers unknown but may be up to 23,000; endangered.

Khiamngan [119] India: Nagaland state, precise location unknown. *Tibeto-Burman*, Konyak language cluster. Number of speakers also unknown, but thought to be endangered.

Khoirao [145] India: northern Manipur state, Senapati district. *Tibeto-Burman*, Zeme language cluster. No census data available; endangered because of language shift to Meithei, the state language of Manipur.

Khowa (*Bugun*) [71] India: Arunachal Pradesh state, West Kameng district, confined to two villages. *Kho-Bwa language cluster*. About 800 speakers; severely endangered.

Khowār [291] Pakistan: Chitral valley and neighbouring valleys. *Indo-European*, Dardic branch. The main language of the valley, spoken by up to 222,800 people; potentially endangered.

Kinnauri [233] India: Himachal Pradesh state, Kinnaur district. *Tibeto-Burman*, West Himalayish branch. In 1981 there were 59,154 ethnic Kinnauri recorded, but proportion of speakers not known; thought to be endangered.

Koch. See **Pānī Koch**

Koḍa [31] India: Maharashtra state, Nagpur district. *Austroasiatic*, North Munda group. A dialect continuum spoken in scattered enclaves, not researched at all but thought to be endangered.

Koḍagu [38] India: Karnataka state, named after the district where it is spoken, otherwise known as Coorg. *Dravidian*, South Dravidian group, related to Malayalam and Tamil. Over 100,000 speakers near the city of Maḍkeri; potentially endangered.

Kohi [205] Nepal: Khoṭāṅ district. *Tibeto-Burman*, Western Kiranti branch. Spoken in one village on the headwaters of the Rāva river. Number of speakers unknown and the language is undescribed; severely endangered.

Kokborok (*Hill Tippera*) [102] India: Tripura state. *Tibeto-Burman*, Bodo-Garo language cluster. Once a majority in the state, the Kokborok speakers now account for just 30 per cent of the population (an estimated 800,000 claim ethnicity, but the majority have abandoned the language) owing to the influx of Bengali speakers. Endangered.

Kolami [51] India: Maharashtra state, Yavatmāḷ and Vardhā districts; Andhra Pradesh, Adilābād district. *Dravidian*, Central Dravidian group. About 70,000 speakers; potentially endangered.

Kom [150] India: Manipur state. *Tibeto-Burman*, Mizo-Kuki-Chin branch. Number of speakers unknown, but rapidly losing ground to Meithei, the state majority language; severely endangered.

Koṇḍa (*Kūbi*) [46] India: Andhra Pradesh state, Viśākhāpaṭnam and Śrīkākulam districts, and Orissa state, Korāpuṭ district. *Dravidian*, Central Dravidian group. Spoken by 15,000 members of the Konda Dora tribe; endangered.

Konyak [116] India: Nagaland state. *Tibeto-Burman*, Konyak group, also called 'Northern Naga'. About 70,000 speakers; endangered.

Koraga [43] India: Karnataka state, Kuṇḍāpura district. *Dravidian*, South Dravidian group. About 1,000 speakers, Untouchables who are bilingual in Kannada. Recently discovered, and severely endangered.

Korku [27] India: Madhya Pradesh and Maharashtra states, mainly in the Satpuḍā and Mahādev hills. *Austroasiatic*, North Munda group. About 200,000 speakers, who are rapidly assimilating with speakers of larger (Indo-Aryan) languages. Potentially endangered.

Korwa (*Koroa, Ernga*) [34] India: Madhya Pradesh state (Rāygaḍh, Sargujā districts), Bihar state (Palāmū and Hazārībāg districts). *Austroasiatic*, North Munda group. A dialect continuum with over 35,000 speakers, widespread bilingualism; potentially endangered.

Kota [35a] India: Tamil Nadu state, Kōttagiri district of Nilgiri Hills. *Dravidian*, South Dravidian group. About 1,000 speakers; endangered.

Kūi (*Kū'i*) [49] India: Orissa state, Gañjām, Baudh-Kondhamāḷ, Korāpuṭ districts; Andhra Pradesh. *Dravidian*, Central Dravidian group. Together with Kūvi, speakers, who are members of the Kondho scheduled tribe, make up half a million. Some writing of missionary tracts in Roman and Oriya scripts; potentially endangered.

Kuluī [304] India: Himachal Pradesh state, Kullu district. *Indo-European*, Western Pahadi branch. Number of speakers may be up to 109,000; potentially endangered.

Kulung [191] Nepal: Solukhumbu and Saṅkhuvā Sabhā district. *Tibeto-Burman*, Central Kiranti group, Khambu language cluster. Number of speakers unknown. Bilingualism in Nepali is general. About 15,000 speakers; endangered.

Kumaoni [314b] India: mainly Uttar Pradesh but also Assam, Bihar, Madhya Pradesh and elsewhere. *Indo-European*, Central Pahadi branch. May be regarded as a dialect continuum rather than a distinct language. Total population over 2 million for speakers of these mutually intelligible dialects, but language is not standardised or generally written and is endangered.

Kum(h)āle [319] Nepal: Gorkhā district. *Indo-Aryan*, further affiliation uncertain. The 1991 census showed 1,413 speakers, a sharp decline in forty years; severely endangered.

Kurru [44] India: a dialect continuum including ***Korava, Yerukula, Yerukala, Kaikudi***. Andhra Pradesh state and adjacent parts of Karnataka and Tamil Nadu. *Dravidian*, South Dravidian group. Total number of speakers, who are nomadic tribesmen, about 100,000. Potentially endangered.

Kurtöp [64a] Bhutan: Lhüntsi district, up to Tibetan border, west of Kurichu river. *Tibeto-Burman*, East Bodish group. About 10,000 speakers, potentially endangered.

333

Kuruba [40] India: Karnataka state, Coorg district. *Dravidian*, South Dravidian group. About 1,000 speakers, consisting of the small Betta-Kuruba tribe, the remainder of the Kuruba tribes having gone over to Kannada. Endangered.

Kurukh (*Kuṛux*, *Oraon*, *Uraon*) [57] India: Bihar state (Choṭā Nāgpur district), Madhya Pradesh, Orissa, West Bengal states; also scattered dialects in Assam and Nepal. In Assam the scattered speakers are referred to as Adibasis ('aborigines'), a term also applied to speakers of unrelated languages. *Dravidian*, North Dravidian group. Approximately 1.5 million speakers of all dialects. Potentially endangered.

Kusunda [6] Nepal: near Damaulī and Gorkhā. *Language Isolate*. Its speakers dispersed in the mid-twentieth century from the four remaining clans. Number of speakers unknown, but moribund.

Kūvi [50] India: Orissa state, Korāpuṭ, Kalāhāṇḍī, Gañjām districts; Andhra Pradesh state, Viśākhāpaṭnam district. *Dravidian*, Central Dravidian group. Together with Kūi, speakers, who are members of the Kondho scheduled tribe, make up half a million. Some writing of missionary tracts in Roman and Oriya scripts; potentially endangered.

Ladakhi (*La-dwags*) [237c] India: Jammu and Kashmir state, Ladakh district. *Tibeto-Burman*, Central Bodish branch. Number of speakers unknown, but may be up to 102,000; declining and endangered.

Lâfûl [13] India: Nicobar Islands, Trinkut island. *Austroasiatic*, Nicobarese group. Number of speakers unknown due to lack of census data, thought to be endangered.

Lakha [249] Bhutan: 'Wangdi Phodr'a district. *Tibeto-Burman*, Central Bodish branch. Number of speakers estimated at 8,000; endangered.

Lakhe [156] India: Mizoram state. *Tibeto-Burman*, Mizo-Kuki-Chin branch. Number of speakers unknown; assimilating into larger Mizo-speaking community; severely endangered.

Lamgang [153] India: Manipur state. *Tibeto-Burman*, Mizo-Kuki-Chin branch. Number of speakers unknown, but rapidly losing ground to Meithei, the state majority language; severely endangered.

Lâmongshé [17] India: Nicobar Islands, Condul. *Austrasiatic*, Nicobarese group. Number of speakers unknown due to lack of census data, thought to be endangered.

'Langthang Tibetan [246] Nepal: near 'Langthang Himāl. *Tibeto-Burman*, Central Bodish branch. Regarded as a dialect of Tibetan in Nepal. Number of speakers unknown; endangered.

Lepcha [69] India: Sikkim, plus Darjeeling district, parts of eastern Nepal, and Samtsi district in southwest Bhutan. A distinct group within *Tibeto-Burman*, with its own script and literary tradition going back at least three centuries. Once the primary language of Sikkim, now giving way everywhere to Nepali, with which bilingualism is the norm. Number of speakers now reduced to a few thousand; highly endangered.

Levai (*Bongro*) **[77]** India: Arunachal Pradesh state, Kameng and Subansiri districts. *Hrusish language cluster.* About 1,000 speakers; severely endangered.

Lhokpu [68] Bhutan: Samtsi district in the southwest. A separate group within *Tibeto-Burman.* Spoken by 2,500 people in two communities, all bilingual in Nepali since the influx of Nepali-speaking settlers. Endangered.

Liangmai [141] India: southwestern Nagaland state. *Tibeto-Burman,* Zeme language cluster. No reliable census information; severely endangered.

Limirong [238] Nepal: Humlā district. *Tibeto-Burman,* Central Bodish branch. Closely related to Tibetan. Number of speakers unknown; endangered.

Lishpa [73] Arunachal Pradesh state: Kameng district. *Kho-Bwa language cluster.* About a thousand speakers, who call themselves 'Monpa'. Severely endangered.

Lohorung [189] Nepal: Saṅkhuvā Sabhā district, upper Arun valley. *Tibeto-Burman,* Eastern Kiranti group, Yakkhaba language cluster. About 4,000 speakers. Bilingualism in Nepali is general; severely endangered because of mass emigration for economic reasons.

'Loke [242] Nepal: Mustang district. *Tibeto-Burman,* Central Bodish branch. Regarded as a dialect of Tibetan in Nepal. Number of speakers unknown; endangered.

Lo'ong [15] India: Nicobar Islands, spoken on coast of Great Nicobar island. *Austroasiatic,* Nicobarese group. Number of speakers unknown due to lack of census data, thought to be endangered.

Lotha [128] India: Nagaland state. *Tibeto-Burman*; the closely related Ao subgroup has a total number of about 65,275, of whom Lotha accounts for about 35,000. Transfer to an Assamese-based creole is general among Ao speakers; severely endangered.

Magar [215] Nepal: Pālpā, Syāṅjā, Tanahŭ and Gorkhā districts. *Tibeto-Burman,* Magaric branch. A relatively numerous and widely dispersed ethnic group, but less than a third of the well over one million ethnic Magar now retain the language, which is giving way to Nepali. Great dialectal variation. Endangered

Mahāsuī [302] India: Himachal Pradesh state, Simla and Solan districts. *Indo-European,* Western Pahadi branch. Part of a dialect continuum which may have a total of half a million speakers, but which is little known and endangered.

Maiyã (*Kohistani*) **[288]** Pakistan: Indus Kohistani district. *Indo-European,* Dardic branch. There may be up to 220,000 speakers; potentially endangered.

Majhi (*Bote*) **[318]** Nepal: several districts along the rivers Nārāyaṇī and Saptagaṇḍakī. *Indo-Aryan,* further affiliation uncertain. Number of speakers according to

1991 census was 11,322, about one fifth of the ethnic group, which is adopting Nepali rapidly. Severely endangered.

Malto [56] India: Bihar state, mainly in the Rājmahal Hills. *Dravidian*, North Dravidian group. Over 100,000 speakers; potentially endangered.

Maluri [136] India: Nagaland state. *Tibeto-Burman*, Angami-Pochuri language cluster. Known also as 'Eastern Rengma', though Rengma is a different language. Number of speakers unknown; moribund or even extinct.

Manchad [229] India: Himachal Pradesh state, Lahul district. *Tibeto-Burman*, West Himalayish branch. About 15,000 speakers, endangered.

Maṇḍa [47] India: Orissa state, Korāpuṭ district. *Dravidian*, Central Dravidian group. About 1,500 speakers; endangered.

Maṇḍeālī [305] India: Himachal Pradesh state, Mandi district. *Indo-European*, Western Pahadi branch. Number of speakers 776,372 in 1991 census, but the language is not in general public use; potentially endangered.

Mao [134] India: northwestern Manipur state, Nagaland state. *Tibeto-Burman*, Angami-Pochuri language cluster. Number of speakers unknown; endangered.

Maram [146] India: Assam and northern Manipur states. *Tibeto-Burman*, Zeme language cluster. Number of ethnic Maram given as 19,968 in 1971 census, but a general shift to Meithei, the state language of Manipur, may have reduced the number of speakers; endangered.

Maring [148] India: northeastern Manipur state. *Tibeto-Burman*, Tangkhul language cluster. No census data available, and the language is not yet extinct.

Mazenderani [259] Iran: Mazandaran province on Caspian littoral. *Indo-European*, Iranian branch. About 3,265,000 speakers, but no institutional support. Potentially endangered.

Meche [108] India: Assam state, Jalpaiguri and Goalpara districts, originally spoken in Nepal and Bhutan. *Tibeto-Burman*, Bodo-Garo language cluster. Now spoken in only a few households and moribund.

Mewahang [190] Nepal: Saṅkhuvā Sabhā district, upper Aruṇ valley. *Tibeto-Burman*, Eastern Kiranti group, Yakkhaba language cluster. Number of speakers unknown. Bilingualism in Nepali is general; severely endangered because of mass immigration into its territory.

Milang [78] India: Arunachal Pradesh state, East Siang district, three villages in the upper Yamne valley. *Tani language cluster*. About 5,000 speakers; endangered.

Miloh [18] India: Nicobar Islands, Milo. *Austroasiatic*, Nicobarese group. Number of speakers unknown due to lack of census data, thought to be endangered.

Minyong [90] India: Arunachal Pradesh state, west bank of lower Siang river. Part of Minyong-Padam subgroup within the *Tani language cluster*. About 20,000 speakers; endangered.

Mishing (*'Plains Miri'*) [96] India: Arunachal Pradesh state, spoken on plains in scattered settlements. Part of Minyong-Padam subgroup within *Tani language cluster*. Fewer than 4,000 speakers; endangered.

Mongsen Ao [125] India: Nagaland state. *Tibeto-Burman*; the closely related Ao subgroup has a total number of about 65,275. Transfer to an Assamese-based creole is general among Ao speakers; severely endangered.

Mru [169] Bangladesh: Chittagong hills. A separate class within *Tibeto-Burman*. Number of speakers estimated at 40,000, but losing ground to Bengali; severely endangered.

Muṇḍārī (*Horo*) [28] India: a dialect continuum including *Hasada?*, *Naguri*, *Latar* and *Kera?*, spoken in Bihar state (Rāñcī, Siṃhabhūm, Manbhūm, Hazārībāg, Palāmū districts), northern Madhya Pradesh and Orissa states. *Austroasiatic*, North Munda group. Total number of speakers about 750,000, bilingualism widespread; potentially endangered.

Munji [275] Afghanistan: Munjan valley. *Indo-European*, Iranian branch. About 2,000 speakers; closely related to Yidgha in Pakistan; endangered.

Mzieme [143] India: southwestern Nagaland state. *Tibeto-Burman*; Zeme language cluster. No reliable census information; severely endangered.

Nachiring [193] Nepal: Khoṭāṅ district. *Tibeto-Burman*, Central Kiranti group, Khambu language cluster. Number of speakers unknown. Bilingualism in Nepali is general; a few hundred elderly speakers, severely endangered because of lack of transfer to younger generation.

Nahali (*Nihali*, *Nehali*) [5] India: Madhya Pradesh, Gawilgarh Hills in Nimar and Ellichpur Districts. *Language Isolate*. Heavily influenced by Korku (Austrasiatic). Less than 2,000 reported speakers. Endangered.

Naiki [51a] India: Maharashtra state, Canda district. *Dravidian*. Central Dravidian group. Spoken by Yerku hill tribesmen, about 1,500 in number. Endangered.

Nancowry [12] India: Nicobar Islands, Nancowry and Camorta islands. *Austroasiatic*, Nicobarese group. Number of speakers unknown due to lack of census data, thought to be endangered.

'Narpa [225c] Nepal: 'Nar and Phu valleys. *Tibeto-Burman*, Manangba branch. About 500 speakers, recorded in 1971; endangered.

Newar [211] Nepal: Kathmandu valley. *Tibeto-Burman*, Newaric branch. Can be divided into four distinct varieties: Kathmandu and Patan; Bhaktapur; Pahari; and Dolakha.

Originally the dominant language of the Kathmandu valley, and with over a million ethnic Newar and a long literary tradition, yet the language is yielding rapidly to Nepali. Endangered.

Ningalāmī [295] Afghanistan: on the Pech river. *Indo-European*, Dardic branch. Spoken in the village of Ningalām, but few, if any, speakers left; thought to be moribund.

Nishi (*Eastern Dafla*) [80] India: Arunachal Pradesh state, Subansiri district. *Tani language cluster.* About 30,000 speakers; endangered. 'Nishi' is also used as a general term for the western Tani languages, such as Tagin and Apatani.

Nocte [122] India: Nagaland state, central Tirap district. *Tibeto-Burman*, Konyak language cluster. About 28,000 speakers; endangered.

Nruanghmei [142] India: northwestern Manipur, Nagaland state. *Tibeto-Burman*; Zeme language cluster. No reliable census information; severely endangered.

Ntenyi [136] India: central Nagaland state. *Tibeto-Burman*, Angami-Pochuri language cluster. Number of speakers unknown, but may be up to 6,600; endangered.

Nupbikha [64c] Bhutan: Bumthang district, area around Trongsa. *Tibeto-Burman*. East Bodish group. Also regarded as the western dialect of **Bumthang** (see entry) and means 'language of the west'. Potentially endangered.

Nupri (*Lārkyā Bhoṭe*) [242] Nepal: Gorkhā district. *Tibeto-Burman*, Central Bodish branch. Regarded as a dialect of Tibetan in Nepal. Number of speakers unknown; endangered.

'Nyenkha (*Henkha, Mangdebi-kha*) [65] Bhutan: Mangde river valley. *Tibeto-Burman*, East Bodish group, highly divergent within the group. About 10,000 speakers; potentially endangered.

'Nyishangba [225a] Nepal: Manang valley. *Tibeto-Burman*, Tamangic branch. Possibly 2,000 or more speakers; endangered.

Ong [16] India: Nicobar Islands, Little Nicobar island. *Austroasiatic*, Nicobarese group. Number of speakers unknown die to lack of census data; thought to be endangered.

Önge [1] India: spoken on Little Andaman, Andaman Islands. *Language Isolate*. One of three surviving Andamanese languages of more than a dozen known during British colonial times. Extremely endangered; ninety-seven speakers recorded in 1981 census of India.

Ormuri [263] Afghanistan: Baraki-Barak area; Pakistan, Kanigram area. *Indo-European*, Iranian branch. There may be as few as fifty speakers left out of an ethnic group of several thousand; severely endangered or moribund.

Padam (*Bor Abor*) **[88]** India: Arunachal Pradesh state, west bank of Siang river. Part of Minyong-Padam sub-group within *Tani language cluster*. About 40,000 speakers; endangered.

Pāḍrī [314] India: Jammu and Kashmir state. *Indo-European*, Western Pahadi branch. Little is known about the language.

Pailibo [85] India: Arunachal Pradesh state, West Siang district, villages on Siyom river. *Tani language cluster*. About a thousand speakers; endangered.

Paite [155] India: Manipur state. *Tibeto-Burman*, Mizo-Kuki-Chin branch. Number of speakers unknown, but rapidly losing ground to Meithei, the state majority language; severely endangered.

Pāñcthare Limbu [183] Eastern Nepal. *Tibeto-Burman*, Limbu group. Total Limbu population about 300,000, but transfer to younger speakers is not taking place. Severely endangered.

Panggi [94] India: Arunachal Pradesh state, lower Yamne valley. Part of Minyong-Padam subgroup within *Tani language cluster*. About 600 speakers; endangered.

Pangvālī [307] India: Himachal Pradesh state, Lahul-Spiti district to border of Chamba district. *Indo-European*, Western Pahadi branch. Number of speakers may be up to 17,000; endangered.

Pānī Koch [11] India: Meghalaya state, western edge of Garo hills. *Tibeto-Burman*, Koch language cluster. The name means 'Water Koch'; speakers also known as Wanang. Only 300 speakers remaining; extremely endangered.

Parācī [262] Afghanistan: Hindu Kush. *Indo-European*, Iranian branch. Spoken in some villages in three valleys. Only one tenth of the ethnic group of up to 6,000 speak the language; endangered.

Pareng (*Gorum*) **[23]** India: Orissa state, Nandpur and Poṭṭangī tālukā, Korāpuṭ. *Austroasiatic*, South Munda group. About 10,000 speakers, bilingualism with majority languages widespread. Potentially endangered.

Parji [53] India: Madhya Pradesh state, Bastar district, near Jagdalpur. *Dravidian*, Central Dravidian group. Approximately 50,000 speakers; potentially endangered.

Pengo [48] India: Orissa state, Kalāhāṇḍī district. *Dravidian*, Central Dravidian group. About 1,500 speakers; endangered.

Phalūṛa [283] Pakistan: lower Chitral valley. *Indo-European*, Dardic branch. Possibly up to 8,600 speakers in about seven villages; endangered.

Phedāppe Limbu [181] Eastern Nepal. *Tibeto-Burman*, Limbu group. The most conservative member of the group. Total Limbu population about 300,000, but transfer to younger speakers is not taking place. Severely endangered.

Phom [118] India: southwestern Nagaland state. *Tibeto-Burman*, Konyak language cluster. About 19,000 speakers; endangered.

Pochuri [135] India: southeastern Nagaland state, Phek district. *Tibeto-Burman*, Angami-Pochuri language cluster. Number of speakers unknown, may be up to 13,000. Endangered.

Powahat [11] India: Nicobar Islands, Bompoka island. *Austroasiatic*, Nicobarese group. Number of speakers unknown due to lack of census data, thought to be endangered.

Prasun [278] Afghanistan: Nuristan, Prasun valley. *Indo-European*, Nuristani branch. Number of speakers about 2,000; endangered.

Pû [8] India: Nicobar Islands, Car Nicobar island. *Austroasiatic*, Nicobarese group. Number of speakers unknown due to lack of census data, thought to be endangered.

Puiron [144] India: Nagaland state. *Tibeto-Burman*, Zeme language cluster. No census data available; severely endangered.

Puma [198] Nepal: Khoṭāṅ district. *Tibeto-Burman*, Southern Kiranti branch. Spoken in only two villages; severely endangered.

Rabha [113] India: Meghalaya and Assam states, along Brahmaputra river. *Tibeto-Burman*, Koch language cluster. Number of speakers is only a small proportion of possibly 375,000 ethnic Rabha; bilingualism in Assamese is general. Endangered.

Raji [219] Nepal: formerly Terai and Pithaurāgaḍh (India) districts, now resettled in Ḍāṅ-Deukhurī district. *Tibeto-Burman*, further affiliation unidentified. A small population (3,274 ethnic Raji in Nepal reported in 1988) which has been resettled and largely lost its ancestral language in the process. Severely endangered or moribund.

Ramo [86] India: Arunachal Pradesh state, West Siang district, upper Siyom valley. *Tani language cluster*. Less than 800 speakers; endangered.

Rangpo (*Rongpo*) [234] India: Cāmolī district. *Tibeto-Burman*, West Himalayish branch. Estimated number of speakers 12,000; endangered.

Raute [220] Nepal: formerly nomadic, now resettled in Ḍāḍeldhurā district. *Tibeto-Burman*, further affiliation unidentified. The Raute (2,878 ethnic members in 1991 census of Nepal) have largely lost their language as a result of resettlement; severely endangered or moribund.

Remo (*Bonda*) [24] India: southern Orissa state, Jayapur hills of Korāpuṭ. *Austroasiatic*, South Munda group. Approximately 2,500 speakers, bilingualism widespread. Endangered.

Rengma [139] India: central Nagaland and Assam and Manipur states. *Tibeto-Burman*, Angami-Pochuri language cluster. Number of speakers uncertain, wide dialectal variation reported; endangered.

Rośanī [265] Afghanistan: Badakhshan province. *Indo-European*, Iranian branch; may be a dialect of Śughnī (q.v.) Number of speakers unknown; endangered.

Rośorvī (*Oroshori*) [267] Afghanistan: Badakhshan province. *Indo-European*, Iranian branch; may be a dialect of Śughnī (q.v.). Number of speakers unknown; endangered.

Ruga (*Rugha*) [112] India: Meghalaya state, southern Garo hills. *Tibeto-Burman*, Koch language cluster. Number of speakers unknown; endangered.

Sak [170] Bangladesh: Chittagong hills up to Burmese border. *Tibeto-Burman*, Kachinic branch, Sak sub-group. Number of speakers was 1,500 in 1981; severely endangered.

Sām [194] Nepal: Saṅkhuvā Sabhā and Bhojpur districts, along Irkhuvā river. *Tibeto-Burman*, Central Kiranti group, Khambu language cluster. Number of speakers unknown, if any; moribund or extinct.

Sampang [192] Nepal: Khoṭāṅ and Bhojpur districts. *Tibeto-Burman*, Central Kiranti group, Khambu language cluster. Number of speakers unknown. Bilingualism in Nepali is general; about a thousand speakers, severely endangered because of lack of transfer to younger generation.

Sanglīcī [272] Afghanistan: Sanglech valley; Tajikistan. *Indo-European*, Iranian branch. Up to 2,000 speakers in Afghanistan and 500 in Tajikistan. Endangered; may be regarded as a single language with Iśkāśmī (q.v.).

Sangtam [126] India: Nagaland state. *Tibeto-Burman*; the closely related Ao subgroup has a total number of about 65,275. Transfer to an Assamese-based creole is general among Ao speakers; severely endangered.

Sariqoli [268] China: southwest Xīnjiāng province. *Indo-European*, Iranian branch. About 20,000 speakers out of an ethnic 'Tajik' group of 33,538 in China (1990). Closely related to Tajik. Endangered.

Sāwī [283a] Pakistan: Chitral valley; originally refugees from Afghanistan. *Indo-European*, Dardic branch. Number of speakers unknown, but up to 3,000 may have returned to Afghanistan in recent years. Endangered.

Seke [224a] Nepal: Kālī Gaṇḍakī river valley. *Tibeto-Burman*, Tamangic branch. Closely related to Thakali and located upstream from it, and with about 7,000 speakers. Potentially endangered.

Sema [138] India: Assam and central and southern Nagaland states. *Tibeto-Burman*, Angami-Pochuri language cluster. The most widely spoken language in this group, with 65,000 speakers estimated; endangered.

341

Semnani [257] Iran: Caspian littoral. *Indo-European*, Iranian branch. Number of speakers unknown; thought to be endangered.

Sentinelese [2] India: spoken on North Sentinel Island, Andaman Islands. *Language Isolate*. One of three surviving Andamanese languages of more than a dozen known during British colonial times. No census data available, but a few speakers may survive. Moribund.

Sherdukpen [74] India: Arunachal Pradesh state, Kameng district. *Kho-Bwa language cluster*; spoken in a few villages by less than 2,000 speakers. Severely endangered.

Sherpa [247] Nepal: Solukhumbu district and around Mt Everest. *Tibeto-Burman*, Central Bodish branch. Regarded as a dialect of Tibetan in Nepal. Number of speakers inside and outside Nepal up to 50,000; potentially endangered as it is not being passed on to younger generation.

Shimong [92] India: Arunachal Pradesh state, Siang district, left bank of Siang river. Part of Minyong-Padam subgroup within *Tani language cluster*. About 2,000 speakers, endangered.

Shingsaba (*Lhomi*) [214] Nepal: Saṅkhuvā Sabhā district as far as Tibetan border. *Tibeto-Burman*, but exact affiliation uncertain. Little is known of the language or the remote and isolated people, of whom there may be around 4,000. State of endangerment unknown.

Shompen [19] India: Nicobar Islands, hinterland of Great Nicobar island. *Austroasiatic*, Nicobarese group, the most divergent of these languages. Number of speakers unknown due to lack of census data; thought to be endangered.

Simte [157] India: southwestern Manipur state. *Tibeto-Burman*, Mizo-Kuki-Chin branch. Number of speakers unknown; severely endangered.

Sirmauḍī [300] India: Himachal Pradesh state. *Indo-European*, Western Pahadi branch. Little is known about the language; it may have up to 14,000 speakers.

Sora (*Saora, Savara*) [22] India: southern Orissa state Korāpuṭ and Gañjām districts, parts of Andhra Pradesh. *Austroasiatic*, South Munda group. Over 300,000 speakers, but bilingualism is widespread. Potentially endangered.

Spiti (*sBi-ti*) [237d] India: Himachal Pradesh state, along Tibetan borders. *Tibeto-Burman*, Central Bodish branch. Regarded as a dialect of Tibetan by some. Number of speakers unknown; potentially endangered.

Śughnī [264] Both sides of Afghanistan-Tajikistan border: Pamir mountains. *Indo-European*, Iranian branch. Possibly 35,000 speakers in Tajikistan and 20,000 in Afghanistan. Endangered.

Sulung (*Puroit*) [72] India: Arunachal Pradesh state, East Kameng and Lower Subansiri districts. *Kho-Bwa language cluster*. Warfare and slavery have reduced the number of speakers, who are semi-nomadic and now number about 4,000. Severely endangered.

Sumāśtī [296] Afghanistan/Pakistan borders: Chitral area. *Indo-European*, Dardic branch. Spoken in part of one village; there may be up to 1,000 speakers; severely endangered.

Sunwar [209] Nepal: Likhu and Khimtī river valleys. *Tibeto-Burman*, Northwestern Kiranti branch. Spoken by a dwindling minority of the 30,000 ethnic Sunwar; severely endangered.

Surel [210] Nepal: Dolakhā district. *Tibeto-Burman*, Northwestern Kiranti branch. Spoken in only one village by a few hundred people; severely endangered.

Tagin [81] India: Arunchal Pradesh state, Subansiri and West Siang districts. *Tani language cluster*. About 25,000 speakers; endangered.

Taihlong [10] India: Nicobar Islands, Teressa island. *Austroasiatic*, Nicobarese group. Number of speakers unknown due to lack of census data, thought to be endangered.

Tai Nora (*Khamyang*) [178] India: Assam state, Sibsagar district. *Tibeto-Burman*, Daic branch. Number of speakers unknown but dwindling; the remaining speakers refer to themselves as Khamyang. Severely endangered.

Tai Phake (*Phākial*) [177] India: Assam state, Tinsukia and Dibrugarh districts. *Tibeto-Burman*, Daic branch. Approximately 2,000 speakers; general bilingualism in Assamese; severely endangered.

Tai Rong (*Tai Long*) [179] India: Assam state, Sibsagar district. *Tibeto-Burman*, Daic branch. A Northern Shan group who migrated from Burma in 1825, now dwindling; number uncertain; severely endangered.

Taleshi [256] Iran and Azerbaijan: on the Caspian littoral. *Indo-European*, Iranian branch. About 112,000 speakers in Iran and 800,000 in Azerbaijan. Potentially endangered.

Tamang [223] Nepal: dispersed throughout central and eastern hills. *Tibeto-Burman*, Tamangic branch. Nearly 90 per cent of over one million ethnic Tamang retain the language, but like all minority Nepalese languages it lacks institutional support; potentially endangered.

Tamarkhole Limbu [184] Eastern Nepal. *Tibeto-Burman*, Limbu group. The total Limbu population is about 300,000, but transfer to younger speakers is not taking place. Severely endangered.

Tangam [89] India: Arunachal Pradesh state, west bank of Siang river. Part of Padam-Minyong subgroup within *Tani language cluster*. Very few speakers left as the community are victims of genocide by neighbouring tribes. Moribund.

Tangkhul [147] India: northeastern Manipur state. *Tibeto-Burman*, Tangkhul language cluster. The 1971 census showed 58,167 ethnic Tangkhul, but owing to a rapid shift to the state language Meithei, it is nearly extinct.

Tangsa [121] India: Nagaland state, Tirap district, Changland and Miao subdivisions. *Tibeto-Burman*, Konyak language cluster; its three dialects, Jogli, Moklum and Lunchang, may be regarded as separate languages. Each dialect has over a thousand speakers, but numbers are declining; endangered.

Taraon [100] India: Arunachal Pradesh state, between Delei, Lati, Kharem and Digaru rivers. One of two members of the *Digarish language cluster*. Estimated to have 6,000 speakers; severely endangered.

Tatet [9] India: Nicobar Islands, Chowra island. *Austroasiatic*, Nicobarese group. Number of speakers unknown due to lack of census data; thought to be endangered.

Tati [253] Iran and Azerbaijan. *Indo-European*, Iranian branch. About 8,000 speakers in Iran, and 22,000 in Azerbaijan (1979). Potentially endangered.

Téhñu [14] India: Nicobar Islands, Katchall island. *Austroasiatic*, Nicobarese group. Number of speakers unknown due to lack of census data; thought to be endangered.

Tengsa [130] India: Nagaland state. *Tibeto-Burman*; the closely related Ao subgroup has a total number of about 65,275. Transfer to an Assamese-based creole is general among Ao speakers; severely endangered.

Thadou [149] India: Manipur state. *Tibeto-Burman*, Mizo-Kuki-Chin branch. Number of speakers unknown, but rapidly losing ground to Meithei, the state majority language; severely endangered.

Thakali [224] Nepal: Kālī Gaṇḍakī river valley. *Tibeto-Burman*, Tamangic branch. According to the 1991 Nepalese census there were 7,113 speakers; the number is declining because of economically motivated emigration from the valley. Potentially endangered.

Thangmi [213] Nepal: Dolakhā and Sindhupālcok districts. *Tibeto-Burman*, Newaric branch. About 30,000 speakers, but not generally being passed to younger generation; endangered.

Thulung [200] Nepal: southern Solukhumbu district. *Tibeto-Burman*, Western Kiranti branch, the only member of the Midwestern subgroup. Estimated number of speakers 8,000, but the language is not being passed on; endangered.

Tiddim Chin [160] India: Mizoram state. *Tibeto-Burman*, Mizo-Kuki-Chin branch; also spoken in Burma. Number of speakers in India unknown; endangered.

Tilung [201] Nepal: Khoṭāṅ district. *Tibeto-Burman*, Western Kiranti branch. Only its name and approximate location are known. Number of speakers unknown but very few remain; moribund.

Tinan [230] India: Himachal Pradesh state, Lahul district. *Tibeto-Burman*, West Himalayish branch. 1,833 speakers in 1981; endangered.

Tirāhī [289] Afghanistan: southeast of Jalalabad. *Indo-European*, Dardic branch. A few speakers left out of an ethnic group of up to 5,000, in a few remaining villages; moribund.

Tiwa (*Lalung*) [103] India: Tripura state, Kamrup and Marigaon districts and in the Karbi Anglong hills. *Tibeto-Burman*, Bodo-Garo language cluster. About 35,000 speakers; endangered.

Toda [36] India: western Tamil Nadu state, Nilgiri Hills, near Ootacamund. *Dravidian*, South Dravidian group, closely related to Tamil and Malayalam. About a thousand speakers; unwritten; endangered.

Torwālī [287] Pakistan: both sides of Swat river, Swat Kohistan. *Indo-European*, Dardic branch, Kohistani group. May have up to 60,000 speakers; endangered.

Toto [114] India: West Bengal, Jalpāīguḍī district, near Bhutanese border. *Tibeto-Burman*, Dhimalish language cluster. Just under a thousand speakers known in 1994, a declining number. Severely endangered.

Tsum [243] Nepal: banks of Shar river. *Tibeto-Burman*, Central Bodish branch. Regarded as a dialect of Tibetan in Nepal. Number of speakers unknown; endangered.

Tuḷu [32] India: Kerala and Karnataka states, coastal areas as far as North Kanarā district. *Dravidian*, South Dravidian group. One of the few minor Dravidian languages committed to writing, using an adapted form of the Grantha script like Malayalam, since 1842. Over one million speakers, but potentially endangered.

Turi [32] India: West Bengal and Bihar (Palāmū, Rāñcī, Siṃhabhūm, Rāygaḍh, Chattīsgaḍh districts). *Austroasiatic*, North Munda group. Number of speakers unknown, but in the thousands; endangered.

Vaiphei [159] India: Assam and southern Manipur states. *Tibeto-Burman*, Mizo-Kuki-Chin branch. Number of speakers unknown, but no more than 21,000; severely endangered.

Vedda [4] Sri Lanka: spoken in a few pockets around Hennanigala and possibly Dambana or Polonnaruwa. *Language Isolate*, first recorded in 1675. The Ceylonese government policy of displacement in the mid-twentieth century accelerated language loss and assimilation into Sinhalese society. Moribund.

345

Waigali [279] Afghanistan: southeast Nuristan, Kunar province. *Indo-European*, Nuristani branch. May be up to 8,000 speakers; endangered.

Wakhi [270] Afghanistan: Pamir mountains. *Indo-European*, Iranian branch. Spoken in villages along the Panj river; number of speakers may be up to 7,000. Endangered.

Wambule (*Ombule*) [202] Nepal: confluence of Dūdhkosī and Sunkosī rivers. *Tibeto-Burman*, Western Kiranti branch, Chaurasiya group. The two Chaurasiya languages have a total of 15,000 speakers; endangered.

Wancho [117] India: Arunachal Pradesh state, Tirap district. *Tibeto-Burman*, Konyak language cluster. About 30,000 speakers; endangered.

Wotapuri-Katarqalai [290] Afghanistan: Nuristan. *Indo-European*, Dardic branch. Spoken by up to 2,000 people in the two towns of Wotapur and Katarqala. Endangered.

Yacham [129] India: Nagaland state. *Tibeto-Burman*; the closely related Ao subgroup has a total number of about 65,275. Transfer to an Assamese-based creole is general among Ao speakers; severely endangered.

Yaghnobi [276] Tajikistan: headwaters of the Yaghnob river. *Indo-European*, Iranian branch. Possibly up to 2,000 speakers; endangered.

Yakkha [185] Nepal: Tehrathum, Saṅkhuva Sabhā, Dhankuṭā districts. *Tibeto-Burman*, Eastern Kiranti group. Spoken by a few households; on the verge of extinction.

Yamphu [188] Nepal: Saṅkhuvā Sabhā district, upper Arun valley. *Tibeto-Burman*, Eastern Kiranti group, Yakkhaba language cluster. Less than 3,000 speakers. Bilingualism in Nepali is general; severely endangered because of mass emigration for economic reasons.

Yazgulami [269] Tajikistan: Gorno-Badakhshan, along Yazgulyam river. *Indo-European*, Iranian branch. Possibly up to 4,000 speakers; endangered.

Yidgha [274] Pakistan: Lutkuh valley. *Indo-European*, Iranian branch. Number of speakers up to 6,000; endangered.

Yimchungrü [127] India: Nagaland state. *Tibeto-Burman*. Transfer to an Assamese-based creole is general among Ao speakers; severely endangered.

Yol-mo (*Ölmo*) [246a] Nepal: Helambū area. *Tibeto-Burman*, Bodish branch. Speakers call themselves Sherpas, but speak a language distinct from the Sherpa of Mt Everest and Solukhumbu. Number of speakers unknown; endangered.

Zaiwa [98] India: Arunachal Pradesh state, near Walong. One of the two languages of the *Midżuish language cluster*. Less than 200 speakers; endangered.

Zangs-dkar (*Z'angkar*) **[237e]** India: Kashmir, Kargil district. *Tibeto-Burman*, Central Bodish branch. Number of speakers unknown, possibly up to 8,000; endangered.

Zēbākī [271] Afghanistan: Sanglech valley. *Indo-European*, Iranian branch. May be a dialect of Sanglīcī, which has up to 2,000 speakers in total; endangered.

Zeme [140] India: northwestern Manipur and southwestern Nagaland states. *Tibeto-Burman*; Zeme language cluster. No reliable census information; severely endangered by assimilation with Meithei, official language of Manipur.

Zemiaki [282] Afghanistan: Kunar province. *Indo-European*, Nuristani branch; identified as a distinct Nuristani language only in 1999. Number of speakers unknown; endangered.

Zo [158] India: Manipur state. *Tibeto-Burman*, Mizo-Kuki-Chin branch. Number of speakers unknown, but may be up to 17,000; severely endangered in India and in Burma, where it is also spoken.

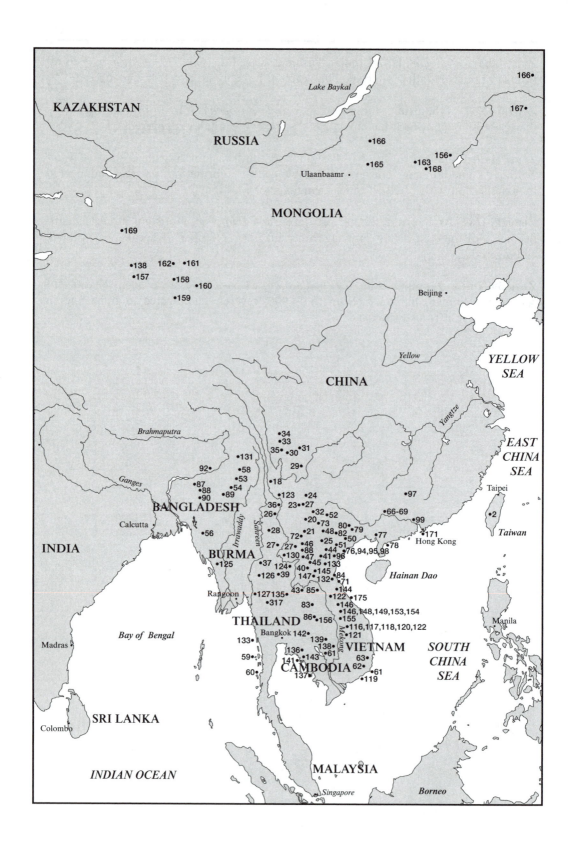

5

East and Southeast Asia[1]

David Bradley

Introduction

This chapter discusses 166 endangered and various recently and not so recently extinct languages of East Asia including China, Mongolia, Japan and Korea, as well as mainland Southeast Asia including Burma, Cambodia, Laos, West or peninsular Malaysia, Thailand and Vietnam, in the context of the surrounding non-endangered languages. As the original indigenous languages of Taiwan are Austronesian, and hence more closely related to the languages of insular Southeast Asia and the Pacific, they are included in the Australasia and the Pacific chapter. Similarly, some of the Tungusic minority languages of northeastern China are more widespread in eastern Russia, and hence are discussed mainly in that chapter. Conversely, there are a few endangered Tai language outliers in northeastern India, all closely related to the Tai languages of East and Southeast Asia, and these are discussed here.

The Sino-Tibetan (ST) languages include the various Sinitic languages and more than 320 Tibeto-Burman (TB) languages. Over 210 identified TB languages are spoken in this area, with the remainder in the South Asian area; a few overlap between the two areas, most notably Tibetan. Of the TB languages in this area, fifty-seven are currently known to be endangered to some degree. Many others in Burma may also be, and there are very many additional TB languages yet to be described or even located in China.

Of some 960 Austronesian (AN) languages, only a small number are spoken on the Asian mainland. This includes four indigenous Malayic languages of West Malaysia, also extending into southern Thailand and the extreme south of Burma. The other AN group here is Chamic, which includes seven languages of southern Vietnam and northeastern Cambodia, with one additional language, Utsat or Tsat, on Hainan Island in China. Of more than eighty other Austro-Thai (AT) languages, over fifty are Thai-Kadai (TK), twenty-seven are Miao-Yao (MY), and a lexical component in Japanese may also fit here. Among these languages, forty or nearly half are endangered to some degree, including eight AN languages, twenty-five TK languages, and seven MY languages.

There are over 130 Austroasiatic (AA) languages, including more than 120 languages of the Mon-Khmer (MK) subgroup, mainly in Southeast Asia but also in southwestern China, and also found in South Asia (languages within Khasi in Meghalaya in northeastern India and the languages of the Nicobar Islands); the other subgroup of AA, the Munda languages, are found only in South Asia. Of over 110 known MK languages in the area covered, fifty-four are now endangered, and most of the rest are at least potentially endangered. There are also certainly more MK languages not yet located, especially in Laos and Burma.

The dubious Altaic group, putatively including Turkic, Mongolic, Tungusic and Japanese/Korean, is more widespread outside this region. In this area there are nine Turkic, at least seven Mongolic, and seven Manchu-Tungus languages as well as Japanese and Korean. Most of the Turkic and Mongolic languages and of course Japanese and Korean are not endangered, but in China all of the Tungusic languages, four Mongolic languages and one Turkic language are endangered.

There is one moribund isolate in northern Japan, Ainu. Various dubious genetic connections have been proposed for it. There are also some non-endangered Indo-European languages, including Russian and Tajik in China, and two endangered indigenous Portuguese creoles.

Population data are from the 2000 census of China, 1997 Ministry of Interior data for Thailand, the 1993 census for Vietnam, data from the 1983 census of Laos retabulated by the Lao Institute of Ethnology, 1999 scholarly estimates[2] based on Malaysian government statistics, and estimates for Burma and Cambodia where recent census information is not available, in all cases supplemented by additional information from a variety of colleagues. For more detailed maps, see Wurm and Hattori (1981), Wurm *et al.* (1987), and especially Moseley and Asher (1994/2006).

History and language areas

This part of the world includes two major and somewhat distinct language areas, within and between each of which there has been long-standing contact and structural convergence: the East Asian linguistic area, the sphere of cultural and linguistic influence of China, and the mainland Southeast Asian linguistic area, where the earlier pattern has been overlain by large and relatively recent migrations and conquests, mainly from the East Asian area to the north. In addition, its current political margin to the west forms part of the Central Asian linguistic area of primarily Turkic, Mongol and some Indo-European and other languages. On its northern fringe, there was formerly the Manchu-Tungus portion of the Siberian linguistic area, now almost entirely Sinicised within northeastern China. Most remaining languages of this group are more widely spoken in Russia, and are discussed in Chapter 3; those two which are entirely restricted to China, the Manchu and Xibo, are considered here.

Among the features of the Southeast Asian linguistic area and of MK languages are verb-medial syntax, extensive prefixation and infixation, widespread phonesthetic reduplication, sesquisyllabic (prefix syllable plus main syllable) word structure, and other phonetic characteristics enumerated in Henderson (1965a).

The East Asian linguistic area has more variety of syntax, with verb-final syntax in nearly all TB and Altaic languages but verb-medial syntax in Chinese, TK and MY. Excluding the Altaic languages, it is characterised by relative lack of agreement morphology, presence of noun classifiers, monosyllabic word structure, presence of pitch-based tonal systems, and so on. Some MK languages such as Vietnamese or AN languages such as Utsat have acquired various East Asian characteristics from Chinese, such as pitch tone systems.

The boundary between these two linguistic areas and the South Asian linguistic area with its verb-final syntax, extensive postpositional agreement and derivational morphology, split ergative case marking, presence of retroflex and voiced 'aspirated' or breathy stops and so on, is also not so hard. There are numerous TB groups on both sides of the borders of Burma and India or Bangladesh, some such as the Arakanese whose migration from Arakan into what is now Bangladesh and parts of Tripura in India over a bit more than 200 years is documented, others probably indigenous on both sides of the modern borders. Furthermore, the MK Khasi in Meghalaya in northeastern India and the indigenous languages of the Nicobar islands have the genetic and some of the structural characteristics of the Southeast Asian linguistic area, while the AA Munda languages of South Asia have been more fully assimilated into the South Asian patterns. One example of structural influence is the spread of classifier systems from the East and Southeast Asian linguistic areas into the northeastern part of the South Asia area, even into Indo-European languages such as Bengali.

Along the long border between Tibet and South Asia, there are many Tibetan and other TB groups who live in India, Nepal and Bhutan; these are discussed in Chapter 4, but it is worth noting that a few such groups live on both sides, and their languages may be more endangered in one nation than in another due to local factors, as in the case of Zaiwa. Before 1904 and from 1962 these borders were notionally closed, and in practical terms they now form an even stronger barrier to regular contact than the main Himalayan range which they follow. As is well known, the South Asian influence on Tibet proper, its religion and its written language was major and with longstanding effects for more than a millennium – a Tibetan response to the series of wars they were waging with various Chinese dynasties on their northeastern and southeastern borders since even earlier, to differentiate and isolate themselves from the related Chinese language and strong cultural influence.

At various periods in their history, the Chinese have come under the domination and strong influence of groups from the north (the Jurchen rulers of the Jin Dynasty, 1115–1234, and the Manchu rulers of the Qing Dynasty, 1644–1911) or from the west (the Mongol rulers of the Yuan Dynasty, 1271–1368). This has even led some scholars such as Hashimoto to suggest that Mandarin, northern Chinese, shows structural influence from Manchu-Tungus and Mongol languages. At many periods, China exerted an extremely strong cultural influence, with or without direct political control, as in Japan, Korea, Vietnam, Mongolia and Tibet. In all cases, this influence persisted long after any direct rule ceased.

Over several millennia, the Chinese majority group has been expanding southwards into all areas of what is now China, assimilating or displacing other groups. This has led to greater or lesser degrees of structural influence of the larger of these languages on regional varieties of Chinese. For example, it is widely recognised that Cantonese shows both lexical and structural influence from a Tai substratum. Conversely, many minority languages have undergone centuries or millennia of linguistic and cultural influence.

The history of mainland Southeast Asia has also been one of repeated dynastic changes over several millennia. It is likely that the main inhabitants of this region at

351

an earlier date were speakers of MK languages; of these, the Vietnamese of what is now northern Vietnam came under the political and cultural domination of China, to such an extent that some linguists used to reject the relationship of Vietnamese with the rest of MK or AA. As a result of Chinese expansion southward, some large groups were displaced and moved into Southeast Asia. This includes the Burmans, who most likely arrived in the valley of Upper Burma as a result of the conquest of the Pyu by the Nanzhao of what is now northwestern Yunnan about 960 AD and subsequently spread into most of Burma. It also includes the Thai, who gradually moved from southwestern Yunnan into what is now Thailand, Laos and northeastern Burma starting a century or so later, displacing and eventually assimilating the local ethnic groups such as the Mon of Haripunjaya (Lamphun) in northern Thailand and Dvaravati in central Thailand, and taking over Khmer-controlled areas of what is now northeastern Thailand. The early history of southern Southeast Asia was dominated by various AN groups, including the Cham of Champa in what is now south-central Vietnam and the Malay of Srivijaya in what is now West Malaysia and the surrounding area, with later Moslem Malay kingdoms after the arrival of Islam.

Genetic linguistic families

The main generally recognised families in this area are ST and AA. Both also extend into South Asia. The other languages are in families whose higher-level classification is a matter of controversy. The AT superfamily proposed by Benedict (1942) includes the TK family (which includes Thai, and is found in southern China as well as Southeast Asia and into the northeastern part of South Asia) and the AN family (mainly in the islands, but also on the coast). Benedict (1975) adds the MY or Hmong-Mien family (mainly in southern China and extending into northern Southeast Asia), and Benedict (1990) proposes to add Japanese as well. More recent proposals by Sagart (2002) based on more solid lexical, phonological and morphological correspondences link AN and ST. An earlier proposed link was of AN and AA in Austric (Schmidt 1906), but this is not widely accepted nowadays. The rather dubious Altaic superfamily is usually said to include Turkic (extending into western China), Mongol (extending into northern China), Manchu-Tungus (extending into northeastern China) and sometimes Japanese and Korean. A couple of Indo-European (IE) languages are spoken in the margins of the area, as well as the Ainu isolate.

Languages of the longer established politically dominant groups within these families have been replacing other related and unrelated languages in central areas for many millennia, leading to greatly reduced linguistic diversity in eastern China and to a lesser extent in Cambodia, coastal areas of Vietnam and Malaysia and the central plains of Thailand and Burma. Marginal upland areas both preserve pre-existing diversity and accommodate migrations from adjacent areas where majority group pressure forces other groups away. This has led to the spread of numerous languages from southwestern China into Southeast Asia.

ST is usually divided into Sinitic (Chinese) and TB. In his chapter in this volume, van Driem (Chapter 4) prefers to refer to ST as Tibeto-Burman. This terminological innovation is based on his suggestion that the Bodic subgroup of TB and Sinitic may form a subgroup within ST. As the language with humanity's longest continuous written tradition, the cluster of varieties within Chinese or Sinitic forms our earliest and some of our most valuable evidence about ST. If we do revise generally accepted genetic linguistic cover terms, we really ought to use autonyms (people's own names for themselves), preferably relatively ancient ones, and recognise the earliest attested languages within each subgroup first; for example, Han for Chinese (though this is actually a dynastic name from just over 2,000 years ago) and Mran for Burmese, giving Han-Mran if we follow van Driem's subgroups and view Tibetan and Chinese as forming a single node.[3] This kind of revision in names of ethnic groups and genetic linguistic groupings has taken place in China and Vietnam since 1950 and more recently for the MY family, renamed Hmong-Mien by some scholars using the autonyms of two large groups at the southwestern edge of the family. Sometimes the order of compound names is reversed, depending on who is doing the naming; for example, the MK languages are called the Khmer-Mon languages in Cambodia.

The centre of gravity of AA is in mainland Southeast Asia, where all subgroups of AA are more closely linked within the MK family, named from two long-established literary languages, Mon and Khmer. This also extends into what is now southern China, both through the presence of some Vietnamese who are the Jing nationality of China in southwestern Guangxi, as well as various Northern MK groups of the Palaungic, Angkuic, Khmuic and Waic subgroups in southwestern Yunnan, and the recently identified Pakanic subgroup, three languages in various areas further east in southwestern China, with one extending into an adjacent area in northern Vietnam.

There are some Chinese in Central Asia, where they are known as Dungan, from the Chinese *Dong'an*, 'east peace', and of course in very substantial and long-established migrant communities throughout Southeast Asia and more recently elsewhere in the world. Substantial migration of majority-group Vietnamese, Khmers, Japanese, Koreans, Thais and others to Western countries is an even more recent phenomenon.

Around the southeastern parts of this area are some languages of the AN family. These include the indigenous non-Chinese languages of Taiwan as discussed by Wurm in Chapter 6 of this volume, and are a major presence in peninsular Malaysia and coastal areas to the north into Thailand and Burma. Furthermore, the Chamic group have long been in what is now southern Vietnam, with a small extension from 982 AD of the Utsat group to Hainan in China, also into northeastern Cambodia a few hundred years ago at the time of the final Vietnamese conquest of southern Vietnam. Subsequently, a few Cham moved from there to Thailand in the mid-nineteenth century (the original silk weavers of the Jim Thompson organisation in Thailand), and after 1975 some Cham came as refugees from Cambodia to Malaysia and various Western countries.

The TK languages were centred in southern China up until a millennium ago, when they expanded southwestward into Southeast Asia and beyond into northeastern South Asia. Within TK, the greatest internal genetic diversity is within the Kadai languages, now scattered across western Guizhou in China and further south, and formerly presumably with much larger speech communities. The Kam-Tai subgroup of TK includes the various Kam-Sui languages of southern Guizhou and northern Guangxi, and the Thai languages, divided into Northern, Central and Southwestern. Northern Tai is mainly found in southern Guizhou, northwestern Guangxi, Hainan; Central Tai groups are in southwestern Guangxi, southeastern Yunnan and into northeastern Vietnam. Southwestern Tai is found in western Yunnan and provided nearly all of the migration into Burma, Laos, Thailand and India.

The MY languages have long been widely distributed in south-central China, including Hunan, Guangdong, Guangxi and Guizhou; the greatest internal diversity is in northern Guangxi and southern Guizhou. These groups have a long history of resistance to the spread of the Chinese majority into these areas, and large groups have moved southwestward away from the advancing Chinese over more than a millennium. They moved long ago into Yunnan, and more recently beyond, into Vietnam, northern Laos and northern Thailand, with a few in northeastern Burma. Since 1975, substantial numbers of the two main diaspora groups, the Hmong (a variety of Western Miao) and the Iu Mien (a variety of Western Yao) moved from Laos to Western countries. These groups don't like the Chinese terms Miao and Yao, and so the MY languages are also called the Hmong-Mien languages using their autonyms.

The genetic position of Japanese and Korean is a matter of dispute. First, because of mutual national antipathy, neither Japanese nor Koreans want to accept a genetic connection, though one seems very clear. Japanese prefer to recognise a southward connection with AN, as proposed in Benedict (1990). Other scholars such as Miller (1971) link them with the Altaic languages, though as discussed in Chapter 3 by Salminen this 'family' is itself highly dubious, based primarily on typological resemblances of Turkic, Mongol and Manchu-Tungus languages, such as vowel harmony, perhaps of areal origin.

In what is now western China, there are various Turkic languages, most of which are more widely spoken in adjacent Central Asian states of the former USSR. A number of Mongol languages are spoken a bit further east, and of course also in Mongolia, as discussed by Salminen. Also present along the borders are small groups of Indo-European speakers, the Russian and Tajik nationalities of China. In addition, there are two endangered Portuguese creoles spoken in former Portuguese coastal enclaves, Melaka in southwestern peninsular Malaysia and Macao in southeastern China. We may also note the extinct Tocharian branch of IE formerly spoken in some areas of what is now far western China.

The sole widely recognised linguistic isolate in this region is Ainu, now moribund in various areas of Hokkaido Island in northern Japan and extinct in former areas such as the Kurile Islands and southern Sakhalin Island. Greenberg (2000) has proposed a link with Japanese and Korean in his Eurasiatic, but this is not widely accepted.

Sino-Tibetan languages

Sinitic

Mandarin Chinese, known in Chinese as *beifang hua*, 'northern speech', is also spoken as a first language by the Dungan nationality of the CIS, most of the (8,612,001) Hui (Moslem) nationality of China, the Kokang nationality of Burma, and the Haw Chinese of northeastern Burma, northern Laos (6,361) and northern Thailand (21,579 in villages, more in towns). It has nearly a billion mother tongue speakers, is well described and not endangered. Varieties of Mandarin are the national languages of China and Taiwan, and one of four national languages of Singapore.

However, the Han Chinese nationality, the 92 per cent majority in China, also includes over 300 million speakers of non-Mandarin varieties of Chinese. While these are all classified as one language in China and use the same characters for writing, the diverse spoken versions of the other six main varieties are not intelligible to speakers of Mandarin.

These non-Mandarin varieties are called *fangyan* – usually translated as 'dialect' in the literature from China. They include Wu (90 million plus, around Shanghai and Zhejiang), Yue or Cantonese (55 million plus, around Hong Kong and Guangzhou), Hakka (45 million, scattered in southeastern China), Min (70 million, mainly in Fujian, also known as Hokkien), Gan (42 million, in Hunan) and Xiang (38 million, in Jiangxi). In addition Taiwan is inhabited mainly by speakers of Min and Hakka, and the majority of overseas Chinese up to 1950 came from the Min, Yue and Hakka regions of the southeastern coast. In particular, nearly all the overseas Chinese in Southeast Asia are of Min, Yue or Hakka origin, apart from some Yunnanese Mandarin speakers in the north of Laos and Thailand and the Shan state of Burma.

The internal diversity of Chinese is very great, especially in phonology and lexicon. Chinese linguists tend to divide this into one *tuyu* 'local vernacular' per county, most of which represent long-standing administrative and social units; there are many thousands of counties. Widespread learning of written Chinese kept the morpho-syntactic differences much less substantial.

As a result of the spread of standard northern Mandarin and major regional varieties of provincial capitals since 1950, many of the smaller *tuyu* are disappearing by being absorbed into a larger regional *fangyan*, which of course may be a subvariety of Mandarin or something else. While much of the effort of Chinese linguists has long been put into studies of *fangyan* and *tuyu*, there remains a lot to be done, especially on morphosyntax, and this is becoming urgent as more and more small local *tuyu* become endangered or lost.

Tibeto-Burman

The only TB languages which now have official national status are Burmese in Burma and Dzongkha (a variety of Tibetan) in Bhutan. In South Asia, Manipuri or Meithei was recently added to Schedule VIII of the Indian constitution as an official language, and various other TB languages have local official status, for example Denzong (another variety of Tibetan very similar to Dzongkha) as well as Lepcha and Limbu in Sikkim. In China, a number of TB languages have local official status alongside Chinese, such as Tibetan in the Tibetan Autonomous Region, Tibetan, Yi, Lisu and so on at the Autonomous Prefecture level, and various other languages at the Autonomous County level.

Bodic

Most members of the Tibetan nationality (total 5,416,021) in China speak a Tibetan dialect: central dBus, south central gTsang, eastern Kham, or northeastern Amdo. As discussed in the following section, almost 300,000 of them speak Tibetan as a second language, with a Qiangic first language; some others in Tibetan areas also speak it, including many Dulong, Pumi, Qiang and Moso (eastern Naxi), and some (western) Naxi, Bai and Lisu. While spoken varieties are not usually mutually intelligible at first, learning can be rapid; spoken Lhasa dialect is used as a lingua franca, and Kham is sometimes used as a lingua franca among herdsmen, even in western Tibet. Literary Tibetan is also widely used, especially for religious purposes, as a diglossic High. Some small local varieties of Tibetan are endangered, but the language as a whole is not.

355

The official classification of Tibetan is much less detailed in China than outside; for example, there are Sherpa in the area north of Mt Everest in China just as there are in northeastern Nepal to its south; but in China they are just regarded as a small local subvariety of south-central Tibetan, while in Nepal they are a separate ethnic group.

Also spoken in southeastern Tibet are two other languages which are Bodic but not Tibetan. Both are included in the Monba nationality (8,923), and both are also more widely spoken south of the border. Cuona Monba or (mɔn^{35} pɑ^{53}) is spoken mainly in Bhutan and Kameng District of Arunachal Pradesh, India, and Motuo Monba or (mon^{13} pa^{55}) is also spoken in Siang District of Arunachal Pradesh in India. Neither is at present endangered.

Qiangic

This subgroup, also known as Northeastern TB, is mainly in western Sichuan and northwestern Yunnan, with one language extending into southern Gansu. Apart from the Bai (1,858,063), Naxi (308,839) and Pumi (33,600) nationalities in northwestern Yunnan and the Qiang nationality (306,072) in northwestern Sichuan, all these groups are included within the Tibetan nationality (overall 5,416,021). Apart from Bai and Naxi, all are within the Tibetan cultural area and use a local spoken Tibetan lingua franca (Kham in the south, Amdo in the north), literary Tibetan for religious purposes, and more recently Chinese. From south to north, the Qiangic languages are the following.

Bai has been heavily influenced by Chinese over more than a millennium. Like Chinese, it has verb-medial main clause word order, but keeps many other typical TB syntactic patterns. In many locations outside its core area in northern Dali Prefecture, the Bai language is extinct or in serious decline, and even in the core area it is heavily and increasingly influenced by Chinese. A very divergent variety of Bai is spoken by about 15,000 of 50,000 Laemae or Lama in parts of Lushui and Lanping counties in southern Nujiang Prefecture, to the northwest of the main Bai concentration.

Naxi comprises two languages: Naxi around Lijiang with two dialects and nearly 300,000 speakers, and Moso with about 40,000 speakers around Luhu Lake in Ninglang County of Yunnan and Muli County and surrounding areas in Sichuan. The Moso in Sichuan are classified as Mongol nationality. Naxi is lexically transitional to Burmic.

Pumi (p^{h}rimi), meaning 'white people', has a wide variety of very distinct dialects from Lanping and Ninglang in Yunnan to Muli in Sichuan. Of nearly 60,000 speakers, over 25,000 in Sichuan are classified as Tibetan nationality.

Continuing northwards in western Sichuan, some members of the Tibetan nationality speak the following, all of which were formerly included in the Chinese category Xifan (Hsifan) and the Tibetan category Hör: Namuyi, about 5,000 speakers, potentially endangered; Shixing, about 1,800 speakers, endangered; Ersu, about 15,000 speakers of several dialects; referred to as Tosu in some foreign literature, and as Lüzi or Lüsu in some Chinese literature, endangered; Muya, about 10,000 speakers, potentiallly endangered; Ergong (sTau in Tibetan), about 35,000 speakers; Choyo (Chinese Queyu), about 7,000 speakers, endangered; Zaba, about 7,700 speakers, potentially endangered; Guichong, 7,000 speakers, endangered; Jiarong, 170,000 speakers, substantial internal dialect differences; also known as rGyarung in Tibetan.

The Qiang nationality includes two extremely distinct languages, Southern with 60,000 speakers and Northern with 70,000 speakers; each includes a wide variety of local dialects, and many other Qiang speak only Chinese. Beyond them to the north are the Baima, 10,000 speakers classified as Tibetan nationality, and endangered by Amdo Tibetan and by Chinese. Some scholars prefer to regard Baima as a local variety of Tibetan, but the very large Tibetan element in Baima is due to contact.

Of the Xifan languages, only Jiarong is moderately well described. Much more work is needed on the rest, especially the endangered languages Shixing, Ersu, Choyo, Guichong and Baima. Work on virtually undescribed and potentially endangered Namuyi, Muya and Zaba is also desirable. The exact genetic position of Bai is a matter of contention. Due to millennia of Chinese influence, this is a difficult issue to resolve. Bai, Naxi and Moso also have some contact lexical links with Burmic languages to their south, but on phonological and morphosyntactic grounds their basic genetic connection is with the Qiangic languages.

Central Tibeto-Burman

WEST ARUNACHAL AND ADI-MISING-NISHI

Formerly known as Abor-Miri-Dafla languages according to now superseded pejorative names, these subbranches of TB are mainly found in Arunachal Pradesh in northeastern India. There are a couple of languages which spread into southeastern Tibet. These are lumped together within the Luoba nationality of 2,965 people. Luoba is from Tibetan, where it means 'savages' and refers specifically to these groups. At times of political stress in China, some Luoba who used to live in China moved to the Indian side. While small in numbers in China, these languages are not endangered because they are also more widely spoken in India. These languages, from west to east, include the very small Sulung group (autonym (poh^{53} ɣut^{33})) who speak a West Arunachal Group language in a distinct subgroup of TB; also the Bugun, Bogar and Damu, which are regarded as varieties of Adi in India.

DIGARISH AND MIJUISH 'MISHMI'

In China there are two small related Digarish TB groups in southeastern Tibet, the 700 Taruang (ta^{31} ʒuaŋ^{55}), known in the Chinese literature as Darang Deng, and the Idu within the Luoba nationality. There is one Taruang village in Burma where they are called Taraung, and a much larger group of Taraon, Tayin or Tain, also known as Digaru Mishmi in India. While endangered in China, Taruang and Idu are not endangered in India.

In the same area of southeastern Tibet, there are two Mijuish TB groups, one of 200 (kɯ^{31} man^{35}), known in the Chinese literature as Geman Deng. The Geman are also known as Kaman or Miju Mishmi in India; their language is likewise endangered in China, but viable in India. There used to be more speakers in China, but many went to India. The other language of this group is endangered Zaiwa, recently located both in Tibet and in India, spoken by under a thousand people with about a third fairly recently arrived in India and the rest still in Tibet. All four of these groups are included in the Indian category 'Mishmi', which is an exonym.

NUNGISH

Among the 28,759 Nu nationality and 7,426 Dulong nationality in China and about 145,000 members of the Rawang ethnic group in far northern Burma, there are eight

357

languages, including one which is actually Burmic, Raorou, spoken by the Nu in Lanping County and discussed further below. The southern Nu in Bijiang County speak three distinct dialects of the Nusu language, with 8,000 speakers overall; some Chinese scholars prefer to classify Nusu as a Burmic language as well. About 7,300 central Nu in southern Fugong County are Anung (Anong in the Chinese literature), but only about 50 to 60 speakers, mostly over forty, remain; there are also several thousand speakers among a slightly larger community in Burma. This language is severely endangered, but has been described by Sun Hongkai. About 6,500 Nu in northern Fugong County in fact speak Dulong, so Dulong has about 12,000 speakers in China, including the Dulong of Gongshan County, north of Fugong.

In Burma there are five distinct varieties of Rawang, as spoken by clan clusters from south to north: 30,000 Lungmi, 50,000 Mvtwang (with Dvmang included), 15,000 Dvngsar or Tangsarr, 35,000 Dvru and 15,000 Zørwang. The Gvnøng supergroup includes the Dvru and the Zørwang. Mvtwang is used for writing, and is spreading at the expense of the others; some, especially the Mvtwang themselves, prefer to regard the other four varieties as dialects of Mvtwang, but the differences are very substantial. Gvnøng (Dvru and Zørwang) is close to Dulong in China and better maintained, but Lungmi and Dvngsar are potentially endangered and undescribed.

Tujia

This nationality has two languages spoken by very few of the 8,028,133 Tujia nationality of northwestern Hunan, southwestern Hubei and eastern Sichuan in south central China. Biji or Northern Tujia is spoken by nearly 60,000, and Mozi or Southern Tujia is spoken by about a thousand, in both cases including children in some limited areas. These totals are down from about 170,000 speakers, 160,000 Biji and 10,000 Mozi, twenty years ago. The Tujia were concealed within the Han Chinese nationality until being identified and recognised in the 1950s. All speakers are bilingual in Chinese, and the two languages are increasingly endangered. Tujia is also very interesting historically because there is so much Chinese contact material superposed on its TB core. Chinese linguists wrongly classify Tujia as part of Burmic, but both languages lack core Burmic features.

Burmic

The Burmic languages comprise the Burmish languages, including Burmese, the Gong language and the Loloish, Yi Branch or Ngwi languages, which can be further subclassified into Northern, Central, Southern and Southeastern. Yi is the post-1950 Chinese term for the largest nationality speaking various languages of this subgroup of TB; the term Yi Branch is used in China to refer to this group of languages, not just the languages of the Yi nationality. Before 1950 the Yi were known as Lolo, whence the term Loloish, but Lolo is now regarded as pejorative by many people in China and avoided. Here the term Ngwi is used, derived from the probable autonym for these Loloish or Yi Branch groups, and itself in turn derived from the TB word for 'silver'.

BURMISH

Burmese, the national language of Burma with about 30 million first language speakers, is the least endangered TB language; however some of its more distinctive 'dialects' are really distinct languages, many of which are becoming endangered as they undergo more and more influence from standard Burmese.

The second largest ethnic group speaking a variety of Burmese is the Arakanese (now known as Rakhine in Burma); its best known feature is the retention of the pronunciation of orthographic 'r'. There are about 1.7 million speakers in Arakan State in the west of the country; in addition there are at least another 100,000 Arakanese locally known as Mogh in southeastern Bangladesh and southern Tripura in India, and another smaller group known as Mrama, Marma or in Burma Mramargyi who are mainly in Bangadesh but a few in India and Burma. The Mrama are a remnant of the Arakanese court who fled over 200 years ago when the Burmans seized Arakan.

In order of size, the following other varieties of Burmese are recognised as separate ethnic groups in Burma: Tavoyan (Dawe, about 400,000 speakers in Tennaserim in the southeast); Beik or Myeik (about 250,000 in the far south); Danu (about 100,000 in the Shan State in the northeast); Intha (about 90,000 around Inle Lake in the southeastern Shan State); Taungyo (about 40,000, also in the Shan State) and Yaw (about 20,000 in west-central Burma). Of these, only Yaw is endangered, though Danu and Taungyo are starting to be, and all are heavily influenced by standard Burmese.

Hpun is a moribund or possibly extinct language along the upper Irrawaddy in the gorges between Myitkyina and Bhamo in north Burma. Survey work in the early 1960s found that the only fluent speakers of the two dialects of Hpun were in their sixties, with some younger semi-speakers. However, if further data could be collected it would be extremely valuable in clarifying the development of the Burmic languages.

The other cluster of Burmic languages is in the northeast of the country and in China. These are Tsaiwa (150,000, including a majority of the 132,143 Jingpo nationality in China; known as Atsi in Jinghpaw and as Zi in Burmese); Langwaw or Langsu (100,000, a few in China; known as Maru in Jinghpaw and Burmese); Lacid (30,000, known as Lashi in Jinghpaw and Burmese); Ngochang (45,000; known as Maingtha in Burmese and as Achang in China where they are a separate nationality of 33,936).[4] The Zaiwa and Lachik are recognised as ethnic groups of the Kachin State of Burma and the Maingtha as an ethnic group of the Shan State there, but the Lawngwaw/Maru are not recognised in Burma. Apart from most Ngochang in China, all of these groups are part of the Kachin culture complex, speak fluent-to-native Jinghpaw Kachin as a lingua franca, and are language-exogamous; so every household has at least two native languages, which may be one Burmish language plus Jinghpaw or two Burmish languages, in which case Jinghpaw is usually a third native language. Commonly encountered marriage patterns are Lacid and Ngochang, Tsaiwa and Langwaw, or any Burmish group and Jinghpaw. A movement for separate literary versions of Ngochang, Lacid, Tsaiwa and Langwaw is starting, but until quite recently the sole language of literacy was Jinghpaw.

There are two severely endangered Burmish languages that are part of this Kachin culture complex: 400 Bola and 70 Chintao (Xiandao in Chinese) who are members of the Achang nationality in China. Chinese linguists have worked on these languages.

GONG

This language, which forms a separate branch within Burmic, was formerly spoken over a wide area of west-central Thailand, along the branches of the River Kwai. It has disappeared from the original area, with the last speakers only recently deceased;

but two communities which migrated to Suphanburi and Uthai Thani provinces to the northeast still maintain distinct dialects of the language; they are classified in the composite Lawa hill tribe of Thailand. Of 500 people in these two villages, about eighty still speak the language: about twenty fluent speakers over fifty years old and additional semi-speakers of varying ability as young as thirty. Thai colleagues and myself are working on this language, which is crucial for the understanding of the Burmic sub-family of TB.

NGWI

Ngwi is divided into four main parts: Northern, Central, Southern and Southeastern (formerly called Tonkin). Northern Ngwi languages are mainly in eastern Yunnan, western Guizhou and southern Sichuan. Central Ngwi is found in west-central Yunnan and to the west. Southern Ngwi languages are located in south-central Yunnan and to the southwest. Southeastern Ngwi is in southeastern Yunnan, Guangxi and northern Vietnam. Phonologically, Southern Ngwi is the most conservative for final consonants, while Northern Ngwi is most conservative for initial consonants. All Ngwi languages share a number of grammatical developments, such as the use of verbs of dimensional extent in question, nominal and adverbial forms. Another widely shared Ngwi pattern is kin group classifiers, which can only be used with a number to refer to a specific group of relatives, such as a father and his children.

Confusingly, Chinese linguists divide the composite Yi nationality of China into six subgroups using similar compass terms, Northern, Eastern, Southeastern, Southern, Central and Western Yi. The Western, Central and Southeastern Yi speak various Central Ngwi languages, along with Lahu, Lisu and so on, while the Eastern, Northern and most Southern Yi speak Northern Ngwi languages; a few Southern Yi speak Southeastern Ngwi languages. No Yi speak Southern Ngwi languages; the largest Southern Ngwi group are the Hani/Akha. Use of the term Ngwi avoids both the pejorative connotations of the former term Loloish, and likely confusion.

The main Ngwi groups in China include the highly composite Yi nationality (7,762,272), the multiple-group Hani nationality (1,439,673 in China, also 12,500 in Vietnam and 727 in Laos; Hani also includes the Akha group, with over 200,000 in Burma, 58,500 in Laos and 56,616 in Thailand), the Lisu nationality (634,912 in China, about 250,000 in Burma, 33,365 in Thailand and 1,200 in India), and the Lahu nationality (453,705 in China, about 250,000 in Burma, 85,845 in Thailand, 15,693 in Laos, and over 1,000 in California), both of which also have substantial internal diversity and include some additional small groups whose languages are endangered, and the Jinuo nationality (20,899).

Hanhi (12,500), Phula (6,500), Lahu (5,400), Lôlô (3,200), Công (1,300) and Sila (600) are recognised ethnic groups of Vietnam, mainly in the northwest of the country. The Lahu of Vietnam are in fact Cosung, a distinct group only integrated into the Lahu nationality in China in 1989. Some of Vietnam's Lôlô are the same as the Nisu, the largest Southern Yi subgroup in China. The Phula speak two Southeastern Ngwi languages also spoken by members of the Yi nationality in China, and the Công speak a language similar to Phunoi or Sinsali of Laos. Cosung, Công and Sila are endangered, as is one of the Phula languages.

In Burma the Lahu and Kwi (Shan word for Lahu Shi or Yellow Lahu) are recognised separately, as are the Lisu and the Kaw (Burmese name for Akha), a part of the

Hani nationality in China. In Laos the Musur (Shan name for the Lahu) and Kwi are also separately recognised, as are the Kaw (Lao name for Akha) and the Sinsali (formerly Phunoi); the Lao list also includes one smaller endangered group, the Sila. In northern Thailand, the official list of hill tribes includes the Lahu (often under the Thai name Muser), the Lisu (as Lisaw), and the Akha (or the former, pejorative Thai term Ikaw). Some of the languages of smaller groups are endangered, and even within the larger groups, many live in urban settings and do not speak their traditional languages. All of these languages are losing domains even in their villages. Conversely, a number of smaller Ngwi and other TB languages are in the process of being replaced by a Yi language, mainly Hani, Lahu, Lisu or a larger Yi language.

Of the recognised groups, the languages of the Jinuo nationality in China, the Sila ethnic group in Vietnam and Laos, the Phin ethnic group of Burma (i.e. Bisu) and one of the languages of the Phula ethnic group of Vietnam (part of the Yi nationality in China) all are endangered. Many other small groups are included in the large nationalities, especially Yi in China but also Hani, Lahu and Lisu; a large number of their languages are endangered.

In addition to the numerous small groups on which data exist, there are many other similar groups classified within the Yi nationality in various areas of Yunnan who most likely speak other endangered languages. In the absence of clear linguistic information, these cannot be included at this time; however, some can be briefly noted here. The Bo of Wenshan Prefecture, Qiubei County, Shupi Township are classified as Yi. Some other examples are the Suan and Pengzi of Yongde County, the Guaigun of Zhenyuan County, the Xiuba of Piangbian County, all with fewer than a thousand people. Larger groups of under 20,000 in Yunnan include the Azong of Jiangcheng Conty, the Ta'er, Naza, Liude, Liwu and Tagu of Yongsheng and Ninglang counties (some of these five probably connected with the Talu and Tazhi nearby), the Long, Ati and Xiqi of Huaning County, the Ani in Mengzi County and the Apu in Jinping County nearby (all five said to be related to Phula and thus presumably Southeastern Ngwi), and nearly twenty more. A few similar groups are also found in adjacent provinces, such as the Yieluo Yi of Yanbian County, Sichuan, various subgroups of Eastern Yi in Weining County of northwest Guizhou, such as Tushu, Lagou, and Guopu, or the various Yi of Tianlin, Xilin and Napo counties in western Guangxi. The literature reports quite a number of these undescribed languages as being endangered, such as Labapho and Asahei in Kaiyuan County. There are of course many other larger groups whose languages may be potentially endangered. And all these are just within the Yi nationality! Given the extreme confusion in the literature about the Yi, all these languages urgently need further research to determine their status.

Part of the confusion of classification of the Yi is due to the Chinese tendency to classify various groups according to their status within the former political system, in which the Black Lolo or Black Yi (Hei Luoluo or Hei Yi) were the feudal lords, with some ruling as local Chinese *tusi* and others maintaining virtual independence up to the 1950s. The White Lolo, now White Yi (Bai Luoluo or Bai Yi) were the more assimilated Yi or the non-noble members of Black Yi communities. The Dry Lolo or Dry Yi (Gan Luoluo or Gan Yi) and the Red Lolo or Red Yi (Hong Luoluo or Hong Yi) were in some cases the servants and serfs of the Black Yi lords, and in other cases distinct groups under political influence from nearby Black Yi lords. Thus these terms refer to quite different groups in different places. For example, of the groups whose languages are endangered, the Aluo are locally referred to as Gan Yi in Chinese; but

361

they are far from the only ones. The relatively assimilated Ayizi and Sanie are locally referred to as Bai Yi, while the Chesu are sometimes locally called Hei Yi; but there are very many other groups for whom the same Chinese terms are used. Among the Samei some claim Hei Yi status, while others prefer to be identified as Bai Yi, which is politically safer.

NORTHERN NGWI

The most numerous Northern Ngwi language clusters are Nosu, 2.25 million in Sichuan and northwestern Yunnan, including a range of languages such as Adur, Suondi, Yinuo and so on; Nasu, about 800,000 including a large range of languages such as Gepo, Aluo and so on in northeastern Yunnan, several in western Guizhou and one in northwestern Guangxi; and Nisu, about 700,000 in south central Yunnan, with 842 in Laos and 3,200 in Vietnam, where they are known as Lôlô. These three groups account for more than half of the Yi nationality (6,578,524) in China, and nearly all of those in Sichuan, Guizhou and Guangxi. Many Nasu, quite a few Nisu and some Nosu do not speak their traditional language, but none of the three main languages is endangered.

Regarded by Chinese linguists as subvarieties of Nasu but linguistically distinct endangered languages are the Ayizi (2,000, but most do not speak it), Samataw (2,808 in one village, but only about 400 speakers), Chesu (6,600, about half speakers), Sanie (17,230, less than half speakers), Samei (28,000, about two thirds speakers) and Aluo (40,000, but fewer speakers). All these languages are spoken within a hundred kilometres of Kunming, the capital of Yunnan and traditional point of origin of the Yi, and are endangered. There are major internal dialect differences in most of them.

Another group speaking a Northern Ngwi language, but of the Southern Yi or Nisu type, are the Kazhuo of Xingmeng township in central Tonghai County, 6,341 members of the Mongol nationality. They are descendants of a Mongol army which probably settled about 700 years ago and married local Nisu women. There are no identfiable vestiges of Mongol in their speech. Within the large Nisu category there are certainly various small endangered languages; no linguistic survey of south-central Yunnan has yet been done so this is not known.

For the major Northern Ngwi languages, there is a long-established written tradition, based on the same principle as Chinese characters, but separate. The earliest surviving inscriptions on stone and on bronze date back about a thousand years, but it is likely that this orthography had its origins in the Cuan kingdoms of eastern Yunnan in the middle of the first millennium AD, if not earlier. Until recently, literacy in these orthographies was the preserve of traditional priests, who transmitted their texts to their chosen sons or nephews; now, some of them have been standardised and put into much wider use. The Nisu tradition of southern Yunnan is relatively unified, as is the Nasu tradition of northern Yunnan and western Guizhou. Both are written from top to bottom (as in traditional Chinese), but Nisu starts from the left. Some Nasu books are written following the usual Chinese practice, starting at the top right. More distinct, both in the form of the characters and in the orientation, is the Nosu tradition of Sichuan, which is written from left to right starting at the top; most Nosu characters are similar to the Nisu and Nasu characters, but rotated ninety degrees clockwise. The literature embodied in these scripts has four main themes: historical texts for recitation at rites of passage, medical knowledge and rituals, astrological and other divinatory texts, and family geneologies. Even though the Nisu, Nasu and Nosu languages are not now endangered, the cultural heritage contained in their traditional literature is very severely endangered, since the only people able to read and understand it fully are traditional priests, most of them very old men.

CENTRAL NGWI

The major non-endangered languages of Central Ngwi are Lisu, Lahu, Lipo and Lolopo. Other smaller groups whose languages are not yet endangered are the Southeastern Yi groups Sani, Axi, Azhe and Azha.

The ethnic classification of the endangered languages within the Central Ngwi subbranch is also quite complex. Jinuo is the sole such group to achieve recognition as a distinct national minority in China, while others are included within the Yi nationality (Hlersu, Lalo, Micha, Naluo, Samatu, Talu, Tanglang and Tazhi), the Lahu nationality (Cosung and Lamu), and the Nu nationality (Raorou).

Jinuo is spoken by less than half of the nationality (20,899); I have never met a young Jinuo who can speak the language. There are two quite distinct dialects. Cosung (Vietnamese term), Kucong (Yunnanese Chinese term, from which the Vietnamese term is derived), Lahu or Lahlu (autonyms) is spoken in various dialects by a population (40,000 in China, 5,400 in Vietnam) widely scattered over south-central Yunnan and northwestern Vietnam; unclassified until the 1980s, they were amalgamated into the Lahu in 1989, although their speech is not mutually intelligible with Lahu. Lamu is severely endangered, with less than a hundred speakers in one valley where they are mingled with Lipo and Lolopo and classified as Lahu, though their speech is more similar to Lisu than to Lahu; the Lipo are classified as Lisu in that area. The Bai group language Laemae is severely endangered by Lisu; their overall population of about 50,000 is partly submerged in Lisu as a clan, but about 15,000 people still speak the language.

All Lolopo (over 500,000) and most Lipo (220,000) are classified as part of the Yi nationality in China, though their languages are quite close genetically to Lisu. About 20,000 Lipo in Luquan County in north-central Yunnan are instead classified as Lisu. The Lolopo are found throughout western and central Chuxiong Prefecture and surrounding areas, extending into southeastern Lijiang Prefecture, eastern Dali Prefecture, and so on. The Lipo are mainly to the northeast of the Lolopo in Chuxiong Prefecture, though they overlap in some areas; they also extend into Panzhihua City in Sichuan and Luquan County in Kunming City. In some areas of northeastern Chuxiong Prefecture just to the west of Luquan, the Lipo have achieved a compromise. They were formerly classified as Yi for all purposes, but now, they are classified as Lisu at the local level, while in all statistics which are sent outside the local area, they are still counted as Yi. Both Lololpo and Lipo are starting to be endangered, and are not spoken by young people in many areas.

A further language in the same cluster, closer to Lipo than to anything else, is Micha; Chinese linguists classify Lipo, Lolopo and endangered Micha together as part of the Central subgroup of the Yi nationality. There are at least 50,000 Micha very widely scattered across western Yunnan, intermingling with the Lalo and Lahu to the southwest, with the Lisu in the northwest, with the Lipo at their northeast, and overlapping with the Lolopo over most of their range. While Micha is moribund or severely endangered in some villages, it is well preserved in others; however it remains

363

completely undescribed. Hlersu (15,000 people, better known as Shansu or Sansu, the Nisu name for this group) is another East-Central Ngwi language, spoken mainly in Xinping County and surrounding areas by a decreasing part of the group.

Sani (120,000) is the dominant local language of Shilin (formerly Lunan) County just southeast of Kunming, and also extends into several neighbouring counties. It is also the vehicle of an endangered indigenous Central Ngwi written tradition, which differs from the written traditions of the various Northern Ngwi groups in that it is also used to write traditional folk stories such as the Ashima story (about a princess who loved a commoner); but like the written traditions of the Nisu, Nasu and Nosu, it is also severely endangered. Axi (100,000) is mainly spoken in the northeastern part of Mile County just to the south of Sani. Azhe (60,000) is spoken mainly in northwestern Mile County, and has its own endangered written tradition. Azha (40,000) is spoken further south in Mile County and some surrounding areas.

South of the main Lisu/Lolopo/Lipo concentration, about 600,000 Lalo live in west-central Yunnan, especially in Wenshan and Nanjian counties, but also in surrounding areas; however, only about half speak the language, which has major internal dialect differences. It is moribund in many peripheral areas and well preserved only in some areas of concentration.

Other endangered Central Ngwi languages in various parts of northwestern Yunnan are Naluo (15,000, moribund in some areas, endangered in others), Samatu (7,500), Talu (over 10,000), Tanglang (947), Tazhi (a few hundred), all in the Yi nationality, and the previously mentioned Raorou (2,100) in the Nu nationality.

SOUTHERN NGWI

The main language cluster within this subbranch is Hani-Akha. Hani is spoken, in a range of quite different dialects, by about 700,000 of the composite Hani nationality (1,439,673) all over south-central Yunnan in China and across the borders in northern Vietnam (12,500) and northeastern Laos (727) where they are known as Hanhi. Very similar are Haoni and Baihong, about 120,000 speakers, to the northwest of Hani in north-central Yunnan. The Akha migrated southwestward about 400 years ago, and about 300,000 now live in the hills of much of southwestern Yunnan, especially Xishuangbanna Prefecture, but also elsewhere further north; and many have also moved on into Laos (58,500), Burma (over 200,000) and Thailand (56,616). Hani and Akha have merged voiceless aspirated and unaspirated stops, with complementary distribution: unaspirated stops occur in syllables with creaky phonation (derived from earlier final stops) and aspirated stops occur in syllables with normal phonation (derived from earlier syllables without final stops); this merger does not take place in Haoni and Baihong.

While Akha is far from endangered, despite ludicrous and often slanderous claims from Matthew McDaniel, there are some smaller languages which fall within its cultural orbit and are being absorbed by it. One example is Akeu (a^{55} $kə^{55}$), spoken by about 5,000 people classified as Akha in Thailand, Burma and northwestern Laos, and as Hani in the southwestern tip of Yunnan in China. Their language is not intelligible to other Akha, though it is quite closely related, and is being replaced by Akha. Another such is Chepya ($tɕe^{11}$ pja^{11}) of northeastern Laos, a small group of about 2,000. A third is Muda (mu^{31} ta^{31}), a group of about 2,000 in Jinghong.

Also within the Hani nationality in China are the somewhat less closely related languages Kaduo (Chinese) or (k^ha tu) and Biyue or (pi jɔ) with about 300,000 speakers together. Both are in southwestern Yunnan, and both are relatively well maintained. A third language similar to Biyue is Mpi, not to be confused with Bisu or the Phunoi subvariety Pisu. This is spoken in one large village near Phrae in northern Thailand; they were transported there from China as war captives about 200 years ago. Mpi is still spoken by most of the 1,200 people in the village, but all are now trilingual, speaking Northern Thai as a diglossic Low and standard Thai as a High. A dictionary exists, but is not very complete; other work is needed here.

There are many other groups within the Hani nationality, widely distributed across southern Yunnan. For some, no reliable linguistic data is available, but the languages may well prove to be endangered. These include Sanda, Duota and Yiche. The Sanda are a group of about a thousand in Menghai County, the Duota are in Yuanjiang and Mojiang counties, and the Yiche are in Honghe County. Even more confusing is the report of two groups with a similar name, Meng: one is included in Hani, lives in Shuangjiang County in western Yunnan, while the other are in Xichou County in southeastern Yunnan.

All languages of the distinctive Bisoid branch of Southern Ngwi are endangered, most of them severely: in China, Laomian in Lancang and Menglian counties and nearby in Burma (7,000, about half speakers), Bisu in Menghai County (known as Laopin), nearby in Burma, (known as Phyin, an official ethnic group of Burma) and transported to northern Thailand (under 3,000 in total in all three countries), Sang-kong (locally known as Buxia in Chinese, under 2,000) in Jinghong, Công of north-western Vietnam (1,300); and endangered to a lesser degree, the six languages within Phunoi[5] or Sinsxali (23,618 in Phongsaly Province, northeastern Laos). Bisu, Laomian and the (law^{33} pan^{11}) variety of Phunoi are quite closely related, but the other five varieties within Phunoi, two called (p^hu^{21} $nɔj^{44}$) and the other three known as ($p^hɔŋ^{33}$ ku^{55}), (law^{21} $sɛŋ^{21}$) and (pi^{33} su^{44}), differ from them and from each other. The Bisoid languages share an unusual sound change: certain prefixed nasals become prenasalised or nonprenasalised voiced stops, for example the widespread TB cognate for 'fire' ([mi] in most languages) becomes (mbi^{21}) or (bi^{21}).

There are two severely endangered languages of another branch of the Southern Ngwi group which are almost completely undescribed: Bana in northern Laos and Sila in northeastern Laos and northwestern Vietnam. The Bana in Laos are included within the Kaw (Akha) ethnic group; in one village in northeastern Laos their language is being replaced by Akha, and in one village in northwestern Laos it is being replaced by Lahu. It is not even clear how many there are; Chazee (1995: 193) says 4,000 in thirty-four villages, but this is clearly a major overestimate. Sila is recognised as an ethnic group in Laos (1,518) and in Vietnam (600); a vocabulary was published by Lefèvre-Pontalis (1892) under the name Asong, and it also sometimes appears in Vietnamese sources as Sida. The same source gives a 'Phana' vocabulary as well, which appears to be Bana. Kingsada and Shintani (1999) give longer vocabularies for these two languages, showing that these languages are both quite distinct from any others in the area. Bana and Sila are being replaced by Lahu, Akha and other sur-rounding languages.

SOUTHEASTERN NGWI

Southeastern Ngwi, formerly known as Tonkin Lolo, includes a number of small groups in southeastern Yunnan and in northern Vietnam, mainly east of the Red

River. Much more descriptive work is needed, and there are almost certainly additional unreported languages yet to be found. The largest group here are the Pula (Chinese term, over 50,000 included in the Yi nationality), Phula (Vietnamese ethnic group; about 5,000 people; also formerly known as Bo Kho Pa there), both from its autonym (pʰu ɬa.) There are various distinct subgroups within Pula, notably (pʰo⁵⁵ lo⁵⁵) and (pʰu⁵⁵). The former is becoming endangered; many young people cannot speak the language.

A pair of closely related endangered languages are Muji (about 50,000 in Mengzi County in China) and Laghuu (about 300 in northern Vietnam, classified as part of the Phula ethnic group, also known as Xa Pho). The local autonyms for Muji are (ɬa³¹ ɣə⁵⁵) or (mu dʑi³³); most Muji speak Pula rather than Muji. Laghuu is spoken in just one village, but there it is well maintained and spoken by children (Edmondson and Lama 2000).

In Funing County of southeastern Yunnan, about 5,000 people of Yi nationality speak (muaŋ⁵¹), or in Chinese Mo'ang, a potentially endangered language which is hardly described. In Guangnan County in the same area, about 5,000 Yi people use (kʌ³³ θu³¹), reported in Chinese as Gasu, also potentially endangered and in need of work.

In summary, there are six or more Southeastern Ngwi languages; several likely additions have been noted above. Five of the six are endangered. Of the eighteen Northern Ngwi languages, seven are endangered. For Central Ngwi it is thirteen endangered out of twenty-one, and for Southern Ngwi eleven endangered out of twenty-two. Thus the Ngwi branch of TB contains both the greatest number of TB languages in the area and the highest proportion of endangered ones. Moreover, as in the case of the MK languages below, it is certain that additional endangered languages remain to be located, especially in China.

Karenic

Karenic can be divided into Southern Karen, mainly Pwo to the south and Sgaw to the north, mainly in the Karen State of Burma and known as Kayin in Burmese and Kariang in Thai; Central Karen, known as Kayah in Burmese and generally as Bwe in Karen, mainly in the Kayah State of Burma; and Northern Karen, including Pa-O (formerly Taungthu in Burmese and still Tawngsu in Thai) and Kayan (formerly Padaung in Burmese), mainly in the Shan State of Burma but some also further south.

The 1983 census for Burma reported 2,122,825 Kayin and 141,028 Kayah. These are extreme underestimates; there are about 5 million Karen there. Many Southern Karen migrated to the western delta region of Burma and a few went further to the islands off southern Burma and even to the Andaman Islands during the British colonial period. There are officially 353,574 Kariang in Thailand, but this is also an underenumeration; others have assimilated into the Thai population. They speak mainly Pho in the west and Sgaw in the northwest; a few thousand in the far northwest speak Central Karen varieties. An additional 120,000 or so are at present in refugee camps, having fled oppression and religious persecution in Burma. Thailand also has 257 Tongsu or Pa-O and a few Kayan.

Twelve Karen ethnic groups are listed under the Karen State in Burma, nine for the Kayah State, and three for the Shan State. Pa-O is listed and counted twice: for the Karen State and for the Shan State. Some of the smaller Central Karen languages within the Kayah ethnic group in Burma are approaching endangerment, with group sizes of about 10,000 for the Manu, Yintale and Geba. Most Central and Northern Karen languages still need linguistic work, which is very difficult at present.

Baric

The core Bodo-Garo or Baric group includes the main TB languages of the plains and low hills of Assam, including Garo, Bodo and so on, and the Northern Naga languages of far northern Nagaland and southeastern Arunachal Pradesh in India, as well as some of the same Naga groups in northwestern Burma. Burling (1983) has expanded the Baric group to include the Luish languages of western Burma and the eastern borders of India, as well as the Jinghpaw language of northern Burma and surrounding areas.

One subgroup of core Baric represented in Burma is Northern Naga in the far northwest, including the Khienmungan (also known as Kalyokengnyu), Htangan, Konyak, Wancho, Haimi, Nocte and Tangsa/Rangpan (which is the same as the Tangsa group of India).[6] These languages go under a bewildering array of alternative names; curiously, none are recognised as separate ethnic groups in Burma; all are simply lumped together as Naga, a pejorative exonym of Indian origin. Apart from Haimi, most groups are also found in India, where there are additional related languages such as Chang and Phom. All, especially those further south or closer to India, are incipiently endangered by Nagamese, an Assamese pidgin which is creolising in Nagaland in India and also spreading into Naga areas of Burma; however, all these languages still have 20,000 or more speakers.

The so-called Luish (from Manipuri *lui*, 'slave') languages of western Burma are almost all extinct or moribund. The only such language not on its last legs is Sak, autonym (atsa?), Burmese name Thet, with nearly 3,000 speakers in Bangladesh and about 1,000 speakers out of an ethnic population of 1,602 in Arakan State of Burma. Kadu was the language of a pre-Burman kingdom in the north of Burma, and is still spoken in north Katha by a couple of thousand from a vestigial ethnic group of about 20,000. Closely related and in the same area is Ganan, with about 500 speakers of an ethnic population of 7,000. Both languages are moribund, but fieldwork is at present impossible. Other Luish languages of northwestern Burma, such as Taman and Malin, may already be extinct, as are several in Manipur. Three Luish languages, Undro (Andro), Chairel and Sekmai (Sengmai), were formerly spoken in villages of these names in southern Manipur State of India, to the southwest of the Taman; the parenthesised names are usually used in the linguistic literature. These languages became extinct nearly a hundred years ago.

A third large group which Burling links with Baric is the Jinghpaw (t$\textsubscript{}$çiŋ^{31} pʰɔʔ^{31}) group of northern Burma, known in Burmese as Kachin. The 1983 census figures for Burma give 465,484 Jinghpaw, but this is an underestimate. As we have seen above, most of the Jingpo nationality of 132,143 in China have a Burmish first language and speak Jinghpaw as a lingua franca; only about 20,000 in China speak Jinghpaw as their first language. There are also about 2,000 Singpho (Jinghpaw) in extreme northeastern India. A reasonable current estimate is that there are at least 600,000 speakers of Jinghpaw, which includes various dialects that are named as separate ethnic groups in Burma: Gauri and so on. There are at least a further 200,000 speakers who know it as an extremely fluent second language, mainly from Burmish groups, and more who use it as a lingua franca, including many Lisu and Nungish TB language speakers. It is

367

replacing some small Burmish languages in China and has recently replaced one Tai language in northeastern India.

Kuki-Chin-Naga

There are many languages in the Kuki-Chin-Naga (KCN) group in South Asia, as well as fifty-four listed among the 135 ethnic groups of Burma: fifty-one in the Chin State and three in Arakan State, all along the western border. Fieldwork is at present very difficult in Burma, so an adequate classification and report on their degree of endangerment is impossible. Chin is a Burmese name; beyond the border, most KCN languages are included in the category Naga in Nagaland, Manipur and Assam, and Kuki in Mizoram and Tripura. The Chin in Burma are generally divided into North Chin, Central Chin and South Chin. For most North and Central Chin, the indigenous name is Zo, and Sho or Asho for most South Chin. The best described variety of North Chin is Tiddim (a town name; Henderson 1965b); there are about 135,000 speakers of this cluster in Burma and some in India. Central Chin is also known as Laizo 'central Zo', and has about 400,000 speakers in Burma, including the Lushai who are now known in India as Mizo, with hundreds of thousands of speakers in Mizoram. South Chin or Sho/Asho has more internal diversity; many of the 250,000 in Burma no longer speak it. Also included here are the Khami/Khumi, about 50,000 in Burma and more in Bangladesh; and probably the Mro or Mru, about 40,000 total, mainly in Arakan in Burma, but also in the southwestern Chin State and in Bangladesh.

In the Chin State of Burma there are also some Meithei or Manipuri, Chawte, Anal and Miram (known in India as Mara or formerly as Lakher), but these languages are concentrated nearby in India and discussed in Chapter 4. Further north are three KCN languages classified as Naga, mainly found in India but with a few in Burma: Maring, Tangkhul and Yimchungrü. These languages have large speaker populations in India and are not endangered.

Austro-Thai

This superfamily was proposed in Benedict (1942) and has gained acceptance by many Asianist linguists, but few Austronesianists. It is based on the observation of about 200 basic vocabulary items which appear to be cognate (Benedict 1975), based on the principle that AN retains two-syllable forms, MY preserves the first syllable, Kam-Tai preserves the second syllable, and some Kadai languages, like AN, retain both syllables but with forms transitional to Kam-Tai. The competing hypothesis among some Chinese linguists is that Kam-Tai (or Zhuang-Dong as they call it) and MY are instead related to Chinese; but the forms proposed to support this hypothesis are mainly contact items borrowed from Chinese into Kam-Tai and MY. Another classification sometimes still seen in the literature is that AN and AA (including MK) form the Austric superfamily proposed by Schmidt (1906). Sagart (2002) links AN and Sino-Tibetan. An extremely conservative view is that AN, TK and MY are three independent families with some contact vocabulary from each other and from various stages and varieties of Chinese. Placing these languages together under AT here is not intended to endorse Benedict's proposals.

Austronesian

Of course the AN language with the largest speech community on the Asian main-land, which is also replacing many endangered languages of Malaysia and Indonesia, is Indonesian/Malay. In slightly different varieties, this is the official language of Malaysia, of Indonesia and of Brunei. Malay is in any case the first language of about two thirds of the population of Peninsular Malaysia and is fluently spoken by nearly all the rest. It has many local dialects, which are receding in the face of standard Malaysian Malay, or of Thai in southern Thailand where there are over a million Malay speakers.

The mainland AN languages which are endangered fall into two genetic subgroups: the Chamic languages, mainly in southern Vietnam but also in northeastern Cambo-dia and one endangered language on the south central coast of Hainan in China, and all the other Malayic languages.

The Chamic languages include the Cham (99,000 in Vietnam, about 100,000 in Cambodia around Kampong Cham, a few thousand refugees in Malaysia and the US), Jarai (242,000 in Vietnam, about 20,000 in Cambodia), Rhade (in Vietnamese Ede, 177,000, about 5,000 more in Cambodia), Northern and Southern Ríoglai (together 72,000; about 55 per cent northern) and Chru (15,000) ethnic groups of Vietnam, and the Haroi (15,000 in Vietnam, not recognised as a separate ethnic group but included in the Jarai total); all of these languages are receding, and Cham, Chru, and the two languages within Ríoglai are becoming endangered. The most endangered Chamic language is Utsat or Tsat, the language of two villages of Hui (Moslem) nationality in southern Hainan. It is typologically interesting because it has become fully tonal, unlike other Chamic languages, due presumably to contact with tonal languages like Chinese which is replacing it.

There are three Malayic group languages which are endangered in the area covered. The dialect chain which includes Moken (2,000) further north and Moklen (4,000) further south is spoken by decreasing groups of seafarers along the coasts of southern Burma and the west coast of southern Thailand as far south as Phuket. Urak Lawoi is spoken by similar groups of about 3,000 ranging southwards from Phuket to beyond the Malaysian border. There are also over 2,000 Duano, Desin Dola, or Orang Kuala along the Malaysian coast just northwest of Singapore, with over 5,000 more in the islands of the Straits of Melaka in Indonesian territory. These are known as Hsaloun in Burmese, as Chaw Thalee, 'sea people', in Thai, and as Orang Laut, 'sea people', in Malay. All these languages have become endangered as these groups settle down; in particular, the Duano are gradually assimilating their speech back into local Malay. Urak Lawoi is well described, but the other two languages still need work.

Thai-Kadai

TK (sometimes just called Kadai) is divided into three subgroups, including Tai with three subgroups, Northern, Central and Southwestern, and Kam-Sui which are quite close to each other and are called Kam-Tai, and the Kadai languages. The term Kadai was coined by Benedict (1942) to refer to this third subgroup, from his reconstructed form of the Kadai word for 'person'. The exact position of some languages in TK (Northern Tai, Kam-Sui or Kadai) is a matter of disagreement between scholars; these include Lajia, Mulao, Li and the 'Ong-Be' language of the Lingao area of Hainan.

369

Chinese scholars refer to Kam-Tai and TK as Zhuang-Dong, from the Chinese name for the largest Thai nationality in China and the largest Kam-Sui nationality, the Dong, which is the Chinese name for the Kam.

The Tai group includes a wide geographical range of languages, classified into ethnic groups quite differently in different countries. In China there are Zhuang (16,178,811), Buyi (2,971,460) and Dai (1,158,989) nationalities; in fact there is a dialect continuum between northern Zhuang as spoken in northwestern Guangxi and Buyi which is mainly spoken in Guizhou, but a major intelligibility break between Northern and Southern Zhuang in Guangxi. Southern Zhuang as spoken in southwestern Guangxi forms a dialect continuum with the languages of closely related ethnic groups in Vietnam, the Nung (705,000), Tay or Tho (1,190,000), and Caolan (60,000). Northern Zhuang or Buyi and Saek are Northern Tai languages, as is Yay or Giay of China, Vietnam and Laos (38,000, also known as Nhang or in Laos as Yang). Southern Zhuang or Nung, Tay and Tho and Caolan are Central Tai languages, and all the rest of the Tai group are Southwestern Tai languages. These include Tai Pong in China (100,000), Yo (50,000), Phuan (80,000) and other small groups in Laos and Thailand, and a variety of larger groups.

The Dai nationality of China speak various Southwestern Tai languages including two large groups with distinct languages and literary traditions which are recognised as distinct ethnic groups in Burma, Laos and Thailand. One is the Tai Lue of northern Laos (102,760), far northern Thailand (6,472), northwestern Vietnam (3,700) and the extreme southwest of Yunnan in China (about 300,000, known as Xi-Dai from Xishuangbanna Dai (in Thai *Sipsongphanna*, '12,000 rice fields') where most Tai Lue in China live). The other is the Tai Mao, part of the Shan (Burmese name) or Tai Yai (own name) group of northeastern Burma and far northwestern Thailand (20,068); in China there are about 350,000 and they are referred to as De-Dai as they live mainly in Dehong. Another large group included within the Dai nationality are the Tai Neua 'northern Tai' in southwest Yunnan along the Lancang (Mekhong) River, about 100,000 speakers; they should not be confused with the similarly named group of eastern Laos.

Also included in the Chinese category of Dai are a few Thai Dam 'black Thai' who are the main component of the Thai ethnic group of northwestern Vietnam (1,040,000), the largest part of the Phu Tai group of Laos, and are known as Lao Song in Thailand. None of these languages is endangered, and all are well described. This Vietnamese Thai category also includes Tai Khaw ('white Tai'), Tai Daeng ('red Tai' and Tai Neua ('north Tai') as in Laos.

Other languages of the Dai nationality of China scattered across western, northern and south-central Yunnan are spoken by various smaller groups in Yongren, Xinping and other counties; linguists from Thailand have been doing extensive fieldwork on these languages since the 1980s.

Apart from a wide range of varieties of Shan, Tai Mao or Tai Yai, the Tai-language groups in Burma include two further languages sometimes viewed as part of Shan but better regarded as distinct languages: Khyn of the eastern Shan State around Kengtung, about 120,000 speakers, with a couple of thousand more nearby in China; and Khamti Shan, 'gold place Shan', of far northwestern Burma and spreading into northeastern India, about 70,000 speakers.

There are three extinct Thai languages formerly spoken in Assam: Ahom, Tairong and Nora; also severely endangered Khamyang with all speakers over forty in one village, and potentially endangered Aiton and Phake (Morey 2002).

The only Northern Tai subgroup language which is severely endangered is Saek, spoken in China by a small number of members of the Zhuang nationality, in Laos (2,459 by ethnicity, not all speak it), and in Thailand. The total group population is about 20,000, but it is now divided into three communities out of contact with each other, and the language is being absorbed into local Lao. It is well described, especially the variety which is moribund in Thailand.

Lao, apart from being the national language of Laos with over 2 million first language speakers and many second language speakers, is also the largest linguistic group in northeastern Thailand, with about 25 million speakers who use it as a diglossic Low. It is also spoken by a few thousand Lao in northeastern Cambodia and by the Lao ethnic group in Vietnam (10,000).

Also in Laos are the Phu Tai (441,497), Nhuon (33,940) and Yang (3,447) groups. The first of these is a group which includes various Southwestern Tai languages very close to Lao, such as Thai Dam 'black Thai' and Tai Khaw 'white Tai' both widely spoken also in Vietnam by the Thai group and in China by part of the Dai nationality; also more or less endangered Tai Daeng 'red Tai', Tai Neua 'northern Tai' (from Samneua Province of Laos) and so on. Each of these has an original territory in northeastern Laos, and they are also found amalgamated in the south where they were moved as war captives some time ago and are losing their original languages. The languages of the Tai Daeng and Tai Neua groups within the Phu Tai category are undescribed and becoming endangered. The second group speak Kham Myang or Northern Thai, as in northern Thailand. The third is the same as the Giay or Nhang group of Vietnam, considered a part of the Zhuang nationality in China.

Other major Southwestern Tai languages include standard central Thai, Pak Tay or Southern Thai, and Kham Myang or Northern Thai. The domains of usage for Kham Myang, Pak Tai and Lao in Thailand are being reduced as standard Thai takes over diglossic High roles, but these languages are vigorous in diglossic Low uses and have many millions of speakers.

The Kam-Sui or Dong subgroup includes five nationalities in China: the Dong (Kam) (2,960,293), mainly in eastern Guizhou; the Li of Hainan (1,247,814, plus about 60,000 more members of the Han Chinese nationality speaking what is locally known as *cunhua*, 'village speech', which is similar to Li); the Shui (Sui) of southeastern Guizhou (406,902); the closely related Maonan of north-central Guangxi (107,166); and the Mulao of northeastern Guangxi (207,356).

Four other Kam-Sui languages are spoken by groups not recognised as separate nationalities in China. There are: the speech of the area around Lingao in northern Hainan, sometimes known as Ong-Be or Be in the Western literature, with over half a million speakers who are members of the Han Chinese nationality; the language of the Rau or Ten (autonyms) or Yanghuang, about 20,000 speakers who are of Buyi nationality in southeastern Guizhou, somewhat endangered but not severely so, and in need of more descriptive work; the language of the Lajia, also known as Lakkia in the Western literature, about 9,000 speakers who are members of the Yao nationality in southeastern Guizhou; moderately endangered, fairly well described but still needing work; and finally the language of the Mak (autonym) or Mo (Mandarin pronunciation of the same), about 5,000 speakers who are members of the Buyi nationality in southeastern Guizhou; quite endangered and in need of more descriptive work.

Unlike the Tai and Kam-Sui subgroups, nearly all languages of the Kadai subgroup are endangered, some very severely so. The only recognised Kadai nationality in

371

China is the Gelao (597,357), three of whose five very distinct languages are moribund and two endangered; the total speaker population in the traditional area in western Guizhou is about 3,000 and rapidly decreasing, and descriptive work is urgently needed. There are also some communities to the south in Guangxi, Yunnan and Vietnam where some of the languages are still spoken by another 2,400 people. From north to south, the five languages are Qaw in Gulin County, Sichuan, and Hakhi or Green Gelao, Tolo or White Gelao, A-uo or Red Gelao and Aqao, the latter four all in west-central Guizhou. Green, White and Red Gelao are all also scattered across western Guangxi, southeastern Yunnan and into Vietnam. The Cíolao ethnic group of Vietnam is underenumerated at 1,500. The speakers of Gelao and other Kadai languages in China outside Guizhou are classified in various nationalities, including Yi, Yao and Zhuang. Curiously, there are more White Gelao and Red Gelao speakers outside Guizhou than in. Between the 1982 and 1990 censuses in China, nearly 380,000 people formerly identified as Han Chinese reclaimed their former Gelao identity; but none of them speaks the language. Of these, 357,226 of them were in seven counties of Zunyi and Tongren Prefectures in northern Guizhou, which returned no Gelao in the 1982 census.

There are several southern outlier Kadai languages in China and Vietnam, all of whose languages are endangered. They include 300 Yerong, a group with Yao nationality in Napo County, Guangxi, and 3,000 Buyang, a group with Zhuang nationality in southeastern Yunnan; 307 Pubiao of Yi nationality in Malipo County, Yunnan, and 1,500 Pupeo, autonym Qabiaw, also known as Laqua in the older literature, which is a recognised ethnic group of Vietnam. Some scholars separate the Paha dialect of Buyang as an additional language, and suggest that the connection between Pubiao and the rest of Buyang is closer than the connection between Paha and the rest of Pubiao. Another similar related pair are the Laji (1,643 with Yi nationality in China), Lachi (7,863, a recognised ethnic group of Vietnam), autonym Lipulio, or Lati in the older literature, with about 5,200 speakers from a combined ethnic group of over 9,500. The Nungven or Ainh group of 200 and the Laha (Vietnamese Klhaphlao) group of 2,100, both in northern Vietnam, are somewhat less endangered than the other Kadai languages, despite the small size of these groups. Apart from Laha and some varieties of Gelao, not enough work has been done on any of these languages.

Miao-Yao

There are four clusters of MY languages, or as they are sometimes now known from the autonyms of the southwesternmost Miao and Yao languages, Hmong-Mien languages: Miao, Yao, Bunu and She, comprising at least eighteen languages. The largest and most complex and internally diverse is the Miao (Chinese), Meo (Vietnamese), Maew (Thai and Lao), Myaing (Burmese) or Hmong (autonym of the best described language included in this subgroup). The total Miao population is China 8,940,116, Vietnam 556,000, Laos 231,168, Thailand 126,300, Burma a few thousand, and over 100,000 refugees from Laos in various Western countries. Miao is divided by Chinese linguists into three clusters: Eastern, mainly in western Hunan and northeastern Guizhou with about 800,000 speakers of two subvarieties; Central or Hmo, mainly in southern Guizhou with about 1.5 million speakers of three subvarieties; and Western or Hmao/Hmong of western Guizhou, Yunnan, Vietnam, Laos, Thailand and Burma, with about 1.8 million speakers in China and nearly a million outside. Hmao/Hmong includes seven subvarieties, one of which is extremely well described: Hmong Dao, 'white Hmong', as spoken in Laos and Mong Njua, 'green Mong', as spoken in Thailand, which are very closely related dialects. There are also many millions of Miao in China who do not speak Miao. Applying the criterion of intelligibility, there are twelve or more Miao languages, most of which need further descriptive work. The smallest speaker populations are 40,000 for two of the Central Miao languages of south-central Guizhou; none of these Maio languages is at present endangered.

Names for all kinds of Miao are extremely confused in the literature, including some place names, descriptive names based on clothing, and various autonyms or exonyms. Often several names refer to the same group, or one name refers to several different groups. The Miao nationality also includes some groups who would like to be separate nationalities, such as the Gedou or Ge, and other formerly unclassified nationality groups amalgamated into the Miao nationality in the 1980s, such as the Laba and Sanqiao; but some Sanqiao who were classified as Dong (a Kam-Sui group) before then retained that nationality.

Somewhat less complex but still including six distinct languages are the Yao (China 2,637,421 including Bunu, Lajia and Yerong or about 2 million without; also Vietnam 474,000, Laos 18,092, Thailand 48,357 and a few thousand refugees from Laos in Western countries; all 50,000 members of the Miao nationality in Hainan actually speak a Yao language). About half those in China speak Yao, and nearly all those outside China. The only well described language is Mien as spoken by the majority in China and most of those outside. Closely related Biaoman and Jinmen as well as more distant Biaomin, Jiaogongmin and Zaomin are much less fully described, but none is really endangered yet.

The approximately 700,000 Bunu (pu nu) are almost all in northwestern Guangxi and are classified as Yao nationality. Most speak one of four core closely related Bunu languages: Bunu, Baonao, Numao and Dongmeng. Bunu, also known as Dongnu, includes Nunu and Bunuo dialects; it is by far the largest group with nearly 600,000 speakers. Baonao is a group of 25,000, also known as Nao Klao, Nao Gelao or Baiku Yao, 'white pants Yao'. Numao with 1,500 speakers and Dongmeng with 600 speakers are endangered. There are also four other Bunu languages which are less close to the four main Bunu languages. Three of these languages, Ngnai (hm nai) with 8,000 speakers, Younuo (ju nɔ) with fewer than 4,000 speakers, and Jiongnai (kjɔŋ nai) with 1,500 speakers, are endangered. Baheng (pa hŋ) is a group of nearly 50,000, mainly in China but also 3,700 in Vietnam, where they are classified as Pa Then. Baheng has two dialects, perhaps different enough to be viewed as languages; they are both potentially endangered. None of these Bunu langages is well described, but work on Dongmeng, the most endangered, is underway.

The She nationality of eastern Guangxi and Guangdong in China has 709,592 members, of whom only about 1,000 still use the (huo nte) language in two small areas near Huizhou in eastern Guangdong; the rest mainly speak Hakka and Cantonese Chinese, and many also know Mandarin. While there has been some work done on She, additional descriptive work is desirable before it disappears.

Austroasiatic

This section will discuss the MK languages which are autochthonous to mainland Southeast Asia. It does not include the Munda languages of eastern South Asia,

373

which form the other component of AA; nor MK Khasi languages of northeastern India or the indigenous MK languages of the Nicobars.

All but three MK languages are at least potentially endangered. One exception is Vietnamese, the national language of Vietnam with nearly 60 million first language speakers in Vietnam, which has been spreading at the expense of MK and other minority languages there for centuries; it is also the language of the 18,915 Jing in China, and substantial groups in Laos who came during the French period and in Thailand who came in the 1940s and early 1950s; as well as the post-1975 refugees in Western countries. The second non-endangered language is Khmer, the national language of Cambodia with at least 10 million speakers, 8 million in Cambodia. While it has been receding in the face of Thai and Vietnamese expansion for more than a millennium, it is still universally spoken in Cambodia and is still replacing some minority MK languages there. There are also 895,000 Khmer in southern Vietnam, a larger number in north-eastern Thailand and 169 in Laos, but not all speak Khmer. Standard Khasi of eastern Meghalaya in India and surrounding areas of India and Bangladesh is the third non-endangered MK language.

Aslian

The fourteen Orang Asli languages of Peninsular Malaysia and southern Thailand are all endangered, mostly severely; some others are already extinct, and some dialects of the surviving languages are also extinct. Northern Aslian includes Maniq/Tonga/Mos/Ten'en (over 300 group members) in southern Thailand, closely related to Kensiu (about 500) on the Thai/Malaysian border. All other Aslian languages are only in Malaysia. The other Northern Aslian languages are Jehai (1,200), Batek (960, many dialects, some extinct) and Chewong (about 400). Kintaq (under 250) is sometimes viewed as a dialect of Kensiu, and Mendriq (about 150) is sometimes viewed as a dialect of Jehai. All are endangered, and all need further descriptive work. Central Aslian includes Lanoh (about 350), Temiar (about 17,000), Semai (about 29,000, many dialects) and Jah Het (about 3,200). Temiar and Semai may appear safe judging from their populations, but even these languages are endangered. Temiar is perhaps the best described Aslian language. Southern Aslian includes Semaq Beri (about 2,500), Semelai (about 4,100) and Besisi (about 2,200), also endangered. Majority community attitudes are very negative.

Katuic-Bahnaric

Katuic

This subgroup of MK is mainly in the inland of central Vietnam and adjacent areas of Laos. It is named after its southeasternmost member, Katu or Kantu, and can be divided into West Katuic (Kuy, So and Bru) and East Katuic (Katu, Kantu, Pacoh, Phuang or Phíuíong, Katang, Kriang, Ta'oih, Ong, Yir and a few others). The largest group included, the Kuy, are the westernmost; they are quite numerous in northern Cambodia and the southeastern part of northeastern Thailand, along the Cambodian border and some in southern Laos. Most are in Thailand; the population in Laos in 1983 was 49,039. There are about 800,000 group members; at least half are speakers of a range of dialects, some mutually unintelligible. They are known as Suai in Thai and

Lao. Another large cluster is the So (160,000) and Bru (45,000) of south-central Laos, extending into central Vietnam and Thailand; many are losing their languages, especially in Thailand. The Bru are also known as Van Kieu in Vietnam.

East Katuic groups include the Katu or Kantu (about 37,000 in Vietnam and 14,676 in Laos, various dialects), the Katang (80,000, including 72,391 in Laos), the Ta'oih (about 50,000 including 24,577 in Laos), the Pacoh (15,000 including 12,923 in Laos), the Phuang (6,000 in Laos and a few in Vietnam known as Phíuíong), the Kriang (autonym), Klor or Ngeh (Lao name, 8,917 in Laos and 1,200 in Vietnam for a total slightly over 10,000), also Ong and Yir, one language, two groups with slightly different dialects (12,000 in Laos).

Three severely endangered East Katuic languages were recently located in Xekong Province of Laos by Theraphan Luangthongkum. One is Chatong, with 580 people in four villages. The others are Dakkang and Triw in the same area, with 1,198 and 1,328 people respectively; all three are undescribed apart from her work, and endangered.

Bahnaric

The Bahnaric languages are quite numerous in southeastern Laos, northwestern Cambodia, the northern part of the central highlands of Vietnam, and the interior of southern Vietnam just northeast of Saigon. The North Bahnaric branch is north of the Chamic languages, West Bahnaric is west of the Chamic groups, and South Bahnaric is south of them; thus clearly the AN Chamic incursion came between them. Despite fairly small populations, a complex dialect situation where various named dialects may lack a superordinate term for the language, and intensive contact with Vietnamese in the eastern part of the area, most of these languages are surviving, though contracting.

West Bahnaric includes Brao/Krung/Kravet/Su in southernmost Laos and northwesternmost Cambodia, a dialect cluster with about 35,000 total, including 350 Brao in Vietnam. Other languages here are Loven or Laven (from the place name for the Boloven plateau in southern Laos) or Jru' (autonym), 28,057 in Laos; Nyaheun, 3,960 in Laos; Oi/Sok/Sapuan/Cheng 25,000 in Laos (Oi 11,194; Cheng 4,540); and Tampuan (15,000 in northeast Cambodia). The most endangered languages in this subbranch are Juk (autonym) or Suai (exonym), 1,500 and Swoeng (autonym) or Lavi (exonym), 492 (or 584 according to the Lao census), both recently located and described by Theraphan Luangthongkum in Xekong Province of Laos.

The Northwest Bahnaric languages, between the West and North Bahnaric languages in southern Laos, include Tarieng or Dakchueng (6,000), Halak (autonym) or Alak (exonym) (13,217), Kaseng (1,200) and Yaeh (3,376 in the census, 4,916 located by Theraphan Luangthongkum in Xekong Province).

Most of the North Bahnaric languages are in the highlands of Vietnam southwest of Danang. These include Takua (6,000), Cua (12,000), Duan (2,500), Katua (4,000), Hre (94,000), Míoníom (6,000), Tíodrah (6,000), Kayíong (25,000), Rengao (18,000); also extending into Laos, Sedang (97,520 of whom 520 in Laos), Jeh (12,000), Halang (15,000) and Khaco' (1,000 in northeastern Cambodia). All are potentially endangered; most of those in Vietnam are fairly well described, but more work is needed in Laos, especially on Kaseng, which is the most endangered language there, and on Khaco' in Cambodia.

The official ethnic classification in Vietnam divides South Bahnaric groups into Chrau in the south, Kíoho and Ma in the east, Stieng in the southwest including into

375

Cambodia, and Mnong in the north, in Vietnam and eastern Cambodia. Census figures for Vietnam are 25,000 Chrau, 92,000 Kíoho, 25,000 for the Ma dialect of Kíoho which is recognised as a separate ethnic group, 50,000 Stieng and 67,000 Mnong; there are probably another 35,000 Stieng and as many as 150,000 Mnong, also known there as Penong, in Cambodia. There are many named varieties of Kíoho and Mnong; linguists divide Mnong into three language clusters, eastern, central and southern. The most endangered language here is Chrau, whose traditional territory just east of Saigon now has a very high proportion of Vietnamese. Many of the smaller dialects of Kíoho and Mnong are also potentially endangered to endangered.

Northern

Palaungic

This branch of MK is sometimes further subdivided into Palaungic, Angkuic and Waic. It is scattered across the southwest of Yunnan and northeastern Burma, and extends into northern Thailand and northwestern Laos.

Palaungic proper has perhaps 350,000 people and includes Riang, Ta-ang (Chinese De'ang, formerly known as Benglong) or Gold Palaung, Ka-ang, Rumai, Pale (Silver Palaung), Na-ang, Na-eang and probably more in Burma. It also includes Lamet of northwestern Laos (14,355), with one village of Khamet near Wiangpapao in Thailand. The De'ang nationality has 17,935 members; a few of them speak Angkuic languages such as U. The population of Palaungic languages in Burma is quite large but unknown. Some villages of Palaung (1,626 people) have recently migrated to Thailand from Burma. Palaungic also includes one endangered language, Danaw, reported to be moribund some time ago, but still spoken by about 1,000 people in one village just west of Inle Lake in the southwestern Shan State of Burma (Robine 2000: 17).

Angkuic comprises Mok (mainly in the Eastern Shan State of Burma where it is known as Tai Loi, Shan for 'hill Tai', also in Thailand near Doi Saket, in Laos, and near Jinghong in China), Angku (Burma), U (also known as Puman; various widely scattered dialects in Shuangjiang County and other areas of west central Yunnan in China), Hu (near Jinghong), and Samtao (2,359) in northwestern Laos. In China U is classified within the De'ang (i.e. Palaung) nationality; some other Angkuic speakers are classified within the Bulang nationality, which also includes Bulang itself, a Waic language. There are additional small unclassified groups such as the Paijiao and Buguo in Menghai County and the Kongge in Jinghong; these may be additional Angkuic languages. Most Angkuic languages are receding and potentially or actually endangered.

Waic languages are very widely spoken in southwestern Yunnan and the Wa areas of the northeastern Shan State in Burma; the total population is approaching 1 million. There are 396,610 members of the Wa nationality in China, and probably a larger number in Burma. The 'standard' dialect selected in China is Paraok, and the Wa nationality also includes La, Va and probably other languages. In recent years substantial numbers of Paraok Wa from northeastern Burma have moved from the northeastern part of the Shan State of Burma to the border region near Chiangdao in northern Chiangmai Province in Thailand, with a few villages actually in Thailand.

Another Waic nationality in China is the Bulang (91,882) in the extreme southwest of Yunnan and nearby in Burma. One variety has been described under the name

Samtao (not the same as the Angkuic Samtao), and another was formerly spoken in Kienka village, near Chiangmai. As in the case of Wa, there are various poorly described languages included here.

Thailand also has its own indigenous endangered Waic languages, Lavüa, spoken by about 20,000 people between Chiangmai and Mae Sariang in northwestern Thailand, and Phalok, west of Mae Rim, just north of Chiangmai. Both are included within the composite Lawa (Thai) or Lua (Northern Thai) hill tribe; the Lavüa of Mae Sariang are the largest group within this category.

Khmuic

The major Khumic language is Khmu itself, with a large number of distinct named dialects covering much of northern Laos (389,694) and spreading into northern Thailand (13,674), northwestern Vietnam (43,000), about 5,000 in Jinghong in south-western Yunnan, and a few in Burma. Some Khmu have relocated as far south as Kanchanaburi in western Thailand. In Laos, Vietnam and Thailand, they are recognised as ethnic groups. In China they are still in the 'unclassified' category, have applied for nationality status, but are unlikely to receive it. The language is not endangered.

Mal, Phay or Pray is a cluster of varieties which lacks a single combined autonym, spoken in Nan Province of northern Thailand (38,823) and across the border in Saignabouri in Laos (13,977). They are locally called Lawa or Lua in Nan Province in northern Thailand, but are officially known as Thin in Thai, a name resented by the community.

The Mlabri are a hunter-gatherer group in the same area as the Mal/Phay/Pray, who are divided into small bands (125 people in Thailand, 24 in Laos). There are substantial lexical and other differences between the speech of different bands, and apparently fairly rapid lexical change. Some dialects are extinct, such as the one called Yumbri in the literature, and others are endangered.

The Pasing, also known as Bit or Kha Bit, are in a few villages in southwestern Phongsaly in northeastern Laos (1,530 people) and even fewer villages (202 people) across the border in Mengla County in China.

Khang and Khao (total about 5,000) are the northeasternmost Khumic groups, in northwestern Vietnam. Further south, on both sides of the Lao/Viet border, are the Ksinmul, also known as Puoc (Laos 2,164, Vietnam 11,000). Thai Then was recently located by Frank Proschan to the east of Luang Phabang in northern Laos. Phong is a local term for a cluster of poorly known Khmuic languages of southern Samneua and northern Xieng Khouang provinces of Laos, not to be confused with the various Pong groups speaking Vietic MK languages. Finally, there is the recently located and endangered Iduh language in east-central Laos on the Vietnamese border, 200 in the group but only thirty speakers. Most of the Khmuic languages other than Khmu are at least potentially endangered, and Mlabri, Iduh and Pasing are particularly so.

Pakanic

This recently-proposed subgroup of MK includes Mang (2,300 in Lai Chau Province, northern Vietnam, 1,216 in Jinping County, China), Lai (autonym Paliu, 1,771 in northwest Guangxi in China) and Pakan (Bugan in Chinese, 3,000 in southeastern

Yunnan). These are the northeasternmost of the MK languages, and all are endangered or severely endangered. There are few if any monolingual speakers; a large proportion of each group does not speak its original language.

Monic

Although Mon is the state language of the Mon State in southeastern Burma, and the Mon ethnic group comprises about 800,000 people, mainly in Burma, the language has been receding under Burmese pressure for nearly 800 years. Many Mon migrants who came from Burma about 200 years ago are settled around Bangkok but nearly all have assimilated and speak only Thai; another wave of Mon refugees came to Thailand in the last twenty years.

Earlier Mon dominance in what is now central Thailand under the Dvaravati kingdom was broken by the Khmer more than a millennium ago. Vestiges of Dvaravati Mon are spoken by the Nyahkur in northeastern Thailand; fewer than 10,000 speakers of three dialects remain, but younger speakers are fewer and less fluent, and in some areas have passive or no knowledge.

Pearic

The Pearic languages are widely distributed in tiny populations across western Cambodia, with small numbers across the border in eastern Thailand and one transported community in western Thailand. Pear is the Khmer word for these groups, who have long been under Khmer dominance. They form a distinct subgroup of MK from Khmer. Curiously, some extremely small communities here have nevertheless maintained their languages, though the Khmer Rouge period further reduced the speaker populations. All are now endangered.

The largest population is speakers of Chong in Thailand along the western border of Cambodia; now about 2,000 people and 500 speakers with the youngest now twenty-two. This language, with three dialects, is the best described Pearic language, but still needs more work. Song or Kasong, usually also known to outsiders as Chong, has a population of about 200 in eastern Thailand, with forty speakers, the youngest of whom is now thirty.

A 'Pear' group – the Khmer word for all these groups; autonym unknown – in Kompong Thom is in 3 to 4 villages, about 250 people, language status unknown but group size reduced from about 1,000 since 1975. East Pearic Samre has a population of about 100 displaced in Pursat Province of Cambodia and another 100 in eastern Thailand, of whom fewer than twenty speak it, the youngest now forty-five. A further group whose autonym is unknown lived in Preah Vihar province before 1975; this 'Pear' language is also endangered.

The group who call themselves Su-ung but are usually called Saoch (which is the Khmer word for a kind of skin disease; obviously this term is unacceptable to the community) have an interesting history. Almost the entire group was transported to western Thailand in 1833, leaving behind a small remnant. Of the remnant in Cambodia, 3 families comprising 17 speakers including children remained in 1993. Among the population in Thailand, now called Khamen Padong 'Padong Khmer' in Thai, the language is severely endangered. It would be very interesting to determine what effect separation since 1833 has had on the two groups, and this is urgent as one of them is severely endangered.

At least one other Pearic language, West Pearic Samre, probably died during the Khmer Rouge period. Samre of Siem Reap Province appears to have become extinct in the 1940s. Several of the other Pearic languages are also on their last legs.

Vietic

The major Vietic language is of course Vietnamese. Most of the small groups speaking Vietic languages in Vietnam are lumped into the single Míuíong ethnic group of 914,000. Many of these no longer speak anything but Vietnamese, and the vast majority of the remainder speak Míuíong itself, which is divided into a number of dialects in three areas. The second largest language of this cluster is Nguon, about 25,000 people, mainly in Vietnam but also 988 in Laos where they are recognised as a separate ethnic group. This language is starting to be endangered.

All other Vietic languages are spoken by tiny groups along the border between south-central Laos and north-central Vietnam, some in areas which are being inundated by dams, and all are endangered, some severely. This includes the very close cluster of Ruc, Sach and May totalling about 2,500 people in Vietnam and Laos; another close cluster of Hung, Pong and Tum with about 6,000 people in Laos and Vietnam; a third cluster of Maleng or Pakatan, Kri and Phong, about 5,000 people in Laos; the Thavung (Ahlao and Ahao dialects), about 1,500 people in Thailand and Laos; the Phonsung or Aheu, 500 in Laos; and the Arem, 1,000 people in Laos. The term Arem is also issued locally in Laos to refer to any of these Vietic groups; in Vietnam they are classified in the Chíut ethnic group, an exonym.

Altaic

Turkic

Turkic nationalities of China, primarily in the Xinjiang Uighur Autonomous Region, are the Uighur (8,399,393), Kazakh (1,250,458), Kirghiz (160,823), Salar (104,503), Uzbek (12,370) and Tatar (4,890). Kazakh, Kirghiz, Uzbek and Tatar are of course far more numerous in the various independent states of the former USSR. Western Yugur or Yellow Uighur in western Gansu has about half the Yugur nationality population (13,719) and about 4,600 speakers; it is the most endangered of these languages. Tatar is also endangered in China. All these languages are moderately well described, though more work on Western Yugur would be desirable.

Mongolic

The Mongolic languages with separate nationalities in China are the Mongol (5,813,947), Santa (513,805, known in Chinese as Dongxiang), Monguor (241,198, known in Chinese as Tu), Dagur (132,394) and Bao'an (16,505). These cover much of Inner Mongolia, northern Qinghai and northern Xinjiang. Of course adjacent areas of Mongolia and eastern Russia also have large numbers of speakers of some of these Mongol languages. Some of the eastern half of the Yugur nationality in Gansu (total 13,719) speak an endangered Mongolic language.

A surprisingly high proportion of the members of the various Mongolic nationalities in China do not speak their traditional languages, and the languages of some smaller nationalities are endangered. For example, Wurm *et al.* (1987: C-2) suggest that only 60,000 of the Dagur speak Dagur, and only 6,000 Bao'an speak Bao'an; however, another 4,000 people speaking Bao'an in Tongren County, Qinghai are misclassified as Monguor nationality, giving a total of 10,000 Bao'an speakers of about 16,000 in the group. Even Mongol is spoken by only about two thirds of the members of the Mongol nationality in China.

The most endangered Mongolic language in China is Kangjia, with about 2,000 speakers who are members of the Hui (Moslem) nationality in Qinghai. Also endangered in China, though of course not in Russia, is Buriat with fewer than 1,000 speakers. Eastern Yugur and Bao'an are also endangered, and Dongxiang or Santa, despite its large group population, is beginning to be endangered. All Mongolic languages which have been recognised as separate nationalities are fairly well described, but work is needed on Kangjia.

Tungusic[7]

In China as in Russia, every Manchu-Tungus language is at least endangered, and most are moribund.

The Jurchen language of the rulers of the Jin Dynasty (1115–1234) is thought to be the precursor of the Manchu language of the rulers of the Qing Dynasty (1644–1911), but despite official support up to 1911, massive literature and a 1990 population of 10,682,262, the language in its homeland of Manchuria is extinct apart from three locations in northwestern Heilongjiang with a few remaining speakers: Sanjiazi village, Fuyu County, a few speakers over fifty; Daxing village, Tailai County, a few speakers over sixty, and Dawujiazi village, Aihui County, a few elderly individuals. These speakers are rather tired of linguistic fieldworkers.

Manchu survives much better in Xinjiang, where the Xibo (sometimes Xibe) nationality is the remainder of Manchu armies moved there during the Qing Dynasty. Within a current population of 188,824 both in northeastern China and in Xinjiang in the northwest, only approximately 26,760 were estimated to speak the language, including some children, in the late 1980s (Wurm *et al.* 1987: C-5); Stary (2003) suggests about half this number now, but still a few children.

The Nanai language, formerly known as Goldi, is known as the Hezhe or Hezhen nationality in China. Of 4,640 Hezhe south of the Amur River in northeast Heilongjiang, about forty (twenty-five in Tongjiang County over sixty, fifteen in Raohe County over fifty) still spoke the language in 1990.

The Ewenki and Oroqen nationalities also form part of the cluster of Tungus languages that includes Evenki in Russia and Mongolia. Janhunen (1997) equates Ewenki with Solon in Russia and indicates that Ewenki and Oroqen are part of the same language cluster, but Whaley *et al.* (1999) suggest that they are distinct languages. Of the Ewenki in China (2000 population 30,505), Wurm *et al.* (1987) suggest that 17,000 still spoke the language in 1982, but Whaley *et al.* (1999) suggest far fewer: 10,000 total including Russia, mostly over fifty. From the 8,196 Oroqen in China in 2000, about 2,240 concentrated in Alihe Oroqen Banner were said to speak the language in the 1980s, but Whaley *et al.* (1999) report fewer now, mainly aged over fifty. Janhunen (1997) gives a more detailed report on the four dialects of Oroqen: Kumarchen is spoken by some children, Orochen has speakers over forty, with perhaps a few children, Selpechen has only speakers over forty, and Birarchen has only a few old speakers.

There has been a great deal of excellent work done on these languages, in China and Russia; but more documentation work on Xibo would be highly useful.

Indo-European

The two nationalities of China speaking Indo-European languages are the Tajik (41,028) and Russian (15,609). These two languages are widely spoken in the former USSR, and the former also in northern Afghanistan. Both are well described and neither is endangered.

Though of course a creole cannot uncontroversially be attributed to its lexical source language, there is one severely endangered 'Portuguese' creole, Papia Kristang of Melaka in Malaysia. This is spoken among a group of former fishermen concentrated in one neighbourhood; the group has about 10,000 people, and the language is still spoken by 2,150 people including most of those over fifty, some younger adults and a few children; the language is being replaced by Malaysian English. It is well described in Baxter (1988).

A second, related creole locally known as Patua is moribund in Macao, which was returned to China by Portugal in 1999; half of the group of 10,000 returned to Portugal then. While some salvage work and some heritage activities in the community are underway, this language is spoken by fewer than fifty people, all over seventy.

Ainu

Ainu was formerly spoken in southern Sakhalin and the Kurile Islands, now under control of Russia, and on the northern part of Honshu Island in Japan, but is now confined to Hokkaido Island in northern Japan and is moribund there.

Ainu leaders claim up to 100,000 Ainu in Hokkaido; but official census statistics suggest only 23,830. Many people of partial Ainu background conceal and deny it because of strongly negative attitudes among the Japanese majority community. Sawai (1998) discusses the current situation and attitudes among the Ainu from an insider's perspective. Of the four original dialects of Ainu, the Sakhalin and Kurile dialects are extinct, the Northeastern Hokkaido dialect is probably extinct,[8] and the Southwestern Hokkaido dialects are moribund despite recent revival efforts. In the Hidaka region which officially has 9,299 Ainu or 39 per cent of the total, the least moribund local variety is the Saru dialect of Hiratori town, with four relatively fluent female speakers in their seventies or older, and probably some slightly younger semi-speakers who will acknowledge their Ainu ability after these elderly ladies die. The Shizunai dialect is in the same area. The Chitose and Horobetsu dialects come from the area about 30km north of Hiratori, now officially having another 7,330 Ainu or nearly 31 per cent of the total. The youngest speakers of any dialect of Ainu who learned it as children are at least sixty. Revival efforts are underway, with language classes for adults and for children and a newsletter in Ainu. Research on all forms of Ainu is extremely urgent, though most surviving dialects are fairly well described.

Extinct languages of the area

There are various extinct languages of the area documented in historical and written sources, representing the TB, TK and MK families.

381

Of the TB languages in this area which survive in written materials but have no modern descendants, the earliest-attested is Bailang, a language of what is now Sichuan, with a song transcribed during the Han period about 2,000 years ago. Pyu, the language of various kingdoms in what is now central Burma, was widely written up to the destruction of these cities around 960 AD and last attested in a multilingual inscription of 1112 AD. Xixia, also known as Tangut, ceased to be written after the conquest of the Xixia by the Yuan Dynasty in the late thirteenth century AD. Zhangzhung, a former language of what is now western Tibet, survives in a curious literary half-life as the liturgical language of Bön, the pre-Buddhist religion of Tibet. The Nam language described by Thomas (1948) may also have been TB.

Of the extinct TK languages, the best attested language is Ahom in northeastern India. Since it ceased to be spoken nearly 200 years ago, a literary tradition has persisted, and a spoken revival is now being attempted. Two other languages of the same area, Nora and Tairong, became extinct during the twentieth century. Chinese historical sources suggest that there were probably more Kadai languages in southern Sichuan which have disappeared without trace, in the same area as Qaw, which is about to die.

Kenaboi, a language of West Malaysia which died about a century ago, is now believed to be a composite of Aslian MK with extensive Malayic AN lexical input and a third component of unknown origin (Hajek forthcoming). Some other southern Aslian languages have also become extinct, replaced by Malay.

There are doubtless many MK languages which have become extinct without scholarly attention. For example, the spread of the Khmer empire and its language must certainly have displaced a large number of indigenous languages of what is now Cambodia; the last vestiges of some of these are the Pearic languages. Similarly, the modern distribution of the Pakanic languages might suggest that there were other MK languages in eastern Yunnan that have now disappeared. The presence of the Khasi in northeastern India, separated from the rest of MK by a large number of TB languages, could also imply the disappearance of other MK languages in between.

The main extinct Tungusic language with written attestation is Jurchen, the dynastic language of the Jin Dynasty. However, it can be argued that Manchu and Xibo are modern descendants of the same language. Of course, it will not be long before spoken Manchu is extinct, and most other Tungusic languages are not far behind it.

Language endangerment and national policy

In China, Vietnam, Laos and Burma there is a rigid official classification of all citizens into ethnic groups: a majority group speaking the national language and a number of minorities. In addition to the majority groups, China has fifty-five national minorities; in Laos there are forty-six, in Vietnam fifty-three, and in Burma 134. The degree of inclusiveness of these categories differs from country to country; in China the tendency is to lump closely related groups into one nationality, amalgamating small groups into larger nationalities speaking related languages; while in Vietnam, Laos and Burma, the categories tend to follow people's own ethnic categories more closely, though not completely. The exceptions to this in Laos and Vietnam are that the ethnic groups most closely related to the majority group are lumped into one category: in Vietnam, the Mường; and in Laos, the Phu Tai. This means that ethnic groups speaking distinct languages which are classified as one nationality in China may be classified into two or more ethnic groups in Vietnam, Laos or Burma. In Thailand there are sixteen recognised tribal groups; there is no official ethnic classification in Cambodia. The following table (Table 5.1) summarises the situation, with percentages of majority language speakers from available census data or other estimates (Table 5.1).

Perhaps the most interesting category in China is the 'other – unclassified' national minority, people not included in any of the fifty-six categories. This comprises small groups who have not (yet) been reclassified as members of some larger national minority. There is reluctance to recognise additional national minorities; the only new one since the 1950s is the Jinuo nationality, recognised in 1978. In most recent cases, groups who applied for nationality status have instead been amalgamated into an existing nationality; for example the Laomian and Cosung into the Lahu. Some cases are still pending, but the authorities now say that very small groups cannot get the status of a separate national minority; this is despite the fact that there are six nationalities recognised in the 1950s with fewer than 10,000 members, including the Luoba with only 2,965.

The Gaoshan nationality with 4,461 members in China is a special case; this is the nationality of the various AN minority groups of Taiwan, who are much more numerous in Taiwan but of course are not enumerated in the mainland census. Most of the other smaller nationalities of China are more numerous in adjacent countries; of the ten smallest groups, only two, Yugur with 13,719 people and Bao'an with 16,505 people, are restricted to China.

The Thai list of *Chaw Khaw*, 'hill tribes', has grown from nine to sixteen over the last thirty years; these are identified groups in the north and west of the country who get special assistance from the Public Welfare Department. In addition to these, there are many small scattered groups speaking MK languages in the northeast, a patchwork of speakers of different Tai languages scattered across the central plain as a result of transportation of war captives from Laos and points north up to about a hundred years ago, also three groups speaking Malayic AN languages and two groups speaking Aslian MK languages in the south.

Cambodia has no official list of minorities; in any case these are relatively small and mainly confined to peripheral areas, especially the northeast of the country. There is also a scattering of endangered MK languages of the Pearic subgroup with extremely small speaker populations in the western half of the country, and some other MK and AN groups in the northeast.

Table 5.1. Ethnic Categories

	ethnic groups	per cent majority	minority categorisation
China	56	92	lumped
Vietnam	54	87	partly split
Laos	47	50.1	partly split
Burma	135	(63?)	split
Thailand	17	over 95	split
Cambodia	–	over 98	none
Malaysia	3	(60+)	lumped

In Peninsular Malaysia the endangered languages are spoken by members of two categories of minority, the *Orang Laut*, 'sea people', who speak various endangered AN languages closely related to Malay, and the *Orang Asli*, 'original people', the indigenous negrito groups with various endangered MK languages. There are *Orang Asli* who do not speak a MK language; some of the southern *Orang Asli* languages are extinct.

Future needs

The most urgent need in this area is comprehensive surveys of the small groups speaking undescribed and endangered languages in China and Burma. It is not even known how many more languages there are in these countries; our recent surveys (Bradley and Bradley 2002; Bradley 2004) covering only a few areas in southwestern China have located literally dozens of previously unknown endangered languages. This lack of information is due to the long-term majority practice in China of under-differentiation in the classification of minority groups. This is reflected in modern government policies in China, and contrasts sharply with the much more atomistic approach in South Asia, where the model of the caste system has led to a classification of tribes which reflects linguistic reality much more directly, if anything with some overdifferentiation. In other mainland Southeast Asian nations, the situation is better known, partly because the policy reflects linguistic reality more or less directly.

Documentation work on the endangered languages of Laos and Cambodia, carried out mainly by foreign scholars, is progressing slowly. Since 1975 there has been much less work on the endangered languages of Vietnam, but more is needed here as well. In Thailand both Thai and foreign scholars have been active over many years, and the documentation situation is fairly good. In West Malaysia there is considerable work underway on the Aslian MK languages, but more could be done on the non-Malay Malayic AN languages.

In terms of genetic classification, there are some macro issues yet to be resolved. One is the solidity or otherwise of the AT construct including TK, AN and possibly MY, and the competing view that AN and ST are linked. Another problem issue is the genetic as opposed to areal relationship if any among the Altaic languages, Turkic, Mongolic and Tungusic, and whether Japanese and Korean are related to Altaic and/ or to AT as a result of contact, genetic relationship or both. Benedict (1990) attempts to prove the case for Japanese links with AT, while Miller (1971) assumes a genetic connection with Altaic. The micro issues of genetic classification are less problematic, though there is still some controversy about the internal classification of TB languages as a whole, including those in South Asia and those in this area. Information from endangered and extinct languages has a role to play here; for example, the key role of the Kadai languages in AT and Sino-Austronesian, or the important information for TB subgrouping available in under-utilised data on extinct languages such as Xixia and Pyu.

By contrast, there has been little detailed investigation of the outcomes of long-term contact and the development of areal and subareal characteristics. This is particularly interesting for endangered languages, where the processes of change are much faster and more profound. For example, Bradley (1992) shows how the Gong tonal system has converged toward the Thai tonal system, losing its non-Thai-like characteristics and gaining a Thai tone.

National issues and language endangerment

Japan is a mainly monolingual society, with substantial regional differentiation within Japanese. The Endangered Languages of the Pacific Rim project has provided the opportunity for Japanese scholars to continue to explore the endangered regional varieties of Japanese including Ryukyuan, as well as endangered languages in many other areas of the region. There is also a long tradition of research on Ainu, by a few Japanese and foreign scholars. Since the enactment of the New Ainu Law in 1997, there has also been more public support for emblematic Ainu culture maintenance, but language revival is starting to look unlikely as Ainu becomes more and more moribund. This has not prevented activists in some areas from setting up school-based programmes, but the materials are more heritage-oriented than serious attempts at revival.

In the two Koreas there is no language endangerment issue, though of course the Korean language has tended to diverge between north and south over the last fifty years. There is increasing influence from English in the south, and a tendency to purism in the north. The Korean minorities in Japan and in China are mainly bilingual, and there is some tendency to lose Korean among parts of these groups.

In China since the 1950s, the spread of *Putonghua*, 'common speech', the spoken standard variety based on the speech of Beijing, has added an additional Chinese variety for most speakers of Sinitic languages. In most of northern and southwestern China, this is quite close genetically to the local Mandarin speech varieties, but in the southeast there is a large area where the difference is more extreme: the Wu speech area around Shanghai, the Min speech area centred on Fujian, Hainan and some surrounding areas and on Taiwan, the Yue or Cantonese speech area of most of Guangdong and eastern Guangxi, the Hakka speech area at the junction of Fujian, Jiangxi and Guangdong, the Gan speech area of Hunan, and the Xiang speech area of Jiangxi. These other six varieties each have very large internal diversity, and none is mutually intelligible with Mandarin. However, all Chinese agree that they form a single historical ethnic group, sharing the use of Chinese characters for writing. The use of *Putonghua* in more and more public domains is not endangering these local varieties of Chinese, as other local domains remain for them. However, there is some loss of local differences within Chinese, as regional subvarieties absorb the local speech of parts of their hinterlands with the expansion of cities.

The persistence of some of the main languages of some national minorities is in doubt. In some cases the battle is lost and the spoken varieties of the languages will soon disappear, as in the case of Manchu, the various languages within the Gelao nationality, She, and so on. In other cases the endangerment is not quite so terminal, and small numbers of children are still learning the languages, though only a very small and decreasing proportion of the ethnic group; this is the case for the two languages within the Tujia nationality, among others. Most such languages are at least fairly well documented, and the choice to stop using them is one which has been made by the speech community or by its leaders on their behalf.

For those smaller groups in China whose separate status has not been recognised, and who are amalgamated into a larger nationality with some other dominant language, the situation is much worse. First, they are not entitled to public support, as their speech is not the 'standard' for their nationality. Second, they are classified together with some larger group and must either use that other group's language or even Chinese to communicate within the nationality area. Third, they tend to be small groups with relatively low local prestige. Thus a very large number of such languages is endangered, and there are doubtless additional endangered languages which have not yet been located, let alone documented. This documentation is a major and urgent undertaking, but this has no priority at all with local authorities, who focus on economic development, and is neglected even by the majority of linguists in China, who prefer to work on varieties of Chinese.

Vietnam is in a similar situation to China: the majority Kinh or Vietnamese language is not endangered; indeed it is also the language of the Jing nationality in China, a substantial group in southeastern Cambodia, smaller groups in southern Laos and northeastern Thailand, and very large post-1975 populations in many Western countries. The Viet language of these Kinh people is the main focus of education and the medium of national life. Even outside Vietnam, the language is relatively well maintained.

Vietnamese is also replacing the languages of other ethnic groups in many domains. Ironically, among the most endangered languages of Vietnam are the most closely related MK languages within the Vietic group. Because of the policy that languages of the other ethnic groups of Vietnam should use romanised orthographies similar to Vietnamese, the systems in use are different from those used by the same groups in surrounding countries, thus reducing the opportunity for transnational contact and reinforcement of language and other aspects of ethnic identity.

Laos is unusual among the nations of this region because its national language, Lao, is the mother tongue of only half the population. Lao is also spoken as a regional diglossic Low by a far larger population in northeastern Thailand, more than ten times the mother-tongue Lao population of Laos. Lao in Laos is inundated by contact with Thai, and has converged markedly toward Thai in the last few decades, despite political antipathy since the communist takeover of all of Laos in 1975. Recent spelling reform has emphasised the difference from Thai by deleting unpronounced consonant clusters, as in the name of the former royal capital, Luang Phabang, formerly written as Luang Phrabang.

Because the communist government of Laos originated in the hills of eastern Laos, some of its leaders are members of non-Lao ethnic groups; however, the languages of these ethnic groups are not a national priority. Indeed, there is strong government resistance to separate educational arrangements or ethnic language maintenance. Popular classification of these ethnic groups into a few large socioeconomically based categories contrasts with the government classification, which follows the former Soviet model also used in China and Vietnam, recognising a great deal of diversity, though not all the distinct ethnolinguistic groups noted in Chazee (1995).

In both Laos and Vietnam, the official classification of ethnic groups has a much lower tendency to lump distinct groups together than in China. Because of this, quite a few groups are recognised as separate groups in Laos and/or in Vietnam, but included in some larger group in China. For example, the Pathen and Cosung or Lahu of Vietnam are separate groups, but in China the Pathen, speakers of an endangered Bunu language, are included in the Yao, and the Cosung are included in the much more broadly defined Lahu.

In Cambodia the government emphasises the promotion of Khmer, the national language and a mother tongue of about 98 per cent of the population, including the local ethnic Chinese and Vietnamese who are mostly bilingual. The various very small minorities in the northeast of the country and scattered elsewhere who still speak other MK or Chamic AN languages are mainly able to speak Khmer as well. However, reports of the death of all these languages may be premature, since some Pearic languages have already persisted among tiny populations in bilingual situations over more than a millennium of Khmer domination. What is certain is that language maintenance for these groups will attract no government interest.

If the regional varieties of the South (Pak Tay), North (Kam Myang) and Northeast (Isan or Lao) and the Thai-speaking Sino-Thai are included, about 95 per cent of Thailand's population uses a variety of Thai as their mother tongue, and everyone uses Central Thai as a standard language, learned in school and used in all aspects of national life. There are substantial groups who also speak the language of an adjacent country: some Khmer and Vietnamese in the northeast and many Malay in the far south. Conversely, the Pak Tay variety of Thai is also spoken by a small number of Buddhists in northeastern peninsular Malaysia, and by the Thai diaspora in Western countries.

The Thai government also recognises a small but gradually increasing number of hill tribes, and makes special provision for their economic and educational development. These hill tribes have also become a focus of tourism. However, there is no government assistance for language maintenance; rather, the tendency is to bring hill tribe children to hostels in Thai towns for education beyond the initial primary school available in most villages; there is also economic migration for work in the towns. Most of the hill tribes arrived over the last century from further north, and are still much more numerous in China or Burma where they originated. There are some small indigenous groups in the north and west of the country speaking MK or TB languages; most of these are lumped into the Thai category Lawa, also known as Lua in Kam Myang (Northern Thai); most of these languages are endangered. Most of the groups included in this Lawa/Lua category do not like and prefer not to use this term.

Scattered across the plains of Thailand, there are isolated pockets of groups transported from elsewhere. Up to the end of the nineteenth century, when Thai armies were in the territory of their neighbours, large groups of local people were relocated back into core Thai-controlled areas in village-sized units, since it was unrealistic to hold remote territory or collect taxes from people there. Other distant groups chose to move into land provided by the Thai government in the plains. In a surprising number of cases, these villages have maintained their language, while of course being fully bilingual in Thai. There are various MK groups, quite a few non-Thai TK groups, and a few TB groups like this. For example, the Lao Song scattered across west-central and the northern part of southern Thailand still can speak Thai Dam, a TK language of northeastern Laos, northwestern Vietnam and adjacent areas of China. These displaced languages have naturally evolved differently from what is spoken in the original area. In some cases, the displaced groups maintain their language better than those left behind.

Burma, or Myanmar as its military government tells us to call it since 1990, promotes Burmese as the national language and uses it exclusively in schools and government. The literary variety of Burmese as studied in schools and written in all government documents is a diglossic High, rather archaic and quite different from the spoken Low, which makes it even harder for minority groups to learn and use. The terminological alternatives for the name of the country are one example: in the literary High, the country is Myanmar (mjəma^{22}) but in the spoken Low it is Bamar (bəma^{22}), whence English Burma. While the government tolerates supplementary education in minority languages, notably through religious institutions such as Buddhist temples, Christian churches and so on, it does not support or promote these other languages in any way. This has already resulted in the Burmanisation of much of the population of the central plain and lower eastern hills, including many Mon, Shan and others.

Throughout Malaysia, Malaysian is the national language and must be learned and used by all citizens. Local varieties of Malay are also the first language of a majority of the population of West Malaysia, especially in non-urban areas. While Malaysian and Indonesian diverged during the colonial period, since independence the two standards have been brought closer together, most notably with a spelling reform in 1972.

Malaysia has a special government department for *Orang Asli* affairs, but this does not work on language maintenance. While most of the main Aslian MK languages are fairly well known, much more work needs to be done, especially to document their internal dialect diversity and the processes of contact between them. The indigenous Malayic AN languages of the groups classified as *Orang Laut*, 'sea people', are widely regarded as just local nonstandard varieties of Malay, and may have a tendency to be absorbed into local Malay varieties over time. The long-term prognosis for all these languages is not good.

Similarly, the government makes little effort to maintain the Chinese and Indian languages spoken by a substantial portion of the population who arrived during the British period, though these communities have been able to make some arrangements for language education. A somewhat longer established community is the Portuguese creole group in Melaka. Among this group, the tendency has been to replace their creole with Malaysian English. However, the recent designation of this creole group as a *bumiputra*, 'indigenous' group of Malaysia and positive discrimination in favour of indigenous groups have led to some efforts for revival.

Future prospects for language maintenance

In addition to the languages listed in this encyclopedia, virtually every language in this area which is not the official majority language of a nation is at least potentially endangered. This means that every AA language in this area apart from Vietnamese and Khmer is at risk. Of the TB languages, all but Burmese are similarly threatened, though some of the larger languages, themselves absorbing some TB and other languages, are less so. Of the mainland AN languages, everything else in Chamic will soon be endangered. Malay is of course safe, and as Chapter 6 indicates, it and its Indonesian variety are replacing a large number of other AN languages in Indonesia. Of the TK languages, most other than Thai are also in varying degrees of danger, even Lao because of extensive influence from Thai. Many more MY languages are becoming endangered too, though some of the larger groups may persist as in the case of the larger TB and TK groups. In all cases, these non-majority languages have already lost many domains to dominant languages, and the proportion of each minority group who can speak their language is decreasing.

The nominal policy in China and Vietnam is supportive of minority language maintenance, but the reality is that the national language is essential for participation in modern national life everywhere in this region. Education in small minority languages is almost completely absent in Cambodia, Laos and West Malaysia, relegated to the non-school sector in Burma, Japan and Thailand, and often neglected, even by minority authorities themselves, in Vietnam and China.

While some communities whose languages are endangered have started language maintenance efforts, this is the exception. Many of the endangered languages of this area, even those where maintenance efforts are underway, will soon disappear. Documentation efforts are urgent, and are fairly advanced in Thailand and Malaysia. Some such work is being done in Laos, Cambodia, Vietnam and China, but far from enough; and very little has been done in Burma.

Notes

1 I am pleased to acknowledge the support of the UNESCO Endangered Languages programme and of the Australian Research Council (A59701122, A59803475, A00001357) and assistance from various institutions in China, especially the Yunnan Academy of Social Sciences, Thailand, especially Mahidol University, and France, especially the Centre National de la Recherche Scientifique. Data from a number of colleagues is included here: 2000 China census figures from Colin Mackerras, information on Ainu from Theresa Savage, on Aslian from Geoffrey Benjamin, on various Mon-Khmer languages from Suwilai Premsrirat, Therphan Luangthongkum and Gérard Diffloth, and on various Kadai and other languages of Vietnam from Jerry Edmondson. Of course all remaining shortcomings and errors and any misunderstandings of information from others are my sole responsibility.
2 In Benjamin forthcoming.
3 In order not to introduce further confusion, I use the term Tibeto-Burman (TB) here in its traditional value, for Sino-Tibetan (ST) languages other than Sinitic or Chinese.
4 There are also individual Ngochang blacksmith families in many Jinghpaw and Shan villages across northern Burma; these are locally known as Tai Sa; my thanks to Jerry Edmondson for this information.
5 Phunoi, 'small men', is a Lue and Lao name also used as an autonym by two of six Phunoi or Sinsali subgroups; the term Sinsali became the new official name for this ethnic group in 1998.
6 An orthography is being developed for the Moshang clan dialect of Rangpan/Tangsa in Burma, also intended for use by Nocte, Haimi and Wancho.
7 My warm thanks to Juha Janhunen and Tapani Salminen for comments concerning this section.
8 The then recent death of the last speaker was reported at the UNESCO International Symposium on Endangered Languages in Tokyo in November 1995.

References

Baxter, Alan N. (1988) *A Grammar of Kristang (Malacca Creole Portuguese)*. Pacific Linguistics B-95. Canberra: Australian National University.
Benedict, Paul K. (1942) Thai, Kadai and Indonesian: a new alignment in Southeastern Asia. *American Anthropologist* 44: 576–601.
——(1975) *Austro-Thai Language and Culture*. New Haven CT: HRAF Press.
——(1990) *Japanese/Austro-Thai*. Ann Arbor MI: Karoma.
Benjamin, Geoffrey (forthcoming) Introduction: endangered languages. In Hein Steinhauer (ed.) *Endangered Languages and Literatures of South-East Asia*. Leiden: Brill.
Bradley, David (1992) Tone alternations in Ugong. In Carol Compton and John Hartmann (eds) *Papers in Tai Languages, Linguistics and Literatures in Honor of William J. Gedney on his 77th Birthday*, 55–64. De Kalb IL: Northern Illinois University Press.
——(2004) Introduction: language policy and language endangerment in China. *International Journal of the Sociology of Language* 170: 1-14.

Bradley, David and Maya Bradley (2002) Language policy and language maintenance: Yi in China. In David Bradley and Maya Bradley (eds) *Language Endangerment and Language Maintenance*, 74–96. London: RoutledgeCurzon.

Burling, Robbins (1983) The Sal languages. *Linguistics of the Tibeto-Burman Area* 7/2: 1–31.

Chazee, Laurent (1995) *Atlas des ethnies et des sous-ethnies du Laos*. Bangkok: Laurent Chazee.

Edmondson, Jerry and Lama Ziwo (2000) Laghuu or Xá Phó, a new language of the Yi group. *Linguistics of the Tibeto-Burman Area* 22/1: 1–10.

Greenberg, Joseph H. (2000) *Indo-European and its Closest Relatives. The Eurasiatic Language Family*. Stanford CA: Stanford University Press.

Hajek, John (forthcoming) The mystery of the Kenaboi. In Hein Steinhauer (ed.) *Endangered Languages and Literatures of South-East Asia*. Leiden: Brill.

Hattaway, Paul (2000) *Operation China*. Pasadena CA: Piquant.

Henderson, Eugénie J. A. (1965a) The topography of certain phonetic and morphological characteristics of South-East Asian languages. *Lingua* 15: 400–34.

——(1965b) *Tiddim Chin: A Descriptive Analysis of Two Texts*. London: Oxford University Press.

Janhunen, Juha (1997) The languages of Manchuria in today's China. In H. Shoji and J. Janhunen (eds) *Northern Minority Languages, Problems of Survival*, 123–46. Senri Ethnological Studies no. 44. Osaka: National Museum of Ethnology.

Kingsada, Thongpheth and Tadahiko Shintani (eds) (1999) *Basic Vocabularies of the Languages Spoken in Phongsaly, Lao P.D.R.* Lao-Japan Project Data Paper 1. Tokyo: Institute for the Study of Languages and Cultures of Asia and Africa.

Krauss, Michael (1997) The indigenous languages of the North: a report on their present state. In H. Shoji and J. Janhunen (eds) *Northern Minority Languages, Problems of Survival*, 1–34. Senri Ethnological Studies no. 44. Osaka: National Museum of Ethnology.

Lefèvre-Pontalis, Pierre (1892) Notes sur quelques populations du nord de l'Indochine. *Journal Asiatique* 19: 237–69.

Miller, Roy Andrew (1971) *Japanese and the Other Altaic Languages*. Chicago IL: University of Chicago Press.

Morey, Stephen (2002) Tai languages of Assam, a progress report – does anything remain of the Tai Ahom language? In David Bradley and Maya Bradley (eds) *Language Endangerment and Language Maintenance*, 98–113. London: RoutledgeCurzon.

Moseley, Christopher and Ronald E. Asher (eds) (1994) *Atlas of the World's Languages*. London: Routledge. Second, revised edition 2006.

Robine, François (2000) *Fils et maîtres du lac. Relations interethniques dans l'Etat Shan de Birmanie*. Paris: Editions CNRS.

Sagart, Laurent (2002) Sino-Tibeto-Austronesian: an updated and improved argument. Paper presented at the Ninth International Conference on Austronesian Linguistics, Canberra 9–11 January 2002. To appear in L. Sagart, R. Blench and A. Sanchez-Mazas (eds) *The Peopling of East Asia: Putting Together Archaeology, Linguistics and Genetics*. London: RoutledgeCurzon.

Sawai, Harumi (1998) The present situation of the Ainu language. In Kazuto Matsumura (ed.) *Studies in Endangered Languages*, 177–89. Tokyo: Hituzi Syobo.

Schmidt, Wilhelm (1906) Die Mon-Khmer Völker: ein Bindeglied zwischen den Volkern Zentral-Asiens und Austronesiens. *Archiv für Anthropologie* n.s. 5: 59–109.

Shoji, Hiroshi and Juha Janhunen (eds) (1997) *Northern Minority Languages, Problems of Survival*. Senri Ethnological Studies no. 44. Osaka: National Museum of Ethnology.

Thomas, F. S. (1948) *Nam, An Ancient Language on the Sino-Tibetan Borderland*. London: Oxford University Press.

Whaley, Lindsay J., Lenore A. Grenoble and Fengxiang Li (1999) Revisiting Tungusic classification from the bottom up: a comparison of Ewenki and Oroqen. *Language* 75/2: 286–321.

Wurm, Stephen A. and Shirô Hattori (eds) (1981) *Language Atlas of the Pacific Area*. Pacific Linguistics C-66.

Wurm, Stephen A., Benjamin K. T'sou, David Bradley, Li Rong, Xiong Zhenghui, Zhang Zhenxing, Fu Maoji, Wang Jun and Dob (eds) (1987) *Language Atlas of China*. Hong Kong: Longman.

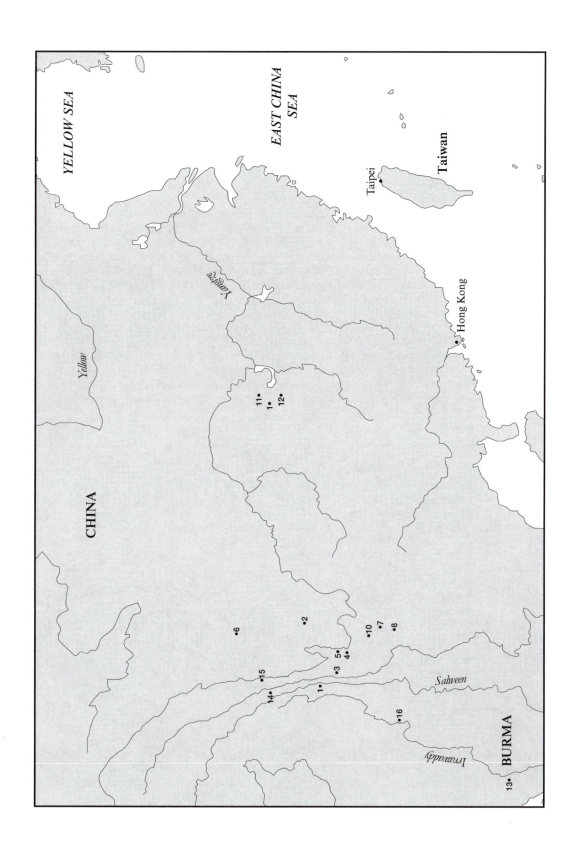

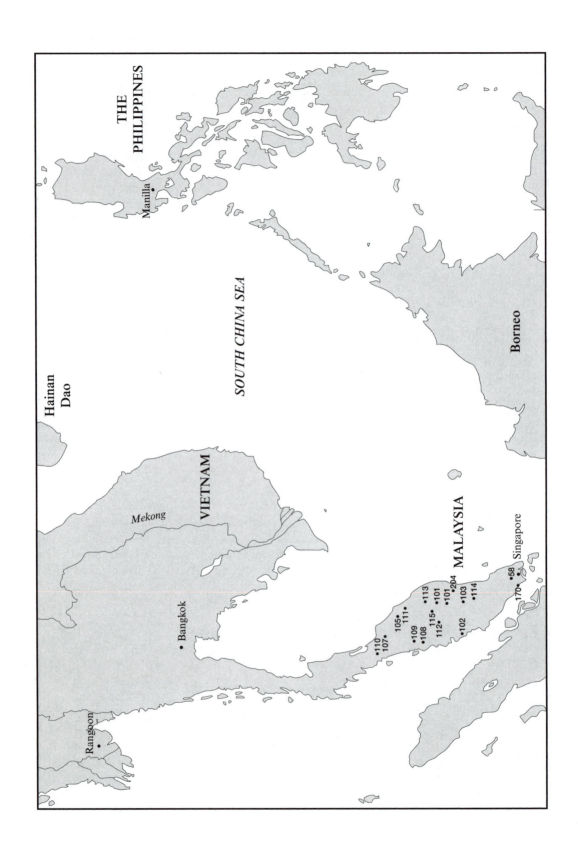

THE PHILIPPINES

Manilla

SOUTH CHINA SEA

Hainan Dao

VIETNAM

Mekong

Bangkok

Rangoon

MALAYSIA

Singapore

Borneo

110
107
105
111
109
108
115
112
113
101
101
204
102
103
114
58
170

Tibeto-Burman Qiangic

Anung (*Anong*) **[1]** China: Yunnan, central Fugong County; Burma: northeastern Kachin State, southeastern Putao. Anong is the same name represented in Chinese pinyin. Classified within the composite Nu nationality in China, along with one other Qiangic language and two Loloish languages, Nusu and Zaozou. In Burma, the (a^{31} $nuŋ^{55}$) are a component of the composite Rawang ethnic group, all speaking Qiangic languages. Approximately 7,300 group members in China, but only about 50 to 60 elderly speakers; a further 10,000 in Burma, about a third speakers and a further third with passive knowledge. Most younger Anung are native speakers of Lisu; they and many other Anung also speak other languages, including Mvtwang Rawang, Jinghpaw Kachin and Burmese in Burma, and Chinese in China. Moribund in China, severely endangered in Burma.

Baima **[2]** China: northern Sichuan, Pingwu, Jiuzhaigou and Songpan counties and Wenxian County, Gansu Province. The group name means 'white horse' in Chinese. There are about 14,000 group members, classified in the Tibetan nationality, and about 10,000 speakers, who also speak local Amdo Tibetan and Chinese. The language is inundated with Tibetan loanwords, to such an extent that some classify it as a variety of Tibetan, and others prefer to include it in the Tibetan rather than the Qiang subgroup of TB. Language in decline and potentially endangered.

Choyo (*Queyu*) **[3]** China: western Sichuan, Yalong, Xinlong and Litang counties. A Xifan group, members of the Tibetan nationality; 7,000 of this group at the borders of these three counties; the Chinese names are both attempts to represent the phonetic value of their autonym. They are Tibetan Buddhists, and use Tibetan as a liturgical language. Endangered.

Ersu (*Luzi*, *Tosu*) **[4]** China: southwestern Sichuan, eastern Jiulong, Mianning, western Puge, Yuexi, and Ganluo and northern Muli counties. There are about 20,000 (lɨ zɨ), meaning 'white people', but only about 15,000 can speak the language. Ersu represents the same name in another dialect; Tosu is a former name seen in old Chinese sources. They are included in the Tibetan nationality, but speak a distinct Xifan language. The eastern part of their traditional territory is now heavily populated with Nuosu, and the language is endangered.

Guichong (*Guiqiong*) **[5]** China: western Sichuan, Kangding Conty, Yutong Township. Some 7,000 (gu^{35} $tɕʰɔ\sim^{55}$), who have Tibetan nationality and are Tibetan Buddhist, speak one of the Xifan group languages and local Tibetan. Potentially endangered.

Laemae **[6]** China: Yunnan, Luobenzhuo Township of Lushui County, northwestern Lanping County, both in southern Nujiang Prefecture. Classified partly in Bai and partly in Lisu nationality; about 15,000 still speak a distinct language closely related to Bai, known as Lama in Lanping and Laemae (in Chinese, Lemei) in Luobenzhuo; others have assimilated and are simply a local clan within the Lisu in other areas, and speak only Lisu. Group population, including that submerged in the Lisu, is about 50,000; but people who identify as members of this group are far fewer, and speakers number only about 15,000, including most children in the core area of Luobenzhuo. Severely endangered, being replaced by Lisu.

Muya (*Minyag*) **[7]** China: western Sichuan, Kangding and Jiulong counties. Living near Minya Konka, a famous Tibetan pilgrimage destination; the name of this mountain contains their ethnonym. The 15,000 Muya are members of the Tibetan nationality and practise Tibetan Buddhism, but most still speak a Xifan language as well. Potentially endangered.

Namuyi **[8]** China: southwestern Sichuan, Jiulong, Mianning, Xichang and Muli counties. One of the Xifan languages, included in the Tibetan nationality, 5,000 ($n\varepsilon^{55}$ mu^{33} $z\Omega^{31}$) group members in the area where these four counties meet. Most also speak Tibetan and some Chinese, and follow Tibetan Buddhism. Potentially endangered.

Shixing (*Xumi*) **[9]** China: southwestern Sichuan, Muli County, Wachang Township. Under 2,000 ($s\textsubscript{l}^{55}$ $h\tilde{i}$) or (ϱu^{33} mu^{55}) people of Tibetan nationality, about 1,800 speak this Xifan language. Endangered.

Zaba (*Zhaba*) **[10]** China: Sichuan, northern Daocheng and southern Yajiang counties. Another Xifan group, own name ($p\varepsilon^{35}$ $ts\Omega^{35}$) but known in Tibetan as ɦDra-pa, whence the name Zaba; or Zhaba; some Guichong are also called by this Tibetan name. The Zaba proper are also included in the Tibetan nationality, following Tibetan Buddhism and using Tibetan as a liturgical language. About 7,700 group members, most can speak but the language is potentially endangered.

Tujia

Tujia, *Northern* (*Biji*) **[11]** China: northwestern Hunan. 8,028,133 members of the nationality in four provinces, recognised only in the 1950s; previously included in the Han Chinese majority though known locally. There are two distinct languages included within this nationality, Northern and Southern Tujia, with different autonyms and very extensive lexical and other structural differences. The autonym for Northern Tujia is (pi^{21} $t\varphi i^{21}$ $k^h a^{21}$), which appears in the Chinese literature in various forms: Bizi, Bizhika and so on. In rapid decline; reported to have been spoken by as many as 170,000 people twenty years ago, but now perhaps 60,000 speakers, plus about half as many with passive knowledge. There are nineteen village clusters on the borders where Longshan, Baoqing, Guzhang and Yongshun counties meet; there, the language is still spoken, in some places mainly by old people but in a few also by some children; all are bilingual in varieties of Chinese. Recently extinct in southeastern Sichuan, northeastern Guizhou and southwestern Hubei provinces, extinct or moribund in most of northwestern Hunan, severely endangered in the remaining areas.

Tujia, *Southern* (*Mozi*) **[12]** China: northwestern Hunan, Luxi County. Population and other background as for Northern Tujia; spoken to the southeast of the remaining Northern Tujia concentration. The Southern Tujia autonym is (m^{21} $dz\Omega^{21}$), represented in Chinese sources as Mozhi or Mozhihei. Earlier reported as still spoken in ten villages in eastern Luxi county, but recently found only in three: Boluozhai where all including children speak the language; Puzhu, where some children can speak; and Xiaqieji, where only adults can speak; in some of the other villages old people still know the language. Fewer than 10,000 speakers, mainly older people. Extinct, moribund or severely endangered in most places; severely endangered in two remaining villages.

Mijuish

***Zaiwa* [13]** China: southeast Tibet, Zayul County, three villages (Songgu, Lading and Tama) in Lower Zayul Township; also India: northeast Arunachal Pradesh, Walong and surrounding villages; for more details see Jacquesson (2001) and Li and Jiang (2001). Those in China have various clan surnames but no group autonym and are included in the Tibetan nationality, while those in India are classified as the Meyor and Zakhring tribes according to their clan names; more recently they have started to use the group name Zaiwa. The Chinese literature refers to them as Zha, from the local Tibetan term for this group, (tsa^{35}), probably derived from the local place name Zayul. Total speaker population under 1,000 (about one third in India), all multilingual. Zaiwa, not to be confused with Burmish Zaiwa (pronounced *tsaiwa*) or Atsi, is closely related to Miju Mishmi or Geman and endangered.

Burmic

Burmish

***Bola* [14]** China: Yunnan, Dehong Prefecture. Well under a thousand in Luxi, Yingjiang and surrounding counties, included in the Jingpo nationality, intermarrying with other groups within this nationality including Zaiwa (Atsi, Zi) and Langsu (Lawngwaw, Maru) as well as Jinghpaw. The Pola are an exogamous patrilineal clan within the Jinghpaw/Kachin, and so all are multilingual, speaking other languages from within the cluster natively, as well as some Chinese and a local Tai language. Endangered, being the second smallest clan language within the group.

***Chintaw* (*Xiantao*) [15]** China: Yunnan, Yingjiang County. Seventy people calling themselves (k^{h}an^{31} taw^{31}) (whence the Chinese term Xiantao) forming all thirty of the population in one relocated village, Meng'erzhai (Meng'er) moved in 1958, and 40 of 49 inhabitants in Xiantaozhai (also known as Mangmian) in the other, moved in 1995. Classified as Achang nationality since 1980, most speak Chinese and Jinghpaw and can understand most of Achang. Those over forty are mainly first-language Chintaw speakers, but there are no monolinguals and no fluent speakers under ten. The language is being replaced by Jinghpaw in Meng'er and by Chinese and Jinghpaw in Mangmian. Severely endangered.

***Hpun* [16]** Burma: Irrawaddy gorge north of Bhamo. About 1,500 members of the ethnic group in about 15 villages; two distinct dialects, called according to place names in the literature: southern (me^{42} tɕo^{11}) moribund by 1959 and now extinct,

395

northern (səmaŋ[42]) then severely endangered, now also very moribund; some older people remember lexical items, but none can speak. Hpun (pʰũ[42]) is the Burmese name; the group's own names were northern (pʰjei[42]) and southern (pʰru[42]). Limited available lexical material indicates that Hpun was the most phonologically conservative Burmish language. Imminently extinct if not already so.

Yaw Burma: west-central. Under 10,000 ethnic Yaw in southwestern Sagaing Division, west of Pakkoku. Most younger members of the group can understand but not speak the language, which is being absorbed into closely related Burmese. Endangered.

Gong

Gong (*Ugong, Kanburi Lawa*) [17] Thailand: northwestern Suphanburi and southwestern Uthai Thani provinces. Own name (goŋ[35]) or similar; Ugong means 'person-Gong'. About 500 group members in the two villages where the language survives, but most of them speak only Thai and/or Lao. Called Lawa in Thai, a composite group which includes various Mon-Khmer groups as well as Gong. The southernmost and most distinctive Burmish language, with some radical sound changes such as *mr > /g/. Extinct in traditional territory in western Kanchanaburi (or Kanburi for short) Province, moribund (youngest fluent speakers over forty, but revival activities underway) in Kok Chiang village in Suphanburi Province, and endangered in Khok Khwai village in Uthai Thani Province, where the Gong have recently lost their land and dispersed into the surrounding forests.

Loloish/Yi/Ni

Northern

Aluo (*Ala, Naluo, Yala, Lila, Laka, Gan Yi*) [18] China: Yunnan, northern Wuding, Luquan and Yuanmou counties; Sichuan, southern Huili and western Miyi counties. About 40,000 group members within the Yi nationality, but far fewer speakers. Known as Gan Yi, 'dry Yi', in Chinese, one of several groups so called, subservient to the Hei Yi, 'black Yi' nobility and Bai Yi, 'white Yi' commoner Nasu and Nosu. Laka was the term used in early missionary contacts; it is the Nasu name for the group. Aluo, Naluo, Ala, Yala and Lila are different local versions of their autonym (ʔa[55] la[33]). Being replaced by Chinese and/or varieties of closely related Nasu. Severely endangered in all three villages in Miyi County, endangered in most other places.

Ayizi [19] China: Yunnan, Shilin, Yiliang and surrounding counties. At least 2,000 people, members of this group within the Yi nationality in widely scattered villages, notably Aimalong village in northwestern Shilin County. Language unstudied, extinct in most places, moribund at best in Aimalong.

Chesu [20] China: Yunnan, along the border of Xinping and Shuangbai counties. Group of about 6,600 included in the Yi nationality. *Su* is a widespread nominalising suffix meaning 'people', seen in the names of many Loloish groups. The language appears to be more closely related to Eastern Yi Nasu further north, rather than to adjacent Hlersu (Central Yi) and Nisu (Southern Yi) with which it is in direct contact. Some Chesu do not speak the language, using Chinese instead; in other areas it is in decline, and becoming endangered.

Kazhuo **[21]** China: Yunnan, central Tonghai County, Xinmeng Township. 6,341 members of the group, but fewer speakers; own name (k^ha^{55} ts^ho^{21}). Classified as Mongol nationality; the group claims descent from a Mongol army left behind in Yunnan during the Yuan Dynasty, and maintains a shrine for Genghis Khan and other Mongol emperors, but they are aware that the language they speak is a Loloish one, and find their speech moderately similar to nearby Nisu. There is no evidence of any Mongol lexical or other material in the language. Most young people are semi-speakers, speaking Chinese instead; endangered, and becoming more so.

Samei **[22]** China: Yunnan, Guandu District of Kunming City, forty-two villages just southeast of the city; also seven villages in northwestern Yiliang County to the east. A group of about 28,000 Yi whose own name is ($s\alpha^{21}$ ni^{53}), but are known in Chinese as Samei. Extinct in some northwestern villages very close to Kunming city, severely endangered to the east in northeastern Guandu and Yiliang, and endangered in Ala Township which is the centre of the Samei distribution and where most villages are entirely or largely Samei. Few fully fluent young speakers, though many children have passive understanding of the language.

Samataw (***Samaduo***) **[23]** China: Yunnan, Kunming City, Guandu District. 2,808 group members of Yi nationality and about 400 speakers in one large village, Zijun (also known as Da'er 'big ear') surrounded by Chinese in the plain just south of Kunming city. Reported to be similar to the speech of the 5,700 Adu of Huaning County in northwest Yunnan, but this is unconfirmed. Own name ($s\alpha^{33}$ $m\alpha^{21}$ $t\alpha w^{21}$); Samaduo is a Chinese rendering of this. The language is similar to Samei and Sanyie but not mutually intelligible; not to be confused with Samatu. No fluent speakers under fifty, severely endangered but some language heritage activities underway in the village school.

Sanie **[24]** China: Yunnan, Xishan District of Kunming City and adjacent areas of southern Fumin and northern Anning counties. 17,230 group members and under 8,000 speakers in seventy-six villages, classified in the Yi nationality; see Bradley (2004a) for details. The only known Loloish language to retain labiovelar clusters, as in the name of the group, ($s\alpha^{21}$ $\eta w\varepsilon^{21}$), but only in the easternmost dialects which are moribund; elsewhere ($s\alpha^{21}$ $\mathrm{\tcommaaccent}\varepsilon^{21}$). In villages closer to Kunming the language is spoken only by the elderly, slightly further away only by adults, but furthest away a few children speak the language, which is being replaced by Chinese in the east and by Chinese and Nasu in the west. Endangered to severely endangered; the most phonologically conservative dialects moribund.

Central

Cosung (***Kucong, Lahu***) **[25]** China: south central Yunnan, Xinping, Jingdong, Zhenyuan, Jinggu, Jinping, Jiangcheng and Mengla counties; Vietnam, Lai Chau Province,

Míuíong Te District. Kucong is a Chinese term for the group, and Cosung is the Vietnamese version of the same. Own name (la ɬu), but despite the similar name, speaking a rather distinctive language close to but not mutually intelligible with Lahu. About 45,000 group members, very widely scattered from north to south, east of the main Lahu concentrations, cultural similarities with adjacent Hani rather than with Lahu. 5,400 in Vietnam, nearly 40,000 in China. Applied for but failed to achieve official nationality status in China in the early 1980s, amalgamated into the Lahu nationality in 1989. Language starting to be replaced by Hani and Chinese; endangered.

Hlersu (*Sansu*, *Shansu*, *Lesu*) [26] China: Yunnan, northwest Xinping County; also scattered in adjacent areas of Shuangbai, Jinping, Shiping, Zhenyuan and Eshan counties. About 15,000 people, classified in the Yi nationality. Shansu (or in local pronunciation Sansu) is the Nisu (and hence the Chinese) name for this group; Lesu is the Chesu name for them. There are some Nisu and Chesu who speak Hlersu, and some Hlersu speak Nisu and/or Chesu. Along with Cosung and Talu, one of the few Central Loloish languages to retain voiceless (ɬ). Genetically rather close to Lolopho. Potentially endangered to endangered, being replaced by Nisu and/or Chinese in some areas.

Jinuo [27] China: Yunnan, northeastern Jinghong County, Youle (Jinuo) Mountain area. 20,899 group members, but difficult to find fluent speakers under thirty. Recognised as a separate nationality in 1979, the only such instance after the 1950s. Relatively complex tone sandhi processes; becoming severely endangered. There is also a fairly distinctive dialect of Jinuo spoken southwest of Jinghong in the Buyuan mountains by about 1,000 within the Jinuo nationality, but most live concentrated in one area.

Lalo [28] China: Yunnan, southwestern Dali Prefecture. The core Lalo area is Nanjian and Weishan counties. A former name for Weishan was Menghua, and so it has also been called 'Menghua Lolo' in the older literature. Over half a million members of this subgroup; many of those living further west, south or east do not speak the language; less than half speakers, not all fluent and not many children. Within (la^{21} lu^{33}) there are several varieties, which Chinese linguists categorise into eastern and western dialects. In many areas it is extinct, moribund or severely endangered, but in other areas it is less so.

Lamu [29] China: Yunnan, northeastern Binchuan County. There are 120 people in two villages, classified as members of the Lahu nationality, but speaking a distinctive language much more similar to Lisu. Intermarried with and all bilingual in Lipho. The Lipho are much more numerous in the area; most also speak Chinese and some Lolopho, also spoken nearby. Severely endangered.

Michal/Miqie (*Minchia*, *Mielang*, *Minglang*) [30] China: Yunnan, scattered locations from Fumin, Luquan and Wuding counties north of Kunming, also in various small clusters in Yongren, Dayao, Yaoan and Nanhua counties in west-central Yunnan, and in Jingdong, Zhenyuan and Jinggu counties further south, along the eastern side of the Mekong. The first two are autonyms, (mi^{21} $tʂ^ha^{55}$) and (mi^{21} $tɕ^hɛ^{55}$); the tones of these names also differ from place to place. The other three names are various local

Chinese terms. Not to be confused with Minjia, a former name for the very large Bai nationality of the Dali area. Also formerly spoken in several villages in southern Anning and southwestern Jinning counties south of Kunming, and as far south as one Lahu village at the northern extremity of Thailand, which intermarried with the Miqie and later moved from Jinggu County to Burma in the early 1950s and in 1971 to Thailand. The group goes under a variety of names and speaks a very diverse range of dialects not in contact with each other. Group population at least 30,000, but far fewer speakers; autonym (mi^{21} tɕʰɛ^{33}) or similar. Classified in the Yi nationality; moderately closely related to Lipho. Extinct in some areas, moribund or severely endangered in others, otherwise endangered.

Naluo (***Naruo***, ***Laluo***, ***Shuitian***, ***Shui Yi***, ***Gan Yi***) **[31]** China: Yunnan, southern Huaping and eastern Yongsheng counties; Sichuan, western Panzhihua City. About 15,000, most in Yunnan and a couple of thousand in Pingjiang and Futian townships of Panzhihua; part of the Yi nationality. Not to be confused with Lalo of southwestern Dali Prefecture. Shuitian, 'irrigated field', is the local Chinese term used in Sichuan; Shui Yi, 'water Yi', and Gan Yi, 'dry Yi', are local Chinese terms used in Yunnan; the other terms are alternative versions of their autonym. Language moribund to extinct in Sichuan, potentially endangered to endangered in Yunnan.

Samatu (***Samadu***) **[32]** China: Yunnan, Zhenkang and Yongde counties. Some 7,500 Yi, mainly in Zhenkang County. Said to be descendants of a Chinese army sent to the area many centuries ago, who married local Yi women. Not to be confused with Samataw, a distinct group near Kunming. Language unstudied and moribund, almost completely replaced by Chinese.

Talu **[33]** China: Yunnan, Yongsheng, Ninglang and Huaping counties. Some 10,138 (tʰɑ^{21} lu̠^{55}) people in the Yi nationality, mainly in four villages of Liude Township in northeastern Yongsheng, also in adjacent parts of Ninglangping Township of southern Ninglang, and Tongda Township in northeastern Huaping. Unusual for Central Yi in having voiceless nasals as well as voiceless lateral. Language closely related to Lolopho and potentially endangered.

Tanglang **[34]** China: Yunnan, southwestern Lijiang County, southern Tai'an Township. There are 947 people in eight villages, classified as members of the Yi nationality; also a few in adjacent areas of Jianchuan County. Most including children can speak the language, called (tʰo^{42} lo^{42}), but also Chinese; long-term Bai cultural influence, also in contact with Naxi. Potentially endangered.

Tazhi **[35]** China: Sichuan, northern Miyi County, Puwei Township. Small group of a few hundred who say they came from northern Yunnan centuries ago, possibly from the Nasu or Bai areas. Language unstudied and moribund to extinct.

Zaozou (***Raoruo***) **[36]** China: Yunnan, Lanping, Lushui and Yunlong counties. There are 2,100 group members, 1,800 in Lanping, most of the rest in Lushui; the group calls itself (zao^{55} zuo^{33}). Old people can speak, but many young people are semi-speakers or do not speak it at all; all also speak other languages including Chinese and often Lisu. One of four groups classified as part of the Nu nationality (28,759 group members), which is a residual category of non-Lisu TB groups in Nujiang Prefecture, including also Loloish Nusu and two Qiangic groups, Dulong who live outside Gongshan County as well as endangered Anung. Endangered.

Southern

Akeu [37] China: Jinghong and Menghai counties; Burma: eastern Shan State, Thailand, northern Chiangrai Province. About 5,000 widely scattered (a^{55} k^{h}ə^{55}) people, classified in the Hani nationality in China and in the Akha group in Burma and Thailand; possibly also in Laos. All speakers also speak Akha, which is replacing Akeu in most places; they also know other dominant languages including some Tai language, and in China, also Chinese. Closely related to Akha, but not mutually intelligible; notable for tone reversal in which Akha high tone corresponds to Akeu low tone, and Akha low tone corresponds to Akeu high tone. Endangered.

Bana (*Pana*) [38] China: Jinghong; Laos, northwestern. There are only a few hundred members of this ethnic group in two villages in Laos; there are also some hundreds nearby in China; some sources report as many as a couple of thousand, but this is unconfirmed. The language is quite closely related to Sila, which is further east. They are included by the Chinese authorities within the Hani nationality and by the Lao authorities within the Akha ethnic group; all are multilingual, speaking Akha and/or Lahu and some Tai language. At the village in Houaysai Province in Laos, the language is being replaced by Lahu; at the one in Namtha Province and in China, it is being replaced by Akha. Severely endangered.

Bisu [39] Thailand: southwestern Chiangrai Province; Burma: Möng Yan area, Eastern Shan State; China: Menghai County. Unclassified for nationality in China but locally called Laopin in Chinese, classified as the Hpyin ethnic group in Burma, and usually included within the Lawa or Lua hill tribe category in Thailand. In Thailand, spoken in two villages, Doi Chomphu and Pui Kham, also known as Doi Pui; in Phadaeng village, the language is moribund, and in Takaw, recently extinct. About 500 group members in the remaining two villages, but not all young people are speakers. Reported as moribund as long ago as 1890 in Burma, but still spoken by a population of about 2,000 in two or three villages, all bilingual in Lahu. In China, spoken in one village of 240 people, Laopinzhai, in Manghong Village Cluster, Mengzhe Township, Menghai County. Maintenance efforts underway; contact has recently been reestablished between the Bisu in these three areas; see Person (2004) for details. Relatively closely related to Laomian and the Lawpan variety of Sinsali, less so to the rest of Sinsali, Công and Sangkong; together these languages form the Bisoid subgroup of Southen Loloish. Endangered.

Chepya [40] Laos: western Phongsaly Province. About 2,000 speakers, included in the Akha ethnic group but speaking a quite distinct language. They call themselves (tɕ^{h}e^{11} p^{h}ja^{11}), and their language is endangered, being replaced by Akha.

Công [41] Vietnam: Lai Chau Province, Míuíong Te District. Closely related to most varieties of Sinsali/Phunoi of Laos, and less so to Bisu of Thailand, Burma and China and to Laomian of China and Burma. 1,300 in Vietnam, recognised as an ethnic group. Only about 450 speak the language, which is endangered.

Laomian [42] China: Yunnan, one cluster of three villages in north central Lancang County and two clusters of three villages in northern Menglian County; also three further villages in Burma to the west of Menglian. The group's name for itself is (gu^{33} ba^{21}) 'our group'; The Chinese name Laomian is derived from the Lahu name (lɔ^{53} mɛ^{21}). Over 5,000 group members in China, and about 2,000 in Burma; in China classified as part of the Lahu nationality since 1990. Most Laomian speak Lahu as well as Chinese and some other local languages. More than half of the remaining Laomian population in China lives mixed in Lahu-majority villages. All three clusters in China (about 480 people in Dongzhu village cluster, Zhutang Township, Lancang County; about 820 people in Nanya village cluster, Nanya Township; and about 600 people in Xinggan village cluster, Fuyan Township, both in Menglian County) have an original village called Laomianzhai, 'Laomian fortified village'. For more details see Xu (2004). According to the local Lahu origin stories, the Laomian were a fairly numerous group in ancient times, but now they are much reduced; many have doubtless simply been absorbed into the local Lahu population. Closely related to Bisu, and more distantly to Sangkong, Công and the Sinsali groups. Not all of the remaining Laomian can speak the language; it is endangered, especially in the most economically advanced village, Nanya in Menglian, where it is being replaced by Chinese and Lahu.

Mpi [43] Thailand: central Phrae Province. One village, Ban Dong, just east of Phrae town, with a recent southern offshoot Ban Dong Tai, 'South Ban Dong'. About 1,200 Mpi live there; all speak Northern Thai and Thai; many young people have passive or no knowledge of Mpi. According to their tradition, they were brought as war captives from what is now Jinghong County in China over 200 years ago; and indeed some closely related non-endangered languages, including Khatu (Chinese term Kaduo) and Piyo (Chinese term Biyue), classified as part of the Hani nationality, are still spoken there. Endangered.

Muda [44] China: Yunnan, southwestern Jinghong County. About 2,000 members of this group in Nanlianshan Township, Nanlian village calling themselves (mu^{31} ta̠^{31}) and included in the Hani nationality. Closely related to Akha but distinct. Potentially endangered.

Phunoi/Sinsali [45] Laos: southwestern Phongsaly Province. Includes five distinct varieties, two types of (pʰu^{21} nɔj^{44}), also (pʰɔŋ^{33} ku^{55}), (law^{21} sɛŋ^{21}), and (pi^{33} su^{44}); total 23,618 members. The official name of this recognised ethnic group of Laos changed from pejorative Phunoi (Lao for 'small man') to Sinsali in the late 1990s. The Phongku variety is closer to Bisu and Laomian; others closer to Công and Sangkong. Potentially endangered, especially so in the case of Phongku, Laoseng and Pisu varieties.

Sangkong [46] China: Jinghong County. Classified as Hani nationality. There are well under 2,000 members of the (saŋ^{55} qʰoŋ^{55}) group, most of whom can speak the language, in three villages in Mangwanwa village cluster, Xiaojie Township and one newer village, Tuanjie, in Menglong Town. It shares the characteristic and unusual sound change seen in Bisu, Công, Phin, Laomian, Laophin and Sinsali, whereby some prefixed initial nasals become prenasalised voiced stops; this characterises the Bisoid subgroup of Southern Loloish; in most of the other languages of this group other than Bisu, the prenasalised stops lose their nasality and become voiced stops. The local Shan name for the group is (pu^{33} ça^{55}), which appears in some Chinese sources as Buxia. Sangkong is losing ground and potentially endangered.

Sila (*Sida, Asong, Kha Pai*) [47] Laos: northern; Vietnam: northwestern. 1,518 in Laos, 600 in Vietnam. Kha Pai, 'white slaves', is a former pejorative name, and Asong is the name under which the earliest data was recorded in the 1890s. Two areas in northeastern Laos: mainly in northeastern Namtha and northern Muangsai provinces, and one village relocated near Luang Phabang; also some in Miuiong Te District of Lai Chau Province in northwestern Vietnam. One of the smallest recognised ethnic groups of Vietnam and Laos. While most members of the ethnic group can speak the language, it has low prestige and is losing domains; potentially endangered.

Southeastern

Gasu [48] China: Yunnan, northeastern Guangnan County; Guangxi, southern Xilin County. There are two very distinctive dialects of (ka^{33} θu^{31}) spoken in Yunnan and nearby in Guangxi. Part of the Yi nationality, about 5,000 people, mainly bilingual. Potentially endangered.

Laghuu (*Xa Pho*) [49] Vietnam: Lao Cai Province. About 1,000 group members in three villages, classified within the Phula ethnic group, own name (la^{21} ɣɯ^{44}); Xa Pho is a former Vietnamese name for the group. Closely related to Muji, but distinct. Language potentially endangered.

Mo'ang [50] China: Yunnan, southwestern Funing County; Guangxi, western Napo County; northern Vietnam. Most of over 5,000 Yi nationality members in four townships of Funing County and three of Napo County speak (mɯɑŋ^{51}), which is virtually undescribed. Reported by Edmondson to be similar to the language of the Lolo ethnic group of Vietnam (3,100 people) in Cao Bang and Ha Giang provinces, autonym (ma^{53} tsi^{53}), briefly described in Edmondson (2003), and to a small nearby group calling themselves (mo^{33} ndi^{31}) across the border in China. Endangered.

Muji [51] China: Yunnan, Mengzi County, Gejiu City and surrounding areas. Over 50,000 people including 1,345 people in Gamadi village, Shuitian Township where the language has been briefly described, own names (ɬa^{31} ɣə^{55}) or (mu^{31} dʑi^{31}), Yi nationality, living together with Phula and speaking Phula and Chinese. Closely related to Laghuu of Vietnam. Only 400 remaining speakers in Gamadi and similarly reduced numbers elsewhere; some children speak it, but it is endangered.

Phula (*Pula, Bo Kho Pa*) [52] China: Yunnan, Honghe Prefecture and western Wenshan Prefecture, Vietnam, Lao Cai Province. About 5,400 in Vietnam (the Phula ethnic group total of 6,424 includes the Laghuu) and over 50,000 in China. Part of the Yi nationality in China, recognised as a separate nationality in Vietnam. Pula is from the Chinese pinyin form of the name; Bo Kho Pa is a former alternative name in

Vietnam. In western Honghe Prefecture (parts of Honghe, Yuanyang, Shiping and Jianshui counties and Gejiu City) and in northwestern Vietnam the ($p^ho^{55} lo^{55}$) variety is spoken, while in eastern Honghe and western Wenshan prefectures (especially Mengzi, but also Yanshan, Kaiyuan, Maguan, Wenshan and Xichou counties), and along the central part of the China/Vietnam border the (p^hu^{55}) variety is spoken; some regard these as two distinct languages. While the eastern Pu variety is not currently endangered, western Phula is potentially endangered, and becoming more so.

Baric

Luish

Ganan [53] Burma: northeast Sagaing Division, Katha District. Some twenty villages around Namza, about 7,000 ethnic group members but at most 500 speakers. The language is severely endangered to moribund, being replaced by Burmese.

Kadu [54] Burma: northeast Sagaing Division, Katha District, north-central Pinlebu and nearby in southern Banmauk. Ethnic group of under 20,000 in sixteen villages who retain this identity, the descendants of a much larger group known in Burmese inscriptions as Kantu, who were rulers of the Tagaung kingdom prior to the Burman conquest of Upper Burma about a millennium ago. The language has been gradually receding ever since. It was already reported as moribund, about to be replaced by Burmese, nearly a hundred years ago, and the Kadu villages are dispersed in an area also inhabited by speakers of Burmese. Unstudied since 1973; presumably moribund, soon to be extinct. Not to be confused with the Katuic Mon-Khmer language Kadu or Kantu of Vietnam and Laos.

Malin [55] Burma: northeast Sagaing Division, Katha District. Closely related to Kadu and Ganan, reported to have become extinct by 1931.

Sak (**Thet**) [56] Burma: northwest Rakhine State; Bangladesh, southeastern Chittagong District. At least 2,000 in Burma, over 3,000 in Bangladesh. Their autonym is (ətsaʔ); Sak is an old Burmese name, already found in early inscriptions, now pronounced ($\theta\epsilon?^{44}$), whence Thet. Fourteen villages reported in Bangladesh, and seventeen in Burma. The least endangered Luish language, but now potentially endangered.

Taman [57] Burma: northwest Sagaing Division, 100km north of Homalin. The 1931 census enumerated 938 speakers, no reliable recent figures. The northernmost Luish language, by now at least severely endangered if not already extinct.

Austronesian

Malayic

Duano (**Desin Dolaq**, **Orang Kuala**) [58] Malaysia: southern peninsular, coast between Johor Baru and Batu Pahat; Indonesia: islands east of northern Sumatra in the Straits of

Malacca. About 7,500 group members, two-thirds in Indonesia and one third in Malaysia. In Malaysia, included in the category Orang Asli 'aboriginal people', along with all the groups who speak or formerly spoke various Austroasiatic languages. The Duano are also categorised as Orang Laut 'sea people' or migratory fishermen, which includes other AN groups further north, such as the Urak Lawoi and Moken/Moklen. The language is currently being absorbed into local Malay, and is endangered to severely endangered.

Moken (Moklen) **[59]** Burma: islands of the southeastern coast from Tavoy to the Thai border; and Thailand: islands off the southwest coast from the Burmese border to Phuket; also a few settlements on the coast. About 4,000 in Burma and about 2,000 in Thailand, some no longer following their traditional migratory fishing lifestyle and some of these not speaking the language. Known as Saloun in Burmese and sometimes as Chao Thalee 'sea people' in Thai; Moken is an autonym used by most dialect groups in Burma. Six dialect groups, from north to south Dung, Jait, Lebi and Niawi in Burma, Jadiak straddling the border, and Moklen in Thailand. There is one Jadiak village south of the Moklen at the southern tip of Phuket Island; but in this village there is extensive contact with Urak Lawoi and Thai and young people no longer speak traditional Moken. Various literacy materials have been prepared, based on Karen, Burmese, Roman and Thai scripts. Many speakers know Burmese, Thai or in some cases both; the language is endangered.

Urak Lawoi **[60]** Thailand: islands off the southwest coast from Phuket to the Malaysian border. About 3,000 group members, mainly migratory fishermen; their name means 'sea people', and is cognate with Orang Laut which means the same in Malay. Most are bilingual in Thai and many also speak Malay. Various Thai-script and romanised literacy materials have been prepared. The language is endangered, often replaced by Thai and/or Malay when members of the group settle down.

Chamic

Cham **[61]** Vietnam: southeast, inland from the coast from Phan Rang half way to Saigon; Cambodia: northeast, around Kampong Cham; small groups from Cambodia in Thailand and Malaysia. Although the ethnic group is numerous, perhaps as many as 250,000, and recognised as an ethnic group of Vietnam, their language is potentially endangered. It was the language of the ancient Champa kingdom in what is now southern Vietnam, but in its traditional territory it is being replaced by Vietnamese. As a result of a substantial migration of Moslem Cham into northeastern Cambodia after the conquest of the last Cham empire by the expanding Vietnamese, by far the largest concentration of Cham is now there, but this was very severely depleted during the Khmer Rouge period (1975–79); all remaining Cham there are bilingual in Khmer, and Cham has no official status in modern Cambodia. Some Khmer Rouge-era Moslem Cham refugees from Cambodia are now settled in Malaysia, where they also speak Malay. There is also an old Cham neighborhood of Bangkok, war captives brought there in the mid-19th century from northeastern Cambodia; they remain Moslem and are aware of their Cham origins, but speak only Thai.

Chru **[62]** Vietnam: southern, inland from Phan Rang around Malam. About 11,000 group members, recognised as the Chíuru ethnic group of Vietnam. Romanised materials prepared pre-1975, not now in use. This language, like Roglai to its northeast, is in decline, being replaced by Vietnamese in many domains, and is potentially endangered.

Ríoglai **[63]** Vietnam: southern; west of Nha Trang to north of Phan Thet inland from the coast About 45,000 ethnic group members speaking two distinct languages, ***Northern Ríoglai*** (25,000) and ***Southern Ríoalai*** (20,000). Romanised materials exist but are not in use. The languages are both potentially endangered by Vietnamese.

Utsat (***Tsat***, ***Huihui***) **[64]** China: Hainan Province, Sanya County, Huihui and Huixin villages. About 5,000 group members and under 4,000 speakers who are Moslem and classified as members of the Hui (non-Turkic Moslem) nationality. Utsat or Tsat is their own name. They arrived by sea from what is now southern Vietnam. Thurgood and Li (2003) date the first migration to 982 AD, with a second migration about 1471 AD. The language is closest to Northern Roglai, but quite divergent from all other Chamic languages, having developed tones under the influence or contact with Chinese. It is potentially endangered, with everyone also speaking Hainanese Min and/or Cantonese Chinese and using Mandarin Chinese for education and other formal purposes.

Tai-Kadai

Kadai

Buyang **[65]** China: Yunnan, Wenshan Prefecture. *Eastern Kadai*. Many of over 3,000 Buyang people classified in the Zhuang nationality speak four quite different varieties of Buyang. In 9 villages of Gula Township of Funing County: 300 in Langjia, 200 in Ecun, 200 in Maguan, 180 in Lagan, 50 in Nongna and so on. Some scholars separate the Paha variety and treat it as the sole language in a separate Central subgroup of Kadai, linking other types of Buyang and Pubiao to each other in the Eastern subgroup and only then with Paha. All types of Buyang are endangered.

Gelao (***Aqaw***, ***Gao***) **[66]** China: western central Guizhou Province. *Western Kadai*. One of the major components of the Golao nationality of China; this is the best-described Kadai language. It is spoken only by a few elderly individuals in various rural areas of Pingba and Puding counties, and formerly in Anshun, Zhijin and Shuicheng counties and Luzhi City. The ethnic group is very much more numerous. Moribund.

Gelao (***Green***, ***Hagei***, ***Ho Ki***) **[67]** China: Guizhou Province, central, from north to south; also in Guangxi and in Ha Giang Province of Vietnam. *Western Kadai*. One of the components of the Gelao nationality of China and the Kíolao ethnic group of Vietnam. There are only about 2,000 speakers split into groups based in Guanling County, and others in Renhuan and Qinglong counties. Nearly all other Green Gelao, elsewhere in China and in Vietnam, speak only other languages; however, there is one village with two elderly speakers in Longlin County, Guangxi Province. Thus, the language is extinct in most locations and severely endangered where it is still spoken.

Gelao (***Red***, ***A-uo***, ***A-ou***, ***Voa De***) **[68]** China: Guizhou Province, northwestern; Vietnam: Ha Giang Province. *Western Kadai*. One of the components of the Gelao nationality

405

of China and the Kíolao ethnic group of Vietnam. Only a few speakers remain in rural areas of Liuzhi City and Zhenning County; in Zhijin, Qianxi and Dafang counties, despite the presence of over 100,000 members of the Gelao nationality; the language has been replaced by Chinese. In Vietnam about 30 semispeakers who call themselves 'Vanto' live in one Kíolao community of 400. The language is extinct in most places and moribund in the few where it is still known.

Gelao (*White, Duoluo, Tu Du*) [69] China: Guizhou Province, Liupanshui City, etc. Vietnam, Ha Giang Province. *Western Kadai.* One of the components of the Gelao nationality of China and the Kíolao ethnic group of Vietnam. About 3,000 speakers remain, including under 1,000 in Guizhou, the Chinese rendering of the name of this group is Duoluo; the Vietnamese term Tu Du derives from the name used by White Gelao in Vietnam. There is one village of speakers in Longlin County, Guangxi Province, and a further cluster of 1,500 group members in Malipo County, Yunnan Province, with 400 more nearby in Vietnam. Whilst being the least endangered Gelao language, it is nevertheless extinct in most places and severely endangered or endangered where it is still spoken.

Lachi (*Lati*) [70] Vietnam: Ha Giang Province. *Western Kadai.* A recognised ethnic group of Vietnam, closely related to the Laji of China. The census total for the Lachi is 7,863, but only about 5,000 can speak the language, concentrated in and around Phung village; it is endangered.

Laha (*Khla Phlao*) [71] Vietnam: Síon La and Lao Cai provinces. *Southern Kadai.* A recognised ethnic group of 2,100 people in Vietnam; their speech has two rather distinct varieties: in one village in Síon La Province, it is moribund, spoken only by those over 50; while in several villages in Lao Cai it is still spoken but potentially endangered.

Laji [72] China: Yunnan Province, Maguan County. *Western Kadai.* A group of 1,643 included in the Yi nationality, closely related to the Lachi who are a recognised ethnic group of Vietnam. Of the Laji, only about 200 still speak the language, which is moribund.

Mulao (*Ayo, Mulao Jia*) [73] China: Guizhou Province, Majiang County and surrounding areas. *Eastern Kadai.* A scattered group of about 20,000 people, in six counties of eastern central Guizhou, mostly in the 'unclassified nationality' group but a few classified in Mulao, the Mulam Kam-Sui nationality of northern Guangxi. Much of the group speaks only Chinese or other minority languages, language uninvestigated and severely endangered.

Nung Ven (*Ainh*) [74] Vietnam: Ha Giang Province. *Eastern Kadai.* One village of 200 in Vietnam speaking a Kadai language which is potentially endangered but better maintained than most other Kadai languages of that country.

Pubiao (*Bubiao, Pu Peo, Ka Beo, Laqua*) [75] China: Yunnan Province, Malipo County; Dong Van district, Ha Giang Province, Vietnam. *Eastern Kadai.* Recognised as the Pupeo ethnic group of Vietnam, included within the Yi nationality of China. Of

307 in China, about 50 speak the language. Of 382 in Vietnam, most can speak it. The language is thus severely endangered in China and endangered in Vietnam.

Qaw **[76]** China: Sichuan Province, Gulin County and Guizhou Province, Bijie County. *Western Kadai*. The northernmost Kadai language, with about 3,000 group members but few if any elderly speakers left. They are classified as members of the Gelao nationality; not to be confused with the TB-speaking members of the Yi nationality elsewhere in Sichuan Province. Moribund or extinct.

Yerong (***Daban Yao***) **[77]** China: Guangxi Province, Napo County. *Eastern Kadai*. This group of over 300 people are classified in the Yao nationality, but speak a Kadai language; some Buyang also speak Yerong. Not related to Yao, including the Daban Yao of southwestern Yunnan who speak Iu Mien Yao. Endangered.

Kam-Sui

Lajia (***Lakkia***) **[78]** China: east central Guangxi Province, Jinxiu County. 12,000 group members, included in Yao nationality, about 9,000 speakers, many also able to speak Chinese, but not nearby languages of the Miao and other Yao nationality members. Endangered.

Mak (***Mo***) **[79]** China: south central Guizhou Province, northwestern part of Libo County. Kam-Sui. 10,000 group members, all classified as part of the Bouyei nationality, but only about 5,000 speakers, also able to speak Bouyei and Chinese. Endangered.

Maonan **[80]** China: north central Guangxi Province, Huanjiang County and surrounding areas. Kam-Sui. A separate recognized nationality, population 107,166, but far fewer speakers. Potentially endangered.

Mulam (***Mulao***) **[81]** China: north central Guangxi Province, mainly Luocheng County. Kam-Sui. One of China's 55 recognised nationalities; population 207,352 but only about 30,000 speakers. Distinct from the Kadai group Mulao, written with a different first character; but a few Kadai Mulao speakers have been included in the Mulam/Mulao nationality. Endangered.

Rao (***Ten***, ***Yanghuang***) **[82]** China: south central Guizhou Province, Pingtang County, also some in Huishui and Dushan counties. Classified within the Bouyei nationality; 25,000 members of the ethnic group, but only about 20,000 speakers; most also speak local Chinese and Bouyei. Yanghuang is the name used by outsiders to refer to the group. Endangered.

Tai

Saek **[83]** Laos: northwestern areas of Khammouane Province; Thailand: 5 villages in the northeast of Nakorn Phanom Province; perhaps also in China. *Northern Tai*. About 20,000 group members, but only about 10,000 speakers, mainly in Laos; transported as war captives several centuries ago from southwestern China into southern Laos, and some later into Thailand. Uncertain whether the language survives in China, severely endangered in Thailand, endangered in Laos.

***Tai Daeng* [84]** Vietnam: western Thanh Hoa Province; Laos: southeastern Houaphan Province. *Southwestern Tai*. About 100,000 or less group members, fewer than 80,000 speakers; the name means 'red Tai'. Classified within the Thai ethnic group of Vietnam group (of which they are a small part; that also includes the much larger Tai Dam 'black Tai' and Tai Khaw 'white Tai' groups) and part of the composite Phu Tai group in Laos, also scattered across southern Laos. Potentially endangered in traditional territory, endangered elsewhere.

***Tai Neua* [85]** Laos: northeastern Houaphan Province, also scattered to the southwest across central Laos and mixed with related groups within the amalgamated but diverse Phu Tai group in southern Laos. *Southwestern Tai*. About 95,000 group members, mainly outside the traditional area, but fewer than 70,000 can speak; most strongly influenced by Lao. Their name means 'northern Tai', and also reflects the name of the capital of Houaphan Province, Samneua, where their traditional territory lies; potentially endangered to endangered. There is another different Southwestern Tai group with the same name in Lincang Prefecture of southwest central Yunnan in China whose quite different language is not endangered.

TAI LANGUAGES OF NE INDIA (ALL ARE SOUTHWESTERN TAI)

***Ahom* [87]** India: Assam, eastern plains. Formerly the language of the Ahom kingdom, which ruled Assam from the 14th century to the 1820s; about a million ethnic group members, including much of the elite and many landowners of eastern Assam. Extinct as a spoken language, having been replaced by Assamese nearly 200 years ago; but many manuscripts survive and a priestly tradition of chanting them continues, for example in several villages just east of Sibsagar. Attempts to revive the spoken language are underway, with the assistance of scholars from the Aiton and Phake communities who speak closely related languages.

***Aiton* (*Sham Doaniya*) [88]** India: Assam, Golaghat and Karbi Anglong districts along Dhonsiri River. Spoken by more than a thousand group members in eight villages, including some non-Aiton who have moved into their villages as labourers. The term Sham Doaniya means 'Shan interpreters' in Assamese, but this term is not now in use; nowadays Doania refers instead to Singpho in Tinsukia District. Many manuscripts survive, and the language is still learned by children. Potentially endangered, but currently undergoing a revival of cultural activity.

***Khamti* (*Khampti*) [89]** Burma: northwestern; India: Assam and Arunachal Pradesh, northeastern. About 25,000 speakers in Burma; some 5,000 in India in about 40 villages, the latter mainly in the southwest of Lohit District near Tezu but south of the Lohit River, and extending into adjacent areas of Tirap District; also at least eight villages in Lakhimpur District of Assam, including one mixed with Phake. Their name means 'gold place'. Khamti is verb-final, unlike all other related languages but like the surrounding TB languages. Potentially endangered; all speakers bilingual.

Khamyang **[90]** India: Assam, Tinsukia District Spoken by about 50 people over 40 in Pawaimukh village, moribund. All speakers are bilingual in Assamese which is replacing Khamyang. Some believe that it is the sole modern remnant of Nora, and indeed the Assamese use the term Nora to refer to the Khamyang.

Nora (*Tai Nora*) **[91]** India: Assam. About 300 speakers remained a century ago; became extinct during 20th century, replaced by Assamese. Khamyang is thought by some to be a modern survivor of Nora.

Phake (*Tai Phakial*) **[92]** India: Assam, Dibrugarh and Tinsukia districts; Arunachal Pradesh, Tirap District. About 2,000 speakers in 11 villages, including children. One village is also partly Khamti. Potentially endangered, but there is a flowering of activity focussed on the numerous Phake traditional manuscripts.

Tairong **[93]** India: Assam, Jorhat and Golaghat districts. Extinct, though limited data were collected in the early 20th century when it was still spoken. However, in its six or more villages this group now speaks a divergent variety of Singpho, a TB language, with some Tai lexicon and a distinctive tone system; so modern spoken Tairong (also known as Turung) should instead be classified within Singpho/Jinghpaw/Jingpo of northern Burma, western Yunnan in China, and northeastern India.

Miao-Yao (Hmong-Mien)

Baheng (*Pa Then*) **[94]** China: SE Guizhou and NE Guangxi provinces; also in Vietnam. About 45,000 in China, of whom 30,000 speak the language, and are classified in the Bunu subgroup of the Yao nationality. One of four languages related to but distinct from Bunu proper; the others are Younuo, Ngnai and Jiongnai. Two distinct dialects or languages, *Northern* as spoken only by about 4,000 people in Liping County, Guizhou Province, and *Southern* as spoken by those in Congjiang and Rongjiang counties of Guizhou, in four counties of NE Guangxi, notably Sanjiang County, and by the 3,700 Pà Then in Vietnam, where they are recognized as a separate ethnic group. Potentially endangered.

Dongmeng **[95]** China: SE Guizhou. About 600 people in Weng'ang, Dongtang and Maolan townships, in the SE of Libo County. One of four core Bunu subgroups; the others are Bunu, Baonao and Numao. Known in Chinese as Changpao Yao 'long skirt Yao', also formerly known as Beidongnuo; not to be confused with the Western Miao subgroup Hmong. Some mutual intelligibility with Numao; classified as Yao nationality; for details see Niederer (2002). Endangered.

Jiongnai **[96]** China: E Guangxi Province, Jinxiu County. One of four languages related to but distinct from Bunu proper. Known as Hualan Yao 'flower blue Yao' in Chinese. About 1,500 group members of Yao nationality, mainly speakers. 'Kiong people'. Endangered.

Ngnai Wunai **[97]** China: SW Hunan, scattered over six counties. One of four languages related to but distinct from Bunu proper. Known as Huayi Yao 'flower shirt Yao' in Chinese. 8,000 group members included in the Yao nationality. Most can speak the language; autonym [hm nai] 'Hm people'. Endangered.

409

Numao [98] China: SE Guizhou Province, Libo County. About 1,500 people in Yaolu Township, E of Libo. One of four core Bunu subgroups, classified in the Yao nationality. Own name [nu hmou], also known in Chinese as Heiku Yao 'black trouser Yao'. Some mutual intelligibility with Dongmeng, but not with other Bunu languages. Endangered.

She [99] China: south central Guangdong Province. 709,592 members of this recognized nationality of China, scattered over the highlands of five southeastern provinces; but only about 1,000 speakers, calling themselves [huo nte] and concentrated in Boluo, Zengcheng, Huidong and Haifeng counties, all within 100 km north or northeast of Hong Kong; the other She mainly speak Hakka Chinese as their first language, and other Chinese languages as well. Extinct in most locations, moribund or severely endangered in all others.

Younuo [100] China: NE Guangxi Province, Longsheng and Xing'an counties. One of four languages related to but distinct from Bunu proper. Known as Hong Yao 'red Yao' in Chinese. About 4,000 members of this group, mainly able to speak their language; own name [ju nuo] 'Yu people'. Endangered.

Austroasiatic

Mon-Khmer

ASLIAN

Batek [101] Malaysia: northeast peninsular, W. Trengganu. *Northern Aslian*. Some 960 group members; various dialects including sw Mintil, SE Batek Igaq, NE Batek Teq, C Batek Deq and far S Batek Nong; also other extinct dialects including far S Batek Hapen. Close contact and intermarriage between dialects and with adjacent Mendriq, Temiar, Semai, Semaq Beri and so on; speakers accommodate readily to other Aslian languages and dialects. All speakers also speak Malay, and many use Temiar as a lingua franca; language endangered.

Besisi (*Mah Meri*) [102] Malaysia, southwest peninsular, along coast of Selangor and formerly as far south as Melaka and as far inland as Kuala Lumpur. *Southern Aslian*. Currently 2,185 group members, but many do not speak the language; northern Betisek and southern Sisik dialects; Mah Meri is an autonym. Swamped by Malay, all speakers are bilingual and the language is severely endangered; several dialects are already extinct.

Chewong [103] Malaysia: central peninsular, E of Raub. *Northern Aslian*. About 400 group members, two dialects, western Kled and eastern Chewong. Some contact with adjacent Jah Het, Batek and Semaq Beri. All speakers also speak Malay; language endangered.

Jah Het [104] Malaysia: central peninsular, near Temerloh and Jerantut. *Central Aslian* (but some prefer to classify it as a fourth independent branch of Aslian). 3,193 group members, to the east of the Batek Nong and Chewong, west of the Semaq Beri and north of the Semelai. The extinct Kenaboi language, an Aslian language with extensive Malay influence, was formerly spoken to its southwest. All speakers also speak Malay; language endangered.

Jehai (*Jahai*) [105] Thailand: southern, sw Narathiwat Province; Malaysia, northeastern peninsular, around Belum. *Northern Aslian*. About 1200 group members, including 1049 in Malaysia. Includes southeastern Batek Teh dialect which is more similar to the rest of Jehai than to the rest of Batek. Close contact and intermarriage between dialects and with adjacent Kensiu, Mendriq and Temiar; speakers accommodate readily to other Aslian languages and dialects. All speakers also speak Malay; language endangered.

Kenaboi [106] Malaysia: central peninsular, SE of Kuala Lumpur. Language extinct late 19th century; the final stage of the language as recorded then showed very extensive Malay lexical influence and an unidentified stratum in one source which was neither Malay nor Aslian, perhaps a taboo language, leading some scholars to classify it as a language isolate. Recent work by Hajek on the available data suggests that it was an Aslian language heavily influenced by Malay; *classification uncertain*, possibly another branch of Aslian or intermediate between Southern and Central.

Kensiu [107] Thailand: southern, Betong; Malaysia: northwest peninsular, near Baling. *Northern Aslian*. About 500 group members, about half each in Thailand and Malaysia, four distinct dialects (Batuq, Siong, Nakil, Bong) of hunter-gatherer bands. Numerous other extinct dialects further west, formerly extending to the coast across from Penang. Close contact and intermarriage between dialects and with adjacent Jehai, Lanoh and Temiar; speakers accommodate readily to other Aslian languages and dialects. All speakers also speak Malay; many in Thailand also speak Southern Thai; language endangered.

Kintaq [108] Malaysia: northwest peninsular, around Baling. *Northern Aslian*. About 235 group members, in close contact with Kensiu of which it is sometimes considered a dialect. Close contact and intermarriage with adjacent Kensiu, Jehai, Lanoh and Temiar; speakers accommodate readily to other Aslian languages and dialects. All speakers also speak Malay; language endangered.

Lanoh [109] Malaysia: northwest peninsular, north of Kota Tampin. *Central Aslian*. About 350 group members. Close contact and intermarriage with adjacent Kensiu, Jehai and Temiar; speakers accommodate readily to other Aslian languages. All speakers also speak Malay, and many use Temiar as a lingua franca; language endangered.

Maniq (*Tonga'*, *Mos*, *Ten'en*) [110] Thailand: southern, Satun Province. *Northern Aslian*. At least 300 group members with five distinct dialects in separate nomadic hunter-gatherer bands. Intermarriage between bands leads to extensive dialect contact. All speakers speak Southern Thai and many speak local Malay, and the language as well as the survival of the communities in their traditional lifestyle is endangered.

Mendriq (*Menriq*) [111] Malaysia: northeast peninsular, Bertam area. *Northern Aslian*. About 145 group members. Sometimes treated as a dialect of Jehai; close contact and intermarriage with adjacent Jehai, Batek, and Temiar; speakers accommodate readily

411

to other Aslian languages and dialects. All speakers also speak Malay, and many use Temiar as a lingua franca; language endangered.

Semai (Senoi, Sengoi) [112] Malaysia: central peninsular, near and south of Cameron Highlands. *Central Aslian*. Nearly 29,000 group members, over 26,000 in traditional areas. Has a very large number of small localised dialects, most with fewer than a thousand speakers, and many extinct dialects further west and south. The Cameron Highlands dialect is used on the radio and is a school language, as well as being the lingua franca of the Aslian military unit in the Malaysian armed forces. All speakers are bilingual in Malay, and the language is endangered.

Semaq Beri [113] Malaysia: eastern highlands, w of Kuantan. *Southern Aslian*. 2,488 group members, but not all speak the language. In contact with Northern Aslian Batek and Chewong to its northwest, and with Central Aslian Jah Het to its southwest. It covers a large territory, as large as that of Semai, but has less dialect differentiation. All speakers are bilingual in Malay, and the language is endangered.

Semelai [114] Malaysia: south central peninsular, southeast of Temerloh. *Southern Aslian*. 4,103 group members. Apart from Semelai proper which has most of the remaining speakers, the Temoq dialect has a few hundred. No longer spoken in some southern and southwestern areas of former traditional territory. All speakers are bilingual in Malay, and the language is endangered.

Temiar [115] Malaysia: north central highlands, NE of Ipoh. *Central Aslian*. About 17,000 group members, including over 15,000 living in traditional areas, with three main dialects: northern, southern and northwestern Lanoh Kobak, which is a dialect of Temiar, not of Lanoh. Intermarriage with other Aslian groups gives some speakers knowledge of other Aslian languages; however Temiar is used as a lingua franca by many Northern Aslian groups and at a government hospital provided for all Aslian groups; it is also a school language with limited literacy materials. All speakers also speak Malay; the language is losing domains, and is potentially endangered although it is the most secure Aslian language.

Katuic-Bahnaric

Katuic

Chatong [116] Laos: Xekong Province, Kaluem District. NE *Katuic*. 580 group members in 4 villages, most speaking this language recently located by Thai linguist Theraphan Luangthongkum. Endangered.

Dakkang [117] Laos: Xekong Province, Dakchueng District. SE *Katuic*. 1,198 group members in 8 villages, mainly able to speak this language recently located by Thai linguist Theraphan Luangthongkum. Endangered.

Triw [118] Laos: Xekong Province, Dakchueng District. SE *Katuic*. 1,328 group members in 9 villages, of whom most speak this language recently located by Thai linguist Theraphan Luangthongkum. Endangered.

Bahnaric

Chrau (*Chíoro*) **[119]** Vietnam: southern. *South Bahnaric*. About 15,000 members of this officially recognized ethnic group, the southernmost Bahnaric language, but far fewer speakers because of its location just to the east of Saigon. Becoming endangered.

Juk (*Suai*) **[120]** Laos: Xekong Province, Thataeng District. *West Bahnaric*. About 1,500 in 3 villages, not the same as the Western Katuic Kui language, also known as Suai in Thai. Most are speakers of this language recently located by Thai linguist Theraphan Luangthongkum. Endangered.

Kaco' **[121]** Cambodia: northeastern Virochey Province. *North Bahnaric*. About 1,000 group members located by Gerard Diffloth; formerly misidentified as Lamam, a clan name among this and some surrounding groups. Endangered.

Swoeng (*Lavi*) **[122]** Laos: Xekong Province, Lamam District. *West Bahnaric*. The Swoeng (autonym) or Lavi should not be confused with the Loven further south. There are 492 group members in 3 villages, mostly speaking this language recently located by Thai linguist Theraphan Luangthongkum. Endangered.

Northern

Angkuic

Hu **[123]** China: Yunnan, Shuangjiang County, Shahe Township. Classified as Bulang nationality, but far from the main concentration of Bulang in Menghai County on the Burmese border further south. About 700 speakers in two villages with about 1,400 people; endangered.

Mok (*Tai Loi*) **[124]** Burma: eastern Shan State; Laos, Namtha Province. Tai Loi means 'hill Tai' in local Tai languages. Scattered in northeastern Kengtung in the eastern Shan State, with one village near Kengtung town and some also further south and in extreme northwestern Namtha Province of Laos, and one village in Thailand. Population uncertain, speakers have very low status locally, language endangered. Also spoken in China, where it is included in the Bulang nationality.

Palaungic

Danau **[125]** Burma: southwestern Shan State, to the northwest of Inle Lake. Also written Danaw. Reported as moribund forty years ago, but still spoken by a few thousand members of this group in three villages: Taungpawhla just northwest of Inle Lake, Esaya on the road from the lake north to Taunggyi, and Kunpawagyi further west, also a few families in other villages such as Nyaungkun near Heho further west. Surrounded, influenced and being replaced by various TB languages. Severely endangered.

413

Waic

Phalok (***Mae Rim Lawa***) **[126]** Thailand: Chiangmai Province, west of Mae Rim District. About 200 group members, but language moribund or extinct.

Lavüa (***Lawa***) **[127]** Thailand: Mae Sariang and Hot districts of southwestern Chiangmai Province. Roughly 20,000 group members, but many do not speak the language, and all are bilingual in Northern Thai, with most also having knowledge of Central Thai. Endangered.

Khmuic

Iduh (***Tai Hat***, ***Hat***) **[128]** Vietnam: western Thanh Hoa Province; Laos: northeastern Xieng Khouang Province. A group of about 200, of whom only some 30 middle-aged and elderly people can still speak the language; believed to be an eastern dialect of Khmu until recent fieldwork by Gerard Diffloth. Severely endangered.

Mlabri (***Phi Tong Luang***, ***Yumbri, Mrabri***) **[129]** Laos: western Saignabouri Province; Thailand: northeastern Nan Province. Phi Tong Luang means 'spirits of the yellow leaves' in Thai and Lao, and refers to their hunter-gatherer lifestyle. Mrabri and Yumbri are other renderings of the group's own name. A group of about 150 speakers, disrupted by conflict along the Thai/Lao border where they lived. Some have now settled down; and are assimilating into nearby Hmong/Meo and Thai/Lao groups. Only about 100 still speak the language, with two lexically-distinct dialects, one much more endangered than the other, and some extinct dialects. Endangered.

Pasing (***Kha Bit***, ***Bit***) **[130]** Laos: one small area in northeastern Luang Namtha Province and one in south central Phongsaly Province; also an even smaller cluster in southeastern Mengla County of Yunnan in China. Group total population 1,732 in Laos and about 500 more in China; speaker population under a thousand. Endangered.

Pakanic

Bugan (***Pakan***, ***Pukan***) **[131]** China: southeast Yunnan, south Guangnan and north Xichou counties. Recently located language, seven villages with a group population of 3,000. Gérard Diffloth suggests it forms a subgroup of MK with Lai and Mang. Endangered.

Lai (***Paliu***) **[132]** China: northwest Guangxi Province, north central Longlin County. Group population 1,771; only about 500 speakers; Paliu is the group's own name. The northeasternmost MK language; a subgroup with Bugan and Mang. Severely endangered.

Mang **[133]** Vietnam: northern Lai Chau Province; China: Yunnan Province, Jinping County, southern Mengla Township. Group population 2,300 in Vietnam, 1,216 in China, but less than half are speakers. Recognised as an ethnic group of Vietnam, unclassified in China. Severely endangered.

Monic

***Mon* [134]** Burma: Mon State; Thailand: central. Various dialects; extensive ancient inscriptions and literature, now at risk. Formerly the dominant language of the Lop-buri and Dvaravati kingdoms of central Thailand, conquered by the Khmers around the 7th century and then by the Thais in the 13th; also the language of the Mon kingdom of Lower Burma, conquered in the 11th century by the Burmans but influencing them greatly. In addition to a very large ethnic group of over a million people (more than 800,000 in Burma and the rest in Thailand), a large part of the Thai population of the central plains and the Burman population of southeastern Burma doubtless has Mon ethnic antecedents. Most of the Mons in central Thailand who retain their ethnic identity migrated from Burma, either in the late 18th and early 19th century to serve the Thai kings, or in the late 20th century escaping turmoil in Burma. Among the former group, the language is moribund to extinct; among the latter, and about half of the ethnic group in Burma, it is surviving with reduced domains and low status, Despite its large speaker population, potentially endangered.

***Nyahkur* [135]** Thailand: northeastern, southern Phetchabun, western Chaiyaphum and northwestern Korat provinces. Ethnic group of about 20,000, very widely dispersed in the low hills between the central plain and the northeastern plateau of Thailand; remnant of the Mon of the Dvaravati kingdom. Spoken by about 10,000 of the ethnic group, including a few children, especially in Chaiyaphum Province; but most of the young are semispeakers at best. Severely endangered.

Pearic

***Chong* [136]** Thailand: Chantaburi Province, Makham and Phongnamrawn districts. Three dialects. Total about 2,000 group members, all speakers of Thai. It has the largest number of contrastive phonation types found in any language, four; most other Pearic languages also have similarly elaborate systems, but they have not been as well described. Severely endangered, about 500 Chong speakers remain, with the youngest speaker of any dialect in their 20s.

***Chu-ng* ('*Sa-och*', *Sa-ong*, *Khamen Padong*) [137]** Cambodia: Kompong Som Province, near Veal Rinh; Thailand: Kanchanaburi Province, Srisawat District, Tha Thungna village. 43 speakers in Cambodia in the early 1880s, 17 speakers (three families) in the 1990s; also 150 in Thailand, including 20 speakers, about half fluent, with the youngest semispeakers now approaching 40. Known as Chu'ung, Sa-ong or Khamen Padong ('Padong Khmer') in Thailand; the Khmer name Sa-och is a kind of skin disease in Khmer, and is greatly resented by the group. The speakers in Thailand were transported as war captives in 1833, but some escaped the Thais and remained behind or later returned. All speakers in Cambodia are bilingual in Khmer, and all in Thailand speak Thai. Despite the very small speaker population, the language is still transmitted to children and used as an in-group language in Cambodia and is only potentially endangered, while in Thailand it is moribund.

***'Pear'* [138]** Cambodia: Preah Vihar Province, Rovieng District. Three or four villages, population reduced from about 1,000 people pre-1975 to perhaps 250 now.

Autonym unknown, but still reported as spoken; likely to be endangered or severely endangered.

***Samre* (*East Pear*) [139]** Cambodia: Pursat Province, west. About 200 group members, half post-1975 refugees in Thailand. Of those in Thailand, fewer than 20 speak the language, the youngest approaching 50. Moribund in Thailand, severely endangered in Cambodia.

***Samre of Siem Riep* [140]** Cambodia: Siem Riep Province. Extinct by the 1940s; replaced by Khmer.

***Samre/Samray* (*West Pear*) [141]** Cambodia: Battambang Province, southwest. Several distinct dialects. 'Reported as nearly exterminated by the Khmer Rouge; two speakers in a refugee camp in Thailand in the early 1980s, present whereabouts unknown. Probably extinct.

***Song* (*Kasong*, *Chong of Trat*) [142]** Thailand: Trat Province, east. Group population 200, 40 speakers, the youngest in their 30s. Distinct language often confused with Chong. Severely endangered, being replaced by Thai.

***Su'ung* (*Souy*) [143]** Cambodia: Kompong Speu Province. Fewer than 500 in group, many non-speakers. Most relocated from Phnom Aural nearer to Kompong Speu in the 1990s. All speakers bilingual in Khmer, endangered.

Vietic

***Arem* [144]** Vietnam: western Quang Binh Province; Laos: eastern Khammouan Province. *Western Vietic*. Under 1,000 group members, fewer than one hundred speakers. Included in the Chíut ethnic minority in Vietnam, formerly hunter-gatherers. Severely endangered.

***Hung* [145]** Vietnam: western Thanh Hoa Province. *Western Vietic*. Fewer than 1,000 group members, about half able to speak. Very closely related to Pong and Tum. Endangered.

***Kri* [146]** Laos: southeastern Borikhan Province. *Western Vietic*. A very small group, estimated at only 31 people; closely related to Maleng/Pakatan and the Vietic Phong. Severely endangered.

***Maleng* (*Pakatan*, 'Harème') [147]** Laos: northeastern Khammouan Province. *Western Vietic*. Under 1,000 group members, about half able to speak it. Pakatan is a village name for one of about ten villages of this group; an old French source also describes this group under the name Harème, derived from the Bru (Katuic) term for all the small Western VM groups; not the same as Arem. Closely related to Kri and the Vietic Phong. Endangered.

***May* [148]** Vietnam: western Quang Binh Province; Laos: eastern Khammouan Province. *Western Vietic*. Over 1,000 group members including 904 in Vietnam, about half speakers. Very closely related to Ruc and Sach. Former hunter-gathers included in the Chíut ethnic minority in Vietnam. Endangered.

***Nguon* [149]** Vietnam: western Quang Binh Province; Laos: southeastern Khammouan Province. *Miuíong subgroup language*. Some 2,000 group members, about half speakers. Potentially endangered.

***Phonsung* (*Aheu*) [150]** Laos: northeastern Khammouan Province, southeastern Borikhan Province. *Western Vietic*. Roughly 500 group members, about half able to speak; Phonsung is the name of a village where they formerly lived. Endangered.

***Phong* [151]** Laos: southeastern Borikhan Province. *Western Vietic*. Small group of a few hundred, only some able to speak. Distinct from various Khmuic groups further north also called Phong, from the Tay Poong who speak a Miuíong subgroup language and are included in the Thô ethnic minority in Vietnam, and from the Pong of the Central Hung/Tum/Pong cluster; this Phong is closely related to Kri and Maleng. Endangered.

***Pong* (*Poong*) [152]** Laos: northeastern Borikhan Province; also adjacent areas of Vietnam. *Western Vietic*. Some 3,000 group members, about half speakers; very closely related to Hung and Tum. Distinct from Khmuic Phong, Miuíong group Tay Poong and the Phong of the Western Vietic Maleng/Phong/Kri cluster. Endangered.

***Ruc* [153]** Vietnam: western Tuyen Hoa Province; Laos: eastern Khammouan Province. *Western Vietic*. About 500 group members including 189 in Vietnam; about half speakers. Very closely related to May and Sach. Included in the Chíut ethnic minority in Vietnam, and formerly hunter-gatherers. Sometimes called Kha Tong Luang ('slaves of the yellow leaves') in Laos, not to be confused with the Mlabri. Endangered.

***Sach* [154]** Vietnam: southwestern Quang Binh Province and adjacent areas of Laos. *Western Vietic*. About 1,000 group members, about half speakers. Very closely related to May and Ruc. Included in the Chu't ethnic minority in Vietnam, former hunter-gatherers; sometimes called Kha Tong Luang in Laos; not to be confused with the Mlabri. Endangered.

***Thavung* (*Ahlao, Ahao*) [155]** Laos: southeastern Borikhan Province; Thailand: Sakorn Nakorn Province, Pathum-wapi Subdistrict, 3 villages. *Western Vietic*. About 1,500 group members, some 450 speakers. Ahlao and Ahao are their autonyms. Severely endangered in Thailand, where they are locally called So (the name of a much larger Katuic group); also endangered in Laos.

***Tum* [156]** Laos: southeastern Borikhan Province. *Western Vietic*. 2,042 group members, about half speakers. Very closely related to Hung and Pong. Endangered.

Ainu

***Ainu* [157]** Japan: Hokkaido; formerly also northern Honshu in Japan, and further north in the Kurile Islands and southern Kamchatka, Russia. *Isolate*. Official census

417

population 23,830 but actual population estimated over 100,000; about ten fluent speakers over 70, some additional semi-speakers over 60, small numbers of younger Ainu learning the language in classes. All southern dialects and probably the north-eastern Hokkaido dialects extinct. Sakhalin dialects displaced to Japan 1945, extinct 1994. Southwestern Hokkaido subdialects (including the Saru variety in the Biratori town area, which has 39 percent of the officially acknowledged Ainu population, and nearby, the Shizunai, Chitose and Horobetsu varieties where a further 31 per cent of the Ainu live) have a few speakers each, but revival efforts are underway, especially since a new 1997 law recognising the cultural rights of the Ainu. Moribund, but with some younger heritage speakers including children.

Mongolic

Bonan (*Bao'an*) **[158]** China: Qinghai and Gansu provinces. Of the 16,505 members of the nationality officially known as Bao'an, fewer than 10,000 can speak the language. About two-thirds live in southwestern Gansu and are Moslem, while one-third live nearby in Tongren County of Qinghai Province and follow Tibetan Buddhism. *Gansu Bonan* is heavily influenced by and being replaced by Chinese; **Qinghai Bonan** is strongly influenced by Tibetan. There is some mutual intelligibility between Bonan, Kangjia and adjacent varieties of southern Monguor (official nationality name Tu). Endangered.

Kangjia [159] China: Qinghai, Tongren County. About half of 2,000 members of the Hui (Moslem) naitonality (also known as Tongren Turen 'original inhabitants of Tongren') in the Kangyang area of Tongren County speak this Mongolic language which is only described very briefly. The name means 'Kang family' and refers to their usual surname, Kang. Very closely related to Bonan and Monguor (Tu). Severely endangered.

Santa (*Dongxiang*) **[160]** China: NW Gansu. The Chinese name for this nationality, Dongxiang, means 'east township'. 513,805 people, but only about 200,000 speakers. This language is losing ground to Chinese more rapidly than nearby Monguor (Tu). Potentially endangered.

Yugur, Eastern (*Shira* or *Enger Yugur*) **[161]** China: Gansu Province. Over 6,000 group members including 4,000 speakers live in Sunun County of northern Gansu and sur-rounding areas. They are officially linked with the Turkic-speaking Western Yugur in the Yugur nationality, with 13,719 people in total. A few Yugur in Dahe Township can speak both the Turkic Western Yugur language and the Mongolic Eastern Yugur language, but this is unusual. Endangered.

Turkic

Yugur, Western (*Saryg Yugur*) **[162]** China: Gansu Province, to north and west of the Eastern Yugur. Over 7,000 group members (part of the 13,719 Yugur nationality) and about 4,600 speakers live in northern and western Sunun County and into the south of Jiuquan city further northwest; sometimes known as Yellow Uighur. Both Yugur groups are Tibetan Buddhist, but also have some indigenous shamanic traditions. Endangered.

Manchu-Tungus (Tungusic)

Ewenk (*Manchurian Reindeer Tungus*) **[163]** China: northeastern Inner Mongolia. Total of 30,505 members of the Ewenke nationality, but most speak varieties of Solon; less than 1,000 of those in the Chen Barag Banner speak Ewenk, which is also spoken in eastern Russia. Some scholars regard this, Khamnigan, Solon and Oroqen as part of a dialect chain extending into eastern Russia. Severely endangered in China.

Hezhe (*Nanai*, *Goldi*) **[164]** China: Heilongjiang Province, northeast. 4,640 group members in China. More widely spoken in eastern Russia where classified as the Nanai nationality, also formerly called Goldi; known as Hezhe in Chinese. Fewer than 40 elderly speakers in three villages in Tongjiang and Raohe counties; about half speak Kilen and half speak Nanai, both with considerably more speakers in eastern Russia. Youngest speakers in China now over 60, moribund in China.

Khamnigan [165] China: northeastern Inner Mongolia; Mongolia: northeastern central. Small population of speakers of dialects of Ewenk, included with Solon and Ewenk proper in Ewenke nationality of China. Speakers also speak Khamnigan Mongol; uncertain whether those in Mongolia still speak Ewenk at all. This is also the Mongol term for all Ewenk. Status unknown in Mongolia, severely endangered in China.

Manchu (*Man*) **[166]** China: Heilongjiang Province. Formerly the dynastic language of the Jurchen rulers of the Jin dynasty of northern China (1115–1234) and of the Qing dynasty (1644–1911), with extensive literary and other documentation. 10,682,262 members of the Man nationality in China, and others assimilated into the Han Chinese population. The distinct Xibo language is a Qing-dynasty offshoot. Manchu is long extinct among the mainly urbanised Manchu, but still studied in an ongoing scholarly tradition. There are about 20 speakers, all over 50, and some semispeakers in three remote villages in the northwest of Heilongjiang Province: two south of Heihe, and one north of Qiqihar. Moribund.

Oroqen (*Orochen*) **[167]** China: northeastern Inner Mongolia and northwestern Heilongjiang Province. MT, Ewenki. 8,196 members of the Oroqen nationality, scattered around the Alihe Oroqen Banner, but only spoken by at most 30 per cent of the group, mainly middle-aged to elderly. Some scholars regard Oroqen, Ewenk and Solon as a dialect chain. Four dialects: *Kumarchen*, *Orochen*, *Selpechen* and *Birarchen*; the first still has some child speakers, but the second and third have no speakers under 50, and the fourth is moribund. Severely endangered.

Solon [168] China: northeastern Inner Mongolia. MT, Ewenk. Included in the Ewenke nationality in China, about 21,000 group members in Morindawa Daur Banner and other areas of northeastern Inner Mongolia west and south of the Oroqen, but fewer than 10,000 speakers, especially over 50; also spoken in Russia. Many speakers also speak Daur Mongol and Chinese. Severely endangered in China.

Xibo (*Xibe*, *Sibo*, *Sibe*) **[169]** China: Xinjiang Province, Qapqal County and various urban areas. About 27,000 members of the Xibo nationality in Xinjiang. Most there

419

still speak the language in the family, including many children. Among the over 160,000 of the 2000 population of 188,824 of Xibo nationality who are in Liaoning Province in northeast China, the language is long extinct. Divergent variety of Manchu spoken by the descendants of a Manchu army sent to Xinjiang in 1764, now the least-endangered MT language of China. Not mutually intelligible with modern spoken Manchu; but very similar to literary Manchu; potentially endangered.

Indo-European Creole

Kristang [170] Malaysia: southwest peninsular, Melaka (Malacca). Portuguese creole. About 10,000 members of this Catholic group from Melaka's time as a Portuguese seaport, with about 2,150 speakers: most of those over 50, about a third of younger adults and some children. Originally derived from Portuguese creole as spoken on the west coast of India, but with extensive local Malay lexical material; being replaced by Malaysian English. However, as a result of the new requirement for members of the group to speak the language in order to gain access to various benefits as bumiputra (indigenous) Malaysians, many non-speakers wish to learn it. Endangered.

Patuá [171] China: Macao. Portuguese creole. Over 10,000 members of this group, but only about 5,000 remain in Macao since its return to China in 1999. Fewer than 50 speakers over 70 years old, but now the object of folkloristic interest among the remaining community; formerly also spoken by the Catholic Portuguese creole community in Hong Kong. For centuries of Portuguese rule, there was continuous decreolisation towards Portuguese. Speakers also use Cantonese Chinese, which is the source of substantial lexical material; there is also Malay and Indian lexicon reflecting the connection with Kristang and other Portuguese Creoles further west. Moribund.

References

Bai, Bibo, personal communication.

Baxter, Alan, personal communication

Benjamin, Geoffrey. 1981. Peninsular Malaysia. In Stephen A. Wurm & Shiro Hattori (eds) *Language Atlas of the Pacific Area,* Map 37. Pacific Linguistics C-66.

——To appear. Introduction: endangered languages. In Hein Steinhauer (ed.) *Endangered Languages and Literatures of South-East Asia.* Leiden.

Bernot, Denise, personal communication.

Bradley, David (2004a) Sanie and language loss in China. *International Journal of the Sociology of Language* 170: 113–24.

——(2004b) Introduction: language policy and language endangerment in China. *International Journal of the Sociology of Language* 170: 1–14.

Brassett, Cecilia and Philip Brasset. 2004. Diachronic and synchronic overview of the Tujia language of Central South China. *International Journal of the Sociology of Language* 170: 55–71.

Diffloth, Gérard, personal communication

Diller, Anthony V. 1992. Tai languages in Assam: Daughters or ghosts? In Carol J. Compton & John F. Hartmann (eds) *Papers on Tai Languages, Linguistics and Literatures,* 5–43. DeKalb IL: Center for Southeast Asian Studies, Northern Illinois University.

Edmondson, Jerold A. 2003. Three Tibeto-Burman languages of Vietnam. In David Bradley, Randy LaPolla, Boyd Michailovsky and Graham Thurgood (eds) *Language Variation and*

Change in the Sinosphere and the Indosphere: A Festschrift for James A. Matisoff. Pacific Linguistics series. Canberra: Australian National University.

——personal communication

Hajek, John. The mystery of the Kenaboi. In Hein Steinhauer (ed.) *Endangered Languages and Literatures of South-East Asia.* Leiden (in press).

Harrell, Stevan. 2001. *Ways of Being Ethnic in Souhwest China.* Seattle WA: University of Washington Press.

Hattaway, Paul. 2000. *Operation China.* Pasadena CA: Piquant.

Janhunen, Juha. 1997. The languages of Manchuria in today's China. In Hiroshi Shoji & Juha Janhunen (eds) *Northern Minority Languages: Problems of survival.* Senri Ethnological Studies no. 44, 123–46. Osaka: National Museum of Ethnology.

——2004. Tungusic: an endangered language family in Northeast Asia. *International Journal of the Sociology of Language* 170:25–38.

Jacquesson, François. 2001. Person-marking in Tibeto-Burman languages, northeastern India. *Linguistics of the Tibeto-Burman Area* 24/1: 113–44.

Li Dalei and Jiang Di. 2001. Zha speech sketch. *Minzu Yuwen* 2001/6: 61–75.

Li Yongxiang, personal communication.

Luangthongkum, Theraphan personal communication

Mackerras, Colin, personal communication.

Morey, Stephen. 2002. Tai languages of Assam, a progress report—Does anything remain of the Tai Ahom language? In David Bradley & Maya Bradley (eds) *Language Endangerment and Language Maintenance,* 98–113. London: RoutledgeCurzon.

——2002. The Tai Languages of Assam—a grammar and texts. PhD thesis, Monas U.

Naw Say Bay. 1995. The phonology of the Dung dialect of Moken. In David Bradley (ed.) *Studies in Burmese Languages,* 193–205. Papers in Southeast Asian Linguistics No. 13. Pacific Linguistics A-83.

Niederer, Barbara. 2002. Introduction to Changpao Yao. *Cahiers de Linguistique, Asie Orientale* 3172: 211–43.

——personal communication

Peiros, Ilia, personal communication

Person, Kirk R. 2004. Language revitalization or dying gasp? Language preservation efforts among the Bisu. *International Journal of the Sociology of Language* 170: 83–102.

Ratliff, Martha. 1998. Ho-ne (She) is Mhongic: one final argument. *Linguistics of the Tibeto-Burman Area* 21/2: 97–109.

Robinne, François. 2000. *Fils et maitres de lac. Relations interethniques dans l'Etat Shan de Birmanie.* Paris: CNRS Editions.

Sagart, Laurent, personal communication.

Salminen, Tapani, personal communication

Savage, Theresa, personal communication

Senna Fernandez, Miguel & Alan Baxter. 2001. *Maquista chapado, vocabulário e expressões do crioulo português de Macau* [Real Maccanese: vocabulary and expressions of the Portuguese Creole of Macao]. Macau: Instituto Internacional de Macau.

Stary, Giovanni. 2003. Sibe: an endangered language. In Mark Janse & Sumen Tol (eds) *Language Death and Language Maintenance: Theoretical, practical and descriptive approaches,* 81–88. Amsterdam: Benjamins.

Sun Hongkai 1999. Zhongguo kongbai yuyan de diaocha yanjiu. [Research on the endangered languages of China]. In *Zhongguo Yuyan de Xintuozhan* [New Developments in Chinese Linguistics], Shi Feng and Pan Wuyun (eds), 3–17. Hong Kong: City University of Hong Kong Press.

Sun Hongkai. 2004. The Anong language: studies of a language in decline. *International Journal of the Sociology of Language* 170: 103–12.

Suwilai, Premsrirat, personal communication

Thurgood, Graham & Li Fengxiang. 2003. Contact-induced variation and syntactic change in the Tsat of Hainan. In David Bradley, Randy LaPolla, Graham Thurgood & Boyd Michailovsky

421

(eds) *Language Variation and Change in the Sinosphere and the Indosphere: A Festschrift for James A. Matisoff.* Pacific-Linguistics. Canberra: Australian National University.

Tsung, Linda and Dai Qingxia. 2004. A vanishing language: the case of Xiandao. *International Journal of the Sociology of Language* 170: 125–31.

Weera Ostapirat, 2000 Proto-Kra. *Linguistics of the Tibeto-Burman Area* 23/1.

Wurm, Stephen A. *et al.* (eds) 1987. *Language Atlas of China.* Hong Kong: Longman.

Wurm, Stephen A. *et al.* (eds) 1987. *Language Atlas of China.* Hong Kong: Longman. Also Chinese edition, Beijing: Academy of Social Sciences Press

Xu Shixuan. 2004. Survey of the current situation of Laomian and Laopin. *International Journal of the Sociology of Language* 170: 71–82.

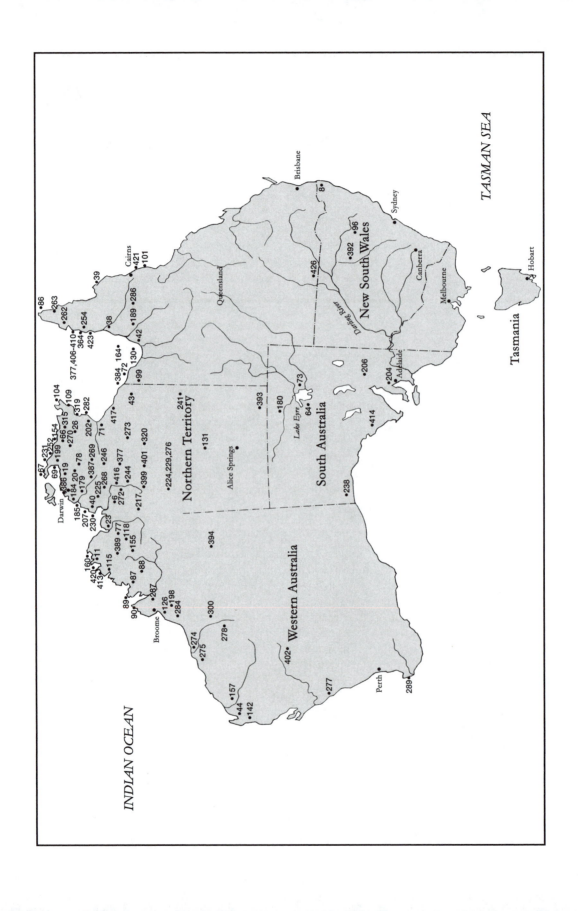

6

Australasia and the Pacific

Stephen A. Wurm

INTRODUCTION

General remarks

For the purpose of this Encyclopedia the Australasia and the Pacific area is deemed to include Australia, New Zealand, Papua New Guinea, Irian Jaya and the other parts of Indonesia, Peninsular Malaysia, and all Pacific islands to the east and northeast of Papua New Guinea. The Philippines and Taiwan also belong linguistically to Australasia and the Pacific (in Taiwan only the original indigenous languages) and will be touched upon here too.

There are four types of indigenous languages in the Australasia and the Pacific area – the very widespread, just under 1,200 interrelated *Austronesian* languages, the about 780 *Papuan* languages of which 710 or a little more belong to five unrelated large groups of languages (with two of these possibly related to each other), and twenty unrelated small groups, with a dozen or so isolated languages. In Australia, interrelated *Aboriginal* languages are found which originally may have numbered 500 or more just before the time of contact. A catastrophic smallpox epidemic which started in Sydney around 1789 and is believed to have swept through many parts of Australia killing a considerable proportion of the Aboriginal population, is likely to have caused the extinction of at least a hundred of the very small local languages. Today, there are about twenty-five fully functional Aboriginal languages, about 120 threatened languages in various stages of endangerment, with at least fifty of them in the last stages of disappearance, with only a few elderly speakers left. In addition, about 170 other languages have become recently or relatively recently extinct, with their last few elderly speakers dying during the last two decades or so. This gives a total of about 320–30 languages to which quite a few long-extinct languages have to be added to arrive at a figure of about 400 languages a short time after the time of contact. Only about a third of those are still surviving today, a good number of them barely. On the positive side, efforts have been, or are being, undertaken to revive, or reinvigorate, some dead or dying Aboriginal languages, with varying degrees of success. By way of contrast, only about fifty languages have become recently or relatively recently extinct in the Pacific (38 Austronesian and 11 Papuan languages), though about 305 are threatened and in various degrees of endangerment, with fifty-nine of them seriously or terminally endangered.

The fourth group in this area are *Austro-Asiatic* languages in Peninsular Malaysia, which constitute a very small portion of the large group of interrelated Austro-Asiatic languages widespread in parts of Southeast Asia. They are not dealt with in this Australasia and the Pacific section.

In addition to these local languages, there were and are forty-four Pidgin and Creole languages in the Australasia and Pacific area, of which eight are now extinct, and eighteen threatened, with ten of them seriously or terminally, whereas eighteen are still functioning.

Diachronic survey of the linguistic development of the area

Austronesian languages

The Austronesian language areas

The Austronesian languages constitute a very widespread large group of interrelated languages in the Indo-Pacific and Australasian area. The number of its member languages is around 1,200, with a total of 230 million speakers. Insular Southeast Asia is its western region and the New Guinea area, Melanesia, Micronesia and Polynesia its eastern one, and it also includes Madagascar. Going from north to south in its western region, the original languages of Taiwan, the languages of the Philippines, Malaysia, and Indonesia are very predominantly Austronesian, with Malagasy on Madagascar also belonging to them. In the New Guinea area there are over 300 Austronesian languages, and the languages of Micronesia and Polynesia are all Austronesian. In addition, Austronesian languages are found in Vietnam, Cambodia, and on Hainan Island in China (the so-called Cham languages), and also in the far south of Myanmar. The speakers of Malagasy migrated 1,000 to 2,000 years ago from southern Borneo to Madagascar via southern India.

Distribution and numbers of Austronesian languages and their speakers

With few exceptions, the Austronesian languages are closely interrelated, and in spite of their very large number and the enormous expanse of the territories occupied by them, it is very easy to recognize their genetic interrelationship. Because of their great similarity to each other, it is often difficult to establish whether various communalects are different languages, or dialects of one language. As a result of this, the total number of Austronesian languages is a contentious issue. Taking this into account, the approximate number of Austronesian languages of given areas, and the number of their speakers in these areas is as follows: *Taiwan*: fifteen living languages, 200,000 speakers; *Philippines*: about 150 languages, about 60 million speakers; *Vietnam, Cambodia and Hainan Island* (*China*): ten languages, about 700,000 speakers; *Madagascar*: one language, 11 million speakers; *Indonesia, Malaysia and Brunei*: about 610 languages, 160 million speakers; *Melanesia* (*without the Indonesian part of the New Guinea area*): about 430 languages, about 1,200,000 speakers; *Micronesia*: twenty living languages, about 300,000 speakers; *Polynesia*: thirty-six living languages, about 700,000 speakers.

Genetic interrelationship, history and classification of Austronesian languages

The recognition of the genetic interrelationship and initial classification of Austronesian languages had its beginnings in the nineteenth century, with good results, but the full recognition of the Austronesian nature of the Malayo-Polynesian languages of Melanesia became evident only later, though Codrington (1885) had already pointed it out. The history of the development of the present-day Austronesian languages is well known today, thanks to the work by eminent Austronesianists such as Dempwolff (1934–8), Pawley (1978), Blust (1978), Ross (1988) and others. Much work was devoted to the successful reconstruction of proto-Austronesian. The development of the Austronesian language picture is believed to have been as follows: from proto-Austronesian, the Taiwanese languages and proto-Malayo-Polynesian developed. From the latter, the Western Malayo-Polynesian languages and the Central and Eastern Malayo-Polynesian proto-language originated. From this, the Central Malayo-Polynesian languages and the Eastern Malayo-Polynesian proto-languages developed. From the latter, the Southern Halmahera Islands and Northwest New Guinea Malayo-Polynesian languages and the Oceanic proto-languages were derived. The present-day Malayo-Polynesian languages of Melanesia, Micronesia and Polynesia are daughter-languages of the latter.

A more detailed classification of the present-day languages derived from proto-Austronesian is as follows: (1) Atayalic; (2) Tsouic; (3) Paiwanic (these are all Taiwanese language groups); (4) Malayo-Polynesian languages. These consist of two large groups: (A) the Western Malayo-Polynesian languages; (B) the Central-Eastern Malayo-Polynesian languages. The group (B) comprises two large subgroups: (1) the Central Malayo-Polynesian languages; (2) the Eastern Malayo-Polynesian languages. The latter has two member groups: (a) the southern Halmahera Islands and north-western New Guinea one; (b) the Oceanic one which consists of eighteen member subgroups. The eighteenth of these, which is called Remote Oceanic, has four sections: Micronesian, Southeastern Oceanic, Central and Northern Vanuatuan, and Central Pacific. The last of these has two sub-sections: one is the Rotuma-Fijian, and the other comprises all the Polynesian languages. It is interesting to note that of the two major groups of the Malayo-Polynesian world, the number of languages constituting the Western Malayo-Polynesian languages is, with about 390 languages, smaller than that of those of the Central and Eastern Malayo-Polynesian languages, which is about 570 languages, while the number of the speakers of the Western languages is about 230 million, but that of the Central and Eastern ones a mere 3 million or so.

Spreading and migrations of the Austronesian languages and their speakers

The past migrations of the Austronesians and their languages are well understood. Their most ancient known original home is the island of Taiwan (formerly known as Formosa) from where they started to move towards the south 7,000 years ago. The languages of the Austronesians who remained on Taiwan, are very archaic and show phonemic differentiations which have disappeared from all the other Austronesian, i.e.

427

the Malayo-Polynesian, languages. From Taiwan, the Malayo-Polynesians penetrated into the Philippine islands and from there into present-day Indonesia, and in some areas, into small parts of continental Southeast Asia and of Hainan Island.

About 1,000–2,000 years ago, a group speaking an ancestral form of today's Ma'anyan language started migrating westwards from southeastern Borneo, and through southern India eventually reached Madagascar where they still live today, speaking the present form of their original language, i.e. Malagasy, which has 11 million speakers. A branch of the Malayo-Polynesians heading towards present-day Indonesia from the north, moved eastwards and about 5,500 years ago reached areas to the west of the New Guinea region. Groups continuing eastwards from there appear to have reached the large semicircle formed by the large islands of New Britain and New Ireland. There the Malayo-Polynesians got into contact with dark-skinned Papuans and mixed with them. Later they migrated from there to the northern shores of New Guinea and its small offshore islands. A part of them moved further east to the western Solomon Islands, and also reached the Vanikoro and Utupua Islands in the Santa Cruz Archipelago, southern Vanuatu, the Loyalty Islands, and New Caledonia. It appears that they settled in those areas about 4,500–4,000 years ago. Most of them are dark-skinned. Malayo-Polynesians continuing to stay west of the New Guinea area remained light-skinned. A part of those migrated eastwards, presumably after the east and southeast migration of the dark-skinned Malayo-Polynesians mentioned above, and occupied the southeastern half of the Solomon Islands, and most of the northern and central islands of Vanuatu. They appeared to have had very much less contact with Papuans and have generally remained more light-skinned than the dark-skinned Malayo-Polynesians mentioned above. A part of them penetrated the Micronesian Islands world, with the exception of Guam, the Chamorro-speaking Mariana Islands, the Palau Islands, and the island of Yap, where today speakers of Western Malayo-Polynesian languages live. The lighter-skinned Malayo-Polynesians also reached the easternmost part, and a portion of the south-eastern coast, of the New Guinea mainland. They remained more light-skinned than their Papuan-speaking neighbours, and their languages are similar to those of the lighter-skinned Malayo-Polynesians of the southeastern Solomon Islands, though some of them show Papuan linguistic influence.

The Malayo-Polynesian languages, spoken by the lighter-skinned Malayo-Polynesians differ in various ways from those spoken by the dark-skinned Malayo-Polynesians mentioned above, and have developed towards the Remote Oceanic type of Oceanic Malayo-Polynesians (see above).

About 3,500 years ago, a migration of lighter-skinned Malayo-Polynesians from central Vanuatu reached the islands of Fiji and Rotuma. Much later a migration of dark-skinned Malayo-Polynesians reached the Fiji Islands, resulting in the present-day Fijians being in part dark-skinned and curly-haired though otherwise their physical anthropological setup is close to that of the Polynesians. Before this last migration, a strong migration from the Fiji Islands reached the easternmost islands of present-day Polynesia, i.e. Tonga and Niue, about 3,000 years ago, and Samoa a little later. On these islands, the proto-Polynesian language developed.

About 2,500 years ago, a number of westward migrations from the Samoan islands took Samoan-type Polynesian languages to central Vanuatu, into the Santa Cruz Archipelago, far-flung small islands adjacent to the main Solomon Islands chain, and to the Wallis and Futuna Islands lying between Samoa and Rotuma. Towards the north, such languages reached the islands of Tuvalu, Tokelau and Pukapuka. About 2,000 years ago, major eastward migrations reached the Cook Islands, Tahiti, the Tuamotu Archipelago, and the Marquesas Islands, where the Eastern Polynesian proto-language developed. About 1,000 years ago, westward migrations from the Cook Islands and Tahiti reached New Zealand where the Maori language arose. About the same time, northward migrations from the Marquesas Islands reached the islands of Hawaii.

Characteristics of Austronesian languages

Phonologically, Austronesian languages are, with few exceptions, fairly simple. A few of them are tone languages, e.g. in New Caledonia, where the phonologies are also quite complex. The Eastern Malayo-Polynesian languages have generally fewer phonemes than the more archaic Taiwanese and Western Malayo-Polynesian ones. In the morphology, prefixes, suffixes and infixes play a larger part in Taiwanese and Western Malayo-Polynesian than in Eastern Malayo-Polynesian. In almost all Austronesian languages, a distinction appears between inclusive (i.e. including the person addressed) and exclusive (i.e. excluding the person addressed) forms of the first person non-singular pronoun forms. In the Eastern Malayo-Polynesian languages, a dual number is present in pronouns, and often also a trial. In Western languages, possession is mostly indicated by possessive suffixes or by possessive pronouns. In Eastern languages, inalienable possession (e.g. with body parts and with certain relationship terms) is indicated by possessive suffixes. Alienable possession, i.e. with things which the owner can dispose of at will, such as food, drinking water, tools etc., possession is indicated by possession words which precede the noun denoting the possessed thing, and are provided with possessive suffixes. In most Eastern languages, there are only very few types of such possession words, e.g. one for edibles, one for drinkable liquids, one for anything else, but in a few, especially Micronesian languages, their number can be much larger, up to dozens. In Polynesian languages, all possessive relations are expressed by possession words, with their character vowel being *o* for inalienable and *a* for all kinds of alienable possession.

In the noun and verb morphology, many prefixes and suffixes and also infixes, appear, and reduplication plays a major role in many languages. Especially in Western languages, many word bases can function as either nouns or verbs according to the affixes with which they are used. In the Eastern languages, especially the Oceanic languages, transitive verbs are provided with special suffixes, to which object suffixes indicating the person and number of the object are added. In Polynesian languages, and also in some other Oceanic languages, indication of the direction of an action, e.g. towards or away from the speaker, is important.

In syntax, a special type, called 'focus' type, is strongly in evidence in the Taiwanese and Philippine languages, and also in some languages in north Borneo and Sulawesi, and also met with to a lesser extent in some other Austronesian languages. With this type, the verb which often begins the sentence is provided with various affixes, which by their differing forms indicate whether the stress, i.e. the focus in the utterance, is on the actor, or the object, or the location of an action, etc. In another frequent sentence-type found in many Malayo-Polynesian languages, the subject usually stands at the beginning of a sentence, and the word order is subject-verb-object. Especially in Oceanic languages, the subject is indicated by a prefix or particle before the verb which marks the person of the actor. In Polynesian languages, the word order is usually verb-subject-object, with the actor indicated by a particle or pronoun after the verb.

Papuan languages

General remarks

About 780 so-called Papuan languages occupy most of the New Guinea mainland and portions of the large islands adjacent to it. In the west, these are the islands of Timor, Alor and Pantar, and the northern part of the Halmaheras. In the east, there are the islands of New Britain, New Ireland and Bougainville. There are also Papuan languages on several islands of the Solomon Islands chain, and to the east of the Solomon Islands they occupy the main island of the Santa Cruz Archipelago, and much of the Reef Islands to the north of it. If the over 350 Malayo-Polynesian languages found in the same regions are added to the 780 Papuan languages, it is evident that close to one fifth of the languages of the world are concentrated in this comparatively very small area. Seeing that the total number of speakers of Papuan languages is only about 3 million, it is evident that the number of speakers of individual Papuan languages is rather small. In fact, over a third of the over 3 million speakers of Papuan languages is taken up by just thirteen large Papuan languages – the largest of these has only 240,000 speakers, and two others have over 100,000 each. The remaining languages have usually only a few thousand speakers each, very many only a few hundred, and quite a few even less speakers.

Establishment of the Papuan language picture

Until the late 1950s, and even later, the impression current among linguists interested in the Pacific area was that the individual Papuan languages were very largely language isolates, and only a few groups of interrelated Papuan languages were recognized, with no interrelationship between such groups discernible. Until then, reasonably good studies and descriptions existed only of a few geographically widely separated Papuan languages, and very little systematic study of Papuan languages had been undertaken. 'Papuan languages' were understood to mean essentially that these were not Malay-Polynesian languages (hence the previously often used term 'non-Austronesian languages') and that they were generally not related to each other except in a few specified cases.

However, it was noted that a number of Papuan languages had quite striking typological and structural similarities. On the initiative of Stephen Wurm, the linguistic research institute (later Department of Linguistics) in the then Research School of Pacific Studies (now Research School of Pacific and Asian Studies) of the Australian National University in Canberra started a multi-year programme after 1960 with the aim to undertake research into the general Papuan language picture and situation, and of individual Papuan languages. Linguists attached to the Summer Institute of Linguistics (SIL) – active in New Guinea – also joined this venture, with a number of its members spending one, two or three years at the Canberra linguistic research institute. In the course of this research programme, it was found that the total number of Papuan languages was much greater than previously assumed. More then seventy families of genetically related languages were established, and a large portion of these were gradually included into a number of language stocks and these then into a very large group of, in part only very distantly, interrelated languages which eventually numbered about 500, with a total of about 2.5 million speakers. It occupies four fifths of the New Guinea mainland, and parts of the islands of Timor, Alor and Pantar to the west of New Guinea. It was named the Trans-New Guinea Phylum.

The lexical comparative work in the establishment of this Phylum was in part made difficult by the presence of word-tabus in many parts of New Guinea which affects the vocabulary of a language, and changes especially nouns. It means that, if a person whose name is a word in the language of a given group dies, that word cannot be used any more and either has to be deliberately altered, or replaced by some other word which has a somewhat related meaning. Seeing that very many languages have only very few speakers, such a vocabulary change would usually be observed by all speakers of that language. Some of the essential early results of this programme were included in the 1,000-page Wurm (ed.) (1975) publication, of which Wurm (1982) is an in part updated summary publication. Wurm and Hattori (1981–3) gives very detailed information on the language picture of the New Guinea area on fourteen large multicoloured maps and the text materials accompanying them.

Some experts such as Foley (1986) regarded the establishment of the Trans-New Guinea Phylum of Papuan languages as controversial. However, recent detailed work involving a large number of its member languages on the basis of much more extensive and better studies than were available over twenty years ago, and establishing sound correspondences between many languages, along with the recognition of far-reaching structural and formal agreements between them, has demonstrated the presence of genetic relationship amongst many member languages of this large Phylum (Pawley 1995; Ross 1995).

In addition to the establishment of the Trans-New Guinea Phylum, the programme has demonstrated that of the remaining Papuan languages, about 100 belonged to the so-called Sepik-Ramu Phylum in the northwestern part of Papua New Guinea, with a total of about 200,000 speakers. About fifty more languages belong to the so-called Torricelli Phylum, which is also located in the northwestern part of Papua New Guinea, with a total of about 80,000 speakers. Furthermore, thirty-one languages are members of the so-called West Papuan Phylum, which takes in the greater northern part of the northwestern peninsula (called 'Bird's Head') of Irian Jaya, and the northern half of the Halmahera Islands, with a total number of about 240,000 speakers. A fifth phylum of fairly closely interrelated languages was a few years ago established as comprising thirty-four languages in the western lowland and western coastal areas of Irian Jaya, with some members of it spoken in near-coastal areas of Cenderawasih Bay which was formerly called Geelvinck Bay. After this, the new phylum was named Geelvinck Bay Phylum.

Thirty-four languages constitute the so-called East Papuan languages, which are scattered over the large islands and island group to the east of the New Guinea mainland, i.e. New Britain, New Ireland, Rossel Island, Bougainville Island, the Solomon Islands chain, and the Santa Cruz Archipelago, with a total of about 70,000 speakers. Several language families have been established within the East Papuan languages, and there seem to be links between these languages, and though combining them into an East Papuan Phylum (Wurm (ed.) 1975; Wurm 1982), the existence of such a phylum is still in question. It appeared that there were no relationship links between the five phyla mentioned above, but recent research seems to suggest the possibility of some relationship between the Torricelli Phylum and the West Papuan Phylum.

Apart from these five large groups and the East Papuan languages, twenty-two further languages belong to four unrelated small phyla (together with a total of about 10,400 speakers). Finally, there are ten small language isolates, possibly languages spoken by refugees from areas where there were now extinct larger languages or language groups.

Apart from this surveying, comparative classifying and general work in Papuan languages over thirty years or so, descriptions, dictionaries, grammars, and other studies of Papuan languages were produced, a large portion of which were published in the large linguistic publication series *Pacific Linguistics* issued by the Department of Linguistics in the Research School of Pacific (and Asian) Studies of the Australian National University in Canberra.

Spreading and migrations of the Papuan languages and their speakers

Very much less is known about the migrations of speakers of Papuan languages and their languages than is the case with the Austronesians. It is certain that they came into New Guinea from the west. It seems that the first immigrants into New Guinea were ancestors of the Australian Aborigines who may have reached it 50,000–40,000 years ago. At that time New Guinea and Australia were interconnected as a single continent and only separated 8,000–10,000 years ago. The ancestral Australian Aborigines spread south into Australia, and eventually most of them left New Guinea under pressure of the later Papuan immigrants before the geographical separation of New Guinea and Australia. There is some linguistic evidence of the former presence of Australian languages in parts of New Guinea (Foley 1986), and there are also some cultural and physical anthropological pointers (such as bloodgroups) in support of this.

It may seem that the first Papuan speakers began to enter New Guinea around 15,000 or so years ago. Perhaps the present-day Papuan speakers whose languages belong to some of the smaller language phyla, to the West Papuan and Torricelli Phyla and the East Papuan languages, are in part descendants of these early Papuan immigrants. There are some vague similarities between their languages, but it has so far not been possible to establish any relationship links between them.

The speakers of languages belonging to the Trans-New Guinea Phylum probably arrived in New Guinea only 5,000–6,000 years ago. In these languages, even in areas which today are far from regions occupied by Austronesian (i.e. Oceanic Malayo-Polynesian) speakers, there are Austronesian loan words which reflect proto-forms which may have been in use in areas not far to the west of New Guinea before Malayo-Polynesian speakers reached New Guinea about 5,500 years ago (see above section on spreading and migration of the Austronesian languages). This makes it appear likely that the ancestors of present-day speakers of Papuan languages lived thousands of years ago in areas to the west of New Guinea where they were met by Malayo-Polynesians moving eastwards, and took over loan words from them. It seems that the Malayo-Polynesians forced them out of those areas, and made them enter New Guinea thereby.

The Trans-New Guinea Phylum speakers spread far and wide through New Guinea, and in this process absorbed a part of the earlier Papuan immigrants. It is probable that they forced the ancestors of the present-day East Papuan language speakers out of New Guinea into the island world to the east of it, because there is an East Papuan substratum in the languages spoken in the eastern peninsula-like end of the New Guinea mainland. There is also evidence of a later strong east-to-west movement of Trans-New Guinea Phylum languages from Huon Gulf area all the way into western Irian Jaya.

Characteristics of Papuan languages

Though the Papuan languages belong to a number of different language phyla and groups which, with one possible exception, do not seem to be related to each other, there are some structural features which are present in many Papuan languages. On the phonological level, it is for instance rare for *l*- and *r*-type consonants to be separate phonemes. Phonemic tonal distinctions occur in many languages, though are predominantly present in Trans-New Guinea Phylum languages. Unusual consonant phonemes are rare, but some very unusual ones do occur, such as dental-labial co-articulated stops, velar stops with bilateral release, bilabial trills, etc.

Structurally, a dual is very widespread. Noun class systems are common, though mainly in Trans-New Guinea languages the class of a noun is not apparent from the noun itself, but is indicated by existential verbs, e.g. 'to be something' which are different with nouns belonging to different classes. In other phyla, class indication through affixes to nouns with concordance in the noun phrase or also through subject and object marking on the verb does occur, as does the marking of the class of a noun through their plural forms. Gender distinction is also fairly widespread.

The grammatical structure is very or even extremely complicated, especially in a number of Trans-New Guinea, Torricelli and East Papuan languages. A distinction between sentence-medial and sentence-final verbs is very widespread in Trans-New Guinea Phylum languages, but also present in several languages belonging to other phyla, etc. This means that of several verbs in a sentence, the person and number of the subject is only marked on the last verb, whereas the sentence-medial verbs are provided with suffixes which indicate the temporal, sequential, etc. relationships between the actions indicated by them and the final verb (e.g. simultaneity, successivity, cause, etc.), and also whether their subjects and that of the final verb are the same or different. If they are different, it is often indicated on the sentence-medial verbs what persons of the subjects of a medial verb and the final verb are involved in a sentence, e.g. whether it is I-you, I-he, you-they, etc. The word order in almost all Papuan languages is subject-object-verb. Many Papuan languages have only a restricted number of numeric words, 'one', 'two', with 'three' = 'one-two'; 'four' = 'two-two'; 'five' = 'hand'; 'twenty' = 'man' (i.e. 'two hands-two feet'). In some languages, numeric words are related to part of or points on (e.g. nose tip, nipples, etc.) the body and can reach thirty or more.

Typical characteristics of many *Trans-New Guinea Phylum* languages are: very great structural complexity especially in the verb morphology, complicated systems of the sentence-medial and sentence-final verb sequences mentioned above, indication of noun classes by existential verbs as mentioned above, relative rarity of gender distinction, distinction of only two persons (speaker and other) in verbal subject markers. The indication of plural with nouns is very rare. The contrast between two sets of consonant phonemes is usually voicing. The many non-phonemic variants (allophones) of consonants are usually fricatives. There are predominantly only five vowels, with little allophonic variation. Phonemic tones are frequent. The word order is always subject-object-verb.

Sepik-Ramu Phylum languages differ markedly from Trans-New Guinea Phylum languages, but show strong influences from the latter in the southern regions of the phylum which are in the vicinity of such languages. In Sepik-Ramu Phylum languages, the contrast between two sets of consonant phonemes is usually prenasalization.

Consonants have few allophonic forms. The number of vowels is predominantly three to five, with strong allophonic variation. Structural complexity is lower than in Trans-New Guinea Phylum languages (except for the members of three separate grammatically aberrant language groups in the phylum, in which complexity is at a very high level). Noun class systems are very widespread, their indication is usually by affixes. Gender indication is very frequent, and appears together with other noun class systems in some languages. The indication of plural with nouns is frequent. With personal pronouns, seven basic forms appear for them in a large part of the phylum, with five to six of them present in any given language. However, the same forms may have different meanings in different languages. For instance, the same pronoun form may mean 'I' in one language, and 'you (one)' in another. The systems of sentence-medial and sentence-final verb forms found in Trans-New Guinea Phylum languages also appear in many of the Sepik-Ramu Phylum ones, but are much simpler than in the former, and often only rudimentary. The word order is always subject-object-verb.

The *Torricelli Phylum* languages are generally close to each other lexically and structurally, which contrasts with the view that the ancestors of their present-day speakers came to New Guinea many thousands of years ago (see above section on spreading of Papuan languages). It seems likely that the great majority of the speakers of ancestral Torricelli Phylum-type languages had given up their languages in favour of other languages, and that the present-day Torricelli Phylum languages are the relatively recent descendants of a single or a few closely related ancestral Torricelli-type languages. There is also physical anthropological evidence for such a possibility.

In the individual Torricelli Phylum languages, five to eight vowel phonemes occur. As a rule, there is no phonemic contrast between voiced and voiceless consonants. There are many fricative phonemes. A very typical feature of the languages is a distinction between two or three grammatical genders. In addition, several of the languages show a noun-class system which has between three and thirteen classes, with a very complicated concordance system, with the class of a given noun marked in pronouns, adjectives, numerals, demonstratives, and the subject and object markers in verbs. The gender or class of a noun is indicated by its ending or by the form of its plural. With adjectives, numerals, demonstratives, etc. the class of the noun to which they refer, is indicated by prefixes or suffixes. The subject, object and indirect object affixes are integral parts of a verb form, and differ for gender and class. In addition, they have also different forms in the different tenses. This and changes of the initial part of a verb stem denote the different tenses. There is no distinction between sentence-medial and sentence-final verb forms. Marking of the dual and plural number is highly complex. The word order is always subject-object-verb.

The *West Papuan Phylum* languages are typologically a little similar to the Torricelli Phylum languages, but are very much simpler than those. Latest research results suggest that there may be relationship links between the languages of the two phyla. Austronesian influence upon the languages of the West Papuan Phylum is strong, both in vocabulary and structure, especially upon the Northern Halmahera languages. The chief characteristics of the West Papuan Phylum languages are as follows: the subject and object are marked by prefixes on verbs, with gender distinctions in the third person singular. Tenses, modes and aspects are indicated by suffixes. There is no distinction between sentence-medial and sentence-final verbs. The verbal complex is generally much simpler than in other Papuan languages which is largely attributable to the strong Austronesian influence upon them. In all languages of this phylum, inclusive and exclusive forms of the non-singular first person pronouns are distinguished, as a result of this influence (see above section on Austronesian language chgaracteristics). Nouns have special plural forms in several of the languages. The word order is sometimes the typical Papuan subject-object-verb, but often it corresponds to the typical Malayo-Polynesian noun-verb-object, which is also due to this influence.

Of the *East Papuan* languages, some are extremely complicated in their phonological setup, but there are also simple to very simple ones. For instance, in the Yele language of Rossel Island to the east of the eastern end of Papua New Guinea, there are eleven oral and eight nasal vowel phonemes, with length also phonemic. The consonantal phonemic setup is also highly complex, with a distinction between dental and alveolar articulation in stops and nasals, prenasalization and nasal release of stops, labial-velar, dental-labial and alveolar-labial co-articulation of stops and of two nasals together, and labialization and palatalization of stops (Henderson 1995). By way of contrast, the Rotokas language on Bougainville Island has only five vowel and six consonant phonemes, but with a large amount of morphophonemic changes and suprasegmental features. Structurally, the East Papuan languages are fairly to very complex. In various languages, there are sometimes very elaborate gender and noun class systems, marked by pre- or suffixes, and mostly accompanied by concordance systems. Nouns often have plural forms. The verb inflection is mostly very complex, but in most of the languages, the individual affixes and formants, though they can be very numerous and separated from each other, are clearly recognizable, with few assimilations and morpho-phonemic changes. Only in very few of the languages, for instance in the Yele language mentioned above, is the complicated verbal morphology rendered even more complex by such morphophonemic changes (as is the case in many Trans-New Guinea Phylum languages). In the verb forms, affixes denote many modes, aspects, tenses, the general direction of actions and their direction and location in relation to the speaker, negation, reversal of the action, effect of an action upon an object, etc. in addition to the subject, object, beneficiary of the action etc. (e.g. Wurm 1992a). Distinction between sentence-medial and sentence-final forms is present in some languages, but is simple.

In some of the languages, e.g. in those of the Santa Cruz Archipelago, Austronesian influence is strongly in evidence in the vocabulary and also in some structural features (e.g. the indication of possession). Some affixes in them are Austronesian in form, but Papuan in function. The word order in East Papuan languages is usually subject-object-verb, but in the Austronesian-influenced ones it is often subject-verb-object.

The languages of the *Small Papuan Phyla* differ structurally in various ways from those of the Large Papuan Phyla. For instance, in some of the languages of the Sko Phylum located in northern central New Guinea in coastal border areas of Papua New Guinea and Irian Jaya, there are complicated phonemic tones which play a part in the elaborate verbal inflection as morphologically significant tones.

Australian languages

General remarks and the Australian language picture and history

The Australian languages constitute a large group of interrelated languages which originally took in all of the Australian continent. The question as to whether the languages of Tasmania, of which the last speaker died in 1877, are related to those of the

Australian continent, is problematic because of the paucity and unreliability of the material available on them. Most of it does not suggest a relationship, be it lexically or structurally – but their separation from continental Australia and its languages happened about 12,000 years ago when the sea levels rose in the Bass Strait and cut off Tasmania. That time-depth may well be enough to obliterate any trace of linguistic relationship which may have been distant even then, especially when materials for comparison are so meagre and poor.

The Australian Aborigines are believed to have first reached New Guinea, which was connected to Australia until about 8,000–10,000 years ago, about 50,000 or more years ago, and spread through Australia in a relatively short time of about 10,000 years. There are some linguistic, physical and cultural traces of them in New Guinea, from where they where probably pushed out by some early Papuan migrations, before the Torres Strait separated New Guinea from Australia. Australia was much wetter, more lush and fertile in its interior for many thousands of years after the arrival of the Australian Aborigines than it is today, and it seems likely that the distribution of Aboriginals and their languages was much more even and differently patterned than at the time of contact.

Today, one very large family of languages, called Pama-Nyungan, occupies seven eighths of Australia, with the exception of most of Arnhem Land in the north and the Kimberleys area to the southwest of it, where 26–7 different, though interrelated, small Australian language families are found, which all differ from Pama-Nyungan too as much or more than they differ from each other. Also, while a number of lexical items appear in many Australian languages, regional vocabularies are found in a number of, mostly near-coastal, regions of Australia, where they tend to be accompanied by structural features which are at variance with some widespread ones in other Pama-Nyungan languages. Also, lexical cognates can be found in widely separated areas, with no occurrence of these cognates in languages located between such areas.

All this, and the existence of the far-flung nature of the Pama-Nyungan family, suggest the following: it is known that the interior of the continent, especially in its western part, started drying thousands of years ago. Before that time, it seems that the Australian language picture may have been more varied on the entire continent, much as it is today in its far north and northwest. With the gradual drying up, the speakers of languages or a language group, apparently the ancestors of the core of the present-day Pama-Nyungan family in the areas most affected, may have started to move outwards, extensively and powerfully, forcing the earlier languages into marginal areas of the continent in the south, east and west, superimposing upon them much of their vocabulary and features, and influencing them until only such vestiges of them remained as are manifested by the regional vocabularies, widely scattered vocabulary cognates, and characteristics reflecting the influence and features of the immigrant languages in aberrant ways.

This was the language picture in Australia shortly after the time of contact, with about 400 languages, or fewer or more, depending on the assessment of language versus dialect. Most of these had only a very small number of speakers, in the hundreds. As a result of the impact of the English language and the attitudes, actions and policies of the white Australians, more than half of these languages have become extinct, as has already been indicated above in the general remarks above, and another fifty or more are heading for extinction soon, with perhaps seventy likely to survive for some length of time, and only about twenty-five or so facing a brighter future.

The positive language policies in Australia during the last decades, and the strong awakening of Aboriginal ethnic self-consciousness and their reawakened interest in their own languages has slowed down the decline, and has led to the reinvigoration and even revival of several moribund or even extinct languages, but most of the large number of languages spoken today by only a handful or less of very old speakers can hardly be saved by this.

Characteristics of Australian languages

With the exception of languages in Cape York Peninsula which have been phonologically influenced by Papuan languages, and with that of a few other languages, the Australian languages are remarkably similar in their phonological setup. Most of them have a large number of phonemically relevant points of articulation with consonants, i.e. labial, interdental, dental, retroflexed, palatal, velar, and rarely, glottal. This applies to stops, nasals and, with the exception of labial, velar and glottal, to *l*, though a velarized *l* occurs. There are two or three *r*-sounds, rolled, fricative and retroflexed. In the majority of the languages, there is no phonemically relevant voicing with stops, and in most languages there are no fricatives. In the great majority of the languages, there are only three vowel phonemes, *a*, *i*, *u*, with *a* very frequent. Structurally, there are two types of Australian languages, languages in which prefixes and suffixes occur, and languages without prefixes, only with suffixes. The forms of subject and object markers which in the first type appear as prefixes, are similar to those in the second type where they appear as suffixes. The prefixing languages are limited to those of twenty-four of the non-Pama-Nyungan families. Many of those languages have two or more noun-classes with concordance, with the classes (or genders) indicated by prefixes. The languages of one of the remaining three non-Pama-Nyungan families have also noun classes, though they are suffixing languages, and such noun classes also occur in a few languages belonging to different groups within the Pama-Nyungan family.

A striking feature of languages of what can be regarded as the core of the Pama-Nyungan family is the so-called affix-transferring, which means that subject (and object) markers are not added to the verbs, but to the first word of a sentence which is often only a catalyst word whose purpose is to carry these suffixes. Tense, aspect and other markers are suffixed to the verbs.

In general, the morphology of Australian languages is rather elaborate. There are many relational markers with nouns (for cases, etc.). The verbal morphology is elaborate, and in a number of languages, sentence-medial and sentence-final verb forms are distinguished, with the former indicating whether the subject of the former is the same as, or different from, that of the latter (as in many Papuan languages). A dual number is often present, and there are often different forms for the inclusive and exclusive first person non-singular pronoun. In some languages, tense is indicated with non-verbs such as pronouns (e.g. in the Baagandji or Darling River group of Pama-Nyungan) or by the form of the direct object verb suffix (e.g. in languages of the Pama-Nyungan Tangic group in the Gulf of Carpentaria area). In some languages of Arnhem Land, the noun object is included in the verb, often in a suppleted form. There are usually only two or three numerals in a language. The word order is very free in some languages, more rigid in others, with the basic word order tending towards subject-object-verb. Even with very closely related languages, the similarities in their vocabulary are of a lower to much lower order than in similar cases in other language groups which may be attributable to the operation of word-taboos, as mentioned above in the section on the Papuan language picture.

A special case are the languages on the islands of Torres Strait. The Meriam language of Darnley Island is a Papuan language closely related to the Gizra language on the south coast of the Trans-Fly area of Papua New Guinea – apparently an immigrant language from there a few centuries ago. The Kala Lagaw language of the other Torres Strait islands has Meriam phonology, and some of its basic vocabulary is Meriam. Structurally, it is more like a Pama-Nyungan Australian language. Racially, its speakers appear to be more Papuan than Australian, and regard themselves as different from Australian Aborigines. It may well be that they were originally Meriam speakers who have incompletely adopted an Australian language.

The Austro-Asiatic Aslian languages of Peninsular Malaysia

General remarks

On Peninsular Malaysia, i.e. the Malay Peninsula, there are 16–19 (depending how the difference between language and dialect is assessed) so-called Aslian languages which constitute a branch of the Mon-Khmer family or group of the Austro-Asiatic languages which are widespread in continental Southeast Asia, and northeastern India, with some also in extreme southwestern China. The language of the Nicobar Islands is also Austro-Asiatic. The Aslian languages belong to three different sections, i.e. North Aslian, South Aslian, and Senoic (or Eastern Aslian). They are largely located in the interior of the Peninsula. It is very likely that they were present in the area before the Austronesians occupied most of the coastal areas and pushed them inland.

Characteristics of Aslian languages

Aslian languages are typical Mon-Khmer languages. They have fixed last-syllable stress, with a large number of possible vowels in the final syllable. A great number and variety of infixes is present in words. In some of the languages almost any consonant can become an infix through a regular morphological process. Also, numerous substitutions of consonants and vowels are possible, to convey gradations of meaning. Apart from such substitutions, partial reduplications, infixed copying of the final consonant of a word, systematic distortions of words, etc. occur with all this reminiscent of deliberate language games. The object is consistently placed after the verb, the possessed stands after the possessor, the attributive adjective after the noun, and demonstratives after the adjective.

Language endangerment and problems of language preservation in the area

General remarks

Language endangerment refers to a situation in which a language is no longer fully functioning within a speech community or other social group, but is falling into disuse and is moving into the direction of eventual extinction. One of the main reasons for this is pressure on a, usually minor, language and its speakers by a dominant, usually major, language and the attitudes of its speakers, which may rank from forcing the speakers of the minor language to use their major language only, to various forms of indirect cultural pressure. For instance, the speakers of a minor language may be placed in economically and socially disadvantaged situations in which knowledge and use of the major language provides economic and social advantages. Even without such indirect pressures, some or many of the speakers of minor languages, especially members of the young generation, and children, tend to be attracted to a readily available major language, and prefer it to their own. Other more dramatic, causes can be: sudden disruption of the life and basis of existence of a small speech community by the intrusion of some economic and exploiting activity from the outside world, such as large-scale logging activities by a major logging company in the area of a small forest-dwelling community, or drilling for oil by an international oil company in the living area of a hunting and gathering community, etc. Other causes are the decimation and subsequent dispersal of the members of a speech community through natural disasters such as volcanic eruptions, tsunamis, or through diseases assuming plague proportions, or wars and genocide, etc.

A good yardstick for recognizing the level of endangerment of a language in the less dramatic situations mentioned above is the use of a threatened language in various generations of a speech community, especially that of children and young adults. If they begin not to learn the language any more and 10–30 per cent do not, the language is *potentially endangered*. If there are only few children speakers left, and the youngest good speakers are young adults, the language is *endangered*. If the youngest good speakers are largely past middle age, the language is *seriously endangered*. If only a handful of mostly old speakers are left, the language is *moribund*. If no speakers seem to be left, the language is believed *extinct*.

It may be mentioned that many languages believed extinct have recently been found to still have speakers; they had become secret, for fear of their speakers of persecution. With the cessation of the reason for their fear, the languages were no longer hidden by them. Some really *extinct* languages have recently been *revived*, e.g. Hebrew, and some Australian Aboriginal languages. This yardstick cannot be used in the more dramatic cases of language endangerment mentioned above. There other factors have to be taken into account. For instance, a perfectly well functioning language of a small forest-dwelling community with children speakers would have to be regarded as endangered or even seriously endangered if it is known that a logging company from a dominant language area is about to move into its territory, inevitably precipitating the total disruption of the life, existence and culture of the forest dwellers. The well functioning language of a small speech community totally dispersed in many directions by the effects of a major volcanic eruption or a major local war must be regarded as probably seriously endangered, etc.

In general, the Australasian and Pacific areas have, at least until very recently, been those areas of the world least affected by widespread language endangerment and death, with the notable exception of Australia, which has ranked very high amongst the countries and parts of the world with the worst records in this. Taiwan (i.e. Formosa) has had a very poor record for a very long time until a few years ago, and New Caledonia had also been a bad area, and Hawaii a very bad one.

Indonesia has, in recent decades, increasingly acquired a bad record of language endangerment through its language policies, especially in Irian Jaya, parts of Maluku, and also in Sulawesi, and its record can be expected to get worse because of them. In all these cases, the large dominant metropolitan language and the attitudes, policies and ignorance of their largely monolingual speakers towards minority languages and their speakers were largely to blame for the language endangerment and death in areas of their physical and political dominance, with their accompanying economic influence. In some other areas of Australasia and the Pacific, e.g. the Philippines, Papua New Guinea, large lingua francas take the place of metropolitan dominant languages, but have a very much less damaging influence upon minority languages and their speakers for reasons set out below. Some missionary lingua francas in the New Guinea area and the Solomon Islands, have led to the endangerment and even to the death of some local languages, with their damaging influence being on the increase in Papua New Guinea also for reasons of changes in the general social patterns there, such as the recent great mobility of the local populations, increasing intermarriage between speakers of different languages, etc. (see below).

Tahitian, as a lingua franca, is endangering some neighbouring Polynesian languages to some extent. It may be pointed out that because of the prevalent bi- and multi-lingualism in many parts of the Australasian and Pacific area, especially on the part of the speakers of numerically small languages, the presence of powerful lingua francas and dominant languages is often less of a threat to the maintenance of numerically small languages than is the case in other parts of the world where the acquisition of a lingua franca and especially a dominant language by speakers of a minority language very often results in the receding and disappearance of the minority language. In multilingual regions of the Pacific area, the speakers of a minority or numerically small language often tend to simply add the knowledge of the major language to their repertory of languages, without much damage, if any, done to their knowledge and mastery of their own language, unless pressure from such a language and its monolingual speakers is aided by official destructive policies and becomes too overwhelming to successfully resist.

In many Pacific areas, especially in the southwestern Pacific and in particular in the New Guinea area, even the speakers of very small languages regard and cling to their languages as a vital symbol of their identity, which aids them also in resisting pressure from a dominant language and its speakers.

However, a numerically very small stable language with only some 100 or even fewer speakers, can – especially in the New Guinea area – become endangered and eventually extinct in an indirect manner. Young men tend to emigrate from their village to centres of employment, mostly large towns, where they usually marry women of different language backgrounds, with a lingua franca becoming the language of the family. The young women left behind in the villages will marry men from other villages and language backgrounds, and while they may pass their own language onto their children, the language of the village of their husbands tends to become dominant in such mixed marriages and the women's (and their children's) language will just linger on for a while. This eventually leads to the disappearance of the language of the village of these women when the older people left behind in their original village die.

In other words, even very small languages in the southwestern Pacific and especially the New Guinea area, can survive as long as the original social fabric of their speakers is maintained, even if they have contacts with speakers of major languages. If original local cultures decay, which is progressively the case in most of this area, local languages tend to survive as indicated above, but they frequently get affected by structural and semantic changes (Wurm 1986; 1992b). Especially the highly complex verb systems of Papuan languages tend to get simplified and omit grammatical forms which reflect culturally significant categories such as certain tenses and aspects in the traditional culture, but are not significant in the new culture taken over, even only in part, by the speakers of such languages. Also, many Papuan languages possess complicated noun class systems with accompanying highly complex concordance features in the sentences. Some of these classes may be based on concepts important in the traditional cultures of the speakers of such languages, e.g. on mythological and other esoteric concepts. With the decay of the local cultures and the resulting disappearance of these concepts, the significance of the relevant classes gets lost, and these classes disappear from the languages concerned.

With some Papuan languages, their entire complex noun class systems are known to have completely disappeared within a few decades, for instance in the Buna and Maprik languages in northern near-coastal areas of Papua New Guinea.

Language endangerment in various parts of Australasia and the Pacific

Indonesia

In Indonesia there is a very large number of small languages, beside quite a number of large ones. The Indonesian language, which originally was nobody's first language in the country, now has over 6 million young first-language speakers, though these are sometimes also conversant with a local language, but usually prefer to use Indonesian. Indonesian exerts great pressure endangering small languages, following a policy pattern common with monolingual speakers of large metropolitan languages in Europe, Siberia, and North and South America, though as yet with much less devastating effects because of the cushioning effect of widespread multilingualism, strong resistance to Indonesian pressure in some areas, and also the comparatively shallow time-depth of the existence of such a policy. For instance, in Central Maluku (the Moluccas) where sixty-six languages were once extant, ten are extinct and three moribund, with eleven others beginning to be endangered, even if the number of the speakers of some of them is considerable.

Large languages, Malay dialects used as lingua francas, and Indonesian itself threaten small languages through increasing pressure. In Sulawesi, the Bugis language, whose speakers settle in many areas as traders, is an important lingua franca which exercises pressure on small languages, in addition to the pressure by Indonesian, and other factors also add to language endangerment, resulting in 36 of the 121 languages on Sulawesi being endangered or even moribund. In Borneo, where about 140 languages are located, some of them quite small, one language is extinct and five (or probably many more) endangered, with about ten more having very small numbers of speakers. Pressure is from Indonesian (and Malay in Sarawak) and some large local languages. On Sumatra, one of the languages on the islands off the southwestern coast is endangered, and one on an island off the northeastern coast is moribund or even extinct. Other, mostly large to very large languages in western Indonesia, are not endangered, though some with comparatively few speakers may soon be. Of the fifty-three languages on Timor Island and areas adjacent to it, six are potentially endangered, two endangered, and one moribund.

However, the situation in East Timor is special. The rampages and massacres there by the militia in late 1999 have had a catastrophic effect on the population and have profoundly changed the language situation in much of it. The moribund language mentioned above, the Papuan language Maku'a, was spoken in a settlement which had

441

been completely razed to the ground and its population killed, scattered or deported to camps in Western Timor. It was feared that the language may have become extinct as a result of this. However, very recent information from Professor James Fox, the Director of the Research School of Pacific and Asian Studies of the Australian National University in Canberra, who had a first-hand opportunity to check on the language situation in parts of East Timor, found a number of Maku'a speakers still alive and even obtained some Maku'a language material from them. A catastrophic fate was feared to have befallen other languages of East Timor, especially some with comparatively few speakers, as a result of actions of the perpetrators of such pernicious acts there. Fortunately, this does not seem to have been the case. The situation for the country's languages since it became independent remains to be seen, the former colonial language, Portugese, has been retained as an official language.

Education everywhere in Indonesia is essentially in Indonesian, though in some of the large languages, such as Javanese, Madurese, Sundanese, Batak on Sumatra, and Gorontalo on Sulawesi, some unofficial use of them in education occurs. In some of them, literacy is widespread. Such languages still have high prestige among speakers of small languages, but are gradually losing it to Indonesian, especially amongst members of the young generation. In several small languages in Irian Jaya and elsewhere in eastern Indonesia, the international SIL organization has established small-scale literacy and produced some small educational publications in them.

Irian Jaya is also a special case in Indonesia. It contains about 250 languages, many of them small to very small. As in Papua New Guinea (see below), the local people have had, and still have, a very strong sense of ethnic identity, with their local language the main symbol of this identity. This has strongly contributed to their languages being very little endangered until Indonesia took over Irian Jaya from the Dutch, under whose administration there was very little pressure on the local languages. The Dutch used a form of Malay for administrative purposes and for some educational purposes, but local languages also had a role in this, especially as used by missions. This changed very considerably with the Indonesian takeover, which resulted in Indonesian becoming the sole language used for all purposes including all education, and the use of local languages being discouraged. A strong transmigration programme brought a large number of settlers, especially from Java, which disadvantaged the local population. The Indonesian language and the attitudes and policies of its speakers have played a role, and had an influence on local languages and their speakers, comparable to that of a metropolitan dominant language in other parts of the world like the Americas, the former USSR, and Australia in the days before many of the negative attitudes and influences turned to positive ones in recent times. In Irian Jaya, this situation led to increasing endangerment of local languages, especially small to very small ones, although also some quite large ones, with tens of thousands of speakers, are now endangered because of the pervading pressure from Indonesian. Sixty-five languages in Irian Jaya are now endangered to some extent, two are extinct, and close to 100 other languages with small to very small numbers of speakers are likely to become endangered in the forseeable future.

Philippines

Here there is relatively very little language endangerment, in spite of a very uneven distribution of the number of speakers of individual languages. Of the 150 languages

442

in the Philippines, ten very large ones have a total number of 50 million speakers, which is about 90 per cent of the population of the Philippines. One of these, the national language Pilipino (Tagalog) has 10 million first-language speakers, over 15 million second-language speakers, and is understood by over 40 million. It is quite apparent that the widespread multilingualism in the Philippines is a good defence against the loss of minority languages there, aided by the accompanying lack of language policies hostile to minority languages. Fourteen small languages in the Philippines are endangered, with three extinct, with the reason for this being mainly pressure from larger languages.

Taiwan

Taiwan (formerly known as Formosa) was originally occupied completely by Austronesian language speakers. Around 1,600AD, a strong immigration of Fukien (Hokkien)-speaking Chinese began into the western lowland areas of the island, which lead to a gradual sinicization of the Austronesians of those areas. Twenty-three languages are known to have existed, of which eight are now extinct and fifteen are still spoken, but six of these are moribund. All of the latter are located in the mountainous eastern half of the island. In the 1950s, a strong influx of further Chinese speakers took place, and Mandarin Chinese became the official language of Taiwan. Chinese language pressure on the Austronesian languages became stronger, and the latter continued to recede before Chinese. This was aided by governmental policies. However, during the last few years, there has been a reversal of governmental language policy with the government now actively supporting the maintenance of the Austronesian minority languages. This has resulted in their revitalization.

Papua New Guinea

Papua New Guinea, with its approximately 850 languages and other peculiarities, is a particularly interesting and special case in the Pacific and requires some elaborate treatment here. Here, language endangerment had been at a very low level until two decades or so ago – it was at the lowest level of all areas in the world containing many small languages. This was largely attributable to the very low role of a metropolitan language, English, in the country. Though it was the official language of the then colonial masters (Australia) of the country, it exercised very little social influence. The number of expatriate English speakers was very low indeed and of necessity, the widespread lingua franca, Tok Pisin, often under the misnomer New Guinea Pidgin, had to be used for virtually every aspect of the colonial administration and face-to-face contact between the expatriates and members of the local population. Another lingua franca used in the former Territory of Papua in the southern part of the country, namely Police Motu (later misnamed Hiri Motu), supplemented it in some areas and smaller local lingua francas were resorted to in some areas in addition. Though English was an instrument of education, the number of members of the local population who had a good command of it remained far too low to have a significant impact on the local language picture, which consists of about 850, mostly small to very small, languages. Only ten languages have now over 50,000 speakers, and only three over 100,000, with the largest local language, Enga in the western part of the highlands area, having 238,000 (Nekitel 1998), an increase from 160,000 or so about twenty years ago (Wurm and Hattori 1981–3). Until less than twenty years ago, and to a considerable extent also today, though with this progressively weakening, Papua New Guineans have, with great pride, regarded their local languages as the main symbol of their local identities.

The large general lingua franca Tok Pisin, which today is known as a second language by about three quarters of the population of the country, and by about half of it twenty years ago, is now looked upon by them as a symbol of their national identity. Until about twenty years ago, it constituted no threat to the local languages. It was very little creolized, with only the children of linguistically mixed marriages in the urban centres learning it as their first language, because of necessity, it had to be the language of the family. Tok Pisin developed over a century ago in the former German New Guinea (Wurm and Mühlhäusler 1985; Wurm *et al.* 1996) and right from the start, functioned as an inter-native lingua franca, and as an European-native means of intercommunication only as a subsidiary function. It developed into a highly complex language with essentially Melanesian-Austronesian grammar, and much of its vocabulary derived from English, but often with changed meanings and a sound system which makes much of it incomprehensible to English speakers. A good portion of its vocabulary has native or German origins. Especially in the past, very few expatriates had a proper command of it and used instead a sort of English jargon, nicknamed 'Tok Masta' by the natives.

The situation as described began to change about twenty years ago, following the independence of Papua New Guinea in 1975. This resulted in a decrease in the importance of the local languages to many members of the local population, especially of the young generation, a preference for the use of Tok Pisin by many, especially young, speakers of small, and some larger, languages, and the increasing endangerment of a number of small, and some not so small, languages, though the level of language endangerment is still far below that prevailing in neighbouring Irian Jaya, and in most other parts of the world.

There have been essentially four main reasons for this development: (1) the greatly increasing mobility of the population of the country; (2) the rapidly rising of the frequency of intermarriage between speakers of many different languages in more and more parts of Papua New Guinea, without the migration of one or both partners to urban centres; (3) the increasing role and importance of electronic media in which, apart from English, Tok Pisin and Hiri Motu and fifteen large local languages are used, and a small number of not so large languages in some regions. This raises the prestige of perhaps two dozen major languages in Papua New Guinea, and sidelines 830 or so others; (4) varying educational policies have been sometimes favourable for the maintenance of local languages, or have sometimes contributed to the endangerment of languages. Up to the middle of the twentieth century, local languages and mission and church lingua francas played an important part in elementary education. Afterwards, the Australian administration favoured the use of English in education more and more, though the results of this were not particularly encouraging, and frowned upon the use of local languages, and especially of Tok Pisin, for this purpose. After the independence of Papua New Guinea in 1975, the small English-educated elite tried to continue this policy, which was not successful because of the communication breakdown, inherent in this approach, between English-speaking expatriate teachers and their pupils who mostly did not know English. Tok Pisin and Hiri Motu, as well as local languages, had to be used to achieve some communication between the teachers and pupils, with the teachers often having little or no knowledge of these languages.

By way of contrast, the SIL has been very active in Papua New Guinea since the mid-1950s, with even better results than in Irian Jaya (see above under Indonesia). Over 270 local languages, predominantly those with not very small numbers of speakers, have until 1997 been studied by SIL members, with their speakers achieving literacy in their own languages. A large amount of literacy materials, manuals of important matters of daily life such as hygiene, health, skills, etc., have been produced by the SIL in these languages, as well as vernacular guide booklets for use in elementary education. This has been in addition to their being engaged in translating Scripture into those local languages. During the 1980s, the education policies of the Papua New Guinea government started turning in the direction of strengthening local traditional cultures and values, together with raising literacy levels in local languages, Tok Pisin, Hiri Motu, and English. In this, the SIL has played a crucial role. More and more provincial vernacular preparatory schools have become established in the various provinces of Papua New Guinea, and in the early 1990s these numbered almost a hundred, with programmes in well over twenty languages. This constituted a modest beginning to renewed elementary education in local languages, which quickly led to cases of reverse language shift and the increased use of local languages by children (Mühlhäusler et al. 1996). Added to this, the efforts of SIL in over 270 languages also constitutes an important contribution to the role of local languages in elementary education. However, all this still leaves out hundreds of other local languages from any role in elementary education. The use of only certain local languages in the basic educational process increases their prestige in the eyes of Papua New Guineans, but their use in the official education system contributes to lowering the respect of the speakers of many other, especially very small, languages for their own languages. The declaration by the Vice-Minister of Education of Papua New Guinea, Dr John Waiko, on 8 September 1997, which made every one of the local languages official languages of the country that could all be used in basic elementary education along with Tok Pisin, Hiri Motu and English, was an important decision for potentially slowing down language endangerment in Papua New Guinea.

However, the problem of the practical implementation of such a policy decision, seems far beyond the capabilities of the country. A radical re-thinking concerning the possibility of some utilization of purely oral instruction for every child in a provincial vernacular preparatory school for an hour or so every day, may help to resolve this problem. In almost every class of such a school there would be children from several different language backgrounds, who are also bi- or multilingual in the language(s) used in the school for basic elementary education and literacy. It is being proposed that such pupils be split into groups according to their mother-tongues and be spoken to by a suitable adult person every day for some period in their own language, providing them with some basic information about their culture and traditions, about hygiene, health, useful skills such as gardening, and other knowledge of value to them, thereby contributing to the maintenance of their languages, and to raising the respect for them in the eyes of the children.

Seventy-seven languages of Papua New Guinea are endangered in varying degrees, with sixteen extinct. Close to 200 languages have rather small to very small numbers of speakers and are likely candidates for endangerment. For instance, catastrophic events like the disastrous tsunami which hit a coastal and lagoon section of the far northwest coast of Papua New Guinea in November 1998, brought several viable small languages to the brink of extinction by killing most of their speakers. In addition to the ninety-three endangered or extinct local languages, there are over a dozen pidgin languages based on local languages, and a German-based Creole. All of these are moribund or extinct, which would bring the total of endangered or extinct languages in Papua New Guinea close to eighty. Efforts are being undertaken to stem the tide of endangerment, especially to influence the young generation not to prefer Tok Pisin when talking to speakers of their own language, with varying success.

Admiralty Islands

While extinct languages on the Admiralty Islands, to the north of Papua New Guinea, have been included in what has been said, the somewhat unusual situation on that island group deserves some remarks. There are thirty-two Melanesian Austronesian languages on the Admiralty Islands, some of them with very few speakers. Several are endangered or on the way to becoming endangered. Pressure on them is exercised by creolized Tok Pisin, because the Admiralty Islands are the only non-urban area in Papua New Guinea with quite a number of first-language creolized Tok Pisin speakers. These have been present for several decades for a number of reasons: the smallness of the local languages and the absence of local lingua francas, frequent intermarriage of speakers of different languages well before this became widespread elsewhere in Papua New Guinea, and the apparent relative weakness of the great value attached to local languages as symbol of local identity by their speakers which has been so strong in other parts of Papua New Guinea and elsewhere in the southwestern Pacific. Creolized Tok Pisin has high prestige in the Admiralty Islands and exercises an influence comparable to that of a metropolitan dominant language spoken by monolinguals.

Solomon Islands

In the Solomon Islands, there are sixty-two Austronesian and seven Papuan languages alive today. The main source of endangerment, especially for small languages, has been the presence of several large lingua francas which were originally mission lingua francas and as such exert more cultural and consciously directed pressure on other, usually smaller, local languages than non-missionary lingua francas in the area which are largely trade languages and exist in the repertory of multilingual speakers of local languages, without exerting cultural pressure. Originally, there were ten Papuan languages in the Solomons, but three became extinct from the pressure of one large missionary lingua franca, Roviana. Twelve of the Austronesian languages and one Papuan are in danger, and some more small ones are likely candidates for this, with increasing pressure from the main Solomon Islands lingua franca, the English-based Solomon Pijin.

Vanuatu

In Vanuatu, 100 Austronesian languages are alive now. Early in the twentieth century, the population was decimated as a result of the introduction of devastating new diseases, in particular smallpox, influenza and leprosy. The numbers of speakers of individual languages was greatly reduced thereby, but only a relatively moderate number of languages, perhaps twenty or so, became extinct then. Today, there are three languages which have become extinct in living memory, and thirty-one are in various stages of endangerment. Most of these have very small numbers of speakers, and are under pressure from larger neighbouring languages, and the main lingua franca and national language Bislama, which is an English-based pidgin with a rather complex un-English grammar, though less elaborate than Tok Pisin in Papua New Guinea.

New Caledonia

New Caledonia is a special case in the southwestern Pacific. With the exception of Australia and New Zealand, it is the only region in this area in which the majority of the inhabitants are monolingual speakers of a metropolitan dominant language, French, and display the cultural aggression characteristic of such speech communities. The French language and the attitudes and policies of its speakers have put the indigenous languages and their speakers under great pressure, leading to only 20,000 of the 55,000 indigenous Melanesians being able to speak one or several of the local aberrant Austronesian languages. In the past, and in part still today, stable multilingualism has been the rule in the New Caledonian linguistic picture. However, until quite recently, it has not been able to protect the local languages against the overwhelming pressure of French and the cultural attitudes of its speakers. Recently there has been a strong reawakening of indigenous ethnic identity feelings in New Caledonia, which has resulted in the revitalization of several local languages. Nevertheless, small local languages are under subtle pressure from larger local languages, which counteracts the traditional stable multilingualism and mutual respect for local languages in the indigenous population. This has led to two of the local languages becoming extinct, and thirteen becoming endangered in various degrees, with two of them moribund.

French Polynesia

The languages of French Polynesia are little endangered. The influence of French is strong in Papeete, the capital of Polynesia, but is weak to very weak in other areas. Until about a decade ago, Tahitian had been strongly receding before French in Papeete, with many young Tahitians gradually losing their command of it. However, there has been a very strong revival and reinvigoration of the language during the 1990s, with increasing use of it in the media. At the same time, other Polynesian languages have been receding before Tahitian in the Tuamotuan, Marquesan and Austral Islands archipelagos, with three languages now potentially endangered or endangered.

Hawaiian Islands

The Hawaiian language was close to extinction a decade or two ago, except on Niihau Island in the northwest of the island chain. This island has been a private property for many years, and visitors have not been permitted on it. This made it possible for the Hawaiian language to survive on that island, with its speakers largely monolingual. On other Hawaiian islands, the language had almost completely given way to pidgin English and English until the 1980s, when a strong move towards the revival of Hawaiian started. Over 2,000 young speakers emerged from Hawaiian language immersion courses. In spite of this, it is still doubtful whether the Hawaiian language will survive outside Niihau Island, because of the abnormal nature of the Hawaiian speech community which consists of grandparents, great-grandparents and young

447

persons, with no parents speaking the language. At the same time, its continued existence is threatened by very strong pressure from English, and even more so by American monolingualist attitudes.

Polynesian outlier languages

Each of the so-called Polynesian outlier languages located to the west of Polynesia in Melanesia has had traditionally only very few speakers, but is not endangered by larger languages, because most of them are very isolated. An exception to this is the Emae language spoken on Emwae Island in Vanuatu which has been influenced by a Melanesian language, and is potentially endangered.

New Zealand

At the beginning of the twentieth century, the Polynesian Maori language in New Zealand was close to extinction. It has had quite an impressive revival since, and now has many thousands of fair to good speakers. However, the young generation has been losing interest in it in recent years, and its ultimate survival may be in doubt.

Easter Island

The Rapanui language of Easter Island came very near to extinction because of the forced removal of most of the speakers from the island to guano collection areas in South America, where most of them perished. Very few returned to their home island, but the population did increase there again. There are now approximately 2,500 speakers of the language. However, the language is endangered because of negative attitudes of the young generation towards it.

Micronesia

The Micronesian languages are not much endangered. Only one of them, Mapia, which was spoken to the southwest of the Micronesian area proper on an island located to the north of western Irian Jaya, has become extinct, quite some time ago, under pressure from Biak, the former Austronesian lingua franca of the area. Biak itself is now in danger due to overwhelming pressure from Indonesian, in spite of having about 40,000 speakers. Two Micronesian languages located outside Micronesia, Tanapag on the west coast of Saipan Island in the northern Mariana Islands, and Tobian in Palau, are respectively endangered and seriously endangered, under pressure from the Chamorro and the Palauan language.

Australia

Some remarks on the endangerment and extinction situation of Australian Aboriginal languages have already been included above in the general remarks on the Australian languages. Many of the languages regarded as extinct became extinct a long time ago, in the nineteenth and the early twentieth century, among others the Iora language of the Sydney area, the Awabakal language of the Lake Macquarie area to the north of Sydney, and the Kaurna language of Adelaide, which ceased to be a language of daily inter-communication in the 1890s, with its last speaker dying in 1927. Causes of this were varied, with epidemic diseases (especially smallpox); genocide, including the poisoning of waterholes by white settlers; the removal of Aboriginal tribes from their traditional hunting and living areas; the concentration of Aborigines of different tribal and language backgrounds on missions and in camps where they were discouraged from speaking their tribal languages and of necessity had to resort to a lingua franca or pidgin English to communicate with each other; the removal of Aboriginal children from their parents and tribes to situations where only English was used, etc.; and in general, the pressure from pidgin English and English used by the increasing white population (Wurm *et al.* 1996). Other languages became extinct more recently for less inhumane reasons, mainly the pressure from English and the assimilation policies of the Australian government, although the removal of Aboriginal children from their parents and their placement in an English-speaking environment, often without the consent of their parents (especially in the case of quarter-cast children, whom they tended to regard as not really Aboriginal), continued until recent decades.

This situation changed in the 1970s when negative governmental policies and practices involving Aborigines and their languages were replaced by positive ones, and assimilation policies gave way to those of multiculturalism. Aboriginal languages still viable were encouraged, and in areas where they were used in daily life, bilingual education was introduced. This policy worked well, though it has recently come under attack in the Northern Territory where most of the viable Aboriginal languages are spoken, with the territory's administrators trying to abolish it in the mistaken belief that bilingual education will adversely affect the children's knowledge of English, though the opposite is the case.

All these situations coincided with a very strong reawakening of a sense of ethnic identity among the Aboriginals, and of interest in their own languages. This resulted in the reinvigoration and revival of several moribund and extinct Aboriginal languages, such as for instance the abovementioned Kaurna language of the Adelaide area. This was revived on the basis of extensive reliable published and other materials on the language obtained from the last speakers prior to its extinction. A teaching course for members of the Kaurna tribe for learning their former language was arranged for at the University of Adelaide, and now there are again a number of speakers of the language who use it daily. Other languages have been similarly revived. This has resulted in the designation of 'extinct' for Australian Aboriginal languages being an uncertain categorization in some particular instances.

Also, a few languages believed extinct have been found to still have speakers – in such cases the languages had sometimes gone underground as secret languages in response to earlier negative government policies.

Peninsular Malaysia

The Aslian languages in Peninsular Malaysia are mostly potentially endangered, because of pressure from Malay, the national language of Malaysia.

Pidgin and Creole languages

As has already been mentioned, there are in addition to the local indigenous languages, forty-six Pidgin and Creole languages, including Trade Pidgins and Trade Jargons, which are or were spoken in the Pacific and Australasia, mainly in various parts of Indonesia, in Papua New Guinea, Micronesia and Polynesia. Eight of these are extinct and twenty-six threatened, with ten of them seriously endangered or moribund. Only twelve are still fully functioning.

Survey of recently extinct languages

Here a survey of recently, or relatively recently extinct, languages is given. Their number is comparatively small, except for Australia. With each language named in the alphabetical list of entries of threatened or extinct languages, information on its location by regions and classification is given. The circumstances of extinction of languages are indicated after the name of the region concerned, or added to the language entries themselves. Notes on their structures are given in the entries.

Taiwan

The Taiwanese autochthonous languages are Austronesian, and constitute the three non-Malayo-Polynesian branches of them (Atayalic, Tsouic, Paiwanic) – the fourth branch comprises all Malayo-Polynesian Austronesian languages. Eight of the Taiwanese Austronesian languages are extinct, three of them became recently or relatively recently extinct. All of them succumbed to pressure from Chinese, and/or of large local languages.

Philippines

All Philippine languages are Western Malayo-Polynesian. The three extinct languages succumbed to pressure by larger languages decades ago. A fourth language, Ata, in Negros Oriental Province, Meso Philippine, Central, for which a few families of speakers were reported in 1973, may now be extinct. It may have succumbed to the large Cebuano language.

Malaysia

There is only one extinct Malayo-Polynesian language in Malaysia, the Seru language in Sarawak on Borneo.

Indonesia

There are relatively few extinct languages in Indonesia, though their number is likely to increase very markedly in the foreseeable future in view of the relentless pressure of Indonesian. The areas within Indonesia which contain extinct languages will be mentioned individually below.

Sumatra (Sumatera)

The Lom (or Belom, or Napor) language, a Western Malayo-Polynesian language on northeast Bangka Island, off southeastern Sumatra, which has been reported to have perhaps fifty speakers, is regarded by some as possibly extinct. If this is the case, the pressure from local Malay, and from Indonesian, would have been the cause.

Sulawesi

The languages of Sulawesi are Western Malayo-Polynesian. One language is definitely extinct, and another, Dampal, possibly extinct by now, under pressure from large neighbouring languages.

Maluku

Most of the many Malayo-Polynesian languages of Maluku belong to the Central-Eastern Malayo-Polynesian language group, and within that to its central section. Of the extinct languages, only Ibu is Papuan and belongs to the West Papuan Phylum. Five Malayo-Polynesian languages are definitely and five probably extinct. Two Creole languages are definitely extinct: a total of about twelve or thirteen. In all cases, they succumbed mostly to pressure from Ambon Malay, the lingua franca of Central Maluku, and pressure from Indonesian has also taken its toll. Pressure from large local languages also resulted in its replacing small languages in some instances.

Nusa Tenggara

The only definitely extinct language here is Timor Creole Portuguese, which used to be spoken around Dili and other centres on Timor, until a few decades ago.

Irian Jaya

There is one definitely extinct Micronesian language in Irian Jaya, one probably extinct Eastern Malayo-Polynesian language, South Halmahera-West New Guinea group, and one probably extinct Papuan language of the Papuan Geelvinck Bay Phylum. They succumbed to pressure from large local and regional languages.

Papua New Guinea

The languages in Papua New Guinea, as in Irian Jaya, belong to two quite different categories. They are either Eastern Malayo-Polynesian of the Western Oceanic type (EMPW), or Papuan languages (P) which belong to several unrelated phyla. Sixteen languages (seven Papuan, nine Malayo-Polynesian) have become recently or relatively recently extinct.

In addition to these, there are eight Papuan-based pidgin languages, discovered in the early 1990s in the interior of the East Sepik Province (Williams 1996), two Papuan-based trade pidgins formerly used between the Motu people of the Port Moresby area and two linguistically different Papuan-speaking communities in the Gulf Province, three pidgin trade languages based on the Malay-Polynesian Mekeo language in the Western near-coastal part of the Central Province, and a German-based Creole in the East New Britain Province. Four of these are extinct, one more probably extinct, the remainder moribund, except for the Mekeo Trade Pidgins which are seriously endangered, and the German-based Creole which is seriously endangered.

451

Solomon Islands

The languages of the Solomon Islands are, as in Papua New Guinea, Eastern Malayo-Polynesian languages of the Western Oceanic (EMPW) or Central-Eastern Oceanic (EMPCE) type, or Papuan languages of the East Papuan type. The great majority of the languages are Malayo-Polynesian. Three of the Papuan languages and two of the Malayo-Polynesian ones are extinct.

Vanuatu

The languages of Vanuatu are all Malayo-Polynesian of the EMPCE type. Perhaps twenty or so of the languages became extinct around the end of the nineteenth and the early twentieth centuries. Three of them have become more recently extinct and will be mentioned in the listings, and at least two more are very close to extinction.

New Caledonia

All the New Caledonian languages are Malayo-Polynesian of the EMPCE, remote Oceanic, New Caledonian type which has some aberrant features. Two of the languages have become relatively recently extinct.

Micronesia

The local languages in Micronesia are largely Micronesian, with three Polynesian, one Western Malayo-Polynesian (Yapese) and one English-and-Micronesian-based Creole. The Micronesian languages are all of the EMPCE, remote Oceanic, Micronesian type. Only one Micronesian language is extinct, the Mapia language spoken forrmerly on Mapia Island north of Irian Jaya (see under Irian Jaya).

Australia

In the latter part of the nineteenth century and the first decades of the twentieth, a considerable number of Australian languages ceased to be languages in daily use, and gradually became extinct, though for many of the languages thus affected, a few speakers, or at least one or two, could be found until well past the middle of the twentieth century, or even today. For a number of languages believed long extinct, speakers or at least semi-speakers were located by persistent linguistic fieldworkers. In several cases, such speakers had not used their languages for several decades, but got back into remembering them quite well when the linguists started working with them systematically. In the late 1970s and the 1980s, many dying languages were known, or believed, to have one, two, or a few more elderly speakers. This situation has changed very markedly since, with these old speakers passing away, resulting in the extinction of their languages. However, there is a high factor of uncertainty in calling an Australian language extinct, when it is known to have had a few, or even only one, speaker(s) not long ago. With remaining speakers of Australian languages frequently scattered over vast areas, often very far from their original tribal region, there is always a chance that a speaker of a language believed extinct still survives somewhere.

Reasons for the massive endangerment and extinction of Australian languages have been given above in the general remarks on Australian languages and in the above section on language endangerment in more detail. It may be added here that in northern parts of Australia, pressure from Kriol, the English-based Australian Creole, has also made Australian languages fall into disuse, especially with children. Aboriginal English, which many Aborigines regard as a symbol of Aboriginal identity, has also contributed to this in many parts of Australia.

Taking all this into consideration, 180 Australian languages mostly believed recently extinct or probably extinct have been listed in the entries of threatened and extinct languages, on the understanding that several of them may well be found to have one or a few speakers, and/or that some more languages may be believed to be recently extinct or probably extinct by the time of the publication of this encyclopedia.

Classification of languages, research priorities, shortcomings in present knowledge and current work, prospects for language maintenance or rescue, and future prospects

Classification of languages

There are relatively few problems with the classification of the languages in Australasia and the Pacific. The classification of the Austronesian languages as given here is generally accepted. With the Papuan languages, the situation is as follows: the large Trans-New Guinea Phylum which was first established by the present writer, C. L. Voorhoeve and K. McElhanon in the mid-1970s (Wurm (ed.) 1975; Wurm 1982; Wurm and Hattori 1981–3), was accepted by some specialists, but regarded by others as requiring further proof. Intensive work during the last few years by a team of linguists has proved beyond doubt that the Trans-New Guinea Phylum is a reality (e.g. Pawley 1995; 1998; Ross 1995). The Sepik-Ramu Phylum established by Laycock (Laycock 1975a) is largely accepted, but a few of the languages included in it as constituting the lower Sepik (Nor-Pondo) subphylum-level stock may actually constitute a small separate phylum. The Torricelli Phylum also established by Laycock (Laycock 1975b) is generally accepted. The West Papuan Phylum tentatively established by Voorhoeve (Voorhoeve 1975a; Wurm 1982) is also generally accepted, and the small East Bird's Head phylum-level stock which Voorhoeve (Voorhoeve 1975b) regarded as a separate phylum, is now known to be part of the West Papuan Phylum. The East Papuan Phylum which the present writer established tentatively (Wurm 1975; 1982) may in fact contain several small unrelated phylic groups. The small additional phyla of Papuan languages are generally accepted. The classification of the Aslian languages, and that of the Australian Aboriginal languages, is also generally accepted.

Research priorities

In the whole of Australasia and the Pacific area, the first research priority is the establishment of which languages are endangered, especially those seriously endangered or moribund, and their study, as detailed as possible, if that has not been done before. The collection of as many data as possible, in writing and through sound recordings, is most important, with adequate translations and explanations, so that a good analysis of the collected materials is possible even after the death of the last speaker of the language.

If there is enough time, i.e. there is more than one surviving speaker, a preliminary grammatical statement should be compiled which is likely to show up gaps in the information which should be filled by subsequent informant work. A list of at least 500–1,000 vocabulary items should be compiled which again will have obvious gaps to be filled. Most importantly, as many texts as possible should be collected, with both interlinear and free translations. This basic descriptive and informative material should then be expanded as far as possible through further collaboration with informants. Work on a range of endangered languages should always take precedence over studying only one language very thoroughly while other endangered languages remain unstudied and disappear. It is very important that even short and sketchy, or incomplete and preliminary, studies and materials be quickly published or made available in some other form to linguists so as to encourage further urgent work in endangered languages. In all this, attention should be focused on small languages, which even in their original un-endangered form had very few speakers. This is necessary because such languages can disappear very quickly once they become endangered, and also because they are less likely than larger ones to have been studied, even superficially, by competent linguists. At the same time it is important that languages selected for study be not very closely related to, or almost dialects of, languages already well studied. In areas with many different languages like New Guinea, small languages sometimes tend to be linguistic isolates, or languages only very distantly related to larger ones.

Shortcomings in present knowledge, and current work

Shortcomings in present knowledge

First, the state of knowledge about the nature, structure, lexicon, etc. of individual Austronesian languages in given areas is briefly reviewed.

LEVEL OF THE KNOWLEDGE OF AUSTRONESIAN LANGUAGES

The majority of them are at least superficially known, many much better. In the various parts of the Austronesian world, the situation is as set out below.

Philippines Many of the languages are quite well known, thanks to the efforts of members of the very active SIL there, of other Philippine linguists, and of outside, mainly American, linguists.

Taiwan The surviving languages are generally quite well known, thanks to intensive work by Taiwanese, Japanese and some other linguists. The extinct ones are in part reasonably well known, but those which became extinct a long time ago, are generally little known, except for some for which good materials are extant, e.g. Siraya, which is being studied by A. Adelaar.

Indonesia and Malaysia Thanks to the efforts of mainly Dutch, and more recently, Indonesian linguists, missionaries, members of the SIL, and others, in various parts of

Indonesia and Malaysia, the following can be said about these two countries: in Sumatra, Java and Bali, most languages, including most of the few small ones there, are well known, thanks to the efforts of Dutch, Indonesian and German linguists. In Borneo where there is a large number of small to quite small languages in addition to some large ones, many are quite well known, others only superficially or only very little. In Sulawesi, most languages, especially large ones, are well known, but a few of the smaller ones only superficially. Some of those are being studied now, especially by the German linguist N. P. Himmelmann. In Maluku where there is a large number of small languages, e.g. on Ceram Island, many of them are only superficially known, though a few have been well studied by now. In Nusa Tenggara, the island chain extending eastwards from Bali to, and including, Timor, some Austronesian languages are well known, some of the smaller ones only superficially. In Irian Jaya, most of the not very numerous Austronesian languages are only known to a limited extent, but a few have been well studied and are well known. In the areas from Borneo to Irian Jaya, Dutch linguists, missionary linguists, and members of the SIL, and some others, e.g. American linguists, have greatly contributed to our knowledge.

Areas further to the east In *Papua New Guinea*, as a result of the efforts of Australian, Papua New Guinean and mission and SIL linguists, and some others, quite a few Austronesian languages are well known, but quite a number of the small ones only superficially. Most of the Austronesian languages in the *Solomon Islands* are reasonably well to well known mainly through the work of missionaries and members of the SIL, and of predominantly Australian linguists. A few of the small ones are only superficially known. The Austronesian languages of the Santa Cruz Archipelago are reasonably well known through the work of Australian linguists and others. In *Vanuatu*, some languages are well known mainly through the work of Australian and French linguists, but quite a few are known only superficially, and others very little. In *New Caledonia* and the *Loyalty Islands*, most languages have been studied quite well, mainly by missionaries and French and Australian scholars, but a few are only superficially known. In the *Fiji* area and *Polynesia*, virtually all languages are well known, thanks to the efforts of New Zealand, French, American and some other scholars, including missionary linguists, and the same is the case in *Micronesia*, where Australian, American and some other scholars have worked, as well as missionary linguists.

LEVEL OF THE KNOWLEDGE OF PAPUAN LANGUAGES

In general, our knowledge of the nature, structures, lexicons, etc. of many of the 780 Papuan languages is quite good, but many are only superficially known, and a good number of them are hardly known at all beyond a list of words and perhaps a few remarks on their nature and grammar. In the various areas in which Papuan languages are spoken, the situation is set out below.

Irian Jaya Quite a few of the Papuan languages are quite well known thanks to the work of Dutch, Australian, German and Indonesian linguists, members of the SIL, missionary linguists, and some others. There is a large number of only superficially known languages, and an even greater number of especially small languages on which there is very little information beyond a wordlist.

Northern Halmahera, and Timor, Alor and Pantar Islands   Most of the Papuan languages of these islands are known to some extent, with some of them well, as a result of the efforts of mainly Dutch and Australian linguists.

Papua New Guinea   A considerable number of the Papuan languages of Papua New Guinea has been studied in some detail, and they are reasonably to well known thanks to the work of mainly Australian and some Papua New Guinean linguists, members of the SIL, missionary linguists, and some others. Many languages are only superficially known, and quite a few are only little or hardly known beyond a wordlist and some notes on their structure.

Solomon Islands   All of the four surviving Papuan languages in the Solomons are reasonably well known due to work by Australian, Canadian and British linguists, missionary linguists and to activities of members of the SIL.

Santa Cruz Archipelago   All three Papuan languages there are reasonably to well known due to work by Australian linguists.

LEVEL OF THE KNOWLEDGE OF AUSTRALIAN LANGUAGES

Australia   Most surviving languages have now been thoroughly studied largely by Australian linguists, and members of the SIL, and are well known. This also applies to languages relatively recently extinct. Some of the languages extinct in the first part of the twentieth century or during the nineteenth century are reasonably well documented and allow a fairly good insight into their nature, structure and lexicon. Of quite a few others, sketchy descriptions exist which give superficial knowledge of them. A large number of languages extinct long ago are only known through wordlists, and perhaps through a few notes on their structure and/or a few short sentences, though some others are quite well documented.

Tasmanian languages   The Tasmanian languages, extinct in the nineteenth century, with the last speaker dying in 1877, are very poorly documented. There were several languages, and their relationship to Australian mainland languages is in question.

LEVEL OF THE KNOWLEDGE OF ASLIAN LANGUAGES IN PENINSULAR MALAYSIA

The Austro-Asiatic languages of the interior of Peninsular Malaysia have been studied by Austro-Asiatic specialists from various countries, and are quite well known.

Current work in languages of Australasia and the Pacific

The information given here dovetails with the cursory information given above on relatively good knowledge of individual languages, and expands on it for activities in recent years. It concentrates on work leading to good knowledge of individual languages.

Philippines   For many years, and continuing unabated, the SIL has been studying individual Philippine languages, publishing large amounts of information on them.

Other academic institutions in the Philippines have also been carrying out such work, and continue to do so. Some American linguists, in part based in Hawaii, have also been working in Philippine linguistics, and still do so.

Taiwan Taiwan linguists attached to the Academia Sinica in Taiwan have been carrying out much work in the Austronesian languages of Taiwan and this work is continuing. Japanese linguists have also been doing such work for a long time. An Australian linguist has been studying one of the now extinct Taiwanese languages on the basis of available materials.

Indonesia In the past, Dutch linguists, including a number of missionary linguists, produced a large number of studies, grammars, dictionaries and other materials on individual languages of Indonesia. This tradition is still continuing for some parts of Indonesia. However, Indonesian research institutions and universities have taken over most of this task, and have been publishing numerous contributions on individual languages. Linguists based in Australia, Hawaii and mainland USA, Germany and elsewhere have worked in, and published on, languages of Maluku, Timor, the Aru Islands, Sulawesi, Borneo, Sumatra and other parts of Indonesia, with this work still continuing. Irian Jaya and the Halmahera Islands constitute a special area which is dealt with below in the following section.

Papua New Guinea, Irian Jaya and the Halmahera Islands Papua New Guinea, Irian Jaya and the Halmahera Islands, which together contain almost 1,200 languages, have presented a formidable task for linguistic study. For *Papua New Guinea*, missionary linguists had provided an impressive number of studies of individual languages in the past. This activity has now largely ceased with the nationalization of mission and church activities. However, the SIL has taken over this task, and has been working in over 270 languages of Papua New Guinea since the mid-1950s, producing a very large number of grammars, dictionaries, etc. on individual languages and studies of some of their special linguistic features which have in part been published by themselves, or in the serial publication *Pacific Linguistics* mentioned below, or elsewhere. This activity is continuing vigorously, and is expanding. While linguists of the University of Sydney had in the past contributed to the study of Papua New Guinea languages, the main centre of such work has been the Department of Linguistics at the Research School of Pacific Studies, recently renamed Research School of Pacific and Asian Studies, of the Australian National University in Canberra since the early 1960s. A very large amount of research into and studies of, individual languages of Papua New Guinea has been carried out at it, or under its auspices, with this activity continuing. The Department's serial publication *Pacific Linguistics*, which has four subseries (Occasional Papers, Monographs, Books, Special Publications), has by now reached 501 published volumes, and has over two dozen more in preparation. Its subseries have now, as from volume 501, been combined into a single series, as *Pacific Linguistics*. It was established by the Department in the early 1960s for the purpose of publishing linguistic research results in the Greater Pacific area and Southeast Asia. Many of its volumes or parts of them are devoted to languages of Papua New Guinea, and there is a special subseries within the Occasional Papers which is devoted to publishing materials on languages in danger of disappearing in the Asia-Pacific region, with one number in it dealing exclusively with Papua New Guinea. The Department of Linguistics of the University of Sydney began vigorous research into languages of Papua New Guinea again a number of years ago, and is continuing with this activity. The Department of Languages and Linguistics of the University of Papua New Guinea in Port Moresby had carried out a number of studies of Papua New Guinea languages and issued the journal *Kivung* which published research results. This journal has ceased appearing, but research by the Department has been continuing and pays special attention to language endangerment.

Irian Jaya For Irian Jaya, Dutch linguists and missionary linguists had provided a number of studies of individual languages in the past. The work by Dutch linguists continues, largely under the auspices of Leiden University, with some of the results published in *Pacific Linguistics* and others by themselves. Work by missionary linguists has largely ceased, but members of the SIL have become very active in the study of individual languages in Irian Jaya and have produced good results. They have published some of these themselves, or in *Pacific Linguistics*. A large amount of research into languages of Irian Jaya has been carried out through the abovementioned Department of Linguistics of the Research School of Pacific and Asian Studies of the Australian National University, with results published in *Pacific Linguistics* or in the Netherlands. The University of Cenderawasih in Jayapura, the capital of Irian Jaya, has also carried out research into Irian Jaya languages, and has paid attention in this also to languages in danger.

Halmahera For Halmahera, much of the work in individual languages was carried out by Dutch linguists in the past, and more recently through the abovementioned Department of Linguistics in Canberra, with results published in *Pacific Linguistics*.

Solomon Islands, Santa Cruz Archipelago, Vanuatu and New Caledonia Most of the work on languages in these areas has been undertaken through the Department of Linguistics, Research School of Pacific and Asian Studies, the Australian National University, and for some parts of them, by members of the SIL and this work is continuing. The University of Sydney, through its Department of Anthropology, did some work in the past but this is no longer the case. Linguists from Canada and Britain also worked on Papuan languages of the Solomons decades ago, and this has now been taken up again by the original Canadian worker for continuation. Most of the work on languages of the Santa Cruz Archipelago has been undertaken through the Department of Linguistics, Research School of Pacific and Asian Studies, Canberra and is continuing. That on languages on Vanuatu, and the Loyalty Islands to the north of New Caledonia, has been through the same Department, and some of it also by French linguists. Most of the work on New Caledonian languages has been carried out by French missionary linguists and through French universities and institutions. All this work is continuing.

Fiji area and Polynesia Much of the work on the languages of the Fiji area has been carried out by linguists from Fiji, Australia, Hawaii and New Zealand. Most of that in the Polynesian area outside French Polynesia was done by linguists from Hawaii and New Zealand, and that of those in French Polynesia by French linguists, with Australians also contributing. The University of Hawaii Press published profusely on individual Polynesian, and also Micronesian, languages, and the French published on those of French Polynesia, especially Tahitian. All this work is continuing. The University of the South Pacific (USP) which has campuses in several Pacific countries such as Fiji, Vanuatu, etc., has also contributed to the study of eastern Pacific languages on a continuing basis.

Micronesia   The study of languages of Micronesia was largely carried out by linguists from Hawaii, through the University of Hawaii, with some of their results published in *Pacific Linguistics*. American linguists have also worked in them. All this work is continuing.

Australia   Work in the Australian Aboriginal languages had a number of decades ago been concentrated on the Universities of Sydney, Western Australia, and Queensland, and was also carried on by missionary linguists. In the last decades, it became an important concern of the Department of Linguistics in the Faculties, The Australian National University, with the abovementioned Department of Linguistics in the Research School of Pacific and Asian Studies of that University also active in that field during the 1960s and 1970s, with *Pacific Linguistics* also publishing a considerable number of works on these languages to the present day, and interest in Australian languages still continuing there to some extent. Within the University, the Centre of Linguistic Typology has also been active in the study of Australian languages on a continuing basis. All these activities at the Australian National University are still continuing, except that the Centre of Linguistic Typology has moved to La Trobe University, Melbourne, at the end of 1999, but is continuing its work on Australian languages there. The governmental Institute of Aboriginal and Torres Strait Islanders Studies in Canberra has for many years devoted much of its activities to work in Aboriginal languages and continues to do so. The departments of linguistics in the University of Melbourne and La Trobe University, both located in Melbourne, have been, and are, doing much work in these languages. The same is the case of the University of Queensland in Brisbane, the University of New England in Armidale, the University of Western Australia and the Edith Cowan University in Perth, the University of Adelaide, and a number of other research and teaching centres in Australia. The SIL has been very active in work in Aboriginal languages, and continues to be so. In the Northern Territory of Australia, bilingual education in an Aboriginal language and English has been available for speakers of a number of Aboriginal languages for many years, but had unfortunately become a political football by the end of 1998.

Aslian languages in Peninsular Malaysia   Work in these languages has been carried out by Austro-Asianists from several countries. In Australia there is expertise in Austro-Asian languages in the Department of Linguistics of La Trobe University in Melbourne.

Work directed specifically at languages in danger

In this section, the discussion is directed at the question of the study of languages in danger, and the establishment of the danger status of languages, i.e. whether they are in danger at all, and if so, whether they are potentially endangered, endangered, seriously endangered, moribund, or (apparently) extinct.

Much of the work and facts mentioned immediately above, and above in the section dealing with endangerment and preservation, touch upon the question of the study of languages in danger. Many of the study activities mentioned involve languages which

459

happen to be in danger, without the study being undertaken primarily because a language which is the object of such a study is in danger of disappearing.

However, there are many language study projects and activities undertaken specifically because the language or languages concerned are in danger of disappearing. Many of the language surveys carried out by the SIL, linguists attached to universities and other organizations, etc., have as their aim to establish the status, and social standing, viability, and the possibility of some endangerment of the languages concerned. The large publication *Ethnologue, Languages of the World* which is issued by the SIL every four years or so (13th edn Grimes 1996; 14th edn 2000, 15th edn 2004) gives a good indication of which languages are in danger, or believed extinct. UNESCO and organizations affiliated with it such as the International Council of Philosophy and Humanistic Studies (CIPSH, UNESCO, Paris) have given special two-year grants to assist the study of languages in danger and continue to do so. Several study projects involving Australasian and Pacific languages have been assisted in this manner. The Permanent International Council of Linguists (CIPL, Leiden) which is affiliated with CIPSH, has also supported study projects specifically directed at languages in danger in Australasia. The Australian Institute of Aboriginal and Torres Strait Islanders Studies mentioned above has undertaken and supported several salvage studies of dying Australian languages, as linguists of several Australian universities have also done.

A project has been started by the present writer in collaboration with members of the Cenderawasih University in Jayapura, Irian Jaya, and linguists of the former Language and Literature Department (now part of a larger school) in the University of Papua New Guinea in Port Moresby, to establish information on language endangerment in New Guinea. Linguists of the University of the South Pacific, which has small campuses in several countries in the South Pacific such as Fiji, Vanuatu and elsewhere, have also carried out work, such as salvage work, specifically aimed at languages in danger of disappearing. Linguists at French universities and research institutions have concerned themselves with languages in danger especially in New Caledonia and Vanuatu. Linguists in New Zealand and Hawaii directed their attention at Maori and Hawaiian. Linguists of the Philippines and also of Hawaii and the USA have been concerned with language endangerment in the Philippines, with some of them, and linguists from Germany, also studying language endangerment in parts of Indonesia. Linguists in Taiwan, Japan and Australia have concerned themselves with endangered and dying Austronesian languages in Taiwan. Serial publications containing information specifically on endangered languages on Australasia and the Pacific such as the subseries in the series D of *Pacific Linguistics* mentioned before, have been established or are planned.

Prospects for maintenance or rescue of individual threatened languages

Prospects for the maintenance or rescue of individual threatened languages in Australasia and the Pacific are varied in different areas, and are determined by three main factors: (1) the attitudes and policies of administrations and governments; (2) the interest of the speakers themselves in their threatened languages; (3) the availability of resources and means for such activities, and the readiness of the speakers and their communities themselves to be actively involved in the maintenance and rescue of their threatened languages. Much of this, especially the matters mentioned under (1) and (2), have been touched upon in various parts of the foregoing.

Philippines

There are only few languages in danger in the Philippines, all of them small to very small ones threatened by larger neighbouring ones. There is no administrative effort against or for their preservation, and generally, their usually multilingual speakers and ethnic groups themselves are not particularly interested in their preservation.

Taiwan

The threatened languages in Taiwan are mostly moribund. The switch of government policies involving the indigenous Austronesian languages in the last few years from negative to supportive has raised the interest of their speakers in them. There are some efforts being made towards the preservation of endangered languages, but it may be too late for most of the moribund ones, though a revival of some of them may occur.

Indonesia including Irian Jaya

There appears to be little hope for halting the endangerment of especially the small languages, considering the negative attitudes of the government and the administration towards local languages and the exclusive fostering of Indonesian everywhere, which for small languages is particularly threatening. In Irian Jaya, the speakers of local languages regard them as symbols of their ethnic identity and take pride in them, as is the case in Papua New Guinea, but this is not enough to counteract the overwhelming pressure of Indonesian. Activities of the SIL in a number of languages, especially in Irian Jaya, act as counterbalance against this for the languages concerned. There is perhaps a possibility that political changes may give certain areas in present-day Indonesia greater freedom in determining their own affairs, which could benefit small local languages there and ensure their survival as a result of increasing self-consciousness and pride in the ethnic identity of their speakers.

Papua New Guinea

In general, the adult generation, especially those over thirty, are keenly interested in the preservation of all local languages, including threatened ones. However, in several areas, many members of the younger generation and the children are more inclined to use Tok Pisin in preference to their own languages, though many of them still have at least a passable or passive knowledge of their language. There have been a number of attempts through educational and propagandistic means, the use of media, etc., in such areas to stem the tide and encourage greater use of local language by members of the younger generation and children, but their success has largely been limited. In other areas most speakers of local, including small, languages are still very interested in preserving their languages as symbols of their ethnic identity. However, what militates against this are factors as discussed in some detail in the section on language endangerment above, such as increasing mobility of the population and increasing intermarriage between speakers of different languages, mounting impact of electronic and other media which use only Tok Pisin, Hiri Motu, a few major regional lingua francas and a limited number of large local languages. The same is the case with basic elementary education, though all languages of Papua New Guinea were in 1997

461

declared official, and therefore admissible for use in educational pursuits. A radical re-thinking of language use in basic elementary education as outlined above in the section on language endangerment would have to be necessary as an oral supplement to current elementary basic educational practices in Papua New Guinea, to constitute a strong factor in the preservation of, especially small, local languages and to stem the tide of their endangerment. The activities of the SIL, which now embrace over 270 local languages, though not really small ones, constitute a strong bulwark against the endangerment of these languages.

Solomon Islands

The government is dominated by an English-educated elite, which is not much interested in the maintenance of threatened languages. Large former mission lingua francas constitute a threat to small languages because of their cultural and social impact, and the general Solomon Islands lingua franca, Solomon Pijin, also constitutes a considerable threat because of the preference for it by the young generation in many areas. Here again, the work of members of the SIL in a number of languages ensure the maintenance of local languages, though they are not particularly interested in endangered languages.

Santa Cruz Archipelago

Of the threatened Melanesian Austronesian languages, none is likely to survive. Their speakers prefer using Solomon Pijin or the two local lingua franca (one of which is also endangered), and seem to have lost interest in maintaining their languages.

Vanuatu

About half a dozen moribund languages are unlikely to survive. The speakers of local languages take some pride in them, but generally not to the degree as encountered in Papua New Guinea. The lingua franca of Vanuatu, Bislama, plays a role with some members of the young generation and children which is similar to that of Tok Pisin in Papua New Guinea, i.e. it tends to be preferred to the local languages by them, but not to the same extent as in Papua New Guinea. Languages which are endangered or even seriously endangered may have a chance to be maintained or reinvigorated from a further strengthening of the feeling of ethnic identity of their speakers. There have been instances of this, but in general not overly successful for language maintenance.

New Caledonia and Loyalty Islands

A very strong reawakening of a sense of ethnic identity has taken place in New Caledonia and the Loyalty Islands in recent times, which has had a beneficial effect on the local Austronesian languages, by way of increased resistance to the influence of the dominant French language. As has been mentioned above in the general remarks on language endangerment, New Caledonia has traditionally had egalitarian multi-lingualism with the local population, with mutual respect for each others' languages. However, in the last decades, several small languages have retreated before large local languages, and at least two are now moribund. Their reinvigoration may perhaps be a

462

possibility, considering the increasing importance attached by the indigenous population to the role of their languages.

Fiji area and Polynesia

As has been mentioned above, the Polynesian Maori language of New Zealand underwent a strong revival early in the twentieth century, but the present young generation is not very interested in it, which may make it a threatened language again. However, when considering the very strong ethnic self-consciousness of the Maori population, the Maori language seems unlikely to be allowed by it to slide down far towards endangerment. The situation of the Hawaiian language has also been mentioned above in the section on endangerment. Though it has now 2,000 or so young speakers, its situation may have to be regarded as somewhat precarious because of the unusual distribution of speakers – children and grandparent speakers, but no parent speakers – and even more so because of Hawaii being in the orbit of US influence, which is one of the very worst situations in the world today for an indigenous language to be in. Of other Polynesian languages, those of the Marquesas and the Austral Islands, and the Tu'amotu Archipelago, are retreating before Tahitian, which has become the Polynesian lingua franca of the area. The Rapanui language of Easter Island, which has recovered from near-extinction, as mentioned above, is moving towards endangerment again because of the declining interest of the young generation and children in it. The Polynesian outlier language Emae located on Emwae Island in Vanuatu, is surrounded by Melanesian Austronesian languages, which have influenced it quite markedly, and its maintenance may be threatened. Vigorous efforts to maintain it are planned.

Australia

The Australian Aboriginal languages fared very badly right from the beginning of European settlement in 1788 until a few decades ago as a result of the attitudes of the white settlers and their deliberately destructive policies. More than half of the originally 400 or so languages have become extinct, and many of the still extant languages are moribund or endangered in various degrees of severity. Only about twenty-five languages are still viable. Around 1970, the turnaround of governmental policies towards Aborigines and their languages from negative to very positive, and the very strong revival of a feeling of ethnic identity in the Aboriginal population (mentioned above in the endangerment section) was accompanied by a steady increase of interest on the part of the Aborigines in their own languages and their maintenance, reinvigoration and revival. This was supported by governmental actions such as the creation of the Australian Institute of Aboriginal and Torres Strait Islanders Studies, a research institute concerned with research and study into Aboriginal matters including culture, art and languages. The introduction of bilingual education in areas where Aboriginal languages were still viable was another such act, as well as support for work in Aboriginal languages and their maintenance and revival through universities and other institutions. This, together with active involvement of Aboriginal communities who were aided in this by linguists, has resulted in the reinvigoration of several moribund languages, and even the revival of others definitely extinct. This trend is continuing and may halt the decline of Aboriginal languages in Australia. The vigor-

463

ous activities of the SIL in a considerable number of Aboriginal languages have been very beneficial, but they concentrate on viable and still partly viable languages, which is of little help to the maintenance of more endangered languages.

Aslian languages in Peninsular Malaysia

Most of these languages are potentially endangered, with some members of the young generation and some children preferring Malay to their own languages. With continuing pressure from Malay, this trend is likely to worsen, unless it can be slowed down or halted through an upsurge in ethnic self-consciousness of their speakers and increased interest by them in their languages and their maintenance.

Future prospects

What has been outlined above pretty well indicates the future prospects of language endangerment and disappearance, as well as those of language maintenance and revival in the various parts of Australasia and the Pacific. To sum up, prospects of only limited, or decelerating endangerment of languages, with good language maintenance, are good to very good in the Philippines (with the exception of some at present moribund or seriously endangered or even only endangered languages), in Taiwan, the Loyalties and New Caledonia, Micronesia and perhaps Polynesia. They are less so in Papua New Guinea and in part depending on the introduction of new oral basic elementary education methods supplementing existing educational practices. They are also less so in the Solomon Islands and Vanuatu and with Aslian languages in Peninsular Malaysia. They are bad for Indonesia including Irian Jaya unless present situations change. They are very bad for the Melanesian Austronesian languages in the Santa Cruz Archipelago. Australia is a special case in having good prospects for languages still viable or not too seriously endangered, but it has a rather large number of moribund languages with a handful or fewer speakers each as a sad heritage from a grim past, with most of these destined to disappear shortly, though a few of them may be reinvigorated and survive, or, if the last speaker(s) die, may be revived and relearned by their descendants eager to do so, as has been happening recently with several Aboriginal languages.

References

Blust, Robert (1978) 'Eastern Malayo-Polynesian: a subgrouping argument'. In: Stephen A. Wurm and Lois Carrington (eds) *Second International Conference on Austronesian Linguistics: Proceedings Fascicle 1*, pp. 181–234. Canberra: Pacific Linguistics Series C-61.

Codrington, Robert H. (1885) *The Melanesian languages.* Oxford. [Reprinted 1974, Amsterdam: Philo Press.]

Dempwolff, Otto (1934–8) *Vergleichende Lautlehre des Austronesischen Wortschatzes.* 3 vols. Berlin: Reimer.

Foley, William A. (1986) *The Papuan languages of New Guinea.* Cambridge: Cambridge University Press.

Grimes, Barbara E. (ed.) (1996) *Ethnologue, languages of the world.* 13th edn. Dallas TX: Summer Institute of Linguistics.

Henderson, James (1995) *Phonology and grammar of Yele, Papua New Guinea.* Canberra: Pacific Linguistics Series B-112.

Laycock, Donald C. (1975a) 'The Sepik-Ramu Phylum'. In: Stephen A. Wurm (ed.) *New Guinea languages and language study, vol. 1: Papuan languages and the New Guinea linguistic scene*. Canberra: Pacific Linguistics Series C-38: pp. 731–63.

——(1975b) 'The Torricelli Phylum'. In: Stephen A. Wurm (ed.) *New Guinea languages and language study, vol. 1: Papuan languages and the New Guinea linguistic scene*. Canberra: Pacific Linguistics Series C-38: pp. 767–80.

Mühlhäusler, Peter, Malcolm Philpott and Rachel Trew (1996) 'Modern media in the Pacific area and their role in intercultural communication'. In: Stephen A. Wurm, Peter Mühlhäusler and Darrell T. Tryon (eds) *Atlas of languages of intercultural communication in the Pacific, Asia, and the Americas*. 3 vols. Berlin and New York: Mouton de Gruyter, pp. 1389–454.

Nekitel, Otto (1998) *Voices of yesterday, today and tomorrow. Language, culture and identity*. New Delhi: UBS Publishers' Distributors Ltd, in association with Nekitelson Pty Ltd, Port Moresby, Papua New Guinea.

Pawley, Andrew (1978) 'The New Guinea Oceanic hypothesis'. *Kivung* 11: pp. 99–151.

——(1995) 'C. L. Voorhoeve and the Trans-New Guinea phylum hypothesis'. In: Connie Baak, Mary Bakker and Dick v.d. Meij (eds) *Tales from a concave world*. Leiden: Leiden University, pp. 83–123.

——(1998) 'The Trans New Guinea Phylum hypothesis: a reassessment'. In: Jelle Miedema, Cecilia Odé and Rien A. C. Dam (eds) *Perspectives on the Bird's Head of Irian Jaya, Indonesia*. Proceedings of the Leiden Conference of 13–17 October 1997. Amsterdam and Atlanta GA: Editions Rodopi, pp. 655–90.

Ross, Malcolm D. (1988) *Proto Oceanic and the Austronesian languages of Western Melanesia*. Canberra: Pacific Linguistics Series C-98.

——(1995) 'The great Papuan pronoun hunt: recalibrating our sights'. In: Connie Baak, Mary Bakker and Dick v.d. Meij (eds) *Tales from a concave world*. Leiden: Leiden University, pp. 139–68.

Voorhoeve, Clemens L. (1975a) 'West Papuan Phylum languages on the mainland of New Guinea'. In: Stephen A. Wurm (ed.) *New Guinea languages and language study, vol. 1: Papuan languages and the New Guinea linguistic scene*. Canberra: Pacific Linguistics Series C-38: pp. 717–28.

——(1975b) 'East Bird's Head, Geelvinck Bay phyla'. In: Stephen A. Wurm (ed.) *New Guinea languages and language study, vol. 1: Papuan languages and the New Guinea linguistic scene*. Canberra: Pacific Linguistics Series C-38: pp. 867–78.

Williams, Jeff (1996) Jeff Williams' contribution on pp. 418–22, in: Peter Mühlhäusler, Tom Dutton, Even Hovdhaugen, Jeff Williams and Stephen A. Wurm, 'Precolonial patterns of intercultural communication in the Pacific Islands', in: Stephen A. Wurm, Peter Mühlhäusler and Darrell T. Tryon (eds) *Atlas of languages of intercultural communication in the Pacific, Asia, and the Americas*. 3 vols. Berlin and New York: Mouton de Gruyter, pp. 401–37.

Wurm, Stephen A. (1975) 'The East Papuan Phylum in general'. In: Stephen A. Wurm (ed.) *New Guinea languages and language study, vol. 1: Papuan languages and the New Guinea linguistic scene*. Canberra: Pacific Linguistics Series C-38: pp. 783–804.

——(1982) *Papuan languages of Oceania*. Tübingen: Gunther Narr Verlag.

——(1986) 'Grammatical decay in Papuan languages'. Canberra: Pacific Linguistics Series A-70: pp. 207–11.

——(1992a) 'Some features of the verb complex in Northern Santa Cruzan, Solomon Islands'. In: Tom Dutton, Malcolm Ross and Darrell Tryon (eds) *The language game: papers in memory of Donald C. Laycock*. Canberra: Pacific Linguistics Series C-110: pp. 527–51.

——(1992b) 'Change of language structure and typology in a Pacific language as a result of culture change'. In: Tom Dutton (ed.) *Culture change, language change*. Canberra: Pacific Linguistics Series C-120: pp. 141–57.

——(2000) 'Threatened languages in the Western Pacific area from Taiwan to, and including, Papua New Guinea'. In Matthias Brenzinger (ed.) *Language endangerment, research and documentation – setting priorities for the 21st century*. Berlin: Mouton de Gruyter.

465

——(2001) 'Language endangerment in the insular Greater Pacific area, and the New Guinea area in particular'. In: Andrew Pawley, Malcolm Ross and Darrell Tryon (eds) *The boy from Bundaberg: Studies in Melanesian linguistics in honour of Tom Dutton.* Canberra: Pacific Linguistics pp. 383–97.

Wurm, Stephen A. (ed.) (1975) *New Guinea languages and language study, vol. 1: Papuan languages and the New Guinea linguistic scene.* Canberra: Pacific Linguistics Series C-38.

Wurm, Stephen A. and Shirô Hattori (eds) (1981–3) *Language atlas of the Pacific area.* Canberra: Australian Academy of the Humanities, in collaboration with the Japan Academy; also as Pacific Linguistics Series C-66: p. 67.

Wurm, Stephen A. and Peter Mühlhäusler (eds) (1985) *Handbook of Tok Pisin (New Guinea Pidgin).* Canberra: Pacific Linguistics Series C-70.

Wurm, Stephen A., Peter Mühlhäusler and Darrell T. Tryon (eds) (1996) *Atlas of languages of intercultural communication in the Pacific, Asia, and the Americas.* 3 vols. Berlin and New York: Mouton de Gruyter.

ALPHABETICAL LIST OF ENTRIES FOR THREATENED AND EXTINCT LANGUAGES

In these entries, summary information is given on each threatened or extinct language in the Pacific area. The name (and alternative name) of the language, the country or region where it is spoken, its location within them, a brief classification, reasons for its threatened status, some remarks on its distinctive structural features, and sometimes additional relevant information will be given in the case of languages in various stages of endangerment. For extinct languages, the information is less elaborate, but the approximate time of extinction is mentioned, but for the reasons of extinction, the reader is referred to the section of the Introduction in which reasons for the extinction of languages in relevant countries or areas are touched upon, unless special conditions have prevailed for given languages.

A number of abbreviations have been used to avoid the frequent repetition of sometimes quite lengthy expressions:

CEMP	Central-Eastern Malayo-Polynesian
CMP	Central Malayo-Polynesian
EMP	Eastern Malayo-Polynesian
EMPCE	Eastern Malayo-Polynesian, Central-Eastern Oceanic
EMPW	Eastern Malayo-Polynesian, Western Oceanic
EP	East Papuan
IJ	Irian Jaya
MP	Malayo-Polynesian
n-MPAUN	non-Malayo-Polynesian Austronesian
NSW	New South Wales (Australia)
NT	Northern Territory (Australia)
P	Papuan
PNG	Papua New Guinea
PNy	Pama-Nyungan (very large Australian language family)
QLD	Queensland (Australia)
SA	South Australia (Australia)
SERP	Sepik-Ramu Phylum
SHWNG	Southern Halmahera-West New Guinea Group (Malayo-Polynesian)
TNGP	Trans-New Guinea Phylum
TRCP	Torricelli Phylum
WA	Western Australia
WMP	Western Malayo-Polynesian
WPAP	West Papuan Phylum

Abaga **[144]** Papua New Guinea: Eastern Highlands Province, eastern part of the Goroka District. Spoken north of Henganofi, around Kisi. P, TNGP, Huon-Finisterre, Finisterre. The speakers appear to have migrated from the southern Huon Peninsula area into the Eastern Highlands where they live in the territory of the large Kamano language. Structurally it corresponds to the TNGP type (see the *Damal* entry). No literacy in it. In the 1960s, there were still about 150 speakers of it, but in 1994 only five were left. They were all bilingual in Kamano and partly also in the Benabena language further west. The language has been under intense pressure from Kamano. It is now moribund.

467

Abai Sungai [110] Malaysia: Sabah. Spoken in the extreme northeast of Sabah, on the lower Kinabatangan River, southeast of Sandakan. WMP, Borneo, northeast Borneo, Paitanic. The speakers are fishermen. It has focusing syntax and verb structure, sharply distinguishing the expression of active and passive in the verb, as a central grammatical feature (see *Nataoran* and *Lengilu* for more details). No literacy in it. Second language is Sabah Malay, and there is shifting to Bahasa Malaysia, the national standard Malay language of Malaysia. In 1982, 500 speakers were reported, but there are fewer today. The language is beginning to be endangered.

Adabe (or *Ataura*) [58] Indonesia: Timor Island area. Spoken on Atauro Island, north of Dili on Timor Island. TNGP, Timor-Alor-Pantar. It is lexically a member of Timor-Alor-Pantar, but has largely Malay-Polynesian structure. Apparently an originally Malay-Polynesian language heavily influenced by Papuan languages of the Timor-Alor-Pantar type, but it has the usual Papuan word order subject-object-verb. No literacy in it. 1,000 speakers in the ethnic group reported in 1981, with the number of speakers lower today. It is potentially endangered.

Adasen (or *Addasen Tinguian*, or *Adasen Itneg*) [10] Philippines. Spoken in northeastern Luzon, in northwestern Abra Province. WMP, Northern Philippine, Northern Luzon. Very high level of bilingualism in Ilocano, young people begin to tend to prefer it to Adasen. The language has focusing syntax and verb structure. See the *Nataoran* entry for details. Fairly high level of literacy, Latin alphabet. 4,000 speakers, but is beginning to be potentially endangered.

Adynyamathanha (or *Wailpi*) [206] Australia: central SA, Flinders Ranges area. PNY, South-West Yura. General features of almost all PNY languages (and of most Australian languages) is a sound system in which stops and nasals have six articulatory points (bilabial, interdental, dental, retroflexed, palatal, velar), but a voiced-voiceless distinction is very rare. Laterals have four of these articulatory points. There are two or three different *r*-sounds, but no fricatives, and mostly only the three vowels *a, i, u*, with *a* being very frequent. Word order is very free. In many languages, the affixes indicating the actor and the object of an action, are not added to the verbs, but to the first word of the sentence. Only suffixes appear in the grammatical structure. Tenses and aspects are indicated by suffixes on the verb. There are mostly no gender or class distinctions. There is no literacy in Adynyamathanha. In 1990, twenty or more speakers were reported, but today there are fewer. The remaining few speakers are bilingual in English. There are efforts to maintain and reinvigorate the language. It is seriously endangered, but in the light of such efforts it may become only endangered.

Aghu Tharnggalu [not mapped] Australia: QLD, southern central Cape York Peninsula. PNY, Paman, Rarmul Pama. Recently extinct.

Agta, Alabat Island (or *Alabat Island Dumagat*) [14] Philippines. Spoken on Alabat Island, southeast of Manila, east of Quezon Province. WMP, Northern Philippine, Northern Luzon. High level of bilingualism in Tagalog. Most speakers have shifted to Tagalog. There were still fifty speakers in 1972, but their number has been decreasing. The language has focusing syntax and verb structure. See the *Nataoran* entry for details. No literacy in it. The language is seriously endangered.

Agta, Camarinas Norte (or *Manide*, or *Agiyan*) **[15]** Philippines. Spoken in southeastern Luzon, at Santa Elena and Labo, in Camarinas Norte. WMP, Northern Philippine, North Luzon. Bilingualism in Tagalog seems to be prevalent. Young people may tend to prefer Tagalog. The language has focusing syntax and verb structure. See the *Nataoran* entry for details. No literacy in it. In 1979, there were 200 speakers of it, but this number is receding. The language is becoming endangered.

Agta, Central Cagayan **[16]** Philippines. Spoken in northeast Luzon. WMP, Northern Philippine, North Luzon. The speakers are Negrito. The language has focusing syntax and verb structure. See the *Nataoran* entry for details. Literacy is present, about 3 per cent of the speakers are literate. Latin alphabet. There were 1,000 speakers reported in 1979, but this number has fallen to 600–700 by 1993, and this trend is continuing, probably due to pressure from the large Ibanag language. The language is moving towards becoming endangered.

Agta, Dicamay **[not mapped]** Philippines: Luzon, in Isabella Province. WMP, Northern Philippine, Northern Luzon. Recently extinct.

Agta, Isarog **[17]** Philippines. Spoken on Mt Isarog, northeast of Naga City, Bicol Province, southeastern Luzon. WMP, Meso Philippines, Central Philippine. Receded from pressure from the large Bicolano language. The language has focusing syntax and verb structure. See the *Nataoran* entry for details. There is no literacy in it. In 1984, there were a few speakers of it in an ethnic group of 1,000. The language is moribund, and almost extinct.

Agta, Mt Iraya (or *Itbeg Rugnot*) **[18]** Philippines: east of Lake Buhi and of Naga City, Bicol Province, southeastern Luzon. WMP, Meso Philippine, Central Philippine. Has heavily borrowed lexical items from the large Central Bicolano language with the result that it now shows 85–90 per cent lexical similarity with it. The language has focusing syntax and verb structure. See the *Nataoran* entry for details. In 1979, there were 200 speakers, but their number is decreasing. No literacy in it. The language is getting lexically swamped by Bicolano, and is endangered.

Agwamin **[286]** Australia: QLD, southern central Cape York Peninsula. PNY, Paman, Southern Pama. Extinct?

Ak **[285]** Papua New Guinea: Sandaun Province. About 40km north of Yellow River ownship, to the east of the Upper Sand River, a northern tributary of the Sepik River, northeast of Yawari. P, SERP, Sepik, Yellow River. It corresponds largely to the usual SERP structural characteristics; the languages are very rarely tonal. Morphological complexity is low to medium, except for the members of four aberrant groups (the Upper Sepik, Nor-Pondo, and Leonard Schultze groups, and also Gapun), where it is high to extreme. Morphology is usually transparent, few morphophonemic changes. Two-gender system in person markers (plus multiple class systems in the aberrant groups), plural marking of nouns is common in the central and eastern parts of the SERP, subject marking on the verbs is common, object marking occurs, but more rarely. Sentence-medial verb forms occur, but are much simpler than in TNGP languages. Word order is always subject-object verb. In Ak, there is no subject marking with the verb, and the morphology is simpler than generally in SERP languages. No literacy in it. In 1981, eighty-three speakers were reported. Now there are less: present reports mention eighty or less speakers. The language is under heavy pressure from neighbouring larger languages of the same group such as Namie, and the children beginning to prefer Tok Pisin, the national language of Papua New Guinea. Ak is now endangered.

Alamblak-Arafundi Trade Pidgin [not mapped] Papua New Guinea: East Sepik Province, lower Karawari and middle Arafundi Rivers area. Consultants in Yimas on other trade pidgin in that general area mentioned that a trade pidgin was once used between the P, SERP, Ramu, Arafundi speaking village of Auwim and the P, SERP, Sepik Hill, Alamblak-speaking village of Chimbut, without further details being available. It is not known whether the language is now moribund, or already extinct.

Alawa (or ***Kallana***) [71] Australia: northern NT, southeastern Arnhem Land, Roper River, Maran, Alawic. For structural information see the ***Jawoyn*** and the ***Yanyuwa*** entries. Alawa is a tonal language, like Mangarayi and Yangman. No literacy in it. In 1991, 17 fluent speakers and four partial speakers were reported. All speakers are bilingual in the English-based pidgin lingua franca Kriol. Young people hardly understand a little Alawa. The language is seriously endangered.

Alngith [not mapped] Australia: QLD, northeastern Cape York Peninsula. PNY, Paman, Northern Pama. Recently extinct.

Alta, Northern (or ***Edimala***, or ***Ditaylin Dumagat***) [23] Philippines: eastern part of the wide neck section of Luzon which is north of Manila, in Aurora Province, to the west of Baler, and well northeast of Cabanatuan. WMP, Northern Philippine, Northern Luzon. The speakers are regarded as Negrito. The language has focussing syntax and verb structure. See the ***Nataoran*** entry for details. It is not closely related to other local languages. In 1992, there were 240 speakers, but they seem to be decreasing under pressure from Tagalog. No literacy in it. Endangered.

Alune (or ***Sapalew***, or ***Patasiwa***, or ***Alfoeren***) [116] Indonesia: Maluku. Spoken inland and on the northern, northwestern and southwestern coasts of West Seram Island. The largest language in West Seram. CEMP, CMP, Central Maluku. Structurally it corresponds to what has been said in the ***Palu'e*** entry about some characteristics of CMP. It may be added that some Central Maluku languages have a living-non-living distinction in the pronoun system. Literacy in it is extant. In 1987, 13,000 to 15,000 speakers were reported. The numbers are less now. The speakers in the interior who are the majority, use the language daily. In the coastal areas, usage is not vigorous. There is pressure from Ambon Malay and standard Indonesian. The language is moving towards being endangered in parts of its area.

Amahai [113] Indonesia: Maluku. Spoken in southwest Seram Island, on the east coast of Piru Bay. CEMP, CMP, Central Maluku. Structurally it corresponds to what is said in the ***Palu'e*** and ***Alune*** entries. No literacy in it. In 1987, fifty speakers were reported. Now they are less. The language has been affected by transmigration and there is pressure from Ambon Malay and Indonesian. The language is moribund.

Amblong [36] Vanuatu. Spoken inland in southeastern Santo. CEMP, EMPCE, remote Oceanic, North and Central Vanuatu. For structural notes see the *Anus* entry. No literacy in it. In 1983, 150 speakers were reported. Today there may be over 100 speakers. Closely related to the neighbouring Narango and Morouas, probably in a dialect chain with them which influences Amblong. Children tend not to learn Amblong. It is now potentially endangered and moving towards being endangered.

Ami (or *Ame*) [22] Australia: northeastern NT, southwest of Darwin, on the southern coast of Anson Bay. Daly, Bringen-Bringen-Wagaydy, Wagaydy. For structural information see the *Jawoyn* entry. No literacy in it. In 1983, 30–5 fluent speakers were reported. The speakers are using the English-based pidgin lingua franca Kriol as second language to which the children are shifting. There are fewer speakers today. The language is getting seriously endangered.

Ampibabo Lauje [120] Indonesia: Sulawesi. A form of the large Lauje language (see Lauje) which is spoken on the east coast of the southern third of the narrow neck connecting the bulk of Sulawesi with its northeastern peninsula. Near Ampibabo. WMP, Sulawesi, Central Sulawesi, Tomini. Structurally it corresponds to the Southern Sulawesi type (see *Bahonsuai*). Some literacy in it. Its general area is heavily populated by speakers of other large languages, such as the Ledo language. There is a strong inclination of Ampibabo Lauje speakers to reside temporarily outside their area for wage work, but there are few opportunities for that at present. There are 6,000 speakers, but the two factors mentioned are driving the language towards being endangered.

Amto [74] Papua New Guinea: Sandaun Province. Spoken in the Amanab Province, south of the Upper Sepik River, toward the headwaters of the Left May River, on the Samaia River. P. Amto-Musian (or Musan) small phylum. Little is known about the structure of Amto, except that a two-gender system exists in the third person singular pronoun. No literacy in it. In 1981, 230 speakers were reported. This number may still be correct, but the speakers are acculturating rapidly. As a result, their language is becoming endangered.

Amurdak (or *Amarag*) [19] Australia: northern NT, Arnhem Land. Yiwadjan, Amaragic. For structural information see the *Jawoyn* entry. No literacy in it. In 1983, it was believed extinct, but is now known to have 2–3 elderly speakers. Moribund.

Andegerebinha [214] Australia: central eastern NT, Hay River and Pituri Creek area. PNY, Arandic. For structural information see the *Adynyamathanha* entry. No literacy in it. In 1981, perhaps ten speakers were reported. Today there are very few. The language is moribund.

Andio (or *Masama*) [41] Indonesia: Sulawesi. Spoken on the southern coast near the eastern head of the eastern peninsula of Sulawesi, by about 1,700 persons. WMP, Sulawesi, Central Sulawesi, east-central Sulawesi. Structurally it corresponds to the Southern Sulawesi type (see *Bahonsuai*). No literacy in it. Under pressure from Indonesian and the large neighbouring languages Saluan and Balantak. The language is potentially endangered.

471

Antakarinya (or *Andagarinya*) **[180]** Australia: northeastern area of SA. PNY, Southwest, Wati (or Western Desert). For structural information see the *Adynyamathanha* entry. There is no literacy in the language. In 1981, possibly fifty speakers were reported, in 1983 only few. The people generally speak Kriol, the English-based pidgin language spoken in many areas of the northern half of Australia and which in a creolized form, is now the first language of well over 10,000 Australian Aborigines. Antakarinya is seriously endangered, becoming moribund.

Anuki (or *Gabobora*) **[119]** Papua New Guinea: Milne Bay Province, Cape Vogel. Spoken on the north coast of Cape Vogel Peninsula, around Tapiosan. CEMP, EMPW, Milne Bay-Central Province languages. For structural notes see the *Anus* entry. No literacy in it. In 1975, 574 speakers were reported. Recent estimates mention 542. The language is under pressure from the related larger Are (Mukawa) language, and the children tend to prefer Tok Pisin. Anuki is now endangered.

Anus **[196]** Indonesia: Irian Jaya. Spoken on one of the Podena islands off the northeast coast of Irian Jaya, northeast of Ahus, east of the Tor River. CEMP, EMPW, Sarmi-Yotafa. Structurally, the EMPW languages in general, show none of the characteristics of WMP as are present in CMP, but only the EMP features mentioned in the *Pa'ela* and *Alune* entries. No literacy in the language declining. It is probably because of pressure from the large Kwesten languages (P, TNGP, Tor) on the opposite coast, and of Indonesian. The language is endangered.

Aore **[29]** Vanuatu: on Aore Island, off southern Santo Island. EMPCE, remote Oceanic, North and Central Vanuatu. Had one old speaker in 1982. Now extinct.

Aputai (or *Welemur*, or *Tutunohan*) **[29]** Indonesia: Maluku. Spoken on the north central and south central coasts of Wetar Island, north of northeast Timor Island. CEMP, CMP, Timor-Flores. Structurally it is similar to what is said in the *Palu'e* entry. No literacy in it. In 1990, 150 speakers were reported. It may be less today. One of its dialects is extinct. There is pressure from the large Talur language and Indonesian. It is endangered.

Arabana **[64]** Australia: northeastern South Australia, at Birdsville, at west side of Lake Eyre to Stuart Range. PNY, Arabana-Wangkangurru. For structural information see the *Adynyamathanha* entry. Very closely related to Wangkangurru. The two can be regarded as dialects of one language. No literacy in Arabana. In 1981, possibly eight speakers were reported. Today, only two or three are left. If Arabana and Wangkangurru are regarded as one language, it would have less than half a dozen speakers. Moribund.

Arafundi-Enga Trade Pidgin **[not mapped]** Papua New Guinea: East Sepik and Enga Provinces. A trade pidgin reported in 1966 as being used between the P, SERP, Ramu, Arafundi speakers of the upper Arafundi River and the P, TNGP, East New Guinea Highlands, West-Central, Enga language in its Maramuni dialect far to the south. It is a simplified Enga with significant lexical input from Arafundi. It contains some structural features which belong to neither of these two languages. It seems to be still extant, but possibly endangered.

Araki [34] Vanuatu: on Araki Island off South Santo. CEMP, EMPCE, remote Oceanic, North and Central Vanuatu. For structural information see the *Anus* entry. No literacy in it. In 1983, 105 speakers were reported. Today there are 60–70 speakers, with very few children speakers. The larger Tangoa language of the neighbouring Tangoa Island puts pressure on it, and children are switching to it. Araki is getting endangered.

Arapesh, Bumbita (or *Weri*) [258] Papua New Guinea: East Sepik Province. Spoken in the northern central part of the East Sepik Province in the Maprik District, in the Torricelli mountains. TRCP, Arapesh. Structurally it is typically TRCP: relatively many different vowels (up to eight), a two- or three-member gender system, plus in several TRCP languages (including Arapesh) a 3–13-member noun class system with a very complicated and comprehensive concordance system involving pronouns, adjectives, numerals, demonstratives, and subject and object marking on the verbs. The indication of the dual and plural numbers on nouns etc. is very complex. There are no sentence-medial verb forms which are common in TNGP and many SERP languages. Word order is always subject-object-verb. There is beginning literacy in Bumbita Arapesh. In 1994, 2,353 speakers were reported in thirteen villages. Middle-aged and older speakers use the language, but except for two villages, younger people mainly use Tok Pisin, the national language of Papua New Guinea. Bumbita Arapesh is now potentially endangered.

Arawum (or *Kom*) [27] Papua New Guinea: Madang Province. Spoken on the southern (Rai) coast of Astrolabe Bay, on the lower Kambara River and the coast west of Rimbo. P, TNGP, Madang, Kabenau Family. Structurally it is TNGP (see the *Damal* entry). No literacy in it. In 1981, seventy-five speakers were reported. It is under pressure from larger languages of the area such as Siroi, and the children prefer Tok Pisin. The language is now endangered.

Areba [**not mapped**] Australia: QLD, southwestern Cape York Peninsula. PNY, Norman Pama. Recently extinct.

Arguni [218] Indonesia: Irian Jaya. Spoken on an island in the Maccluer Gulf off the northwest coast of the Bomberai Peninsula, which is south of the Bird's Head Peninsula. CEMP, CMP, North Bomberai. Structurally similar to what is said in the *Pa'ela* and *Alune* entries. No literacy in it. In 1977, 200 speakers were reported. Likely to be less today because of pressure from the larger CEMP and CMP languages Bedoanas and Sekar, the larger P, TNGP Iha and Baham languages nearby, and of Indonesian. It is potentially endangered.

Arhâ [123] New Caledonia: spoken in West-Central New Caledonia, inland from Poya, in the upper southern valleys. CEMP, EMPCE, New Caledonian, Southern. For structural notes see the *Arhö* entry. No literacy in it. In 1974, 250 speakers were reported. Now they are very much fewer. The language is under pressure from two large neighbouring New Caledonian languages, Ajië and Paicî, and from French. It is now seriously endangered.

Arhö (or *Aro*) [122] New Caledonia, central southwestern coast, on the coast and inland, around Poya town. CEMP, EMPCE, Oceanic, New Caledonian, Southern. Structurally,

473

the New Caledonian languages correspond to the EMP pattern (see the *Anus* entry), but are grammatically simpler than most EMP languages. They lack the indication of transitive verbs by a suffix, and do not indicate the tense in the verbs. Few affixes occur, mostly particles are used to express grammatical functions. However, their sound systems are exceedingly complex. The languages are tonal, which is unusual in Malayo-Polynesian languages, though occurring sporadically outside New Caledonia. They have some very unusual sounds like for instance a nasalized rolled *r*. There is no literacy in Arhö. In 1982, 10–100 speakers were reported. Now it is only a small number. The language is under pressure from two large neighbouring New Caledonian languages, Ajië (in which the Arhö speakers are bilingual) in the southeast and Paicî in the northwest, and from French. It is moribund.

Ari [107] Papua New Guinea: Western Province, Aramia River Area, north of the Lower Fly River. Spoken in the area of the confluence of the Upper Aramia and the Soari Rivers, around Ari. P, TNGP, Gogodala-Suki. A dialect of the Ari-Waruna language. Its structure is typically TNGP (see the *Damal* entry). A special feature of the Gogodala-Suki languages is the obligatory appearance of a transitive suffix on the verb if a person-object suffix is present in it. No literacy in Ari. In 1976, about eighty speakers were reported. This is still the same. Speakers are using Gogodala and begin to shift to it. Ari is now endangered.

Aribwatsa [not mapped] Papua New Guinea: in the Lae town area in the northeast of Papua New Guinea. EMPW, Siassi Section. The last speaker died in 1997. The speakers shifted to the Bukawa (Bugawag, EMPW) language. Recently extinct.

Arta [21] Philippines: southeastern part of the head portion of northern Luzon, Quirino Province. The few speakers are scattered in villages, with twelve in Villa Santiago, and three or four in the town of Nagtipunan. They are Negrito. WMP, Northern Philippine, Northern Luzon. The language has focusing syntax and verb structure. See the *Nataoran* entry for details. It is not linguistically close to any other language in the general area. In 1992, there were seventeen speakers, but their numbers decreased since. Moribund, almost extinct.

As [211] Indonesia: Irian Jaya. Spoken on the north coast of the Western Bird's Head Peninsula. CEMP, EMP, SHWNG. Structurally it is as for the *Gebe* entry. No literacy in it. In 1988, 250 speakers were reported. There is pressure from the large P, WPAP languages Abun and Moi and of Indonesian. It is potentially endangered.

Asumboa (or *Asumbuo*) [59] Solomon Islands, Santa Cruz Archipelago, Utupua Island. CEMP, EMPCE, Oceanic, Utupua. Structurally similar to what has been said in the *Anus* entry. Speakers of Nyisunggu (or Tanimbili) have been shifting to it. It is one of the two lingua francas of Utupua Island, but has been under pressure from Amba (or Nembao), the other larger lingua franca to which Asumboa speakers are shifting, and from Solomon Pijin. Asumboa speakers use Amba, Nyisunggu or Solomon Pijin as second languages, and there is 25 to 50 per cent literacy. In 1990, sixty speakers were reported. Recent reports mention only twenty speakers, amongst them four child-speakers, the youngest ten years old. The language is now seriously endangered.

Ata [not mapped] Philippines: in Negros Oriental Province, at the northern end of Negros Island, Meso Philippine, Central Philippine. In 1973, a few families of speakers were reported. It may by now have succumbed to the large Cebuano language. Probably extinct.

Atampaya [not mapped] Australia: QLD, extreme northern Cape York Peninsula. PNY, Paman, Northern Pama. Recently extinct.

Atemble (or *Atemple*) [9] Papua New Guinea: Madang Province. Spoken on the right side of the Ramu River, northwest of Aiome and upstream from Annaberg. P, TNGP, Adelbert Range, Wanang Family. Structurally it is TNGP (see the *Damal* entry). No literacy in it. In 1981, sixty-five speakers were reported. Today it is still close to that figure, but it is under pressure from large related languages such as Angaua, and from Tok Pisin. It is now endangered.

Atta Faire (or *Southern Atta*) [115] Philippines: extreme central north of the head portion of Luzon, southwest of Pamplona, Cagayan Province. WMP, Northern Philippine, Northern Luzon. The language has focussing syntax and verb structure. See the *Nataoran* entry for details. The speakers are largely bilingual in the large Ibanag language and the Atta Pamplona language next to them. They are Negrito. In 1981, 400–550 speakers were reported. The numbers are decreasing. Literacy work is said to be needed. The language is getting endangered.

Auye [114] Indonesia: Irian Jaya. Spoken in the northwestern part of the Central Highlands, in the mountains southeast of Cenderawasih Bay, on a mountain slope, on the Siriwo River. P, TNGP, Wissel Lakes-Kemandoga. Closely related to the very large Ekari language. See the *Damal* entry for structural notes. There is 5–15 per cent literacy in it. In 1992, about 500 speakers were reported, in 1995 only 350. Under pressure from Ekari and Indonesian. It is potentially endangered.

Awabakal [not mapped] Australia: NSW, south from Newcastle. PNY, Yuin-Kuric, Kuri. Long extinct, but there are attempts at revival.

Awera [216] Indonesia: Irian Jaya. Spoken at the mouth of the Wapoga River, southwest of the centre of the east coast of Cenderawasih Bay in western Irian Jaya. P, Geelvinck Bay Phylum, Lakes Plain, Awera. A structural characteristic of the Geelvinck Bay Phylum languages on the Irian Jaya mainland is the lack of distinction between masculine and feminine gender which is found in the Yawa language of the Geelvinck Bay Phylum as spoken in the central part of the large Yapen Island in northeastern Cenderawasih Bay. In all languages of this phylum, suffixes and postposed particles play a very major role. Many have implosive stop consonants and are tonal. The general direction of an action, and its direction in relation to the subject, are indicated in the verb complex. A large number of aspects are found in the verb. The negative is marked by a suffix plus a postposed particle. Word order is the usual Papuan subject-object-verb. There is no literacy in Awera. In 1987, approximately 100 speakers were reported. This number may well be less today, because there are about 100 speakers of the large CEMP, EMP, SHWNG Ansus language living in the same community, and their language and Indonesian are widely used in the community, with the children preferring the latter. Awera is getting endangered.

Awyi (or *Nyao*) [102] Indonesia: Irian Jaya. Spoken near the northeastern Irian Jaya-Papua New Guinea border, about 50km south of Jayapura. P, TNGP, Border Stock. Though they belong to the TNGP, the languages of the Border Stock have some structural features which differ from those commonly found in the majority of TNGP languages (see the *Damal* entry). For instance, the class of nouns is marked in Border Stock languages by verb prefixes, whereas in TNGP languages they tend to be indicated by auxiliary verbs. No number is distinguished in personal pronouns, whereas TNGP languages usually have singular, dual and plural. The typical TNGP distinction between sentence-medial and sentence-final verb is lacking in Border Stock languages. There is no literacy in Awyi. In 1978, 400 speakers were reported. Because of the relative nearness of Awyi to the capital Jayapura, it is subject to very strong pressure from Indonesian. It has to be regarded as potentially endangered.

Ayabadhu [not mapped] Australia: QLD, Northeastern Cape York Peninsula, south of Coen. PNY, Paman, Middle Pama. Recently extinct?

Ayta, Bataan (or *Bataan Sambal*) [45] Philippines: in the central part of the wide neck-section of Luzon which is north of Manila. It is in Bataan Province. WMP, Northern Philippine, Bashiic-Central Luzon-Mindoro (Central Luzon). The language has focussing syntax and verb structure. See the *Nataoran* entry for details. The speakers who are Negrito, are fairly bilingual in Tagalog. No literacy in it. In 1986, 572 speakers were reported, but their number is decreasing from pressure of the large Botolan Sambal language, and of Tagalog. It is beginning to get endangered.

Ayta, Sorsogon [76] Philippines: extreme southern end of Luzon, near Sorsogon town, Sorsogon Province. WMP, Meso Philippine, Central Philippine. The language has focussing syntax and verb structure. See *Nataoran* entry for details. Frequent inter-marriage of the speakers with members of other groups to the detriment of the language. No literacy in it. In 1984, forty speakers were reported, but their number has been decreasing since. It is moribund.

Ayta, Tayabas [not mapped] Philippines: Luzon, in Quezon Province. WMP, Tayabas Bay, Meso Philippine, Central Philippine. Recently extinct.

Baadi (or *Bardi*) [90] Australia: northwestern WA, Dampier Land, at Beagle Bay. Nyulnyulan. For structural information see the *Jawoyn* entry. The Nyulnyulan languages are non-classifying. In 1990, 100 speakers were reported. Children and adolescents use English as their language now. Many of them seem to understand Baadi but never speak it. The adults are all bilingual in English. The number of speakers is lower now. The language is endangered and is moving towards being seriously endangered.

Babuza (or *Favorlang*, or *Poavosa*) [428] Taiwan. Spoken on the western central coast of Taiwan and along the Tatu and Choshui rivers. n-MPAUN, Paiwanic group. The language has been under pressure from Chinese. The members of the ethnic group have mostly shifted to Chinese. The language has a focussing syntax and verb structure. See the *Nataoran* entry for details. No literacy in it. Moribund. A few elderly speakers.

Badala [**not mapped**] Australia: southeast QLD, Frazer Island. PNY, Waka-Kabic, Kabi, Than. Last native speaker died 1960. One secondary speaker still exists.

Badjiri [**not mapped**] Australia: southwestern QLD, north of Cunnamulla. PNY, Karnic, Ngura. Recently extinct.

Bagupi [**92**] Papua New Guinea: Madang Province. Spoken at the headwaters of the Gogol River, west of Mabanob, northwest of Madang town. P, TNGP, Madang, Hanseman Family. Structurally it is TNGP (see the ***Damal*** entry). No literacy in it. In 1981 fifty-eight speakers were reported. Today, the figure is still around sixty, but the language is under pressure from neighbouring large languages such as Garuh, and Tok Pisin, which is taking its toll. It is now endangered.

Bahonsuai [**4**] Indonesia: Sulawesi. Spoken in southeastern Sulawesi, on the northeastern coast of its eastern peninsula-like part extending southward from the central portion of Sulawesi. WMP, Sulawesi, Central Sulawesi, Bungku-Mori. Its structure is like that found in most Southern Sulawesi languages, which is similar to Malayic (see ***Enggano***) with some EMP features, i.e. complicated differentiation between intransitve and transitive verbs, marking of the verb subject and object by pre- and suffixes, but following Malayic in marking possession by noun suffixes, and the relatively simple distinction between active and passive expression in the verb. No literacy in it. In 1991, 200 speakers were reported. There are fewer now. It is getting endangered.

Baki [**95**] Vanuatu. Spoken on western Epi Island. CEMP, EMPCE, remote Oceanic, North and Central Vanuatu. For structural notes see the ***Anus*** entry. Five to fifteen per cent literacy in it. In 1981, 200 speakers were reported. Today there may be about 150. There is pressure from the English-based pidgin lingua franca and national language Bislama. Baki is now potentially endangered.

Baleasang (or ***Baleasan***) [**127**] Indonesia: Sulawesi. Spoken on Marimbayu Peninsula on the southern third of the west coast of the narrow neck connecting the bulk of Central Sulawesi with its northeastern peninsula. WMP, Sulawesi, Central Sulawesi, Tomini. Structurally, it corresponds to the Southern Sulawesi type (see ***Bahonsuai***). No literacy in it. In 1979, it was spoken in five villages, with 4,000 inhabitants. In 1995 there were only three, with about 3,200 inhabitants. However, these three are almost entirely populated by Baleasang speakers, though the 15–30 year-olds study in towns where they bring back Indonesian as their preferred language. This makes the language endangered, though it still may have close to 3,000 speakers.

Bandjalang [**8**] Australia: northeastern corner of NSW. PNY, Bandjalangic. For structural information see the ***Adynyamathanha*** entry, but the affixing of person markers is little in evidence. However, it has noun classes indicated by suffixes. There is some literacy in it. In 1983, ten speakers were reported. Today there are fewer. The speakers are bilingual in English. The language is now moribund.

Bandjigali [**not mapped**] Australia: northwestern NSW. PNY, Baagandji. Recently extinct.

477

Bandyin [**not mapped**] Australia: northeastern QLD, Hitchinbrook Island, northeast of Ingham. PNY, Dyirbalic. Extinct for some time.

Banggarla [**not mapped**] Australia: SA, Spencer Gulf. PNY, South-West, Yura. Extinct?

Baras (or ***Ende***) [**210**] Indonesia: Sulawesi, near the northwestern coast of the main geographical bulk of Sulawesi, between the Lariang and Budong-Budong Rivers. WMP, Sulawesi, Central Sulawesi, Kaili-Pamona. Structurally it corresponds to the Southern Sulawesi type (see ***Bahonsuai***). No literacy in it. Some of its speakers think that the language will die out. In 1987, 250 speakers were reported, but the language is receding under pressure from the large Kaili language and of Indonesian. It is now endangered.

Barrow Point [**not mapped**] Australia: QLD, Cape York Peninsula, Princess Charlotte Bay. PNY, Barrow Point. Recently extinct.

Basay (or ***Kawanuwan***) [**not mapped**] Northern tip area of Taiwan. n-MPAUN, Paiwanic. Old people remember a few words. Recently extinct.

Batak (or ***Babuyan, Palawan Batak***) [**57**] Philippines: spoken in north-central Palawan Island. WMP, Meso Philippine, Palawano. The language has focussing syntax and verb structure. See the ***Nataoran*** entry for details on that. The preferred word order in the sentence is verb-object-subject. In Philippine languages, the verb is often sentence-initial, but the subject follows it. The speakers are Negrito. There is some literacy in it. In 1984, 300 speakers were reported. Their number is decreasing from pressure of the large Palawano and Tagbanwa languages. It is beginning to be endangered.

Bayali (or ***Darumbal***, or ***Darawal***) [**not mapped**] Australia: southeastern QLD, coast and hinterland, Gladstone to Rockhampton. PNY, Waka-Kabic, Kingkel. Extinct for several decades.

Bayungu (or ***Giong***, or ***Mulgarnoo***) [**not mapped**] Australia: WA, West Pilbara. PNY, South-West, Kanyara. Recently extinct?

Bedoanas [**219**] Indonesia: Irian Jaya. Spoken on the northwest coast of the Bomberai Peninsula, which is south of the Bird's Head. CEMP, EMP, SHWNG, Bomberai. Structurally as for the ***Gebe*** entry. No literacy in it. In 1977, 250 speakers were reported. There is pressure from the CMP Sekar language, the larger P, TNGP Iha and Baham languages, and from Indonesian, with speaker numbers declining, especially with the young generation, and children not using it any more. It is now potentially endangered and heading towards being endangered.

Benggoi (or ***Uhei-Kaclakin***) [**24**] Indonesia: Maluku. Spoken on the north coast of East Seram Island. CEMP, CMP, Central Maluku. Structurally like the remarks given in the ***Palu'e*** and ***Alune*** entries. No literacy in it. In 1989, 350 speakers were reported. Pressure from Ambon Malay and Indonesian. It is potentially endangered.

Bepour [**60**] Papua New Guinea: Madang Province. Spoken in the northeastern part of Madang Province, just south of the lower Kumil River, due south of Sikor. P, TNGP, Adelbert

Range, Kumilan Family. Structurally it is TNGP (see the ***Damal*** entry). No literacy in it. In 1981, fifty-seven speakers were reported. Today it is still close to that figure, but it is under pressure from large languages such as its northern neighbour Mauwake (or Ulingan) to which it is closely related, and from Tok Pisin. It is now endangered.

Besoa (or ***Behoa***) **[12]** Indonesia: Sulawesi. Spoken somewhat to the east of the centre of the bulk of Sulawesi, near Watutau, to the northwest of Lake Poso by about 3,000. There is some literacy in it. WMP, Sulawesi, Central Sulawesi, Kaili-Pamona. Structurally it corresponds to the Southern Sulawesi type (see ***Bahonsuai***). Almost everybody can speak Indonesian, and the young generation is beginning to prefer it to Besoa, especially the children. The language is potentially endangered.

Biak (or ***Biak-Numfor***) **[195]** Indonesia: Irian Jaya. Spoken on Biak and Numfor to the north of Cenderawasih Bay and east of the Bird's Head Peninsula, and also on numerous small islands east and west of the Bird's Head, including Mapia Island to the north of the eastern Bird's Head. CEMP, EMP, SHWNG. Structurally it is as in the ***Gebe*** entry. Fairly widespread literacy in it. In 1981, 40,000 first language speakers were reported. It is a widespread lingua franca, with up to 100,000 second language speakers reported in 1991. However, it has been under very heavy pressure from Indonesian, and the young generation is losing its command of it, with quite a few preferring Indonesian to it. It is now potentially quite endangered.

Bidyara **[not mapped]** Australia: central QLD, Warrego River. PNY, Maric, Mari. Recently extinct?

Bierebo **[94]** Vanuatu. Spoken on western Epi Island. CEMP, EMPCE, remote Oceanic, North and Central Vanuatu. For structural notes, see the ***Anus*** entry. No literacy in it. In 1983, 483 speakers were reported. Today there may be under 350. Many speakers are ilingual in the neighbouring closely related Baki where language work has been carried out by the Summer Institute of Linguistics and where there is some literacy. It puts pressure on Bierebo, which is losing children speakers. It is now potentially endangered.

Bieria (or ***Vovo***) **[97]** Vanuatu. Spoken on southwestern Epi Island. CEMP, EMPCE, remote Oceanic, North and Central Vanuatu. For structural information see the ***Anus*** entry. Five to fifteen per cent literacy in it. In 1981, 170 speakers were reported. Today there may be about 120. Speakers are bilingual in Baki, to which some children may be switching. Bieria is now potentially endangered.

Biladaba **[not mapped]** Australia: SA, Lake Callabonna in the middle-northeast of SA. PNY, Karnic, Karna. Recently extinct.

Bilakura **[74]** Papua New Guinea: Madang Province. Spoken in northeastern Madang Province, on the headwaters of the Gilagil River, due east of Kosilanta. P, TNGP, Adelbert Range, Numugenan Family. Structurally it is TNGP (see the ***Damal*** entry). No literacy in it. In 1981, thirty-five speakers were reported. Recent reports still mention thirty-four. Under pressure from closely related larger languages such as Parawen, and from Tok Pisin. It is now seriously endangered.

Bina [not mapped] Papua New Guinea: eastern part of central Province, southeastern hinterland. EMPW, Milne-Bay-Central Province Section. Magoric. In 1981, there were two non-primary speakers of it. It is now extinct.

Biri [not mapped] Australia: QLD, southeast of Charters Towers. PNY, Maric, Mari. Recently extinct? There are attempts at reviving it.

Blablanga (or *Gema*, or *Goi*) [33] Solomon Islands: Santa Isabel Island, northeastern and southwestern coast of the southern central part of the island. CEMP, EMPW, Santa Isabel Group. For structural notes see the *Anus* entry. No literacy in it. In 1990, 600 speakers were reported. That figure may still be valid today. Speakers are bilingual in the large Cheke Holo (or Maringhe) language which is the southeastern neighbour of Blablanga, and puts pressure on it. The language is now potentially endangered.

Boano (or *Bolano*) [121] Indonesia: Sulawesi, on the south coast of the northeastern peninsula of Sulawesi, in its extreme western part where it joins the narrow neck which links the peninsula to the bulk of Sulawesi, in a single village with about 2,700 inhabitants, near Borneo. In 1990, 2,350 speakers were reported. WMP, Sulawesi, Central Sulawesi, Tomini. Structurally, it corresponds to the Southern Sulawesi type (see *Bahonsuai*). Their village has no space for new migrants to settle there, and Boano is the daily language used there. However, their children receive their primary school instruction in Indonesian, and Boano has to be regarded as potentially endangered.

Bonerif [150] Indonesia: Irian Jaya, in the inland central north coast area, east of the Upper Tor River. P, TNGP, Tor. Structurally the Tor languages correspond to the TNGP type, but have rudimentary gender distinction in verb forms, and directional markers. There is number marking in nouns. There is no literacy in Bonerif. In 1994, four speakers were reported, but some other estimates go up to forty. The speakers intermarry with those of the much larger Tor language Berik, their western neighbours, and Berik is used as a second language. The language is at least seriously endangered and heading towards being moribund.

Bonggo [177] Indonesia: Irian Jaya. Spoken on the northeast coast east of Sarmi and west of Demta. CEMP, EMPW, Sarmi-Yotafa. For structural notes see the *Anus* entry. No literacy in it. In 1975, 432 speakers were reported, but now it would be around 200. It has been under pressure from Indonesian, to which children are switching. It is now endangered.

Bosilewa [124] Papua New Guinea: Milne Bay Province. Spoken on the central north coast of Fergusson Island. CEMP, EMPW, Milne Bay-Central Province languages, Dobuan. For structural notes see the *Anus* entry. No literacy in it. In 1972, 350 speakers were reported. Now they would be about 250. The speakers are bilingual in the large Dobu language to which children are switching. Bosilewa is potentially endangered.

Bothar (or *Rema*) [187] Papua New Guinea: Western Province, Morehead District. Spoken in the extreme southwestern part of the Western Province, on the Morehead and Upper Bensbach Rivers. Apparently a dialect of Tonda, or a closely related language. P, TNGP, Trans-Fly, Morehead and Upper Maro Rivers Family, Tonda. For structural notes see the *Moraori* and *Dorro* entries. No literacy in it. In the 1980 census, sixty-eight speakers were reported. There may be less today. The language is under pressure from Tonda and other larger local languages, and from Tok Pisin. It is now endangered.

Broome Pearling Lugger Pidgin (or ***Broome Creole***, or ***Japanese Pidgin English***) **[not mapped]** Australia: northwestern WA, at Broome, Beagle Bay, La Grange, One Arm Point and Derby. A Malay-based pidgin language with only second language speakers. Contains some Japanese and Kriol (the English-based pidgin lingua franca of much of northern Australia) words. It is lingua franca on pearling boats, used for communication between Malays, Japanese, Chinese, and Aborigines. There are about 40–50 or more speakers, predominantly Aborigines. It is potentially endangered.

Budibud **[47]** Papua New Guinea: Milne Bay Province. Spoken on the Lachlan Islands, 150km east of Woodlark Island. CEMP, EMPW, Milne Bay-Central Province languages, Kilivila. For structural notes see the *Anus* entry. No literacy in it. In 1970, 170 speakers were reported. Today there would be about 120. The speakers are bilingual in Muyuw, to which children are switching. Budibud is getting potentially endangered.

Budong-Budong (or ***Tangkou***) **[117]** Indonesia: Sulawesi. Spoken near to the central-western coast of the bulk of Sulawesi, on the lower Budung-Budung River. WMP, Sulawesi, South Sulawesi. Structurally it corresponds to the Southern Sulawesi type (see *Bahonsuai*). No literacy in it. In 1988, seventy or fewer speakers were reported, now they are fewer. Some intermarriage and bilingualism with the large Topoiyo language and pressure from it. The language is now seriously endangered.

Bugunidja **[not mapped]** Australia: northern NT, between the upper South Alligator and the Nourlangie Rivers, south of Jim Jim Crossing. Related to Umbugarla and Ngurmbur (or Ngumbur). Extinct for some time.

Bukiyip (or ***Arapesh Abu'***, or ***Mountain Arapesh***, or ***Arapesh Buki***, or ***Kavu***) **[257]** Papua New Guinea: East Sepik Province. Spoken in the northern central part of the East Sepik Province, in the Yangoru District, Torricelli mountains, northeast of Bumbita Arapesh. For the location and structural notes see the *Arapesh Bumbita* entry. There is some literacy in it. In 1995, about 12,000 speakers (including 5,000 coastal Arapesh) were reported. Latest reports mention 10,304. The problem with the language is that many children are unwilling to speak it, and quite a few of them do not know it at all, or not properly. Even many adults are unwilling to speak it. There is a decided shift of the speakers to Tok Pisin. The language is now potentially endangered and moving towards being endangered.

Bulgebi **[136]** Papua New Guinea: Madang Province. Spoken inland on the eastern end of the southern (Rai) coast of Astrolabe Bay, on the lower Nankina River, about 15km south of Saidor. P, TNGP, Huon-Finisterre, Finisterre, Warup Family. Structurally it is TNGP (see the *Damal* entry). No literacy in it. In 1981, fifty-two speakers were reported. The figure still stands around fifty, but the language is under pressure from

481

closely related neighbouring larger languages such as Dahating, and from Tok Pisin, the Papua New Guinea national language. It is now endangered.

***Bulinya* [not mapped]** Australia: coastal western WA, north of Geraldton, on Greenbough River. PNY, South-West, Kardu. Recently extinct.

Bunaba* [87]** Australia: northeastern WA, Fitzroy crossing area. Bunaban. For structural information see the ***Jawoyn entry. There is no literacy in it. In 1990, 50–100 speakers were reported. Today only old people speak Bunaba, a few tens of them. The children know only a few words. Their first language is the English-derived pidgin lingua franca Kriol in its creolized form. The language is endangered and moving towards being seriously endangered.

Burate* [133]** Indonesia: Irian Jaya. Spoken at the mouth of the Wapoga River, east coast of Cenderawasih Bay, near Awera (see Awera). Structurally typical mainland Geelvinck Bay language (see the ***Awera entry). P. Geelvinck Bay, Eastern Geelvinck Bay. No literacy in it. In 1987, approximately 100 speakers were reported. The speakers are seminomadic. The language is regarded as endangered.

***Burduna* [not mapped]** Australia: WA, Henry and Upper Lyndon Rivers. PNY, South-West Kanyara. Recently extinct?

Busoa* [221]** Indonesia: Sulawesi. Spoken on the extreme southwest coast of Buton Island which is southeast of the southeastern peninsula of Sulawesi near Masiri. There were 500 speakers reported in 1991. WMP, Sulawesi, Muna-Buton (Muna). Structurally it corresponds to the Southern Sulawesi type (see ***Bahonsuai). No literacy in it. Under pressure of the large Wolio and Cia-Cia languages, and of Indonesian. At least potentially endangered, moving towards being endangered.

***Butam* [not mapped]** Papua New Guinea: East New Britain Province, in the Gazelle Peninsula. P, East Papuan, Baining-Taulil Section, dialect of Taulil. Extinct since 1981.

Bwatoo* [125]** New Caledonia. Spoken a third of the length of New Caledonia from its northwestern end, on the southwestern coast at Oundjo, and further south near Poya. CEMP, EMPCE, New Caledonian, Northern. For structural notes see the ***Arhö entry. No literacy in it. It may be a dialect of Haveke. In 1982, 300 speakers were reported. Today their number is somewhat less, and children are beginning not to learn it. It is under pressure from the two large neighbouring New Caledonian languages Ajië and Paicî, and from French. It is getting potentially endangered.

Dabra* (or *Bok*, or *Taria*) [135]** Indonesia: Irian Jaya. Spoken on the south side of the lower Idenburg River, near Megambilis. Geelvinck Bay Phylum, Lakes Plain, East Lakes Plain. For structural features see the ***Awera entry. No literacy in it. In 1978, 100 speakers were reported. The language is under some pressure from Indonesian and heading towards being endangered.

***Dagoman* [not mapped]** Australia: northern NT, Katherine area, on Fergusson River. Gunwinyguan, Yangmanic, Nolgin. Extinct for some time.

Dakka [227] Indonesia: Sulawesi. Spoken in the southeastern part of the non-peninsular bulk of Sulawesi. WMP, Sulawesi, south Sulawesi. Structurally it corresponds to the Southern Sulawesi type (see the *Bahonsuai* entry). No literacy in it. In 1986, 1,500 speakers were reported. The language is under pressure from larger neighbouring languages such as Rampi, and from Indonesian. It is potentially endangered.

Dalabon. See *Ngalkbun*

Damal (also known as *Uhunduni*) [50] Indonesia: Irian Jaya. Spoken northeast of Mt Jaya, the highest peak of the Carstens Mountains. It is actually one of the dialects of the very large Uhunduni language which is a lingua franca beyond its borders, but is now also showing signs of becoming potentially endangered. P, TNGP, Wissel Lakes-Kemandoga. Main structural features of TNGP languages are the presence of phonologically relevant tones in many of them, complicated verb morphology which is often veiled by extensive sound changes in the conjugations, rarity of gender systems, dual numbers in pronouns, and subject and object marking in verbs, no number marking on nouns, presence of sentence-medial verb forms different from sentence-final ones. One other typical TNGP feature is mentioned in the *Awyi* entry. There is some literacy in Damal. It has 4,000 to 5,000 speakers. Children are beginning to prefer Indonesian. Potentially endangered.

Dampal [28] Indonesia: Sulawesi, on the northwestern coast of the northern part of the narrow neck connecting the central bulk of Sulawesi with its northeastern peninsula, near Bangkir. WMP, Sulawesi, Central Sulawesi, Tomini. Structurally it corresponds to the Southern Sulawesi type (see *Bahonsuai*). No literacy in it. The ethnic group numbered about 300 in 1995. Most of them had intermarried with immigrant Bugis from South Sulawesi and do not speak Dampal any more. There were two good speakers and a few semi-speakers left in 1995, with one of the former dying in 1996. The language is moribund and almost extinct, or just about extinct now.

Dampelas [223] Indonesia: Sulawesi, on the west coast of the narrow neck connecting the central bulk of Sulawesi with its northeastern peninsula. Close to Sabang. WMP, Sulawesi, Central Sulawesi, Tomini. Structurally it corresponds to the Southern Sulawesi type (see *Bahonsuai*). No literacy in it. Spoken in eight villages, but in seven of these, there are strong migrant communities, and the everyday language used publicly is only Indonesia. The population of the eighth village is 99 per cent Dampelas, who are well off. Many of their children go to Palu town further south to school and university, and when they come home, they prefer Indonesian to Dampelas. Indonesian is used increasingly in families who want their children to have higher education. The ethnic group is around 10,000 or more, but only about 2,000 have still a good command of the language, which is rapidly receding before Indonesian and is endangered.

Darabal (or *Dharabal*) [not mapped] Australia: eastern coastal QLD, on the Fitzroy River, from Rockhampton north to Marlborough and Shoalwater Bay. PNy, Waka-Kabic, Kingkel. Extinct for several decades.

Darkinyung Australia: Sydney area. See *Iyora*

Darling (*Southern Baagandji*, or *Baagandji*, or *Paakantji*) **[134]** Australia: western NSW, southern part of the Darling River Basin. PNy, Baagandji. For structural information see the *Adnyamathanha* entry. However, in some of the Baagandji dialects, tenses are indicated by changing the initial consonant of the personal pronouns. There is no literacy in the language. In 1970, five or more fluent speakers were reported, but there are only one or two left now who have some knowledge of the vocabulary. However, there are efforts to revitalize and revive the language. In its present state, it is moribund, practically extinct.

Dayi (or *Dhay'yi*) **[111]** Australia: northern NT, southeastern Arnhem Land. Spoken at Roper River, Yirrkala, Lake Evella, Galiwinku, and Numbulwa. PNy, Yuulngu. For structural information see the *Adnyamathanha* entry. No literacy in it. In 1983, 200 speakers were reported. The position of the language has been adversely affected by the scattering of children, who now speak other languages. All remaining speakers are bilingual in English. The language is now endangered.

Demisa **[245]** Indonesia: Irian Jaya. Spoken on the east coast of Cenderawasih Bay and inland. Lingua franca of most of the eastern side of Cenderawasih Bay, and of seminomadic people in the interior. Geelvinck Bay Phylum, East Geelvinck Bay. For structural notes see the *Awera* entry. No literacy in it. In 1993, 500 speakers were reported. It is under pressure from Indonesian and the large CEMP, EMP, SHWNG Waropen language, and is potentially endangered.

Dengalu **[203]** Papua New Guinea: Morobe Province. Spoken inland to the southwest of the western extremity of the Huon Gulf. CEMP, EMPW, Markham Family, Buang. Technically, it is a member of the dialect chain which constitutes the large Mumeng language. See the *Anus* entry for structural information. No literacy in it. In 1978, 140 speakers were reported. They are likely to be fewer today. The language is under pressure from other larger dialects of the large Mumeng language, and of Tok Pisin. It is now endangered.

Dhalandji **[44]** Australia: northwestern WA, head of Exmouth Gulf, inland to Ashburton River, West Pilbara. PNy, South-West, Kanyara. For information on structural features see the *Adynyamathanha* entry. No literacy in it. In 1981, twenty speakers were reported. Today there are only a few. The language is moribund.

Dhangu (or *Yolngu-Matha*) **[105]** Australia: extreme northern NT, northeastern Arnhem Land, Elcho Island. PNy, Yuulngu. For structural information see the *Adynyamathanha* entry. Some literacy in it. In 1983, 350 speakers were reported. There has been some reduction in this, especially through the loss of children speakers to other languages. Speakers are bilingual in the large language Djambarrpuyngu, which is a major Aboriginal lingua franca in the area. Dhangu is getting potentially endangered.

Dhargari (or *Thargarri*, or *Targari*) **[142]** Australia: northwestern WA, Kennedy Range, upper Minilya and Lower Lyons Rivers, West Pilbara. PNy, South-West, Kanyara. For structural information see the *Adynyamathanha* entry. No literacy in it. In 1981, six speakers were reported. There may be one or two speakers left now. The language is moribund or perhaps already extinct.

Dharuk: Australia: Sydney area. See *Iyora*

Dhurga [not mapped] Australia: NSW, Coastal, Jervis Bay. PNy, Yuin-Kuric, Yuin. Extinct for decades.

Dieri (or *Diyari*) [73] Australia: SA, east of Lake Eyre North. PNy, Karnic, Karna. For structural information, see the *Adynyamathanha* entry. There used to be some literacy in it. In 1981, twelve speakers were reported. One or two may be left today. Dieri is moribund, or perhaps already extinct.

Dirari [not mapped] Australia: SA, east of Lake Eyre North. PNy, Karnic, Karma. Recently extinct.

Dixon Reef [63] Vanuatu; central southwest Malekula, coastal and inland. CEMP, EMPCE, remote Oceanic, north and central Vanuatu, Malekula Interior. Small Nambas Group. Structurally similar to what has been said in the *Anus* entry. No literacy in it. In 1982, fifty speakers were reported. They are likely to be fewer today. It is under pressure from related larger neighbouring languages such as Katbol and Labo, its northern and southern neighbours. It is now endangered and moving towards being seriously endangered.

Djamindjung [40] Australia: northwestern NT, Victoria River. Djaminjungan. For structural information, see the *Jawoyn* entry. There is no literacy in it. In 1990, thirty speakers were reported. Speakers are bilingual in the PNy Ngarinman language of the same area, and in the English-based pidgin language Kriol. There are fewer speakers today, and the language is seriously endangered.

Djangun [not mapped] Australia: northern QLD, central southern Cape York Peninsula, between the Upper Mitchell and Walsh Rivers, as far west as the Lynd River. PNy, Yalandyic. Recently extinct.

Djawi [89] Australia: WA, King Sound to Brunswick Bay. Nyulnyulan.

Djendewal [not mapped] Australia: southeastern corner of QLD, North and South Stradbroke Island, east of Brisbane. PNy, Durrubulic. Closely related to Yagara. Extinct for two decades.

Djinang [104] Australia: extreme northern NT, northeastern Arnhem Land, Ramingining, Goyder and Blyth Rivers. PNy, Yuulngu. For structural information, see the *Adynyamathanha* entry. Some literacy in it. In 1982, 250 or more speakers were reported. Speakers are in varying degrees bilingual in the very large Gupapuyngu language, in the lingua franca Djambarrpuyngu, or in Dhuwal. There is increasing use of English. The language is getting potentially endangered.

Djinba [109] Australia: extreme northern NT, northeastern Arnhem Land, Ngangalala. Southeastern neighbour of the Djinang language. PNy, Yuulngu. For structural information see the *Adynyamathanha* entry. No literacy in it. In 1983, 60–90 speakers were reported. Their number may have decreased somewhat. Speakers intermarry with the

Djinang speakers, and some are bilingual in Djinang, others in the large lingua franca Djamparrpuyngu. Djinba is potentially endangered.

Djingili* [43]** Australia: northern central NT, at Newcastle Waters, Ash Burton Range, Elliot. West Barkly Tablelands Group. Jingalic. The languages of this group are not PNY, but employ only suffixes. They have noun classes as they are found in many non-PNY languages (see the ***Jawoyn entry), but they are indicated by suffixes. No literacy in Djingili. In 1983, twenty or fewer fluent first language speakers were reported. Today there are very few. The speakers are bilingual in the English-based pidgin lingua franca Kriol. Djingili is moribund.

***Djiwarli* [not mapped]** Australia: northwestern WA, north of Mt Augustus in the Walburg Ranges, due east 400km inland from Cape Cuvier and Lake McLeod. PNY, southwest, coastal Ngayarda. Recently extinct.

Doga (or ***Magabara***) **[215]** Papua New Guinea: Milne Bay Province. Spoken on the northern coast of Cape Vogel. CEMP, EMPW, Milne Bay-Central Province languages. For structural information see the ***Anus*** entry. Most young people are literate in English or another language. In 1975, 200 speakers were reported. Today there may be less. Over 60 per cent of the young people know English, others are bilingual in neighbouring larger local languages such as Anuki. English and Tok Pisin exert pressure on the language, which is at least potentially endangered.

Dondo* [222]** Indonesia: Sulawesi. Spoken by both a west coastal and a middle hill population of a total of about 13,000 (reported in 1991 as 15,000 or fewer) in the extreme western part of the northeastern peninsula of Sulawesi, where it joins the narrow neck which links it to the bulk of Sulawesi. Today the middle hill people all live in resettlement projects and small hamlets near the coast. WMP, Sulawesi, Central Sulawesi, Tomini. Structurally, it corresponds to the Southern Sulawesi type (see ***Bahonsuai). Most of the middle hill Dondo interact socially with the Dondo coastal population which reinforces the use of Dondo in a variety of functions. Only their children, who receive their primary school instruction in Indonesian, constitute a possible threat to the language, which may therefore be potentially endangered.

***Dororo* [79]** Solomon Islands: on western New Georgia, inland. P. East Papuan, Kazukuru Family. The speakers shifted to the EMPW Roviana language, the church language of the island, and lingua franca of much of the Western Solomons. Extinct for several decades.

Dorro (or ***Tais***) **[184]** Papua New Guinea: Western Province. Spoken on the western third of the south coast, around Mari, west of Tais. P, TNGP, Trans-Fly, Morehead and Upper Maro Rivers Family. Structurally the languages of the Morehead and Upper Maro Rivers Family show a number of agreements with the TNGP type (see the ***Damal*** entry), but also have some aberrant features, such as the absence of sentence-medial verb forms, and changes in the initial syllable of verb forms for tense. The personal pronoun systems are defective and one form indicates two or more different pronouns. There is no literacy in Dorro. In 1980 and 1981, numbers of speakers ranging from 66 to 80 were reported. The figure of eighty is still correct now, but the language is under pressure from large closely related neighbouring languages, especially the Nambu language to the north, and also from Tok Pisin. It is now endangered.

Doutai (or ***Dou, Dou-Fou, Taori***) **[140]** Indonesia: Irian Jaya. Spoken at the confluence of the Dou (Tariku) and Fou (Muyabu) Rivers, tributaries of the upper Rouffaer River in the western central part of the eastern main bulk of Irian Jaya, west of Taiyeve. Geelvinck Bay Phylum, Lakes Plain, Tariku East. See the ***Awera*** entry for remarks on its structure. No literacy in it. In 1993, 335 speakers were reported, but the latest information from Irian Jaya puts their number at only seventy. It is under such pressure from Indonesian, that it is now endangered.

Dubu **[80]** Indonesia: Irian Jaya. Spoken near the Papua New Guinea border, south of the Pai River about 150km south of Jayapura. P, TNGP, Pauwasi. Structurally somewhat aberrant from the TNGP type. No literacy in it. In 1978, 130 speakers were reported. Under some pressure from Indonesian. Potentially endangered.

Dumun (or ***Bai***) **[1]** Papua New Guinea: Madang Province. Spoken on the southern (Rai) coast of Astrolabe Bay, on the coast at the mouth of the Gowar River west of Dein, and on its lower course. P, TNGP, Madang, Yaganon Family. Structurally it is TNGP (see the ***Damal*** entry). No literacy in it. In 1981, forty-two speakers were reported. At present, their number is still near forty, but the language is under strong pressure from related neighbouring larger languages such as Saep and Siroi, and from Tok Pisin, the Papua New Guinea national language. It is now seriously endangered.

Duriankere (or ***Esaro***, or ***Sailen***) **[75]** Indonesia: Irian Jaya. Spoken on a small island at the southern end of the strait between the western end of the Bird's Head Peninsula and Salawati Island. P, TNGP, Timor-Alor-Pantar, South Bird's Head, Inawatan. Structurally somewhat like what is detailed in the ***Maku'a*** entry, but more complex. No literacy in it. In 1988, 100 speakers were reported. Under heavy pressure from the WPAP, Bird's Head Moi and Seget languages, and of Indonesian. Now speakers are much fewer, with the only speakers elderly. The language is seriously endangered.

Dusner **[51]** Indonesia: Irian Jaya, around Dusner town, west coast of Cenderawasih Bay, Wandamen Bay area. EMP, South Halmahera – West New Guinea group. Biakic Section. It had six elderly speakers in 1978, but is now probably extinct because of pressure from the neighbouring large Wandamen language of the same group.

Duungidjawu **[not mapped]** Australia: southeastern QLD. PNY, Waka-Kabic, Miyan Waka. Last native speaker died in 1965. Two secondary speakers still exist. See the ***Wakawaka*** entry.

Duwet **[201]** Papua New Guinea: Morobe Province. Spoken inland from the Huon Gulf, north of Lae, in the lower Busu River area. CEMP, EMPW, Markham languages. For structural notes see the ***Anus*** entry. No literacy in it. In 1988, 398 speakers were reported. Now there may be about 300. It is under pressure from large related languages, e.g. Wampar, and from Tok Pisin which children prefer, and is potentially endangered.

Dyaabugay **[98]** Australia: northeast QLD, southeastern coast of Cape York Peninsula, Barron River, from south of Mareeba to Kuranda, north to Port Douglas. PNY, Yidinic. For structural information see the *Adynyamathanha* entry. No literacy in it. In 1981, three speakers were reported, and the language was heading for extinction. However, in the 1980s and later, a strong revival of the language was undertaken among the Dyaabugay people with the help of linguists, relying on the last few speakers, and the language has since been in daily use among members of the ethnic group as a symbol of their identity. It is certainly not moribund now, but may be classed as seriously endangered to endangered, depending on the direction of the further development of the revivalist trend among the young generation.

Dyaberdyaber **[not mapped]** Australia: WA, northwest coast, south of Beagle Bay and inland. Nyulnyulan. Recently extinct.

Dyangadi (or *Thangatti*) **[not mapped]** Australia: NSW, northeastern coast and hinterland, Kempsey area. PNY, Yuin-Kuric, Kuri. Extinct for two decades.

Dyirbal **[101]** Australia: northeast QLD, in the extreme southeastern part of Cape York Peninsula, Herberton, south to the headwaters of Herbert River, at Ravenshoe and Woodleigh, east to Tully Falls. PNY, Dyirbalic. For structural information see the *Adynyamathanha* entry. However, it has noun classes indicated by suffixes. No literacy in it. In 1983, 40–50 speakers were reported. Today there are only few. The language is moribund.

Dyugun **[not mapped]** Australia: northwestern WA coast around Broome and inland. Nyulnyulan. Recently extinct.

East Makian (or *Makian Dalam*, or *Taba*) **[37]** Indonesia: Maluku. Spoken on East Makian Island, Mori Island, Kayoa Island, Ternate Island, Malifut on Halmahera, the west coast of South Halmahera, on Dacau and Obi Islands, etc., in north Maluku. CEMP, EMP, SHWNG. For structural information, see the *Gebe* entry. 25–50 per cent literacy. In 1983, 20,000 or more speakers were reported. However, a volcanic eruption on Makian Island, transmigrations, the presence of speakers of several other languages in East Makian speaking areas, and the pressure from these and from Indonesian, have taken their toll. It is receding and falling into disuse in several of its areas, and generally undergoing marked structural changes. It is now potentially endangered to endangered.

Eleman Hiri Trade Pidgin **[not mapped]** Papua New Guinea: coastal Gulf Province area from east of the Purari River Delta to Cape Possession further southeast. This language was used by the EMP, EMPW Motu language speakers of the present-day Port Moresby area and by their trading partners, the speakers of the P, TNGP, Eleman languages in the Gulf District area mentioned above during the Motuans' annual trading voyages there. The language is a pidgin, based in its structure on several different languages of the Papuan Eleman Family. Its vocabulary is 80 per cent from the same sources, and 20 per cent from Motu. The language fell into disuse with European contact and the consequent cessation of the annual trade voyages. It is now extinct.

Emae (or *Emwae*) [2] Vanuatu: Emwae Island. Spoken on Emwae Island, to the north of northeast Efate Island. CEMP, EMP, Oceanic, remote Oceanic, Polynesian (Western). For structural information see the *Maori* entry, but Emwae is influenced by the CEMP, EMPCE, Oceanic, remote Oceanic, North and Central Vanuatuan North Efate language spoken in the northern part of Efate Island. This influence has affected its structure. For the structural features of the Vanuatu languages to which North Efate belongs, see the *Anus* entry. There is no literacy in Emae. In 1981, about 200 speakers were reported. They are all bilingual in the North Efate language. This and the English-based lingua franca Bislama, which is the national language of Vanuatu, puts pressure on Emae. Emae language use is quite vigorous, but it is becoming potentially endangered.

Emplawas [3] Indonesia: Maluku. Spoken on southwest Babar Island in South Maluku, northeast from the northeastern tip of Timor Island. CEMP, CMP, Timor-Flores (South Maluku). Structurally as per the *Palu'e* and *Alune* entries. No literacy in it. In 1989, 250 speakers were reported. Under pressure from the large language of the island (Babar) and Indonesian. The language may be potentially endangered.

Enggano [5] Indonesia: Sumatra, on Enggano Island, southwest of Sumatra and on four smaller nearby islands. WMP, Sundic, Sumatra. Not closely related to any other language of the area. It is rather Malayic in structure, with subject-verb-object word order, many affixes in the word formation and noun and verb inflection, little focussing and simple active-passive contrast. It is aberrant in several ways and shows features from languages further east. No literacy in it. In 1981 it still had 1,000 speakers, but there is pressure from Sumatran Malay and from Indonesian, and their number is decreasing, and the language is heading towards being endangered.

Erokwanas [220] Indonesia: Irian Jaya, on the northwest coast of Bomberai Peninsula. CEMP, EMP, SHWNG, Bomberai. Structurally it is as per the *Gebe* entry. No literacy in it. In 1977, 250 speakers were reported; now there are probably fewer. Under pressure from the large TNGP, West Bomberai Baham language, and from Indonesian. Children tend not to use it. It is potentially endangered.

Erre [not mapped] Australia: NT, northern central Arnhem Land, south of Oenpelli. Mangerrian, Urninganggic. Recently extinct.

Faghani [55] Solomon Islands: northwestern part of San Cristobal (Makira) Island. CEMP, EMPCE remote Oceanic, Southeast Solomons languages. For structural information see the *Anus* entry. A fair amount of literacy in it. In 1981, 300 speakers were reported. There may be 200–250 today. Bilingualism in the large Roviana lingua franca is widespread. It puts some pressure on Faghani and children switch to it. Faghani is potentially endangered.

Faita [13] Papua New Guinea: Madang Province. Spoken on the Upper Ramu River, near Usino. P, TNGP, Adelbert Range. Structurally it is TNGP (see the *Damal* entry). No literacy in it. In 1981, fifty-seven speakers were reported. There are still fifty or more speakers today, but the language is under pressure from large related neighbouring languages such as Usino, and of Tok Pisin, the Papua New Guinea national language. Faita is now endangered.

489

Fayu (or *Sehudate*) **[6]** Indonesia: Irian Jaya. Spoken west of the confluence of the Tariku (Dou) and Muyabu (Fou) rivers in the western central part of the main bulk of Irian Jaya. Lingua franca of the Western Lakes Plain. Geelvinck Bay Phylum, Lakes Plain, Tariku, West. See the *Awera* entry for remarks on its structure. Some literacy in it. In 1991, 400 speakers were reported. Four nomadic groups. Coming under pressure from Indonesian, which the children tend to prefer. It is potentially endangered.

Flinders Island **[not mapped]** Australia: QLD, Cape York Peninsula, Flinders Island, Princess Charlotte Bay. PNY, Flinders Island. Recently extinct.

Foya **[7]** Indonesia: Irian Jaya. Spoken on the upper Bu River, in the upper Tor River area, inland from the central north coast area. P, TNGP, Tor. For notes on its structure see the *Bonerif* entry. There is no literacy in it. In 1993, it was said that there could possibly be about fifty speakers. Speakers are shifting to the neighbouring Mander language, which also has few native speakers. The number of Foya speakers is likely to be considerably less than fifty. It has been seriously endangered before, but is now more likely to be moribund.

Gadhang (or *Kattang*, or *Worrimi*) **[not mapped]** Australia: central coast and hinterland of NSW, Taree area. PNY, Yuin-Kuric, Kuri. Recently extinct.

Gadjerawang **[11]** Australia: northeastern WA and northwestern NT, north coast from Wyndham eastwards to the mouth of Victoria River, and inland. Djeragan, Miriwungic. For structural information see the *Jawoyn* entry. No literacy in it. In 1981, perhaps three spreakers were reported. Still not extinct, a few elderly speakers extant. Moribund.

Gagadu (or *Kakatu*, or *Kakadju*) **[20]** Australia: northern NT, central Arnhem Land, Oenpelli. Gagadjuan. For structural information see the *Jawoyn* entry. No literacy in it. In 1981, six speakers were reported, who were all bilingual in another Aboriginal language. Today Gagadu is moribund, with one speaker left.

Gambera **[not mapped]** Australia: WA, Admiralty Gulf, far northern Kimberleys area. Wororan, Wunambalic. Recently extinct?

Ganggalida (or *Yukulta*) **[99]** Australia: northwest corner of QLD, west of Burketown, Gulf of Carpentaria coast and hinterland south to Doomadgee. PNY, Tangkic. For structural information see the *Adynyamathanha* and *Kayardild* entries. No literacy in it. In 1981 possibly five speakers were reported. Now half a dozen semi-speakers and possibly one full speaker are reported. Moribund.

Gangulu **[not mapped]** Australia: QLD. Isaac River, west of Marlborough. PNY, Maric, Mari. Recently extinct.

Gao **[35]** Solomon Islands: southeastern Isabel Island, around Tatamba. CEMP, EMPW, East Isabel Group. For structural notes see the *Anus* entry. In 1990, 550 speakers were reported. This may still be valid today, but there is an increasing number of mixed marriages, and the home language of children tends to become increasingly the large neighbouring closely related Cheke Holo (or Maringhe) language. There is some literacy in Cheke Holo. There is also bilingualism in the Bughotu language, the southeastern neighbour of Gao. Solomon Pijin is also used. The language is becoming endangered under these circumstances.

Gapun (or *Taiap*) [25] Papua New Guinea: northeastern corner of the East Sepik Province. Spoken inland, south of the Sepik River mouth. Gapun is the name of the village, but is used in literature for the language whose real name is Taiap. P, SERP, but possibly originally unrelated to it, but heavily influenced by it. Structurally aberrant when compared with the usual SERP characteristics (see the *Ak* entry). Complex verb morphology, with subject marking through suffixes. No noun classification, but there is a two-gender system in third person pronoun. No number marking on nouns. No literacy in it. In 1987, 89 speakers were reported. No speakers under 10–12 years old then. More recent estimates mention seventy-four, mostly middle-aged or older. Heavy pressure from surrounding languages such as Abu (Adjora) and Tok Pisin. It is now seriously endangered. Some regard it as moribund.

Garawa [72] Australia: northeastern NT at Borroloola and in the adjacent part of northwestern QLD at Doomadgee. Garawan. Though it is non-Pama-Nyungan, it is a suffixing language. There is some literacy in it. In 1990, 200 or more speakers were reported. Speakers intermarry with the neighbouring Yanyuwa speakers. There are likely to be fewer speakers today. The language is now heading towards being endangered.

Garlali [not mapped] Australia: southwestern QLD, between Thargomindah on the Bulloo River and Eulo on the upper Paroo River. PNY, Karnic, Ngura. Recently extinct.

Garringbal [not mapped] Australia: northeastern inland QLD, at the headwaters of rivers running north into the Fairbairn Reservoir. South of Springsure. PNY, Maric, Mari. Extinct for some time.

Garuwahi [26] Papua New Guinea: Milne Bay Province. Spoken on the northern part of the eastern extremity of the Papua New Guinea mainland, near East Cape. CEMP, EMPW, Milne Bay-Central Province languages. For structural information, see the *Anus* entry. No literacy in it. In 1972, 225 speakers were reported. Today there are likely to be less. The speakers are bilingual in the large related Wedau language, their western neighbour, and there is pressure from Tok Pisin. The language is potentially endangered.

Gebe [30] Indonesia: Maluku (north). Spoken on Gebe Island and the two nearby smaller islands of Yu (or Yoi'umiyal) and Gag, lying between South Halmahera and Waigeo Island (which belongs to Irian Jaya). CEMP, EMP, South Halmahera-West New Guinea. Structurally the South Halmahera-West New Guinea type languages, though they are classified as belonging to EMP, deviate quite markedly in their features from what has been said in the *Palu'e* entry about EMP characteristics. They have some EMP features, but also some WMP ones, as is the case with CMP languages. As a special feature, the number of nouns is marked by suffixes, with a living/non-living distinction. With the indication of possession, that of permanent possession is rarely used, and with non-permanent, it is indicated whether the possessed is living or non-living, and also whether it is one or several. The almost universally present distinction in the Malayo-Polynesian languages, between the inclusive (i.e. including the person addressed) and exclusive (i.e. excluding the person addressed) in non-singular forms of the first person pronoun, is only present in the dual number. The subject of a verb is marked by prefixes in some and by infixes in others, whereas in EMP languages usually only prefixes appear. Some other verb prefixes which are frequent in WMP, are found occasionally, but are in general lacking in other EMP languages. No literacy in it. In 1983, 1,000 to 3,000 speakers were reported. Mining operations started in the language area which led to more schooling of the children and increasing use of Indonesian and bilingualism in it. The language is potentially endangered.

Getmata [not mapped] Papua New Guinea: in West New Britain Province. EMPW, New Britain Section, southwest New Britain. Extinct since the 1950s.

Giya Australia: northeastern coastal QLD, northwest of Mackay, at Collinsville and Bloomsbury. PNY, Maric, Mari. Extinct for quite some time.

Giyug [not mapped] Australia: NT, southwest of Darwin, on Peron Islands in Anson Bay. Daly, Bringen-Wagaydy. Recently extinct.

Gorap [31] Indonesia: North Maluku. Spoken on Morotai Island (the northernmost large island of North Halmahera) and on the southern coast and hinterland of Kau Bay in central eastern North Halmahera. Malayo-Polynesian creole, with a mixed vocabulary which also contains words from Malay, Indonesian and from the large West Papuan, North Halmahera lingua franca Ternate. Its word order is different from both Malayo-Polynesian and North Halmahera Papuan languages. The speakers are believed to have come from Sulawesi. In 1992, 1,000 were reported, but they may be less now under strong pressure from the languages from which the majority of its vocabulary seems to have originated. It is now endangered.

Gorovu (or *Yerani*) [32] Papua New Guinea: extreme southeastern corner of the East Sepik Province. Spoken on the lower Ramu River, southeast of Komtina. P, SERP, Ramu, Grass Family. The Ramu languages of the SERP have simpler morphologies than those of the Sepik, or standard SERP, type (see the *Ak* entry). There is often no person marking in verbs in Ramu languages, or it is only rudimentary. Plural forms of nouns occur fairly frequently, but their forms are usually predictable and regular. Noun classification and two-gender systems are rare in them. They lack sentence-medial verb forms. There is no literacy in Gorovu. In 1981, fifty speakers were reported, but now there only are twenty or less. The speakers are shifting to the large related Banaro language, the western neighbour of Gorovu. It is now seriously endangered and moving towards being moribund.

Gugadj [not mapped] Australia: QLD, southern end of Gulf of Carpentaria coast of Cape York Peninsula. PNY, Paman, Flinders Pama. Recently extinct.

Gugu Badhun [not mapped] Australia: northern QLD, inland from Ingham near Einasleigh. Recently extinct. PNY, Maric, Mari. There are attempts at reviving it.

Gugu Warra [not mapped] Australia: QLD, central eastern Cape York Peninsula, west bank of Normanby River. PNY, Paman, Lamalamic. Recently extinct.

Gugubera (or *Koko Bera*) [38] Australia: northern QLD, central west coast of Cape York Peninsula, around the mouth of Mission River, and at Mitchell River. PNY, Paman, Coastal Pama. For structural information see the *Adynyamathanha* entry. There is no literacy in it. In 1991, fifteen fluent speakers were reported out of an ethnic group of fifty. The language of those who did not know Gugubera was Torres Strait Creole (or Broken), and most of the group speak Kunjen as second language. Today there are fewer speakers, and Torres Strait Creole is taking over. The language is seriously endangered.

Guguyimidjir (or *Kukuyimidjir*, or *Guugu Yimithirr*) [39] Australia: northeastern Queensland, central eastern Cape York Peninsula, Hopevale. PNY, Yalandyic. For structural information see the *Adynyamathanha* entry. There is some literacy in it. In 1991, 20–30 fluent speakers were reported, 200–300 were said to know and understand the language, but preferred English. There is a total of 400 in the ethnic group. Children did understand the language, but only spoke it a little, and mainly used Aboriginal English. Today the situation is deteriorating, with fewer fluent speakers, and less knowledge of the language by others in the ethnic group. The language is endangered.

Guliguli [not mapped] Solomon Islands. Same area and Family as Dororo. P, extinct for several decades, same reason as with Dororo.

Gungabula [not mapped] Australia: Inland southeastern QLD, near Injune. PNY, Maric, Mari. Extinct.

Gungalanya [not mapped] Australia: southwestern corner of QLD, near Bedouri and Lake Philippi. PNY, Karnic, Palku. Extinct for several decades.

Gunian (or *Gooniyandi*) [88] Australia: northwestern WA, Fitzroy Crossing area. Bunaban. For structural information, see the *Jawoyn* entry. No literacy in it. In 1990, 100 speakers were reported. The speakers now generally speak the English-based pidgin lingua franca Kriol. Only the elderly speak Gunian. The language is now seriously endangered and getting towards being moribund.

Gunya [not mapped] Australia: central southern QLD, near Wyandra. PNY, Maric, Mari. Recently extinct.

Guragone (or *Gun-Guragone*) [66] Australia: northern NT, northeastern Arnhem Land, south of Maningrida, along the Mann River. Burraran. For structural information see the *Jawoyn* entry. No literacy in it. In 1990, twenty speakers were reported. They are likely to be fewer today. All speakers are bilingual in Burarra or Gunwinygu, which exerts pressure on their Guragone. The language is seriously endangered and is heading towards being moribund.

Guramalum [not mapped] Papua New Guinea: in New Ireland Province. EMPW, New Ireland-Tolai Section, Patpatar-Tolai Subsection. It had three or four speakers in 1987, but is now probably extinct.

493

Gurdjar [42] Australia: Northwestern corner area of QLD, on the northeastern side of the Norman River, at Normanton. PNy, Paman, Norman Pama. For structural information see the *Adynyamathanha* entry. No literacy in it. In 1981, possibly thirty speakers were reported. Gurdjar was in daily use by older people, but children preferred English. The situation today is much less favourable for the language, which has now only one or two surviving speakers and is now moribund.

Gureng Gureng [not mapped] Australia: PNy, Waka-Kabic, QLD, Than. Extinct for some time.

Guringgai Australia: Sydney area. See **Iyora**

Gurinji (or *Gurindji*) [118] Australia: northwestern NT, Victoria River and Wave Hill, Kalkaringi. PNy, South-West, Ngumbin. For structural notes see the *Adynyamathanha* entry. Some literacy in it. In 1983, 250 fluent first language speakers were reported, with a total of 400 including partial speakers. All speakers are bilingual in Kriol, the English-based pidgin lingua franca. Today the speaker numbers are lower, especially because the children use only Kriol. However, language maintenance activities are being undertaken. The language is potentially endangered.

Gurnu [not mapped] Australia: northwestern NSW, on the Darling River at Louth, as far as Bourke, and northwards beyond Enngonia. PNy, Baagandji. Extinct for three decades.

Guwamu [not mapped] Australia: Inland southeastern QLD, near St George. PNy, Maric, Mari. Extinct for three decades.

Guyani [not mapped] Australia: eastern central SA, north and west of Lake Torrens, around Andamooka and north to Maree, and almost to Lake Eyre South. PNy, South-West, Yura. Extinct for decades.

Habu [56] Indonesia: East Timor Island. Spoken in the central part of East Timor Island. CEMP, CMP, Waima'a. The Waima'a languages deviate in the pronominal and possessive system, and some verb forms, from the other Malay-Polynesian languages of Timor. There is no literacy in it. In 1981, 1,000 speakers were reported, but now there would be rather fewer speakers. It has many loan words from the neighbouring Papuan TNGP Timor-Alor-Pantar languages, which put pressure on it. It is potentially endangered.

Haeke (or *Haeake*) [46] New Caledonia. A third of the length of New Caledonia from the northwestern end, on the southwestern coast, near Koné town. CEMP, EMPCE, Oceanic, New Caledonian, Haekic. For structural notes see the *Arhö* entry. There is no literacy in Haeke. In 1982, 100 or fewer speakers were reported. Now there are only a few. The language has been under pressure from the large Paicî language, its southwestern neighbour, and from French. It is moribund.

Hauna Trade Pidgin [not mapped] Papua New Guinea: western East Sepik Province, the upper Sepik River and the lower Leonard Schultze River. This trade pidgin developed between the P, SERP, Sepik, Upper Sepik, Iwam language-speaking village of Hauna on the upper Sepik River and the P, SERP, Leonard Schultze, Walio language-speaking village of Wasiak on the lower Leonard Schultze River. The language is a simplified variety of Iwam with input from Walio. About 40 per cent of the lexicon is Walio-derived, as well as three important grammatical elements. It may be potentially endangered.

Haveke **[48]** New Caledonia. Spoken about a third of the length of New Caledonia from its western end, on the southwestern coast from Gatope towards the southeast. CEMP, EMPCE, New Caledonian, Northern. For structural notes see the *Arhö* entry. No literacy in it. In 1982, 300 speakers were reported. Now they are much less, with virtually no children speakers. It is under pressure from the large neighbouring New Caledonian Paicî language, and from French. It is now endangered.

Hawaiian **[49]** Hawaiian Islands. CEMP, EMP, Oceanic, remote Oceanic, Polynesian (Eastern). For structural information see the *Maori* entry. Hawaiian has one of the simplest sound systems of all the languages in the world, with eight consonants and five vowels. Literacy in Hawaiian is widespread amongst the speakers. The language was heading for extinction outside Ni'ihau Island until a few decades ago, when revival efforts started in other parts of the Hawaiian Islands. Ni'ihau Island has been a private property to which entry by outsiders is forbidden, and the largely monolingual Hawaiian speakers there, were and are sheltered from the destructive influence of English and English monolingualist American attitudes. Today there are 2,000 mother tongue speakers, and 8,000 can speak and understand Hawaiian. There is a problem with a considerable number of young speakers being trained in the language through immersion courses, and also of very old speakers being available, but there are relatively few adult and middle-aged speakers, which results in a lack of communication situations for the active use of the Hawaiian language. Because of what has been said above, the language can be regarded as endangered.

Helong (or *Semau*) **[52]** Indonesia: Timor Island. Spoken on the southwestern tip of Timor Island near the port of Tenau, and in the majority of the villages on the nearby coast of Semau Island. CEMP, CMP, Timor-Flores. Unlike many of the other CMP languages near it, it does not inflect vowel-initial verb roots for person and number, has long and short vowels, and a glottal stop. No literacy in it. Speakers of the variety of Helong spoken on Semau Island, are beginning to shift to Kupang Malay under pressure from speakers of it from outside, especially from Roti and Sawu islands. Standard Indonesian also puts pressure on Helong. In 1996, 9,000 speakers were reported. This number may be reduced now. The language is potentially endangered.

Hermit (or *Agomes*, or *Luf*, or *Maron*) **[not mapped]** Papua New Guinea: in Admiralty Islands, Western Manus Province, Luf and Maron Islands in the Hermit Islands. EMPW, Eastern Admiralty Islands Section. May still have a few speakers, but is either in the last moribund stage, or already extinct.

Hiw (or *Torres*) **[53]** Vanuatu: Torres Islands, Hiw Island. CEMP, EMPCE, remote Oceanic, North and Central Vanuatu. Similar in structure to what has been said in the *Anus* entry. Some literacy in it. In 1983, 120 speakers were reported, though in 1981,

495

only fifty were said to exist. There may be fewer today. Speaker numbers are dwindling. The influence of the national language Bislama may be a reason for this, as may emigration. It is now endangered.

Hmwaveke [54] New Caledonia. Spoken less than a third of the length of New Caledonia from its western end, inland from Vuh around Tieta. CEMP, EMPCE, New Caledonian, Northern. For structural notes see the *Arhö* entry. No literacy in it. In 1982, 300 speakers were reported. Now they are much less, with virtually no children speakers. It is under pressure from the large neighbouring New Caledonian Paicî language, and from French. It is now endangered.

Hoava [61] Solomon Islands: New Georgia, North Marovo lagoon, on the central northern coast of the main New Georgia Island. CEMP, EMPW, New Georgia Group. For structural notes see the *Anus* entry. In 1981, 600 speakers were reported. Speakers are bilingual in the large lingua franca and church language Roviana, their southern neighbour language. The language is now potentially endangered.

Hoti [not mapped] Indonesia: Maluku, on East Seram Island. CEMP, CMP, central Maluku. There were still about ten elderly speakers in 1987, but it is now probably extinct.

Hukumina (or *Bambaa*) [not mapped] Indonesia: Maluku, on northwestern Buru Island. CEMP, CMP, central Maluku. In 1989, there was at least one eighty-year-old speaker, but it is now extinct.

Hulung [62] Indonesia: Maluku, on West Seram Island. CEMP, CMP, central Maluku. Still spoken in 1991 by less than ten persons, but is now probably extinct.

Iatmul Jargon [not mapped] Papua New Guinea: East Sepik Province, Middle Sepik River area. A simplified P, SERP, Sepik, Middle Sepik, Ndu, Iatmul language used throughout the Middle-Sepik region before as a lingua franca. It is now extinct.

Ibu [65] Indonesia: Maluku, Halmahera, on the northern Halmahera Island, at the mouth of the Ibu River. P, WPAP. In 1987 there were a few elderly speakers, but it is now probably extinct. There are 50 to 200 in the ethnic group.

Ifo [not mapped] Vanuatu: on northeastern Erromanga Island. EMPCE, South Vanuatu Section. Relatively recently extinct.

Ilgar (or *Garig*) [67] Australia: northern NT, northern Arnhem Land, on Croker Island, Cobourg Peninsula. Yiwaidjan, Yiwaidjic. For some of the structural information see the *Jawoyn* entry. However, it has, like Iwaidja, some aberrant features. For instance, it has kinship verbs, inflected prepositions, distinct forms of the personal pronouns for neutral position, moving towards, or away from the speaker, etc. No literacy in it. Only three or four speakers are left, the others have shifted to Iwaidja. Moribund.

Iresim [186] Indonesia: Irian Jaya. Spoken on the coast and inland in the southernmost Cenderawasih Bay area, in the eastern part of the neck portion of the Bird's Head Peninsula, as far inland as Yamur Lake. CEMP, EMP, SHWNG. For notes on its

496

structure see the **Kao** entry. No literacy in it. In 1977, about 100 speakers were reported. There may be fewer today. Pressure is mainly from Indonesian, to which the children are shifting. It is now endangered.

Isirawa (or *Saberi*, or *Okwasar*) **[68]** Indonesia: Irian Jaya. Spoken on the western part of the north coast, and inland, west of Sarmi. Traditionally the lingua franca on the western central north coast. P, TNGP, Dani-Kwerba, Northern Division. Structurally, the languages of the Northern (Kwerba Division of Dani-Kwerba) correspond to those of the TNGP as mentioned in the **Damal** and **Awyi** entries, but they also show aberrant features, such as a rudimentary two-gender system only appearing in markers with the verbs, not with pronouns. There is considerable literacy in it, up to 15 per cent of the speakers. In 1993, 2,000 speakers were reported. Language use is vigorous, but Isirawa is losing its lingua franca and trade language status to Indonesian, and the children are beginning to prefer Indonesian to it. It is potentially endangered.

Itik (or *Betef*) **[149]** Indonesia: Irian Jaya. Spoken inland from the north coast, east of the Tor River and west of the upper Biri River, at Itik. P, TNGP, Tor. For remarks on its structure see the **Bonerif** entry. No literacy in it. In 1978, about 100 speakers were reported. It is under pressure from Indonesian and is potentially endangered.

Iwaidja (or *Jiwaidja*) **[69]** Australia: extreme northern NT, Arnhem Land, Croker Island. Yiwaidjan, Yiwaidjic. For structural information see the **Ilgar** entry, but it has also some additional aberrant features. Limited use of written material on Croker Island. In 1983, 180 speakers were reported. All speakers are bilingual in English. The speaker numbers are lower today, about 150, with speakers shifting to English or Kunwinjku. The language is potentially endangered.

Iyora (or *Yora*) **[not mapped]** Australia: Sydney area, north to Newcastle and Muswellbrook, inland to Mudgee and beyond Bathurst. Name of one subgroup of the PNY, Yuin-Kuri Group. It comprised five languages, Darkinyung in the northwest, Awabakal in the north, Dharuk in the west, Guringgai in the northwestern Sydney area, and Iyora in the present Sydney City area. They are all long extinct, but at least Awabakal, Guringgai and Iyora are well remembered names.

Jarnango (or *Yanangu*, or *Nangu*) **[70]** Australia: northern NT, northern Arnhem Land, on two of the most western Crocodile Islands, adjacent to Cape Stewart, Maningrida and Millingimbi. PNY, Yuulngu. For structural notes see the **Adynyamathanha** entry. No literacy in the language. In 1983, possibly forty speakers were reported. The speakers generally speak the closely related large lingua franca Djambarrpuyngu, or the also closely related Gupapuyngu, or Burarra. The number of speakers has been decreasing, and the language is seriously endangered.

Jaru (or *Djaru*) **[77]** Australia: northwestern WA, Halls Creek, southwestern Kimberley region. PNY, South-West, Ngumbin. For structural information see the **Adynyamathanha** entry. There is some limited literacy. In 1981, 250 speakers were reported. The children speak the English-based pidgin lingua franca Kriol or Aboriginal English, and the number of Jaru speakers has been decreasing. The language is endangered.

Javindo |**not mapped**| Indonesia: Java, Semarang. A creolized media lingua with a predominantly Javanese grammar and a mixed Dutch-Javanese vocabulary. See the *Peco'* entry for the origin of such creolized forms of Dutch. There may still be a few second-language speakers and even some very few first-language speakers of it. It is moribund.

Jawoyn (or *Jawony*, or *Djauan*) |**78**| Australia: extreme northern NT, northeastern Arnhem Land, Bamyili settlement, and at Katherine. Gunwinyguan, Jawoynic. Non-PNY languages of northern Australia in and south of Arnhem Land, the Kimberleys and adjacent areas, except for the West Barkly Tablelands languages, differ structurally from the PNY languages in having prefixes on verbs, mainly for the indication of the person and number of actors and the objects. However, the forms of these prefixed person markers are comparable to suffixes indicating persons and objects in PNY languages. Also, the majority of these non-PNY languages distinguish two or several genders and/or classes of nouns, with a concordance, indicating the gender or class of the noun referred to running through a sentence. A number of these languages lack this gender and class distinction. There is no literacy in Jawoyn. In 1983, possibly 100 speakers were reported. All speakers are bilingual in Kriol, the English-derived pidgin lingua franca, and some also in English, and some in Ngalkbun, another larger Gunwinyguan language. All education is in Kriol and English. The number of speakers is much lower today, and even aged people use it only rarely. Jawoyn is seriously endangered.

Kadai |**81**| Indonesia: North Maluku, Sula Islands, Taliabu Island. Spoken in the interior mountainous area of Taliabu Island and possibly also of Mangole (Sulabesi) Island. CEMP, CMP, Central Maluku. Structurally as per the *Palu'e* and *Alune* entries. No literacy in it. In 1982, 300 speakers were reported. Now considerably less. There is extensive logging in the language area and the government is resettling the speakers along the coast, disrupting the speech community. The language is endangered.

Kaibobo |**82**| Indonesia: Maluku. Spoken in West Seram Island, at Piru Bay. CEMP, CMP, Central Maluku. Structurally it corresponds to what is detailed in the *Palu'e* and *Alune* entries. No literacy in it. In 1983, 500 speakers were reported. There would be much fewer now, because in several villages the speakers have been shifting to Ambon Malay. The language is endangered.

Kaiep |**83**| Papua New Guinea: East Sepik Province. Spoken on the central coast of the province around Taul. CEMP, EMPW, Siassi languages. For structural information see the *Anus* entry. No literacy in it. In 1993, 300 speakers were reported. Now there may be about 250. It is under pressure from the very large Manam language to which it is very closely related. It is potentially endangered.

Kairui-Midiki |**84**| Indonesia: East Timor Island. Spoken in the central part of East Timor Island. CEMP, CMP, Waima'a. What is said in the *Habu* entry about its structure and mixed nature, applies fully to Kairui-Midiki. No literacy in it. In 1981, about 2,000 speakers were reported, with rather fewer speakers today. It is potentially endangered.

Kaiy (or *Taori-Kei*, or *Todi*) |**85**| Indonesia: Irian Jaya. Spoken on the lower Rouffaer River, to the east of the confluence of the van Daalen River and the lower Rouffaer

River, in the western central part of the eastern main bulk of Irian Jaya. Geelvinck Bay Phylum, Lakes Plain, Tariku, East. For notes on its structure, see the *Awera* entry. No literacy in it. In 1991, about 250 speakers were reported. It is under pressure from Indonesian, which is favoured by children. The language is potentially endangered.

Kaki Ae (or *Raepa Tati*, or *Tate*) [182] Papua New Guinea: coastal eastern part of the Gulf Province. Spoken southeast of Kerema. P, TNGP, Eleman (doubtful), Tate. Structurally deviating from usual TNGP (see the *Damal* entry) in some features, e.g. particles are more common than affixes, the subject is not indicated on the verb, and medial verb forms are not highly developed. There is no literacy in the language. In 1993, 310 speakers were reported. More recent estimates mention 266. The speakers are bilingual in the very large Toaripi language whose speakers surround them, and the language is under pressure from it. It is now potentially endangered.

Kala Lagaw Ya (or *Kala Lagau Langgus*, or *Mabuiag*) [86] Australia: insular northern QLD, western Torres Strait Islands. A language classified as PNY Australia, but with a phonology corresponding largely to that of the Papuan TNGP, Trans-Fly-Bulaka River, Eastern Trans-Fly, Meriam language further east in Torres Strait, and with some vocabulary from the same source. Probably its speakers were originally Papuans from the Trans-Fly area of what is today Papua New Guinea who adopted an Australian language. There are about 4,000 or so fluent speakers in the Torres Strait area. Others have moved to the Queensland mainland, particularly to cities such as Townsville and Brisbane. Outside the Kala Lagaw Ya language area, those younger than thirty are likely to speak Torres Strait Creole. Kala Lagaw Ya is now potentially endangered.

Kalao (or *Kalatoa*) [89] Indonesia: Sulawesi. Spoken on eastern Kalao Island, south of Salayar Island which is located south of the southeastern tip of the southern peninsula of Sulawesi. WMP, Sulawesi, Muna-Buton. Structurally it corresponds to the Southern Sulawesi type (see *Bahonsuai*). No literacy in it. In 1988, 500 speakers were reported; there are probably less today. Under pressure from the large Bonerate language and Indonesian. It is potentially endangered.

Kalarko [not mapped] Australia: WA, southeastern corner. PNY, Southwest, Mirning. Recently extinct.

Kalkatungu [not mapped] Australia: QLD, Mt Isa area. PNY, Galgadungic. Recently extinct.

Kamarian (or *Seruawan*) [91] Indonesia: Maluku, on West Seram Island. CEMP, CMP, central Maluku. Had less than ten speakers in 1987, but is now probably extinct.

Kamasa [93] Papua New Guinea: southwestern corner of the Morobe Province. Spoken by some individuals in three separate villages, northeast of Menyamnya township. P, TNGP, Angan Family. Structurally, the Angan languages are much like the TNGP type, but have all a two-gender system, and verb prefixes where standard TNGP languages have verb suffixes. There is no literacy in Kamasa. In 1978, twenty speakers were reported, but now there are less than ten. It is under pressure from other large Angan languages, especially Menya. It is now moribund.

Kamilaroi (or *Gamilaraay*) [96] Australia: Central northern NSW. PNY, Wiradhuric. Recently extinct in its original form, but is spoken by many as a mixture of English and Kamilaroi. Attempts are being made to restore an approximation to the original form.

Kamu (or *Gamor*) [not mapped] Australia: northwestern NT, due south of Darwin, northeast of the lower Daly River, on the lower Douglas River. Daly, Malagmalag, Daly Proper. Recently extinct.

Kanakanabu (or *Kanabu*) [430] Taiwan. Spoken in southern central Taiwan around the town of Minchuan. n-MPAUN, Tsouic group, southern branch of it. The language has been under pressure from the large Bunun language of the Taiwan Austronesian Paiwanic group, and from Taiwanese Chinese. Most of the members of the ethnic group have shifted to these two languages. The language has focussing syntax and verb structure. See the *Nataoran* entry for details. No literacy in it. Moribund. A few old speakers.

Kandas [100] Papua New Guinea: New Ireland Province. Spoken on the southwest coast of New Ireland. CEMP, EMPW, New Ireland-Tolai languages. For structural information see the *Anus* entry. No literacy in it. In 1972, 400 speakers were reported. Today there may be about 300 or so speakers. It is under pressure from the very large Tolai language, and is potentially endangered.

Kaniet [not mapped] Papua New Guinea: Admiralty Islands, Manus Province, Anchorite and Kaniet Islands. EMPW. Western Admiralty Islands Section. Extinct since the 1950s.

Kaningara (or *Kaningra*) [103] Papua New Guinea: southern central East Sepik Province. Spoken near the Kuvanmas Lake, between the middle Korosamen and Karawari Rivers, west of Amboin. P, SERP, Sepik Hill, Alamblak Family. The Sepik Hill languages have SERP structural features (see the *Ak* entry), but have been influenced in their structure by TNGP languages and show some TNGP features (for those see the *Damal* entry). No literacy in it. In 1981, 359 speakers were reported. More recent reports mention 327. The speakers are highly bilingual in Tok Pisin, which puts pressure on the language, especially with young speakers. It is now potentially endangered.

Kanju (or *Kaantyu*) [263] Australia: northern QLD, central Cape York Peninsula. PNY, Paman, Northeastern Pama. For structural notes, see the *Adynyamathanha* entry. No literacy in it. In 1981, possibly fifty speakers were reported. The number of speakers has been decreasing considerably since. The language is seriously endangered.

Kanowit [106] Malaysia: Sarawak. Spoken on the Middle Rejang River, in the third administrative division. WMP, Borneo, Rejang-Baram. It has focussing syntax and verb structure (see *Nataoran* for details), and the distinction between the active and passive way of expression in the verb is a fundamental feature (see *Lengilu* for more details). No literacy in it. The language is receding before Iban. In 1981, there were still 170 speakers, but they are much less now and the young generation prefers Iban. Lots of Iban borrowings. The language is endangered.

Kao [108] Indonesia: North Maluku. Spoken on the northwestern coast of Kao Bay, North Halmahera, around the town of Kao, near the mouth of the Kao River. WPAP,

North Halmahera. Structurally, the North Halmahera WPAP Papuan languages are fairly simple, and show strong influence from Malayo-Polynesian. Kao is even simpler than other WPAP languages. Salient characteristics of them are a pervading distinction between masculine and feminine gender which is indicated with adjectives, the possessive particles added to nouns, and the subject prefixes added to verbs. With object prefixes to verbs there is a living and non-living distinction. The subject prefixes have different forms in different tenses, and according to the person of the object. Malay-Polynesian influence is for instance noticeable in the first person plural pronoun having inclusive (i.e. including the person addressed) and exclusive (i.e. excluding the person addressed) forms, and in the word order subject-verb-object which is contrasting with the usual Papuan subject-object-verb order. There is 50–70 per cent literacy. In 1983, 200 or some more speakers were reported, but this number would be fewer today, because the speakers have been affected by transmigration. The language is now endangered.

Kapori [112] Indonesia: Irian Jaya. Spoken in one village on the upper Idenburg River, in the northeastern inland part of Irian Jaya. P, TNGP? Kaure Stock, Kapori Family-level isolate. Little is known about its structure, but what is known corresponds to the TNGP type. No literacy in it. In 1978, sixty speakers were reported. There are probably fewer now. Pressure from Indonesian is making itself felt. The language has been regarded as endangered, but may be moving towards being soon seriously endangered.

Karadjeri (or *Garadyari*) [126] Australia: northwestern WA, Roebuck Bay to about 100km inland, Broome. PNY, South-West, Marngu. For structural notes see the *Adynyamathanha* entry. No literacy in it. In 1991, twelve speakers were reported. The children speak Aboriginal English. The number of speakers has been dropping since. The language is heading towards being moribund.

Karami [not mapped] Papua New Guinea: in the Gulf Province, on the border of the Western Province. P, TNGP, Inland Gulf Family. Extinct since the 1950s.

Karas [128] Indonesia: Irian Jaya. Spoken on Karas Island, off the southwest coast of the Bomberai Peninsula, which is south of Bird's Head Peninsula. The island is southeast of Fakfak. P, TNGP, West Bomberai. See the *Damal* and *Awyi* entries for structural notes. In addition, noun class systems with concordance occur in some Bomberai languages, and plural forms of nouns are found. No literacy in Karas. In 1978, 200 speakers were reported, but more recent estimates mention only about 100. The language is under pressure from the local lingua franca, the large TNGP, West Bomberai Iha language, and of Indonesian. It is now endangered.

Kariyarra [not mapped] Australia: northwestern WA, inland from Port Hedland. PNY, Southwest, Coastal Ngayarda. Last speaker died in 1991. Some people still know some words.

Karore [not mapped] Papua New Guinea: in West New Britain Province, Kandrian District. EMPW, New Britain Section, Southwest New Britain. CEMP, EMPW, southwest New Britain. According to a 1995 report (Grimes 1996), it has 500–600 speakers. However, University of Papua New Guinea linguists engaged in assessing language endangerment in Papua New Guinea, regard it as extinct since the 1950s. There is obviously some confusion. A language apparently called Karore appears to have become extinct in the area, and another language in the same area which still has hundreds of speakers, seems to be known by the same name – unless there is some misunderstanding.

Katabaga **[not mapped]** Philippines: Luzon, on the Bondoc Peninsula. WMP, unclassified, probably Meso Philippine. Recently extinct.

Kaurna **[204]** Australia: SA, Adelaide area. PNY, Southwest, Yura. Ceased to be a daily language in the 1890s. The last speaker died in 1927. Now nearly fully revived, with over fifty speakers. Still endangered.

Kavalan (or ***Kuwarawan***, or ***Kibalan***, or ***Shekwan***) **[not mapped]** Taiwan. Originally spoken in the northeastern coastal area of Taiwan from north of Toucheng southwards through Ilan to Sanhsing and inland on the Lanyang River. No speakers left in the original area, only migrant speakers in the village of Hualien in the Nataoran language area, and by a few in the area of the large Atayal language. N-MPAUN, Paiwanic group. Most of the speakers have shifted to Chinese. The language has focussing syntax and verb structure. See the ***Nataoran*** entry for details. No literacy in it. Moribund. A few old speakers.

Kawacha (or ***Kawatsa***) **[129]** Papua New Guinea: southwestern corner of the Morobe Province. Spoken around Katsiong, northeast of Menyamnya township. P, TNGP, Angan Family. For its structure see the ***Kamasa*** entry. No literacy in it. In 1978, thirty speakers were reported. Now there are fifteen or less. The speakers are bilingual in Yagwoia, a large Angan language which is the western neighbour of Kawacha, and which exerts pressure on it. It is now moribund.

Kayardild (or ***Gayardilt***) **[130]** Australia: northwestern QLD, on Bentinck Island in the southeastern corner of the Gulf of Carpentaria. PNY, Tangkic. For some points in its structure, see the ***Adynyamathanha*** entry. However, there are some very special features of Tangkic languages. For instance, most nouns in a sentence, except the subject, are inflected for tense and mood. There is a complicated system of demonstratives to indicate the location or movement in terms of cardinal points of the compass, e.g. a man in the west, or coming from the east, etc. There are limited materials prepared for school. In 1981, about fifty speakers were reported. There has been a rapid shift to English by the speakers since they were taken from Bentinck Island and brought to Mornington Island Mission in 1940, with children prevented from seeing their parents and kept in dormitories. With few exceptions, Kayardild speakers are bilingual in English. There are only five full speakers left. The language is now heading towards being moribund.

Kayeli **[not mapped]** Indonesia: Maluku, at Namlea Bay, Buru Island. CEMP, CMP, central Maluku. There were still four old speakers in 1989. The language of the original Kayeli speakers is now Ambon Malay or the large Buru Island language Lisela. Extinct.

Kaytetye (or ***Kaidjitj***, or ***Gaidjidj***) **[131]** Australia: southern NT, north of Alice Springs. PNY, Arandic. In 1983, 200 speakers were reported. It is under pressure from the much larger closely related Alyawarra language, and from Kriol, the English-derived pidgin lingua franca, which the Kaytetye speak generally. The number of speakers is likely to be considerably lower today. Kaytetye is potentially endangered and heading towards being endangered.

***Kayupulau* [181]** Indonesia: Irian Jaya. Spoken in two island villages in Jayapura harbour. CEMP, EMPW, Sarmi-Yotafa. It may be a dialect of Tobati (Yotafa). For notes on its structure see the *Anus* entry. There is no literacy in it. In 1978, 573 speakers were reported. However, recent estimates indicate that there are now no more than fifty speakers, all of them over fifty years of age. The nearness of the language to the capital Jayapura with its overwhelming Indonesian pressure, and Kayupulau being surrounded by speakers of the closely related Tobati (Yotafa) language, which is now also seriously endangered, has taken its toll. The language is now seriously endangered.

***Kazukuru* [not mapped]** Solomon Islands. Same area and Family as Dororo and Guliguli which were possibly dialects of Kazukuru. P. Extinct for several decades, same reason as with Dororo and Guliguli.

Keder* [132]** Indonesia: Irian Jaya. Spoken on the west-central north coast, east of the Tor River mouth. P, TNGP, Tor. For structural notes see the ***Bonerif entry. No literacy in it. In 1973, 200 to 600 speakers were reported, but recent estimates speak of 200 or less. It is under pressure from the larger TNGP, Tor language Kwesten, and from Indonesian. It is now endangered.

***Kembra* [137]** Indonesia: Irian Jaya. Spoken close to the Papua New Guinea border, east of the Sogber River (tributary of the upper Idenburg River). P, unclassified. Structure unknown. No literacy in it. In 1991, thirty speakers were reported. Believed to be moribund.

Kitja* (or *Gidja*) [77]** Australia: northwestern WA, near Hall's Creek and Turkey Creek. Djeragan, Kitjic. For structural notes see the ***Jawoyn entry. Some literacy in it. In 1983, 100 or more still nomadic speakers were reported. The mother tongue of the children is the English-based pidgin lingua franca Kriol, in which all adults are bilingual. The number of the speakers has decreased since, and the language is endangered.

Kodeoha* (or *Kondeha*) [138]** Indonesia: Sulawesi. Spoken on the central west coast of the southeastern peninsula of Sulawesi, near Lasusua. WMP, Sulawesi, Central Sulawesi, Bungku-Mori. Structurally it corresponds to the Southern Sulawesi type (see ***Bahonsuai). No literacy in it. There are conflicting reports on the number of speakers: in 1989, 300; and in 1991, 1,500. The very large Bugis language is generally used as second language, and there is pressure from Indonesian. The language is potentially endangered.

***Kofei* [139]** Indonesia: Irian Jaya. Spoken about the middle of the eastern side of Cenderawasih Bay, inland near the Sirami River. A dialect of the much larger Barapasi (Baropasi) language. Geelvink Bay Phylum, East Geelvink Bay. For structural notes see the *Awera* entry. No literacy in it. In 1987, about 100 speakers were reported, but there may be more living semi-nomadically in the interior. Under pressure from Barapasi and in part from Indonesian. It is now endangered.

Koiari, *Grass* (or *Koiari*) [141] Papua New Guinea: Central Province. Spoken east of Port Moresby around Sirinumu Dam, as far inland as Goldie River settlement and Kailakinumu. P, TNGP, Eastern TNGP, Koiarian Family. Structural features of the Eastern TNGP languages correspond largely to standard TNGP ones. Deviations from that are: the paucity of tonal languages, the marking of the object on verbs through suffixes rather than through prefixes, the less elaborate nature of the sentence-medial verb forms, and the less significant development of the indication of noun classes through auxiliary verbs. There is some literacy in the language. In 1973, 1,800 speakers were reported. This figure is still valid, but the language is under pressure from both Tok Pisin and Hiri Motu (the southern lingua franca of Papua New Guinea). The young speakers begin to prefer Tok Pisin. The language is now potentially endangered.

Koitabu (or *Koita*) [143] Papua New Guinea: Central Province, around and west of Port Moresby, and inland as far as the Goldie and Brown rivers. P, TNGP, Eastern TNGP, Koiarian Family. For structural notes see the *Koiari*, *Grass* entry. No literacy in it. In 1989, 3,000 speakers were reported. That figure is still valid. However, it is under pressure from the CEMP, EMPW Motu language of Port Moresby, from Hiri Motu (the southern lingua franca of Papua New Guinea), Tok Pisin, and English. There is considerable bilingualism in one of these languages, and also multilingualism. Young speakers tend to prefer Tok Pisin or English. The language is now potentially endangered.

Kokata (or *Gugada*) [not mapped] Australia: central northern SA, near Coober Pedy. PNY, South-West, Wati. Recently extinct.

Kokota [146] Solomon Islands: Santa Isabel Island, northeastern and southwestern coast of the central part of the island. CEMP, EMPW, Santa Isabel Group. For structural notes see the *Anus* entry. No literacy in it. In 1990, 200 speakers were reported. There may be fewer now. Speakers are bilingual in the large Cheke Holo (or Maringhe) language and also in the Zabana (or Kia) language which is not a neighbouring language. Solomon Pijin is also used. The language is becoming endangered.

Koneraw [147] Indonesia: Irian Jaya. Spoken on the western part of the south coast of the large Frederik Hendrik Island, in southeastern Irian Jaya. P, TNGP, Central and South New Guinea, Mombum. The structural features of the languages of the Mombum Family correspond largely to those of the TNGP in general (see the *Damal* and *Awyi* entries), but substratum features are in evidence such as the presence of two genders in the third person pronouns, the appearance of subject and object suffixes with the verb, and a low-level elaboration of sentence-medial verb forms. No literacy in it. In 1978, 300 speakers were reported. There may well be fewer now. It is under pressure from the large P, TNGP, Kolopom, Kimaghama language, its northern neighbour, and from Indonesian. It is now potentially endangered.

Koriki Hiri Trade Pidgin [not mapped] Papua New Guinea: coastal Gulf Province, around the delta of the Purari River. Used by the EMP, EMPW Motu language speakers and their P, TNGP, Koriki speaking trading partners during the Motuans' annual trading voyages there. It is essentially simplified Koriki with some Motu elements in it. It is now extinct (see also the ***Eleman Hiri Trade Pidgin*** entry).

Koro [148] Vanuatu: on Santa Maria (or Gaua) Island in the Banks Islands. CEMP, EMPCE, remote Oceanic, North and Central Vanuatu. Structurally similar to what is detailed in the ***Anus*** entry. No literacy in it. In 1983, 105 speakers were reported. There may well be fewer today. The language has been under pressure from larger related languages on the island such as the Lakona and Numa languages, and from the very much larger Ambae West (or Opa) on West Ambae (or Aoba) Island to the south of Gaua Island. It is now endangered.

Koroni [151] Indonesia: Sulawesi. Spoken in the northeastern coastal hinterland area of the southeastern peninsula of Sulawesi. WMP, Sulawesi, Central Sulawesi, Bungku-Mori. Structurally it corresponds to the Southern Sulawesi type (see ***Bahonsuai***). No literacy in it. In 1991, about 500 speakers were reported. Probably fewer now. There is pressure from Indonesian. The language is potentially endangered.

Kowaki [152] Papua New Guinea: northeastern Madang Province. Spoken south of the Kumil River, about 10km from the coast, south of Sikor and of Malala Harbour. P, TNGP, Adelbert Range, Tiboran Family. Structurally it is TNGP (see the ***Damal*** entry). No literacy in it. In 1981, thirty-one speakers were reported. Now there are still about thirty, but it is under pressure from large neighbouring languages such as Mauwake (or Ulingan). It is now seriously endangered.

Kowiai (or ***Kaiwai***) [153] Indonesia: Irian Jaya, on the southwest coast at Kaimana, opposite the Bomberai Peninsula, and on several islands in Kamrau Bay. Traditionally the lingua franca of the area. CEMP, CMP, South Bomberai. See the ***Pa'ela*** and ***Alune*** entries for structural notes. No literacy in it. In 1984, 600 speakers were reported. It is losing its lingua franca status to Indonesian and Irianese Malay (Pasar Malay). There is pressure on it by them and widespread bilingualism. It is now potentially endangered.

Kukatja (or ***Gugadja***) [155] Australia: northwestern WA, south of Hall's Creek, at Balgo, Lake Gregory and the area to the east. PNY, South-West, Wati. For structural notes, see the ***Adynyamathanha*** entry. There is no literacy in it. In 1983, 300 speakers were reported. They are bilingual in the large languages Pintupi-Luritja, Ngaa-nyatjarra, Martu Wangka or Walmajarri, which put pressure on it. The language is potentially endangered.

Kuku-Manck [not mapped] Australia: QLD, west coast of Cape York Peninsula, south of Aurukun. PNY, Paman, Middle Pama. Recently extinct.

Kuku-Mu'inh [not mapped] Australia: QLD, west coast of Cape York Peninsula, south of Aurukun. PNY, Paman, Middle Pama. Recently extinct?

Kuku-Muminh (or ***Wik-Muminh***) [254] Australia: northern QLD, west coast of Cape York Peninsula, south of Aurukun. PNY, Paman, Middle Pama. For structural notes see the ***Adynyamathanha*** entry. No literacy in it. In 1981, thirty-one speakers were reported. Today there are considerably less. The language is under pressure from the closely related large lingua franca Wik Mungkan, its northern neighbour. It is now seriously endangered.

Kuku-Ugbanh **[not mapped]** Australia: QLD, west coast of Cape York Peninsula, below Aurukun. PNY, Paman, Middle Pama. Recently extinct?

Kuku-Uwanh **[255]** Australia: northern Queensland, west coast of Cape York Peninsula, south of Aurukun. PNY, Paman, Middle Pama. For structural information see the ***Adynyamathanha*** entry. No literacy in it. In 1981, forty speakers were reported. Today there are much fewer. The language is under pressure from the closely related large lingua franca Wik Mungkan, its northern neighbour. It is seriously endangered.

Kuku-Ya'u (or ***Kuuku-Ya'u***) **[262]** Australia: northern QLD, northeastern Cape York Peninsula, south of Temple Bay. PNY, Paman, Northeastern Pama. For structural information see the ***Adynyamathanha*** entry. However, several languages in the northern part of Cape York Peninsula have been heavily influenced in their sound systems by Papuan languages from New Guinea with whose speakers they had contacts. This resulted in the sound systems of these languages being quite un-Australian, though their original Australian sound systems can be reconstructed through comparative linguistics. There is no literacy in Kuku-Ya'u. In 1981, about 100 speakers were reported. Today there are fewer. The speakers are bilingual in Torres Strait Creole (or Broken), which is the language of most children today. Kuku-Ya'u is endangered.

Kumbainggar (or ***Gumbainggiri***) **[not mapped]** Australia: northeastern NSW, Grafton and north coast. PNY, Gumbainggiric. Recently extinct.

Kunbarlang (or ***Gunbalang***) **[154]** Australia: extreme northern NT, central northern Arnhem Land, at Oenpelli, Maningrida, and Goulburn Island. Gunwinyguan, Gunwinygic. For structural notes see the ***Jawoyn*** entry. No literacy in it. In 1983, 50–100 speakers were reported. The number of speakers has been decreasing. People generally speak the closely related large lingua franca Kunwinjku which puts pressure on Kunbarlang. There are perhaps twenty speakers left today. It is now seriously endangered.

Kungarakany **[not mapped]** Australia: NT, south of Darwin. Gungaraganyan. Last full speaker died in 1989.

Kunggara **[not mapped]** Australia: QLD, extreme southwest of Cape York Peninsula, near Normanton, Delta. PNY, Paman, Norman Pama. Recently extinct?

Kunggari (or ***Gungari***) **[not mapped]** Australia: central southern QLD near Stonehenge, PNY, Mari, Maric, Kapu. Recently extinct?

Kunjen (or ***Kukuminjen***) **[189]** Australia: northern QLD, central Cape York Peninsula, at Wrotham Park, Kowanyama, Edward River. PNY, Paman, Central Pama. For structural notes see the ***Adynyamathanha*** entry. Some literacy in it. In 1991, 20 to 25 fluent speakers and forty with some knowledge of the language were reported out of about

300 in the ethnic group. The ethnic group speaks mainly Torres Strait Creole (or Broken), and most of them are bilingual in other Aboriginal languages, English, or the English-based pidgin lingua franca Kriol. All this puts pressure on Kunjen, which has been losing speakers since 1991. It is seriously endangered.

Kuot (or *Panaras*) [156] Papua New Guinea: central New Ireland, mainly coastal on east and west coast. P, East Papuan, Kuot. Structurally the East Papuan languages have mostly gender and class systems with concord, which are indicated by particles or affixes on nouns and adjuncts (adjectives, demonstratives, numerals, in verbs with subjects and objects). Number marking with nouns is widespread. Verb morphology is usually elaborate, but mostly quite transparent. There is some literacy in Kuot. In 1985, 1,000 speakers were reported. This has not changed much, but Kuot is under pressure from neighbouring larger languages, especially the CEMP, EMPW Nalik (its northwestern neighbour), and also from Tok Pisin which children tend to prefer. Kuot is now potentially endangered.

Kurrama (or *Gurama*, or *Karama*) [157] Australia: northwestern WA, southeast of Pannawonica. PNY, South-West, coastal Ngayarda. For structural information see the *Adynyamathanha* entry. No literacy in it. In 1981, perhaps fifty speakers were reported. Today there are much fewer. All are bilingual in English. The language is endangered and is moving towards being seriously endangered.

Kuthant [not mapped] Australia: QLD, extreme southeast of Cape York Peninsula, north of Karumba and Normanton. PNY, Paman, Norman Pama. Recently extinct.

Kuuk Yak [not mapped] Australia: northern QLD, inland from the mid-western coast of Cape York Peninsula, between the Edward and Coleman rivers. PNY, Paman, Western Pama. Recently extinct.

Kuwama (or *Pungupungu*) [not mapped] Australia: NT, southwest of Darwin, near mouth of Muldiva River. Daly, Bringen-Wagaydy. Recently extinct.

Kwansu [158] Indonesia: Irian Jaya. Spoken in near-coastal northeastern Irian Jaya, west of Lake Sentani. TNGP, Nimboran. Structurally the Nimboran Family languages correspond in general to the TNGP languages, with some aberrant features such as the precise marking of the location and direction of actions with the verb. No literacy in it. In 1977, 350 speakers were reported. There may well be fewer now. They are bilingual in Indonesian, and the language is under pressure from it. Kwansu is now potentially endangered.

Kwerisa (or *Taogwe*) [159] Indonesia: Irian Jaya. Spoken on the lower Rouffaer River in central eastern Irian Jaya. Geelvinck Bay Phylum, Lakes Plain, Tariku (East). See the *Awera* entry for structural notes. No literacy in it. There is confusion in the number of speakers. In 1987, the possibility of some elderly speakers was mentioned. In 1992, fifteen speakers were reported, and in 1993, possibly fifty-five. The language is under pressure from the larger Geelvinck Bay Phylum Kaiy language which is potentially endangered, and from Indonesian. Most of the speakers have shifted to Kaiy. The language is now moribund.

Kwini (or *Gwiini*, or *Kunan*) **[160]** Australia: northwestern WA, coastal western Kimberley area, at Kalumburu. Wororan, Wunambalic. The extinct Gambera language (see *Gambera* entry) was probably a dialect of Kwini. For structural information see the *Jawoyn* entry. No literacy in it. Kwini is the name of the people. They refer to their language as **Kunan**. In 1979, fifty or more speakers were reported. Children used to know something of the language, but most of them spoke Aboriginal English as their first language. The latter is now universally the case, and Aboriginal English is taking over generally. The number of Kwini speakers has dropped very much, and the language is now seriously endangered.

Labo (or *Mewun*) **[161]** Vanuatu: spoken at the Southwest Bay, southwestern Malekula. CEMP, EMPCE, remote Oceanic, North and Central Vanuatu, Malekula Interior. For structural notes see the *Anus* entry. Some literacy in it. In 1981, 350 speakers were reported. There may be still close to that many speakers, but children are beginning not to learn the language. It is beginning to be potentially endangered.

Laghu (or *Korighole*, or *Katova*) **[162]** Solomon Islands: central southwestern coast of Santa Isabel island. ECMP, EMPW, Santa Isabel Group. For structural notes see the *Anus* entry. No literacy in it. In 1981, five speakers were reported, now it is only three. The language has succumbed to pressure from large related neighbouring languages, such as Zabana (or Kia), its northwestern neighbour. It is moribund.

Laiyolo (or *Da'ang*) **[163]** Indonesia: Sulawesi. Spoken on the southern tip of Selayar Island, which is located south of the southeastern tip of the southern tip of Sulawesi. There are two rather different dialects, Laiyolo and Barang-Barang. WMP, Sulawesi, Muna-Buton. Structurally, it corresponds to the Southern Sulawesi type (see *Bahonsuai*). No literacy in it. In 1988, 600 speakers were reported for the Laiyolo dialect, and 450 for the Barang-Barang dialect. In the latter, language use was vigorous then, but in the Laiyolo dialect, children were not using the language. The number of speakers of the language is probably considerably less now. The large Selayar language is used as second language, and there is pressure from Indonesian too. The language is heading towards being endangered.

Lamu-Lamu (or *Lamalama*) **[not mapped]** Australia: QLD, northeastern Cape York Peninsula, near Coen. PNY, Paman, Lamalamic. Recently extinct.

Laragia (or *Larakiya*) **[not mapped]** Australia: NT, Darwin area. Laragiyan. Recently extinct?

Lardil **[164]** Australia: northeastern QLD, on Mornington Island in the southeastern corner of the Gulf of Carpentaria. PNY, Tangkic. For structural information see the *Adynyamathanha* and *Gayardilt* entries. The inflection of the noun object of a verb for tense as mentioned in the latter entry is a prominent feature of Lardil. Limited written materials exist for use in the local school. In 1981, possibly fifty speakers were reported. The speakers use more English than Lardil, a tendency which has been increasing over the years because the missionaries had been discouraging the use of the language. Children do not know the language. There are now only three to four full speakers left, but more semi-speakers. The language is moving towards being moribund.

Laua [not mapped] Papua New Guinea: eastern part of the central Province. P, TNGP, Eastern part, Mailuan Family. In 1987, one speaker was left; now probably extinct.

Lauje [165] Indonesia: Sulawesi. The main form of Lauje, which has about 38,000 speakers (for the *Ampibabo* form of it, see that entry), is spoken in the northern third of the narrow neck linking the northeastern peninsula of Sulawesi to the bulk of Sulawesi, in the area around Tinombo on the eastern coast. The Lauje live on the coast, in the middle hills, and the inner hills. WMP, Sulawesi, Central Sulawesi, Tomini. Structurally it corresponds to the Southern Sulawesi type (see *Bahonsuai*). The coastal villages are overcrowded and relatively poor. Steep mountains are very close to the coast, leaving little land for rice fields and gardens, and no incentive for immigrants. In Tinombo, 60 per cent of the population is Lauje, with strong Kaili and Gorontalo communities. There is less tendency to language shift than in other provincial capitals. Coastal Lauje interact regularly with middle hill Lauje among whom they have relatives, speaking only Lauje on these occasions. There is no space for the resettlement projects close to the coast for the inner hill Lauje which also contributes to the maintenance of Lauje. There is some literacy in it. Only the children who receive their primary school instructions in Indonesian constitute a possible threat to the language, which may therefore be potentially endangered.

Laxudumau [166] Papua New Guinea: New Ireland Province. Spoken in the village of Lakudumau on the central east coast of New Ireland, on the border between the large CEMP, EMPW Nalik and Kara languages. CEMP, EMPCE, New Ireland-Tolai languages. For structural notes see the *Anus* entry. The language is different from both Nalik and Kara. It has only recently been discovered and may be a transitional dialect between Nalik and Kara, or a separate language. There are about 500 speakers today, but the language is under heavy pressure from Tok Pisin, as well as from Nalik and Kara, and is potentially endangered.

Legenyem (or *Laganyan*) [212] Indonesia: Irian Jaya. Spoken on Waigeo Island (in the Raja Ampat Islands, northwest of the western end of the Bird's Head Peninsula), in the northwest and on the south coast of the island. CEMP, EMP, SHWNG. For structural notes see the *Gebe* entry. No literacy in it. In 1993, about 300 speakers were reported. Under pressure from the larger CEMP, EMP, SHWNG language Maya and Indonesian. It is now potentially endangered.

Lehalurup (or *Lehali*, or *Ureparapara*) [167] Vanuatu: Banks Islands, Ureparapara Island. CEMP, EMPCE, remote Oceanic, North and Central Vanuatu. Similar in structure to what has been said in the *Anus* entry. No literacy in it. In 1983, ninety speakers were reported. Recent reports mention around 100, of which thirty are children, with the mean age of the youngest speakers eight years. It appears to be in a healthy state, but there is pressure from the larger Vatrata language on the large Vanua Lava Island immediately to the south of it. It is getting potentially endangered.

Lemolang (or *Baebunta*) [168] Indonesia: Sulawesi. Spoken in the central western part of the bulk of Sulawesi. WMP, Sulawesi, South Sulawesi. Structurally, it corresponds to the Southern Sulawesi type (see *Bahonsuai*). No literacy in it. There are reports that some children do not speak the language. A dialect of the very large Tae language is

509

the dominant language of the area. That and Indonesian exert pressure on Lemolang, for which 2,000 speakers were reported in 1995. This may well be less now. The language is potentially endangered.

Lengilu* [169]** Indonesia: Kalimantan (Indonesian Borneo). Spoken in the western part of the extreme northeastern extension of Kalimantan, close to the Sarawak border. WMP, Borneo, Apo-Duat. It has focussing syntax and verb structure (see ***Nataoran for details). The distinction between active and passive expression in the verb is a central feature. Word order is subject-verb-object, in the passive it is object-subject-verb. Receding under pressure from the Lundayeh language. In 1981, there seem to have been ten speakers left, today it is less. It is moribund, almost extinct.

Leningitij (or ***Linngithig***) **[not mapped]** Australia: QLD, northeastern Cape York Peninsula, southeast of Weipa. PNY, Paman, Northern Pama. Recently extinct.

Liki* [176]** Indonesia: Irian Jaya. Spoken on Like Island, to the north of Sarmi on the western north coast of Irian Jaya. One of the dialects of Sobei. CEMP, EMPW, Sarmi-Yotafa. See the ***Anus entry for structural notes. No literacy in it. In 1954, twenty-five speakers were reported. It is still surviving now, but is getting moribund.

Likum* [170]** Papua New Guinea: Manus Province. Spoken in the western part of Manus Island, Admiralty Islands. CEMP, EMPW, Admiralty Islands languages. For structural information, see the ***Anus entry. No literacy in it. In 1977, 100 speakers were reported. There may be fewer today. The speakers are bilingual in the large neighbouring Nyindrou (or Lindrou) language. This and the creolized Tok Pisin of the Admiralty Islands exerts pressure on Likum, which is now getting endangered.

Liliali (or ***Leliali***) **[not mapped]** Indonesia: Maluku, on northeastern Buru Island. CEMP, CMP, central Maluku. The last speaker died in 1989. Extinct.

Limilngan (or ***Manadja***, or ***Minitji***) **[not mapped]** Australia: NT, Arnhem Land, east of Darwin, between Mary rivers and West Alligator River. *Unclassified*. Recently extinct.

Lisela (or ***Buru***, or ***Wayapo***) **[191]** Indonesia: Maluku. Spoken on northern and eastern coastal strips of the large Buru Island. CEMP, CMP, Central Maluku. Structurally it corresponds to what is said in the ***Palu'e*** and ***Alune*** entries. No literacy in it. In 1989, 11,900 speakers were reported, but they are much fewer now. Language use is not vigorous, and a shift to Ambon Malay is in process. The language is now endangered.

Lola* [228]** Indonesia: Southeast Maluku. Spoken in three villages on three islands east of Kobroor and Baun Islands in the Aru Islands, to the south of the neck portion of the Bird's Head Peninsula of Irian Jaya. CEMP, CMP, Southeast Maluku. Structurally the language is similar to what has been said in the ***Pa'ela and ***Alune*** entries. No literature in it. In 1995, 830 speakers were reported. There are probably fewer now. In one of the three villages, language use is quite vigorous. In another one, young people are beginning to use Ambon Malay among themselves. In the third, there are many non-Aru people, and Ambon Malay is commonly used. The language is now potentially endangered.

Lolak [172] Indonesia: Sulawesi. Spoken on the eastern part of the north coast of the northeastern peninsula of Sulawesi. WMP, Sulawesi, Mongondow-Gorontalic. The language has focussing syntax and verb structure. See the *Nataoran* entry for details. In its detailed structure, it is close to the very large Gorontalo language, but has heavily borrowed lexical items from the very large Mongondow language. No literacy in it. It is completely surrounded by Mongondow, which is the second language of all Lolak speakers and puts great pressure on Lolak. There are fifty speakers left, and the language is seriously endangered.

Lom (or *Belom, Mapor*) [173] Indonesia: Sumatra, on northeast Bangka Island, Belinyu District. WMP, Sundic (Sumatra). Not closely related to any other language of the area. However, its structure is likely to be Malayic, with subject-verb-object word order. Contradictory reports say that there are still about fifty speakers, whereas others say that it is possibly extinct. In any case, it is at least seriously endangered or moribund, or possibly extinct.

Lorediakarkar [175] Vanuatu. Spoken on the central east coast of Espiritu Santo Island. CEMP, EMPCE, remote Oceanic, North and Central Vanuatu, East Santo. Structurally similar to what has been said in the *Anus* entry. No literacy in it. In 1972, fifty speakers were reported. There are probably fewer today. The language has been under pressure from related neighbouring larger languages, especially the Shark Bay language to which it is closely related and to which speakers have shifted. It is now seriously endangered.

Loun [178] Indonesia: Maluku. Spoken on the north coast of West Seram Island. CEMP, CMP, Central Maluku. Structurally it is as per the *Palu'e* and *Alune* entries. No literacy in it. Very few speakers left. The language has succumbed to pressure from larger local languages, Ambon Malay, and Indonesian. It is moribund.

Lumaete (or *Mumaite*, or *Lumara*) [not mapped] Indonesia: Maluku, around Kayelik on Southern Namlea Bay, eastern Buru Island. CEMP, CMP, central Maluku. Apparently a dialect of Kayali. Recently extinct.

Madhimadhi [not mapped] Australia: northwestern Victoria and southwestern NSW. Between the Murray River and the Balranald district of NSW and as far north as the Lachlan River. PNY, Kulinic. The last speaker died over three decades ago. Extinct.

Madngele (or *Matngala*) [179] Australia: northeastern NT, south of Darwin and south of the Daly River, on the west bank of the Muldiva River. Daly Group, Malagmalag, Daly Proper. In 1983, 15 to 20 speakers were reported. For structural notes, see the *Jawoyn* entry. There is no literacy in Madngele. There are very few speakers left today. The language is moribund.

Mafea (or *Mavea*) [183] Vanuatu: East Espiritu Santo Island, on Mafea and Ais Islands off the southeastern coast of Santo Island. CEMP, EMPCE, remote Oceanic, North and Central Vanuatu. Similar in structure to what has been said in the *Anus* entry. No literacy in it. In 1981, fifty speakers were reported. Recent reports speak of seventy, with ten of them children with a mean age of eight years. Appears to be

511

healthy, but there is pressure from the closely related larger Shark Bay language on the coast opposite, and inland from the coast. The language is getting potentially endangered.

Magadige* [185]** Australia: northwestern NT, southwest of Darwin, inland from Anson Bay, south of Maridjabin. Daly, Bringen-Wagaydy, Bringen. For structural notes see the ***Jawoyn entry. No literacy in it. In 1983, perhaps thirty speakers were reported. Today there are very much less. The language is under pressure from the English-based pigdin lingua franca Kriol, and from English, and is seriously endangered. It is heading towards being moribund.

Magori* [188]** Papua New Guinea: eastern part of the Central Province. Spoken at the eastern end of Table Bay, on the lower Bailebo-Tavenei River. CEMP, EMPW, Milne Bay-Central Province languages. For structural information, see the ***Anus entry, but the vocabulary of Magori is very heavily influenced by the neighbouring large Mailu language which is a TNGP, eastern TNGP Papuan language. No literacy in it. In 1971, 200 speakers were reported, but their number is decreasing. Most Magori speakers are bilingual or trilingual in the large Suau language, Mailu or Hiri Motu, the third official language of Papua New Guinea, and second general lingua franca of southern Papua New Guinea. The language is at least potentially endangered.

***Mahigi* [not mapped]** Papua New Guinea: in the Western Province, Upper Ramu River area. P, TNGP, Inland Gulf Family. Extinct for a few decades.

***Makolkol* [190]** Papua New Guinea: East New Britain Province, Gazelle Peninsula. P, East Papuan, Baining-Taulil. Seven elderly speakers in 1988. Now probably extinct.

***Maku'a* (or *Lovaea* or *Lovaya*) [191]** Indonesia: Timor Island. Spoken on the northeastern tip of Timor Island. TNGP, Timor-Alor-Pantar. Not closely related to other Timor-Alor-Pantar languages. It corresponds in general to the structure of the Timor-Alor-Pantar languages which is simpler than that of most other TNGP Papuan languages and shows influences from WPAP and Malayo-Polynesian languages. (The Lovaea (or Lovaya) dialect shows even more Malayo-Polynesian influences in its vocabulary than Maku'a proper.) However, Maku'a (and Lovaea) have a complicated noun class system in which the noun classes are marked by suffixes, and which is absent from other languages of the group. No literacy in it. The speakers have almost all shifted to the large Fataluku language, which is also a Timor-Alor-Pantar language. In 1981, about fifty speakers were reported. Since the East Timor massacres and deportations before independence there are probably very many fewer. The area where Maku'a was spoken was very much affected by the rampages and killings by the militia. It was feared that the last speakers of Maku'a may have perished as a result of this. However, as was mentioned above in the section on language endangerment, it is now known that there are still some surviving speakers of Maku'a. The language is moribund.

Malalamai* [192]** Papua New Guinea: Madang Province. Spoken on the Rai Coast of Astrolabe Bay, near Saidor. CEMP, EMPCE, Siassi languages. For structural notes see the ***Anus entry. No literacy in it. In 1977, 341 speakers were reported. Today there may be about 150 or so. The language is under pressure from neighbouring related languages such as Malasanga, and from Tok Pisin, which the children prefer. It is now endangered.

Malgana **[not mapped]** Australia: WA, central western coast, south of Shark Bay. PNY, South-West, Kardu. Extinct for several decades.

Malmariv **[193]** Vanuatu: northern central Espiritu Santo Island, on the middle Jordan River. CEMP, EMPCE, remote Oceanic, North and Central Vanuatu. Structurally similar to what has been said in the *Anus* entry. No literacy in it. In 1983, 150 speakers were reported. This figure is still valid according to recent reports, which mention that, of the 150, thirty-five are children speakers, with a mean age of eight years. The language appears to be healthy, but is under pressure from the closely related larger Tolomako language, its northern neighbour, and the less closely related, but much larger Sakao language, its eastern neighbour. It is now potentially endangered.

Malyangaba **[not mapped]** Australia: central eastern SA, between Lake Frome and the NSW border, middle and lower Eurimilla Creek, and extending into adjacent areas of NSW. PNY, Karnic, Yarli. Extinct for over three decades.

Manambu-Kwoma Trade Pidgin **[not mapped]** Papua New Guinea: East Sepik Province, middle Sepik area. A trade pidgin reported in 1932 as being used between the P, SERP, Sepik, Middle Sepik, Ndu, Manambu language speakers around Ambunti, and the P, SERP, Middle Sepik, Nukuma, Kwoma language speakers further east on the Sepik River and north of it. It is said to be lexically an amalgam of both languages. It is not known whether it is still extant.

Manda **[194]** Australia: northwestern NT, near the coast southwest of Anson Bay, southwest of Darwin. Daly, Bringen-Wagaydy, Wagaydy. In 1983, perhaps twenty-five speakers were reported. They were all bilingual in the English-based pidgin lingua franca Kriol, or in English. The speakers are very few today. The language is moribund.

Mandandanyi **[not mapped]** Australia: Inland southeastern QLD, around Roma. PNY, Maric, Mari. Recently extinct.

Mander **[197]** Indonesia: Irian Jaya. Spoken inland in the central north coast area, on the Upper Bu River, a tributary of the Upper Tor River. P, TNGP, Tor. Some of the Foyu speakers have shifted to it. For structural notes see the *Bonerif* entry. No literacy in it. In 1991, twenty speakers were reported. Speakers intermarry with the speakers of the much larger TNGP, Tor language Berik who are their western neighbours, and speak Berik as a second language. The speakers are nomadic. The language is now seriously endangered.

Mangala (or *Mangarla*) **[198]** Australia: northwestern WA, southeast of Broome, on the Jurgurra Creek, at the Edgar Range, West Pilbara. PNY, South-West, Marngu. For structural notes see the *Adynyamathanha* entry. No literacy in it. In 1981, possibly twenty speakers were reported, all of them elderly. Children knew a few words, but spoke the English-based pidgin langua franca Kriol or Aboriginal English. Today there are very few speakers left. The language is moribund.

Mangarayi (or *Mangarai*) **[199]** Australia: extreme northern NT, northern central Arnhem Land, at Mataranka and Elsey stations. Gunwinyguan, Mangarayic. For structural notes see the *Jawoyn* entry. Mangarayi is a tonal language, like Yangman and Alawa. No literacy in it. In 1983, fifty or fewer speakers were reported. People generally speak the English-based pidgin lingua franca Kriol, which puts pressure on their language. There are fewer speakers today, and the language is endangered or seriously endangered.

Mangareva **[not mapped]** French Polynesia: Gambier Islands, Mangareva Island. CEMP, EMP, Oceanic, remote Oceanic, Polynesian (Eastern). For structural information see the *Maori* entry. There is some literacy in it. In 1987, 1,600 speakers were reported. Today there are very much less, at best 300–400. The speakers are bilingual in Tahitian, which exerts great pressure on Mangareva. The language is now endangered and heading towards getting seriously endangered.

Mangerr (or *Mangerei*) **[not mapped]** Australia: NT, northern Arnhem Land, around Oenpelli. Mangerian, Mangerric. Recently extinct.

Mansim (or *Borai*): Indonesia: Irian Jaya. Spoken at the northeastern tip of the Bird's Head Peninsula, south of Manokwari. WPAP, Bird's Head Peninsula. Structurally similar to the Kao (see the *Kao* entry). The WPAP languages of the Bird's Head show somewhat less MP influence than those of northern Halmahera, but still have the MP word order subject-verb-object. Subject and object are indicated in the verb by prefixes. There is no literacy in Mansim. In the ethnic group of 1,000, 100 speakers were believed to exist until not long ago. However, it is evident that there are now only five speakers left, with most of these not having a full command of the language. Pressure from the large neighbouring related Hatam language and especially from Indonesian has taken its toll. The language is moribund and almost extinct.

Maori **[not mapped]** New Zealand: CEMP, EMP, Oceanic, remote Oceanic, Polynesian (Eastern). The Polynesian languages have basically EMP characteristics (see the *Anus* entry), but differ from other EMP languages in employing mostly particles in their grammatical structure. Prefixes and suffixes are very few. The typical EMP distinction between non-alienable and alienable possession is expressed by the particles *o* and *a* after the object possessed. Indication of the direction and location of an action, towards or near the speakers and away from the speakers, plays an important role. The sound systems of Polynesian languages are simpler than those of other EMP Oceanic languages. Literacy in Maori is almost universal. The language was heading toward extinction at the beginning of the twentieth century, but had a spectacular revival after that. In 1991, 50,000 to 70,000 speakers, and 100,000 who understood it, were reported out of a total Maori population of 310,000 or more. All speakers are bilingual in English. In 1995, 30,000 to 50,000 adult speakers over fifteen years old were reported. Recently, there has been increasing reluctance by members of the young generation to use Maori, in spite of the existence of over 300 government-funded Maori language schools, including schools for pre-school children. The language is now potentially endangered, and heading towards being endangered.

Mapia [not mapped] Indonesia: Irian Jaya. Formerly spoken on Mapia Island, north of the eastern part of the Bird's Head Peninsula. EMP, remote Oceanic, Micronesian. Comparatively recently its speakers shifted to the large Biak language, the lingua franca of the area. Extinct.

Mara [202] Australia: northern NT, southwestern Arnhem Land, in the Roper River area. Maran, Mara. For structural notes, see the *Jawoyn* entry. No literacy in it. In 1991, fifteen or fewer speakers were reported. The speakers intermarry with the Yanyuwa speakers. Most of the Mara people speak the English-based pidgin lingua franca Kriol and are also bilingual in English. This puts pressure on the Mara language, with the speakers getting fewer. The language is seriously endangered and is heading towards being moribund.

Maragus [205] Vanuatu: central North Malekula Island. EMPCE, EMP, remote Oceanic, North and Central Vanuatu. Had ten speakers in 1971. Now probably extinct.

Maranunggu [207] Australia: northwestern NT, southwest of Darwin, inland from Anson Bay. Daly, Bringen-Wagaydy, Wagaydy. For structural notes see the *Jawoyn* entry. No literacy in it. In 1983, 15–20 speakers were reported. Young people spoke the English-based pidgin lingua franca Kriol then. Now this is becoming general, and there are few speakers of Maranunggu left. The language is moribund.

Maremgi [208] Indonesia: Irian Jaya. Spoken inland from the central north coast, south of Anus, east of Lake Tahoen. P, TNGP, Tor. For structural notes see the *Bonerif* entry. No literacy in it. In 1975, forty-seven speakers were reported. There are probably fewer now. It is under pressure from neighbouring TNGP, Tor languages. It is still regarded as only endangered.

Margany [not mapped] Australia: southern central QLD, between Quilpie and Wyandra, and the Bulloo and Paroo rivers. PNY, Maric, Mari. Recently extinct.

Mari (*Dorro* dialect?) [213] Papua New Guinea: Western Province. Spoken on the western third of the south coast, around the Tais settlement, and inland about 15km. P, TNGP, Trans-Fly, Morehead and Upper Moro Rivers Family. May be a dialect of Dorro (Tais). For its structure see the *Dorro* entry. No literacy in Mari. In the 1980 census, eighty-four speakers were reported. Now it may be around eighty. It is under pressure from the closely related Nambu language, its northern neighbour, and from Tok Pisin. It is now endangered.

Maridan (or *Meradan*) [209] Australia: northwestern NT, southwest of Darwin, north of Moyle River, east of Magadige. Daly Bringen-Wagaydy, Bringen. For structural information see the *Jawoyn* entry. No literacy in it. In 1981, perhaps twenty speakers were reported. Today there are only a few speakers left. The English-based pidgin lingua franca Kriol is taking over. The language is moribund.

Maridjabin [217] Australia: northwestern NT, southwest of Darwin, inland from Anson Bay, south of the Mariyedi and Manda languages. Daly, Bringen-Wagaydy, Bringen. For structural information see the *Jawoyn* entry. There is no literacy in it. In

515

1970, twenty speakers were reported. The English-based pidgin lingua franca Kriol has been taking over, and there are now very few speakers left. Maridjabin is moribund.

Marimanindji **[224]** Australia: northwestern NT, southwest of Darwin and the Daly River, west of the Muldiva River, near its headwaters. Daly, Bringen-Wagaydy, Bringen. For structural information see the ***Jawoyn*** entry. No literacy in it. In 1983, perhaps fifteen speakers were reported. Now they are only very few. The English-based pidgin lingua franca Kriol has been taking over. The language is moribund.

Maringarr **[225]** Australia: northwestern NT, southwest of Darwin, south of the Moyle River. Daly, Bringen-Waygaydy, Bringen. For structural information see the ***Jawoyn*** entry. No literacy in it. In 1983, 30 to 40 speakers were reported. Today there are much fewer, because speakers have shifted to the English-based pidgin lingua franca Kriol. It is now seriously endangered.

Marithiel (or ***Bringen***, or ***Brinken***) **[229]** Australia: northwestern NT, southwest of Darwin. 50–80km south of the Daly River and the Central Daly River, at the Daly River Mission, Bagot and Delissaville. Daly, Bringen-Waygaydy, Bringen. For structural information see the ***Jawoyn*** entry. There is no literacy in Marithiel. In 1983, twenty-five fluent speakers and fifty second language users were reported. The number of speakers has gone down since through speakers shifting to the English-based pidgin lingua franca Kriol. Marithiel is endangered.

Mariyedi **[230]** Australia: northwestern NT, southwest of Darwin, south of the Manda language (see the ***Manda*** entry). Daly, Bringen-Wagaydy, Bringen. For structural information see the ***Jawoyn*** entry. No literacy in it. In 1981, perhaps twenty speakers were reported. Today there are only a few, because speakers have shifted to the English-based pidgin lingua franca Kriol. Mariyedi is moribund.

Marrgu (or ***Margu***, or ***Yaako***) **[231]** Australia: northern Arnhem Land, northern NT, on Croker Island. Yiwaidjan, Margic. For structural information see the ***Jawoyn*** entry. No literacy in it. In 1981, possibly four speakers were reported. Now only one speaker remaining. Moribund.

Martuthunira **[not mapped]** Australia: northwestern coast of WA, southwest of Dampier. PNy, South-West, Coastal Ngayarda. Recently extinct?

Massep **[232]** Indonesia: Irian Jaya. Spoken east of the mouth of the Apauwar River which is east of the mouth of the large Mamberamo River in the far west of the north coast of Irian Jaya, east of the eastern top end of Cenderawasih Bay. The language is now regarded as P, TNGP, Dani-Kwerba, Kwerba, Northern Division, though when its existence was discovered in 1955, it was said to be quite different from the neighbouring languages of the Kwerba Family. For structural notes see the ***Isirawa*** entry. No literacy in it. In 1978, about forty speakers were reported. They are likely to be rather fewer now. It is under pressure from the larger neighbouring P, TNGP, Kwerba languages such as Isirawa and Samarokena, and from Indonesian. It is now seriously endangered.

Maung **[233]** Australia: extreme northern NT, northern Arnhem Land, Goulburn Island. Yiwaidjan, Yiwaidjic. For structural information see the *Jawoyn* entry. Some literacy in it. In 1983, 200 speakers were reported. The speakers are bilingual in English or Gunwinygu. The children are beginning not to use Maung. It is getting potentially endangered.

Mawak **[234]** Papua New Guinea: Madang Province. Spoken south of the upper Kumil River, southwest of Sikor and Malala Harbour. P, TNGP, Adelbert Range, Tiboran Family. Structurally it is TNGP (see the *Damal* entry). There is no literacy in it. In 1981, thirty-one speakers were reported. Recent estimates still mention about thirty, but the language is under pressure from neighbouring large languages such as Miani (or Tani), its northern neighbour, and from Tok Pisin. It is now seriously endangered.

Mayaguduna **[not mapped]** Australia: Inland from northern QLD, Gulf of Carpentaria coast, between Leichhardt River and Flinders River. PNY, Paman, Mayabic. Recently extinct.

Maykulan (or *Maygulan*) **[not mapped]** Australia: Inland from the eastern corner of the QLD coast of the Gulf of Carpentaria. PNY, Paman, Mayabic. Extinct for several decades.

Mbara **[not mapped]** Australia: northern central QLD, south of Cape York Peninsula, north of the Stawell River. PNY, Paman, Southern Pama. Recently extinct.

Mbariman-Gudhinma **[not mapped]** Australia: QLD, eastern Cape York Peninsula, southwest coast of Princess Charlotte Bay. PNY, Paman, Lamalamic. Recently extinct.

Mea **[235]** New Caledonia. Spoken inland in southern central New Caledonia, in the upper valleys around Méa-Mébara and Méchin, on the northeastern side of New Caledonia. CEMP, EMPCE, New Caledonian, southern. For structural notes see the *Arhö* entry. Not much literacy in it. In 1982, 300 speakers have been reported. Now they are much less, with virtually no children speakers. It is under pressure from the larger neighbouring New Caledonian Tiri language, and from French. It is now endangered.

Mekeo Trade Pidgins **[not mapped]** Papua New Guinea: northwestern coastal Central Province. Three of such languages are known which constitute closely similar varieties. They grew out of contacts between speakers of different dialects of the EMP, EMPW Mekeo language and their northern neighbours, speakers of the P, TNGP, Eastern TNGP, Goilalan, Kunimaipa language. Most of the structure of these languages is derived from Mekeo. In their vocabulary, personal pronouns, some numerals, postpositions, verbs and a few nouns are from Mekeo, whereas demonstrative and interrogative pronouns, some numerals, the adjectives and most nouns are from Kunimaipa. One of these trade pidgins varieties became extinct some time ago, but the other two are still extant, although endangered to seriously endangered.

Melanesian-Chinese Mixed Pidgin English in Nauru **[not mapped]** Micronesia: Nauru Island. A mixture of a Melanesian and a Chinese type of pidgin English. In spite of its low social status it remains a viable everyday language in Nauru, used in a commercial context, mainly in Chinese-run trade stores and restaurants. The total number of its

517

speakers would be several thousand, i.e. most of the population of Nauru. It is just beginning to be superseded by English and is potentially endangered.

Meriam (or *Miriam-Mer*) **[237]** Papua New Guinea and Australia. On Darnley Island in the eastern part of Torres Strait in Australian territory in QLD, and on some islands and areas in Papua New Guinea territory. Not an Australian language, but P. TNGP. Trans-Fly-Bulaka River, Eastern Trans-Fly. Very closely related to the Gizra language spoken on the south coast of the Western Province of Papua New Guinea, and inland, east of the lower Pahoturi River, with limited mutual intelligibility. The Meriam speakers in Australian territory appear to be comparatively recent immigrants, a few centuries or so ago, from the area east of the Pahoturi River in what is today south-western Papua New Guinea. For structural information see the *Dorro* entry. Some literacy in it especially on the Papua New Guinea side. In 1991, 300 to 400 speakers were reported in the Australian territory, with the total number being about 700 speakers. The language is healthy in both areas, but in the Australian territory most speakers are bilingual in Torres Strait Creole (or Broken) with some children giving preference to it. Meriam is heading towards becoming potentially endangered in Australia.

Midhaga **[not mapped]** Australia: southwestern QLD, on the Lower Diamantina River, at Lake Machattie and the Bilpa Morea Claypan. PNy, Karnic, Palku. Extinct for several decades.

Mindiri **[391]** Papua New Guinea: Madang Province. Spoken on the southern (Rai) coast of Astrolabe Bay, west of Saidor, and immediately west of Dein. CEMP, EMPW, Siassi. For structural notes see the *Anus* entry. No literacy in Mindiri. In 1981, ninety-three speakers were reported. There may be about ninety today. Under pressure from neighbouring non-MP languages such as Ganglau and Tok Pisin, which the young speakers prefer. It is now endangered.

Mingin **[not mapped]** Australia: northwestern corner of QLD, inland from the southeastern extremity of the Gulf of Carpentaria. PNy, Tangkic. Extinct for a considerable time.

Miriwung **[236]** Australia: extreme northeastern corner of WA, at Kununurra, southeast of Wyndham and north of Lake Argyle. Also at Turkey Creek further south. Djeragan, Miriwungic. For structural information see the *Jawoyn* entry. No literacy in it. In 1990, 10 to 20 fluent speakers were reported, and 350 partial speakers in 1983. Young people only use the English-based pidgin lingua franca Kriol today, and some old people still speak Miriwung. Most of them speak Kriol. The language is seriously endangered and is heading towards being moribund.

Mirning **[238]** Australia: southwestern corner of SA and westwards in southern WA as far as Rawlinna. Coastal, and inland as far as Ooldea in SA, and Forrest and Rawlinna in WA, on the Nullarbor Plain. PNy, South-West, Wati. For structural information, see the *Adynyamathanha* entry. No literacy in it. It was believed recently extinct, but one speaker is reported to be living in Perth. Moribund.

Miwa **[not mapped]** Australia: WA, far northern Kimberleys area. Wororan, Wunambalic. Recently extinct?

Miyan [not mapped] Australia: northeastern inland QLD. Between the upper Torrens Creek and the upper Torrens River, south of Pentland. PNY, Maric, Mari. Extinct for some time.

Moere [239] Papua New Guinea: Madang Province. Spoken south of the Kumil River, about 6km from the coast, south of Sikor and the Malala Harbour. P, TNGP, Adelbert Range, Kumilan Family. Structurally it is TNGP (see the *Damal* entry). There is no literacy in it. In 1981, fifty-six speakers were reported. This figure is still valid, but Moere is under pressure from neighbouring large languages such as Bunabun, and from Tok Pisin. It is now endangered.

Moksela (or *Opselan*) [not mapped] Maluku, near Kayeli on eastern Buru Island. CEMP, CMP, central Maluku. Extinct since 1974.

Momuna (or *Somahai*) [240] Indonesia: Irian Jaya. Spoken in the lowlands just south of the main ranges in eastern central Irian Jaya, on the middle Vriendschap River and on the Catalina (Eilanden) River. P, TNGP, Central and South New Guinea. Traditional lingua franca of the area. Structurally it seems most closely to the Ok Family languages of the Central and South New Guinea Stock. It is structurally close to the general TNGP type (see the *Damal* entry), but has some aberrant features such as a two-gender distinction in pronouns, and object affixes with the verb. Some nouns have plural forms. In 1987, 2,700 speakers were reported, but latest estimates speak of only 2,000. The speakers are 5–15 per cent literate in Momuna. They are in contact with speakers of the very large Dani language, who have been learning Momuna as a contact language. However, it has been losing its contact language status to Indonesian and is under pressure from it. It is now potentially endangered.

Mor₂ [241] Indonesia: Irian Jaya. Spoken in the northeast Bomberai Peninsula, on the coast of Bintuni Bay. (The added '2' is used because there is another *Mor₁* in Irian Jaya, a non- endangered CEMP, EMP, SHWNG language spoken on the Mor Islands in east Cenderawasih Bay.) Mor₂ is P, TNGP, Mor₂. For structural information see the *Damal* entry. No literacy in it. In 1977, sixty speakers were reported, but there are fewer now. The language is under pressure from the large TNGP, West Bomerai languages Iha and Baham, and from Indonesian. It is now seriously endangered.

Moraori [242] Indonesia: Irian Jaya. Spoken in the extreme southwestern corner area of Irian Jaya, close to the Papua New Guinea border, east of Merauke. P, TNGP, Trans-Fly, Moraori. Languages of the Trans-Fly type have TNGP structured characteristics (see the *Damal* entry), but lack sentence-medial verb forms. They have defective pronoun systems and a rudimentary two-gender system only indicated with the third person object with verbs, but not in the pronouns themselves. In some languages, including Moraori, verb stem changes occur to indicate non-singularity of the object. Moraori is special in having a full pronoun system, and has a full negative conjugation. There is no literacy in Moraori. The number of its speakers is estimated to be about fifty. It seems to remain steady, but the language is under pressure from the large Marind language, whose speakers surround the Moraori speakers, and from Indonesian. It is regarded as only endangered.

519

Mosimo **[243]** Papua New Guinea: Madang Province. Spoken about 30km inland from the east coast north of Alexishafen, straight west from Garu and Yoidik settlements. P, TNGP, Madang, Hanseman Family. Structurally it is TNGP (see the *Damal* entry). No literacy in it. In 1981, fifty-eight speakers were reported. There are still around fifty or so, but the language is under pressure from large neighbouring languages, especially Garus, its eastern neighbour. Tok Pisin also takes its toll. It is now endangered.

Mudbura **[244]** Australia: northwestern NT, Victoria River to Barkly Tablelands. PNY, South-West, Ngumbin. For structural information see the *Adynyamathanha* entry. No literacy in it. In 1983, possibly fifty speakers were reported. Most speakers are bilingual in English and other Aboriginal languages. Speaker numbers are decreasing. The language is endangered and becoming seriously endangered.

Mulaha **[not mapped]** Papua New Guinea: central Province, coastal. P, TNGP, Eastern part, Kwalean Family. Extinct since the 1950s.

Mullukmulluk (or *Malak-Malak*) **[246]** Australia: northwestern NT, southwest of Darwin, on the northern bank of the Daly River. Daly, Malagmalag, Malagmalag Proper. For structural information see the *Jawoyn* entry. In 1988, 9 to 11 fully fluent speakers were reported. The people generally speak the English-based pidgin lingua franca Kriol, and speaker numbers have been falling. The language is now moribund.

Muluridyi **[not mapped]** Australia. QLD, southeastern corner of Cape York Peninsula, west of Cairns at Mareeba. PNY, Yalandyic. Recently extinct.

Murik (or *Nor*, or *Nor-Murik Lakes*) **[355]** Papua New Guinea: East Sepik Province, Angoram District. Spoken on the coast west of the mouth of the Sepik River. P, SERP, Nor Pondo, Nor Family. The Nor-Pondo languages constitute one of the three aberrant groups of the SERP (see the *Suarmin* entry), which may originally not have been members of it, but had a SERP lexical element laid over them. Structurally they are different from the general SERP type (see the *Yimas* entry). However, while the complex noun classification system with extensive concordance mentioned in the Yimas entry was reported for Murik (and another member of the Nor Family), it had vanished from daily use from both of them by 1970. There is no literacy in Murik. In 1977, 1,476 speakers were reported, it was down to 1,256 in the 1990 census, and is likely to be considerably lower today. The language is under pressure from Tok Pisin, which the young speakers prefer. It is now potentially endangered.

Muruwari (or *Murawari*) **[not mapped]** Australia: QLD and NSW central border, from Bourke in the south to Bollon in the north. PNY, Muruwaric. Recently extinct.

Musan (or *Musian*) **[370]** Papua New Guinea: Sandaun Province. Spoken about 50km east of the Irian Jaya border, about 10km south of the Upper Sepik River. It is located northeast of the related Amto language (see the *Amto* entry). Amto-Musian (or Musan) small phylum. Little is known about the structure of Musan, except that there is a two-gender system in the third person singular pronoun. No literacy in it. In 1981, seventy-five speakers were reported. This number may still be correct, but the speakers are acculturating rapidly. Because of this, the language is becoming endangered.

Musom (or *Misatik*) [247] Papua New Guinea: Morobe Province, eastern Markham Valley. Spoken in the southwestern corner of the Huon Peninsula, north-northwest of Lae town, on the western bank of the Busu River. CEMP, EMPW, Markham Family. See the *Anus* entry for structural notes. No literacy in it. In 1989, 264 speakers were reported. Recent estimates mention 219. There is much intermarriage of Musom speakers with speakers of other languages, strong presence of Tok Pisin, the national language of Papua New Guinea, and of the CEMP, EMPW Yabim, the former Lutheran church lingua franca (still used by persons over forty years of age), the nearness of Lae and the influence of city life, education of children in English, long absences of adult males for work – all factors detrimental to the language, which is now endangered.

Mussau-Emira (or *Mussau*, or *Emira*) [248] Papua New Guinea: Mussau or St Matthias Islands, northwest of the northwestern end of New Ireland. CEMP, EMPW, Mussau. For structural notes see the *Anus* entry. The language is lexically aberrant. There is some literacy in it. In 1992, 4,200 to 5,000 speakers were reported. Recent reports mention 3,651. The language is under pressure from Tok Pisin, which tends to be preferred by young speakers and children. It is now potentially endangered, and is heading towards being endangered.

Mwatebu [249] Papua New Guinea: Milne Bay Province. Spoken on the northern central coast of Normanby Island. CEMP, EMPW, Milne Bay-Central Coast languages, Dobuan. For structural information see the *Anus* entry. There is little literacy in it. In 1972, 166 speakers were reported, but their number is lower now. The speakers are bilingual in the large Normanby Islands lingua franca Duau and the larger Dobu language, the lingua franca of the d'Entrecastaux Archipelago. They exert pressure on the language which is at least potentially endangered.

Naati [250] Vanuatu. Spoken in the southwestern corner area of Malekula. CEMP, EMPCE, remote Oceanic, North and Central Vanuatu, Malekula Coastal. One of the languages mentioned in the Southwest Bay entry (see *Southwest Bay*). Structurally similar to what is said in the *Anus* entry. No literacy in it. In the latest 1998 report on it, the members of just one family are mentioned as the last speakers, only a handful. The language is moribund.

Nafi (*Sirak*) [251] Papua New Guinea: Morobe Province. Spoken to the north of Lae on the Busu River. CEMP, EMPW, Markham languages. For structural notes see the *Anus* entry. No literacy in it. In 1988, 157 speakers were reported. Now there may be below 100 speakers. It is under pressure from neighbouring large related languages such as Wampar, and from Tok Pisin which the children prefer. It is potentially endangered and moving towards being endangered.

Naka'ela (or *Patakai*) [not mapped] Indonesia: Maluku, on northwestern Seram Island. CEMP, CMP, central Maluku. Had five old speakers in 1985. Now extinct.

521

Nakara [252] Australia. Extreme northern NT, northeastern Arnhem Land, Maningrida, Goulburn Island. Burarran. For structural information see the *Jawoyn* entry. No literacy in it. In 1983, 75 to 100 speakers were reported. People generally are bilingual in the neighbouring larger languages Burarra and Djeebanna. The language is getting endangered.

Napu (or *Pekurehua*) [253] Indonesia: Sulawesi. Spoken in the northeastern part of the bulk of Sulawesi, east of Lake Lindu. WMP, Sulawesi, Central Sulawesi, Kaili-Pamona. Structurally it corresponds to the Southern Sulawesi type (see *Bahonsuai*). There is some literacy in it. Nearly all speakers use Indonesian as second language. In 1995, 6,000 speakers were reported; only 4,000 in 1996. Young speakers tend to use Indonesian. Potentially endangered.

Narau [256] Indonesia: Irian Jaya. Spoken on the upper Idenburg River and north as far as the upper Nawa River, in the northeastern inland part of Irian Jaya. P, TNGP, Kaure Stock, Kaure. Little is known about its structure, but what is known corresponds in general to the TNGP type (see the *Damal* entry). No literacy in it. In 1993, about 100 speakers were reported. There are probably fewer now, because of pressure from its larger eastern neighbour Kaure of the same Family, and of Indonesian. It is now endangered.

Narrinyeri (or *Ngarinyeri*) [not mapped] Australia: southeastern coast of SA, from Naracoorte to beyond Murray Bridge. PNy, Ngarinyeric-Yithayithic. Recently extinct.

Narungga (or *Narranga*) [not mapped] Australia: SA, west of Adelaide, on the Yorke Peninsula. PNy, South-West, Yura. Believed to have become extinct in 1936, but probably only became so much later.

Nasarian [259] Vanuatu: southern central Malekula Island. CEMP, EMPCE, remote Oceanic, North and Central Vanuatu, Malekula Interior. Structurally similar to what has been said in the *Anus* entry. No literacy in it. In 1983, twenty speakers were reported. Now there will be considerably fewer. The language has succumbed to pressure from related larger languages such as Letemboi, its southern neighbour, and Labo, its eastern neighbour. Its speakers have largely shifted to them. It is now moribund.

Nataoran (or *Sakizaya*, or *Sakiray*, or *Amis*, *Nataoran*) [429] Taiwan. Spoken in villages in the Hualien area in central eastern coastal Taiwan. n-MPAUN, Paiwanic group. Closely related to the large Amis language spoken further south. The language has been under pressure from Amis, and of Chinese. No literacy in it. Like all Taiwanese Austronesian languages, it has a focussing syntax and verb structure in which the verb forms differ according to whether the agent, the patient, the location or the beneficiary (or instrument) of the action is in focus, i.e. regarded as most important. Moribund. A few elderly speakers.

Naueti [260] Indonesia: East Timor. Spoken on the southern coast of northeastern Timor Island. CEMP, CMP, Timor-Flores. Contains many loanwords from the Papuan Timor-Alor-Pantar languages, especially from the large Makasai language. They put pressure on it, as does Indonesian. No literacy in it. In 1981, about 1,000 speakers were reported. The language is potentially endangered.

Nauna [261] Papua New Guinea: Manus Province. Spoken on Nauna Island, east of Manus Island in the Admiralty Islands. CEMP, EMPW, Admiralty Islands languages. For structural information, see the *Anus* entry. No literacy in it. In 1977, 130 speakers were reported. There are probably fewer today. The speakers are bilingual in the large Titan language spoken on an island to the west of Nauna Island, and there is pressure on the Nauna language from the creolized Tok Pisin of the Admiralty Islands. It is now potentially endangered.

Nauruan [not mapped] on Nauru Island. CEMP, EMP, Oceanic, remote Oceanic, Micronesian. Apart from showing typical features of EMPCE languages (see the *Anus* entry) Micronesian languages are characterized by possessing highly complex class systems mainly in their numerical systems, with usually dozens of different classes for different counted objects. Also, they have complex sound systems containing some very unusual sounds, and elaborate pronoun systems. The literacy level is high. Almost all Nauruans are bilingual in English. Nauruan is used as a second language by speakers of Kiribati, Tuvalu, Kosraean and Marshallese living on Nauru. Nauruan children tend not to learn Nauruan any more. The language is potentially endangered and is moving towards being endangered.

Navwien [264] Vanuatu: southwestern corner of Malekula, near Malfaxal settlement. CEMP, EMPCE, remote Oceanic, North and Central Vanuatu, Malekula Coastal. Structurally similar to what is said in the *Anus* entry. No literacy in it. A recent report mentions five speakers. The language has succumbed to pressure from other local languages, and from Bislama. The speakers have almost all shifted to these. It is moribund.

Neku [265] New Caledonia. Spoken inland and on the coast in southwestern central New Caledonia, around Bourail. CEMP, EMPCE, New Caledonian, Southern. For structural notes see the *Arhö* entry. No literacy in it. In 1982, 200 speakers were reported. Now they are very much fewer. Neku is under pressure from the larger New Caledonian languages Ajië and Tiri, and from French. It is now seriously endangered.

Nemi [266] New Caledonia. Spoken in the northern quarter of New Caledonia, on the coast and inland on the northeastern side, mainly in the upper valleys, and also on the southwestern coast at Voh. CEMP, EMPCE, New Caledonian, Northern. For structural notes, see the *Arhö* entry. Not much literacy in it. In 1982, 600 speakers were reported which may have been exaggerated, because a recent report mentions only 325, but the language is only potentially endangered, with children beginning not to learn the language. It is under pressure from the neighbouring larger closely related languages Jawe and Fwâi, and from French, which has led to it being potentially endangered.

Ngadjunmaya [not mapped] Australia: central southern near coastal WA, centred around Balladonia. PNY, South-West, Mirning. Recently extinct?

Ngaduk (or *Ngarduk*) [not mapped] Australia: northern NT, between the mouths of the Lower South Alligator and the Lower East Alligator rivers. *Unclassified*. Extinct for some time.

Ngalakan [267] Australia: NT, southeastern Arnhem Land, north of Roper River. Gunwinyguan, Ngalakanic. For structural information see the *Jawoyn* entry. No literacy in it. In 1981, possibly ten speakers were reported. Now several speakers still remain. Moribund.

Ngaliwuru [268] Australia: northeastern NT, Victoria River, due south of Darwin. Djaminguan. Very closely related to Djamindjung, or a dialect of it. In 1980, it was said that the two are so closely linked that only some elderly speakers could distinguish them. For structural information, see the *Jawoyn* entry. No literacy in it. Its speaker number was included in the thirty reported for Djamindjung in 1990. Today there would be hardly any distinguishable speakers left. Ngaliwuru is moribund.

Ngalkbun (or *Dalabon*, or *Dangbon*, or *Buwan*) [269] Australia: northern NT, in Arnhem Land at Oenpelli, and further south in the Northern Territory, in the Katherine area. Gunwinyguan, Gunwinygic. For structural information see the *Jawoyn* entry. A small amount of vernacular material was produced in the early 1980s. In 1983, 100 to 200 speakers were reported. Most speakers are bilingual in the English-based pidgin lingua franca Kriol, and some in the closely related Rembarrunga or the Gunwinygu languages. Some Rembarrunga speakers use Ngalkbun as a second language. Young Ngalkbun speakers are shifting to Kriol and others to Kunwinjku. The number of speakers has dropped drastically, and there are only about twenty full speakers left today. The language is getting seriously endangered.

Ngamini [not mapped] Australia: northeastern SA, around Warburton Creek. PNy, Karnic, Karna. Recently extinct.

Ngandi [270] Australia: northern NT, central eastern Arnhem Land. Gunwinyguan, Ngandic. For structural information see the *Jawoyn* entry. No literacy in it. Believed extinct for some time, but now it seems that some speakers may still remain. Moribund.

Ngangikurungkurr (or *Nangikurrunggurr*) [271] Australia: northwestern NT, south-southwest of Darwin, at the junction of the Daly and Flora Rivers, at the Daly River Mission, and at Tipperary Station. Daly, Moil. For structural information see the *Jawoyn* entry. No literacy in it. It is the main language in the Daly River group. In 1988, 275 speakers were reported. The speakers are bilingual in the English-based pidgin lingua franca Kriol or in English, and some young speakers are shifting to it. The language is getting potentially endangered.

Nganyaywana [not mapped] Australia: northeastern NSW, between Inverell and Glen Innes. PNy, Yuin-Kuric, Kuri. Extinct for some time.

Ngardi [not mapped] Australia: northwestern WA, close to the NT border, southeast of Balgo, northwest of Lake White. PNy, South-West, Ngarga. Probably extinct.

Ngarinman [272] Australia: northwestern NT, Victoria River around Jasper Creek. PNy, South-West, Ngumbin. For structural information see the *Adynyamathanha* entry.

No literacy in it. In 1983, possibly 170 speakers were reported. Speakers generally speak Kriol, the English-based pidgin lingua franca, to which the children are shifting. The number of Ngarinman speakers is considerably less today. The language is at least potentially endangered.

Ngarinyin (or *Ungarinyin*) **[273]** Australia: northwestern WA, Kimberley, Derby to the King River. Wororan, Ungarinjinic. For structural information see the *Jawoyn* entry. Some literacy in it. In 1981, possibly eighty-two speakers were reported. Most children speak the English-based pidgin language Kriol as their first language. Some children know a little of the language. The number of speakers is lessening, with Kriol taking over. The language is at least endangered.

Ngarla (or *Ngarlawanga*) **[274]** Australia: northwestern WA, inland from Port Hedland. PNY, South-West, Inland Ngayarda. For structural information, see the *Adynyamathanha* entry. No literacy in it. In 1991, eight fluent speakers and ten partial speakers were reported. Today there are fewer. The language is moribund.

Ngarluma **[275]** Australia: northwest coast of WA, southwest of Port Hedland, around Roebourne and inland. PNY, South-West, Coastal Ngayarda. For structural information, see the *Adynyamathanha* entry. No literacy in it. In 1970, seventy speakers were reported. Speakers are bilingual in English. The speaker numbers have been lessening since, and the language is endangered.

Ngarndji **[not mapped]** Australia: NT, Barkly Tableland, northeast of Lake Wood. West Barkly, Wambayan. Recently extinct.

Ngatikese Men's Creole **[not mapped]** Eastern Micronesia, on Ngatik (Sapuahfik) Atoll, southwest of Ponape. It is a mixed English-Ponapean creole spoken by older Sapuahfik men among themselves. It resulted from the massacre in 1837 of all adult males on Ngatik by the crew of a British ship. It is understood by women and children. The number of speakers is around 700. All of them are bilingual in the Sapuahfik dialect of Ponapean. The language is getting potentially endangered.

Ngawun **[not mapped]** Australia: northwestern QLD, between Flinders River and Norman River. PNY, Paman, Mayabic. Recently extinct.

Ngayawung **[not mapped]** Australia: southeastern SA, west of the lower Murray River at Morgan and Swan Reach. In the Robertstown area. PNY, Ngarinyeric-Yithayithic. Extinct for a very considerable time, but its former existence is still in living memory.

Ngenkiwumerri **[276]** Australia: northwestern NT, south-southeast of Darwin, south of the middle Daly River. PNY, Daly, Moil. For structural information, see the *Jawoyn* entry. No literacy in it. In 1981, perhaps fifty speakers were reported. The language is under pressure from the larger neighbouring closely related Nangikurrunggur language, and of the English-based pidgin lingua franca Kriol. There are fewer speakers now. The language is endangered and moving towards being seriously endangered.

Ngunbudj [not mapped] Australia: northern NT, between the Lower West Alligator and the Lower South Alligator rivers. *Unclassified*. Extinct for some time.

Ngunnawal [not mapped] Australia: southeastern NSW, west of Yass, northeast of Canberra. PNY, Yuin-kuric, Yuin. Extinct for decades.

Ngura [not mapped] Australia: northwestern NSW and southwestern QLD. Ngura is the name of the group. PNY, Karnic, Ngura. In 1981, there was still one speaker of the Garlali (or Kalali) member of it, four of Wangkumarra, two of Badjiri, and one of Punthamara (or Bundhamara). These members are on the borderline between language and dialect. Today the whole group is probably extinct, as is, probably, the language.

Nguri [not mapped] Australia: southeastern inland QLD, between the uppermost Warrego and Maranoa Rivers, east of Augathella. PNY, Maric, Mari. Extinct for some time.

Ngurmbur (or *Ngumbur*) [not mapped] Australia. Related to Bugunidja and Umbugarla. NT, northwestern Arnhem Land, between the West and the South Alligator rivers, north of Jim Jim Crossing. *Unclassified*. Recently extinct.

Nhanda [277] Australia: coastal Western WA, northeast of Geraldton, on Murchison River. PNY, South-West, Kardu. For structural information, see the *Adynyamathanha* entry. No literacy in it. In 1995, a few speakers were reported. Some are still surviving. The language is moribund.

Nhuwala [not mapped] Australia: coastal Ngayarda, northwestern coast of WA, and on Barrow and Montebello Islands. PNY, South-West. Recently extinct?

Nijadali (or *Nyiyabali*, or *Palygu*) [278] Australia: northwestern WA, at Marble Bar and possibly some at Nullagine, southeast of Port Hedland. PNY, South-West, Wati. For structural information, see the *Adynyamathanha* entry. No literacy in it. In 1990, six speakers were reported. The people generally speak Aboriginal English or the large language Nyangumarta, their northwestern neighbour. There are very few speakers left. The language is moribund, if not extinct.

Nila [279] Indonesia: Maluku. Now spoken in a transmigration area on south-central Seram Island. They came from Nila Island, north of Babar Island, in south Central Maluku, but have been moved to Seram Island, because of volcanic activity on their island. CEMP, CMP, Timor-Flores (southwest Maluku). Structurally, it is as per the *Palu'e* and *Alune* entries. No literacy in it. In 1989, 1,800 speakers were reported. There are likely to be fewer now as a result of their transmigration. The language is potentially endangered.

Nimanbur [not mapped] Australia: northwestern coastal WA, northeast of Broome, on King Sound inland. Nyulnyulan. Recently extinct.

Nisvai (or *Vetbong*) [280] Vanuatu: southeastern corner area of Malekula, south of Lamap settlement, in the area assumed to be that of the Port Sandwich language.

Probably a dialect of it, or a closely related language. CEMP, EMPCE, remote Oceanic, North and Central Vanuatu, Malekula Coastal. Structurally similar to what is mentioned in the *Anus* entry. No literacy in it. In a recent report, twenty speakers are mentioned, two of them children, eight years old. The language is under pressure from related neighbouring languages and from Bislama. It is endangered or seriously endangered.

Norfolkese and *Pitcairnese* [not mapped] Eastern Australia: Norfolk Island, and southeastern Pacific, Pitcairn Island. An English-Tahitian cant developed by mutineers of the British ship *Bounty* settling on Pitcairn Island in 1790, with some of them removed to Norfolk Island in 1859. It is an in-group language used to assist in the preservation of identity. The language is getting impoverished and anglicized on Pitcairn Island among the fifty inhabitants, a remnant of 225 in 1940. It is holding on Norfolk Island, with 580 speakers. The language is in a diglossic relationship with Standard British English. On Pitcairn Island it is endangered.

Nugunu (or *Nukunu*) [not mapped] Australia: eastern SA, on northernmost extension of Spencer Gulf, between Port Augusta and Whyalla. PNy, South-West, Yura. Recently extinct.

Numbami (*Siboma*) [281] Papua New Guinea: Morobe Province. Spoken in one village on the southern coast of the Huon Peninsula, east of Lae. CEMP, EMPW, Siassi languages. For structural notes see the *Anus* entry. No literacy in it. In 1978, 270 speakers were reported. Today there may be about 200 speakers. It is under pressure from the neighbouring large related Bugawac (Bukawac) language, and from Tok Pisin. It is potentially endangered.

Nungali [not mapped] Australia: northwestern NT, east of Wyndham and southeast of Port Keats, in the Upper Daly (Aroona) River area. Djamindjungan. Recently extinct.

Nunggubuyu [282] Australia: northeastern NT, southeastern Arnhem Land, north of Numbulwar. Gunwinyguan, Nunggubuan. For structural information, see the *Jawoyn* entry. Some literacy in it. In 1991, 300 fluent speakers and 400 partial or second language speakers were reported. These figures are still essentially valid, but children only understand the language, while speaking the English-based pidgin lingua franca Kriol. Because of this, the language is heading towards being potentially endangered.

Nusa Laut [283] Maluku: on Nusa Laut and the Lease Islands. CEMP, CMP, central Maluku. Had possibly about ten speakers in 1987, but is now probably extinct. The speakers have shifted to Malay.

Nyamal (or *Nyamarl*) [284] Australia: northwestern WA, around Bamboo Creek, Marble Bar, Nullagine, to the coast just east of Port Hedland. PNy, South-West, Inland Ngayarda. For structural information see the *Adynyamathanha* entry. No literacy in it. In 1991, 20 to 30 speakers were reported. The children speak the large neighbouring language Nyangumarta or English. The speakers are becoming fewer. The language is endangered and heading towards being seriously endangered.

Nyangga [not mapped] Australia: extreme northwestern coastal corner of QLD and adjacent part of the NT coastal area. PNY, Tangkic. May be the same as Ganggalida (Yukulta). Recently extinct.

Nyawaygi [not mapped] Australia: northeastern coastal QLD between Ingham and Townsville. PNY, Nyawaygic. Recently extinct.

Nyigina [287] Australia: northwestern WA, on the lower Fitzroy River, inland east of Broome. Nyulnyulan. For structural information see the *Jawoyn* entry. No literacy in it. In 1981, possibly fifty speakers were reported. Most of the speakers are bilingual in the large PNY, South-West, Ngumbin language Walmajarri spoken by their south-eastern neighbours. The children speak the English-based pidgin lingua franca Kriol or Aboriginal English as their first language. The language is endangered and heading towards being seriously endangered.

Nyisunggu (or *Tanimbili*) [288] Solomon Islands, Santa Cruz Archipelago, eastern Utupua Island. CEMP, EMPCE, Santa Cruz, Utupua. Structurally similar to what is detailed in the *Anus* entry. No literacy in it. In 1990, 150 speakers were reported. Recent reports mention only fifty, of whom ten are children of around ten years of age. Amba, Asumboa and Pijin are second languages to which the speakers have been shifting. The language is now endangered.

Nyulnyul [not mapped] Australia: extreme northwestern coast of WA, south of the Kimberleys, at Beagle Bay. Nyulnyulan. Recently extinct?

Nyunga (or *Nyungar*) [289] Australia: extreme southwestern part of WA. PNY, South-West, Nyungar. Recently extinct. About 8,000 people descended from speakers of the now extinct former Nyungar languages speak a mixture of English and Nyunga, the 'Neo-Nyunga'.

Obokuitai (or *Obogwitai*, or *Ati*, or *Aliki*) [290] Indonesia: Irian Jaya. Spoken just north of the middle Rouffaer River, in one village in central eastern Irian Jaya. Geelvinck Bay Phylum, Lakes Plain, Tariku, East. For structural notes see the *Awera* entry. About 15 per cent of the speakers are literate in Obokuitai. In 1996, 130 speakers were reported. The language is holding its own well, but the children are coming under Indonesian influence and pressure. The language is becoming potentially endangered.

Oirata (or *Maaro*) [291] Indonesia: South Maluku. Spoken on southeast Kisar Island, north of the northeastern tip of Timor Island. TNGP, Timor-Alor-Pantar. Structurally it corresponds to what is said in the *Maku'a* entry, but it has no noun class system, only a masculine-feminine two-gender system, and its verbal system is rather complex. No literacy in it. In 1981, 1,200 speakers were reported, but they are very much fewer now. The Oirata are socially heavily disadvantaged and looked down upon as inferior by the large Kisar language speakers inhabiting the remainder of Kisar Island. This has a very negative influence on the Oirata language, which is now endangered.

Onin [292] Indonesia: Irian Jaya. Spoken on the northwestern coast of northwestern Bomberai Peninsula, which is south of the Bird's Head. CEMP, CMP, North Bomberai.

For structural notes see the *Pa'ela* and *Alune* entries. No literacy in it. In 1978, 600 speakers were reported. That figure may be lower now. The language is under pressure from the large P, TNGP, Western Bomberai language Iha, and from Indonesian. It is now potentially endangered.

Onjab (or *Onjob*) **[293]** Papua New Guinea: Oro Province. Spoken less than 10km inland from the east coast of Collingwood Bay, inland from Wanigela settlement, in Naukwata and Koreat. P, TNGP, Eastern TNGP, Dagan Family. For structural notes see the *Koiari* entry. Speakers are literate in English and the CEMP, EMPW Ubir language spoken further southeast on the coast of Collingwood Bay as a church lingua franca. In 1981, 160 speakers were reported. Recent estimates mention a similar figure, but the language is under pressure from Ubir, English and Tok Pisin, and is now endangered.

Ormu **[294]** Indonesia: Irian Jaya. Spoken in the northeastern north coast area, just west of Jayapura. CEMP, EMPW, Sarmi-Yotafa. For structural notes see the *Anus* entry. No literacy in it. In 1995, 600 speakers were reported, but the most recent estimates mention 500 speakers. The speakers are largely bilingual in Indonesian, and the language is under pressure from it. It is now potentially endangered.

Oroha (or *Oraha*) **[295]** Solomon Islands: southern end of South Malaita Island. CEMP, EMPCE, remote Oceanic, Malaita Group, southeast Solomons. For structural notes see the *Anus* entry. No literacy in it. In 1981, about 100 speakers were reported. This figure may still be reasonably accurate. The speakers are bilingual in the large related Sa'a language, the northern neighbour of Oroha, and are shifting to it. Oroha is now endangered.

Ouma **[296]** Papua New Guinea: central Province, southeastern coastal area near Labu. EMPW, Milne Bay-central Province Section, Oumic. Had four speakers in 1970. Now probably extinct.

Padoe (or *Soroako*, or *Tambe'e*, or *Ajo*, or *Alalao*) **[297]** Indonesia: Sulawesi. Spoken in the southeastern part of the bulk of Sulawesi, and the extreme northern part of the southeastern peninsula of Sulawesi, west of Lake Towuti. WMP, Sulawesi, Central Sulawesi, Bungku-Mori. Structurally it corresponds to the Southern Sulawesi type (see *Bahonsuai*). Some limited literacy in it. In 1987, 7,000–10,000 speakers were reported, and 6,000 in 1991. There is vigorous language use, but an increasing number of speakers are shifting to Indonesian. The language is potentially endangered.

Pakanha **[not mapped]** Australia: QLD, central Cape York Peninsula, south of Coleman River. PNY, Paman, Middle Pama. Recently extinct?

Palu'e **[298]** Indonesia: Nusa Tenggara, Flores Island area. Spoken on Palu Island, north of central Flores Island. It is on the borderline of being a separate language or an aberrant dialect of the large Li'o language spoken on the coast opposite it. CEMP, CMP, Bima-Sumba. No literacy in it. Like many CMP languages, Palu'e (and Li'o) are structurally transitional between WMP and EMP, but closer to the latter. For instance, the distinction between permanent and non-permanent possession, typical of all EMP languages, is found in many CMP languages. The WMP feature of words indicating the class and nature of nouns appearing between numerals and nouns is found in some CMP languages. The EMP distinction between transitive and intransitive verbs is found in a number of CMP languages. In many of them, the subject and object, and their number, is marked by prefixes and by suffixes, as is typical of EMP, etc. In 1981, 3,000 speakers of Palu'e were reported, but there has been a strong earthquake on the island which caused the population to scatter on parts of Flores Island, which affected the language badly. It is now endangered.

Palumata (or **Balamata**) **[not mapped]** Indonesia: Maluku, on northwest Buru Island. CEMP, CMP, central Maluku. Now extinct.

Panasuan [299] Indonesia: Sulawesi. Spoken in the southwestern part of the bulk of Sulawesi. WMP, Sulawesi, South Sulawesi. Structurally it corresponds to the Southern Sulawesi type (see **Bahonsuai**). Perhaps some little literacy in it. In 1988, 900 or more speakers were reported. In 1984, only 645 were reported. Under some pressure from the larger Kalumpang and Seko languages, and from Indonesian. The language is potentially endangered.

Panytyima [300] Australia: northwestern WA, east-southeast of Tom Price, a long way southeast of Port Hedland. PNY, South-West, Inland Ngayarda. For structural information see the **Adynyamathanha** entry. No literacy in it. In 1972, fifty speakers were reported. Speakers are bilingual in the large related neighbouring language Yindji-barndi, or in English. There are much fewer speakers today. The language is seriously endangered.

Papapana [301] Papua New Guinea: North Solomons Province. Spoken on the northern part of the east coast of Bougainville Island. CEMP, EMPW, Bougainville languages. For structural information see the **Anus** entry. No literacy in it. In 1977, 150 speakers were reported. Possibly fewer now. The language is under pressure from large related languages such as Vasui (or Tinputz) and of Tok Pisin. It is now at least potentially endangered, or possibly endangered.

Papi (or **Paupe**) **[317]** Papua New Guinea: Sandaun Province. Spoken south of the Upper Sepik, in one village on the lower Frieda River, a southern tributary of the Upper Sepik, southeast of the May River settlement. P, SERP, Leonard Schultze, Papi Family. For its classification and structural features see the **Suarmin** entry. There is some literacy in it. In 1981, seventy-five speakers were reported. This figure is still valid. All the speakers know at least some Tok Pisin, which puts pressure on the language. It is now endangered.

Papuan Pidgin English [not mapped] Southern central and southeastern Papua New Guinea. An English-based, relatively unstable pidgin in use in the former Territory of Papua since the 1880s mainly for intercommunication between indigenes and Europeans. It was superseded by **Police Motu** (later called **Hiri Motu**, see that entry in the list of viable threatened and recently extinct pidgin and creole languages in the Pacific and Australia) in 1920 in administration and as the language of the police force. It lingered on, and became extinct only recently, with a few remnants of it remembered by some old men today.

Paulohi [302] Indonesia: Maluku. Spoken on the west coast of Elpaputih Bay in southwest Seram Island. CEMP, CMP, Central Maluku. Structurally it corresponds to what is said in the ***Palu'e*** and ***Alune*** entries. No literacy in it. In 1982, fifty possible speakers were reported. Now there would be only very few left. They suffered from a severe earthquake and tidal wave, and were decimated by disease. The language is moribund and almost extinct.

Pauwi [303] Indonesia: Irian Jaya. Spoken on the west side of the lower Mamberamo River by Lake Rombebai, in the northeast of non-pensinular Irian Jaya. *Language isolate*. Nothing much is known of its structure. No literacy in it. In 1975, about 100 speakers were reported. It seems that it is under pressure from the larger Warembori language which is also a language isolate. It may be potentially endangered.

Pazeh (or ***Shekhoan***, ***Lekhwan***) [not mapped] In the lower western part of the top third of Taiwan: n-MPAUN, Paiwanic. Still used as home language in the 1930s. Became extinct in the mid-1990s, i.e. recently extinct.

Peco' [not mapped] Indonesia: Jakarta. A creolized hybrid form of Dutch developed by people of mixed Indonesian-Dutch descent during Dutch colonial times in their endeavour to adapt to the Dutch ruling class. It is a sort of media lingua with a predominantly Malay vocabulary and a Dutch vocabulary, with Malay and Sundanese elements in it. There are still second-language speakers and some first-language speakers of it, but it is moribund.

Pendau (or ***Ndau*** or ***Umalasa***) [304] Indonesia: Sulawesi. The Pendau language area has traditionally been the middle and inner hill areas of much of the central part of the narrow neck which links the bulk of Sulawesi with its northeastern peninsula. WMP, Sulawesi, Central Sulawesi, Tomini. Structurally, it corresponds to the Southern Sulawesi type (see ***Bahonsuai***). Today most Pendau speakers live in resettlement projects or small hamlets close to coastal villages, along a 150km stretch of the west coast. The total number of speakers is about 3,200 today. In 1991, 2,000 to 5,000 were reported. The Pendau keep much to themselves and tend not to enter into close social relationships with speakers of another language. Pendau is the everyday language in their settlements. They use Indonesian only if they have to, e.g. to outside officials. However, their children receive instruction in the primary schools in Indonesian, and the non-Pendau coastal population is socially dominant. The language must therefore be regarded as potentially endangered.

Penrhyn (or ***Tongareva***) [not mapped] Northern Cook Islands, Penrhyn Island. CEMP, EMP, Oceanic, remote Oceanic, Polynesian (Eastern). For structural information see the ***Maori*** entry. There is no literacy in it. In 1981, 600 speakers were reported. Today there are much fewer. The language is being supplanted by Rarotongan and is disappearing rapidly. It is now endangered and rapidly moving towards being seriously endangered.

Pije [305] New Caledonia. Spoken in the northern quarter of New Caledonia, mainly inland on the northeastern side, around Tiendanite. CEMP, EMPCE, New Caledonian, Northern. For structural notes see the *Arhö* entry. Not much literacy in it. In 1982, 100 speakers were reported. Today there are many fewer. The language is under pressure from the neighbouring large and closely related Fwâi language and from French. It is now seriously endangered.

Pini [not mapped] Australia: southwestern WA, Three Rivers area. PNY, South-West, Wati. Recently extinct?

Pinigura [not mapped] Australia: northwestern WA, on Duck River, inland from Exmouth Gulf. PNY, South-West, Coastal Ngayarda. Recently extinct?

Piru [306] Indonesia: Maluku, on West Seram Island. CEMP, CMP, central Maluku. Had less than ten speakers in 1989. Now probably extinct.

Pitta Pitta (or *Bidha Bidha*) [not mapped] Australia: western Queensland (the QLD area which is north of northeastern SA). North of Boulia. PNY, Karnic, Palku. Recently extinct.

Piu (or *Sanbiau*, or *Lanzog*, or *Kuruko*) [307] Papua New Guinea: Morobe Province. Spoken to the west of the western extremity of the Huon Gulf on the upper Watut River. CEMP, EMPW, Markham Family, Buang. For structural information see the *Anus* entry. No literacy in it. In 1970, 130 speakers were reported. There are likely to be less today. The language is under pressure from the neighbouring large related Mumeng language, and from Tok Pisin. It is now endangered.

Polonombauk [308] Vanuatu. Spoken in the southeast interior of Santo. CEMP, EMPCE, remote Oceanic, North and Central Vanuatu, East Santo, South. Structurally similar to what is detailed in the *Anus* entry. No literacy in it. In 1983, 225 speakers were reported. Today there may be around 120. Very few children learn the language. It is under pressure from the neighbouring related Butmas-tur language. Polonombauk is getting endangered.

Portuguese Pidjin and *Creole* [not mapped] Indonesia. Various forms of this were spoken in Indonesia, for instance on Timor Island as Timor Creole Portuguese around Dili and other centres, in Jakarta, on Flores Island, on Sumatra, in Kalimantan, on Sulawesi, in Maluku on Ambon, and in a few other areas. It is extinct in Indonesia, but is still spoken in Malacca (Peninsular Malaysia), Sri Lanka, etc. See also the *Ternateño* entry.

Puari [309] Papua New Guinea: Sandaun Province. Spoken on the coast west of the Warapu language area mentioned in the Warapu entry. Sko Phylum, Krisa Family. For structural information see the *Warapu* entry. No literacy in Puari. In 1981, 371 speakers were reported. Language use was vigorous then. However, the tsunami mentioned in the Sissano and Warapu entries also hit the area inhabited by Puari speakers and annihilated most of them. It is not known how many survived, largely by being elsewhere at that time, but they are probably only in the tens. The language is now seriously endangered.

Punan Batu **[310]** Malaysia: Central Sarawak. Spoken on the Lower Linau River (southern arm of the Upper Rejang River). West of Long Geng, southeast of Belaga. WMP, Borneo, Rejang-Baram. The speakers are hunter-gatherers. The language has focussing syntax and verb structure, and the distinction between active and passive expression in the verb is a basic feature (see ***Nataoran*** and ***Lengilu*** for more details). No literacy in it. In 1981, fifty speakers were reported. There are probably fewer today. The language is seriously endangered.

Punthamara (or ***Bundhamara***) **[not mapped]** Australia: southwestern QLD, near Thargomindah. PNy, Karnic, Ngura. Recently extinct.

Pwaamei **[311]** New Caledonia. Spoken in the northern quarter of New Caledonia, inland on the southwestern side, around and northeast of Temata, inland from Voh. CEMP, EMPCE, New Caledonian, Northern. For structural notes see the ***Arhö*** entry. No literacy in it. In 1974, 325 speakers were reported. Today the speakers are somewhat less, and the children are beginning not to learn the language. It is under pressure from the neighbouring large Jawe language and from French. It is getting potentially endangered.

Pwapwâ **[312]** New Caledonia. Spoken in the northern quarter of New Caledonia, on the coast and hinterland on the southwestern side, around Boyen. CEMP, EMPCE, New Caledonian, Northern. For structural notes see the ***Arhö*** entry. No literacy in it. In 1982, 130 speakers were reported. Today they are much fewer. The language is under pressure from the neighbouring large New Caledonian languages Jawe and Yuaga, and from French. It is now seriously endangered.

Queensland Canefield English (or ***Kanaka English***) **[not mapped]** Australia: eastern coastal Queensland, near Cairns, Townsville, Mackay and Bundaberg. It developed from the nineteenth-century Pacific Pidgin English among indentured Melanesian labour on the Queensland sugar-cane plantations as from the middle of the nineteenth century, with many thousands of speakers. Most of the Melanesian Islander labourers were repatriated after the turn of the century, but a few stayed behind and continued using the language, referred to in Queensland as Kanaka English. There are still some speakers of it today, but it is moribund.

Rahambuu (or ***Wiau***) **[313]** Indonesia: Sulawesi. Spoken on the northern west coast of the southeastern peninsula of Sulawesi, north of Lasusua. WMP, Sulawesi, Central Sulawesi, Bungku-Mori. It corresponds tro the Southern Sulawesi type (see ***Bahonsuai***). No literacy in it. There are conflicting reports on the number of speakers: in 1989, 500; and in 1991, 5,000. Apparently a misprint in one of the sources. The very large language Bugis is used as second language, and there is pressure from Indonesian. The language is potentially endangered.

Rapa (or ***Rapan***) **[not mapped]** French Polynesia, Austral Islands, Rapa Island. CEMP, EMP, Oceanic, remote Oceanic, Polynesian (Eastern). For structural information see the ***Maori*** entry. There is no literacy in it. In 1977, 400 speakers were reported. Today there are much fewer because the language is being rapidly supplanted by Tahitian. It is now endangered, and moving towards being seriously endangered.

533

Rapanui (or *Easter Island*) [not mapped] Chile: Easter Island. CEMP, EMP, Oceanic, remote Oceanic, Polynesian (Eastern). For structural information see the *Maori* entry. There is 25–50 per cent literacy. The language had become almost extinct in the early twentieth century when the speakers were taken from the island to work collecting guano on South American coastal locations. Very few survived and returned to their island. Today there are 2,400–2,500 speakers again, of whom 2,200 are on Easter Island. Language use has been vigorous, but is now declining. Bilingualism in Spanish is universal, and members of the young generation are losing interest in the language. Reinvigoration efforts are in progress. The language is now endangered.

Rarotongan (or *Cook Island Maori*) [not mapped] Cook Islands. CEMP, EMP, Oceanic, remote Oceanic, Polynesian (Eastern). For structural information see the *Maori* entry. Trade language. Wide literacy. More than half the speakers live in New Zealand. The speakers were reported as totalling 43,000 one to two decades ago. However, language use and speaker numbers are rapidly decreasing, especially in the diaspora, and English is the preferred language of members of the young generation. The language is potentially endangered and becoming endangered.

Ratagnon (or *Datagnon* or *Latan*) [314] Philippine. Spoken on the southern tip of Mindoro Island. WMP, Meso Philippine, Central Philippine (Bisayan). The speakers have largely shifted to Tagalog, and the process is continuing. No literacy in it. There are very few speakers left. It is moribund.

Rembarrunga (or *Rembarrnga*) [315] Australia: northern NT, central Arnhem Land, north of the upper Roper River, also further north at Maningrida and outstations, and the Katherine area. Gunwinyguan, Rembargic. For structural information, see the *Jawoyn* entry. No literacy in it. In 1983, 150 speakers were reported. Many are bilingual in the English-based pidgin lingua franca Kriol, or the related languages Ngalkbun or Gunwinygu. Few children learn the language. The language is getting endangered.

Repanbitip [316] Vanuatu. Spoken inland on southeast Malekula Island. CEMP, EMPCE, remote Oceanic, North and Central Vanuatu, Malekula Interior, Small Nambas. Structurally similar to what has been said in the *Anus* entry. No literacy in it. In 1983, ninety speakers were reported. There may be fewer today. The language has been under pressure from related neighbouring languages, and from Bislama. It is now endangered.

Ririo [318] Solomon Islands: northern third of the northeastern coast of central Choiseul Island. CEMP, EMPW, Choiseul Group. For structural notes, see the *Anus* entry. No literacy in it. In 1977, 200 speakers were reported. Now there are only eighteen, four of whom are children of about ten years of age. The language has been under pressure from the large related trade language and lingua franca Babatana, its southern neighbour, to which the speakers have been shifting. Ririo is now seriously endangered.

Ritarungo (or *Ritharrngu*) [319] Australia: northern NT, eastern Arnhem Land at the Rose River and the Roper River. PNY, Yuulngu. For structural information, see the

Adynyamathanha entry. No literacy in it. In 1983, 300 or more speakers were reported. Some of the speakers are bilingual in the English-based pidgin lingua franca Kriol, and some in the related Djinba. The use of Kriol has been increasing, especially among members of the young generation. The language is slowly moving towards being potentially endangered.

Saaroa (or *Rarua*, or *Pachien*, or *Sisyaban*) [320] Taiwan, in southern central Taiwan, southeast of Minchuan and of the Kanakanabu language area, on the Laonung River. n-MPAUN, Tsouic group, southern branch of it. Has been under pressure of the large Bunun language of the Taiwan Austronesian Paiwanic group, and of Taiwanese Chinese. Most of the ethnic group has shifted to these two languages. The language has focussing syntax and verb structure. See the *Nataoran* entry for details. No literacy in it. Moribund. A few old speakers.

Saisiyat (or *Amutoura*, or *Bouiok*) [321] Taiwan. Spoken in northwestern Taiwan, in the western mountains, to the west of the large Atayal language area. Its northern dialect is located to the west of Wufeng, and its southern to the south of Mt Wuchih. n-MPAUN, Paiwanic group. The northern dialect speakers have almost assimilated to Atayal, and only a few can still speak their language. The speakers of the southern dialect use their language more actively, but many young people are shifting to Hakka Chinese. The language has focussing syntax and verb structure. See the *Nataoran* entry for details. No literacy in it. In 1978, 3,200 speakers of Saisiyat were reported, but the language is now endangered.

Salas (or *Salas Gunung*) [322] Indonesia: Maluku. Spoken in the Waru Bay area, southeastern Seram Island. CEMP, CMP, Central Maluku. Structurally it corresponds to what is said in the *Palu'e* and *Alune* entries. No literacy in it. In 1982, fifty speakers were reported, likely to be less now. Most use the Masiwang language of the area as second language and they are shifting to it. The language is seriously endangered.

Saluan, Kahumamahon (or *Interior Saluan*) [323] Indonesia: Sulawesi. Spoken on the east-central part of the eastern peninsula of Sulawesi. WMP, Sulawesi, Central Sulawesi, East-Central Sulawesi. Structurally it corresponds to the Southern Sulawesi type (see *Bahonsuai*). No literacy in it. In 1995, 2,000 speakers were reported. Under pressure from the large coastal Saluan language and from Indonesian. The language is potentially endangered.

Samosa [324] Papua New Guinea: Madang Province. Spoken about 30km inland from Alexishafen on the headwaters of a northern tributary of the Gogol River. P, TNGP, Madang, Hanseman Family. It is TNGP (see the *Damal* entry). No literacy in it. In 1981, ninety-four speakers were reported. This figure is still valid, but the language is under pressure from larger languages of the same Family, such as Garus and Garuh (or Nobanob), its eastern neighbour, and of Tok Pisin. It is now endangered.

Saparua [325] Indonesia: Maluku. Spoken on Saparua Island and the opposite coast of southwestern Seram Island. CEMP, CMP, Central Malulu. Structurally it is as per the

Palu'e and *Alune* entries. Some little literacy in it. In 1989, 10,200 speakers were reported. Now probably much fewer, because the speakers are shifting to Ambon Malay. The language is now endangered.

Saponi [326] Indonesia: Irian Jaya. Spoken in a village inland from the central part of the eastern coast of Cenderawasih Bay. P, Geelvinck Bay Phylum, Lakes Plain, Rasawa-Saponi. For structural information see the *Awera* entry. No literacy in it. In 1987, ten or fewer speakers were reported. The language is under pressure from larger related languages of the area such as the related Rasawa, and of Indonesian. It is moribund, possibly extinct.

Sauri [327] Indonesia: Irian Jaya. Spoken on the central eastern coast of Cenderawasih Bay, northeast of Waren. Probably a dialect of the larger Baropasi language. Geelvinck Bay Phylum, East Geelvinck Bay. For structural notes see the *Awera* entry. No literacy in it. In 1987, about 300 speakers were reported. Under some pressure from the large CEMP, EMP, SHWNG Waropen language spoken around Waren, and from Indonesian. Getting potentially endangered.

Sause [328] Indonesia: Irian Jaya. Spoken about 100km southwest of Lake Sentani, in northeastern Irian Jaya, on the Upper Nawa River, south of Lereh. Formerly assumed to be a Family-level isolate in the P, TNGP, Kaure Stock, but now regarded as being P, TNGP, Tor. For structural notes see the *Bonerif* entry. No literacy in it. In 1993, about 300 speakers were reported. Under pressure from Indonesian because of the nearness of Lereh town. It is now endangered.

Savo (or *Savosavo*) [329] Solomon Islands. Spoken on Savo Island, north of north-western Guadalcanal Island. EP, Solomon Islands Family. For structural information see the *Taulil* entry. There is no literacy in Savo. In 1976, 1,147 speakers were reported. Today there are considerably less, because the use of Savo has been declining among the members of the younger generation, in favour of Solomon Pijin and English, with this trend accelerating. The language is now endangered.

Seke [330] Vanuatu. Spoken on central Pentecost (Raga) Island. CEMP, EMPCE, remote Oceanic, North and Central Vanuatu, East Vanuatu. For structural information see the *Anus* entry. No literacy in it. In 1983, 300 speakers were reported. The speaker numbers may not be much less now, but children are beginning not to learn Seke. The language is under pressure from the neighbouring related large Apma language. It is beginning to be potentially endangered.

Sene [331] Papua New Guinea: Morobe Province, eastern end of Huon Peninsula. P, TNGP, Huon-Finisterre. Seven speakers left in 1978. Now probably extinct.

Senggi [332] Indonesia: Irian Jaya. Spoken about 100 km due south of Jayapura, near the border of Papua New Guinea, in northeastern Irian Jaya, near Senggi town. P, TNGP, Border Stock. For structural notes see the *Awyi* entry. No literacy in it. In 1978, 120 speakers were reported. Probably fewer now. It is under pressure from Indonesian, because of the nearness of Senggi town. It is now potentially endangered.

Sengseng **[333]** Papua New Guinea: West New Britain Province. Spoken in the south-west interior, in the Amgen River area. CEMP, EMPW, New Britain languages. For structural notes, see the ***Anus*** entry. Some literacy in it. In 1982, 453 speakers were reported. There may still be 400 or more speakers, but only just over half the children learn the language. Sengseng is becoming potentially endangered.

Sepa **[334]** Papua New Guinea: Madang Province. Spoken on the coast south of Manam Island around Bogia. CEMP, EMPW, Siassi languages. For structural notes see the ***Anus*** entry. No literacy in it. In 1981, 268 speakers were reported. Today there may be about 200. There is pressure on the language from the large related Manam language. It is potentially endangered.

Sera **[403]** Papua New Guinea: Sandaun Province. Spoken in one village on the northwestern coast of Papua New Guinea, to the west of the area originally occupied by the Sissano language (see the ***Sissano*** entry). CEMP, EMPW, Siassi Family. See the ***Anus*** entry for structural information. No literacy in it. In 1981, 432 speakers were reported. However, the same tsunami which hit the Sissano language area in November 1998, also annihilated most of the Sera-speaking population. Only a small number of speakers were left. The language is now seriously endangered.

Serili **[335]** Indonesia: South Maluku. Spoken on northeast Masela Island, southeast of Babar Island. CEMP, CMP, Timor-Flores (South Maluku). Structurally it is as per the ***Pa'une*** and ***Alune*** entries. No literacy in it. In 1980, 328 speakers were reported. It is under pressure from the larger Masela language and Indonesian. The language is potentially endangered.

Seru **[not mapped]** Malaysia: Formerly in Kabong, in western central Sarawak, in the 2nd Division. Western Malayo-Polynesian, Borneo, Rejang, Melanau. Comparatively recently extinct, under pressure from a larger local language.

Shark Bay **[336]** Vanuatu. Spoken in East Santo on Litaro (Pilot) Island and on the coast and in the hinterland of Shark Bay. CEMP, EMPCE, remote Oceanic, North and Central Vanuatu, East Santo, South. Structurally similar to what has been said in the ***Anus*** entry. No literacy in it. In 1981, 225 speakers were reported. Today they may be about 200 or somewhat less. The children are beginning not to learn the language any more. There is pressure from Bislama on the language. It is beginning to be potentially endangered.

Sian **[337]** Malaysia: Central Sarawak, east of Belaga, 7th Division. Neighbouring on Punan Batu, and may be mutually intelligible with it. WMP, Borneo, Rejang-Baram. The language has focussing syntax and verb structure, and the distinction of the active-passive expression in the verb is fundamental (see ***Nataoran*** and ***Lengilu*** for more details). No literacy in it. In 1981, seventy speakers were reported. Probably there are fewer today. The language is endangered.

Siraya (or ***Baksa, Pepohoan***) **[not mapped]** In the southwestern part of the bottom third of Taiwan. N-MPAUN, Paiwanic. Still spoken in the early 1900s. Well documented. Extinct.

Sissano* [404]** Papua New Guinea: Sandaun Province. Spoken on a long stretch of the northwestern coast of Papua New Guinea between Vanimo and Aitape. CEMP, EMPW, Siassi Family. See the ***Anus entry for structural notes. No literacy in it. In 1990, 4,776 speakers were reported. Language use was vigorous then. However, in November 1998, a terrible tsunami was caused by a violent sea-quake only 25km off the coast and hit the coast with tremendous force, almost completely annihilating the population within the disaster area. There were only very few survivors, and almost the only speakers left were those who happened to be absent from the disaster area. It is hard to estimate the number of surviving speakers, but it is unlikely to exceed a few hundred or so. The language is now seriously endangered.

Sobei (or ***Biga***, or ***Imasi***) **[338]** Indonesia: Irian Jaya. Spoken on the central north coast of Irian Jaya, at Ahus and at Sarmi, and in various dialectal forms on islands to the north of Sobei and Sarmi. CEMP, EMPW, Sarmi-Yotafa. For structurally notes see the ***Anus*** entry. In 1987, 1,850 speakers were reported. There are probably fewer speakers now. The children are bilingual in Indonesian and tend to prefer it to Sobei. Intermarriage with members of other language groups is increasing, and Irianese Malay (Pasar Malay) is used with people from other language areas. Sobei speakers are beginning to shift to it. The language is now endangered.

Somm* [339]** Papua New Guinea: Morobe Province. Spoken in the northern part of the western end of the Huon Peninsula, on the middle Som River, a tributary of the Uruwa River, east of the Wantoat settlement. P, TNGP, Finisterre, Uruwa Family. It is TNGP (see the ***Damal entry). No literacy in it. In 1978, eighty-eight speakers were reported. Recent reports mention eighty. It is under pressure from large neighbouring languages, especially the related Wantoat, its western neighbour, and of Tok Pisin. It is now endangered.

Sösörian* [340]** Vanuatu: southeastern corner of Malekula, north of Lamap settlement, in the area assumed to be that of the Port Sandwich language (see the ***Nisvai entry). CEMP, EMPCE, remote Oceanic, North and Central Vanuatu, Malekula Coastal. Structurally similar to what is mentioned in the ***Anus*** entry. No literacy in it. In a recent report, four speakers are mentioned. The language succumbed to pressure from related neighbouring languages, and from Bislama. It is moribund.

Southwest Bay (***Ninde***, ***Sinesip*** [***Nahara***], ***Naati***) **[341]** Vanuatu: southwestern corner area of Malekula. CEMP, EMPCE, remote Oceanic, North and Central Vanuatu, Malekula Coastal. Structurally similar to what is said in the ***Anus*** entry. Some literacy in Ninde and Sinesip. Ninde has close to 1,000 speakers. 500 speakers are reported for Sinesip, which seems healthy, but is under pressure from closely related larger neighbouring languages, especially Malfaxal (Naha'ai), its southern neighbour, and is under pressure from Bislama. Naati is spoken by only 25 speakers, all members of a single extended family.

Sowa* [342]** Vanuatu: west coast of central southern Pentecost Island. CEMP, EMPCE, remote Oceanic, North and Central Vanuatu. Structurally similar to what has been said in the ***Anus entry. No literacy in it. In 1971, twenty speakers were reported. Now there will be considerably less. The language has been succumbing to the quite large related Apma language which surrounds it in the north and east. Its speakers have largely shifted to it. It is now moribund.

Suarmin (or ***Duranmin***, or ***Akiapmin***) **[343]** Papua New Guinea: Sandaun Province, Telefomin District. Spoken in a few hamlets on the Kenu (Hok) River, a tributary of the Om River, in the Central Range area, not very far from the Irian Jaya border. Leonard Schultze, Papi Family. The Leonard Schultze languages constitute one of the three aberrant groups of the SERP which may originally not have been members of it, but had a SERP lexical element overlaid over them. Structurally they are different from the general SERP type (see the ***Ak*** entry) in having a multiple noun class system. Class markers are added to adjectives, demonstratives, numerals, etc., according to the class of the noun to which they belong, but the class is not indicated by markers on the nouns themselves. Pronouns are also different from those regularly found in SERP languages. There is no literacy in Suarmin. In 1979, 188 were reported in a census, but recent information mentions 145. Young people are quite bilingual in the large Telefol language, the western neighbour of Suarmin, which puts pressure upon it. It is now endangered.

Sumariup (or ***Sogoba***, or ***Latoma***) **[344]** Papua New Guinea: southern central East Sepik Province. Spoken south of the uppermost Karawari River, southeast of Amboin settlement. P, SERP, Sepik Hill, Bahinemo Family. For structural features see the ***Kaningara*** entry. No literacy in it. In 1993, eighty speakers were reported. This figure is still valid. The speakers are bilingual in Tok Pisin and the large related language Alamblak, which is the northern neighbour of Sumariup, which is under pressure from these two languages. It is now endangered.

Susuami **[345]** Papua New Guinea: Morobe Province. Spoken in the upper Watut River valley, outside Bulolo town. P, TNGP, Angan Family. For its structure see the ***Kawasa*** entry. No literacy in it. In 1990, fifteen speakers were reported, but now it would be less than ten. The speakers use the large Angan language Angaatiha as second language, and most of them have shifted to it. The surviving speakers have lost interest in their language, which is now moribund.

Taap **[346]** Papua New Guinea: Morobe Province. Spoken by a few elderly persons in the central dialect area of the large Wantoat language (P, TNGP, Finisterre, Wantoat Family) and may be a dialect of it. The Finisterre Family languages are structurally TNGP (see the ***Damal*** entry). No literature in Taap. Recently, about ten or fewer speakers were reported. Most of the speakers have shifted to Wantoat. Taap is moribund.

Taikat (or ***Arso***) **[347]** Indonesia: Irian Jaya. Spoken about 50km south of Jayapura on the Upper Tami River around Arso town near the Papua New Guinea border. P, TNGP, Border Stock. For structural notes see the ***Awyi*** entry. No literarcy in it. In 1978, 600 speakers were reported. There are probably fewer now. The language is under pressure from Indonesian because of its nearness to Arso, and to the capital Jayapura. Especially the children are under strong pressure from Indonesian. It is now potentially endangered.

Taje [348] Indonesia: Sulawesi. On the east coast of the extreme southern end of the narrow neck connecting the central bulk of Sulawesi with its northeastern peninsula. Close to Ampibabo and Parigi. WMP, Sulawesi, Central Sulawesi, Tomini. Structurally it corresponds to the Southern Sulawesi type (see *Bahonsuai*). No literacy in it. About 200 persons whose parents were both Taje live in a village near Parigi. Considerably more know some Taje because one of their parents was Taje. However, most speakers do not know the language well, except for one old man. The language is heavily influenced by neighbouring languages. One hundred and fifty more had to be resettled near Ampibabo, 50km north of Parigi, and about thirty more even further north. The language was regarded as nearly extinct in 1902 by a visiting linguist, and is now certainly moribund and nearly extinct.

Tajio [349] Indonesia: Sulawesi. Spoken on the east coast of the central part of the narrow neck connecting the bulk of Sulawesi with its northeastern peninsula, with a total of about 12,000 speakers today. In 1991, 18,000 speakers were reported. One part of them is located near Kasimbar, and another further north near Tada. WMP, Sulawesi, Central Sulawesi, Tomini. Structurally, it corresponds to the Southern Sulawesi type (see *Bahonsuai*). No literacy in it. Near Kasimbar, the Tajio villages are surrounded by villages of speakers of other languages. Near Tada, there is no space for new migrants to settle there, and relatively few of the children go to towns for further education and bring back Indonesian linguistic influence, at least for the time being. There the language is safe now, but would have to be regarded as potentially endangered.

Taloki [350] Indonesia: Sulawesi. Spoken on the northwest coast of Buton Island located to the south of the southeastern peninsula of Sulawesi. WMP, Sulawesi, Central Sulawesi, Bungku-Mori. It corresponds to the Southern Sulawesi type (see *Bahonsuai*). No literacy in it. In 1995, 500 speakers were reported, and 400 before that. High level of bilingualism in the large Muna language, and there is pressure from Indonesian. The language is potentially endangered.

Talondo' [351] Indonesia: Sulawesi. Spoken in the southwestern part of the non-peninsular bulk of Sulawesi. WMP, Sulawesi, South Sulawesi. Structurally it corresponds to the Southern Sulawesi type (see the *Bahonsuai* entry). In 1986, 500 speakers were reported. It is under pressure from larger neighbouring languages such as Mamuju, and from Indonesian. It is now potentially endangered.

Tambotalo [352] Vanuatu: inland of southeast Espiritu Santo Island. CEMP, EMPCE, remote Oceanic, North and Central Vanuatu, West Santo. Structurally similar to what has been said in the *Anus* entry. No literacy in it. In 1981, fifty speakers were reported. There will be fewer today. The language has been under pressure from the closely related larger languages Tutuba in the east, Naranggo in the south, and the less closely related Shark Bay language in the north, to which speakers have shifted. It is now seriously endangered.

Tanapag [not mapped] On the west central coast of Saipan Island, northern Mariana Islands. CEMP, EMP, Oceanic, remote Oceanic, Micronesian. For structural information see the *Nauru* entry. There is some literacy. There are some hundred speakers, but members of the ethnic group under thirty years of age do not speak Tanapag, but the

WMP language Chamorro. The language is endangered, but there is work in progress to promote its use.

Tandia **[353]** Indonesia: Irian Jaya, Bird's Head neck area just south of Wandamen Peninsula. EMP, South Halmahera-West New Guinea. Cenderawasih Bay Section. Had two elderly speakers in 1991, but is now probably extinct with the speakers shifting to the Wandamen language.

Tanema **[354]** Solomon Islands: Temotu Province, Vanikoro Island. EMPCE, Santa Cruz, Vanikoro. Old people remember a few words. The ethnic group numbers 150. The speakers shifted to Solomon Pijin or the EMPCE Buma (or Teanu) language, the main language of Vanikoro. Recently extinct.

Tarpia (or ***Sufrai***) **[356]** Indonesia: Irian Jaya. Spoken in the northeastern coast area of Irian Jaya, west of Sentani Lake. CEMP, EMPW, Sarmi-Yotafa. For structural notes see the ***Anus*** entry. No literacy in it. In 1978, 564 speakers were reported, but now it is much less. It has been under pressure from the neighbouring large TNGP Papuan language Sentani, and especially from Indonesian. It is now endangered.

Taulil **[357]** Papua New Guinea: East New Britain Province, Gazelle Peninsula. Spoken in the northern central part of the Gazelle Peninsula, EP, New Britain, Baining-Taulil Family. For structural notes see the ***Kuot*** entry. In 1982, 826 speakers were reported, and recent estimates mention about 800. The speakers are bilingual in the very large CEMP, EMPW Tolai (or Kuanua) language, which puts pressure on Taulil. It is now potentially endangered.

Tause (or ***Doa***, or ***Darha***) **[358]** Indonesia: Irian Jaya. Spoken northeast of the juncture of the Tariku (Dou) and Muyabe (Fou) rivers, north of the upper Rouffaer River, around Deraposi, in the western central part of non-peninsular Irian Jaya. Geelvinck Bay Phylum, Lakes Plain, Tariku, West. For structural notes see the ***Awera*** entry. No literacy in it. In 1993, 350 speakers were reported. Bilingualism in Fayu is present especially with the young generation, and pressure is exerted upon the language by it. No Indonesian spoken. The language is in the process of becoming potentially endangered.

Taworta **[359]** Indonesia: Irian Jaya. Spoken on the south side of the lower Idenburg River, east of Taive, in the western central part of non-peninsular Irian Jaya. Geelvinck Bay Phylum, Lakes Plain, East Lakes Plain. For structural notes see the ***Awera*** entry. No literacy in it. In 1993, 150 speakers were reported. Under some pressure from Indonesian. It is beginning to become potentially endangered.

Te Parau Tinito **[not mapped]** French Polynesia: Tahiti. A pidgin Tahitian which has been predominantly spoken by Chinese living in Tahiti, especially in the capital Papeete. 'Tinito' is the Tahitian word for 'Chinese', and 'te parau' means 'the speech'. It has been receding before standard Tahitian and French, and is today only spoken by elderly Chinese. It is seriously endangered.

Teanu (or ***Buma***) **[360]** Solomon Islands, Santa Cruz Archipelago, northeastern Vanikoro Island. CEMP, EMPCE, Santa Cruz, Vanikoro. Structurally similar to what is

541

detailed in the *Anus* entry. Some literacy in it. In 1989, 350 speakers including 170 adults were reported. Recent reports mention only sixty speakers including twenty children. Their second language is Solomon Pijin, to which the speakers have been shifting. The language is now endangered.

Tenis (or ***Tench***) **[361]** Papua New Guinea: New Ireland Province, Tench Island. CEMP, EMPW, New Ireland, Tolai. For structural notes see the *Anus* entry. No literacy in it. In 1972, forty-nine speakers were reported. There still may be about forty speakers. All are highly bilingual in Mussau-Emira, which puts pressure on it, with speakers shifting to it. The language is now seriously endangered.

Ternateño **[not mapped]** Indonesia: North Maluku, on Ternate Island, west of Halmahera Island. It is a Portuguese-based creole, with Spanish lexicon. Extinct for quite some time.

Te'un **[362]** Indonesia: Maluku (south central). Now spoken in a transmigration area in south and central Seram Island (originally on Te'un Island in south central Maluku). CEMP, CMP, Timor-Flores (southwest Maluku). Structurally it is as per the *Palu'e* and *Alune* entries. No literacy in it. In 1990, 1,200 speakers were reported. Now rather less. They were moved to Seram Island because of volcanic activity on Te'un Island. This transmigration put pressure on the language, as did Ambon Malay. It is now endangered.

Thao (or ***Chuihwan***, or ***Vulung***) **[363]** Taiwan. Spoken in central Taiwan, around Sun Moon Lake (Lake Jihyüeh). n-MPAUN, Paiwani group. The language is under pressure from Taiwanese Chinese (Minnan), and most of its speakers have shifted to it. The language has focussing syntax and verb structure. See the *Nataoran* entry for details. No literacy in it. Moribund. A few old speakers out of an ethnic group of 300.

Thayore (or ***Kuuk Thaayoorre***) **[364]** Australia: northern QLD, inland from the midwestern coast of Cape York Peninsula, between Edward River and Coleman River, inland from Edward River settlement. PNY, Paman, Western Pama. For structural information see the *Adynyamathanha* entry. Some literacy in it. In 1991, 150 speakers were reported, out of an ethnic group of 350. The number of speakers has been going down slowly. The language is endangered.

Thaypan **[not mapped]** Australia: QLD, central Cape York Peninsula, Coleman River. PNY, Paman, Rarmul Pama. Recently extinct.

Thurawal (or ***Dharawal***) **[not mapped]** Australia: NSW, southern coast, around Wollongong, Nowra and inland to Bowral. Lower Shoalhaven River. PNY, Yuin-Kuric, Yuin. Recently extinct.

Tialo (or ***Tomini***) **[365]** Indonesia: Sulawesi, on the south coast of the northeastern peninsula of Sulawesi, in its extreme western part where it joins the narrow neck which links the peninsula to the bulk of Sulawesi. One part of Tialo is spoken east of Tomini town, the other to the west of Moutong town. WMP, Sulawesi, Central Sulawesi, Tomini. Structurally it corresponds to the Southern Sulawesi type (see *Bahonsuai*). No literacy in it. The total of its speakers is now about 30,000. In 1992, it was reported to be 42,000. There are very large transmigration projects right behind many Tialo villages, with the transmigrants outnumbering the Tialo. So far, this pattern of settlement has not affected Tialo language usage very much, but is likely to do so with improved transportation facilities. Tialo is to be regarded as potentially endangered.

Tjurruru **[not mapped]** Australia: northwestern WA, inland from Exmouth Gulf, on Hardey River, southwest of Tom Price. PNY, South-West, Inland Ngayarda. Extinct for some time.

Tobada' (or ***Bada***) **[not mapped]** Indonesia: Sulawesi. On the headwaters of the Budong-Budong River, in the central northeastern part of the main body of Sulawesi. WMP, Sulawesi, South Sulawesi. There was one speaker of it in 1985, but it is now extinct. The ethnic group of 1,000–2000 has switched to the neighbouring Topoiyo language. Extinct.

Tobati (or ***Yotafa***) **[366]** Indonesia: Irian Jaya. Spoken in Jayapura Bay, close to Jayapura, the capital of Irian Jaya, especially southeast of it. CEMP, EMPW, Sarmi-Yotafa. For structural notes see the ***Anus*** entry. No literacy in it. In 1975, 2,462 speakers were reported, but now there are less than 100. It has been under very great pressure from Indonesian, due to its closeness to the capital. It is now seriously endangered.

Tobian (or ***Tobi***, or ***Hatobohei***) **[not mapped]** on Tobi (or Hatobohei) Island in Palau (the Republic of Belau). CEMP, EMP, Oceanic, remote Oceanic, Micronesian. For structural information see the ***Nauru*** entry. No literacy in it. In 1995, twenty-two or more speakers were reported. The language is seriously endangered.

Tofamna **[367]** Indonesia: Irian Jaya. Spoken in a village about 100km south-southwest of Jayapura just east of the Nawa River, just north ot its junction with the Upper Idenburg River, in northeastern Irian Jaya. P, TNGP, Tofamna. Little is known about its structure, but what is known, agrees with the TNGP type (see the ***Damal*** entry) in general. No literacy in it. In 1993, about 100 speakers were reported. It is geographically close to the larger Kaure language, and may be under pressure from it and perhaps from Indonesian. It may be on the way to become potentially endangered.

Tolomako **[368]** Vanuatu. Spoken on central northern Santo, around the southern coast of Big Bay. CEMP, EMPCE, remote Oceanic, North and Central Vanuatu, West Santo. For structural information see the **Anus** entry. Some literacy in it. In 1983, 450 speakers were reported. The number of speakers may be little less today, but the children are beginning not to learn the language. It is beginning to be potentially endangered.

Tomadino **[369]** Indonesia: Sulawesi. Spoken on the northern part of the east coast of the southeastern peninsula of Sulawesi near Bungku town. WMP, Sulawesi, Central Sulawesi, Bungku-Mori. Structurally, it corresponds to the Southern Sulawesi type (see ***Bahonsuai***). No literacy in it. In 1991, 600 speakers were reported. People tend to use the large Bungku language as mother tongue and are shifting to it. The language is endangered.

Tombelala **[370]** Indonesia: Sulawesi. Spoken on the far northern parts of the east coast of the southeastern peninsula of Sulawesi. WMP, Sulawesi, Central Sulawesi, Kaili-Pamona. Structurally, it corresponds to the Southern Sulawesi type (see ***Bahonsuai***). No literacy in it. In 1995, 1,100 speakers were reported. Indonesian is much used as a second language and puts pressure on it, and the Tombelala consider themselves as Pamona who speak the large Pamona language, though Tombelala has only 66–76 per cent lexical similarity to the various Pamona dialects. The language is potentially endangered.

Toratán (or ***Ratahan***) **[371]** Indonesia: Sulawesi. Spoken in the northeastern section of the northern peninsula of Sulawesi, extending to the southern coast of the northern peninsula. WMP, Sulawesi, Sangir-Minahasan, Sangiric. It is located in the middle of the Minahasa region, but belongs to the Sangiric languages. Structurally it has focussing syntax and verb structure. See the ***Nataoran*** entry for details. It has some syntactic features differing from that language type as also represented by Philippine languages, and has an elaborate system of spatial demonstrative. There is some literacy in it. In 1989, 30,000 Toratán were reported, which was probably the ethnic group. A report from 1999 estimates that there are only 500 good speakers, most of them over sixty years old, and a few thousand semi-speakers. The language is evidently on the way to being seriously endangered from pressure of Minahasan languages surrounding it.

Totoli (or ***Tolitoli***, or ***Gage***) **[372]** Indonesia: Sulawesi, in the extreme western part of the northern peninsula of Sulawesi, on the western coast above the northern end of the narrow neck connecting Northern Sulawesi with the central bulk of Sulawesi, near Tolitoli and further north. WMP, Sulawesi, Central Sulawesi, Tomini. Structurally, it corresponds to the Southern Sulawesi type (see ***Bahonsuai***). No literacy in it. In 1991, the ethnic group was reported to be 28,000 in twenty-nine villages or parts of villages; in 1996 it was about 25,000 in fewer villages, with four of these about 80km northeast of Tolitoli town. That town of more than 30,000 inhabitants consists of four villages, with less than half of the inhabitants ethnic Totoli in three of them. In the fourth village, the language is in part still used as everyday language, but quite a few of the young people from it received university education outside, and often got government jobs. Their daily language is Indonesian. Many of them return regularly to that village and influence language use there. In the other villages of Tolitoli, most fluent speakers of Totoli are over fifty. The Totoli language is definitely endangered there. The same is the case in six other villages in the Tolitoli plain, outside the town of Tolitoli, where under the influence of outsiders, the Totoli speakers shift to Indonesian. However, the four Totoli villages 80km northeast have no space for new migrants to settle there, and not many children go to towns for education. There Totoli is safe now, but potentially endangered.

Tuamotuan (or ***Pa'umotu***) **[not mapped]** French Polynesia: Tuamotuan Islands. CEMP, EMP, Oceanic, remote Oceanic, Polynesian (Eastern). For structural information see the ***Maori*** entry. There is no literacy in it. In 1987, 14,400 speakers were reported of whom 8,000 to 9,000 were on Tuamotuan Islands, and over 2,000 in Tahiti. The speaker numbers are likely to be considerably lower today. Bilingualism in Tahitian is widespread, and many speakers have been shifting to it. It is now endangered.

Tubuai-Rurutu (or *Austral*) **[not mapped]** French Polynesia: Austral Islands. CEMP, EMP, Oceanic, remote Oceanic, Polynesian (Eastern). For structural notes see the *Maori* entry. There is no literacy in it. In 1987, 8,000 speakers were reported. There is extensive bilingualism in Tahitian, and there is a tendency of speakers to shift to it. It is now endangered.

Turaka **[373]** Papua New Guinea: Milne Bay Province. Spoken inland, west of the central coast of Goodenough Bay, on the southernmost arm of the Ruaba River, a few kilometres south of Ruaba. P, TNGP, Eastern TNGP, Dagan Family. For structural notes see the *Koiari* entry. No literacy in it. In 1981, thirty-five speakers were reported. There are still about thirty speakers now, but the language is under pressure from large neighbouring related languages, especially the Daga language. It is now seriously endangered.

Tutuba **[374]** Vanuatu. Spoken on Tutuba Island off the southeastern coast of Santo. CEMP, EMPCE, remote Oceanic, North and Central Vanuatu, West Santo. For structural information see the *Anus* entry. No literacy in it. In 1983, 150 speakers were reported. Today there may be about 120 speakers, and the children are beginning not to learn the language. Tutuba is potentially endangered.

Tyaraity (or *Djeradj*) **[not mapped]** Australia: NT, originally southwest of Darwin, at the mouth of the Reynolds River. Later at Delissavile, NT. Daly, Malagmalag. Recently extinct?

Uhunduni **[375]** Indonesia: Irian Jaya. Spoken in the central highlands of Irian Jaya, around Mt Jaya. About 14,000 active speakers in 1991. See the *Damal* entry. Uhunduni shows signs of becoming potentially endangered.

Ujir (or *Udjir*) **[376]** Indonesia: southern Maluku (Aru Islands). Spoken on Ujir Island in the northwest corner of the Aru Islands, and on the end of the western peninsula on Wokam Island there. CEMP, CMP, Southeast Maluku. Structurally it corresponds to what is said in the *Palu'e* and *Alune* entries. No literacy in it. In 1995, 975 speakers were reported. Their number is decreasing, and language use is declining because of the influence of Malay used by an increasing number of outsiders. The language is now endangered.

Umbindhamu **[not mapped]** Australia: QLD, northern Cape York Peninsula, north of Coen. PNY, Paman, Lamalamic. Recently extinct?

Umbugarla **[not mapped]** Australia: NT, east of Darwin, between Mary River and South Alligator River. Related to Bugunidja and Ngurmbur (or Ngumbur). Recently extinct.

Umbuygamu **[not mapped]** Australia: QLD, northern Cape York Peninsula, east coast of Princess Charlotte Bay. PNY, Paman, Lamalamic. Recently extinct?

Umpila **[377]** Australia: northern QLD, coastal northeastern Cape York Peninsula. PNY, Paman, Northeastern Pama. For structural information see the *Adynyamathanha* entry. No literacy in it. In 1981, possibly 100 speakers were reported. Today only a few older people know the language well, the middle generation has a varying proficiency, and the young generation speaks Torres Strait Creole (or Broken). The language is seriously endangered and moving towards being moribund.

Unserdeutsch (or *Rabaul Creole German*) **[not mapped]** Papua New Guinea. It is a creolized form of an originally pidgin German which developed in the Gazelle Peninsula of New Britain during German colonial times among the Catholic mixed-race community. In 1981, 100 or fewer fluent speakers were reported, of whom fifteen were in New Britain, a few in other parts of Papua New Guinea, and the rest in southeastern Queensland, Australia. There are much fewer speakers today because of intermarriage and increased mobility. Most of the speakers are past middle age, though there are still younger members of the community who can understand it. All speakers are fluent in at least two other languages, i.e. standard German, English or Tok Pisin. Some also speak the large local EMP, EMPW, Oceanic language Tolai (or Kuanua). Unserdeutsch is now seriously endangered.

Ura **[378]** Vanuatu: South Vanuatu, northern part of Erromanga Island. CEMP, EMPCE, South Vanuatu. The South Vanuatuan languages are much more complicated than the other EMPCE languages in their structures. For instance, verbs have different verb stems in different tenses, the person and number of the object are indicated by complicated suffix systems and there are large-scale sound changes in the inflexion which veil the grammatical forms. There is no literacy in Ura. In 1977, ten or fewer speakers were reported. Recent reports mention seven aged speakers. The language succumbed to pressure from its much larger southern neighbour, the related Erromanga language. It is moribund.

Uradhi **[not mapped]** Australia: QLD, northeast Cape York Peninsula, North Alice Creek. PNY, Paman, Northern Pama. Recently extinct.

Urningangg **[not mapped]** Australia: NT, northwestern Arnhem Land, upper reaches of East Alligator River. Mangerrian, Urninganggic. Recently extinct?

Uruava **[379]** Papua New Guinea: North Solomons Province, on the northeastern coast of Bougainville Island. EMPW, Bougainville. Had five or fewer speakers in 1977. Now probably extinct.

Usku **[380]** Indonesia: Irian Jaya. Spoken in a village about 50km south of Jayapura. P, TNGP, Usku. Little is known about its structure, but it does seem to correspond in part to the TNGP type (see the *Damal* entry). No literacy in it. Information concerning the number of speakers is contradictory, and ranges from 160 (1991, which may be the ethnic group or the population of the village), to as low as twenty. The language seems to be under great pressure from Indonesian, and is considered to be seriously endangered by Indonesian linguists.

Uya (or *Usu* or *Sausi*) **[381]** Papua New Guinea: Madang Province. Spoken on the Upper Ramu River, about 40km southwest of the westernmost point of the Astrolabe Bay, near Koropa. A dialect of the Sausi language. P, TNGP, Madang, Evapia Family. It is TNGP (see the *Damal* entry). No literacy in it. In 1987, ninety-three speakers were reported. That figure is still valid, but the dialect is under pressure from the main part of the Sausi language. It is now endangered.

Vamale* [382]** New Caledonia. Spoken on the northeastern coast, a third of the length of New Caledonia from its northwestern end, around Téganpaik. CEMP, EMPCE, New Caledonian, Northern. For structural notes see the ***Arhö entry. No literacy in it. In 1982, 150 speakers were reported. Now they are considerably less, with virtually no children speakers. The language is under pressure from the large neighbouring New Caledonian languages Fwâi and Cemuhi, and from French. It is now endangered.

***Vano* [not mapped]** Solomon Islands: Temotu Province, Vanikoro Island. EMPCE, Santa Cruz, Vanikoro. Old people remember a few words. The ethnic group numbers 120. The speakers shifted to Solomon Pijin or the Buma (or Teanu) language. Recently extinct.

Vehes (or ***Buasi***) **[383]** Papua New Guinea: Morobe Province. Spoken inland from the westernmost extremity of the Huon Gulf. CEMP, EMPW, Markham Family, Buang. See the ***Anus*** entry for structural notes. No literacy in it. In 1978, 100 speakers were reported. This is likely to be less today. The language is under pressure from the large languages Buang Mapos and Buang Mangga, which are its northern and southwestern neighbours and to which it is related, and from Tok Pisin. It is now endangered.

***Waamwang* [not mapped]** New Caledonia: in northwestern New Caledonia. EMPCE, Oceanic, New Caledonian, Northern. Extinct for several decades.

Waanyi (or ***Wanji***) **[384]** Australia: extreme northwestern corner of QLD in the Nicholson River area, to the west of Doomadgee, and overlapping into extreme northeastern NT. Garawan, Waanyi. For structural information, see the ***Jawoyn*** entry. No literacy in it. In 1981, perhaps ten speakers were reported. Today there are two semi-speakers, and a full speaker has recently been discovered in the extreme south-western corner of QLD, more than 1,200 km south of his homeland. The language is moribund.

Wab (or ***Som***) **[385]** Papua New Guinea: Madang Province. Spoken on the north coast of the Huon Peninsula, near Saidor. CEMP, EMPW, Siassi languages. For structural notes, see the ***Anus*** entry. No literacy in Wab. In 1977, 142 speakers were reported. There may be fewer today, because the language is under pressure from the neighbouring larger closely related Biliau (or Awad Bing) language, and especially from Tok Pisin because of its nearness to Saidor. It is at least potentially endangered.

***Wadjalang* [not mapped]** Australia: southern central QLD, on the uppermost Bulloo River, north of Quilpie. PNY, Maric, Mari. Extinct for some time.

Wadjiginy (or ***Wagaydy***) **[386]** Australia: northwestern NT, southwest of Darwin along the coast and inland along the Finniss River, Daly, Bringen-Wagaydy. For structural information see the ***Jawoyn*** entry. No literacy in it. In 1988, twelve fluent speakers were reported. The members of the ethnic group understand the language when old

547

people speak it, but they only speak the English-based lingua franca Kriol. There are fewer speakers today. The language is now moribund.

Wadjigu [not mapped] Australia: eastern central QLD, southwest of Fairbairn Reservoir. PNY, Maric, Mari. Recently extinct.

Wagaya [not mapped] Australia: eastern NT, at Wonarah, east of Tennant Creek. PNY, Wagaya-Warluwaric, Wagaya. Recently extinct?

Wageman (or ***Wagiman***) [387] Australia: northern NT, northwest of Katherine, in the upper Daly River area, and at Pine Creek. Gunwinyguan, Yangmanic. For structural information see the ***Jawoyn*** entry. No literacy in it. In 1983, perhaps fifty speakers were reported. The use of the English-based pidgin lingua franca Kriol has been increasing, and the speakers have become much fewer. The language is now seriously endangered.

Waima'a [388] Indonesia: East Timor. Spoken inland from the northeastern coast of East Timor Island. CEMP, CMP, Waima'a. It is the major language of the Waima'a group to which also Habu and Kairui-Midiki belong. What is said in the ***Habu*** entry about its structure and mixed nature, applies fully to Waima'a. No literacy in it. In 1981, about 3,000 speakers were reported. It is under pressure from the neighbouring Papuan Timor-Alor-Pantar languages, especially Makasai. It is now potentially endangered.

Wakawaka (or ***Wakka***) [not mapped] Australia. The Wagawaga dialect was located in southeastern QLD, 200km inland from the southern end of Fraser Island. PNY, Waka-Kabic, Miyan, Waka. It has been extinct for decades. For the Duungidjawu dialect, see the ***Duungidjawu*** entry.

Walmajarri (or ***Walmatjari***) [389] Australia: northwestern WA, in the area along the Fitzroy River valley, at Lake Gregory and La Grange. PNY, South-West, Ngumbin. For structural information see the ***Adynyamathanha*** entry. Some literacy in it. In 1990, 1,000 speakers were reported. Some children still understand and respond to Walmajarri today, but the first language of all children is the English-based pidgin lingua franca Kriol. The language is beginning to become endangered.

Wambaya [390] Australia: northern NT, Barkly Tableland, headwaters of the Limmen Bight and McArthur Rivers, and east of Lake Woods. West Barkly, Wambayan. For structural information see the ***Djingili*** entry. No literacy in it. In 1983, up to eighty speakers were reported, which may have been excessive. The second language of the Wambaya is the English-based pidgin lingua franca Kriol. The number of speakers is very low now, only two or three. The language is moribund.

Wamin [not mapped] Australia: northern QLD, in central base of Cape York Peninsula, northwest of Einasleigh. PNY, Paman, Southern Pama. Recently extinct.

Wandarang [not mapped] Australia: NT, southwestern Arnhem Land, between Rose River and Phelp River, near Numbulwar. Maran, Mara. Extinct for some time. Speakers shifted to Kriol, the English-based Pidgin creole language.

Wangaaybuwan-Ngiyambaa (or ***Wongaibon-Ngiyambaa***) **[392]** Australia: northwestern NSW, southeast of the Darling River, on the Barwon and Bogan Rivers. PNY, Wiradhuric, Gamilaraayic. For structural information see the ***Adynyamathanha*** entry. No literacy in it. In 1981, perhaps twelve speakers were reported. Now there are very few left. The language is moribund.

Wanggamala **[not mapped]** Australia: southeastern corner of the NT, Hay River. PNY, Karnic, Palku. Recently extinct.

Wanggumara **[not mapped]** Australia: southwestern corner of QLD, northwest from Thargomindah. PNY, Karnic, Ngura. Closely related to Garlali. Recently extinct.

Wangkangurru **[393]** Australia: southeastern corner of the NT. PNY, Karnic, Arabana-Wangkangurru. For structural information see the ***Adynyamathanha*** entry. Very closely related to Arabana. The two can be regarded as dialects of one language. No literacy in it. In 1981, eight speakers were reported. Today, only one or two are left. If Wangkangurru and Arabana are regarded as dialects of one language, it would have less than half a dozen speakers. Moribund.

Wanman (or ***Warnman***) **[394]** Australia: northern WA, Marble Bar area. PNY, Southwest, Wati. In 1973, twenty speakers were reported. The people generally speak English, or the closely related large language Martu Wanka, or the large also related language Nyangumarta. This puts pressure on Wanman, and the speaker number is considerably lower today. It is seriously endangered.

Wano **[395]** Indonesia: Irian Jaya. Spoken in the central highlands area, on the Upper Tariku (Dou) River which is there known as the Yamo River. Lingua franca and trade language in the area. P, TNGP, Dani-Kwerba, Dani, southern section. For structural notes see the ***Isirawa*** entry. There is some literacy in Wano. In 1993, 3,500 speakers were reported. Wano is under pressure from the neighbouring very large Western Dani language, and is also losing its trade language status. Indonesian is also beginning to play a role. Wano is now potentially endangered.

Warapu **[396]** Papua New Guinea: Sandaun Province. Spoken on a part of the northwestern coast of Papua New Guinea on the northwest peninsula of the Sissano lagoon which is between Vanimo and Aitape. Sko Phylum, Krisa Family. Sko languages are tonal, with tonal morphological processes. Pronoun systems are elaborate, with various combinations of the sex of persons referred to expressed through different forms. With verbs, only a masculine-feminine contrast is found with verbal subject prefixes. Verb inflection is very complicated. There is no literacy in Warapu. In 1983, 1,602 speakers were reported, including 442 non-residents. Language use was vigorous then. However, in November 1998, the terrible tsunami mentioned in the Sissano entry, almost completely annihilated the population in the disaster area and there were hardly any Warapu speaking survivors in that area, and almost the only Warapu speakers were those who were absent from the area, i.e. non-resident speakers living elsewhere. Their number may be a few hundred. The language is now endangered, or even seriously endangered in view of the scattered nature of the surviving Warapu speakers.

549

Waray (or *Warrai*) [not mapped] Australia: NT, western Arnhem Land, upper Adelaide River area, at Adelaide River township. (Gunwinyguan?). Warayan. *Family-level isolate.* Recently extinct?

Wardaman (or *Wadaman*) [397] Australia: northern NT, upper Daly River. Gunwinyguan, Yangmanic. For structural information see the *Jawoyn* entry. No literacy in it. In 1983, perhaps fifty speakers were reported. The Wardaman generally speak the English-based pidgin lingua franca Kriol. The number of speakers is lower now. The language is endangered and is moving towards being seriously endangered.

Wari (or *Weretai*) [398] Indonesia: Irian Jaya. Spoken on the Lakes Plain near Taive, on a southern tributary of the lower Idenburg River which joins the latter about 10km east of where the Rouffaer River joins the Idenburg River. Geelvinck Bay Phylum, Lakes Plain, Tariku, East. For structural notes see the *Awera* entry. No literacy in it. There are conflicting reports of the number of its speakers, which range from 50–75 to about 300 (1993). The language is under pressure from Indonesian, especially the children. It is now getting endangered.

Wariyangga [not mapped] Australia: WA, West Pilbara, Walburg Range, east of Mount Augustus. PNY, South-West, inland Ngayarda (or Mantharda group). Extinct for several decades.

Warlmanpa (or *Walmala*) [399] Australia: northwestern WA, near the NT border. Mt Leichhardt area. PNY, South-West, Ngarga. For structural information, see the *Adynyamathanha* entry. No literacy in it. In 1981, perhaps fifty speakers were reported. The people generally speak the English-based pidgin lingua franca Kriol to which speakers are shifting. The number of speakers is lower today. The language is endangered and becoming seriously endangered.

Warluwara [not mapped] Australia: extreme western central QLD on Georgina River, at Urandangi. PNY, Wagaya-Warluwaric, Warluwara-Thawa. Recently extinct.

Warrgamay [not mapped] Australia: northeastern QLD coast at Ingham and on lower Herbert River. PNY, Dyirbalic. Recently extinct.

Warrungu (or *Warungu*) [not mapped] Australia: northeastern QLD, just south of the southeastern base of Cape York Peninsula. Northeast of Einasleigh. PNY, Maric, Mari. Recently extinct. There are attempts at reviving it.

Waru (or *Mopute*) [400] Indonesia: Sulawesi. Spoken in the hinterland of the northern part of the east coast of the southeastern peninsula of Sulawesi, not far from Bungku town. WMP, Sulawesi, Central Sulawesi, Bungku-Mori. Structurally, it corresponds to the Southern Sulawesi type (see *Bahonsuai*). No literacy in it. In 1991, 350 speakers were reported. Under pressure from larger neighbouring languages and Indonesian. It is potentially endangered.

Warumungu (or *Warramunga*) [401] Australia: central NT, Tennant Creek area. PNY, Warumungic. For structural information see the *Adynyamathanha* entry. No literacy in it. In 1983, 200 speakers were reported. The people generally speak the English-based pidgin lingua franca Kriol, which the children prefer and some speak as first language. The language is heading towards being endangered.

Warwa [not mapped] Australia: northwestern WA, around the mouth of the Fitzroy River, Derby area. Nyulnyulan. Extinct for some time.

Watjari [402] Australia: western central WA, northeast of Geraldton, Mt Magnet to Geraldton. PNy, South-west, Watjari. For structural information see the *Adynyamathanha* entry. No literacy in it. In 1981, fifty or fewer fluent speakers were reported out of an ethnic group of fewer than 200. The people generally speak English, and the number of speakers is considerably lower today. The language is endangered and moving towards being seriously endangered.

Wembawemba (dialects) [not mapped] Australia: most of western Victoria, including the Melbourne area, and extending into southwestern New South Wales in the Swan Hill area. The main dialect, called Wembawemba, was spoken in the Lake Hindmarsh area in far western Victoria, and also in the Swan Hill area. PNy, Kulinic, Kulin. For general structural features see the *Adynyamathanha* entry, but it has aberrant features such as pronouns consisting of bases to which possessive suffixes indicating the person are added. Verbs have subject and object suffixes whose forms change extensively when they are combined with each other. There is no literacy in it. Some knowledge of the language survived with some former speakers until less than three decades ago. It is now extinct.

Wergaia [not mapped] Australia: northwestern Victoria from Dimboola to Lake Hindmarsh and Lake Albacuyta along the Wimmera River, and from Yanac to Warracknabeal. PNy, Kulin, Kulinic. The last fluent speaker died in 1954. Extinct for close to half a century.

Wetamut [405] Vanuatu: southeastern part of Santa Maria (or Gaua) Island in the Banks Islands. CEMP, EMPCE, remote Oceanic, North and Central Vanuatu. Structurally similar to what has been said in the *Anus* entry. No literacy in it. In 1970, seventy speakers were reported. They may well be fewer today. The language has been under pressure from larger related languages on the island, in particular from the Lakona and Nume languages. It is now endangered.

Wikalkan (or *Wikngatara*, or *Wik-Ngatharra*) [406] Australia: northern QLD, northwestern coastal Cape York Peninsula, south of Aurukun. PNy, Paman, Middle Pama. For structural information see the *Adynyamathanha* entry. No literacy in it. In 1981, eighty-six speakers were reported. The young generation speaks the large neighbouring closely related lingua franca Wik-Munkan, which puts pressure on Wikalkan. There are fewer speakers today, and the language is endangered.

Wik-Epa [not mapped] Australia: QLD, northern Cape York Peninsula, southeast of Aurukun. PNy, Paman, Middle Pama. Recently extinct.

Wik-Iiyanh [407] Australia: northern QLD, northern central Cape York Peninsula, southwest of Coen. PNy, Paman, Middle Pama. For structural information see the

Adynyamathanha entry. No literacy in it. In 1981, forty speakers were reported. The large related lingua franca Wik-Munkan exerts pressure on it. There are fewer speakers today. The language is getting seriously endangered.

***Wik-Keyagan* [not mapped]** Australia: QLD, northern Cape York Peninsula, southeast of Aurukun. PNY, Paman, Middle Pama. Recently extinct.

***Wik-Me'anha* [408]** Australia: northern QLD, northwestern Cape York Peninsula, southeast of Aurukun. PNY, Paman, Middle Pama. For structural information see the *Adynyamathanha* entry. No literacy in it. In 1981, twelve speakers were reported. Today the speakers are fewer. The language is moribund.

***Wik-Ngathana* [409]** Australia: northern QLD, northwest coast of Cape York Peninsula, below Aurukun. PNY, Paman, Middle Pama. For structural information see the *Adynyamathanha* entry. No literacy in it. In 1981, 126 speakers were reported. There is pressure on the language from the large neighbouring closely related lingua franca Wik-Munkan. The number of speakers is less now. The language is potentially endangered.

***Wikngenchera* (or *Ngandjara*, or *Nantjara*, or *Kugu Nganchara*) [410]** Australia: northern QLD, northwest coast of Cape York Peninsula, south of Aurukun. PNY, Paman, Middle Pama. For structural information see the *Adynyamathanha* entry. No literacy in it. In 1970, fifty speakers were reported. Now all young people speak the large closely related lingua franca Wik-Mungkan. All adults are bilingual in it. Under pressure from it, the number of speakers has dropped significantly. The language is now seriously endangered.

***Wilawila* [not mapped]** Australia: WA, central Kimberleys. Wororan, Ungarinjic. Recently extinct.

***Wiradhuri* [not mapped]** Australia: southeastern inland NSW. From Murray River northwards, to Murrumbidgee River and Lachlan River, and further north beyond Dubbo. PNY, Wiradhuric. Recently extinct? Attempts at partial revival.

***Wirangu* [411]** Australia: central western SA, from coast between Streaky Bay and Yalata, and north to Ooldea region. PNY, South-West, Wati. For structural information, see the *Adynyamathanha* entry. No literacy in it. In 1981, perhaps two speakers were reported. Today there are only two semi-speakers left. Moribund, nearly extinct.

***Woria* [412]** Indonesia: Irian Jaya. Spoken by very few in Botawa village, inland from the middle of the east coast of Cenderawasih Bay. Geelvinck Bay Phylum, East Geelvinck Bay. For structural notes see the *Awera* entry. No literacy in it. In 1987, twelve speakers were reported. There are probably fewer now. The languages of the village is the Geelvinck Bay Phylum, East Geelvinck Bay, Demisa language, and the large CEMP, EMP, SHWNG Waropen language, which both put pressure on it. It is now moribund, almost extinct.

***Worimi* (or *Warrimi*, or *Kattang* or *Gadhang*) [not mapped]** Australia: central coast of NSW, from Forster inland to Maitland. PNY, Yuin-Kuric, Kuri. Recently extinct.

Worora (or *Worrorran*) **[413]** Australia: northwestern WA, Kimberleys, Derby area, Colier Bay. Wororan, Wororic. For structural information, see the *Jawoyn* entry. One peculiarity of the Wororan languages is that the classes in their class systems are indicated by suffixes, not by prefixes. Some literacy in it. In 1990, twenty fluent speakers were reported. In 1983, 150 second-language speakers were reported, reflecting the former status of Worora as a lingua franca. Many of the speakers were, and are even more today, bilingual in English, Aboriginal English, or the English-based pidgin lingua franca Kriol. Some children know a little of the language. There are fewer speakers today, and the language is seriously endangered.

Wotu **[414]** Indonesia: Sulawesi. Spoken on the south coast at the extreme northern part of Bone Bay which separates the southern and southeastern peninsulas of Sulawesi around Wotu town. WMP, Sulawesi, Muna-Buton. Structurally, it corresponds to the Southern Sulawesi type (see *Bahonsuai*). Some limited literacy in it. In 1987, 5,000 speakers were reported; there may be less now. The Luwu dialect of the very large Bugis language is dominant in the area and puts pressure on it, as does Indonesian. The language is potentially endangered.

Wuliwuli **[not mapped]** Australia: southeastern QLD, inland from Bundaberg, on Dawson River, around Theodore, Banana and Baralaba. PNy, Waka-Kabic, Miyan. Extinct for several decades.

Wulna **[not mapped]** Australia: NT, Arnhem Land around Darwin, mouth of Adelaide River and inland. Laragiyan. Recently extinct.

Wunambal (or *Unambal*) **[415]** Australia: northwestern WA, Kimberley, Mowanjum, Wyndham and Kalumburu. Wororan, Wunambalic. For structural information, see the *Jawoyn* and *Worora* entries. No literacy in it. In 1990, twenty speakers were reported. People generally speak the English-based pidgin lingua franca Kriol. Some children know a little of the language, but most speak Kriol, Aboriginal English or standard English as their mother tongue. The number of speakers is lower now. The language is seriously endangered and heading towards being moribund.

Yabula-Yabula **[not mapped]** Australia: NSW and Victoria border area, on both sides of the Murray River, to the north of the Yorta-Yorta language area (see the *Yorta-Yorta* entry). PNy, Yota-Yotic. Extinct early in the twentieth century, but in living memory.

Yagara **[not mapped]** Australia: southeastern corner of QLD, south of Brisbane, south to Gold Coast, inland almost as far as Toowoomba and Warwick. PNy, Durrubulic. Extinct for over four decades.

Yalarnnga **[not mapped]** Australia: northwestern QLD, south of Mt Isa, around Dajarra. PNy, Galgadungic-Yalarnngic. Extinct for decades.

Yandruwandha **[not mapped]** Australia: northeastern SA, around Moomba, and extending into Queensland. PNy, Karnic, Karna. Recently extinct. Old people remember some words.

553

Yangkal [not mapped] Australia: northwest corner of QLD, Carpentaria Gulf coast, and Forsyth Island. PNY, Tangkic. Very closely related to Kayardild and Yukulta. Some old people have a passive knowedge of it, but it is now practically extinct.

Yangman [416] Australia: northern NT, at Elsey Creek (an upper tributary of the Roper River), southeast of Katherine, and at Katherine itself. Gunwinyguan, Yangmanic, Nolgin. For structural information see the *Jawoyn* entry. Yangman is a tonal language like Alawa and Mangarayi. No literacy in it. In 1983, ten speakers were reported, out of an ethnic group of fifty. Now the ethnic group speaks English or the English-based pidgin lingua franca Kriol. There are fewer speakers today. The language is moribund.

Yanyuwa (or *Yanyula*) [417] Australia: northeastern corner of the NT, at Borooloola, and at Doomadgee in the northwestern corner area of QLD. Regarded as a non-PNY Family isolate. Though it is a prefixing language with a multiple-classifying system with extensive concord, it has been suggested that it may be a Pama-Nyungan language. For structural information see the *Jawoyn* entry. There is some literacy in it. In 1990, 70–100 speakers were reported. The speakers are all bilingual in the English-based pidgin lingua franca Kriol or in English, and some in the neighbouring non-PNY Garawa language. Speakers intermarry with the Garawa or the also non-PNY speaking Mara. Children usually speak the mother's language, but at puberty the boys learn and afterwards speak the father's language. Through this, Yanyuwa has been losing young speakers and is now getting endangered.

Yapunda (or *Reiwo*) [418] Papua New Guinea: Sandaun Province. Spoken in the eastern part of Sandaun Province, about 40km south-southeast of Aitape, on the upper Om River. P, TRCP, Wapei Family. For structural notes see the *Arapesh*, *Bumbita* entry. No literacy in it. In 1981, sixty-nine speakers were reported. That figure is still valid, but the language is under pressure from neighbouring related larger languages, such as Aiku, its southern neighbour. It is now endangered.

Yarawi [419] Papua New Guinea: Morobe Province. May be a dialect of the one of the two P, TNGP Binanderean languages Yekora or Suena. Yekora is spoken on the central northeastern coast between Morobe town and Hercules Bay, and also inland southwest of Morobe, on the Upper Mo River at Posei, and Suena is its northwestern coastal neighbour, around Morobe. The Binanderean languages are structurally TNGP, with a few aberrant features, e.g. verb stem suppletion to indicate a change of tense. There is no literacy in Yarawi (or in Yekora). There is one surviving speaker of Yarawi now, with most speakers having shifted to Yekora. Yarawi is moribund, almost extinct.

Yardliwarra [not mapped] Australia: eastern SA, east of Lake Torrens and southwest of Lake Frome, north of Carrieton. PNY, Karnic, Yarli. Extinct for several decades.

Yarluyandi [not mapped] Australia: extreme southwestern corner of QLD and adjacent areas in northwestern SA and the extreme southeastern corner of the NT. PNY, Karnic, Palku. Extinct for several decades.

Yawarawarga [not mapped] Australia: northeastern corner of SA, overlapping into QLD. PNY, Karnic, Karna. Recently extinct.

Yawuru [not mapped] Australia: northwestern WA, south of the Kimberleys. On the coast south of Broome. Nyulnyulan. Recently extinct.

Yaygir [not mapped] Australia: far north coast of NSW, between Coffs Harbour and Yamba, east of Grafton. PNy, Yaygiran, Yaygiric. Extinct for more than four decades.

Yeidji [420] Australia: northeastern corner of WA, Kimberley, in the Wyndham area. Wororan, Wunambalic. Appears to be in a dialect chain with Miwa, Kwini, Gambera and Wunambal. For structural information, see the *Jawoyn* and *Wororan* entries. No literacy in it. In 1983, 400 or fewer speakers were reported, probably an exaggerated figure. Their number is very much smaller today, perhaps fifty or less. The English-based pidgin lingua franca and Aboriginal English and English have taken their toll, with the young generation speaking these as their mother tongue. The language is endangered and getting seriously endangered.

Yidiny (or *Yidin*) [421] Australia: northeast QLD, formerly in the Atherton region, west of Cairns, last speakers on the Palm Islands, Babinda. PNy, Yidinic. For structural information, see the *Adynyamathanha* entry. No literacy in it. In 1981, perhaps twelve speakers were reported. Now there are very few. The language is moribund.

Yilba [not mapped] Australia: northeastern inland QLD, west of the headwaters of Torrens Creek, at Torrens Creek settlement. PNy, Maric, Mari. Extinct for some time.

Yiman [not mapped] Australia: southeastern inland QLD, upper Dawson River, north of Taroom. PNy, Maric, Mari. Extinct for some time.

Yimas [422] Papua New Guinea: East Sepik Province. Spoken in the southeastern part of the East Sepik Province on the lower Arafundi River, a southern tributary of the middle Karawari River, itself a southern tributary of the middle Sepik River. SERP, Nor-Pondo, Pondo Family. See the *Murik* entry about remarks on the classification and aberrant character of the Nor-Pondo languages. The Pondo Family languages have preserved the original structural features of the Nor-Pondo languages, which are: a complex noun classification system, which involves adjectives, demonstratives, numerals, possessive pronouns, and prefixes and suffixes with the verbs which all take different markers according to the twelve classes of Yimas nouns, but it does not affect the personal pronouns, with no separate gender system present. Nouns have very irregular dual and plural forms. There is no literacy in Yimas. In 1981, 350 speakers were reported. Now there are about 300. The language is under pressure from larger related languages such as Tabriak (or Karawari), its northern neighbour, and of Tok Pisin which the young speakers tend to prefer. Yimas is now potentially endangered.

Yimas-Alamblak Trade Pidgin [not mapped] Papua New Guinea: East Sepik Province, middle Arafundi and middle Karawari Rivers. Used between Yimas village and the P. SERP, Sepik Hill, Alamblak language speaking village of Chimbut. It is very much simplified Yimas, with much of its lexicon derived from the P. SERP? Nor-Pondo, Pondo, Tabriak (or Karawari) language. There is one surviving active speaker, and several passive speakers. The language is moribund.

555

Yimas-Arafundi Trade Pidgin **[not mapped]** Papua New Guinea: East Sepik Province, middle Arafundi River area. Used between the P. SERP?, Nor-Pondo, Pondo, Yimas language speaking village of Yimas and the P, SERP, Ramu, Arafundi speaking village of Auwim. It is simplified Yimas (see the ***Yimas*** entry for the Yimas language) with lexical input from Arafundi. It has very few speakers left and is moribund.

Yimas-Iatmul Trade Pidgin **[not mapped]** Papua New Guinea: East Sepik Province, middle Arafundi and lower Sepik Rivers. Used between Yimas village and the P, SERP Sepik, Iatmul speaking villages Mindimbit and Angriman on the lower Sepik River. There is one Yimas man left with any knowledge of this language, which is in the last stage of becoming extinct.

Yimas-Tabriak (or ***Karawari***) ***Trade Pidgin*** **[not mapped]** Papua New Guinea: East Sepik Province, middle Arafundi and middle Karawari Rivers. Used between Yimas village and the Tabriak (or Karawari) speaking villages along the Karawari River. Yimas and Tabriak are closely related members of the Pondo Family of P, SERP? Nor-Pondo, Pondo. Tabriak has had an important influence on the grammar of pidginized Yimas in the Yimas-Tabriak Trade Pidgin. There are a few surviving speakers. The language is moribund.

Yindjilandji **[not mapped]** Australia: northeastern NT, Barkly Tableland, north of Avon Downs. PNY, Wagaya-Warluwaric, Warluwara-Thawa. Recently extinct.

Yinggarda **[not mapped]** Australia: WA, inland northwest of Shark Bay, between Gascoyne and Lyons Rivers. PNY, South-West, Kardu. Recently extinct?

Yir Tangedl **[not mapped]** Australia: northern QLD, inland from the mid-western coast of Cape York Peninsula, south of Coleman River. PNY, Paman, Western Pama. Recently extinct.

Yir-Yoront **[423]** Australia: northern QLD, west central Cape York Peninsula, southeast of Edward River. PNY, Paman, Western Pama. In 1991, fifteen fluent speakers and some second-language speakers were reported. Most members of the ethnic group speak Torres Strait Creole (or Broken). There are fewer speakers today. The language is seriously endangered.

Yoba **[424]** Papua New Guinea: Central Province, southeastern hinterland. EMPW, Milne Bay-Central Province, Magoric. Two non-primary speakers observed in 1970 and 1981. Now probably extinct.

Yoki **[425]** Indonesia: Irian Jaya. Spoken on the east side of the mouth of the Mamberamo River, on the western coast of non-peninsular Irian Jaya. *Unclassified*, probably a Papuan language isolate. Very little is known about its structure. No literacy in it. In 1978, forty speakers were reported. It is under pressure from the larger Warembori language of the area, which is also a Papuan language isolate. Yoki is now seriously endangered.

Yorta-Yorta (or ***Yota-Yota***, or ***Bangerang***) **[not mapped]** Australia: NSW and Victoria border area, from the junction of the Murray and Goulburn rivers, on both sides of the Murray River from west of Echuca to the east, beyond Tocumwal and Cobram, and to the southeast along the Goulburn River to the Shepparton area and further south along the Goulburn River. PNY, Yota-Yotic. Extinct for about four decades, but some vocabulary is remembered by several persons. There are attempts at reviving the language.

Yugambal (or *Yugumbal*) **[not mapped]** Australia: northeastern inland NSW, around Tenterfield. PNY, Yuin-Kuric, Kuri. Extinct for some time.

Yukulta **[not mapped]** Australia. See *Ganggalida*

Yuru **[not mapped]** Australia: northeastern coast of QLD, between Ayr and Bowen, east of the Burdekin River. PNY, Nyawaygic. Extinct for several decades.

Yuwaalaraay **[not mapped]** Australia: far northern central NSW, on Narran Lake and at Lightning Ridge, south and east to the Barwon River. PNY, Wiradhuric, Gamilaraayic. Extinct for several decades.

Yuwaaliyaay **[not mapped]** Australia: far southern central QLD, close to the NSW border, on the middle Moonie and Bokhara rivers, at Hebel, Dirranbandi and Nindigulli. PNY, Wiradhuric, Gamilaraayic. For structural information see the *Adynyamathanha* entry. No literacy in it. In 1985 three speakers were reported, now it is one, plus semi-speakers. Moribund.

Yuwibara **[426]** Australia: northeastern coastal QLD, Mackay area. PNY, Maric, Mari. Extinct for quite some time.

Yuyu **[not mapped]** Australia: extreme southeastern inland SA and in a small adjacent part of Victoria. In the Karoond and Lameroo area in SA, and the Murrayville area in Victoria. PNY, Ngarinyeric-Yithayithic. Extinct for a very considerable time, but its former existence is still in living memory.

Zazao (or *Kilokaka*) **[427]** Solomon Islands: Santa Isabel Island. Spoken on the central southwestern coast of the island. CEMP, EMPW, Santa Isabel Group. For structural notes see the *Anus* entry. No literacy in it. In 1990, 166 speakers were reported, which is about what the speaker numbers are now. Speakers are bilingual in the related large Cheke Holo (or Maringhe) and the Zabana (or Kia) languages. It is getting endangered.

Zire **[not mapped]** New Caledonia: on the central southwestern coast of New Caledonia. EMPCE, Oceanic, New Caledonian, Southern. Extinct for several decades. It is being revived, and according to recent reports thirty or so have learned it as a second language.

Sources and persons consulted for the alphabetical list of entries for threatened and extinct languages

Austin, Peter (1992) *A Dictionary of Gamilaraay, Northern New South Wales.* Melbourne: University of Melbourne.

Austin, Peter, Corinne Williams and Stephen A. Wurm (1980) 'The Linguistic Situation in North Central New South Wales'. Canberra: Pacific Linguistics Series A-59: 167–80.

Blake, Barry J. (1998) *Wathawurrung and the Colac Language of Southern Victoria*. Canberra: Pacific Linguistics Series C-147.

Bowe, Heather and Stephen Morey (1999) 'The Yorta Yorta (Bangerang) Language of the Murray Goulburn, Southeast Australia – including Yabula Yabula'. Canberra: Pacific Linguistics Series C-154.

Breen, Gavan (1990) 'Salvage Studies of Western Queensland Aboriginal Languages'. Canberra: Pacific Linguistics Series B-105.

Bright, William (ed.) (1992) *International Encyclopedia of Linguistics* (4 vols). New York/Oxford: Oxford University Press.

Capell, Arthur (1944) 'Peoples and Languages of Timor'. *Oceania* 14(3): 191–219; 14(4): 311–37; 15(1): 19–48.

Carrington, Lois (1996) 'A Linguistic Bibliography of the New Guinea Area'. Canberra: Pacific Linguistics Series D-90.

Dixon, Robert M. W. (1980) *The Languages of Australia*. Cambridge Language Surveys, Cambridge: Cambridge University Press.

Dutton, Thomas E. (1969 [reprinted 1970, 1971]) 'The Peopling of Central Papua: Some Preliminary Observations'. Canberra: Pacific Linguistics Series B-9.

——(1973) 'A Checklist of Languages and Present-day Villages of Central and South-East Mainland Papua'. Canberra: Pacific Linguistics Series B-24.

——(1975 [reprinted 1978]) 'Studies in Languages of Central and South-East Papua'. Canberra: Pacific Linguistics Series C-29.

Dutton, Thomas E. (ed.) (1992) 'Culture Change, Language Change: Case Studies from Melanesia'. Canberra: Pacific Linguistics Series C-120.

Dutton, Thomas, Malcolm Ross and Darrell Tryon (eds) (1993) 'The Language Game: Papers in Memory of Donald C. Laycock'. Canberra: Pacific Linguistics Series C-110.

Evans, Nicholas D. (1992) *Kayardild, Dictionary and Thesaurus*. Melbourne: University of Melbourne, Department of Linguistics and Language Studies.

——(1995) *A Grammar of Kayardild*. Berlin/New York: Mouton de Gruyter.

Franklin, Karl (ed.) (1975) 'The Linguistic Situation in the Gulf District and Adjacent Areas'. Canberra: Pacific Linguistics Series C-26.

Grimes, Barbara F. (ed.) (1996) *Ethnologue: Languages of the World* (13th edn.) Dallas TX: Summer Institute of Linguistics.

Grimes, Charles E., Tom Therik, Barbara Dix Grimes and Max Jacob (1997) *A Guide to the People and Languages of Nusa Tenggara*. Kupang: Artha Wacana Press.

Grimes, Joseph E. (1995) 'Language Endangerment in the Pacific'. *Oceanic Linguistics*, 34(1): 1–11.

Hercus, Luise A. (1986) 'Victorian Languages: A Late Survey'. Canberra: Pacific Linguistics Series B-77.

Himmelmann, Nikolaus P. and John U. Wolff (2000) *Toratán (Ratahan). Languages of the World/Materials 150*. Munich: Lincom Europa.

Holmer, Nils M. (1988) 'Notes on Some Queensland Languages'. Canberra: Pacific Linguistics Series D-79.

Holzknecht, Suzanne (1989) 'The Markham Languages of Papua New Guinea'. Canberra: Pacific Linguistics Series C-115.

King, Julia K. and John Wayne King (eds) (1984 [reprinted 1992, 1997]) 'Languages of Sabah: A Survey Report'. Canberra: Pacific Linguistics Series C-78.

Laycock, Donald C. (1973) 'Sepik Languages – Checklist and Preliminary Classification'. Canberra: Pacific Linguistics Series B-25.

Lynch, John (ed.) (1983) 'Studies in the Languages of Erromango'. Canberra: Pacific Linguistics Series C-79.

McElhanon, Ken A. and C. L. Voorhoeve (1978) 'The Trans-New Guinea Phylum: Explorations in Deep-level Genetic Relationships'. Canberra: Pacific Linguistics Series B-16.

McGregor, William (1988) 'Handbook of Kimberley Languages, vol. I: General Information'. Canberra: Pacific Linguistics Series C-105.

Merrifield, Scott and Martinus Salea (1996) *North Sulawesi Language Survey.* Dallas TX: Summer Institute of Linguistics.

Nekitel, Otto I. M. S. (1998) *Voices of Yesterday, Today and Tomorrow. Language, Culture and Identity.* New Delhi: UBS Publishers' Distributors Ltd/Port Moresby, Papua New Guinea: Nekitelson Pty Ltd.

Prentice, David J. (1970) 'The Linguistic Situation in Northern Borneo'. In: Wurm, S. A. and D. L. Laycock (eds) 'Pacific Linguistic Studies in Honour of Arthur Capell'. Canberra: Pacific Linguistics Series C-13: 369–408.

Reesinck, Ger P. (1999) 'A Grammar of Hatam, Irian Jaya, Indonesia'. Canberra: Pacific Linguistics Series C-146.

Ross, Malcolm (1996) 'Languages of New Britain and New Ireland, vol. 1: Austronesian Languages of the North New Guinea Cluster in Northwestern New Britain'. Canberra: Pacific Linguistics Series C-135.

Schmidt, Annette (1990) *The Loss of Australia's Aboriginal Language Heritage.* Canberra: Aboriginal Studies Press for the Australian Institute of Aboriginal and Torres Strait Islander Studies.

Stockhof, Wim A. L. (1975) 'Preliminary Notes on the Alor and Pantar Languages (East Indonesia)'. Canberra: Pacific Linguistics Series B-43.

Thieberger, Nicholas (1993) 'Western Australian Aboriginal Languages South of the Kimberleys Region'. Canberra: Pacific Linguistics Series C-124.

Tryon, Darrell T. (1976 [reprinted 1980]) 'New Hebrides Languages: An Internal Classification'. Canberra: Pacific Linguistics Series C-50.

——(1980) 'Daly Family Languages, Australia'. Canberra: Pacific Linguistics Series C-32.

Tryon, Darrell T. and Bryan D. Hackmann (1983) 'Solomon Islands Languages: An Internal Classification'. Canberra: Pacific Linguistics Series C-72.

Voorhoeve, C. L. (1975) 'Languages of Irian Jaya: Checklist. Preliminary Classification, Language Maps, Wordlists'. Canberra: Pacific Linguistics Series B-31.

——(1987) 'The Languages of the North-Halmaheran Stock'. Canberra: Pacific Linguistics Series A-76: 181–209.

Williams, Jeff (1996) Jeff Williams' contribution in vol. II/1, on pp. 418–22. In: Mühlhäusler, Peter, Tom Dutton, Even Hovdhaugen, Jeff Williams and Stephen A. Wurm, 'Precolonial Patterns of Intercultural Communication in the Pacific Islands' in Stephen A. Wurm, Peter Mühlhäusler and Darrell T. Tryon (eds) (1996) *Atlas of Languages of Intercultural Communication in the Pacific, Asia, and the Americas* (3 vols). Berlin and New York: Mouton de Gruyter, pp. 401–37.

Wurm, Stephen A. (1972) *Languages of Australia and Tasmania. Janua Linguarum, Series Critica.* vol. 1. The Hague/Paris: Mouton.

——(1982) *Papuan Languages of Oceania. Ars Linguistica* 7. Tübingen: Gunter Narr Verlag.

——(1998a) 'Methods of Language Maintenance and Revival, with Selected Cases of Language Endangerment in the World'. In: Kazuto Matsumura (ed.) *Studies in Endangered Languages.* Tokyo: Hituzi Syobo, pp. 191–211.

——(1998b) 'Language Endangerment and Death in the Central and Southwestern Pacific, with Notes on the Western'. In: Mark Janse (ed.) *Productivity and Creativity, Studies in General and Descriptive Linguistics in Honor of E. M. Uhlenbeck. Trends in Linguistics. Studies and Monographs, 116.* Berlin/New York: Mouton de Gruyter, pp. 479–91.

——(2000) 'Language Endangerment in the Insular Greater Pacific Area, and the New Guinea Area in Particular'. In: Wurm, Stephen A. (forthcoming(a)) *Tentative Map Of Languages In Danger, Pacific, General Overview.* Paris/Canberra: UNESCO Publishing/Pacific Linguistics. A new revised and enlarged edition of Wurm, Stephen A. (ed.) (1996) *Atlas of the World's Languages in Danger of Disappearing*. Paris/Canberra: UNESCO Publishing/Pacific Linguistics.

——(forthcoming(a)) *Tentative Map of Languages in Danger, Pacific, General Overview*. To be published in a new revised and enlarged edition of Wurm, Stephen A. (ed.) (1996) *Atlas of the World's Languages in Danger of Disappearing*. Paris/Canberra: UNESCO Publishing/Pacific Linguistics.

——(forthcoming(b)) *Atlas of Threatened and Recently Extinct Languages in the Pacific Area*.

——(forthcoming(c)) *Threatened Languages in the Western Pacific Area from Taiwan to, and Including, Papua New Guinea*. Berlin and New York: Mouton de Gruyter.

Wurm, Stephen A. (ed.) (1975) 'New Guinea Area Languages and Language Study, vol. 1: Papuan Languages and the New Guinea Linguistic Scenes'. Canberra: Pacific Linguistics Series C-38.

——(1976) 'New Guinea Area Languages and Language Study, vol. 2: Austronesian Languages'. Canberra: Pacific Linguistics Series C-39.

——(1996) *Atlas of the World's Languages in Danger of Disappearing*. Paris/Canberra: UNESCO Publishing/Pacific Linguistics.

——(1997) 'Materials on Languages in Danger of Disappearing in the Asia-Pacific Region, no. 1: Some Endangered Languages of Papua New Guinea: Kaki Ae, Musom, and Aribwatsa'. Canberra: Pacific Linguistics Series D-89.

Wurm, Stephen A. and Shirô Hattori (eds) (1981–3) *Language Atlas of the Pacific Area*. Canberra: Australian Academy of the Humanities in collaboration with the Japan Academy. Also as Canberra: Pacific Linguistics Series C-66–7.

Wurm, Stephen A., Peter Mühlhäusler and Darrell T. Tryon (eds) (1996) *Atlas of Languages of Intercultural Communication in the Pacific, Asia, and the Americas* (3 vols). Berlin and New York: Mouton de Gruyter (many relevant contributions).

Zgraggen, John A. (1975 [reprinted 1979]) 'The Languages of the Madang District, Papua New Guinea'. Canberra: Pacific Linguistics Series B-41.

Hundreds of volumes of *Pacific Linguistics* which contain snippets or more of relevant information.

The present writer's extensive fieldnotes of languages of Papua New Guinea and the New Guinea area, the Solomon Islands, of the Santa Cruz Archipelago, of Polynesian languages, languages of Australia, some Western and Central Malayo-Polynesian languages, etc.

Personal communications from: Adelaar, Alexander; Austin, Peter; Blake, Barry; Blust, Robert; Bowden, John; Boulan-Smit, Christine; Bradley, David; Capell, Arthur, the late; Chowning, Ann; de Vries, James; Donohue, Mark; Dutton, Tom; Eklund, Robert; Evans, Nicholas; Fox, James; Franklin, Karl; Grimes, Charles; Hackmann, Bryan; Hale, Ken; Hercus, Luise; Himmelmann, Nikolaus; Holzknecht, Suzanne; Kamene, Sakarepe; Kanasa, Biama; Kulick, Don; Laycock, Donald, the late; Li, Paul Jen-Kuei; Lindström, Eva; Mühlhäusler, Peter; Nekitel, Otto; Osmond, Meredith; Pawley, Andy; Purba, Theodorus; Reesinck, Ger; Ross, Malcolm; Soaba, Russel; Stockhof, Wim; Thiebergen, Nicholas; Thomas, Dicks; Todd, Evelyn; Tryon, Darrell; Voorhoeve, Bert; and the Summer Institute of Linguistics at Ukarumpa, Papua New Guinea; and others.

LIST OF THE LANGUAGES OF THE PACIFIC AREA

In this section Austronesian, Papuan, Australian, and Pidgin and Creole languages have been listed under the headings of the various genetic groups to which they belong. The names of languages which are threatened in any form, or have in living memory become extinct, or probably extinct, are given in italics. Alternative names for them are given in italics after the main name, in parentheses. The language names (and alternative names) under which they are listed are followed by a code letter which indicates the level of their endangerment, or mark them as extinct. These letters are as follows: P = potentially endangered; E = endangered; S = seriously endangered, M = moribund; D = extinct ('dead'). For a definition of these terms, and for the main hallmark of the various levels of endangerment, see the Introduction above, in the section dealing with endangerment. Some long extinct languages have been mentioned, especially when such languages had some special significance in the past. The code LD ('long dead') has been added to them. Alternative names have been added in parentheses to the main names of languages in many cases, especially to names given in italics. It may be mentioned here again, as has been pointed out in the section on endangerment in the Introduction, that a language can be endangered or even seriously endangered even if it has children speakers and is functioning apparently quite healthily. This would for instance be the case if the total number of speakers is very small, say 20–30, and the speakers are in imminent danger of being exposed to major interference by members of a metropolitan civilization, such as a mining operation, oil drilling, logging, or some other major interference with their environment, life style and livelihood, or are even threatened by physical extinction – the latter could also be the result of a natural catastrophe such as an earthquake, volcanic eruption, tsunami, major fires, flooding, and serious consequences of the El Niño phenomenon.

Austronesian languages

Non-Malayo-Polynesian Austronesian languages

Languages of Taiwan (in the literature known as Formosan languages)

Amis ■ *Babuza (Favorlang, Poavosa)* M ■ *Basay (Kawanuwan)* D ■ Bunun ■ *Hoanya* LD ■ *Kanakanabu (Kanabu)* M ■ *Kavalan (Kuwarawan, Kibalan, Shekwan)* M ■ *Ketangalan* LD ■ *Kulun* LD ■ *Nataoran (Amis Nataoran, Sakizaya, Sakiray)* M ■ Paiwan ■ *Papora* LD ■ *Pazeh (Shekhoan, Lekwhan)* D ■ Pyuma ■ Rukai ■ *Saaroa (Rarua, Pachien, Sisyaban)* M ■ *Saisiyat (Amutoura, Bouiok)* E ■ *Siraiya (Baksa, Pepohoan)* D ■ *Taokas* LD ■ Taroko ■ Tayal ■ *Thao (Chuihwan, Vulung)* M ■ Tsou.

Malayo-Polynesian Austronesian languages

Western Malayo-Polynesian languages

Isolates in the Northern Mariana Islands, in Palau, and Micronesia

Chamorro ■ Palauan ■ Yapese.

Philippine languages

NORTHERN PHILIPPINE LANGUAGES

Bashiic-Central Luzon – Northern Mindoro languages   Agta, Remontado ■ Alangan ■ Ayta, Abenlen ■ Ayta, Ambala ■ *Ayta, Bataan (Bataan Sambal)* E ■ Ayta, Mag-Anchi ■ Ayta, Mag-Indi ■ Bolinao ■ Ibatan ■ Iraya ■ Ivatan ■ Pampangan ■ Sambal, Botolan ■ Sambal, Tina ■ Tadyawan ■ Yami (Botel Tobago).

North Luzon languages   *Adasen (Addasen Tinguian, Adasen Itneg)* P ■ *Agta, Alabat Island (Alabat Island Dumagat)* S ■ *Agta, Camarines Norte (Manide, Agiyan)* E ■ Agta, Casiguran Dumagat ■ *Agta, Central Cagayan* E ■ *Agta, Dicamay* D ■ Agta, Eastern Cagayan ■ Agta, Umiray Dumagat ■ Agta, Villaviciosa ■ *Alta, Northern (Edimala, Ditaylin Dumagat)* E ■ Alta, Southern ■ *Arta* M ■ *Atta, Faire (Southern Atta)* E ■ Atta, Pamplona ■ Atta, Pudtol ■ Balangao ■ Bontoc, Central ■ Bontoc, Eastern ■ Ga'dang ■ Gaddang ■ Ibaloi ■ Ibanag ■ Ifugao, Amganad ■ Ifugao, Ayangan ■ Ifugao, Kiangan ■ Ifugao, Mayoyao ■ Ilocano ■ Ilongot ■ Isinai ■ Isnag ■ Itawit ■ Itneg, Binongan ■ Itneg, Inlaod ■ Itneg, Masadiit ■ Itneg, Southern ■ Kalinga, Butbut ■ Kalinga, Limos ■ Kalinga, Lower Tanudan ■ Kalinga, Lubuagan ■ Kalinga, Mabaka Valley ■ Kalinga, Madukayang ■ Kalinga, Southern ■ Kalinga, Upper Tanudan ■ Kallahan, Kayapa ■ Kallahan, Keley-I ■ Kallahan, Tinoc ■ Kankanaey ■ Kankanay, Northern ■ Karao ■ Kasiguranin ■ Pangasinan ■ Paranan ■ Yogad.

MESO-PHILIPPINE LANGUAGES

Central Philippine languages   *Agta, Isarog* M ■ *Agta, Mt. Iraya (Itbeg Rugnot)* E ■ Agta, Mt. Iriga ■ Aklanon ■ *Ata₁* D ■ Ati ■ *Ayta, Sorsogon* M ■ *Ayta, Tayabas* D ■ Bantoanon ■ Bicolano, Albay ■ Bicolano, Central ■ Bicolano, Iriga ■ Bicolano, Northern Catanduanes ■ Bicolano, Southern Catanduanes ■ Butuanon ■ Caluyanun ■ Capiznon ■ Cebuano ■ Cuyonon ■ Davaweño ■ Hiligaynon ■ Kalagan ■ Kalagan, Kagan ■ Kalagan, Tagakaulu ■ Kamayo ■ Karolanos ■ *Katabaga* D ■ Kinaray-A ■ Loocnon ■ Magahat ■ Malaynon ■ Mamanwa ■ Mandaya, Cataelano ■ Mandaya, Karaga ■ Mandaya, Sangab ■ Mansaka ■ Masbatenyo ■ Porohanon ■ *Ratagnon (Datagnon, Latan)* M ■ Romblomanon ■ Sorsogon, Masbate ■ Sorsogon, Waray ■ Sulod ■ Surigaonon ■ Tagalog ■ Tausug ■ Waray-Waray.

Kalamian languages   Agutaynen ■ Tagbanwa, Calamian ■ Tagbanwa, Central.

Palawano languages   Banggi ■ *Batak (Babuyan, Palawan Batak)* E ■ Molbog ■ Palawano, Brooke's Point ■ Palawano, Central ■ Palawano, Southwest ■ Tagbanwa.

South Mangyan languages   Buhid ■ Hanunoo ■ Tawbuid.

SOUTH MINDANAO LANGUAGES

Bagobo ■ Blaan, Koronadal ■ Blaan, Sarangani ■ Tboli ■ Tiruray.

SOUTH PHILIPPINE LANGUAGES

Agusan ■ Ata₂ ■ Binukid ■ Bukidnon, Western ■ Cinamiguin ■ Cotabato ■ Dibabawon ■ Higaonon ■ Ilanun ■ Ilianen ■ Kagayanen ■ Magindanaon ■ Maranao ■ Matig-Salug ■ Obo ■ Sarangani ■ Tagabawa ■ Subanun, Central ■ Subanun, Lapuyan ■ Subanun, Tuboy ■ Subanun, Western.

Sundic languages

GAYO ISOLATED LANGUAGE

Gayo.

MADURESE ISOLATE LANGUAGE

Madurese.

BALI-SASAK LANGUAGES

Balinese ■ Sasak ■ Sumbawa.

JAVANESE LANGUAGES

Javanese ■ Javanese, Caribbean ■ Osing ■ Tengger.

SUNDANESE LANGUAGES

Badui ■ Sunda.

LAMPUNGIC LANGUAGES

Abung ■ Komering ■ Krui ■ Lampung ■ Pesisir, Southern ■ Pubian ■ Sungkai.

MALAYIC LANGUAGES

Aceh ■ Balau ■ Banjar ■ Basa Kupang (Kupang Malay) ■ Bengkulu ■ Brunei ■ Cham, Eastern ■ Cham, Western ■ Chru ■ Dayak, Malayic ■ Duano' ■ Haroi ■ Huihui ■ Iban ■ Indonesian ■ Jakun ■ Jarai ■ Kendayan ■ Keninjal ■ Kerinci ■ Kubu ■ Larantuka ■ Lembak ■ Lintang ■ Loncong ■ Lubu ■ Madurese isolate ■ Malay, Ambonese ■ Malay, Baba ■ Malay, Bacanese ■ Malay, Berau ■ Malay, Bukit ■ Malay, Cocos Islands ■ Malay, Kedah ■ Malay, Kutai ■ Malay, Negeri Sembilan ■ Malay, North Moluccan ■ Malay, Pattani ■ Malay, Standard ■ Milikin ■ Minangkabau ■ Moken ■ Moklen ■ Mualang ■ Musi ■ Ogan ■ *Orang Kanaq* s ■ Orang Seletar ■ Palembang ■ Pasemah ■ Peranakan ■ Rade ■ Rejang ■ Roglai, Cacgai ■ Roglai, Northern ■ Roglai, Southern ■ Sebuyau ■ Selako ■ Semendo ■ Serawai ■ Temuan ■ Urak Lawoi'.

SUMATRAN LANGUAGES

Batak Alas-Kluet ■ Batak Angkolo ■ Batak Dairi ■ Batak Karo ■ Batak Mandailing ■ Batak Simalungan ■ Batak Toba ■ *Enggano* E ■ *Lom* (*Belom*, *Mapor*) S, M, or D ■ Mentawai ■ Nias ■ Sikule ■ Simeulue.

Borneo languages

APO DUAT LANGUAGES

Kelabit ■ *Lengilu* M ■ Lundayeh ■ Putoh ■ Sa'ban.

BARITO LANGUAGES

Ampanang ■ Bakumpai ■ Dohoi ■ Dusun Deyah ■ Dusun Malang ■ Dusun Witu ■ Kahayan ■ Katingan ■ Lawangan ■ Ma'anyan ■ Malagasy ■ Ngaju ■ Paku ■ Siang ■ Tawoyan ■ Tunjung.

KAYAN-KENYAH LANGUAGES

Aoheng ■ Bahau ■ Bukat ■ Hovongan ■ Kayan, Baram ■ Kayan, Busang ■ Kayan, Kayan River ■ Kayan, Mahakam ■ Kayan, Mendalam ■ Kayan, Murik ■ Kayan, Rejang ■ Kayan, Wahau ■ Kenyah, Bahau River ■ Kenyah, Bakung ■ Kenyah, Kayan River ■ Kenyah, Kelinyau ■ Kenyah, Mahakam ■ Kenyah, Sebob ■ Kenyah, Tutoh ■ Kenyah, Upper Baram ■ Kenyah, Wahau ■ Kenyah, Western ■ Kereho-Uheng ■ Madang ■ Modang ■ Punan Aput ■ Punan Merah ■ Punan-Nibong ■ Punan Tubu ■ Segai.

LAND DAYAK LANGUAGES

Ahe ■ Bekati' ■ Benyadu' ■ Biatah ■ Bukar Sadong ■ Dayak, Land ■ Djongkang ■ Jagoi ■ Kembayan ■ Lara' ■ Nyadu ■ Ribun ■ Sanggau ■ Sara ■ Semandang ■ Silakau ■ Singgi ■ Tringus.

MBALOH LANGUAGES

Embaloh ■ Taman.

NORTHEAST BORNEO LANGUAGES

Abai Sungai E ■ Baukan ■ Bisaya, Brunei ■ Bisaya, Sabah ■ Bisaya, Sarawak ■ Bolongan ■ Dumpas ■ Dusun, Central ■ Dusun, Kuala Monsok ■ Dusun, Segama ■ Dusun, Tambunan ■ Dusun, Tempasuk ■ Gana ■ Kadazan, Coastal ■ Kadazan, Eastern ■ Kadazan, Klias River ■ Kadazan, Sugut ■ Kimaragang ■ Kinabatangan Sungai ■ Kinabatangan, Upper ■ Kota Marudu Talantang ■ Kota Marudu Tinagas ■ Kuijau ■ Lingkabau ■ Lobu, Lanas ■ Lobu, Tampias ■ Lotud ■ Minokok ■ Murut, Beaufort ■ Murut, Dusun ■ Murut, Kalabakan ■ Murut, Keningau ■ Murut, Pandewan ■ Murut, Selungai ■ Murut, Sembakung ■ Murut, Serudung ■

Murut, Tagal ■ Murut, Timugon ■ Okolod ■ Paluan ■ Papar ■ Rungus ■ Sinabu ■ Sonsogon ■ Tatana ■ Tebilung ■ Tengara ■ Tidong ■ Tombonuo ■ Tutong 1.

REJANG-BARAM LANGUAGES

Basap ■ Berawan ■ Bintulu ■ Bukitan ■ Burusu ■ Daro-Matu ■ Kajaman ■ *Kanowit* E ■ Kiput ■ Lahanan ■ Lelak ■ Melanau ■ Narom ■ Punan Bah-Biau ■ *Punan Batu* S ■ Punan Merap ■ Sajau Basap ■ Sekapan ■ *Seru* D ■ *Sian* E ■ Sibu ■ Tanjong ■ Tutong ■ Ukit.

Sama-Bajaw languages

Bajaw, Indonesian ■ Bajaw, West Coast ■ Mapun ■ Sama, Abaknon ■ Sama, Balangingi ■ Sama, Central ■ Sama, Pangutaran ■ Sama, Southern ■ Yakan.

Sulawesi languages

ISOLATE

Bingkokak.

CENTRAL SULAWESI LANGUAGES

Isolates   Balaesan ■ Banggai.

Bungku-Mori languages   *Bahonsuai* E ■ Bungku ■ *Kodeoha* (*Kondeha*) P ■ *Koroni* P ■ Kulisusu ■ Mekongga ■ Mori ■ Moronene ■ *Padoe* (*Soroako, Tambe'e, Ajo, Alalao*) P ■ *Rahambuu* P ■ *Taloki* P ■ Tolaki ■ *Tomadino* E ■ Tulambatu ■ *Waru* (*Mopute*) P.

East-Central Sulawesi languages   *Andio* (*Masama*) P ■ Balantak ■ Saluan, Coastal ■ *Saluan, Kahumamahon* (*Interior Saluan*) P.

Kaili-Pamona languages   Bada ■ *Baras* (*Ende*) E ■ *Besoa* (*Behaa*) P ■ Kaili ■ Ledo ■ Lindu ■ Moma ■ *Napu* (*Bara, Pekurehua*) P ■ Pamona ■ Rampi ■ Sedoa ■ *Tombelala* P ■ Topoiyo ■ Uma.

Tomini languages   *Ampibao Lauje* P ■ *Baleasang* (*Baleasan*) E ■ *Boano* (*Bolano*) P ■ *Dampal* M(D?) ■ *Dampelas* (*Dampelasa*) E ■ *Dondo* P ■ *Lauje* P ■ *Pendau* (*Ndau, Umalasa*) P ■ *Taje* M ■ *Tajio* P ■ *Totoli* (*Tolitoli, Gage*) P ■ *Tialo* (*Tomini*) P.

MONGONDOW-GORONTALIC LANGUAGES

Atinggola ■ Bintauna ■ Bolango ■ Buol ■ Gorontalo ■ Kaidipang ■ *Lolak* S ■ Mongondow ■ Ponosakan ■ Suwawa.

MUNA-BUTON LANGUAGES

Bonerate ■ *Busoa* E ■ Cia-Cia ■ Kaimbulawa ■ *Kalao* (*Kalaotoa*) P ■ Kamaru ■ Kioko-Ueesi ■ *Laiyolo* (*Da'ang*) E ■ Lasalimu ■ Liabuku ■ Muna ■ Pancana ■ Tukangbesi ■ Wolio ■ *Wotu* P.

565

SANGIR-MINAHASAN LANGUAGES

Bantik ∎ Sangil ∎ Sangir ∎ Tahulandang ∎ Talaud ∎ Tombulu ∎ Tondano ∎ Tonsawang ∎ Tonsea ∎ Tontemboan ∎ *Toratán* (*Ratahan*) s.

SOUTH SULAWESI LANGUAGES

Aralle-Tabulahan ∎ Bentong ∎ *Budong-Budong* (*Tangkou*) s ∎ Bugis ∎ Campalagian ∎ *Dakka* p ∎ Kalumpang ∎ Konjo, Coastal ∎ Konjo, Highland ∎ *Lemolang* (*Baebunta*) p ∎ Makassar ∎ Malimpung ∎ Mamasa ∎ Mamuju ∎ Mandar ∎ Massenrempulu ∎ *Panasuan* p ∎ Pannei ∎ Pattae' ∎ Pattinjo ∎ Pitu Ulunna Salu ∎ Rongkong ∎ Seko Padang ∎ Seko Tengah ∎ Selayar ∎ Ta'e ∎ *Talondo'* p ∎ Toala' ∎ *Tobada'* d ∎ Toraja-Sa'dan ∎ Ulumanda'.

Central Malayo-Polynesian languages

BIMA-SUMBA LANGUAGES

Anakalangu ∎ Bima ∎ Ende ∎ Kodi ∎ Lamboya ∎ Li'o ∎ Mamboru ∎ Manggarai ∎ Ndao ∎ Ngada ∎ *Palu'e* e ∎ Riung ∎ Sawu ∎ Sumba ∎ Wanukaka ∎ Weyewa.

CENTRAL MALUKU LANGUAGES

Alune (*Alfoeren, Patasiwa, Sapalew*) e ∎ *Amahai* m ∎ Ambelau ∎ *Aputai* (*Tutunohan, Welemur*) e ∎ Asilulu ∎ Atamanu ∎ Banda ∎ Bati ∎ *Benggoi* (*Uhei-Kaclakin, Isal*) p ∎ Boano ∎ Buru ∎ Elpaputih ∎ *Emplawas* p ∎ Geser ∎ Haruku ∎ Hila-Kaitetu ∎ Hitu ∎ Horuru ∎ *Hoti* d ∎ Huaulu ∎ *Hukumina* d ∎ *Hulung* d ∎ Iha ∎ *Kadai* e ∎ *Kaibobo* e ∎ Kamarian ∎ *Kayeli* d ∎ Laha ∎ Larike-Wakasihu ∎ Latu ∎ Liambata ∎ *Liliali* (*Leliali*) d ∎ Lisabata-Nuniali ∎ *Lisela* (*Buru, Wayapo*) e ∎ *Loun* m ∎ Luhu ∎ Mangei ∎ Mangole ∎ Manipa ∎ Manusela ∎ Masiwang ∎ *Moksela* d ∎ *Naka'ela* d ∎ *Nila* p ∎ Nuaulu, North ∎ Nuaulu, South ∎ *Nusa Laut* d ∎ *Palumata* d ∎ *Paulohi* m ∎ *Piru* d ∎ *Salas* (*Salas Gunung*) s ∎ Saleman ∎ *Saparua* e ∎ Sepa ∎ *Serili* p ∎ Seti ∎ Sula ∎ Taliabu ∎ *Te'un* e ∎ Teluti ∎ Tulehu ∎ Watubela ∎ Wemale, North ∎ Wemale, South ∎ Werinama.

SOUTHEAST MALUKU LANGUAGES

Barakai ∎ Batuley ∎ Dobel ∎ Fordata ∎ Karey ∎ Kei ∎ Koba ∎ Kola ∎ Kompane ∎ Kur ∎ *Lola* p ∎ Lorang ∎ Mariri ∎ Selaru ∎ Seluwasan ∎ Tarangan, East ∎ Tarangan, West ∎ Teor ∎ *Ujir* e ∎ Wokam ∎ Yamdena.

TIMOR-FLORES LANGUAGES

Babar, North ∎ Babar, Southeast ∎ Dai ∎ Damar, North ∎ Damar, South ∎ Dawera-Daweloor ∎ Galoli ∎ Hahutan ∎ *Helong* (*Semau*) p ∎ Idate ∎ Iliun ∎ Imroing ∎ Kedang ∎ Kemak ∎ Kisar ∎ Lakalei ∎ Lamaholot ∎ Limera ∎ Luang ∎ Mambai ∎ Masela, Central ∎ Masela, East ∎ *Naueti* p ∎ *Palu'e* e ∎ Perai ∎ Roma ∎ Roti ∎ Serua ∎ Sikka ∎ Talur ∎ Tela-Masbuar ∎ Tetun ∎ Timor ∎ Tugun ∎ Tukudede.

WAIMA'A LANGUAGES

Habu P ■ *Kairui-Midiki* P ■ *Waima'a* P.

NORTH AND SOUTH BOMBERAI PENINSULA MALAYO-POLYNESIAN LANGUAGES

Arguni P ■ *Kowiai* (*Kaiwai*) P ■ *Onin* P ■ Sekar ■ Uruangnirin.

Eastern Malayo-Polynesian languages

South Halmahera–West New Guinea languages

Ambai ■ Amber ■ Ansus ■ *As* P ■ *Bedoanas* P-E ■ *Biak* P ■ Buli ■ Busami ■ *Dusner* D ■ *Erokwanas* P ■ Gane ■ *Gebe* P ■ Irarutu ■ *Iresim* E ■ Kawe ■ Kurudu ■ *Legenyem* P ■ Maba ■ Maden ■ *Makian, East* (*Taba*) E-S ■ Marau ■ Matbat ■ Ma'ya ■ Meoswar ■ *Mor$_2$* S ■ Munggui ■ Nabi ■ Palamul ■ Papuma ■ Patani ■ Pom ■ Roon ■ Sawai ■ Serui-Laut ■ Tandia ■ Wandamen ■ Waropen ■ Woi ■ Woriasi ■ Yaur ■ Yeretuar.

Oceanic languages

SARMI-YOTAFA LANGUAGES

Anus E ■ *Bonggo* E ■ *Kayupulau* S ■ *Liki* M ■ *Ormu* P ■ *Sobei* E ■ *Tarpia* E ■ *Tobati* S.

MARKHAM LANGUAGES

Adzera ■ Buang, Central ■ Buang, Mangga ■ Dangal ■ *Dengalu* E ■ *Duwet* (*Guwot*) P ■ Hote ■ Mari ■ Misim ■ Mumeng ■ *Musom* (*Misatik*) E ■ *Nafi* (*Sirak*) P-E ■ Ngariawan ■ Patep ■ *Piu* E ■ Silisili ■ Sirasira ■ Sukurum ■ *Vehes* (*Buasi*) E ■ Wampar ■ Wampur ■ Watut, Middle ■ Yalu ■ Yamap ■ Yanta ■ Zenang.

SIASSI LANGUAGES

Aribwatsa D ■ Arop ■ Bariai ■ Barim ■ Biem ■ Bilbil ■ Biliau ■ Bukawac ■ Dami ■ Gedaged ■ Gitua ■ Iwal ■ *Kaiep* P ■ Kairiru ■ Kaliai ■ Kela ■ Kis ■ Kove ■ Labu ■ Lukep ■ *Malalamai* E ■ Malasanga ■ Maleu-Kilenge ■ Malon ■ Manam ■ Mangap ■ Matukar ■ Medebur ■ Megiar ■ *Mindiri* E ■ Mutu ■ Nengaya ■ *Numbami* ■ Roinji ■ *Sepa* P ■ *Sera* S ■ *Siboma* P ■ Sio ■ *Sissano* S ■ Suain ■ Takia ■ Tami ■ Terebu ■ Tumleo ■ *Wab* P ■ Wogeo ■ Yabim ■ Yakamul.

MUSSAU-EMIRA LANGUAGE

Mussau-Emira (*Mussau, Emira*) P-E.

MILNE BAY-CENTRAL PROVINCE LANGUAGES

Anuki E ■ Are ■ Arifama-Miniafia ■ Auhelawa ■ *Bina* D ■ Boanaki ■ *Bosilewa* P ■ *Budibud* P ■ Buhutu ■ Bunama ■ Bwaidoka ■ Dawawa ■ Diodio ■ Dobu ■ *Doga*

(*Magabara*) P ■ Doura ■ Duau ■ Galeya ■ Gapapaiwa ■ *Garuwahi* P ■ Gumasi ■ Hula ■ Iamalele ■ Iduna ■ Igora ■ Kabadi ■ Kalokalo ■ Keopara ■ Kilivila (Kiriwina) ■ Kuni ■ *Magori* P ■ Mekeo ■ Mineveha ■ Misima-Paneati ■ Morima ■ Motu ■ Muyuw ■ *Mwatebu* P ■ Nara ■ Nimowa ■ *Ouma* D ■ Sewa Bay ■ Sinagoro ■ Sinaki ■ Suau ■ Tagula ■ Taupota ■ Tawala ■ Tubetube ■ Ubir ■ Wagawaga ■ Waima ■ Wataluma ■ Wedau ■ *Yoba* D.

ADMIRALTY ISLANDS LANGUAGES

Andra-Hus ■ Baluan-Pam ■ Bipi ■ Bohuai ■ Elu ■ Ere ■ *Hermit* D ■ *Kaniet* D ■ Kele ■ Koro ■ Kurti ■ Leipon ■ Lele ■ Lenkau ■ Levei-Ndrehet ■ *Likum* E ■ Lindrou ■ Loniu ■ Lou ■ Mokerang ■ Mondropolon ■ Nali ■ *Nauna* P ■ Okro ■ Pak-Tong ■ Papitalai ■ Penchal ■ Ponam ■ Seimat ■ Sori-Harengan ■ Titan ■ Wuvulu-Aua.

NEW IRELAND-TOLAI LANGUAGES

Barok ■ Bilur ■ *Guramalum* D ■ *Kandas* P ■ Kara ■ Konomala ■ Label ■ Lavatbura-Lamusong ■ *Laxudumau* P ■ Lihir ■ Mandak ■ Mandara ■ Nalik ■ Notsi ■ Patpatar ■ Ramoaaina ■ Siar ■ Sursurunga ■ Tangga ■ *Tenis* S ■ Tiang ■ Tigak ■ Tolai ■ Tungak.

NEW BRITAIN LANGUAGES

Aiklep ■ Akolet ■ Apalik ■ Aria (Bibling) ■ Arove ■ Avau ■ Bao ■ Bebeli ■ Gimi ■ *?Karore* D? ■ Kaulong ■ Lamogai ■ Lesing-Atui ■ Lote ■ Mamusi ■ Mangsing ■ Mengen ■ Miu ■ Mok ■ Pulie-Rauto ■ *Sengseng* P ■ Tomoip.

KIMBE LANGUAGES (NEW BRITAIN)

Bali-Vitu ■ Bola ■ Bulu ■ Harua ■ Meramera ■ Nakanai.

BOUGAINVILLE ISLAND LANGUAGES

Banoni ■ Hahon ■ Hakö ■ Halia ■ Minigir ■ Mono ■ Nagarige ■ Nehan ■ *Papapana* P-E ■ Petats ■ Saposa ■ Solos ■ Teop ■ Torau ■ *Uruawa* D ■ Vasui (Tinputz).

CHOISEUL ISLAND LANGUAGES

Babatana ■ *Ririo* S ■ Tavula ■ Varese.

NEW GEORGIA ISLAND LANGUAGES

Bareke-Vangunu ■ Duke ■ *Hoava* P ■ Kusaghe ■ Lungga ■ Marovo ■ Roviana ■ Ughele.

SANTA ISABEL ISLAND LANGUAGES

Blablanga P ■ *Gao* E ■ *Kokota* E ■ *Laghu* M ■ Maringe ■ Zabana ■ *Zazao* E.

REMOTE OCEANIC LANGUAGES

Southeast Solomons languages   Are'are ■ Arosi ■ Bauro ■ Birao ■ Bughotu ■ Dori'o ■ *Faghani* P ■ Fataleka ■ Gela ■ Ghari ■ Gula'alaa ■ Kahua ■ Kwaio ■ Kwara'ae ■ Langalanga ■ Lau ■ Lengo ■ Longgu ■ Malango ■ *Oroha* E ■ Sa'a ■ Talise ■ To'abaita.

North and Central Vanuatu languages   Akei ■ Ambae, East ■ Ambae, West ■ *Amblong* P-E ■ Ambrym, North ■ Ambryn, Southeast ■ *Aore* D ■ Apma ■ *Araki* E ■ Aulua ■ Axamb ■ Baetora ■ *Baki* P ■ *Bierebo* P ■ *Bieria* P ■ Big Nambas ■ Burmbar ■ Butmas-Tur ■ Dakaka ■ *Dixon Reef* S ■ Efate, North ■ Efate, South ■ Fortsenal ■ Hano ■ *Hiw* E ■ Katbol ■ *Koro* E ■ *Labo* P ■ Lakona ■ Lamenu ■ Lametin ■ Larevat ■ Lehali ■ *Lehalurup* P ■ Letemboi ■ Lewo ■ Lingarak ■ Litzlitz ■ Lonwolwol ■ *Lorediakarkar* S ■ Mae ■ Maewo ■ *Mafea* P ■ Maii ■ Malfaxal ■ *Malmariv* P ■ Malo ■ Malua Bay ■ *Maragus* D ■ Marino ■ Maskelynes ■ Merlav ■ Morouas ■ Mosina ■ Mota ■ Motlav ■ Mpotovoro ■ *Naati* M ■ Namakura ■ Narango ■ *Nasarian* M ■ Navut ■ *Navwien* M ■ *Nisvai* E-S ■ Nokuku ■ Nume ■ Paama ■ Piamatsina ■ *Polonombauk* E ■ Port Sandwich ■ Port Vato ■ *Repanbitip* E ■ Rerep ■ Roria ■ Sa ■ Sakao ■ *Seke* P ■ *Shark Bay* P ■ *Sösörian* M ■ *Southwest Bay* E-S ■ *Sowa* M ■ *Tambotalo* S ■ Tangoa ■ Tasmate ■ Toga ■ *Tolomako* P ■ *Tutuba* P ■ Unua ■ Uripiv-Wala-Rano-Atchin ■ Valpei ■ Vao ■ Vatrata ■ Vinmavis ■ Vunapu ■ Wailapa ■ *Wetamut* E ■ Wusi.

Rotuman-Fijian languages   Rotuman ■ Fijian.

Polynesian languages   Anuta ■ *Emae* (*Emwae*) P ■ Futunan, East ■ Futunan, West, and Aniwan ■ *Hawaiian* E ■ Kapingamarangi ■ Luangiua ■ Mangarevan ■ Manihiki-Rakahanga ■ *Maori* P-E ■ Marquesan, North ■ Marquesan, South ■ Mele-Fila ■ Niuafo'ou ■ Niuean ■ Nukumanu ■ Nukuoro ■ Nukuria ■ Penrhyn ■ Pileni ■ Pukapukan ■ *Rapa* (*Rapan*) E-S ■ *Rapanui* E ■ Rarotongan ■ Rennellese-Bellonese ■ Samoan ■ Sikaiana ■ Tahitian ■ Takuu ■ Tikopia ■ Tokelauan ■ Tongan ■ *Tuamotuan* (*Paumotu*) E ■ *Tubuai-Rurutu* (*Austral*) P ■ Tuvaluan ■ Uvean, East ■ Uvean, West.

Micronesian languages   Carolinian ■ Ikiribati (Kiribati, Gilbertese) ■ Kusaie ■ *Mapia* D ■ Marshallese ■ Mokil ■ Mortlock ■ Namonuito ■ *Nauruan* E ■ Ngatik ■ Pááfang ■ Pingelap ■ Ponapean ■ Puluwat ■ Satawal ■ Sonsorol ■ *Tanapag* (*Talabwog*) E ■ *Tobian* (*Tobi, Hatobohei*) S ■ Truk (Ruk, Chuuk) ■ Ulithi ■ Woleaian.

SANTA CRUZ LANGUAGES

Amba (Nembao) ■ *Asumboa* (*Asumbuo*) S ■ *Nyisunggu* (*Tanimbili*) E ■ *Tanema* D ■ *Teanu* E ■ *Vano* D.

SOUTH VANUATU LANGUAGES

Aneityum ■ *Ifo* D ■ Kwamera ■ Lenakel ■ Sie ■ Tanna, North ■ Tanna, Southwest ■ *Ura* M ■ Whitesands.

569

LOYALTY ISLANDS LANGUAGES

Dehu (Lifu) ■ Iaai (Iai) ■ Nengone (Maré).

NEW CALEDONIA LANGUAGES

Ajië ■ *Arhâ* s ■ *Arhö* (*Aro*) m ■ *Bwatoo* p ■ Caac ■ Cemuhi ■ Dumbea ■ Fwâi ■ *Haeke* m ■ *Haveke* e ■ *Hmwaveke* e ■ Jawe ■ Kumak ■ *Mea* e ■ *Neku* s ■ *Nemi* p ■ Numee ■ Nyâlayu ■ Orowe ■ Paicî ■ *Pije* s ■ *Pwaamei* p ■ *Pwapwâ* s ■ Tiri ■ *Vamale* e ■ *Waamwang* d ■ Xaracuu ■ Xaragure ■ Yuaga ■ *Zire* d.

Papuan languages

Trans-New Guinea Phylum languages

Main Central and West Trans-New Guinea Phylum languages

HUON-FINISTERRE LANGUAGES

Abaga m ■ Asat ■ Bam ■ Bonkiman ■ *Bulgebi* e ■ Burum-Mindik ■ Dahating ■ Dedua ■ Degenan ■ Domung ■ Finungwa ■ Forak ■ Gabutamon ■ Gira ■ Guiarak ■ Gusan ■ Irumu ■ Kâte ■ Kewieng ■ Kinalakna ■ Komba ■ Komutu ■ Kosorong ■ Kovai ■ Kumukio ■ Mamaa ■ Mape ■ Mebu ■ Mesem ■ Migabac ■ Momare ■ Mongi ■ Morafa ■ Munkip ■ Nabak ■ Nahu ■ Nakama ■ Nankina ■ Nek ■ Nekgini ■ Neko ■ Ngaing ■ Nimi ■ Nokopo ■ Nomu ■ Nuk ■ Numanggang ■ Ono ■ Rawa ■ Sakam ■ Sauk ■ Selepet ■ *Sene* d ■ Sialum ■ *Som* e ■ *Taap* m ■ Timbe ■ Tobo ■ Ufim ■ Uri ■ Wandabong ■ Wantoat ■ Weliki ■ Yagawak ■ Yagomi ■ Yau ■ Yupna.

MADANG LANGUAGES

Amele ■ Anjam ■ *Arawum* e ■ Asas ■ *Bagupi* e ■ Baimak ■ Bau ■ Bemal ■ Bongu ■ Danaru ■ Duduela ■ Dumpu ■ *Dumun* s ■ Gal ■ Ganglau ■ Garuh ■ Garus ■ Girawa ■ Gumalu ■ Isebe ■ Jilim ■ Kamba ■ Kare ■ Kesawai ■ Kolom ■ Kwato ■ Lemio ■ Male (Koliku) ■ Matepi ■ Mawan ■ *Mosimo* e ■ Munit ■ Murupi ■ Nake ■ Nobanob ■ Ogea ■ Panim ■ Pulabu ■ Rapting ■ Rempi ■ Rerau ■ Saep ■ *Samosa* e ■ Saruga ■ Sausi ■ Sihan ■ Silopi ■ Sinsauru ■ Siroi ■ Songum ■ Sumau ■ Urigina ■ Usino ■ Utu ■ *Uya* (*Usu*) e ■ Wagi ■ Wamas ■ Yabong ■ Yangulam ■ Yoidik.

ADELBERT RANGE LANGUAGES

Abasakur ■ Amaimon ■ Apal ■ *Atemble* e ■ Bargam ■ *Bepour* e ■ *Bilakura* s ■ Biyom ■ Bunabun ■ Dimir ■ *Faita* e ■ Hinihon ■ Ikundun ■ Isabi ■ Katiati ■ Koguman ■ Korak ■ *Kowaki* s ■ Maia ■ Maiani ■ Mala ■ Malas ■ Mauwake ■ *Mawak* s ■ Miani ■ *Moere* e ■ Moresada ■ Musak ■ Musar ■ Nent ■ Osum ■ Parawen ■ Paynamar ■ Pondoma ■ Sileibi ■ Tauya ■ Ukuriguma ■ Usan ■ Wadaginam ■ Wanambre ■ Wasembo ■ Waskia ■ Yaben ■ Yarawata.

EAST NEW GUINEA HIGHLANDS LANGUAGES

Agarabi ■ Alekano (Gahuku) ■ Angal, East ■ Angal Heneng, South ■ Angal Heneng, West ■ Asaro, Upper ■ Awa ■ Awiyaana (Auyana) ■ Benabena ■ Binumarien ■ Bisorio ■ Chuave ■ Dom ■ Enga ■ Fore ■ Gadsup ■ Gants ■ Gende ■ Gimi ■ Golin (Gumine) ■ Huli ■ Imbongu (Imbo Ungu) ■ Inoke-Yate (Inoke, Yate) ■ Ipili ■ Kalam ■ Kamano ■ Kambaira ■ Kandawo (Ganja) ■ Kanite ■ Kenati (Aziana) ■ Kewa, East ■ Kewa, South ■ Kewa, West ■ Keyagana ■ Kobon ■ Kosena ■ Kumai (Mid Wahgi) ■ Kuman ■ Kyaka ■ Lembena ■ Maring ■ Mbo-Ung (Miyemu, Tembogia, Tembalo, Tetalo) ■ Medlpa ■ Narak ■ Nembi ■ Nete ■ Nii ■ Nomane ■ Owenia (Owena) ■ Salt-Yui ■ Samberigi ■ Siane ■ Sinasina ■ Tai ■ Tairora ■ Tokano (Zuhuzuho, Yufiyufa) ■ Umbu-Ungu (Kaugel, Gawigl) ■ Usarufa ■ Waffa ■ Wahgi ■ Wiru (Witu) ■ Yagaria ■ Yaweyuha (Yabiyufa).

ANGAN LANGUAGES

Ampeeli-Wojokeso (Safeyoka, Wojokeso) ■ Angaatiha ■ Angoya ■ Ankave ■ Baruya ■ Hamtai ■ *Kamasa* M ■ *Kawacha (Kawatsa)* M ■ Menya ■ Simbari ■ *Susuami* M ■ Tainae (Ivori) ■ Yagwoia.

CENTRAL AND SOUTH NEW GUINEAN LANGUAGES

Agala ■ Aghu ■ Aimele ■ Asienara ■ Asmat, Casuarina Coast ■ Asmat, Central ■ Asmat, Yaosakor ■ Awin ■ Awyu ■ Bainapi ■ Beami ■ Bimin ■ Bogaya ■ Bosavi ■ Citak ■ Citak, Tamnim ■ Duna ■ Etoro ■ Faiwol ■ Gobasi ■ Iria ■ Iwur ■ Kaeti ■ Kalamo ■ Kamoro ■ Kamula ■ Kasua ■ Kati, Northern ■ Kati, Southern ■ Kauwol ■ Kombai ■ Konai ■ *Koneraw* P ■ Korowai ■ Kotogüt ■ Kware ■ Mianmin ■ Mombum ■ *Momuna (Somahai)* P ■ Ngalum ■ Ninggerum ■ Onabasulu ■ Pare ■ Pisa ■ Samo-Kubo ■ Sawi ■ Sempan ■ Setaman ■ Siagha-Yenimu ■ Sonia ■ Suganga ■ Telefol ■ Tifal ■ Tomu ■ Urapmin ■ Wambon ■ Wanggom ■ Yair ■ Yonggom.

DANI-KWERBA LANGUAGES

Airoran ■ Bagusa ■ Dani, Lower Grand Valley ■ Dani, Mid Grand Valley (Tulem) ■ Dani, Upper Grand Valley ■ Dani, Western (Timorini) ■ Hupla (Soba) ■ *Isirawa (Okwasar)* P ■ Kauwerawec ■ Kwerba ■ *Massep* S ■ Nduga (Pesechem) ■ Nggem ■ Nopuk ■ Samarokena ■ Silimo (South Ngalik) ■ Walak (Lower Pyramid, Wodo) ■ *Wano* P ■ Yali, Angguruk (Yalimo) ■ Yali, Ninia (North Ngalik).

WISSEL LAKES-KEMANDOGA LANGUAGES

Auye P ■ *Damal (Uhunduni)* P ■ Ekari (Kapauku, Ekagi) ■ Moni ■ Wolani (Woda).

BORDER LANGUAGES

Ainbai ■ Amanab ■ *Awyi* P ■ Daonda ■ Kilmeri ■ Manem ■ Ningera ■ Pagi ■ *Senggi* P ■ Simog ■ Sowanda ■ *Taikat* P ■ Umeda ■ Waris.

SENTANI LANGUAGES

Demta ■ Nafri ■ Sentani ■ Tabla.

TOR LANGUAGES

Berik ■ *Bonerif* M ■ Dabe ■ *Foya* S-M ■ *Itik* P ■ *Keder* E ■ Kwesten ■ *Mander* S ■ *Maremgi* E ■ Mawes ■ Orya ■ Wares ■ *Sause* E.

GOGODALA-SUKI LANGUAGES

Ari E ■ Gogodala ■ Suki.

MARIND LANGUAGES

Boazi ■ Marind ■ Marind, Bian ■ Warkay-Bipim (Bipim) ■ Yaqay ■ Zimakani (Dea).

KAYAGAR LANGUAGES

Atohwaim (Kaugat) ■ Kaygir ■ Tamagario.

MAIRASI-TANAHMERAH LANGUAGES

Mairasi ■ Mer ■ Semimi ■ Tanahmerah.

WEST BOMERAI LANGUAGES

Baham ■ Iha ■ *Karas* E.

East Trans-New Guinea Phylum languages

BINANDEREAN LANGUAGES

Aeka ■ Ambasi ■ Baruga ■ Binandere ■ Dogoro ■ Ewage-Notu ■ Gaina ■ Hunjara ■ Korafe ■ Mawae ■ Orokaiva ■ Suena ■ Yekora ■ *Yarawi* M ■ Zia.

CENTRAL AND SOUTHEASTERN TRANS-NEW GUINEA LANGUAGES

Dagan languages   Daga ■ Ginuman ■ Jimajima (Dima) ■ Kanasi ■ Maiwa ■ Mapena ■ *Onjab* (*Onjob*) E ■ *Turaka* S.

Goilalan languages   Biangai ■ Fuyuge ■ Kunimaipa ■ Tauade ■ Weri.

Koiarian languages   Barai ■ Koiali, Moutain ■ *Koiari, Grass* (*Koiari*) P ■ *Koitabu* (*Koita*) P ■ Managalasi ■ ömie.

Kwalean languages   Humene ■ Kwale ■ *Mulaha* D.

Mailuan languages   Bauwaki ■ Binahari ■ Domu ■ *Laua* ᴅ ■ Mailu (Mage) ■ Morawa.

Manubaran languages   Doromu ■ Maria.

Yareban languages   Aneme Wake ■ Bariji ■ Moikodi ■ Nawaru ■ Yareba.

Trans-New Guinea Phylum languages not belonging to the Central and West or the East Trans-New Guinea Phylum languages

TEBERAN-PAWAIAN LANGUAGES

Dadibi (Daribi, Karimui) ■ Folopa (Podopa) ■ Pawaia.

TRANS-FLY-BULAKA RIVER LANGUAGES

Agöb ■ Aramba (Upper Morehead) ■ Aturu ■ Bamu ■ Bine ■ *Bothar* (*Rema*) ᴇ ■ *Dorro* (*Tais*) ᴇ ■ Gidra ■ Gizra ■ Idi ■ Kanum ■ Kerewo ■ Kiwai, Northeast ■ Kiwai, Southern ■ Kiwai, Wabuda ■ Lewada-Dewara ■ Maklew ■ *Mari* (*Dorro*) ᴇ ■ Meriam (Miriam-Mir) ■ *Moraori* ᴇ ■ Morigi ■ Mutum ■ Nambu ■ Peremka (Kunja) ■ Rouku (Ara, Tokwasa) ■ Tirio ■ Tonda ■ Waia ■ Yei (Yey) ■ Yelmek.

TURAMA-KIKORIAN LANGUAGES

Ikobi-Mena ■ Kairi (Dumu) ■ Omati.

ELEMAN LANGUAGES

?Kaki Ae (*Tate, Raepa Tati*) ᴘ ■ Keuru ■ Koriki (Purari) ■ Opao ■ Orokolo ■ Toaripi ■ Uaripi.

INLAND GULF LANGUAGES

Ipiko ■ *Karami* ᴅ ■ Minanibai ■ Tao-Suamato.

KAURE LANGUAGES

Kapori ᴇ-ꜱ ■ Kaure ■ Kosadle (Kosare) ■ *Narau* ᴇ.

KOLOPOM LANGUAGES

Kimaghama ■ Ndom ■ Riantana.

MEK LANGUAGES

Eipomek ■ Gilika ■ Hmanggona (Naltje) ■ Ketengban ■ Korupun ■ Nipsan (Yaly, Abenago) ■ Sela ■ Una (Goliath) ■ Yale, Kosarek (Kosarek).

NIMBORAN LANGUAGES

Gresi ■ Kemtuik ■ *Kwansu* P ■ Mekwei ■ Nimboran.

PAUWASI LANGUAGES

Dubu P ■ Emumu ■ Towei ■ Yafi.

SENAGI LANGUAGES

Angor (Senagi) ■ Kamberataro.

SOUTH BIRD'S HEAD LANGUAGES

Arandai ■ *Duriankere* S ■ Inawatan (Suabo) ■ Kais (Kampung Baru, Aiso, Atori) ■ Kokoda (Samalek, Oderago) ■ Kemberano (Kalitami) ■ Konda (Ogit) ■ Puragi (Mogao) ■ Tarof (Nebes) ■ Yahadian (Nerigo).

TIMOR-ALOR-PANTAR LANGUAGES

Abui ■ *Adabe* P ■ Blagar ■ Bunak ■ Fataluku ■ Kabola ■ Kafoa ■ Kelon ■ Kolana ■ Kui ■ Lamma ■ Makasai ■ *Maku'a* (*Lovaea*) M ■ Nedebang ■ *Oirata* (*Maaro*) E ■ Tanglapui ■ Tewa ■ Woisika.

Isolated languages belonging to the Trans-New Guinea Phylum

Dem ■ Molof ■ *Mor*$_2$ S ■ Morwap (Janggu) ■ Oksapmin ■ *Tofamna* P ■ *Usku* S.

Sepik-Ramu Phylum languages

Main language stocks

SEPIK LANGUAGES

Abau ■ *Ak* E ■ Alamblak ■ Amal ■ Ambulas ■ Awun ■ Bahinemo ■ Bikaru ■ Biksi ■ Bisis (Yambiyambi) ■ Bitara ■ Boikin ■ Bouye ■ Burui ■ Chenapian ■ Gaikundi ■ Hewa ■ Iatmul ■ Iwam ■ Iwam, Sepik ■ Kalou ■ Kamnum ■ *Kaningra* (*Kaningara*) P ■ Kapriman ■ Karawa ■ Kimki ■ Koiwat ■ Kwanga ■ Kwasengen ■ Kwoma ■ Manambu ■ Mari ■ Mehek ■ Namia ■ Ngala ■ Niksek ■ Pahi ■ Pasi ■ Piame ■ Saniyo-Hiyowe ■ Sawos ■ Sengo ■ *Sumariup* (*Sogoba*) E ■ Wamsak ■ Watakataui ■ Wogamusin ■ Yelogu ■ Yerakai ■ Yessan-Mayo.

RAMU LANGUAGES

Abu ■ Aiome ■ Aion ■ Akrukay ■ Andarum ■ Anor ■ Arafundi ■ Awar ■ Banaro ■ Biwat ■ Borei ■ Bosngun ■ Botin ■ Breri ■ Bun ■ Changriwa ■ *Gorovu* (*Yerani*) S ■ Hagahai ■ Haruai ■ Igana ■ Igom ■ Itutang ■ Kaian ■ Kire ■

Kominimung ■ Kyenele ■ Langam ■ Maramba ■ Mekmek ■ Midsivindi ■ Mikarew ■ Miyak ■ Mongol ■ Pinai ■ Rao ■ Romkun ■ Sepen ■ Tanggu ■ Tanguat ■ Wapi ■ Watam ■ Yaul.

Aberrant language stocks

GAPUN LANGUAGE

Gapun (*Taiap*) S(-M?).

LEONARD SCHULTZE LANGUAGES

Papi (*Paupe*) E ■ Pei ■ *Suarmin* (*Duranmin, Akiapmin*) E ■ Tuwari ■ Walio ■ Yabio.

NOR-PONDO LANGUAGES

Angoram ■ Chambri ■ Kopar ■ *Murik* (*Nor, Nor-Murik Lakes*) P ■ Tabriak (Karawari) *Yimas* P.

Torricelli Phylum languages

Agi ■ Aiku ■ Alatil ■ *Arapesh, Bumbita* P ■ Arapesh, Southern (Muhiang, Mufian) ■ Aruek ■ Aruop ■ Au ■ Aunalei ■ Beli ■ Bragat (Alauagat, Yauan) ■ *Bukiyip* (*Bukiyup, Mountain Arapesh, Kavu*) P-E ■ Buna ■ Bungain ■ Dia ■ Eitiep ■ Elepi ■ Elkei ■ Gnau ■ Kamasau ■ Kombio ■ Laeko-Libuat ■ Lilau ■ Mandi ■ Mitang ■ Monumbo ■ Muniwara ■ Ningil ■ Olo ■ Seta ■ Seti ■ Siliput ■ Sinagen ■ Torricelli ■ Urat ■ Urim ■ Urimo ■ Valman ■ Wanap ■ Wanib (Arinua) ■ Wiaki ■ Wom ■ Yahang ■ Yambes ■ *Yapunda* (*Reiwo*) E ■ Yau ■ Yil ■ Yis.

Geelvinck Bay Phylum languages

Awera E ■ Bapu ■ Barapasi (Baropasi) ■ Bauzi ■ Biritai ■ *Burate* E ■ *Dabra* (*Bok, Taria*) E ■ *Demisa* P ■ *Doutai* (*Taori, Tolitai, Dou, Dou-Fou*) E ■ Duvle ■ Edopi (Dou) ■ Eritai (Barua) ■ *Fayu* (*Sehudate*) P ■ Foau ■ Iau (Foi, Turu) ■ *Kaiy* (*Todi, Taori-kei*) P ■ Kirikiri ■ *Kofei* E ■ *Kwerisa* (*Taogwe*) M ■ Nisa (Bonefa, Kerema) ■ *Obokuitai* (*Ati, Aliki, Obogwitai*) P ■ Papasena ■ Rasawa ■ *Saponi* (M-)D ■ *Sauri* P ■ Saweru ■ Sikaritai ■ *Tause* (*Doa, Darha*) P ■ *Taworta* P ■ Tefaro (Demba) ■ Tunggare (Tarunggare) ■ *Wari* (*Weretai*) E ■ *Woria* M ■ Yawa.

West Papuan Phylum languages

Abun ■ Galela ■ Gamkonora ■ Hattam ■ *Ibu* D? ■ Kalabra ■ *Kao* E ■ Karon Dori ■ Kuwani ■ Loloda ■ Mai Brat ■ Makian, West ■ *Mansim* (*Borai*) M ■ Mantion (Manikion) ■ Meah (Mansibaber) ■ Modole ■ Moi ■ Moraid ■ Moskona (Sabena) ■ Mpur ■ Pagu ■ Sahu ■ Seget ■ Tehit ■ Ternate ■ Tidore ■ Tobaru ■ Tobelo ■ Tugutil ■ Waioli.

575

East Papuan languages

Anem ■ Ayiwo (Reefs) ■ Baniata ■ Bilua ■ Buin (Telei) ■ *Butam* D ■ *Dororo* (*Doriri*) D ■ Eivo ■ *Guliguli* D ■ Kairak ■ *Kazukuru* D ■ Keriaka ■ Kol ■ Koromira ■ Kunua ■ *Kuot* (*Panaras*) P ■ Lavukaleve ■ *Makolkol* D ■ Mali (Gaktai) ■ Nagovisi ■ Nanggu ■ Nasioi ■ Pele-Ata (Wasi) ■ Qaqet ■ Rotokas ■ Santa Cruz (Natügu, Nendö, Löndäi) ■ *Savo* (*Savosavo*) E ■ Simbali ■ Siwai ■ Sulka ■ *Taulil* P ■ Uisai ■ Ura (Uramat) ■ Yele (Yeletnye).

Sko Phylum languages

Krisa ■ *Puari* S ■ Rawo ■ Sangke ■ Sko ■ Vanimo ■ *Warapu* E-S ■ Wutung.

Left May (Arai) Phylum languages

Ama (Waniabu) ■ Bo (Po) ■ Iteri (Yinibu) ■ Nimo ■ Owiniga (Arai) ■ Rocky Peak.

Kwomtari-Baibai Phylum languages

Baibai ■ Fas ■ Guriaso ■ Kwomtari ■ Nai (Biaka, Amini) ■ Pyu.

Amto-Musian Phylum languages

Amto E ■ *Musan* (*Musian*) E.

Isolated Papuan languages not belonging to any group, and not related to each other

Baso ■ Burmeso (Taurap) ■ Busa ■ Karkar-Yuri (Karkar, Yuri) ■ *?Kembra* M ■ Kibiri (Porome) ■ *Pauwi* P ■ Warembori (Warenbori) ■ Yale (Nagatman) ■ *Yoki* S ■

Australian languages

This list only includes languages which are healthy, threatened, recently extinct or extinct languages whose former existence is still in living memory, though it may have become extinct long ago.

Pama-Nyungan languages

Arandic languages

Alyawarra ■ *Andegerebinha* M ■ Anmatjirra ■ Aranda, Eastern (Eastern Arrernte) ■ Aranda, Western ■ *Kaytetye* (*Gaididj, Kaititj*) P-E.

Baagandji languages

Baarundji D ■ *Bandjigali* D ■ *Gurnu* D ■ *Darling* (*Southern Baagandji*) M.

Bandjalang language

Bandjalang M.

Barrow Point language

Barrow Point D.

Bunaban languages

Bunaba E-S ■ *Gunian* S.

Durrubulan languages

Djendewal D ■ *Yagara* D.

Dyirbalic languages

Bandyin D ■ *Dyirbal* M ■ *Warrgamay* D.

Flinders Island language

Flinders Island D.

Galgadungic languages

Kalkutung (Kalkatung, Galgadung) D ■ *Yalarnnga* D.

Kala Lagaw Ya language

Kala Lagaw Ya (Kala Yagaw Ya, Mabuiag) P.

Karnic languages

Arabana M ■ *Badjiri* D ■ *Biladaba* D ■ *Dieri* M-D? ■ *Dirari* D ■ *Garlali* D ■ *Gunga-lanya* D ■ *Malyangaba* D ■ *Midhaga* D ■ *Ngamini* D ■ *Ngura* D ■ *Pitta Pitta* D ■ *Punthamara (Bundhamara)* D ■ *Wanggamala* D ■ *Wangkangurru* D ■ *Wanggumara* D ■ *Yandruwandha* D ■ *Yardliwarra* D ■ *Yarluyandi* D ■ *Yawarawarga* M.

Kulinic languages

Wembawemba D.

577

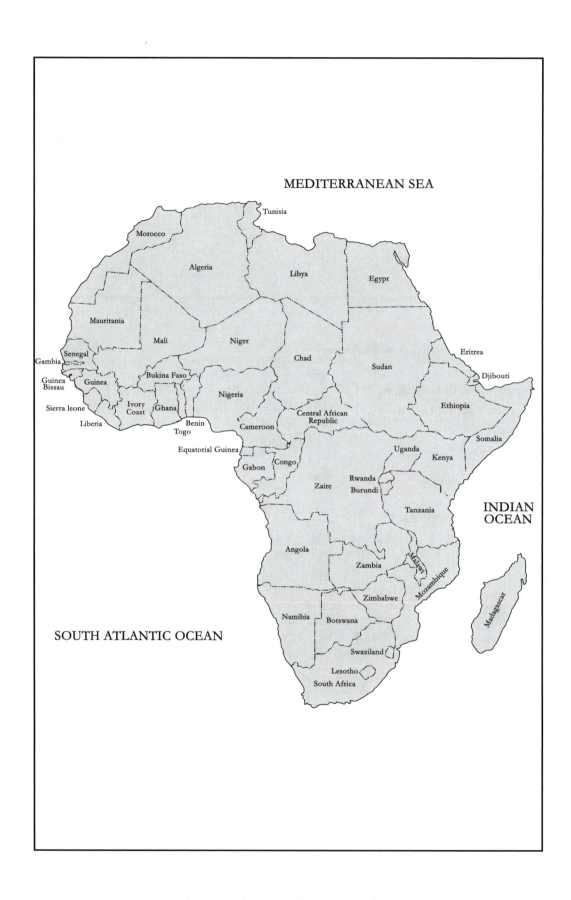

7

Africa[1]

Gerrit J. Dimmendaal and F. K. Erhard Voeltz

There will still be ample time and opportunity to do all the theorizing any linguist's heart might desire. But if considerable numbers of linguists are not willing to take temporary leave of their desks, blackboards and computers for an urgent stint of fieldwork, there will be incalculably fewer data and texts for their successors to measure future theoretical models against.

(Nancy Dorian, 1994: 802, review of *Endangered Languages* by R. H. Robins and E. M. Uhlenbeck)

Language families

At least 25 per cent of the world's languages spoken today are situated in Africa, the continent from which modern humans – and presumably human language – originated. As a linguistic area, Africa is still characterized, not only by a large number of languages, but also by considerable genetic heterogeneity. According to a widely accepted genetic classification of African languages, that of Greenberg (1963a), there are four major phyla: Afroasiatic, Khoisan, Niger-Congo, and Nilo-Saharan. Greenberg's views present a synthesis of more than a century of scholarly work in the area of genetic classification. Though widely accepted, his classification has also led to some reclassification; moreover, in a sequel to his seminal work it has been suggested that there may be representatives of additional language families. The historical background to Greenberg's scholarly work, as well as of studies by scholars following up on his insights, is discussed below.

The core of Afroasiatic, formerly known as Hamito-Semitic, was recognized long prior to Greenberg's classificatory work. The unity of the relatedness of the Semitic languages, for example, was recognized by Jewish scholars as early as the tenth century (cf. Versteegh 1983). The genetic links between Semitic and Ancient Egyptian, the language of pharaonic times, gradually became clear after Champollion's decipherment of hieroglyphic Egyptian in the 1820s. Egyptian survived in a more recent form called Coptic, which probably became extinct in the sixteenth century, but which is still used as the liturgical language of the Monophysite Christian church in Egypt. The long extinct Semitic language Akkadian was rediscovered and identified as a Semitic language in the 1850s. Müller (1877) probably was the first to propose Hamito-Semitic as a genetic grouping including Egyptian and Semitic, as well as Berber (Libyco-Berber) and the then-known Cushitic languages of northeastern Africa. The term 'afroasiatique' probably was coined by Delafosse (1914).

In his pioneering series of studies on the genetic classification of African languages published between 1949 and 1954 and reprinted as a monograph in 1955, Joseph Greenberg accepted this phylum as a valid genetic grouping. But he also added a branch, Chadic, which included languages spreading out in various directions from Lake Chad. As pointed out by Greenberg (1955), the term Hamito-Semitic should be avoided, for Semitic constituted but one of the five branches; moreover, the concept 'Hamitic' had developed racist connotations during preceding decades, in particular after Meinhof's (1912) publication *Die Sprachen der Hamiten*, which constituted a mixture of genetic and typological as well as of (physical) anthropological criteria; Hamitic languages, according to Meinhof, were spoken originally by stock-keeping peoples of Caucasian stock.

In a sequel to Greenberg's revised classification of African languages published in 1963, Fleming (1969) proposed to excise one group then called West Cushitic from Cushitic and to accord it the status of a separate primary branch within Afroasiatic, called Omotic (after a major river in the area, the Omo). Although its Afroasiatic affiliation has been disputed, the allocation of Omotic within Afroasiatic is now well established, based on the attestation of classic morphological properties of Afroasiatic. These grammatical properties, e.g. the form of pronominal markers, case, and verbal derivational markers, are summarized in Hayward (2000). Given the considerable time-depth involved for Afroasiatic (the oldest documents for members of the Semitic branch dating back some four millennia) of course one only expects to find a minimum of reconstructable lexical roots. As grammatical features tend to be less subject to innovation, they constitute more crucial diagnostic features for genetic relationships. According to Hayward (2000), the subgrouping for Afroasiatic is as shown in Table 7.1.

During the nineteenth century, European missionaries and explorers also set out to study the vast number of languages south of the Sahara. The same era saw the commencement of comparative studies in which the historical relationships between these languages became a central issue. One of the genetic groupings emerging from this research, and situated in southern Africa, were the so-called Click languages, which

Table 7.1. The classification of Afroasiatic

1.	Berber (Lybico-Berber)	5.	Cushitic
2.	Chadic		5.1. Northern
	a. West Chadic		5.2. Central
	b. Biu-Mandara		5.3. Highland East Cushitic
	c. East Chadic		5.4. Lowland East Cushitic
	d. Masa		5.5. Dullay
3.	Egyptian		5.6. Southern Cushitic
4.	Semitic	6.	Omotic
	4.1. North-east		6.1. North Omotic
	4.2. North-west		6.2. South Omotic
	4.3. South Semitic		

received their name after a prominent typological feature; alternatively, these languages were also known as Bushmen and Hottentot languages. The modern term Khoisan (or Khoisan) probably was coined by Schultze (1928: 211) from the word for 'person', kxoe, in languages spoken by 'Hottentot' groups, and their name for foraging 'Bushmen' groups, San. The widely accepted genetic division of languages spoken by these groups into a Northern group, a Central group, and a Southern group, goes back to Bleek (1929); the Central group consists of "Bushmen" languages as well as "Hottentot" languages. Trombetti (1910) probably was the first author to hint at a possible link between Central Khoisan languages and a language spoken in Tanzania, Sandawe. It was Bleek (1929) apparently who first suggested that another language spoken in modern Tanzania, Hadza (also known as Tindiga or Kiindiga), should be considered as being related to the Khoisan languages of southern Africa. Greenberg (1963a: 66–75) tried to substantiate these claims for a common genetic origin through an additional listing of a series of grammatical properties as well as lexical similarities.

Khoisan languages once probably covered larger parts of present-day Southern Africa, possibly extending into East Africa, where Hadza and Sandawe are still spoken today (both in modern Tanzania). Most of the extinct languages of South Africa probably belonged to Southern Khoisan (see, for example, Köhler 1975 and Winter 1981 for surveys of Khoisan languages that have become extinct over the past centuries); today, this branch essentially consists of one member, the !Xu dialect cluster.

Khoisan probably is the one group on the African continent that has been affected most severely percentage-wise by cases of language shift and language death. According to Güldemann and Vossen (2000: 99), the number of languages and dialects may well have exceeded 100 in the past, but only thirty or so still exist today. Since many of them disappeared without having been documented (as was the case for Australian languages), historical-comparative work in this area is seriously hampered. The small number of scholars today working on these languages appear to treat Khoisan primarily as an areal, rather than a genetic, grouping. This position, whereby up to eight distinct families have been assumed, has been defended most vigorously by Westphal, e.g. in Westphal (1962). Vossen (1997), however, has provided further grammatical evidence in favour of Central Khoisan and Sandawe as a genetic relationship; moreover, his pioneering study is a first attempt to work out sound correspondences for Central Khoisan using classical neogrammarian methods.

In their survey of Khoisan, Güldemann and Vossen (2000:102) present the following grouping (Table 7.2) (which includes extinct languages such as Kwadi, once spoken in Angola, and possibly related to Central Khoisan and Sandawe).

Amongst the genetic groupings established by nineteenth-century comparativists was another group of languages also spoken in southern Africa, and extending northwards across a vast area towards Cameroon and Kenya. This group of languages

Table 7.2. The classification of Khoisan

1. Non-Khoe	3. Sandawe
1.1. Ju (Northern)	4. Kwadi
1.2. !Ui-Taa (Southern)	5. Hadza
1.3. ≠Hõã (isolate)	
2. Khoe (Central)	
2.1. Khoekhoe	
2.2. Kalahari Khoe	

is known today as Bantu, a label coined by Bleek (1862–9) after a common word for 'people' in these languages. Additional genetic groupings for Africa as a whole were established through the work of Sigismund Koelle's *Polyglotta Africana* (1854). Koelle, who was based as a missionary in Freetown, worked with speakers of over 150 different African languages, mostly expatriate-slaves from West Africa who had resettled in Sierra Leone after having been liberated. Koelle posited a number of (primarily geographical, but partially also genetic/typological) groupings in the West African region, e.g. Kru, West Atlantic ('Westatlantisch') and Mande (Manding), which were recognized by subsequent generations of scholars as genetic units themselves belonging to a larger family, later to be called Niger-Congo.

Languages south of the Sahara had also come to be known as 'Sudanic' languages after the Arabic expression for the lands of 'the blacks'. But whereas in the case of the West African members of this zone clear-cut evidence for genetic relationship was gradually forthcoming during the next decades, those in the north-central and eastern parts of the continent did not. This led Westermann (1927) to a postulation of three groups of 'Sudanic' languages: Western Sudanic, Central Sudanic, and Eastern Sudanic. The same author also was the first to observe that those languages in the western parts of the continent showed affinities with an already established language group known as Bantu.

In his series of groundbreaking comparative studies of African languages, published between 1949 and 1954 and reprinted in a monograph published in 1955, Greenberg proposed the name Niger-Congo for a genetic unit involving the so-called Western Sudanic languages and Bantu. According to Greenberg's classification, however, the vast number of Bantu languages covering major parts of central and southern Africa constitute but a subgroup within the Bantoid branch of Benue-Congo, one the six primary branches of Niger-Congo. Greenberg (1955) also included a group of languages spoken in a region between Nigeria and Sudan, called Adamawa Eastern, in this larger genetic grouping. In a follow-up to this classification, Greenberg (1963a) further included the Kordofan languages of north-central Sudan into a still larger phylum, called Niger-Kordofanian. (See also Gregersen 1977: 74–141, for further details on the classificatory history of African language phyla including Niger-Kordofanian.)

In more recent studies (e.g. Williamson 1989) the label Niger-Kordofanian has come to be replaced by Niger-Congo. Whereas many scholars accept the validity of Niger-Congo as a genetic grouping, its existence has not yet been proven on the basis of classical comparative methods of sound correspondences, although scholars like John Stewart have initiated this type of research through a series of publications (e.g. Stewart 1983). There has been relatively little discussion ever since the days of Sigismund Koelle on the validity of the various smaller units within this phylum. On the other hand, there is no consensus on the subclassification of Niger-Congo as a whole. One of the more recent subclassifications of the Niger-Congo language family, that of Williamson and Blench (2000) is repeated below in Table 7.3.

The Volta-Congo contains a West Volta-Congo branch, with Kru, Gur and Adamawa as well as Ubangian languages, and an East Volta-Congo group. The latter contains Kwa as well as Benue-Congo languages.

In the same groundbreaking comparative study of African languages referred to above, Greenberg (1955) further postulated the existence of a new family termed Macro-Sudanic. Since many of the languages included in this family were located in the watersheds of the Chari River and the Nile or in the areas in between them,

Table 7.3. The classification of Niger-Congo

1. Kordofanian
2. Mande-Atlantic-Congo
   a. Atlantic
   b. Mande
   c. Ijo-Congo
      i. Ijoid
      ii. Dogon-Congo
         1. Dogon
         2. Volta-Congo

Macro-Sudanic was subsequently redesignated as Chari-Nile, also in order to avoid possible confusion with the term 'Sudanic' as used by some of Greenberg's intellectual predecessors. The Chari-Nile family included, amongst others, a Central Sudanic and an Eastern Sudanic branch. The latter were coterminous with, but not entirely identical with Westermann's Central Sudanic and Eastern Sudanic, since specific languages and language groups were added or excluded from these groups by Greenberg. In his classificatory work, Greenberg further followed the lead of scholars such as Bryan, Conti Rossini, Johnston, Lukas, Murray, Stevenson, and Tucker, whose pioneering descriptive and comparative work had resulted in more detailed knowledge of the language map of eastern and central Africa.

In the follow-up study published in 1963, purporting a new and comprehensive genetic classification of all African languages, Greenberg postulated the Nilo-Saharan family. This superstock, constituting the fourth phylum on the African continent next to Afroasiatic, Niger-Kordofanian (Niger-Congo) and Khoisan, was essentially the earlier Chari-Nile family together with certain languages or groups formerly assigned by Greenberg and others to independent and historically isolated units (Koman, Fur, Mimi, Maban, (Central) Saharan). The different groups, constituting the Nilo-Saharan family according to Greenberg (1963a), are presented below in Table 7.4 with some nomenclature amendments proposed by different scholars in later studies.

Meroitic, a language surviving only in inscriptions as it became extinct after the Meroe kingdom (or Kingdom of Kush) fell to the expanding Ethiopian empire of Aksum in the fourth century AD, has also been claimed to be a Nilo-Saharan language. Meroitic was written in a consonantal alphabet partly derived from Egyptian with some additional symbols of indigenous origin. In the first decade of the twentieth century the script was partly deciphered by the Egyptologist Griffith.

As was the case with Niger-Congo, the Nilo-Saharan phylum has also been subject to various attempts at subclassification, e.g. by Bender (2000) and Ehret (2001). In these studies, lower-level units established in earlier work are usually retained, but, it is argued, Chari-Nile does not constitute a valid unit within Nilo-Saharan. Ehret (2001: 88–9), for example, divides Nilo-Saharan into two major subgroups:

1 Koman
2 Sudanic with Central Sudanic and Northern Sudanic; the latter contains all the remaining subgroups distinguished by Greenberg, i.e. Eastern Sudanic (called Eastern Sahelian by Ehret), Fur, Kunama, Maban, Nera, Saharan, and Songhai.

Table 7.4. The classification of Nilo-Saharan

	Current label
1. Songhai	Songhai
2. Saharan	Saharan
3. Maba	Maban
4. Fur	Fur
5. Chari-Nile	Chari-Nile
A. Eastern Sudanic	Eastern Sudanic
1. Nubian	Nubian
2. Murle etc.	Surmic
3. Barea	Barea
4. Ingassana	Eastern Jebel
5. Nyima, Afitti	Nyimang, Afitti
6. Temein, Teis-um-Danab	Temein, Keiga Jirru
7. Merarit, Tama, Sungor	Taman
8. Dagu of Darfur etc.	Daju
9. Nilotic	Nilotic
10. Nyangiya, Teuso	Kuliak
B. Kunama	Kunama
C. Berta	Nera
D. Central Sudanic	Central Sudanic
6. KomaKoman	

In Greenberg's 1963 comparative study of African languages, the Kadu languages were classified as members of the Kordofanian group, the latter forming the Niger-Kordofanian phylum together with Niger-Congo. Greenberg also pointed out, however, that the Kadu group showed considerable divergence from the rest. Today, it is widely assumed that Kadu (a label coined after the common word for 'person' in these languages) is part of Nilo-Saharan (compare Bender 2000). According to Ehret (2001: 68), the Kadu languages do not belong to Nilo-Saharan proper, although they 'may possibly be related at some deeper level to Nilo-Saharan as a whole'.

A number of Africanists have expressed their reservations about the genetic affiliation of the Ubangian branch within Adamawa-Ubangian or even as a proper member of Niger-Congo (e.g. Erhard Voeltz); others have expressed their doubts about Mande's affiliation to Niger-Congo, or Songhai to Nilo-Saharan. A number of Africanists have expressed their doubt about the genetic unity of Atlantic as a separate branch within Niger-Congo, as the genetic distances between several of the languages involved at times is huge (Voeltz 1996; Wilson f.c.). Since most of the languages classified as Atlantic have retained the archaic noun-class system, it may in fact have been this latter (typological) feature, lacking for example in neighbouring Mande languages, which led to their subgrouping as members of one primary branch within Niger-Congo. It has also been claimed that Niger-Congo and Nilo-Saharan may form a still larger genetic unit, called Kongo-Saharan (compare Gregersen 1972, Creissels 1981, Blench 1995). The present author also adheres to this view of a larger genetic grouping, with the Songhai cluster and Mande probably constituting early splits from this macro-family; conjectural evidence in favour of this hypothesis is to be found in rather specific morphological features (compare, for example, Dimmendaal 2001a).

As a result of more recent research, it has become clear that in the West African area there are a number of languages possibly constituting early splits from Niger-Congo. This appears to apply to isolated languages such as Mbre (Pre) in the Ivory Coast, and Mpre, a language once spoken in Ghana which appears to have become extinct. More problematic in terms of genetic classification is a language known as Laal, which is spoken in Chad. As pointed out by Williamson and Blench (2000: 36), it contains 'substantial Chadic and Adamawa elements as well as a core vocabulary of unknown provenance'. In situations where the source languages for specific borrowings, and the relative chronology in which they entered specific languages, cannot be traced back, and where closely related languages have become extinct, the limitations of our comparative methods do not allow us to distinguish retentions from innovation through borrowing in such genetic isolates. This of course complicates classificatory work to a considerable extent. It is easy to see how a situation such as that reported for Laal, for example, could come about historically. If, a thousand years from now, English were the only Indo-European language left – all other members of the family having disappeared without any trace – we would find a language with lexical strata of all kinds: words like 'potato' or 'tomato' would point towards Amerindian languages (assuming they would still be spoken, and words like 'cipher' and 'algebra' would show a link with Semitic languages, if these retained reflexes of these words. But there would not be enough evidence to allow English to be classified with any known language family. In the case of English we know that we are dealing with borrowings; moreover, the relative chronology of these lexical strata is clear. But for languages without earlier written sources – such as Laal – which share lexical items with languages belonging to distinct genetic groupings, it is clear that the lexicon will not provide any clues on genetic relationship. (See also Dimmendaal 1995 for a discussion.)

There appear to be a number of other still unclarified cases for genetic subgrouping on the African continent. In, for example southwestern Ethiopia, there are – what appear to be – two linguistic isolates, both of which are highly endangered as well: Biraile (Ongota), and Shabo (Mekeyir). In addition, the former language of the Jalabe in northeastern Nigeria may constitute a linguistic isolate according to Kleinewillinghöfer (2001). It is possible of course that these languages represent the last members of an otherwise extinct African language family.

As pointed out above, most Khoisan specialists appear to treat this proposed phylum as an areal, rather than a genetic, grouping. This would imply that languages such as Hadza (in Tanzania) constitute additional linguistic isolates. The genetic classification of these African languages cannot be clarified until in-depth studies become available of their grammatical structure, and of morphological features in particular. The latter tend to be more resilient to change; consequently, these morphological properties potentially constitute important diagnostic properties for genetic relationships.

What these various problematic classifications with respect to Biraile, Jalabe, the Kadu group, the Koman group, Laal, Shabo, or the Ubanguian group (and possibly Mande) seem to tell us is that there is still more genetic variation on the African continent than we may have been led to believe by earlier investigations.

Linguistic development of the area

Whereas most Niger-Congo languages are spoken over a largely contiguous area, Nilo-Saharan languages have a rather fragmented distribution. The desertification of the Sahel region over the past six millennia probably had a more pervasive effect on human population, and consequently on the linguistic map in the area, than any other factor. The relatively small number of Nilo-Saharan languages (around 100 compared to over 1,000 Niger-Congo languages) may also be an exponent of the fact that many of them, in particular those situated in the western zones, are spoken in areas where human population has now become scarce as a result of gradual changes in geographical conditions.

As pointed out by Pachur and Kröpelin (1987), there is paleoclimatic evidence that between 9,000 and 4,000 BC the Sahara was more humid, held numerous lakes, and teemed with savanna fauna, e.g. giraffes and other larger mammals. At that period the southern edge of the eastern Sahara was some 500 kilometres further north than today, whereas there was a river system characterized by numerous ground water outlets and freshwater lakes with an overall length of more than 2,700km, and flowing eastwards from Eastern Chad and entering the Nile between the third and fourth cataracts. Also Lake Chad and the Mali lakes record high levels of rainfall and humid phases between 9,500 and 4,500 years ago. There is archaeological evidence that during this period, 'Saharans' began to tend cattle and make pottery, and then started to keep sheep and goats, and they may also have been beginning to domesticate sorghum and millet. Saharan pastoralism thus preceded the earliest known date (5,200 BC) for the arrival of food production in Egypt.

The gradual desertification, which started some 6,000 years ago, forced people to withdraw into areas with sufficient water supplies and where possibilities for food production were still available. During the same period also the drier areas of the Arabian Peninsula emerged. In the Middle East, people concentrated their settlements in the vicinity of major rivers such as the Euphrates and the Tigris. The gradual desertification in the Saharan region resulted in a concentration of settlement along remaining water sources. Thus, in the border area between Chad and Sudan, a region characterized by mountains and watersheds, one finds a plethora of languages even today. In this area, genetically isolated Nilo-Saharan languages (compare Greenberg's classification above), such as Fur are found, as well as the closely related Amdang language, the Maba-Mimi languages, Eastern Sudanic groups belonging to the Daju cluster, the Tama cluster and the Nubian cluster, Central Sudanic languages such as Sinyar, Saharan languages such as Berti and Zaghawa, as well as Arabic-speaking groups. What kind of languages these earlier inhabitants of the Saharan region spoke is a question which can no longer be answered. But the present-day situation with mainly isolated Nilo-Saharan languages and language groups being scattered over this area suggests that at least some of these languages may have belonged to this phylum. Also, the distribution of specific typological features in these various languages suggests that some of the geographically isolated groups in the Sahel region were once part of a larger linguistic area, characterized by common typological features. At the phonological level, the presence of vowel harmony is one such characteristic pointing towards areal links with languages spoken in an area which is not or no longer geographically contiguous with these Nilo-Saharan languages. This type of vowel harmony (of the cross-height type; cf. Stewart 1967) appears to be found, for example, in the Tama group, a group of Nilo-Saharan languages spoken in the border area between Chad and Sudan. The same type of vowel harmony is attested in a wide range of languages much further towards the south and ranging from Senegal all the way towards Ethiopia (see also Dimmendaal 2001b). These latter languages belong to Niger-Congo, Nilo-Saharan as well as the Chadic and Omotic branch within Afro-asiatic. Vowel harmony of the cross-height type thus clearly is an areal phenomenon.

586

Its presence in the geographically isolated Tama languages is hard to explain unless some type of areal contact with languages further towards the south is assumed at some point in history. The alternative explanation, retention of this phonological property in the Tama group from a common Nilo-Saharan ancestor, also implies some historical explanation, namely inheritance from a common ancestor, which had this kind of vowel harmony. Cross-height vowel harmony of the type found in the Tama languages is indeed attested in other Eastern Sudanic groups, e.g. Surmic or Nilotic; speakers of these languages today are found mainly in the southern Sudan and adjacent regions of Uganda, Kenya, and Ethiopia. In either case, the gradual desertification of the Sahara region helps to explain why the vowel harmony band is now discontinuous in the north central African region.

The Tama languages and other Nilo-Saharan languages in the north-central African region, such as the Maban group, Fur or Nyimang (the latter being spoken in the Nuba Mountains of north-central Sudan), also share various morpho-syntactic features with languages further towards the east and southeast. For example, they all have a verb-final syntax with its concomitant properties (in terms of the relative position of auxiliary verbs and the common use of postpositions or postnominal modifiers). Also, the use of converbs and verbal compounding appears to be common in languages in a region ranging from northern Nigeria and Niger eastwards towards Ethiopia (cf. Amha and Dimmendaal 2006 for further details).

Verb-final languages are found mainly in northeastern Africa, in particular in the Omotic and Cushitic branch of Afroasiatic. Today, Nilo-Saharan groups such as the Tama languages, Maban, and Fur are spoken in geographically isolated areas of the Saharan region, far away from the Cushitic or Omotic region in northeastern Africa. Moreover, each of these groups probably constitutes a genetically relatively isolated unit within Nilo-Saharan. Consequently, these common typological features are not easily explained as the result of areal diffusion in more recent times. Clearly, an explanation in terms of areal contact or diffusion between these Nilo-Saharan groups and Cushitic and/or Omotic (i.e. Afroasiatic) groups at a much earlier point in history is a more plausible hypothesis. The former presence of a major river system flowing from eastern Chad towards the Nile in modern Sudan provides a natural ecological environment where such areal diffusion of linguistic features may have occurred. The geographical discontinuity with respect to this typological feature would be a natural consequence of the gradual desertification of the area.

Whereas a gradual geographical isolation or retraction towards less arid zones in the area may have been one outcome of the desertification, migration – for either ecological or political reasons – may have constituted an alternative scenario. The Nuba Mountains in Sudan, for example, appear to have functioned as a refugium area in this respect. This region is characterized by a large number of languages (over forty in fact), belonging to different Niger-Saharan groups (Kadu, Nubian, Nyimang, Temein) as well as to the Kordofanian branch within Niger-Congo. The large number of languages in the Nuba Mountains, and the at times considerable genetic distance between them (e.g. between the Kordofanian languages, which form a subgroup within Niger-Congo), suggests that we are dealing with an area where groups have been settled over a considerable period of time. The typological differences between different languages in the Nuba Mountains, which range from verb-initial to verb-final, again suggests that we are not dealing with an ancient diffusion area, but rather with a region to where groups migrated at different points in time over the past millennia. Of course, this is supported by the fact that the various languages belong to different language families. For a number of them, closely related languages are found outside the Nuba mountain region. This again supports the hypotheses concerning the historical scenario sketched above. Nubian languages, for example, are spoken in other parts of the Sudan as well as in Egypt. Apart from 'Hill' Nubian, there are Nubian languages which are spoken along the banks of the Nile (in northern Sudan and Egypt); in addition, there are two varieties, Midob and Birked, which are spoken in Dar Fur Province, northern Sudan. These latter languages and the Nubian languages spoken in the vicinity of the Nile presumably represent ancient instances of linguistic dispersion related to the desertification in the Wadi Howar region (discussed above). There is also historical evidence (from ancient sources) of migrations of Nubian groups living along the Nile further north into the Nuba Mountains. During the destruction of the Nubian kingdoms by the Arabs between the thirteenth and sixteenth centuries, some of the Nubian groups dispersed into the hill country of Kordofan, north-central Sudan, taking their name with them. By extension, the name Nubii (or variants of this name) came to be used to designate other peoples of this region as well. The variant name 'Nuba' is therefore primarily a geographical term, referring to the inhabitants of the region known today as the Nuba Mountains. Historically, however, the name is erroneous in view of the diversity of languages and cultures which the inhabitants of these hills present.

Another such retreat area is found in the area north of the upper Benue River, Nigeria (Kleinewillinghöfer 2001: 239). Also, the Ethiopian highlands appeared to have constituted another refugium of sorts over the past millennia. This at least is suggested by the great number of languages and language families found in the area compared to many other regions across the continent. First, there are Omotic languages; given the fact that virtually all Omotic languages are all situated in this area, their common linguistic ancestor probably was spoken in these highlands. But in addition, there are Cushitic and Semitic languages spoken in this area. Third, there are Nilo-Saharan languages. And, rather strikingly, there are two languages already referred to above which either form a language family of their own, or, alternatively, constitute early split-offs from Nilo-Saharan (or Afroasiatic), namely Biraile (Ongota) and Shabo (Mekeyir). Apart from Omotic and the two isolates, all other genetic groups are represented in various other parts of east and central Africa. This again suggests that the highland area probably functioned as a niche providing ecological (or social-political) advantages in historical times.

The historical processes leading to the situation as it is found today thus appear to have been multivalued. On the one hand, an expansion and historical diversification of languages must have taken place in certain areas (e.g. for Omotic, Nilotic or Surmic), often resulting in contact processes with other language groups or families. There is also evidence for a reduction (probably as a result of climatological changes) of human habitation in certain areas, e.g. in the eastern Sahel region. In addition, and related to the desertification phenomena, one can identify refugium areas.

The geographical expansion of language groups may have been gradual in some cases, e.g. for Omotic, with languages being spread over a relatively contiguous region; the at times considerable historical differences between these Omotic languages suggests that great time depths are involved in the historical divergence for this Afroasiatic branch. Alternatively, the considerable structural homogeneity with a high number of cognate forms in the case of the approximately 400 Bantu languages, which are spread over a large region, suggests that here a rather rapid expansion may have occurred. Bantu languages, which form a lower-level subgroup within the large Niger-Congo family, are spread over an area ranging from Cameroon towards Kenya and south of this area. The fact that they are relatively closely related suggest that punctuation was involved, i.e. a rapid expansion which probably started from the border area between Cameroon and Nigeria (where their closest relatives within the Benue-Congo group, the subgroup to which they belong, are spoken). Such rapid expansions usually are related to cultural (technological) innovations. Possibly, the use of iron led to improved food production techniques and higher population densities, as well as new political organizations during the early periods of the Bantu expansion. In their eastward and southward expansion, speakers of Bantu languages must have met with pygmy groups already inhabiting the forested regions. Whether these pygmy groups spoke languages belonging to one of the four phyla proposed by Greenberg or to still other phyla that have disappeared since, is something we will never know. As pointed out by Vansina (1986), it is probably wrong to assume that invading farmers speaking Bantu languages engulfed the pygmy homeland. Instead, Vansina (1986: 435–6) proposes the following scenario:

> The way in which this occurred can be visualized by postulating a model of farming villages (all farmers in the forest lived in villages) surrounded by bands of hunter-gatherers, often speaking different languages among themselves. The villages became hubs in social and economic relationships and their languages became linguae francae. That is, bilingualism was more common among hunter-gatherers than among farmers. In the long run the smaller units of hunter-gatherers, unit by unit, will lose their languages. The villagers will not, although in the whole interacting region their number may be smaller than that of all hunter-gatherers combined. Add to it the necessary prestige which smelters of iron and purveyors of bananas and salt enjoyed and it is not surprising that all pygmy languages disappeared.

Today, and this presumably holds for the past as well, there are pygmy farmers, and Negro hunter-gatherers for example. Characteristically, however, pygmy groups speak languages belonging to widely distinct language families, suggesting that language shift may have occurred amongst them as part of a social adaptation strategy towards their non-pygmy neighbours time and again. The Baka in Cameroon speak a variant of Ngbaka (Adamawa Ubangian; Niger-Congo), whereas the Aka (Central African Republic, Congo-Kinshasa) speak a Bantu language (Benue-Congo); the Mamvu in Congo (Congo-Kinshasa) speak a Central Sudanic (Nilo-Saharan) language, etc. This situation appears to have parallels elsewhere in the world; compare, for example, Malaysian Negritos and Philippine Negritos, who adopted Austroasiatic and Austronesian languages, respectively, from the farmers who came to surround them.

Further towards the south and southeast, speakers of Bantu languages came into contact with Khoisan groups. This social interaction appears to have been characterized by peaceful co-existence, as evidenced for example through intermarriage. Although Khoisan languages appear to have disappeared as a result of contact with Bantu, it was mainly the arrival of Europeans from the seventeenth century onwards which led to the extinction of so many Khoisan languages, also as a result of genocide.

The picture emerging from these various historical scenarios sketched above is one characterized by gradual expansion or regression of languages and language families, accompanied occasionally by language shift; in individual cases, there may have been rapid language shift as well. What should be avoided, since there appears to be no empirical evidence for this, is a 'Clapham Junction theory of African history', where people are assumed to have been on the move all the time, migrating across the continent like ping-pong balls millennium after millennium. As shown next, the presence of large convergence areas further suggests that these historical developments were mostly gradual in nature; the distribution of various typological properties is best explained as a result of relatively stable linguistic situations lasting over considerable periods of time, and allowing for the gradual spreading of typological features between languages that were either genetically related or not.

Linguistic areas, spread zones and residual zones

Africa south of the Sahara constitutes a linguistic zone with respect to specific phonological features such as the prominence of tone. Also, features such as vowel harmony are widespread, covering an area ranging from Senegal all the way towards Ethiopia, as pointed out in the preceding section. These and other features (such as nasalized vowels, labial-velar stops, and clicks) are indicative of ancient convergence areas, resulting from long-term multilingualism, a situation that is still common today, as many Africans are polyglots. At the same time, there is also considerable typological variation, with specific phonological, as well as morphological, syntactic and semantic features clustering around smaller linguistic areas. In view of the genetic heterogeneity and the absence of lingua francas covering larger areas of the continent, this type of typological diversity of course is what one should expect. A number of these smaller convergence zones are discussed next, also in relation to patterns of bilingualism and language shift.

In a continent-wide word order typology of African languages, Heine (1976) has argued that there are four common constituent order types with their concomitant features on the continent:

1 Type A (with SVO order; corresponding to type I in Greenberg's 1966 typology)
2 Type B (with SAUX OV order, sometimes alternating with SVO, and postpositions; this type was set up as an additional type by Heine 1976)
3 Type C (with VSO order; corresponding to type III in Greenberg 1966)
4 Type D (with SOV order; corresponding to type II in Greenberg 1966)

Type C and type D languages constitute each other's mirror image in terms of head/modifier order, in that in the former prepositions, rather than postpositions, tend to be used, with auxiliaries preceding rather than following main verbs.

The areal distribution of these types does not necessarily reflect larger convergence areas. The region where type A languages are spoken, for example, does not reflect one homogeneous syntactic type, as Heine (1976) has pointed out already. Type A languages in the central and southern African region (where Bantu languages are spoken) are characterized by extensive morphologies, whereas many of the type A languages spoken in the region between Nigeria and the Ivory Coast are more analytical in nature. Consequently, these languages classified as type A, based on the relative position of subject, verb and object, belong to different subtypes otherwise.

Such areal properties, often cutting across genetic boundaries, may point towards a diffusion of morphosyntactic (as well as phonological) properties. One of the best known convergence areas on the African continent is that of Ethiopian Semitic, first described by Leslau (1945; 1952). During the past two millennia (and starting probably some 2,500 years ago), Ethiopian Semitic languages, themselves originating from the Middle East, probably started to converge from a type C (i.e. verb-initial) towards a type D (verb-final) language. Whereas the validity of Ethiopia at large as a convergence area has been criticized (cf. Tosco 2000), the type D languages in the area do share a number of striking typological properties. The verb-final type is attested in Ethiopian Cushitic as well as Omotic languages. These various verb-final languages in northeastern Africa form an areal zone extending west towards Chad, also including a range of Nilo-Saharan languages. As argued in Amha and Dimmendaal (2006), this Nilo-Saharan zone coincides with a former river system in the southeastern Sahara, the lower Wadi Howar.

Another such convergence area, as described and defined by Heine (1976), is found in the border area between Ethiopia, Sudan, Uganda, and Kenya. Here, a series of verb-initial languages are found belonging to the Surmic and Nilotic branch as well as the Kuliak branch within Nilo-Saharan. Whereas Nilotic and Surmic are closely related, Kuliak probably constitutes a much earlier split-off from Nilo-Saharan. There is ample evidence for contact between speakers of these distinct languages, not only in terms of mutual borrowing, but also because of various cultural features shared by these groups (cf. Dimmendaal 1984; 1998).

There are a number of other verb-initial languages in eastern Africa, e.g. the Kadu languages in the Nuba Mountains of north-central Sudan, and the linguistic isolate (or Khoisan language) Hadza in Tanzania. Whether these once were part of a larger zone of verb-initial languages in East Africa cannot or can no longer be tested, since other indications of contact, e.g. lexical borrowing, appear to be missing. A verb-initial syntax is also attested for Berber, and for Ancient Egyptian Semitic languages of the Middle East, as well as for a number of languages belonging to the Chadic branch within Afroasiatic. Whether the verb-initial structure of these languages is due to the fact that they once constituted a linguistic diffusion zone of verb-initial languages again remains hypothetical. Given the limited number of constituent order types found cross-linguistically, the areal distribution observed today could equally well be due to independent development. In the same way, southern African Central Khoisan languages with SOV order probably constitute a separate linguistic zone from the verb-final type found in northeastern Africa.

As may be expected, given several decades of subsequent research, the typology proposed by Heine (1976) is in need of further refinement for a number of reasons. First, as new data became available for various languages in eastern Africa, it also became clear that there are a number of languages where the universally rare constituent order OVS may be argued to be basic. See, for example, Andersen 1988 for the Nilotic language Päri; similarly, it has been claimed that other languages closely related to Päri, may have a basic OVS constituent order, e.g. Anywa (Reh 1996), and Shilluk (Miller and Gilley 2001).

Second, there are languages in northeastern Africa with a strong tendency towards a verb-second constituent order whereby the initial constituent tends to be a topic (with variable syntactic functions, e.g. subject, object, or adjunct; compare Andersen 1992 for a description of the Nilotic language, Dinka, in this respect.

Third, constituent order constitutes but one parameter for cross-linguistic variation. Languages with similar or identical basic word order may differ in the way syntactic relations are expressed. For example, in the Ijo group within Niger-Congo as well as in the Saharan group within Nilo-Saharan, the basic position of the verb is sentence-final. But, whereas in the Ijo group syntactic relations are expressed periphrastically, e.g. through the use of serial verb constructions, the Saharan languages use case marking on noun phrases as well as verbal morphology in order to express syntactic cohesion.

Additional properties which are relevant for typological classifications, also from an areal point of view, involve the marking of syntactic relations either on phrasal or clausal heads (i.e. through head-marking) or on phrasal or clausal modifiers (i.e. through dependent-marking), as pointed out by Nichols (1986; 1992). Indeed, various strategies for the coding of syntactic relations in African languages have a clear-cut areal distribution. For example, the use of serial verbs in order to express an adjunctival role such as instrument, location, or benefactive, is common in an area ranging from the Ivory Coast eastwards towards the border area between Nigeria and Cameroon. Languages in this area belong to distinct Niger-Congo subgroups, such as Kwa, Benue-Congo, Gur, Mande and Ijo (Dimmendaal 2001b).

What is the relevance of these observations on areal types for a chapter on endangered languages in Africa? First, these cases of areal convergence show us that areal diffusion of features with relative stable (compound) bilingualism constitutes a clear-cut alternative to language shift and language loss. Second, there are spread zones in certain areas on the African continent (e.g. Bantu, Nilotic), characterized by a low degree of structural diversity and reflecting relatively shallow time depth (due to a relatively recent expansion over a larger area). Alternatively, there are residual zones, characterized by considerable genetic variation as well as a variation in linguistic types (cf. Nichols 1992 for a definition of spread zones and residual zones).

It is rather striking, when plotting endangered African languages on a map, that several endangered languages are found at the edge of so-called spread zones, e.g. where Nilotic borders on Kuliak or Southern Cushitic, or where Bantu has been encroaching upon Khoisan. Spread zones often seem to result from cultural innovations (or punctuation in the sense of Dixon 1997), and contacts between groups with different production modes indeed appear to constitute one trigger for language shift, as shown in the next section.

Whereas shift from a Khoisan language towards Bantu appears to have been common in areas where representatives from these groups got into contact with each other, the Khoisan region itself clearly constitutes a residual zone, with languages having coexisted next to each other over considerable periods of time. Güldemann (1998) has shown that the Kalahari Basin differs significantly in many features from these larger areas in Africa as a whole, or other parts of the world; also, the genetic density in this area is three times that for the rest of Africa. Central Khoisan languages are characterized according to Güldemann by head marking on the verb. There is also a rather extensive system of nominal and pronominal person-gender number system, as compared to Southern Khoisan and Northern Khoisan. Northern Khoisan is much more analytical in its morphosyntactic structure, with tense aspect mood as we as focus and negation markers occurring between the subject and the verb (Güldemann and Vossen 2000: 109). Clearly, then, we are dealing with a residual zone, which is best explained historically as an ancient area of dispersal of genetically related languages as well as of language groups which cannot or no longer be shown to belong to the same phylum.

The picture emerging from the linguistic data in the Khoisan area corresponds, in an interesting way, with physical anthropological variation. With almost 200 distinct features, the Khoisan area constitutes the most concentrated mix of ancient human genes, as argued by Soodyall and Jenkins (1998). The same authors have shown (using mitochondrial DNA sequence data from extant Khoisan people) that some of the mitochondrial DNA lineages found in Khoisan populations have diverged from a common ancestor between 73,000 and 112,000 years ago. Both the linguistic and the genetic situation point towards an equilibrium state where communities coexisted next to each other, without major languages absorbing others, and without any of them functioning as lingua francas for larger areas or absorbing other languages.

In the region north of the Khoisan area in southern Africa a spread zone with a relatively homogeneous set of Bantu languages is spoken, resulting from relatively recent expansions from the central African region. But in the Rift Valley area further towards the north, starting in Tanzania and extending towards the Red Sea, one again finds high genetic density combined with considerable structural-linguistic diversity. Apart from Bantu (Niger-Congo), one finds representatives from Nilo-Saharan (e.g. Kuliak, Surmic, Nilotic and other groups), from Afroasiatic (Omotic, Cushitic, and Semitic), as well as a number of possible linguistic isolates, e.g. Hadza (Tanzania), Biraile (Ethiopia), and Shabo (Ethiopia) in this area. The expansion of modern human beings appears to have started from southern Africa in a northern direction across the East African Rift Valley, and out of Africa into the Middle East over the past 100,000 years or so. Consequently, the genetic diversity may simply be the outcome of the great antiquity and co-existence of a number of indigenous linguistic stocks in the area. Nevertheless, language shift through ethnic fission and fusion appears to have been part and parcel of the cultural history of this area as well. These and other factors resulting in language shift are discussed in greater detail next.

The social background to language shift

There appears to be a widespread view among social scientists and linguists that language constitutes the most important identifying property in the social symbolization of ethnic identity. At the same time, it has been argued by Schlee (1989) as well as other social anthropologists, that specific social groups in eastern Africa often see their clan identity (based on a putative group descent line) as much more pervasive than ethnic identity. Interestingly, however, such clans are often distributed over distinct ethnic groups speaking distinct languages. Unseth and Abbink (1998) discuss the distribution of the clan name 'Mela', which is found among Surmic (Nilo-Saharan) speaking groups such as the Me'en and Suri, as well as the Omotic (Afroasiatic) Dizi. Such situations are best explained, as argued by Unseth and Abbink (1998: 104), if one assumes that there are connections between these ethnic groups in terms of migrating clans or lineages, which have been absorbed into another ethnic group. Many ethnic groups in eastern Africa, in particular those with a pastoral subsistence economy, appear to constitute amalgamations of formerly distinct groups (Dimmendaal 1989). Such shifts in ethnic identity (accompanied by language shift while at the same time retaining clan membership) appear to have been a common theme in the cultural history of eastern Africa. This at least is suggested by numerous case studies in the literature of submerged groups amongst various ethnic groups in eastern Africa.

Language shift of the type described above must have been common across Africa, either as a gradual process occasionally involving entire speech communities, or alternatively, through radical and sudden shift (without decay). Tosco (1998) has referred to this latter scenario, brought about by political factors such as invasions or by natural disasters, as the 'catastrophe theory'. When white settlers first appeared in southern Africa after 1600, for example, a radical decline in the number of Khoisan languages set in as a result of genocide as well as new diseases such as smallpox. Such scenarios appear to constitute the exception rather than the rule as far as Africa is concerned; instead gradual shift as well as ethnic fusion appear to have constituted the norm. Although no concrete evidence can be adduced to this end, given the lack of historical sources and the time depth involved, it seems logical – by extension of the argument – to assume that the desertification of the Sahel region caused people to abandon specific areas and to regroup themselves, with consequential shifts in language choice in intra-group communication, and occasionally with replacement of languages.

The historical development of Semitic, where written sources go back at least 3,000 years, shows us how complex and intricate in fact the history of languages may be; moreover, its development also shows us that language shift is but one historical outcome of language contact, next to convergence and creolization. Compare, for example, one of the earliest attested cases of language death, that of a Northeastern Semitic language, Akkadian, spoken by one of the earliest urban civilizations in Mesopotamia, and used as a language next to the linguistic isolate Sumerian. It is clear from the sources available on this extinct language that Akkadian strongly converged towards the target language Sumerian before it disappeared ultimately. There are various reports on other Semitic languages that have become extinct, e.g. Hadrami, Minaan, Qatabanian and Sabaean on the Arabian Peninsula, as well as the Ethiopian Semitic language Ge'ez. The latter language ceased to be a spoken language around 1000 AD, but Ge'ez developed into a liturgical language subsequently. Another, more recent case of language death of an Ethiopian Semitic language, is that of Gafat; Leslau met with – what appear to have been – four terminal speakers in 1947 (Leslau 1956). And then there is the remarkable history of Hebrew, at one point a virtually extinct language, now revived and renovated. In addition there are creolized forms of Semitic languages such as (Ki)Nubi, the Arabic-based Creole which emerged as a contact language amongst soldiers of the Mahdi in Sudan; today, most of its speakers are based in Uganda and Kenya.

Whether languages are pidginized and creolized, or whether they are abandoned in contact situations, of course depends on the nature of the social interaction. Pidginized languages typically emerge when incomplete access to the target language occurs. Language shift typically occurs in situations where one moves from integral bilingualism, i.e. a situation where one functions more or less in two languages, towards regressive (residual) bilingualism, i.e. towards a situation where the new target language is dominant. This latter situation is characteristic, for example, for second- or third-generation immigrant communities.

With respect to many endangered African languages, it is clear that it is not necessarily major lingua francas of the region, or national languages, which triggered language shift. Instead, assimilation to larger, more powerful or prestigious neighbouring groups may cause a shift in language solidarity. As observed, for example, by Connell (1998) with respect to the Mambila region in the border area between Nigeria and

Cameroon, it is essentially neighbouring languages, not African lingua francas or European languages, replacing local vernaculars. Alternatively, assimilation to smaller but culturally dominant groups may take place. Blench (1998:198) mentions such a case, that of the Fali language of the Fali Plateau (Cameroon/Nigeria) which has yielded to Ndoro, a language which is in retreat elsewhere.

The number of speakers appears to be but one factor, at times playing only a minor role as a determining factor in language stability. And here lies a fundamental problem in trying to determine the status of many African languages as being endangered or not. In her survey of endangered languages in Africa, Sommer (1992) took the small number of speakers (say less than 500) as an important parameter for language stability and language shift. But as Batibo and Tsonope (2000: xv) have observed, for example, with respect to the Khoisan languages of Botswana, 'one should avoid generalizing on the endangered Khoisan languages, as the smallness of a language in terms of numbers of speakers does not indicate that the language would die within a short time'. The authors compare the case of Zaramo (Tanzania), with over 200,000 'speakers' now loosing ground rapidly in favour of Swahili, with the case of the Tshabon Nama with hardly 200 speakers but still enjoying vitality. Such major shifts in language solidarity affecting large speech communities can be found all over the African continent, e.g. in Nigeria where the Edoid (Niger-Congo) language with 1 million speakers is developing into an endangered language, as speakers are shifting towards other languages such as Nigerian Pidgin English. Consequently, several of the languages listed in Sommer (1992) as being endangered have not been included in the present survey, whereas other languages at times involving several tens of thousands of (former) speakers are included in the list below.

Such divergent outcomes point towards the need for a sociolinguistic model, which distinguishes between different types of attitudes towards outside groups and their languages. A highly useful model in this respect, because of its explanatory value, is the one proposed by Malcolm Ross in a number of publications. According to Ross (2001) speech communities may be characterized, in terms of their external relationships, as 'closed' or 'open'. The former are characterized by few relationships links to speakers in other groups, whereas open groups have many such links. In addition, the latter may be either loose-knit or tight-knit in terms of their internal relationships. 'A loose-knit group is one where speakers are not bound together by tight bonds of linguistic solidarity, whilst a tight-knit group is one where they are', as pointed out by Ross (2001: 155).

Such differences in terms of social behaviour clearly have consequences for language behaviour as well. In the southern Sudan, for example, there is a small speech community of a few thousand people known as the Tennet, whose language belongs to the Surmic group within Nilo-Saharan. The Tennet often work as blacksmiths among neighbouring ethnic groups such as the Lotuxo or Toposa, whose languages they tend to use on a day-to-day basis. Because of this sociolinguistic situation, Dimmendaal (1982b) contended that Tennet might be endangered. However, as subsequent research has made clear, the Tennet appear to form an open but tight-knit society with a strong sense of ethnic identity; their own language clearly plays an important role in this self-identification. Open groups which are loose-knit presumably are prone to shift language solidarity more easily than tight-knit groups. By implication, African speech communities with relatively few speakers may keep their language when they constitute a closed group in terms of their external relationships, or, alternatively, when they constitute an open but tight-knit society. And here lies a major problem in estimating the language vitality of various groups. Where such studies on language attitudes are missing – and this is the case for many parts of Africa – we can only make an educated guess in determining whether a language is actually endangered or not. Moreover, social networks may change relatively fast. For example, the sociolinguistic situation for the Nubian (Nilo-Saharan) languages Kunuz and Fadicca in Egypt was relatively stable for several centuries, but experienced a sudden 'tip' when the Aswan Dam was built in the 1960s; part of the process involved a resettlement of about 50,000 people. This in turn resulted in new social networks, as a result of which many Nubian speakers preferred to use Arabic for its integrative role (in order to participate in Arab or Muslim culture), but also because a good command of Arabic was a sine qua non for a better economical position (Rouchdy 1989).

Traditionally, most regions in Africa are characterized by a multitude of languages. The multilingual situation was compounded by the addition of languages imported during the colonial period. Although, for example, Great Britain and France differed in their policies towards their colonies, their national languages played a major role in the administration of the overseas territories of both colonial powers. During the colonial period, the French instituted a 'French only' policy in their overseas colonies. The British colonial language policy on the other hand has always been non-monolingual, allowing the use of more than one language in the school system, even though the emphasis has differed from time to time. The most important effect of this approach has been the development of a multilingual pattern of national communication in different countries where English plays a role. Nevertheless, English continues to be the official language of Ghana, for example, and Ghanaian languages are used in other ways. Consequently, the scale of political dependence on the former imperial languages in African countries is much larger than in Asia, also with respect to the educational system. As pointed out by Bamgboṣe (1991: 49), the production of books in African languages represents only 16 per cent of total book production. But the impact of these languages on processes of language shift at the local, regional or national level appears to have been less pervasive than the role played by indigenous languages, at least until fairly recently. It is only more recently that Nigerian Pidgin English and Ghanaian English have begun to play an increasingly important role on a day-to-day basis in the southern parts of Nigeria and Ghana, to the extent that they may begin to replace indigenous languages as primary means of communication, especially in areas where no other lingua franca is available.

As Mazrui and Mazrui (1998: 82) have pointed out, 'Africa invented language; Asia sacralized language; and Europe universalized it'. The authors are referring to languages such as English or French, which have turned into global successes. However, in sharp contrast to the 'fourth world' situation in the Americas or Australia, where indigenous communities occasionally were turned into guests in their own countries, and were sometimes forced to give up their first language, the impact of European languages in the language shift process in Africa appears to have been limited both during colonial as well as in postcolonial times. In countries such as Ghana, Nigeria and Zambia English continued to be the sole official language of the country, whereas in Mali or the Ivory Coast French occupied this role. In countries like Kenya the official language English is used next to the national language Swahili at various public levels of communication. None of these languages it would seem, however, were ever used as an instrument or tool in order to direct language behaviour, e.g. in order to eliminate the use of other languages.

For most states in postcolonial Africa there were no indigenous languages that could play the role of a politically neutral language to be invoked in furthering national integration. There are only a few virtually monolingual countries, Burundi, Lesotho, Madagascar, Mauritius, Rwanda, Seychelles, Somalia, and Swaziland. And as the more recent political history of some of these countries shows, a one-language nation is not an absolute guarantee for national integration, or 'nationism' (i.e. of political integration and efficiency in running a country), as Bamgboṣe (1991) has called it.

One of the few African countries where an indigenous language has become the national language after independence is Tanzania with Swahili. The latter language had developed from a minority language into a widespread lingua franca in East Africa already during the nineteenth century. Swahili has been characterized as a 'preponderant language' by Mazrui and Mazrui (1998: 125), i.e. as an indigenous language which is very widespread as a second language but whose native speakers are not numerous enough or otherwise dominant or powerful enough in society to be politically threatening. By contrast, dominant languages such as Bambara in Mali or Moore in Burkina Fasso, and Hausa in Nigeria, were never considered as languages of national integration, since they are not politically neutral languages. Promoting one of these as the national language, e.g. Hausa in Nigeria, would have constituted a serious political mistake. Nevertheless, one may observe an ever-increasing role in daily interaction for major lingua francas such as Swahili, but also for Hausa and other languages, in spite of differences in their external setting (in terms of Sasse's 1992a, 1992b model of language shift). Swahili is beginning to replace other languages as a primary language in particular in coastal regions of Tanzania, and Hausa is replacing various languages in northern Nigeria. As shown in an elegant contribution by Haruna (1997), there have been various social and historical factors contributing to the rapid spread of Hausa. The latter developed into a functional language associated with progress, because of its role in the educational system of the region, its association with a powerful religion (Islam), its status as a lingua franca (and related to that, producing for a market economy), as well as other factors.

Ethiopia was never colonized by a European country, and consequently European languages never played a major role in the administrative or educational system. Whereas Amharic was the dominant language during Haile Selassie's reign, the use of languages other than the national language Amharic became a regular feature of the education system after 1974, when the Derg regime overthrew the emperor Haile Selassie. In this respect, the new government followed a major trend in the postcolonial period of many African countries characterized by a move in the direction of extending the use of African languages for initial literacy and as media of instruction. More recent surveys show that the political decision to teach literacy in fifteen languages in Ethiopia has not been implemented effectively, since almost all the resources of the state ended up being allocated to the three major languages Amharic, Tigrigna and Oromo. It is also to be kept in mind that the minor languages were, for the most part, scarcely used for written communication before the campaigns. Nevertheless, the important role of these major languages in the educational system does have some effect on language attitudes. For example, knowledge of Amharic is generally considered to be important in Ethiopia because it enhances social mobility within the country. But language shift, e.g. towards Amharic as a first language, for example, is not more common than shifts towards other Ethiopian languages with a more regional distribution.

The effect of the educational system on language attitudes in this respect accordingly appears to be minor.

'Africans south of the Sahara are nationalistic about their race, and often about their land; and of course many are nationalistic about their particular "tribe". But nationalism about African languages is relatively weak as compared with India, the Middle East or France', according to Mazrui and Mazrui (1998: 5). The explanation is to be found, according to the authors, not only in linguistic diversity and linguistic scale, but also in the distinction between the oral tradition and the written (Mazrui and Mazrui 1998: 5). The presence of a long written tradition (with sacred literature) helps to deepen a propensity for linguistic nationalism; this is obvious, for example, when looking at Arab nationalism. Consequently, it is not language by itself that matters but rather the symbolism attached to it.

We thus see that several factors may affect language behaviour, e.g. existing patterns of multilingualism, the colonial legacy, the educational policy during colonial and post-colonial times, more specifically the relative importance given to the use of African languages in the media. These days, urbanization results in new networks with consequential effects on patterns of language use and language behaviour; more specifically it may result in the displacement of other languages, especially those spoken by open and loose-knit groups. Languages such as Arabic, Hausa, Swahili or other major lingua francas spread particularly fast in urbanized areas, developing into primary languages for an ever widening group of people, whereas in rural areas local networks with local languages continue to play a more important role; such differences obviously have to do with different degrees of exposure to these major lingua francas in schools, the media and public administration. It has been shown by Hammad (2002) in a detailed study of language attitudes in greater Khartoum (Sudan), that mother tongue shift towards Arabic is progressing at a significant rate among the various languages groups investigated, especially the younger generations. Apart from age, other parameters, e.g. ethnic background, inter-ethnic marriage, level of education and job status, determine the role played by Arabic in daily interaction; also, the tendency towards language shift appears to be stronger with females than with males. Arabic was reported to be very important for education, social interaction, religious purposes and economic privileges (in this order). At the same time, ethnic languages are viewed as important symbols of ethnic identities and cultural heritage. Language areas as spoken by southerners and Beja are still among the healthiest in Sudan in general as well as in the greater Khartoum area. There is, however, a significant discrepancy, between the positive attitudes towards ethnic languages and their actual maintenance by the communities studied by Hammad, i.e. in spite of the fact that such languages are held to be important for symbolic reasons, they may nevertheless be given up as primary means of communication. Lack of institutional support for ethnic languages and intermarriage are seen as important causal factors in this respect.

On the whole, language death appears to be less dramatic on the African continent than in other parts of the world. Although national governments may have other priorities – quite understandably so – there are initiatives both from within these African countries as well as from abroad, to help document endangered languages. Most African countries are open to such research plans. There was a period in the postcolonial history of Tanzania when local authorities did not welcome research on languages other than Swahili. Establishing Swahili as the national language had been a core ideological ingredient of Tanzania's national language policy after the country's independence. Today, research on minority languages, endangered or otherwise, is welcomed in countries like Tanzania and elsewhere. Consequently, there are initiatives for salvage linguistics, sometimes supported by European or American organizations, e.g. the Volkswagen Foundation, Unison, or the Dutch National Science Foundation (which issued a special programme in 2001 for the documentation of endangered languages). As the list of endangered languages below helps to show, there are various scholars (e.g. in Ethiopia and Ghana) who are in the process of documenting languages that are likely to disappear within the next few generations.

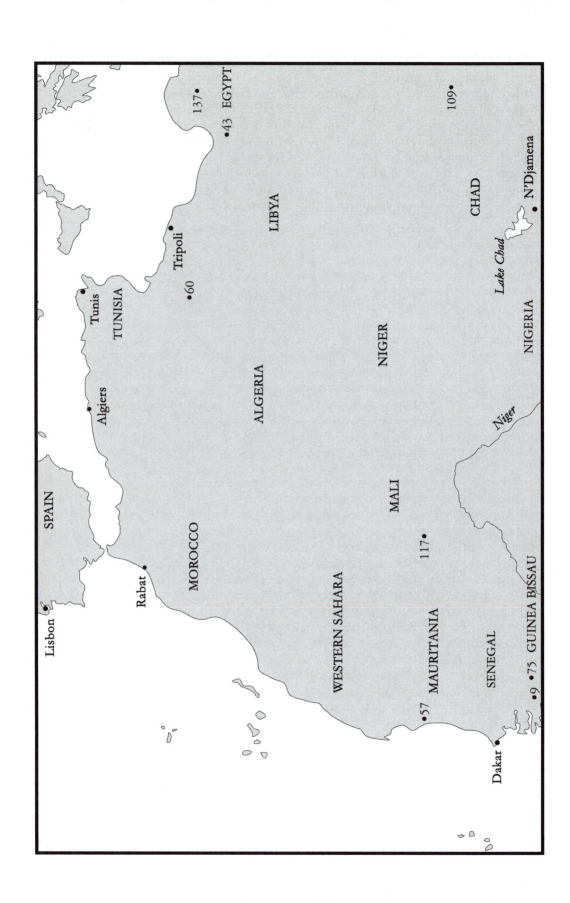

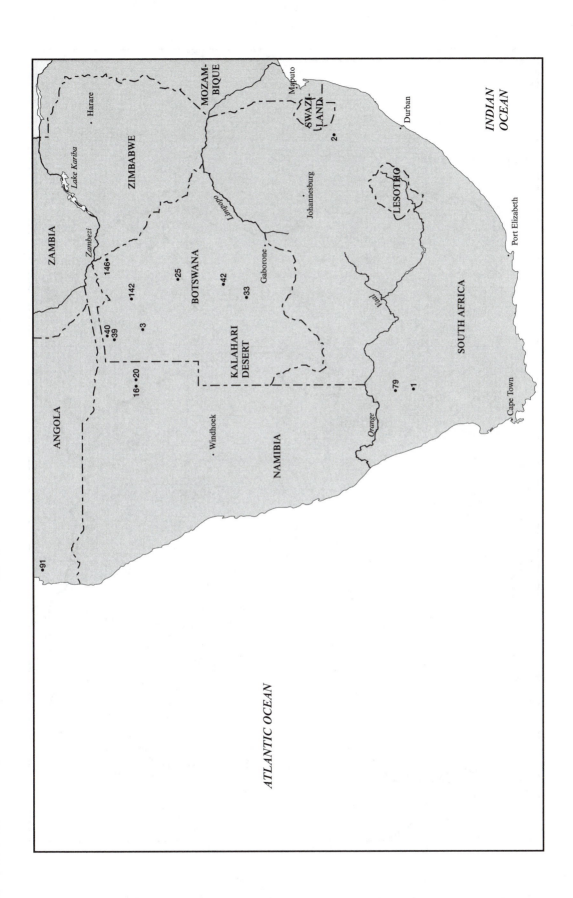

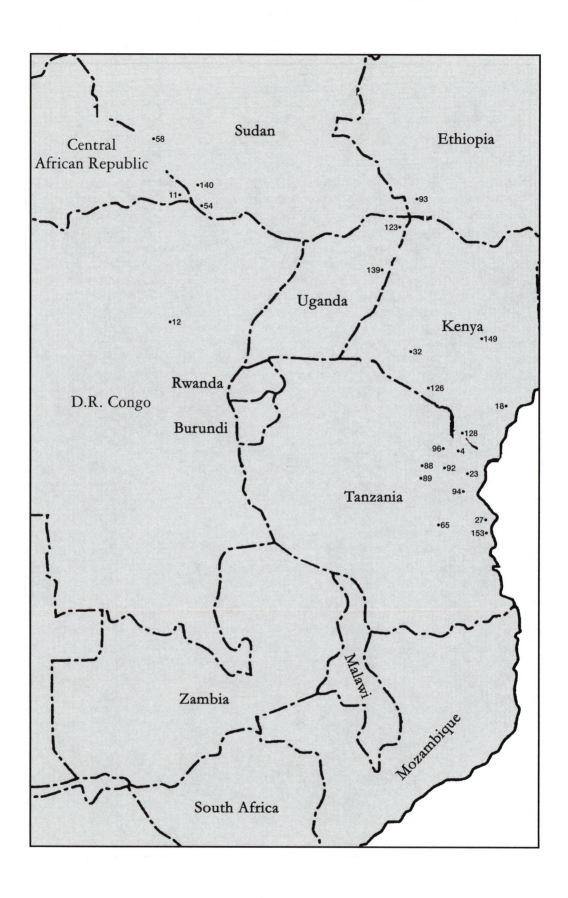

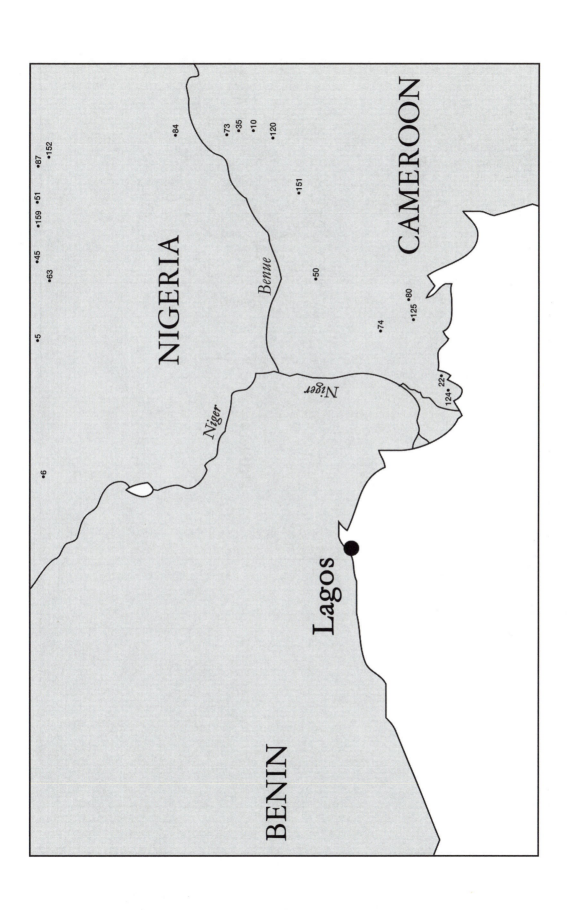

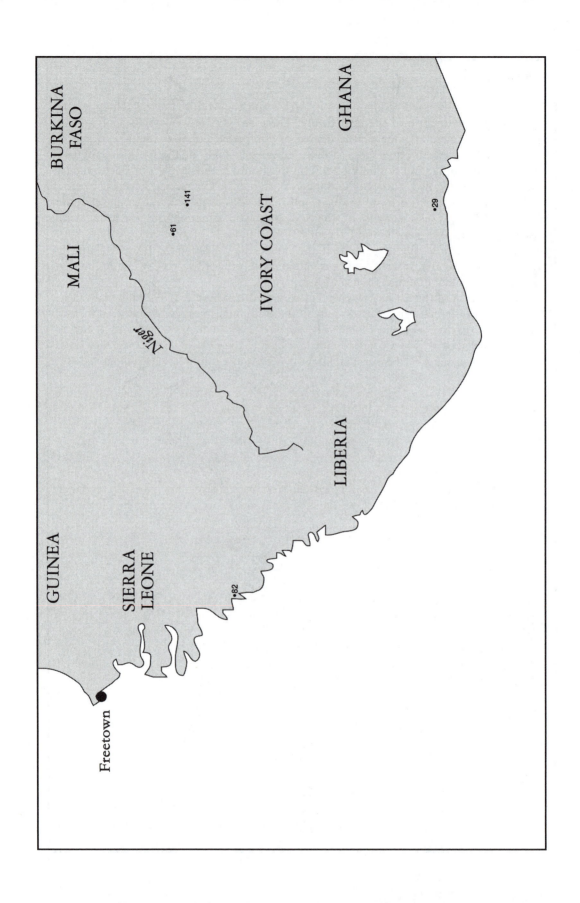

Language list

Below, a list is presented of languages in Africa and the Middle East which appear to be faced with extinction in the near future. There are very few reliable sociolinguistic studies on language attitude or the degree of competence also in relation to age or generation for African languages; to date, Zelealem's study of the Cushitic language Qemant in Ethiopia, and Sommer (1995) on the Bantu language Yeyi in Botswana are among the few detailed studies of endangered languages. Consequently, the list below at times constitutes little more than an informed guess. Also, investigators at times arrive at different assessments of the sociolinguistic situation, in particular with respect to languages which, until recently, had hundreds of thousands of speakers. Thus, whereas some might claim that the Nilo-Saharan language Bura Mabang in eastern Chad and the western Sudan is endangered, other observers would argue that there are still a few hundred thousand fluent speakers left.

A comparison of the list below with that compiled by Sommer (1992) will make clear that there are differences in the assessment of the sociolinguistic situation between the two sources. Not only were languages added below, also several languages classified as endangered in Sommer (1992) were not included as such in the present survey. Sommer takes the number of speakers to be a crucial factor in determining the health of a language. But we now know that small but close-knit communities may hold on to their language, whereas languages may become endangered within a few generations even when they are spoken by a few hundred thousand people forming rather loose-knit societies. It is to be noted that the concept 'small' implies a few thousand speakers in an African context, whereas for Australian or Brazilian standards this probably would mean a few hundred.

A number of other phenomena may be pointed out as complicating factors in the assessment of the number of actually endangered languages on the African continent. Whereas for a number of countries detailed surveys with language maps have been prepared, for others detailed knowledge on the linguistic situation is lacking. For example, according to some official figures there are twelve languages in Mali. But as pointed out by Geoffrey Heath (personal communication), there may be as many as fifty distinct languages sometimes spoken in just a few villages. Detailed surveys usually result in the 'discovery' of additional languages, as shown in the detailed survey by Voeltz (1996) for Guinea. For some areas with extreme linguistic heterogeneity, e.g. in Nigeria, where three distinct phyla (Afroasiatic, Niger-Congo and Nilo-Saharan languages) meet, detailed surveys are lacking, although a number of linguists (e.g. Blench 1998; Connell 1998; Kleinewillinghöfer 1996; Shimizu 1982; Storch 1998) have made important contributions in this respect. In areas for which such information is lacking, minority languages may disappear without their existence ever having been observed in the scientific literature. Moreover, if languages are associated with separate ethnic identities, they are more likely to be distinguished as separate languages in the literature. However, language and ethnicity often are not isomorphic, and so speakers may identify themselves in various ways to the outside world. Kleinewillinghöfer (1996) presents examples of this with respect to northeastern Nigeria, where people speaking distinct and at times genetically unrelated languages, e.g. Adamawa (Niger-Congo) languages and Chadic (Afroasiatic) languages, may still form one ethnic group.

A number of languages thought to be extinct may still have some speakers left. This may be true, for example, for the Cushitic language Aasáx in Tanzania. Because of their explicit or implicit stigmatization in social interaction, Aasáx speakers may identify themselves as Maasai, and thereby become 'invisible', e.g. in interview situations. Also, some of the cases of language death discussed below in actual fact may be instances of dialect loss; where intelligibility studies are lacking, this problem (separate languages versus dialects of the same language) cannot be avoided.

Finally, patterns of multilingualism may change rapidly, e.g. in northern Nigeria, where numerous Chadic and Benue-Congo languages may vanish in the near future. The interested reader may therefore want to consult the present list in combination with studies in Brenzinger (1992; 1998), as well as Grimes (1996 or later versions). For the complicated situation in the Khoisan area, the interested reader is referred to Winter (1981). A more general survey of sociolinguistic issues in Sub-Saharan Africa with special focus on minority languages can be found in the special issue of the *International Journal of the Sociology of Language* 125 (1997).

Below, we will essentially refer to lower-level units as well as to the phylum to which particular endangered languages belong, as far their genetic classification is concerned, since these appear to be well established; genetic classifications for intermediate levels seem to change all the time, and reference to them is therefore avoided here. Details on the overall classification of these languages may be found in the Appendix.

Endangered languages

ǀAnda [39] is a Central Khoisan language belonging to the Khoe cluster within this family. It is spoken traditionally north of the Okavango Delta, northwestern Botswana. Data on the language can be found in Vossen (1997).

≠Haba [3] is a Central Khoisan language, more specifically a member of the //Ana group. It is spoken traditionally in an area south of the Okavango Delta, northwestern Botswana. Vossen (1997) provides data on this language.

≠Hõã and Tshasi [33] possibly Southern Khoisan languages spoken by some 400 adults in Khudumelapye, Salajwe, Tsia and Bodungwe, Botswana. Also Tshwa, Shuakwe, Kua and !Xaise all Khoe languages spoken in the Nata area by people who were traditionally subjugated to the Bolata (serfdom) system. 1,000 to 1,500 (GR). Southern Kalahari Desert, Kweneng District. Linguistic affiliation: Khoisan, Southern Africa, Southern, Hua. Reported to be diminishing in numbers. Related to !Xoo.

Aasáx [4] is a Southern Cushitic language, whose former speakers are scattered among the Nilotic (Nilo-Saharan) Maa in northern Tanzania. It is not clear whether the language has become completely extinct, or whether there are still some (rusty) speakers left. The social background to language reduction among the ethnic Aasáx has been described by Winter (1979).

Ahlon [24] also known as *Achlo, Igo*, is an endangered Togo-Remnant language (Niger-Congo) language spoken in the border area between southern Ghana and Togo. It is closely related to Kposo and Bowiri. The official name for the language is Ahlon, whereas its speakers, who number around 6,3000, call themselves Igo. The Kwa language Ewe is becoming more and more of a first language for the Igo people.

606

Aka [52], also known as *Sillok* (Silak) after the name of the hill region in northern Sudan where it is spoken, may still have a few hundred speakers. The name **Fa-c-aka** is a selfname for the Aka people most of whom live west of the Berta-speaking people, by whom they have been strongly influenced. Aka belongs to a cluster of languages, known as (Eastern) Jebel, one of the smaller subgroups within the Nilo-Saharan phylum. Two other members of this group, Kelo and Molo, are also endangered, only the third member Ingassana being a thriving language. As is the case with other groups in northern Sudan, the Aka people have become heavily arabicized.

Aka (*Bayaka*, *Nyoyaka*, *Beká*, *Pygmée De Mongoumba*, *Pygmée De La Lobaye*, *Pygmées De La Sanghas*, *'babinga'*, *'bambenga'*, *'négrille'*) [19] is spoken in the dense forest area that forms the border between the Central African Republic and Congo-Brazzaville. While there are general indications that Aka is a distant dialect of Lingala, including many loan words from neighbouring Bantu and Ubangian languages, there is a possiblity that this complex consists of two or even more languages distantly related. Preliminary investigations of the Aka spoken around Mongoumba and the Bayaka of Nola, for example, show some major differences in vocabulary and grammatical structure, suggesting that they may not be mutually intelligible (Voeltz ms).

While population figures estimate the Aka population at 30,000 there are good reasons to believe that the language/dialect(s) as a whole is at risk of disappearing. Progressively Aka/Bayaka-speakers are leaving the confines of the forest areas and are settling in the vicinity of smaller settlements in hope of day labour or medical assistance. Often it is exactly due to the effort of 'helping' the forest populations that they are being drawn out of their original environment. Frequently the consequence of these noble efforts is destitution, illness and the loss of their language in favour of Sango, in the Central African Republic and Lingala in the Congo.

Akiek [32] is a Southern Nilotic (Nilo-Saharan) language spoken in Kenya by a small number of people. The so-called Akiek of Kinare in Kenya now speak Kikuyu as a first language; there may still be a few rememberers left (Dimmendaal 1989). Its former speakers are also referred to as Ndorobo, a derogatory term used for various (former) hunter-gatherer groups living in eastern Africa, e.g. the Elmolo along Lake Turkana (Kenya), who now speak a variety of the Nilotic language Maa, but who spoke the Cushitic language Elmolo in former times. The name Akie(k) (or Ndorobo) is also used for an ethnic group in northern Tanzania who now speak the Eastern Nilotic language Maasai as a first language. The Akiek groups in Tanzania and Kenya, who speak the same language basically, apparently are not in contact with each other. The names Suiei and Sogoo appear to refer to dialects of the same language.

Alagwa [88], also known as *Alagwase*, *Alawa*, *Asi*, *Chasi*, *Wasi*, is a Southern Cushitic (Afroasiatic) language closely related to Iraqw. The ethnic group consists of about 10,000 people (Mous 1992). Kondoa District, Tanzania. Adult members of the ethnic group still appear to have a fairly good command of the language. Nearly all are bilingual in the Bantu language Rangi, which has become the dominant language among Alagwa children.

Anyimere [31], also known as *Animere*, *Kunda*, refers to an ethnic group of about 500 people in Ghana. There are only a few fluent speakers left of this so-called Togo-Remnant (Niger-Congo) language, all of whom are over forty. The language is used in only a limited set of functional domains (Marshall Lewis, personal communication). The Kwa language Twi (Akan), spoken by many Anyimere as a second language, appears to be becoming increasingly important as a first language for the Anyimere.

Anfillo [77], also known as *Southern Mao* (the term Mao being an ethnonymic label used to denote various groups in the area speaking different languages), is an Omotic language still spoken by about 500 speakers out of an ethnic group of approximately 1,000 people living in western Ethiopia, west of Dembi-Dollo (Yigezu 1995). Most Anfillo have switched to the Cushitic language (Western) Oromo, which became more and more of a dominant language in the area from the sixteenth century onwards.

Awjilah [43], also known as *Augila*, *Aoudjila*, is a variety of Berber spoken by some 2,000 people in eastern Libya. Most men are bilingual in Awjilah and Arabic, but many women appear to speak only Awjilah.

Baka (*Pygmée*, *Bebayaka*, *Bebayaga*, *Bibaya*, *Pygmees De L'est*, *Babinga*) **[161]** is an Ubangian language of Cameroon, closely related to Ngbaka-Mab'o. A good portion of the vocabulary is borrowed from neighbouring Bantu languages as well as from Lingala. While population figures of around 25,000 are given for the Baka population, there are strong indications that they will share the fate of their cultural neighbours, the Aka and will abandon their traditional way of life for a squatter existence on the fringe of society waiting for the next handout from the next humanitarian organization. With this process they are also likely to abandon their language in favour of Fang, the lingua franca of the Southern part of Cameroon.

Baldamu [56], also known as *Mbazla*, belongs to the Biu-Mandara branch within Chadic. Its current number of speakers, who live in northern Cameroon, is not known. The Atlantic (Niger-Congo) language Fulfulde appears to play an increasingly important role in the area.

Basa-Kaduna [5], also known as *Basa-Gumna*, *Basa Kuta*, *Gwadara Basa*, is a Kainji (Niger-Congo) language spoken in northern Nigeria. Its existence is currently under pressure due to the increasing role played by the lingua franca in the area, the Chadic language Hausa. There may be no fluent speakers left.

Basa-Kontagora [6] is one of various endangered Kainji (Niger-Congo) languages spoken in northwestern Nigeria. There may be less than ten speakers left for this language.

Bathari [103], also known as *Bautahari*, *Bothari*, belongs to the South-Semitic branch (Afroasiatic). It probably has some 300 speakers left (according to Morris, quoted in Simeone-Senelle 1997:379) on the southern coast of Oman. Its speakers are known as the Batahira (Botahara). Bathari is closely related to Mehri, a language with well over

70,000 speakers according to Johnstone (1987), who calls it a dialect of the same language.

Bati [7], also known as ***Bati ba Ngong, Bati de Brousse***, refers to a speech community that consisted of some 800 people in the 1970s living to the right of the Sanaga River between the Sambasa and Bakoko, Cameroon. Their language belongs to Guthrie's zone A.40, and is closely related to Nomaande and Yambeta. The Bantu languages Basaa, Bakoko and Yambassa play an important role for most Bati people on a day-to-day basis.

Bayot [9] is an Atlantic (Niger-Congo) language spoken in southwestern Senegal. The imminent disappearance of the language appears to be due mainly to the fact that Bayot speakers have been disseminated into foreign areas, as a result of the long lasting conflicts and rebellion against the Senegalese government in their home area. In the diaspora Bayot people apparently avoid using their first language.

Bayso [8] probably has approximately 3,200 speakers left (Brenzinger 1995). It is also known as ***Alkali***, after the Bayso name for Gidiccho Island, Ethiopia, where most Bayso speakers live. In addition, speakers may be found on Welege Island, which is situated towards the northern end of Lake Abbaya in the southern Ethiopian Rift Valley, on Golmakka Island in Lake Abaya, as well as on the western shore of the lake. Bayso is a Cushitic (Afro-Asiatic) language. The people are bilingual in Wolaytta and/or Oromo, also as a result of recent resettlement programmes, which resulted in modified patterns of bilingualism.

Beeke [12] or ***Ibeke*** is a member of the Lega-Kalanga (D.20) group within Bantu (Niger-Congo). There may be some 1,000 speakers left for this language in the Ituri region of Congo (Kinshasa). Beeke is losing ground in favour of Ndaka, a Bantu language belonging to a different subgroup within Bantu, the Bira-Huku group (D.30).

Bete [10] is a language about which very little is known. It may still have a few speakers left out of a population of around 3,000 people, living at the foot of Bete Mountain, Nigeria, who now speak a Jukun language. The genetic classification of Bete has not been clarified. It is reported to have been close to a language called Bibi and Lufu, whose genetic classification also remains to be solved. The name Bete is not to be confused with a language by the same name spoken in southeastern Nigeria. This latter language belongs to the Cross-River branch within Niger-Congo.

Birgid (*Bergit, Berguid, Kajjara, Murgi*) [38] belongs to the Nubian cluster within Nilo-Saharan. The language used to be spoken in northern Sudan, as well as in north Kordofan south of El Obeid. It is not clear whether there are still speakers left in the linguistically complex border area between Chad and Sudan.

Birri [11] refers to a language belonging to the Central Sudanic branch within Nilo-Saharan. It is closely related to languages like Bagirmi and the Sara cluster. The names Mboto and Munga refer to dialects of Birri. The language may be extinct in the Sudan, but there appear to be speakers left in the southeastern corner of the

Central African Republic. The people are bilingual in Zande. They may be assimilated by the larger Zande people through marriage. Birri is different from the Adamawa-Ubangian language Bviri, also known as Belanda, which is spoken in the Southern Sudan. Belanda does not appear to be endangered, although many Belanda are assimilated by the neighbouring Zande through marriage.

Bobongo [13] is spoken in a few hamlets in the area of Nola-Bayanga, Central African Republic. Along with Pande it is part of the westernmost expansion of the Lingala complex (Bantu C.30 group). Sango and neighbouring Gbaya and Banda play an ever increasing role as means of communication, especially for the children.

Bodo [41] is very likely nearly extinct. In the Central African Republic a few individuals admitting to be Bodo could be identified, but all of them spoke only Zande. There is a possibility that there are still a few speakers scattered in the Sudan. Bodo is said to be a Bantu language belonging to the Bira-Huku (D.30) group.

Boni [34], also known as *Aweer(a)*, *Ogoda*, *Sanye*, *Wa(a)ta(-Bala)*, is spoken by probably less than 200 people in Kenya, near the Somali border, although ethnic Boni seem to number around 5,000. Many of its former speakers have switched to the Cushitic language Orma or Somali, or to Swahili. Traditionally, the Boni lived as hunter-gatherers in the forest hinterland behind Lamu Island and the Tana River.

Boro [76], also known as *Bworo*, *Shinasha*, *Scinacia*, is an Omotic (Afroasiatic) language of Ethiopia spoken by an ethnic group consisting of some 4,000 people The names **Amuru**, **Gamila**, **Guba** and **Wambera** are names of Boro dialects. The people use Amharic or Oromo as second languages.

Bubbure [159] is a West Chadic language spoken mainly in Bure village, northern Nigeria, which probably has less than fifty fluent speakers left. Most Bubbure people have switched to the Chadic language Hausa as a first language; also, many Bubbure speak Fulfulde (Atlantic; Niger-Congo), another major lingua franca in the area.

Buga [40] refers to a Central Khoisan language also known by a variety of other names, e.g. *Buka-Khwe*, *Boga-Kwe*, *River Bushman*. Buga is spoken in Botswana; there may also be speakers in Angola. Data on the language may be found in Vossen's (1997) comparative study of Central Khoisan.

Bung [14] is the name of a language of Cameroon which probably has become extinct or is nearly extinct (Connell 1998: 216). Bung probably is a Mambiloid lect, i.e. a member of a Northern Bantoid subgroup within Niger-Congo, once spoken in a village with the same name in the Tikar Plain, Adamawa Province, Cameroon (Connell 1998). Its speakers have switched to Fulfulde, a major lingua franca in the area, as well as to another Mambiloid variety, the Ndung lect within Kwanja.

Burunge [89] is a Southern Cushitic language, also known as *Bulunge*, *Mbulugwe*, and spoken in Central Province, Tanzania. Although the ethnic Burunge number at least 30,000, there appear to be only a few hundred fluent speakers left.

Bussa [21] belongs to the Konsoid group within Lowland East Cushitic (Afroasiatic), and is spoken mainly in an area southwest of Lake Chamo, Ethiopia. The present number of speakers is estimated at around 1,500 (Wondwosen Tesfae, personal communication). The Bussa are abandoning their language in favour of other Cushitic languages such as Oromo and Konso, which are the dominant languages of the area.

Cambap [15] is spoken by a group of people in the Adamawa Province, Cameroon, close to the Nigerian border. The people call themselves **Camba**. The language belongs to the Mambiloid cluster within Northern Bantoid (Niger-Congo). Its speakers are bilingual in another variety of Mambiloid, Kwanja, which is now spoken as a first language (Connell 1998: 212). There are probably less than 1,000 speakers of Cambap left.

Camo [160] is one of various Kainji (Niger-Congo) languages on the Jos Plateau, Nigeria, currently endangered. Camo is also the name of one of the two dialects, the other one being *Kudu* (*Kuda*). The community consists of 2,000 to 4,000 people.

Cara [111], also known by a variety of other names, e.g. *(N)Fachara*, *Pakara*, *Tariya*, *Ter(i)a*, refers to an endangered Niger-Congo language belonging to the Central Plateau group. It is spoken in the Bassa LGA, Plateau State, Nigeria.

Cara [16], self name **Cárá-dàm**, refers to a Central Khoisan language, more specifically a member of the Shua cluster, Central Khoisan group. Languages of this cluster are spoken in northeastern Namibia. Data on Cara can be found in Vossen (1997).

Cassanga (or *Kasanga*) **[17]**, own name **Guhaaca**, is an Atlantic language once spoken astride the border of Guinea Bissau and the Casamance Province of Senegal. There may be a few elderly speakers left, most younger people having switched to the lingua franca of the area, Mandinka.

Dahalo [18] is also known as *Sanye*, the preferred name since the name Dahalo is derogatory. It should be noted, however, that the name Sanye is also used for a different language in the area, Waata. Alternatively, Dahalo is referred to as **Guo Garimani**. The ethnic group consists of some 3,000 people living mainly near the mouth of the Tana River along the Kenyan coast. Dahalo is a Cushitic (Afroasiatic) language with a click sound in its phonological inventory; the latter unit possibly entered the language through contact with Khoisan-speaking groups in the distant past. Dahalo people are bilingual in Swahili, which is becoming their primary language.

Danisi [20], also referred to as *Danisa*, *Demisane*, *Madenassa*, *Madenassena*, is a language belonging to the Shua cluster within Central Khoisan, and spoken in northeastern Namibia. Vossen (1997) provides data on this little-known Khoisan language.

Dar el Kabira. See **Kamdang** and **Tulishi**

Defaka [22] is a Niger-Congo language forming a subgroup together with the Ijo group. All languages belonging to this relatively isolated genetic subgroup within Niger-Congo are spoken in the Niger Delta of Nigeria. Defaka, which is also known as *Afakani*, is essentially spoken in the town of Nkoroo by approximately 1,000 people or possibly less. Its speakers are multilingual in languages spoken in the Eastern Delta Fringe, in particular Nkoroo, and to a lesser extent Benue-Congo languages like Igbo, Obolo and Kana.

Denderoko [23] refers to a coastal Bantu (Niger-Congo) language spoken in Tanzania. As with other communities in the area, e.g. the Digo, the Denderoko people are shifting towards Swahili as a primary language.

Deti [25], also known as *Tete*, *Teti*, *Tletle*, is a Central Khoisan language spoken in Botswana. The names **K'ere-Khwe** and **Tsh'erekhwe** refer to dialects of this language. It is currently being replaced by Nambya, a Bantu (Niger-Congo) language belonging to the Shona cluster (Chris Collins quoted in Batibo 1998: 277).

Dimbong (*Kaaloŋ*, *Mboŋ*, *Bape*, *Palong*) [78] is spoken in two villages, Mbong and Dii in the Canton Yambetta. Dimbong, closely related to Rikpa (Bafia), is a Bantu language grouped as A.52.

Dimme [26], also known as *Dima*, is a South Omotic language (Afroasiatic) language spoken in Ethiopia. The autonym for the language is Dim-af or Dim-ap. The Dimme speech community is estimated at around 5,000 (Yilma and Siebert 1995: 2). The Omotic language Aari as well as the lingua franca of the region Amharic play an important role in their daily communication.

Doe [27] refers to a Bantu language spoken along the Tanzanian coast, belonging to zone G in Guthrie's classification, more specifically to the Zigula-Zaramo cluster (G.30). For the Doe speech community, consisting of some 24,000 people, Swahili is becoming more and more important in daily interaction.

Duli [28] is an endangered Adamawa (Niger-Congo) language in Cameroon's North Province. In this area the Atlantic (Niger-Congo) language Fulani plays an important role as a lingua franca as well as the new primary language for many people in the area. It is not clear whether the Duli language is extinct already, or whether there are some speakers left.

Ega [29], a language spoken in the Ivory Coast, also known as *Dies*. It is the most western of the Kwa languages, surrounded by Dida, a language of the Kru family. There are only a few elderly speakers left for Ega, which is being replaced by the surrounding Dida speaking population.

El Hugeirat [30] refers to a Nubian (Nilo-Saharan) language in the El Hugeirat (Hagerat) Hills, north-central Sudan. Tucker and Bryan (1956: 76) give a figure of 202 speakers, but they also observe that this Hill Nubian lect is known only through a wordlist dating back to the 1930s. Speakers of other languages in the area interviewed in Khartoum by the first author of the present contribution, e.g. speakers of Dilling or Nyimang, were not aware of a separate language in the area by this name. This variety of Hill Nubian may therefore be extinct already.

Elmolo [36] refers to an ethnic group living along the shores of Lake Turkana (Kenya) as well as the neighbouring semi-arid desert area. Among the 4,000 ethnic Elmolo, who now speak Samburu, a Nilotic (Nilo-Saharan) language, there may still be a few elderly people speaking the former language of the group, a Cushitic (Afroasiatic) language also known as Elmolo. The Elmolo language is closely related to Daasanech, which is spoken north of Lake Turkana.

Fali of Baissa [35] refers to a nearly extinct language in the Plateau region, Nigeria, whose genetic classification is not clear (Crozier and Blench 1992). Most likely, it belongs to the Benue-Congo group within Niger-Congo.

Fam [73] is a Bantoid language, more specifically classified as a member of the Mambiloid group within Northern Bantoid (Niger-Congo) with 1,000 or few speakers who live southeast and north of the Mambila Plateau, Nigeria.

Fongoro (also *Gele, Kole*) **[85]** refers to an ethnic group of approximately 1,000 people living on both sides of the border between Chad and Sudan. Their language belongs to the Sara-Bagirmi group within Central Sudanic (Nilo-Saharan). Fongoro people have shifted to Fur linguistically and culturally, although there may be a few elderly speakers left in isolated places.

Fumu [37], also known as *Ifumu, Mfumu*, was spoken once to the north of Brazzaville (Congo), but may be extinct today. In the 1950s there were still speakers around for this language, which belongs to the Teke group (B.70) within narrow Bantu (Niger-Congo).

Gabake-Ntshori [42], also known by a variety of other names, e.g. *G!abakethsori, Hiechware, Chuware, Masarwa, Tati, Tati Bushman*, is a Central Khoisan language spoken in Botswana. It forms a co-dialect with Kwe-Etshori. The actual number of speakers is not known.

Gafat [44] is a South Semitic language spoken in the Blue Nile region, Ethiopia, which may have become extinct already. Its former speakers appear to have shifted to the dominant language in the area and the national language of the country, Amharic.

Gana [45] also known as *Ganawa, SiGana*, belongs to the Kainji group within Niger-Congo in Nigeria. It is one of several languages in the area whose existence is currently under pressure as a result of the growing importance of Hausa in the region. In addition, the Jarawan Bantu language Gura appears to play a role at least in one Gana village. The language appears to be the same as a language known as Rishi or Ishi (or Rusancii in the dominant language of the area, Hausa). Data on the Gana language can be found in Shimizu (1982).

Ganjule (*Ganjawle*) **[46]** refers to an Omotic (Afroasiatic) language with probably less than fifty speakers left living mainly west of Lake Ch'amo, Ethiopia. The language used to be spoken on a small island called Ganjule Island on the northwestern tip of Lake Chamo, but its speakers have recently relocated to Shela-Mela on the west shore of Lake Chamo. The name **Ganta** seems to refer to a dialect of Ganjule. The language is closely related to Harro and Gats'ame. Some Ganjule are bilingual in Wolaytta. The

Ethiopian linguist Hirut Woldemariam is currently documenting this group of closely related languages or dialects.

Gats'ame [69] also *Kachama, Makka, Get'eme* (which is the name of the southern most island in Lake Abaya, Ethiopia, where Gats'ame people used to live in the past) is still spoken today, probably by some 1,000 speakers living mainly in Ugayo and Mole village, west of Lake Abaya in Ethiopia. The language is closely related to Ganjule and Harro, which probably are dialects of the same language (although no common name exists for this cluster). This cluster of endangered languages is currently being documented by the Ethiopian linguist Hirut Woldemariam.

Gbayi (*Kpasiya*) [47] spoken in the Mingala Prefecture, Central African Republic. While there are estimates of around 5,000 speakers, the language is at risk of being replaced by Banda. Gbayi is an Ubangian language, fairly closely related to Ngbandi and Sango. It should not be confused with **Kpatiri**, q.v.

Geme (*Jeme, Ngba*) [48] is spoken north of Ndele (CAR) in and around Aliou, where the large majority of inhabitants speak Togbo, a Banda dialect. It is an Ubangian language, fairly closely related to Nzakara and Zande.

Gey [49] also known as *Gewe, Gueve*, refers to a group consisting of some 1,900 people in an area east of Pitoa, Cameroon. Their language, which is now assumed to be extinct, belonged to the Adamawa branch within the Adamawa-Ubangi group (Niger-Congo). Ethnic Gey appear to have shifted to Fulfulde as their first language.

Goemai [84] (also known as *Ankwe*) is one of several Chadic (Afroasiatic) languages in Plateau State, central Nigeria, currently being replaced by Hausa as a first language. The community itself consists of about 150,000 people, but transmission of the Goemai language to younger generations appears to be limited.

Gule [not mapped] refers to a Koman (Nilo-Saharan) language in Sudan, which still had a few older speakers, left in 1979 (Bender 2000: 48). The language probably has become extinct. Its name is derived from a mountain by the same name. The people are also referred to as **Funj** or **Fungi** (a name applied to the former political state of Funj). The self-name appears to have been **Anej** or **Hamej Feca**. The people have shifted towards Sudanese Arabic as their first language.

Gwara [50] probably is a dialect of the Chadic (Afroasiatic) language Margi of eastern Nigeria. Whereas this latter language is not endangered as such, the Gwara lect appears to be endangered (compare Wolff 1974–5).

Gyem (*Gema*) [51] is a Benue-Congo language belonging to the Jos group of the Eastern Kainji branch. Last demographic data (1971) indicate 100 speakers (Crozier and Blench 1992). Spoken to the north of Jos, Nigeria, it is systematically being replaced by Hausa.

Hadza [96] also known as *Hatsa, Hadzapi, Kangeju (Wa)Kindiga, Tindiga*, is spoken by some 800 people (de Voogt 1992: 6) southeast of Lake Victoria, near Lake Eyasi,

Tanzania. Neighbouring groups such as the Nilotic Tatoga, the Cushitic Iraqw and the Bantu group Sukuma appear to be encroaching upon their traditional territory. The Hadza appear to form a rather close-knit society traditionally, as a result of which their language may remain an important symbol of their ethnic identity for the coming generations. Sander Steeman is preparing an in-depth study of this language, whose genetic relationship with Khoisan cannot be discounted, but whose genetic relationships with Northern, Central, or Southern Khoisan (or Sandawe) in any case would be remote.

Haraza [not mapped], also known as *Jebel Haraza* after a mountain in the area approximately 200km west of Khartoum, is the name of a Nubian (Nilo-Saharan) language. In the 1970s there were still a few elderly people whom one might have characterized as 'rememberers'. These days, the Haraza community speaks Sudanese Arabic as a first language.

Harro (*Haro*) [51] is spoken by some 150 people on Gidiccho Island in Lake Abaya, Ethiopia, and is part of the Ometo group within Omotic (Afroasiatic). The name **Gidiccho** is also used as a name for the inhabitants of the island with the same name. In addition to Harro, however, Bayso and Oromo (both Cushitic languages) are spoken on Gidiccho Island. These latter languages are gradually replacing Harro. This endangered language has been described by Woldemariam (2004).

Harsusi [105], also called *Harsiyyat*, *Hars*, is a South-Semitic (Afroasiatic) language spoken in Oman, which had an estimated 700 speakers left in the 1970s. The speech community consisted of some 600 Harasis and 100 <Ifar or <Afar. This estimate was made, however, during a period when many people had left their region to work in oil wells. The actual number of speakers may therefore be higher. Harsusi is closely related to Mehri, which plays an important role in daily interaction, as does Arabic.

Hijuk [53] is spoken by only a part of the population of the village of Batanga, Cameroon. It seems to belong to the Bafia subgroup (Bantu A.50). No published material on the language is known.

Hobyot [101], also known as *Kalam Rifi*, is spoken by a few hundred people in Oman as well as across the border in Yemen. Hobyot belongs to South Semitic, as does Mehri, of which it may be a dialect (cf. Johnstone 1987).

Homa [54] refers to a (Narrow) Bantu language once spoken in the Southern Sudan around the towns of Mopoi and Tambura, but now probably extinct. It belonged to zone D, more specifically to the Bira-Huku cluster (D.30), a group whose speakers are found mainly in northeastern Congo (Kinshasa, the former Zaïre).

Hone [55] is an endangered Jukun language, spoken mainly by people over forty, although in some remote settlements children may still learn Hone as a first language. It is also known by a variety of other names, e.g. (*Wapan*) *Gwana*, *Gaateri*, *Kona Jukun*, *Pindiga-Jukun*; the names Wapan and Kona also refer to closely related Central-Jukunoid languages. Hone is one of several northern Jukun languages vanishing under the strong influence of Hausa as well as a result of interethnic marriage. The language is documented by Storch (1998).

Hulaulá [not mapped] is an Aramaic lect also known as *'Aramit*, *Galiglu*, *Jabali*, *Judeo-Aramaic*, *Kurdit*, *Lishana Noshan*, *Lishana Axni*. It is still spoken by some 9,500 mainly older people, of which around 9,000 live in Israel and around 300–400 in the Kurdistan region in Iran, according to Mutzafi (quoted in Grimes 2000). The names Saqiz, Kerend, Sanandaj and Suleimaniya refer to dialects of this Aramaic language.

Imeraguen [57] is spoken by a few isolated people to the North of Nouakchott along the Atlantic seaboard. The language is unclassified; it is reported (p.c. from O. M. Diagana) to be a variety of Hassaniyya with a strong Soninke (Saraxole) substrate element.

Indri [58] is spoken by some 700 speakers in the Southern Sudan, in a small area around Raga. It belongs to the Feroge group of Ubangian languages. Speakers are reported to be bilingual in Arabic and Feroge.

Isubu (*Bimbia*, *Isuwu*, *Su*) **[59]** was one of the earliest Sub-Saharan languages to receive the attention of European researchers. Today it is spoken by only a few speakers, including some children, in three villages on the coast and the islands on the foot of Mount Cameroon. Isubu belongs to the Duala group of Bantu languages (A.23).

Jeri (selfname **Jerikuo**) **[61]** is spoken by some 1,500 speakers around Korhogo in the northern Ivory Coast. Ethnic Jeri consist of some 20,000 people. The Jeri language belongs to the Central branch within Mande. Kastenholz (1998) has observed that its speakers are often leatherworkers among the Sienare Senufo (who speak a Gur language). The latter language, as well as Manding, play an increasingly important role in daily interaction among the Jeri.

Jilbe [62], also known as **Zoulbou**, is a Chadic (Afroasiatic) language, which probably has 2,000 or fewer speakers mainly living in Jilbe town, a settlement on the border of Cameroon and Nigeria across from the town of Dabanga. It may be the same language as Ziziliveken. Jilbe is a genetically rather distinct member of the Kotoko (Lagwan) group, an ethnic group speaking a Chadic language, which comprises some 38,500 people living in the border area between Cameroon, Chad and Nigeria.

Ju [63] is a West Chadic language spoken probably by less than 1,000 people in Bauchi State, Nigeria. Apart from another Chadic language, Guruntum, which functions as a dominant neighbouring language, Hausa plays a pervasive role as a primary means of communication in the area.

Judeo-Berber [not mapped] is a variety of Moroccan Berber (Afroasiatic) still spoken by some 2,000 mainly elderly speakers in the High Atlas range of Morocco (Podolsky, quoted in Grimes 2000). Monolingual communities in the country may have disappeared before 1930 as a result of the dominant role of Moroccan Arabic. Also, some speakers went to Israel from 1950 to 1960.

Kaka (*Sanga-Sanga*) **[64]** is spoken around Bayanga, Central African Republic. Kaka, not to be confused with Kako (Bantu A.90), is possibly closely related to Mpiemo and the Maka-Njem complex (Bantu A.80). Very few speakers, documented only in early word lists (cf. Ouzilleau 1911)

Kamdang [95] is a member of the Kadu group within Nilo-Saharan, spoken in the hills south of the Nuba Mountains (Sudan) by some 3,000 people. More specifically, its speakers and those of related dialects such as Dar el Kabira (Turu, Logoke, Minjimmina) and Tulishi live on Jebel Tulishi, Jebel Kamdang, and south of Tulishi. (See also **Tulishi**.)

Kami [65] refers to a Bantu language in Tanzania, classified as a member of the Zigula-Zaramo cluster G.30 by Guthrie. It is one of various Bantu languages in the coastal area whose speakers are switching to Swahili as a first language.

Kande [66], also known as *Okande* (a name referring to the people speaking Kande) probably has 1,000 or fewer speakers. Kande is a Bantu language spoken west of Booue in Gabon, and classified as a member of the Tsogo cluster (i.e. the B.30 group in Guthrie's grouping of Bantu languages; Guthrie 1976–81). The other language belonging to the same subgroup as Kande is Tsogo, also known as Apindji.

Kanga [67], also known as *Kufo*, *Kufa*, is a member of the Kadu group within Nilo-Saharan, spoken by approximately 8,000 people in the Miri Hills (Sudan). Dialects: **Abu Sinun**, **Chiroro-Kursi**, **Kufa-Lima**. As is the case with many other small languages spoken in the Nuba Mountains, its current linguistic situation is unclear, due to the fact that many speakers have settled in the greater Khartoum area, where Arabic is becoming more and more of a first language among migrants.

Kari (*Kare*, *Li-kari-li*, *A-khale*) **[68]** may be nearly extinct. In the early 1990s only a few individuals all over seventy years of age still could remember a few words or phrases in the Zemio-Obo-Dimbia area of the CAR. It is likely that there are a few more speakers left on the other side of the border in the northern part of the Congo. Kari is grouped by Bastin (1978) as belonging (with Bodo) to the Bira-Huku group (Bantu D.38).

Kasabe [not mapped] is a member of the Mambila cluster (Northern Bantu), once spoken close to the Nigerian border, Cameroon. The language may be extinct already. According to Connell (1998) the last known speaker may have died in 1995. The people now speak Mvop, another variety of the Mambila cluster within Northern Bantoid.

Kazibati [70], also known as *Ganzibati*, *Hadjibatie*, *Kasiboti*, is spoken by a small group of people (numbering probably less than 400) near Makolo (Congo-Kinshasa). It probably belongs to the Baya, Ngbaka-Manzi group within Ubangi (Niger-Congo), and is known essentially through a study by Costermans (1938).

Kelo [71], also referred to as *Tornasi* (after the name of the hill region where it used to be spoken), is an Eastern Jebel (Nilo-Saharan) language spoken in northern Sudan, west of Berta. The name Beni Sheko probably refers to a dialect of Kelo; the selfname of the language is Ndu-faa-Keelo. Two other Eastern Jebel languages, Aka and Molo, are also endangered; the only other remaining member of the Eastern Jebel cluster, Gaam (Ingessana, Tabi), on the other hand is a thriving language with some 30,000 speakers.

K'emantney [72], also referred to as *Kemanat, Kimant, Qimant*, is one of the few endangered languages on the African continent for which there is a detailed study available, not only of the language structure, but also of the external setting (in terms of Sasse's 1992a, 1992b model of language shift) for the obsolescence process through Leyew's (2001) study. K'emantney is a Northern Cushitic language spoken north of Lake Tana, Ethiopia. Whereas some seventy years ago, the language was spoken by thousands of people, it is currently spoken by some 1,600 people as a first language; the number of second-language speakers is estimated at around 3,400. K'emantney is gradually giving way to Amharic, the national lingua franca of Ethiopia. Zelealem (2003) contains a description of K'emantney, including observations on structural variation within the language as a result of language contraction.

Kiong [74] also known as *Oko(n)yong, Iyoniyong, Akoiyang*, belongs to the Upper Cross group within Cross River (Niger-Congo) and is still spoken by a few elderly people in Cross River State, Nigeria. Most Kiong people today speak another Cross River language, Efik, which has been a major language in the area for several centuries.

Kobiana [75], own name **Guboy**, also known as *Buy, Uboi*, is an Atlantic language spoken in Guinea Bissau and Senegal; the language, which has around 400 speakers left (Vanderaa 1991), may already have disappeared in Senegal. Guboy is closely related to Banyun and Kasanga. Speakers are bilingual in Mandyak, which appears to have become the dominant first language of the group.

Koi-Sanjaq [not mapped] is the name of a Aramaic (Semitic, Afroasiatic) variety spoken in northern Iraq by some 800 to 1,000 people in a town with the same name, as well as in a nearby village called Armota.

Korana [79] also known as *!Kora, Koraqua*, 50 speakers in South Africa out of an ethnic group of 10,000 (Barrett 1972). Western. Possibly also found in Botswana. Khoisan, Southern Africa, Central, Nama. Nomads. Slowly dying out. May be extinct.

Korop (also known as *D(y)urop, Ododop, Erorup*) **[80]** is an Upper Cross (Niger-Congo) language closely related to Kiong, and endangered as is its closest relative. Among the ethnic group, which consists of at least 12,500 people living in the border area of Cameroon's South West Province and the neighbouring area across the border in Nigeria, Efik appears to have become a dominant language.

Kpatiri (*Kpatili, Patri*) **[81]** is an Ubangian (Niger-Congo) language spoken in Mingala Prefecture, Central African Republic. The language is systematically being replaced by Nzakara, with which it is fairly closely related.

618

Krim (*Kim, Kimi, Kirim, Kittim*) **[82]** is spoken along the Krim River, Sierra Leone, surrounded by Vai and Sherbro. Of some 10,000 individuals claiming to be Krim, only about 5 per cent still speak the language, but these do include a good number of children. Other Krim now mostly speak Mende. Krim is an Atlantic language, belonging to the southern Mel subgroup.

Kubi [83], also known as *Kuba* (**Kuba-wa** being the name for its speakers) is a variety of Bole, a Chadic (Afroasiatic) language spoken northeast of Bauchi town, Nigeria, by some 1,500 people. The Bole group as a whole has around 100,000 speakers. For many speakers Hausa appears to have become a dominant language.

Kudu [86], also known as *Kuda(wa)*, refers to a Kainji (Niger-Congo) language, spoken in central Nigeria. It forms a dialect cluster with Camo, which also appears to be vanishing (see also under **Camo**). Kudu belongs to the Kainji group within Niger-Congo. The ethnic group consists of 2,000 to 4,000 people.

Kupto [87], also known as *Kutto*, is a member of the Tangale group within Chadic (Afroasiatic), which may have some 3,000 or less speakers left. It is closely related to languages like Kushi, Kwaami, Pero, Piya and Tangale. Its role appears to be diminishing as a result of the growing importance of Hausa in the area of Northeastern Nigeria where it is spoken.

Kwadi [91] refers to a Khoisan language (also known as *Cuanhoca, Cuepe, Curoca, Koroka*), which has probably become extinct. The ethnic Kwadi live mainly in southwestern Angola, south of Moçamedes, and seem to speak a Bantu language these days.

K'wadza [92], also known as *Kwadza, Ng'omvia, Qwadza*, refers to a Southern Cushitic (Afroasiatic) language in Tanzania. The people have shifted towards the Bantu language Gogo. There may be a few speakers left in the area of Itiso and Solwu (Tanzania; Derek Elderkin, personal communication, quoted in Sommer 1992: 366).

Kwegu [93], also known as *Koegu, Kwegi, Bacha, Menja*, is a Surmic (Nilo-Saharan) language spoken in scattered villages along the Omo River, southwestern Ethiopia. Many Kwegu live in a symbiotic relationship as hunter-gatherers with neighbouring pastoral groups such as the Me'en and Bodi (who also speak Surmic languages) as well as the Dizi, an Omotic group with a strong focus on agriculture. These neighbouring languages play an increasingly important role in the daily lives of Kwegu speakers. A first description of the language is to be found in Hieda (1998). The names Yidinit or Yidinich, as well as Muguji, refer to dialects of the same language.

Kwere [94] is a Bantu language also known as *Kwele* or *Ng'were*. It belongs to the Zigula-Zaramo, i.e. the G.30 group within Bantu (Niger-Congo), according to Guthrie. Although the ethnic group consists of some 100,000 people living mainly in the coastal regions of Tanzania (also among the Zaramo and Ruguru), the language apparently is endangered as a result of the growing importance of Swahili in the area. The people in fact refer to themselves as Waswahili 'in their desire to identify themselves with the coastal culture' (Batibo 1992: 89).

Kwisi [not mapped], a Bantu (Niger-Congo) language also known as *Kwandu* or *Mbundyu*, probably has become extinct, but it was still spoken by a few elderly people in the 1960s, according to Westphal (1965: 135) who refers to the language as a 'remnant of a pre-Kuvale primitive Bantu language, spoken by few very old people. Its affiliations are tentatively placed with languages as far east as Barotseland.' It was spoken in Southwest Zambia, near the Angolana and Namibian borders.

Laro [97], also known as *Larawa*, *Laranchi*, *Laru*, refers to a Kainji (Niger-Congo) language spoken amongst an ethnic group of some 5,000 people along the banks of the Niger River, northwestern Nigeria. They are reported to be assimilating to Bisã language and culture.

Likpe [98] also known as *Sekpele* or *Mu*, is an endangered Togo-Remnant (Niger-Congo) language spoken in southeastern Ghana. It is losing ground in favour of the dominant language in the area, Ewe, which is becoming more and more of a primary language for the Likpe people. The names **Sekwa** and **Sekpele** refer to dialects of the same language for the approximately 15,000 ethnic Likpe. Felix Ameka is currently documenting the language.

Lishana Deni [not mapped] also known by a variety of other names (e.g. *Judeo-Aramaic*, *Kurdit*, *Lashon Targum*, *Lishan Hozaye*, *Lishan Hudaye*) is an Aramaic (Semitic, Afroasiatic) language originally from northwest Iraqi Kurdistan. Many speakers, most of whom are over forty-five years old, live in Israel these days. The names **Amadiya**, **Atrush**, **Bet-Tanure**, **Dohuk**, **Kara**, **Nerwa**, and **Zakho** refer to dialects of the same language.

Lishanán [not mapped], also known by a variety of other names (*Judeo-Aramaic* or *Jewish Aramaic*, *Nash Didan*, *Lishana Didan*, *Kurdit Azerbaijanit*, *Lishana Shel Imrani*, *Persian Azerbaijan*, *Galigalu*, *Lakhlókhi*, *Lishanit Targum*) refers to the language of an ethnic group of approximately 5,300 people, most of whom now live in Israel. Originally, it was spoken in Iranian Azerbaijan and southeast Turkey. There are small communities of around 500 people in Georgia, 300 in Azerbaijan, and fifty or less in Kazakhstan.

Logba [99] is an endangered Togo-Remnant (Niger-Congo) language spoken by an ethnic group of about 5,000 people in southern Ghana. It belongs to a cluster comprising Avatime, Logba and Nyagbo-Tafi. For many ethnic Logba, Ewe and (Ghanaian) English become more and more of a primary language in daily communication. G. E. Kofi is currently documenting the language.

Lomon [100], also known as *Lumun* or *Kuku-Lumun*, is a member of the Talodi group within Kordofanian (Niger-Congo), and spoken in the Moro Hills (Kordofan) in north-central Sudan. No current figures are available for the number of Lomon speakers.

Lorkoti [not mapped] refers to a dialect of the Maa cluster (Nilotic), which is part of Nilo-Saharan. It may have disappeared already (possibly a case of dialect death accordingly). There is still an ethnic group called Lorokoti in the Leroghi Plateau (Kenya); they all appear to speak a different Maa lect, Samburu, these days.

Lufu [102] refers to an unclassified language with probably a few elderly speakers left. The ethnic group, which consists of 2,000 to 3,000 people, now speaks a variety of Jukun (Niger-Congo), a language cluster involving some 40,000 people in eastern Nigeria and the neighbouring border area of Cameroon. The name Jukun refers to a group of related languages, whose speakers were once united in a centralized state known as Kororofa. The Lufu language is reported to have been close to Bete and Bibi, both of which are endangered or already extinct.

Luri [104] refers to a Chadic language in Bauchi State (Nigeria), which had around thirty speakers left according to a survey carried out in 1973 by the Summer Institute of Linguistics. Its proper position within the Chadic branch of Afroasiatic is not known. Its former speakers appear to have shifted to Hausa as a primary means of communication.

Mandaic [not mapped] is the name of an Aramaic (Semitic) language which is also known as *Mandaean*, *Mandaayi*, *Mandi*, *Subbi*, *Sa'iba*. It still has some 800 to 1,000 speakers in Iran. Ethnic Mandaeans number around 5,000 in the Khuzistan area in Iran and speak Western Farsi, whereas the 23,000 ethnic Mandaeans in Iraq all speak Arabic, with some older people being bilingual. Ethnic Mandaeans in Iraq appear to have shifted to Arabic as their first language. The language may still be in use by small immigrant communities in the United States (where they are known as 'Yokhana-naye') as well as Australia. The names **Ahwaz (Ahvaz)** and **Shushtar** refer to dialects of Mandaic.

Mangas [106] is spoken in Bauchi State, Nigeria. The few speakers still reported (180, SIL 1971; Crozier and Blench 1992) may well have opted for Hausa, the dominant language in all of the area. Mangas is West Chadic.

Maslam [107] or *Maltam* belongs to the Kotoko cluster within Chadic (Afroasiatic), and is spoken by 5,000 or fewer people in Cameroon, and a few hundred people in Chad. The name **Sao (Sahu)** refers to a dialect of the same language.

Mboŋa (*Mboa*) **[108]** is the easternmost Jarawan language recorded. It is reported to be spoken in the vicinity of Betare-Oya, Lom-and-Djerem Division, Cameroon. The only reliable data on the language are to be found in Strümpell (1910). The language is very likely to be extinct.

Mimi [109] refers to 5,000 speakers out of an ethnic group of some 50,000 people in scattered communities mainly around Darfur. Their language belongs to the Maban group within Nilo-Saharan. The majority, however, speaks Shuwa Arabic as a first language. The linguistic label Mimi is not be confused with the name Mimi as used in reference to other ethnic groups in the area speaking different languages, e.g. the Andang (Amdang, also known as Biltine, Mima or Mututu). The latter speak a language closely related to Fur, and forms a separate genetic unit within Nilo-Saharan.

Mlahsó [not mapped] is the name of an Aramaic (Semitic, Afroasiatic) variety which was still spoken by a small number of people in Turkey during the 1970s. There may be a few elderly speakers left.

621

Molo [110], also known as *Malkan*, or *Tvra-ka-Molo* ('the speech of Molo') probably had some one hundred speakers left in the 1980s (Bender 1988) around the Jebel Malkan region south of the Blue Nile in northern Sudan, near the Ethiopian border. Molo belongs to a cluster of closely related languages, known as the Eastern Jebel group within Nilo-Saharan. Two other members of this cluster, Aka and Kelo, are endangered as well. Its speakers are reported to be bilingual in Arabic and the Nilo-Saharan language Berta.

Mser [112], also known as (*Kotoko*) *Kuseri*, *Mandage*, is a member of the Kotoko cluster within Chadic, spoken by some 2,100 people in northern Cameroon and Chad. Shuwa Arabic appears to play an increasingly important role in the Chad region. Mser appears to be closely related varieties such as Gawi, Kalo (Kalakafra), Houlouf and Kabe.

Muguji. See **Kwegu**

Mvanip [113] is a language belonging to the Mambiloid cluster within Northern Bantoid (Niger-Congo), which probably has fewer than 1,000 speakers left in eastern Nigeria. Mvanip is also known as *Mvanon*, *Magu*, or *Mvanlip*. It is mentioned by Blench (1998) as a language 'which may be prove to be endangered in the short to medium term', like other smaller languages in the area such as Fam, Mbongo, according to the same author. These latter languages, as well as other smaller languages belonging to the same (Mambiloid) cluster, have not been included in the present list, basically because the number of speakers is not a crucial criterion for endangerment, as argued in the introductory remarks to the present list. Mvanip is mentioned here as an exemplary case of a relatively small community whose language may or may not be endangered in the near future.

Nagumi (also *Bama*, *Mbama*) **[114]** is a Jarawan Bantu (Niger-Congo) language in Cameroon, which may be extinct already. According to Voegelin and Voegelin (1977: 55) this was the same language as a language known by the name of Ngong. The latter language is still spoken by a few people living in a village by the same name south of Garoua, Cameroon.

Nayi [115], also known as *Na'o*, is an Omotic (Afroasiatic) language, forming a subgroup with Dizi and Sheko. The ethnic group consists of some 12,000 people living in southwestern Ethiopia. Yilma and Siebert (1995: 4), in their report on the sociolinguistic situation in the area observed that more than any other language, 'Kaffa is the language which is most frequently named as the first language of the interviewees' spouses. This is even more often the case with the interviewees' children. From this, a gradual shift from Nayi to Kaffa seems impending.' *Kaffo*, also known as *Kaficho*, is the lingua franca of the region.

Ndai (*Galke*, *Pormi*) **[116]** is very nearly extinct. Only a few speakers are left in and around Tchollire, Mayo-Rey Division, North Province, Cameroon. Ndai is an Adamawa 6 language. Some documentation can be found in Baudelaire (1944) and Lacroix (1962).

622

Nemadi (*Ikoku*, *Namadi*, *Nimadi*, *Nomadi*) **[117]** is spoken in the area between Tidjikdja and Tichit, Mauritania and extending towards Timbuktu in Mali. No data exists on this language, no classification has been proposed. It is not unlikely that the language can be linked to Azer, Zenaga, Soninke and/or Hassaniyya. No information is available on which lingua franca they use, although it is likely to be Hassaniyya.

Ngbinda [118] is a Bantu (Niger-Congo) language, closely related to Bira-Huku (Guthrie's zone D.30) with which it forms a subgroup. The area in Congo-Kinshasa where the language is spoken is known as Bungbinda, whereas its speakers are called Bangbinda. There appear to be only a few speakers left in scattered spots in the region; there may also be a few speakers left in Sudan.

Ngong. See **Nagumi**

Njanga [119] is the name of a Kwanja lect, i.e. of a Mambiloid (Northern Bantoid) language, spoken in the village of Mbondjanga, Adamawa Province, Cameroon, close to the Nigerian border. The people often intermarry with the Sundani, another Kwanja group whose language plays an increasingly important role in the area.

Njerep [120], also known as *Njerup*, is spoken by a few people in Cameroon, close to the Nigerian border, more specifically in the Ba Mambila village of Somié (compare Connell 1998). Njerep is closely related to Kasabe, which is also endangered. Apparently, the Njerep language is no longer used for communication. Instead, people now use the language of the surrounding community, Ba or Mvop, which is another Mambila lect.

Nkondi (*Ngondi*) **[121]** spoken in isolated hamlets in the area of Nola-Bayanga, Central African Republic. Nkondi belongs to the Lingala complex (Bantu C.30 group). It is being replaced by Sango and encroaching Gbaya and Banda.

Nyagbo-Tafi [122] is a Togo-Remnant language spoken in the Ghana-Togo frontier. It is closely related to Logba, another endangered Togo-Remnant language, as well as to Avatime. As is the case with a number of other Togo-Remnant languages, the language is endangered because speakers are switching towards more dominant languages like Ewe and (Ghanaian) English. James Essegbey is currently documenting Nyagbo-Tafi.

Nyang'i [123], also known as *Nyangiya*, *Nipori*, *Ngapore*, *Upale*, belongs to the Kuliak group within Nilo-Saharan, which further consists of the endangered language Soo, as well as Ik (or Teuso). The ethnic Nyang'i live in the Napore Hills, northeastern Uganda. Their dominant language is a variety of the Nilotic language Karimojong, known as Dodos. Only a few elderly people still speak Nyang'i as a first language.

Obulum [124], also known as *Abuloma*, is spoken in and around Abuloma town, Rivers State, Nigeria. It belongs to the Central-Delta group within Cross River (Niger-Congo), together with Kugbo. Obulum is endangered, probably like other smaller Cross-River languages in the region, because of the dominant role of Nigerian Pidgin English and major languages like Ijo in the area.

Odut [125], a language once spoken in southeastern Nigeria in a region where the Cross-River (Niger-Congo) language Efik is dominant. Odut has been classified as a member of the Upper Cross group within Cross-River (Niger-Congo). According to Forde and Jones (1950) there were around 700 speakers at the time, but the language may be extinct by now.

Okiek. See **Akie**

Omotik [126] also known as ***Laamoot***, is a Southern Nilotic language of southern Kenya which is closely related to Datooga. There may be as few as fifty speakers left, all over forty years old. The Laamoot people are also known as '*(N)Dorobo*', a derogatory cover term used for several small hunter or forest groups in eastern Africa speaking different languages (e.g. the Elmolo, the Yaaku, and the Akie). Most Laamoot (Omotik) now use the Nilotic language Maasai as a primary means of communication. Data on the language called Omotik (which is not to be confused with a sub-branch of the Afroasiatic family known by the same name) can be found in Rottland (1982).

Omo-Murle [127] is the name of a variety of **Murle**, i.e. a Surmic (Nilo-Saharan) language in southwestern Ethiopia as well as across the border in Sudan. The Omo-Murle people have become absorbed into the Nilotic Nyangatom people (also known as the Bume). There may still be a few elderly people left with some knowledge of their former language. The closely related Murle language is still spoken by at least 60,000 people in Sudan.

Ongamo [128], also known as ***Ngasa***, is a Nilotic language with 200 to 300 mostly elderly speakers out of an ethnic group of 2,500 people, most of whom live on the eastern slopes of Mount Kilimanjaro. Ongamo forms a genetic subgroup with Maa within the Eastern Nilotic branch of Nilotic, which is part of the Nilo-Saharan phylum. Younger people now tend to speak Chaga, a Bantu (Niger-Congo) language.

Ongota [129], alternatively known as ***Birale***, ***Biraile***, is a genetic isolate spoken in the linguistically complex southwestern corner of Ethiopia. Its speakers are gradually shifting towards the Cushitic language Ts'amay; interestingly, many Ts'amay are now in the process of shifting their language solidarity towards the Cushitic language Konso or the Omotic language Hamar. There is also some knowledge of Konso as well as another dominant Cushitic language in the area, Oromo, among the Ongota. In addition, some Ongota speak the Omotic language Hamar-Banna. Savà and Tosco (2000) have presented a first survey of the Ongota language.

Pande [130], a Bantu language spoken around Nola, Central African Republic. Preliminary lexical information (Voeltz ms.) indicates that the language constitutes one of the furthest western extensions of the Lingala complex (Bantu C.30 group). Sango, the lingua franca of the area, and encroaching Gbaya and Banda, tend to be replacing Pande.

Putai (*Western Margi*) [131] is spoken in central eastern Nigeria. Its speakers are quite numerous as a population, but no longer speak the language itself, having opted for

Kanuri in recent years. Putai is classified as Chadic, Biu-Mandara. It is possible that Putai is a dialect of Margi.

Qwarenya [132] is the name of an Agaw or Central Cushitic (Afroasiatic) language spoken in a region to the northwest and west of Lake Tana, Ethiopia. It is also known as *Qwaräsa*, the language of the Qwara, *Falashan*, since it was the major language of the Falashas or 'Black Jews' in Ethiopia. The Falasha traditionally referred to themselves as Betä Israel; the greater part emigrated to Israel in the 1990s. For most Falashas in Ethiopia, Amharic and Tigrinya had already become the dominant languages. There may be a few elderly speakers left (Appleyard 1998); a closely related dialect or variety and known as **Kailiña** appears to have become extinct already.

Rishi. See **Gana**

Sele [133], also known as *Sentrokofi* or *Santrokofi* (which is the name for its speakers) is a Togo Remnant (Niger-Congo) language spoken by some 6,000 people in southeastern Ghana. Ewe is becoming more and more of a dominant, first language in the area, as a result of which Sele as well as a number of other Togo Remnant languages are becoming obsolescent.

Senaya [not mapped] is the name of an Aramaic variety spoken by approximately fifty people in the Kurdistan region of Iran. There may be additional speakers elsewhere in the world, e.g. as immigrants in the United States, Australia and Western Europe. Senaya speakers use Assyrian Neo-Aramaic as a second language.

Shabo [134], also known as *Mekeyir*, or *Mikeyir*, is the name for a small ethnic group with between 400 and 1,000 people in southwestern Ethiopia who live among the Majang (Surmic, Nilo-Saharan) as well as among the Shakacho, who speak an Omotic (Afroasiatic) language. The Shabo live in a symbiotic relationship with these two groups, whose languages function as important second languages for the Shabo. The genetic position of Shabo is not clear; it may constitute a linguistic isolate.

Sheni [135], also known as *Asennize*, *Shani*, *Shaini*, refers to a nearly extinct Kainji (Niger-Congo) language in the Jos Plateau region, Nigeria. The only source on the language, which may have a few hundred speakers left, is Shimizu (1982).

Shiki [136], also known as *Gubi*, *Guba(wa)*, refers to a Jarawan Bantu (Niger-Congo) language in Nigeria, with less than 1,000 speakers. The name Gubi probably refers to a dialect of this language, as does the name Guru.

Singa (*Lusinga*, *Cula*) **[not mapped]** spoken on Rusinga Island, Lake Victoria, Uganda, may be extinct. According to Johnston (1919: 73), Singa is a 'dialect of Luwanga ... mixed with Lu-ganda and Ku-kerebe'. Whiteley, as cited in Bryan (1959: 109), claims that the people on this and the neighbouring islands speak Luo, but that there are a few people remaining speaking an 'archaic form of Ganda'.

Siwi [137], also called *Siwa* (after the name for the oasis where the Siwi people live), *Sioua*, *Oasis Berber*, or *Zenati*, is a Berber (Afroasiatic) language spoken in Egypt.

625

Most ethnic Siwi, a group consisting of some 5,000 people, appear to have shifted to Arabic as a first language.

Somyev [138], also known as *Kila* (after the term for blacksmith in Fulfulde), is spoken in two villages; one in Cameroon (Torbi) and one in Nigeria (Kila Yang). Its speakers call themselves **Somyewe**. Fulfulde is a lingua franca. The primary language of their community is a Mambila lect, Maberem.

Soo [139], also known as *Tepeth* or *Tepes*, is a Kuliak (Nilo-Saharan) language spoken in northern Uganda. There are three dialects spoken on three different mountains in the area, Mount Moroto, where the Tepes dialect is spoken, Mount Kadam where the Kadam dialect is spoken, and Mount Napak. The number of ethnic Soo is estimated at around 5,000, although the number of Soo speakers lies at the most around the 100 mark (Carlin 1993: 5). Most Soo speakers are over fifty. Younger people speak the Nilotic (Nilo-Saharan) language Karimojong as a primary language; in the Kadam area the Nilotic language Päkoot plays an important role. The name Kuliak derives from a stem referring to 'poor people, people without cattle' in Karimojong and other Eastern Nilotic languages. Soo is closely related to Nyang'i, which is also endangered, as well as Ik (Teuso).

Suba [not mapped] is the name of an administrative division in Tanzania where several Bantu languages are spoken, more specifically *Kihacha*, *Kisimbiti*, *Sweta*, *Surwa* which appears to be endangered (compare also Kihore 2000). Ethnic Suba these days speak the Nilotic language Luo.

Tati. See **Gabake-Ntshori**

Thuri [140], also known as *Wada Thuri* or *Shatt*, but distinct from the Daju language Shatt. *Dhe Thuri* means 'mouth of the Thuri'; the *Jo Thuri* ('Thuri people') numbered 6,600 according to Tucker and Bryan (1956). Southern Sudan between Wau and Aweil, between the Jur and Lol rivers, on the Raga-Nyamlell road, and on the Wau-Deim Zubeir road. Thuri belongs to the Western Nilotic branch within Nilo-Saharan. Dialects: Bodho (Dembo, Demen, Dombo), Colo (Shol), Manangeer. It is reported that all Thuri groups speak Dinka or Luwo and are nearly absorbed into Dinka groups.

Tima, known as *Domurik* by its speakers, refers to a language spoken in the Nuba Mountains, Sudan. There are still around 5000 ethnic Tima, but the Tima language is seriously endangered as a result of the encroaching role of Sudanese Arabic. Though classified as a Kordofanian language by Greenberg (1963), Tima appears to constitute a linguistic isolate together with Julud and Katla.

Tonjon [141] possibly has no fluent speakers left. According to Kastenholz (1998: 260) there are only rememberers for this Western Mande (Niger-Congo) language in the Ivory Coast. The people call themselves Numu (the word for blacksmith in the lingua franca of the region, Manding). The replacing languages in the area are Dyula, a Mande language, and Jimini-Senufo, a Gur language (Kastenholz 1998).

Ts'ixa [142], a Shua language spoken in Mababe area (Botswana), of which little is known; see Batibo 1998: 277.

Tulishi (*Tulesh*, *Thulishi*) [143] is spoken by approximately 2,500 people in a region south of the Nuba Mountains in Sudan. Their language belongs to the Kadu group within Nilo-Saharan. It forms a dialect cluster together with Dar el Kabira and Kamdang, which are also endangered languages. See also **Kamdang**.

Tuotom (*Ponek*, *Bonek*) [144] A few speakers can be found in Bonek near Ndikine-meki, Cameroon. The Botomp now tend rather to speak Tunen. Tuotom is classified as Bantoid, belonging to the Western Mbam-Nkam subgroup.

Turoyo [not mapped] refers to an almost extinct Aramaic variety in Turkey. Kurdish appears to have become the dominant or first language in the area. There may still be speakers of this distinct variety of Aramaic in countries such as Germany or the Scandinavian lands.

Twendi [145] belongs to the Mambiloid group within Northern Bantoid (Niger-Congo). It probably has 1,000 or fewer speakers left in western Cameroon. Twendi speakers are switching towards Kwanja or Konja, another variety of the Mambila-Konja cluster within Mambiloid.

Tyua [146] is a Khoe (Central Khoisan) language once spoken along the Zimbabwe border in Botswana, but possibly without any speakers left today. It is also known as *Masarwa* or *Basarwa*, which is a general name used in the Setswana language for Khoisan groups.

Wawa [147] is one of several Mambiloid (Bantoid, Niger-Congo) varieties, which appears to be endangered. The approximately 3,000 speakers live mainly west of Banyo in Cameroon with a possible extension into the neighbouring region of Nigeria. Fulani plays an important role as a second language in the area.

Wela [148], or *Hwela*, refers to the language of a special caste of blacksmiths living among the Kulango-Abron (who speak a Gur language) in northeastern Ivory Coast. Wela, also known as *Numu*, is a Western Mande (Niger-Congo) language. There probably are not more than 1,500 speakers for Wela.

Yaaku [149], also known as *Mogogodo*, *Mukogodo*, *Siegu*, is an East Cushitic (Afroasiatic) language spoken in Kenya. The people are also referred to as 'Ndorobo', which is a derogatory cover term for several small hunter or forest groups in Kenya and Tanzania, speaking a variety of distinct languages not linguistically related. In the 1980s there were some fifty speakers left (all over forty years old) out of an ethnic group of approximately 250. For ethnic Yaaku, the Nilotic language Maa has become the dominant language these days.

Yashi [150] spoken by around 400 (SIL, Crozier and Blench 1992) in Akwanga LGA, Plateau State, Nigeria. It is classified as a Western Plateau language, belonging to the Southwestern subgroup. No known documentation exists for this language.

Yeni [not mapped] is a Mambila lect, i.e. a Northern Bantoid (Niger-Congo) language, which used to be spoken in western Cameroon, but which may be extinct already. Yeni is closely related to Cambap, Njerep and Kasabe, all of which are endangered as well. The people have switched to Langa, another Mambila variety.

Yidinit. See **Kwegu**

Yukuben [151] is a Jukunoid language spoken in eastern Nigeria as well as on the other side of the border in western Cameroon. Ethnic Yukuben count around 16,000. It is closely related to Kuteb and Kapya and is grouped as belonging to Central Jukunoid, Plateau Platoid.

Zangwal [152] is found in Bauchi State, Nigeria. According to Grimes 2000 only about 100 speakers remained in 1993. Zangwal is a West Chadic language, belonging to the Guruntum subgroup. The language does not seem to be documented.

Zaramo [153], also known as *Zalamo*, *Zaramu*, *Saramo*, *Myagatwa*, is a Bantu (Niger-Congo) language (belonging to the G.30 zone in Guthrie's classification). Although the ethnic group may consist of 200,000 people, most Zaromo tend to speak Swahili as a first language these days. It is now reported that only a few elderly people speak the language (Brenzinger *et al.* 1991). Most Zaramo live along the Tanzanian coast between Bagamoyo and Dar es Salaam.

Zargulla [154], also known as *Zergulla*, is an Omotic (Afroasiatic) language, which has around 300 speakers. Its speakers, who live mainly west of Lake Chamo, Ethiopia, are in the process of shifting to another Omotic language, Zaysse, a major language in the area with around 12,000 speakers at present. Azeb Amha is currently documenting Zargulla.

Zay [155], also known as *Zway* or *Zoay*, after the name of the lake along whose shores the people live. Zay is a Gurage lect or variant, i.e. an Ethiopian Semitic (Afroasiatic) language, whose number of speakers appears to be decreasing because of the dominant role of Amharic.

Ziriya [156] is the name of a Kainji (Niger-Congo) language in the Jos area, Nigeria, which lost ground in favour of the contact language in the area, Hausa.

Ziziliveken [157], also *Zizilivakan*, *Ziliva*, *Fali of Jilbu*, is a Chadic language classified as a member of the Kotoko cluster, and spoken by a few hundred people in the border area between Nigeria and Cameroon, according to Crozier and Blench (1992: 112).

Zumaya [158] is reported to have only a dozen speakers left in one location, Ouro-Lamordé, Maroua, Cameroon in 1983 (Dieu and Renaud 1983). It is said to be close to Masa, a Chadic language. Speakers of Zumaya seem to have shifted to Fulfulde.

Notes

1 Part of the research for this chapter was carried out in the context of the Collaborative Research Project 389 'Arid Climate, Adaptation and Cultural Innovation in Africa'. Gerrit Dimmendaal would like to thank the Deutsche Forschungsgemeinschaft for supporting this

interdisciplinary project, and for its financial support for fieldwork in the Sudan. He would also like to thank members of the Centre for Advanced Study and the Research Centre for Linguistic Typology, La Trobe University (Melbourne), in particular Sasha Aikhenvald and Bob Dixon, for the support and encouragement during the final preparation of the present contribution. Erhard Voeltz would like to thank the Deutsche Forschungsgemeinschaft for support. Special thanks are also due to Al-Amin Abu-Manga and Leoma Gilley (Institute of African and Asian Studies, University of Khartoum) for making this fieldwork possible, and to Marshall Lewis for his briefing on a number of endangered languages.

References

Andersen, Torben (1988) Consonant alternation in the verbal morphology of Päri. *Afrika und Übersee* 71.1: 63–113.

——(1992) Subject and topic in Dinka. *Studies in Language* 15: 265–94.

Amha, Azeb and Gerrit J. Dimmendaal (2006) Converbs from an African perspective. In Felix Ameka, Alan Dench and Nicholas Evans (eds) *Catching Grammar*, pp. 93–442. Berlin: Mouton de Gruyter.

Appleyard, David L. (1998) Language death: The case of Qwarenya (Ethiopia). In M. Brenzinger (ed.) *Endangered Languages in Africa*. Cologne: Rüdiger Köppe, pp. 143–59.

Bamgboṣe, Ayo (1991) *Language and the Nation: The Language Question in Sub-Saharan Africa*. Edinburgh: Edinburgh University Press.

Bastin, Yvonne (1978) Les langues bantoues. In: Daniel Barreteau (ed.) *Inventaire des études linguistiques sur les pays d'Afrique Noire d'expression française et sur Madagascar*, pp. 123–85. Paris: Conseil International de la Langue Française.

Batibo, Herman M. (1997) Double allegiance between nationalism and Western modernization in language choice: The case of Botswana and Tanzania. In: Martin Pütz (ed.) *Language Choices: Conditions, Constraints, and Consequences*, pp. 195–205. Amsterdam: John Benjamins.

——(1998) The fate of the Khoesan languages of Botswana. In M. Brenzinger (ed.) *Endangered Languages in Africa*. Cologne: Rüdiger Köppe, pp. 267–84.

——(1992) The fate of the ethnic languages of Tanzania. In M. Brenzinger (ed.), *Language Death: Factual and Theoretical Explorations with Special Reference to East Africa*, pp. 85–98. Berlin: Mouton de Gruyter.

Batibo, H. M. and J. Tsonope (eds) (2000) *The State of Khoesan Languages in Botswana*. Mogoditshane, Botswana: Tasalls Publishing and Books.

Baudelaire, H. (1944) La numération de 1 à 10 dans les dialectes Habé de Garoua, Guider, Poli et Rey Bouba. *Bulletin de la Société d'études Camerounaises* 5: 23–30.

Bender, M. Lionel (2000) Nilo-Saharan. In Bernd Heine and Derek Nurse (eds) *African Languages: An Introduction*, pp. 43–73. Cambridge: Cambridge University Press.

Bleek, Dorothea F. (1929) *Comparative Vocabularies of Bushman Languages*. Cambridge: Cambridge University Press.

Bleek, Wilhelm Heinrich Immanuel (1862–9) *A Comparative Grammar of South African Languages*, vol. 1, London: Trubner.

Blench, Roger (1995) Is Niger-Congo simply a branch of Nilo-Saharan? In Robert Nicolaï and Franz Rottland (eds) *Actes du cinquème colloque de linguistique nilo-saharienne, Nice, 1992*, pp. 83–130. Cologne: Rüdiger Köppe.

——(1998) The status of the languages of Central Nigeria. In Matthias Brenzinger (ed.) *Engandered languages in Africa*, pp. 187–206. Köln: Köppe Verlag.

Brenzinger, Matthias (1995) The 'islanders' of Lake Abaya and Lake Ch'amo: Harro, Ganjule, Gats'ame and Bayso. *Survey of the Little-Known Languages of Ethiopia* 26: 2–36.

Brenzinger, Matthias (ed.) (1992) *Language Death, Factual and Theoretical Explorations with Special Reference to East Africa*, Berlin: Mouton de Gruyter (*Contributions to the Sociology of Language* 64).

——(1998) *Endangered Languages in Africa*. Cologne: Rüdiger Köppe.

Brenzinger, Matthias, Bernd Heine and Gabriele Sommer (1991) Language death in Africa. In Robert H. Robins and Eugenius M. Uhlenbeck (eds) *Endangered languages*, pp. 19–44. Oxford and New York: Berg.

Bryan, Margaret Arminel (1959) *The Bantu Languages of Africa*. London: Oxford University Press for International African Institute. (*Handbook of African Languages*).

Carlin, Eithne (1993) *The So Language*. Cologne: Institut für Afrikanistik. (*Afrikanistische Monographien, 2*).

Connell, Bruce (1998) Moribund languages of the Nigeria-Cameroon borderland. In Matthias Brenzinger (ed.) *Endangered Languages in Africa*, pp. 207–25. Cologne: Rüdiger Köppe.

Costermans, B. J. (1938) De Kazibati. *Kongo-Overzee* 4: 177–84.

Creissels, Denis (1981) De la possibilité de rapprochements entre le songhay et les langues niger-congo (en particulier mandé). In Thilo C. Schadeberg and Lionel M. Bender (eds) *Nilo-Saharan, proceedings of the first Nilo-Saharan Linguistics Colloquium, Leiden, September 8–10, 1980*, pp. 307–27. Dordrecht: Foris.

Crozier, D. H. and Roger M. Blench (eds) (1992) *An Index of Nigerian Languages, second* edition, Dallas TX: Summer Institute of Linguistics.

Delafosse, Maurice (1914) *Esquisse générale des langues de l'Afrique et plus particulièrement de l'Afrique française*. Paris: Maisonneuve.

de Voogt, A. J. (1992) Some phonetic aspects of Hatsa and Sandawe clicks. MA thesis, Leiden University, the Netherlands.

Dieu, Michel and Patrick Renaud (1983) *Situation linguistique en Afrique centrale. Inventaire préliminaire. Le Cameroun*. Paris: ACCT. (*Atlas Linguistique de L'Afrique Centrale*).

Dimmendaal, Gerrit J. (1984) Tenet (Surma): Ein Fall partiellen Sprachwechsels. In Rainer Voßen and Ulrike Claudi (eds) *Sprache, Geschichte und Kultur in Afrika. Vorträge gehalten auf dem III. Afrikanistentag, Köln, 14/15. Oktober 1982*, pp. 331–44. Hamburg: Helmut Buske.

——(1989) On language death in eastern Africa. In Nancy Dorian (ed.) *Investigating Obsolescence: Studies in Language Contraction and Language Death*, pp. 13–31. Cambridge: Cambridge University Press.

——(1995) Do some languages have a multi-genetic or non-genetic origin? An exercise in taxonomy. In Robert Nicolaï and Franz Rottland (eds) *Proceedings of the Fifth Nilo-Saharan Linguistics Colloquium*, pp. 357–72. Cologne: Rüdiger Köppe.

——(1998) Language contraction versus other types of contact-induced change. In M. Brenzinger (ed.) *Endangered Languages in Africa*, pp. 71–117. Cologne: Rüdiger Köppe.

——(2001a) Logophoric marking and represented speech in African languages as evidential hedging strategies. *Australian Journal of Linguistics* 21.2: 131–57.

——(2001b) Language diffusion and genetic relationship: An African perspective. In Alexandra Aikhenvald and R. M. W. Dixon (eds) *Areal Diffusion and Genetic Inheritance*, pp. 358–98. Oxford: Oxford University Press.

Dixon, R. M. W (1997) *The Rise and Fall of Languages*. Cambridge: Cambridge University Press.

Dorian, Nancy (1994) Review of *Endangered Languages* (Robins and Uhlenbeck). *Language* 70: 797–802.

Ehret, Christopher (2001) *A Historical-Comparative Reconstruction of Nilo-Saharan*. Cologne: Rüdiger Köppe.

Fleming, Harold (1969) The classification of West Cushitic within Hamito-Semitic. In Daniel McCall *et al.* (eds) *Eastern African History*, pp. 3–27. New York: Praeger.

Forde, D. and G. I. Jones (1950) *The Ibo and Ibibio-speaking Peoples of South-Eastern Nigeria*. London: Oxford University Press for the International African Institute. (*Ethnographic Survey of Africa, Western Africa, Part I*).

Greenberg, Joseph H. (1955) *Studies in African Linguistic Classification*. New Haven CT: Compass Publishing.

——(1963a) *The Languages of Africa*. Bloomington IN: Indiana University Press. (*International Journal of American Linguistics*, Vol. 29.1, *Part II*).

——(1963b) Some universals of grammar with particular reference to the order of meaningful elements. In Joseph H. Greenberg (ed.) *Universals of language*, pp. 58–90. Cambridge MA: MIT Press.

Gregersen, Edgar A. (1972) Kongo-Saharan. *Journal of African Languages* 11: 69–89.

——(1977) *Language in Africa. An Introductory Survey*. New York: Gordon and Breach.

Grimes, Barbara F. (ed.) (2000) *Ethnologue*, 14th edn, Dallas TX: SIL International.

Güldemann, Tom (1998) The Kalahari basin as an object of areal typology: A first approach. In Matthias Schladt (ed.) *Language, Identity and Conceptualization*, pp. 137–69. *Quellen zur Khoisan Forschung, 13*. Cologne: Rüdiger Köppe.

Güldemann, Tom and Rainer Vossen (2000) Khoisan. In Bernd Heine and Derek Nurse (eds) *African Languages: An Introduction*, pp. 99–122. Cambridge: Cambridge University Press.

Guthrie, Malcolm (1976–81) *Comparative Bantu*. Farnborough: Gregg International Publishers.

Hammad, Abdel Rahim Hamid Mugadam (2002) Language maintenance and shift in Sudan: The case of ethnic minority groups in Greater Khartoum. Ph.D. dissertation, Khartoum: University of Khartoum.

Haruna, Andrew (1997) Factors responsible for the spread of Hausa in the Southern Bauchi area, Northern Nigeria. *Studies of the Department of African Languages and Cultures* 22: 5–31.

Hayward, Richard J. (2000) Afroasiatic. In Bernd Heine and Derek Nurse (eds) *African Languages: An Introduction*, pp. 74–98. Cambridge: Cambridge University Press.

Heine, Bernd (1976) *A Typology of African Languages Based on the Order of Meaningful Elements*. Berlin: Dietrich Reimer. (*Kölner Beiträge zur Afrikanistik 4*).

Heine, Bernd and Derek Nurse (eds) (2000) *African Languages: An Introduction*. Cambridge: Cambridge University Press.

Hieda, Osamu (1998) A sketch of Keogu grammar: Towards reconstructing Proto-Southeastern Surmic. In Dimmendaal and Last (eds.), pp. 345–436. Dimmendaal Gerrit J. and Marco Last (eds.) 1998. *Surmic Languages and Cultures*. Cologne: Rüdiger Köppe.

Johnston, Harry Hamilton (1919) *A Comparative Study of the Bantu and Semi-Bantu Languages*. Oxford: Clarendon Press.

Johnstone, T. M. (1987) *Mehri Lexicon and English-Mehri Word-list*. London: SOAS.

Kastenholz, Raimund (1998) Language shift and language death among Mande blacksmiths and leatherworkers in the diaspora. In Matthias Brenzinger, *Endangered languages in Africa*, pp. 253–66. Cologne: Rüdiger Köppe.

Kihore (2000) Historical syntactic aspects of Kihacha. In Kuyikoyela Kahigi *et al.* (eds) *Lugha za Tanzania/Languages of Tanzania*, pp. 67–80. Leiden: CNWS. (CNWS Publications no. 89).

Kleinewillinghöfer, Ulrich (1996) Die nordwestlichen Adamawa-Sprachen: Eine Übersicht. *Frankfurter Afrikanistische Blätter* 8: 80–104.

——(2001) Jalaa – an almost forgotten language of northeastern Nigeria: A language isolate? *Sprache und Geschichte in Afrika* 16/17: 239–71.

Koelle, Sigismund Wilhelm (1854) *Polyglotta Africana*. London: Church Missionary House.

Köhler, O. (1975) Geschichte und Probleme der Gliederung der Sprachen Afrikas. Von den Anfängen bis zur Gegenwart. In H. Baumann (ed.) *Die Völker Afrikas und ihre traditionellen Kulturen Teil 1, Allgemeiner Teil und südliches Afrika*, pp. 135–373. Wiesbaden.

Lacroix, Pierre-Francis (1962) Note sur la langue galke (ndai). *Journal of African Languages* 1.2: 94–121.

Leslau, Wolf (1945) The influence of Cushitic on the Semitic languages of Ethiopia: A problem of substratum. *Word* 1: 59–82.

——(1952) The influence of Sidamo on the Ethiopic language of Gurage. *Language* 28: 63–81.

——(1956) Additional notes on Kambatta of Southern Ethiopia. *Anthropos* 51: 985–93.

Leyew, Zelealem (2003) *The Kemantney Language: A Sociolinguistic and Grammatical Study of Language Replacement*. Cologne: Rüdiger Köppe.

631

Mazrui, Ali A. and Alamin Mazrui (1998) *The Power of Babel: Language and Governance in the African Experience*. Oxford: James Currey.

Meinhof, Carl (1912) *Die Sprachen der Hamiten*. Hamburg: L. Friederichsen. (*Abhandlungen des hamburgischen Kolonialinstituts, Band IX, Reihe B, Völkerkunde, Kulturgeschichte und Sprachen, Band 6*).

Miller, Catherine and Al-Amin Abu-Manga (1992) *Language Change and National Integration: Rural Migrants in Khartoum*. Khartoum: Khartoum University Press.

Miller, Cynthia and Leoma G. Gilley (2001) Evidence for ergativity in Shilluk. *Journal of African Languages and Linguistics* 22.1: 33–68.

Mous, Maarten (1992) *A Grammar of Iraqw*. Leiden: University of Leiden Press.

Müller, Friedrich (1877) *Grundriss der Sprachwissenschaft*. Vienna: A. Hölder.

Nichols, Johanna (1986) Head-marking and dependent-marking grammar. *Language* 62: 56–119.

——(1992) *Lingistic Diversity in Time and Space*. Chicago, IL: University of Chicago Press.

Ouzilleau, Docteur (1911) Notes sur la langue des pygmées de la Sanga, suivies de vocabulaires. *Revue d'Ethnographie et de Sociologie* 2: 69–92.

Pachur, H.-J. and S. Kröpelin (1987) Wadi Howar: Paleoclimatic evidence from an extinct river system in the southeastern Sahara. *Science* 237: 298–300.

Reh, Mechthild (1996) *Anywa language. Description and internal reconstruction*. Cologne: Rüdiger Köppe.

Robins, Robert H. and Eugenius M. Uhlenbeck (1992) *Endangered Languages*. Oxford and New York: Berg Publishers.

Ross, Malcolm (2001) Contact-induced change in Oceanic languages in north-west Melanesia. In Alexandra Y. Aikhenvald and R. M. W. Dixon (eds) *Areal Diffusion and Genetic Inheritance: Problems in Comparative Lingustics*, pp. 134–66. Oxford: Oxford University Press.

Rottland, Franz (1982) *Die südnilotischen Sprachen. Beschreibung, Vergleichung und Rekonstruktion*. Berlin: Dietrich Reimer. (*Kölner Beiträge zur Afrikanistik 7*).

Rouchdy, Aleya (1989) Persistence or tip in Egyptian Nubian. In Nancy C. Dorian (ed.) *Investigating Obsolescence: Studies in Language Contraction and Death*, pp. 91–102. Cambridge: Cambridge University Press.

Sasse, Hans-Jürgen (1992a) Language decay and contact-induced change: Similarities and differences. In Matthias Brenzinger (ed.) *Language Death: Factual and Theoretical Explorations with Special Reference to East Africa*, pp. 59–80. Berlin: Mouton de Gruyter.

——(1992b) Theory of language death. In Matthias Brenzinger (ed.) *Language Death: Factual and Theoretical Explorations with Special Reference to East Africa*, pp. 7–30. Berlin: Mouton de Gruyter.

Savà, Graziano and Mauro Tosco (2000) A sketch of Ongota, a dying language of southwest Ethiopia. *Studies in African Linguistics* 29.2.59–136.

Schlee, Günter (1989) *Identities on the Move: Clanship and Pastoralism in Northern Kenya*. Nairobi: Gideon's Press.

Schultze, Leonard (1928) *Zur Kenntnis des Körpers der Hottentotten und Buschmänner*. Jena: G. Fischer.

Shimizu Kiyoshi (1982) Die Nord-Jos-Gruppe der Plateau-Sprachen Nigerias. *Afrika und Übersee* 65(2): 161–210.

Simeone-Senelle, Marie-Claude (1997) *The Modern South Arabian Languages. The Semitic Languages*. R. Hetzron (ed.) London: Routledge, 378–423.

Sommer, Gabriele (1992) A survey on language death in Africa. In Matthias Brenzinger (ed.) *Language Death, Factual and Theoretical Explorations with Special Reference to East Africa*, pp. 301–417. Berlin: Mouton de Gruyter.

——(1995) *Ethnographie des Sprachwechsels: So zialer Wandel und Sprachverhalten bei den Yeyi (Botswana)*. Cologne: Rüdiger Köppe.

Soodyall, H. and T. Jenkins (1998) Khoisan prehistory: The evidence of the genes. In A. Banks *et al.* (eds) *Proceedings of the Khoisan identities and cultural heritage conference*, pp. 374–82. Cape Town: Institute for Historical Research.

Stewart, John M. (1967) Tongue root position in Akan vowel harmony. *Phonetica* 16: 185–204.

——(1983) The high unadvanced vowels of Proto-Tano-Congo. *Journal of West African Languages* 12.1: 19–36.

Storch, Anne (1998) *Das Hone und seine Stellung im Zentral-Jukunoid*. Frankfurt am Main: Johann Wolfgang von Goethe Universität (inaugural dissertation).

Strümpell, F. (1910) Vergleichendes Wörterverzeichnis der Sprachen Adamauas. *Zeitschrift für Ethnologie* 42: 444–88.

Tosco, Mauro (1998) 'People who are not the language they speak': On language shift without language decay in East Africa. In Matthias Brenzinger (ed.) *Endangered Languages in Africa*, pp. 119–42. Cologne: Rüdiger Köppe.

——(2000) Is there an 'Ethiopian language area'? *Anthropological Linguistics* 42: 329–65.

Traill, Anthony and H. Nakagawa (2000) A historical !xóõ-|gui contact zone: Linguistic and other relations. In H. M. Batibo and J. Tsonope (eds) *The state of Khoesan languages in Botswana*, pp. 1–17. Gaberone: University of Botswana.

Trombetti, A (1910) *La Lingua degli Ottentotti e la lingua dei Wa-Sandawi*. Bologna: Gamberini & Parmoggiani.

Tucker, A. N. and M. A. Bryan (1956) *The Non-Bantu Languages of North-Eastern Africa. (Handbook of African Languages Part III)*. London: Oxford University Press for International African Institute.

Unseth, Peter and Jon Abbink (1998) Cross-ethnic clan identities among Surmic groups and their neighbours: The case of the Mela. In Gerrit J. Dimmendaal and Marco Last (eds) *Surmic Languages and Cultures*, pp. 103–11. Cologne: Rüdiger Köppe.

Vanderaa, Larry (1991) *A Survey for Christian Reformed World Missions of Missions and Churches in West Africa*. Grand Rapids: Christian Reformed World Missions.

Vansina, Jan (1986) Do pygmies have a history? *Sprache und Geschichte in Afrika* 7.1: 431–45.

Versteegh, Cornelis H. M. (1983) *The History of Linguistics in the Near East*. Amsterdam: John Benjamins.

Voegelin, C. F. and F. M. Voegelin (1977) *Classification and Index of the World's Languages*. New York: Elsevier.

Voeltz, Erhard (ed.) (1996) *Les langues de la Guinée*. Conakry: Faculty of Literature and Humanities, University of Conakry.

Vossen, Rainer (1997) *Die Khoe-Sprachen: Ein Beitrag zur Erforschung der Sprachgeschichte Afrikas*. Cologne: Rüdiger Köppe. (*Quellen zur Khoisan-Forschung 12.*)

Westermann, Dietrich (1927) *Die westlichen Sudansprachen und ihre Beziehungen zum Bantu*. Berlin: de Gruyter. (*Mitteilungen des Seminars für orientalische Sprachen, Beiheft 30.*)

Westphal, Ernst Oswald J. (1962) A re-classification of Southern African Non-Bantu languages. *Journal of African Languages* 1: 1–8.

——(1965) Linguistic research in S.W.A. and Angola. In *Die ethnischen Gruppen in Südwest-Afrika*, pp. 125–44. Windhoek: S.W.A. Wissenschaftliche Gesellschaft.

Williamson, Kay (1989) Niger-Congo overview. In John T. Bendor-Samuel and Rhonda L. Hartell (eds) *The Niger-Congo Languages: A Classification and Description of Africa's Largest Language Family*, pp. 3–45. Lanham MD: University Press of America.

Williamson, Kay, and Roger Blench (2000) Niger-Congo. In Bernd Heine and Derek Nurse (eds) *African Languages: An Introduction*, pp. 11–42. Cambridge: Cambridge University Press.

Wilson, W. A. A. (f.c.) *Guinea Languages of the Atlantic Group: Description and Internal Classification*, ed. Anne Storch with a contribution by John M. Stewart.

Winter, J. C. (1979) Language shift among the Aasáx, a hunter-gatherer tribe in Tanzania: An historical and sociolinguistic case-study. *Sprache und Geschichte in Afrika* 1: 175–204.

——(1981) Khoisan. In B. Heine, Thilo C. Schadeberg and E. Wolff (eds) *Die Sprachen Afrikas*, pp. 329–74. Hamburg: Buske.

Woldemariam, Hirut (2004) *The grammer of Haro with comparative notes on the ometo group.* Ph.D. Dissertation. Addis Ababa University.

Wolff, Ekkehard (1974–5) Sprachwandel und Sprachwechsel in Nordostnigeria. *Afrika und Übersee 58.3–4*: 187–212.

Yigezu, Moges (1995) Dying twice: The case of Anfillo languages. *Afrikanistische Arbeitspapiere 43*: 67–95.

Yilma, Aklilu and Ralph Siebert (1995) Survey of Chara, Dime, Melo and Nayi. *Survey of little-known languages of Ethiopia 25*: 1–8.

Zelealem, Liyew (2001) Some structural signs of obsolescence in K'emant. Ph.D. dissertation (to be published by Rüdiger Köppe, Cologne).

Index of languages

654